Massachusetts Municipal Profiles

2010

D1403758

F62 .M37
Massachusetts municipal
profiles.

39090014937060

State & Municipal Profiles Series

WITHDRAWN

Massachusetts Municipal Profiles

2010

State & Municipal Profiles Series

information publications
Woodside, California

Books from Information Publications

State & Municipal Profiles Series

Almanac of the 50 States

California Cities, Towns & Counties

Florida Cities, Towns & Counties

The New Jersey Municipal Data Book

Connecticut Municipal Profiles

Massachusetts Municipal Profiles

American Profiles Series

Asian Americans: A Statistical Sourcebook and Guide to Government Data

Black Americans: A Statistical Sourcebook and Guide to Government Data

Hispanic Americans: A Statistical Sourcebook and Guide to Government Data

Essential Topics Series

Energy, Transportation & the Environment:
A Statistical Sourcebook and Guide to Government Data

Health in America:
A Statistical Sourcebook and Guide to Government Data

ISBN 978-0-911273-50-2 Paper
ISBN 978-0-911273-51-9 CD
Massachusetts Municipal Profiles 2010

©2010 Information Publications, Inc.
Printed in the United States of America

All rights reserved. No part of this book may be reproduced or transmitted in any form or by any means, including but not limited to electronic or mechanical photocopying, recording, or any information storage and retrieval system without written permission from the publisher.

Information Publications, Inc.
2995 Woodside Rd., Suite 400-182
Woodside, CA 94062-2446

www.informationpublications.com
info@informationpublications.com

Toll Free Phone 877.544.INFO (4636)
Toll Free Fax 877.544.4635

Direct Dial Phone 650.568.6170
Direct Dial Fax 650.568.6150

Table of Contents

©2010 Information Publications, Inc. All rights reserved. Photocopying prohibited. For additional copies, contact the publisher at www.informationpublications.com or (877)544-INFO (4636)

©2010 Information Publications, Inc. All rights reserved. Photocopying prohibited. For additional copies, contact the publisher at www.informationpublications.com or (877)544-INFO (4636)

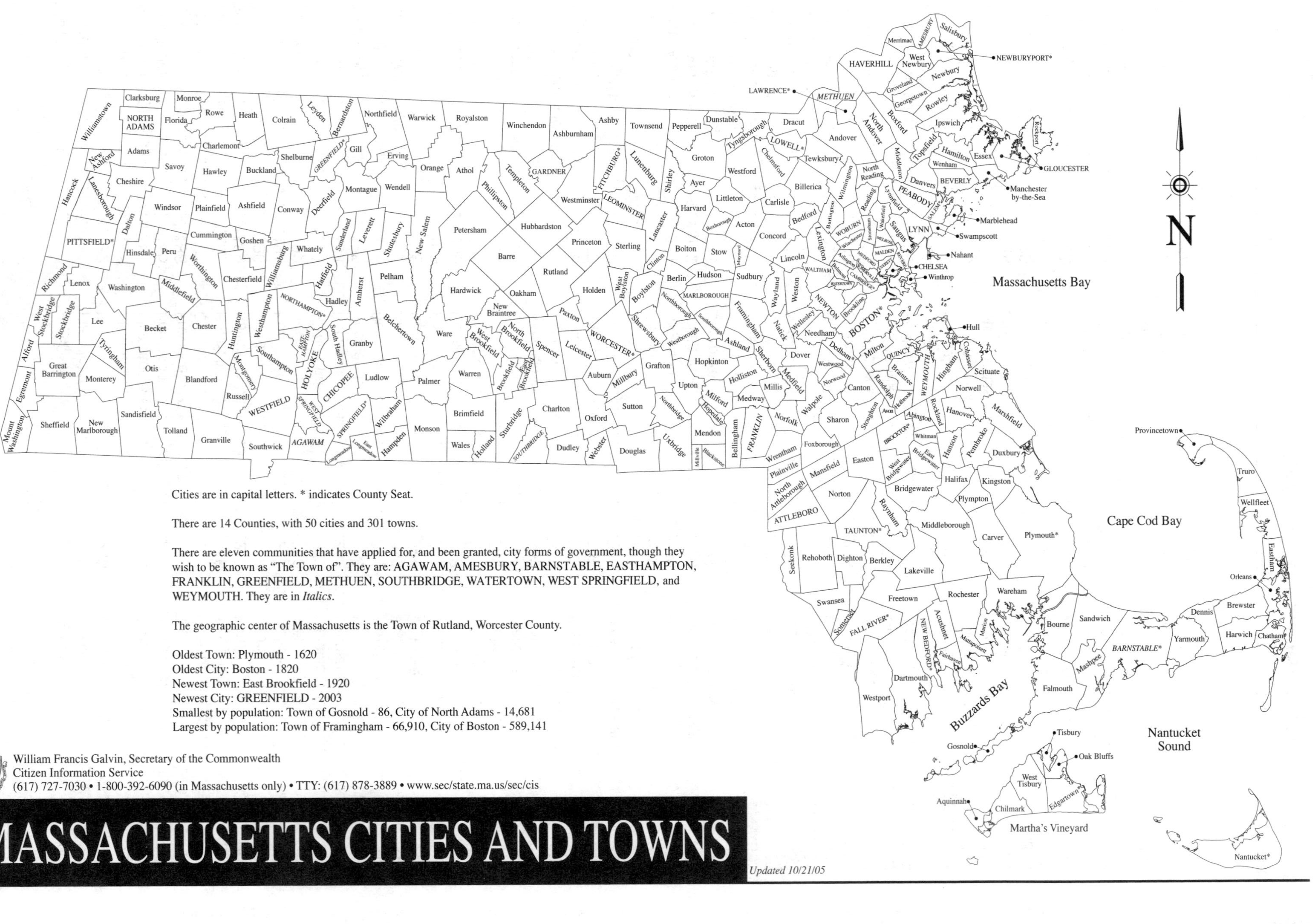

Cities are in capital letters. * indicates County Seat.

There are 14 Counties, with 50 cities and 301 towns.

There are eleven communities that have applied for, and been granted, city forms of government, though they wish to be known as "The Town of". They are: AGAWAM, AMESBURY, BARNSTABLE, EASTHAMPTON, FRANKLIN, GREENFIELD, METHUEN, SOUTHBRIDGE, WATERTOWN, WEST SPRINGFIELD, and WEYMOUTH. They are in *Italics*.

The geographic center of Massachusetts is the Town of Rutland, Worcester County.

Oldest Town: Plymouth - 1620
Oldest City: Boston - 1820
Newest Town: East Brookfield - 1920
Newest City: GREENFIELD - 2003
Smallest by population: Town of Gosnold - 86, City of North Adams - 14,681
Largest by population: Town of Framingham - 66,910, City of Boston - 589,141

William Francis Galvin, Secretary of the Commonwealth
Citizen Information Service
(617) 727-7030 • 1-800-392-6090 (in Massachusetts only) • TTY: (617) 878-3889 • www.sec/state.ma.us/sec/cis

MASSACHUSETTS CITIES AND TOWNS

Updated 10/21/05

Massachusetts Municipal Profiles

2010

Massachusetts Municipal Profiles is an annual reference book published by Information Publications since 1986. It is part of the **State & Municipal Profiles Series**, which also includes the ***Almanac of the 50 States***, as well as municpal and county profile books on California, Connecticut, Florida, and New Jersey. Drawing from a variety of established sources, ***Massachusetts Municipal Profiles*** provides concise, comprehensive one-page profiles for all 351 incorporated places (cities, towns and villages) in Massachusetts.

This book contains a one-page profile for every Massachusetts municipality, and several supplemental data appendices. Within the municipal profiles sections, these pages are arranged alphabetically by municipal name, without various prefixes such as city, town or village. Each page organizes the data into nine categories to allow rapid access to data and easy comparisons: **Demographics & Socioeconomic Characteristics**, **General Information**, **Voters & Government Information**, **Housing & Construction**, **Public Library**, **Municipal Finance**, **Taxation**, **Police & Crime**, and **Local School District**.

Introduction to the Data

The information in this volume has been obtained from a variety of sources. To aid researchers with questions about the methodology behind the data or the terms used, we have identified the source for each piece of data. These questions can best be answered by the original collectors of the data, who are cited in the **Explanation of the Categories**.

With the exception of the names of local and county officials, almost all of the information was originally collected by an agency of the state or federal government. Using such information assures a high level of accuracy, reliability, and comprehensiveness. However, not all the information collected by government agencies has been published, nor is it necessarily readily available. Many government agencies collect information largely for their own internal use, and the data remains stored in the original materials used for collection. We have selected the most appropriate items from the available information.

Information Publications conducted a series of mail, phone, email, and online surveys in March 2010 through April 2010 to obtain the current names of **government officials**, **police chiefs**, **fire chiefs**, **librarians**, and **school superintendents**. Information gathered from the surveys is used to supplement other sources to provide complete and up-to-date information.

The notation "NA" stands for "not available." Although we strive to obtain all available data, there are several reasons for data not being available. Many agencies only provide data for places of a certain size or population, so data is not available for many of the smaller municipalities. Other times, "NA" indicates that the information was never sent to the data-collecting agency, or was not available to the agency at press time. Reporting is often voluntary, and some towns have chosen not to report. Finally, sometimes the category or descriptor simply does not apply to the town (as in the case of towns without police or fire chiefs).

Readers should also note that the numbers for subcategories do not always add up to the total shown. In some cases, this is due to rounding error in the original data collection; other times, only certain subgroups of a larger category are presented.

Explanation of the Categories

Demographics & Socioeconomic Characteristics

All information in this category, with a few exceptions, comes from the 2000 US Census. The exceptions are: **2008 population estimates**, which come from the Census Bureau's annual population estimates; the **population projections** for **2010** and **2020**, released in December 2003 by the Massachusetts State Data Center, part of MISER (Massachusetts Institute for Social and Economic Research at Amherst, Massachusetts); and **2008** and **December 2009 labor** and **unemployment rate** figures, which come from the Massachusetts Department Labor and Workforce Development.

Race, as used by the Bureau of the Census, is not meant to denote any scientific or biological concept of race. The subgroups displayed here represent the self-categorization of respondents. It should also be noted that **Hispanic origin** is not a racial category. Persons may be of any race, and be of Hispanic origin as well. As a result, only the seven subgroups under race add to the total 2000 population.

Educational Attainment applies to persons who are 25 years or older. College graduates are persons with at least a four-year degree.

Income and Poverty as reported by the 2000 US Census is of the previous year, 1999.

A **household** includes all the persons occupying a housing unit. A **family household** includes a householder and one or more other persons living in the same household who are related to the householder by birth, marriage, or adoption. The number of family households always equals the number of families; however, a family household may also include non-relatives living with the family. Not all persons live in households. Some, for example, are members of the armed forces, or are inmates of institutions, or live in group

©2010 Information Publications, Inc. All rights reserved. Photocopying prohibited. For additional copies, contact the publisher at www.informationpublications.com or (877)544-INFO (4636)

quarters. As a result, the total number of persons in a city or town can be greater than the number of persons living in all households of that town. The subgroups displayed here under households were selected for potential interest and by no means represent a full breakdown of all types of households. Readers should also note that there is overlap between types of households. For example, the same household may have both members under 18 years of age and members over 65.

Total civilian labor force includes all persons 16 years old and older, who are not members of the armed forces, who are either employed or unemployed. **Self-employed workers** refers to workers in their own non-incorporated businesses.

One more US Census program warrants mentioning: the **American Community Survey (ACS)**, a monthly sample of the US population. The ACS is beginning to track much of the information previously only measured by the Decennial Census. Currently the ACS provides single-year data on a nationwide and statewide level, as well as for cities and counties with populations over 65,000. Beginning with the 2007 ACS, the coverage has expanded to include 3-year (2005-2007) averages for communities with populations greater than 20,000. (By 2010, the Bureau of the Census hopes to use the ACS to track all the information currently collected in the long form of the Decennial Census.) The 2008 ACS provides 1-year estimates for Massachusetts' 14 counties, as well as 1-year estimates for 15 of its 351 municipalities, and 3-year estimates for 67 of 351 municipalities. A selection of the ACS data is included in **Appendix C** for counties (1-year estimates for 2008), and **Appendix D** (1-year estimates for 2008) and **Appendix E** (3-year estimates for 2005-2008) for municipalities. You can find more information about the ACS at http://www.census.gov/acs/www.

One caution in using the ACS data is that, owing to the margin of error inherent in any sampling process, the ACS provides different figures for the total population from the Census Bureau's Population Division statistics. In order to avoid confusion, information obtained from the two sources should never be presented together.

General Information

The **address** and **telephone number** shown are for the central location of municipal business; i.e., the city hall or city administrative offices, and were obtained from surveys done by Information Publications. Other information, such as **website** or **email address**, was also obtained from the surveys. **Land area** and **water area** are from the 2000 US Census. **Population density** for **2008** is calculated by Information Publications based on the **2008 population estimates** from the Census Bureau and the **land area** measurement from the 2000 US Census. It should be noted that land area measurement as reported by the 2000 US Census is in square meters. It has been converted into square miles in the profiles, using a conversion factor of 2,589,988 square meters per square mile.

Voters & Government Information

Government type lists the form of local government in use. **Number of selectmen** lists the number of members on the board of selectmen or town council. **Government type** and **number of governing body members** were obtained from the surveys. **US Congressional District(s)** come from the Census Bureau.

Registered Voters was compiled from a list provided by the state Board of Elections, reflecting voter registration as of October 2008, and is the latest released by the Board.

All **local officials'** names were gathered from our surveys, or obtained from the municipality's website. Many municipal functions are presided over by advisory boards, instead of individual officials. In such cases, the chairperson of a given board is listed with the abbreviation "Chr."

Housing and Construction

Statistics for **new privately-owned housing units authorized by building permit** come from the 2006–2008 annual reports from the US Bureau of the Census' Manufacturing, Mining, and Construction Statistics division. Places that issue building permits are asked to report monthly to the Bureau. Estimates are revised periodically, so the data presented here may differ slightly from the most recent information on the Census Bureau's website.

Parcel count by property class comes from the Massachusetts Department of Revenue, accessible through the Department of Local Services' Massachusetts Municipal Data Bank.

Public Library

Address, **phone number** and **director/librarian name** are from the online Massachusetts Public Library Directory, supplemented with information from our surveys.

All library statistics come from the **2008 Data Files** provided by the Massachusetts Board of Library Commissioners. **Population** estimates used in calculating per capita figures are from 2008. **Holdings** is the total number of library materials. For towns with multiple independent libraries, the address, **librarian**, and **internet** information are given for the largest library only (in terms of population served or size of budget). **Per capita income**, **expenditures**, and **holdings** data is pooled across all of the libraries.

©2010 Information Publications, Inc. All rights reserved. Photocopying prohibited. For additional copies, contact the publisher at www.informationpublications.com or (877)544-INFO (4636)

Property Taxation and Average Single Family Tax Bill

Information in this section comes from the Massachusetts Department of Revenue, Division of Local Services, Massachusetts Municipal Data Bank.

Taxation rates are per $1,000 of **assessed valuation**. Although cities and towns are required to assess all real property at 100% of true value, this may not be the final result. Readers are cautioned that a house in town X selling for $200,000 may have a different tax bill from a house in town Y selling for $200,000 even if both towns have the same tax rates. A variety of factors affect this, most notably the date of the last revaluation. **Average single family tax bills** are calculated by the Massachusetts Department of Revenue from the **single family assessed value, single-family parcels**, and the **residential tax rate**.

Municipal Finance

Information in this section comes from the Massachusetts Department of Revenue, Division of Local Services, Massachusetts Municipal Data Bank. The Department of Revenue collects finance data on a form known as Schedule A, which is meant to account for a municipality's revenues, expenditures and other financing sources, uses, changes in fund balance and certain balance sheet account information. Data included here comes from the Schedule A **General Fund Revenues** and **General Fund Expenditures** files.

Police & Crime

The **number of officers**, **violent crimes**, and **property crimes** data comes from "Crime in the United States, 2008," a joint report by the Federal Bureau of Investigation and the state law enforcement agencies. **Violent crime** is defined as murder, forcible rape, robbery and aggravated assault. **Property crime** is defined as burglary, larceny, and motor vehicle theft.

School System

Information displayed under headings for this section comes from reports of the Massachusetts Department of Education, derived from annual statistical reports completed by all school systems and filed with the department.

The profile pages present data for only **local school districts**, which are administered by a city or town school committee, with expenses paid by that city or town. Resident pupils may attend local schools free of charge while other pupils (if any) are charged tuition (which is usually paid by their town of residence). Not every town operates a school system, and among those that do, not all operate a system which includes every grade. In most cases, the city or town is a member of a regional system.

There are five types of public school systems which can relate to an individual community's educational offering. There are **local school districts**, which are listed on the profile pages. In addition, there are two types of regional school systems: **academic regional districts**, and **vocational-technical regional districts**. Both regional system types are administered by regional school committees, and the expenses of the system are divided according to pre-arranged formula between member cities and towns. There are also **independent vocational school systems** (administered by a board of trustees with the expenses paid by the city in which they are located), and **county agricultural school systems** (administered by a board of trustees, with expenses paid by county tax assessments). Information on these types of regional school districts is located in **Appendix F**.

Some towns rely on a combination of local and regional schools to serve their needs. For example, Acton operates a PK-6 local school district. It sends resident pupils in grades 7-8 to academic regional school district Acton-Boxborough, and grades 9-12 to either Acton-Boxborough, or to the Minuteman regional vocational-technical district. Information about the local school district is found on the Acton page; the **other school districts** item lists any applicable regional systems found in **Appendix F**.

Name, address, telephone number and **superintendent** of the public school system come from the Massachusetts Department of Education, supplemented by responses from our own surveys. All other data is for the school year 2007-08 except where indicated.

Under **grade plan**, all grade ranges included in the local system are shown, from lowest to highest. Thus a grade plan K-12 includes elementary schools, middle schools, and high schools. K-6 means the local system only includes kindergarten through sixth grade. This section uses the standard abbreviations of "K" for kindergarten, and "PK" for pre-kindergarten school programs.

Total enrollment shows enrollment in all district programs. **Graduation rate** refers to the percent of a cohort (the students entering 9th grade at the same time) who graduate within 4 years. **Dropout rate** indicates the percentage of students in grades 9-12 who dropped out of school between July 1 and June 30 prior to the listed year and who did not return to school by the following October 1. Dropouts are defined as students who leave school prior to graduation for reasons other than transfer to another school.

©2010 Information Publications, Inc. All rights reserved. Photocopying prohibited. For additional copies, contact the publisher at www.informationpublications.com or (877)544-INFO (4636)

Per-pupil expenditures were computed by the Massachusetts Department of Education; numbers are for all students, including special needs students.

Average teacher salary was provided by the Massachusetts Department of Education for teachers in regular day programs. Note that this average has nothing at all to do with teachers' wage and salary agreements, or contracts with teachers' organizations.

Student/teacher ratio shows the total number of students divided by the total number of classroom teachers. **Students per computer** shows the total number of students per computer in the classroom. **Highly-qualified teachers** meet the Federal **No Child Left Behind** requirements of having at least a bachelor's degree and a Massachusetts teaching license at some level, as well as having shown mastery of the subjects they are teaching. **Licensed teachers** refers to those with a license in the particular subject they teach.

The **Massachusetts Competency Assessment System (MCAS)** is designed to meet the requirements of the Education Reform Law in 1993, and currently forms a large part of Massachusetts' compliance with the federal **No Child Left Behind** program. All public school students in Massachusetts are required to take these tests. Students in grades 3-8 and 10 take tests in English Language Arts (ELA) and mathematics (students in some grades also take tests in science and history/social science). In addition, students must pass grade 10 assessments as a condition of eligibility for a high school diploma. At the **proficient** level, students demonstrate a solid understanding of challenging subject matter and solve a wide variety of problems. In this publication, the heading **% proficient** indicates the percent of students scoring at proficient levels or higher. Another important measure is the **Composite Performance Index (CPI)**, a measure, ranging from 0-100, of the student performance in a school relative to attaining grade-level proficiency. The **CPI** measures are an important part of determining whether a district or school is making enough progress towards meeting federally-mandated standards.

The goals of education are complex, and standardized tests measure the degree of attainment of only a few of those goals. Standardized test scores should not be the only criteria used to evaluate an educational program. The reader must realize that only a small amount of the information that is required for a total evaluation is provided in district profiles. For a more in-depth look, interested readers should talk with the districts directly and do extensive research of all data available from the schools, the districts, and the Massachusetts Department of Education.

Appendices

In addition to the main profile section, Massachuetts Municipal Profiles contains several appendices of supplemental data. Information in the appendices comes from the same source as the corresponding item on the profile page unless otherwise noted below.

Appendix A is the profile for the Commonwealth of Massachusetts, taken from the 2010 edition of the ***Almanac of the 50 States*** (ISBN: 978-0-929960-62-3, paper; 978-0-929960-63-0, hardcover), also published by Information Publications. Please refer to that volume for similar information on each of the 50 states, the District of Columbia, and the United States in summary.

Appendix B lists Massachusetts' municipalities by county.

Appendix C provides brief profiles of Massachusetts' 14 counties, using data from the 2000 Decennial Census, 2008 American Community Survey, University of Massachusetts, and Massachusetts Department of Revenue.

Appendix D provides American Community Survey 1-year estimates for the 15 Massachusetts municipalities with populations over 65,000.

Appendix E provides American Community Survey 3-year averages for 2006-2008 for the 67 Massachusetts municipalities with populations over 20,000.

Appendix F provides information on the 85 regional school systems in Massachusetts, with the same information as the local school districts listed in the profile pages.

Appendix G provides comparative tables for counties and municipalities in Massachusetts.

Appendix H lists Massachusetts' State and Congressional representatives.

©2010 Information Publications, Inc. All rights reserved. Photocopying prohibited. For additional copies, contact the publisher at www.informationpublications.com or (877)544-INFO (4636)

Abbreviations

-	Zero or not applicable / not available
Actg	Acting
Admin	Administrator
Assn	Association
Avg	Average
Bd of Sel	Board of Selectmen
CAFO	Chief Administrative & Financial Officer
CFO	Chief Financial Officer
Chr	Chairperson
Comm	Community
(County)	Services provided by County
CPI	Composite Performance Index
Dep	Deputy
Dev	Development
Dir	Director
est	estimates
FCCIP	Franklin County Cooperative Inspection Program
FRCOG	Franklin County Regional Council of Governments
FY	Fiscal year ended in June 30
H'holds	Households
Hi-Lo ranking	Ranking from highest to lowest
Int	Interim
Lib	Library
MCAS	Massachusetts Competency Assessment System
Mgr	Manager
MISER	Massachusetts Institute for Social and Economic Research
NA	Not Applicable or Not Available
Prof	Proficient
Svcs	Services
Superint	Superintendent
Treas	Treasurer

Disclaimer

Massachusetts Municipal Profiles contains thousands of pieces of information. Reasonable precautions, along with a good deal of care, were taken in its preparation. Despite all efforts, it is possible that some of the information contained in this book may not be accurate. Some errors may be due to errors in the original source materials, others may have been made by the compilers of this volume. An incorrect spelling may occur, a figure may be inverted and similar mistakes may exist. The compilers, editors, typist, printers, and others are all human, and in a work of this magnitude the possibility of error can never be fully eliminated.

If any piece of information is believed to be inaccurate, please contact the publisher. We are eager to eliminate any errors from coming editions and we will be pleased to check a piece of information.

The publisher is also aware that some users may apply the data in this book in various remunerative projects. Although we have taken reasonable and responsible measures to insure total accuracy, we cannot take responsibility for liability or losses suffered by users of the data. The information provided here is believed to be correct at the time of publication. No other guarantees are made or implied.

The publisher assumes no liability for losses incurred by users, and warrants only that diligence and due care were used in the production of this volume.

A Final Word

In order to continue to meet its goals, ***Massachusetts Municipal Profiles*** is revised and updated on an annual basis. The best suggestions for improvement in a ready-reference source such as this come from the regular users of the work. Therefore, we actively solicit your comments and ideas. If you know how this book could become more useful to you, please contact us.

The Editors
Massachusetts Municipal Profiles
Information Publications, Inc.
2995 Woodside Road, Suite 400-182
Woodside, CA 94062

www.informationpublications.com
info@informationpublications.com

Toll Free Phone: 877-544-4636
Toll Free Fax: 877-544-4635

Publisher: Eric Weiner
Editors: Beth Ann Allen and Jeff Brenion

©2010 Information Publications, Inc. All rights reserved. Photocopying prohibited. For additional copies, contact the publisher at www.informationpublications.com or (877)544-INFO (4636)

Massachusetts Municipal Profiles

2010

Demographics & Socio-Economic Characteristics

Population

1990	13,817
2000	14,605
Male	7,131
Female	7,474
2008	16,689
2010 (projected)††	14,869
2020 (projected)††	14,919

Race & Hispanic Origin, 2000

Race	
White	14,237
Black/African American	111
American Indian/Alaska Native	17
Asian	71
Hawaiian Native/Pacific Islander	1
Other Race	47
Two or more races	121
Hispanic origin	103

Age & Nativity, 2000

Under 5 years	1,012
18 years and over	10,867
21 years and over	10,389
65 years and over	1,779
85 years and over	250
Median Age	36.7
Native-born	14,219
Foreign-born	386

Age, 2020 (projected)††

Under 5 years	873
5 to 19 years	2,677
20 to 39 years	3,645
40 to 64 years	4,904
65 years and over	2,820

Educational Attainment, 2000

Population 25 years and over	9,864
High School graduates or higher	89.8%
Bachelor's degree or higher	22.0%
Graduate degree	6.0%

Income & Poverty, 1999

Per capita income,	$23,380
Median household income	$57,100
Median family income	$68,826
Persons in poverty	519
H'holds receiving public assistance	63
H'holds receiving social security	1,313

Households, 2000

Total households	5,263
With persons under 18	1,972
With persons over 65	1,229
Family households	3,746
Single person households	1,212
Persons per household	2.7
Persons per family	3.3

Labor & Employment, 2000

Civilian labor force	8,132
Unemployment rate	2.4%
Civilian labor force, 2008†	9,307
Unemployment rate†	6.7%
Civilian labor force, 12/09†	9,348
Unemployment rate†	9.8%
Employed persons 16 years and over, by occupation:	
Managers & professionals	2,833
Service occupations	1,076
Sales & office occupations	2,293
Farming, fishing & forestry	10
Construction & maintenance	751
Production & transportation	977
Self-employed persons	445

Most demographic data is from the 2000 Decennial Census
† Massachusetts Department of Revenue
†† University of Massachusetts, MISER

General Information

Town of Abington
500 Gliniewicz Way
Abington, MA 02351
781-982-2100

Elevation	121 ft.
Land area (square miles)	9.9
Water area (square miles)	0.2
Population density, 2008 (est)	1,685.8
Year incorporated	1712
Website	abingtonmass.com

Voters & Government Information

Government type	Open Town Meeting
Number of Selectmen	5
US Congressional District(s)	10

Registered Voters, October 2008

Total	10,346
Democrats	3,097
Republicans	1,149
Unaffiliated/other	6,026

Local Officials, 2010

Chair, Bd. of Sel.	Thomas Corbett
Manager	Phillip L. Warren Jr
Town Clerk	Linda C. Adams
Finance Director	Leo E. Provost Jr
Tax Collector	Leo E. Provost Jr
Tax Assessor	Paul Zakrzewski
Attorney	Kopelman & Paige
Public Works	NA
Building	NA
Comm Dev/Planning	Wayne Smith
Police Chief	David Majenski
Emerg/Fire Chief	Arthur Pelland

Housing & Construction

New Privately Owned Housing Units Authorized by Building Permit

	Single Family	Total Bldgs	Total Units
2006	29	37	95
2007	27	39	151
2008	18	18	18

Parcel Count by Property Class, 2010

Total	5,442
Single family	3,687
Multiple units	279
Apartments	75
Condos	690
Vacant land	320
Open space	0
Commercial	204
Industrial	68
Misc. residential	25
Other use	94

Public Library

Abington Public Library
600 Gliniewicz Way
Abington, MA 02351
(781)982-2139

Director .... Deborah Grimmett (Actg)

Library Statistics, FY 2008

Population served, 2007	16,365
Registered users	6,977
Circulation	105,571
Reference transactons	9,739
Total program attendance	70,921
per capita:	
Holdings	4.14
Operating income	$28.56
Internet Access	
Internet computers available	14
Weekly users	287

Municipal Finance

Debt at year end 2008	$18,325,009
Moody's rating, July 2009	A3

Revenues, 2008

Total	$38,266,360
From all taxes	23,775,954
Federal aid	222,777
State aid	10,583,046
From other governments	0
Charges for services	224,133
Licenses, permits & fees	503,165
Fines & forfeits	68,067
Interfund transfers	1,700,526
Misc/other/special assessments	594,346

Expenditures, 2008

Total	$38,219,670
General government	1,302,463
Public safety	4,773,011
Other/fixed costs	6,089,027
Human services	304,628
Culture & recreation	687,922
Debt Service	3,087,708
Education	19,221,481
Public works	2,368,177
Intergovernmental	385,253

Taxation, 2010

Property type	Valuation	Rate
Total	$1,841,792,600	-
Residential	1,576,227,669	13.86
Open space	0	0.00
Commercial	206,441,931	13.86
Industrial	21,988,800	13.86
Personal	37,134,200	13.86

Average Single Family Tax Bill, 2010

Avg. assessed home value	$312,264
Avg. single fam. tax bill	$4,328
Hi-Lo ranking	112/301

Police & Crime, 2008

Number of police officers	28
Violent crimes	56
Property crimes	360

Local School District

(school data 2007-08, except as noted)

Abington
1 Ralph Hamlin Lane
Abington, MA 02351
781-982-2150

Superintendent	Peter Schafer
Grade plan	PK-12
Total enrollment '09-10	2,189
Grade 12 enrollment, '09-10	145
Graduation rate	88.4%
Dropout rate	5.4%
Per-pupil expenditure	$9,910
Avg teacher salary	$59,807
Student/teacher ratio '08-09	15.8 to 1
Highly-qualified teachers, '08-09	92.8%
Teachers licensed in assigned subject	96.1%
Students per computer	4.7

Massachusetts Competency Assessment System (MCAS), 2009 results

	English		Math	
	% Prof	CPI	% Prof	CPI
Gr 4	49%	79	37%	74.9
Gr 6	71%	89.7	59%	79.5
Gr 8	87%	95.8	44%	72
Gr 10	80%	93	80%	92.6

Other School Districts (see Appendix D for data)
South Shore Vocational Tech

©2010 Information Publications, Inc. All rights reserved. Photocopying prohibited. For additional copies, contact the publisher at www.informationpublications.com or (877)544-INFO (4636)

Demographics & Socio-Economic Characteristics

Population

1990	17,872
2000	20,331
Male	10,020
Female	10,311
2008	20,797
2010 (projected)††	19,871
2020 (projected)††	18,435

Race & Hispanic Origin, 2000

Race	
White	17,982
Black/African American	142
American Indian/Alaska Native	15
Asian	1,758
Hawaiian Native/Pacific Islander	5
Other Race	130
Two or more races	299
Hispanic origin	360

Age & Nativity, 2000

Under 5 years	1,507
18 years and over	14,339
21 years and over	13,970
65 years and over	1,701
85 years and over	189
Median Age	37.9
Native-born	17,416
Foreign-born	2,915

Age, 2020 (projected)††

Under 5 years	982
5 to 19 years	3,433
20 to 39 years	4,635
40 to 64 years	6,281
65 years and over	3,104

Educational Attainment, 2000

Population 25 years and over	13,500
High School graduates or higher	97.8%
Bachelor's degree or higher	69.3%
Graduate degree	33.9%

Income & Poverty, 1999

Per capita income,	$41,901
Median household income	$91,624
Median family income	$108,189
Persons in poverty	590
H'holds receiving public assistance	58
H'holds receiving social security	1,203

Households, 2000

Total households	7,495
With persons under 18	3,288
With persons over 65	1,162
Family households	5,540
Single person households	1,601
Persons per household	2.7
Persons per family	3.2

Labor & Employment, 2000

Civilian labor force	11,276
Unemployment rate	2.0%
Civilian labor force, 2008†	11,650
Unemployment rate†	4.0%
Civilian labor force, 12/09†	11,623
Unemployment rate†	5.8%
Employed persons 16 years and over, by occupation:	
Managers & professionals	7,219
Service occupations	752
Sales & office occupations	2,320
Farming, fishing & forestry	27
Construction & maintenance	321
Production & transportation	415
Self-employed persons	907

Most demographic data is from the 2000 Decennial Census
† Massachusetts Department of Revenue
†† University of Massachusetts, MISER

General Information

Town of Acton
472 Main St
Acton, MA 01720
978-264-9615

Elevation	268 ft.
Land area (square miles)	20.0
Water area (square miles)	0.3
Population density, 2008 (est)	1,039.9
Year incorporated	1735
Website	www.acton-ma.gov

Voters & Government Information

Government type	Open Town Meeting
Number of Selectmen	5
US Congressional District(s)	5

Registered Voters, October 2008

Total	14,016
Democrats	3,886
Republicans	1,693
Unaffiliated/other	8,386

Local Officials, 2010

Chair, Bd. of Sel.	Lauren S. Rosenzweig
Manager	Steven L. Ledoux
Clerk	Eva K. Taylor
Finance Director	Stephen Barrett
Tax Collector	John Murray III
Tax Assessor	Brian McMullen
Attorney	Stephen Anderson
Public Works	Bruce Stamski
Building	Frank Ramsbottom
Planning	Roland Bartl
Police Chief	Francis Widmayer
Emerg/Fire Chief	Robert Craig

Housing & Construction

New Privately Owned Housing Units Authorized by Building Permit

	Single Family	Total Bldgs	Total Units
2006	71	71	71
2007	70	70	70
2008	49	49	49

Parcel Count by Property Class, 2010

Total	8,362
Single family	4,877
Multiple units	99
Apartments	46
Condos	2,239
Vacant land	561
Open space	0
Commercial	330
Industrial	112
Misc. residential	15
Other use	83

Public Library

Acton Memorial Library
486 Main St.
Acton, MA 01720
(978)264-9641

Library Director	Marcia Rich

Library Statistics, FY 2008

Population served, 2007	20,753
Registered users	17,115
Circulation	594,647
Reference transactons	18,701
Total program attendance	240,397
per capita:	
Holdings	7.13
Operating income	$46.48
Internet Access	
Internet computers available	12
Weekly users	424

Municipal Finance

Debt at year end 2008	$50,563,845
Moody's rating, July 2009	Aa1

Revenues, 2008

Total	$73,791,936
From all taxes	62,055,889
Federal aid	0
State aid	7,268,889
From other governments	160,382
Charges for services	89,970
Licenses, permits & fees	666,602
Fines & forfeits	0
Interfund transfers	53,000
Misc/other/special assessments	1,748,602

Expenditures, 2008

Total	$69,933,105
General government	4,334,352
Public safety	6,211,685
Other/fixed costs	5,152,458
Human services	321,017
Culture & recreation	1,545,096
Debt Service	3,142,783
Education	46,758,705
Public works	2,120,813
Intergovernmental	211,478

Taxation, 2010

Property type	Valuation	Rate
Total	$3,741,421,414	-
Residential	3,257,545,318	17.12
Open space	0	0.00
Commercial	321,119,694	17.12
Industrial	97,872,285	17.12
Personal	64,884,117	17.12

Average Single Family Tax Bill, 2010

Avg. assessed home value	$512,103
Avg. single fam. tax bill	$8,767
Hi-Lo ranking	15/301

Police & Crime, 2008

Number of police officers	33
Violent crimes	21
Property crimes	273

Local School District

(school data 2007-08, except as noted)

Acton
16 Charter Road
Acton, MA 01720
978-264-4700

Superintendent	Stephen Mills
Grade plan	PK-6
Total enrollment '09-10	2,614
Grade 12 enrollment, '09-10	0
Graduation rate	NA
Dropout rate	NA
Per-pupil expenditure	$10,283
Avg teacher salary	$68,880
Student/teacher ratio '08-09	18.7 to 1
Highly-qualified teachers, '08-09	100.0%
Teachers licensed in assigned subject	100.0%
Students per computer	NA

Massachusetts Competency Assessment System (MCAS), 2009 results

	English		Math	
	% Prof	CPI	% Prof	CPI
Gr 4	79%	91.9	71%	90
Gr 6	90%	96.8	86%	94.6
Gr 8	NA	NA	NA	NA
Gr 10	NA	NA	NA	NA

Other School Districts (see Appendix D for data)

Acton-Boxborough Regional, Minuteman Vocational Tech

©2010 Information Publications, Inc. All rights reserved. Photocopying prohibited. For additional copies, contact the publisher at www.informationpublications.com or (877)544-INFO (4636)

See Introduction for an explanation of all data sources.

Demographics & Socio-Economic Characteristics

Population

1990	9,554
2000	10,161
Male	4,975
Female	5,186
2008	10,368
2010 (projected)††	10,462
2020 (projected)††	10,650

Race & Hispanic Origin, 2000

Race	
White	9,876
Black/African American	43
American Indian/Alaska Native	17
Asian	17
Hawaiian Native/Pacific Islander	2
Other Race	79
Two or more races	127
Hispanic origin	80

Age & Nativity, 2000

Under 5 years	511
18 years and over	7,787
21 years and over	7,417
65 years and over	1,514
85 years and over	136
Median Age	39.7
Native-born	9,121
Foreign-born	1,040

Age, 2020 (projected)††

Under 5 years	488
5 to 19 years	1,769
20 to 39 years	2,440
40 to 64 years	3,937
65 years and over	2,016

Educational Attainment, 2000

Population 25 years and over	7,090
High School graduates or higher	72.6%
Bachelor's degree or higher	13.0%
Graduate degree	2.8%

Income & Poverty, 1999

Per capita income,	$21,753
Median household income	$51,500
Median family income	$58,722
Persons in poverty	386
H'holds receiving public assistance	105
H'holds receiving social security	1,251

Households, 2000

Total households	3,793
With persons under 18	1,350
With persons over 65	1,094
Family households	2,837
Single person households	802
Persons per household	2.7
Persons per family	3.1

Labor & Employment, 2000

Civilian labor force	5,430
Unemployment rate	2.9%
Civilian labor force, 2008†	5,852
Unemployment rate†	8.1%
Civilian labor force, 12/09†	5,886
Unemployment rate†	11.0%
Employed persons 16 years and over, by occupation:	
Managers & professionals	1,252
Service occupations	887
Sales & office occupations	1,342
Farming, fishing & forestry	14
Construction & maintenance	688
Production & transportation	1,092
Self-employed persons	297

Most demographic data is from the 2000 Decennial Census
† Massachusetts Department of Revenue
†† University of Massachusetts, MISER

General Information

Town of Acushnet
122 Main St
Acushnet, MA 02743
508-998-0200

Elevation	46 ft.
Land area (square miles)	18.5
Water area (square miles)	0.5
Population density, 2008 (est)	560.4
Year incorporated	1860
Website	www.acushnet.ma.us

Voters & Government Information

Government type	Open Town Meeting
Number of Selectmen	3
US Congressional District(s)	4

Registered Voters, October 2008

Total	7,898
Democrats	2,991
Republicans	557
Unaffiliated/other	4,305

Local Officials, 2010

Chair, Bd. of Sel.	David E. Wojnar
Manager/Town Admin.	Alan Coutinho
Clerk	Pamela A. Labonte
Finance Director	Cathy Doane
Tax Collector	Kristie Costa
Tax Assessor	Kelly Koska (Asst)
Attorney	Kopelman & Paige
Public Works	Paul Sylvia
Building	James Marot
Planning	Henry Young
Police Chief	Michael G. Alves
Emerg/Fire Chief	Kevin Gallagher

Housing & Construction

New Privately Owned Housing Units Authorized by Building Permit

	Single Family	Total Bldgs	Total Units
2006	14	14	14
2007	9	9	9
2008	10	10	10

Parcel Count by Property Class, 2010

Total	4,454
Single family	3,204
Multiple units	165
Apartments	14
Condos	0
Vacant land	670
Open space	0
Commercial	61
Industrial	44
Misc. residential	143
Other use	153

Public Library

Russell Memorial Library
88 Main St.
Acushnet, MA 02743
(508)998-0270

Director	Jayme Viveiros

Library Statistics, FY 2008

Population served, 2007	10,443
Registered users	3,762
Circulation	58,075
Reference transactons	0
Total program attendance	0
per capita:	
Holdings	2.73
Operating income	$20.30
Internet Access	
Internet computers available	3
Weekly users	0

Municipal Finance

Debt at year end 2008	$17,630,698
Moody's rating, July 2009	A2

Revenues, 2008

Total	$21,772,047
From all taxes	12,813,693
Federal aid	44,011
State aid	8,334,842
From other governments	8,695
Charges for services	89,661
Licenses, permits & fees	108,529
Fines & forfeits	5,620
Interfund transfers	250,000
Misc/other/special assessments	58,498

Expenditures, 2008

Total	$21,740,540
General government	1,171,756
Public safety	2,417,340
Other/fixed costs	2,247,152
Human services	301,152
Culture & recreation	270,933
Debt Service	279,157
Education	13,612,419
Public works	1,278,314
Intergovernmental	162,317

Taxation, 2010

Property type	Valuation	Rate
Total	$1,191,724,554	-
Residential	1,103,317,207	10.47
Open space	0	0.00
Commercial	33,640,063	12.81
Industrial	28,612,200	12.81
Personal	26,155,084	12.81

Average Single Family Tax Bill, 2010

Avg. assessed home value	$300,340
Avg. single fam. tax bill	$3,145
Hi-Lo ranking	219/301

Police & Crime, 2008

Number of police officers	17
Violent crimes	24
Property crimes	173

Local School District

(school data 2007-08, except as noted)

Acushnet
708 Middle Road, Suite 1
Acushnet, MA 02743
508-998-0260

Superintendent	Stephen Donovan
Grade plan	PK-8
Total enrollment '09-10	996
Grade 12 enrollment, '09-10	0
Graduation rate	NA
Dropout rate	NA
Per-pupil expenditure	$9,817
Avg teacher salary	$49,020
Student/teacher ratio '08-09	13.9 to 1
Highly-qualified teachers, '08-09	100.0%
Teachers licensed in assigned subject	100.0%
Students per computer	2.3

Massachusetts Competency Assessment System (MCAS), 2009 results

	English		Math	
	% Prof	CPI	% Prof	CPI
Gr 4	63%	82.7	45%	80.4
Gr 6	68%	87.3	56%	80.6
Gr 8	87%	95.9	54%	75.9
Gr 10	NA	NA	NA	NA

Other School Districts (see Appendix D for data)

Sends grades 9-12 to Fairhaven, New Bedford and Old Colony Vocational Tech, Bristol County Agricultural

©2010 Information Publications, Inc. All rights reserved. Photocopying prohibited. For additional copies, contact the publisher at www.informationpublications.com or (877)544-INFO (4636)

See Introduction for an explanation of all data sources.

Demographics & Socio-Economic Characteristics

Population

1990	9,445
2000	8,809
Male	4,154
Female	4,655
2008	8,295
2010 (projected)††	7,902
2020 (projected)††	7,182

Race & Hispanic Origin, 2000

Race	
White	8,635
Black/African American	32
American Indian/Alaska Native	7
Asian	21
Hawaiian Native/Pacific Islander	4
Other Race	24
Two or more races	86
Hispanic origin	72

Age & Nativity, 2000

Under 5 years	460
18 years and over	6,832
21 years and over	6,548
65 years and over	1,800
85 years and over	230
Median Age	41.3
Native-born	8,703
Foreign-born	106

Age, 2020 (projected)††

Under 5 years	347
5 to 19 years	1,053
20 to 39 years	1,672
40 to 64 years	2,456
65 years and over	1,654

Educational Attainment, 2000

Population 25 years and over	6,263
High School graduates or higher	77.4%
Bachelor's degree or higher	15.6%
Graduate degree	5.7%

Income & Poverty, 1999

Per capita income,	$18,572
Median household income	$32,161
Median family income	$40,559
Persons in poverty	904
H'holds receiving public assistance	104
H'holds receiving social security	1,453

Households, 2000

Total households	3,992
With persons under 18	1,147
With persons over 65	1,358
Family households	2,433
Single person households	1,390
Persons per household	2.2
Persons per family	2.8

Labor & Employment, 2000

Civilian labor force	4,486
Unemployment rate	7.9%
Civilian labor force, 2008†	4,395
Unemployment rate†	9.0%
Civilian labor force, 12/09†	4,434
Unemployment rate†	11.6%
Employed persons 16 years and over, by occupation:	
Managers & professionals	1,154
Service occupations	724
Sales & office occupations	1,067
Farming, fishing & forestry	13
Construction & maintenance	401
Production & transportation	771
Self-employed persons	264

Most demographic data is from the 2000 Decennial Census
† Massachusetts Department of Revenue
†† University of Massachusetts, MISER

General Information

Town of Adams
8 Park St
Adams, MA 01220
413-743-8300

Elevation	799 ft.
Land area (square miles)	22.9
Water area (square miles)	0.0
Population density, 2008 (est)	362.2
Year incorporated	1778
Email	phutchin@town.adams.ma.us

Voters & Government Information

Government type	Rep. Town Meeting
Number of Selectmen	5
US Congressional District(s)	1

Registered Voters, October 2008

Total	6,076
Democrats	2,207
Republicans	482
Unaffiliated/other	3,337

Local Officials, 2010

Chair, Bd. of Sel.	Donald Sommer
Manager/Admin	Jonathan Butler
Town Clerk	Paul Hutchinson
Finance Director	Holly Denault
Tax Collector	NA
Tax Assessor	Donna Aitken MacDonald
Attorney	Edmund R. St. John III
Public Works	Thomas Satico
Building	NA
Comm Dev/Planning	Donna Cesan
Police Chief	Donald Poirot
Emerg/Fire Chief	Stephen Brown

Housing & Construction

New Privately Owned Housing Units Authorized by Building Permit

	Single Family	Total Bldgs	Total Units
2006	9	9	9
2007	6	6	6
2008	3	3	3

Parcel Count by Property Class, 2010

Total	3,476
Single family	2,148
Multiple units	458
Apartments	109
Condos	20
Vacant land	370
Open space	0
Commercial	144
Industrial	71
Misc. residential	48
Other use	108

Public Library

Adams Free Library
92 Park Street
Adams, MA 01220
(413)743-8345

Director	Deborah Bruneau

Library Statistics, FY 2008

Population served, 2007	8,214
Registered users	8,233
Circulation	70,089
Reference transactons	1,642
Total program attendance	0
per capita:	
Holdings	5.36
Operating income	$36.56
Internet Access	
Internet computers available	2
Weekly users	33

Municipal Finance

Debt at year end 2008	$5,704,777
Moody's rating, July 2009	NA

Revenues, 2008

Total	$13,154,439
From all taxes	8,539,713
Federal aid	0
State aid	2,659,700
From other governments	30,077
Charges for services	143,468
Licenses, permits & fees	79,419
Fines & forfeits	31,108
Interfund transfers	761,452
Misc/other/special assessments	454,751

Expenditures, 2008

Total	$12,037,113
General government	1,221,184
Public safety	1,471,188
Other/fixed costs	1,835,680
Human services	305,291
Culture & recreation	617,777
Debt Service	805,677
Education	3,873,019
Public works	1,858,844
Intergovernmental	38,453

Taxation, 2010

Property type	Valuation	Rate
Total	$494,010,962	-
Residential	410,355,404	15.33
Open space	0	0.00
Commercial	34,389,186	18.19
Industrial	27,448,200	18.19
Personal	21,818,172	18.19

Average Single Family Tax Bill, 2010

Avg. assessed home value	$141,746
Avg. single fam. tax bill	$2,173
Hi-Lo ranking	290/301

Police & Crime, 2008

Number of police officers	16
Violent crimes	39
Property crimes	251

Local School District

(school data 2007-08, except as noted)

Adams (non-op)
125 Savoy Road
Cheshire, MA 01225
413-743-2939

Superintendent	Alfred Skrocki

Non-operating district.
Resident students are sent to the Other School Districts listed below.

Grade plan	NA
Total enrollment '09-10	NA
Grade 12 enrollment, '09-10	NA
Graduation rate	NA
Dropout rate	NA
Per-pupil expenditure	NA
Avg teacher salary	NA
Student/teacher ratio '08-09	NA
Highly-qualified teachers, '08-09	NA
Teachers licensed in assigned subject	NA
Students per computer	NA

Other School Districts (see Appendix D for data)
Adams-Cheshire Regional, Northern Berkshire Vocational Tech

©2010 Information Publications, Inc. All rights reserved. Photocopying prohibited. For additional copies, contact the publisher at www.informationpublications.com or (877)544-INFO (4636)

See Introduction for an explanation of all data sources.

Demographics & Socio-Economic Characteristics*

Population

1990	27,323
2000	28,144
Male	13,369
Female	14,775
2008	28,091
2010 (projected)††	27,641
2020 (projected)††	27,046

Race & Hispanic Origin, 2000

Race	
White	27,217
Black/African American	257
American Indian/Alaska Native	48
Asian	275
Hawaiian Native/Pacific Islander	3
Other Race	120
Two or more races	224
Hispanic origin	514

Age & Nativity, 2000

Under 5 years	1,560
18 years and over	21,931
21 years and over	21,056
65 years and over	4,703
85 years and over	813
Median Age	40.3
Native-born	26,642
Foreign-born	1,502

Age, 2020 (projected)††

Under 5 years	1,294
5 to 19 years	3,999
20 to 39 years	6,303
40 to 64 years	8,839
65 years and over	6,611

Educational Attainment, 2000

Population 25 years and over	20,158
High School graduates or higher	87.5%
Bachelor's degree or higher	21.4%
Graduate degree	6.4%

Income & Poverty, 1999

Per capita income,	$22,562
Median household income	$49,390
Median family income	$59,088
Persons in poverty	1,537
H'holds receiving public assistance	170
H'holds receiving social security	3,253

Households, 2000

Total households	11,260
With persons under 18	3,481
With persons over 65	3,043
Family households	7,462
Single person households	3,157
Persons per household	2.4
Persons per family	3.0

Labor & Employment, 2000

Civilian labor force	15,511
Unemployment rate	4.1%
Civilian labor force, 2008†	15,821
Unemployment rate†	6.2%
Civilian labor force, 12/09†	15,933
Unemployment rate†	8.7%
Employed persons 16 years and over, by occupation:	
Managers & professionals	4,939
Service occupations	2,102
Sales & office occupations	4,531
Farming, fishing & forestry	22
Construction & maintenance	1,184
Production & transportation	2,093
Self-employed persons	919

Most demographic data is from the 2000 Decennial Census
* see Appendix E for American Community Survey data
† Massachusetts Department of Revenue
†† University of Massachusetts, MISER

General Information

City of Agawam
36 Main St
Agawam, MA 01001
413-786-0400

Elevation	88 ft.
Land area (square miles)	23.2
Water area (square miles)	1.0
Population density, 2008 (est)	1,210.8
Year incorporated	1855
Website	www.agawam.ma.us

Voters & Government Information

Government type	Mayor-Council
Number of Councilpersons	11
US Congressional District(s)	2

Registered Voters, October 2008

Total	20,269
Democrats	6,259
Republicans	3,161
Unaffiliated/other	10,697

Local Officials, 2010

Mayor	Richard A. Cohen
Council President	Donald Rheault
Clerk	Richard M. Theroux
Finance Director	Laurel Placzek
Tax Collector	Laurel Placzek
Tax Assessor	Linda Morneau
Attorney	Christopher Johnson
Public Works	Anthony Sylvia
Building	D. Gachas
Planning	Debbie Dachos
Police Chief	Vincent Gioscia
Emerg/Fire Chief	Steven Martin

Housing & Construction

New Privately Owned Housing Units Authorized by Building Permit

	Single Family	Total Bldgs	Total Units
2006	58	59	60
2007	33	34	35
2008	20	20	20

Parcel Count by Property Class, 2010

Total	11,196
Single family	7,640
Multiple units	431
Apartments	61
Condos	1,597
Vacant land	768
Open space	0
Commercial	317
Industrial	160
Misc. residential	15
Other use	207

Public Library

Agawam Public Library
750 Cooper Street
Agawam, MA 01001
(413)789-1550

Director	Judith Clini

Library Statistics, FY 2008

Population served, 2007	28,333
Registered users	19,566
Circulation	364,023
Reference transactons	14,704
Total program attendance	297,440
per capita:	
Holdings	5.63
Operating income	$38.68
Internet Access	
Internet computers available	25
Weekly users	609

Municipal Finance

Debt at year end 2008	$26,301,607
Moody's rating, July 2009	Aa3

Revenues, 2008

Total	$69,518,627
From all taxes	45,548,314
Federal aid	0
State aid	20,665,537
From other governments	6,785
Charges for services	604,559
Licenses, permits & fees	230,025
Fines & forfeits	8,715
Interfund transfers	45,000
Misc/other/special assessments	1,204,846

Expenditures, 2008

Total	$66,396,927
General government	5,867,330
Public safety	7,232,031
Other/fixed costs	10,313,924
Human services	1,003,982
Culture & recreation	1,078,549
Debt Service	2,821,958
Education	32,480,781
Public works	4,444,999
Intergovernmental	453,732

Taxation, 2010

Property type	Valuation	Rate
Total	$2,796,296,393	-
Residential	2,224,622,388	12.94
Open space	0	0.00
Commercial	237,753,135	27.07
Industrial	230,388,360	27.07
Personal	103,532,510	27.07

Average Single Family Tax Bill, 2010

Avg. assessed home value	$226,851
Avg. single fam. tax bill	$2,935
Hi-Lo ranking	243/301

Police & Crime, 2008

Number of police officers	48
Violent crimes	43
Property crimes	325

Local School District

(school data 2007-08, except as noted)

Agawam
1305 Springfield St, Suite 1
Feeding Hills, MA 01030
413-821-0548

Superintendent	Mary Czajkowski
Grade plan	PK-12
Total enrollment '09-10	4,273
Grade 12 enrollment, '09-10	304
Graduation rate	83.1%
Dropout rate	8.6%
Per-pupil expenditure	$11,159
Avg teacher salary	$59,323
Student/teacher ratio '08-09	13.4 to 1
Highly-qualified teachers, '08-09	99.9%
Teachers licensed in assigned subject	98.8%
Students per computer	4.6

Massachusetts Competency Assessment System (MCAS), 2009 results

	English		Math	
	% Prof	CPI	% Prof	CPI
Gr 4	55%	83.1	55%	84.5
Gr 6	68%	85.5	59%	79.1
Gr 8	85%	94.1	58%	81.3
Gr 10	83%	93.7	77%	90.6

Other School Districts (see Appendix D for data)
None

©2010 Information Publications, Inc. All rights reserved. Photocopying prohibited. For additional copies, contact the publisher at www.informationpublications.com or (877)544-INFO (4636)

©2010 Information Publications, Inc. All rights reserved. Photocopying prohibited. For additional copies, contact the publisher at www.informationpublications.com or (877)544-INFO (4636)

Demographics & Socio-Economic Characteristics

Population

1990	418
2000	399
Male	188
Female	211
2008	392
2010 (projected)††	374
2020 (projected)††	357

Race & Hispanic Origin, 2000

Race	
White	395
Black/African American	3
American Indian/Alaska Native	0
Asian	0
Hawaiian Native/Pacific Islander	0
Other Race	0
Two or more races	1
Hispanic origin	0

Age & Nativity, 2000

Under 5 years	12
18 years and over	316
21 years and over	309
65 years and over	64
85 years and over	7
Median Age	49.6
Native-born	375
Foreign-born	18

Age, 2020 (projected)††

Under 5 years	13
5 to 19 years	34
20 to 39 years	41
40 to 64 years	134
65 years and over	135

Educational Attainment, 2000

Population 25 years and over	303
High School graduates or higher	96.7%
Bachelor's degree or higher	51.5%
Graduate degree	28.7%

Income & Poverty, 1999

Per capita income,	$40,412
Median household income	$49,632
Median family income	$62,344
Persons in poverty	16
H'holds receiving public assistance	0
H'holds receiving social security	52

Households, 2000

Total households	171
With persons under 18	40
With persons over 65	47
Family households	114
Single person households	51
Persons per household	2.3
Persons per family	2.9

Labor & Employment, 2000

Civilian labor force	205
Unemployment rate	2.9%
Civilian labor force, 2008†	223
Unemployment rate†	3.1%
Civilian labor force, 12/09†	223
Unemployment rate†	4.5%
Employed persons 16 years and over, by occupation:	
Managers & professionals	91
Service occupations	22
Sales & office occupations	48
Farming, fishing & forestry	0
Construction & maintenance	18
Production & transportation	20
Self-employed persons	42

Most demographic data is from the 2000 Decennial Census
† Massachusetts Department of Revenue
†† University of Massachusetts, MISER

General Information

Town of Alford
5 Alford Ctr Rd
Alford, MA 01230
413-528-4536

Elevation	NA
Land area (square miles)	11.6
Water area (square miles)	0.0
Population density, 2008 (est)	33.8
Year incorporated	1775
Website	www.townofalford.org

Voters & Government Information

Government type	Open Town Meeting
Number of Selectmen	3
US Congressional District(s)	1

Registered Voters, October 2008

Total	400
Democrats	149
Republicans	43
Unaffiliated/other	206

Local Officials, 2010

Chair, Bd. of Sel.	Charles Ketchen
Manager/Admin	NA
Clerk	Paula Doyle
Finance Director	Beth Hull
Tax Collector	Roxanne Germain
Tax Assessor	Francis Lauria
Attorney	Lucy Prashker
Public Works	Monty Green
Building	Tom Race
Planning	Carl Stewart
Police Chief	Richard Robarge
Emerg/Fire Chief	Stephen Berkel

Housing & Construction

New Privately Owned Housing Units Authorized by Building Permit

	Single Family	Total Bldgs	Total Units
2006	2	2	2
2007	0	0	0
2008	3	3	3

Parcel Count by Property Class, 2010

Total	478
Single family	291
Multiple units	4
Apartments	0
Condos	0
Vacant land	126
Open space	0
Commercial	1
Industrial	0
Misc. residential	10
Other use	46

Public Library

Alford Free Public Library
5 Alford Center Road
Alford, MA 01230
(413)528-4536

Librarian	Lois Milligan

Library Statistics, FY 2008

Population served, 2007	394
Registered users	0
Circulation	37
Reference transactons	0
Total program attendance	200
per capita:	
Holdings	2.98
Operating income	$0.00
Internet Access	
Internet computers available	0
Weekly users	0

Municipal Finance

Debt at year end 2008	$0
Moody's rating, July 2009	NA

Revenues, 2008

Total	$1,203,273
From all taxes	1,107,911
Federal aid	0
State aid	16,794
From other governments	1,460
Charges for services	5,990
Licenses, permits & fees	23,591
Fines & forfeits	0
Interfund transfers	8,101
Misc/other/special assessments	19,713

Expenditures, 2008

Total	$1,043,030
General government	135,795
Public safety	56,319
Other/fixed costs	71,883
Human services	8,915
Culture & recreation	749
Debt Service	0
Education	498,608
Public works	269,725
Intergovernmental	1,036

Taxation, 2010

Property type	Valuation	Rate
Total	$249,106,377	-
Residential	242,919,097	4.50
Open space	0	0.00
Commercial	2,051,781	4.50
Industrial	27,499	4.50
Personal	4,108,000	4.50

Average Single Family Tax Bill, 2010

Avg. assessed home value	$652,551
Avg. single fam. tax bill	$2,936
Hi-Lo ranking	241/301

Police & Crime, 2008

Number of police officers	NA
Violent crimes	NA
Property crimes	NA

Local School District

(school data 2007-08, except as noted)

Alford (non-op)
PO Box 339
Sheffield, MA 01257
413-229-8778

Superintendent	Michael Singleton

Non-operating district.
Resident students are sent to the Other School Districts listed below.

Grade plan	NA
Total enrollment '09-10	NA
Grade 12 enrollment, '09-10	NA
Graduation rate	NA
Dropout rate	NA
Per-pupil expenditure	NA
Avg teacher salary	NA
Student/teacher ratio '08-09	NA
Highly-qualified teachers, '08-09	NA
Teachers licensed in assigned subject	NA
Students per computer	NA

Other School Districts (see Appendix D for data)
Southern Berkshire Regional

See Introduction for an explanation of all data sources.

Demographics & Socio-Economic Characteristics

Population

1990	14,997
2000	16,450
Male	7,932
Female	8,518
2008	16,584
2010 (projected)††	17,292
2020 (projected)††	18,315

Race & Hispanic Origin, 2000

Race	
White	15,988
Black/African American	105
American Indian/Alaska Native	37
Asian	95
Hawaiian Native/Pacific Islander	4
Other Race	40
Two or more races	181
Hispanic origin	156

Age & Nativity, 2000

Under 5 years	1,100
18 years and over	12,157
21 years and over	11,715
65 years and over	1,969
85 years and over	294
Median Age	36.7
Native-born	15,883
Foreign-born	514

Age, 2020 (projected)††

Under 5 years	1,130
5 to 19 years	3,055
20 to 39 years	4,641
40 to 64 years	6,244
65 years and over	3,245

Educational Attainment, 2000

Population 25 years and over	11,158
High School graduates or higher	87.6%
Bachelor's degree or higher	26.4%
Graduate degree	9.3%

Income & Poverty, 1999

Per capita income,	$24,103
Median household income	$51,906
Median family income	$62,875
Persons in poverty	951
H'holds receiving public assistance	186
H'holds receiving social security	1,454

Households, 2000

Total households	6,380
With persons under 18	2,324
With persons over 65	1,320
Family households	4,228
Single person households	1,713
Persons per household	2.5
Persons per family	3.1

Labor & Employment, 2000

Civilian labor force	8,889
Unemployment rate	3.6%
Civilian labor force, 2008†	8,645
Unemployment rate†	6.1%
Civilian labor force, 12/09†	8,549
Unemployment rate†	8.9%
Employed persons 16 years and over, by occupation:	
Managers & professionals	3,396
Service occupations	1,073
Sales & office occupations	2,155
Farming, fishing & forestry	31
Construction & maintenance	767
Production & transportation	1,149
Self-employed persons	593

Most demographic data is from the 2000 Decennial Census
† Massachusetts Department of Revenue
†† University of Massachusetts, MISER

General Information

Town of Amesbury
62 Friend St
Amesbury, MA 01913
978-388-8121

Elevation	150 ft.
Land area (square miles)	12.4
Water area (square miles)	1.2
Population density, 2008 (est)	1,337.4
Year incorporated	1668
Website	www.amesburyma.gov

Voters & Government Information

Government type	Mayor
Number of Councilpersons	9
US Congressional District(s)	6

Registered Voters, October 2008

Total	11,950
Democrats	3,406
Republicans	1,643
Unaffiliated/other	6,786

Local Officials, 2010

Mayor	Thatcher W. Kezer III
Manager/Admin	NA
Clerk	Bonnijo Kitchin
Finance Director	Michael Basque
Tax Collector	Donna Cornoni
Tax Assessor	Mary Marino
Attorney	Kopelman & Paige
Public Works	Robert Desmarais
Building	Dennis Nadeau
Planning	Joseph Fahey
Police Chief	Michael Cronin
Emerg/Fire Chief	Jonathan Brickett (Actg)

Housing & Construction

New Privately Owned Housing Units Authorized by Building Permit

	Single Family	Total Bldgs	Total Units
2006	29	29	29
2007	23	23	23
2008	17	17	17

Parcel Count by Property Class, 2010

Total	6,206
Single family	3,354
Multiple units	434
Apartments	59
Condos	1,442
Vacant land	350
Open space	0
Commercial	214
Industrial	94
Misc. residential	40
Other use	219

Public Library

Amesbury Public Library
149 Main St.
Amesbury, MA 01913
(978)388-8149

Director	Patty DiTullio (Actg)

Library Statistics, FY 2008

Population served, 2007	16,429
Registered users	14,954
Circulation	159,449
Reference transactons	6,923
Total program attendance	56,857
per capita:	
Holdings	4.65
Operating income	$35.96
Internet Access	
Internet computers available	3
Weekly users	150

Municipal Finance

Debt at year end 2008	$33,126,188
Moody's rating, July 2009	A3

Revenues, 2008

Total	$47,335,417
From all taxes	32,132,198
Federal aid	0
State aid	12,861,711
From other governments	100,954
Charges for services	356,524
Licenses, permits & fees	265,992
Fines & forfeits	0
Interfund transfers	905,300
Misc/other/special assessments	356,369

Expenditures, 2008

Total	$47,111,090
General government	2,048,195
Public safety	6,336,795
Other/fixed costs	4,254,783
Human services	396,319
Culture & recreation	749,996
Debt Service	2,333,436
Education	25,217,645
Public works	2,782,589
Intergovernmental	2,638,130

Taxation, 2010

Property type	Valuation	Rate
Total	$1,907,592,445	-
Residential	1,632,389,706	17.77
Open space	0	0.00
Commercial	143,902,844	17.77
Industrial	95,158,230	17.77
Personal	36,141,665	17.77

Average Single Family Tax Bill, 2010

Avg. assessed home value	$319,201
Avg. single fam. tax bill	$5,672
Hi-Lo ranking	55/301

Police & Crime, 2008

Number of police officers	31
Violent crimes	46
Property crimes	291

Local School District

(school data 2007-08, except as noted)
Amesbury
10 Congress Street
Amesbury, MA 01913
978-388-0507

Superintendent	David Jack
Grade plan	PK-12
Total enrollment '09-10	2,424
Grade 12 enrollment, '09-10	161
Graduation rate	85.1%
Dropout rate	7.7%
Per-pupil expenditure	$11,568
Avg teacher salary	$61,540
Student/teacher ratio '08-09	14.1 to 1
Highly-qualified teachers, '08-09	97.5%
Teachers licensed in assigned subject	98.5%
Students per computer	6

Massachusetts Competency Assessment System (MCAS), 2009 results

	English		Math	
	% Prof	CPI	% Prof	CPI
Gr 4	62%	86.8	54%	81.3
Gr 6	71%	87.1	53%	75.7
Gr 8	82%	92.1	51%	75.8
Gr 10	87%	94.7	81%	91.1

Other School Districts (see Appendix D for data)
Whittier Vocational Tech

©2010 Information Publications, Inc. All rights reserved. Photocopying prohibited. For additional copies, contact the publisher at www.informationpublications.com or (877)544-INFO (4636)

See Introduction for an explanation of all data sources.

Demographics & Socio-Economic Characteristics

Population

1990	35,228
2000	34,874
Male	16,764
Female	18,110
2008	35,565
2010 (projected)††	36,583
2020 (projected)††	36,840

Race & Hispanic Origin, 2000

Race	
White	27,665
Black/African American	1,780
American Indian/Alaska Native	74
Asian	3,144
Hawaiian Native/Pacific Islander	33
Other Race	1,009
Two or more races	1,169
Hispanic origin	2,159

Age & Nativity, 2000

Under 5 years	993
18 years and over	30,398
21 years and over	19,944
65 years and over	2,314
85 years and over	392
Median Age	21.8
Native-born	30,268
Foreign-born	4,605

Age, 2020 (projected)††

Under 5 years	1,027
5 to 19 years	9,449
20 to 39 years	16,527
40 to 64 years	5,678
65 years and over	4,159

Educational Attainment, 2000

Population 25 years and over	12,926
High School graduates or higher	95.1%
Bachelor's degree or higher	68.7%
Graduate degree	41.7%

Income & Poverty, 1999

Per capita income,	$17,427
Median household income	$40,017
Median family income	$61,237
Persons in poverty	4,530
H'holds receiving public assistance	199
H'holds receiving social security	1,639

Households, 2000

Total households	9,174
With persons under 18	2,578
With persons over 65	1,654
Family households	4,547
Single person households	2,620
Persons per household	2.5
Persons per family	3.0

Labor & Employment, 2000

Civilian labor force	20,090
Unemployment rate	8.2%
Civilian labor force, 2008†	19,444
Unemployment rate†	3.5%
Civilian labor force, 12/09†	19,430
Unemployment rate†	4.7%
Employed persons 16 years and over, by occupation:	
Managers & professionals	9,238
Service occupations	3,111
Sales & office occupations	4,596
Farming, fishing & forestry	79
Construction & maintenance	376
Production & transportation	1,033
Self-employed persons	1,037

Most demographic data is from the 2000 Decennial Census
† Massachusetts Department of Revenue
†† University of Massachusetts, MISER

General Information

Town of Amherst
4 Boltwood Ave
Amherst, MA 01002
413-259-3002

Elevation	356 ft.
Land area (square miles)	27.7
Water area (square miles)	0.0
Population density, 2008 (est)	1,283.9
Year incorporated	1775
Website	amherstma.gov

Voters & Government Information

Government type	Rep. Town Meeting
Number of Selectmen	5
US Congressional District(s)	1

Registered Voters, October 2008

Total	18,956
Democrats	9,343
Republicans	1,076
Unaffiliated/other	8,257

Local Officials, 2010

Chair, Bd. of Sel.	Stephanie J. O'Keeffe
Manager	Laurence R. Shaffer
Town Clerk	Sandra J. Burgess
Finance Director	John Musante
Tax Collector	Claire McGinnis
Tax Assessor	David W. Burgess
Attorney	Kopelman & Paige
Public Works	Guilford Mooring
Building	B. Weeks
Comm Dev/Planning	Jonathan Tucker
Police Chief	Scott Livingstone
Fire Chief	Lindsay Stromgren (Actg)

Housing & Construction

New Privately Owned Housing Units Authorized by Building Permit

	Single Family	Total Bldgs	Total Units
2006	24	26	68
2007	33	35	44
2008	24	24	24

Parcel Count by Property Class, 2010

Total	6,816
Single family	4,073
Multiple units	362
Apartments	147
Condos	1,006
Vacant land	559
Open space	0
Commercial	339
Industrial	30
Misc. residential	53
Other use	247

Public Library

Jones Library Inc
43 Amity Street
Amherst, MA 01002
(413)259-3090

Director	Bonnie Isman

Library Statistics, FY 2008

Population served, 2007	35,962
Registered users	18,637
Circulation	541,424
Reference transactons	42,256
Total program attendance	350,000
per capita:	
Holdings	6.72
Operating income	$61.39
Internet Access	
Internet computers available	49
Weekly users	1,171

Municipal Finance

Debt at year end 2008	$10,988,385
Moody's rating, July 2009	Aa3

Revenues, 2008

Total	$62,641,456
From all taxes	35,977,858
Federal aid	0
State aid	16,828,559
From other governments	0
Charges for services	1,421,375
Licenses, permits & fees	888,616
Fines & forfeits	151,062
Interfund transfers	2,831,724
Misc/other/special assessments	2,271,131

Expenditures, 2008

Total	$58,036,117
General government	3,284,271
Public safety	8,417,276
Other/fixed costs	5,733,102
Human services	760,445
Culture & recreation	2,800,788
Debt Service	958,973
Education	32,439,294
Public works	1,605,854
Intergovernmental	2,036,114

Taxation, 2010

Property type	Valuation	Rate
Total	$2,127,375,010	-
Residential	1,918,464,577	16.95
Open space	0	0.00
Commercial	154,294,823	16.95
Industrial	4,563,700	16.95
Personal	50,051,910	16.95

Average Single Family Tax Bill, 2010

Avg. assessed home value	$334,327
Avg. single fam. tax bill	$5,667
Hi-Lo ranking	56/301

Police & Crime, 2008

Number of police officers	48
Violent crimes	86
Property crimes	470

Local School District

(school data 2007-08, except as noted)

Amherst
170 Chestnut Street
Amherst, MA 01002
413-362-1805

Superintendent	Maria Geryk
Grade plan	PK-6
Total enrollment '09-10	1,321
Grade 12 enrollment, '09-10	0
Graduation rate	NA
Dropout rate	NA
Per-pupil expenditure	$15,169
Avg teacher salary	$59,376
Student/teacher ratio '08-09	10.1 to 1
Highly-qualified teachers, '08-09	94.4%
Teachers licensed in assigned subject	97.6%
Students per computer	3

Massachusetts Competency Assessment System (MCAS), 2009 results

	English		Math	
	% Prof	CPI	% Prof	CPI
Gr 4	56%	78.9	55%	80.5
Gr 6	78%	90.9	69%	83.8
Gr 8	NA	NA	NA	NA
Gr 10	NA	NA	NA	NA

Other School Districts (see Appendix D for data)
Amherst-Pelham Regional

©2010 Information Publications, Inc. All rights reserved. Photocopying prohibited. For additional copies, contact the publisher at www.informationpublications.com or (877)544-INFO (4636)

See Introduction for an explanation of all data sources.

Demographics & Socio-Economic Characteristics

Population

1990	29,151
2000	31,247
Male	15,050
Female	16,197
2008	33,418
2010 (projected)††	31,112
2020 (projected)††	29,955

Race & Hispanic Origin, 2000

Race	
White	28,621
Black/African American	234
American Indian/Alaska Native	19
Asian	1,791
Hawaiian Native/Pacific Islander	11
Other Race	262
Two or more races	309
Hispanic origin	567

Age & Nativity, 2000

Under 5 years	2,052
18 years and over	22,259
21 years and over	21,506
65 years and over	3,831
85 years and over	558
Median Age	39.5
Native-born	28,077
Foreign-born	3,170

Age, 2020 (projected)††

Under 5 years	1,624
5 to 19 years	5,746
20 to 39 years	6,730
40 to 64 years	10,131
65 years and over	5,724

Educational Attainment, 2000

Population 25 years and over	20,897
High School graduates or higher	95.5%
Bachelor's degree or higher	62.5%
Graduate degree	29.9%

Income & Poverty, 1999

Per capita income,	$41,133
Median household income	$87,683
Median family income	$104,820
Persons in poverty	1,205
H'holds receiving public assistance	151
H'holds receiving social security	2,624

Households, 2000

Total households	11,305
With persons under 18	4,692
With persons over 65	2,630
Family households	8,490
Single person households	2,447
Persons per household	2.7
Persons per family	3.2

Labor & Employment, 2000

Civilian labor force	15,499
Unemployment rate	2.3%
Civilian labor force, 2008†	17,021
Unemployment rate†	4.8%
Civilian labor force, 12/09†	16,829
Unemployment rate†	7.0%
Employed persons 16 years and over, by occupation:	
Managers & professionals	9,691
Service occupations	944
Sales & office occupations	3,369
Farming, fishing & forestry	0
Construction & maintenance	506
Production & transportation	635
Self-employed persons	1,270

Most demographic data is from the 2000 Decennial Census
† Massachusetts Department of Revenue
†† University of Massachusetts, MISER

General Information

Town of Andover
36 Bartlet St
Andover, MA 01810
978-623-8200

Elevation	150 ft.
Land area (square miles)	31.0
Water area (square miles)	1.1
Population density, 2008 (est)	1,078.0
Year incorporated	1646
Website	andoverma.gov

Voters & Government Information

Government type	Open Town Meeting
Number of Selectmen	5
US Congressional District(s)	5

Registered Voters, October 2008

Total	22,907
Democrats	6,170
Republicans	3,905
Unaffiliated/other	12,756

Local Officials, 2010

Chair, Bd. of Sel.	Alex J. Vispoli
Manager	Reginald S. Stapczynski
Town Clerk	Randall L. Hanson
Finance Director	Anthony J. Torrisi
Tax Collector	David Reilly
Tax Assessor	David A. Billard
Attorney	Thomas J. Urbelis
Public Works	Jack Petkus
Building	Joseph R. Piantedosi
Comm Dev/Planning	Paul Materazzo
Police Chief	Brian J. Pattullo
Emerg/Fire Chief	Michael B. Mansfield

Housing & Construction

New Privately Owned Housing Units Authorized by Building Permit

	Single Family	Total Bldgs	Total Units
2006	22	28	63
2007	21	23	29
2008	14	19	30

Parcel Count by Property Class, 2010

Total	11,528
Single family	8,484
Multiple units	256
Apartments	59
Condos	1,570
Vacant land	499
Open space	57
Commercial	260
Industrial	139
Misc. residential	21
Other use	183

Public Library

Memorial Hall Library
2 North Main Street
Andover, MA 01810
(978)623-8401

Director	Beth Mazia

Library Statistics, FY 2008

Population served, 2007	33,284
Registered users	32,991
Circulation	569,281
Reference transactons	64,323
Total program attendance	414,323
per capita:	
Holdings	7.61
Operating income	$76.27
Internet Access	
Internet computers available	40
Weekly users	1,055

Municipal Finance

Debt at year end 2008	$89,486,634
Moody's rating, July 2009	Aa1

Revenues, 2008

Total	$125,228,050
From all taxes	99,684,306
Federal aid	0
State aid	11,773,313
From other governments	0
Charges for services	2,519,291
Licenses, permits & fees	1,961,902
Fines & forfeits	475,184
Interfund transfers	6,595,496
Misc/other/special assessments	1,109,279

Expenditures, 2008

Total	$112,710,313
General government	7,913,534
Public safety	14,839,562
Other/fixed costs	5,283,661
Human services	802,288
Culture & recreation	4,536,334
Debt Service	12,722,575
Education	57,612,168
Public works	6,046,680
Intergovernmental	2,852,501

Taxation, 2010

Property type	Valuation	Rate
Total	$6,837,657,244	-
Residential	5,462,980,161	13.19
Open space	10,866,600	13.19
Commercial	566,418,366	21.33
Industrial	624,853,500	21.33
Personal	172,538,617	21.33

Average Single Family Tax Bill, 2010

Avg. assessed home value	$548,860
Avg. single fam. tax bill	$7,239
Hi-Lo ranking	31/301

Police & Crime, 2008

Number of police officers	52
Violent crimes	10
Property crimes	441

Local School District

(school data 2007-08, except as noted)

Andover
36 Bartlet Street
Andover, MA 01810
978-623-8501

Superintendent	Claudia Bach
Grade plan	PK-12
Total enrollment '09-10	6,163
Grade 12 enrollment, '09-10	426
Graduation rate	95.1%
Dropout rate	1.1%
Per-pupil expenditure	$12,536
Avg teacher salary	$69,934
Student/teacher ratio '08-09	13.7 to 1
Highly-qualified teachers, '08-09	97.1%
Teachers licensed in assigned subject	98.6%
Students per computer	3.1

Massachusetts Competency Assessment System (MCAS), 2009 results

	English		Math	
	% Prof	CPI	% Prof	CPI
Gr 4	80%	93.5	74%	91.1
Gr 6	89%	96.3	83%	93.4
Gr 8	94%	98.4	73%	88.7
Gr 10	94%	97.8	93%	97

Other School Districts (see Appendix D for data)
Greater Lawrence Vocational Tech

©2010 Information Publications, Inc. All rights reserved. Photocopying prohibited. For additional copies, contact the publisher at www.informationpublications.com or (877)544-INFO (4636)

See Introduction for an explanation of all data sources.

Demographics & Socio-Economic Characteristics

Population

1990 201
2000 344
Male 169
Female 175
2008 357
2010 (projected)†† 405
2020 (projected)†† 466

Race & Hispanic Origin, 2000

Race
White 184
Black/African American 1
American Indian/Alaska Native 126
Asian 0
Hawaiian Native/Pacific Islander 0
Other Race 3
Two or more races 30
Hispanic origin 4

Age & Nativity, 2000

Under 5 years 20
18 years and over 257
21 years and over 244
65 years and over 35
85 years and over 5
Median Age 37.1
Native-born 361
Foreign-born 3

Age, 2020 (projected)††

Under 5 years 16
5 to 19 years 51
20 to 39 years 138
40 to 64 years 166
65 years and over 95

Educational Attainment, 2000

Population 25 years and over 233
High School graduates or higher . . . 95.7%
Bachelor's degree or higher 41.6%
Graduate degree 12.0%

Income & Poverty, 1999

Per capita income, ... $21,420
Median household income $45,208
Median family income $46,458
Persons in poverty 26
H'holds receiving public assistance 5
H'holds receiving social security 22

Households, 2000

Total households 141
With persons under 18 49
With persons over 65 28
Family households 89
Single person households 43
Persons per household 2.4
Persons per family 3.0

Labor & Employment, 2000

Civilian labor force 190
Unemployment rate 4.2%
Civilian labor force, 2008† 214
Unemployment rate† 8.9%
Civilian labor force, 12/09† 218
Unemployment rate† 9.6%
Employed persons 16 years and over, by occupation:
Managers & professionals 61
Service occupations 31
Sales & office occupations 34
Farming, fishing & forestry 5
Construction & maintenance 27
Production & transportation 24
Self-employed persons 34

Most demographic data is from the 2000 Decennial Census
† Massachusetts Department of Revenue
†† University of Massachusetts, MISER

General Information

Town of Aquinnah
65 State Rd
Aquinnah, MA 02535
508-645-2300

Elevation . . . . . NA
Land area (square miles) 5.4
Water area (square miles) 35.4
Population density, 2008 (est) 66.1
Year incorporated 1870
Website . . . . . aquinnah-ma.gov

Voters & Government Information

Government type . . . . . Open Town Meeting
Number of Selectmen 3
US Congressional District(s) 10

Registered Voters, October 2008

Total 398
Democrats 129
Republicans 15
Unaffiliated/other 252

Local Officials, 2010

Chair, Bd. of Sel. . . . . . James Newman
Manager/Exec. . . . . . Jeffrey Burgoyne
Clerk . . . . . Carolyn Feltz
Finance . . . . . Judith Jardin
Tax Collector . . . . . Wenonah Madison
Tax Assessor . . . . . Hugh Taylor
Attorney . . . . . NA
Public Works . . . . . NA
Building . . . . . NA
Comm Dev/Planning . . . . . NA
Police Chief . . . . . Randhi P. Belain
Emerg/Fire Chief . . . . . Walter Delaney

Housing & Construction

New Privately Owned Housing Units Authorized by Building Permit

	Single Family	Total Bldgs	Total Units
2006	6	6	6
2007	9	9	9
2008	7	7	7

Parcel Count by Property Class, 2010

Total 822
Single family 379
Multiple units 0
Apartments 0
Condos 6
Vacant land 394
Open space 0
Commercial 10
Industrial 0
Misc. residential 29
Other use 4

Public Library

Aquinnah Public Library
One Church Street
Aquinnah, MA 02535
(508)645-2314

Director . . . . . Jennifer Christy

Library Statistics, FY 2008

Population served, 2007 354
Registered users 1,026
Circulation 12,412
Reference transactons 452
Total program attendance 3,900

per capita:

Holdings 26.71
Operating income $211.26

Internet Access

Internet computers available 3
Weekly users 43

Municipal Finance

Debt at year end 2008 . . . . . $512,235
Moody's rating, July 2009 . . . . . NA

Revenues, 2008

Total $3,131,165
From all taxes 2,419,220
Federal aid 0
State aid 4,761
From other governments 0
Charges for services 270,817
Licenses, permits & fees 45,431
Fines & forfeits 5,016
Interfund transfers 50,686
Misc/other/special assessments 167,617

Expenditures, 2008

Total $2,894,042
General government 561,994
Public safety 648,293
Other/fixed costs 236,849
Human services 50,235
Culture & recreation 152,811
Debt Service 92,330
Education 966,777
Public works 126,741
Intergovernmental 58,012

Taxation, 2010

Property type	Valuation	Rate
Total	$709,977,649	-
Residential	696,049,084	3.79
Open space	0	0.00
Commercial	6,807,115	3.79
Industrial	0	0.00
Personal	7,121,450	3.79

Average Single Family Tax Bill, 2010

Avg. assessed home value $1,248,895
Avg. single fam. tax bill $4,733
Hi-Lo ranking 90/301

Police & Crime, 2008

Number of police officers 4
Violent crimes 0
Property crimes 7

Local School District

(school data 2007-08, except as noted)

Aquinnah (non-op)
RR2, Box 261, 4 Pine Street
Vineyard Haven, MA 02568
508-693-2007

Superintendent . . . . . James Weiss

Non-operating district.
Resident students are sent to the Other School Districts listed below.

Grade plan . . . . . NA
Total enrollment '09-10 . . . . . NA
Grade 12 enrollment, '09-10 . . . . . NA
Graduation rate . . . . . NA
Dropout rate . . . . . NA
Per-pupil expenditure . . . . . NA
Avg teacher salary . . . . . NA
Student/teacher ratio '08-09 . . . . . NA
Highly-qualified teachers, '08-09 . . . . . NA
Teachers licensed in assigned subject . . . . . NA
Students per computer . . . . . NA

Other School Districts (see Appendix D for data)
Marthas Vineyard and Up-Island Regionals

©2010 Information Publications, Inc. All rights reserved. Photocopying prohibited. For additional copies, contact the publisher at www.informationpublications.com or (877)544-INFO (4636)

See Introduction for an explanation of all data sources.

Demographics & Socio-Economic Characteristics*

Population

1990	44,630
2000	42,389
Male	19,679
Female	22,710
2008	40,993
2010 (projected)††	38,579
2020 (projected)††	35,192

Race & Hispanic Origin, 2000

Race	
White	38,561
Black/African American	719
American Indian/Alaska Native	57
Asian	2,107
Hawaiian Native/Pacific Islander	6
Other Race	279
Two or more races	660
Hispanic origin	787

Age & Nativity, 2000

Under 5 years	2,562
18 years and over	34,605
21 years and over	33,898
65 years and over	7,130
85 years and over	990
Median Age	39.5
Native-born	36,443
Foreign-born	5,946

Age, 2020 (projected)††

Under 5 years	1,510
5 to 19 years	4,782
20 to 39 years	8,751
40 to 64 years	12,846
65 years and over	7,303

Educational Attainment, 2000

Population 25 years and over	32,436
High School graduates or higher	91.7%
Bachelor's degree or higher	52.8%
Graduate degree	28.2%

Income & Poverty, 1999

Per capita income,	$34,399
Median household income	$64,344
Median family income	$78,741
Persons in poverty	1,714
H'holds receiving public assistance	192
H'holds receiving social security	5,209

Households, 2000

Total households	19,011
With persons under 18	4,592
With persons over 65	5,313
Family households	10,779
Single person households	6,501
Persons per household	2.2
Persons per family	2.9

Labor & Employment, 2000

Civilian labor force	24,544
Unemployment rate	2.2%
Civilian labor force, 2008†	24,289
Unemployment rate†	4.3%
Civilian labor force, 12/09†	24,110
Unemployment rate†	6.2%
Employed persons 16 years and over, by occupation:	
Managers & professionals	14,623
Service occupations	2,029
Sales & office occupations	5,173
Farming, fishing & forestry	21
Construction & maintenance	1,061
Production & transportation	1,104
Self-employed persons	1,884

Most demographic data is from the 2000 Decennial Census
* see Appendix E for American Community Survey data
† Massachusetts Department of Revenue
†† University of Massachusetts, MISER

General Information

Town of Arlington
730 Massachusetts Ave
Arlington, MA 02476
781-316-3000

Elevation	50 ft.
Land area (square miles)	5.2
Water area (square miles)	0.3
Population density, 2008 (est)	7,883.3
Year incorporated	1807
Website	www.arlingtonma.gov

Voters & Government Information

Government type	Rep. Town Meeting
Number of Selectmen	5
US Congressional District(s)	7

Registered Voters, October 2008

Total	30,083
Democrats	14,602
Republicans	2,337
Unaffiliated/other	12,981

Local Officials, 2010

Chair, Bd. of Sel.	Kevin F. Greeley
Manager	Brian Sullivan
Town Clerk	Corinne M. Rainville
Finance Director	Ruth Lewis
Tax Collector	Stephen J. Gilligan
Tax Assessor	Robert Greeley
Attorney	Juliana Rice
Public Works	John Bean
Building	Michael Byrne
Comm Dev/Planning	Carol Kowalski
Police Chief	Frederick Ryan
Emerg/Fire Chief	Robert Jefferson

Housing & Construction

New Privately Owned Housing Units Authorized by Building Permit

	Single Family	Total Bldgs	Total Units
2006	11	31	69
2007	10	23	48
2008	3	14	52

Parcel Count by Property Class, 2010

Total	14,650
Single family	7,978
Multiple units	2,648
Apartments	147
Condos	3,033
Vacant land	337
Open space	0
Commercial	389
Industrial	23
Misc. residential	13
Other use	82

Public Library

Robbins Library
700 Massachusetts Avenue
Arlington, MA 02476
(781)316-3200

Library Director	Maryellen Loud

Library Statistics, FY 2008

Population served, 2007	41,144
Registered users	24,962
Circulation	573,948
Reference transactons	74,265
Total program attendance	0
per capita:	
Holdings	5.73
Operating income	$50.49
Internet Access	
Internet computers available	20
Weekly users	1,296

Municipal Finance

Debt at year end 2008	$54,904,865
Moody's rating, July 2009	Aa2

Revenues, 2008

Total	$130,604,194
From all taxes	82,464,899
Federal aid	385,218
State aid	18,614,805
From other governments	54,483
Charges for services	818,604
Licenses, permits & fees	2,285,960
Fines & forfeits	360,666
Interfund transfers	874,211
Misc/other/special assessments	12,372,674

Expenditures, 2008

Total	$101,329,099
General government	4,561,264
Public safety	11,953,110
Other/fixed costs	11,633,940
Human services	671,263
Culture & recreation	2,787,743
Debt Service	18,594,386
Education	40,199,933
Public works	7,560,056
Intergovernmental	2,622,634

Taxation, 2010

Property type	Valuation	Rate
Total	$6,892,736,257	-
Residential	6,482,931,507	12.11
Open space	0	0.00
Commercial	294,051,850	12.11
Industrial	20,969,800	12.11
Personal	94,783,100	12.11

Average Single Family Tax Bill, 2010

Avg. assessed home value	$477,218
Avg. single fam. tax bill	$5,779
Hi-Lo ranking	51/301

Police & Crime, 2008

Number of police officers	61
Violent crimes	55
Property crimes	661

Local School District

(school data 2007-08, except as noted)

Arlington
869 Massachusetts Avenue
Arlington, MA 02476
781-316-3523

Superintendent	Kathleen Bodie
Grade plan	PK-12
Total enrollment '09-10	4,713
Grade 12 enrollment, '09-10	266
Graduation rate	90.7%
Dropout rate	3.3%
Per-pupil expenditure	$11,685
Avg teacher salary	$57,636
Student/teacher ratio '08-09	13.8 to 1
Highly-qualified teachers, '08-09	97.3%
Teachers licensed in assigned subject	97.8%
Students per computer	NA

Massachusetts Competency Assessment System (MCAS), 2009 results

	English		Math	
	% Prof	CPI	% Prof	CPI
Gr 4	80%	92.4	75%	92.3
Gr 6	85%	94.4	74%	89.2
Gr 8	88%	95.3	70%	85
Gr 10	92%	96.8	86%	93.6

Other School Districts (see Appendix D for data)
Minuteman Vocational Tech

©2010 Information Publications, Inc. All rights reserved. Photocopying prohibited. For additional copies, contact the publisher at www.informationpublications.com or (877)544-INFO (4636)

See Introduction for an explanation of all data sources.

Demographics & Socio-Economic Characteristics

Population

1990	5,433
2000	5,546
Male	2,817
Female	2,729
2008	5,974
2010 (projected)††	5,993
2020 (projected)††	6,658

Race & Hispanic Origin, 2000

Race	
White	5,416
Black/African American	12
American Indian/Alaska Native	2
Asian	34
Hawaiian Native/Pacific Islander	0
Other Race	17
Two or more races	65
Hispanic origin	92

Age & Nativity, 2000

Under 5 years	332
18 years and over	3,940
21 years and over	3,737
65 years and over	492
85 years and over	38
Median Age	37.3
Native-born	5,311
Foreign-born	235

Age, 2020 (projected)††

Under 5 years	404
5 to 19 years	1,268
20 to 39 years	1,752
40 to 64 years	2,279
65 years and over	955

Educational Attainment, 2000

Population 25 years and over	3,583
High School graduates or higher	90.0%
Bachelor's degree or higher	26.1%
Graduate degree	9.0%

Income & Poverty, 1999

Per capita income,	$21,659
Median household income	$55,568
Median family income	$58,993
Persons in poverty	350
H'holds receiving public assistance	10
H'holds receiving social security	350

Households, 2000

Total households	1,929
With persons under 18	853
With persons over 65	339
Family households	1,541
Single person households	301
Persons per household	2.9
Persons per family	3.2

Labor & Employment, 2000

Civilian labor force	2,970
Unemployment rate	3.2%
Civilian labor force, 2008†	3,126
Unemployment rate†	7.8%
Civilian labor force, 12/09†	3,106
Unemployment rate†	11.3%
Employed persons 16 years and over, by occupation:	
Managers & professionals	1,110
Service occupations	439
Sales & office occupations	623
Farming, fishing & forestry	0
Construction & maintenance	299
Production & transportation	403
Self-employed persons	235

Most demographic data is from the 2000 Decennial Census
† Massachusetts Department of Revenue
†† University of Massachusetts, MISER

General Information

Town of Ashburnham
32 Main St
Ashburnham, MA 01430
978-827-4104

Elevation	1,028 ft.
Land area (square miles)	38.7
Water area (square miles)	2.3
Population density, 2008 (est)	154.4
Year incorporated	1765
Website	www.ashburnham-ma.gov

Voters & Government Information

Government type	Open Town Meeting
Number of Selectmen	3
US Congressional District(s)	1

Registered Voters, October 2008

Total	4,307
Democrats	1,039
Republicans	609
Unaffiliated/other	2,601

Local Officials, 2010

Chair, Bd. of Sel.	Edward Vitone, Jr.
Town Administrator	Douglas Briggs
Town Clerk	Linda A. Ramsdell
Treasurer	Anne Cervantes
Tax Collector	Carla H. Clifford
Tax Assessor	Richard Coswell
Attorney	Deborah Phillips
Public Works	Steven Nims
Building	Michael Gallant
Comm Dev/Planning	None
Police Chief	Loring Barrett Jr
Emerg/Fire Chief	Paul Zbikowski

Housing & Construction

New Privately Owned Housing Units Authorized by Building Permit

	Single Family	Total Bldgs	Total Units
2006	17	17	17
2007	21	21	21
2008	18	19	24

Parcel Count by Property Class, 2010

Total	3,725
Single family	2,374
Multiple units	44
Apartments	4
Condos	0
Vacant land	1,089
Open space	0
Commercial	43
Industrial	28
Misc. residential	48
Other use	95

Public Library

Stevens Memorial Library
20 Memorial Dr.
Ashburnham, MA 01430
(978)827-4115

Director .... Cheryl Paul-Bradley

Library Statistics, FY 2008

Population served, 2007	5,959
Registered users	2,846
Circulation	26,220
Reference transactons	0
Total program attendance	52,510
per capita:	
Holdings	7.39
Operating income	$44.51
Internet Access	
Internet computers available	5
Weekly users	117

Municipal Finance

Debt at year end 2008	$6,769,012
Moody's rating, July 2009	A3

Revenues, 2008

Total	$12,651,770
From all taxes	9,462,106
Federal aid	0
State aid	1,002,280
From other governments	14,668
Charges for services	236,824
Licenses, permits & fees	110,565
Fines & forfeits	1,541
Interfund transfers	443,378
Misc/other/special assessments	690,204

Expenditures, 2008

Total	$11,979,345
General government	1,031,666
Public safety	1,673,910
Other/fixed costs	813,507
Human services	64,668
Culture & recreation	210,290
Debt Service	317,555
Education	6,540,499
Public works	1,225,530
Intergovernmental	57,227

Taxation, 2010

Property type	Valuation	Rate
Total	$627,539,382	-
Residential	600,605,155	16.15
Open space	0	0.00
Commercial	14,494,445	16.15
Industrial	4,947,700	16.15
Personal	7,492,082	16.15

Average Single Family Tax Bill, 2010

Avg. assessed home value	$228,072
Avg. single fam. tax bill	$3,683
Hi-Lo ranking	159/301

Police & Crime, 2008

Number of police officers	10
Violent crimes	6
Property crimes	45

Local School District

(school data 2007-08, except as noted)

Ashburnham (non-op)
11 Oakmont Drive
Ashburnham, MA 01430
978-874-1501

Superintendent.......... Michael Zapantis

Non-operating district.
Resident students are sent to the Other School Districts listed below.

Grade plan	NA
Total enrollment '09-10	NA
Grade 12 enrollment, '09-10	NA
Graduation rate	NA
Dropout rate	NA
Per-pupil expenditure	NA
Avg teacher salary	NA
Student/teacher ratio '08-09	NA
Highly-qualified teachers, '08-09	NA
Teachers licensed in assigned subject	NA
Students per computer	NA

Other School Districts (see Appendix D for data)
Ashburnham-Westminster Regional, Montachusett Vocational Tech

©2010 Information Publications, Inc. All rights reserved. Photocopying prohibited. For additional copies, contact the publisher at www.informationpublications.com or (877)544-INFO (4636)

See Introduction for an explanation of all data sources.

Demographics & Socio-Economic Characteristics

Population

1990	2,717
2000	2,845
Male	1,428
Female	1,417
2008	2,927
2010 (projected)††	2,864
2020 (projected)††	2,925

Race & Hispanic Origin, 2000

Race	
White	2,789
Black/African American	8
American Indian/Alaska Native	6
Asian	10
Hawaiian Native/Pacific Islander	0
Other Race	3
Two or more races	29
Hispanic origin	24

Age & Nativity, 2000

Under 5 years	166
18 years and over	2,047
21 years and over	1,936
65 years and over	271
85 years and over	23
Median Age	38.2
Native-born	2,768
Foreign-born	77

Age, 2020 (projected)††

Under 5 years	165
5 to 19 years	505
20 to 39 years	718
40 to 64 years	1,048
65 years and over	489

Educational Attainment, 2000

Population 25 years and over	1,869
High School graduates or higher	90.9%
Bachelor's degree or higher	25.5%
Graduate degree	10.0%

Income & Poverty, 1999

Per capita income,	$21,648
Median household income	$61,000
Median family income	$64,900
Persons in poverty	143
H'holds receiving public assistance	8
H'holds receiving social security	243

Households, 2000

Total households	978
With persons under 18	420
With persons over 65	203
Family households	783
Single person households	148
Persons per household	2.9
Persons per family	3.3

Labor & Employment, 2000

Civilian labor force	1,580
Unemployment rate	3.8%
Civilian labor force, 2008†	1,564
Unemployment rate†	6.8%
Civilian labor force, 12/09†	1,588
Unemployment rate†	11.6%
Employed persons 16 years and over, by occupation:	
Managers & professionals	514
Service occupations	162
Sales & office occupations	417
Farming, fishing & forestry	4
Construction & maintenance	195
Production & transportation	228
Self-employed persons	139

Most demographic data is from the 2000 Decennial Census
† Massachusetts Department of Revenue
†† University of Massachusetts, MISER

General Information

Town of Ashby
895 Main St
Ashby, MA 01431
978-386-2424

Elevation	900 ft.
Land area (square miles)	23.8
Water area (square miles)	0.4
Population density, 2008 (est)	123.0
Year incorporated	1767
Website	www.ci.ashby.ma.us

Voters & Government Information

Government type	Open Town Meeting
Number of Selectmen	3
US Congressional District(s)	1

Registered Voters, October 2008

Total	2,408
Democrats	418
Republicans	327
Unaffiliated/other	1,647

Local Officials, 2010

Chair, Bd. of Sel.	Peter McMurray
Manager/Admin	(vacant)
Town Clerk	Lorraine Pease
Finance Director	Kate Stacy
Tax Collector	Beth Ann Scheid
Tax Assessor	Harald Scheid
Attorney	Kopelman & Paige
Public Works	William Davis
Building	Tony Ammendolia
Comm Dev/Planning	Andrew Leonard
Constable	William Davis
Emerg/Fire Chief	William Seymour Jr

Housing & Construction

New Privately Owned Housing Units Authorized by Building Permit

	Single Family	Total Bldgs	Total Units
2006	7	7	7
2007	7	7	7
2008	6	6	6

Parcel Count by Property Class, 2010

Total	1,620
Single family	1,063
Multiple units	16
Apartments	1
Condos	0
Vacant land	368
Open space	0
Commercial	21
Industrial	4
Misc. residential	14
Other use	133

Public Library

Ashby Free Public Library
PO Box 279
Ashby, MA 01431
(978)386-5377

Director ..... Mary Murtland

Library Statistics, FY 2008

Population served, 2007	2,944
Registered users	1,183
Circulation	15,806
Reference transactons	1,326
Total program attendance	7,302
per capita:	
Holdings	6.70
Operating income	$25.37
Internet Access	
Internet computers available	5
Weekly users	11

Municipal Finance

Debt at year end 2008	$0
Moody's rating, July 2009	NA

Revenues, 2008

Total	$5,151,031
From all taxes	4,368,295
Federal aid	0
State aid	582,796
From other governments	1,261
Charges for services	93,827
Licenses, permits & fees	46,450
Fines & forfeits	16,836
Interfund transfers	16
Misc/other/special assessments	20,775

Expenditures, 2008

Total	$4,975,148
General government	427,031
Public safety	765,439
Other/fixed costs	418,517
Human services	22,578
Culture & recreation	72,315
Debt Service	0
Education	2,810,592
Public works	438,292
Intergovernmental	20,384

Taxation, 2010

Property type	Valuation	Rate
Total	$319,193,905	-
Residential	303,045,953	13.64
Open space	0	0.00
Commercial	8,945,276	13.64
Industrial	1,007,700	13.64
Personal	6,194,976	13.64

Average Single Family Tax Bill, 2010

Avg. assessed home value	$242,536
Avg. single fam. tax bill	$3,308
Hi-Lo ranking	202/301

Police & Crime, 2008

Number of police officers	6
Violent crimes	NA
Property crimes	NA

Local School District

(school data 2007-08, except as noted)

Ashby (non-op)
23 Main Street
Townsend, MA 01469
978-597-8713

Superintendent ..... Maureen Marshall

Non-operating district.
Resident students are sent to the Other School Districts listed below.

Grade plan	NA
Total enrollment '09-10	NA
Grade 12 enrollment, '09-10	NA
Graduation rate	NA
Dropout rate	NA
Per-pupil expenditure	NA
Avg teacher salary	NA
Student/teacher ratio '08-09	NA
Highly-qualified teachers, '08-09	NA
Teachers licensed in assigned subject	NA
Students per computer	NA

Other School Districts (see Appendix D for data)

North Middlesex Regional, Montachusett Vocational Tech

©2010 Information Publications, Inc. All rights reserved. Photocopying prohibited. For additional copies, contact the publisher at www.informationpublications.com or (877)544-INFO (4636)

See Introduction for an explanation of all data sources.

Demographics & Socio-Economic Characteristics

Population

1990	1,715
2000	1,800
Male	883
Female	917
2008	1,822
2010 (projected)††	1,847
2020 (projected)††	1,928

Race & Hispanic Origin, 2000

Race	
White	1,752
Black/African American	11
American Indian/Alaska Native	2
Asian	6
Hawaiian Native/Pacific Islander	0
Other Race	1
Two or more races	28
Hispanic origin	8

Age & Nativity, 2000

Under 5 years	95
18 years and over	1,372
21 years and over	1,322
65 years and over	209
85 years and over	25
Median Age	41.8
Native-born	1,748
Foreign-born	53

Age, 2020 (projected)††

Under 5 years	74
5 to 19 years	220
20 to 39 years	422
40 to 64 years	652
65 years and over	560

Educational Attainment, 2000

Population 25 years and over	1,290
High School graduates or higher	94.5%
Bachelor's degree or higher	46.5%
Graduate degree	22.2%

Income & Poverty, 1999

Per capita income,	$26,483
Median household income	$52,875
Median family income	$56,739
Persons in poverty	137
H'holds receiving public assistance	11
H'holds receiving social security	159

Households, 2000

Total households	741
With persons under 18	249
With persons over 65	155
Family households	501
Single person households	178
Persons per household	2.4
Persons per family	2.9

Labor & Employment, 2000

Civilian labor force	1,087
Unemployment rate	3.2%
Civilian labor force, 2008†	1,093
Unemployment rate†	4.0%
Civilian labor force, 12/09†	1,091
Unemployment rate†	5.5%
Employed persons 16 years and over, by occupation:	
Managers & professionals	542
Service occupations	114
Sales & office occupations	173
Farming, fishing & forestry	23
Construction & maintenance	101
Production & transportation	99
Self-employed persons	207

Most demographic data is from the 2000 Decennial Census
† Massachusetts Department of Revenue
†† University of Massachusetts, MISER

General Information

Town of Ashfield
PO Box 560
Ashfield, MA 01330
413-628-4441

Elevation	1,244 ft.
Land area (square miles)	40.3
Water area (square miles)	0.1
Population density, 2008 (est)	45.2
Year incorporated	1765
Website	NA

Voters & Government Information

Government type	Open Town Meeting
Number of Select Board Members	3
US Congressional District(s)	1

Registered Voters, October 2008

Total	1,333
Democrats	403
Republicans	113
Unaffiliated/other	804

Local Officials, 2010

Chair, Bd. of Sel.	Lynn Dole
Manager/Admin	Andrea Llamas
Town Clerk	Maryellen Cranston
Finance	Laura Blakesley
Tax Collector	Laura Blakesley
Tax Assessor	Lenny Roberts
Attorney	Donna MacNicol
Public Works	Tom Poissont
Building	Jim Hawkins
Comm Dev/Planning	NA
Police Chief	John Svoboda
Emerg/Fire Chief	Douglas Field

Housing & Construction

New Privately Owned Housing Units Authorized by Building Permit

	Single Family	Total Bldgs	Total Units
2006	6	6	6
2007	5	5	5
2008	3	3	3

Parcel Count by Property Class, 2010

Total	1,365
Single family	602
Multiple units	37
Apartments	3
Condos	0
Vacant land	268
Open space	0
Commercial	17
Industrial	6
Misc. residential	19
Other use	413

Public Library

Belding Memorial Library
PO Box 407
Ashfield, MA 01330
(413)628-4414

Librarian/Trustee ....Anne C. Judson

Library Statistics, FY 2008

Population served, 2007	1,815
Registered users	1,600
Circulation	24,867
Reference transactons	0
Total program attendance	0
per capita:	
Holdings	9.43
Operating income	$26.80
Internet Access	
Internet computers available	1
Weekly users	50

Municipal Finance

Debt at year end 2008	$1,443,269
Moody's rating, July 2009	NA

Revenues, 2008

Total	$4,019,718
From all taxes	3,025,883
Federal aid	0
State aid	404,189
From other governments	27,736
Charges for services	78,431
Licenses, permits & fees	34,730
Fines & forfeits	0
Interfund transfers	127,135
Misc/other/special assessments	160,807

Expenditures, 2008

Total	$3,477,764
General government	209,413
Public safety	181,385
Other/fixed costs	198,050
Human services	39,545
Culture & recreation	47,718
Debt Service	109,688
Education	2,005,826
Public works	613,473
Intergovernmental	72,654

Taxation, 2010

Property type	Valuation	Rate
Total	$221,102,925	-
Residential	205,203,932	13.54
Open space	0	0.00
Commercial	8,655,416	13.54
Industrial	969,334	13.54
Personal	6,274,243	13.54

Average Single Family Tax Bill, 2010

Avg. assessed home value	$238,932
Avg. single fam. tax bill	$3,235
Hi-Lo ranking	211/301

Police & Crime, 2008

Number of police officers	2
Violent crimes	3
Property crimes	16

Local School District

(school data 2007-08, except as noted)

Ashfield (non-op)
24 Ashfield Road
Shelburne Falls, MA 01370
413-625-0192
Superintendent........ Michael Buoniconti

Non-operating district.
Resident students are sent to the Other School Districts listed below.

Grade plan	NA
Total enrollment '09-10	NA
Grade 12 enrollment, '09-10	NA
Graduation rate	NA
Dropout rate	NA
Per-pupil expenditure	NA
Avg teacher salary	NA
Student/teacher ratio '08-09	NA
Highly-qualified teachers, '08-09	NA
Teachers licensed in assigned subject	NA
Students per computer	NA

Other School Districts (see Appendix D for data)
Mohawk Trail Regional

See Introduction for an explanation of all data sources.

©2010 Information Publications, Inc. All rights reserved. Photocopying prohibited. For additional copies, contact the publisher at www.informationpublications.com or (877)544-INFO (4636)

Demographics & Socio-Economic Characteristics

Population

1990	12,066
2000	14,674
Male	7,100
Female	7,574
2008	15,807
2010 (projected)††	17,602
2020 (projected)††	20,894

Race & Hispanic Origin, 2000

Race	
White	13,482
Black/African American	262
American Indian/Alaska Native	15
Asian	363
Hawaiian Native/Pacific Islander	4
Other Race	245
Two or more races	303
Hispanic origin	428

Age & Nativity, 2000

Under 5 years	1,153
18 years and over	10,967
21 years and over	10,653
65 years and over	1,432
85 years and over	93
Median Age	37.4
Native-born	13,241
Foreign-born	1,433

Age, 2020 (projected)††

Under 5 years	1,363
5 to 19 years	3,742
20 to 39 years	5,288
40 to 64 years	7,102
65 years and over	3,399

Educational Attainment, 2000

Population 25 years and over	10,282
High School graduates or higher	94.8%
Bachelor's degree or higher	45.6%
Graduate degree	19.1%

Income & Poverty, 1999

Per capita income,	$31,641
Median household income	$68,392
Median family income	$77,611
Persons in poverty	295
H'holds receiving public assistance	65
H'holds receiving social security	1,079

Households, 2000

Total households	5,720
With persons under 18	2,131
With persons over 65	1,061
Family households	4,023
Single person households	1,296
Persons per household	2.6
Persons per family	3.0

Labor & Employment, 2000

Civilian labor force	8,676
Unemployment rate	4.3%
Civilian labor force, 2008†	9,467
Unemployment rate†	4.7%
Civilian labor force, 12/09†	9,648
Unemployment rate†	7.2%
Employed persons 16 years and over, by occupation:	
Managers & professionals	3,989
Service occupations	929
Sales & office occupations	2,244
Farming, fishing & forestry	9
Construction & maintenance	586
Production & transportation	548
Self-employed persons	672

Most demographic data is from the 2000 Decennial Census
† Massachusetts Department of Revenue
†† University of Massachusetts, MISER

General Information

Town of Ashland
101 Main St
Ashland, MA 01721
508-881-0100

Elevation	188 ft.
Land area (square miles)	12.4
Water area (square miles)	0.5
Population density, 2008 (est)	1,274.8
Year incorporated	1846
Website	www.ashlandmass.com

Voters & Government Information

Government type	Open Town Meeting
Number of Selectmen	5
US Congressional District(s)	3

Registered Voters, October 2008

Total	10,571
Democrats	3,062
Republicans	1,316
Unaffiliated/other	6,157

Local Officials, 2010

Chair, Bd. of Sel.	Paul D. Monaco
Town Manager	John D. Petrin
Clerk	Tara M. Ward
Finance Director	Mark J. Purple
Tax Collector	Christine Brodeur
Tax Assessor	Richard Ball
Attorney	Lisa Mead
Public Works	Doug Small
Building	Ed Morini
Planning	Stephen Kerlin
Police Chief	Scott Rohmer
Fire Chief	William Kee

Housing & Construction

New Privately Owned Housing Units Authorized by Building Permit

	Single Family	Total Bldgs	Total Units
2006	36	40	52
2007	21	27	45
2008	22	24	38

Parcel Count by Property Class, 2010

Total	6,345
Single family	3,687
Multiple units	176
Apartments	48
Condos	1,757
Vacant land	387
Open space	9
Commercial	168
Industrial	60
Misc. residential	14
Other use	39

Public Library

Ashland Public Library
66 Front St.
Ashland, MA 01721
(508)881-0134

Director	Paula Bonetti

Library Statistics, FY 2008

Population served, 2007	15,796
Registered users	5,081
Circulation	154,224
Reference transactons	1,002
Total program attendance	0
per capita:	
Holdings	3.22
Operating income	$19.33
Internet Access	
Internet computers available	14
Weekly users	205

Municipal Finance

Debt at year end 2008	$56,794,226
Moody's rating, July 2009	A1

Revenues, 2008

Total	$52,869,866
From all taxes	33,529,722
Federal aid	0
State aid	6,819,001
From other governments	12,353
Charges for services	0
Licenses, permits & fees	1,021,118
Fines & forfeits	43,165
Interfund transfers	1,710,909
Misc/other/special assessments	4,866,799

Expenditures, 2008

Total	$45,198,859
General government	1,957,516
Public safety	4,824,986
Other/fixed costs	6,621,722
Human services	300,791
Culture & recreation	364,800
Debt Service	4,288,300
Education	22,217,228
Public works	1,219,046
Intergovernmental	604,470

Taxation, 2010

Property type	Valuation	Rate
Total	$2,200,543,850	-
Residential	2,006,673,000	15.10
Open space	321,300	15.10
Commercial	111,666,000	15.10
Industrial	42,063,300	15.10
Personal	39,820,250	15.10

Average Single Family Tax Bill, 2010

Avg. assessed home value	$373,619
Avg. single fam. tax bill	$5,642
Hi-Lo ranking	57/301

Police & Crime, 2008

Number of police officers	27
Violent crimes	20
Property crimes	163

Local School District

(school data 2007-08, except as noted)

Ashland
87 West Union Street
Ashland, MA 01721
508-881-0150

Superintendent	Perry Davis
Grade plan	PK-12
Total enrollment '09-10	2,640
Grade 12 enrollment, '09-10	173
Graduation rate	92.9%
Dropout rate	5.5%
Per-pupil expenditure	$11,332
Avg teacher salary	$61,775
Student/teacher ratio '08-09	15.3 to 1
Highly-qualified teachers, '08-09	99.6%
Teachers licensed in assigned subject	99.4%
Students per computer	4.1

Massachusetts Competency Assessment System (MCAS), 2009 results

	English		Math	
	% Prof	CPI	% Prof	CPI
Gr 4	64%	86.2	50%	80.9
Gr 6	75%	92.3	74%	87.6
Gr 8	91%	96.4	64%	81
Gr 10	93%	96.9	88%	94.3

Other School Districts (see Appendix D for data)
South Middlesex Vocational Tech

©2010 Information Publications, Inc. All rights reserved. Photocopying prohibited. For additional copies, contact the publisher at www.informationpublications.com or (877)544-INFO (4636)

Demographics & Socio-Economic Characteristics

Population

1990	11,451
2000	11,299
Male	5,469
Female	5,830
2008	11,570
2010 (projected)††	11,288
2020 (projected)††	11,412

Race & Hispanic Origin, 2000

Race	
White	10,884
Black/African American	74
American Indian/Alaska Native	40
Asian	48
Hawaiian Native/Pacific Islander	3
Other Race	83
Two or more races	167
Hispanic origin	222

Age & Nativity, 2000

Under 5 years	648
18 years and over	8,424
21 years and over	8,012
65 years and over	1,940
85 years and over	335
Median Age	38.6
Native-born	10,988
Foreign-born	311

Age, 2020 (projected)††

Under 5 years	636
5 to 19 years	1,937
20 to 39 years	2,735
40 to 64 years	3,819
65 years and over	2,285

Educational Attainment, 2000

Population 25 years and over	7,507
High School graduates or higher	80.0%
Bachelor's degree or higher	13.3%
Graduate degree	4.2%

Income & Poverty, 1999

Per capita income,	$16,845
Median household income	$33,475
Median family income	$41,061
Persons in poverty	1,038
H'holds receiving public assistance	131
H'holds receiving social security	1,492

Households, 2000

Total households	4,487
With persons under 18	1,520
With persons over 65	1,277
Family households	2,970
Single person households	1,274
Persons per household	2.5
Persons per family	3.0

Labor & Employment, 2000

Civilian labor force	5,336
Unemployment rate	4.5%
Civilian labor force, 2008†	5,208
Unemployment rate†	9.0%
Civilian labor force, 12/09†	5,397
Unemployment rate†	12.7%
Employed persons 16 years and over, by occupation:	
Managers & professionals	1,249
Service occupations	845
Sales & office occupations	1,201
Farming, fishing & forestry	3
Construction & maintenance	413
Production & transportation	1,385
Self-employed persons	303

Most demographic data is from the 2000 Decennial Census
† Massachusetts Department of Revenue
†† University of Massachusetts, MISER

General Information

Town of Athol
584 Main St
Athol, MA 01331
978-249-2368

Elevation	535 ft.
Land area (square miles)	32.6
Water area (square miles)	0.8
Population density, 2008 (est)	354.9
Year incorporated	1762
Website	www.athol-ma.gov

Voters & Government Information

Government type	Open Town Meeting
Number of Selectmen	5
US Congressional District(s)	1

Registered Voters, October 2008

Total	6,948
Democrats	1,645
Republicans	914
Unaffiliated/other	4,321

Local Officials, 2010

Chair, Bd. of Sel.	Alan Dodge
Town Manager	David Ames
Town Clerk	Nancy Burnham
Treasurer	Ben Feldman
Tax Collector	Karen Stoddard
Tax Assessor	Lisa Aldrich
Attorney	Mark Goldstein
Public Works	Douglas Walsh
Building	Jeffrey Cooke
Comm Dev/Planning	Phil Delorey
Police Chief	Timothy Anderson
Emerg/Fire Chief	James Wright

Housing & Construction

New Privately Owned Housing Units Authorized by Building Permit

	Single Family	Total Bldgs	Total Units
2006	43	44	45
2007	22	22	22
2008	14	14	14

Parcel Count by Property Class, 2010

Total	5,256
Single family	3,393
Multiple units	354
Apartments	80
Condos	103
Vacant land	932
Open space	0
Commercial	217
Industrial	57
Misc. residential	21
Other use	99

Public Library

Athol Public Library
568 Main St.
Athol, MA 01331
(978)249-9515

Director .... Debra A. Blanchard

Library Statistics, FY 2008

Population served, 2007	11,601
Registered users	11,976
Circulation	133,370
Reference transactons	1,814
Total program attendance	0
per capita:	
Holdings	4.76
Operating income	$36.05
Internet Access	
Internet computers available	29
Weekly users	284

Municipal Finance

Debt at year end 2008	$7,459,697
Moody's rating, July 2009	A3

Revenues, 2008

Total	$16,779,963
From all taxes	9,656,990
Federal aid	0
State aid	3,146,112
From other governments	27,170
Charges for services	2,941,665
Licenses, permits & fees	145,911
Fines & forfeits	0
Interfund transfers	317,403
Misc/other/special assessments	272,356

Expenditures, 2008

Total	$13,086,659
General government	1,116,902
Public safety	2,817,715
Other/fixed costs	2,894,553
Human services	324,284
Culture & recreation	456,333
Debt Service	656,270
Education	3,342,629
Public works	1,416,440
Intergovernmental	60,513

Taxation, 2010

Property type	Valuation	Rate
Total	$724,403,038	-
Residential	639,640,253	13.30
Open space	0	0.00
Commercial	50,961,347	13.30
Industrial	15,265,600	13.30
Personal	18,535,838	13.30

Average Single Family Tax Bill, 2010

Avg. assessed home value	$154,121
Avg. single fam. tax bill	$2,050
Hi-Lo ranking	293/301

Police & Crime, 2008

Number of police officers	17
Violent crimes	47
Property crimes	291

Local School District

(school data 2007-08, except as noted)

Athol (non-op)
P.O.Box 968
Athol, MA 01331
978-249-2400

Superintendent .... Anthony Polito

Non-operating district.
Resident students are sent to the Other School Districts listed below.

Grade plan	NA
Total enrollment '09-10	NA
Grade 12 enrollment, '09-10	NA
Graduation rate	NA
Dropout rate	NA
Per-pupil expenditure	NA
Avg teacher salary	NA
Student/teacher ratio '08-09	NA
Highly-qualified teachers, '08-09	NA
Teachers licensed in assigned subject	NA
Students per computer	NA

Other School Districts (see Appendix D for data)
Athol-Royalston Regional, Montachusett Vocational Tech

See Introduction for an explanation of all data sources.

©2010 Information Publications, Inc. All rights reserved. Photocopying prohibited. For additional copies, contact the publisher at www.informationpublications.com or (877)544-INFO (4636)

Demographics & Socio-Economic Characteristics*

Population

1990	38,383
2000	42,068
Male	20,441
Female	21,627
2008	42,833
2010 (projected)††	44,773
2020 (projected)††	48,170

Race & Hispanic Origin, 2000

Race	
White	38,410
Black/African American	691
American Indian/Alaska Native	67
Asian	1,367
Hawaiian Native/Pacific Islander	15
Other Race	765
Two or more races	753
Hispanic origin	1,805

Age & Nativity, 2000

Under 5 years	2,942
18 years and over	31,394
21 years and over	30,150
65 years and over	5,422
85 years and over	749
Median Age	36.1
Native-born	38,323
Foreign-born	3,745

Age, 2020 (projected)††

Under 5 years	3,123
5 to 19 years	8,506
20 to 39 years	13,017
40 to 64 years	15,907
65 years and over	7,617

Educational Attainment, 2000

Population 25 years and over	28,635
High School graduates or higher	81.9%
Bachelor's degree or higher	23.5%
Graduate degree	6.5%

Income & Poverty, 1999

Per capita income,	$22,660
Median household income	$50,807
Median family income	$59,112
Persons in poverty	2,539
H'holds receiving public assistance	365
H'holds receiving social security	3,894

Households, 2000

Total households	16,019
With persons under 18	5,707
With persons over 65	3,579
Family households	10,921
Single person households	4,117
Persons per household	2.6
Persons per family	3.1

Labor & Employment, 2000

Civilian labor force	22,907
Unemployment rate	3.7%
Civilian labor force, 2008†	24,261
Unemployment rate†	8.2%
Civilian labor force, 12/09†	24,241
Unemployment rate†	11.0%
Employed persons 16 years and over, by occupation:	
Managers & professionals	7,403
Service occupations	2,698
Sales & office occupations	5,863
Farming, fishing & forestry	23
Construction & maintenance	1,785
Production & transportation	4,291
Self-employed persons	1,144

Most demographic data is from the 2000 Decennial Census
* see Appendix E for American Community Survey data
† Massachusetts Department of Revenue
†† University of Massachusetts, MISER

General Information

City of Attleboro
77 Park St
Attleboro, MA 02703
508-223-2222

Elevation	130 ft.
Land area (square miles)	27.5
Water area (square miles)	0.8
Population density, 2008 (est)	1,557.6
Year incorporated	1694
Website	www.cityofattleboro.us

Voters & Government Information

Government type	Mayor-Council
Number of Councilpersons	11
US Congressional District(s)	3

Registered Voters, October 2008

Total	26,688
Democrats	6,946
Republicans	3,397
Unaffiliated/other	16,132

Local Officials, 2010

Mayor	Kevin J. Dumas
Budget & Admin	Barry K. LaCasse
City Clerk	Elizabeth A. Shockroo
Treasurer	Ethel Sandbach
Tax Collector	Debora Marcoccio
Tax Assessor	Stanley Nacewicz
Attorney	Robert Mangiaratti
Public Works	John Clover
Building	Douglas Semple
Comm Dev/Planning	Gary Ayrassian
Police Chief	Richard Pierce
Emerg/Fire Chief	Ronald Churchill

Housing & Construction

New Privately Owned Housing Units Authorized by Building Permit

	Single Family	Total Bldgs	Total Units
2006	100	105	110
2007	54	58	68
2008	45	47	49

Parcel Count by Property Class, 2010

Total	14,233
Single family	9,298
Multiple units	1,385
Apartments	211
Condos	1,211
Vacant land	1,236
Open space	0
Commercial	456
Industrial	237
Misc. residential	77
Other use	122

Public Library

Attleboro Public Library
74 North Main Street
Attleboro, MA 02703
(508)222-0157

Director	Walter B. Stitt

Library Statistics, FY 2008

Population served, 2007	43,113
Registered users	20,500
Circulation	253,597
Reference transactons	11,119
Total program attendance	184,000
per capita:	
Holdings	2.44
Operating income	$25.89
Internet Access	
Internet computers available	8
Weekly users	1,531

Municipal Finance

Debt at year end 2008	$115,380,653
Moody's rating, July 2009	A3

Revenues, 2008

Total	$102,660,912
From all taxes	52,948,761
Federal aid	0
State aid	41,443,854
From other governments	218,508
Charges for services	3,244,565
Licenses, permits & fees	926,821
Fines & forfeits	135,222
Interfund transfers	1,031,815
Misc/other/special assessments	1,355,683

Expenditures, 2008

Total	$87,812,733
General government	3,373,523
Public safety	12,986,892
Other/fixed costs	4,116,463
Human services	3,300,520
Culture & recreation	2,601,413
Debt Service	7,180,020
Education	48,605,254
Public works	2,584,778
Intergovernmental	3,063,870

Taxation, 2010

Property type	Valuation	Rate
Total	$4,267,810,373	-
Residential	3,548,851,803	11.20
Open space	0	0.00
Commercial	372,303,132	18.28
Industrial	228,492,900	18.28
Personal	118,162,538	18.28

Average Single Family Tax Bill, 2010

Avg. assessed home value	$281,562
Avg. single fam. tax bill	$3,153
Hi-Lo ranking	218/301

Police & Crime, 2008

Number of police officers	82
Violent crimes	143
Property crimes	956

Local School District

(school data 2007-08, except as noted)

Attleboro
100 Rathbun Willard Drive
Attleboro, MA 02703
508-222-0012

Superintendent	Pia Durkin
Grade plan	PK-12
Total enrollment '09-10	5,933
Grade 12 enrollment, '09-10	404
Graduation rate	76.4%
Dropout rate	13.0%
Per-pupil expenditure	$10,878
Avg teacher salary	$69,120
Student/teacher ratio '08-09	15.0 to 1
Highly-qualified teachers, '08-09	96.2%
Teachers licensed in assigned subject	97.7%
Students per computer	6.5

Massachusetts Competency Assessment System (MCAS), 2009 results

	English		Math	
	% Prof	CPI	% Prof	CPI
Gr 4	57%	83.5	55%	83.7
Gr 6	58%	85.1	48%	76.3
Gr 8	81%	92.6	50%	74.8
Gr 10	77%	91.3	73%	88.9

Other School Districts (see Appendix D for data)
Bristol County Agricultural

©2010 Information Publications, Inc. All rights reserved. Photocopying prohibited. For additional copies, contact the publisher at www.informationpublications.com or (877)544-INFO (4636)

See Introduction for an explanation of all data sources.

Demographics & Socio-Economic Characteristics

Population

1990 15,005
2000 15,901
  Male 7,572
  Female 8,329
2008 16,222
2010 (projected)†† 15,555
2020 (projected)†† 15,083

Race & Hispanic Origin, 2000

Race
  White 15,510
  Black/African American 92
  American Indian/Alaska Native 18
  Asian 142
  Hawaiian Native/Pacific Islander 4
  Other Race 37
  Two or more races 98
Hispanic origin 166

Age & Nativity, 2000

Under 5 years 847
18 years and over 12,285
21 years and over 11,881
65 years and over 2,882
85 years and over 374
  Median Age 40.9
Native-born 15,347
Foreign-born 554

Age, 2020 (projected)††

Under 5 years 694
5 to 19 years 2,306
20 to 39 years 3,290
40 to 64 years 5,329
65 years and over 3,464

Educational Attainment, 2000

Population 25 years and over 11,469
  High School graduates or higher .. 88.8%
  Bachelor's degree or higher 24.2%
  Graduate degree 8.7%

Income & Poverty, 1999

Per capita income, ... $23,802
Median household income $51,753
Median family income $60,805
Persons in poverty 516
H'holds receiving public assistance 91
H'holds receiving social security 2,110

Households, 2000

Total households 6,346
  With persons under 18 1,933
  With persons over 65 2,029
  Family households 4,406
  Single person households 1,634
Persons per household 2.5
Persons per family 3.0

Labor & Employment, 2000

Civilian labor force 8,443
  Unemployment rate 2.4%
Civilian labor force, 2008† 8,675
  Unemployment rate† 5.4%
Civilian labor force, 12/09† 8,861
  Unemployment rate† 8.5%
Employed persons 16 years and over, by occupation:
  Managers & professionals 3,049
  Service occupations 1,053
  Sales & office occupations 2,376
  Farming, fishing & forestry 0
  Construction & maintenance 815
  Production & transportation 951
  Self-employed persons 552

Most demographic data is from the 2000 Decennial Census
† Massachusetts Department of Revenue
†† University of Massachusetts, MISER

©2010 Information Publications, Inc. All rights reserved. Photocopying prohibited. For additional copies, contact the publisher at www.informationpublications.com or (877)544-INFO (4636)

General Information

Town of Auburn
104 Central St
Auburn, MA 01501
508-832-7701

Elevation .... 600 ft.
Land area (square miles) 15.4
Water area (square miles) 1.0
Population density, 2008 (est) 1,053.4
Year incorporated 1778
Website .... auburnguide.com

Voters & Government Information

Government type .... Rep. Town Meeting
Number of Selectmen 5
US Congressional District(s) 3

Registered Voters, October 2008

Total 11,504
Democrats 3,590
Republicans 1,360
Unaffiliated/other 6,494

Local Officials, 2010

Chair, Bd. of Sel. .... Robert D. Grossman
Manager/Admin .... Charles O'Connor Jr
Town Clerk .... Ellen Gaboury
Finance Director .... Edward Kazanovicz
Tax Collector .... Theresa Lolax
Tax Assessor .... Cynthia Cosgrove
Attorney .... Robert Henningan
Public Works .... Darlene N. Wood Belsito
Building .... Donald Miller
Comm Dev/Planning .... Shelia Conroy
Police Chief .... Andrew Sluckis Jr
Emerg/Fire Chief .... William Whynot

Housing & Construction

New Privately Owned Housing Units Authorized by Building Permit

	Single Family	Total Bldgs	Total Units
2006	45	45	45
2007	35	35	35
2008	24	24	24

Parcel Count by Property Class, 2010

Total 6,585
Single family 4,958
Multiple units 253
Apartments 16
Condos 416
Vacant land 414
Open space 0
Commercial 285
Industrial 124
Misc. residential 41
Other use 78

Public Library

Auburn Public Library
369 Southbridge St.
Auburn, MA 01501
(508)832-7790

Director .... Joan F. Noonan

Library Statistics, FY 2008

Population served, 2007 16,259
Registered users 8,783
Circulation 212,258
Reference transactons 7,151
Total program attendance 0
per capita:
Holdings 6.64
Operating income $34.60
Internet Access
Internet computers available 4
Weekly users 116

Municipal Finance

Debt at year end 2008 .... $26,571,000
Moody's rating, July 2009 .... A2

Revenues, 2008

Total $44,081,610
From all taxes 32,482,353
Federal aid 0
State aid 7,691,678
From other governments 152,738
Charges for services 996,722
Licenses, permits & fees 558,774
Fines & forfeits 33,945
Interfund transfers 1,299,924
Misc/other/special assessments 432,738

Expenditures, 2008

Total $38,271,064
General government 2,666,461
Public safety 5,275,533
Other/fixed costs 1,720,485
Human services 609,571
Culture & recreation 824,949
Debt Service 3,117,394
Education 20,995,195
Public works 2,140,924
Intergovernmental 619,076

Taxation, 2010

Property type	Valuation	Rate
Total	$1,862,433,986	-
Residential	1,326,664,929	14.34
Open space	0	0.00
Commercial	341,714,197	24.06
Industrial	140,535,600	24.06
Personal	53,519,260	23.95

Average Single Family Tax Bill, 2010

Avg. assessed home value $225,198
Avg. single fam. tax bill $3,229
Hi-Lo ranking 212/301

Police & Crime, 2008

Number of police officers .... NA
Violent crimes .... NA
Property crimes 503

Local School District

(school data 2007-08, except as noted)

Auburn
5 West Street
Auburn, MA 01501
508-832-7755

Superintendent .... Maryellen Brunelle
Grade plan PK-12
Total enrollment '09-10 2,399
Grade 12 enrollment, '09-10 196
Graduation rate 90.2%
Dropout rate 6.7%
Per-pupil expenditure $11,526
Avg teacher salary $59,995
Student/teacher ratio '08-09 .... 14.0 to 1
Highly-qualified teachers, '08-09 .... 96.6%
Teachers licensed in assigned subject .. 97.0%
Students per computer 3.6

Massachusetts Competency Assessment System (MCAS), 2009 results

	English		Math	
	% Prof	CPI	% Prof	CPI
Gr 4	67%	86.3	52%	82.8
Gr 6	76%	90.2	58%	80.8
Gr 8	83%	93.8	52%	77.7
Gr 10	88%	95	83%	93.5

Other School Districts (see Appendix D for data)
Southern Worcester County Vocational Tech

See Introduction for an explanation of all data sources.

Demographics & Socio-Economic Characteristics

Population

1990 4,558
2000 4,443
Male 2,126
Female 2,317
2008 4,300
2010 (projected)†† 4,025
2020 (projected)†† 3,569

Race & Hispanic Origin, 2000

Race
White 4,152
Black/African American 166
American Indian/Alaska Native 12
Asian 41
Hawaiian Native/Pacific Islander 0
Other Race 34
Two or more races 38
Hispanic origin 64

Age & Nativity, 2000

Under 5 years 243
18 years and over 3,442
21 years and over 3,302
65 years and over 780
85 years and over 73
Median Age 40.2
Native-born 4,288
Foreign-born 155

Age, 2020 (projected)††

Under 5 years 153
5 to 19 years 511
20 to 39 years 788
40 to 64 years 1,302
65 years and over 815

Educational Attainment, 2000

Population 25 years and over 3,116
High School graduates or higher .. 90.6%
Bachelor's degree or higher 21.2%
Graduate degree 6.6%

Income & Poverty, 1999

Per capita income, ... $24,410
Median household income $50,305
Median family income $60,625
Persons in poverty 292
H'holds receiving public assistance 25
H'holds receiving social security 620

Households, 2000

Total households 1,705
With persons under 18 521
With persons over 65 568
Family households 1,220
Single person households 401
Persons per household 2.6
Persons per family 3.1

Labor & Employment, 2000

Civilian labor force 2,319
Unemployment rate 3.5%
Civilian labor force, 2008† 2,297
Unemployment rate† 7.4%
Civilian labor force, 12/09† 2,298
Unemployment rate† 10.6%
Employed persons 16 years and over, by occupation:
Managers & professionals 807
Service occupations 247
Sales & office occupations 680
Farming, fishing & forestry 0
Construction & maintenance 187
Production & transportation 316
Self-employed persons 116

Most demographic data is from the 2000 Decennial Census
† Massachusetts Department of Revenue
†† University of Massachusetts, MISER

General Information

Town of Avon
Buckley Center
Avon, MA 02322
508-588-0414

Elevation .... 250 ft.
Land area (square miles) 4.4
Water area (square miles) 0.2
Population density, 2008 (est) 977.3
Year incorporated 1888
Email .... MMcCue@avonmass.org

Voters & Government Information

Government type .... Open Town Meeting
Number of Selectmen 3
US Congressional District(s) 9

Registered Voters, October 2008

Total 3,030
Democrats 1,062
Republicans 289
Unaffiliated/other 1,664

Local Officials, 2010

Chair, Bd. of Sel. .... Francis A. Hegarty
Manager/Admin .... Mike McCue
Clerk .... Jean Kopke
Finance Director .... Jean Kopke
Tax Collector .... Michael A. Depesa
Tax Assessor .... Warren Lane
Attorney .... Joseph S. Lalli
Public Works .... NA
Building .... Robert Borden
Comm Dev/Planning .... NA
Police Chief .... Warren Phillips
Emerg/Fire Chief .... Robert Spurr

Housing & Construction

New Privately Owned Housing Units Authorized by Building Permit

	Single Family	Total Bldgs	Total Units
2006	5	5	5
2007	5	5	5
2008	4	4	4

Parcel Count by Property Class, 2010

Total 1,836
Single family 1,275
Multiple units 114
Apartments 10
Condos 36
Vacant land 151
Open space 0
Commercial 92
Industrial 124
Misc. residential 15
Other use 19

Public Library

Avon Public Library
280 West Main St.
Avon, MA 02322
(508)583-0378

Director .... Karen Johnson

Library Statistics, FY 2008

Population served, 2007 4,303
Registered users 2,650
Circulation 46,122
Reference transactons 946
Total program attendance 49,872

per capita:

Holdings 10.76
Operating income $79.70

Internet Access

Internet computers available 5
Weekly users 30

Municipal Finance

Debt at year end 2008 .... $10,862,020
Moody's rating, July 2009 .... A2

Revenues, 2008

Total $17,579,205
From all taxes 13,932,469
Federal aid 0
State aid 1,776,373
From other governments 87,743
Charges for services 399,367
Licenses, permits & fees 223,997
Fines & forfeits 0
Interfund transfers 287,272
Misc/other/special assessments 435,992

Expenditures, 2008

Total $16,422,612
General government 782,274
Public safety 2,791,368
Other/fixed costs 2,668,344
Human services 158,198
Culture & recreation 370,063
Debt Service 1,732,149
Education 6,144,452
Public works 1,520,824
Intergovernmental 140,095

Taxation, 2010

Property type	Valuation	Rate
Total	$845,197,825	-
Residential	435,120,611	10.88
Open space	0	0.00
Commercial	144,621,689	23.07
Industrial	208,189,300	23.07
Personal	57,266,225	22.96

Average Single Family Tax Bill, 2010

Avg. assessed home value $284,629
Avg. single fam. tax bill $3,097
Hi-Lo ranking 228/301

Police & Crime, 2008

Number of police officers 15
Violent crimes 6
Property crimes 195

Local School District

(school data 2007-08, except as noted)

Avon
Patrick Clark Drive
Avon, MA 02322
508-588-0230

Superintendent .... Margaret Frieswyk
Grade plan PK-12
Total enrollment '09-10 748
Grade 12 enrollment, '09-10 48
Graduation rate 73.4%
Dropout rate 14.1%
Per-pupil expenditure $12,097
Avg teacher salary $54,627
Student/teacher ratio '08-09 .... 12.0 to 1
Highly-qualified teachers, '08-09 .... 99.0%
Teachers licensed in assigned subject .. 98.4%
Students per computer 2.3

Massachusetts Competency Assessment System (MCAS), 2009 results

	English		Math	
	% Prof	CPI	% Prof	CPI
Gr 4	53%	79.2	47%	78.8
Gr 6	70%	90.6	52%	79.1
Gr 8	86%	94.5	45%	70.7
Gr 10	84%	93.8	63%	83.9

Other School Districts (see Appendix D for data)

Blue Hills Vocational Tech, Norfolk County Agricultural

©2010 Information Publications, Inc. All rights reserved. Photocopying prohibited. For additional copies, contact the publisher at www.informationpublications.com or (877)544-INFO (4636)

See Introduction for an explanation of all data sources.

©2010 Information Publications, Inc. All rights reserved. Photocopying prohibited. For additional copies, contact the publisher at www.informationpublications.com or (877)544-INFO (4636)

Demographics & Socio-Economic Characteristics

Population

1990 . . . 6,871
2000 . . . 7,287
Male . . . 3,585
Female . . . 3,702
2008 . . . 7,399
2010 (projected)†† . . . 7,328
2020 (projected)†† . . . 7,257

Race & Hispanic Origin, 2000

Race
White . . . 6,261
Black/African American . . . 415
American Indian/Alaska Native . . . 19
Asian . . . 211
Hawaiian Native/Pacific Islander . . . 10
Other Race . . . 166
Two or more races . . . 205
Hispanic origin . . . 342

Age & Nativity, 2000

Under 5 years . . . 513
18 years and over . . . 5,539
21 years and over . . . 5,220
65 years and over . . . 876
85 years and over . . . 140
Median Age . . . 34.8
Native-born . . . 6,594
Foreign-born . . . 693

Age, 2020 (projected)††

Under 5 years . . . 442
5 to 19 years . . . 1,370
20 to 39 years . . . 1,854
40 to 64 years . . . 2,276
65 years and over . . . 1,315

Educational Attainment, 2000

Population 25 years and over . . . 5,002
High School graduates or higher . . 88.7%
Bachelor's degree or higher . . . 25.9%
Graduate degree . . . 9.8%

Income & Poverty, 1999

Per capita income, . . . $26,400
Median household income . . . $46,619
Median family income . . . $61,968
Persons in poverty . . . 765
H'holds receiving public assistance . . . 71
H'holds receiving social security . . . 645

Households, 2000

Total households . . . 2,982
With persons under 18 . . . 952
With persons over 65 . . . 558
Family households . . . 1,773
Single person households . . . 979
Persons per household . . . 2.3
Persons per family . . . 2.9

Labor & Employment, 2000

Civilian labor force . . . 4,089
Unemployment rate . . . 3.2%
Civilian labor force, 2008† . . . 4,216
Unemployment rate† . . . 5.9%
Civilian labor force, 12/09† . . . 4,311
Unemployment rate† . . . 9.9%
Employed persons 16 years and over, by occupation:
Managers & professionals . . . 1,500
Service occupations . . . 567
Sales & office occupations . . . 937
Farming, fishing & forestry . . . 13
Construction & maintenance . . . 393
Production & transportation . . . 549
Self-employed persons . . . 140

Most demographic data is from the 2000 Decennial Census
† Massachusetts Department of Revenue
†† University of Massachusetts, MISER

General Information

Town of Ayer
1 Main St
PO Box 308
Ayer, MA 01432
978-772-8215

Elevation . . . 240 ft.
Land area (square miles) . . . 9.0
Water area (square miles) . . . 0.6
Population density, 2008 (est) . . . 822.1
Year incorporated . . . 1871
Website . . . ayer.ma.us

Voters & Government Information

Government type . . . Open Town Meeting
Number of Selectmen . . . 5
US Congressional District(s) . . . 5

Registered Voters, October 2008

Total . . . 4,536
Democrats . . . 1,183
Republicans . . . 617
Unaffiliated/other . . . 2,700

Local Officials, 2010

Chair, Bd. of Sel. . . . Cornelius F. Sullivan
Town Administrator . . . Shaun Suhoski
Clerk . . . John Canney II
Treasurer . . . M. Stephanie Gintner
Tax Collector . . . John Canney II
Tax Assessor . . . Ed Cornellier
Attorney . . . Kopelman & Paige
Public Works . . . Daniel F. Nason
Building . . . Gabriel Vellante
Comm Dev/Planning . . . Christopher Ryan
Police Chief . . . William A. Murray
Emerg/Fire Chief . . . Robert Pedrazzi

Housing & Construction

New Privately Owned Housing Units Authorized by Building Permit

	Single Family	Total Bldgs	Total Units
2006	14	22	30
2007	24	31	38
2008	26	28	32

Parcel Count by Property Class, 2010

Total . . . 2,986
Single family . . . 1,421
Multiple units . . . 261
Apartments . . . 71
Condos . . . 434
Vacant land . . . 406
Open space . . . 0
Commercial . . . 183
Industrial . . . 104
Misc. residential . . . 37
Other use . . . 69

Public Library

Ayer Public Library
26 E. Main St., PO Box 135
Ayer, MA 01432
(978)772-8250

Director . . . Mary Anne Lucht

Library Statistics, FY 2008

Population served, 2007 . . . 7,369
Registered users . . . 4,800
Circulation . . . 72,255
Reference transactons . . . 25,000
Total program attendance . . . 80,000
per capita:
Holdings . . . 9.40
Operating income . . . $58.98
Internet Access
Internet computers available . . . 9
Weekly users . . . 300

Municipal Finance

Debt at year end 2008 . . . $21,075,352
Moody's rating, July 2009 . . . A2

Revenues, 2008

Total . . . $22,678,517
From all taxes . . . 15,219,492
Federal aid . . . 63,837
State aid . . . 4,774,827
From other governments . . . 42,088
Charges for services . . . 120,100
Licenses, permits & fees . . . 227,655
Fines & forfeits . . . 0
Interfund transfers . . . 984,984
Misc/other/special assessments . . . 622,767

Expenditures, 2008

Total . . . $20,629,733
General government . . . 1,599,798
Public safety . . . 2,655,360
Other/fixed costs . . . 4,217,643
Human services . . . 193,187
Culture & recreation . . . 544,989
Debt Service . . . 1,464,731
Education . . . 8,900,409
Public works . . . 970,294
Intergovernmental . . . 83,322

Taxation, 2010

Property type	Valuation	Rate
Total	$972,743,450	-
Residential	627,463,300	11.49
Open space	0	0.00
Commercial	93,092,300	25.54
Industrial	145,299,000	25.54
Personal	106,888,850	25.54

Average Single Family Tax Bill, 2010

Avg. assessed home value . . . $275,964
Avg. single fam. tax bill . . . $3,171
Hi-Lo ranking . . . 215/301

Police & Crime, 2008

Number of police officers . . . 17
Violent crimes . . . 24
Property crimes . . . 148

Local School District

(school data 2007-08, except as noted)

Ayer
141 Washington Street
Ayer, MA 01432
978-772-8600

Superintendent . . . George Frost
Grade plan . . . PK-12
Total enrollment '09-10 . . . 1,197
Grade 12 enrollment, '09-10 . . . 101
Graduation rate . . . 95.5%
Dropout rate . . . 4.5%
Per-pupil expenditure . . . $11,199
Avg teacher salary . . . $56,857
Student/teacher ratio '08-09 . . . 12.6 to 1
Highly-qualified teachers, '08-09 . . . 97.4%
Teachers licensed in assigned subject . . 97.9%
Students per computer . . . 3

Massachusetts Competency Assessment System (MCAS), 2009 results

	English		Math	
	% Prof	CPI	% Prof	CPI
Gr 4	51%	77.1	46%	76.8
Gr 6	65%	85.6	54%	75
Gr 8	76%	89.5	43%	66
Gr 10	81%	93	67%	84.2

Other School Districts (see Appendix D for data)
Receives students from Shirley

See Introduction for an explanation of all data sources.

Demographics & Socio-Economic Characteristics*

Population

1990	40,949
2000	47,821
Male	22,864
Female	24,957
2008	46,184
2010 (projected)††	56,368
2020 (projected)††	65,953

Race & Hispanic Origin, 2000

Race	
White	43,925
Black/African American	1,309
American Indian/Alaska Native	283
Asian	387
Hawaiian Native/Pacific Islander	18
Other Race	799
Two or more races	1,100
Hispanic origin	812

Age & Nativity, 2000

Under 5 years	2,509
18 years and over	37,323
21 years and over	36,094
65 years and over	9,599
85 years and over	1,106
Median Age	42.3
Native-born	44,499
Foreign-born	3,322

Age, 2020 (projected)††

Under 5 years	3,246
5 to 19 years	9,702
20 to 39 years	14,030
40 to 64 years	21,620
65 years and over	17,355

Educational Attainment, 2000

Population 25 years and over	34,695
High School graduates or higher	90.4%
Bachelor's degree or higher	32.2%
Graduate degree	11.9%

Income & Poverty, 1999

Per capita income,	$25,554
Median household income	$46,811
Median family income	$54,026
Persons in poverty	4,173
H'holds receiving public assistance	333
H'holds receiving social security	6,886

Households, 2000

Total households	19,626
With persons under 18	5,689
With persons over 65	6,566
Family households	13,005
Single person households	5,437
Persons per household	2.4
Persons per family	2.9

Labor & Employment, 2000

Civilian labor force	23,810
Unemployment rate	4.8%
Civilian labor force, 2008†	25,233
Unemployment rate†	7.6%
Civilian labor force, 12/09†	24,498
Unemployment rate†	9.5%
Employed persons 16 years and over, by occupation:	
Managers & professionals	8,016
Service occupations	4,536
Sales & office occupations	5,915
Farming, fishing & forestry	83
Construction & maintenance	2,381
Production & transportation	1,746
Self-employed persons	2,746

Most demographic data is from the 2000 Decennial Census
* see Appendix E for American Community Survey data
† Massachusetts Department of Revenue
†† University of Massachusetts, MISER

General Information

City of Barnstable
367 Main St
Hyannis, MA 02601
508-862-4610

Elevation	50 ft.
Land area (square miles)	60.0
Water area (square miles)	16.2
Population density, 2008 (est)	769.7
Year incorporated	1639
Website	www.town.barnstable.ma.us

Voters & Government Information

Government type	Manager-Council
Number of Councilpersons	13
US Congressional District(s)	10

Registered Voters, October 2008

Total	32,386
Democrats	8,242
Republicans	5,836
Unaffiliated/other	18,073

Local Officials, 2010

Council President	Frederick Cheigotis
Town Manager	John Klimm
City Clerk	Linda Hutchenrider
Finance Director	Mark Milne
Tax Collector	Maureen Niemi
Tax Assessor	Jeff Rudziak
Attorney	Ruth Weil
Public Works	Mark Ells
Building	Thomas Perry
Comm Dev/Planning	Thomas Geiler
Police Chief	Paul McDonald (Actg)
Emerg/Fire Chief	NA

Housing & Construction

New Privately Owned Housing Units Authorized by Building Permit

	Single Family	Total Bldgs	Total Units
2006	77	78	93
2007	51	51	51
2008	37	37	37

Parcel Count by Property Class, 2010

Total	27,702
Single family	20,577
Multiple units	301
Apartments	142
Condos	1,656
Vacant land	2,209
Open space	0
Commercial	1,847
Industrial	110
Misc. residential	610
Other use	250

Public Library

Hyannis Public Library Association
401 Main St.
Hyannis, MA 02601
(508)771-5124

Director	Ann-Louise Harries

Library Statistics, FY 2008

Population served, 2007	16,097
Registered users	12,085
Circulation	111,609
Reference transactons	1,872
Total program attendance	0
per capita:	
Holdings	3.63
Operating income	$35.16
Internet Access	
Internet computers available	18
Weekly users	530

Municipal Finance

Debt at year end 2008	$143,232,336
Moody's rating, July 2009	Aa1

Revenues, 2008

Total	$126,083,409
From all taxes	94,490,775
Federal aid	904,183
State aid	14,882,347
From other governments	0
Charges for services	2,863,331
Licenses, permits & fees	1,629,876
Fines & forfeits	358,560
Interfund transfers	6,947,551
Misc/other/special assessments	2,003,393

Expenditures, 2008

Total	$117,618,261
General government	10,756,818
Public safety	12,525,168
Other/fixed costs	7,796,225
Human services	1,461,360
Culture & recreation	2,993,387
Debt Service	10,485,056
Education	62,459,225
Public works	4,736,832
Intergovernmental	3,931,168

Taxation, 2010

Property type	Valuation	Rate
Total	$13,360,218,025	-
Residential	11,822,832,710	7.77
Open space	0	0.00
Commercial	1,279,251,935	6.87
Industrial	81,780,400	6.87
Personal	176,352,980	6.87

Average Single Family Tax Bill, 2010

Avg. assessed home value	NA
Avg. single fam. tax bill	NA
Hi-Lo ranking	NA

Police & Crime, 2008

Number of police officers	114
Violent crimes	372
Property crimes	1,638

Local School District

(school data 2007-08, except as noted)

Barnstable
P O Box 955, 230 South Street
Hyannis, MA 02601
508-862-4952

Superintendent	Patricia Grenier
Grade plan	PK-12
Total enrollment '09-10	4,293
Grade 12 enrollment, '09-10	387
Graduation rate	79.5%
Dropout rate	9.5%
Per-pupil expenditure	$12,654
Avg teacher salary	$66,872
Student/teacher ratio '08-09	13.0 to 1
Highly-qualified teachers, '08-09	98.0%
Teachers licensed in assigned subject	98.3%
Students per computer	4

Massachusetts Competency Assessment System (MCAS), 2009 results

	English		Math	
	% Prof	CPI	% Prof	CPI
Gr 4	64%	86.8	54%	84.6
Gr 6	NA	NA	NA	NA
Gr 8	79%	92	50%	75.9
Gr 10	82%	93.1	75%	89.2

Other School Districts (see Appendix D for data)
Cape Cod Vocational Tech

©2010 Information Publications, Inc. All rights reserved. Photocopying prohibited. For additional copies, contact the publisher at www.informationpublications.com or (877)544-INFO (4636)

See Introduction for an explanation of all data sources.

©2010 Information Publications, Inc. All rights reserved. Photocopying prohibited. For additional copies, contact the publisher at www.informationpublications.com or (877)544-INFO (4636)

Demographics & Socio-Economic Characteristics

Population

1990	4,546
2000	5,113
Male	2,506
Female	2,607
2008	5,431
2010 (projected)††	5,435
2020 (projected)††	5,961

Race & Hispanic Origin, 2000

Race	
White	4,992
Black/African American	26
American Indian/Alaska Native	5
Asian	17
Hawaiian Native/Pacific Islander	0
Other Race	15
Two or more races	58
Hispanic origin	41

Age & Nativity, 2000

Under 5 years	320
18 years and over	3,661
21 years and over	3,526
65 years and over	647
85 years and over	73
Median Age	37.1
Native-born	5,065
Foreign-born	48

Age, 2020 (projected)††

Under 5 years	402
5 to 19 years	1,134
20 to 39 years	1,480
40 to 64 years	1,992
65 years and over	953

Educational Attainment, 2000

Population 25 years and over	3,363
High School graduates or higher	85.3%
Bachelor's degree or higher	20.4%
Graduate degree	7.7%

Income & Poverty, 1999

Per capita income,	$20,476
Median household income	$50,553
Median family income	$56,069
Persons in poverty	176
H'holds receiving public assistance	21
H'holds receiving social security	601

Households, 2000

Total households	1,889
With persons under 18	730
With persons over 65	475
Family households	1,378
Single person households	431
Persons per household	2.7
Persons per family	3.2

Labor & Employment, 2000

Civilian labor force	2,637
Unemployment rate	5.7%
Civilian labor force, 2008†	2,800
Unemployment rate†	8.9%
Civilian labor force, 12/09†	2,863
Unemployment rate†	11.4%
Employed persons 16 years and over, by occupation:	
Managers & professionals	954
Service occupations	302
Sales & office occupations	542
Farming, fishing & forestry	13
Construction & maintenance	296
Production & transportation	381
Self-employed persons	148

Most demographic data is from the 2000 Decennial Census
† Massachusetts Department of Revenue
†† University of Massachusetts, MISER

General Information

Town of Barre
Box 697
40 West St
Barre, MA 01005
978-355-2504

Elevation	620 ft.
Land area (square miles)	44.3
Water area (square miles)	0.3
Population density, 2008 (est)	122.6
Year incorporated	1774
Website	townofbarre.com

Voters & Government Information

Government type	Open Town Meeting
Number of Selectmen	3
US Congressional District(s)	1

Registered Voters, October 2008

Total	3,419
Democrats	913
Republicans	506
Unaffiliated/other	1,962

Local Officials, 2010

Chair, Bd. of Sel.	Richard Jankauskas
Administrator	David Battistoni
Town Clerk	Ellen Glidden
Finance Dir.	D. Haynes/B. Pellegrino
Tax Collector	Marcia Langelier
Tax Assessor	John Meilus
Attorney	James Baird
Public Works	Richard Wheeler
Building	George Ricker
Comm Dev/Planning	NA
Police Chief	Erik Demetropoulos (Actg)
Emerg/Fire Chief	Joseph Rogowski

Housing & Construction

New Privately Owned Housing Units Authorized by Building Permit

	Single Family	Total Bldgs	Total Units
2006	27	27	27
2007	19	19	19
2008	6	6	6

Parcel Count by Property Class, 2010

Total	2,785
Single family	1,528
Multiple units	148
Apartments	20
Condos	4
Vacant land	738
Open space	0
Commercial	56
Industrial	24
Misc. residential	39
Other use	228

Public Library

Woods Memorial Library
19 Pleasant St., PO Box 489
Barre, MA 01005
(978)355-2533

Director	Stephanie Carpenter

Library Statistics, FY 2008

Population served, 2007	5,419
Registered users	5,002
Circulation	33,703
Reference transactons	3,757
Total program attendance	46,352
per capita:	
Holdings	6.88
Operating income	$36.73
Internet Access	
Internet computers available	9
Weekly users	81

Municipal Finance

Debt at year end 2008	$5,074,635
Moody's rating, July 2009	A3

Revenues, 2008

Total	$8,454,795
From all taxes	5,935,215
Federal aid	0
State aid	1,147,198
From other governments	16,953
Charges for services	776,041
Licenses, permits & fees	140,585
Fines & forfeits	0
Interfund transfers	378,975
Misc/other/special assessments	29,914

Expenditures, 2008

Total	$8,366,685
General government	541,088
Public safety	1,262,082
Other/fixed costs	425,688
Human services	168,849
Culture & recreation	206,365
Debt Service	314,537
Education	4,106,248
Public works	1,138,883
Intergovernmental	202,945

Taxation, 2010

Property type	Valuation	Rate
Total	$451,387,618	-
Residential	408,641,210	12.35
Open space	0	0.00
Commercial	24,450,643	12.35
Industrial	5,972,100	12.35
Personal	12,323,665	12.35

Average Single Family Tax Bill, 2010

Avg. assessed home value	$215,574
Avg. single fam. tax bill	$2,662
Hi-Lo ranking	269/301

Police & Crime, 2008

Number of police officers	8
Violent crimes	20
Property crimes	72

Local School District

(school data 2007-08, except as noted)

Barre (non-op)
872 South Street
Barre, MA 01005
978-355-4668

Superintendent	Maureen Marshall

Non-operating district.
Resident students are sent to the Other School Districts listed below.

Grade plan	NA
Total enrollment '09-10	NA
Grade 12 enrollment, '09-10	NA
Graduation rate	NA
Dropout rate	NA
Per-pupil expenditure	NA
Avg teacher salary	NA
Student/teacher ratio '08-09	NA
Highly-qualified teachers, '08-09	NA
Teachers licensed in assigned subject	NA
Students per computer	NA

Other School Districts (see Appendix D for data)
Quabbin Regional, Montachusett Vocational Tech

See Introduction for an explanation of all data sources.

Demographics & Socio-Economic Characteristics

Population

1990	1,481
2000	1,755
Male	883
Female	872
2008	1,801
2010 (projected)††	1,887
2020 (projected)††	2,043

Race & Hispanic Origin, 2000

Race	
White	1,710
Black/African American	12
American Indian/Alaska Native	3
Asian	9
Hawaiian Native/Pacific Islander	0
Other Race	2
Two or more races	19
Hispanic origin	19

Age & Nativity, 2000

Under 5 years	87
18 years and over	1,341
21 years and over	1,292
65 years and over	228
85 years and over	18
Median Age	40.6
Native-born	1,707
Foreign-born	44

Age, 2020 (projected)††

Under 5 years	104
5 to 19 years	299
20 to 39 years	399
40 to 64 years	735
65 years and over	506

Educational Attainment, 2000

Population 25 years and over	1,235
High School graduates or higher	87.6%
Bachelor's degree or higher	23.9%
Graduate degree	11.5%

Income & Poverty, 1999

Per capita income,	$21,861
Median household income	$46,806
Median family income	$53,417
Persons in poverty	79
H'holds receiving public assistance	8
H'holds receiving social security	187

Households, 2000

Total households	692
With persons under 18	231
With persons over 65	169
Family households	505
Single person households	152
Persons per household	2.5
Persons per family	2.9

Labor & Employment, 2000

Civilian labor force	916
Unemployment rate	5.0%
Civilian labor force, 2008†	1,003
Unemployment rate†	6.4%
Civilian labor force, 12/09†	1,028
Unemployment rate†	10.3%
Employed persons 16 years and over, by occupation:	
Managers & professionals	302
Service occupations	143
Sales & office occupations	193
Farming, fishing & forestry	9
Construction & maintenance	99
Production & transportation	124
Self-employed persons	91

Most demographic data is from the 2000 Decennial Census
† Massachusetts Department of Revenue
†† University of Massachusetts, MISER

General Information

Town of Becket
557 Main St
Becket, MA 01223
413-623-8934

Elevation	1,574 ft.
Land area (square miles)	46.3
Water area (square miles)	1.5
Population density, 2008 (est)	38.9
Year incorporated	1765
Website	www.townofbecket.org

Voters & Government Information

Government type	Open Town Meeting
Number of Selectmen	3
US Congressional District(s)	1

Registered Voters, October 2008

Total	1,292
Democrats	358
Republicans	151
Unaffiliated/other	773

Local Officials, 2010

Chair, Bd. of Sel.	William F. Cavanaugh
Town Administrator	Tony Blair
Town Clerk	Jeanne Pryor
Finance Director	Michael Falk
Tax Collector	Kathleen Hayn Burtt
Tax Assessor	Susan Donnelly
Attorney	Sarah Bell
Public Works	Leonard Tisdale
Building	William Girard
Comm Dev/Planning	Gale LaBelle (Chr)
Police Chief	William H. Elovirta
Emerg/Fire Chief	John Hall

Housing & Construction

New Privately Owned Housing Units Authorized by Building Permit

	Single Family	Total Bldgs	Total Units
2006	28	28	28
2007	23	23	23
2008	11	11	11

Parcel Count by Property Class, 2010

Total	NA
Single family	NA
Multiple units	NA
Apartments	NA
Condos	NA
Vacant land	NA
Open space	NA
Commercial	NA
Industrial	NA
Misc. residential	NA
Other use	NA

Public Library

Becket Athenaeum, Inc.
PO Box 9
Becket, MA 01223
(413)623-5483

Director	Zina Jayne

Library Statistics, FY 2008

Population served, 2007	1,797
Registered users	736
Circulation	12,600
Reference transactons	780
Total program attendance	0
per capita:	
Holdings	9.43
Operating income	$42.69
Internet Access	
Internet computers available	2
Weekly users	15

Municipal Finance

Debt at year end 2008	$0
Moody's rating, July 2009	NA

Revenues, 2008

Total	$4,863,257
From all taxes	4,256,335
Federal aid	0
State aid	274,440
From other governments	16,423
Charges for services	100,870
Licenses, permits & fees	70,815
Fines & forfeits	0
Interfund transfers	122,500
Misc/other/special assessments	10,937

Expenditures, 2008

Total	$4,508,234
General government	567,954
Public safety	555,821
Other/fixed costs	443,134
Human services	29,369
Culture & recreation	58,964
Debt Service	0
Education	2,011,972
Public works	801,668
Intergovernmental	39,352

Taxation, 2010

Property type	Valuation	Rate
Total	NA	-
Residential	NA	NA
Open space	NA	NA
Commercial	NA	NA
Industrial	NA	NA
Personal	NA	NA

Average Single Family Tax Bill, 2010

Avg. assessed home value	NA
Avg. single fam. tax bill	NA
Hi-Lo ranking	NA

Police & Crime, 2008

Number of police officers	2
Violent crimes	2
Property crimes	50

Local School District

(school data 2007-08, except as noted)

Becket (non-op)
PO Box 299
Dalton, MA 01227
413-684-0320

Superintendent	James Stankiewicz

Non-operating district.
Resident students are sent to the Other School Districts listed below.

Grade plan	NA
Total enrollment '09-10	NA
Grade 12 enrollment, '09-10	NA
Graduation rate	NA
Dropout rate	NA
Per-pupil expenditure	NA
Avg teacher salary	NA
Student/teacher ratio '08-09	NA
Highly-qualified teachers, '08-09	NA
Teachers licensed in assigned subject	NA
Students per computer	NA

Other School Districts (see Appendix D for data)
Central Berkshire Regional

©2010 Information Publications, Inc. All rights reserved. Photocopying prohibited. For additional copies, contact the publisher at www.informationpublications.com or (877)544-INFO (4636)

See Introduction for an explanation of all data sources.

Demographics & Socio-Economic Characteristics

Population

- 1990 ... 12,996
- 2000 ... 12,595
  - Male ... 6,275
  - Female ... 6,320
- 2008 ... 13,545
- 2010 (projected)†† ... 12,433
- 2020 (projected)†† ... 11,805

Race & Hispanic Origin, 2000

- Race
  - White ... 11,486
  - Black/African American ... 208
  - American Indian/Alaska Native ... 28
  - Asian ... 680
  - Hawaiian Native/Pacific Islander ... 0
  - Other Race ... 43
  - Two or more races ... 150
- Hispanic origin ... 227

Age & Nativity, 2000

- Under 5 years ... 843
- 18 years and over ... 9,623
- 21 years and over ... 9,402
- 65 years and over ... 2,311
- 85 years and over ... 381
  - Median Age ... 42.1
- Native-born ... 11,379
- Foreign-born ... 1,216

Age, 2020 (projected)††

- Under 5 years ... 613
- 5 to 19 years ... 1,958
- 20 to 39 years ... 2,060
- 40 to 64 years ... 3,536
- 65 years and over ... 3,638

Educational Attainment, 2000

- Population 25 years and over ... 9,096
  - High School graduates or higher ... 94.9%
  - Bachelor's degree or higher ... 57.4%
  - Graduate degree ... 27.3%

Income & Poverty, 1999

- Per capita income, ... $39,212
- Median household income ... $87,962
- Median family income ... $101,081
- Persons in poverty ... 300
- H'holds receiving public assistance ... 56
- H'holds receiving social security ... 1,307

Households, 2000

- Total households ... 4,621
  - With persons under 18 ... 1,636
  - With persons over 65 ... 1,342
  - Family households ... 3,419
  - Single person households ... 1,007
- Persons per household ... 2.6
- Persons per family ... 3.0

Labor & Employment, 2000

- Civilian labor force ... 6,490
  - Unemployment rate ... 2.3%
- Civilian labor force, 2008† ... 6,801
  - Unemployment rate† ... 4.8%
- Civilian labor force, 12/09† ... 6,843
  - Unemployment rate† ... 6.2%
- Employed persons 16 years and over, by occupation:
  - Managers & professionals ... 4,076
  - Service occupations ... 497
  - Sales & office occupations ... 1,198
  - Farming, fishing & forestry ... 0
  - Construction & maintenance ... 287
  - Production & transportation ... 280
  - Self-employed persons ... 509

Most demographic data is from the 2000 Decennial Census
† Massachusetts Department of Revenue
†† University of Massachusetts, MISER

General Information

Town of Bedford
10 Mudge Way
Bedford, MA 01730
781-275-0083

- Elevation ... 135 ft.
- Land area (square miles) ... 13.7
- Water area (square miles) ... 0.1
- Population density, 2008 (est) ... 988.7
- Year incorporated ... 1729
- Website ... www.bedfordma.gov

Voters & Government Information

- Government type ... Open Town Meeting
- Number of Selectmen ... 5
- US Congressional District(s) ... 6

Registered Voters, October 2008

- Total ... 9,435
- Democrats ... 2,612
- Republicans ... 1,332
- Unaffiliated/other ... 5,460

Local Officials, 2010

- Chair, Bd. of Sel. ... Michael Rosenberg
- Town Manager ... Richard Reed
- Clerk ... Doreen Tremblay
- Finance Director ... Peter Naum
- Tax Collector ... Victor Garofalo
- Tax Assessor ... (vacant)
- Attorney ... Michael Lehane
- Public Works ... Richard Warrington
- Building ... Chris Laskey
- Planning ... Richard Joly
- Police Chief ... James Hicks
- Fire Chief ... David Grunes

Housing & Construction

New Privately Owned Housing Units Authorized by Building Permit

	Single Family	Total Bldgs	Total Units
2006	28	32	114
2007	35	41	223
2008	20	24	36

Parcel Count by Property Class, 2010

- Total ... 4,497
- Single family ... 3,318
- Multiple units ... 298
- Apartments ... 9
- Condos ... 444
- Vacant land ... 154
- Open space ... 27
- Commercial ... 124
- Industrial ... 71
- Misc. residential ... 17
- Other use ... 35

Public Library

Bedford Free Public Library
7 Mudge Way
Bedford, MA 01730
(781)275-9440

- Library Director ... Richard Callaghan

Library Statistics, FY 2008

- Population served, 2007 ... 13,146
- Registered users ... 10,736
- Circulation ... 338,948
- Reference transactons ... 11,742
- Total program attendance ... 0

per capita:

- Holdings ... 8.55
- Operating income ... $85.96

Internet Access

- Internet computers available ... 10
- Weekly users ... 883

Municipal Finance

- Debt at year end 2008 ... $50,675,201
- Moody's rating, July 2009 ... Aa1

Revenues, 2008

- Total ... $65,753,759
- From all taxes ... 45,531,325
- Federal aid ... 0
- State aid ... 6,700,940
- From other governments ... 170,790
- Charges for services ... 3,756,108
- Licenses, permits & fees ... 1,322,590
- Fines & forfeits ... 0
- Interfund transfers ... 4,863,062
- Misc/other/special assessments ... 1,704,472

Expenditures, 2008

- Total ... $64,287,583
- General government ... 3,183,547
- Public safety ... 5,405,563
- Other/fixed costs ... 7,161,256
- Human services ... 1,081,151
- Culture & recreation ... 1,204,407
- Debt Service ... 7,337,702
- Education ... 28,720,867
- Public works ... 7,267,206
- Intergovernmental ... 2,925,884

Taxation, 2010

Property type	Valuation	Rate
Total	$2,755,935,570	-
Residential	2,115,408,335	13.08
Open space	4,837,900	9.81
Commercial	271,250,635	29.51
Industrial	293,984,600	29.51
Personal	70,454,100	29.51

Average Single Family Tax Bill, 2010

- Avg. assessed home value ... $506,620
- Avg. single fam. tax bill ... $6,627
- Hi-Lo ranking ... 38/301

Police & Crime, 2008

- Number of police officers ... 28
- Violent crimes ... 4
- Property crimes ... 185

Local School District

(school data 2007-08, except as noted)

Bedford
97 McMahon Road
Bedford, MA 01730
781-275-7588

- Superintendent ... Maureen Lacroix
- Grade plan ... PK-12
- Total enrollment '09-10 ... 2,429
- Grade 12 enrollment, '09-10 ... 162
- Graduation rate ... 90.8%
- Dropout rate ... 2.2%
- Per-pupil expenditure ... $14,634
- Avg teacher salary ... $67,622
- Student/teacher ratio '08-09 ... 12.5 to 1
- Highly-qualified teachers, '08-09 ... 96.8%
- Teachers licensed in assigned subject ... 98.2%
- Students per computer ... 2.7

Massachusetts Competency Assessment System (MCAS), 2009 results

	English		Math	
	% Prof	CPI	% Prof	CPI
Gr 4	70%	87.9	66%	86.8
Gr 6	85%	93.8	77%	90.7
Gr 8	88%	95.8	73%	87.4
Gr 10	92%	96.9	90%	95

Other School Districts (see Appendix D for data)

Shawsheen Valley Vocational Tech

©2010 Information Publications, Inc. All rights reserved. Photocopying prohibited. For additional copies, contact the publisher at www.informationpublications.com or (877)544-INFO (4636)

See Introduction for an explanation of all data sources.

Demographics & Socio-Economic Characteristics

Population

1990	10,579
2000	12,968
Male	6,313
Female	6,655
2008	14,233
2010 (projected)††	15,825
2020 (projected)††	19,658

Race & Hispanic Origin, 2000

Race

White	12,467
Black/African American	105
American Indian/Alaska Native	25
Asian	125
Hawaiian Native/Pacific Islander	6
Other Race	71
Two or more races	169
Hispanic origin	204

Age & Nativity, 2000

Under 5 years	888
18 years and over	9,429
21 years and over	9,033
65 years and over	1,142
85 years and over	104
Median Age	36.3
Native-born	12,544
Foreign-born	424

Age, 2020 (projected)††

Under 5 years	1,243
5 to 19 years	3,326
20 to 39 years	5,676
40 to 64 years	6,267
65 years and over	3,146

Educational Attainment, 2000

Population 25 years and over	8,555
High School graduates or higher	89.9%
Bachelor's degree or higher	31.5%
Graduate degree	13.1%

Income & Poverty, 1999

Per capita income,	$21,938
Median household income	$52,467
Median family income	$60,830
Persons in poverty	763
H'holds receiving public assistance	144
H'holds receiving social security	1,037

Households, 2000

Total households	4,886
With persons under 18	1,969
With persons over 65	858
Family households	3,519
Single person households	991
Persons per household	2.7
Persons per family	3.1

Labor & Employment, 2000

Civilian labor force	7,613
Unemployment rate	4.9%
Civilian labor force, 2008†	8,183
Unemployment rate†	5.2%
Civilian labor force, 12/09†	8,150
Unemployment rate†	7.0%
Employed persons 16 years and over, by occupation:	
Managers & professionals	2,713
Service occupations	1,126
Sales & office occupations	1,854
Farming, fishing & forestry	62
Construction & maintenance	729
Production & transportation	758
Self-employed persons	541

Most demographic data is from the 2000 Decennial Census
† Massachusetts Department of Revenue
†† University of Massachusetts, MISER

General Information

Town of Belchertown
2 Jabish St
PO Box 670
Belchertown, MA 01007
413-323-0403

Elevation	613 ft.
Land area (square miles)	52.7
Water area (square miles)	2.6
Population density, 2008 (est)	270.1
Year incorporated	1761
Website	www.belchertown.org

Voters & Government Information

Government type	Open Town Meeting
Number of Selectmen	5
US Congressional District(s)	1

Registered Voters, October 2008

Total	9,651
Democrats	2,880
Republicans	1,344
Unaffiliated/other	5,337

Local Officials, 2010

Chair, Bd. of Sel.	James Barry
Town Administrator	Gary Brougham
Clerk	William Barnett
Accountant	Jill Panto
Treas/Collector	Lisa Banner
Tax Assessor	John Whelihem
Attorney	Kopelman & Paige
Public Works	Steven Williams
Building	Paul Adzima
Planning	Douglas Albertson
Police Chief	Francis R. Fox Jr
Fire Chief	Edward Bock

Housing & Construction

New Privately Owned Housing Units Authorized by Building Permit

	Single Family	Total Bldgs	Total Units
2006	68	68	68
2007	59	59	59
2008	18	18	18

Parcel Count by Property Class, 2010

Total	6,065
Single family	4,185
Multiple units	173
Apartments	21
Condos	154
Vacant land	873
Open space	0
Commercial	105
Industrial	50
Misc. residential	23
Other use	481

Public Library

Clapp Memorial Library
PO Box 627
Belchertown, MA 01007
(413)323-0417

Director	Owen Maloney

Library Statistics, FY 2008

Population served, 2007	13,971
Registered users	8,741
Circulation	123,057
Reference transactons	5,720
Total program attendance	84,240
per capita:	
Holdings	2.06
Operating income	$27.67
Internet Access	
Internet computers available	7
Weekly users	204

Municipal Finance

Debt at year end 2008	$43,160,066
Moody's rating, July 2009	NA

Revenues, 2008

Total	$39,302,931
From all taxes	20,703,325
Federal aid	249,885
State aid	16,141,410
From other governments	48,605
Charges for services	267,521
Licenses, permits & fees	166,172
Fines & forfeits	10,396
Interfund transfers	495,481
Misc/other/special assessments	610,068

Expenditures, 2008

Total	$37,837,668
General government	2,105,668
Public safety	2,729,991
Other/fixed costs	5,256,587
Human services	549,648
Culture & recreation	642,439
Debt Service	3,782,264
Education	20,542,361
Public works	1,337,781
Intergovernmental	845,175

Taxation, 2010

Property type	Valuation	Rate
Total	$1,377,547,114	-
Residential	1,274,165,607	14.86
Open space	0	0.00
Commercial	65,929,215	14.86
Industrial	12,274,110	14.86
Personal	25,178,182	14.86

Average Single Family Tax Bill, 2010

Avg. assessed home value	$256,549
Avg. single fam. tax bill	$3,812
Hi-Lo ranking	150/301

Police & Crime, 2008

Number of police officers	24
Violent crimes	19
Property crimes	164

Local School District

(school data 2007-08, except as noted)

Belchertown
PO Box 841
Belchertown, MA 01007
413-323-0456

Superintendent	Judith Houle
Grade plan	PK-12
Total enrollment '09-10	2,610
Grade 12 enrollment, '09-10	160
Graduation rate	89.4%
Dropout rate	3.7%
Per-pupil expenditure	$9,748
Avg teacher salary	$56,708
Student/teacher ratio '08-09	15.5 to 1
Highly-qualified teachers, '08-09	97.7%
Teachers licensed in assigned subject	99.4%
Students per computer	4.1

Massachusetts Competency Assessment System (MCAS), 2009 results

	English		Math	
	% Prof	CPI	% Prof	CPI
Gr 4	60%	82	49%	79.1
Gr 6	59%	85	56%	77.7
Gr 8	78%	90.6	58%	77.7
Gr 10	95%	97.9	91%	96.2

Other School Districts (see Appendix D for data)

Pathfinder Vocational Tech

©2010 Information Publications, Inc. All rights reserved. Photocopying prohibited. For additional copies, contact the publisher at www.informationpublications.com or (877)544-INFO (4636)

See Introduction for an explanation of all data sources.

Demographics & Socio-Economic Characteristics

Population

1990	14,877
2000	15,314
Male	7,503
Female	7,811
2008	15,900
2010 (projected)††	14,690
2020 (projected)††	14,166

Race & Hispanic Origin, 2000

Race	
White	14,844
Black/African American	140
American Indian/Alaska Native	19
Asian	131
Hawaiian Native/Pacific Islander	5
Other Race	46
Two or more races	129
Hispanic origin	184

Age & Nativity, 2000

Under 5 years	1,077
18 years and over	11,204
21 years and over	10,811
65 years and over	1,483
85 years and over	97
Median Age	36.3
Native-born	14,822
Foreign-born	492

Age, 2020 (projected)††

Under 5 years	862
5 to 19 years	2,438
20 to 39 years	3,564
40 to 64 years	4,942
65 years and over	2,360

Educational Attainment, 2000

Population 25 years and over	10,362
High School graduates or higher	88.2%
Bachelor's degree or higher	22.0%
Graduate degree	6.3%

Income & Poverty, 1999

Per capita income,	$25,047
Median household income	$64,496
Median family income	$72,074
Persons in poverty	384
H'holds receiving public assistance	100
H'holds receiving social security	1,171

Households, 2000

Total households	5,557
With persons under 18	2,246
With persons over 65	1,076
Family households	4,282
Single person households	1,010
Persons per household	2.8
Persons per family	3.2

Labor & Employment, 2000

Civilian labor force	8,939
Unemployment rate	3.6%
Civilian labor force, 2008†	9,471
Unemployment rate†	7.3%
Civilian labor force, 12/09†	9,577
Unemployment rate†	10.8%
Employed persons 16 years and over, by occupation:	
Managers & professionals	2,934
Service occupations	1,170
Sales & office occupations	2,883
Farming, fishing & forestry	20
Construction & maintenance	709
Production & transportation	904
Self-employed persons	360

Most demographic data is from the 2000 Decennial Census
† Massachusetts Department of Revenue
†† University of Massachusetts, MISER

General Information

Town of Bellingham
10 Mechanic St
Bellingham, MA 02019
508-657-2800

Elevation	293 ft.
Land area (square miles)	18.5
Water area (square miles)	0.5
Population density, 2008 (est)	859.5
Year incorporated	1719
Website	www.bellinghamma.org

Voters & Government Information

Government type	Open Town Meeting
Number of Selectmen	5
US Congressional District(s)	2

Registered Voters, October 2008

Total	10,558
Democrats	3,034
Republicans	1,395
Unaffiliated/other	6,080

Local Officials, 2010

Chair, Bd. of Sel.	Dawn M. Davies
Manager/Admin	Denis Fraine
Town Clerk	Ann L. Odabashian
Finance Director	Marilyn A. Mathieu
Tax Collector	Grace L. Devitt
Tax Assessor	Mary Ellen Hutchins
Attorney	Blatman, Bobrowski & Mead
Public Works	Donald F. DiMartino
Building	Stuart S. LeClaire
Comm Dev/Planning	Stacey J. Wetstein
Police Chief	Gerard Daigle Jr
Emerg/Fire Chief	Richard Ranieri

Housing & Construction

New Privately Owned Housing Units Authorized by Building Permit

	Single Family	Total Bldgs	Total Units
2006	43	46	53
2007	15	15	15
2008	9	10	11

Parcel Count by Property Class, 2010

Total	6,340
Single family	4,505
Multiple units	227
Apartments	11
Condos	702
Vacant land	448
Open space	0
Commercial	198
Industrial	107
Misc. residential	29
Other use	113

Public Library

Bellingham Public Library
100 Blackstone St.
Bellingham, MA 02019
(508)966-1660

Director .... Bernadette Rivard

Library Statistics, FY 2008

Population served, 2007	15,908
Registered users	8,429
Circulation	128,465
Reference transactons	1,496
Total program attendance	103,205
per capita:	
Holdings	3.89
Operating income	$31.91
Internet Access	
Internet computers available	10
Weekly users	253

Municipal Finance

Debt at year end 2008	$45,185,612
Moody's rating, July 2009	Aa3

Revenues, 2008

Total	$46,086,268
From all taxes	29,334,197
Federal aid	97,566
State aid	13,079,940
From other governments	96,610
Charges for services	537,379
Licenses, permits & fees	247,492
Fines & forfeits	168,920
Interfund transfers	1,633,924
Misc/other/special assessments	445,120

Expenditures, 2008

Total	$40,172,115
General government	2,431,958
Public safety	4,483,310
Other/fixed costs	1,981,039
Human services	291,103
Culture & recreation	603,753
Debt Service	5,275,236
Education	22,122,600
Public works	2,159,085
Intergovernmental	824,031

Taxation, 2010

Property type	Valuation	Rate
Total	$2,206,813,918	-
Residential	1,576,023,742	11.96
Open space	0	0.00
Commercial	214,819,039	16.79
Industrial	117,129,690	16.79
Personal	298,841,447	16.61

Average Single Family Tax Bill, 2010

Avg. assessed home value	$275,984
Avg. single fam. tax bill	$3,301
Hi-Lo ranking	203/301

Police & Crime, 2008

Number of police officers	30
Violent crimes	NA
Property crimes	NA

Local School District

(school data 2007-08, except as noted)

Bellingham
60 Harpin Street
Bellingham, MA 02019
508-883-1706

Superintendent	David Fischer
Grade plan	PK-12
Total enrollment '09-10	2,635
Grade 12 enrollment, '09-10	194
Graduation rate	84.8%
Dropout rate	5.6%
Per-pupil expenditure	$10,399
Avg teacher salary	$59,749
Student/teacher ratio '08-09	14.6 to 1
Highly-qualified teachers, '08-09	94.7%
Teachers licensed in assigned subject	97.3%
Students per computer	2.7

Massachusetts Competency Assessment System (MCAS), 2009 results

	English		Math	
	% Prof	CPI	% Prof	CPI
Gr 4	60%	85.1	59%	86.1
Gr 6	64%	87	44%	71.8
Gr 8	74%	91.2	58%	78.4
Gr 10	82%	93	76%	91

Other School Districts (see Appendix D for data)
Blackstone Valley Vocational Tech, Norfolk County Agricultural

See Introduction for an explanation of all data sources.

©2010 Information Publications, Inc. All rights reserved. Photocopying prohibited. For additional copies, contact the publisher at www.informationpublications.com or (877)544-INFO (4636)

Demographics & Socio-Economic Characteristics*

Population

1990	24,720
2000	24,194
Male	11,292
Female	12,902
2008	23,291
2010 (projected)††	22,393
2020 (projected)††	20,741

Race & Hispanic Origin, 2000

Race	
White	22,062
Black/African American	266
American Indian/Alaska Native	31
Asian	1,393
Hawaiian Native/Pacific Islander	2
Other Race	100
Two or more races	340
Hispanic origin	440

Age & Nativity, 2000

Under 5 years	1,415
18 years and over	18,707
21 years and over	18,268
65 years and over	4,049
85 years and over	649
Median Age	40.4
Native-born	20,621
Foreign-born	3,573

Age, 2020 (projected)††

Under 5 years	914
5 to 19 years	3,094
20 to 39 years	5,474
40 to 64 years	7,031
65 years and over	4,228

Educational Attainment, 2000

Population 25 years and over	17,586
High School graduates or higher	94.6%
Bachelor's degree or higher	63.1%
Graduate degree	36.7%

Income & Poverty, 1999

Per capita income,	$42,485
Median household income	$80,295
Median family income	$95,057
Persons in poverty	1,058
H'holds receiving public assistance	90
H'holds receiving social security	2,653

Households, 2000

Total households	9,732
With persons under 18	3,121
With persons over 65	2,860
Family households	6,454
Single person households	2,524
Persons per household	2.5
Persons per family	3.0

Labor & Employment, 2000

Civilian labor force	13,016
Unemployment rate	2.3%
Civilian labor force, 2008†	12,734
Unemployment rate†	3.9%
Civilian labor force, 12/09†	12,716
Unemployment rate†	6.3%
Employed persons 16 years and over, by occupation:	
Managers & professionals	8,635
Service occupations	942
Sales & office occupations	2,358
Farming, fishing & forestry	7
Construction & maintenance	425
Production & transportation	352
Self-employed persons	1,084

Most demographic data is from the 2000 Decennial Census
* see Appendix E for American Community Survey data
† Massachusetts Department of Revenue
†† University of Massachusetts, MISER

General Information

Town of Belmont
455 Concord Ave
Box 56
Belmont, MA 02478
617-993-2600

Elevation	58 ft.
Land area (square miles)	4.7
Water area (square miles)	0.0
Population density, 2008 (est)	4,955.5
Year incorporated	1859
Website	www.town.belmont-ma.gov

Voters & Government Information

Government type	Rep. Town Meeting
Number of Selectmen	3
US Congressional District(s)	7

Registered Voters, October 2008

Total	16,086
Democrats	5,870
Republicans	1,601
Unaffiliated/other	8,568

Local Officials, 2010

Chair, Bd. of Sel.	Ralph T. Jones
Town Administrator	Thomas Younger
Town Clerk	Ellen O'Brien Cushman
Town Accountant	Barbara Hagg
Treasurer	Floyd Carman
Tax Assessor	Richard D. Simmons Jr
Attorney	NA
Public Works	Peter Castanino
Building	Glenn Clancy
Comm Dev/Planning	Glenn Clancy
Police Chief	Richard McLaughlin
Fire Chief	David L. Frizzell

Housing & Construction

New Privately Owned Housing Units Authorized by Building Permit

	Single Family	Total Bldgs	Total Units
2006	42	42	42
2007	1	2	3
2008	15	15	15

Parcel Count by Property Class, 2010

Total	8,097
Single family	4,516
Multiple units	1,816
Apartments	37
Condos	1,366
Vacant land	111
Open space	0
Commercial	194
Industrial	10
Misc. residential	5
Other use	42

Public Library

Belmont Public Library
336 Concord Ave.
Belmont, MA 02478
(617)489-2000

Library Director	Maureen Conners

Library Statistics, FY 2008

Population served, 2007	23,356
Registered users	15,638
Circulation	592,049
Reference transactons	42,307
Total program attendance	309,686
per capita:	
Holdings	6.81
Operating income	$81.41
Internet Access	
Internet computers available	18
Weekly users	606

Municipal Finance

Debt at year end 2008	$36,286,136
Moody's rating, July 2009	Aaa

Revenues, 2008

Total	$77,209,659
From all taxes	62,406,817
Federal aid	291,374
State aid	8,045,696
From other governments	7,726
Charges for services	1,443,627
Licenses, permits & fees	746,872
Fines & forfeits	195,409
Interfund transfers	1,269,086
Misc/other/special assessments	1,401,526

Expenditures, 2008

Total	$63,380,827
General government	3,794,375
Public safety	8,834,309
Other/fixed costs	4,448,407
Human services	692,515
Culture & recreation	2,668,699
Debt Service	4,390,744
Education	32,135,253
Public works	4,918,320
Intergovernmental	1,498,205

Taxation, 2010

Property type	Valuation	Rate
Total	$5,291,129,740	-
Residential	4,978,131,700	12.16
Open space	0	0.00
Commercial	258,278,600	12.16
Industrial	15,023,000	12.16
Personal	39,696,440	12.16

Average Single Family Tax Bill, 2010

Avg. assessed home value	$757,904
Avg. single fam. tax bill	$9,216
Hi-Lo ranking	11/301

Police & Crime, 2008

Number of police officers	47
Violent crimes	38
Property crimes	263

Local School District

(school data 2007-08, except as noted)

Belmont
644 Pleasant Street
Belmont, MA 02478
617-993-5401

Superintendent	George Entwistle
Grade plan	PK-12
Total enrollment '09-10	3,974
Grade 12 enrollment, '09-10	277
Graduation rate	92.7%
Dropout rate	2.1%
Per-pupil expenditure	$11,301
Avg teacher salary	$66,366
Student/teacher ratio '08-09	15.6 to 1
Highly-qualified teachers, '08-09	96.5%
Teachers licensed in assigned subject	97.7%
Students per computer	4.3

Massachusetts Competency Assessment System (MCAS), 2009 results

	English		Math	
	% Prof	CPI	% Prof	CPI
Gr 4	85%	94.6	72%	89.6
Gr 6	86%	95.3	78%	90.5
Gr 8	96%	97.7	75%	89.4
Gr 10	95%	98.2	95%	97.6

Other School Districts (see Appendix D for data)
Minuteman Vocational Tech

©2010 Information Publications, Inc. All rights reserved. Photocopying prohibited. For additional copies, contact the publisher at www.informationpublications.com or (877)544-INFO (4636)

See Introduction for an explanation of all data sources.

Demographics & Socio-Economic Characteristics

Population

1990 4,237
2000 5,749
Male 2,855
Female 2,894
2008 6,462
2010 (projected)†† 7,679
2020 (projected)†† 10,397

Race & Hispanic Origin, 2000

Race
White 5,561
Black/African American 32
American Indian/Alaska Native 8
Asian 21
Hawaiian Native/Pacific Islander 2
Other Race 61
Two or more races 64
Hispanic origin 55

Age & Nativity, 2000

Under 5 years 449
18 years and over 3,998
21 years and over 3,804
65 years and over 373
85 years and over 31
Median Age 34.7
Native-born 5,585
Foreign-born 164

Age, 2020 (projected)††

Under 5 years 771
5 to 19 years 2,165
20 to 39 years 2,932
40 to 64 years 3,527
65 years and over 1,002

Educational Attainment, 2000

Population 25 years and over 3,700
High School graduates or higher . . . 85.7%
Bachelor's degree or higher 20.8%
Graduate degree 6.6%

Income & Poverty, 1999

Per capita income, ... $21,652
Median household income $66,295
Median family income $69,222
Persons in poverty 145
H'holds receiving public assistance 6
H'holds receiving social security 319

Households, 2000

Total households 1,843
With persons under 18 946
With persons over 65 275
Family households 1,567
Single person households 199
Persons per household 3.1
Persons per family 3.4

Labor & Employment, 2000

Civilian labor force 3,210
Unemployment rate 1.9%
Civilian labor force, 2008† 3,831
Unemployment rate† 6.9%
Civilian labor force, 12/09† 3,806
Unemployment rate† 9.4%
Employed persons 16 years and over, by occupation:
Managers & professionals 1,041
Service occupations 408
Sales & office occupations 782
Farming, fishing & forestry 15
Construction & maintenance 416
Production & transportation 486
Self-employed persons 235

Most demographic data is from the 2000 Decennial Census
† Massachusetts Department of Revenue
†† University of Massachusetts, MISER

General Information

Town of Berkley
1 North Main St
Berkley, MA 02779
508-822-3348

Elevation . . . . 77 ft.
Land area (square miles) 16.5
Water area (square miles) 0.8
Population density, 2008 (est) 391.6
Year incorporated 1735
Website . . . . NA

Voters & Government Information

Government type . . . . Open Town Meeting
Number of Selectmen 3
US Congressional District(s) 4

Registered Voters, October 2008

Total 4,098
Democrats 983
Republicans 521
Unaffiliated/other 2,568

Local Officials, 2010

Chair, Bd. of Sel. . . . . Julie Taylor Jr
Manager/Admin . . . . NA
Clerk . . . . Carolyn Awalt
Treasurer . . . . Carolyn Awalt
Tax Collector . . . . Wendy Cochrane
Tax Assessor . . . . George Moitoza
Attorney . . . . Gay, Gay & Field
Public Works . . . . Scott Fournier
Building . . . . Joseph Lawrence
Planning . . . . Steven Leary
Police Chief . . . . Scott Labonte
Emerg/Fire Chief . . . . John Franco

Housing & Construction

New Privately Owned Housing Units Authorized by Building Permit

	Single Family	Total Bldgs	Total Units
2006	19	25	35
2007	15	15	15
2008	16	17	20

Parcel Count by Property Class, 2010

Total . . . . NA
Single family . . . . NA
Multiple units . . . . NA
Apartments . . . . NA
Condos . . . . NA
Vacant land . . . . NA
Open space . . . . NA
Commercial . . . . NA
Industrial . . . . NA
Misc. residential . . . . NA
Other use . . . . NA

Public Library

Berkley Public Library
1 North Main Street
Berkley, MA 02779
(508)822-3329

Director . . . . William Schneller

Library Statistics, FY 2008

Population served, 2007 6,433
Registered users 2,557
Circulation 31,924
Reference transactons 250
Total program attendance 0

per capita:

Holdings 3.65
Operating income $18.80

Internet Access

Internet computers available 2
Weekly users 25

Municipal Finance

Debt at year end 2008 . . . . $14,580,000
Moody's rating, July 2009 . . . . A3

Revenues, 2008

Total $16,508,821
From all taxes 7,327,727
Federal aid 0
State aid 7,752,939
From other governments 2,955
Charges for services 118,989
Licenses, permits & fees 96,450
Fines & forfeits 50,650
Interfund transfers 933,423
Misc/other/special assessments 112,844

Expenditures, 2008

Total $15,303,824
General government 459,335
Public safety 1,148,338
Other/fixed costs 388,630
Human services 21,626
Culture & recreation 108,200
Debt Service 1,520,621
Education 10,371,382
Public works 645,395
Intergovernmental 422,154

Taxation, 2010

Property type	Valuation	Rate
Total	NA	-
Residential	NA	NA
Open space	NA	NA
Commercial	NA	NA
Industrial	NA	NA
Personal	NA	NA

Average Single Family Tax Bill, 2010

Avg. assessed home value . . . . NA
Avg. single fam. tax bill . . . . NA
Hi-Lo ranking . . . . NA

Police & Crime, 2008

Number of police officers 6
Violent crimes 7
Property crimes 75

Local School District

(school data 2007-08, except as noted)

Berkley
21 North Main Street
Berkley, MA 02779
508-822-5220

Superintendent . . . . Thomas Lynch
Grade plan PK-8
Total enrollment '09-10 921
Grade 12 enrollment, '09-10 0
Graduation rate . . . . NA
Dropout rate . . . . NA
Per-pupil expenditure $9,342
Avg teacher salary $59,311
Student/teacher ratio '08-09 . . . . 14.8 to 1
Highly-qualified teachers, '08-09 . . . . 98.0%
Teachers licensed in assigned subject . . 99.3%
Students per computer 2.5

Massachusetts Competency Assessment System (MCAS), 2009 results

	English		Math	
	% Prof	CPI	% Prof	CPI
Gr 4	31%	72.1	35%	74.3
Gr 6	69%	88.7	61%	81.6
Gr 8	87%	95.2	55%	78.5
Gr 10	NA	NA	NA	NA

Other School Districts (see Appendix D for data)

Sends grades 9-12 to Somerset and Bristol-Plymouth Vocational Tech, Bristol County Agricultural

©2010 Information Publications, Inc. All rights reserved. Photocopying prohibited. For additional copies, contact the publisher at www.informationpublications.com or (877)544-INFO (4636)

See Introduction for an explanation of all data sources.

Demographics & Socio-Economic Characteristics

Population

1990	2,293
2000	2,380
Male	1,189
Female	1,191
2008	2,853
2010 (projected)††	2,325
2020 (projected)††	2,210

Race & Hispanic Origin, 2000

Race	
White	2,323
Black/African American	4
American Indian/Alaska Native	2
Asian	23
Hawaiian Native/Pacific Islander	0
Other Race	9
Two or more races	19
Hispanic origin	12

Age & Nativity, 2000

Under 5 years	172
18 years and over	1,784
21 years and over	1,723
65 years and over	295
85 years and over	29
Median Age	39.5
Native-born	2,326
Foreign-born	54

Age, 2020 (projected)††

Under 5 years	116
5 to 19 years	362
20 to 39 years	445
40 to 64 years	790
65 years and over	497

Educational Attainment, 2000

Population 25 years and over	1,626
High School graduates or higher	88.3%
Bachelor's degree or higher	36.4%
Graduate degree	10.5%

Income & Poverty, 1999

Per capita income,	$28,915
Median household income	$65,667
Median family income	$76,419
Persons in poverty	92
H'holds receiving public assistance	0
H'holds receiving social security	227

Households, 2000

Total households	872
With persons under 18	326
With persons over 65	215
Family households	666
Single person households	163
Persons per household	2.7
Persons per family	3.1

Labor & Employment, 2000

Civilian labor force	1,265
Unemployment rate	1.0%
Civilian labor force, 2008†	1,545
Unemployment rate†	5.9%
Civilian labor force, 12/09†	1,547
Unemployment rate†	8.1%
Employed persons 16 years and over, by occupation:	
Managers & professionals	565
Service occupations	78
Sales & office occupations	286
Farming, fishing & forestry	15
Construction & maintenance	164
Production & transportation	144
Self-employed persons	110

Most demographic data is from the 2000 Decennial Census
† Massachusetts Department of Revenue
†† University of Massachusetts, MISER

General Information

Town of Berlin
23 Linden St
Berlin, MA 01503
978-838-2442

Elevation	300 ft.
Land area (square miles)	12.9
Water area (square miles)	0.2
Population density, 2008 (est)	221.2
Year incorporated	1812
Website	townofberlin.com

Voters & Government Information

Government type	Open Town Meeting
Number of Selectmen	3
US Congressional District(s)	5

Registered Voters, October 2008

Total	1,914
Democrats	379
Republicans	277
Unaffiliated/other	1,245

Local Officials, 2010

Chair, Bd. of Sel.	Valary Bradley
Manager/Admin	NA
Town Clerk	Eloise E. Salls
Treasurer	Dennis A. Fearebay
Tax Collector	Richard Sardell
Tax Assessor	Howard H. Spaulding
Attorney	Brackett & Lucas
Public Works	Dennis A. Bartlett
Building	Lawrence Brandt
Planning	Ronald Vavruska (Chr)
Police Chief	Otto F. Rhode Jr
Fire Director	Bruce Ricard

Housing & Construction

New Privately Owned Housing Units Authorized by Building Permit

	Single Family	Total Bldgs	Total Units
2006	6	6	6
2007	67	67	67
2008	25	25	25

Parcel Count by Property Class, 2010

Total	1,422
Single family	784
Multiple units	40
Apartments	5
Condos	147
Vacant land	228
Open space	0
Commercial	48
Industrial	25
Misc. residential	20
Other use	125

Public Library

Berlin Public Library
23 Carter St.
Berlin, MA 01503
(978)838-2812

Director	Suzanne McGuire

Library Statistics, FY 2008

Population served, 2007	2,699
Registered users	1,451
Circulation	18,128
Reference transactons	0
Total program attendance	0
per capita:	
Holdings	7.69
Operating income	$40.21
Internet Access	
Internet computers available	3
Weekly users	20

Municipal Finance

Debt at year end 2008	$6,658,137
Moody's rating, July 2009	A2

Revenues, 2008

Total	$8,895,953
From all taxes	6,903,275
Federal aid	0
State aid	1,357,094
From other governments	40,159
Charges for services	16,116
Licenses, permits & fees	10,083
Fines & forfeits	225
Interfund transfers	235,363
Misc/other/special assessments	166,819

Expenditures, 2008

Total	$8,612,316
General government	650,461
Public safety	1,018,540
Other/fixed costs	709,919
Human services	19,537
Culture & recreation	109,981
Debt Service	1,032,389
Education	4,316,578
Public works	570,571
Intergovernmental	135,952

Taxation, 2010

Property type	Valuation	Rate
Total	$559,301,500	-
Residential	419,829,150	13.37
Open space	0	0.00
Commercial	118,624,830	13.37
Industrial	9,549,600	13.37
Personal	11,297,920	13.37

Average Single Family Tax Bill, 2010

Avg. assessed home value	$383,436
Avg. single fam. tax bill	$5,127
Hi-Lo ranking	71/301

Police & Crime, 2008

Number of police officers	7
Violent crimes	0
Property crimes	18

Local School District

(school data 2007-08, except as noted)
Berlin
215 Main Street
Boylston, MA 01505
508-869-2837

Superintendent	Brian McDermott
Grade plan	PK-6
Total enrollment '09-10	212
Grade 12 enrollment, '09-10	0
Graduation rate	NA
Dropout rate	NA
Per-pupil expenditure	$14,774
Avg teacher salary	$73,547
Student/teacher ratio '08-09	13.0 to 1
Highly-qualified teachers, '08-09	100.0%
Teachers licensed in assigned subject	100.0%
Students per computer	2.9

Massachusetts Competency Assessment System (MCAS), 2009 results

	English		Math	
	% Prof	CPI	% Prof	CPI
Gr 4	67%	85.3	51%	80.1
Gr 6	66%	87.1	65%	84.6
Gr 8	NA	NA	NA	NA
Gr 10	NA	NA	NA	NA

Other School Districts (see Appendix D for data)
Berlin-Boylston Regional, Assabet Valley Vocational Tech

©2010 Information Publications, Inc. All rights reserved. Photocopying prohibited. For additional copies, contact the publisher at www.informationpublications.com or (877)544-INFO (4636)

See Introduction for an explanation of all data sources.

Demographics & Socio-Economic Characteristics

Population

1990	2,048
2000	2,155
Male	1,055
Female	1,100
2008	2,230
2010 (projected)††	2,158
2020 (projected)††	2,194

Race & Hispanic Origin, 2000

Race	
White	2,134
Black/African American	2
American Indian/Alaska Native	0
Asian	0
Hawaiian Native/Pacific Islander	1
Other Race	4
Two or more races	14
Hispanic origin	10

Age & Nativity, 2000

Under 5 years	88
18 years and over	1,662
21 years and over	1,589
65 years and over	349
85 years and over	45
Median Age	42.1
Native-born	2,139
Foreign-born	18

Age, 2020 (projected)††

Under 5 years	81
5 to 19 years	281
20 to 39 years	452
40 to 64 years	773
65 years and over	607

Educational Attainment, 2000

Population 25 years and over	1,531
High School graduates or higher	91.9%
Bachelor's degree or higher	19.5%
Graduate degree	6.0%

Income & Poverty, 1999

Per capita income,	$20,959
Median household income	$45,259
Median family income	$53,125
Persons in poverty	94
H'holds receiving public assistance	15
H'holds receiving social security	263

Households, 2000

Total households	848
With persons under 18	289
With persons over 65	244
Family households	604
Single person households	187
Persons per household	2.5
Persons per family	3.0

Labor & Employment, 2000

Civilian labor force	1,193
Unemployment rate	3.9%
Civilian labor force, 2008†	1,214
Unemployment rate†	6.4%
Civilian labor force, 12/09†	1,215
Unemployment rate†	8.2%
Employed persons 16 years and over, by occupation:	
Managers & professionals	342
Service occupations	168
Sales & office occupations	303
Farming, fishing & forestry	15
Construction & maintenance	157
Production & transportation	162
Self-employed persons	102

Most demographic data is from the 2000 Decennial Census
† Massachusetts Department of Revenue
†† University of Massachusetts, MISER

General Information

Town of Bernardston
38 Church St
PO Box 504
Bernardston, MA 01337
413-648-5401

Elevation	NA
Land area (square miles)	23.4
Water area (square miles)	0.0
Population density, 2008 (est)	95.3
Year incorporated	1762
Website	www.town.bernardston.ma.us

Voters & Government Information

Government type	Open Town Meeting
Number of Selectmen	3
US Congressional District(s)	1

Registered Voters, October 2008

Total	1,579
Democrats	287
Republicans	188
Unaffiliated/other	1,093

Local Officials, 2010

Chair, Bd. of Sel.	Robert Raymond
Manager/Admin	Rebecca Jurek
Town Clerk	Judy Knight
Treasurer	Joy Grover
Tax Collector	Mona Minor
Tax Assessor	Jill Watrous
Attorney	Kopelman & Paige
Public Works	Gary Wetherby
Building	James Hawkins
Comm Dev/Planning	NA
Police Chief	James Palmeri
Emerg/Fire Chief	Peter Shedd

Housing & Construction

New Privately Owned Housing Units Authorized by Building Permit

	Single Family	Total Bldgs	Total Units
2006	11	11	11
2007	4	4	4
2008	4	4	4

Parcel Count by Property Class, 2010

Total	1,272
Single family	731
Multiple units	33
Apartments	4
Condos	0
Vacant land	302
Open space	0
Commercial	38
Industrial	11
Misc. residential	31
Other use	122

Public Library

Cushman Library
PO Box 248
Bernardston, MA 01337
(413)648-5402

Librarian	Karen Stinchfield

Library Statistics, FY 2008

Population served, 2007	2,225
Registered users	798
Circulation	18,632
Reference transactons	575
Total program attendance	9,692
per capita:	
Holdings	8.35
Operating income	$25.78
Internet Access	
Internet computers available	3
Weekly users	10

Municipal Finance

Debt at year end 2008	$2,635,132
Moody's rating, July 2009	NA

Revenues, 2008

Total	$4,333,642
From all taxes	3,468,527
Federal aid	0
State aid	625,669
From other governments	0
Charges for services	6,387
Licenses, permits & fees	25,570
Fines & forfeits	53,218
Interfund transfers	29,067
Misc/other/special assessments	62,602

Expenditures, 2008

Total	$4,185,921
General government	220,878
Public safety	328,241
Other/fixed costs	214,315
Human services	40,769
Culture & recreation	50,539
Debt Service	361,654
Education	2,577,189
Public works	376,944
Intergovernmental	15,392

Taxation, 2010

Property type	Valuation	Rate
Total	$212,301,511	-
Residential	190,479,498	15.47
Open space	0	0.00
Commercial	13,610,650	15.47
Industrial	3,513,167	15.47
Personal	4,698,196	15.47

Average Single Family Tax Bill, 2010

Avg. assessed home value	$215,080
Avg. single fam. tax bill	$3,327
Hi-Lo ranking	197/301

Police & Crime, 2008

Number of police officers	3
Violent crimes	3
Property crimes	24

Local School District

(school data 2007-08, except as noted)

Bernardston (non-op)
97 F Sumner Turner Rd
Northfield, MA 01360
413-498-2911

Superintendent.............Dayle Doiron

Non-operating district.
Resident students are sent to the Other School Districts listed below.

Grade plan	NA
Total enrollment '09-10	NA
Grade 12 enrollment, '09-10	NA
Graduation rate	NA
Dropout rate	NA
Per-pupil expenditure	NA
Avg teacher salary	NA
Student/teacher ratio '08-09	NA
Highly-qualified teachers, '08-09	NA
Teachers licensed in assigned subject	NA
Students per computer	NA

Other School Districts (see Appendix D for data)
Pioneer Valley Regional, Franklin County Vocational Tech

See Introduction for an explanation of all data sources.

©2010 Information Publications, Inc. All rights reserved. Photocopying prohibited. For additional copies, contact the publisher at www.informationpublications.com or (877)544-INFO (4636)

Demographics & Socio-Economic Characteristics*

Population

1990	38,195
2000	39,862
Male	18,851
Female	21,011
2008	39,343
2010 (projected)††	39,759
2020 (projected)††	39,447

Race & Hispanic Origin, 2000

Race	
White	38,257
Black/African American	413
American Indian/Alaska Native	70
Asian	511
Hawaiian Native/Pacific Islander	12
Other Race	207
Two or more races	392
Hispanic origin	720

Age & Nativity, 2000

Under 5 years	2,504
18 years and over	31,207
21 years and over	29,450
65 years and over	6,230
85 years and over	1,049
Median Age	38.3
Native-born	37,767
Foreign-born	2,095

Age, 2020 (projected)††

Under 5 years	2,090
5 to 19 years	6,730
20 to 39 years	9,904
40 to 64 years	12,817
65 years and over	7,906

Educational Attainment, 2000

Population 25 years and over	27,633
High School graduates or higher	90.8%
Bachelor's degree or higher	36.5%
Graduate degree	13.2%

Income & Poverty, 1999

Per capita income,	$28,626
Median household income	$53,984
Median family income	$66,486
Persons in poverty	2,163
H'holds receiving public assistance	431
H'holds receiving social security	4,288

Households, 2000

Total households	15,750
With persons under 18	4,817
With persons over 65	4,037
Family households	9,907
Single person households	4,703
Persons per household	2.4
Persons per family	3.0

Labor & Employment, 2000

Civilian labor force	22,131
Unemployment rate	6.9%
Civilian labor force, 2008†	21,677
Unemployment rate†	5.8%
Civilian labor force, 12/09†	21,371
Unemployment rate†	8.0%
Employed persons 16 years and over, by occupation:	
Managers & professionals	8,733
Service occupations	2,711
Sales & office occupations	5,958
Farming, fishing & forestry	22
Construction & maintenance	1,331
Production & transportation	1,854
Self-employed persons	1,519

Most demographic data is from the 2000 Decennial Census
* see Appendix E for American Community Survey data
† Massachusetts Department of Revenue
†† University of Massachusetts, MISER

General Information

City of Beverly
191 Cabot St
Beverly, MA 01915
978-921-6000

Elevation	44 ft.
Land area (square miles)	16.6
Water area (square miles)	6.1
Population density, 2008 (est)	2,370.1
Year incorporated	1668
Website	www.beverlyma.gov

Voters & Government Information

Government type	Mayor-Council
Number of Councilpersons	9
US Congressional District(s)	6

Registered Voters, October 2008

Total	25,615
Democrats	7,145
Republicans	3,074
Unaffiliated/other	15,252

Local Officials, 2010

Mayor	William F. Scanlon Jr
Manager/Admin	NA
City Clerk	Frances Macdonald
Finance Director	John Dunn
Tax Collector	Kathleen Kileen Robble
Tax Assessor	Frank Golden
Attorney	Roy Gelineau
Public Works	Michael Collins
Building	Steve Frederickson
Comm Dev/Planning	Tina Cassidy
Police Chief	Mark Ray
Emerg/Fire Chief	Richard Pierce

Housing & Construction

New Privately Owned Housing Units Authorized by Building Permit

	Single Family	Total Bldgs	Total Units
2006	38	38	38
2007	13	13	13
2008	13	13	13

Parcel Count by Property Class, 2010

Total	12,305
Single family	8,366
Multiple units	1,086
Apartments	249
Condos	1,310
Vacant land	506
Open space	0
Commercial	436
Industrial	109
Misc. residential	47
Other use	196

Public Library

Beverly Public Library
32 Essex St.
Beverly, MA 01915
(978)921-6062

Director	Pat Cirone

Library Statistics, FY 2008

Population served, 2007	39,198
Registered users	28,768
Circulation	396,100
Reference transactons	15,496
Total program attendance	288,256
per capita:	
Holdings	8.41
Operating income	$43.94
Internet Access	
Internet computers available	21
Weekly users	1,318

Municipal Finance

Debt at year end 2008	$70,305,923
Moody's rating, July 2009	A1

Revenues, 2008

Total	$97,411,089
From all taxes	71,956,859
Federal aid	1,155,201
State aid	17,256,472
From other governments	106,547
Charges for services	2,285,425
Licenses, permits & fees	620,184
Fines & forfeits	47,038
Interfund transfers	2,959,417
Misc/other/special assessments	511,973

Expenditures, 2008

Total	$87,045,120
General government	4,190,573
Public safety	13,186,576
Other/fixed costs	7,276,415
Human services	1,205,245
Culture & recreation	2,844,757
Debt Service	7,121,057
Education	45,539,974
Public works	3,855,135
Intergovernmental	1,825,388

Taxation, 2010

Property type	Valuation	Rate
Total	$5,650,101,694	-
Residential	4,820,965,219	11.63
Open space	712,875	11.63
Commercial	529,349,630	20.58
Industrial	160,128,580	20.58
Personal	138,945,390	20.58

Average Single Family Tax Bill, 2010

Avg. assessed home value	$430,457
Avg. single fam. tax bill	$5,006
Hi-Lo ranking	75/301

Police & Crime, 2008

Number of police officers	69
Violent crimes	122
Property crimes	695

Local School District

(school data 2007-08, except as noted)

Beverly
502 Cabot St
Beverly, MA 01915
978-921-6100

Superintendent	James Hayes
Grade plan	PK-12
Total enrollment '09-10	4,269
Grade 12 enrollment, '09-10	318
Graduation rate	85.7%
Dropout rate	7.1%
Per-pupil expenditure	$11,488
Avg teacher salary	$62,703
Student/teacher ratio '08-09	14.3 to 1
Highly-qualified teachers, '08-09	99.0%
Teachers licensed in assigned subject	98.5%
Students per computer	4.1

Massachusetts Competency Assessment System (MCAS), 2009 results

	English		Math	
	% Prof	CPI	% Prof	CPI
Gr 4	54%	80.5	53%	80.6
Gr 6	76%	89.6	55%	76.4
Gr 8	81%	92	45%	72.1
Gr 10	79%	90.9	73%	87.1

Other School Districts (see Appendix D for data)
North Shore Vocational Tech

©2010 Information Publications, Inc. All rights reserved. Photocopying prohibited. For additional copies, contact the publisher at www.informationpublications.com or (877)544-INFO (4636)

See Introduction for an explanation of all data sources.

Demographics & Socio-Economic Characteristics

Population

1990	37,609
2000	38,981
Male	19,823
Female	19,158
2008	41,844
2010 (projected)††	37,893
2020 (projected)††	36,067

Race & Hispanic Origin, 2000

Race	
White	36,906
Black/African American	432
American Indian/Alaska Native	39
Asian	1,074
Hawaiian Native/Pacific Islander	16
Other Race	127
Two or more races	387
Hispanic origin	600

Age & Nativity, 2000

Under 5 years	2,689
18 years and over	28,947
21 years and over	27,730
65 years and over	3,260
85 years and over	294
Median Age	35.9
Native-born	36,519
Foreign-born	2,426

Age, 2020 (projected)††

Under 5 years	2,002
5 to 19 years	6,266
20 to 39 years	9,418
40 to 64 years	12,346
65 years and over	6,035

Educational Attainment, 2000

Population 25 years and over	26,041
High School graduates or higher	89.1%
Bachelor's degree or higher	23.4%
Graduate degree	7.8%

Income & Poverty, 1999

Per capita income,	$24,953
Median household income	$67,799
Median family income	$72,102
Persons in poverty	1,414
H'holds receiving public assistance	132
H'holds receiving social security	2,930

Households, 2000

Total households	12,919
With persons under 18	5,309
With persons over 65	2,392
Family households	10,245
Single person households	2,113
Persons per household	2.9
Persons per family	3.3

Labor & Employment, 2000

Civilian labor force	21,403
Unemployment rate	3.1%
Civilian labor force, 2008†	23,141
Unemployment rate†	5.8%
Civilian labor force, 12/09†	23,333
Unemployment rate†	8.9%
Employed persons 16 years and over, by occupation:	
Managers & professionals	7,282
Service occupations	2,715
Sales & office occupations	6,002
Farming, fishing & forestry	0
Construction & maintenance	2,212
Production & transportation	2,521
Self-employed persons	1,040

Most demographic data is from the 2000 Decennial Census
† Massachusetts Department of Revenue
†† University of Massachusetts, MISER

General Information

Town of Billerica
Town Hall
365 Boston Rd
Billerica, MA 01821
978-671-0942

Elevation	250 ft.
Land area (square miles)	25.9
Water area (square miles)	0.5
Population density, 2008 (est)	1,615.6
Year incorporated	1655
Website	www.town.billerica.ma.us

Voters & Government Information

Government type	Rep. Town Meeting
Number of Selectmen	5
US Congressional District(s)	5

Registered Voters, October 2008

Total	24,363
Democrats	7,662
Republicans	2,973
Unaffiliated/other	13,553

Local Officials, 2010

Chair, Bd. of Sel.	Marc T. Lombardo Jr
Manager	William Williams
Town Clerk	Shirley E. Schult
Finance	John Clark
Tax Collector	John Clark
Tax Assessor	Richard Scanlon
Attorney	NA
Public Works	Abdul H. Alkhatib
Building	Milton H. Kinney Jr
Comm Dev/Planning	Peter Kennedy
Police Chief	Daniel Rosa Jr
Emerg/Fire Chief	Anthony Capaldo

Housing & Construction

New Privately Owned Housing Units Authorized by Building Permit

	Single Family	Total Bldgs	Total Units
2006	90	95	246
2007	58	58	58
2008	39	39	39

Parcel Count by Property Class, 2010

Total	14,576
Single family	10,722
Multiple units	596
Apartments	34
Condos	1,072
Vacant land	1,139
Open space	0
Commercial	402
Industrial	469
Misc. residential	51
Other use	91

Public Library

Billerica Public Library
25 Concord Rd.
Billerica, MA 01821
(978)671-0948

Director	Barbara Flaherty

Library Statistics, FY 2008

Population served, 2007	42,038
Registered users	38,846
Circulation	312,860
Reference transactons	26,758
Total program attendance	223,146
per capita:	
Holdings	3.15
Operating income	$31.29
Internet Access	
Internet computers available	25
Weekly users	715

Municipal Finance

Debt at year end 2008	$62,738,990
Moody's rating, July 2009	Aa3

Revenues, 2008

Total	$123,047,288
From all taxes	87,259,834
Federal aid	0
State aid	24,298,666
From other governments	0
Charges for services	8,741,964
Licenses, permits & fees	850,266
Fines & forfeits	188,415
Interfund transfers	40,125
Misc/other/special assessments	834,009

Expenditures, 2008

Total	$110,938,540
General government	3,716,733
Public safety	14,142,370
Other/fixed costs	9,260,268
Human services	1,053,284
Culture & recreation	1,552,122
Debt Service	6,500,240
Education	56,627,486
Public works	13,826,077
Intergovernmental	4,019,637

Taxation, 2010

Property type	Valuation	Rate
Total	$5,453,285,443	-
Residential	4,173,919,992	12.53
Open space	0	0.00
Commercial	285,073,046	28.47
Industrial	836,441,405	28.47
Personal	157,851,000	28.47

Average Single Family Tax Bill, 2010

Avg. assessed home value	$325,397
Avg. single fam. tax bill	$4,077
Hi-Lo ranking	130/301

Police & Crime, 2008

Number of police officers	63
Violent crimes	NA
Property crimes	NA

Local School District

(school data 2007-08, except as noted)

Billerica
365 Boston Rd
Billerica, MA 01821
978-436-9500

Superintendent	Anthony Serio
Grade plan	PK-12
Total enrollment '09-10	5,940
Grade 12 enrollment, '09-10	351
Graduation rate	88.5%
Dropout rate	3.5%
Per-pupil expenditure	$11,166
Avg teacher salary	$58,426
Student/teacher ratio '08-09	14.0 to 1
Highly-qualified teachers, '08-09	95.3%
Teachers licensed in assigned subject	96.5%
Students per computer	3.9

Massachusetts Competency Assessment System (MCAS), 2009 results

	English		Math	
	% Prof	CPI	% Prof	CPI
Gr 4	51%	82.1	45%	79
Gr 6	67%	86.5	60%	82.2
Gr 8	81%	93.2	55%	79.6
Gr 10	81%	92	83%	92.3

Other School Districts (see Appendix D for data)
Shawsheen Valley Vocational Tech

©2010 Information Publications, Inc. All rights reserved. Photocopying prohibited. For additional copies, contact the publisher at www.informationpublications.com or (877)544-INFO (4636)

See Introduction for an explanation of all data sources.

Demographics & Socio-Economic Characteristics

Population

1990	8,023
2000	8,804
Male	4,363
Female	4,441
2008	9,021
2010 (projected)††	9,625
2020 (projected)††	10,626

Race & Hispanic Origin, 2000

Race	
White	8,574
Black/African American	29
American Indian/Alaska Native	21
Asian	67
Hawaiian Native/Pacific Islander	1
Other Race	21
Two or more races	91
Hispanic origin	91

Age & Nativity, 2000

Under 5 years	557
18 years and over	6,361
21 years and over	6,064
65 years and over	890
85 years and over	90
Median Age	35.4
Native-born	8,564
Foreign-born	240

Age, 2020 (projected)††

Under 5 years	657
5 to 19 years	1,894
20 to 39 years	3,067
40 to 64 years	3,538
65 years and over	1,470

Educational Attainment, 2000

Population 25 years and over	5,663
High School graduates or higher	80.7%
Bachelor's degree or higher	16.3%
Graduate degree	4.4%

Income & Poverty, 1999

Per capita income,	$20,936
Median household income	$55,163
Median family income	$61,633
Persons in poverty	327
H'holds receiving public assistance	79
H'holds receiving social security	707

Households, 2000

Total households	3,235
With persons under 18	1,328
With persons over 65	651
Family households	2,355
Single person households	725
Persons per household	2.7
Persons per family	3.2

Labor & Employment, 2000

Civilian labor force	4,830
Unemployment rate	1.8%
Civilian labor force, 2008†	5,197
Unemployment rate†	8.1%
Civilian labor force, 12/09†	5,236
Unemployment rate†	11.3%
Employed persons 16 years and over, by occupation:	
Managers & professionals	1,364
Service occupations	680
Sales & office occupations	1,351
Farming, fishing & forestry	0
Construction & maintenance	598
Production & transportation	748
Self-employed persons	241

Most demographic data is from the 2000 Decennial Census
† Massachusetts Department of Revenue
†† University of Massachusetts, MISER

General Information

Town of Blackstone
15 St Paul St
Blackstone, MA 01504
508-883-1500

Elevation	186 ft.
Land area (square miles)	10.9
Water area (square miles)	0.3
Population density, 2008 (est)	827.6
Year incorporated	1845
Website	www.townofblackstone.org

Voters & Government Information

Government type	Open Town Meeting
Number of Selectmen	5
US Congressional District(s)	2

Registered Voters, October 2008

Total	6,120
Democrats	1,814
Republicans	638
Unaffiliated/other	3,631

Local Officials, 2010

Chair, Bd. of Sel.	NA
Town Administrator	Kanneth Bianchi
Town Clerk	Marianne Staples
Finance Director	(vacant)
Tax Collector	Diane Warren
Tax Assessor	Pat Salamone
Attorney	Pat Costello
Public Works	(vacant)
Building	Gerald Rivet
Town Planner	(vacant)
Police Chief	Ross Atstupenas
Emerg/Fire Chief	Michael Sweeney

Housing & Construction

New Privately Owned Housing Units Authorized by Building Permit

	Single Family	Total Bldgs	Total Units
2006	19	19	19
2007	13	13	13
2008	10	10	10

Parcel Count by Property Class, 2010

Total	NA
Single family	NA
Multiple units	NA
Apartments	NA
Condos	NA
Vacant land	NA
Open space	NA
Commercial	NA
Industrial	NA
Misc. residential	NA
Other use	NA

Public Library

Blackstone Public Library
86 Main St.
Blackstone, MA 01504
(508)883-1931

Director	Cyndee Marcoux

Library Statistics, FY 2008

Population served, 2007	9,042
Registered users	4,911
Circulation	91,320
Reference transactons	6,175
Total program attendance	50,170
per capita:	
Holdings	4.65
Operating income	$35.43
Internet Access	
Internet computers available	22
Weekly users	306

Municipal Finance

Debt at year end 2008	$17,942,317
Moody's rating, July 2009	NA

Revenues, 2008

Total	$15,941,346
From all taxes	13,157,193
Federal aid	0
State aid	1,751,587
From other governments	0
Charges for services	15,044
Licenses, permits & fees	170,838
Fines & forfeits	39,649
Interfund transfers	490,069
Misc/other/special assessments	158,483

Expenditures, 2008

Total	$15,419,306
General government	1,125,713
Public safety	2,056,459
Other/fixed costs	852,562
Human services	208,678
Culture & recreation	455,665
Debt Service	1,678,866
Education	7,673,464
Public works	1,295,119
Intergovernmental	42,067

Taxation, 2010

Property type	Valuation	Rate
Total	NA	-
Residential	NA	NA
Open space	NA	NA
Commercial	NA	NA
Industrial	NA	NA
Personal	NA	NA

Average Single Family Tax Bill, 2010

Avg. assessed home value	NA
Avg. single fam. tax bill	NA
Hi-Lo ranking	NA

Police & Crime, 2008

Number of police officers	16
Violent crimes	20
Property crimes	145

Local School District

(school data 2007-08, except as noted)

Blackstone (non-op)
175 Lincoln Street
Blackstone, MA 01504
508-883-4400

Superintendent..... Kimberly Shaver-Hood

Non-operating district.
Resident students are sent to the Other School Districts listed below.

Grade plan	NA
Total enrollment '09-10	NA
Grade 12 enrollment, '09-10	NA
Graduation rate	NA
Dropout rate	NA
Per-pupil expenditure	NA
Avg teacher salary	NA
Student/teacher ratio '08-09	NA
Highly-qualified teachers, '08-09	NA
Teachers licensed in assigned subject	NA
Students per computer	NA

Other School Districts (see Appendix D for data)
Blackstone-Millville Regional, Blackstone Valley Vocational Tech

©2010 Information Publications, Inc. All rights reserved. Photocopying prohibited. For additional copies, contact the publisher at www.informationpublications.com or (877)544-INFO (4636)

See Introduction for an explanation of all data sources.

Demographics & Socio-Economic Characteristics

Population

1990	1,187
2000	1,214
Male	607
Female	607
2008	1,270
2010 (projected)††	1,232
2020 (projected)††	1,235

Race & Hispanic Origin, 2000

Race	
White	1,199
Black/African American	6
American Indian/Alaska Native	2
Asian	3
Hawaiian Native/Pacific Islander	0
Other Race	0
Two or more races	4
Hispanic origin	4

Age & Nativity, 2000

Under 5 years	69
18 years and over	921
21 years and over	884
65 years and over	117
85 years and over	8
Median Age	40.3
Native-born	1,187
Foreign-born	27

Age, 2020 (projected)††

Under 5 years	55
5 to 19 years	176
20 to 39 years	290
40 to 64 years	471
65 years and over	243

Educational Attainment, 2000

Population 25 years and over	840
High School graduates or higher	88.6%
Bachelor's degree or higher	25.8%
Graduate degree	8.5%

Income & Poverty, 1999

Per capita income,	$24,285
Median household income	$52,935
Median family income	$59,375
Persons in poverty	41
H'holds receiving public assistance	7
H'holds receiving social security	102

Households, 2000

Total households	456
With persons under 18	163
With persons over 65	89
Family households	350
Single person households	89
Persons per household	2.7
Persons per family	3.0

Labor & Employment, 2000

Civilian labor force	699
Unemployment rate	3.9%
Civilian labor force, 2008†	734
Unemployment rate†	5.2%
Civilian labor force, 12/09†	746
Unemployment rate†	7.8%
Employed persons 16 years and over, by occupation:	
Managers & professionals	229
Service occupations	99
Sales & office occupations	156
Farming, fishing & forestry	2
Construction & maintenance	68
Production & transportation	118
Self-employed persons	45

Most demographic data is from the 2000 Decennial Census
† Massachusetts Department of Revenue
†† University of Massachusetts, MISER

General Information

Town of Blandford
102 Main St
Blandford, MA 01008
413-848-2782

Elevation	1,452 ft.
Land area (square miles)	51.7
Water area (square miles)	1.8
Population density, 2008 (est)	24.6
Year incorporated	1741
Email	blandfordselectmen@hughes.net

Voters & Government Information

Government type	Open Town Meeting
Number of Selectmen	3
US Congressional District(s)	1

Registered Voters, October 2008

Total	910
Democrats	165
Republicans	175
Unaffiliated/other	561

Local Officials, 2010

Chair, Bd. of Sel.	Chester Broughton
Manager/Admin	NA
Town Clerk	Staci Iglesias
Finance	Anne Holliday
Tax Collector	Leeann Thompson
Tax Assessor	Lauralee Bertram
Attorney	NA
Public Works	Brad Curry
Building	Thomas Lagodich
Comm Dev/Planning	Julie Mueller
Police Chief	Ron Brown
Emerg/Fire Chief	Don Carpenter

Housing & Construction

New Privately Owned Housing Units Authorized by Building Permit

	Single Family	Total Bldgs	Total Units
2006	8	8	8
2007	7	7	7
2008	7	7	7

Parcel Count by Property Class, 2010

Total	1,022
Single family	499
Multiple units	9
Apartments	0
Condos	0
Vacant land	356
Open space	0
Commercial	4
Industrial	5
Misc. residential	13
Other use	136

Public Library

Porter Memorial Library
PO Box 797
Blandford, MA 01008
(413)848-2853

Director	Mary Jo Place

Library Statistics, FY 2008

Population served, 2007	1,279
Registered users	947
Circulation	9,037
Reference transactons	142
Total program attendance	0
per capita:	
Holdings	9.30
Operating income	$30.67
Internet Access	
Internet computers available	2
Weekly users	15

Municipal Finance

Debt at year end 2008	$4,812,365
Moody's rating, July 2009	NA

Revenues, 2008

Total	$2,131,545
From all taxes	1,804,094
Federal aid	0
State aid	208,199
From other governments	13,330
Charges for services	0
Licenses, permits & fees	69,052
Fines & forfeits	0
Interfund transfers	0
Misc/other/special assessments	18,435

Expenditures, 2008

Total	$2,453,921
General government	204,850
Public safety	69,696
Other/fixed costs	86,919
Human services	20,977
Culture & recreation	36,648
Debt Service	29,321
Education	1,602,028
Public works	403,482
Intergovernmental	0

Taxation, 2010

Property type	Valuation	Rate
Total	$169,714,215	-
Residential	148,381,285	12.62
Open space	0	0.00
Commercial	6,947,592	12.62
Industrial	404,100	12.62
Personal	13,981,238	12.62

Average Single Family Tax Bill, 2010

Avg. assessed home value	$223,957
Avg. single fam. tax bill	$2,826
Hi-Lo ranking	252/301

Police & Crime, 2008

Number of police officers	NA
Violent crimes	NA
Property crimes	NA

Local School District

(school data 2007-08, except as noted)

Blandford (non-op)
12 Littleville Road
Huntington, MA 01050
413-685-1011

Superintendent	David Hopson

Non-operating district.
Resident students are sent to the Other School Districts listed below.

Grade plan	NA
Total enrollment '09-10	NA
Grade 12 enrollment, '09-10	NA
Graduation rate	NA
Dropout rate	NA
Per-pupil expenditure	NA
Avg teacher salary	NA
Student/teacher ratio '08-09	NA
Highly-qualified teachers, '08-09	NA
Teachers licensed in assigned subject	NA
Students per computer	NA

Other School Districts (see Appendix D for data)
Gateway Regional

©2010 Information Publications, Inc. All rights reserved. Photocopying prohibited. For additional copies, contact the publisher at www.informationpublications.com or (877)544-INFO (4636)

See Introduction for an explanation of all data sources.

Demographics & Socio-Economic Characteristics

Population

1990	3,134
2000	4,148
Male	2,082
Female	2,066
2008	4,530
2010 (projected)††	4,974
2020 (projected)††	5,546

Race & Hispanic Origin, 2000

Race	
White	4,055
Black/African American	8
American Indian/Alaska Native	2
Asian	54
Hawaiian Native/Pacific Islander	1
Other Race	8
Two or more races	20
Hispanic origin	33

Age & Nativity, 2000

Under 5 years	331
18 years and over	2,885
21 years and over	2,824
65 years and over	258
85 years and over	15
Median Age	38.3
Native-born	3,904
Foreign-born	244

Age, 2020 (projected)††

Under 5 years	404
5 to 19 years	1,355
20 to 39 years	1,087
40 to 64 years	1,971
65 years and over	729

Educational Attainment, 2000

Population 25 years and over	2,768
High School graduates or higher	97.6%
Bachelor's degree or higher	67.3%
Graduate degree	28.9%

Income & Poverty, 1999

Per capita income,	$42,542
Median household income	$102,798
Median family income	$108,967
Persons in poverty	75
H'holds receiving public assistance	0
H'holds receiving social security	180

Households, 2000

Total households	1,424
With persons under 18	651
With persons over 65	185
Family households	1,202
Single person households	159
Persons per household	2.9
Persons per family	3.2

Labor & Employment, 2000

Civilian labor force	2,372
Unemployment rate	3.4%
Civilian labor force, 2008†	2,585
Unemployment rate†	4.5%
Civilian labor force, 12/09†	2,584
Unemployment rate†	7.0%
Employed persons 16 years and over, by occupation:	
Managers & professionals	1,579
Service occupations	104
Sales & office occupations	429
Farming, fishing & forestry	20
Construction & maintenance	80
Production & transportation	80
Self-employed persons	230

Most demographic data is from the 2000 Decennial Census
† Massachusetts Department of Revenue
†† University of Massachusetts, MISER

General Information

Town of Bolton
663 Main St
Bolton, MA 01740
978-779-2771

Elevation	387 ft.
Land area (square miles)	19.9
Water area (square miles)	0.1
Population density, 2008 (est)	227.6
Year incorporated	1738
Website	www.townofbolton.com

Voters & Government Information

Government type	Open Town Meeting
Number of Selectmen	3
US Congressional District(s)	5

Registered Voters, October 2008

Total	3,246
Democrats	675
Republicans	653
Unaffiliated/other	1,914

Local Officials, 2010

Chair, Bd. of Sel.	Kenneth Troup
Town Administrator	Donald Lowe
Town Clerk	Pamela H. Powell
Treasurer	Donna Madden
Tax Collector	Donna Madden
Tax Assessor	Jeffrey Nichols
Attorney	Brackett & Lucas
Public Works	Harold Brown
Building	NA
Comm Dev/Planning	Jennifer A. Burney
Police Chief	Vincent Alfano
Emerg/Fire Chief	John Stephenson

Housing & Construction

New Privately Owned Housing Units Authorized by Building Permit

	Single Family	Total Bldgs	Total Units
2006	24	24	24
2007	20	20	20
2008	6	6	6

Parcel Count by Property Class, 2010

Total	2,229
Single family	1,568
Multiple units	12
Apartments	1
Condos	130
Vacant land	370
Open space	0
Commercial	22
Industrial	13
Misc. residential	10
Other use	103

Public Library

Bolton Public Library
PO Box 188
Bolton, MA 01740
(978)779-2839

Director	Kelly Collins

Library Statistics, FY 2008

Population served, 2007	4,481
Registered users	2,846
Circulation	52,615
Reference transactons	0
Total program attendance	22,105
per capita:	
Holdings	6.66
Operating income	$46.09
Internet Access	
Internet computers available	2
Weekly users	20

Municipal Finance

Debt at year end 2008	$13,190,000
Moody's rating, July 2009	Aa3

Revenues, 2008

Total	$17,401,486
From all taxes	15,308,879
Federal aid	0
State aid	886,249
From other governments	53,178
Charges for services	149,467
Licenses, permits & fees	125,398
Fines & forfeits	585
Interfund transfers	349,540
Misc/other/special assessments	264,095

Expenditures, 2008

Total	$16,394,966
General government	958,107
Public safety	1,453,400
Other/fixed costs	556,985
Human services	59,819
Culture & recreation	213,712
Debt Service	1,629,176
Education	10,221,347
Public works	1,285,508
Intergovernmental	16,912

Taxation, 2010

Property type	Valuation	Rate
Total	$931,523,796	-
Residential	841,525,762	17.61
Open space	0	0.00
Commercial	45,727,538	17.61
Industrial	13,091,400	17.61
Personal	31,179,096	17.61

Average Single Family Tax Bill, 2010

Avg. assessed home value	$485,135
Avg. single fam. tax bill	$8,543
Hi-Lo ranking	16/301

Police & Crime, 2008

Number of police officers	10
Violent crimes	2
Property crimes	61

Local School District

(school data 2007-08, except as noted)

Bolton (non-op)
50 Mechanic Street
Bolton, MA 01740
978-779-0539

Superintendent	Michael Wood

Non-operating district.
Resident students are sent to the Other School Districts listed below.

Grade plan	NA
Total enrollment '09-10	NA
Grade 12 enrollment, '09-10	NA
Graduation rate	NA
Dropout rate	NA
Per-pupil expenditure	NA
Avg teacher salary	NA
Student/teacher ratio '08-09	NA
Highly-qualified teachers, '08-09	NA
Teachers licensed in assigned subject	NA
Students per computer	NA

Other School Districts (see Appendix D for data)
Nashoba Regional, Minuteman Vocational Tech

©2010 Information Publications, Inc. All rights reserved. Photocopying prohibited. For additional copies, contact the publisher at www.informationpublications.com or (877)544-INFO (4636)

Demographics & Socio-Economic Characteristics*

Population

1990	574,283
2000	589,141
Male	283,588
Female	305,553
2008	609,023
2010 (projected)††	619,081
2020 (projected)††	649,395

Race & Hispanic Origin, 2000

Race	
White	320,944
Black/African American	149,202
American Indian/Alaska Native	2,365
Asian	44,284
Hawaiian Native/Pacific Islander	366
Other Race	46,102
Two or more races	25,878
Hispanic origin	85,089

Age & Nativity, 2000

Under 5 years	32,046
18 years and over	472,582
21 years and over	432,815
65 years and over	61,336
85 years and over	8,507
Median Age	31.1
Native-born	437,305
Foreign-born	151,836

Age, 2020 (projected)††

Under 5 years	37,255
5 to 19 years	121,960
20 to 39 years	236,568
40 to 64 years	179,242
65 years and over	74,370

Educational Attainment, 2000

Population 25 years and over	377,574
High School graduates or higher	78.9%
Bachelor's degree or higher	35.6%
Graduate degree	15.3%

Income & Poverty, 1999

Per capita income,	$23,353
Median household income	$39,629
Median family income	$44,151
Persons in poverty	109,128
H'holds receiving public assistance	9,766
H'holds receiving social security	44,831

Households, 2000

Total households	239,528
With persons under 18	61,428
With persons over 65	45,350
Family households	115,096
Single person households	88,944
Persons per household	2.3
Persons per family	3.2

Labor & Employment, 2000

Civilian labor force	308,107
Unemployment rate	7.2%
Civilian labor force, 2008†	304,652
Unemployment rate†	6.0%
Civilian labor force, 12/09†	307,797
Unemployment rate†	8.3%
Employed persons 16 years and over, by occupation:	
Managers & professionals	123,850
Service occupations	50,839
Sales & office occupations	73,199
Farming, fishing & forestry	223
Construction & maintenance	14,118
Production & transportation	23,630
Self-employed persons	12,988

Most demographic data is from the 2000 Decennial Census
* see Appendix D and E for American Community Survey data
† Massachusetts Department of Revenue
†† University of Massachusetts, MISER

General Information

City of Boston
1 City Hall Sq
Boston, MA 02201
617-635-4000

Elevation	10 ft.
Land area (square miles)	48.4
Water area (square miles)	41.2
Population density, 2008 (est)	12,583.1
Year incorporated	1630
Website	www.cityofboston.gov

Voters & Government Information

Government type	Mayor-Council
Number of Councilpersons	13
US Congressional District(s)	8, 9

Registered Voters, October 2008

Total	381,013
Democrats	209,710
Republicans	27,541
Unaffiliated/other	140,601

Local Officials, 2010

Mayor	Thomas M. Menino
Manager/Admin	Lisa C. Signori
Clerk	Rosaria Salerno
Finance Director	Lisa C. Signori
Tax Collector	NA
Tax Assessor	Ronald Rakow
Attorney	William Sinnott
Public Works	Dennis Royer
Building	William Good
Planning	Charlotte Goler-Richie
Police Chief	Edward Davis
Emerg/Fire Chief	Roderick Fraser Jr

Housing & Construction

New Privately Owned Housing Units Authorized by Building Permit

	Single Family	Total Bldgs	Total Units
2006	94	282	2419
2007	48	150	1041
2008	23	79	513

Parcel Count by Property Class, 2010

Total	143,734
Single family	30,437
Multiple units	31,643
Apartments	5,138
Condos	56,652
Vacant land	7,272
Open space	0
Commercial	8,061
Industrial	697
Misc. residential	1,595
Other use	2,239

Public Library

Boston Public Library
700 Boylston Street
Boston, MA 02116
(617)536-5400

President	Amy Ryan

Library Statistics, FY 2008

Population served, 2007	599,351
Registered users	552,797
Circulation	3,159,087
Reference transactons	1,090,826
Total program attendance	3,534,700
per capita:	
Holdings	26.93
Operating income	$65.47
Internet Access	
Internet computers available	513
Weekly users	14,071

Municipal Finance

Debt at year end 2008	$870,373,413
Moody's rating, July 2009	Aa1

Revenues, 2008

Total	$2,463,311,428
From all taxes	1,484,384,318
Federal aid	0
State aid	638,921,542
From other governments	9,377,951
Charges for services	35,639,046
Licenses, permits & fees	47,576,958
Fines & forfeits	63,776,197
Interfund transfers	12,140,770
Misc/other/special assessments	85,747,323

Expenditures, 2008

Total	$2,247,372,997
General government	121,340,509
Public safety	494,653,281
Other/fixed costs	329,574,621
Human services	103,710,918
Culture & recreation	46,054,489
Debt Service	119,387,502
Education	794,628,715
Public works	107,780,292
Intergovernmental	128,275,628

Taxation, 2010

Property type	Valuation	Rate
Total	$87,256,532,047	-
Residential	56,279,025,448	11.88
Open space	0	0.00
Commercial	25,931,406,498	29.38
Industrial	798,981,631	29.38
Personal	4,247,118,470	29.38

Average Single Family Tax Bill, 2010

Avg. assessed home value	NA
Avg. single fam. tax bill	NA
Hi-Lo ranking	NA

Police & Crime, 2008

Number of police officers	2,213
Violent crimes	6,676
Property crimes	22,429

Local School District

(school data 2007-08, except as noted)

Boston
26 Court Street
Boston, MA 02108
617-635-9050

Superintendent	Carol Johnson
Grade plan	PK-12
Total enrollment '09-10	55,371
Grade 12 enrollment, '09-10	4,070
Graduation rate	59.9%
Dropout rate	21.5%
Per-pupil expenditure	$17,151
Avg teacher salary	$76,108
Student/teacher ratio '08-09	12.8 to 1
Highly-qualified teachers, '08-09	95.9%
Teachers licensed in assigned subject	97.9%
Students per computer	3.6

Massachusetts Competency Assessment System (MCAS), 2009 results

	English		Math	
	% Prof	CPI	% Prof	CPI
Gr 4	31%	64.7	28%	65
Gr 6	43%	72.2	33%	60.6
Gr 8	59%	81.5	28%	56.9
Gr 10	64%	84.6	62%	81.2

Other School Districts (see Appendix D for data)
None

©2010 Information Publications, Inc. All rights reserved. Photocopying prohibited. For additional copies, contact the publisher at www.informationpublications.com or (877)544-INFO (4636)

See Introduction for an explanation of all data sources.

Demographics & Socio-Economic Characteristics

Population

1990	16,064
2000	18,721
Male	9,223
Female	9,498
2008	19,392
2010 (projected)††	21,712
2020 (projected)††	25,130

Race & Hispanic Origin, 2000

Race	
White	17,732
Black/African American	261
American Indian/Alaska Native	100
Asian	132
Hawaiian Native/Pacific Islander	2
Other Race	185
Two or more races	309
Hispanic origin	273

Age & Nativity, 2000

Under 5 years	1,171
18 years and over	14,630
21 years and over	13,775
65 years and over	3,299
85 years and over	378
Median Age	39.2
Native-born	18,127
Foreign-born	585

Age, 2020 (projected)††

Under 5 years	1,381
5 to 19 years	3,946
20 to 39 years	5,218
40 to 64 years	7,812
65 years and over	6,773

Educational Attainment, 2000

Population 25 years and over	12,902
High School graduates or higher	92.6%
Bachelor's degree or higher	27.2%
Graduate degree	9.1%

Income & Poverty, 1999

Per capita income,	$22,092
Median household income	$45,113
Median family income	$51,603
Persons in poverty	1,261
H'holds receiving public assistance	151
H'holds receiving social security	2,372

Households, 2000

Total households	7,439
With persons under 18	2,241
With persons over 65	2,252
Family households	5,013
Single person households	1,990
Persons per household	2.4
Persons per family	2.9

Labor & Employment, 2000

Civilian labor force	9,173
Unemployment rate	7.2%
Civilian labor force, 2008†	9,852
Unemployment rate†	7.9%
Civilian labor force, 12/09†	9,644
Unemployment rate†	10.3%
Employed persons 16 years and over, by occupation:	
Managers & professionals	2,601
Service occupations	1,487
Sales & office occupations	2,518
Farming, fishing & forestry	34
Construction & maintenance	1,117
Production & transportation	754
Self-employed persons	781

Most demographic data is from the 2000 Decennial Census
† Massachusetts Department of Revenue
†† University of Massachusetts, MISER

General Information

Town of Bourne
24 Perry Ave
Bourne, MA 02532
508-759-0600

Elevation	50 ft.
Land area (square miles)	40.9
Water area (square miles)	11.9
Population density, 2008 (est)	474.1
Year incorporated	1884
Website	www.townofbourne.com

Voters & Government Information

Government type	Open Town Meeting
Number of Selectmen	5
US Congressional District(s)	10

Registered Voters, October 2008

Total	12,996
Democrats	3,027
Republicans	2,080
Unaffiliated/other	7,829

Local Officials, 2010

Chair, Bd. of Sel.	John F. Ford
Admin	Thomas Guerino
Town Clerk	Barry H. Johnson
Finance Director	Linda Marzelli
Tax Collector	Kathleen Burgess
Tax Assessor	Donna Barakauskas
Attorney	Robert S. Troy
Public Works	Rickie Tellier
Building	Roger La Porte
Comm Dev/Planning	Coreen Moore
Police Chief	Earl Baldwin
Fire Chief	Daniel Doucette (Actg)

Housing & Construction

New Privately Owned Housing Units Authorized by Building Permit

	Single Family	Total Bldgs	Total Units
2006	73	73	73
2007	62	63	65
2008	23	24	51

Parcel Count by Property Class, 2010

Total	11,270
Single family	7,627
Multiple units	121
Apartments	22
Condos	1,107
Vacant land	1,310
Open space	0
Commercial	667
Industrial	46
Misc. residential	201
Other use	169

Public Library

Jonathan Bourne Public Library
19 Sandwich Road
Bourne, MA 02532
(508)759-0644

Director	Patrick Marshall

Library Statistics, FY 2008

Population served, 2007	19,023
Registered users	10,779
Circulation	148,672
Reference transactons	2,756
Total program attendance	104,872
per capita:	
Holdings	3.46
Operating income	$31.27
Internet Access	
Internet computers available	8
Weekly users	218

Municipal Finance

Debt at year end 2008	$34,572,693
Moody's rating, July 2009	Aa3

Revenues, 2008

Total	$52,027,046
From all taxes	33,823,359
Federal aid	168,138
State aid	9,508,564
From other governments	3,428
Charges for services	1,273,953
Licenses, permits & fees	554,284
Fines & forfeits	129,064
Interfund transfers	5,464,334
Misc/other/special assessments	550,961

Expenditures, 2008

Total	$42,637,686
General government	3,038,475
Public safety	5,896,396
Other/fixed costs	3,164,026
Human services	748,787
Culture & recreation	703,258
Debt Service	4,468,237
Education	20,820,425
Public works	2,008,747
Intergovernmental	1,789,335

Taxation, 2010

Property type	Valuation	Rate
Total	$4,609,880,940	-
Residential	4,085,719,149	7.54
Open space	0	0.00
Commercial	394,574,831	7.54
Industrial	33,374,510	7.54
Personal	96,212,450	7.54

Average Single Family Tax Bill, 2010

Avg. assessed home value	$446,624
Avg. single fam. tax bill	$3,368
Hi-Lo ranking	187/301

Police & Crime, 2008

Number of police officers	36
Violent crimes	63
Property crimes	580

Local School District

(school data 2007-08, except as noted)

Bourne
36 Sandwich Rd
Bourne, MA 02532
508-759-0660

Superintendent	Edmond LaFleur
Grade plan	PK-12
Total enrollment '09-10	2,372
Grade 12 enrollment, '09-10	161
Graduation rate	87.7%
Dropout rate	7.5%
Per-pupil expenditure	$11,642
Avg teacher salary	$57,570
Student/teacher ratio '08-09	14.7 to 1
Highly-qualified teachers, '08-09	95.0%
Teachers licensed in assigned subject	96.7%
Students per computer	2.6

Massachusetts Competency Assessment System (MCAS), 2009 results

	English		Math	
	% Prof	CPI	% Prof	CPI
Gr 4	45%	77.9	38%	73.6
Gr 6	75%	89.7	58%	79.3
Gr 8	77%	90.8	47%	72.6
Gr 10	87%	95.5	85%	93.9

Other School Districts (see Appendix D for data)
Upper Cape Cod Vocational Tech

©2010 Information Publications, Inc. All rights reserved. Photocopying prohibited. For additional copies, contact the publisher at www.informationpublications.com or (877)544-INFO (4636)

See Introduction for an explanation of all data sources.

Demographics & Socio-Economic Characteristics

Population

1990	3,343
2000	4,868
Male	2,483
Female	2,385
2008	5,081
2010 (projected)††	5,668
2020 (projected)††	6,273

Race & Hispanic Origin, 2000

Race	
White	4,324
Black/African American	16
American Indian/Alaska Native	1
Asian	413
Hawaiian Native/Pacific Islander	0
Other Race	18
Two or more races	96
Hispanic origin	55

Age & Nativity, 2000

Under 5 years	358
18 years and over	3,381
21 years and over	3,287
65 years and over	230
85 years and over	16
Median Age	36.7
Native-born	4,254
Foreign-born	614

Age, 2020 (projected)††

Under 5 years	355
5 to 19 years	1,171
20 to 39 years	2,027
40 to 64 years	1,995
65 years and over	725

Educational Attainment, 2000

Population 25 years and over	3,115
High School graduates or higher	98.0%
Bachelor's degree or higher	72.1%
Graduate degree	32.4%

Income & Poverty, 1999

Per capita income,	$40,794
Median household income	$87,618
Median family income	$110,572
Persons in poverty	137
H'holds receiving public assistance	8
H'holds receiving social security	168

Households, 2000

Total households	1,853
With persons under 18	813
With persons over 65	177
Family households	1,271
Single person households	480
Persons per household	2.6
Persons per family	3.3

Labor & Employment, 2000

Civilian labor force	2,820
Unemployment rate	3.0%
Civilian labor force, 2008†	2,976
Unemployment rate†	4.3%
Civilian labor force, 12/09†	2,969
Unemployment rate†	6.4%
Employed persons 16 years and over, by occupation:	
Managers & professionals	1,730
Service occupations	204
Sales & office occupations	601
Farming, fishing & forestry	4
Construction & maintenance	88
Production & transportation	108
Self-employed persons	217

Most demographic data is from the 2000 Decennial Census
† Massachusetts Department of Revenue
†† University of Massachusetts, MISER

General Information

Town of Boxborough
29 Middle Rd
Boxborough, MA 01719
978-263-1116

Elevation	300 ft.
Land area (square miles)	10.4
Water area (square miles)	0.0
Population density, 2008 (est)	488.6
Year incorporated	1783
Website	www.town.boxborough.ma.us

Voters & Government Information

Government type	Open Town Meeting
Number of Selectmen	5
US Congressional District(s)	5

Registered Voters, October 2008

Total	3,448
Democrats	853
Republicans	471
Unaffiliated/other	2,114

Local Officials, 2010

Chair, Bd. of Sel.	Rebecca Neville
Manager/Admin	Selina Shaw
Town Clerk	Elizabeth Markiewicz
Finance Director	Margaret Dennehy
Tax Collector	Mary P. Shemowat
Tax Assessor	Duane Adams
Attorney	Kopelman & Paige
Public Works	Thomas Garmon
Building	John Field
Comm Dev/Planning	Elizabeth Hughes
Police Chief	Richard Vance
Emerg/Fire Chief	Geoffrey Neagle

Housing & Construction

New Privately Owned Housing Units Authorized by Building Permit

	Single Family	Total Bldgs	Total Units
2006	10	10	10
2007	2	2	2
2008	5	5	5

Parcel Count by Property Class, 2010

Total	2,372
Single family	1,167
Multiple units	15
Apartments	5
Condos	801
Vacant land	137
Open space	0
Commercial	80
Industrial	44
Misc. residential	3
Other use	120

Public Library

Sargent Memorial Library
427 Massachusetts Ave.
Boxborough, MA 01719
(978)263-4680

Director	Maureen Strapko

Library Statistics, FY 2008

Population served, 2007	5,097
Registered users	3,955
Circulation	117,512
Reference transactons	6,324
Total program attendance	72,727
per capita:	
Holdings	9.74
Operating income	$57.61
Internet Access	
Internet computers available	12
Weekly users	540

Municipal Finance

Debt at year end 2008	$8,544,500
Moody's rating, July 2009	Aa3

Revenues, 2008

Total	$18,489,311
From all taxes	15,714,551
Federal aid	0
State aid	2,043,631
From other governments	48,120
Charges for services	274,534
Licenses, permits & fees	59,311
Fines & forfeits	0
Interfund transfers	0
Misc/other/special assessments	174,582

Expenditures, 2008

Total	$18,781,696
General government	821,161
Public safety	2,052,659
Other/fixed costs	1,702,549
Human services	73,666
Culture & recreation	304,361
Debt Service	1,406,412
Education	11,449,844
Public works	971,044
Intergovernmental	0

Taxation, 2010

Property type	Valuation	Rate
Total	$961,330,741	-
Residential	722,063,119	16.53
Open space	0	0.00
Commercial	81,176,198	16.53
Industrial	138,354,394	16.53
Personal	19,737,030	16.53

Average Single Family Tax Bill, 2010

Avg. assessed home value	$506,349
Avg. single fam. tax bill	$8,370
Hi-Lo ranking	18/301

Police & Crime, 2008

Number of police officers	NA
Violent crimes	11
Property crimes	52

Local School District

(school data 2007-08, except as noted)
Boxborough
493 Massachusetts Avenue
Boxborough, MA 01719
978-263-4569

Superintendent	Curtis Bates
Grade plan	PK-6
Total enrollment '09-10	495
Grade 12 enrollment, '09-10	0
Graduation rate	NA
Dropout rate	NA
Per-pupil expenditure	$11,627
Avg teacher salary	$67,377
Student/teacher ratio '08-09	13.4 to 1
Highly-qualified teachers, '08-09	100.0%
Teachers licensed in assigned subject	100.0%
Students per computer	2.8

Massachusetts Competency Assessment System (MCAS), 2009 results

	English		Math	
	% Prof	CPI	% Prof	CPI
Gr 4	86%	93.8	83%	93.8
Gr 6	91%	96.9	83%	93.2
Gr 8	NA	NA	NA	NA
Gr 10	NA	NA	NA	NA

Other School Districts (see Appendix D for data)
Acton-Boxborough Regional, Minuteman Vocational Tech

©2010 Information Publications, Inc. All rights reserved. Photocopying prohibited. For additional copies, contact the publisher at www.informationpublications.com or (877)544-INFO (4636)

See Introduction for an explanation of all data sources.

Demographics & Socio-Economic Characteristics

Population

1990	6,266
2000	7,921
Male	3,939
Female	3,982
2008	8,131
2010 (projected)††	8,338
2020 (projected)††	8,280

Race & Hispanic Origin, 2000

Race	
White	7,713
Black/African American	27
American Indian/Alaska Native	9
Asian	96
Hawaiian Native/Pacific Islander	2
Other Race	23
Two or more races	51
Hispanic origin	67

Age & Nativity, 2000

Under 5 years	589
18 years and over	5,370
21 years and over	5,183
65 years and over	740
85 years and over	57
Median Age	39.4
Native-born	7,535
Foreign-born	386

Age, 2020 (projected)††

Under 5 years	533
5 to 19 years	1,840
20 to 39 years	1,630
40 to 64 years	2,813
65 years and over	1,464

Educational Attainment, 2000

Population 25 years and over	5,016
High School graduates or higher	99.2%
Bachelor's degree or higher	62.8%
Graduate degree	28.5%

Income & Poverty, 1999

Per capita income,	$48,846
Median household income	$113,212
Median family income	$119,491
Persons in poverty	108
H'holds receiving public assistance	8
H'holds receiving social security	554

Households, 2000

Total households	2,568
With persons under 18	1,276
With persons over 65	516
Family households	2,255
Single person households	248
Persons per household	3.1
Persons per family	3.3

Labor & Employment, 2000

Civilian labor force	3,939
Unemployment rate	1.5%
Civilian labor force, 2008†	4,163
Unemployment rate†	4.5%
Civilian labor force, 12/09†	4,097
Unemployment rate†	6.4%
Employed persons 16 years and over, by occupation:	
Managers & professionals	2,403
Service occupations	227
Sales & office occupations	1,000
Farming, fishing & forestry	0
Construction & maintenance	134
Production & transportation	115
Self-employed persons	403

Most demographic data is from the 2000 Decennial Census
† Massachusetts Department of Revenue
†† University of Massachusetts, MISER

General Information

Town of Boxford
7A Spofford Road
Boxford, MA 01921
978-887-6000

Elevation	100 ft.
Land area (square miles)	24.0
Water area (square miles)	0.6
Population density, 2008 (est)	338.8
Year incorporated	1685
Website	www.town.boxford.ma.us

Voters & Government Information

Government type	Open Town Meeting
Number of Selectmen	5
US Congressional District(s)	6

Registered Voters, October 2008

Total	5,969
Democrats	974
Republicans	1,420
Unaffiliated/other	3,547

Local Officials, 2010

Chair, Bd. of Sel.	Barbara Jessel
Manager/Admin	Alan Benson
Town Clerk	Robin Phelan (Int)
Finance Director	Kathleen Benevento
Tax Collector	Ellen Guerin
Tax Assessor	David F. Benson (Chr)
Attorney	NA
Public Works	John Dold
Building	Jay Nies
Comm Dev/Planning	Ross Povenmire
Police Chief	Gordon Russell Jr
Emerg/Fire Chief	Kerry Stickney

Housing & Construction

New Privately Owned Housing Units Authorized by Building Permit

	Single Family	Total Bldgs	Total Units
2006	10	10	10
2007	3	3	3
2008	9	9	9

Parcel Count by Property Class, 2010

Total	3,008
Single family	2,638
Multiple units	0
Apartments	1
Condos	3
Vacant land	289
Open space	0
Commercial	13
Industrial	9
Misc. residential	7
Other use	48

Public Library

Boxford Town Library
10 Elm St.
Boxford, MA 01921
(978)887-8920

Director	Diane Giarrusso

Library Statistics, FY 2008

Population served, 2007	8,074
Registered users	8,143
Circulation	99,287
Reference transactons	13,533
Total program attendance	39,955
per capita:	
Holdings	7.99
Operating income	$52.84
Internet Access	
Internet computers available	9
Weekly users	43

Municipal Finance

Debt at year end 2008	$13,723,172
Moody's rating, July 2009	Aa2

Revenues, 2008

Total	$26,027,887
From all taxes	22,036,610
Federal aid	0
State aid	2,763,240
From other governments	77,859
Charges for services	303,509
Licenses, permits & fees	260,998
Fines & forfeits	0
Interfund transfers	13,571
Misc/other/special assessments	286,050

Expenditures, 2008

Total	$26,006,610
General government	1,339,351
Public safety	2,103,877
Other/fixed costs	2,353,735
Human services	275,798
Culture & recreation	414,686
Debt Service	1,575,623
Education	15,728,924
Public works	2,059,894
Intergovernmental	154,722

Taxation, 2010

Property type	Valuation	Rate
Total	$1,746,156,477	-
Residential	1,686,610,900	12.37
Open space	0	0.00
Commercial	13,348,500	12.37
Industrial	1,121,700	12.37
Personal	45,075,377	12.37

Average Single Family Tax Bill, 2010

Avg. assessed home value	$618,372
Avg. single fam. tax bill	$7,649
Hi-Lo ranking	26/301

Police & Crime, 2008

Number of police officers	13
Violent crimes	0
Property crimes	65

Local School District

(school data 2007-08, except as noted)

Boxford
28 Middleton Road
Boxford, MA 01921
978-887-0771

Superintendent	Bernard Creeden
Grade plan	PK-6
Total enrollment '09-10	917
Grade 12 enrollment, '09-10	0
Graduation rate	NA
Dropout rate	NA
Per-pupil expenditure	$10,746
Avg teacher salary	$67,331
Student/teacher ratio '08-09	13.6 to 1
Highly-qualified teachers, '08-09	100.0%
Teachers licensed in assigned subject	100.0%
Students per computer	2.8

Massachusetts Competency Assessment System (MCAS), 2009 results

	English		Math	
	% Prof	CPI	% Prof	CPI
Gr 4	78%	90.1	61%	86.4
Gr 6	91%	96.7	88%	95.9
Gr 8	NA	NA	NA	NA
Gr 10	NA	NA	NA	NA

Other School Districts (see Appendix D for data)

Masconomet Regional, North Shore Vocational Tech

©2010 Information Publications, Inc. All rights reserved. Photocopying prohibited. For additional copies, contact the publisher at www.informationpublications.com or (877)544-INFO (4636)

Demographics & Socio-Economic Characteristics

Population

1990	3,517
2000	4,008
Male	1,994
Female	2,014
2008	4,264
2010 (projected)††	4,100
2020 (projected)††	4,112

Race & Hispanic Origin, 2000

Race	
White	3,876
Black/African American	27
American Indian/Alaska Native	9
Asian	55
Hawaiian Native/Pacific Islander	0
Other Race	10
Two or more races	31
Hispanic origin	23

Age & Nativity, 2000

Under 5 years	238
18 years and over	3,034
21 years and over	2,959
65 years and over	491
85 years and over	39
Median Age	39.8
Native-born	3,800
Foreign-born	208

Age, 2020 (projected)††

Under 5 years	200
5 to 19 years	629
20 to 39 years	950
40 to 64 years	1,502
65 years and over	831

Educational Attainment, 2000

Population 25 years and over	2,863
High School graduates or higher	93.0%
Bachelor's degree or higher	37.7%
Graduate degree	15.4%

Income & Poverty, 1999

Per capita income,	$32,274
Median household income	$67,703
Median family income	$77,604
Persons in poverty	111
H'holds receiving public assistance	10
H'holds receiving social security	393

Households, 2000

Total households	1,573
With persons under 18	540
With persons over 65	355
Family households	1,141
Single person households	350
Persons per household	2.6
Persons per family	3.0

Labor & Employment, 2000

Civilian labor force	2,106
Unemployment rate	0.9%
Civilian labor force, 2008†	2,259
Unemployment rate†	5.3%
Civilian labor force, 12/09†	2,346
Unemployment rate†	9.0%
Employed persons 16 years and over, by occupation:	
Managers & professionals	1,076
Service occupations	208
Sales & office occupations	459
Farming, fishing & forestry	6
Construction & maintenance	174
Production & transportation	163
Self-employed persons	96

Most demographic data is from the 2000 Decennial Census
† Massachusetts Department of Revenue
†† University of Massachusetts, MISER

General Information

Town of Boylston
221 Main St
Boylston, MA 01505
508-869-0143

Elevation	519 ft.
Land area (square miles)	16.0
Water area (square miles)	3.6
Population density, 2008 (est)	266.5
Year incorporated	1786
Website	www.boylston-ma.gov

Voters & Government Information

Government type	Open Town Meeting
Number of Selectmen	3
US Congressional District(s)	3

Registered Voters, October 2008

Total	3,132
Democrats	629
Republicans	461
Unaffiliated/other	2,028

Local Officials, 2010

Chair, Bd. of Sel.	James Stanton
Manager/Admin	Nancy Colbert
Town Clerk	Sandra Bourassa
Finance Director	Aylice Johns
Tax Collector	Aylice Ellen Johns
Tax Assessor	Carl Cravedi
Attorney	Steve Madaus (Int)
Public Works	NA
Building	Mark Bertonassi
Comm Dev/Planning	NA
Police Chief	Anthony Sahagian
Emerg/Fire Chief	Joe Flanagan

Housing & Construction

New Privately Owned Housing Units Authorized by Building Permit

	Single Family	Total Bldgs	Total Units
2006	21	24	27
2007	9	9	9
2008	8	8	8

Parcel Count by Property Class, 2010

Total	1,969
Single family	1,341
Multiple units	60
Apartments	15
Condos	163
Vacant land	279
Open space	0
Commercial	30
Industrial	24
Misc. residential	13
Other use	44

Public Library

Boylston Public Library
695 Main St.
Boylston, MA 01505
(508)869-2371

Director	Nicholas Langhart

Library Statistics, FY 2008

Population served, 2007	4,266
Registered users	2,314
Circulation	22,186
Reference transactons	0
Total program attendance	11,285
per capita:	
Holdings	7.62
Operating income	$36.26
Internet Access	
Internet computers available	2
Weekly users	10

Municipal Finance

Debt at year end 2008	$6,473,178
Moody's rating, July 2009	A2

Revenues, 2008

Total	$11,816,014
From all taxes	9,564,317
Federal aid	0
State aid	1,318,984
From other governments	18,215
Charges for services	208,704
Licenses, permits & fees	144,607
Fines & forfeits	0
Interfund transfers	310,315
Misc/other/special assessments	125,436

Expenditures, 2008

Total	$11,262,668
General government	814,619
Public safety	1,299,513
Other/fixed costs	902,997
Human services	75,726
Culture & recreation	185,602
Debt Service	885,310
Education	6,320,908
Public works	430,666
Intergovernmental	347,327

Taxation, 2010

Property type	Valuation	Rate
Total	$688,997,540	-
Residential	619,934,921	12.82
Open space	0	0.00
Commercial	37,255,519	12.82
Industrial	19,153,100	12.82
Personal	12,654,000	12.82

Average Single Family Tax Bill, 2010

Avg. assessed home value	$389,418
Avg. single fam. tax bill	$4,992
Hi-Lo ranking	77/301

Police & Crime, 2008

Number of police officers	10
Violent crimes	2
Property crimes	32

Local School District

(school data 2007-08, except as noted)
Boylston
215 Main Street
Boylston, MA 01505
508-869-2837

Superintendent	Brian McDermott
Grade plan	PK-6
Total enrollment '09-10	377
Grade 12 enrollment, '09-10	0
Graduation rate	NA
Dropout rate	NA
Per-pupil expenditure	$11,267
Avg teacher salary	$62,383
Student/teacher ratio '08-09	14.0 to 1
Highly-qualified teachers, '08-09	100.0%
Teachers licensed in assigned subject	100.0%
Students per computer	9.2

Massachusetts Competency Assessment System (MCAS), 2009 results

	English		Math	
	% Prof	CPI	% Prof	CPI
Gr 4	67%	87.5	42%	80.2
Gr 6	93%	97.1	84%	93
Gr 8	NA	NA	NA	NA
Gr 10	NA	NA	NA	NA

Other School Districts (see Appendix D for data)
Berlin-Boylston Regional

See Introduction for an explanation of all data sources.

©2010 Information Publications, Inc. All rights reserved. Photocopying prohibited. For additional copies, contact the publisher at www.informationpublications.com or (877)544-INFO (4636)

Demographics & Socio-Economic Characteristics*

Population

1990	33,836
2000	33,828
Male	15,935
Female	17,893
2008	35,294
2010 (projected)††	32,687
2020 (projected)††	30,653

Race & Hispanic Origin, 2000

Race	
White	31,784
Black/African American	398
American Indian/Alaska Native	36
Asian	1,062
Hawaiian Native/Pacific Islander	11
Other Race	216
Two or more races	321
Hispanic origin	394

Age & Nativity, 2000

Under 5 years	2,084
18 years and over	26,230
21 years and over	25,298
65 years and over	6,137
85 years and over	839
Median Age	40.0
Native-born	31,105
Foreign-born	2,723

Age, 2020 (projected)††

Under 5 years	1,414
5 to 19 years	5,061
20 to 39 years	6,878
40 to 64 years	10,493
65 years and over	6,807

Educational Attainment, 2000

Population 25 years and over	24,088
High School graduates or higher	91.0%
Bachelor's degree or higher	31.8%
Graduate degree	10.0%

Income & Poverty, 1999

Per capita income,	$28,683
Median household income	$61,790
Median family income	$73,417
Persons in poverty	1,247
H'holds receiving public assistance	149
H'holds receiving social security	4,212

Households, 2000

Total households	12,652
With persons under 18	4,058
With persons over 65	4,075
Family households	8,912
Single person households	3,087
Persons per household	2.6
Persons per family	3.2

Labor & Employment, 2000

Civilian labor force	17,628
Unemployment rate	2.5%
Civilian labor force, 2008†	18,445
Unemployment rate†	6.0%
Civilian labor force, 12/09†	18,567
Unemployment rate†	8.6%
Employed persons 16 years and over, by occupation:	
Managers & professionals	6,955
Service occupations	2,218
Sales & office occupations	5,147
Farming, fishing & forestry	15
Construction & maintenance	1,529
Production & transportation	1,323
Self-employed persons	993

Most demographic data is from the 2000 Decennial Census
* see Appendix E for American Community Survey data
† Massachusetts Department of Revenue
†† University of Massachusetts, MISER

General Information

Town of Braintree
1 JFK Memorial Dr
Braintree, MA 02184
781-794-8000

Elevation	70 ft.
Land area (square miles)	13.9
Water area (square miles)	0.6
Population density, 2008 (est)	2,539.1
Year incorporated	1640
Website	www.townofbraintreegov.org

Voters & Government Information

Government type	Mayor-Council
Number of Councilpersons	9
US Congressional District(s)	9

Registered Voters, October 2008

Total	24,824
Democrats	9,640
Republicans	2,912
Unaffiliated/other	12,138

Local Officials, 2010

Mayor	Joseph C. Sullivan
Manager/Admin	Peter J. Morin
Town Clerk	Joseph F. Powers
Finance Director	Edward Spellman Jr
Tax Collector	NA
Tax Assessor	Robert M. Cusack
Attorney	Carolyn M. Murray
Public Works	Thomas Whalen
Building	Mary E. McGrath
Comm Dev/Planning	Christine Stickney
Police Chief	Paul H. Frazier
Emerg/Fire Chief	Kevin J. Murphy

Housing & Construction

New Privately Owned Housing Units Authorized by Building Permit

	Single Family	Total Bldgs	Total Units
2006	16	35	214
2007	21	64	359
2008	10	11	24

Parcel Count by Property Class, 2010

Total	12,355
Single family	8,995
Multiple units	576
Apartments	76
Condos	1,459
Vacant land	509
Open space	0
Commercial	497
Industrial	142
Misc. residential	31
Other use	70

Public Library

Thayer Public Library
798 Washington Street
Braintree, MA 02184
(781)848-0405

Director	Elizabeth Wolfe

Library Statistics, FY 2008

Population served, 2007	34,422
Registered users	18,526
Circulation	354,008
Reference transactons	23,560
Total program attendance	0
per capita:	
Holdings	4.50
Operating income	$39.11
Internet Access	
Internet computers available	19
Weekly users	588

Municipal Finance

Debt at year end 2008	$27,951,263
Moody's rating, July 2009	Aa3

Revenues, 2008

Total	$90,616,661
From all taxes	66,481,025
Federal aid	7,017
State aid	15,870,393
From other governments	674,242
Charges for services	2,268,871
Licenses, permits & fees	2,575,511
Fines & forfeits	0
Interfund transfers	944,536
Misc/other/special assessments	897,533

Expenditures, 2008

Total	$83,416,871
General government	3,032,111
Public safety	14,656,812
Other/fixed costs	5,946,040
Human services	770,439
Culture & recreation	2,078,350
Debt Service	2,050,227
Education	45,765,764
Public works	5,383,559
Intergovernmental	3,593,911

Taxation, 2010

Property type	Valuation	Rate
Total	$5,359,518,266	-
Residential	4,151,406,685	9.67
Open space	0	0.00
Commercial	932,243,691	21.72
Industrial	192,792,100	21.72
Personal	83,075,790	21.65

Average Single Family Tax Bill, 2010

Avg. assessed home value	$365,241
Avg. single fam. tax bill	$3,532
Hi-Lo ranking	169/301

Police & Crime, 2008

Number of police officers	74
Violent crimes	45
Property crimes	912

Local School District

(school data 2007-08, except as noted)

Braintree
348 Pond Street
Braintree, MA 02184
781-380-0130

Superintendent	Peter Kurzberg
Grade plan	PK-12
Total enrollment '09-10	5,377
Grade 12 enrollment, '09-10	349
Graduation rate	95.0%
Dropout rate	1.3%
Per-pupil expenditure	$10,445
Avg teacher salary	$61,682
Student/teacher ratio '08-09	14.2 to 1
Highly-qualified teachers, '08-09	99.9%
Teachers licensed in assigned subject	99.2%
Students per computer	6

Massachusetts Competency Assessment System (MCAS), 2009 results

	English		Math	
	% Prof	CPI	% Prof	CPI
Gr 4	66%	87.9	53%	84.3
Gr 6	77%	91.9	78%	91.9
Gr 8	88%	96.2	65%	86.3
Gr 10	88%	95.8	87%	95.6

Other School Districts (see Appendix D for data)
Blue Hills Vocational Tech, Norfolk County Agricultural

©2010 Information Publications, Inc. All rights reserved. Photocopying prohibited. For additional copies, contact the publisher at www.informationpublications.com or (877)544-INFO (4636)

Demographics & Socio-Economic Characteristics

Population

1990 . . . 8,440
2000 . . . 10,094
Male . . . 4,685
Female . . . 5,409
2008 . . . 9,936
2010 (projected)†† . . . 12,130
2020 (projected)†† . . . 14,483

Race & Hispanic Origin, 2000

Race
White . . . 9,815
Black/African American . . . 77
American Indian/Alaska Native . . . 23
Asian . . . 77
Hawaiian Native/Pacific Islander . . . 3
Other Race . . . 35
Two or more races . . . 64
Hispanic origin . . . 107

Age & Nativity, 2000

Under 5 years . . . 353
18 years and over . . . 7,988
21 years and over . . . 7,757
65 years and over . . . 2,647
85 years and over . . . 451
Median Age . . . 46.9
Native-born . . . 9,740
Foreign-born . . . 354

Age, 2020 (projected)††

Under 5 years . . . 541
5 to 19 years . . . 1,628
20 to 39 years . . . 2,670
40 to 64 years . . . 4,650
65 years and over . . . 4,994

Educational Attainment, 2000

Population 25 years and over . . . 7,544
High School graduates or higher . . 94.2%
Bachelor's degree or higher . . . 40.6%
Graduate degree . . . 15.1%

Income & Poverty, 1999

Per capita income, . . . $24,638
Median household income . . . $49,276
Median family income . . . $57,174
Persons in poverty . . . 360
H'holds receiving public assistance . . . 47
H'holds receiving social security . . . 1,646

Households, 2000

Total households . . . 4,124
With persons under 18 . . . 1,121
With persons over 65 . . . 1,575
Family households . . . 2,854
Single person households . . . 1,023
Persons per household . . . 2.3
Persons per family . . . 2.8

Labor & Employment, 2000

Civilian labor force . . . 4,851
Unemployment rate . . . 2.5%
Civilian labor force, 2008† . . . 5,329
Unemployment rate† . . . 7.4%
Civilian labor force, 12/09† . . . 5,226
Unemployment rate† . . . 10.1%
Employed persons 16 years and over, by occupation:
Managers & professionals . . . 1,759
Service occupations . . . 834
Sales & office occupations . . . 1,312
Farming, fishing & forestry . . . 28
Construction & maintenance . . . 491
Production & transportation . . . 308
Self-employed persons . . . 754

Most demographic data is from the 2000 Decennial Census
† Massachusetts Department of Revenue
†† University of Massachusetts, MISER

General Information

Town of Brewster
2198 Main St
Brewster, MA 02631
508-896-3701

Elevation . . . 39 ft.
Land area (square miles) . . . 23.0
Water area (square miles) . . . 2.5
Population density, 2008 (est) . . . 432.0
Year incorporated . . . 1803
Website . . . www.town.brewster.ma.us

Voters & Government Information

Government type . . . Open Town Meeting
Number of Selectmen . . . 5
US Congressional District(s) . . . 10

Registered Voters, October 2008

Total . . . 8,442
Democrats . . . 2,081
Republicans . . . 1,500
Unaffiliated/other . . . 4,788

Local Officials, 2010

Chair, Bd. of Sel. . . . Dyanne Cooney
Town Administrator . . . Charles Sumner
Town Clerk . . . Mildred Unger
Treasurer . . . Lisa Souve
Tax Collector . . . Lisa Vitale
Tax Assessor . . . David Tately
Attorney . . . Edward Veara
Public Works . . . Robert Bersin
Building . . . Victor Staley
Comm Dev/Planning . . . Susan Leven
Police Chief . . . Richard Koch
Fire Chief . . . Roy Jones III

Housing & Construction

New Privately Owned Housing Units Authorized by Building Permit

	Single Family	Total Bldgs	Total Units
2006	38	38	38
2007	31	31	31
2008	19	19	19

Parcel Count by Property Class, 2010

Total . . . 8,348
Single family . . . 5,461
Multiple units . . . 48
Apartments . . . 7
Condos . . . 1,486
Vacant land . . . 903
Open space . . . 0
Commercial . . . 171
Industrial . . . 27
Misc. residential . . . 112
Other use . . . 133

Public Library

Brewster Ladies Library
1822 Main Street
Brewster, MA 02631
(508)896-3913

Director . . . Suzanne Teuteberg

Library Statistics, FY 2008

Population served, 2007 . . . 10,023
Registered users . . . 11,113
Circulation . . . 147,705
Reference transactons . . . 4,246
Total program attendance . . . 110,210

per capita:

Holdings . . . 6.08
Operating income . . . $63.38

Internet Access

Internet computers available . . . 14
Weekly users . . . 0

Municipal Finance

Debt at year end 2008 . . . $23,478,605
Moody's rating, July 2009 . . . A1

Revenues, 2008

Total . . . $37,454,515
From all taxes . . . 23,200,002
Federal aid . . . 0
State aid . . . 2,725,357
From other governments . . . 3,638
Charges for services . . . 3,833,464
Licenses, permits & fees . . . 638,019
Fines & forfeits . . . 11,164
Interfund transfers . . . 60,821
Misc/other/special assessments . . . 3,491,025

Expenditures, 2008

Total . . . $31,289,775
General government . . . 1,726,758
Public safety . . . 3,596,431
Other/fixed costs . . . 3,522,861
Human services . . . 368,898
Culture & recreation . . . 2,464,534
Debt Service . . . 2,789,034
Education . . . 14,413,887
Public works . . . 1,845,944
Intergovernmental . . . 561,428

Taxation, 2010

Property type	Valuation	Rate
Total	$3,752,841,370	-
Residential	3,539,749,545	6.20
Open space	0	0.00
Commercial	164,629,445	6.20
Industrial	10,086,100	6.20
Personal	38,376,280	6.20

Average Single Family Tax Bill, 2010

Avg. assessed home value . . . $500,612
Avg. single fam. tax bill . . . $3,104
Hi-Lo ranking . . . 226/301

Police & Crime, 2008

Number of police officers . . . 19
Violent crimes . . . 16
Property crimes . . . 129

Local School District

(school data 2007-08, except as noted)

Brewster
78 Eldredge Pkwy
Orleans, MA 02653
508-255-8800

Superintendent . . . Richard Hoffmann
Grade plan . . . PK-5
Total enrollment '09-10 . . . 503
Grade 12 enrollment, '09-10 . . . 0
Graduation rate . . . NA
Dropout rate . . . NA
Per-pupil expenditure . . . $13,707
Avg teacher salary . . . $59,934
Student/teacher ratio '08-09 . . . 11.5 to 1
Highly-qualified teachers, '08-09 . . . 100.0%
Teachers licensed in assigned subject . 100.0%
Students per computer . . . 3.9

Massachusetts Competency Assessment System (MCAS), 2009 results

	English		Math	
	% Prof	CPI	% Prof	CPI
Gr 4	88%	94.6	68%	91
Gr 6	NA	NA	NA	NA
Gr 8	NA	NA	NA	NA
Gr 10	NA	NA	NA	NA

Other School Districts (see Appendix D for data)
Nauset Regional, Cape Cod Vocational Tech

©2010 Information Publications, Inc. All rights reserved. Photocopying prohibited. For additional copies, contact the publisher at www.informationpublications.com or (877)544-INFO (4636)

See Introduction for an explanation of all data sources.

Demographics & Socio-Economic Characteristics

Population

1990	21,249
2000	25,185
Male	13,233
Female	11,952
2008	25,774
2010 (projected)††	28,704
2020 (projected)††	32,575

Race & Hispanic Origin, 2000

Race	
White	21,982
Black/African American	1,017
American Indian/Alaska Native	59
Asian	271
Hawaiian Native/Pacific Islander	5
Other Race	1,569
Two or more races	282
Hispanic origin	693

Age & Nativity, 2000

Under 5 years	1,559
18 years and over	19,420
21 years and over	17,493
65 years and over	2,168
85 years and over	223
Median Age	33.6
Native-born	24,040
Foreign-born	1,127

Age, 2020 (projected)††

Under 5 years	1,981
5 to 19 years	6,755
20 to 39 years	10,014
40 to 64 years	9,419
65 years and over	4,406

Educational Attainment, 2000

Population 25 years and over	15,736
High School graduates or higher	86.8%
Bachelor's degree or higher	29.6%
Graduate degree	9.0%

Income & Poverty, 1999

Per capita income,	$23,105
Median household income	$65,318
Median family income	$73,953
Persons in poverty	746
H'holds receiving public assistance	140
H'holds receiving social security	1,689

Households, 2000

Total households	7,526
With persons under 18	3,097
With persons over 65	1,570
Family households	5,587
Single person households	1,474
Persons per household	2.8
Persons per family	3.3

Labor & Employment, 2000

Civilian labor force	13,330
Unemployment rate	6.6%
Civilian labor force, 2008†	13,177
Unemployment rate†	5.9%
Civilian labor force, 12/09†	13,061
Unemployment rate†	8.4%
Employed persons 16 years and over, by occupation:	
Managers & professionals	4,567
Service occupations	1,847
Sales & office occupations	3,720
Farming, fishing & forestry	33
Construction & maintenance	940
Production & transportation	1,348
Self-employed persons	515

Most demographic data is from the 2000 Decennial Census
† Massachusetts Department of Revenue
†† University of Massachusetts, MISER

General Information

Town of Bridgewater
25 South St
Bridgewater, MA 02324
508-697-0919

Elevation	104 ft.
Land area (square miles)	27.5
Water area (square miles)	0.7
Population density, 2008 (est)	937.2
Year incorporated	1656
Website	bridgewaterma.org

Voters & Government Information

Government type	Open Town Meeting
Number of Selectmen	5
US Congressional District(s)	9

Registered Voters, October 2008

Total	15,366
Democrats	4,227
Republicans	2,047
Unaffiliated/other	8,998

Local Officials, 2010

Chair, Bd. of Sel.	Christopher Flynn
Manager/Admin	Troyl clarkson
Clerk	Ronald Adams
Finance	Douglas Dorr
Tax Collector	Douglas Dorr
Tax Assessor	John Welby
Attorney	Mark Gildea
Public Works	Andy Bagas
Building	David Moore
Planning	David Matton
Police Chief	Michael Bots
Fire Chief	George Rogers

Housing & Construction

New Privately Owned Housing Units Authorized by Building Permit

	Single Family	Total Bldgs	Total Units
2006	56	57	60
2007	46	46	46
2008	30	30	30

Parcel Count by Property Class, 2010

Total	7,904
Single family	5,204
Multiple units	406
Apartments	44
Condos	867
Vacant land	844
Open space	0
Commercial	269
Industrial	107
Misc. residential	26
Other use	137

Public Library

Bridgewater Public Library
15 South St.
Bridgewater, MA 02324
(508)697-3331

Director	(vacant)

Library Statistics, FY 2008

Population served, 2007	25,514
Registered users	15,609
Circulation	104,748
Reference transactons	4,410
Total program attendance	46,224
per capita:	
Holdings	5.46
Operating income	$21.02
Internet Access	
Internet computers available	9
Weekly users	29

Municipal Finance

Debt at year end 2008	$29,484,385
Moody's rating, July 2009	Baa2

Revenues, 2008

Total	$39,633,221
From all taxes	30,495,363
Federal aid	0
State aid	5,505,856
From other governments	195,087
Charges for services	1,148,040
Licenses, permits & fees	330,680
Fines & forfeits	62,134
Interfund transfers	609,661
Misc/other/special assessments	643,200

Expenditures, 2008

Total	$37,249,204
General government	1,701,230
Public safety	6,273,449
Other/fixed costs	4,187,973
Human services	314,048
Culture & recreation	579,306
Debt Service	2,191,781
Education	20,232,009
Public works	1,334,370
Intergovernmental	435,038

Taxation, 2010

Property type	Valuation	Rate
Total	$2,445,667,180	-
Residential	2,147,538,115	12.31
Open space	0	0.00
Commercial	166,446,655	12.31
Industrial	68,650,400	12.31
Personal	63,032,010	12.31

Average Single Family Tax Bill, 2010

Avg. assessed home value	$327,645
Avg. single fam. tax bill	$4,033
Hi-Lo ranking	135/301

Police & Crime, 2008

Number of police officers	34
Violent crimes	51
Property crimes	236

Local School District

(school data 2007-08, except as noted)

Bridgewater (non-op)
687 Pleasant Street
Raynham, MA 02767
508-824-2730

Superintendent	Jacqueline Forbes

Non-operating district.
Resident students are sent to the Other School Districts listed below.

Grade plan	NA
Total enrollment '09-10	NA
Grade 12 enrollment, '09-10	NA
Graduation rate	NA
Dropout rate	NA
Per-pupil expenditure	NA
Avg teacher salary	NA
Student/teacher ratio '08-09	NA
Highly-qualified teachers, '08-09	NA
Teachers licensed in assigned subject	NA
Students per computer	NA

Other School Districts (see Appendix D for data)
Bridgewater-Raynham Regional, Bristol-Plymouth Vocational Tech

©2010 Information Publications, Inc. All rights reserved. Photocopying prohibited. For additional copies, contact the publisher at www.informationpublications.com or (877)544-INFO (4636)

See Introduction for an explanation of all data sources.

Demographics & Socio-Economic Characteristics

Population

1990	3,001
2000	3,339
Male	1,654
Female	1,685
2008	3,708
2010 (projected)††	3,786
2020 (projected)††	4,402

Race & Hispanic Origin, 2000

Race	
White	3,262
Black/African American	17
American Indian/Alaska Native	12
Asian	2
Hawaiian Native/Pacific Islander	2
Other Race	24
Two or more races	20
Hispanic origin	43

Age & Nativity, 2000

Under 5 years	202
18 years and over	2,427
21 years and over	2,311
65 years and over	367
85 years and over	46
Median Age	38.9
Native-born	3,296
Foreign-born	43

Age, 2020 (projected)††

Under 5 years	272
5 to 19 years	814
20 to 39 years	977
40 to 64 years	1,512
65 years and over	827

Educational Attainment, 2000

Population 25 years and over	2,243
High School graduates or higher	85.6%
Bachelor's degree or higher	27.9%
Graduate degree	9.2%

Income & Poverty, 1999

Per capita income,	$23,711
Median household income	$50,181
Median family income	$59,943
Persons in poverty	145
H'holds receiving public assistance	21
H'holds receiving social security	353

Households, 2000

Total households	1,250
With persons under 18	471
With persons over 65	291
Family households	886
Single person households	289
Persons per household	2.7
Persons per family	3.2

Labor & Employment, 2000

Civilian labor force	1,782
Unemployment rate	3.0%
Civilian labor force, 2008†	1,992
Unemployment rate†	5.4%
Civilian labor force, 12/09†	2,053
Unemployment rate†	9.5%
Employed persons 16 years and over, by occupation:	
Managers & professionals	593
Service occupations	259
Sales & office occupations	371
Farming, fishing & forestry	18
Construction & maintenance	217
Production & transportation	271
Self-employed persons	177

Most demographic data is from the 2000 Decennial Census
† Massachusetts Department of Revenue
†† University of Massachusetts, MISER

General Information

Town of Brimfield
21 Main St
Brimfield, MA 01010
413-245-4112

Elevation	660 ft.
Land area (square miles)	34.7
Water area (square miles)	0.5
Population density, 2008 (est)	106.9
Year incorporated	1731
Website	brimfieldma.org

Voters & Government Information

Government type	Open Town Meeting
Number of Selectmen	3
US Congressional District(s)	2

Registered Voters, October 2008

Total	2,545
Democrats	589
Republicans	430
Unaffiliated/other	1,504

Local Officials, 2010

Chair, Bd. of Sel.	Diane M. Panaccione
Manager/Admin	NA
Clerk	Pamela Beall
Finance	Kirsten Weldon
Tax Collector	Susan S. Hilker
Tax Assessor	Duane Adams
Attorney	NA
Public Works	NA
Building	NA
Comm Dev/Planning	NA
Police Chief	Charles Kuss
Emerg/Fire Chief	Stephen Denning

Housing & Construction

New Privately Owned Housing Units Authorized by Building Permit

	Single Family	Total Bldgs	Total Units
2006	19	19	19
2007	17	17	17
2008	9	9	9

Parcel Count by Property Class, 2010

Total	2,426
Single family	1,268
Multiple units	9
Apartments	0
Condos	0
Vacant land	628
Open space	0
Commercial	89
Industrial	8
Misc. residential	23
Other use	401

Public Library

Brimfield Public Library
PO Box 377
Brimfield, MA 01010
(413)245-3518

Director	Rebecca Wells-Mullen

Library Statistics, FY 2008

Population served, 2007	3,695
Registered users	1,418
Circulation	18,015
Reference transactons	800
Total program attendance	6,770
per capita:	
Holdings	4.85
Operating income	$22.55
Internet Access	
Internet computers available	2
Weekly users	30

Municipal Finance

Debt at year end 2008	$1,800,000
Moody's rating, July 2009	NA

Revenues, 2008

Total	$8,856,147
From all taxes	5,654,317
Federal aid	22,210
State aid	2,022,125
From other governments	17,774
Charges for services	90,094
Licenses, permits & fees	200,121
Fines & forfeits	0
Interfund transfers	10,118
Misc/other/special assessments	419,694

Expenditures, 2008

Total	$8,110,352
General government	539,828
Public safety	349,930
Other/fixed costs	499,418
Human services	130,097
Culture & recreation	236,281
Debt Service	377,506
Education	5,326,493
Public works	626,350
Intergovernmental	24,449

Taxation, 2010

Property type	Valuation	Rate
Total	$443,946,757	-
Residential	399,235,005	11.93
Open space	0	0.00
Commercial	27,274,142	11.93
Industrial	4,809,400	11.93
Personal	12,628,210	11.93

Average Single Family Tax Bill, 2010

Avg. assessed home value	$262,139
Avg. single fam. tax bill	$3,127
Hi-Lo ranking	222/301

Police & Crime, 2008

Number of police officers	NA
Violent crimes	NA
Property crimes	NA

Local School District

(school data 2007-08, except as noted)

Brimfield
320A Brookfield Rd
Fiskdale, MA 01518
508-347-3077

Superintendent	Daniel Durgin
Grade plan	PK-6
Total enrollment '09-10	344
Grade 12 enrollment, '09-10	0
Graduation rate	NA
Dropout rate	NA
Per-pupil expenditure	$12,472
Avg teacher salary	$55,809
Student/teacher ratio '08-09	11.7 to 1
Highly-qualified teachers, '08-09	100.0%
Teachers licensed in assigned subject	100.0%
Students per computer	3.9

Massachusetts Competency Assessment System (MCAS), 2009 results

	English		Math	
	% Prof	CPI	% Prof	CPI
Gr 4	63%	83.3	63%	84.8
Gr 6	73%	89.1	69%	85.4
Gr 8	NA	NA	NA	NA
Gr 10	NA	NA	NA	NA

Other School Districts (see Appendix D for data)
Tantasqua Regional

©2010 Information Publications, Inc. All rights reserved. Photocopying prohibited. For additional copies, contact the publisher at www.informationpublications.com or (877)544-INFO (4636)

See Introduction for an explanation of all data sources.

Demographics & Socio-Economic Characteristics*

Population

1990	92,788
2000	94,304
Male	45,206
Female	49,098
2008	93,007
2010 (projected)††	94,123
2020 (projected)††	93,924

Race & Hispanic Origin, 2000

Race	
White	57,989
Black/African American	16,811
American Indian/Alaska Native	338
Asian	2,066
Hawaiian Native/Pacific Islander	34
Other Race	9,728
Two or more races	7,338
Hispanic origin	7,552

Age & Nativity, 2000

Under 5 years	6,846
18 years and over	68,050
21 years and over	64,299
65 years and over	11,064
85 years and over	1,573
Median Age	34.0
Native-born	76,960
Foreign-born	17,344

Age, 2020 (projected)††

Under 5 years	6,660
5 to 19 years	19,316
20 to 39 years	25,699
40 to 64 years	27,962
65 years and over	14,287

Educational Attainment, 2000

Population 25 years and over	59,428
High School graduates or higher	75.9%
Bachelor's degree or higher	14.0%
Graduate degree	4.4%

Income & Poverty, 1999

Per capita income,	$17,163
Median household income	$39,507
Median family income	$46,235
Persons in poverty	13,390
H'holds receiving public assistance	1,878
H'holds receiving social security	8,668

Households, 2000

Total households	33,675
With persons under 18	13,171
With persons over 65	7,820
Family households	22,748
Single person households	8,950
Persons per household	2.7
Persons per family	3.4

Labor & Employment, 2000

Civilian labor force	45,620
Unemployment rate	6.7%
Civilian labor force, 2008†	45,186
Unemployment rate†	8.2%
Civilian labor force, 12/09†	45,142
Unemployment rate†	11.8%
Employed persons 16 years and over, by occupation:	
Managers & professionals	10,178
Service occupations	7,654
Sales & office occupations	12,755
Farming, fishing & forestry	9
Construction & maintenance	3,291
Production & transportation	8,673
Self-employed persons	1,617

Most demographic data is from the 2000 Decennial Census
* see Appendix D and E for American Community Survey data
† Massachusetts Department of Revenue
†† University of Massachusetts, MISER

General Information

City of Brockton
45 School St
Brockton, MA 02301
508-580-7114

Elevation	100 ft.
Land area (square miles)	21.5
Water area (square miles)	0.1
Population density, 2008 (est)	4,325.9
Year incorporated	1874
Website	www.brockton.ma.us

Voters & Government Information

Government type	Mayor-Council
Number of Councilpersons	11
US Congressional District(s)	9

Registered Voters, October 2008

Total	52,062
Democrats	26,316
Republicans	4,612
Unaffiliated/other	20,726

Local Officials, 2010

Mayor	Linda Balzotti
Manager/Admin	NA
City Clerk	Anthony Zeoli
Finance	John Condon
Tax Collector	James Martelli
Tax Assessor	Bernard Siegel
Attorney	Phil Nesseralla
Public Works	Mike Thoreson
Building	James Casieri
Comm Dev/Planning	(vacant)
Police Chief	William Conlon
Emerg/Fire Chief	Richard Francis

Housing & Construction

New Privately Owned Housing Units Authorized by Building Permit

	Single Family	Total Bldgs	Total Units
2006	85	110	147
2007	51	53	57
2008	28	31	34

Parcel Count by Property Class, 2010

Total	25,905
Single family	16,381
Multiple units	3,518
Apartments	391
Condos	2,043
Vacant land	1,525
Open space	0
Commercial	1,522
Industrial	293
Misc. residential	75
Other use	157

Public Library

Brockton Public Library System
304 Main St.
Brockton, MA 02301
(508)580-7890

Director	Harry Williams

Library Statistics, FY 2008

Population served, 2007	93,092
Registered users	36,486
Circulation	282,725
Reference transactons	32,448
Total program attendance	0
per capita:	
Holdings	2.31
Operating income	$23.63
Internet Access	
Internet computers available	51
Weekly users	898

Municipal Finance

Debt at year end 2008	$238,041,163
Moody's rating, July 2009	A2

Revenues, 2008

Total	$278,458,551
From all taxes	101,247,906
Federal aid	1,043,054
State aid	154,535,433
From other governments	25,705
Charges for services	698,012
Licenses, permits & fees	1,627,104
Fines & forfeits	700,511
Interfund transfers	8,472,326
Misc/other/special assessments	5,054,250

Expenditures, 2008

Total	$229,878,462
General government	10,125,534
Public safety	36,515,833
Other/fixed costs	13,684,567
Human services	1,433,899
Culture & recreation	2,027,400
Debt Service	13,520,833
Education	139,136,498
Public works	7,874,054
Intergovernmental	4,963,785

Taxation, 2010

Property type	Valuation	Rate
Total	$5,868,201,889	-
Residential	4,553,399,820	13.77
Open space	0	0.00
Commercial	931,408,442	28.24
Industrial	199,506,867	28.24
Personal	183,886,760	28.24

Average Single Family Tax Bill, 2010

Avg. assessed home value	$197,037
Avg. single fam. tax bill	$2,713
Hi-Lo ranking	262/301

Police & Crime, 2008

Number of police officers	184
Violent crimes	NA
Property crimes	NA

Local School District

(school data 2007-08, except as noted)

Brockton
43 Crescent Street
Brockton, MA 02301
508-580-7511

Superintendent	Matthew Malone
Grade plan	PK-12
Total enrollment '09-10	15,502
Grade 12 enrollment, '09-10	885
Graduation rate	72.8%
Dropout rate	16.0%
Per-pupil expenditure	$12,814
Avg teacher salary	$64,315
Student/teacher ratio '08-09	13.8 to 1
Highly-qualified teachers, '08-09	90.7%
Teachers licensed in assigned subject	94.2%
Students per computer	3.5

Massachusetts Competency Assessment System (MCAS), 2009 results

	English		Math	
	% Prof	CPI	% Prof	CPI
Gr 4	34%	68.4	31%	69.2
Gr 6	50%	77.6	42%	70.1
Gr 8	70%	87.2	27%	59.1
Gr 10	74%	89.1	57%	78.8

Other School Districts (see Appendix D for data)
Southeastern Vocational Tech

©2010 Information Publications, Inc. All rights reserved. Photocopying prohibited. For additional copies, contact the publisher at www.informationpublications.com or (877)544-INFO (4636)

Demographics & Socio-Economic Characteristics

Population

1990 . . . 2,968
2000 . . . 3,051
Male . . . 1,499
Female . . . 1,552
2008 . . . 3,007
2010 (projected)†† . . . 3,367
2020 (projected)†† . . . 3,796

Race & Hispanic Origin, 2000

Race
White . . . 2,993
Black/African American . . . 6
American Indian/Alaska Native . . . 16
Asian . . . 9
Hawaiian Native/Pacific Islander . . . 0
Other Race . . . 1
Two or more races . . . 26
Hispanic origin . . . 18

Age & Nativity, 2000

Under 5 years . . . 178
18 years and over . . . 2,260
21 years and over . . . 2,166
65 years and over . . . 412
85 years and over . . . 30
Median Age . . . 38.9
Native-born . . . 3,008
Foreign-born . . . 43

Age, 2020 (projected)††

Under 5 years . . . 225
5 to 19 years . . . 635
20 to 39 years . . . 899
40 to 64 years . . . 1,274
65 years and over . . . 763

Educational Attainment, 2000

Population 25 years and over . . . 2,080
High School graduates or higher . . 83.2%
Bachelor's degree or higher . . . 16.8%
Graduate degree . . . 6.1%

Income & Poverty, 1999

Per capita income, . . . $20,144
Median household income . . . $45,655
Median family income . . . $54,519
Persons in poverty . . . 187
H'holds receiving public assistance . . . 17
H'holds receiving social security . . . 324

Households, 2000

Total households . . . 1,204
With persons under 18 . . . 417
With persons over 65 . . . 299
Family households . . . 857
Single person households . . . 287
Persons per household . . . 2.5
Persons per family . . . 3.0

Labor & Employment, 2000

Civilian labor force . . . 1,665
Unemployment rate . . . 4.1%
Civilian labor force, 2008† . . . 1,678
Unemployment rate† . . . 7.5%
Civilian labor force, 12/09† . . . 1,714
Unemployment rate† . . . 11.1%
Employed persons 16 years and over, by occupation:
Managers & professionals . . . 494
Service occupations . . . 219
Sales & office occupations . . . 369
Farming, fishing & forestry . . . 3
Construction & maintenance . . . 163
Production & transportation . . . 348
Self-employed persons . . . 95

Most demographic data is from the 2000 Decennial Census
† Massachusetts Department of Revenue
†† University of Massachusetts, MISER

General Information

Town of Brookfield
6 Central St
Brookfield, MA 01506
508-867-2930

Elevation . . . 700 ft.
Land area (square miles) . . . 15.5
Water area (square miles) . . . 1.1
Population density, 2008 (est) . . . 194.0
Year incorporated . . . 1673
Website . . . brookfieldma.us

Voters & Government Information

Government type . . . Open Town Meeting
Number of Selectmen . . . 3
US Congressional District(s) . . . 2

Registered Voters, October 2008

Total . . . 2,342
Democrats . . . 516
Republicans . . . 309
Unaffiliated/other . . . 1,484

Local Officials, 2010

Chair, Bd. of Sel. . . . James Allen
Admin Assistant . . . Donna Neylon
Clerk . . . Linda Lincoln
Treasurer . . . James Dunbar
Tax Collector . . . Lois Moores
Tax Assessor . . . Phillip Peirce
Attorney . . . Kopelman & Paige
Public Works . . . Herbert Chaffe
Building . . . Jeffrey Taylor
Planning . . . Daniel Leahy
Police Chief . . . Ross Ackerman
Emerg/Fire Chief . . . Peter Martell

Housing & Construction

New Privately Owned Housing Units Authorized by Building Permit

	Single Family	Total Bldgs	Total Units
2006	5	5	5
2007	4	4	4
2008	3	3	3

Parcel Count by Property Class, 2010

Total . . . 1,449
Single family . . . 907
Multiple units . . . 61
Apartments . . . 5
Condos . . . 40
Vacant land . . . 297
Open space . . . 0
Commercial . . . 28
Industrial . . . 6
Misc. residential . . . 35
Other use . . . 70

Public Library

Merrick Public Library
PO Box 528
Brookfield, MA 01506
(508)867-6339

Director . . . Brenda Metterville

Library Statistics, FY 2008

Population served, 2007 . . . 3,030
Registered users . . . 3,345
Circulation . . . 26,244
Reference transactons . . . 1,890
Total program attendance . . . 14,008
per capita:
Holdings . . . 8.74
Operating income . . . $35.61
Internet Access
Internet computers available . . . 5
Weekly users . . . 291

Municipal Finance

Debt at year end 2008 . . . $3,425,800
Moody's rating, July 2009 . . . NA

Revenues, 2008

Total . . . $7,528,112
From all taxes . . . 4,354,076
Federal aid . . . 0
State aid . . . 2,417,686
From other governments . . . 25,318
Charges for services . . . 158,091
Licenses, permits & fees . . . 27,418
Fines & forfeits . . . 0
Interfund transfers . . . 297,233
Misc/other/special assessments . . . 124,145

Expenditures, 2008

Total . . . $7,141,170
General government . . . 495,522
Public safety . . . 579,237
Other/fixed costs . . . 541,591
Human services . . . 32,151
Culture & recreation . . . 126,372
Debt Service . . . 758,217
Education . . . 3,983,412
Public works . . . 505,264
Intergovernmental . . . 119,404

Taxation, 2010

Property type	Valuation	Rate
Total	$293,133,163	-
Residential	274,153,545	14.28
Open space	0	0.00
Commercial	10,704,727	14.28
Industrial	2,155,477	14.28
Personal	6,119,414	14.28

Average Single Family Tax Bill, 2010

Avg. assessed home value . . . $236,930
Avg. single fam. tax bill . . . $3,383
Hi-Lo ranking . . . 184/301

Police & Crime, 2008

Number of police officers . . . 4
Violent crimes . . . NA
Property crimes . . . NA

Local School District

(school data 2007-08, except as noted)

Brookfield
320 Brookfield Rd
Fiskdale, MA 01518
508-347-3077

Superintendent . . . Daniel Durgin
Grade plan . . . PK-6
Total enrollment '09-10 . . . 304
Grade 12 enrollment, '09-10 . . . 0
Graduation rate . . . NA
Dropout rate . . . NA
Per-pupil expenditure . . . $12,478
Avg teacher salary . . . $60,958
Student/teacher ratio '08-09 . . . 10.9 to 1
Highly-qualified teachers, '08-09 . . . 100.0%
Teachers licensed in assigned subject . 100.0%
Students per computer . . . 3.4

Massachusetts Competency Assessment System (MCAS), 2009 results

	English		Math	
	% Prof	CPI	% Prof	CPI
Gr 4	60%	81.3	55%	80.6
Gr 6	67%	89.7	64%	85.9
Gr 8	NA	NA	NA	NA
Gr 10	NA	NA	NA	NA

Other School Districts (see Appendix D for data)
Tantasqua Regional

©2010 Information Publications, Inc. All rights reserved. Photocopying prohibited. For additional copies, contact the publisher at www.informationpublications.com or (877)544-INFO (4636)

See Introduction for an explanation of all data sources.

Demographics & Socio-Economic Characteristics*

Population

1990	54,718
2000	57,107
Male	25,832
Female	31,275
2008	54,896
2010 (projected)††	59,229
2020 (projected)††	62,423

Race & Hispanic Origin, 2000

Race	
White	46,304
Black/African American	1,566
American Indian/Alaska Native	71
Asian	7,325
Hawaiian Native/Pacific Islander	16
Other Race	578
Two or more races	1,247
Hispanic origin	2,018

Age & Nativity, 2000

Under 5 years	2,639
18 years and over	47,604
21 years and over	45,876
65 years and over	7,108
85 years and over	1,335
Median Age	34.5
Native-born	41,887
Foreign-born	15,174

Age, 2020 (projected)††

Under 5 years	2,802
5 to 19 years	8,913
20 to 39 years	23,102
40 to 64 years	18,769
65 years and over	8,837

Educational Attainment, 2000

Population 25 years and over	41,060
High School graduates or higher	96.3%
Bachelor's degree or higher	76.9%
Graduate degree	45.3%

Income & Poverty, 1999

Per capita income,	$44,327
Median household income	$66,711
Median family income	$92,993
Persons in poverty	5,177
H'holds receiving public assistance	273
H'holds receiving social security	4,811

Households, 2000

Total households	25,594
With persons under 18	5,805
With persons over 65	5,161
Family households	12,227
Single person households	9,395
Persons per household	2.2
Persons per family	2.9

Labor & Employment, 2000

Civilian labor force	33,902
Unemployment rate	3.5%
Civilian labor force, 2008†	32,825
Unemployment rate†	3.7%
Civilian labor force, 12/09†	32,007
Unemployment rate†	4.8%
Employed persons 16 years and over, by occupation:	
Managers & professionals	23,582
Service occupations	2,302
Sales & office occupations	5,787
Farming, fishing & forestry	0
Construction & maintenance	354
Production & transportation	688
Self-employed persons	2,722

Most demographic data is from the 2000 Decennial Census
* see Appendix E for American Community Survey data
† Massachusetts Department of Revenue
†† University of Massachusetts, MISER

General Information

Town of Brookline
333 Washington St.
Brookline, MA 02445
617-730-2000

Elevation	40 ft.
Land area (square miles)	6.8
Water area (square miles)	0.0
Population density, 2008 (est)	8,072.9
Year incorporated	1705
Website	www.brookline.ma.gov

Voters & Government Information

Government type	Rep. Town Meeting
Number of Selectmen	5
US Congressional District(s)	4

Registered Voters, October 2008

Total	41,158
Democrats	20,020
Republicans	3,277
Unaffiliated/other	17,653

Local Officials, 2010

Chair, Bd. of Sel.	Nancy Daly
Town Administrator	Richard Kelliher
Town Clerk	Patrick Ward
Finance Director	Stephen E. Cirillo
Treas/Collector	Stephen E. Cirillo
Tax Assessor	Gary McCabe
Attorney	Jennifer Dopazo
Public Works	Andrew M. Pappastergion
Building	Walter White (Actg)
Comm Dev/Planning	Jeffrey R. Levine
Police Chief	Daniel O'Leary
Emerg/Fire Chief	Peter Skerry

Housing & Construction

New Privately Owned Housing Units Authorized by Building Permit

	Single Family	Total Bldgs	Total Units
2006	17	18	22
2007	6	11	53
2008	6	11	50

Parcel Count by Property Class, 2010

Total	17,007
Single family	4,540
Multiple units	1,431
Apartments	335
Condos	9,545
Vacant land	290
Open space	0
Commercial	473
Industrial	9
Misc. residential	266
Other use	118

Public Library

Brookline Public Library
361 Washington St.
Brookline, MA 02445
(617)730-2370

Town Librarian	James C. Flaherty

Library Statistics, FY 2008

Population served, 2007	54,809
Registered users	44,530
Circulation	1,288,576
Reference transactons	42,729
Total program attendance	698,227
per capita:	
Holdings	7.32
Operating income	$66.66
Internet Access	
Internet computers available	77
Weekly users	2,600

Municipal Finance

Debt at year end 2008	$97,328,175
Moody's rating, July 2009	Aaa

Revenues, 2008

Total	$190,178,161
From all taxes	141,235,060
Federal aid	348
State aid	19,535,712
From other governments	8,970
Charges for services	4,760,023
Licenses, permits & fees	3,579,782
Fines & forfeits	4,555,358
Interfund transfers	7,753,612
Misc/other/special assessments	4,374,648

Expenditures, 2008

Total	$177,590,033
General government	9,033,466
Public safety	26,095,307
Other/fixed costs	33,501,489
Human services	1,803,336
Culture & recreation	5,554,348
Debt Service	13,824,443
Education	67,700,921
Public works	10,311,994
Intergovernmental	5,410,405

Taxation, 2010

Property type	Valuation	Rate
Total	$14,841,644,460	-
Residential	13,453,462,600	10.97
Open space	0	0.00
Commercial	1,236,446,900	17.80
Industrial	13,522,800	17.80
Personal	138,212,160	17.80

Average Single Family Tax Bill, 2010

Avg. assessed home value	NA
Avg. single fam. tax bill	NA
Hi-Lo ranking	NA

Police & Crime, 2008

Number of police officers	132
Violent crimes	NA
Property crimes	861

Local School District

(school data 2007-08, except as noted)
Brookline
333 Washington Street
Brookline, MA 02445
617-730-2403

Superintendent	William Lupini
Grade plan	PK-12
Total enrollment '09-10	6,472
Grade 12 enrollment, '09-10	437
Graduation rate	94.2%
Dropout rate	2.5%
Per-pupil expenditure	$15,431
Avg teacher salary	$78,308
Student/teacher ratio '08-09	12.9 to 1
Highly-qualified teachers, '08-09	96.2%
Teachers licensed in assigned subject	99.6%
Students per computer	4.8

Massachusetts Competency Assessment System (MCAS), 2009 results

	English		Math	
	% Prof	CPI	% Prof	CPI
Gr 4	72%	89.4	69%	89.2
Gr 6	88%	95.8	80%	91.1
Gr 8	93%	97.5	75%	88.5
Gr 10	91%	97.1	88%	96

Other School Districts (see Appendix D for data)
Norfolk County Agricultural

©2010 Information Publications, Inc. All rights reserved. Photocopying prohibited. For additional copies, contact the publisher at www.informationpublications.com or (877)544-INFO (4636)

See Introduction for an explanation of all data sources.

©2010 Information Publications, Inc. All rights reserved. Photocopying prohibited. For additional copies, contact the publisher at www.informationpublications.com or (877)544-INFO (4636)

Demographics & Socio-Economic Characteristics

Population

1990 1,928
2000 1,991
Male 994
Female 997
2008 1,989
2010 (projected)†† 1,889
2020 (projected)†† 1,792

Race & Hispanic Origin, 2000

Race
White 1,922
Black/African American 9
American Indian/Alaska Native 9
Asian 13
Hawaiian Native/Pacific Islander 0
Other Race 10
Two or more races 28
Hispanic origin 23

Age & Nativity, 2000

Under 5 years 97
18 years and over 1,494
21 years and over 1,406
65 years and over 264
85 years and over 37
Median Age 39.6
Native-born 1,964
Foreign-born 34

Age, 2020 (projected)††

Under 5 years 75
5 to 19 years 248
20 to 39 years 451
40 to 64 years 622
65 years and over 396

Educational Attainment, 2000

Population 25 years and over 1,375
High School graduates or higher 89.8%
Bachelor's degree or higher 25.2%
Graduate degree 8.7%

Income & Poverty, 1999

Per capita income, ... $20,033
Median household income $45,833
Median family income $51,420
Persons in poverty 137
H'holds receiving public assistance 31
H'holds receiving social security 213

Households, 2000

Total households 772
With persons under 18 276
With persons over 65 188
Family households 543
Single person households 168
Persons per household 2.6
Persons per family 3.0

Labor & Employment, 2000

Civilian labor force 1,162
Unemployment rate 4.2%
Civilian labor force, 2008† 1,105
Unemployment rate† 3.3%
Civilian labor force, 12/09† 1,085
Unemployment rate† 3.5%
Employed persons 16 years and over, by occupation:
Managers & professionals 360
Service occupations 149
Sales & office occupations 244
Farming, fishing & forestry 8
Construction & maintenance 102
Production & transportation 250
Self-employed persons 157

Most demographic data is from the 2000 Decennial Census
† Massachusetts Department of Revenue
†† University of Massachusetts, MISER

General Information

Town of Buckland
17 State St
Buckland, MA 01370
413-625-6330

Elevation .... 420 ft.
Land area (square miles) 19.6
Water area (square miles) 0.2
Population density, 2008 (est) 101.5
Year incorporated 1779
Website .... NA

Voters & Government Information

Government type .... Open Town Meeting
Number of Selectmen 3
US Congressional District(s) 1

Registered Voters, October 2008

Total 1,288
Democrats 329
Republicans 114
Unaffiliated/other 839

Local Officials, 2010

Chair, Bd. of Sel. .... Stefan Racz
Town Administrator .... Andrea Llamas
Clerk .... Janice Purington
Finance .... Linda Marcott
Tax Collector .... Linda Marcott
Tax Assessor .... Marion Scott
Attorney .... Kopelman & Paige
Public Works .... Steve Daby
Building .... James Hawkins
Comm Dev/Planning .... John Gould
Police Chief .... James Hicks
Emerg/Fire Chief .... R. Scott/R. Scott

Housing & Construction

New Privately Owned Housing Units Authorized by Building Permit

	Single Family	Total Bldgs	Total Units
2006	3	3	3
2007	2	2	2
2008	1	1	1

Parcel Count by Property Class, 2010

Total 1,132
Single family 594
Multiple units 60
Apartments 8
Condos 4
Vacant land 165
Open space 0
Commercial 40
Industrial 9
Misc. residential 33
Other use 219

Public Library

Buckland Public Library
PO Box 149
Buckland, MA 01338
(413)625-9412

Director .... Liz Jacobson-Carroll

Library Statistics, FY 2008

Population served, 2007 1,990
Registered users 376
Circulation 21,818
Reference transactons 50
Total program attendance 0

per capita:

Holdings 4.83
Operating income $17.31

Internet Access

Internet computers available 1
Weekly users 18

Municipal Finance

Debt at year end 2008 .... $668,853
Moody's rating, July 2009 .... NA

Revenues, 2008

Total $3,674,791
From all taxes 3,019,073
Federal aid 90,029
State aid 369,694
From other governments 355
Charges for services 56,082
Licenses, permits & fees 38,888
Fines & forfeits 10,673
Interfund transfers 26,835
Misc/other/special assessments 31,581

Expenditures, 2008

Total $3,373,917
General government 321,846
Public safety 208,818
Other/fixed costs 161,832
Human services 59,056
Culture & recreation 61,376
Debt Service 128,842
Education 1,864,715
Public works 531,765
Intergovernmental 35,667

Taxation, 2010

Property type	Valuation	Rate
Total	$216,886,891	-
Residential	175,528,250	13.78
Open space	0	0.00
Commercial	8,585,801	13.78
Industrial	26,839,380	13.78
Personal	5,933,460	13.78

Average Single Family Tax Bill, 2010

Avg. assessed home value $218,605
Avg. single fam. tax bill $3,012
Hi-Lo ranking 233/301

Police & Crime, 2008

Number of police officers 2
Violent crimes 7
Property crimes 17

Local School District

(school data 2007-08, except as noted)

Buckland (non-op)
24 Ashfield Rd
Shelburne Falls, MA 01370
413-625-0192

Superintendent .... Michael Buoniconti

Non-operating district.
Resident students are sent to the Other School Districts listed below.

Grade plan .... NA
Total enrollment '09-10 .... NA
Grade 12 enrollment, '09-10 .... NA
Graduation rate .... NA
Dropout rate .... NA
Per-pupil expenditure .... NA
Avg teacher salary .... NA
Student/teacher ratio '08-09 .... NA
Highly-qualified teachers, '08-09 .... NA
Teachers licensed in assigned subject .... NA
Students per computer .... NA

Other School Districts (see Appendix D for data)

Mohawk Trail Regional, Franklin County Vocational Tech

See Introduction for an explanation of all data sources.

Demographics & Socio-Economic Characteristics*

Population

1990	23,302
2000	22,876
Male	11,265
Female	11,611
2008	24,985
2010 (projected)††	21,632
2020 (projected)††	19,662

Race & Hispanic Origin, 2000

Race	
White	19,836
Black/African American	312
American Indian/Alaska Native	16
Asian	2,436
Hawaiian Native/Pacific Islander	5
Other Race	74
Two or more races	197
Hispanic origin	296

Age & Nativity, 2000

Under 5 years	1,575
18 years and over	17,483
21 years and over	16,887
65 years and over	3,174
85 years and over	233
Median Age	38.3
Native-born	19,478
Foreign-born	3,398

Age, 2020 (projected)††

Under 5 years	961
5 to 19 years	3,276
20 to 39 years	4,533
40 to 64 years	6,676
65 years and over	4,216

Educational Attainment, 2000

Population 25 years and over	16,020
High School graduates or higher	92.3%
Bachelor's degree or higher	42.6%
Graduate degree	15.8%

Income & Poverty, 1999

Per capita income,	$30,732
Median household income	$75,240
Median family income	$82,072
Persons in poverty	434
H'holds receiving public assistance	79
H'holds receiving social security	2,270

Households, 2000

Total households	8,289
With persons under 18	2,890
With persons over 65	2,286
Family households	6,371
Single person households	1,587
Persons per household	2.8
Persons per family	3.2

Labor & Employment, 2000

Civilian labor force	12,786
Unemployment rate	2.7%
Civilian labor force, 2008†	14,200
Unemployment rate†	4.8%
Civilian labor force, 12/09†	14,228
Unemployment rate†	7.2%
Employed persons 16 years and over, by occupation:	
Managers & professionals	6,064
Service occupations	1,294
Sales & office occupations	3,403
Farming, fishing & forestry	22
Construction & maintenance	722
Production & transportation	936
Self-employed persons	558

Most demographic data is from the 2000 Decennial Census
* see Appendix E for American Community Survey data
† Massachusetts Department of Revenue
†† University of Massachusetts, MISER

General Information

Town of Burlington
29 Center St
Burlington, MA 01803
781-270-1600

Elevation	220 ft.
Land area (square miles)	11.8
Water area (square miles)	0.1
Population density, 2008 (est)	2,117.4
Year incorporated	1799
Website	www.burlington.org

Voters & Government Information

Government type	Rep. Town Meeting
Number of Selectmen	5
US Congressional District(s)	6

Registered Voters, October 2008

Total	16,511
Democrats	5,181
Republicans	1,761
Unaffiliated/other	9,516

Local Officials, 2010

Chair, Bd. of Sel.	Ralph Patuto
Manager/Admin	Robert Mercier
Town Clerk	Jane Chew
Treasurer	Brian Curtin
Tax Collector	Brian Curtin
Tax Assessor	Russell Washburn
Attorney	Kopelman & Paige
Public Works Supt	John Sanchez
Building	John Clancy
Comm Dev/Planning	Anthony Fields
Police Chief	Michael Kent
Emerg/Fire Chief	Lee Callahan

Housing & Construction

New Privately Owned Housing Units Authorized by Building Permit

	Single Family	Total Bldgs	Total Units
2006	60	60	60
2007	21	24	34
2008	13	13	13

Parcel Count by Property Class, 2010

Total	7,873
Single family	6,538
Multiple units	13
Apartments	13
Condos	484
Vacant land	279
Open space	0
Commercial	364
Industrial	153
Misc. residential	15
Other use	14

Public Library

Burlington Public Library
22 Sears Street
Burlington, MA 01803
(781)270-1690

Director	Lori Hodgson

Library Statistics, FY 2008

Population served, 2007	25,034
Registered users	19,039
Circulation	397,939
Reference transactons	24,375
Total program attendance	145,733
per capita:	
Holdings	4.26
Operating income	$47.86
Internet Access	
Internet computers available	15
Weekly users	584

Municipal Finance

Debt at year end 2008	$28,127,588
Moody's rating, July 2009	Aa2

Revenues, 2008

Total	$91,346,516
From all taxes	74,370,438
Federal aid	180,193
State aid	8,809,422
From other governments	11,985
Charges for services	3,476,427
Licenses, permits & fees	1,360,273
Fines & forfeits	14,189
Interfund transfers	1,719,607
Misc/other/special assessments	701,991

Expenditures, 2008

Total	$84,768,451
General government	3,789,843
Public safety	12,641,075
Other/fixed costs	11,969,294
Human services	1,233,479
Culture & recreation	2,451,997
Debt Service	4,128,701
Education	39,276,231
Public works	8,746,211
Intergovernmental	531,620

Taxation, 2010

Property type	Valuation	Rate
Total	$4,519,333,825	-
Residential	2,938,363,015	10.90
Open space	0	0.00
Commercial	1,267,650,950	29.70
Industrial	176,476,500	29.70
Personal	136,843,360	29.70

Average Single Family Tax Bill, 2010

Avg. assessed home value	$383,265
Avg. single fam. tax bill	$4,178
Hi-Lo ranking	123/301

Police & Crime, 2008

Number of police officers	63
Violent crimes	23
Property crimes	688

Local School District

(school data 2007-08, except as noted)
Burlington
123 Cambridge Street
Burlington, MA 01803
781-270-1801

Superintendent	Eric Conti
Grade plan	PK-12
Total enrollment '09-10	3,711
Grade 12 enrollment, '09-10	248
Graduation rate	95.8%
Dropout rate	1.9%
Per-pupil expenditure	$13,023
Avg teacher salary	$65,581
Student/teacher ratio '08-09	12.3 to 1
Highly-qualified teachers, '08-09	93.0%
Teachers licensed in assigned subject	95.5%
Students per computer	5.3

Massachusetts Competency Assessment System (MCAS), 2009 results

	English		Math	
	% Prof	CPI	% Prof	CPI
Gr 4	62%	85.2	54%	82.5
Gr 6	75%	89.7	70%	85.8
Gr 8	87%	95.3	59%	81.6
Gr 10	86%	95	80%	91.4

Other School Districts (see Appendix D for data)
Shawsheen Valley Vocational Tech

©2010 Information Publications, Inc. All rights reserved. Photocopying prohibited. For additional copies, contact the publisher at www.informationpublications.com or (877)544-INFO (4636)

See Introduction for an explanation of all data sources.

Demographics & Socio-Economic Characteristics*

Population

1990 ... 95,802
2000 ... 101,355
  Male ... 49,674
  Female ... 51,681
2008 ... 105,596
2010 (projected)†† ... 104,709
2020 (projected)†† ... 107,118

Race & Hispanic Origin, 2000

Race
  White ... 69,022
  Black/African American ... 12,079
  American Indian/Alaska Native ... 290
  Asian ... 12,036
  Hawaiian Native/Pacific Islander ... 77
  Other Race ... 3,230
  Two or more races ... 4,621
Hispanic origin ... 7,455

Age & Nativity, 2000

Under 5 years ... 4,125
18 years and over ... 87,908
21 years and over ... 79,078
65 years and over ... 9,282
85 years and over ... 1,233
  Median Age ... 30.4
Native-born ... 75,137
Foreign-born ... 26,218

Age, 2020 (projected)††

Under 5 years ... 4,804
5 to 19 years ... 17,541
20 to 39 years ... 42,959
40 to 64 years ... 28,798
65 years and over ... 13,016

Educational Attainment, 2000

Population 25 years and over ... 66,315
  High School graduates or higher ... 89.5%
  Bachelor's degree or higher ... 65.1%
  Graduate degree ... 38.5%

Income & Poverty, 1999

Per capita income, ... $31,156
Median household income ... $47,979
Median family income ... $59,423
Persons in poverty ... 11,295
H'holds receiving public assistance ... 932
H'holds receiving social security ... 7,221

Households, 2000

Total households ... 42,615
  With persons under 18 ... 8,056
  With persons over 65 ... 7,218
  Family households ... 17,595
  Single person households ... 17,649
Persons per household ... 2.0
Persons per family ... 2.8

Labor & Employment, 2000

Civilian labor force ... 59,909
  Unemployment rate ... 6.1%
Civilian labor force, 2008† ... 58,460
  Unemployment rate† ... 3.9%
Civilian labor force, 12/09† ... 57,773
  Unemployment rate† ... 5.5%
Employed persons 16 years and over, by occupation:
  Managers & professionals ... 37,581
  Service occupations ... 5,011
  Sales & office occupations ... 10,025
  Farming, fishing & forestry ... 35
  Construction & maintenance ... 1,187
  Production & transportation ... 2,402
  Self-employed persons ... 3,415

Most demographic data is from the 2000 Decennial Census
* see Appendix D and E for American Community Survey data
† Massachusetts Department of Revenue
†† University of Massachusetts, MISER

©2010 Information Publications, Inc. All rights reserved. Photocopying prohibited. For additional copies, contact the publisher at www.informationpublications.com or (877)544-INFO (4636)

General Information

City of Cambridge
795 Massachusetts Ave
Cambridge, MA 02139
617-349-4000

Elevation ... 10 ft.
Land area (square miles) ... 6.4
Water area (square miles) ... 0.7
Population density, 2008 (est) ... 16,499.4
Year incorporated ... 1636
Website ... cambridgema.gov

Voters & Government Information

Government type ... Council-Manager
Number of Councilpersons ... 9
US Congressional District(s) ... 8

Registered Voters, October 2008

Total ... 64,727
Democrats ... 37,822
Republicans ... 3,280
Unaffiliated/other ... 22,935

Local Officials, 2010

Mayor ... E. Denise Simmons
Manager ... Robert Healy
City Clerk ... Margaret Drury
Finance Director ... Louis DePasquale
Tax Collector ... Louis DePasquale
Tax Assessor ... Robert Reardon
Attorney ... Donald Drisdell
Public Works ... Lisa Peterson
Building ... Ranjit Singanayagam
Comm Dev/Planning ... Beth Rubenstein
Police Commissioner ... Robert Haas
Emerg/Fire Chief ... Gerald Reardon

Housing & Construction

New Privately Owned Housing Units Authorized by Building Permit

	Single Family	Total Bldgs	Total Units
2006	12	23	54
2007	25	30	611
2008	12	13	36

Parcel Count by Property Class, 2010

Total ... 23,891
Single family ... 3,771
Multiple units ... 3,973
Apartments ... 862
Condos ... 13,253
Vacant land ... 179
Open space ... 0
Commercial ... 1,171
Industrial ... 201
Misc. residential ... 152
Other use ... 329

Public Library

Cambridge Public Library
359 Broadway
Cambridge, MA 02139
(617)349-4040

Director of Libraries ... Susan Flannery

Library Statistics, FY 2008

Population served, 2007 ... 101,388
Registered users ... 52,161
Circulation ... 1,139,732
Reference transactons ... 189,163
Total program attendance ... 0

per capita:

Holdings ... 3.74
Operating income ... $61.93

Internet Access

Internet computers available ... 51
Weekly users ... 1,842

Municipal Finance

Debt at year end 2008 ... $280,085,759
Moody's rating, July 2009 ... Aaa

Revenues, 2008

Total ... $416,424,645
From all taxes ... 260,197,708
Federal aid ... 826,681
State aid ... 46,748,709
From other governments ... 0
Charges for services ... 50,725,094
Licenses, permits & fees ... 14,072,085
Fines & forfeits ... 136,950
Interfund transfers ... 24,883,330
Misc/other/special assessments ... 9,417,044

Expenditures, 2008

Total ... $336,616,033
General government ... 22,130,706
Public safety ... 60,570,553
Other/fixed costs ... 35,990,480
Human services ... 9,714,542
Culture & recreation ... 13,557,181
Debt Service ... 37,492,223
Education ... 99,972,663
Public works ... 17,417,021
Intergovernmental ... 39,567,157

Taxation, 2010

Property type	Valuation	Rate
Total	$24,271,700,606	-
Residential	14,894,312,603	7.72
Open space	0	0.00
Commercial	5,560,488,691	18.75
Industrial	2,905,823,212	18.75
Personal	911,076,100	18.75

Average Single Family Tax Bill, 2010

Avg. assessed home value ... NA
Avg. single fam. tax bill ... NA
Hi-Lo ranking ... NA

Police & Crime, 2008

Number of police officers ... 275
Violent crimes ... 414
Property crimes ... 3,138

Local School District

(school data 2007-08, except as noted)

Cambridge
159 Thorndike Street
Cambridge, MA 02141
617-349-6494

Superintendent ... Jeffrey Young
Grade plan ... PK-12
Total enrollment '09-10 ... 5,950
Grade 12 enrollment, '09-10 ... 352
Graduation rate ... 88.3%
Dropout rate ... 4.4%
Per-pupil expenditure ... $25,187
Avg teacher salary ... $71,185
Student/teacher ratio '08-09 ... 11.1 to 1
Highly-qualified teachers, '08-09 ... 93.7%
Teachers licensed in assigned subject ... 95.6%
Students per computer ... 2.7

Massachusetts Competency Assessment System (MCAS), 2009 results

	English		Math	
	% Prof	CPI	% Prof	CPI
Gr 4	50%	76.7	48%	77.8
Gr 6	62%	83.8	51%	74.4
Gr 8	77%	91.4	42%	67.2
Gr 10	70%	87.4	63%	83.3

Other School Districts (see Appendix D for data)
None

See Introduction for an explanation of all data sources.

Demographics & Socio-Economic Characteristics

Population

1990	18,530
2000	20,775
Male	9,805
Female	10,970
2008	22,048
2010 (projected)††	21,732
2020 (projected)††	21,918

Race & Hispanic Origin, 2000

Race	
White	19,220
Black/African American	598
American Indian/Alaska Native	24
Asian	626
Hawaiian Native/Pacific Islander	5
Other Race	105
Two or more races	197
Hispanic origin	296

Age & Nativity, 2000

Under 5 years	1,319
18 years and over	15,869
21 years and over	15,363
65 years and over	3,505
85 years and over	628
Median Age	39.8
Native-born	18,984
Foreign-born	1,791

Age, 2020 (projected)††

Under 5 years	1,049
5 to 19 years	3,726
20 to 39 years	4,620
40 to 64 years	7,588
65 years and over	4,935

Educational Attainment, 2000

Population 25 years and over	14,702
High School graduates or higher	93.2%
Bachelor's degree or higher	44.7%
Graduate degree	17.4%

Income & Poverty, 1999

Per capita income,	$33,510
Median household income	$69,260
Median family income	$82,904
Persons in poverty	690
H'holds receiving public assistance	59
H'holds receiving social security	2,466

Households, 2000

Total households	7,952
With persons under 18	2,586
With persons over 65	2,352
Family households	5,548
Single person households	2,022
Persons per household	2.6
Persons per family	3.1

Labor & Employment, 2000

Civilian labor force	10,934
Unemployment rate	3.3%
Civilian labor force, 2008†	11,711
Unemployment rate†	5.6%
Civilian labor force, 12/09†	11,725
Unemployment rate†	7.8%
Employed persons 16 years and over, by occupation:	
Managers & professionals	5,140
Service occupations	1,226
Sales & office occupations	2,780
Farming, fishing & forestry	21
Construction & maintenance	809
Production & transportation	592
Self-employed persons	725

Most demographic data is from the 2000 Decennial Census
† Massachusetts Department of Revenue
†† University of Massachusetts, MISER

General Information

Town of Canton
801 Washington St
Canton, MA 02021
781-821-5000

Elevation	100 ft.
Land area (square miles)	18.9
Water area (square miles)	0.6
Population density, 2008 (est)	1,166.6
Year incorporated	1797
Website	town.canton.ma.us

Voters & Government Information

Government type	Open Town Meeting
Number of Selectmen	5
US Congressional District(s)	9

Registered Voters, October 2008

Total	15,490
Democrats	5,325
Republicans	1,921
Unaffiliated/other	8,192

Local Officials, 2010

Chair, Bd. of Sel.	Salvatori Gerald
Manager/Exec.	William Friel
Town Clerk	Tracy Kenney
Finance Director	Jim Murgia
Tax Collector	Jim Murgia
Tax Assessor	Daniel Flood
Attorney	Paul DeRensis
Public Works	Michael Trotta
Building	Edward Walsh
Comm Dev/Planning	NA
Police Chief	Kenneth Berkowitz
Emerg/Fire Chief	Doody Charles III

Housing & Construction

New Privately Owned Housing Units Authorized by Building Permit

	Single Family	Total Bldgs	Total Units
2006	18	32	131
2007	14	29	134
2008	9	22	123

Parcel Count by Property Class, 2010

Total	NA
Single family	NA
Multiple units	NA
Apartments	NA
Condos	NA
Vacant land	NA
Open space	NA
Commercial	NA
Industrial	NA
Misc. residential	NA
Other use	NA

Public Library

Canton Public Library
786 Washington St.
Canton, MA 02021
(781)821-5027

Director	Mark Lague

Library Statistics, FY 2008

Population served, 2007	21,916
Registered users	11,016
Circulation	261,512
Reference transactons	8,450
Total program attendance	138,800
per capita:	
Holdings	6.26
Operating income	$44.12
Internet Access	
Internet computers available	29
Weekly users	423

Municipal Finance

Debt at year end 2008	$58,805,160
Moody's rating, July 2009	Aa2

Revenues, 2008

Total	$62,796,301
From all taxes	50,003,319
Federal aid	0
State aid	7,091,326
From other governments	7,853
Charges for services	381,643
Licenses, permits & fees	669,240
Fines & forfeits	167,237
Interfund transfers	2,055,779
Misc/other/special assessments	1,209,952

Expenditures, 2008

Total	$53,097,412
General government	2,585,250
Public safety	7,823,446
Other/fixed costs	3,837,242
Human services	551,778
Culture & recreation	1,295,618
Debt Service	5,938,069
Education	26,263,621
Public works	3,865,754
Intergovernmental	894,634

Taxation, 2010

Property type	Valuation	Rate
Total	NA	-
Residential	NA	NA
Open space	NA	NA
Commercial	NA	NA
Industrial	NA	NA
Personal	NA	NA

Average Single Family Tax Bill, 2010

Avg. assessed home value	NA
Avg. single fam. tax bill	NA
Hi-Lo ranking	NA

Police & Crime, 2008

Number of police officers	41
Violent crimes	54
Property crimes	301

Local School District

(school data 2007-08, except as noted)

Canton
960 Washington Street
Canton, MA 02021
781-821-5060

Superintendent	John D'Auria
Grade plan	PK-12
Total enrollment '09-10	3,125
Grade 12 enrollment, '09-10	217
Graduation rate	85.9%
Dropout rate	5.2%
Per-pupil expenditure	$11,324
Avg teacher salary	$66,265
Student/teacher ratio '08-09	13.5 to 1
Highly-qualified teachers, '08-09	99.3%
Teachers licensed in assigned subject	98.1%
Students per computer	3.4

Massachusetts Competency Assessment System (MCAS), 2009 results

	English		Math	
	% Prof	CPI	% Prof	CPI
Gr 4	71%	90.1	72%	91.2
Gr 6	78%	90.6	68%	84.9
Gr 8	91%	96.4	61%	82.4
Gr 10	91%	96.6	87%	95

Other School Districts (see Appendix D for data)

Blue Hills Vocational Tech, Norfolk County Agricultural

©2010 Information Publications, Inc. All rights reserved. Photocopying prohibited. For additional copies, contact the publisher at www.informationpublications.com or (877)544-INFO (4636)

See Introduction for an explanation of all data sources.

©2010 Information Publications, Inc. All rights reserved. Photocopying prohibited. For additional copies, contact the publisher at www.informationpublications.com or (877)544-INFO (4636)

Demographics & Socio-Economic Characteristics

Population

1990 4,333
2000 4,717
Male 2,338
Female 2,379
2008 4,874
2010 (projected)†† 4,591
2020 (projected)†† 4,188

Race & Hispanic Origin, 2000

Race
White 4,409
Black/African American 8
American Indian/Alaska Native 3
Asian 228
Hawaiian Native/Pacific Islander 2
Other Race 6
Two or more races 61
Hispanic origin 56

Age & Nativity, 2000

Under 5 years 340
18 years and over 3,272
21 years and over 3,177
65 years and over 395
85 years and over 37
Median Age 41.9
Native-born 4,149
Foreign-born 568

Age, 2020 (projected)††

Under 5 years 239
5 to 19 years 803
20 to 39 years 762
40 to 64 years 1,452
65 years and over 932

Educational Attainment, 2000

Population 25 years and over 3,146
High School graduates or higher 99.4%
Bachelor's degree or higher 83.4%
Graduate degree 39.1%

Income & Poverty, 1999

Per capita income, ... $59,559
Median household income $129,811
Median family income $142,350
Persons in poverty 111
H'holds receiving public assistance 0
H'holds receiving social security 297

Households, 2000

Total households 1,618
With persons under 18 764
With persons over 65 289
Family households 1,372
Single person households 184
Persons per household 2.9
Persons per family 3.2

Labor & Employment, 2000

Civilian labor force 2,385
Unemployment rate 0.7%
Civilian labor force, 2008† 2,555
Unemployment rate† 4.7%
Civilian labor force, 12/09† 2,547
Unemployment rate† 6.6%
Employed persons 16 years and over, by occupation:
Managers & professionals 1,759
Service occupations 96
Sales & office occupations 386
Farming, fishing & forestry 0
Construction & maintenance 45
Production & transportation 83
Self-employed persons 290

Most demographic data is from the 2000 Decennial Census
† Massachusetts Department of Revenue
†† University of Massachusetts, MISER

General Information

Town of Carlisle
66 Westford St
Carlisle, MA 01741
978-369-6155

Elevation .... 200 ft.
Land area (square miles) 15.4
Water area (square miles) 0.2
Population density, 2008 (est) 316.5
Year incorporated 1805
Website .... www.carlislema.gov

Voters & Government Information

Government type .... Open Town Meeting
Number of Selectmen 5
US Congressional District(s) 5

Registered Voters, October 2008

Total 3,737
Democrats 941
Republicans 600
Unaffiliated/other 2,182

Local Officials, 2010

Chair, Bd. of Sel. .... Timothy Hult
Town Admin .... Timothy D. Goddard
Town Clerk .... Charlene Hinton
Town Accountant .... Pricscilla Dumka
Treas/Collector .... M. Lawrence Barton
Tax Assessor .... John Speidel
Attorney .... Deutsch Williams
Public Works .... Gary Davis
Building Commissioner .... John Minty
Planning Admin. .... George Mansfield
Police Chief .... John Sullivan
Fire Chief .... David Flannery

Housing & Construction

New Privately Owned Housing Units Authorized by Building Permit

	Single Family	Total Bldgs	Total Units
2006	12	12	12
2007	7	7	7
2008	2	2	2

Parcel Count by Property Class, 2010

Total 1,987
Single family 1,638
Multiple units 13
Apartments 0
Condos 21
Vacant land 226
Open space 0
Commercial 7
Industrial 2
Misc. residential 7
Other use 73

Public Library

Gleason Public Library
22 Bedford Road, Box 813
Carlisle, MA 01741
(978)369-4898

Director .... Angela Mollet

Library Statistics, FY 2008

Population served, 2007 4,882
Registered users 4,949
Circulation 133,145
Reference transactons 1,237
Total program attendance 0

per capita:

Holdings 13.24
Operating income $104.34

Internet Access

Internet computers available 7
Weekly users 225

Municipal Finance

Debt at year end 2008 .... $8,565,000
Moody's rating, July 2009 .... Aa2

Revenues, 2008

Total $21,890,746
From all taxes 19,568,038
Federal aid 0
State aid 1,474,045
From other governments 8,325
Charges for services 0
Licenses, permits & fees 74,958
Fines & forfeits 13,346
Interfund transfers 239,948
Misc/other/special assessments 256,043

Expenditures, 2008

Total $21,432,165
General government 1,028,738
Public safety 1,722,373
Other/fixed costs 1,415,390
Human services 184,477
Culture & recreation 592,316
Debt Service 1,150,132
Education 13,916,708
Public works 1,046,876
Intergovernmental 65,555

Taxation, 2010

Property type	Valuation	Rate
Total	$1,385,741,490	-
Residential	1,361,355,522	14.62
Open space	0	0.00
Commercial	9,859,060	14.62
Industrial	1,320,700	14.62
Personal	13,206,208	14.62

Average Single Family Tax Bill, 2010

Avg. assessed home value $771,254
Avg. single fam. tax bill $11,276
Hi-Lo ranking 5/301

Police & Crime, 2008

Number of police officers 10
Violent crimes 2
Property crimes 15

Local School District

(school data 2007-08, except as noted)

Carlisle
83 School Street
Carlisle, MA 01741
978-369-6550

Superintendent .... Marie Doyle
Grade plan PK-8
Total enrollment '09-10 698
Grade 12 enrollment, '09-10 0
Graduation rate .... NA
Dropout rate .... NA
Per-pupil expenditure $13,477
Avg teacher salary $72,000
Student/teacher ratio '08-09 .... 11.7 to 1
Highly-qualified teachers, '08-09 .... 92.1%
Teachers licensed in assigned subject .. 99.0%
Students per computer 2.1

Massachusetts Competency Assessment System (MCAS), 2009 results

	English		Math	
	% Prof	CPI	% Prof	CPI
Gr 4	84%	94.9	73%	91.1
Gr 6	83%	94.3	76%	89.1
Gr 8	97%	98.2	87%	94.3
Gr 10	NA	NA	NA	NA

Other School Districts (see Appendix D for data)

Concord-Carlisle Regional, Minuteman Vocational Tech

See Introduction for an explanation of all data sources.

Demographics & Socio-Economic Characteristics

Population

1990 . . . 10,590
2000 . . . 11,163
Male . . . 5,455
Female . . . 5,708
2008 . . . 11,574
2010 (projected)†† . . . 12,816
2020 (projected)†† . . . 14,714

Race & Hispanic Origin, 2000

Race
White . . . 10,692
Black/African American . . . 136
American Indian/Alaska Native . . . 11
Asian . . . 34
Hawaiian Native/Pacific Islander . . . 1
Other Race . . . 107
Two or more races . . . 182
Hispanic origin . . . 91

Age & Nativity, 2000

Under 5 years . . . 726
18 years and over . . . 8,118
21 years and over . . . 7,738
65 years and over . . . 1,650
85 years and over . . . 151
Median Age . . . 37.4
Native-born . . . 10,839
Foreign-born . . . 324

Age, 2020 (projected)††

Under 5 years . . . 831
5 to 19 years . . . 2,336
20 to 39 years . . . 3,418
40 to 64 years . . . 4,511
65 years and over . . . 3,618

Educational Attainment, 2000

Population 25 years and over . . . 7,343
High School graduates or higher . . 85.5%
Bachelor's degree or higher . . . 13.8%
Graduate degree . . . 3.5%

Income & Poverty, 1999

Per capita income, . . . $20,398
Median household income . . . $53,506
Median family income . . . $61,738
Persons in poverty . . . 557
H'holds receiving public assistance . . . 62
H'holds receiving social security . . . 1,280

Households, 2000

Total households . . . 3,984
With persons under 18 . . . 1,572
With persons over 65 . . . 1,180
Family households . . . 3,010
Single person households . . . 786
Persons per household . . . 2.8
Persons per family . . . 3.2

Labor & Employment, 2000

Civilian labor force . . . 5,843
Unemployment rate . . . 3.1%
Civilian labor force, 2008† . . . 6,385
Unemployment rate† . . . 8.2%
Civilian labor force, 12/09† . . . 6,298
Unemployment rate† . . . 9.8%
Employed persons 16 years and over, by occupation:
Managers & professionals . . . 1,479
Service occupations . . . 879
Sales & office occupations . . . 1,790
Farming, fishing & forestry . . . 7
Construction & maintenance . . . 720
Production & transportation . . . 784
Self-employed persons . . . 258

Most demographic data is from the 2000 Decennial Census
† Massachusetts Department of Revenue
†† University of Massachusetts, MISER

General Information

Town of Carver
108 Main St
Carver, MA 02330
508-866-3400

Elevation . . . 96 ft.
Land area (square miles) . . . 37.5
Water area (square miles) . . . 2.3
Population density, 2008 (est) . . . 308.6
Year incorporated . . . 1790
Website . . . www.carverma.org

Voters & Government Information

Government type . . . Open Town Meeting
Number of Selectmen . . . 5
US Congressional District(s) . . . 10

Registered Voters, October 2008

Total . . . 8,679
Democrats . . . 2,189
Republicans . . . 1,175
Unaffiliated/other . . . 5,252

Local Officials, 2010

Chair, Bd. of Sel. . . . John H. Angley
Manager/Town Admin . . . Richard LaFond
Clerk . . . Jean F. McGillicuddy
Finance Director . . . Scott A. McCaig
Tax Collector . . . John K. Franey
Tax Assessor . . . Karen Bell
Attorney . . . Kopelman & Paige
Public Works . . . William Halunen
Building . . . Michael Mendoza
Planning . . . Jack Hunter
Police Chief . . . Arthur Parker
Emerg/Fire Chief . . . Craig Weston

Housing & Construction

New Privately Owned Housing Units Authorized by Building Permit

	Single Family	Total Bldgs	Total Units
2006	64	64	64
2007	23	23	23
2008	20	20	20

Parcel Count by Property Class, 2010

Total . . . 4,362
Single family . . . 3,043
Multiple units . . . 59
Apartments . . . 2
Condos . . . 91
Vacant land . . . 417
Open space . . . 0
Commercial . . . 164
Industrial . . . 50
Misc. residential . . . 38
Other use . . . 498

Public Library

Carver Public Library
2 Meadowbrook Way
Carver, MA 02330
(508)866-3415

Director . . . Carole Julius

Library Statistics, FY 2008

Population served, 2007 . . . 11,547
Registered users . . . 8,790
Circulation . . . 103,703
Reference transactons . . . 0
Total program attendance . . . 0
per capita:
Holdings . . . 5.18
Operating income . . . $32.24
Internet Access
Internet computers available . . . 19
Weekly users . . . 200

Municipal Finance

Debt at year end 2008 . . . $4,536,201
Moody's rating, July 2009 . . . A3

Revenues, 2008

Total . . . $35,120,827
From all taxes . . . 16,807,227
Federal aid . . . 0
State aid . . . 12,425,904
From other governments . . . 0
Charges for services . . . 296,979
Licenses, permits & fees . . . 105,777
Fines & forfeits . . . 23,406
Interfund transfers . . . 811,926
Misc/other/special assessments . . . 2,324,804

Expenditures, 2008

Total . . . $32,874,043
General government . . . 1,896,131
Public safety . . . 2,709,384
Other/fixed costs . . . 1,737,469
Human services . . . 421,404
Culture & recreation . . . 374,296
Debt Service . . . 2,822,068
Education . . . 21,308,073
Public works . . . 1,227,691
Intergovernmental . . . 295,208

Taxation, 2010

Property type	Valuation	Rate
Total	$1,166,102,780	-
Residential	999,553,425	13.49
Open space	0	0.00
Commercial	92,555,985	19.34
Industrial	30,893,000	19.34
Personal	43,100,370	19.34

Average Single Family Tax Bill, 2010

Avg. assessed home value . . . $282,701
Avg. single fam. tax bill . . . $3,814
Hi-Lo ranking . . . 149/301

Police & Crime, 2008

Number of police officers . . . 17
Violent crimes . . . 20
Property crimes . . . 100

Local School District

(school data 2007-08, except as noted)

Carver
3 Carver Square Blvd.
Carver, MA 02330
508-866-6160

Superintendent . . . Elizabeth Sorrell
Grade plan . . . PK-12
Total enrollment '09-10 . . . 1,847
Grade 12 enrollment, '09-10 . . . 119
Graduation rate . . . 81.6%
Dropout rate . . . 11.6%
Per-pupil expenditure . . . $11,350
Avg teacher salary . . . $59,809
Student/teacher ratio '08-09 . . . 13.8 to 1
Highly-qualified teachers, '08-09 . . . 97.9%
Teachers licensed in assigned subject . . 98.6%
Students per computer . . . 4.5

Massachusetts Competency Assessment System (MCAS), 2009 results

	English		Math	
	% Prof	CPI	% Prof	CPI
Gr 4	45%	76.7	42%	75.5
Gr 6	45%	75.5	49%	74.2
Gr 8	78%	91.7	55%	77.1
Gr 10	91%	97.5	82%	93

Other School Districts (see Appendix D for data)
Old Colony Vocational Tech

©2010 Information Publications, Inc. All rights reserved. Photocopying prohibited. For additional copies, contact the publisher at www.informationpublications.com or (877)544-INFO (4636)

See Introduction for an explanation of all data sources.

Demographics & Socio-Economic Characteristics

Population

1990 . . . 1,249
2000 . . . 1,358
Male . . . 668
Female . . . 690
2008 . . . 1,378
2010 (projected)†† . . . 1,424
2020 (projected)†† . . . 1,506

Race & Hispanic Origin, 2000

Race
White . . . 1,291
Black/African American . . . 4
American Indian/Alaska Native . . . 9
Asian . . . 10
Hawaiian Native/Pacific Islander . . . 1
Other Race . . . 6
Two or more races . . . 37
Hispanic origin . . . 27

Age & Nativity, 2000

Under 5 years . . . 68
18 years and over . . . 1,017
21 years and over . . . 964
65 years and over . . . 157
85 years and over . . . 17
Median Age . . . 38.4
Native-born . . . 1,355
Foreign-born . . . 36

Age, 2020 (projected)††

Under 5 years . . . 81
5 to 19 years . . . 253
20 to 39 years . . . 339
40 to 64 years . . . 551
65 years and over . . . 282

Educational Attainment, 2000

Population 25 years and over . . . 943
High School graduates or higher . . . 89.9%
Bachelor's degree or higher . . . 29.0%
Graduate degree . . . 10.6%

Income & Poverty, 1999

Per capita income, . . . $19,577
Median household income . . . $46,548
Median family income . . . $50,962
Persons in poverty . . . 144
H'holds receiving public assistance . . . 10
H'holds receiving social security . . . 150

Households, 2000

Total households . . . 524
With persons under 18 . . . 175
With persons over 65 . . . 125
Family households . . . 353
Single person households . . . 132
Persons per household . . . 2.5
Persons per family . . . 3.0

Labor & Employment, 2000

Civilian labor force . . . 788
Unemployment rate . . . 5.3%
Civilian labor force, 2008† . . . 766
Unemployment rate† . . . 5.7%
Civilian labor force, 12/09† . . . 770
Unemployment rate† . . . 8.2%
Employed persons 16 years and over, by occupation:
Managers & professionals . . . 251
Service occupations . . . 118
Sales & office occupations . . . 178
Farming, fishing & forestry . . . 10
Construction & maintenance . . . 77
Production & transportation . . . 112
Self-employed persons . . . 102

Most demographic data is from the 2000 Decennial Census
† Massachusetts Department of Revenue
†† University of Massachusetts, MISER

General Information

Town of Charlemont
157 Main St
PO Box 677
Charlemont, MA 01339
413-339-4335

Elevation . . . NA
Land area (square miles) . . . 26.1
Water area (square miles) . . . 0.3
Population density, 2008 (est) . . . 52.8
Year incorporated . . . 1765
Website . . . charlemont-ma.us

Voters & Government Information

Government type . . . Open Town Meeting
Number of Selectmen . . . 3
US Congressional District(s) . . . 1

Registered Voters, October 2008

Total . . . 882
Democrats . . . 197
Republicans . . . 81
Unaffiliated/other . . . 595

Local Officials, 2010

Chair, Bd. of Sel. . . . Winston Healy
Manager/Admin . . . Kathy A. Reynolds
Town Clerk . . . Linda Wagner
Finance . . . Norma Lynch
Tax Collector . . . Lynn Hathaway
Tax Assessor . . . Carol Rice (Chr)
Attorney . . . Kopelman & Paige
Public Works . . . Gordon Hathaway
Building . . . Jim Hawkins (Chr)
Comm Dev/Planning . . . Gisela Walker
Police Chief . . . Jared Bellows
Fire Chief . . . Ken Hall

Housing & Construction

New Privately Owned Housing Units Authorized by Building Permit

	Single Family	Total Bldgs	Total Units
2006	5	5	5
2007	3	3	3
2008	6	6	6

Parcel Count by Property Class, 2010

Total . . . 908
Single family . . . 403
Multiple units . . . 18
Apartments . . . 6
Condos . . . 8
Vacant land . . . 306
Open space . . . 0
Commercial . . . 22
Industrial . . . 5
Misc. residential . . . 44
Other use . . . 96

Public Library

Tyler Memorial Library
PO Box 518
Charlemont, MA 01339
(413)339-4355 x1

Librarian . . . Bambi Miller

Library Statistics, FY 2008

Population served, 2007 . . . 1,367
Registered users . . . 925
Circulation . . . 11,619
Reference transactons . . . 620
Total program attendance . . . 8,401

per capita:

Holdings . . . 12.37
Operating income . . . $14.72

Internet Access

Internet computers available . . . 1
Weekly users . . . 12

Municipal Finance

Debt at year end 2008 . . . $480,995
Moody's rating, July 2009 . . . NA

Revenues, 2008

Total . . . $2,771,586
From all taxes . . . 2,093,948
Federal aid . . . 0
State aid . . . 362,978
From other governments . . . 0
Charges for services . . . 73,022
Licenses, permits & fees . . . 41,444
Fines & forfeits . . . 7,020
Interfund transfers . . . 74,000
Misc/other/special assessments . . . 59,587

Expenditures, 2008

Total . . . $2,697,205
General government . . . 228,115
Public safety . . . 189,368
Other/fixed costs . . . 157,284
Human services . . . 28,363
Culture & recreation . . . 22,023
Debt Service . . . 35,694
Education . . . 1,599,019
Public works . . . 421,514
Intergovernmental . . . 15,825

Taxation, 2010

Property type	Valuation	Rate
Total	$132,465,578	-
Residential	116,234,537	15.79
Open space	0	0.00
Commercial	9,693,084	15.79
Industrial	796,900	15.79
Personal	5,741,057	15.79

Average Single Family Tax Bill, 2010

Avg. assessed home value . . . $199,973
Avg. single fam. tax bill . . . $3,158
Hi-Lo ranking . . . 217/301

Police & Crime, 2008

Number of police officers . . . NA
Violent crimes . . . 0
Property crimes . . . 10

Local School District

(school data 2007-08, except as noted)

Charlemont (non-op)
24 Ashfield Rd
Shelburne Falls, MA 01370
413-625-0192

Superintendent . . . Michael Buoniconti

Non-operating district.
Resident students are sent to the Other School Districts listed below.

Grade plan . . . NA
Total enrollment '09-10 . . . NA
Grade 12 enrollment, '09-10 . . . NA
Graduation rate . . . NA
Dropout rate . . . NA
Per-pupil expenditure . . . NA
Avg teacher salary . . . NA
Student/teacher ratio '08-09 . . . NA
Highly-qualified teachers, '08-09 . . . NA
Teachers licensed in assigned subject . . . NA
Students per computer . . . NA

Other School Districts (see Appendix D for data)
Hawlemont and Mohawk Trail Regionals

©2010 Information Publications, Inc. All rights reserved. Photocopying prohibited. For additional copies, contact the publisher at www.informationpublications.com or (877)544-INFO (4636)

See Introduction for an explanation of all data sources.

Demographics & Socio-Economic Characteristics

Population

1990	9,576
2000	11,263
Male	5,515
Female	5,748
2008	12,585
2010 (projected)††	13,518
2020 (projected)††	16,582

Race & Hispanic Origin, 2000

Race	
White	11,047
Black/African American	26
American Indian/Alaska Native	23
Asian	52
Hawaiian Native/Pacific Islander	7
Other Race	38
Two or more races	70
Hispanic origin	110

Age & Nativity, 2000

Under 5 years	810
18 years and over	7,887
21 years and over	7,558
65 years and over	867
85 years and over	177
Median Age	35.4
Native-born	11,086
Foreign-born	177

Age, 2020 (projected)††

Under 5 years	1,153
5 to 19 years	3,116
20 to 39 years	4,620
40 to 64 years	5,322
65 years and over	2,371

Educational Attainment, 2000

Population 25 years and over	7,275
High School graduates or higher	86.8%
Bachelor's degree or higher	26.4%
Graduate degree	10.5%

Income & Poverty, 1999

Per capita income,	$23,626
Median household income	$63,033
Median family income	$70,208
Persons in poverty	620
H'holds receiving public assistance	68
H'holds receiving social security	673

Households, 2000

Total households	3,788
With persons under 18	1,830
With persons over 65	527
Family households	3,045
Single person households	551
Persons per household	2.9
Persons per family	3.2

Labor & Employment, 2000

Civilian labor force	6,019
Unemployment rate	2.2%
Civilian labor force, 2008†	6,791
Unemployment rate†	6.6%
Civilian labor force, 12/09†	6,968
Unemployment rate†	9.3%
Employed persons 16 years and over, by occupation:	
Managers & professionals	2,400
Service occupations	583
Sales & office occupations	1,439
Farming, fishing & forestry	27
Construction & maintenance	670
Production & transportation	765
Self-employed persons	302

Most demographic data is from the 2000 Decennial Census
† Massachusetts Department of Revenue
†† University of Massachusetts, MISER

General Information

Town of Charlton
37 Main St
Charlton, MA 01507
508-248-2200

Elevation	895 ft.
Land area (square miles)	42.5
Water area (square miles)	1.2
Population density, 2008 (est)	296.1
Year incorporated	1754
Website	www.townofcharlton.net

Voters & Government Information

Government type	Open Town Meeting
Number of Selectmen	5
US Congressional District(s)	2

Registered Voters, October 2008

Total	9,839
Democrats	2,097
Republicans	1,599
Unaffiliated/other	6,063

Local Officials, 2010

Chair, Bd. of Sel.	Frederick C. Swensen
Manager/Admin	Robin L. Craver
Town Clerk	Susan Nichols
Town Accountant	Joan Walker
Town Collector	Lucia Blanchette
Principal Assessor	Debbie Ceccarini
Attorney	James Cosgrove
Highway Supt	Gerry Foskett
Building Commissioner	Curtis Meskus
Comm Dev/Planning	Alan Gordon
Police Chief	James Pervier
Emerg/Fire Chief	Charles Cloutier Jr

Housing & Construction

New Privately Owned Housing Units Authorized by Building Permit

	Single Family	Total Bldgs	Total Units
2006	62	62	62
2007	30	31	32
2008	25	25	25

Parcel Count by Property Class, 2010

Total	6,098
Single family	3,937
Multiple units	66
Apartments	38
Condos	153
Vacant land	1,426
Open space	0
Commercial	139
Industrial	52
Misc. residential	21
Other use	266

Public Library

Charlton Public Library
40 Main St.
Charlton, MA 01507
(508)248-0452

Director	Cheryl Hansen

Library Statistics, FY 2008

Population served, 2007	12,576
Registered users	4,820
Circulation	91,194
Reference transactons	490
Total program attendance	0
per capita:	
Holdings	2.75
Operating income	$27.19

Internet Access

Internet computers available	21
Weekly users	155

Municipal Finance

Debt at year end 2008	$20,438,184
Moody's rating, July 2009	A3

Revenues, 2008

Total	$20,573,175
From all taxes	16,915,328
Federal aid	0
State aid	1,797,046
From other governments	91,833
Charges for services	87,022
Licenses, permits & fees	154,377
Fines & forfeits	0
Interfund transfers	1,139,083
Misc/other/special assessments	194,243

Expenditures, 2008

Total	$17,773,233
General government	1,589,041
Public safety	3,438,957
Other/fixed costs	1,762,758
Human services	187,779
Culture & recreation	411,347
Debt Service	602,712
Education	8,546,172
Public works	1,194,123
Intergovernmental	40,344

Taxation, 2010

Property type	Valuation	Rate
Total	$1,482,114,942	-
Residential	1,296,650,232	10.24
Open space	0	0.00
Commercial	81,880,605	10.24
Industrial	53,305,855	10.24
Personal	50,278,250	10.24

Average Single Family Tax Bill, 2010

Avg. assessed home value	$276,208
Avg. single fam. tax bill	$2,828
Hi-Lo ranking	251/301

Police & Crime, 2008

Number of police officers	19
Violent crimes	15
Property crimes	131

Local School District

(school data 2007-08, except as noted)

Charlton (non-op)
68 Dudley Oxford Road
Dudley, MA 01571
508-943-6888

Superintendent	Sean Gilrein

Non-operating district.
Resident students are sent to the Other School Districts listed below.

Grade plan	NA
Total enrollment '09-10	NA
Grade 12 enrollment, '09-10	NA
Graduation rate	NA
Dropout rate	NA
Per-pupil expenditure	NA
Avg teacher salary	NA
Student/teacher ratio '08-09	NA
Highly-qualified teachers, '08-09	NA
Teachers licensed in assigned subject	NA
Students per computer	NA

Other School Districts (see Appendix D for data)
Dudley-Charlton Regional, Southern Worcester County Vocational Tech

©2010 Information Publications, Inc. All rights reserved. Photocopying prohibited. For additional copies, contact the publisher at www.informationpublications.com or (877)544-INFO (4636)

See Introduction for an explanation of all data sources.

Demographics & Socio-Economic Characteristics

Population

1990	6,579
2000	6,625
Male	3,126
Female	3,499
2008	6,701
2010 (projected)††	6,732
2020 (projected)††	6,877

Race & Hispanic Origin, 2000

Race	
White	6,362
Black/African American	117
American Indian/Alaska Native	12
Asian	18
Hawaiian Native/Pacific Islander	1
Other Race	61
Two or more races	54
Hispanic origin	66

Age & Nativity, 2000

Under 5 years	193
18 years and over	5,746
21 years and over	5,615
65 years and over	2,273
85 years and over	360
Median Age	53.9
Native-born	6,337
Foreign-born	343

Age, 2020 (projected)††

Under 5 years	145
5 to 19 years	531
20 to 39 years	832
40 to 64 years	2,191
65 years and over	3,178

Educational Attainment, 2000

Population 25 years and over	5,458
High School graduates or higher	93.3%
Bachelor's degree or higher	42.7%
Graduate degree	16.1%

Income & Poverty, 1999

Per capita income,	$28,594
Median household income	$45,519
Median family income	$56,750
Persons in poverty	311
H'holds receiving public assistance	14
H'holds receiving social security	1,639

Households, 2000

Total households	3,160
With persons under 18	514
With persons over 65	1,491
Family households	1,887
Single person households	1,097
Persons per household	2.0
Persons per family	2.5

Labor & Employment, 2000

Civilian labor force	2,943
Unemployment rate	4.5%
Civilian labor force, 2008†	3,227
Unemployment rate†	7.4%
Civilian labor force, 12/09†	3,170
Unemployment rate†	9.9%
Employed persons 16 years and over, by occupation:	
Managers & professionals	1,028
Service occupations	534
Sales & office occupations	705
Farming, fishing & forestry	179
Construction & maintenance	225
Production & transportation	140
Self-employed persons	730

Most demographic data is from the 2000 Decennial Census
† Massachusetts Department of Revenue
†† University of Massachusetts, MISER

General Information

Town of Chatham
549 Main St
Chatham, MA 02633
508-945-5100

Elevation	46 ft.
Land area (square miles)	16.2
Water area (square miles)	8.2
Population density, 2008 (est)	413.6
Year incorporated	1712
Website	www.chatham-ma.gov

Voters & Government Information

Government type	Open Town Meeting
Number of Selectmen	5
US Congressional District(s)	10

Registered Voters, October 2008

Total	5,783
Democrats	1,161
Republicans	1,389
Unaffiliated/other	3,201

Local Officials, 2010

Chair, Bd. of Sel.	Leonard M. Sussman
Manager	William G. Hinchey
Clerk	Julie S. Smith
Finance Director	Jennifer Petit
Tax Collector	Louise Redfield
Tax Assessor	Andrew Machado
Attorney	Bruce Gilmore
Public Works	Jeff Colby
Building	Kevin McDonald
Planning	Kevin McDonald
Police Chief	Mark R. Pawlina
Emerg/Fire Chief	Michael Ambriscoe

Housing & Construction

New Privately Owned Housing Units Authorized by Building Permit

	Single Family	Total Bldgs	Total Units
2006	58	60	65
2007	54	54	54
2008	32	32	32

Parcel Count by Property Class, 2010

Total	7,728
Single family	5,694
Multiple units	49
Apartments	9
Condos	457
Vacant land	658
Open space	0
Commercial	284
Industrial	116
Misc. residential	321
Other use	140

Public Library

Eldredge Public Library
564 Main St.
Chatham, MA 02633
(508)945-5170

Director .... Irene B. Gillies

Library Statistics, FY 2008

Population served, 2007	6,390
Registered users	10,700
Circulation	132,857
Reference transactons	4,206
Total program attendance	176,544
per capita:	
Holdings	8.94
Operating income	$102.04
Internet Access	
Internet computers available	17
Weekly users	644

Municipal Finance

Debt at year end 2008	$34,714,722
Moody's rating, July 2009	Aa3

Revenues, 2008

Total	$34,015,991
From all taxes	25,516,924
Federal aid	0
State aid	2,132,824
From other governments	3,128
Charges for services	2,537,644
Licenses, permits & fees	877,674
Fines & forfeits	55,706
Interfund transfers	1,711,321
Misc/other/special assessments	590,385

Expenditures, 2008

Total	$30,661,018
General government	2,401,417
Public safety	5,608,342
Other/fixed costs	3,076,795
Human services	898,310
Culture & recreation	1,480,020
Debt Service	5,094,474
Education	8,830,391
Public works	2,331,037
Intergovernmental	808,704

Taxation, 2010

Property type	Valuation	Rate
Total	$6,364,049,234	-
Residential	5,949,895,817	3.82
Open space	0	0.00
Commercial	347,898,048	3.82
Industrial	35,056,635	3.82
Personal	31,198,734	3.82

Average Single Family Tax Bill, 2010

Avg. assessed home value	$861,926
Avg. single fam. tax bill	$3,293
Hi-Lo ranking	205/301

Police & Crime, 2008

Number of police officers	18
Violent crimes	5
Property crimes	191

Local School District

(school data 2007-08, except as noted)

Chatham
425 Crowell Rd
Chatham, MA 02633
508-945-5130

Superintendent	Mary Ann Lanzo
Grade plan	PK-12
Total enrollment '09-10	674
Grade 12 enrollment, '09-10	39
Graduation rate	91.4%
Dropout rate	5.2%
Per-pupil expenditure	$14,660
Avg teacher salary	$62,891
Student/teacher ratio '08-09	10.3 to 1
Highly-qualified teachers, '08-09	98.5%
Teachers licensed in assigned subject	100.0%
Students per computer	1.4

Massachusetts Competency Assessment System (MCAS), 2009 results

	English		Math	
	% Prof	CPI	% Prof	CPI
Gr 4	52%	82.1	58%	84.6
Gr 6	84%	93	68%	85
Gr 8	91%	96	46%	75.9
Gr 10	92%	98.6	92%	97.6

Other School Districts (see Appendix D for data)
Cape Cod Vocational Tech

See Introduction for an explanation of all data sources.

©2010 Information Publications, Inc. All rights reserved. Photocopying prohibited. For additional copies, contact the publisher at www.informationpublications.com or (877)544-INFO (4636)

Demographics & Socio-Economic Characteristics

Population

1990	32,383
2000	33,858
Male	16,364
Female	17,494
2008	34,409
2010 (projected)††	33,151
2020 (projected)††	31,602

Race & Hispanic Origin, 2000

Race	
White	31,520
Black/African American	266
American Indian/Alaska Native	23
Asian	1,563
Hawaiian Native/Pacific Islander	3
Other Race	177
Two or more races	306
Hispanic origin	418

Age & Nativity, 2000

Under 5 years	2,264
18 years and over	25,403
21 years and over	24,576
65 years and over	4,418
85 years and over	534
Median Age	38.9
Native-born	31,440
Foreign-born	2,418

Age, 2020 (projected)††

Under 5 years	1,653
5 to 19 years	5,599
20 to 39 years	6,921
40 to 64 years	10,881
65 years and over	6,548

Educational Attainment, 2000

Population 25 years and over	23,654
High School graduates or higher	93.0%
Bachelor's degree or higher	44.0%
Graduate degree	18.1%

Income & Poverty, 1999

Per capita income,	$30,465
Median household income	$70,207
Median family income	$82,676
Persons in poverty	938
H'holds receiving public assistance	168
H'holds receiving social security	3,328

Households, 2000

Total households	12,812
With persons under 18	4,647
With persons over 65	3,171
Family households	9,307
Single person households	2,963
Persons per household	2.6
Persons per family	3.1

Labor & Employment, 2000

Civilian labor force	18,668
Unemployment rate	2.7%
Civilian labor force, 2008†	18,860
Unemployment rate†	5.1%
Civilian labor force, 12/09†	18,904
Unemployment rate†	7.9%
Employed persons 16 years and over, by occupation:	
Managers & professionals	9,583
Service occupations	1,872
Sales & office occupations	4,330
Farming, fishing & forestry	19
Construction & maintenance	1,109
Production & transportation	1,254
Self-employed persons	985

Most demographic data is from the 2000 Decennial Census
† Massachusetts Department of Revenue
†† University of Massachusetts, MISER

General Information

Town of Chelmsford
50 Billerica Rd
Chelmsford, MA 01824
978-250-5201

Elevation	150 ft.
Land area (square miles)	22.6
Water area (square miles)	0.5
Population density, 2008 (est)	1,522.5
Year incorporated	1655
Website	www.townofchelmsford.us

Voters & Government Information

Government type	Rep. Town Meeting
Number of Selectmen	5
US Congressional District(s)	5

Registered Voters, October 2008

Total	23,644
Democrats	5,897
Republicans	3,178
Unaffiliated/other	14,427

Local Officials, 2010

Chair, Bd. of Sel.	Clare L. Jeannotte
Town Manager	Paul E. Cohen
Clerk	Elizabeth L. Delaney
Finance Director	John B. Sousa Jr
Tax Collector	John B. Sousa Jr
Tax Assessor	Frank T. Reen Jr
Attorney	Kopelman & Paige
Public Works	James Pearson
Building	Scott Hammond
Planning	Evan Belansky
Police Chief	James Murphy
Fire Chief	John E. Parow

Housing & Construction

New Privately Owned Housing Units Authorized by Building Permit

	Single Family	Total Bldgs	Total Units
2006	65	72	182
2007	23	23	23
2008	12	12	12

Parcel Count by Property Class, 2010

Total	13,285
Single family	8,998
Multiple units	232
Apartments	40
Condos	2,591
Vacant land	668
Open space	0
Commercial	424
Industrial	238
Misc. residential	13
Other use	81

Public Library

Chelmsford Public Library
25 Boston Rd.
Chelmsford, MA 01824
(978)256-5521

Director	Becky Herrmann

Library Statistics, FY 2008

Population served, 2007	34,128
Registered users	49,245
Circulation	633,795
Reference transactons	19,851
Total program attendance	217,354
per capita:	
Holdings	4.35
Operating income	$47.18
Internet Access	
Internet computers available	47
Weekly users	1,025

Municipal Finance

Debt at year end 2008	$99,444,732
Moody's rating, July 2009	Aa3

Revenues, 2008

Total	$98,743,163
From all taxes	75,259,807
Federal aid	266,858
State aid	16,651,184
From other governments	179,718
Charges for services	282,244
Licenses, permits & fees	1,047,245
Fines & forfeits	68,221
Interfund transfers	2,292,600
Misc/other/special assessments	1,347,643

Expenditures, 2008

Total	$94,944,821
General government	3,695,637
Public safety	9,725,140
Other/fixed costs	15,467,276
Human services	695,612
Culture & recreation	1,719,719
Debt Service	11,677,861
Education	44,613,228
Public works	5,878,240
Intergovernmental	1,472,108

Taxation, 2010

Property type	Valuation	Rate
Total	$4,855,429,025	-
Residential	3,913,682,175	15.15
Open space	0	0.00
Commercial	399,855,510	15.15
Industrial	391,746,900	15.15
Personal	150,144,440	15.15

Average Single Family Tax Bill, 2010

Avg. assessed home value	$347,659
Avg. single fam. tax bill	$5,267
Hi-Lo ranking	64/301

Police & Crime, 2008

Number of police officers	50
Violent crimes	45
Property crimes	651

Local School District

(school data 2007-08, except as noted)

Chelmsford
230 North Road
Chelmsford, MA 01824
978-251-5100

Superintendent	Donald Yeoman
Grade plan	PK-12
Total enrollment '09-10	5,418
Grade 12 enrollment, '09-10	389
Graduation rate	93.3%
Dropout rate	1.8%
Per-pupil expenditure	$10,070
Avg teacher salary	$61,998
Student/teacher ratio '08-09	15.8 to 1
Highly-qualified teachers, '08-09	99.4%
Teachers licensed in assigned subject	99.4%
Students per computer	5

Massachusetts Competency Assessment System (MCAS), 2009 results

	English		Math	
	% Prof	CPI	% Prof	CPI
Gr 4	75%	89.9	63%	85.6
Gr 6	86%	93.7	71%	86.8
Gr 8	91%	96.1	59%	79.9
Gr 10	91%	96.8	86%	94.3

Other School Districts (see Appendix D for data)
Nashoba Valley Vocational Tech

©2010 Information Publications, Inc. All rights reserved. Photocopying prohibited. For additional copies, contact the publisher at www.informationpublications.com or (877)544-INFO (4636)

See Introduction for an explanation of all data sources.

Demographics & Socio-Economic Characteristics*

Population

1990	28,710
2000	35,080
Male	17,617
Female	17,463
2008	41,577
2010 (projected)††	43,858
2020 (projected)††	56,077

Race & Hispanic Origin, 2000

Race	
White	20,328
Black/African American	2,544
American Indian/Alaska Native	170
Asian	1,647
Hawaiian Native/Pacific Islander	32
Other Race	8,049
Two or more races	2,310
Hispanic origin	16,984

Age & Nativity, 2000

Under 5 years	2,829
18 years and over	25,512
21 years and over	24,062
65 years and over	3,933
85 years and over	641
Median Age	31.3
Native-born	22,406
Foreign-born	12,674

Age, 2020 (projected)††

Under 5 years	4,859
5 to 19 years	13,297
20 to 39 years	17,991
40 to 64 years	15,118
65 years and over	4,812

Educational Attainment, 2000

Population 25 years and over	21,597
High School graduates or higher	59.5%
Bachelor's degree or higher	10.0%
Graduate degree	3.0%

Income & Poverty, 1999

Per capita income,	$14,628
Median household income	$30,161
Median family income	$32,130
Persons in poverty	7,921
H'holds receiving public assistance	864
H'holds receiving social security	2,882

Households, 2000

Total households	11,888
With persons under 18	4,843
With persons over 65	2,589
Family households	7,614
Single person households	3,421
Persons per household	2.9
Persons per family	3.5

Labor & Employment, 2000

Civilian labor force	14,212
Unemployment rate	7.3%
Civilian labor force, 2008†	13,467
Unemployment rate†	8.7%
Civilian labor force, 12/09†	15,620
Unemployment rate†	10.9%
Employed persons 16 years and over, by occupation:	
Managers & professionals	2,361
Service occupations	3,324
Sales & office occupations	3,330
Farming, fishing & forestry	108
Construction & maintenance	966
Production & transportation	3,084
Self-employed persons	429

Most demographic data is from the 2000 Decennial Census
* see Appendix E for American Community Survey data
† Massachusetts Department of Revenue
†† University of Massachusetts, MISER

General Information

City of Chelsea
500 Broadway
Chelsea, MA 02150
617-466-4000

Elevation	10 ft.
Land area (square miles)	2.2
Water area (square miles)	0.3
Population density, 2008 (est)	18,898.6
Year incorporated	1739
Website	chelseama.gov

Voters & Government Information

Government type	Manager-Council
Number of Councilpersons	11
US Congressional District(s)	8

Registered Voters, October 2008

Total	12,752
Democrats	7,053
Republicans	807
Unaffiliated/other	4,797

Local Officials, 2010

Council President	Leo Robinson
City Manager	Jay Ash
Clerk	Deborah A. Clayman
CFO	Ned Keefe
Tax Collector	Robert Boulrice
Tax Assessor	Philip Waterman
Attorney	Cheryl Watson
Public Works	Joseph Foti
Building	Joe Cooney
Planning	John DePriest
Police Chief	Brian Kyes
Emerg/Fire Chief	Herbert C. Fothergill Jr

Housing & Construction

New Privately Owned Housing Units Authorized by Building Permit

	Single Family	Total Bldgs	Total Units
2006	0	3	6
2007	0	3	6
2008	0	8	239

Parcel Count by Property Class, 2010

Total	6,413
Single family	848
Multiple units	2,137
Apartments	325
Condos	1,844
Vacant land	480
Open space	0
Commercial	479
Industrial	159
Misc. residential	14
Other use	127

Public Library

Chelsea Public Library
569 Broadway
Chelsea, MA 02150
(617)466-4350

Director	Robert Collins

Library Statistics, FY 2008

Population served, 2007	38,203
Registered users	14,391
Circulation	56,316
Reference transactons	360
Total program attendance	0
per capita:	
Holdings	2.02
Operating income	$9.48
Internet Access	
Internet computers available	14
Weekly users	270

Municipal Finance

Debt at year end 2008	$62,670,438
Moody's rating, July 2009	Baa1

Revenues, 2008

Total	$115,936,053
From all taxes	35,440,767
Federal aid	1,141,169
State aid	67,727,068
From other governments	0
Charges for services	1,556,479
Licenses, permits & fees	1,884,347
Fines & forfeits	1,792,603
Interfund transfers	2,248,364
Misc/other/special assessments	2,072,628

Expenditures, 2008

Total	$110,031,785
General government	4,106,057
Public safety	16,485,109
Other/fixed costs	11,653,684
Human services	731,894
Culture & recreation	380,877
Debt Service	10,009,919
Education	58,958,144
Public works	3,681,084
Intergovernmental	4,021,544

Taxation, 2010

Property type	Valuation	Rate
Total	$2,131,640,190	-
Residential	1,448,984,874	12.09
Open space	0	0.00
Commercial	452,809,866	29.00
Industrial	144,812,300	29.00
Personal	85,033,150	29.00

Average Single Family Tax Bill, 2010

Avg. assessed home value	NA
Avg. single fam. tax bill	NA
Hi-Lo ranking	NA

Police & Crime, 2008

Number of police officers	91
Violent crimes	669
Property crimes	1,635

Local School District

(school data 2007-08, except as noted)

Chelsea
500 Broadway Street, c/o City Hall Room 216
Chelsea, MA 02150
617-466-4477

Superintendent	Thomas Kingston
Grade plan	PK-12
Total enrollment '09-10	5,638
Grade 12 enrollment, '09-10	253
Graduation rate	49.9%
Dropout rate	25.5%
Per-pupil expenditure	$12,409
Avg teacher salary	$58,243
Student/teacher ratio '08-09	13.7 to 1
Highly-qualified teachers, '08-09	99.6%
Teachers licensed in assigned subject	99.5%
Students per computer	4.4

Massachusetts Competency Assessment System (MCAS), 2009 results

	English		Math	
	% Prof	CPI	% Prof	CPI
Gr 4	40%	72.6	42%	76.8
Gr 6	44%	74.1	35%	65.4
Gr 8	57%	78.8	27%	57.2
Gr 10	48%	77.6	43%	67.2

Other School Districts (see Appendix D for data)
Northeast Metro Vocational Tech

See Introduction for an explanation of all data sources.

©2010 Information Publications, Inc. All rights reserved. Photocopying prohibited. For additional copies, contact the publisher at www.informationpublications.com or (877)544-INFO (4636)

Demographics & Socio-Economic Characteristics

Population

1990	3,479
2000	3,401
Male	1,706
Female	1,695
2008	3,314
2010 (projected)††	3,329
2020 (projected)††	3,249

Race & Hispanic Origin, 2000

Race	
White	3,340
Black/African American	13
American Indian/Alaska Native	3
Asian	21
Hawaiian Native/Pacific Islander	0
Other Race	2
Two or more races	22
Hispanic origin	15

Age & Nativity, 2000

Under 5 years	171
18 years and over	2,606
21 years and over	2,487
65 years and over	486
85 years and over	52
Median Age	40.6
Native-born	3,311
Foreign-born	90

Age, 2020 (projected)††

Under 5 years	153
5 to 19 years	492
20 to 39 years	723
40 to 64 years	1,130
65 years and over	751

Educational Attainment, 2000

Population 25 years and over	2,402
High School graduates or higher	87.9%
Bachelor's degree or higher	20.5%
Graduate degree	7.2%

Income & Poverty, 1999

Per capita income,	$19,156
Median household income	$41,981
Median family income	$53,885
Persons in poverty	223
H'holds receiving public assistance	18
H'holds receiving social security	417

Households, 2000

Total households	1,367
With persons under 18	445
With persons over 65	346
Family households	986
Single person households	316
Persons per household	2.5
Persons per family	2.9

Labor & Employment, 2000

Civilian labor force	1,828
Unemployment rate	5.7%
Civilian labor force, 2008†	1,947
Unemployment rate†	8.4%
Civilian labor force, 12/09†	1,925
Unemployment rate†	10.2%
Employed persons 16 years and over, by occupation:	
Managers & professionals	612
Service occupations	279
Sales & office occupations	427
Farming, fishing & forestry	6
Construction & maintenance	189
Production & transportation	211
Self-employed persons	103

Most demographic data is from the 2000 Decennial Census
† Massachusetts Department of Revenue
†† University of Massachusetts, MISER

General Information

Town of Cheshire
80 Church St
Cheshire, MA 01225
413-743-1690

Elevation	963 ft.
Land area (square miles)	26.9
Water area (square miles)	0.6
Population density, 2008 (est)	123.2
Year incorporated	1793
Email	admin@cheshire-ma.gov

Voters & Government Information

Government type	Open Town Meeting
Number of Selectmen	3
US Congressional District(s)	1

Registered Voters, October 2008

Total	2,358
Democrats	676
Republicans	223
Unaffiliated/other	1,446

Local Officials, 2010

Chair, Bd. of Sel.	Daniel J. Delorey III
Administrator	Tom Webb
Clerk	Christine B. Emerson
Treasurer	Rebecca Herzog
Tax Collector	Rebecca Herzog
Tax Assessor	Everett Martin
Attorney	Edmund St. John III
Public Works	Peter LeFebvre
Building	Stanley Zarek
Planning	Bernard Bator
Police Chief	Timothy Garner
Emerg/Fire Chief	Thomas Francesconi

Housing & Construction

New Privately Owned Housing Units Authorized by Building Permit

	Single Family	Total Bldgs	Total Units
2006	6	6	6
2007	1	2	3
2008	6	6	6

Parcel Count by Property Class, 2010

Total	1,635
Single family	1,096
Multiple units	51
Apartments	7
Condos	0
Vacant land	206
Open space	0
Commercial	36
Industrial	14
Misc. residential	104
Other use	121

Public Library

Cheshire Public Library
PO Box 740
Cheshire, MA 01225
(413)743-4746

Director	Judy Bender

Library Statistics, FY 2008

Population served, 2007	3,299
Registered users	1,648
Circulation	6,199
Reference transactons	0
Total program attendance	0
per capita:	
Holdings	2.88
Operating income	$7.72
Internet Access	
Internet computers available	1
Weekly users	4

Municipal Finance

Debt at year end 2008	$825,000
Moody's rating, July 2009	NA

Revenues, 2008

Total	$5,835,277
From all taxes	4,002,513
Federal aid	0
State aid	1,173,182
From other governments	7,188
Charges for services	386,844
Licenses, permits & fees	24,754
Fines & forfeits	0
Interfund transfers	0
Misc/other/special assessments	120,398

Expenditures, 2008

Total	$4,309,537
General government	283,830
Public safety	155,826
Other/fixed costs	286,111
Human services	34,189
Culture & recreation	24,444
Debt Service	181,564
Education	2,368,503
Public works	933,229
Intergovernmental	40,348

Taxation, 2010

Property type	Valuation	Rate
Total	$304,883,087	-
Residential	277,107,178	9.33
Open space	0	0.00
Commercial	18,676,763	9.33
Industrial	1,548,370	9.33
Personal	7,550,776	9.33

Average Single Family Tax Bill, 2010

Avg. assessed home value	$209,708
Avg. single fam. tax bill	$1,957
Hi-Lo ranking	295/301

Police & Crime, 2008

Number of police officers	NA
Violent crimes	0
Property crimes	12

Local School District

(school data 2007-08, except as noted)

Cheshire (non-op)
125 Savoy Road
Cheshire, MA 01225
413-743-2939

Superintendent	Alfred Skrocki

Non-operating district.
Resident students are sent to the Other School Districts listed below.

Grade plan	NA
Total enrollment '09-10	NA
Grade 12 enrollment, '09-10	NA
Graduation rate	NA
Dropout rate	NA
Per-pupil expenditure	NA
Avg teacher salary	NA
Student/teacher ratio '08-09	NA
Highly-qualified teachers, '08-09	NA
Teachers licensed in assigned subject	NA
Students per computer	NA

Other School Districts (see Appendix D for data)
Adams-Cheshire Regional

©2010 Information Publications, Inc. All rights reserved. Photocopying prohibited. For additional copies, contact the publisher at www.informationpublications.com or (877)544-INFO (4636)

See Introduction for an explanation of all data sources.

Demographics & Socio-Economic Characteristics

Population

1990 . . . 1,280
2000 . . . 1,308
Male . . . 673
Female . . . 635
2008 . . . 1,287
2010 (projected)†† . . . 1,338
2020 (projected)†† . . . 1,390

Race & Hispanic Origin, 2000

Race
White . . . 1,285
Black/African American . . . 2
American Indian/Alaska Native . . . 6
Asian . . . 1
Hawaiian Native/Pacific Islander . . . 0
Other Race . . . 4
Two or more races . . . 10
Hispanic origin . . . 17

Age & Nativity, 2000

Under 5 years . . . 72
18 years and over . . . 981
21 years and over . . . 934
65 years and over . . . 150
85 years and over . . . 12
Median Age . . . 39.4
Native-born . . . 1,289
Foreign-born . . . 17

Age, 2020 (projected)††

Under 5 years . . . 80
5 to 19 years . . . 247
20 to 39 years . . . 325
40 to 64 years . . . 507
65 years and over . . . 231

Educational Attainment, 2000

Population 25 years and over . . . 866
High School graduates or higher . . . 87.0%
Bachelor's degree or higher . . . 17.4%
Graduate degree . . . 6.1%

Income & Poverty, 1999

Per capita income, . . . $18,098
Median household income . . . $43,816
Median family income . . . $51,932
Persons in poverty . . . 76
H'holds receiving public assistance . . . 14
H'holds receiving social security . . . 122

Households, 2000

Total households . . . 500
With persons under 18 . . . 187
With persons over 65 . . . 106
Family households . . . 361
Single person households . . . 106
Persons per household . . . 2.6
Persons per family . . . 3.1

Labor & Employment, 2000

Civilian labor force . . . 717
Unemployment rate . . . 5.6%
Civilian labor force, 2008† . . . 733
Unemployment rate† . . . 8.6%
Civilian labor force, 12/09† . . . 742
Unemployment rate† . . . 12.1%
Employed persons 16 years and over, by occupation:
Managers & professionals . . . 162
Service occupations . . . 123
Sales & office occupations . . . 144
Farming, fishing & forestry . . . 7
Construction & maintenance . . . 92
Production & transportation . . . 149
Self-employed persons . . . 71

Most demographic data is from the 2000 Decennial Census
† Massachusetts Department of Revenue
†† University of Massachusetts, MISER

General Information

Town of Chester
15 Middlefield Rd
Chester, MA 01011
413-354-7760

Elevation . . . NA
Land area (square miles) . . . 36.7
Water area (square miles) . . . 0.4
Population density, 2008 (est) . . . 35.1
Year incorporated . . . 1783
Website . . . townofchester.net

Voters & Government Information

Government type . . . Open Town Meeting
Number of Selectmen . . . 3
US Congressional District(s) . . . 1

Registered Voters, October 2008

Total . . . 970
Democrats . . . 207
Republicans . . . 150
Unaffiliated/other . . . 606

Local Officials, 2010

Chair, Bd. of Sel. . . . Michael W. Crochiere
Manager/Admin . . . NA
Clerk . . . Cheryl A. Baldasaro
Finance . . . Lisa Edinger
Tax Collector . . . Mary Ann T. Pease
Tax Assessor . . . Pamela Anderson
Attorney . . . NA
Public Works . . . NA
Building . . . NA
Comm Dev/Planning . . . Richard B. Holzman
Police Chief . . . Dan Ilnicky
Emerg/Fire Chief . . . Richard Small

Housing & Construction

New Privately Owned Housing Units Authorized by Building Permit

	Single Family	Total Bldgs	Total Units
2006	1	1	1
2007	4	4	4
2008	3	3	3

Parcel Count by Property Class, 2010

Total . . . 1,049
Single family . . . 489
Multiple units . . . 26
Apartments . . . 1
Condos . . . 0
Vacant land . . . 338
Open space . . . 0
Commercial . . . 17
Industrial . . . 6
Misc. residential . . . 13
Other use . . . 159

Public Library

Hamilton Memorial Library
15 Middlefield Road
Chester, MA 01011
(413)354-7808

Librarian . . . Gale S. Andrade

Library Statistics, FY 2008

Population served, 2007 . . . 1,296
Registered users . . . 1,181
Circulation . . . 7,577
Reference transactons . . . 234
Total program attendance . . . 2,145
per capita:
Holdings . . . 5.99
Operating income . . . $40.07
Internet Access
Internet computers available . . . 1
Weekly users . . . 9

Municipal Finance

Debt at year end 2008 . . . $905,945
Moody's rating, July 2009 . . . NA

Revenues, 2008

Total . . . $3,037,683
From all taxes . . . 2,120,637
Federal aid . . . 0
State aid . . . 373,991
From other governments . . . 8,773
Charges for services . . . 82,281
Licenses, permits & fees . . . 13,034
Fines & forfeits . . . 0
Interfund transfers . . . 231,679
Misc/other/special assessments . . . 103,644

Expenditures, 2008

Total . . . $2,743,407
General government . . . 215,754
Public safety . . . 96,041
Other/fixed costs . . . 140,492
Human services . . . 26,054
Culture & recreation . . . 30,307
Debt Service . . . 115,402
Education . . . 1,681,713
Public works . . . 430,205
Intergovernmental . . . 3,749

Taxation, 2010

Property type	Valuation	Rate
Total	$127,534,262	-
Residential	118,633,574	16.74
Open space	0	0.00
Commercial	4,830,998	16.74
Industrial	571,400	16.74
Personal	3,498,290	16.74

Average Single Family Tax Bill, 2010

Avg. assessed home value . . . $176,269
Avg. single fam. tax bill . . . $2,951
Hi-Lo ranking . . . 238/301

Police & Crime, 2008

Number of police officers . . . NA
Violent crimes . . . NA
Property crimes . . . NA

Local School District

(school data 2007-08, except as noted)

Chester (non-op)
12 Littleville Road
Huntington, MA 01050
413-685-1011
Superintendent . . . David Hopson

Non-operating district.
Resident students are sent to the Other School Districts listed below.

Grade plan . . . NA
Total enrollment '09-10 . . . NA
Grade 12 enrollment, '09-10 . . . NA
Graduation rate . . . NA
Dropout rate . . . NA
Per-pupil expenditure . . . NA
Avg teacher salary . . . NA
Student/teacher ratio '08-09 . . . NA
Highly-qualified teachers, '08-09 . . . NA
Teachers licensed in assigned subject . . . NA
Students per computer . . . NA

Other School Districts (see Appendix D for data)
Gateway Regional

©2010 Information Publications, Inc. All rights reserved. Photocopying prohibited. For additional copies, contact the publisher at www.informationpublications.com or (877)544-INFO (4636)

See Introduction for an explanation of all data sources.

Demographics & Socio-Economic Characteristics

Population

1990	1,048
2000	1,201
Male	599
Female	602
2008	1,288
2010 (projected)††	1,228
2020 (projected)††	1,256

Race & Hispanic Origin, 2000

Race	
White	1,185
Black/African American	0
American Indian/Alaska Native	0
Asian	3
Hawaiian Native/Pacific Islander	3
Other Race	1
Two or more races	9
Hispanic origin	1

Age & Nativity, 2000

Under 5 years	74
18 years and over	892
21 years and over	860
65 years and over	117
85 years and over	11
Median Age	39.5
Native-born	1,182
Foreign-born	19

Age, 2020 (projected)††

Under 5 years	66
5 to 19 years	201
20 to 39 years	270
40 to 64 years	423
65 years and over	296

Educational Attainment, 2000

Population 25 years and over	812
High School graduates or higher	91.6%
Bachelor's degree or higher	24.9%
Graduate degree	6.2%

Income & Poverty, 1999

Per capita income,	$19,220
Median household income	$49,063
Median family income	$57,361
Persons in poverty	68
H'holds receiving public assistance	5
H'holds receiving social security	102

Households, 2000

Total households	447
With persons under 18	168
With persons over 65	84
Family households	325
Single person households	84
Persons per household	2.7
Persons per family	3.1

Labor & Employment, 2000

Civilian labor force	709
Unemployment rate	3.5%
Civilian labor force, 2008†	754
Unemployment rate†	5.2%
Civilian labor force, 12/09†	749
Unemployment rate†	6.0%
Employed persons 16 years and over, by occupation:	
Managers & professionals	215
Service occupations	86
Sales & office occupations	145
Farming, fishing & forestry	11
Construction & maintenance	115
Production & transportation	112
Self-employed persons	85

Most demographic data is from the 2000 Decennial Census
† Massachusetts Department of Revenue
†† University of Massachusetts, MISER

General Information

Town of Chesterfield
422 Main Road
PO Box 299
Chesterfield, MA 01012
413-296-4771

Elevation	1,427 ft.
Land area (square miles)	31.1
Water area (square miles)	0.2
Population density, 2008 (est)	41.4
Year incorporated	1762
Website	www.townofchesterfieldma.com

Voters & Government Information

Government type	Open Town Meeting
Number of Selectmen	3
US Congressional District(s)	1

Registered Voters, October 2008

Total	869
Democrats	190
Republicans	108
Unaffiliated/other	564

Local Officials, 2010

Chair, Bd. of Sel.	Robert W. Recos
Manager/Admin	Charlene L. Nardi
Town Clerk	Sandra Wickland
Finance Director	Bernard Berube
Tax Collector	Lenora Pittsinger
Tax Assessor	Ed Severance
Attorney	Kopelman & Paige
Public Works	NA
Building	Paul Tacy
Comm Dev/Planning	Charles Valencik
Police Chief	Gary Wickland
Emerg/Fire Chief	David Hewes

Housing & Construction

New Privately Owned Housing Units Authorized by Building Permit

	Single Family	Total Bldgs	Total Units
2006	5	5	5
2007	4	4	4
2008	3	3	3

Parcel Count by Property Class, 2010

Total	912
Single family	539
Multiple units	8
Apartments	1
Condos	0
Vacant land	225
Open space	0
Commercial	8
Industrial	14
Misc. residential	3
Other use	114

Public Library

Chesterfield Public Library
PO Box 305
Chesterfield, MA 01012
(413)296-4735

Librarian	Cynthia Squier

Library Statistics, FY 2008

Population served, 2007	1,273
Registered users	0
Circulation	6,997
Reference transactons	416
Total program attendance	0
per capita:	
Holdings	7.63
Operating income	$21.77
Internet Access	
Internet computers available	3
Weekly users	15

Municipal Finance

Debt at year end 2008	$707,898
Moody's rating, July 2009	NA

Revenues, 2008

Total	$2,660,044
From all taxes	2,029,294
Federal aid	167
State aid	342,996
From other governments	1,425
Charges for services	50,660
Licenses, permits & fees	0
Fines & forfeits	0
Interfund transfers	31,250
Misc/other/special assessments	102,126

Expenditures, 2008

Total	$2,415,563
General government	212,305
Public safety	77,193
Other/fixed costs	135,885
Human services	12,063
Culture & recreation	27,702
Debt Service	106,919
Education	1,397,973
Public works	423,774
Intergovernmental	21,749

Taxation, 2010

Property type	Valuation	Rate
Total	$144,472,810	-
Residential	136,074,778	15.26
Open space	0	0.00
Commercial	2,563,722	15.26
Industrial	2,213,100	15.26
Personal	3,621,210	15.26

Average Single Family Tax Bill, 2010

Avg. assessed home value	$223,423
Avg. single fam. tax bill	$3,409
Hi-Lo ranking	183/301

Police & Crime, 2008

Number of police officers	NA
Violent crimes	NA
Property crimes	NA

Local School District

(school data 2007-08, except as noted)

Chesterfield (non-op)
19 Stage Rd
Westhampton, MA 01027
413-527-7200

Superintendent	Craig Jurgensen

Non-operating district.
Resident students are sent to the Other School Districts listed below.

Grade plan	NA
Total enrollment '09-10	NA
Grade 12 enrollment, '09-10	NA
Graduation rate	NA
Dropout rate	NA
Per-pupil expenditure	NA
Avg teacher salary	NA
Student/teacher ratio '08-09	NA
Highly-qualified teachers, '08-09	NA
Teachers licensed in assigned subject	NA
Students per computer	NA

Other School Districts (see Appendix D for data)
Chesterfield-Goshen and Hampshire Regionals

©2010 Information Publications, Inc. All rights reserved. Photocopying prohibited. For additional copies, contact the publisher at www.informationpublications.com or (877)544-INFO (4636)

See Introduction for an explanation of all data sources.

Demographics & Socio-Economic Characteristics*

Population

1990	56,632
2000	54,653
Male	25,994
Female	28,659
2008	54,941
2010 (projected)††	52,914
2020 (projected)††	51,483

Race & Hispanic Origin, 2000

Race	
White	49,089
Black/African American	1,244
American Indian/Alaska Native	107
Asian	474
Hawaiian Native/Pacific Islander	57
Other Race	2,679
Two or more races	1,003
Hispanic origin	4,790

Age & Nativity, 2000

Under 5 years	2,986
18 years and over	42,284
21 years and over	40,190
65 years and over	9,638
85 years and over	1,042
Median Age	38.7
Native-born	50,191
Foreign-born	4,462

Age, 2020 (projected)††

Under 5 years	2,578
5 to 19 years	8,182
20 to 39 years	12,902
40 to 64 years	17,316
65 years and over	10,505

Educational Attainment, 2000

Population 25 years and over	37,695
High School graduates or higher	74.9%
Bachelor's degree or higher	12.3%
Graduate degree	4.3%

Income & Poverty, 1999

Per capita income,	$18,646
Median household income	$35,672
Median family income	$44,136
Persons in poverty	6,608
H'holds receiving public assistance	968
H'holds receiving social security	7,841

Households, 2000

Total households	23,117
With persons under 18	6,660
With persons over 65	7,052
Family households	14,139
Single person households	7,560
Persons per household	2.3
Persons per family	3.0

Labor & Employment, 2000

Civilian labor force	27,112
Unemployment rate	4.8%
Civilian labor force, 2008†	27,514
Unemployment rate†	8.0%
Civilian labor force, 12/09†	27,733
Unemployment rate†	10.9%
Employed persons 16 years and over, by occupation:	
Managers & professionals	5,892
Service occupations	4,312
Sales & office occupations	7,067
Farming, fishing & forestry	40
Construction & maintenance	2,447
Production & transportation	6,046
Self-employed persons	955

Most demographic data is from the 2000 Decennial Census
* see Appendix E for American Community Survey data
† Massachusetts Department of Revenue
†† University of Massachusetts, MISER

General Information

City of Chicopee
17 Springfield St
Chicopee, MA 01013
413-594-1500

Elevation	93 ft.
Land area (square miles)	22.9
Water area (square miles)	1.0
Population density, 2008 (est)	2,399.2
Year incorporated	1848
Website	www.chicopeema.gov

Voters & Government Information

Government type	Mayor-Council
Number of Aldermen	13
US Congressional District(s)	2

Registered Voters, October 2008

Total	34,959
Democrats	14,751
Republicans	3,759
Unaffiliated/other	16,162

Local Officials, 2010

Mayor	Michael Bissonnette
Manager/Admin	NA
Clerk	Keith W. Rattell
Treasurer	Ernest LaFlamme Jr
Tax Collector	Carole Jendrysik-Harms
Tax Assessor	Stanley Iwanicki
Attorney	Susan Phillips
Public Works	Stanley Kulig
Building	Joseph Viamari
Planning	Kate Brown
Police Chief	John Ferraro
Emerg/Fire Chief	Stephen Burkott

Housing & Construction

New Privately Owned Housing Units Authorized by Building Permit

	Single Family	Total Bldgs	Total Units
2006	31	36	43
2007	64	72	80
2008	38	40	42

Parcel Count by Property Class, 2010

Total	17,867
Single family	10,957
Multiple units	2,146
Apartments	412
Condos	1,775
Vacant land	1,232
Open space	0
Commercial	696
Industrial	333
Misc. residential	62
Other use	254

Public Library

Chicopee Public Library
449 Front Street
Chicopee, MA 01013
(413)594-1800

Director	Nancy Contois

Library Statistics, FY 2008

Population served, 2007	53,876
Registered users	25,574
Circulation	344,234
Reference transactons	20,644
Total program attendance	257,991
per capita:	
Holdings	2.33
Operating income	$28.80
Internet Access	
Internet computers available	72
Weekly users	1,314

Municipal Finance

Debt at year end 2008	$29,953,499
Moody's rating, July 2009	A2

Revenues, 2008

Total	$134,674,619
From all taxes	61,696,690
Federal aid	0
State aid	63,120,238
From other governments	51,287
Charges for services	3,564,411
Licenses, permits & fees	737,024
Fines & forfeits	314,779
Interfund transfers	0
Misc/other/special assessments	2,595,095

Expenditures, 2008

Total	$127,334,342
General government	5,115,842
Public safety	18,193,390
Other/fixed costs	25,390,367
Human services	1,832,726
Culture & recreation	3,320,071
Debt Service	3,482,731
Education	63,060,109
Public works	5,557,940
Intergovernmental	1,307,177

Taxation, 2010

Property type	Valuation	Rate
Total	$3,665,344,340	-
Residential	2,922,419,960	13.63
Open space	0	0.00
Commercial	366,882,540	28.95
Industrial	244,570,900	28.95
Personal	131,470,940	28.95

Average Single Family Tax Bill, 2010

Avg. assessed home value	$182,709
Avg. single fam. tax bill	$2,490
Hi-Lo ranking	281/301

Police & Crime, 2008

Number of police officers	135
Violent crimes	323
Property crimes	1,678

Local School District

(school data 2007-08, except as noted)

Chicopee
180 Broadway
Chicopee, MA 01020
413-594-3410

Superintendent	Richard Rege
Grade plan	PK-12
Total enrollment '09-10	7,845
Grade 12 enrollment, '09-10	621
Graduation rate	65.9%
Dropout rate	21.3%
Per-pupil expenditure	$11,567
Avg teacher salary	$58,932
Student/teacher ratio '08-09	12.6 to 1
Highly-qualified teachers, '08-09	94.2%
Teachers licensed in assigned subject	94.9%
Students per computer	3.3

Massachusetts Competency Assessment System (MCAS), 2009 results

	English		Math	
	% Prof	CPI	% Prof	CPI
Gr 4	35%	71.9	32%	71.3
Gr 6	57%	78.4	42%	67.7
Gr 8	67%	85.3	33%	61.7
Gr 10	66%	85.3	51%	74.2

Other School Districts (see Appendix D for data)
None

©2010 Information Publications, Inc. All rights reserved. Photocopying prohibited. For additional copies, contact the publisher at www.informationpublications.com or (877)544-INFO (4636)

See Introduction for an explanation of all data sources.

Demographics & Socio-Economic Characteristics

Population

1990	650
2000	843
Male	413
Female	430
2008	971
2010 (projected)††	997
2020 (projected)††	1,164

Race & Hispanic Origin, 2000

Race	
White	824
Black/African American	3
American Indian/Alaska Native	1
Asian	3
Hawaiian Native/Pacific Islander	0
Other Race	6
Two or more races	6
Hispanic origin	7

Age & Nativity, 2000

Under 5 years	39
18 years and over	668
21 years and over	657
65 years and over	158
85 years and over	22
Median Age	45.6
Native-born	783
Foreign-born	45

Age, 2020 (projected)††

Under 5 years	49
5 to 19 years	134
20 to 39 years	242
40 to 64 years	391
65 years and over	348

Educational Attainment, 2000

Population 25 years and over	642
High School graduates or higher	97.7%
Bachelor's degree or higher	57.2%
Graduate degree	21.2%

Income & Poverty, 1999

Per capita income,	$30,029
Median household income	$41,917
Median family income	$63,750
Persons in poverty	63
H'holds receiving public assistance	0
H'holds receiving social security	99

Households, 2000

Total households	382
With persons under 18	103
With persons over 65	110
Family households	238
Single person households	113
Persons per household	2.2
Persons per family	2.7

Labor & Employment, 2000

Civilian labor force	449
Unemployment rate	2.4%
Civilian labor force, 2008†	537
Unemployment rate†	3.9%
Civilian labor force, 12/09†	557
Unemployment rate†	5.4%
Employed persons 16 years and over, by occupation:	
Managers & professionals	159
Service occupations	69
Sales & office occupations	99
Farming, fishing & forestry	14
Construction & maintenance	71
Production & transportation	26
Self-employed persons	123

Most demographic data is from the 2000 Decennial Census
† Massachusetts Department of Revenue
†† University of Massachusetts, MISER

General Information

Town of Chilmark
401 Middle Rd
PO Box 119
Chilmark, MA 02535
508-645-2100

Elevation	NA
Land area (square miles)	19.1
Water area (square miles)	81.3
Population density, 2008 (est)	50.8
Year incorporated	1694
Website	www.ci.chilmark.ma.us

Voters & Government Information

Government type	Open Town Meeting
Number of Selectmen	3
US Congressional District(s)	10

Registered Voters, October 2008

Total	859
Democrats	366
Republicans	74
Unaffiliated/other	409

Local Officials, 2010

Chair, Bd. of Sel.	J.B. Riggs Parker
Executive Secretary	Timothy R. Carroll
Town Clerk	Jennifer L. Christy
Town Accountant	Thomas Wilson
Tax Collector	Jessica Bradlee
Tax Assessor	Clarissa Allen
Attorney	Ronald Rappaport
Public Works	Keith Emin
Building	Leonard Jason Jr
Comm Dev/Planning	Janet Weidner (Chr)
Police Chief	Brian Cioffi
Emerg/Fire Chief	David Norton

Housing & Construction

New Privately Owned Housing Units Authorized by Building Permit

	Single Family	Total Bldgs	Total Units
2006	39	39	39
2007	30	30	30
2008	21	21	21

Parcel Count by Property Class, 2010

Total	2,252
Single family	1,057
Multiple units	0
Apartments	0
Condos	0
Vacant land	945
Open space	0
Commercial	22
Industrial	2
Misc. residential	209
Other use	17

Public Library

Chilmark Free Public Library
PO Box 180
Chilmark, MA 02535
(508)645-3360

Library Director	Ebba Hierta

Library Statistics, FY 2008

Population served, 2007	963
Registered users	6,157
Circulation	63,904
Reference transactons	1,650
Total program attendance	54,080
per capita:	
Holdings	29.88
Operating income	$275.53
Internet Access	
Internet computers available	8
Weekly users	74

Municipal Finance

Debt at year end 2008	$5,220,000
Moody's rating, July 2009	NA

Revenues, 2008

Total	$6,816,450
From all taxes	5,997,748
Federal aid	0
State aid	8,517
From other governments	1,740
Charges for services	513,165
Licenses, permits & fees	55,320
Fines & forfeits	9,376
Interfund transfers	38,412
Misc/other/special assessments	96,086

Expenditures, 2008

Total	$6,517,690
General government	950,578
Public safety	969,606
Other/fixed costs	675,824
Human services	152,836
Culture & recreation	587,258
Debt Service	443,365
Education	1,816,287
Public works	536,343
Intergovernmental	385,593

Taxation, 2010

Property type	Valuation	Rate
Total	$3,060,583,926	-
Residential	2,993,327,596	2.03
Open space	0	0.00
Commercial	28,388,504	2.03
Industrial	1,133,800	2.03
Personal	37,734,026	2.03

Average Single Family Tax Bill, 2010

Avg. assessed home value	$1,841,890
Avg. single fam. tax bill	$3,739
Hi-Lo ranking	156/301

Police & Crime, 2008

Number of police officers	4
Violent crimes	1
Property crimes	16

Local School District

(school data 2007-08, except as noted)

Chilmark (non-op)
RR2, Box 261, 4 Pine Street
Vineyard Haven, MA 02568
508-693-2007

Superintendent	James Weiss

Non-operating district.
Resident students are sent to the Other School Districts listed below.

Grade plan	NA
Total enrollment '09-10	NA
Grade 12 enrollment, '09-10	NA
Graduation rate	NA
Dropout rate	NA
Per-pupil expenditure	NA
Avg teacher salary	NA
Student/teacher ratio '08-09	NA
Highly-qualified teachers, '08-09	NA
Teachers licensed in assigned subject	NA
Students per computer	NA

Other School Districts (see Appendix D for data)
Marthas Vineyard and Up-Island Regionals

©2010 Information Publications, Inc. All rights reserved. Photocopying prohibited. For additional copies, contact the publisher at www.informationpublications.com or (877)544-INFO (4636)

Demographics & Socio-Economic Characteristics

Population

1990	1,745
2000	1,686
Male	838
Female	848
2008	1,619
2010 (projected)††	1,512
2020 (projected)††	1,311

Race & Hispanic Origin, 2000

Race	
White	1,683
Black/African American	1
American Indian/Alaska Native	0
Asian	0
Hawaiian Native/Pacific Islander	0
Other Race	2
Two or more races	0
Hispanic origin	4

Age & Nativity, 2000

Under 5 years	72
18 years and over	1,302
21 years and over	1,248
65 years and over	278
85 years and over	20
Median Age	41.3
Native-born	1,669
Foreign-born	17

Age, 2020 (projected)††

Under 5 years	53
5 to 19 years	196
20 to 39 years	264
40 to 64 years	488
65 years and over	310

Educational Attainment, 2000

Population 25 years and over	1,188
High School graduates or higher	80.1%
Bachelor's degree or higher	15.2%
Graduate degree	4.1%

Income & Poverty, 1999

Per capita income,	$19,389
Median household income	$43,362
Median family income	$47,411
Persons in poverty	111
H'holds receiving public assistance	11
H'holds receiving social security	237

Households, 2000

Total households	659
With persons under 18	220
With persons over 65	198
Family households	512
Single person households	120
Persons per household	2.6
Persons per family	2.9

Labor & Employment, 2000

Civilian labor force	902
Unemployment rate	4.7%
Civilian labor force, 2008†	918
Unemployment rate†	6.4%
Civilian labor force, 12/09†	955
Unemployment rate†	11.3%
Employed persons 16 years and over, by occupation:	
Managers & professionals	253
Service occupations	161
Sales & office occupations	205
Farming, fishing & forestry	4
Construction & maintenance	102
Production & transportation	135
Self-employed persons	55

Most demographic data is from the 2000 Decennial Census
† Massachusetts Department of Revenue
†† University of Massachusetts, MISER

General Information

Town of Clarksburg
111 River Rd
Clarksburg, MA 01247
413-663-7940

Elevation	1,051 ft.
Land area (square miles)	12.8
Water area (square miles)	0.1
Population density, 2008 (est)	126.5
Year incorporated	1798
Website	NA

Voters & Government Information

Government type	Open Town Meeting
Number of Selectmen	3
US Congressional District(s)	1

Registered Voters, October 2008

Total	1,132
Democrats	241
Republicans	96
Unaffiliated/other	787

Local Officials, 2010

Chair, Bd. of Sel.	Deb Lefave
Manager/Admin	Michael Canales
Town Clerk	Carol Jammalo
Finance Director	Marie Allard
Tax Collector	Melissa McGovern
Tax Assessor	Gustel Progulske
Attorney	NA
Public Works	NA
Building	Vincent Lively
Comm Dev/Planning	David Delano
Police Chief	Michael Williams
Emerg/Fire Chief	Carlyle Chesbro Jr

Housing & Construction

New Privately Owned Housing Units Authorized by Building Permit

	Single Family	Total Bldgs	Total Units
2006	3	3	3
2007	4	4	4
2008	3	3	3

Parcel Count by Property Class, 2010

Total	NA
Single family	NA
Multiple units	NA
Apartments	NA
Condos	NA
Vacant land	NA
Open space	NA
Commercial	NA
Industrial	NA
Misc. residential	NA
Other use	NA

Public Library

Clarksburg Town Library
711 West Cross Road
Clarksburg, MA 01247
(413)664-6050

Director	Lynn DePaoli

Library Statistics, FY 2008

Population served, 2007	1,631
Registered users	835
Circulation	22,705
Reference transactons	925
Total program attendance	11,648
per capita:	
Holdings	7.17
Operating income	$40.60
Internet Access	
Internet computers available	7
Weekly users	100

Municipal Finance

Debt at year end 2008	$804,652
Moody's rating, July 2009	NA

Revenues, 2008

Total	$3,412,827
From all taxes	1,173,784
Federal aid	0
State aid	2,167,158
From other governments	0
Charges for services	10,718
Licenses, permits & fees	2,509
Fines & forfeits	0
Interfund transfers	25,000
Misc/other/special assessments	16,829

Expenditures, 2008

Total	$3,442,051
General government	244,678
Public safety	93,698
Other/fixed costs	256,308
Human services	9,832
Culture & recreation	62,803
Debt Service	53,554
Education	2,391,115
Public works	218,805
Intergovernmental	92,758

Taxation, 2010

Property type	Valuation	Rate
Total	NA	-
Residential	NA	NA
Open space	NA	NA
Commercial	NA	NA
Industrial	NA	NA
Personal	NA	NA

Average Single Family Tax Bill, 2010

Avg. assessed home value	NA
Avg. single fam. tax bill	NA
Hi-Lo ranking	NA

Police & Crime, 2008

Number of police officers	NA
Violent crimes	NA
Property crimes	NA

Local School District

(school data 2007-08, except as noted)

Clarksburg
98 Church Street
North Adams, MA 01247
413-664-9292

Superintendent	Jon Lev
Grade plan	K-8
Total enrollment '09-10	175
Grade 12 enrollment, '09-10	0
Graduation rate	NA
Dropout rate	NA
Per-pupil expenditure	$10,290
Avg teacher salary	$63,662
Student/teacher ratio '08-09	13.8 to 1
Highly-qualified teachers, '08-09	96.4%
Teachers licensed in assigned subject	93.1%
Students per computer	2.5

Massachusetts Competency Assessment System (MCAS), 2009 results

	English		Math	
	% Prof	CPI	% Prof	CPI
Gr 4	21%	68.8	42%	81.3
Gr 6	57%	84.5	57%	77.4
Gr 8	59%	89.2	39%	70.4
Gr 10	NA	NA	NA	NA

Other School Districts (see Appendix D for data)

Sends grades 9-12 to North Adams and Northern Berkshire Vocational Tech

©2010 Information Publications, Inc. All rights reserved. Photocopying prohibited. For additional copies, contact the publisher at www.informationpublications.com or (877)544-INFO (4636)

See Introduction for an explanation of all data sources.

Demographics & Socio-Economic Characteristics

Population

1990	13,222
2000	13,435
Male	6,472
Female	6,963
2008	13,965
2010 (projected)††	13,583
2020 (projected)††	13,796

Race & Hispanic Origin, 2000

Race	
White	11,849
Black/African American	346
American Indian/Alaska Native	29
Asian	120
Hawaiian Native/Pacific Islander	6
Other Race	799
Two or more races	286
Hispanic origin	1,558

Age & Nativity, 2000

Under 5 years	803
18 years and over	10,342
21 years and over	9,912
65 years and over	2,012
85 years and over	265
Median Age	37.1
Native-born	12,138
Foreign-born	1,297

Age, 2020 (projected)††

Under 5 years	756
5 to 19 years	2,091
20 to 39 years	3,714
40 to 64 years	4,818
65 years and over	2,417

Educational Attainment, 2000

Population 25 years and over	9,393
High School graduates or higher	83.7%
Bachelor's degree or higher	23.0%
Graduate degree	9.3%

Income & Poverty, 1999

Per capita income,	$22,764
Median household income	$44,740
Median family income	$53,308
Persons in poverty	949
H'holds receiving public assistance	122
H'holds receiving social security	1,598

Households, 2000

Total households	5,597
With persons under 18	1,689
With persons over 65	1,470
Family households	3,400
Single person households	1,850
Persons per household	2.4
Persons per family	3.1

Labor & Employment, 2000

Civilian labor force	7,243
Unemployment rate	5.1%
Civilian labor force, 2008†	7,623
Unemployment rate†	8.2%
Civilian labor force, 12/09†	7,778
Unemployment rate†	11.3%
Employed persons 16 years and over, by occupation:	
Managers & professionals	2,155
Service occupations	984
Sales & office occupations	1,802
Farming, fishing & forestry	7
Construction & maintenance	549
Production & transportation	1,374
Self-employed persons	368

Most demographic data is from the 2000 Decennial Census
† Massachusetts Department of Revenue
†† University of Massachusetts, MISER

General Information

Town of Clinton
242 Church St
Clinton, MA 01510
978-365-4120

Elevation	325 ft.
Land area (square miles)	5.7
Water area (square miles)	1.6
Population density, 2008 (est)	2,450.0
Year incorporated	1850
Website	www.clintonma.gov

Voters & Government Information

Government type	Open Town Meeting
Number of Selectmen	5
US Congressional District(s)	3

Registered Voters, October 2008

Total	9,299
Democrats	3,383
Republicans	1,015
Unaffiliated/other	4,820

Local Officials, 2010

Chair, Bd. of Sel.	Mary Rose Dickhaut
Manager/Admin	Michael Ward
Town Clerk	Philip Boyce
Treasurer	Patrick McIntyre
Tax Collector	Kathy O'Malley
Tax Assessor	David J. Baird (Chr)
Attorney	Robert Gibbons
Public Works	Christopher McGown
Building	Tony Zahariadis
Planning	Clifford J. Thompson
Police Chief	Mark Laverdure
Fire Chief	Richard Hart

Housing & Construction

New Privately Owned Housing Units Authorized by Building Permit

	Single Family	Total Bldgs	Total Units
2006	27	27	27
2007	16	16	16
2008	19	19	19

Parcel Count by Property Class, 2010

Total	4,586
Single family	2,301
Multiple units	725
Apartments	107
Condos	865
Vacant land	241
Open space	0
Commercial	162
Industrial	80
Misc. residential	49
Other use	56

Public Library

Bigelow Free Public Library
54 Walnut St.
Clinton, MA 01510
(978)365-4160

Director .... Christine M. Flaherty

Library Statistics, FY 2008

Population served, 2007	14,030
Registered users	15,325
Circulation	135,037
Reference transactons	4,651
Total program attendance	78,677
per capita:	
Holdings	13.82
Operating income	$25.12
Internet Access	
Internet computers available	10
Weekly users	320

Municipal Finance

Debt at year end 2008	$31,388,583
Moody's rating, July 2009	Baa1

Revenues, 2008

Total	$33,035,343
From all taxes	16,961,865
Federal aid	0
State aid	15,262,143
From other governments	23,800
Charges for services	313,258
Licenses, permits & fees	226,435
Fines & forfeits	10,452
Interfund transfers	31,500
Misc/other/special assessments	102,945

Expenditures, 2008

Total	$32,860,768
General government	1,071,049
Public safety	4,104,327
Other/fixed costs	4,769,551
Human services	372,293
Culture & recreation	566,246
Debt Service	2,607,482
Education	17,572,539
Public works	1,205,597
Intergovernmental	550,762

Taxation, 2010

Property type	Valuation	Rate
Total	$1,164,793,537	-
Residential	1,007,095,178	13.35
Open space	0	0.00
Commercial	67,432,292	24.52
Industrial	62,616,900	24.52
Personal	27,649,167	24.52

Average Single Family Tax Bill, 2010

Avg. assessed home value	$232,076
Avg. single fam. tax bill	$3,098
Hi-Lo ranking	227/301

Police & Crime, 2008

Number of police officers	27
Violent crimes	4
Property crimes	122

Local School District

(school data 2007-08, except as noted)

Clinton
150 School Street
Clinton, MA 01510
978-365-4200

Superintendent	Terrance Ingano
Grade plan	PK-12
Total enrollment '09-10	1,996
Grade 12 enrollment, '09-10	122
Graduation rate	89.9%
Dropout rate	5.1%
Per-pupil expenditure	$10,838
Avg teacher salary	$62,164
Student/teacher ratio '08-09	14.4 to 1
Highly-qualified teachers, '08-09	96.0%
Teachers licensed in assigned subject	97.2%
Students per computer	3.5

Massachusetts Competency Assessment System (MCAS), 2009 results

	English		Math	
	% Prof	CPI	% Prof	CPI
Gr 4	42%	73.5	43%	75.3
Gr 6	44%	77.7	44%	73.2
Gr 8	75%	90	39%	69.4
Gr 10	74%	90	74%	89.5

Other School Districts (see Appendix D for data)
None

©2010 Information Publications, Inc. All rights reserved. Photocopying prohibited. For additional copies, contact the publisher at www.informationpublications.com or (877)544-INFO (4636)

See Introduction for an explanation of all data sources.

©2010 Information Publications, Inc. All rights reserved. Photocopying prohibited. For additional copies, contact the publisher at www.informationpublications.com or (877)544-INFO (4636)

Demographics & Socio-Economic Characteristics

Population

1990	7,075
2000	7,261
Male	3,500
Female	3,761
2008	7,169
2010 (projected)††	6,899
2020 (projected)††	6,063

Race & Hispanic Origin, 2000

Race	
White	7,130
Black/African American	13
American Indian/Alaska Native	5
Asian	55
Hawaiian Native/Pacific Islander	2
Other Race	14
Two or more races	42
Hispanic origin	50

Age & Nativity, 2000

Under 5 years	532
18 years and over	5,236
21 years and over	5,115
65 years and over	1,114
85 years and over	134
Median Age	40.9
Native-born	6,925
Foreign-born	336

Age, 2020 (projected)††

Under 5 years	296
5 to 19 years	1,135
20 to 39 years	1,178
40 to 64 years	2,081
65 years and over	1,373

Educational Attainment, 2000

Population 25 years and over	5,055
High School graduates or higher	97.2%
Bachelor's degree or higher	60.7%
Graduate degree	20.7%

Income & Poverty, 1999

Per capita income,	$42,909
Median household income	$84,156
Median family income	$100,137
Persons in poverty	201
H'holds receiving public assistance	16
H'holds receiving social security	728

Households, 2000

Total households	2,673
With persons under 18	1,009
With persons over 65	761
Family households	2,014
Single person households	585
Persons per household	2.7
Persons per family	3.2

Labor & Employment, 2000

Civilian labor force	3,564
Unemployment rate	1.5%
Civilian labor force, 2008†	3,645
Unemployment rate†	4.3%
Civilian labor force, 12/09†	3,593
Unemployment rate†	6.3%
Employed persons 16 years and over, by occupation:	
Managers & professionals	2,008
Service occupations	303
Sales & office occupations	949
Farming, fishing & forestry	14
Construction & maintenance	108
Production & transportation	127
Self-employed persons	333

Most demographic data is from the 2000 Decennial Census
† Massachusetts Department of Revenue
†† University of Massachusetts, MISER

General Information

Town of Cohasset
41 Highland Ave
Cohasset, MA 02025
781-383-4100

Elevation	50 ft.
Land area (square miles)	9.9
Water area (square miles)	21.6
Population density, 2008 (est)	724.1
Year incorporated	1710
Website	www.townofcohasset.org

Voters & Government Information

Government type	Open Town Meeting
Number of Selectmen	5
US Congressional District(s)	10

Registered Voters, October 2008

Total	5,380
Democrats	1,199
Republicans	1,197
Unaffiliated/other	2,972

Local Officials, 2010

Chair, Bd. of Sel.	Paul Carlson
Town Manager	William Griffin
Clerk	Marion Douglas
Finance Director	Michael Buckley
Tax Collector	Linda Litchfield
Tax Assessor	Elsa Miller
Attorney	Paul DeRensis
Public Works	Carl Sestito
Building	Robert Egan
Planning	Alfred Moore
Police Chief	Brian Noonan (Actg)
Emerg/Fire Chief	Robert Silvia

Housing & Construction

New Privately Owned Housing Units Authorized by Building Permit

	Single Family	Total Bldgs	Total Units
2006	8	8	8
2007	5	5	5
2008	3	4	19

Parcel Count by Property Class, 2010

Total	3,050
Single family	2,263
Multiple units	88
Apartments	8
Condos	211
Vacant land	278
Open space	0
Commercial	113
Industrial	3
Misc. residential	41
Other use	45

Public Library

Paul Pratt Memorial Library
35 Ripley Road
Cohasset, MA 02025
(781)383-1348

Director	Jacqueline S. Rafferty

Library Statistics, FY 2008

Population served, 2007	7,182
Registered users	5,804
Circulation	180,031
Reference transactons	5,408
Total program attendance	132,563
per capita:	
Holdings	9.23
Operating income	$76.09
Internet Access	
Internet computers available	29
Weekly users	310

Municipal Finance

Debt at year end 2008	$58,876,020
Moody's rating, July 2009	Aa2

Revenues, 2008

Total	$32,821,277
From all taxes	26,601,240
Federal aid	0
State aid	2,854,620
From other governments	5,115
Charges for services	1,106,255
Licenses, permits & fees	343,110
Fines & forfeits	43,085
Interfund transfers	311,480
Misc/other/special assessments	778,186

Expenditures, 2008

Total	$32,130,482
General government	1,456,716
Public safety	3,958,811
Other/fixed costs	3,807,409
Human services	318,367
Culture & recreation	632,596
Debt Service	4,659,982
Education	13,877,311
Public works	2,120,255
Intergovernmental	1,298,537

Taxation, 2010

Property type	Valuation	Rate
Total	$2,438,739,752	-
Residential	2,265,856,922	11.22
Open space	0	0.00
Commercial	144,324,020	11.22
Industrial	9,809,100	11.22
Personal	18,749,710	11.22

Average Single Family Tax Bill, 2010

Avg. assessed home value	$858,006
Avg. single fam. tax bill	$9,627
Hi-Lo ranking	9/301

Police & Crime, 2008

Number of police officers	NA
Violent crimes	7
Property crimes	128

Local School District

(school data 2007-08, except as noted)

Cohasset
143 Pond Street
Cohasset, MA 02025
781-383-6112

Superintendent	Denise Walsh
Grade plan	PK-12
Total enrollment '09-10	1,496
Grade 12 enrollment, '09-10	91
Graduation rate	92.9%
Dropout rate	4.8%
Per-pupil expenditure	$13,102
Avg teacher salary	$62,404
Student/teacher ratio '08-09	13.2 to 1
Highly-qualified teachers, '08-09	97.1%
Teachers licensed in assigned subject	99.1%
Students per computer	1.8

Massachusetts Competency Assessment System (MCAS), 2009 results

	English		Math	
	% Prof	CPI	% Prof	CPI
Gr 4	73%	90.2	67%	89.6
Gr 6	81%	91.1	80%	90.1
Gr 8	92%	97.4	83%	93.6
Gr 10	97%	98.6	96%	98.4

Other School Districts (see Appendix D for data)

South Shore Vocational Tech, Norfolk County Agricultural

See Introduction for an explanation of all data sources.

Demographics & Socio-Economic Characteristics

Population

1990 1,757
2000 1,813
Male 921
Female 892
2008 1,879
2010 (projected)†† 1,802
2020 (projected)†† 1,807

Race & Hispanic Origin, 2000

Race
White 1,783
Black/African American 6
American Indian/Alaska Native 0
Asian 6
Hawaiian Native/Pacific Islander 0
Other Race 2
Two or more races 16
Hispanic origin 18

Age & Nativity, 2000

Under 5 years 116
18 years and over 1,310
21 years and over 1,265
65 years and over 222
85 years and over 19
Median Age 37.8
Native-born 1,776
Foreign-born 23

Age, 2020 (projected)††

Under 5 years 89
5 to 19 years 267
20 to 39 years 455
40 to 64 years 659
65 years and over 337

Educational Attainment, 2000

Population 25 years and over 1,203
High School graduates or higher . . 85.3%
Bachelor's degree or higher 24.7%
Graduate degree 9.8%

Income & Poverty, 1999

Per capita income, ... $18,948
Median household income $40,076
Median family income $46,518
Persons in poverty 122
H'holds receiving public assistance 19
H'holds receiving social security 210

Households, 2000

Total households 686
With persons under 18 255
With persons over 65 167
Family households 478
Single person households 163
Persons per household 2.6
Persons per family 3.1

Labor & Employment, 2000

Civilian labor force 978
Unemployment rate 4.9%
Civilian labor force, 2008† 976
Unemployment rate† 7.0%
Civilian labor force, 12/09† 980
Unemployment rate† 9.3%
Employed persons 16 years and over, by occupation:
Managers & professionals 308
Service occupations 152
Sales & office occupations 173
Farming, fishing & forestry 11
Construction & maintenance 114
Production & transportation 172
Self-employed persons 107

Most demographic data is from the 2000 Decennial Census
† Massachusetts Department of Revenue
†† University of Massachusetts, MISER

General Information

Town of Colrain
55 Main Rd
Colrain, MA 01340
413-624-3454

Elevation . . . . . NA
Land area (square miles) 43.4
Water area (square miles) 0.1
Population density, 2008 (est) 43.3
Year incorporated 1761
Email . . . . . coltnclk@mtdata.com

Voters & Government Information

Government type . . . . . Open Town Meeting
Number of Selectmen 3
US Congressional District(s) 1

Registered Voters, October 2008

Total 1,164
Democrats 282
Republicans 112
Unaffiliated/other 760

Local Officials, 2010

Chair, Bd. of Sel. . . . . . Michael J. Beausoleil
Town Coordinator . . . . . Fred Rees
Town Clerk . . . . . Judith D. Sullivan
Finance Director . . . . . Robert Szafran
Tax Collector . . . . . Leah C. Coburn
Tax Assessor . . . . . Nicholas Anzuoni
Attorney . . . . . Kopelman & Paige
Public Works . . . . . Robert E. White
Building . . . . . Shawn Kimberley
Comm Dev/Planning . . . . . Terrence Maloneyl
Police Chief . . . . . Jason Haskins
Fire Chief . . . . . David V. Celino

Housing & Construction

New Privately Owned Housing Units Authorized by Building Permit

	Single Family	Total Bldgs	Total Units
2006	9	9	9
2007	7	7	7
2008	5	5	5

Parcel Count by Property Class, 2010

Total . . . . . NA
Single family . . . . . NA
Multiple units . . . . . NA
Apartments . . . . . NA
Condos . . . . . NA
Vacant land . . . . . NA
Open space . . . . . NA
Commercial . . . . . NA
Industrial . . . . . NA
Misc. residential . . . . . NA
Other use . . . . . NA

Public Library

Griswold Memorial Library
PO Box 33
Colrain, MA 01340
(413)624-3619

Librarian . . . . . Betty Johnson

Library Statistics, FY 2008

Population served, 2007 1,840
Registered users 807
Circulation 18,475
Reference transactons 0
Total program attendance 7,565
per capita:
Holdings 6.94
Operating income $24.29
Internet Access
Internet computers available 3
Weekly users 30

Municipal Finance

Debt at year end 2008 . . . . . $204,510
Moody's rating, July 2009 . . . . . NA

Revenues, 2008

Total $3,118,651
From all taxes 2,370,969
Federal aid 98,913
State aid 380,944
From other governments 6,150
Charges for services 39,034
Licenses, permits & fees 22,152
Fines & forfeits 1,935
Interfund transfers 160,000
Misc/other/special assessments 19,277

Expenditures, 2008

Total $2,778,803
General government 183,713
Public safety 88,481
Other/fixed costs 166,452
Human services 26,255
Culture & recreation 37,771
Debt Service 58,118
Education 1,750,044
Public works 454,455
Intergovernmental 13,514

Taxation, 2010

Property type	Valuation	Rate
Total	NA	-
Residential	NA	NA
Open space	NA	NA
Commercial	NA	NA
Industrial	NA	NA
Personal	NA	NA

Average Single Family Tax Bill, 2010

Avg. assessed home value . . . . . NA
Avg. single fam. tax bill . . . . . NA
Hi-Lo ranking . . . . . NA

Police & Crime, 2008

Number of police officers . . . . . NA
Violent crimes . . . . . NA
Property crimes . . . . . NA

Local School District

(school data 2007-08, except as noted)

Colrain (non-op)
24 Ashfield Rd
Shelburne Falls, MA 01370
413-625-0192
Superintendent . . . . . Michael Buoniconti

Non-operating district.
Resident students are sent to the Other School Districts listed below.

Grade plan . . . . . NA
Total enrollment '09-10 . . . . . NA
Grade 12 enrollment, '09-10 . . . . . NA
Graduation rate . . . . . NA
Dropout rate . . . . . NA
Per-pupil expenditure . . . . . NA
Avg teacher salary . . . . . NA
Student/teacher ratio '08-09 . . . . . NA
Highly-qualified teachers, '08-09 . . . . . NA
Teachers licensed in assigned subject . . . . NA
Students per computer . . . . . NA

Other School Districts (see Appendix D for data)
Mohawk Trail Regional, Franklin County Vocational Tech

©2010 Information Publications, Inc. All rights reserved. Photocopying prohibited. For additional copies, contact the publisher at www.informationpublications.com or (877)544-INFO (4636)

See Introduction for an explanation of all data sources.

Demographics & Socio-Economic Characteristics

Population

1990	17,076
2000	16,993
Male	8,511
Female	8,482
2008	17,450
2010 (projected)††	15,650
2020 (projected)††	13,529

Race & Hispanic Origin, 2000

Race	
White	15,572
Black/African American	380
American Indian/Alaska Native	16
Asian	492
Hawaiian Native/Pacific Islander	4
Other Race	361
Two or more races	168
Hispanic origin	475

Age & Nativity, 2000

Under 5 years	979
18 years and over	12,730
21 years and over	12,406
65 years and over	2,810
85 years and over	441
Median Age	42.2
Native-born	15,594
Foreign-born	1,399

Age, 2020 (projected)††

Under 5 years	520
5 to 19 years	2,006
20 to 39 years	2,942
40 to 64 years	4,290
65 years and over	3,771

Educational Attainment, 2000

Population 25 years and over	12,052
High School graduates or higher	93.7%
Bachelor's degree or higher	66.1%
Graduate degree	34.7%

Income & Poverty, 1999

Per capita income	$51,477
Median household income	$95,897
Median family income	$115,839
Persons in poverty	612
H'holds receiving public assistance	38
H'holds receiving social security	1,567

Households, 2000

Total households	5,948
With persons under 18	2,263
With persons over 65	1,758
Family households	4,440
Single person households	1,308
Persons per household	2.6
Persons per family	3.1

Labor & Employment, 2000

Civilian labor force	7,618
Unemployment rate	2.0%
Civilian labor force, 2008†	7,701
Unemployment rate†	4.3%
Civilian labor force, 12/09†	7,633
Unemployment rate†	5.9%
Employed persons 16 years and over, by occupation:	
Managers & professionals	4,958
Service occupations	438
Sales & office occupations	1,597
Farming, fishing & forestry	8
Construction & maintenance	235
Production & transportation	231
Self-employed persons	976

Most demographic data is from the 2000 Decennial Census
† Massachusetts Department of Revenue
†† University of Massachusetts, MISER

General Information

Town of Concord
22 Monument Square
PO Box 535
Concord, MA 01742
978-318-3100

Elevation	130 ft.
Land area (square miles)	24.9
Water area (square miles)	1.0
Population density, 2008 (est)	700.8
Year incorporated	1635
Website	www.concordma.gov

Voters & Government Information

Government type	Open Town Meeting
Number of Selectmen	5
US Congressional District(s)	5

Registered Voters, October 2008

Total	12,312
Democrats	4,319
Republicans	1,860
Unaffiliated/other	6,079

Local Officials, 2010

Chair, Bd. of Sel.	Stanly Black
Manager	Christopher Whelan
Town Clerk	Anita Tekle
Finance Director	Anthony Logalbo
Tax Collector	Anthony Logalbo
Tax Assessor	Lynn Masson
Attorney	William Lahey
Public Works	Richard Reine
Building	John Minty
Comm Dev/Planning	Marcia Rasmussen
Police Chief	Leonard Wetherbee
Emerg/Fire Chief	Mark Cotreau

Housing & Construction

New Privately Owned Housing Units Authorized by Building Permit

	Single Family	Total Bldgs	Total Units
2006	20	23	28
2007	27	27	27
2008	14	14	14

Parcel Count by Property Class, 2010

Total	6,324
Single family	4,568
Multiple units	122
Apartments	26
Condos	733
Vacant land	339
Open space	0
Commercial	337
Industrial	37
Misc. residential	64
Other use	98

Public Library

Concord Free Public Library
129 Main Street
Concord, MA 01742
(978)318-3301

Library Director	Kerry Cronin

Library Statistics, FY 2008

Population served, 2007	16,840
Registered users	13,453
Circulation	422,170
Reference transactons	34,100
Total program attendance	254,684
per capita:	
Holdings	16.22
Operating income	$115.59
Internet Access	
Internet computers available	22
Weekly users	1,500

Municipal Finance

Debt at year end 2008	$55,091,156
Moody's rating, July 2009	Aaa

Revenues, 2008

Total	$72,580,986
From all taxes	61,627,749
Federal aid	0
State aid	4,400,172
From other governments	10,675
Charges for services	1,033,692
Licenses, permits & fees	898,517
Fines & forfeits	175,542
Interfund transfers	1,841,745
Misc/other/special assessments	1,296,447

Expenditures, 2008

Total	$63,845,706
General government	3,462,424
Public safety	6,838,374
Other/fixed costs	2,657,349
Human services	589,481
Culture & recreation	1,860,686
Debt Service	5,327,794
Education	38,910,138
Public works	3,339,531
Intergovernmental	365,050

Taxation, 2010

Property type	Valuation	Rate
Total	$5,026,552,229	-
Residential	4,554,723,932	13.09
Open space	0	0.00
Commercial	389,617,284	13.09
Industrial	31,051,000	13.09
Personal	51,160,013	13.09

Average Single Family Tax Bill, 2010

Avg. assessed home value	$835,697
Avg. single fam. tax bill	$10,939
Hi-Lo ranking	7/301

Police & Crime, 2008

Number of police officers	35
Violent crimes	13
Property crimes	273

Local School District

(school data 2007-08, except as noted)

Concord
120 Meriam Rd
Concord, MA 01742
978-318-1500

Superintendent	Diana Rigby
Grade plan	PK-8
Total enrollment '09-10	1,894
Grade 12 enrollment, '09-10	0
Graduation rate	NA
Dropout rate	NA
Per-pupil expenditure	$15,928
Avg teacher salary	$72,540
Student/teacher ratio '08-09	12.4 to 1
Highly-qualified teachers, '08-09	98.0%
Teachers licensed in assigned subject	99.3%
Students per computer	1.6

Massachusetts Competency Assessment System (MCAS), 2009 results

	English		Math	
	% Prof	CPI	% Prof	CPI
Gr 4	78%	92.7	70%	90.1
Gr 6	89%	95.1	64%	82
Gr 8	94%	97.5	68%	85.4
Gr 10	NA	NA	NA	NA

Other School Districts (see Appendix D for data)
Concord-Carlisle Regional, Minuteman Vocational Tech

©2010 Information Publications, Inc. All rights reserved. Photocopying prohibited. For additional copies, contact the publisher at www.informationpublications.com or (877)544-INFO (4636)

See Introduction for an explanation of all data sources.

Demographics & Socio-Economic Characteristics

Population

1990	1,529
2000	1,809
Male	895
Female	914
2008	1,896
2010 (projected)††	1,975
2020 (projected)††	2,240

Race & Hispanic Origin, 2000

Race	
White	1,786
Black/African American	3
American Indian/Alaska Native	4
Asian	9
Hawaiian Native/Pacific Islander	0
Other Race	2
Two or more races	5
Hispanic origin	17

Age & Nativity, 2000

Under 5 years	83
18 years and over	1,354
21 years and over	1,306
65 years and over	171
85 years and over	16
Median Age	40.5
Native-born	1,769
Foreign-born	40

Age, 2020 (projected)††

Under 5 years	121
5 to 19 years	316
20 to 39 years	594
40 to 64 years	756
65 years and over	453

Educational Attainment, 2000

Population 25 years and over	1,261
High School graduates or higher	94.2%
Bachelor's degree or higher	46.9%
Graduate degree	22.9%

Income & Poverty, 1999

Per capita income,	$25,605
Median household income	$56,094
Median family income	$62,917
Persons in poverty	63
H'holds receiving public assistance	6
H'holds receiving social security	141

Households, 2000

Total households	692
With persons under 18	267
With persons over 65	119
Family households	513
Single person households	130
Persons per household	2.6
Persons per family	3.0

Labor & Employment, 2000

Civilian labor force	1,109
Unemployment rate	4.1%
Civilian labor force, 2008†	1,150
Unemployment rate†	4.3%
Civilian labor force, 12/09†	1,148
Unemployment rate†	6.4%
Employed persons 16 years and over, by occupation:	
Managers & professionals	506
Service occupations	126
Sales & office occupations	218
Farming, fishing & forestry	3
Construction & maintenance	109
Production & transportation	101
Self-employed persons	189

Most demographic data is from the 2000 Decennial Census
† Massachusetts Department of Revenue
†† University of Massachusetts, MISER

General Information

Town of Conway
PO Box 240
Conway, MA 01341
413-369-4235

Elevation	558 ft.
Land area (square miles)	37.7
Water area (square miles)	0.1
Population density, 2008 (est)	50.3
Year incorporated	1767
Website	www.townofconway.com

Voters & Government Information

Government type	Open Town Meeting
Number of Selectmen	3
US Congressional District(s)	1

Registered Voters, October 2008

Total	1,551
Democrats	594
Republicans	164
Unaffiliated/other	771

Local Officials, 2010

Chair, Bd. of Sel.	John V. Lochhead
Administrator	Tom Spiro
Clerk	Virginia Knowlton
Treasurer	Elizabeth Braccia
Tax Collector	Elizabeth Braccia
Tax Assessor	Natelie Whitcomb
Attorney	John Fitzgibbon
Public Works	Robert Baker
Building	James Hawkins
Comm Dev/Planning	NA
Police Chief	Kenneth Ouimette
Fire Chief	Robert Baker

Housing & Construction

New Privately Owned Housing Units Authorized by Building Permit

	Single Family	Total Bldgs	Total Units
2006	5	6	7
2007	5	5	5
2008	4	4	4

Parcel Count by Property Class, 2010

Total	1,060
Single family	592
Multiple units	44
Apartments	0
Condos	0
Vacant land	232
Open space	0
Commercial	16
Industrial	10
Misc. residential	26
Other use	140

Public Library

Field Memorial Library
PO Box 189
Conway, MA 01341
(413)369-4646

Librarian	Stephen Thibault

Library Statistics, FY 2008

Population served, 2007	1,884
Registered users	886
Circulation	14,497
Reference transactons	475
Total program attendance	5,430
per capita:	
Holdings	7.97
Operating income	$35.68
Internet Access	
Internet computers available	1
Weekly users	10

Municipal Finance

Debt at year end 2008	$808,215
Moody's rating, July 2009	Baa1

Revenues, 2008

Total	$4,752,873
From all taxes	3,346,433
Federal aid	8,032
State aid	1,101,394
From other governments	3,825
Charges for services	30,739
Licenses, permits & fees	39,068
Fines & forfeits	0
Interfund transfers	54,214
Misc/other/special assessments	84,584

Expenditures, 2008

Total	$4,131,438
General government	239,640
Public safety	121,268
Other/fixed costs	449,547
Human services	134,325
Culture & recreation	7,991
Debt Service	227,841
Education	2,502,639
Public works	350,924
Intergovernmental	97,263

Taxation, 2010

Property type	Valuation	Rate
Total	$259,788,153	-
Residential	236,375,980	13.12
Open space	0	0.00
Commercial	5,642,832	13.12
Industrial	10,554,600	13.12
Personal	7,214,741	13.12

Average Single Family Tax Bill, 2010

Avg. assessed home value	$300,939
Avg. single fam. tax bill	$3,948
Hi-Lo ranking	139/301

Police & Crime, 2008

Number of police officers	NA
Violent crimes	NA
Property crimes	NA

Local School District

(school data 2007-08, except as noted)

Conway
219 Christian Ln RFD1
South Deerfield, MA 01373
413-665-1155

Superintendent	Regina Nash
Grade plan	PK-6
Total enrollment '09-10	175
Grade 12 enrollment, '09-10	0
Graduation rate	NA
Dropout rate	NA
Per-pupil expenditure	$12,704
Avg teacher salary	$56,493
Student/teacher ratio '08-09	12.4 to 1
Highly-qualified teachers, '08-09	100.0%
Teachers licensed in assigned subject	100.0%
Students per computer	2.9

Massachusetts Competency Assessment System (MCAS), 2009 results

	English		Math	
	% Prof	CPI	% Prof	CPI
Gr 4	94%	97.2	94%	98.6
Gr 6	83%	94.8	71%	92.7
Gr 8	NA	NA	NA	NA
Gr 10	NA	NA	NA	NA

Other School Districts (see Appendix D for data)

Frontier Regional, Franklin County Vocational Tech

©2010 Information Publications, Inc. All rights reserved. Photocopying prohibited. For additional copies, contact the publisher at www.informationpublications.com or (877)544-INFO (4636)

Demographics & Socio-Economic Characteristics

Population

1990 . . . 785
2000 . . . 978
Male . . . 495
Female . . . 483
2008 . . . 964
2010 (projected)†† . . . 1,111
2020 (projected)†† . . . 1,269

Race & Hispanic Origin, 2000

Race
White . . . 943
Black/African American . . . 6
American Indian/Alaska Native . . . 4
Asian . . . 3
Hawaiian Native/Pacific Islander . . . 0
Other Race . . . 5
Two or more races . . . 17
Hispanic origin . . . 32

Age & Nativity, 2000

Under 5 years . . . 36
18 years and over . . . 705
21 years and over . . . 669
65 years and over . . . 110
85 years and over . . . 10
Median Age . . . 38.1
Native-born . . . 978
Foreign-born . . . 26

Age, 2020 (projected)††

Under 5 years . . . 61
5 to 19 years . . . 313
20 to 39 years . . . 240
40 to 64 years . . . 393
65 years and over . . . 262

Educational Attainment, 2000

Population 25 years and over . . . 675
High School graduates or higher . . 94.4%
Bachelor's degree or higher . . . 40.3%
Graduate degree . . . 18.1%

Income & Poverty, 1999

Per capita income, . . . $21,553
Median household income . . . $42,250
Median family income . . . $48,750
Persons in poverty . . . 59
H'holds receiving public assistance . . . 14
H'holds receiving social security . . . 101

Households, 2000

Total households . . . 382
With persons under 18 . . . 98
With persons over 65 . . . 85
Family households . . . 239
Single person households . . . 107
Persons per household . . . 2.3
Persons per family . . . 2.8

Labor & Employment, 2000

Civilian labor force . . . 493
Unemployment rate . . . 1.4%
Civilian labor force, 2008† . . . 516
Unemployment rate† . . . 6.8%
Civilian labor force, 12/09† . . . 516
Unemployment rate† . . . 8.9%
Employed persons 16 years and over, by occupation:
Managers & professionals . . . 216
Service occupations . . . 63
Sales & office occupations . . . 95
Farming, fishing & forestry . . . 13
Construction & maintenance . . . 44
Production & transportation . . . 55
Self-employed persons . . . 113

Most demographic data is from the 2000 Decennial Census
† Massachusetts Department of Revenue
†† University of Massachusetts, MISER

General Information

Town of Cummington
33 Main St
Cummington, MA 01026
413-200-5011

Elevation . . . 1,000 ft.
Land area (square miles) . . . 23.1
Water area (square miles) . . . 0.0
Population density, 2008 (est) . . . 41.7
Year incorporated . . . 1779
Website . . . www.cummington-ma.gov

Voters & Government Information

Government type . . . Open Town Meeting
Number of Selectmen . . . 3
US Congressional District(s) . . . 1

Registered Voters, October 2008

Total . . . 661
Democrats . . . 161
Republicans . . . 57
Unaffiliated/other . . . 436

Local Officials, 2010

Chair, Bd. of Sel. . . . Russell Sears III
Manager/Admin . . . NA
Clerk . . . Susan Forgea
Treasurer . . . Susan Warriner
Tax Collector . . . Susan Warriner
Tax Assessor . . . Audrey Marcoux
Attorney . . . Michael Siddall
Public Works . . . NA
Building . . . James Cerone
Planning . . . Benjamin Forbes
Police Chief . . . Dennis Forgea
Fire Chief . . . Bernard Forgea

Housing & Construction

New Privately Owned Housing Units Authorized by Building Permit

	Single Family	Total Bldgs	Total Units
2006	2	2	2
2007	2	2	2
2008	2	2	2

Parcel Count by Property Class, 2010

Total . . . 753
Single family . . . 337
Multiple units . . . 18
Apartments . . . 2
Condos . . . 0
Vacant land . . . 249
Open space . . . 0
Commercial . . . 8
Industrial . . . 6
Misc. residential . . . 21
Other use . . . 112

Public Library

Bryant Free Library
455 Berkshire Trail
Cummington, MA 01026
(413)634-0109

Director . . . Mark DeMaranville

Library Statistics, FY 2008

Population served, 2007 . . . 974
Registered users . . . 631
Circulation . . . 4,089
Reference transactons . . . 208
Total program attendance . . . 1,805

per capita:

Holdings . . . 10.15
Operating income . . . $7.46

Internet Access

Internet computers available . . . 1
Weekly users . . . 3

Municipal Finance

Debt at year end 2008 . . . $249,071
Moody's rating, July 2009 . . . NA

Revenues, 2008

Total . . . $1,240,025
From all taxes . . . 907,890
Federal aid . . . 0
State aid . . . 186,393
From other governments . . . 10,170
Charges for services . . . 43,759
Licenses, permits & fees . . . 19,267
Fines & forfeits . . . 0
Interfund transfers . . . 0
Misc/other/special assessments . . . 36,273

Expenditures, 2008

Total . . . $1,841,695
General government . . . 116,335
Public safety . . . 62,392
Other/fixed costs . . . 70,712
Human services . . . 6,685
Culture & recreation . . . 24,650
Debt Service . . . 39,235
Education . . . 1,125,389
Public works . . . 388,681
Intergovernmental . . . 1,322

Taxation, 2010

Property type	Valuation	Rate
Total	$127,188,208	-
Residential	113,347,267	11.92
Open space	0	0.00
Commercial	7,407,661	11.92
Industrial	1,371,200	11.92
Personal	5,062,080	11.92

Average Single Family Tax Bill, 2010

Avg. assessed home value . . . $223,110
Avg. single fam. tax bill . . . $2,659
Hi-Lo ranking . . . 270/301

Police & Crime, 2008

Number of police officers . . . NA
Violent crimes . . . NA
Property crimes . . . NA

Local School District

(school data 2007-08, except as noted)

Cummington (non-op)
254 Hinsdale Road, Box 299
Dalton, MA 01227
413-684-0320

Superintendent . . . James Stankiewicz

Non-operating district.
Resident students are sent to the Other School Districts listed below.

Grade plan . . . NA
Total enrollment '09-10 . . . NA
Grade 12 enrollment, '09-10 . . . NA
Graduation rate . . . NA
Dropout rate . . . NA
Per-pupil expenditure . . . NA
Avg teacher salary . . . NA
Student/teacher ratio '08-09 . . . NA
Highly-qualified teachers, '08-09 . . . NA
Teachers licensed in assigned subject . . . NA
Students per computer . . . NA

Other School Districts (see Appendix D for data)
Central Berkshire Regional

©2010 Information Publications, Inc. All rights reserved. Photocopying prohibited. For additional copies, contact the publisher at www.informationpublications.com or (877)544-INFO (4636)

See Introduction for an explanation of all data sources.

Demographics & Socio-Economic Characteristics

Population

1990	7,155
2000	6,892
Male	3,293
Female	3,599
2008	6,593
2010 (projected)††	6,476
2020 (projected)††	6,056

Race & Hispanic Origin, 2000

Race	
White	6,739
Black/African American	35
American Indian/Alaska Native	8
Asian	49
Hawaiian Native/Pacific Islander	0
Other Race	30
Two or more races	31
Hispanic origin	70

Age & Nativity, 2000

Under 5 years	388
18 years and over	5,116
21 years and over	4,900
65 years and over	1,152
85 years and over	148
Median Age	40.1
Native-born	6,777
Foreign-born	115

Age, 2020 (projected)††

Under 5 years	290
5 to 19 years	964
20 to 39 years	1,352
40 to 64 years	2,001
65 years and over	1,449

Educational Attainment, 2000

Population 25 years and over	4,689
High School graduates or higher	90.0%
Bachelor's degree or higher	28.0%
Graduate degree	12.0%

Income & Poverty, 1999

Per capita income,	$23,634
Median household income	$47,891
Median family income	$59,717
Persons in poverty	185
H'holds receiving public assistance	17
H'holds receiving social security	866

Households, 2000

Total households	2,712
With persons under 18	927
With persons over 65	782
Family households	1,859
Single person households	730
Persons per household	2.5
Persons per family	3.0

Labor & Employment, 2000

Civilian labor force	3,529
Unemployment rate	2.0%
Civilian labor force, 2008†	3,730
Unemployment rate†	5.7%
Civilian labor force, 12/09†	3,735
Unemployment rate†	8.5%
Employed persons 16 years and over, by occupation:	
Managers & professionals	1,224
Service occupations	566
Sales & office occupations	958
Farming, fishing & forestry	0
Construction & maintenance	281
Production & transportation	431
Self-employed persons	163

Most demographic data is from the 2000 Decennial Census
† Massachusetts Department of Revenue
†† University of Massachusetts, MISER

General Information

Town of Dalton
462 Main St
Town Hall
Dalton, MA 01226
413-684-6111

Elevation	1,150 ft.
Land area (square miles)	21.8
Water area (square miles)	0.0
Population density, 2008 (est)	302.4
Year incorporated	1784
Website	www.dalton-ma.gov

Voters & Government Information

Government type	Open Town Meeting
Number of Select Board Member	5
US Congressional District(s)	1

Registered Voters, October 2008

Total	4,679
Democrats	1,407
Republicans	575
Unaffiliated/other	2,679

Local Officials, 2010

Chair, Bd. of Sel.	John F. Boyle
Town Manager	Kenneth E. Walto
Clerk	Barbara L. Suriner
Treasurer	Sharon M. Messenger
Tax Collector	Jane A. Carman
Tax Assessor	Michael J. Britton
Attorney	Kopelman & Paige
Public Works	David E. Laviolette
Building Inspector	Richard G. Haupt
Planning	Louisa M. Horth
Police Chief	John W. Bartels Jr
Emerg/Fire Chief	Richard D. Kardasen

Housing & Construction

New Privately Owned Housing Units Authorized by Building Permit

	Single Family	Total Bldgs	Total Units
2006	15	15	15
2007	12	12	12
2008	9	9	9

Parcel Count by Property Class, 2010

Total	2,692
Single family	1,948
Multiple units	190
Apartments	32
Condos	109
Vacant land	188
Open space	0
Commercial	67
Industrial	39
Misc. residential	15
Other use	104

Public Library

Dalton Free Public Library
462 Main Street
Dalton, MA 01226
(413)684-6112

Librarian .... Doris Lamica

Library Statistics, FY 2008

Population served, 2007	6,582
Registered users	2,170
Circulation	53,260
Reference transactons	0
Total program attendance	47,844
per capita:	
Holdings	7.26
Operating income	$29.39
Internet Access	
Internet computers available	5
Weekly users	69

Municipal Finance

Debt at year end 2008	$1,305,103
Moody's rating, July 2009	A2

Revenues, 2008

Total	$13,262,912
From all taxes	9,923,883
Federal aid	0
State aid	1,608,437
From other governments	28,992
Charges for services	805,967
Licenses, permits & fees	39,445
Fines & forfeits	33,619
Interfund transfers	24,405
Misc/other/special assessments	399,082

Expenditures, 2008

Total	$12,553,035
General government	752,891
Public safety	1,153,867
Other/fixed costs	1,208,601
Human services	144,970
Culture & recreation	268,039
Debt Service	456,387
Education	7,022,911
Public works	1,509,922
Intergovernmental	35,447

Taxation, 2010

Property type	Valuation	Rate
Total	$615,400,197	-
Residential	517,069,288	15.80
Open space	0	0.00
Commercial	26,603,639	15.80
Industrial	55,748,300	15.80
Personal	15,978,970	15.80

Average Single Family Tax Bill, 2010

Avg. assessed home value	$213,020
Avg. single fam. tax bill	$3,366
Hi-Lo ranking	190/301

Police & Crime, 2008

Number of police officers	11
Violent crimes	21
Property crimes	84

Local School District

(school data 2007-08, except as noted)

Dalton (non-op)
PO Box 299
Dalton, MA 01227
413-684-0320

Superintendent .... James Stankiewicz

Non-operating district.
Resident students are sent to the Other School Districts listed below.

Grade plan	NA
Total enrollment '09-10	NA
Grade 12 enrollment, '09-10	NA
Graduation rate	NA
Dropout rate	NA
Per-pupil expenditure	NA
Avg teacher salary	NA
Student/teacher ratio '08-09	NA
Highly-qualified teachers, '08-09	NA
Teachers licensed in assigned subject	NA
Students per computer	NA

Other School Districts (see Appendix D for data)
Central Berkshire Regional

©2010 Information Publications, Inc. All rights reserved. Photocopying prohibited. For additional copies, contact the publisher at www.informationpublications.com or (877)544-INFO (4636)

See Introduction for an explanation of all data sources.

Demographics & Socio-Economic Characteristics*

Population

1990	24,174
2000	25,212
Male	11,721
Female	13,491
2008	26,762
2010 (projected)††	24,754
2020 (projected)††	23,938

Race & Hispanic Origin, 2000

Race	
White	24,638
Black/African American	87
American Indian/Alaska Native	25
Asian	281
Hawaiian Native/Pacific Islander	4
Other Race	55
Two or more races	122
Hispanic origin	210

Age & Nativity, 2000

Under 5 years	1,391
18 years and over	19,370
21 years and over	18,607
65 years and over	4,331
85 years and over	618
Median Age	40.4
Native-born	24,095
Foreign-born	1,117

Age, 2020 (projected)††

Under 5 years	1,084
5 to 19 years	3,548
20 to 39 years	5,631
40 to 64 years	8,101
65 years and over	5,574

Educational Attainment, 2000

Population 25 years and over	17,777
High School graduates or higher	90.3%
Bachelor's degree or higher	33.0%
Graduate degree	10.8%

Income & Poverty, 1999

Per capita income,	$26,852
Median household income	$58,779
Median family income	$70,565
Persons in poverty	711
H'holds receiving public assistance	82
H'holds receiving social security	2,898

Households, 2000

Total households	9,555
With persons under 18	3,168
With persons over 65	2,744
Family households	6,562
Single person households	2,537
Persons per household	2.5
Persons per family	3.1

Labor & Employment, 2000

Civilian labor force	13,405
Unemployment rate	3.3%
Civilian labor force, 2008†	14,033
Unemployment rate†	6.4%
Civilian labor force, 12/09†	14,486
Unemployment rate†	8.6%
Employed persons 16 years and over, by occupation:	
Managers & professionals	5,356
Service occupations	1,885
Sales & office occupations	3,599
Farming, fishing & forestry	4
Construction & maintenance	1,123
Production & transportation	996
Self-employed persons	766

Most demographic data is from the 2000 Decennial Census
* see Appendix E for American Community Survey data
† Massachusetts Department of Revenue
†† University of Massachusetts, MISER

General Information

Town of Danvers
1 Sylvan St
Danvers, MA 01923
978-777-0001

Elevation	39 ft.
Land area (square miles)	13.3
Water area (square miles)	0.8
Population density, 2008 (est)	2,012.2
Year incorporated	1752
Website	danvers.govoffice.com

Voters & Government Information

Government type	Rep. Twn. Mtg. (125)
Number of Selectmen	5
US Congressional District(s)	6

Registered Voters, October 2008

Total	17,930
Democrats	4,270
Republicans	2,256
Unaffiliated/other	11,298

Local Officials, 2010

Chair, Bd. of Sel.	Gardner S. Trask III
Manager	Wayne Marquis
Clerk	Joseph Collins
Treasurer	Joseph Collins
Tax Collector	Joseph Collins
Tax Assessor	Marlene Locke
Attorney	Murphy, Hesse, Toomey & LeHane
Public Works	David Lane
Building	Richard Maloney
Planning	Karen Nelson
Police Chief	Neil Ouellette
Fire Chief	James Tutko

Housing & Construction

New Privately Owned Housing Units Authorized by Building Permit

	Single Family	Total Bldgs	Total Units
2006	95	117	500
2007	59	60	61
2008	11	11	11

Parcel Count by Property Class, 2010

Total	9,129
Single family	6,077
Multiple units	551
Apartments	90
Condos	1,377
Vacant land	219
Open space	0
Commercial	537
Industrial	149
Misc. residential	29
Other use	100

Public Library

Peabody Institute Library
15 Sylvan St.
Danvers, MA 01923
(978)774-0554

Director	Douglas Rendell

Library Statistics, FY 2008

Population served, 2007	26,736
Registered users	17,750
Circulation	223,518
Reference transactons	26,806
Total program attendance	0
per capita:	
Holdings	5.42
Operating income	$43.79
Internet Access	
Internet computers available	21
Weekly users	714

Municipal Finance

Debt at year end 2008	$35,643,052
Moody's rating, July 2009	Aa2

Revenues, 2008

Total	$73,771,788
From all taxes	56,661,531
Federal aid	0
State aid	9,493,251
From other governments	163,450
Charges for services	944,030
Licenses, permits & fees	2,122,624
Fines & forfeits	0
Interfund transfers	1,723,190
Misc/other/special assessments	1,331,856

Expenditures, 2008

Total	$70,751,311
General government	8,633,103
Public safety	9,748,644
Other/fixed costs	11,318,977
Human services	482,842
Culture & recreation	1,605,894
Debt Service	3,425,762
Education	29,470,348
Public works	5,201,762
Intergovernmental	842,879

Taxation, 2010

Property type	Valuation	Rate
Total	$4,096,958,924	-
Residential	3,050,092,607	12.22
Open space	0	0.00
Commercial	755,881,445	17.92
Industrial	199,003,850	17.92
Personal	91,981,022	17.92

Average Single Family Tax Bill, 2010

Avg. assessed home value	$374,517
Avg. single fam. tax bill	$4,577
Hi-Lo ranking	96/301

Police & Crime, 2008

Number of police officers	47
Violent crimes	52
Property crimes	945

Local School District

(school data 2007-08, except as noted)

Danvers
64 Cabot Road
Danvers, MA 01923
978-777-4539

Superintendent	Lisa Dana
Grade plan	PK-12
Total enrollment '09-10	3,617
Grade 12 enrollment, '09-10	260
Graduation rate	84.6%
Dropout rate	9.2%
Per-pupil expenditure	$12,061
Avg teacher salary	$64,693
Student/teacher ratio '08-09	13.3 to 1
Highly-qualified teachers, '08-09	97.8%
Teachers licensed in assigned subject	96.9%
Students per computer	4

Massachusetts Competency Assessment System (MCAS), 2009 results

	English		Math	
	% Prof	CPI	% Prof	CPI
Gr 4	64%	86.7	46%	81.4
Gr 6	72%	88.9	58%	81.3
Gr 8	85%	94.3	47%	74.7
Gr 10	87%	94.6	82%	91.8

Other School Districts (see Appendix D for data)
North Shore Vocational Tech

©2010 Information Publications, Inc. All rights reserved. Photocopying prohibited. For additional copies, contact the publisher at www.informationpublications.com or (877)544-INFO (4636)

See Introduction for an explanation of all data sources.

Demographics & Socio-Economic Characteristics

Population

1990	27,244
2000	30,666
Male	15,155
Female	15,511
2008	33,899
2010 (projected)††	32,434
2020 (projected)††	34,195

Race & Hispanic Origin, 2000

Race	
White	27,836
Black/African American	325
American Indian/Alaska Native	60
Asian	363
Hawaiian Native/Pacific Islander	10
Other Race	1,570
Two or more races	502
Hispanic origin	461

Age & Nativity, 2000

Under 5 years	1,370
18 years and over	24,404
21 years and over	21,900
65 years and over	4,763
85 years and over	601
Median Age	38.2
Native-born	26,594
Foreign-born	4,072

Age, 2020 (projected)††

Under 5 years	1,564
5 to 19 years	6,602
20 to 39 years	8,231
40 to 64 years	10,822
65 years and over	6,976

Educational Attainment, 2000

Population 25 years and over	20,091
High School graduates or higher	75.3%
Bachelor's degree or higher	24.6%
Graduate degree	10.2%

Income & Poverty, 1999

Per capita income,	$24,326
Median household income	$50,742
Median family income	$60,401
Persons in poverty	1,242
H'holds receiving public assistance	149
H'holds receiving social security	3,548

Households, 2000

Total households	10,555
With persons under 18	3,650
With persons over 65	3,374
Family households	7,817
Single person households	2,349
Persons per household	2.6
Persons per family	3.1

Labor & Employment, 2000

Civilian labor force	16,296
Unemployment rate	12.0%
Civilian labor force, 2008†	15,688
Unemployment rate†	7.9%
Civilian labor force, 12/09†	15,872
Unemployment rate†	11.0%
Employed persons 16 years and over, by occupation:	
Managers & professionals	4,457
Service occupations	2,082
Sales & office occupations	4,004
Farming, fishing & forestry	63
Construction & maintenance	1,673
Production & transportation	2,069
Self-employed persons	1,041

Most demographic data is from the 2000 Decennial Census
† Massachusetts Department of Revenue
†† University of Massachusetts, MISER

General Information

Town of Dartmouth
400 Slocum Rd
Dartmouth, MA 02747
508-910-1800

Elevation	43 ft.
Land area (square miles)	61.6
Water area (square miles)	36.3
Population density, 2008 (est)	550.3
Year incorporated	1664
Website	www.town.dartmouth.ma.us

Voters & Government Information

Government type	Rep. Town Meeting
Number of Selectmen	5
US Congressional District(s)	4

Registered Voters, October 2008

Total	22,993
Democrats	8,903
Republicans	2,243
Unaffiliated/other	11,709

Local Officials, 2010

Chair, Bd. of Sel.	Joe Muchaud
Exec Admin	David G. Cressman
Town Clerk	Lynn M. Medeiros
Finance	NA
Tax Collector	Deborah Piva
Tax Assessor	Paul Bergman
Attorney	Anthony C. Savastano
Public Works	David Hickox
Building	Joel Reed
Comm Dev/Planning	Donald Perry
Police Chief	Gary Soares (Actg)
Emerg Mgmt Dir	Ed Pimental

Housing & Construction

New Privately Owned Housing Units Authorized by Building Permit

	Single Family	Total Bldgs	Total Units
2006	68	68	68
2007	54	54	54
2008	28	29	30

Parcel Count by Property Class, 2010

Total	13,679
Single family	9,679
Multiple units	382
Apartments	38
Condos	330
Vacant land	2,094
Open space	0
Commercial	527
Industrial	117
Misc. residential	131
Other use	381

Public Library

Dartmouth Public Libraries
732 Dartmouth St.
Dartmouth, MA 02748
(508)999-0726

Director	Dolores Tansey (Int)

Library Statistics, FY 2008

Population served, 2007	31,241
Registered users	13,863
Circulation	268,279
Reference transactons	64,766
Total program attendance	0
per capita:	
Holdings	3.32
Operating income	$30.87
Internet Access	
Internet computers available	18
Weekly users	1,202

Municipal Finance

Debt at year end 2008	$74,623,442
Moody's rating, July 2009	A1

Revenues, 2008

Total	$66,641,803
From all taxes	44,043,575
Federal aid	333,022
State aid	15,604,401
From other governments	0
Charges for services	470,752
Licenses, permits & fees	959,190
Fines & forfeits	159,619
Interfund transfers	2,916,966
Misc/other/special assessments	1,077,139

Expenditures, 2008

Total	$57,747,759
General government	2,969,052
Public safety	6,051,669
Other/fixed costs	4,646,130
Human services	795,465
Culture & recreation	1,059,362
Debt Service	5,688,237
Education	33,311,217
Public works	2,427,494
Intergovernmental	691,555

Taxation, 2010

Property type	Valuation	Rate
Total	$5,292,640,560	-
Residential	4,431,609,385	7.85
Open space	0	0.00
Commercial	660,620,515	11.99
Industrial	86,940,200	11.99
Personal	113,470,460	11.92

Average Single Family Tax Bill, 2010

Avg. assessed home value	$377,859
Avg. single fam. tax bill	$2,966
Hi-Lo ranking	236/301

Police & Crime, 2008

Number of police officers	65
Violent crimes	74
Property crimes	1,069

Local School District

(school data 2007-08, except as noted)

Dartmouth
8 Bush Street
Dartmouth, MA 02748
508-997-3391

Superintendent	Stephen Russell
Grade plan	PK-12
Total enrollment '09-10	4,017
Grade 12 enrollment, '09-10	314
Graduation rate	88.9%
Dropout rate	6.3%
Per-pupil expenditure	$9,421
Avg teacher salary	$64,414
Student/teacher ratio '08-09	15.6 to 1
Highly-qualified teachers, '08-09	97.8%
Teachers licensed in assigned subject	98.1%
Students per computer	3.1

Massachusetts Competency Assessment System (MCAS), 2009 results

	English		Math	
	% Prof	CPI	% Prof	CPI
Gr 4	61%	85.1	50%	81.8
Gr 6	66%	87	65%	85.1
Gr 8	88%	95.5	45%	75.5
Gr 10	84%	93.9	77%	89.7

Other School Districts (see Appendix D for data)
Greater New Bedford Vocational Tech, Bristol County Agricultural

©2010 Information Publications, Inc. All rights reserved. Photocopying prohibited. For additional copies, contact the publisher at www.informationpublications.com or (877)544-INFO (4636)

See Introduction for an explanation of all data sources.

Demographics & Socio-Economic Characteristics*

Population

1990	23,782
2000	23,464
Male	11,329
Female	12,135
2008	24,630
2010 (projected)††	21,921
2020 (projected)††	20,090

Race & Hispanic Origin, 2000

Race	
White	22,175
Black/African American	362
American Indian/Alaska Native	37
Asian	439
Hawaiian Native/Pacific Islander	10
Other Race	188
Two or more races	253
Hispanic origin	567

Age & Nativity, 2000

Under 5 years	1,435
18 years and over	18,256
21 years and over	17,683
65 years and over	3,905
85 years and over	484
Median Age	39.6
Native-born	21,311
Foreign-born	2,199

Age, 2020 (projected)††

Under 5 years	951
5 to 19 years	3,218
20 to 39 years	4,748
40 to 64 years	7,142
65 years and over	4,031

Educational Attainment, 2000

Population 25 years and over	16,972
High School graduates or higher	87.9%
Bachelor's degree or higher	33.0%
Graduate degree	12.9%

Income & Poverty, 1999

Per capita income,	$28,199
Median household income	$61,699
Median family income	$72,330
Persons in poverty	1,037
H'holds receiving public assistance	87
H'holds receiving social security	2,773

Households, 2000

Total households	8,654
With persons under 18	2,795
With persons over 65	2,676
Family households	6,146
Single person households	2,065
Persons per household	2.6
Persons per family	3.1

Labor & Employment, 2000

Civilian labor force	12,088
Unemployment rate	2.7%
Civilian labor force, 2008†	12,523
Unemployment rate†	5.6%
Civilian labor force, 12/09†	12,696
Unemployment rate†	7.6%
Employed persons 16 years and over, by occupation:	
Managers & professionals	4,777
Service occupations	1,401
Sales & office occupations	3,487
Farming, fishing & forestry	30
Construction & maintenance	1,234
Production & transportation	830
Self-employed persons	708

Most demographic data is from the 2000 Decennial Census
* see Appendix E for American Community Survey data
† Massachusetts Department of Revenue
†† University of Massachusetts, MISER

General Information

Town of Dedham
26 Bryant St
Dedham, MA 02026
781-751-9100

Elevation	200 ft.
Land area (square miles)	10.5
Water area (square miles)	0.2
Population density, 2008 (est)	2,345.7
Year incorporated	1636
Website	www.dedham-ma.gov

Voters & Government Information

Government type	Rep. Town Meeting
Number of Selectmen	5
US Congressional District(s)	9

Registered Voters, October 2008

Total	16,522
Democrats	6,163
Republicans	1,680
Unaffiliated/other	8,580

Local Officials, 2010

Chair, Bd. of Sel.	Sarah MacDonald Jr
Town Administrator	William Keegan Jr
Town Clerk	Paul M. Munchbach
Finance Director	M. Murphy
Tax Collector	Robin Reyes
Tax Assessor	John Duffy
Attorney	Kopelman & Paige
Public Works	Joseph M. Flanagan
Building	Kenneth R. Cimeno
Comm Dev/Planning	Chris Ryan
Police Chief	Michael J. Weir
Emerg/Fire Chief	William Cullinane

Housing & Construction

New Privately Owned Housing Units Authorized by Building Permit

	Single Family	Total Bldgs	Total Units
2006	12	14	297
2007	60	63	136
2008	11	12	13

Parcel Count by Property Class, 2010

Total	8,576
Single family	6,550
Multiple units	579
Apartments	46
Condos	567
Vacant land	365
Open space	0
Commercial	298
Industrial	67
Misc. residential	29
Other use	75

Public Library

Dedham Public Library
43 Church St.
Dedham, MA 02026
(781)751-9280

Director	Patricia Lambert

Library Statistics, FY 2008

Population served, 2007	24,132
Registered users	9,901
Circulation	288,872
Reference transactons	91,000
Total program attendance	0
per capita:	
Holdings	4.73
Operating income	$45.68
Internet Access	
Internet computers available	13
Weekly users	425

Municipal Finance

Debt at year end 2008	$35,618,443
Moody's rating, July 2009	NA

Revenues, 2008

Total	$79,131,686
From all taxes	60,697,337
Federal aid	0
State aid	8,307,140
From other governments	123,037
Charges for services	532,582
Licenses, permits & fees	4,178,393
Fines & forfeits	0
Interfund transfers	1,614,749
Misc/other/special assessments	1,839,224

Expenditures, 2008

Total	$73,381,684
General government	4,020,140
Public safety	10,806,649
Other/fixed costs	11,198,890
Human services	580,280
Culture & recreation	2,160,083
Debt Service	5,589,475
Education	30,920,507
Public works	6,061,631
Intergovernmental	2,044,029

Taxation, 2010

Property type	Valuation	Rate
Total	$4,005,879,086	-
Residential	3,239,639,379	13.57
Open space	0	0.00
Commercial	607,473,987	28.87
Industrial	44,401,980	28.87
Personal	114,363,740	28.87

Average Single Family Tax Bill, 2010

Avg. assessed home value	$385,198
Avg. single fam. tax bill	$5,227
Hi-Lo ranking	67/301

Police & Crime, 2008

Number of police officers	60
Violent crimes	37
Property crimes	593

Local School District

(school data 2007-08, except as noted)
Dedham
100 Whiting Avenue
Dedham, MA 02026
781-326-5622

Superintendent	June Doe
Grade plan	PK-12
Total enrollment '09-10	2,910
Grade 12 enrollment, '09-10	161
Graduation rate	83.0%
Dropout rate	8.7%
Per-pupil expenditure	$13,893
Avg teacher salary	$67,269
Student/teacher ratio '08-09	12.8 to 1
Highly-qualified teachers, '08-09	98.5%
Teachers licensed in assigned subject	98.7%
Students per computer	2.3

Massachusetts Competency Assessment System (MCAS), 2009 results

	English		Math	
	% Prof	CPI	% Prof	CPI
Gr 4	62%	85.2	49%	80.5
Gr 6	74%	90.3	62%	83.8
Gr 8	83%	94.5	58%	81.4
Gr 10	81%	93.6	86%	94.8

Other School Districts (see Appendix D for data)
Blue Hills Vocational Tech, Norfolk County Agricultural

©2010 Information Publications, Inc. All rights reserved. Photocopying prohibited. For additional copies, contact the publisher at www.informationpublications.com or (877)544-INFO (4636)

See Introduction for an explanation of all data sources.

Demographics & Socio-Economic Characteristics

Population

1990	5,018
2000	4,750
Male	2,339
Female	2,411
2008	4,694
2010 (projected)††	4,620
2020 (projected)††	4,467

Race & Hispanic Origin, 2000

Race	
White	4,619
Black/African American	23
American Indian/Alaska Native	5
Asian	41
Hawaiian Native/Pacific Islander	0
Other Race	23
Two or more races	39
Hispanic origin	74

Age & Nativity, 2000

Under 5 years	239
18 years and over	3,683
21 years and over	3,566
65 years and over	654
85 years and over	69
Median Age	41.3
Native-born	4,499
Foreign-born	251

Age, 2020 (projected)††

Under 5 years	218
5 to 19 years	702
20 to 39 years	1,048
40 to 64 years	1,513
65 years and over	986

Educational Attainment, 2000

Population 25 years and over	3,420
High School graduates or higher	89.3%
Bachelor's degree or higher	35.4%
Graduate degree	15.4%

Income & Poverty, 1999

Per capita income,	$24,555
Median household income	$49,764
Median family income	$64,909
Persons in poverty	213
H'holds receiving public assistance	25
H'holds receiving social security	510

Households, 2000

Total households	1,965
With persons under 18	593
With persons over 65	470
Family households	1,310
Single person households	513
Persons per household	2.4
Persons per family	2.9

Labor & Employment, 2000

Civilian labor force	2,770
Unemployment rate	3.8%
Civilian labor force, 2008†	2,783
Unemployment rate†	5.5%
Civilian labor force, 12/09†	2,815
Unemployment rate†	8.4%
Employed persons 16 years and over, by occupation:	
Managers & professionals	1,103
Service occupations	308
Sales & office occupations	727
Farming, fishing & forestry	6
Construction & maintenance	235
Production & transportation	287
Self-employed persons	102

Most demographic data is from the 2000 Decennial Census
† Massachusetts Department of Revenue
†† University of Massachusetts, MISER

General Information

Town of Deerfield
8 Conway St
South Deerfield, MA 01373
413-665-1400

Elevation	150 ft.
Land area (square miles)	32.3
Water area (square miles)	1.1
Population density, 2008 (est)	145.3
Year incorporated	1673
Website	www.deerfieldma.us

Voters & Government Information

Government type	Open Town Meeting
Number of Selectmen	3
US Congressional District(s)	1

Registered Voters, October 2008

Total	3,756
Democrats	1,116
Republicans	408
Unaffiliated/other	2,190

Local Officials, 2010

Chair, Bd. of Sel.	Mark Gilmore
Manager/Admin	Bernard Kubiak
Town Clerk	Mary Stokarski
Treasurer	Mary Stokarski
Tax Collector	Mary Stokarski
Tax Assessor	Richard Stellman
Attorney	NA
Public Works	Harold Eaton Jr
Building	Bruce Austin
Comm Dev/Planning	NA
Police Chief	Michael Wozniakewicz
Fire Chief	G. Stokarski/C. Stokarski

Housing & Construction

New Privately Owned Housing Units Authorized by Building Permit

	Single Family	Total Bldgs	Total Units
2006	4	4	4
2007	6	6	6
2008	2	2	2

Parcel Count by Property Class, 2010

Total	2,998
Single family	1,403
Multiple units	110
Apartments	16
Condos	164
Vacant land	562
Open space	0
Commercial	174
Industrial	45
Misc. residential	12
Other use	512

Public Library

Tilton Library
75 North Main Street
South Deerfield, MA 01373
(413)665-4683

Director	Sara Woodbury

Library Statistics, FY 2008

Population served, 2007	4,731
Registered users	1,742
Circulation	39,799
Reference transactons	0
Total program attendance	0
per capita:	
Holdings	4.79
Operating income	$30.78
Internet Access	
Internet computers available	2
Weekly users	38

Municipal Finance

Debt at year end 2008	$1,630,000
Moody's rating, July 2009	A1

Revenues, 2008

Total	$11,475,369
From all taxes	8,698,820
Federal aid	19,915
State aid	1,965,879
From other governments	92,436
Charges for services	211,084
Licenses, permits & fees	133,956
Fines & forfeits	1,025
Interfund transfers	70,818
Misc/other/special assessments	140,718

Expenditures, 2008

Total	$10,631,386
General government	660,992
Public safety	647,368
Other/fixed costs	988,882
Human services	69,332
Culture & recreation	177,968
Debt Service	503,546
Education	6,495,557
Public works	924,877
Intergovernmental	162,864

Taxation, 2010

Property type	Valuation	Rate
Total	$685,685,457	-
Residential	520,553,312	11.86
Open space	0	0.00
Commercial	68,600,642	11.86
Industrial	80,724,833	11.86
Personal	15,806,670	11.86

Average Single Family Tax Bill, 2010

Avg. assessed home value	$283,854
Avg. single fam. tax bill	$3,367
Hi-Lo ranking	189/301

Police & Crime, 2008

Number of police officers	8
Violent crimes	NA
Property crimes	NA

Local School District

(school data 2007-08, except as noted)

Deerfield
219 Christian Ln RFD1
South Deerfield, MA 01373
413-665-1155

Superintendent	Regina Nash
Grade plan	PK-6
Total enrollment '09-10	490
Grade 12 enrollment, '09-10	0
Graduation rate	NA
Dropout rate	NA
Per-pupil expenditure	$11,153
Avg teacher salary	$53,851
Student/teacher ratio '08-09	13.0 to 1
Highly-qualified teachers, '08-09	100.0%
Teachers licensed in assigned subject	100.0%
Students per computer	4.2

Massachusetts Competency Assessment System (MCAS), 2009 results

	English		Math	
	% Prof	CPI	% Prof	CPI
Gr 4	74%	90.9	58%	84.4
Gr 6	62%	86.9	53%	76.6
Gr 8	NA	NA	NA	NA
Gr 10	NA	NA	NA	NA

Other School Districts (see Appendix D for data)
Frontier Regional, Franklin County Vocational Tech

©2010 Information Publications, Inc. All rights reserved. Photocopying prohibited. For additional copies, contact the publisher at www.informationpublications.com or (877)544-INFO (4636)

See Introduction for an explanation of all data sources.

Demographics & Socio-Economic Characteristics

Population

1990	13,864
2000	15,973
Male	7,367
Female	8,606
2008	15,349
2010 (projected)††	17,695
2020 (projected)††	19,811

Race & Hispanic Origin, 2000

Race	
White	15,173
Black/African American	308
American Indian/Alaska Native	59
Asian	59
Hawaiian Native/Pacific Islander	0
Other Race	140
Two or more races	234
Hispanic origin	264

Age & Nativity, 2000

Under 5 years	607
18 years and over	13,276
21 years and over	12,919
65 years and over	4,542
85 years and over	446
Median Age	49.4
Native-born	15,178
Foreign-born	795

Age, 2020 (projected)††

Under 5 years	686
5 to 19 years	2,043
20 to 39 years	3,008
40 to 64 years	6,605
65 years and over	7,469

Educational Attainment, 2000

Population 25 years and over	12,544
High School graduates or higher	91.5%
Bachelor's degree or higher	31.0%
Graduate degree	12.1%

Income & Poverty, 1999

Per capita income,	$25,428
Median household income	$41,598
Median family income	$50,478
Persons in poverty	1,119
H'holds receiving public assistance	181
H'holds receiving social security	3,398

Households, 2000

Total households	7,504
With persons under 18	1,532
With persons over 65	3,208
Family households	4,581
Single person households	2,499
Persons per household	2.1
Persons per family	2.7

Labor & Employment, 2000

Civilian labor force	7,309
Unemployment rate	4.9%
Civilian labor force, 2008†	7,827
Unemployment rate†	9.5%
Civilian labor force, 12/09†	7,700
Unemployment rate†	12.5%
Employed persons 16 years and over, by occupation:	
Managers & professionals	2,217
Service occupations	1,426
Sales & office occupations	2,082
Farming, fishing & forestry	25
Construction & maintenance	713
Production & transportation	487
Self-employed persons	914

Most demographic data is from the 2000 Decennial Census
† Massachusetts Department of Revenue
†† University of Massachusetts, MISER

General Information

Town of Dennis
PO Box 2060
South Dennis, MA 02660
508-394-8300

Elevation	24 ft.
Land area (square miles)	20.6
Water area (square miles)	1.6
Population density, 2008 (est)	745.1
Year incorporated	1793
Website	www.town.dennis.ma.us

Voters & Government Information

Government type	Open Town Meeting
Number of Selectmen	5
US Congressional District(s)	10

Registered Voters, October 2008

Total	11,873
Democrats	3,013
Republicans	1,930
Unaffiliated/other	6,858

Local Officials, 2010

Chair, Bd. of Sel.	Paul McCormick
Manager/Admin	Richard White
Clerk	Theresa Bunce
Finance Director	Rosemary Moriarty
Tax Collector	Rosemary Moriarty (Actg)
Tax Assessor	Scott Fahle
Attorney	Kopelman & Paige
Public Works	David Johansen
Building	Brian Florence
Planning	Daniel Fortier
Police Chief	Michael Whalen
Emerg/Fire Chief	Mark Dellner

Housing & Construction

New Privately Owned Housing Units Authorized by Building Permit

	Single Family	Total Bldgs	Total Units
2006	50	51	54
2007	56	56	56
2008	36	36	36

Parcel Count by Property Class, 2010

Total	16,582
Single family	11,516
Multiple units	385
Apartments	18
Condos	1,581
Vacant land	1,548
Open space	34
Commercial	995
Industrial	70
Misc. residential	285
Other use	150

Public Library

Dennis Public Library
5 Hall Street
Dennis Port, MA 02639
(508)760-6219

Library Director	Jessica Langlois

Library Statistics, FY 2008

Population served, 2007	3,095
Registered users	10,484
Circulation	66,446
Reference transactons	9,620
Total program attendance	105,000
per capita:	
Holdings	8.63
Operating income	$101.91
Internet Access	
Internet computers available	8
Weekly users	325

Municipal Finance

Debt at year end 2008	$16,911,212
Moody's rating, July 2009	A1

Revenues, 2008

Total	$44,172,196
From all taxes	31,764,050
Federal aid	0
State aid	1,054,124
From other governments	0
Charges for services	3,972,760
Licenses, permits & fees	3,273,875
Fines & forfeits	64,405
Interfund transfers	3,133,042
Misc/other/special assessments	454,970

Expenditures, 2008

Total	$41,555,305
General government	3,675,162
Public safety	8,540,721
Other/fixed costs	3,584,545
Human services	666,873
Culture & recreation	2,748,261
Debt Service	3,389,464
Education	14,677,528
Public works	3,460,026
Intergovernmental	653,223

Taxation, 2010

Property type	Valuation	Rate
Total	$6,311,438,960	-
Residential	5,841,481,823	5.27
Open space	596,600	5.27
Commercial	370,363,207	5.27
Industrial	23,827,200	5.27
Personal	75,170,130	5.27

Average Single Family Tax Bill, 2010

Avg. assessed home value	$423,534
Avg. single fam. tax bill	$2,232
Hi-Lo ranking	288/301

Police & Crime, 2008

Number of police officers	40
Violent crimes	79
Property crimes	518

Local School District

(school data 2007-08, except as noted)

Dennis (non-op)
296 Station Avenue
South Yarmouth, MA 02664
508-398-7605

Superintendent	Carol Woodbury

Non-operating district.
Resident students are sent to the Other School Districts listed below.

Grade plan	NA
Total enrollment '09-10	NA
Grade 12 enrollment, '09-10	NA
Graduation rate	NA
Dropout rate	NA
Per-pupil expenditure	NA
Avg teacher salary	NA
Student/teacher ratio '08-09	NA
Highly-qualified teachers, '08-09	NA
Teachers licensed in assigned subject	NA
Students per computer	NA

Other School Districts (see Appendix D for data)
Dennis-Yarmouth Regional, Cape Cod Vocational Tech

©2010 Information Publications, Inc. All rights reserved. Photocopying prohibited. For additional copies, contact the publisher at www.informationpublications.com or (877)544-INFO (4636)

See Introduction for an explanation of all data sources.

Demographics & Socio-Economic Characteristics

Population

1990	5,631
2000	6,175
Male	3,037
Female	3,138
2008	6,724
2010 (projected)††	6,261
2020 (projected)††	6,308

Race & Hispanic Origin, 2000

Race	
White	6,039
Black/African American	33
American Indian/Alaska Native	12
Asian	30
Hawaiian Native/Pacific Islander	1
Other Race	17
Two or more races	43
Hispanic origin	66

Age & Nativity, 2000

Under 5 years	357
18 years and over	4,561
21 years and over	4,364
65 years and over	792
85 years and over	95
Median Age	38.0
Native-born	5,857
Foreign-born	318

Age, 2020 (projected)††

Under 5 years	316
5 to 19 years	1,053
20 to 39 years	1,497
40 to 64 years	2,229
65 years and over	1,213

Educational Attainment, 2000

Population 25 years and over	4,127
High School graduates or higher	85.8%
Bachelor's degree or higher	25.1%
Graduate degree	8.3%

Income & Poverty, 1999

Per capita income,	$22,600
Median household income	$58,600
Median family income	$64,792
Persons in poverty	159
H'holds receiving public assistance	23
H'holds receiving social security	586

Households, 2000

Total households	2,201
With persons under 18	891
With persons over 65	555
Family households	1,718
Single person households	414
Persons per household	2.8
Persons per family	3.2

Labor & Employment, 2000

Civilian labor force	3,443
Unemployment rate	4.5%
Civilian labor force, 2008†	3,907
Unemployment rate†	6.7%
Civilian labor force, 12/09†	3,861
Unemployment rate†	8.8%
Employed persons 16 years and over, by occupation:	
Managers & professionals	1,141
Service occupations	512
Sales & office occupations	776
Farming, fishing & forestry	0
Construction & maintenance	435
Production & transportation	425
Self-employed persons	175

Most demographic data is from the 2000 Decennial Census
† Massachusetts Department of Revenue
†† University of Massachusetts, MISER

General Information

Town of Dighton
979 Somerset Ave
Dighton, MA 02715
508-669-5411

Elevation	48 ft.
Land area (square miles)	22.4
Water area (square miles)	0.5
Population density, 2008 (est)	300.2
Year incorporated	1712
Email	smedeiros@townofdighton.com

Voters & Government Information

Government type	Open Town Meeting
Number of Selectmen	3
US Congressional District(s)	4

Registered Voters, October 2008

Total	4,601
Democrats	1,271
Republicans	586
Unaffiliated/other	2,699

Local Officials, 2010

Chair, Bd. of Sel.	Nancy Goulart
Manager/Admin	NA
Clerk	Susana Medeiros
Finance Director	Mary Hathaway
Tax Collector	Mary Hathaway
Tax Assessor	Carol Beauregard
Attorney	NA
Public Works	Thomas Ferry
Building	Joseph Lawrence
Comm Dev/Planning	NA
Police Chief	Robert MacDonald
Emerg/Fire Chief	Antone Roderick Jr

Housing & Construction

New Privately Owned Housing Units Authorized by Building Permit

	Single Family	Total Bldgs	Total Units
2006	39	39	39
2007	26	27	28
2008	21	21	21

Parcel Count by Property Class, 2010

Total	NA
Single family	NA
Multiple units	NA
Apartments	NA
Condos	NA
Vacant land	NA
Open space	NA
Commercial	NA
Industrial	NA
Misc. residential	NA
Other use	NA

Public Library

Dighton Public Library
395 Main St.
Dighton, MA 02715
(508)669-6421

Director	Jocelyn Tavares

Library Statistics, FY 2008

Population served, 2007	6,748
Registered users	2,015
Circulation	43,745
Reference transactons	2,904
Total program attendance	13,144
per capita:	
Holdings	3.76
Operating income	$27.69
Internet Access	
Internet computers available	5
Weekly users	7

Municipal Finance

Debt at year end 2008	$625,022
Moody's rating, July 2009	NA

Revenues, 2008

Total	$13,355,112
From all taxes	11,234,320
Federal aid	0
State aid	934,299
From other governments	1,605
Charges for services	221,884
Licenses, permits & fees	116,509
Fines & forfeits	430
Interfund transfers	710,737
Misc/other/special assessments	67,664

Expenditures, 2008

Total	$12,436,580
General government	722,720
Public safety	1,740,475
Other/fixed costs	910,659
Human services	166,970
Culture & recreation	182,135
Debt Service	123,828
Education	7,475,851
Public works	972,524
Intergovernmental	116,418

Taxation, 2010

Property type	Valuation	Rate
Total	NA	-
Residential	NA	NA
Open space	NA	NA
Commercial	NA	NA
Industrial	NA	NA
Personal	NA	NA

Average Single Family Tax Bill, 2010

Avg. assessed home value	NA
Avg. single fam. tax bill	NA
Hi-Lo ranking	NA

Police & Crime, 2008

Number of police officers	10
Violent crimes	13
Property crimes	27

Local School District

(school data 2007-08, except as noted)

Dighton (non-op)
2700 Regional Road
North Dighton, MA 02764
508-252-5000

Superintendent	Kathleen Montagano

Non-operating district.
Resident students are sent to the Other School Districts listed below.

Grade plan	NA
Total enrollment '09-10	NA
Grade 12 enrollment, '09-10	NA
Graduation rate	NA
Dropout rate	NA
Per-pupil expenditure	NA
Avg teacher salary	NA
Student/teacher ratio '08-09	NA
Highly-qualified teachers, '08-09	NA
Teachers licensed in assigned subject	NA
Students per computer	NA

Other School Districts (see Appendix D for data)
Dighton-Rehoboth Regional, Bristol County Agricultural

©2010 Information Publications, Inc. All rights reserved. Photocopying prohibited. For additional copies, contact the publisher at www.informationpublications.com or (877)544-INFO (4636)

Demographics & Socio-Economic Characteristics

Population

1990	5,438
2000	7,045
Male	3,534
Female	3,511
2008	7,955
2010 (projected)††	9,370
2020 (projected)††	12,591

Race & Hispanic Origin, 2000

Race	
White	6,859
Black/African American	34
American Indian/Alaska Native	9
Asian	45
Hawaiian Native/Pacific Islander	5
Other Race	20
Two or more races	73
Hispanic origin	67

Age & Nativity, 2000

Under 5 years	581
18 years and over	4,960
21 years and over	4,730
65 years and over	543
85 years and over	66
Median Age	34.2
Native-born	6,798
Foreign-born	247

Age, 2020 (projected)††

Under 5 years	1,017
5 to 19 years	2,873
20 to 39 years	3,487
40 to 64 years	3,976
65 years and over	1,238

Educational Attainment, 2000

Population 25 years and over	4,520
High School graduates or higher	90.8%
Bachelor's degree or higher	24.0%
Graduate degree	6.6%

Income & Poverty, 1999

Per capita income,	$23,036
Median household income	$60,529
Median family income	$67,210
Persons in poverty	325
H'holds receiving public assistance	60
H'holds receiving social security	405

Households, 2000

Total households	2,476
With persons under 18	1,120
With persons over 65	408
Family households	1,937
Single person households	429
Persons per household	2.9
Persons per family	3.2

Labor & Employment, 2000

Civilian labor force	3,965
Unemployment rate	1.9%
Civilian labor force, 2008†	4,507
Unemployment rate†	5.9%
Civilian labor force, 12/09†	4,616
Unemployment rate†	8.9%
Employed persons 16 years and over, by occupation:	
Managers & professionals	1,236
Service occupations	504
Sales & office occupations	1,031
Farming, fishing & forestry	9
Construction & maintenance	517
Production & transportation	591
Self-employed persons	238

Most demographic data is from the 2000 Decennial Census
† Massachusetts Department of Revenue
†† University of Massachusetts, MISER

General Information

Town of Douglas
29 Depot St
Douglas, MA 01516
508-476-4000

Elevation	580 ft.
Land area (square miles)	36.4
Water area (square miles)	1.3
Population density, 2008 (est)	218.5
Year incorporated	1746
Website	www.douglasma.org

Voters & Government Information

Government type	Open Town Meeting
Number of Selectmen	5
US Congressional District(s)	2

Registered Voters, October 2008

Total	6,004
Democrats	1,229
Republicans	1,087
Unaffiliated/other	3,637

Local Officials, 2010

Chair, Bd. of Sel.	Michael D. Hughes
Administrator	Michael Guzinski
Clerk	Christine E.G. Furno
Finance Director	Todd G. Bari
Tax Collector	Pamela Carter
Tax Assessor	John Blatchford Jr
Attorney	Kopelman & Paige
Public Works	John J. Furno
Building	Adelle Reynolds
Planning	Richard VandenBerg
Police Chief	Patrick Foley
Emerg/Fire Chief	Donald Gonynor

Housing & Construction

New Privately Owned Housing Units Authorized by Building Permit

	Single Family	Total Bldgs	Total Units
2006	26	26	26
2007	27	28	29
2008	18	18	18

Parcel Count by Property Class, 2010

Total	3,996
Single family	2,566
Multiple units	114
Apartments	24
Condos	136
Vacant land	850
Open space	0
Commercial	49
Industrial	78
Misc. residential	49
Other use	130

Public Library

Simon Fairfield Public Library
PO Box 607
Douglas, MA 01516
(508)476-2695

Director . . . . Ann D. Carlsson

Library Statistics, FY 2008

Population served, 2007	7,924
Registered users	2,820
Circulation	35,301
Reference transactons	1,352
Total program attendance	0
per capita:	
Holdings	3.18
Operating income	$24.31
Internet Access	
Internet computers available	2
Weekly users	20

Municipal Finance

Debt at year end 2008	$21,979,377
Moody's rating, July 2009	A2

Revenues, 2008

Total	$21,614,707
From all taxes	11,264,001
Federal aid	84,863
State aid	9,017,459
From other governments	12,322
Charges for services	102,802
Licenses, permits & fees	105,582
Fines & forfeits	23,375
Interfund transfers	590,249
Misc/other/special assessments	207,027

Expenditures, 2008

Total	$21,687,134
General government	1,342,493
Public safety	2,054,476
Other/fixed costs	3,156,119
Human services	173,949
Culture & recreation	222,864
Debt Service	2,016,586
Education	11,409,092
Public works	988,447
Intergovernmental	316,559

Taxation, 2010

Property type	Valuation	Rate
Total	$939,198,196	-
Residential	884,961,996	11.77
Open space	0	0.00
Commercial	19,916,319	11.77
Industrial	17,906,800	11.77
Personal	16,413,081	11.77

Average Single Family Tax Bill, 2010

Avg. assessed home value	$283,419
Avg. single fam. tax bill	$3,336
Hi-Lo ranking	196/301

Police & Crime, 2008

Number of police officers	15
Violent crimes	12
Property crimes	34

Local School District

(school data 2007-08, except as noted)

Douglas
21 Davis Street
Douglas, MA 01516
508-476-7901

Superintendent	Nancy Lane
Grade plan	PK-12
Total enrollment '09-10	1,771
Grade 12 enrollment, '09-10	87
Graduation rate	85.8%
Dropout rate	6.2%
Per-pupil expenditure	$8,438
Avg teacher salary	$53,703
Student/teacher ratio '08-09	15.7 to 1
Highly-qualified teachers, '08-09	100.0%
Teachers licensed in assigned subject	100.0%
Students per computer	3.1

Massachusetts Competency Assessment System (MCAS), 2009 results

	English		Math	
	% Prof	CPI	% Prof	CPI
Gr 4	63%	85.1	47%	80.5
Gr 6	62%	84.7	43%	73.3
Gr 8	86%	94	48%	71.3
Gr 10	91%	96.6	73%	89.3

Other School Districts (see Appendix D for data)
Blackstone Valley Vocational Tech

©2010 Information Publications, Inc. All rights reserved. Photocopying prohibited. For additional copies, contact the publisher at www.informationpublications.com or (877)544-INFO (4636)

See Introduction for an explanation of all data sources.

Demographics & Socio-Economic Characteristics

Population

1990	4,915
2000	5,558
Male	2,711
Female	2,847
2008	5,644
2010 (projected)††	5,599
2020 (projected)††	5,130

Race & Hispanic Origin, 2000

Race	
White	5,290
Black/African American	23
American Indian/Alaska Native	2
Asian	202
Hawaiian Native/Pacific Islander	1
Other Race	3
Two or more races	37
Hispanic origin	66

Age & Nativity, 2000

Under 5 years	422
18 years and over	3,804
21 years and over	3,700
65 years and over	624
85 years and over	50
Median Age	40.2
Native-born	5,095
Foreign-born	463

Age, 2020 (projected)††

Under 5 years	310
5 to 19 years	1,167
20 to 39 years	993
40 to 64 years	1,793
65 years and over	867

Educational Attainment, 2000

Population 25 years and over	3,586
High School graduates or higher	98.9%
Bachelor's degree or higher	77.8%
Graduate degree	34.3%

Income & Poverty, 1999

Per capita income,	$64,899
Median household income	$141,818
Median family income	$157,168
Persons in poverty	165
H'holds receiving public assistance	4
H'holds receiving social security	429

Households, 2000

Total households	1,849
With persons under 18	865
With persons over 65	436
Family households	1,568
Single person households	236
Persons per household	3.0
Persons per family	3.3

Labor & Employment, 2000

Civilian labor force	2,736
Unemployment rate	1.2%
Civilian labor force, 2008†	2,848
Unemployment rate†	3.8%
Civilian labor force, 12/09†	2,797
Unemployment rate†	5.1%
Employed persons 16 years and over, by occupation:	
Managers & professionals	1,780
Service occupations	153
Sales & office occupations	616
Farming, fishing & forestry	9
Construction & maintenance	84
Production & transportation	60
Self-employed persons	413

Most demographic data is from the 2000 Decennial Census
† Massachusetts Department of Revenue
†† University of Massachusetts, MISER

General Information

Town of Dover
5 Springdale Ave
PO Box 250
Dover, MA 02030
508-785-0032

Elevation	149 ft.
Land area (square miles)	15.3
Water area (square miles)	0.1
Population density, 2008 (est)	368.9
Year incorporated	1784
Website	doverma.org

Voters & Government Information

Government type	Open Town Meeting
Number of Selectmen	3
US Congressional District(s)	4

Registered Voters, October 2008

Total	3,919
Democrats	757
Republicans	1,098
Unaffiliated/other	2,053

Local Officials, 2010

Chair, Bd. of Sel.	Joseph Melican
Manager	David Ramsay
Town Clerk	Barrie Clough
Finance Director	Gerard R. Lane Jr
Tax Collector	Gerard R. Lane Jr
Tax Assessor	William Baranick
Attorney	Anderson & Kreiger
Public Works	Craig Hughes
Building	Anthony Calo
Comm Dev/Planning	Sue Hall
Police Chief	Joseph Griffin
Fire Chief	John Hughes III

Housing & Construction

New Privately Owned Housing Units Authorized by Building Permit

	Single Family	Total Bldgs	Total Units
2006	11	11	11
2007	11	11	11
2008	13	13	13

Parcel Count by Property Class, 2010

Total	2,378
Single family	1,752
Multiple units	26
Apartments	1
Condos	81
Vacant land	345
Open space	0
Commercial	10
Industrial	20
Misc. residential	51
Other use	92

Public Library

Dover Town Library
56 Dedham St., PO Box 669
Dover, MA 02030
(508)785-8113

Director . . . Cheryl Abdullah

Library Statistics, FY 2008

Population served, 2007	5,627
Registered users	3,741
Circulation	157,763
Reference transactons	20,956
Total program attendance	102,595
per capita:	
Holdings	12.00
Operating income	$89.57
Internet Access	
Internet computers available	9
Weekly users	360

Municipal Finance

Debt at year end 2008	$17,045,402
Moody's rating, July 2009	Aaa

Revenues, 2008

Total	$27,050,711
From all taxes	23,910,789
Federal aid	0
State aid	1,576,979
From other governments	15,743
Charges for services	585,445
Licenses, permits & fees	263,368
Fines & forfeits	0
Interfund transfers	120,785
Misc/other/special assessments	288,801

Expenditures, 2008

Total	$25,682,901
General government	1,576,097
Public safety	2,228,703
Other/fixed costs	2,133,326
Human services	133,312
Culture & recreation	718,347
Debt Service	1,841,768
Education	15,282,820
Public works	1,768,528
Intergovernmental	0

Taxation, 2010

Property type	Valuation	Rate
Total	$2,291,620,903	-
Residential	2,233,599,387	10.92
Open space	0	0.00
Commercial	17,358,276	10.92
Industrial	7,372,900	10.92
Personal	33,290,340	10.92

Average Single Family Tax Bill, 2010

Avg. assessed home value	$1,071,801
Avg. single fam. tax bill	$11,704
Hi-Lo ranking	3/301

Police & Crime, 2008

Number of police officers	16
Violent crimes	4
Property crimes	21

Local School District

(school data 2007-08, except as noted)

Dover
157 Farm Street
Dover, MA 02030
508-785-0036

Superintendent	Valerie Spriggs
Grade plan	K-5
Total enrollment '09-10	572
Grade 12 enrollment, '09-10	0
Graduation rate	NA
Dropout rate	NA
Per-pupil expenditure	$15,084
Avg teacher salary	$77,088
Student/teacher ratio '08-09	14.2 to 1
Highly-qualified teachers, '08-09	100.0%
Teachers licensed in assigned subject	100.0%
Students per computer	2.7

Massachusetts Competency Assessment System (MCAS), 2009 results

	English		Math	
	% Prof	CPI	% Prof	CPI
Gr 4	69%	89.3	67%	87.8
Gr 6	NA	NA	NA	NA
Gr 8	NA	NA	NA	NA
Gr 10	NA	NA	NA	NA

Other School Districts (see Appendix D for data)
Dover-Sherborn Regional, Minuteman Vocational Tech, Norfolk County Agricultural

©2010 Information Publications, Inc. All rights reserved. Photocopying prohibited. For additional copies, contact the publisher at www.informationpublications.com or (877)544-INFO (4636)

See Introduction for an explanation of all data sources.

Demographics & Socio-Economic Characteristics

Population

1990 . . . 25,594
2000 . . . 28,562
Male . . . 14,007
Female . . . 14,555
2008 . . . 29,501
2010 (projected)†† . . . 31,664
2020 (projected)†† . . . 35,035

Race & Hispanic Origin, 2000

Race
White . . . 27,170
Black/African American . . . 222
American Indian/Alaska Native . . . 27
Asian . . . 737
Hawaiian Native/Pacific Islander . . . 9
Other Race . . . 123
Two or more races . . . 274
Hispanic origin . . . 443

Age & Nativity, 2000

Under 5 years . . . 1,935
18 years and over . . . 21,271
21 years and over . . . 20,380
65 years and over . . . 3,305
85 years and over . . . 229
Median Age . . . 36.1
Native-born . . . 27,009
Foreign-born . . . 1,553

Age, 2020 (projected)††

Under 5 years . . . 2,138
5 to 19 years . . . 6,326
20 to 39 years . . . 9,557
40 to 64 years . . . 11,710
65 years and over . . . 5,304

Educational Attainment, 2000

Population 25 years and over . . . 19,175
High School graduates or higher . . 83.9%
Bachelor's degree or higher . . . 20.1%
Graduate degree . . . 6.5%

Income & Poverty, 1999

Per capita income, . . . $23,750
Median household income . . . $57,676
Median family income . . . $65,633
Persons in poverty . . . 1,055
H'holds receiving public assistance . . . 75
H'holds receiving social security . . . 2,546

Households, 2000

Total households . . . 10,451
With persons under 18 . . . 4,059
With persons over 65 . . . 2,443
Family households . . . 7,736
Single person households . . . 2,185
Persons per household . . . 2.7
Persons per family . . . 3.2

Labor & Employment, 2000

Civilian labor force . . . 15,780
Unemployment rate . . . 3.1%
Civilian labor force, 2008† . . . 16,682
Unemployment rate† . . . 6.7%
Civilian labor force, 12/09† . . . 16,542
Unemployment rate† . . . 9.3%
Employed persons 16 years and over, by occupation:
Managers & professionals . . . 5,243
Service occupations . . . 1,878
Sales & office occupations . . . 4,416
Farming, fishing & forestry . . . 9
Construction & maintenance . . . 1,505
Production & transportation . . . 2,233
Self-employed persons . . . 784

Most demographic data is from the 2000 Decennial Census
† Massachusetts Department of Revenue
†† University of Massachusetts, MISER

General Information

Town of Dracut
62 Arlington St
Dracut, MA 01826
978-452-1908

Elevation . . . 160 ft.
Land area (square miles) . . . 20.9
Water area (square miles) . . . 0.5
Population density, 2008 (est) . . . 1,411.5
Year incorporated . . . 1702
Website . . . dracut-ma.us

Voters & Government Information

Government type . . . Open Town Meeting
Number of Selectmen . . . 5
US Congressional District(s) . . . 5

Registered Voters, October 2008

Total . . . 20,138
Democrats . . . 6,746
Republicans . . . 2,252
Unaffiliated/other . . . 11,015

Local Officials, 2010

Chair, Bd. of Sel. . . . George Malliaros
Manager . . . Dennis Piendak
Clerk . . . Kathleen Graham
Finance Director . . . Ann Vandal
Tax Collector . . . Debra Barton
Tax Assessor . . . Kathleen Roark
Attorney . . . James A. Hall
Public Works Supt . . . Michael Buxton
Building Inspector . . . Daniel McLaughlin
Town Planner . . . Glen Edwards
Police Chief . . . Kevin Richardson
Fire Chief . . . Leo Gaudette

Housing & Construction

New Privately Owned Housing Units Authorized by Building Permit

	Single Family	Total Bldgs	Total Units
2006	51	51	51
2007	65	66	68
2008	33	33	33

Parcel Count by Property Class, 2010

Total . . . 11,522
Single family . . . 7,359
Multiple units . . . 324
Apartments . . . 47
Condos . . . 1,997
Vacant land . . . 1,156
Open space . . . 0
Commercial . . . 391
Industrial . . . 68
Misc. residential . . . 22
Other use . . . 158

Public Library

Moses Greeley Parker Memorial Library
28 Arlington St.
Dracut, MA 01826
(978)454-5474

Director . . . Dana Mastroianni

Library Statistics, FY 2008

Population served, 2007 . . . 29,498
Registered users . . . 20,086
Circulation . . . 239,107
Reference transactons . . . 16,705
Total program attendance . . . 153,779
per capita:
Holdings . . . 3.21
Operating income . . . $25.79
Internet Access
Internet computers available . . . 20
Weekly users . . . 450

Municipal Finance

Debt at year end 2008 . . . $65,338,442
Moody's rating, July 2009 . . . A2

Revenues, 2008

Total . . . $60,070,475
From all taxes . . . 35,724,580
Federal aid . . . 0
State aid . . . 22,959,287
From other governments . . . 54,953
Charges for services . . . 463,482
Licenses, permits & fees . . . 327,294
Fines & forfeits . . . 25
Interfund transfers . . . 473,746
Misc/other/special assessments . . . 33,554

Expenditures, 2008

Total . . . $53,011,123
General government . . . 2,088,303
Public safety . . . 6,696,950
Other/fixed costs . . . 3,305,863
Human services . . . 644,352
Culture & recreation . . . 921,687
Debt Service . . . 4,555,474
Education . . . 29,789,870
Public works . . . 5,008,624
Intergovernmental . . . 0

Taxation, 2010

Property type	Valuation	Rate
Total	$2,952,877,574	-
Residential	2,674,178,755	11.81
Open space	0	0.00
Commercial	146,432,445	11.81
Industrial	50,201,200	11.81
Personal	82,065,174	11.81

Average Single Family Tax Bill, 2010

Avg. assessed home value . . . $284,026
Avg. single fam. tax bill . . . $3,354
Hi-Lo ranking . . . 193/301

Police & Crime, 2008

Number of police officers . . . 43
Violent crimes . . . 32
Property crimes . . . 280

Local School District

(school data 2007-08, except as noted)

Dracut
2063 Lakeview Avenue
Dracut, MA 01826
978-957-2660

Superintendent . . . Elaine Espindle
Grade plan . . . PK-12
Total enrollment '09-10 . . . 4,107
Grade 12 enrollment, '09-10 . . . 291
Graduation rate . . . 82.6%
Dropout rate . . . 11.3%
Per-pupil expenditure . . . $9,231
Avg teacher salary . . . $61,290
Student/teacher ratio '08-09 . . . 16.8 to 1
Highly-qualified teachers, '08-09 . . . 99.2%
Teachers licensed in assigned subject . 100.0%
Students per computer . . . 13.8

Massachusetts Competency Assessment System (MCAS), 2009 results

	English		Math	
	% Prof	CPI	% Prof	CPI
Gr 4	55%	80.6	35%	73.3
Gr 6	70%	89.1	56%	80.1
Gr 8	66%	86	35%	65
Gr 10	85%	94.1	82%	91.6

Other School Districts (see Appendix D for data)
Greater Lowell Vocational Tech

©2010 Information Publications, Inc. All rights reserved. Photocopying prohibited. For additional copies, contact the publisher at www.informationpublications.com or (877)544-INFO (4636)

See Introduction for an explanation of all data sources.

Demographics & Socio-Economic Characteristics

Population

1990 . . . 9,540
2000 . . . 10,036
Male . . . 4,973
Female . . . 5,063
2008 . . . 11,073
2010 (projected)†† . . . 10,387
2020 (projected)†† . . . 10,824

Race & Hispanic Origin, 2000

Race
White . . . 9,718
Black/African American . . . 49
American Indian/Alaska Native . . . 23
Asian . . . 74
Hawaiian Native/Pacific Islander . . . 0
Other Race . . . 75
Two or more races . . . 97
Hispanic origin . . . 202

Age & Nativity, 2000

Under 5 years . . . 588
18 years and over . . . 7,556
21 years and over . . . 7,005
65 years and over . . . 1,284
85 years and over . . . 137
Median Age . . . 35.9
Native-born . . . 9,480
Foreign-born . . . 556

Age, 2020 (projected)††

Under 5 years . . . 606
5 to 19 years . . . 2,048
20 to 39 years . . . 2,893
40 to 64 years . . . 3,540
65 years and over . . . 1,737

Educational Attainment, 2000

Population 25 years and over . . . 6,489
High School graduates or higher . . . 83.4%
Bachelor's degree or higher . . . 21.0%
Graduate degree . . . 7.4%

Income & Poverty, 1999

Per capita income, . . . $21,546
Median household income . . . $48,602
Median family income . . . $59,309
Persons in poverty . . . 537
H'holds receiving public assistance . . . 108
H'holds receiving social security . . . 1,049

Households, 2000

Total households . . . 3,737
With persons under 18 . . . 1,374
With persons over 65 . . . 948
Family households . . . 2,669
Single person households . . . 880
Persons per household . . . 2.6
Persons per family . . . 3.0

Labor & Employment, 2000

Civilian labor force . . . 5,507
Unemployment rate . . . 4.6%
Civilian labor force, 2008† . . . 5,908
Unemployment rate† . . . 7.3%
Civilian labor force, 12/09† . . . 6,039
Unemployment rate† . . . 10.2%
Employed persons 16 years and over, by occupation:
Managers & professionals . . . 1,676
Service occupations . . . 808
Sales & office occupations . . . 1,322
Farming, fishing & forestry . . . 13
Construction & maintenance . . . 502
Production & transportation . . . 931
Self-employed persons . . . 245

Most demographic data is from the 2000 Decennial Census
† Massachusetts Department of Revenue
†† University of Massachusetts, MISER

General Information

Town of Dudley
Dudley Municipal Complex
71 W Main St
Dudley, MA 01571
508-949-8000

Elevation . . . 650 ft.
Land area (square miles) . . . 21.1
Water area (square miles) . . . 1.0
Population density, 2008 (est) . . . 524.8
Year incorporated . . . 1732
Website . . . www.dudleyma.gov

Voters & Government Information

Government type . . . Open Town Meeting
Number of Selectmen . . . 5
US Congressional District(s) . . . 2

Registered Voters, October 2008

Total . . . 7,212
Democrats . . . 2,143
Republicans . . . 849
Unaffiliated/other . . . 4,152

Local Officials, 2010

Chair, Bd. of Sel. . . . Paul M. Joseph
Town Administrator . . . Peter Jankowski
Clerk . . . Ora E. Finn
Treasurer . . . Richard A. Carmignani Jr
Tax Collector . . . Denise Zoschak
Tax Assessor . . . Conrad Allen
Attorney . . . Brackett & Lucas
Public Works . . . Daniel Gion
Building . . . Daniel Heney
Planning . . . Nancy Runkle
Police Chief . . . Stephen Wojnar
Emerg/Fire Chief . . . Jeffrey E. Phelps

Housing & Construction

New Privately Owned Housing Units Authorized by Building Permit

	Single Family	Total Bldgs	Total Units
2006	32	34	36
2007	34	34	34
2008	20	21	22

Parcel Count by Property Class, 2010

Total . . . 4,915
Single family . . . 3,090
Multiple units . . . 242
Apartments . . . 93
Condos . . . 129
Vacant land . . . 1,069
Open space . . . 0
Commercial . . . 87
Industrial . . . 45
Misc. residential . . . 18
Other use . . . 142

Public Library

Pearle L. Crawford Memorial Library
1 Village St.
Dudley, MA 01571
(508)949-8021

Director . . . Matthew Hall

Library Statistics, FY 2008

Population served, 2007 . . . 10,780
Registered users . . . 5,578
Circulation . . . 44,285
Reference transactons . . . 0
Total program attendance . . . 56,492

per capita:

Holdings . . . 2.40
Operating income . . . $17.32

Internet Access

Internet computers available . . . 5
Weekly users . . . 72

Municipal Finance

Debt at year end 2008 . . . $8,377,634
Moody's rating, July 2009 . . . A2

Revenues, 2008

Total . . . $12,543,826
From all taxes . . . 9,316,156
Federal aid . . . 18,286
State aid . . . 2,051,865
From other governments . . . 37,146
Charges for services . . . 341,949
Licenses, permits & fees . . . 399,649
Fines & forfeits . . . 0
Interfund transfers . . . 138,377
Misc/other/special assessments . . . 120,199

Expenditures, 2008

Total . . . $11,324,584
General government . . . 868,532
Public safety . . . 1,962,140
Other/fixed costs . . . 1,089,618
Human services . . . 74,384
Culture & recreation . . . 171,612
Debt Service . . . 723,622
Education . . . 5,488,275
Public works . . . 801,973
Intergovernmental . . . 33,015

Taxation, 2010

Property type	Valuation	Rate
Total	$907,845,917	-
Residential	842,226,207	9.57
Open space	0	0.00
Commercial	31,451,893	9.57
Industrial	21,113,600	9.57
Personal	13,054,217	9.57

Average Single Family Tax Bill, 2010

Avg. assessed home value . . . $226,508
Avg. single fam. tax bill . . . $2,168
Hi-Lo ranking . . . 291/301

Police & Crime, 2008

Number of police officers . . . 11
Violent crimes . . . 23
Property crimes . . . 52

Local School District

(school data 2007-08, except as noted)

Dudley (non-op)
68 Dudley Oxford Road
Dudley, MA 01571
508-943-6888

Superintendent . . . Sean Gilrein

Non-operating district.
Resident students are sent to the Other School Districts listed below.

Grade plan . . . NA
Total enrollment '09-10 . . . NA
Grade 12 enrollment, '09-10 . . . NA
Graduation rate . . . NA
Dropout rate . . . NA
Per-pupil expenditure . . . NA
Avg teacher salary . . . NA
Student/teacher ratio '08-09 . . . NA
Highly-qualified teachers, '08-09 . . . NA
Teachers licensed in assigned subject . . . NA
Students per computer . . . NA

Other School Districts (see Appendix D for data)

Dudley-Charlton Regional, Southern Worcester County Vocational Tech

©2010 Information Publications, Inc. All rights reserved. Photocopying prohibited. For additional copies, contact the publisher at www.informationpublications.com or (877)544-INFO (4636)

See Introduction for an explanation of all data sources.

Demographics & Socio-Economic Characteristics

Population

1990	2,236
2000	2,829
Male	1,398
Female	1,431
2008	3,323
2010 (projected)††	3,348
2020 (projected)††	3,770

Race & Hispanic Origin, 2000

Race	
White	2,758
Black/African American	3
American Indian/Alaska Native	1
Asian	43
Hawaiian Native/Pacific Islander	0
Other Race	2
Two or more races	22
Hispanic origin	15

Age & Nativity, 2000

Under 5 years	236
18 years and over	1,948
21 years and over	1,883
65 years and over	193
85 years and over	14
Median Age	37.3
Native-born	2,732
Foreign-born	97

Age, 2020 (projected)††

Under 5 years	241
5 to 19 years	813
20 to 39 years	891
40 to 64 years	1,295
65 years and over	530

Educational Attainment, 2000

Population 25 years and over	1,837
High School graduates or higher	94.2%
Bachelor's degree or higher	44.2%
Graduate degree	18.9%

Income & Poverty, 1999

Per capita income,	$30,608
Median household income	$86,633
Median family income	$92,270
Persons in poverty	55
H'holds receiving public assistance	4
H'holds receiving social security	152

Households, 2000

Total households	923
With persons under 18	458
With persons over 65	145
Family households	798
Single person households	95
Persons per household	3.1
Persons per family	3.3

Labor & Employment, 2000

Civilian labor force	1,598
Unemployment rate	1.9%
Civilian labor force, 2008†	1,864
Unemployment rate†	5.2%
Civilian labor force, 12/09†	1,837
Unemployment rate†	5.7%
Employed persons 16 years and over, by occupation:	
Managers & professionals	843
Service occupations	132
Sales & office occupations	343
Farming, fishing & forestry	4
Construction & maintenance	131
Production & transportation	115
Self-employed persons	120

Most demographic data is from the 2000 Decennial Census
† Massachusetts Department of Revenue
†† University of Massachusetts, MISER

General Information

Town of Dunstable
511 Main St
Dunstable, MA 01827
978-649-4514

Elevation	225 ft.
Land area (square miles)	16.5
Water area (square miles)	0.2
Population density, 2008 (est)	201.4
Year incorporated	1673
Website	www.dunstable-ma.gov

Voters & Government Information

Government type	Open Town Meeting
Number of Selectmen	3
US Congressional District(s)	5

Registered Voters, October 2008

Total	2,172
Democrats	421
Republicans	368
Unaffiliated/other	1,371

Local Officials, 2010

Chair, Bd. of Sel.	Wes Goss
Manager/Admin	NA
Clerk	Carol A. Skerrett
Finance Director	Ronald Mikol
Tax Collector	Bonnie Ricardelli
Tax Assessor	Robert Ricardelli
Attorney	Richard Larkin
Public Works	Michael Martin
Building	Dana Barnes
Planning	Brett A. Rock
Police Chief	James Downes III
Emerg/Fire Chief	Charles Rich

Housing & Construction

New Privately Owned Housing Units Authorized by Building Permit

	Single Family	Total Bldgs	Total Units
2006	24	24	24
2007	18	18	18
2008	12	12	12

Parcel Count by Property Class, 2010

Total	1,371
Single family	1,018
Multiple units	10
Apartments	0
Condos	0
Vacant land	157
Open space	0
Commercial	6
Industrial	10
Misc. residential	0
Other use	170

Public Library

Dunstable Free Public Library
588 Main St., PO Box 219
Dunstable, MA 01827
(978)649-7830

Director	Mary Beth Pallis

Library Statistics, FY 2008

Population served, 2007	3,290
Registered users	1,826
Circulation	32,989
Reference transactons	832
Total program attendance	11,039
per capita:	
Holdings	11.58
Operating income	$52.26
Internet Access	
Internet computers available	3
Weekly users	20

Municipal Finance

Debt at year end 2008	$3,077,607
Moody's rating, July 2009	Baa1

Revenues, 2008

Total	$7,311,920
From all taxes	6,665,675
Federal aid	1,997
State aid	321,845
From other governments	16,750
Charges for services	34,446
Licenses, permits & fees	41,713
Fines & forfeits	0
Interfund transfers	188,884
Misc/other/special assessments	20,305

Expenditures, 2008

Total	$7,195,424
General government	329,532
Public safety	794,910
Other/fixed costs	292,961
Human services	25,157
Culture & recreation	151,792
Debt Service	469,663
Education	4,543,508
Public works	571,017
Intergovernmental	2,314

Taxation, 2010

Property type	Valuation	Rate
Total	$493,855,899	-
Residential	472,882,340	13.79
Open space	0	0.00
Commercial	5,011,659	13.79
Industrial	4,072,800	13.79
Personal	11,889,100	13.79

Average Single Family Tax Bill, 2010

Avg. assessed home value	$416,275
Avg. single fam. tax bill	$5,740
Hi-Lo ranking	53/301

Police & Crime, 2008

Number of police officers	7
Violent crimes	NA
Property crimes	NA

Local School District

(school data 2007-08, except as noted)

Dunstable (non-op)
P O Box 729
Groton, MA 01450
978-448-5505

Superintendent	Alan Genovese

Non-operating district.
Resident students are sent to the Other School Districts listed below.

Grade plan	NA
Total enrollment '09-10	NA
Grade 12 enrollment, '09-10	NA
Graduation rate	NA
Dropout rate	NA
Per-pupil expenditure	NA
Avg teacher salary	NA
Student/teacher ratio '08-09	NA
Highly-qualified teachers, '08-09	NA
Teachers licensed in assigned subject	NA
Students per computer	NA

Other School Districts (see Appendix D for data)
Groton-Dunstable Regional, Greater Lowell Vocational Tech

©2010 Information Publications, Inc. All rights reserved. Photocopying prohibited. For additional copies, contact the publisher at www.informationpublications.com or (877)544-INFO (4636)

See Introduction for an explanation of all data sources.

Demographics & Socio-Economic Characteristics

Population

1990 . . . 13,895
2000 . . . 14,248
Male . . . 6,840
Female . . . 7,408
2008 . . . 14,496
2010 (projected)†† . . . 14,473
2020 (projected)†† . . . 14,243

Race & Hispanic Origin, 2000

Race
White . . . 13,934
Black/African American . . . 91
American Indian/Alaska Native . . . 14
Asian . . . 92
Hawaiian Native/Pacific Islander . . . 1
Other Race . . . 37
Two or more races . . . 79
Hispanic origin . . . 102

Age & Nativity, 2000

Under 5 years . . . 1,001
18 years and over . . . 10,036
21 years and over . . . 9,671
65 years and over . . . 1,707
85 years and over . . . 311
Median Age . . . 40.3
Native-born . . . 13,790
Foreign-born . . . 458

Age, 2020 (projected)††

Under 5 years . . . 847
5 to 19 years . . . 2,956
20 to 39 years . . . 2,538
40 to 64 years . . . 4,368
65 years and over . . . 3,534

Educational Attainment, 2000

Population 25 years and over . . . 9,365
High School graduates or higher . . . 97.2%
Bachelor's degree or higher . . . 59.6%
Graduate degree . . . 22.6%

Income & Poverty, 1999

Per capita income, . . . $40,242
Median household income . . . $97,124
Median family income . . . $106,245
Persons in poverty . . . 322
H'holds receiving public assistance . . . 42
H'holds receiving social security . . . 1,212

Households, 2000

Total households . . . 4,946
With persons under 18 . . . 2,128
With persons over 65 . . . 1,190
Family households . . . 3,943
Single person households . . . 876
Persons per household . . . 2.9
Persons per family . . . 3.3

Labor & Employment, 2000

Civilian labor force . . . 6,924
Unemployment rate . . . 1.6%
Civilian labor force, 2008† . . . 7,321
Unemployment rate† . . . 4.8%
Civilian labor force, 12/09† . . . 7,231
Unemployment rate† . . . 7.3%
Employed persons 16 years and over, by occupation:
Managers & professionals . . . 3,823
Service occupations . . . 455
Sales & office occupations . . . 2,028
Farming, fishing & forestry . . . 26
Construction & maintenance . . . 279
Production & transportation . . . 202
Self-employed persons . . . 749

Most demographic data is from the 2000 Decennial Census
† Massachusetts Department of Revenue
†† University of Massachusetts, MISER

General Information

Town of Duxbury
878 Tremont St
Duxbury, MA 02332
781-934-1100

Elevation . . . 36 ft.
Land area (square miles) . . . 23.8
Water area (square miles) . . . 13.9
Population density, 2008 (est) . . . 609.1
Year incorporated . . . 1637
Website . . . www.town.duxbury.ma.us

Voters & Government Information

Government type . . . Open Town Meeting
Number of Selectmen . . . 3
US Congressional District(s) . . . 10

Registered Voters, October 2008

Total . . . 11,108
Democrats . . . 2,236
Republicans . . . 2,545
Unaffiliated/other . . . 6,277

Local Officials, 2010

Chair, Bd. of Sel. . . . Shawn Dahlen
Manager . . . Richard MacDonald
Town Clerk . . . Nancy Oates
Finance Director . . . John Madden
Treas/Collector . . . Elizabeth Conway
Tax Assessor . . . Richard Finnegan
Attorney . . . NA
Public Works . . . Peter Buttkus
Building . . . Scott Lambiase
Comm Dev/Planning . . . Christine Stickney
Police Chief . . . Mark DeLuca
Emerg/Fire Chief . . . Kevin Nord

Housing & Construction

New Privately Owned Housing Units Authorized by Building Permit

	Single Family	Total Bldgs	Total Units
2006	26	26	26
2007	41	41	41
2008	22	24	31

Parcel Count by Property Class, 2010

Total . . . 6,064
Single family . . . 4,814
Multiple units . . . 23
Apartments . . . 9
Condos . . . 339
Vacant land . . . 526
Open space . . . 0
Commercial . . . 108
Industrial . . . 3
Misc. residential . . . 126
Other use . . . 116

Public Library

Duxbury Free Library
77 Alden Street
Duxbury, MA 02332
(781)934-6605

Director . . . Elaine Winquist

Library Statistics, FY 2008

Population served, 2007 . . . 14,444
Registered users . . . 11,516
Circulation . . . 277,813
Reference transactons . . . 6,857
Total program attendance . . . 0
per capita:
Holdings . . . 8.42
Operating income . . . $83.54
Internet Access
Internet computers available . . . 16
Weekly users . . . 500

Municipal Finance

Debt at year end 2008 . . . $23,406,022
Moody's rating, July 2009 . . . Aa2

Revenues, 2008

Total . . . $55,362,500
From all taxes . . . 40,768,623
Federal aid . . . 177,929
State aid . . . 5,071,663
From other governments . . . 0
Charges for services . . . 2,888,876
Licenses, permits & fees . . . 1,697,494
Fines & forfeits . . . 37,250
Interfund transfers . . . 878,223
Misc/other/special assessments . . . 1,921,221

Expenditures, 2008

Total . . . $47,596,952
General government . . . 2,414,167
Public safety . . . 6,086,587
Other/fixed costs . . . 2,736,777
Human services . . . 469,551
Culture & recreation . . . 1,928,345
Debt Service . . . 4,743,122
Education . . . 26,068,307
Public works . . . 2,876,548
Intergovernmental . . . 251,748

Taxation, 2010

Property type	Valuation	Rate
Total	$3,502,291,940	-
Residential	3,374,398,059	11.81
Open space	0	0.00
Commercial	89,418,341	11.81
Industrial	2,233,500	11.81
Personal	36,242,040	11.81

Average Single Family Tax Bill, 2010

Avg. assessed home value . . . $611,353
Avg. single fam. tax bill . . . $7,220
Hi-Lo ranking . . . 32/301

Police & Crime, 2008

Number of police officers . . . NA
Violent crimes . . . NA
Property crimes . . . NA

Local School District

(school data 2007-08, except as noted)

Duxbury
130 St. George Street
Duxbury, MA 02332
781-934-7600

Superintendent . . . Susan Skeiber
Grade plan . . . PK-12
Total enrollment '09-10 . . . 3,298
Grade 12 enrollment, '09-10 . . . 262
Graduation rate . . . 93.2%
Dropout rate . . . 3.0%
Per-pupil expenditure . . . $10,169
Avg teacher salary . . . $67,259
Student/teacher ratio '08-09 . . . 15.1 to 1
Highly-qualified teachers, '08-09 . . . 99.8%
Teachers licensed in assigned subject . . 98.7%
Students per computer . . . 4

Massachusetts Competency Assessment System (MCAS), 2009 results

	English		Math	
	% Prof	CPI	% Prof	CPI
Gr 4	67%	87.1	61%	85.9
Gr 6	86%	94.7	80%	91
Gr 8	94%	98.7	73%	89.5
Gr 10	96%	98.6	91%	96.5

Other School Districts (see Appendix D for data)
None

©2010 Information Publications, Inc. All rights reserved. Photocopying prohibited. For additional copies, contact the publisher at www.informationpublications.com or (877)544-INFO (4636)

See Introduction for an explanation of all data sources.

Demographics & Socio-Economic Characteristics

Population

1990	11,104
2000	12,974
Male	6,349
Female	6,625
2008	13,996
2010 (projected)††	14,271
2020 (projected)††	15,508

Race & Hispanic Origin, 2000

Race	
White	12,573
Black/African American	129
American Indian/Alaska Native	22
Asian	62
Hawaiian Native/Pacific Islander	4
Other Race	43
Two or more races	141
Hispanic origin	97

Age & Nativity, 2000

Under 5 years	918
18 years and over	9,364
21 years and over	8,960
65 years and over	1,311
85 years and over	165
Median Age	35.9
Native-born	12,485
Foreign-born	489

Age, 2020 (projected)††

Under 5 years	963
5 to 19 years	2,999
20 to 39 years	3,915
40 to 64 years	5,127
65 years and over	2,504

Educational Attainment, 2000

Population 25 years and over	8,451
High School graduates or higher	88.6%
Bachelor's degree or higher	22.2%
Graduate degree	6.0%

Income & Poverty, 1999

Per capita income,	$23,532
Median household income	$60,311
Median family income	$67,307
Persons in poverty	523
H'holds receiving public assistance	77
H'holds receiving social security	1,069

Households, 2000

Total households	4,344
With persons under 18	1,881
With persons over 65	877
Family households	3,391
Single person households	758
Persons per household	3.0
Persons per family	3.4

Labor & Employment, 2000

Civilian labor force	6,929
Unemployment rate	2.5%
Civilian labor force, 2008†	7,617
Unemployment rate†	7.1%
Civilian labor force, 12/09†	7,554
Unemployment rate†	9.3%
Employed persons 16 years and over, by occupation:	
Managers & professionals	2,167
Service occupations	896
Sales & office occupations	2,001
Farming, fishing & forestry	5
Construction & maintenance	687
Production & transportation	997
Self-employed persons	545

Most demographic data is from the 2000 Decennial Census
† Massachusetts Department of Revenue
†† University of Massachusetts, MISER

General Information

Town of East Bridgewater
175 Central St
East Bridgewater, MA 02333
508-378-1601

Elevation	40 ft.
Land area (square miles)	17.2
Water area (square miles)	0.3
Population density, 2008 (est)	813.7
Year incorporated	1823
Website	eastbridgewaterma.org

Voters & Government Information

Government type	Open Town Meeting
Number of Selectmen	3
US Congressional District(s)	9

Registered Voters, October 2008

Total	9,216
Democrats	2,265
Republicans	1,382
Unaffiliated/other	5,516

Local Officials, 2010

Chair, Bd. of Sel.	Peter Hamilton
Manager/Town Admin.	George Samia
Town Clerk	Marcia Weidenfeller
Finance Director	Martin Crowley
Tax Collector	Marilyn Thompson
Tax Assessor	Cheryl Pooler
Attorney	Collins, Loughran & Peloquin
Public Works	John Haines
Building	Robert Lundberg
Comm Dev/Planning	Edward Garner
Police Chief	John Cowan
Emerg/Fire Chief	Ryon Pratt

Housing & Construction

New Privately Owned Housing Units Authorized by Building Permit

	Single Family	Total Bldgs	Total Units
2006	56	56	56
2007	58	58	58
2008	25	25	25

Parcel Count by Property Class, 2010

Total	5,614
Single family	3,658
Multiple units	168
Apartments	31
Condos	402
Vacant land	890
Open space	0
Commercial	131
Industrial	128
Misc. residential	25
Other use	181

Public Library

East Bridgewater Public Library
32 Union St.
East Bridgewater, MA 02333
(508)378-1616

Director	Manuel Leite

Library Statistics, FY 2008

Population served, 2007	13,879
Registered users	10,647
Circulation	110,139
Reference transactons	6,781
Total program attendance	0
per capita:	
Holdings	4.50
Operating income	$32.42
Internet Access	
Internet computers available	4
Weekly users	77

Municipal Finance

Debt at year end 2008	$15,589,311
Moody's rating, July 2009	A2

Revenues, 2008

Total	$35,660,168
From all taxes	19,449,260
Federal aid	0
State aid	13,201,511
From other governments	14,168
Charges for services	1,500
Licenses, permits & fees	402,215
Fines & forfeits	27,270
Interfund transfers	926,970
Misc/other/special assessments	818,637

Expenditures, 2008

Total	$34,614,658
General government	2,159,978
Public safety	4,026,697
Other/fixed costs	5,895,269
Human services	332,357
Culture & recreation	433,944
Debt Service	2,131,453
Education	17,849,575
Public works	1,557,746
Intergovernmental	221,502

Taxation, 2010

Property type	Valuation	Rate
Total	$1,615,344,350	-
Residential	1,442,576,108	12.38
Open space	0	0.00
Commercial	91,096,622	12.38
Industrial	43,966,400	12.38
Personal	37,705,220	12.38

Average Single Family Tax Bill, 2010

Avg. assessed home value	$329,440
Avg. single fam. tax bill	$4,078
Hi-Lo ranking	129/301

Police & Crime, 2008

Number of police officers	23
Violent crimes	23
Property crimes	206

Local School District

(school data 2007-08, except as noted)

East Bridgewater
11 Plymouth Street
East Bridgewater, MA 02333
508-378-8200

Superintendent	Susan Cote
Grade plan	PK-12
Total enrollment '09-10	2,375
Grade 12 enrollment, '09-10	154
Graduation rate	90.9%
Dropout rate	6.4%
Per-pupil expenditure	$9,051
Avg teacher salary	$61,226
Student/teacher ratio '08-09	16.7 to 1
Highly-qualified teachers, '08-09	98.9%
Teachers licensed in assigned subject	99.3%
Students per computer	7.5

Massachusetts Competency Assessment System (MCAS), 2009 results

	English		Math	
	% Prof	CPI	% Prof	CPI
Gr 4	55%	83	45%	78.9
Gr 6	81%	92.9	76%	91
Gr 8	82%	94.1	62%	83.1
Gr 10	88%	95.7	81%	92.9

Other School Districts (see Appendix D for data)
Southeastern Vocational Tech

©2010 Information Publications, Inc. All rights reserved. Photocopying prohibited. For additional copies, contact the publisher at www.informationpublications.com or (877)544-INFO (4636)

See Introduction for an explanation of all data sources.

Demographics & Socio-Economic Characteristics

Population

1990 ... 2,033
2000 ... 2,097
Male ... 1,042
Female ... 1,055
2008 ... 2,057
2010 (projected)†† ... 2,097
2020 (projected)†† ... 2,070

Race & Hispanic Origin, 2000

Race
White ... 2,066
Black/African American ... 9
American Indian/Alaska Native ... 5
Asian ... 3
Hawaiian Native/Pacific Islander ... 0
Other Race ... 3
Two or more races ... 11
Hispanic origin ... 16

Age & Nativity, 2000

Under 5 years ... 124
18 years and over ... 1,560
21 years and over ... 1,497
65 years and over ... 279
85 years and over ... 33
Median Age ... 38.6
Native-born ... 2,063
Foreign-born ... 34

Age, 2020 (projected)††

Under 5 years ... 112
5 to 19 years ... 377
20 to 39 years ... 448
40 to 64 years ... 736
65 years and over ... 397

Educational Attainment, 2000

Population 25 years and over ... 1,428
High School graduates or higher ... 83.6%
Bachelor's degree or higher ... 16.2%
Graduate degree ... 6.0%

Income & Poverty, 1999

Per capita income, ... $22,629
Median household income ... $51,860
Median family income ... $57,500
Persons in poverty ... 82
H'holds receiving public assistance ... 9
H'holds receiving social security ... 218

Households, 2000

Total households ... 778
With persons under 18 ... 282
With persons over 65 ... 201
Family households ... 600
Single person households ... 147
Persons per household ... 2.7
Persons per family ... 3.1

Labor & Employment, 2000

Civilian labor force ... 1,159
Unemployment rate ... 2.1%
Civilian labor force, 2008† ... 1,168
Unemployment rate† ... 6.3%
Civilian labor force, 12/09† ... 1,188
Unemployment rate† ... 9.3%
Employed persons 16 years and over, by occupation:
Managers & professionals ... 317
Service occupations ... 163
Sales & office occupations ... 327
Farming, fishing & forestry ... 1
Construction & maintenance ... 120
Production & transportation ... 207
Self-employed persons ... 67

Most demographic data is from the 2000 Decennial Census
† Massachusetts Department of Revenue
†† University of Massachusetts, MISER

General Information

Town of East Brookfield
122 Connie Mack Dr
East Brookfield, MA 01515
508-867-6769

Elevation ... 620 ft.
Land area (square miles) ... 9.8
Water area (square miles) ... 0.5
Population density, 2008 (est) ... 209.9
Year incorporated ... 1920
Website ... www.eastbrookfieldma.us

Voters & Government Information

Government type ... Open Town Meeting
Number of Selectmen ... 3
US Congressional District(s) ... 2

Registered Voters, October 2008

Total ... 1,524
Democrats ... 355
Republicans ... 235
Unaffiliated/other ... 918

Local Officials, 2010

Chair, Bd. of Sel. ... Leo Fayard
Manager/Admin ... NA
Town Clerk ... Virginia Allen
Finance Director ... Rae Ann Barnes
Tax Collector ... Sandra Kady
Tax Assessor ... Linda LeBlanc
Attorney ... Kopelman & Paige
Public Works ... Robert Allen
Building ... John Couture
Comm Dev/Planning ... Mark Violette
Police Chief ... William Cournoyer
Emerg/Fire Chief ... Peter Livermore

Housing & Construction

New Privately Owned Housing Units Authorized by Building Permit

	Single Family	Total Bldgs	Total Units
2006	2	2	2
2007	2	2	2
2008	2	2	2

Parcel Count by Property Class, 2010

Total ... 1,257
Single family ... 764
Multiple units ... 51
Apartments ... 4
Condos ... 2
Vacant land ... 323
Open space ... 0
Commercial ... 35
Industrial ... 9
Misc. residential ... 12
Other use ... 57

Public Library

East Brookfield Public Library
PO Box 90
East Brookfield, MA 01515
(508)867-7928

Director ... Wendy Payette

Library Statistics, FY 2008

Population served, 2007 ... 2,069
Registered users ... 2,586
Circulation ... 11,220
Reference transactons ... 920
Total program attendance ... 6,047
per capita:
Holdings ... 9.29
Operating income ... $35.37
Internet Access
Internet computers available ... 2
Weekly users ... 10

Municipal Finance

Debt at year end 2008 ... $1,456,000
Moody's rating, July 2009 ... A3

Revenues, 2008

Total ... $3,901,602
From all taxes ... 2,863,352
Federal aid ... 0
State aid ... 465,008
From other governments ... 24,065
Charges for services ... 204,416
Licenses, permits & fees ... 17,538
Fines & forfeits ... 0
Interfund transfers ... 122,559
Misc/other/special assessments ... 102,332

Expenditures, 2008

Total ... $3,636,196
General government ... 334,104
Public safety ... 562,162
Other/fixed costs ... 261,367
Human services ... 21,950
Culture & recreation ... 84,939
Debt Service ... 145,252
Education ... 1,700,158
Public works ... 507,721
Intergovernmental ... 18,543

Taxation, 2010

Property type	Valuation	Rate
Total	$234,719,181	-
Residential	213,223,128	12.19
Open space	0	0.00
Commercial	14,854,323	12.19
Industrial	2,176,100	12.19
Personal	4,465,630	12.19

Average Single Family Tax Bill, 2010

Avg. assessed home value ... $242,309
Avg. single fam. tax bill ... $2,954
Hi-Lo ranking ... 237/301

Police & Crime, 2008

Number of police officers ... 3
Violent crimes ... 6
Property crimes ... 49

Local School District

(school data 2007-08, except as noted)

East Brookfield (non-op)
306 Main Street
Spencer, MA 01562
508-885-8500
Superintendent ... Ralph Hicks

Non-operating district.
Resident students are sent to the Other School Districts listed below.

Grade plan ... NA
Total enrollment '09-10 ... NA
Grade 12 enrollment, '09-10 ... NA
Graduation rate ... NA
Dropout rate ... NA
Per-pupil expenditure ... NA
Avg teacher salary ... NA
Student/teacher ratio '08-09 ... NA
Highly-qualified teachers, '08-09 ... NA
Teachers licensed in assigned subject ... NA
Students per computer ... NA

Other School Districts (see Appendix D for data)
Spencer-East Brookfield Regional

©2010 Information Publications, Inc. All rights reserved. Photocopying prohibited. For additional copies, contact the publisher at www.informationpublications.com or (877)544-INFO (4636)

See Introduction for an explanation of all data sources.

©2010 Information Publications, Inc. All rights reserved. Photocopying prohibited. For additional copies, contact the publisher at www.informationpublications.com or (877)544-INFO (4636)

Demographics & Socio-Economic Characteristics

Population

1990	13,367
2000	14,100
Male	6,707
Female	7,393
2008	15,332
2010 (projected)††	14,029
2020 (projected)††	13,705

Race & Hispanic Origin, 2000

Race	
White	13,750
Black/African American	105
American Indian/Alaska Native	6
Asian	124
Hawaiian Native/Pacific Islander	7
Other Race	34
Two or more races	74
Hispanic origin	130

Age & Nativity, 2000

Under 5 years	786
18 years and over	10,609
21 years and over	10,205
65 years and over	2,654
85 years and over	388
Median Age	41.4
Native-born	13,486
Foreign-born	614

Age, 2020 (projected)††

Under 5 years	698
5 to 19 years	2,399
20 to 39 years	2,721
40 to 64 years	4,450
65 years and over	3,437

Educational Attainment, 2000

Population 25 years and over	9,834
High School graduates or higher	90.4%
Bachelor's degree or higher	32.8%
Graduate degree	13.0%

Income & Poverty, 1999

Per capita income,	$27,659
Median household income	$62,680
Median family income	$70,571
Persons in poverty	477
H'holds receiving public assistance	48
H'holds receiving social security	1,838

Households, 2000

Total households	5,248
With persons under 18	1,878
With persons over 65	1,767
Family households	3,986
Single person households	1,132
Persons per household	2.7
Persons per family	3.1

Labor & Employment, 2000

Civilian labor force	7,140
Unemployment rate	2.6%
Civilian labor force, 2008†	7,653
Unemployment rate†	5.1%
Civilian labor force, 12/09†	7,837
Unemployment rate†	7.0%
Employed persons 16 years and over, by occupation:	
Managers & professionals	2,892
Service occupations	786
Sales & office occupations	2,001
Farming, fishing & forestry	0
Construction & maintenance	462
Production & transportation	814
Self-employed persons	472

Most demographic data is from the 2000 Decennial Census
† Massachusetts Department of Revenue
†† University of Massachusetts, MISER

General Information

Town of East Longmeadow
60 Center Sq
East Longmeadow, MA 01028
413-525-5400

Elevation	226 ft.
Land area (square miles)	13.0
Water area (square miles)	0.0
Population density, 2008 (est)	1,179.4
Year incorporated	1894
Website	www.eastlongmeadowma.gov

Voters & Government Information

Government type	Open Town Meeting
Number of Selectmen	3
US Congressional District(s)	2

Registered Voters, October 2008

Total	11,095
Democrats	3,201
Republicans	2,139
Unaffiliated/other	5,707

Local Officials, 2010

Chair, Bd. of Sel.	Enrico J. Villamaino III
Manager/Admin	NA
Town Clerk	Thomas P. Florence
Finance Director	Thomas P. Florence
Tax Collector	Thomas P. Florence
Tax Assessor	J. William Johnston
Attorney	James Donohue
Public Works	David Gromaskie
Building	Daniel Hellyer
Planning	Micheal S. Przybylowicz
Police Chief	Douglas Mellis
Emerg/Fire Chief	Richard J. Brady

Housing & Construction

New Privately Owned Housing Units Authorized by Building Permit

	Single Family	Total Bldgs	Total Units
2006	51	52	181
2007	35	39	79
2008	18	19	148

Parcel Count by Property Class, 2010

Total	6,570
Single family	5,265
Multiple units	53
Apartments	4
Condos	123
Vacant land	651
Open space	0
Commercial	288
Industrial	88
Misc. residential	10
Other use	88

Public Library

East Longmeadow Public Library
60 Center Square STE 2
East Longmeadow, MA 01028
(413)525-5400

Director . . . Susan Peterson

Library Statistics, FY 2008

Population served, 2007	15,222
Registered users	11,060
Circulation	203,829
Reference transactons	1,950
Total program attendance	0
per capita:	
Holdings	5.28
Operating income	$40.88
Internet Access	
Internet computers available	16
Weekly users	825

Municipal Finance

Debt at year end 2008	$34,849,414
Moody's rating, July 2009	A1

Revenues, 2008

Total	$42,817,807
From all taxes	31,388,638
Federal aid	0
State aid	7,518,845
From other governments	3,949
Charges for services	109,023
Licenses, permits & fees	358,661
Fines & forfeits	36,783
Interfund transfers	1,513,482
Misc/other/special assessments	944,213

Expenditures, 2008

Total	$41,674,831
General government	1,412,235
Public safety	2,758,463
Other/fixed costs	6,248,782
Human services	242,223
Culture & recreation	748,723
Debt Service	4,341,334
Education	22,510,346
Public works	3,412,725
Intergovernmental	0

Taxation, 2010

Property type	Valuation	Rate
Total	$1,795,002,834	-
Residential	1,491,832,118	17.38
Open space	0	0.00
Commercial	152,065,606	17.38
Industrial	114,846,400	17.38
Personal	36,258,710	17.38

Average Single Family Tax Bill, 2010

Avg. assessed home value	$260,660
Avg. single fam. tax bill	$4,530
Hi-Lo ranking	98/301

Police & Crime, 2008

Number of police officers	24
Violent crimes	23
Property crimes	369

Local School District

(school data 2007-08, except as noted)

East Longmeadow
180 Maple Street
East Longmeadow, MA 01028
413-525-5450

Superintendent	Elaine Santaniello
Grade plan	PK-12
Total enrollment '09-10	2,850
Grade 12 enrollment, '09-10	229
Graduation rate	92.6%
Dropout rate	2.5%
Per-pupil expenditure	$10,156
Avg teacher salary	$61,676
Student/teacher ratio '08-09	14.1 to 1
Highly-qualified teachers, '08-09	100.0%
Teachers licensed in assigned subject	100.0%
Students per computer	3.5

Massachusetts Competency Assessment System (MCAS), 2009 results

	English		Math	
	% Prof	CPI	% Prof	CPI
Gr 4	64%	85.1	51%	81.3
Gr 6	73%	89.5	53%	78.3
Gr 8	87%	95.3	51%	77.2
Gr 10	89%	96.5	85%	94.1

Other School Districts (see Appendix D for data)
None

See Introduction for an explanation of all data sources.

Demographics & Socio-Economic Characteristics

Population

1990	4,462
2000	5,453
Male	2,637
Female	2,816
2008	5,438
2010 (projected)††	6,202
2020 (projected)††	7,029

Race & Hispanic Origin, 2000

Race	
White	5,252
Black/African American	81
American Indian/Alaska Native	8
Asian	17
Hawaiian Native/Pacific Islander	2
Other Race	16
Two or more races	77
Hispanic origin	45

Age & Nativity, 2000

Under 5 years	208
18 years and over	4,488
21 years and over	4,365
65 years and over	1,419
85 years and over	105
Median Age	47.6
Native-born	5,246
Foreign-born	207

Age, 2020 (projected)††

Under 5 years	199
5 to 19 years	644
20 to 39 years	1,226
40 to 64 years	2,485
65 years and over	2,475

Educational Attainment, 2000

Population 25 years and over	4,201
High School graduates or higher	93.4%
Bachelor's degree or higher	35.3%
Graduate degree	16.2%

Income & Poverty, 1999

Per capita income,	$24,642
Median household income	$42,618
Median family income	$51,269
Persons in poverty	378
H'holds receiving public assistance	32
H'holds receiving social security	1,056

Households, 2000

Total households	2,396
With persons under 18	568
With persons over 65	959
Family households	1,635
Single person households	610
Persons per household	2.2
Persons per family	2.7

Labor & Employment, 2000

Civilian labor force	2,424
Unemployment rate	4.9%
Civilian labor force, 2008†	2,691
Unemployment rate†	10.1%
Civilian labor force, 12/09†	2,678
Unemployment rate†	14.0%
Employed persons 16 years and over, by occupation:	
Managers & professionals	668
Service occupations	371
Sales & office occupations	664
Farming, fishing & forestry	20
Construction & maintenance	420
Production & transportation	163
Self-employed persons	432

Most demographic data is from the 2000 Decennial Census
† Massachusetts Department of Revenue
†† University of Massachusetts, MISER

General Information

Town of Eastham
2500 State Hwy
Eastham, MA 02642
508-240-5900

Elevation	48 ft.
Land area (square miles)	14.0
Water area (square miles)	13.3
Population density, 2008 (est)	388.4
Year incorporated	1651
Website	www.eastham-ma.gov

Voters & Government Information

Government type	Open Town Meeting
Number of Selectmen	5
US Congressional District(s)	10

Registered Voters, October 2008

Total	4,307
Democrats	1,235
Republicans	745
Unaffiliated/other	2,311

Local Officials, 2010

Chair, Bd. of Sel.	Linda Burt
Manager/Admin	Sheila Vanderhoef
Town Clerk	Lillian Lamperti
Finance Director	NA
Tax Collector	Joan Plante
Tax Assessor	Gail Fitzback
Attorney	NA
Public Works	NA
Building	NA
Comm Dev/Planning	Sarah Reposa
Police Chief	Edward Kulhawik
Emerg/Fire Chief	Glenn Olson

Housing & Construction

New Privately Owned Housing Units Authorized by Building Permit

	Single Family	Total Bldgs	Total Units
2006	33	33	33
2007	52	57	62
2008	12	13	14

Parcel Count by Property Class, 2010

Total	6,377
Single family	5,060
Multiple units	117
Apartments	4
Condos	268
Vacant land	571
Open space	0
Commercial	126
Industrial	19
Misc. residential	140
Other use	72

Public Library

Eastham Public Library
190 Samoset Road
Eastham, MA 02642
(508)240-5950

Director	Martha Magane

Library Statistics, FY 2008

Population served, 2007	5,445
Registered users	8,685
Circulation	107,897
Reference transactons	4,299
Total program attendance	0
per capita:	
Holdings	8.97
Operating income	$49.87
Internet Access	
Internet computers available	11
Weekly users	500

Municipal Finance

Debt at year end 2008	$12,569,629
Moody's rating, July 2009	A1

Revenues, 2008

Total	$19,593,313
From all taxes	16,130,364
Federal aid	0
State aid	590,570
From other governments	53,748
Charges for services	1,364,458
Licenses, permits & fees	430,539
Fines & forfeits	8,467
Interfund transfers	493,799
Misc/other/special assessments	260,684

Expenditures, 2008

Total	$18,493,898
General government	2,033,135
Public safety	3,329,153
Other/fixed costs	2,383,520
Human services	511,213
Culture & recreation	510,130
Debt Service	1,545,617
Education	6,720,815
Public works	958,003
Intergovernmental	502,312

Taxation, 2010

Property type	Valuation	Rate
Total	$2,897,862,240	-
Residential	2,780,889,462	5.51
Open space	0	0.00
Commercial	83,440,708	5.51
Industrial	8,149,000	5.51
Personal	25,383,070	5.51

Average Single Family Tax Bill, 2010

Avg. assessed home value	$486,521
Avg. single fam. tax bill	$2,681
Hi-Lo ranking	266/301

Police & Crime, 2008

Number of police officers	15
Violent crimes	0
Property crimes	80

Local School District

(school data 2007-08, except as noted)

Eastham
78 Eldredge Pkwy
Orleans, MA 02653
508-255-8800

Superintendent	Richard Hoffmann
Grade plan	K-5
Total enrollment '09-10	225
Grade 12 enrollment, '09-10	0
Graduation rate	NA
Dropout rate	NA
Per-pupil expenditure	$15,688
Avg teacher salary	$66,775
Student/teacher ratio '08-09	10.0 to 1
Highly-qualified teachers, '08-09	100.0%
Teachers licensed in assigned subject	100.0%
Students per computer	2.2

Massachusetts Competency Assessment System (MCAS), 2009 results

	English		Math	
	% Prof	CPI	% Prof	CPI
Gr 4	93%	98.3	83%	95
Gr 6	NA	NA	NA	NA
Gr 8	NA	NA	NA	NA
Gr 10	NA	NA	NA	NA

Other School Districts (see Appendix D for data)

Nauset Regional, Cape Cod Vocational Tech

©2010 Information Publications, Inc. All rights reserved. Photocopying prohibited. For additional copies, contact the publisher at www.informationpublications.com or (877)544-INFO (4636)

See Introduction for an explanation of all data sources.

Demographics & Socio-Economic Characteristics

Population

1990	15,537
2000	15,994
Male	7,687
Female	8,307
2008	16,195
2010 (projected)††	15,747
2020 (projected)††	15,401

Race & Hispanic Origin, 2000

Race	
White	15,260
Black/African American	102
American Indian/Alaska Native	23
Asian	275
Hawaiian Native/Pacific Islander	1
Other Race	180
Two or more races	153
Hispanic origin	336

Age & Nativity, 2000

Under 5 years	854
18 years and over	12,612
21 years and over	12,112
65 years and over	2,262
85 years and over	274
Median Age	38.6
Native-born	15,334
Foreign-born	660

Age, 2020 (projected)††

Under 5 years	730
5 to 19 years	2,207
20 to 39 years	3,755
40 to 64 years	5,499
65 years and over	3,210

Educational Attainment, 2000

Population 25 years and over	11,457
High School graduates or higher	86.0%
Bachelor's degree or higher	24.0%
Graduate degree	8.8%

Income & Poverty, 1999

Per capita income,	$21,922
Median household income	$45,185
Median family income	$54,312
Persons in poverty	1,414
H'holds receiving public assistance	198
H'holds receiving social security	1,831

Households, 2000

Total households	6,854
With persons under 18	1,954
With persons over 65	1,691
Family households	4,170
Single person households	2,085
Persons per household	2.3
Persons per family	2.9

Labor & Employment, 2000

Civilian labor force	9,356
Unemployment rate	4.1%
Civilian labor force, 2008†	9,424
Unemployment rate†	5.7%
Civilian labor force, 12/09†	9,550
Unemployment rate†	8.4%
Employed persons 16 years and over, by occupation:	
Managers & professionals	3,004
Service occupations	1,581
Sales & office occupations	2,104
Farming, fishing & forestry	5
Construction & maintenance	724
Production & transportation	1,553
Self-employed persons	547

Most demographic data is from the 2000 Decennial Census
† Massachusetts Department of Revenue
†† University of Massachusetts, MISER

General Information

City of Easthampton
50 Payson Ave
Easthampton, MA 01027
413-529-1470

Elevation	188 ft.
Land area (square miles)	13.4
Water area (square miles)	0.2
Population density, 2008 (est)	1,208.6
Year incorporated	1785
Website	www.easthampton.org

Voters & Government Information

Government type	Mayor-Council
Number of Councilpersons	9
US Congressional District(s)	1

Registered Voters, October 2008

Total	11,601
Democrats	4,117
Republicans	1,027
Unaffiliated/other	6,327

Local Officials, 2010

Mayor	Michael Tautznik
Manager/Admin	NA
City Clerk	Barbara LaBombard
Finance Director	Bruce Turner
Tax Collector	Elizabeth Gendron
Tax Assessor	Mark Dimauro
Attorney	Green, Miles, Lipton & Fitzgibbon
Public Works	Joseph Pipczynski
Building	Joseph Fydenkevez
Comm Dev/Planning	Stuart Beckley
Police Chief	Bruce McMahon
Fire Chief	David Mottor

Housing & Construction

New Privately Owned Housing Units Authorized by Building Permit

	Single Family	Total Bldgs	Total Units
2006	66	66	66
2007	35	37	39
2008	15	15	15

Parcel Count by Property Class, 2010

Total	6,013
Single family	3,958
Multiple units	614
Apartments	158
Condos	395
Vacant land	477
Open space	0
Commercial	190
Industrial	103
Misc. residential	15
Other use	103

Public Library

Emily Williston Memorial Lib. and Museum
9 Park Street
Easthampton, MA 01027
(413)527-1031

Director	Francis DiMenno

Library Statistics, FY 2008

Population served, 2007	16,064
Registered users	8,235
Circulation	111,426
Reference transactons	390
Total program attendance	78,000
per capita:	
Holdings	3.65
Operating income	$18.07
Internet Access	
Internet computers available	7
Weekly users	144

Municipal Finance

Debt at year end 2008	$9,587,101
Moody's rating, July 2009	A3

Revenues, 2008

Total	$33,568,638
From all taxes	17,228,354
Federal aid	0
State aid	11,779,027
From other governments	47,968
Charges for services	81,030
Licenses, permits & fees	333,919
Fines & forfeits	0
Interfund transfers	1,859,606
Misc/other/special assessments	1,119,367

Expenditures, 2008

Total	$32,261,357
General government	1,472,953
Public safety	4,662,051
Other/fixed costs	5,859,212
Human services	367,232
Culture & recreation	459,965
Debt Service	1,289,235
Education	15,152,108
Public works	1,454,577
Intergovernmental	1,469,024

Taxation, 2010

Property type	Valuation	Rate
Total	$1,391,081,830	-
Residential	1,230,655,563	12.41
Open space	0	0.00
Commercial	78,497,267	12.41
Industrial	45,919,600	12.41
Personal	36,009,400	12.41

Average Single Family Tax Bill, 2010

Avg. assessed home value	$229,151
Avg. single fam. tax bill	$2,844
Hi-Lo ranking	248/301

Police & Crime, 2008

Number of police officers	27
Violent crimes	43
Property crimes	179

Local School District

(school data 2007-08, except as noted)

Easthampton
50 Payson Avenue, Second Floor
Easthampton, MA 01027
413-529-1500

Superintendent	Deborah Carter
Grade plan	PK-12
Total enrollment '09-10	1,575
Grade 12 enrollment, '09-10	103
Graduation rate	85.7%
Dropout rate	6.1%
Per-pupil expenditure	$10,587
Avg teacher salary	$56,937
Student/teacher ratio '08-09	12.3 to 1
Highly-qualified teachers, '08-09	100.0%
Teachers licensed in assigned subject	99.3%
Students per computer	2.4

Massachusetts Competency Assessment System (MCAS), 2009 results

	English		Math	
	% Prof	CPI	% Prof	CPI
Gr 4	43%	77.3	56%	85.3
Gr 6	56%	82.1	55%	78.1
Gr 8	70%	89	44%	73
Gr 10	74%	90	66%	84

Other School Districts (see Appendix D for data)
None

©2010 Information Publications, Inc. All rights reserved. Photocopying prohibited. For additional copies, contact the publisher at www.informationpublications.com or (877)544-INFO (4636)

See Introduction for an explanation of all data sources.

Demographics & Socio-Economic Characteristics

Population

1990 . . . 19,807
2000 . . . 22,299
  Male . . . 10,840
  Female . . . 11,459
2008 . . . 23,209
2010 (projected)†† . . . 24,638
2020 (projected)†† . . . 26,691

Race & Hispanic Origin, 2000

Race
  White . . . 20,501
  Black/African American . . . 354
  American Indian/Alaska Native . . . 10
  Asian . . . 309
  Hawaiian Native/Pacific Islander . . . 2
  Other Race . . . 920
  Two or more races . . . 203
Hispanic origin . . . 352

Age & Nativity, 2000

Under 5 years . . . 1,457
18 years and over . . . 16,848
21 years and over . . . 15,163
65 years and over . . . 2,095
85 years and over . . . 236
  Median Age . . . 35.5
Native-born . . . 21,278
Foreign-born . . . 1,021

Age, 2020 (projected)††

Under 5 years . . . 1,636
5 to 19 years . . . 5,875
20 to 39 years . . . 6,749
40 to 64 years . . . 8,185
65 years and over . . . 4,246

Educational Attainment, 2000

Population 25 years and over . . . 13,942
  High School graduates or higher . . 93.9%
  Bachelor's degree or higher . . . 39.6%
  Graduate degree . . . 14.1%

Income & Poverty, 1999

Per capita income, . . . $30,732
Median household income . . . $69,144
Median family income . . . $82,190
Persons in poverty . . . 401
H'holds receiving public assistance . . . 159
H'holds receiving social security . . . 1,623

Households, 2000

Total households . . . 7,489
  With persons under 18 . . . 2,958
  With persons over 65 . . . 1,474
  Family households . . . 5,575
  Single person households . . . 1,551
Persons per household . . . 2.7
Persons per family . . . 3.2

Labor & Employment, 2000

Civilian labor force . . . 12,806
  Unemployment rate . . . 3.1%
Civilian labor force, 2008† . . . 13,276
  Unemployment rate† . . . 5.9%
Civilian labor force, 12/09† . . . 13,168
  Unemployment rate† . . . 8.0%
Employed persons 16 years and over, by occupation:
  Managers & professionals . . . 5,495
  Service occupations . . . 1,536
  Sales & office occupations . . . 3,791
  Farming, fishing & forestry . . . 19
  Construction & maintenance . . . 739
  Production & transportation . . . 823
  Self-employed persons . . . 746

Most demographic data is from the 2000 Decennial Census
† Massachusetts Department of Revenue
†† University of Massachusetts, MISER

General Information

Town of Easton
136 Elm St
Easton, MA 02356
508-230-0500

Elevation . . . 195 ft.
Land area (square miles) . . . 28.4
Water area (square miles) . . . 0.7
Population density, 2008 (est) . . . 817.2
Year incorporated . . . 1725
Website . . . www.easton.ma.us

Voters & Government Information

Government type . . . Open Town Meeting
Number of Selectmen . . . 5
US Congressional District(s) . . . 9

Registered Voters, October 2008

Total . . . 15,161
Democrats . . . 4,153
Republicans . . . 2,506
Unaffiliated/other . . . 8,409

Local Officials, 2010

Chair, Bd. of Sel. . . . Colleen A. Corona
Administrator . . . David Colton
Town Clerk . . . Jeremy P. Gillis
Finance Director . . . Teresa DeSilva
Tax Collector . . . Teresa DeSilva
Tax Assessor . . . Robert Alford
Attorney . . . Brackett & Lucas
Public Works . . . Wayne P. Southworth
Building . . . D. Mark Trivett
Comm Dev/Planning . . . Alice Savage
Police Chief . . . Allan Krajcik
Emerg/Fire Chief . . . Thomas Stone

Housing & Construction

New Privately Owned Housing Units Authorized by Building Permit

	Single Family	Total Bldgs	Total Units
2006	56	56	56
2007	38	39	40
2008	17	18	19

Parcel Count by Property Class, 2010

Total . . . 8,283
Single family . . . 5,525
Multiple units . . . 180
Apartments . . . 35
Condos . . . 1,415
Vacant land . . . 601
Open space . . . 0
Commercial . . . 230
Industrial . . . 156
Misc. residential . . . 23
Other use . . . 118

Public Library

Ames Free Library of Easton, Inc.
15 Barrows Street
North Easton, MA 02356
(508)238-2000

Director . . . Madeline Miele Holt

Library Statistics, FY 2008

Population served, 2007 . . . 22,969
Registered users . . . 10,081
Circulation . . . 118,929
Reference transactons . . . 0
Total program attendance . . . 0

per capita:

Holdings . . . 3.28
Operating income . . . $47.83

Internet Access

Internet computers available . . . 11
Weekly users . . . 83

Municipal Finance

Debt at year end 2008 . . . $47,152,519
Moody's rating, July 2009 . . . A2

Revenues, 2008

Total . . . $58,278,206
From all taxes . . . 40,451,176
Federal aid . . . 0
State aid . . . 13,249,746
From other governments . . . 51,843
Charges for services . . . 928,556
Licenses, permits & fees . . . 613,334
Fines & forfeits . . . 4,836
Interfund transfers . . . 1,902,729
Misc/other/special assessments . . . 537,993

Expenditures, 2008

Total . . . $57,147,545
General government . . . 1,930,604
Public safety . . . 6,666,830
Other/fixed costs . . . 9,344,425
Human services . . . 646,835
Culture & recreation . . . 513,410
Debt Service . . . 4,698,408
Education . . . 29,603,900
Public works . . . 2,960,908
Intergovernmental . . . 687,964

Taxation, 2010

Property type	Valuation	Rate
Total	$3,058,665,160	-
Residential	2,652,565,868	13.49
Open space	0	0.00
Commercial	252,177,682	13.49
Industrial	108,077,100	13.49
Personal	45,844,510	13.49

Average Single Family Tax Bill, 2010

Avg. assessed home value . . . $394,948
Avg. single fam. tax bill . . . $5,328
Hi-Lo ranking . . . 60/301

Police & Crime, 2008

Number of police officers . . . 33
Violent crimes . . . 15
Property crimes . . . 211

Local School District

(school data 2007-08, except as noted)

Easton
PO Box 359
North Easton, MA 02356
508-230-3200

Superintendent . . . Michael Green
Grade plan . . . PK-12
Total enrollment '09-10 . . . 3,906
Grade 12 enrollment, '09-10 . . . 283
Graduation rate . . . 92.4%
Dropout rate . . . 4.2%
Per-pupil expenditure . . . $9,608
Avg teacher salary . . . $60,456
Student/teacher ratio '08-09 . . . 15.0 to 1
Highly-qualified teachers, '08-09 . . . 99.5%
Teachers licensed in assigned subject . . 99.6%
Students per computer . . . 3.4

Massachusetts Competency Assessment System (MCAS), 2009 results

	English		Math	
	% Prof	CPI	% Prof	CPI
Gr 4	64%	85.7	62%	86.3
Gr 6	76%	90.6	73%	87.6
Gr 8	90%	96.1	61%	81.5
Gr 10	89%	96	84%	93.4

Other School Districts (see Appendix D for data)

Southeastern Vocational Tech, Bristol County Agricultural

©2010 Information Publications, Inc. All rights reserved. Photocopying prohibited. For additional copies, contact the publisher at www.informationpublications.com or (877)544-INFO (4636)

Demographics & Socio-Economic Characteristics

Population

1990	3,062
2000	3,779
Male	1,912
Female	1,867
2008	3,932
2010 (projected)††	4,683
2020 (projected)††	5,619

Race & Hispanic Origin, 2000

Race	
White	3,527
Black/African American	67
American Indian/Alaska Native	17
Asian	20
Hawaiian Native/Pacific Islander	2
Other Race	58
Two or more races	88
Hispanic origin	44

Age & Nativity, 2000

Under 5 years	220
18 years and over	2,936
21 years and over	2,826
65 years and over	477
85 years and over	37
Median Age	40.3
Native-born	3,451
Foreign-born	328

Age, 2020 (projected)††

Under 5 years	309
5 to 19 years	947
20 to 39 years	1,364
40 to 64 years	1,943
65 years and over	1,056

Educational Attainment, 2000

Population 25 years and over	2,716
High School graduates or higher	89.1%
Bachelor's degree or higher	35.7%
Graduate degree	10.1%

Income & Poverty, 1999

Per capita income,	$25,740
Median household income	$50,407
Median family income	$55,153
Persons in poverty	158
H'holds receiving public assistance	7
H'holds receiving social security	373

Households, 2000

Total households	1,582
With persons under 18	473
With persons over 65	367
Family households	957
Single person households	476
Persons per household	2.4
Persons per family	2.9

Labor & Employment, 2000

Civilian labor force	2,095
Unemployment rate	4.0%
Civilian labor force, 2008†	2,394
Unemployment rate†	9.1%
Civilian labor force, 12/09†	2,513
Unemployment rate†	12.5%
Employed persons 16 years and over, by occupation:	
Managers & professionals	603
Service occupations	382
Sales & office occupations	523
Farming, fishing & forestry	17
Construction & maintenance	346
Production & transportation	141
Self-employed persons	348

Most demographic data is from the 2000 Decennial Census
† Massachusetts Department of Revenue
†† University of Massachusetts, MISER

General Information

Town of Edgartown
70 Main St
Edgartown, MA 02539
508-627-6180

Elevation	NA
Land area (square miles)	27.0
Water area (square miles)	95.7
Population density, 2008 (est)	145.6
Year incorporated	1671
Website	edgartown-ma.us

Voters & Government Information

Government type	Open Town Meeting
Number of Selectmen	3
US Congressional District(s)	10

Registered Voters, October 2008

Total	3,177
Democrats	1,094
Republicans	508
Unaffiliated/other	1,550

Local Officials, 2010

Chair, Bd. of Sel.	Michael Donaroma
Manager/Exec.	Pamela Dolby
Town Clerk	Wanda Williams
Finance Director	Sharon Willoughby
Tax Collector	Melissa Kuehne
Tax Assessor	Laurence A. Mercier
Attorney	Ronald Rappaport
Public Works	Stuart Fuller
Building	Leonard Jason
Comm Dev/Planning	Fred Masado
Police Chief	Paul Condlin
Emerg/Fire Chief	Peter G. Shemeth

Housing & Construction

New Privately Owned Housing Units Authorized by Building Permit

	Single Family	Total Bldgs	Total Units
2006	63	63	63
2007	50	50	50
2008	30	32	35

Parcel Count by Property Class, 2010

Total	6,076
Single family	3,371
Multiple units	47
Apartments	3
Condos	133
Vacant land	1,423
Open space	0
Commercial	366
Industrial	5
Misc. residential	621
Other use	107

Public Library

Edgartown Free Public Library
PO Box 5249
Edgartown, MA 02539
(508)627-4221

Director . . . Felicia Cheney

Library Statistics, FY 2008

Population served, 2007	3,920
Registered users	7,273
Circulation	49,673
Reference transactons	5,000
Total program attendance	42,018
per capita:	
Holdings	9.56
Operating income	$115.22
Internet Access	
Internet computers available	15
Weekly users	300

Municipal Finance

Debt at year end 2008	$25,907,963
Moody's rating, July 2009	Aa3

Revenues, 2008

Total	$25,502,615
From all taxes	20,772,966
Federal aid	0
State aid	1,858,010
From other governments	7,865
Charges for services	1,713,697
Licenses, permits & fees	443,147
Fines & forfeits	55,302
Interfund transfers	117,500
Misc/other/special assessments	267,064

Expenditures, 2008

Total	$24,177,643
General government	1,723,445
Public safety	3,833,212
Other/fixed costs	2,958,672
Human services	506,559
Culture & recreation	752,773
Debt Service	2,564,451
Education	8,185,572
Public works	2,081,740
Intergovernmental	1,571,219

Taxation, 2010

Property type	Valuation	Rate
Total	$6,748,455,465	-
Residential	6,252,150,137	3.09
Open space	0	0.00
Commercial	397,987,193	3.09
Industrial	3,887,800	3.09
Personal	94,430,335	3.09

Average Single Family Tax Bill, 2010

Avg. assessed home value	$1,148,542
Avg. single fam. tax bill	$3,549
Hi-Lo ranking	167/301

Police & Crime, 2008

Number of police officers	15
Violent crimes	8
Property crimes	103

Local School District

(school data 2007-08, except as noted)

Edgartown
4 Pine St.
Vineyard Haven, MA 02568
508-693-2007

Superintendent	James Weiss
Grade plan	PK-8
Total enrollment '09-10	328
Grade 12 enrollment, '09-10	0
Graduation rate	NA
Dropout rate	NA
Per-pupil expenditure	$19,065
Avg teacher salary	$65,593
Student/teacher ratio '08-09	8.6 to 1
Highly-qualified teachers, '08-09	89.8%
Teachers licensed in assigned subject	96.8%
Students per computer	2.9

Massachusetts Competency Assessment System (MCAS), 2009 results

	English		Math	
	% Prof	CPI	% Prof	CPI
Gr 4	72%	90.3	50%	87.5
Gr 6	77%	92.9	68%	87.5
Gr 8	81%	91	46%	74.3
Gr 10	NA	NA	NA	NA

Other School Districts (see Appendix D for data)
Marthas Vineyard Regional

©2010 Information Publications, Inc. All rights reserved. Photocopying prohibited. For additional copies, contact the publisher at www.informationpublications.com or (877)544-INFO (4636)

See Introduction for an explanation of all data sources.

Demographics & Socio-Economic Characteristics

Population

1990 1,229
2000 1,345
Male 646
Female 699
2008 1,351
2010 (projected)†† 1,263
2020 (projected)†† 1,158

Race & Hispanic Origin, 2000

Race
White 1,323
Black/African American 1
American Indian/Alaska Native 1
Asian 4
Hawaiian Native/Pacific Islander 0
Other Race 4
Two or more races 12
Hispanic origin 14

Age & Nativity, 2000

Under 5 years 45
18 years and over 1,099
21 years and over 1,074
65 years and over 269
85 years and over 23
Median Age 47.4
Native-born 1,282
Foreign-born 65

Age, 2020 (projected)††

Under 5 years 25
5 to 19 years 85
20 to 39 years 173
40 to 64 years 412
65 years and over 463

Educational Attainment, 2000

Population 25 years and over 1,028
High School graduates or higher .. 93.2%
Bachelor's degree or higher 43.2%
Graduate degree 21.3%

Income & Poverty, 1999

Per capita income, ... $41,702
Median household income $50,000
Median family income $60,104
Persons in poverty 69
H'holds receiving public assistance 14
H'holds receiving social security 192

Households, 2000

Total households 609
With persons under 18 148
With persons over 65 198
Family households 408
Single person households 168
Persons per household 2.2
Persons per family 2.7

Labor & Employment, 2000

Civilian labor force 748
Unemployment rate 2.8%
Civilian labor force, 2008† 838
Unemployment rate† 4.8%
Civilian labor force, 12/09† 827
Unemployment rate† 4.7%
Employed persons 16 years and over, by occupation:
Managers & professionals 331
Service occupations 118
Sales & office occupations 155
Farming, fishing & forestry 8
Construction & maintenance 67
Production & transportation 48
Self-employed persons 157

Most demographic data is from the 2000 Decennial Census
† Massachusetts Department of Revenue
†† University of Massachusetts, MISER

General Information

Town of Egremont
Box 368
S Egremont, MA 01258
413-528-0182

Elevation .... NA
Land area (square miles) 18.8
Water area (square miles) 0.1
Population density, 2008 (est) 71.9
Year incorporated 1775
Website .... www.egremont-ma.gov

Voters & Government Information

Government type .... Open Town Meeting
Number of Selectmen 3
US Congressional District(s) 1

Registered Voters, October 2008

Total 963
Democrats 342
Republicans 121
Unaffiliated/other 494

Local Officials, 2010

Chair, Bd. of Sel. .... Bruce Cumsky
Manager/Admin .... Mary Brazie
Clerk .... Margaret Muskrat
Treasurer .... Patricia Mielke
Tax Collector .... Patricia Mielke
Tax Assessor .... Mary Minehan
Legal Counsel .... Jeremia Pollard
Public Works .... James Noe
Building Inspector .... Tom Race
Comm Dev/Planning .... Charles Proctor
Police Chief .... Reena Bucknell
Fire Chief .... William Turner

Housing & Construction

New Privately Owned Housing Units Authorized by Building Permit

	Single Family	Total Bldgs	Total Units
2006	4	4	4
2007	7	7	7
2008	0	0	0

Parcel Count by Property Class, 2010

Total 1,136
Single family 737
Multiple units 15
Apartments 2
Condos 0
Vacant land 220
Open space 0
Commercial 18
Industrial 0
Misc. residential 34
Other use 110

Public Library

Egremont Free Library
PO Box 246
South Egremont, MA 01258
(413)528-1474

Librarian .... Sally Caldwell

Library Statistics, FY 2008

Population served, 2007 1,350
Registered users 295
Circulation 7,891
Reference transactons 106
Total program attendance 3,972

per capita:

Holdings 6.26
Operating income $19.74

Internet Access

Internet computers available 2
Weekly users 15

Municipal Finance

Debt at year end 2008 .... $1,152,423
Moody's rating, July 2009 .... NA

Revenues, 2008

Total $3,786,586
From all taxes 2,962,620
Federal aid 0
State aid 260,764
From other governments 46,755
Charges for services 21,675
Licenses, permits & fees 16,258
Fines & forfeits 0
Interfund transfers 55,000
Misc/other/special assessments 211,757

Expenditures, 2008

Total $3,081,417
General government 353,372
Public safety 386,158
Other/fixed costs 302,044
Human services 63,885
Culture & recreation 40,321
Debt Service 43,010
Education 1,311,989
Public works 569,827
Intergovernmental 0

Taxation, 2010

Property type	Valuation	Rate
Total	$443,037,371	-
Residential	414,837,561	6.94
Open space	0	0.00
Commercial	20,105,935	6.94
Industrial	5,200	6.94
Personal	8,088,675	6.94

Average Single Family Tax Bill, 2010

Avg. assessed home value $435,307
Avg. single fam. tax bill $3,021
Hi-Lo ranking 231/301

Police & Crime, 2008

Number of police officers 3
Violent crimes 2
Property crimes 22

Local School District

(school data 2007-08, except as noted)

Egremont (non-op)
PO Box 339
Sheffield, MA 01257
413-229-8778
Superintendent .... Michael Singleton

Non-operating district.
Resident students are sent to the Other School Districts listed below.

Grade plan .... NA
Total enrollment '09-10 .... NA
Grade 12 enrollment, '09-10 .... NA
Graduation rate .... NA
Dropout rate .... NA
Per-pupil expenditure .... NA
Avg teacher salary .... NA
Student/teacher ratio '08-09 .... NA
Highly-qualified teachers, '08-09 .... NA
Teachers licensed in assigned subject .... NA
Students per computer .... NA

Other School Districts (see Appendix D for data)
Southern Berkshire Regional

©2010 Information Publications, Inc. All rights reserved. Photocopying prohibited. For additional copies, contact the publisher at www.informationpublications.com or (877)544-INFO (4636)

See Introduction for an explanation of all data sources.

Demographics & Socio-Economic Characteristics

Population

1990	1,372
2000	1,467
Male	738
Female	729
2008	1,552
2010 (projected)††	1,499
2020 (projected)††	1,507

Race & Hispanic Origin, 2000

Race	
White	1,420
Black/African American	2
American Indian/Alaska Native	12
Asian	2
Hawaiian Native/Pacific Islander	0
Other Race	6
Two or more races	25
Hispanic origin	13

Age & Nativity, 2000

Under 5 years	79
18 years and over	1,131
21 years and over	1,087
65 years and over	202
85 years and over	21
Median Age	38.7
Native-born	1,434
Foreign-born	30

Age, 2020 (projected)††

Under 5 years	67
5 to 19 years	225
20 to 39 years	364
40 to 64 years	564
65 years and over	287

Educational Attainment, 2000

Population 25 years and over	1,036
High School graduates or higher	84.5%
Bachelor's degree or higher	11.6%
Graduate degree	3.3%

Income & Poverty, 1999

Per capita income,	$19,107
Median household income	$40,039
Median family income	$47,212
Persons in poverty	98
H'holds receiving public assistance	11
H'holds receiving social security	179

Households, 2000

Total households	600
With persons under 18	191
With persons over 65	152
Family households	400
Single person households	160
Persons per household	2.5
Persons per family	2.9

Labor & Employment, 2000

Civilian labor force	809
Unemployment rate	5.4%
Civilian labor force, 2008†	838
Unemployment rate†	7.2%
Civilian labor force, 12/09†	850
Unemployment rate†	11.2%
Employed persons 16 years and over, by occupation:	
Managers & professionals	142
Service occupations	155
Sales & office occupations	194
Farming, fishing & forestry	10
Construction & maintenance	89
Production & transportation	175
Self-employed persons	50

Most demographic data is from the 2000 Decennial Census
† Massachusetts Department of Revenue
†† University of Massachusetts, MISER

General Information

Town of Erving
12 East Main St
Erving, MA 01344
413-422-2800

Elevation	474 ft.
Land area (square miles)	13.9
Water area (square miles)	0.5
Population density, 2008 (est)	111.7
Year incorporated	1838
Website	www.erving-ma.org

Voters & Government Information

Government type	Open Town Meeting
Number of Selectmen	3
US Congressional District(s)	1

Registered Voters, October 2008

Total	1,119
Democrats	253
Republicans	110
Unaffiliated/other	750

Local Officials, 2010

Chair, Bd. of Sel.	Andrew T. Tessier
Administrator	Thomas Sharp
Town Clerk	Richard Newton
Finance Director	Margaret Sullivan
Tax Collector	Shirley Deane
Tax Assessor	James Carpenter (Chr)
Attorney	Donna MacNicol
Public Works	Paul Prest
Building	FRCOG
Comm Dev/Planning	FRCOG
Police Chief	Christopher Blair
Emerg/Fire Chief	Almon Meattey

Housing & Construction

New Privately Owned Housing Units Authorized by Building Permit

	Single Family	Total Bldgs	Total Units
2006	1	1	1
2007	4	4	4
2008	0	0	0

Parcel Count by Property Class, 2010

Total	880
Single family	505
Multiple units	39
Apartments	5
Condos	24
Vacant land	133
Open space	19
Commercial	53
Industrial	45
Misc. residential	15
Other use	42

Public Library

Erving Public Library
17 Moore Street
Erving, MA 01344
(413)423-3348

Librarian/Trustee Chr .. Barbara Friedman

Library Statistics, FY 2008

Population served, 2007	1,537
Registered users	453
Circulation	11,791
Reference transactons	227
Total program attendance	4,652
per capita:	
Holdings	4.72
Operating income	$26.53
Internet Access	
Internet computers available	3
Weekly users	14

Municipal Finance

Debt at year end 2008	$4,610,250
Moody's rating, July 2009	Baa1

Revenues, 2008

Total	$9,338,593
From all taxes	6,663,196
Federal aid	0
State aid	1,896,872
From other governments	30,410
Charges for services	17,511
Licenses, permits & fees	31,905
Fines & forfeits	746
Interfund transfers	288,279
Misc/other/special assessments	204,837

Expenditures, 2008

Total	$6,471,857
General government	503,055
Public safety	380,527
Other/fixed costs	879,849
Human services	69,690
Culture & recreation	89,307
Debt Service	913,889
Education	2,865,956
Public works	371,154
Intergovernmental	398,430

Taxation, 2010

Property type	Valuation	Rate
Total	$619,262,929	-
Residential	121,791,060	7.01
Open space	519,100	7.01
Commercial	7,227,231	12.14
Industrial	295,631,498	12.14
Personal	194,094,040	12.14

Average Single Family Tax Bill, 2010

Avg. assessed home value	$186,613
Avg. single fam. tax bill	$1,308
Hi-Lo ranking	299/301

Police & Crime, 2008

Number of police officers	3
Violent crimes	6
Property crimes	38

Local School District

(school data 2007-08, except as noted)

Erving
18 Pleasant Street
Erving, MA 01344
413-423-3337

Superintendent	Joan Wickman
Grade plan	PK-6
Total enrollment '09-10	174
Grade 12 enrollment, '09-10	0
Graduation rate	NA
Dropout rate	NA
Per-pupil expenditure	$13,699
Avg teacher salary	$52,623
Student/teacher ratio '08-09	14.5 to 1
Highly-qualified teachers, '08-09	98.5%
Teachers licensed in assigned subject	97.0%
Students per computer	2.1

Massachusetts Competency Assessment System (MCAS), 2009 results

	English		Math	
	% Prof	CPI	% Prof	CPI
Gr 4	50%	81.8	36%	79.5
Gr 6	81%	95.2	62%	79.8
Gr 8	NA	NA	NA	NA
Gr 10	NA	NA	NA	NA

Other School Districts (see Appendix D for data)

Gill-Montague Regional, Franklin County Vocational Tech

©2010 Information Publications, Inc. All rights reserved. Photocopying prohibited. For additional copies, contact the publisher at www.informationpublications.com or (877)544-INFO (4636)

See Introduction for an explanation of all data sources.

Demographics & Socio-Economic Characteristics

Population

1990	3,260
2000	3,267
Male	1,606
Female	1,661
2008	3,333
2010 (projected)††	3,241
2020 (projected)††	3,288

Race & Hispanic Origin, 2000

Race	
White	3,218
Black/African American	5
American Indian/Alaska Native	4
Asian	14
Hawaiian Native/Pacific Islander	1
Other Race	7
Two or more races	18
Hispanic origin	30

Age & Nativity, 2000

Under 5 years	181
18 years and over	2,475
21 years and over	2,397
65 years and over	443
85 years and over	40
Median Age	40.2
Native-born	3,078
Foreign-born	189

Age, 2020 (projected)††

Under 5 years	196
5 to 19 years	571
20 to 39 years	774
40 to 64 years	1,093
65 years and over	654

Educational Attainment, 2000

Population 25 years and over	2,280
High School graduates or higher	90.9%
Bachelor's degree or higher	36.3%
Graduate degree	13.5%

Income & Poverty, 1999

Per capita income,	$31,613
Median household income	$59,554
Median family income	$70,152
Persons in poverty	215
H'holds receiving public assistance	16
H'holds receiving social security	337

Households, 2000

Total households	1,313
With persons under 18	434
With persons over 65	327
Family households	888
Single person households	351
Persons per household	2.5
Persons per family	3.0

Labor & Employment, 2000

Civilian labor force	1,748
Unemployment rate	1.9%
Civilian labor force, 2008†	1,858
Unemployment rate†	6.3%
Civilian labor force, 12/09†	1,844
Unemployment rate†	8.2%
Employed persons 16 years and over, by occupation:	
Managers & professionals	701
Service occupations	263
Sales & office occupations	376
Farming, fishing & forestry	42
Construction & maintenance	142
Production & transportation	191
Self-employed persons	222

Most demographic data is from the 2000 Decennial Census
† Massachusetts Department of Revenue
†† University of Massachusetts, MISER

General Information

Town of Essex
30 Martin St
Essex, MA 01929
978-768-6531

Elevation	26 ft.
Land area (square miles)	14.2
Water area (square miles)	1.8
Population density, 2008 (est)	234.7
Year incorporated	1819
Website	essexma.org

Voters & Government Information

Government type	Open Town Meeting
Number of Selectmen	3
US Congressional District(s)	6

Registered Voters, October 2008

Total	2,704
Democrats	572
Republicans	538
Unaffiliated/other	1,588

Local Officials, 2010

Chair, Bd. of Sel.	Jeffrey Jones
Manager/Admin	Brendhan Zubricki
Clerk	Sally A. Soucy
Finance Director	Virginia Boutchie
Tax Collector	Virginia Boutchie
Tax Assessor	Richard Cairns
Attorney	Kopelman & Paige
Public Works	Paul Goodwin
Building	William Sanborn
Comm Dev/Planning	NA
Police Chief	Peter Silva
Emerg/Fire Chief	Daniel Doucette

Housing & Construction

New Privately Owned Housing Units Authorized by Building Permit

	Single Family	Total Bldgs	Total Units
2006	13	15	19
2007	7	8	9
2008	1	2	3

Parcel Count by Property Class, 2010

Total	1,796
Single family	981
Multiple units	120
Apartments	7
Condos	78
Vacant land	387
Open space	0
Commercial	53
Industrial	22
Misc. residential	49
Other use	99

Public Library

T.O.H.P. Burnham Free Library
Martin St.
Essex, MA 01929
(978)768-7410

Director	Deborah French

Library Statistics, FY 2008

Population served, 2007	3,323
Registered users	2,653
Circulation	32,037
Reference transactons	0
Total program attendance	0
per capita:	
Holdings	5.39
Operating income	$24.40
Internet Access	
Internet computers available	3
Weekly users	25

Municipal Finance

Debt at year end 2008	$24,002,866
Moody's rating, July 2009	NA

Revenues, 2008

Total	$10,314,048
From all taxes	9,330,861
Federal aid	22,603
State aid	337,709
From other governments	6,100
Charges for services	264,968
Licenses, permits & fees	131,567
Fines & forfeits	10,501
Interfund transfers	98,123
Misc/other/special assessments	55,808

Expenditures, 2008

Total	$9,599,909
General government	649,294
Public safety	1,293,584
Other/fixed costs	757,587
Human services	145,858
Culture & recreation	75,006
Debt Service	192,912
Education	5,603,961
Public works	830,036
Intergovernmental	51,671

Taxation, 2010

Property type	Valuation	Rate
Total	$829,856,573	-
Residential	745,199,020	12.26
Open space	0	0.00
Commercial	57,807,831	12.26
Industrial	15,784,656	12.26
Personal	11,065,066	12.26

Average Single Family Tax Bill, 2010

Avg. assessed home value	$545,337
Avg. single fam. tax bill	$6,686
Hi-Lo ranking	37/301

Police & Crime, 2008

Number of police officers	7
Violent crimes	NA
Property crimes	NA

Local School District

(school data 2007-08, except as noted)

Essex (non-op)
36 Lincoln Street, P. O. Box 1407
Manchester, MA 01944
978-526-4919

Superintendent	Marcia O'Neil

Non-operating district.
Resident students are sent to the Other School Districts listed below.

Grade plan	NA
Total enrollment '09-10	NA
Grade 12 enrollment, '09-10	NA
Graduation rate	NA
Dropout rate	NA
Per-pupil expenditure	NA
Avg teacher salary	NA
Student/teacher ratio '08-09	NA
Highly-qualified teachers, '08-09	NA
Teachers licensed in assigned subject	NA
Students per computer	NA

Other School Districts (see Appendix D for data)
Manchester Essex Regional, North Shore Vocational Tech

©2010 Information Publications, Inc. All rights reserved. Photocopying prohibited. For additional copies, contact the publisher at www.informationpublications.com or (877)544-INFO (4636)

Demographics & Socio-Economic Characteristics*

Population

1990	35,701
2000	38,037
Male	18,119
Female	19,918
2008	37,353
2010 (projected)††	39,405
2020 (projected)††	41,383

Race & Hispanic Origin, 2000

Race	
White	30,321
Black/African American	2,386
American Indian/Alaska Native	120
Asian	1,236
Hawaiian Native/Pacific Islander	26
Other Race	1,898
Two or more races	2,050
Hispanic origin	3,617

Age & Nativity, 2000

Under 5 years	2,244
18 years and over	29,806
21 years and over	28,505
65 years and over	5,602
85 years and over	704
Median Age	35.6
Native-born	29,714
Foreign-born	8,323

Age, 2020 (projected)††

Under 5 years	2,467
5 to 19 years	7,196
20 to 39 years	12,422
40 to 64 years	13,478
65 years and over	5,820

Educational Attainment, 2000

Population 25 years and over	26,399
High School graduates or higher	76.2%
Bachelor's degree or higher	14.7%
Graduate degree	4.6%

Income & Poverty, 1999

Per capita income,	$19,845
Median household income	$40,661
Median family income	$49,876
Persons in poverty	4,456
H'holds receiving public assistance	552
H'holds receiving social security	4,347

Households, 2000

Total households	15,435
With persons under 18	4,658
With persons over 65	4,134
Family households	9,551
Single person households	4,833
Persons per household	2.5
Persons per family	3.1

Labor & Employment, 2000

Civilian labor force	19,184
Unemployment rate	5.0%
Civilian labor force, 2008†	18,975
Unemployment rate†	6.6%
Civilian labor force, 12/09†	19,155
Unemployment rate†	9.5%
Employed persons 16 years and over, by occupation:	
Managers & professionals	4,531
Service occupations	3,487
Sales & office occupations	5,671
Farming, fishing & forestry	31
Construction & maintenance	1,987
Production & transportation	2,524
Self-employed persons	840

Most demographic data is from the 2000 Decennial Census
* see Appendix E for American Community Survey data
† Massachusetts Department of Revenue
†† University of Massachusetts, MISER

General Information

City of Everett
484 Broadway
Everett, MA 02149
617-389-2100

Elevation	10 ft.
Land area (square miles)	3.4
Water area (square miles)	0.3
Population density, 2008 (est)	10,986.2
Year incorporated	1870
Website	www.cityofeverett.com

Voters & Government Information

Government type	Mayor-Council
Number of Bicameral Cncl.	18-Jul
US Congressional District(s)	7

Registered Voters, October 2008

Total	19,167
Democrats	9,970
Republicans	975
Unaffiliated/other	8,099

Local Officials, 2010

Mayor	Carlo DeMaria Jr
Auditor	Lawrence DeCoste
City Clerk	Michael Matarazzo
Treasurer	Domenico D'Angelo
Tax Collector	Domenico D'Angelo
Tax Assessor	(vacant)
Attorney	Colleen Mejia
City Services	Brian Zaniboni
Building	James Sheehan
Comm Dev/Planning	Marzie Galazka
Police Chief	Steven Mazzie
Fire Chief	David Butler

Housing & Construction

New Privately Owned Housing Units Authorized by Building Permit

	Single Family	Total Bldgs	Total Units
2006	40	56	142
2007	31	47	135
2008	21	36	127

Parcel Count by Property Class, 2010

Total	9,506
Single family	2,720
Multiple units	3,796
Apartments	308
Condos	1,446
Vacant land	281
Open space	0
Commercial	524
Industrial	227
Misc. residential	40
Other use	164

Public Library

Parlin Memorial Library
410 Broadway
Everett, MA 02149
(617)394-2300

Director . . . . Deborah Abraham

Library Statistics, FY 2008

Population served, 2007	37,269
Registered users	23,776
Circulation	135,835
Reference transactons	14,383
Total program attendance	0
per capita:	
Holdings	4.03
Operating income	$23.74
Internet Access	
Internet computers available	19
Weekly users	936

Municipal Finance

Debt at year end 2008	$72,148,113
Moody's rating, July 2009	A2

Revenues, 2008

Total	$131,753,960
From all taxes	72,154,639
Federal aid	0
State aid	41,251,056
From other governments	0
Charges for services	11,890,114
Licenses, permits & fees	926,440
Fines & forfeits	1,367,717
Interfund transfers	112,744
Misc/other/special assessments	2,025,625

Expenditures, 2008

Total	$118,569,854
General government	5,135,793
Public safety	18,472,307
Other/fixed costs	10,816,479
Human services	1,842,539
Culture & recreation	1,000,097
Debt Service	8,718,441
Education	46,800,379
Public works	18,210,584
Intergovernmental	7,468,292

Taxation, 2010

Property type	Valuation	Rate
Total	$3,707,402,590	-
Residential	2,331,177,875	13.51
Open space	0	0.00
Commercial	417,812,915	37.02
Industrial	736,864,600	37.02
Personal	221,547,200	37.02

Average Single Family Tax Bill, 2010

Avg. assessed home value	NA
Avg. single fam. tax bill	NA
Hi-Lo ranking	NA

Police & Crime, 2008

Number of police officers	99
Violent crimes	188
Property crimes	1,352

Local School District

(school data 2007-08, except as noted)

Everett
121 Vine Street
Everett, MA 02149
617-389-7950

Superintendent	Frederick Foresteire
Grade plan	PK-12
Total enrollment '09-10	5,889
Grade 12 enrollment, '09-10	465
Graduation rate	72.6%
Dropout rate	15.1%
Per-pupil expenditure	$11,329
Avg teacher salary	$64,822
Student/teacher ratio '08-09	13.3 to 1
Highly-qualified teachers, '08-09	98.8%
Teachers licensed in assigned subject	98.8%
Students per computer	5.1

Massachusetts Competency Assessment System (MCAS), 2009 results

	English		Math	
	% Prof	CPI	% Prof	CPI
Gr 4	35%	70.4	32%	70
Gr 6	53%	78.7	41%	69.2
Gr 8	71%	88.8	28%	60.4
Gr 10	65%	85.9	50%	75.3

Other School Districts (see Appendix D for data)
None

See Introduction for an explanation of all data sources.

©2010 Information Publications, Inc. All rights reserved. Photocopying prohibited. For additional copies, contact the publisher at www.informationpublications.com or (877)544-INFO (4636)

Demographics & Socio-Economic Characteristics

Population

1990	16,132
2000	16,159
Male	7,628
Female	8,531
2008	16,112
2010 (projected)††	15,905
2020 (projected)††	15,744

Race & Hispanic Origin, 2000

Race	
White	15,565
Black/African American	97
American Indian/Alaska Native	42
Asian	71
Hawaiian Native/Pacific Islander	3
Other Race	192
Two or more races	189
Hispanic origin	135

Age & Nativity, 2000

Under 5 years	757
18 years and over	12,653
21 years and over	12,171
65 years and over	3,150
85 years and over	533
Median Age	41.2
Native-born	15,243
Foreign-born	916

Age, 2020 (projected)††

Under 5 years	716
5 to 19 years	2,279
20 to 39 years	3,497
40 to 64 years	5,407
65 years and over	3,845

Educational Attainment, 2000

Population 25 years and over	11,663
High School graduates or higher	76.8%
Bachelor's degree or higher	16.9%
Graduate degree	5.5%

Income & Poverty, 1999

Per capita income,	$20,986
Median household income	$41,696
Median family income	$52,298
Persons in poverty	1,423
H'holds receiving public assistance	159
H'holds receiving social security	2,236

Households, 2000

Total households	6,622
With persons under 18	2,004
With persons over 65	2,120
Family households	4,251
Single person households	2,017
Persons per household	2.4
Persons per family	3.0

Labor & Employment, 2000

Civilian labor force	8,229
Unemployment rate	3.9%
Civilian labor force, 2008†	8,556
Unemployment rate†	8.4%
Civilian labor force, 12/09†	8,583
Unemployment rate†	11.1%
Employed persons 16 years and over, by occupation:	
Managers & professionals	2,353
Service occupations	1,103
Sales & office occupations	2,176
Farming, fishing & forestry	118
Construction & maintenance	750
Production & transportation	1,405
Self-employed persons	499

Most demographic data is from the 2000 Decennial Census
† Massachusetts Department of Revenue
†† University of Massachusetts, MISER

General Information

Town of Fairhaven
40 Center St
Fairhaven, MA 02719
508-979-4104

Elevation	11 ft.
Land area (square miles)	12.4
Water area (square miles)	1.7
Population density, 2008 (est)	1,299.4
Year incorporated	1812
Website	www.fairhaven-ma.gov

Voters & Government Information

Government type	Rep. Town Meeting
Number of Selectmen	3
US Congressional District(s)	4

Registered Voters, October 2008

Total	10,936
Democrats	3,965
Republicans	877
Unaffiliated/other	6,014

Local Officials, 2010

Chair, Bd. of Sel.	Brian K. Bowcock
Executive Secretary	Jeffrey W. Osuch
Town Clerk	Eileen M. Lowney
Finance	John L. Nunes
Tax Collector	Carol Brandolini
Tax Assessor	Paul Matheson
Attorney	Thomas P. Crotty
Public Works	William Fitzgerald
Building	Wayne Fostin
Comm Dev/Planning	William D. Roth Jr
Police Chief	Michael J. Myers
Emerg/Fire Chief	Timothy Francis

Housing & Construction

New Privately Owned Housing Units Authorized by Building Permit

	Single Family	Total Bldgs	Total Units
2006	43	43	43
2007	21	21	21
2008	8	8	8

Parcel Count by Property Class, 2010

Total	7,441
Single family	5,373
Multiple units	431
Apartments	47
Condos	206
Vacant land	912
Open space	0
Commercial	283
Industrial	23
Misc. residential	45
Other use	121

Public Library

Millicent Library
PO Box 30
Fairhaven, MA 02719
(508)992-5342

Director	Carolyn Longworth

Library Statistics, FY 2008

Population served, 2007	16,124
Registered users	8,315
Circulation	145,742
Reference transactons	0
Total program attendance	0
per capita:	
Holdings	4.77
Operating income	$40.09
Internet Access	
Internet computers available	4
Weekly users	400

Municipal Finance

Debt at year end 2008	$26,482,510
Moody's rating, July 2009	A1

Revenues, 2008

Total	$39,631,737
From all taxes	22,347,552
Federal aid	0
State aid	11,991,513
From other governments	0
Charges for services	1,902,787
Licenses, permits & fees	369,082
Fines & forfeits	7,035
Interfund transfers	1,404,484
Misc/other/special assessments	804,642

Expenditures, 2008

Total	$33,608,099
General government	1,613,285
Public safety	4,670,239
Other/fixed costs	2,631,927
Human services	715,626
Culture & recreation	786,575
Debt Service	2,113,786
Education	18,356,045
Public works	2,428,369
Intergovernmental	292,247

Taxation, 2010

Property type	Valuation	Rate
Total	$2,129,465,251	-
Residential	1,816,496,043	8.89
Open space	0	0.00
Commercial	249,034,838	17.87
Industrial	25,049,460	17.87
Personal	38,884,910	17.87

Average Single Family Tax Bill, 2010

Avg. assessed home value	$284,772
Avg. single fam. tax bill	$2,532
Hi-Lo ranking	279/301

Police & Crime, 2008

Number of police officers	32
Violent crimes	51
Property crimes	558

Local School District

(school data 2007-08, except as noted)

Fairhaven
128 Washington Street
Fairhaven, MA 02719
508-979-4000

Superintendent	Robert Baldwin
Grade plan	PK-12
Total enrollment '09-10	1,986
Grade 12 enrollment, '09-10	147
Graduation rate	81.6%
Dropout rate	12.1%
Per-pupil expenditure	$11,044
Avg teacher salary	$54,834
Student/teacher ratio '08-09	13.6 to 1
Highly-qualified teachers, '08-09	97.5%
Teachers licensed in assigned subject	98.0%
Students per computer	4.4

Massachusetts Competency Assessment System (MCAS), 2009 results

	English		Math	
	% Prof	CPI	% Prof	CPI
Gr 4	69%	87.2	49%	82.3
Gr 6	64%	85.2	48%	75
Gr 8	75%	88.5	49%	72.9
Gr 10	78%	91	80%	91

Other School Districts (see Appendix D for data)

Receives students from Acushnet; sends to Greater New Bedford Vocational Tech, Bristol County Agricultural

©2010 Information Publications, Inc. All rights reserved. Photocopying prohibited. For additional copies, contact the publisher at www.informationpublications.com or (877)544-INFO (4636)

See Introduction for an explanation of all data sources.

Demographics & Socio-Economic Characteristics*

Population

1990	92,703
2000	91,938
Male	42,953
Female	48,985
2008	90,931
2010 (projected)††	90,280
2020 (projected)††	89,430

Race & Hispanic Origin, 2000

Race	
White	83,815
Black/African American	2,283
American Indian/Alaska Native	172
Asian	1,987
Hawaiian Native/Pacific Islander	25
Other Race	1,311
Two or more races	2,345
Hispanic origin	3,040

Age & Nativity, 2000

Under 5 years	5,846
18 years and over	69,759
21 years and over	66,343
65 years and over	15,572
85 years and over	2,321
Median Age	35.7
Native-born	73,722
Foreign-born	18,216

Age, 2020 (projected)††

Under 5 years	4,956
5 to 19 years	14,597
20 to 39 years	24,287
40 to 64 years	29,517
65 years and over	16,073

Educational Attainment, 2000

Population 25 years and over	61,177
High School graduates or higher	56.6%
Bachelor's degree or higher	10.7%
Graduate degree	3.2%

Income & Poverty, 1999

Per capita income,	$16,118
Median household income	$29,014
Median family income	$37,671
Persons in poverty	15,421
H'holds receiving public assistance	2,534
H'holds receiving social security	11,673

Households, 2000

Total households	38,759
With persons under 18	12,467
With persons over 65	10,949
Family households	23,558
Single person households	13,247
Persons per household	2.3
Persons per family	3.0

Labor & Employment, 2000

Civilian labor force	42,647
Unemployment rate	7.0%
Civilian labor force, 2008†	44,403
Unemployment rate†	12.7%
Civilian labor force, 12/09†	45,019
Unemployment rate†	16.9%
Employed persons 16 years and over, by occupation:	
Managers & professionals	8,870
Service occupations	7,364
Sales & office occupations	9,855
Farming, fishing & forestry	109
Construction & maintenance	3,841
Production & transportation	9,635
Self-employed persons	1,312

Most demographic data is from the 2000 Decennial Census
* see Appendix D and E for American Community Survey data
† Massachusetts Department of Revenue
†† University of Massachusetts, MISER

General Information

City of Fall River
One Government Center
Fall River, MA 02722
508-324-2000

Elevation	140 ft.
Land area (square miles)	31.0
Water area (square miles)	7.2
Population density, 2008 (est)	2,933.3
Year incorporated	1803
Website	www.fallriverma.org

Voters & Government Information

Government type	Mayor-Council
Number of Councilpersons	9
US Congressional District(s)	3, 4

Registered Voters, October 2008

Total	49,763
Democrats	28,731
Republicans	3,436
Unaffiliated/other	17,163

Local Officials, 2010

Mayor	William A. Flanagan
City Administrator	Adam Chapdelaine
City Clerk	Alison M. Brett
Fiscal Svcs Dir/Treasurer	Daniel Patten
Tax Collector	Shannon Lyonnaise
Assessor	Pamela Davis
Corporation Counsel	Arthur Frank
Public Works	Kenneth Pacheco
Code Enforcement	Joseph M. Biszko
Planning Director	James K. Hartnett
Police Chief	John M. Souza
Fire Chief	Paul Ford

Housing & Construction

New Privately Owned Housing Units Authorized by Building Permit

	Single Family	Total Bldgs	Total Units
2006	133	150	181
2007	133	145	168
2008	42	46	55

Parcel Count by Property Class, 2010

Total	NA
Single family	NA
Multiple units	NA
Apartments	NA
Condos	NA
Vacant land	NA
Open space	NA
Commercial	NA
Industrial	NA
Misc. residential	NA
Other use	NA

Public Library

Fall River Public Library
104 North Main St.
Fall River, MA 02720
(508)324-2700

Administrator	Paula Costa Cullen

Library Statistics, FY 2008

Population served, 2007	90,905
Registered users	30,578
Circulation	201,227
Reference transactons	27,637
Total program attendance	165,830
per capita:	
Holdings	2.20
Operating income	$13.15
Internet Access	
Internet computers available	32
Weekly users	910

Municipal Finance

Debt at year end 2008	$217,013,601
Moody's rating, July 2009	Baa1

Revenues, 2008

Total	$224,239,183
From all taxes	70,765,997
Federal aid	3,705,244
State aid	133,221,684
From other governments	487,830
Charges for services	7,467,400
Licenses, permits & fees	1,552,192
Fines & forfeits	0
Interfund transfers	4,196,092
Misc/other/special assessments	1,421,372

Expenditures, 2008

Total	$188,274,290
General government	5,474,772
Public safety	39,022,705
Other/fixed costs	14,220,071
Human services	3,405,779
Culture & recreation	2,506,341
Debt Service	15,711,466
Education	95,801,176
Public works	9,313,312
Intergovernmental	1,757,780

Taxation, 2010

Property type	Valuation	Rate
Total	NA	-
Residential	NA	NA
Open space	NA	NA
Commercial	NA	NA
Industrial	NA	NA
Personal	NA	NA

Average Single Family Tax Bill, 2010

Avg. assessed home value	NA
Avg. single fam. tax bill	NA
Hi-Lo ranking	NA

Police & Crime, 2008

Number of police officers	240
Violent crimes	1,088
Property crimes	3,528

Local School District

(school data 2007-08, except as noted)

Fall River
417 Rock Street
Fall River, MA 02720
508-675-8420

Superintendent	Margery Mayo-Brown
Grade plan	PK-12
Total enrollment '09-10	9,886
Grade 12 enrollment, '09-10	529
Graduation rate	56.0%
Dropout rate	31.8%
Per-pupil expenditure	$12,121
Avg teacher salary	$63,381
Student/teacher ratio '08-09	13.8 to 1
Highly-qualified teachers, '08-09	93.8%
Teachers licensed in assigned subject	93.9%
Students per computer	9.4

Massachusetts Competency Assessment System (MCAS), 2009 results

	English		Math	
	% Prof	CPI	% Prof	CPI
Gr 4	29%	64.7	28%	63.9
Gr 6	39%	71.9	34%	62.4
Gr 8	63%	84	26%	57.2
Gr 10	65%	86.5	46%	74.4

Other School Districts (see Appendix D for data)
Greater Fall River Vocational Tech, Bristol County Agricultural

See Introduction for an explanation of all data sources.

©2010 Information Publications, Inc. All rights reserved. Photocopying prohibited. For additional copies, contact the publisher at www.informationpublications.com or (877)544-INFO (4636)

Demographics & Socio-Economic Characteristics

Population

1990 27,960
2000 32,660
Male 15,252
Female 17,408
2008 33,123
2010 (projected)†† 36,389
2020 (projected)†† 40,543

Race & Hispanic Origin, 2000

Race
White 30,502
Black/African American 593
American Indian/Alaska Native 168
Asian 300
Hawaiian Native/Pacific Islander 5
Other Race 469
Two or more races 623
Hispanic origin 417

Age & Nativity, 2000

Under 5 years 1,466
18 years and over 25,896
21 years and over 25,135
65 years and over 7,338
85 years and over 863
Median Age 45.0
Native-born 30,763
Foreign-born 1,897

Age, 2020 (projected)††

Under 5 years 1,483
5 to 19 years 4,527
20 to 39 years 6,755
40 to 64 years 13,393
65 years and over 14,385

Educational Attainment, 2000

Population 25 years and over 24,416
High School graduates or higher .. 90.4%
Bachelor's degree or higher 36.0%
Graduate degree 15.7%

Income & Poverty, 1999

Per capita income, ... $27,548
Median household income $48,191
Median family income $57,422
Persons in poverty 2,238
H'holds receiving public assistance 215
H'holds receiving social security 5,437

Households, 2000

Total households 13,859
With persons under 18 3,661
With persons over 65 4,971
Family households 8,976
Single person households 4,136
Persons per household 2.3
Persons per family 2.8

Labor & Employment, 2000

Civilian labor force 15,711
Unemployment rate 5.1%
Civilian labor force, 2008† 17,162
Unemployment rate† 7.2%
Civilian labor force, 12/09† 16,725
Unemployment rate† 9.2%
Employed persons 16 years and over, by occupation:
Managers & professionals 6,049
Service occupations 2,519
Sales & office occupations 3,694
Farming, fishing & forestry 77
Construction & maintenance 1,484
Production & transportation 1,088
Self-employed persons 1,743

Most demographic data is from the 2000 Decennial Census
† Massachusetts Department of Revenue
†† University of Massachusetts, MISER

General Information

Town of Falmouth
59 Town Hall Square
Falmouth, MA 02540
508-548-7611

Elevation .... 18 ft.
Land area (square miles) 44.2
Water area (square miles) 10.2
Population density, 2008 (est) 749.4
Year incorporated 1694
Website .... www.falmouthmass.us

Voters & Government Information

Government type .... Rep. Town Meeting
Number of Selectmen 5
US Congressional District(s) 10

Registered Voters, October 2008

Total 25,881
Democrats 7,828
Republicans 3,631
Unaffiliated/other 14,271

Local Officials, 2010

Chair, Bd. of Sel. .... Mary Pat Flynn
Town Manager .... Robert L. Whritenour
Town Clerk .... Michael C. Palmer
Treasurer .... Carol Martin
Tax Collector .... Patricia O'Connell
Tax Assessor .... David Bailey
Attorney .... Frank Duffy
Public Works .... Ray Jack
Building .... Eladio Gore
Comm Dev/Planning .... Brian Currie
Police Chief .... Anthony Riello
Fire Chief .... Paul Brodeur

Housing & Construction

New Privately Owned Housing Units Authorized by Building Permit

	Single Family	Total Bldgs	Total Units
2006	111	118	158
2007	97	112	176
2008	63	69	116

Parcel Count by Property Class, 2010

Total 23,799
Single family 18,080
Multiple units 275
Apartments 63
Condos 1,301
Vacant land 2,297
Open space 282
Commercial 920
Industrial 121
Misc. residential 259
Other use 201

Public Library

Falmouth Public Library
300 Main Street
Falmouth, MA 02540
(508)457-2555

Director .... Leslie Morrissey

Library Statistics, FY 2008

Population served, 2007 33,247
Registered users 29,763
Circulation 408,039
Reference transactons 43,304
Total program attendance 0
per capita:
Holdings 4.44
Operating income $49.37
Internet Access
Internet computers available 52
Weekly users 4,524

Municipal Finance

Debt at year end 2008 .... $91,884,998
Moody's rating, July 2009 .... Aa2

Revenues, 2008

Total $103,338,540
From all taxes 74,490,476
Federal aid 15,881
State aid 9,863,228
From other governments 84,178
Charges for services 10,553,046
Licenses, permits & fees 1,339,649
Fines & forfeits 132,134
Interfund transfers 0
Misc/other/special assessments 3,429,974

Expenditures, 2008

Total $99,792,310
General government 4,381,729
Public safety 12,331,560
Other/fixed costs 14,238,167
Human services 1,239,859
Culture & recreation 2,661,192
Debt Service 9,875,468
Education 42,658,819
Public works 9,146,554
Intergovernmental 1,775,359

Taxation, 2010

Property type	Valuation	Rate
Total	$11,175,752,766	-
Residential	10,288,846,988	6.75
Open space	3,877,700	6.75
Commercial	611,416,088	6.75
Industrial	76,338,300	6.75
Personal	195,273,690	6.75

Average Single Family Tax Bill, 2010

Avg. assessed home value $492,809
Avg. single fam. tax bill $3,326
Hi-Lo ranking 198/301

Police & Crime, 2008

Number of police officers 61
Violent crimes 125
Property crimes 1,110

Local School District

(school data 2007-08, except as noted)

Falmouth
340 Teaticket Hwy
East Falmouth, MA 02536
508-548-0151

Superintendent .... Marc Dupuis
Grade plan PK-12
Total enrollment '09-10 3,750
Grade 12 enrollment, '09-10 253
Graduation rate 84.0%
Dropout rate 10.9%
Per-pupil expenditure $13,086
Avg teacher salary $66,242
Student/teacher ratio '08-09 .... 11.9 to 1
Highly-qualified teachers, '08-09 ... 100.0%
Teachers licensed in assigned subject .. 99.7%
Students per computer 4.1

Massachusetts Competency Assessment System (MCAS), 2009 results

	English		Math	
	% Prof	CPI	% Prof	CPI
Gr 4	65%	86.3	69%	88.9
Gr 6	74%	89.4	67%	85.4
Gr 8	79%	92	49%	75.8
Gr 10	88%	94.8	85%	92.8

Other School Districts (see Appendix D for data)
Upper Cape Cod Vocational Tech

©2010 Information Publications, Inc. All rights reserved. Photocopying prohibited. For additional copies, contact the publisher at www.informationpublications.com or (877)544-INFO (4636)

See Introduction for an explanation of all data sources.

©2010 Information Publications, Inc. All rights reserved. Photocopying prohibited. For additional copies, contact the publisher at www.informationpublications.com or (877)544-INFO (4636)

Demographics & Socio-Economic Characteristics*

Population

1990	41,194
2000	39,102
Male	18,659
Female	20,443
2008	40,239
2010 (projected)††	38,863
2020 (projected)††	38,837

Race & Hispanic Origin, 2000

Race	
White	32,007
Black/African American	1,426
American Indian/Alaska Native	138
Asian	1,668
Hawaiian Native/Pacific Islander	13
Other Race	2,652
Two or more races	1,198
Hispanic origin	5,852

Age & Nativity, 2000

Under 5 years	2,637
18 years and over	28,998
21 years and over	26,958
65 years and over	5,713
85 years and over	869
Median Age	34.1
Native-born	35,875
Foreign-born	3,227

Age, 2020 (projected)††

Under 5 years	2,536
5 to 19 years	7,620
20 to 39 years	11,442
40 to 64 years	11,239
65 years and over	6,000

Educational Attainment, 2000

Population 25 years and over	24,863
High School graduates or higher	75.4%
Bachelor's degree or higher	15.4%
Graduate degree	6.1%

Income & Poverty, 1999

Per capita income,	$17,256
Median household income	$37,004
Median family income	$43,291
Persons in poverty	5,627
H'holds receiving public assistance	877
H'holds receiving social security	4,598

Households, 2000

Total households	14,943
With persons under 18	5,038
With persons over 65	3,903
Family households	9,363
Single person households	4,526
Persons per household	2.5
Persons per family	3.1

Labor & Employment, 2000

Civilian labor force	19,142
Unemployment rate	8.4%
Civilian labor force, 2008†	18,342
Unemployment rate†	9.2%
Civilian labor force, 12/09†	18,311
Unemployment rate†	13.0%
Employed persons 16 years and over, by occupation:	
Managers & professionals	4,777
Service occupations	2,981
Sales & office occupations	4,509
Farming, fishing & forestry	11
Construction & maintenance	1,504
Production & transportation	3,754
Self-employed persons	644

Most demographic data is from the 2000 Decennial Census
* see Appendix E for American Community Survey data
† Massachusetts Department of Revenue
†† University of Massachusetts, MISER

General Information

City of Fitchburg
718 Main St
Fitchburg, MA 01420
978-345-9550

Elevation	458 ft.
Land area (square miles)	27.8
Water area (square miles)	0.3
Population density, 2008 (est)	1,447.4
Year incorporated	1764
Website	www.ci.fitchburg.ma.us

Voters & Government Information

Government type	Mayor-Council
Number of Councilpersons	11
US Congressional District(s)	1

Registered Voters, October 2008

Total	21,873
Democrats	7,529
Republicans	2,305
Unaffiliated/other	11,810

Local Officials, 2010

Mayor	Lisa A. Wong
Manager/Admin	NA
Clerk	Anna Farrell
Finance Director	Richard Sarasin
Tax Collector	Brian Doheny
Tax Assessor	Thomas Caputi
Attorney	Michael Ciota
Public Works	Lenny Laakso
Building	Michael Gallant
Planning	Larry Casassa
Police Chief	NA
Emerg/Fire Chief	Kevin Roy

Housing & Construction

New Privately Owned Housing Units Authorized by Building Permit

	Single Family	Total Bldgs	Total Units
2006	136	137	138
2007	107	107	107
2008	20	20	20

Parcel Count by Property Class, 2010

Total	12,760
Single family	6,410
Multiple units	2,267
Apartments	372
Condos	1,134
Vacant land	1,383
Open space	0
Commercial	740
Industrial	223
Misc. residential	39
Other use	192

Public Library

Fitchburg Public Library
610 Main St.
Fitchburg, MA 01420
(978)345-9639

Chief Librarian	Sharon Bernard

Library Statistics, FY 2008

Population served, 2007	39,835
Registered users	24,184
Circulation	194,660
Reference transactons	0
Total program attendance	0
per capita:	
Holdings	4.35
Operating income	$37.69
Internet Access	
Internet computers available	10
Weekly users	0

Municipal Finance

Debt at year end 2008	$85,831,596
Moody's rating, July 2009	Baa1

Revenues, 2008

Total	$98,550,676
From all taxes	38,609,965
Federal aid	0
State aid	51,702,021
From other governments	49,985
Charges for services	2,921,233
Licenses, permits & fees	622,155
Fines & forfeits	312,935
Interfund transfers	1,600,000
Misc/other/special assessments	1,366,191

Expenditures, 2008

Total	$83,129,149
General government	2,935,583
Public safety	13,203,995
Other/fixed costs	9,559,515
Human services	738,003
Culture & recreation	1,474,517
Debt Service	5,203,501
Education	44,680,189
Public works	5,062,605
Intergovernmental	0

Taxation, 2010

Property type	Valuation	Rate
Total	$2,443,382,008	-
Residential	1,993,453,635	14.44
Open space	0	0.00
Commercial	235,972,456	20.13
Industrial	117,636,400	20.13
Personal	96,319,517	20.13

Average Single Family Tax Bill, 2010

Avg. assessed home value	$186,056
Avg. single fam. tax bill	$2,687
Hi-Lo ranking	264/301

Police & Crime, 2008

Number of police officers	80
Violent crimes	NA
Property crimes	1,182

Local School District

(school data 2007-08, except as noted)

Fitchburg
376 South Street
Fitchburg, MA 01420
978-345-3200

Superintendent	Andre Ravenelle
Grade plan	PK-12
Total enrollment '09-10	4,997
Grade 12 enrollment, '09-10	330
Graduation rate	72.0%
Dropout rate	18.6%
Per-pupil expenditure	$11,782
Avg teacher salary	$65,382
Student/teacher ratio '08-09	13.6 to 1
Highly-qualified teachers, '08-09	97.6%
Teachers licensed in assigned subject	98.7%
Students per computer	6

Massachusetts Competency Assessment System (MCAS), 2009 results

	English		Math	
	% Prof	CPI	% Prof	CPI
Gr 4	31%	68.3	27%	65.7
Gr 6	45%	74	36%	65
Gr 8	66%	85.4	28%	59.9
Gr 10	60%	82.9	52%	77.5

Other School Districts (see Appendix D for data)
Montachusett Vocational Tech

See Introduction for an explanation of all data sources.

Demographics & Socio-Economic Characteristics

Population

1990	742
2000	676
Male	353
Female	323
2008	675
2010 (projected)††	601
2020 (projected)††	537

Race & Hispanic Origin, 2000

Race	
White	659
Black/African American	4
American Indian/Alaska Native	3
Asian	3
Hawaiian Native/Pacific Islander	0
Other Race	2
Two or more races	5
Hispanic origin	3

Age & Nativity, 2000

Under 5 years	31
18 years and over	506
21 years and over	484
65 years and over	94
85 years and over	5
Median Age	39.8
Native-born	681
Foreign-born	8

Age, 2020 (projected)††

Under 5 years	25
5 to 19 years	81
20 to 39 years	110
40 to 64 years	202
65 years and over	119

Educational Attainment, 2000

Population 25 years and over	454
High School graduates or higher	80.4%
Bachelor's degree or higher	15.0%
Graduate degree	6.6%

Income & Poverty, 1999

Per capita income,	$16,979
Median household income	$43,000
Median family income	$52,500
Persons in poverty	40
H'holds receiving public assistance	1
H'holds receiving social security	64

Households, 2000

Total households	265
With persons under 18	90
With persons over 65	70
Family households	197
Single person households	60
Persons per household	2.6
Persons per family	3.0

Labor & Employment, 2000

Civilian labor force	364
Unemployment rate	2.2%
Civilian labor force, 2008†	396
Unemployment rate†	8.3%
Civilian labor force, 12/09†	406
Unemployment rate†	10.6%
Employed persons 16 years and over, by occupation:	
Managers & professionals	86
Service occupations	48
Sales & office occupations	95
Farming, fishing & forestry	2
Construction & maintenance	53
Production & transportation	72
Self-employed persons	21

Most demographic data is from the 2000 Decennial Census
† Massachusetts Department of Revenue
†† University of Massachusetts, MISER

General Information

Town of Florida
379 Mohawk Trail
Drury, MA 01343
413-662-2448

Elevation	1,895 ft.
Land area (square miles)	24.4
Water area (square miles)	0.2
Population density, 2008 (est)	27.7
Year incorporated	1805
Email	townadmin@floridamass.net

Voters & Government Information

Government type	Open Town Meeting
Number of Selectmen	3
US Congressional District(s)	1

Registered Voters, October 2008

Total	547
Democrats	125
Republicans	43
Unaffiliated/other	376

Local Officials, 2010

Chair, Bd. of Sel.	Neil Oleson
Manager/Admin	Christine Dobbert
Clerk	Lisa Brown
Finance Director	Lisa Tanner
Tax Collector	Linda Haggerty
Tax Assessor	Margo Van Peterson
Attorney	Kopelman & Paige
Public Works	Glen Burdick
Building	Vincent Lively
Planning	Timothy Zelezo
Police Chief	David Burdick
Emerg/Fire Chief	Michael Bedini

Housing & Construction

New Privately Owned Housing Units Authorized by Building Permit

	Single Family	Total Bldgs	Total Units
2006	6	6	6
2007	3	3	3
2008	1	1	1

Parcel Count by Property Class, 2010

Total	648
Single family	292
Multiple units	0
Apartments	1
Condos	0
Vacant land	267
Open space	0
Commercial	6
Industrial	11
Misc. residential	60
Other use	11

Public Library

Florida Free Library
56 North County Road
Florida, MA 01247
(413)664-0153 x14

Director	Alicia Daniels (Actg)

Library Statistics, FY 2008

Population served, 2007	678
Registered users	284
Circulation	15,849
Reference transactons	0
Total program attendance	9,000
per capita:	
Holdings	17.07
Operating income	$34.15
Internet Access	
Internet computers available	2
Weekly users	23

Municipal Finance

Debt at year end 2008	$58,328
Moody's rating, July 2009	NA

Revenues, 2008

Total	$2,454,843
From all taxes	1,886,084
Federal aid	0
State aid	318,950
From other governments	6,385
Charges for services	112,054
Licenses, permits & fees	4,867
Fines & forfeits	0
Interfund transfers	88,825
Misc/other/special assessments	18,839

Expenditures, 2008

Total	$2,516,586
General government	192,706
Public safety	37,650
Other/fixed costs	385,809
Human services	19,593
Culture & recreation	21,920
Debt Service	13,194
Education	1,297,362
Public works	508,830
Intergovernmental	22,273

Taxation, 2010

Property type	Valuation	Rate
Total	$123,288,702	-
Residential	62,060,304	8.00
Open space	0	0.00
Commercial	1,093,387	23.31
Industrial	45,885,800	23.31
Personal	14,249,211	23.31

Average Single Family Tax Bill, 2010

Avg. assessed home value	$159,507
Avg. single fam. tax bill	$1,276
Hi-Lo ranking	300/301

Police & Crime, 2008

Number of police officers	NA
Violent crimes	NA
Property crimes	NA

Local School District

(school data 2007-08, except as noted)

Florida
56 North County Rd
Florida, MA 01247
413-664-6023

Superintendent	Jon Lev
Grade plan	PK-8
Total enrollment '09-10	115
Grade 12 enrollment, '09-10	0
Graduation rate	NA
Dropout rate	NA
Per-pupil expenditure	$11,744
Avg teacher salary	$34,252
Student/teacher ratio '08-09	9.0 to 1
Highly-qualified teachers, '08-09	96.3%
Teachers licensed in assigned subject	98.4%
Students per computer	2.3

Massachusetts Competency Assessment System (MCAS), 2009 results

	English		Math	
	% Prof	CPI	% Prof	CPI
Gr 4	NA	NA	NA	NA
Gr 6	45%	77.5	50%	77.5
Gr 8	43%	75	21%	58.9
Gr 10	NA	NA	NA	NA

Other School Districts (see Appendix D for data)

Receives students from Monroe; sends grades 9-12 to North Adams and Northern Berkshire Vocational Tech

©2010 Information Publications, Inc. All rights reserved. Photocopying prohibited. For additional copies, contact the publisher at www.informationpublications.com or (877)544-INFO (4636)

See Introduction for an explanation of all data sources.

©2010 Information Publications, Inc. All rights reserved. Photocopying prohibited. For additional copies, contact the publisher at www.informationpublications.com or (877)544-INFO (4636)

Demographics & Socio-Economic Characteristics

Population

1990 . . . 14,637
2000 . . . 16,246
Male . . . 7,949
Female . . . 8,297
2008 . . . 16,347
2010 (projected)†† . . . 16,683
2020 (projected)†† . . . 16,738

Race & Hispanic Origin, 2000

Race
White . . . 15,774
Black/African American . . . 134
American Indian/Alaska Native . . . 18
Asian . . . 199
Hawaiian Native/Pacific Islander . . . 2
Other Race . . . 32
Two or more races . . . 87
Hispanic origin . . . 172

Age & Nativity, 2000

Under 5 years . . . 1,118
18 years and over . . . 11,948
21 years and over . . . 11,577
65 years and over . . . 1,933
85 years and over . . . 187
Median Age . . . 38.1
Native-born . . . 15,487
Foreign-born . . . 759

Age, 2020 (projected)††

Under 5 years . . . 937
5 to 19 years . . . 3,015
20 to 39 years . . . 3,881
40 to 64 years . . . 5,766
65 years and over . . . 3,139

Educational Attainment, 2000

Population 25 years and over . . . 11,018
High School graduates or higher . . 92.5%
Bachelor's degree or higher . . . 37.5%
Graduate degree . . . 14.3%

Income & Poverty, 1999

Per capita income, . . . $32,294
Median household income . . . $64,323
Median family income . . . $78,811
Persons in poverty . . . 503
H'holds receiving public assistance . . . 39
H'holds receiving social security . . . 1,457

Households, 2000

Total households . . . 6,141
With persons under 18 . . . 2,277
With persons over 65 . . . 1,390
Family households . . . 4,395
Single person households . . . 1,437
Persons per household . . . 2.6
Persons per family . . . 3.2

Labor & Employment, 2000

Civilian labor force . . . 8,935
Unemployment rate . . . 3.0%
Civilian labor force, 2008† . . . 9,214
Unemployment rate† . . . 5.9%
Civilian labor force, 12/09† . . . 9,166
Unemployment rate† . . . 8.0%
Employed persons 16 years and over, by occupation:
Managers & professionals . . . 4,058
Service occupations . . . 1,045
Sales & office occupations . . . 2,137
Farming, fishing & forestry . . . 14
Construction & maintenance . . . 649
Production & transportation . . . 765
Self-employed persons . . . 599

Most demographic data is from the 2000 Decennial Census
† Massachusetts Department of Revenue
†† University of Massachusetts, MISER

General Information

Town of Foxborough
40 South St
Foxborough, MA 02035
508-543-1200

Elevation . . . 300 ft.
Land area (square miles) . . . 20.1
Water area (square miles) . . . 0.8
Population density, 2008 (est) . . . 813.3
Year incorporated . . . 1778
Website . . . www.foxboroughma.gov

Voters & Government Information

Government type . . . Open Town Meeting
Number of Selectmen . . . 5
US Congressional District(s) . . . 4

Registered Voters, October 2008

Total . . . 11,489
Democrats . . . 2,851
Republicans . . . 1,733
Unaffiliated/other . . . 6,864

Local Officials, 2010

Chair, Bd. of Sel. . . . Paul R. Feeney
Town Manager . . . Andrew Gala Jr
Town Clerk . . . Robert E. Cutler Jr
Finance Director . . . William Scollins III
Treas/Collector . . . Lisa J. Sinkus
Chief Assessor . . . Hannelore Simonds
Attorney . . . Paul DeRensis
Public Works . . . R. Swanson/L. Potter
Building . . . William J. Casbarra
Planning . . . Mark Resnick
Police Chief . . . Edward T. O'Leary
Emerg/Fire Chief . . . Roger P. Hatfield

Housing & Construction

New Privately Owned Housing Units Authorized by Building Permit

	Single Family	Total Bldgs	Total Units
2006	63	63	63
2007	23	23	23
2008	17	28	275

Parcel Count by Property Class, 2010

Total . . . NA
Single family . . . NA
Multiple units . . . NA
Apartments . . . NA
Condos . . . NA
Vacant land . . . NA
Open space . . . NA
Commercial . . . NA
Industrial . . . NA
Misc. residential . . . NA
Other use . . . NA

Public Library

Boyden Library
10 Bird St.
Foxborough, MA 02035
(508)543-1245

Director . . . Jerry M. Cirillo

Library Statistics, FY 2008

Population served, 2007 . . . 16,298
Registered users . . . 11,094
Circulation . . . 230,051
Reference transactons . . . 4,180
Total program attendance . . . 129,236

per capita:

Holdings . . . 6.61
Operating income . . . $56.70

Internet Access

Internet computers available . . . 8
Weekly users . . . 200

Municipal Finance

Debt at year end 2008 . . . $28,832,078
Moody's rating, July 2009 . . . Aa3

Revenues, 2008

Total . . . $50,315,326
From all taxes . . . 35,040,571
Federal aid . . . 50,560
State aid . . . 10,486,544
From other governments . . . 0
Charges for services . . . 370,496
Licenses, permits & fees . . . 2,159,740
Fines & forfeits . . . 98,341
Interfund transfers . . . 947,978
Misc/other/special assessments . . . 580,548

Expenditures, 2008

Total . . . $45,374,958
General government . . . 1,544,231
Public safety . . . 5,676,188
Other/fixed costs . . . 6,873,532
Human services . . . 508,123
Culture & recreation . . . 958,489
Debt Service . . . 2,339,272
Education . . . 23,988,406
Public works . . . 1,789,895
Intergovernmental . . . 1,696,822

Taxation, 2010

Property type	Valuation	Rate
Total	NA	-
Residential	NA	NA
Open space	NA	NA
Commercial	NA	NA
Industrial	NA	NA
Personal	NA	NA

Average Single Family Tax Bill, 2010

Avg. assessed home value . . . NA
Avg. single fam. tax bill . . . NA
Hi-Lo ranking . . . NA

Police & Crime, 2008

Number of police officers . . . 31
Violent crimes . . . NA
Property crimes . . . NA

Local School District

(school data 2007-08, except as noted)

Foxborough
60 South Street, C/O Igo Administration Building
Foxborough, MA 02035
508-543-1660

Superintendent . . . Christopher Martes
Grade plan . . . PK-12
Total enrollment '09-10 . . . 2,867
Grade 12 enrollment, '09-10 . . . 227
Graduation rate . . . 89.5%
Dropout rate . . . 5.9%
Per-pupil expenditure . . . $10,542
Avg teacher salary . . . $62,089
Student/teacher ratio '08-09 . . . 14.2 to 1
Highly-qualified teachers, '08-09 . . . 99.5%
Teachers licensed in assigned subject . . 99.5%
Students per computer . . . NA

Massachusetts Competency Assessment System (MCAS), 2009 results

	English		Math	
	% Prof	CPI	% Prof	CPI
Gr 4	65%	85.6	46%	80.3
Gr 6	80%	91.9	64%	83.3
Gr 8	90%	96.4	70%	85.2
Gr 10	89%	96.4	85%	94.6

Other School Districts (see Appendix D for data)

Southeastern Vocational Tech, Norfolk County Agricultural

See Introduction for an explanation of all data sources.

Demographics & Socio-Economic Characteristics*

Population

1990 64,989
2000 66,910
Male 31,942
Female 34,968
2008 64,885
2010 (projected)†† 66,903
2020 (projected)†† 66,727

Race & Hispanic Origin, 2000

Race
White 53,373
Black/African American 3,409
American Indian/Alaska Native 116
Asian 3,527
Hawaiian Native/Pacific Islander 27
Other Race 4,195
Two or more races 2,263
Hispanic origin 7,265

Age & Nativity, 2000

Under 5 years 4,324
18 years and over 52,575
21 years and over 50,053
65 years and over 8,691
85 years and over 1,353
Median Age 36.2
Native-born 52,760
Foreign-born 14,150

Age, 2020 (projected)††

Under 5 years 3,966
5 to 19 years 12,310
20 to 39 years 19,134
40 to 64 years 20,916
65 years and over 10,401

Educational Attainment, 2000

Population 25 years and over 46,871
High School graduates or higher 87.1%
Bachelor's degree or higher 42.3%
Graduate degree 17.0%

Income & Poverty, 1999

Per capita income, ... $27,758
Median household income $54,288
Median family income $67,420
Persons in poverty 5,130
H'holds receiving public assistance 616
H'holds receiving social security 6,122

Households, 2000

Total households 26,153
With persons under 18 8,065
With persons over 65 5,772
Family households 16,573
Single person households 7,504
Persons per household 2.4
Persons per family 3.0

Labor & Employment, 2000

Civilian labor force 37,028
Unemployment rate 3.5%
Civilian labor force, 2008† 36,948
Unemployment rate† 4.8%
Civilian labor force, 12/09† 37,178
Unemployment rate† 6.8%
Employed persons 16 years and over, by occupation:
Managers & professionals 16,115
Service occupations 5,668
Sales & office occupations 8,710
Farming, fishing & forestry 36
Construction & maintenance 2,100
Production & transportation 3,098
Self-employed persons 2,488

Most demographic data is from the 2000 Decennial Census
* see Appendix D and E for American Community Survey data
† Massachusetts Department of Revenue
†† University of Massachusetts, MISER

General Information

Town of Framingham
150 Concord St
Framingham, MA 01702
508-532-5400

Elevation .... 163 ft.
Land area (square miles) 25.1
Water area (square miles) 1.3
Population density, 2008 (est) 2,585.1
Year incorporated 1700
Website .... www.framinghamma.gov

Voters & Government Information

Government type .... Rep. Town Meeting
Number of Selectmen 5
US Congressional District(s) 7

Registered Voters, October 2008

Total 36,673
Democrats 13,373
Republicans 3,798
Unaffiliated/other 19,225

Local Officials, 2010

Chair, Bd. of Sel. .... A. Ginger Esty
Manager/Admin .... Julian Suso
Town Clerk .... Valerie Mulvey
Finance Director .... Mary E. Kelley
Tax Collector .... Stephen Price
Tax Assessor .... Daniel Dargon
Attorney .... Christopher J. Petrini
Public Works .... Peter A. Sellers
Building .... Michael Foley
Planning/Dev. .... Alison Steinfeld
Police Chief .... Stephen Carl
Emerg/Fire Chief .... Gary Daugherty

Housing & Construction

New Privately Owned Housing Units Authorized by Building Permit

	Single Family	Total Bldgs	Total Units
2006	33	36	39
2007	24	26	28
2008	15	15	15

Parcel Count by Property Class, 2010

Total 19,518
Single family 13,343
Multiple units 1,229
Apartments 255
Condos 2,927
Vacant land 539
Open space 0
Commercial 871
Industrial 116
Misc. residential 76
Other use 162

Public Library

Framingham Public Library
49 Lexington Street
Framingham, MA 01702
(508)532-5570

Director .... Mark Contois

Library Statistics, FY 2008

Population served, 2007 64,786
Registered users 40,825
Circulation 898,953
Reference transactons 100,549
Total program attendance 363,035

per capita:
Holdings 4.49
Operating income $42.32

Internet Access
Internet computers available 22
Weekly users 515

Municipal Finance

Debt at year end 2008 .... $63,721,741
Moody's rating, July 2009 .... A1

Revenues, 2008

Total $193,784,713
From all taxes 148,621,710
Federal aid 2,007,697
State aid 30,629,620
From other governments 83,752
Charges for services 2,055,945
Licenses, permits & fees 2,950,960
Fines & forfeits 509,056
Interfund transfers 2,453,577
Misc/other/special assessments 2,236,198

Expenditures, 2008

Total $163,183,984
General government 7,094,948
Public safety 22,567,719
Other/fixed costs 12,075,648
Human services 1,027,086
Culture & recreation 5,028,882
Debt Service 8,018,241
Education 91,169,144
Public works 12,653,111
Intergovernmental 3,549,205

Taxation, 2010

Property type	Valuation	Rate
Total	$7,934,481,314	-
Residential	5,981,560,227	14.52
Open space	0	0.00
Commercial	1,433,528,853	33.65
Industrial	249,292,200	33.65
Personal	270,100,034	33.65

Average Single Family Tax Bill, 2010

Avg. assessed home value $342,887
Avg. single fam. tax bill $4,979
Hi-Lo ranking 80/301

Police & Crime, 2008

Number of police officers 118
Violent crimes 196
Property crimes 1,600

Local School District

(school data 2007-08, except as noted)

Framingham
14 Vernon Street, Suite 201
Framingham, MA 01701
508-626-9117

Superintendent .... Steven Hiersche
Grade plan PK-12
Total enrollment '09-10 8,153
Grade 12 enrollment, '09-10 515
Graduation rate 87.6%
Dropout rate 5.3%
Per-pupil expenditure $14,621
Avg teacher salary $68,259
Student/teacher ratio '08-09 .... 12.8 to 1
Highly-qualified teachers, '08-09 .... 98.9%
Teachers licensed in assigned subject 99.1%
Students per computer 3.7

Massachusetts Competency Assessment System (MCAS), 2009 results

	English		Math	
	% Prof	CPI	% Prof	CPI
Gr 4	50%	77.7	47%	76.9
Gr 6	65%	83.8	49%	72.1
Gr 8	76%	89.2	50%	74
Gr 10	79%	90.8	80%	89.7

Other School Districts (see Appendix D for data)
South Middlesex Vocational Tech

©2010 Information Publications, Inc. All rights reserved. Photocopying prohibited. For additional copies, contact the publisher at www.informationpublications.com or (877)544-INFO (4636)

See Introduction for an explanation of all data sources.

Demographics & Socio-Economic Characteristics*

Population

1990	22,095
2000	29,560
Male	14,487
Female	15,073
2008	32,148
2010 (projected)††	35,062
2020 (projected)††	41,150

Race & Hispanic Origin, 2000

Race	
White	28,364
Black/African American	318
American Indian/Alaska Native	43
Asian	491
Hawaiian Native/Pacific Islander	9
Other Race	87
Two or more races	248
Hispanic origin	318

Age & Nativity, 2000

Under 5 years	2,774
18 years and over	20,595
21 years and over	19,462
65 years and over	2,418
85 years and over	254
Median Age	34.8
Native-born	27,998
Foreign-born	1,562

Age, 2020 (projected)††

Under 5 years	3,028
5 to 19 years	8,980
20 to 39 years	11,088
40 to 64 years	13,203
65 years and over	4,851

Educational Attainment, 2000

Population 25 years and over	18,736
High School graduates or higher	92.9%
Bachelor's degree or higher	42.7%
Graduate degree	13.7%

Income & Poverty, 1999

Per capita income,	$27,849
Median household income	$71,174
Median family income	$81,826
Persons in poverty	820
H'holds receiving public assistance	131
H'holds receiving social security	2,000

Households, 2000

Total households	10,152
With persons under 18	4,690
With persons over 65	1,775
Family households	7,881
Single person households	1,858
Persons per household	2.9
Persons per family	3.3

Labor & Employment, 2000

Civilian labor force	15,664
Unemployment rate	4.2%
Civilian labor force, 2008†	16,776
Unemployment rate†	5.5%
Civilian labor force, 12/09†	16,833
Unemployment rate†	8.2%
Employed persons 16 years and over, by occupation:	
Managers & professionals	7,010
Service occupations	1,592
Sales & office occupations	3,921
Farming, fishing & forestry	25
Construction & maintenance	1,250
Production & transportation	1,210
Self-employed persons	843

Most demographic data is from the 2000 Decennial Census
* see Appendix E for American Community Survey data
† Massachusetts Department of Revenue
†† University of Massachusetts, MISER

General Information

City of Franklin
355 East Central St
Franklin, MA 02038
508-528-7900

Elevation	303 ft.
Land area (square miles)	26.7
Water area (square miles)	0.3
Population density, 2008 (est)	1,204.0
Year incorporated	1778
Website	www.franklin.ma.us

Voters & Government Information

Government type	Council-Manager
Number of Councilpersons	9
US Congressional District(s)	3

Registered Voters, October 2008

Total	19,911
Democrats	4,744
Republicans	3,078
Unaffiliated/other	12,005

Local Officials, 2010

Chair, Town Council	Scott Mason
Administrator	Jeffrey Nutting
Clerk	Deborah Pellegri
CFO	Jim Dacey
Tax Collector	James Dacey
Tax Assessor	Kevin Doyle
Attorney	Mark Cerel
Public Works	Robert Cantoreggi
Building	David Roche
Planning	Bryan Taberner
Police Chief	Steven T. Williams
Emerg/Fire Chief	Gary McCarraher

Housing & Construction

New Privately Owned Housing Units Authorized by Building Permit

	Single Family	Total Bldgs	Total Units
2006	75	80	128
2007	87	89	101
2008	53	57	216

Parcel Count by Property Class, 2010

Total	10,779
Single family	7,577
Multiple units	315
Apartments	58
Condos	1,582
Vacant land	602
Open space	0
Commercial	226
Industrial	204
Misc. residential	37
Other use	178

Public Library

Franklin Public Library
118 Main Street
Franklin, MA 02038
(508)520-4940

Library Director: Felicia Oti

Library Statistics, FY 2008

Population served, 2007	31,381
Registered users	15,865
Circulation	360,713
Reference transactons	14,106
Total program attendance	213,394
per capita:	
Holdings	3.24
Operating income	$31.67
Internet Access	
Internet computers available	12
Weekly users	1,549

Municipal Finance

Debt at year end 2008	$58,826,821
Moody's rating, July 2009	A1

Revenues, 2008

Total	$93,570,817
From all taxes	53,237,143
Federal aid	408,006
State aid	31,827,061
From other governments	89,342
Charges for services	1,235,302
Licenses, permits & fees	1,077,087
Fines & forfeits	43,390
Interfund transfers	3,296,324
Misc/other/special assessments	1,178,581

Expenditures, 2008

Total	$88,880,100
General government	3,888,479
Public safety	8,743,776
Other/fixed costs	6,185,227
Human services	424,445
Culture & recreation	1,279,873
Debt Service	5,338,703
Education	55,739,686
Public works	3,663,178
Intergovernmental	3,616,733

Taxation, 2010

Property type	Valuation	Rate
Total	$4,354,757,148	-
Residential	3,399,580,062	12.03
Open space	0	0.00
Commercial	333,182,926	12.03
Industrial	489,851,380	12.03
Personal	132,142,780	12.03

Average Single Family Tax Bill, 2010

Avg. assessed home value	$368,736
Avg. single fam. tax bill	$4,436
Hi-Lo ranking	103/301

Police & Crime, 2008

Number of police officers	46
Violent crimes	3
Property crimes	96

Local School District

(school data 2007-08, except as noted)

Franklin
355 East Central Street
Franklin, MA 02038
508-541-5243

Superintendent	Maureen Sabolinski
Grade plan	PK-12
Total enrollment '09-10	6,120
Grade 12 enrollment, '09-10	398
Graduation rate	94.4%
Dropout rate	3.1%
Per-pupil expenditure	$9,751
Avg teacher salary	$66,361
Student/teacher ratio '08-09	15.7 to 1
Highly-qualified teachers, '08-09	94.1%
Teachers licensed in assigned subject	98.0%
Students per computer	6.1

Massachusetts Competency Assessment System (MCAS), 2009 results

	English		Math	
	% Prof	CPI	% Prof	CPI
Gr 4	74%	90.7	72%	91
Gr 6	85%	94.5	74%	89.4
Gr 8	91%	96.9	68%	84.8
Gr 10	89%	96.6	86%	94.5

Other School Districts (see Appendix D for data)
Tri County Vocational Tech, Norfolk County Agricultural

©2010 Information Publications, Inc. All rights reserved. Photocopying prohibited. For additional copies, contact the publisher at www.informationpublications.com or (877)544-INFO (4636)

See Introduction for an explanation of all data sources.

Demographics & Socio-Economic Characteristics

Population

1990	8,522
2000	8,472
Male	4,259
Female	4,213
2008	9,027
2010 (projected)††	8,699
2020 (projected)††	8,747

Race & Hispanic Origin, 2000

Race	
White	8,146
Black/African American	61
American Indian/Alaska Native	16
Asian	55
Hawaiian Native/Pacific Islander	1
Other Race	92
Two or more races	101
Hispanic origin	62

Age & Nativity, 2000

Under 5 years	458
18 years and over	6,387
21 years and over	6,058
65 years and over	767
85 years and over	71
Median Age	38.0
Native-born	7,923
Foreign-born	549

Age, 2020 (projected)††

Under 5 years	396
5 to 19 years	1,431
20 to 39 years	2,018
40 to 64 years	3,223
65 years and over	1,679

Educational Attainment, 2000

Population 25 years and over	5,683
High School graduates or higher	82.4%
Bachelor's degree or higher	21.7%
Graduate degree	6.3%

Income & Poverty, 1999

Per capita income,	$24,237
Median household income	$64,576
Median family income	$69,368
Persons in poverty	417
H'holds receiving public assistance	36
H'holds receiving social security	618

Households, 2000

Total households	2,932
With persons under 18	1,179
With persons over 65	552
Family households	2,391
Single person households	413
Persons per household	2.9
Persons per family	3.1

Labor & Employment, 2000

Civilian labor force	4,991
Unemployment rate	2.1%
Civilian labor force, 2008†	5,498
Unemployment rate†	7.4%
Civilian labor force, 12/09†	5,508
Unemployment rate†	9.5%
Employed persons 16 years and over, by occupation:	
Managers & professionals	1,673
Service occupations	856
Sales & office occupations	1,198
Farming, fishing & forestry	7
Construction & maintenance	454
Production & transportation	700
Self-employed persons	311

Most demographic data is from the 2000 Decennial Census
† Massachusetts Department of Revenue
†† University of Massachusetts, MISER

General Information

Town of Freetown
PO Box 438
3 North Main St
Assonet, MA 02702
508-644-2001

Elevation	32 ft.
Land area (square miles)	36.6
Water area (square miles)	1.7
Population density, 2008 (est)	246.6
Year incorporated	1683
Website	www.freetownma.gov

Voters & Government Information

Government type	Open Town Meeting
Number of Selectmen	3
US Congressional District(s)	4

Registered Voters, October 2008

Total	6,314
Democrats	1,768
Republicans	711
Unaffiliated/other	3,788

Local Officials, 2010

Chair, Bd. of Sel.	Jean C. Fox
Manager/Admin	John Healey
Town Clerk	Jacqueline A. Brown
Treasurer	Anita L. Howland
Tax Collector	Stephen G. Curran
Tax Assessor	Richard Field (Chr)
Attorney	Kopelman & Paige
Highway Surveyor	Charles J. Macomber
Building Inspector	Paul R. Bourgeois
Planning	Robert N. Raymond (Chr)
Police Chief	Carlton E. Abbott Jr
Fire Chief	Gary Silvia

Housing & Construction

New Privately Owned Housing Units Authorized by Building Permit

	Single Family	Total Bldgs	Total Units
2006	22	22	22
2007	18	18	18
2008	15	15	15

Parcel Count by Property Class, 2010

Total	4,012
Single family	2,936
Multiple units	71
Apartments	0
Condos	13
Vacant land	579
Open space	0
Commercial	87
Industrial	42
Misc. residential	38
Other use	246

Public Library

James White Memorial Library
5 Washburn Road
East Freetown, MA 02717
(508)763-5344

Director .... Dorothy Stanley-Ballard

Library Statistics, FY 2008

Population served, 2007	8,935
Registered users	1,784
Circulation	34,939
Reference transactons	1,393
Total program attendance	12,580
per capita:	
Holdings	3.34
Operating income	$13.97
Internet Access	
Internet computers available	8
Weekly users	19

Municipal Finance

Debt at year end 2008	$8,691,000
Moody's rating, July 2009	NA

Revenues, 2008

Total	$19,838,783
From all taxes	14,413,614
Federal aid	0
State aid	3,599,737
From other governments	71,295
Charges for services	885,308
Licenses, permits & fees	173,717
Fines & forfeits	0
Interfund transfers	475,356
Misc/other/special assessments	109,878

Expenditures, 2008

Total	$19,456,349
General government	844,855
Public safety	2,601,972
Other/fixed costs	2,660,388
Human services	157,202
Culture & recreation	113,846
Debt Service	669,603
Education	11,020,943
Public works	952,411
Intergovernmental	235,129

Taxation, 2010

Property type	Valuation	Rate
Total	$1,260,402,840	-
Residential	1,043,173,361	10.30
Open space	0	0.00
Commercial	63,941,609	16.48
Industrial	98,995,300	16.48
Personal	54,292,570	16.48

Average Single Family Tax Bill, 2010

Avg. assessed home value	$312,786
Avg. single fam. tax bill	$3,222
Hi-Lo ranking	213/301

Police & Crime, 2008

Number of police officers	17
Violent crimes	17
Property crimes	163

Local School District

(school data 2007-08, except as noted)

Freetown
98 Howland Rd
Lakeville, MA 02347
508-923-2000

Superintendent	John McCarthy
Grade plan	PK-4
Total enrollment '09-10	533
Grade 12 enrollment, '09-10	0
Graduation rate	NA
Dropout rate	NA
Per-pupil expenditure	$12,470
Avg teacher salary	$57,259
Student/teacher ratio '08-09	17.6 to 1
Highly-qualified teachers, '08-09	95.8%
Teachers licensed in assigned subject	96.6%
Students per computer	2.4

Massachusetts Competency Assessment System (MCAS), 2009 results

	English		Math	
	% Prof	CPI	% Prof	CPI
Gr 4	55%	80.6	46%	77.2
Gr 6	NA	NA	NA	NA
Gr 8	NA	NA	NA	NA
Gr 10	NA	NA	NA	NA

Other School Districts (see Appendix D for data)
Freetown-Lakeville Regional, Bristol County Agricultural

©2010 Information Publications, Inc. All rights reserved. Photocopying prohibited. For additional copies, contact the publisher at www.informationpublications.com or (877)544-INFO (4636)

See Introduction for an explanation of all data sources.

©2010 Information Publications, Inc. All rights reserved. Photocopying prohibited. For additional copies, contact the publisher at www.informationpublications.com or (877)544-INFO (4636)

Demographics & Socio-Economic Characteristics*

Population

1990	20,125
2000	20,770
Male	10,645
Female	10,125
2008	20,682
2010 (projected)††	21,429
2020 (projected)††	22,303

Race & Hispanic Origin, 2000

Race	
White	19,343
Black/African American	476
American Indian/Alaska Native	70
Asian	284
Hawaiian Native/Pacific Islander	16
Other Race	253
Two or more races	328
Hispanic origin	848

Age & Nativity, 2000

Under 5 years	1,244
18 years and over	15,841
21 years and over	15,171
65 years and over	3,341
85 years and over	510
Median Age	37.5
Native-born	19,301
Foreign-born	1,469

Age, 2020 (projected)††

Under 5 years	1,206
5 to 19 years	3,400
20 to 39 years	6,458
40 to 64 years	7,329
65 years and over	3,910

Educational Attainment, 2000

Population 25 years and over	14,286
High School graduates or higher	78.2%
Bachelor's degree or higher	15.2%
Graduate degree	5.0%

Income & Poverty, 1999

Per capita income,	$18,624
Median household income	$37,334
Median family income	$47,164
Persons in poverty	1,863
H'holds receiving public assistance	265
H'holds receiving social security	2,537

Households, 2000

Total households	8,282
With persons under 18	2,694
With persons over 65	2,286
Family households	5,086
Single person households	2,687
Persons per household	2.4
Persons per family	3.0

Labor & Employment, 2000

Civilian labor force	10,080
Unemployment rate	4.6%
Civilian labor force, 2008†	9,900
Unemployment rate†	9.7%
Civilian labor force, 12/09†	9,682
Unemployment rate†	12.1%
Employed persons 16 years and over, by occupation:	
Managers & professionals	2,757
Service occupations	1,626
Sales & office occupations	2,519
Farming, fishing & forestry	19
Construction & maintenance	618
Production & transportation	2,080
Self-employed persons	420

Most demographic data is from the 2000 Decennial Census
* see Appendix E for American Community Survey data
† Massachusetts Department of Revenue
†† University of Massachusetts, MISER

General Information

City of Gardner
95 Pleasant St
Gardner, MA 01440
978-632-1900

Elevation	1,190 ft.
Land area (square miles)	22.2
Water area (square miles)	0.8
Population density, 2008 (est)	931.6
Year incorporated	1785
Website	www.gardner-ma.gov

Voters & Government Information

Government type	Mayor-Council
Number of Councilpersons	11
US Congressional District(s)	1

Registered Voters, October 2008

Total	11,909
Democrats	4,222
Republicans	1,362
Unaffiliated/other	6,186

Local Officials, 2010

Mayor	Mark P. Hawke
Manager/Admin	NA
Clerk	Alan L. Agnelli
Treasurer	Charline Daigle
Tax Collector	Charline Daigle
Tax Assessor	Dennis W. Comee
Attorney	John Flick
Public Works	Dane Arnold
Building	Richard Reynolds
Planning	Robert Hubbard
Police Chief	Neil Erickson
Fire Chief	Ronald Therrien

Housing & Construction

New Privately Owned Housing Units Authorized by Building Permit

	Single Family	Total Bldgs	Total Units
2006	35	35	35
2007	29	29	29
2008	21	21	21

Parcel Count by Property Class, 2010

Total	6,715
Single family	3,895
Multiple units	876
Apartments	183
Condos	546
Vacant land	598
Open space	0
Commercial	305
Industrial	143
Misc. residential	75
Other use	94

Public Library

Levi Heywood Memorial Library
55 West Lynde St.
Gardner, MA 01440
(978)632-5298

Director	Gail P. Landy

Library Statistics, FY 2008

Population served, 2007	20,613
Registered users	12,694
Circulation	196,554
Reference transactons	17,088
Total program attendance	0
per capita:	
Holdings	5.84
Operating income	$34.65
Internet Access	
Internet computers available	6
Weekly users	262

Municipal Finance

Debt at year end 2008	$37,312,514
Moody's rating, July 2009	Baa1

Revenues, 2008

Total	$46,425,851
From all taxes	18,113,485
Federal aid	269,449
State aid	25,382,005
From other governments	145,054
Charges for services	431,880
Licenses, permits & fees	198,583
Fines & forfeits	98,867
Interfund transfers	577,300
Misc/other/special assessments	604,614

Expenditures, 2008

Total	$40,008,461
General government	1,977,919
Public safety	5,174,460
Other/fixed costs	3,557,389
Human services	776,249
Culture & recreation	1,238,745
Debt Service	2,339,668
Education	21,441,667
Public works	2,489,676
Intergovernmental	1,011,574

Taxation, 2010

Property type	Valuation	Rate
Total	$1,202,156,961	-
Residential	1,017,805,088	14.86
Open space	0	0.00
Commercial	98,461,512	14.86
Industrial	54,698,200	14.86
Personal	31,192,161	14.86

Average Single Family Tax Bill, 2010

Avg. assessed home value	$180,050
Avg. single fam. tax bill	$2,676
Hi-Lo ranking	267/301

Police & Crime, 2008

Number of police officers	31
Violent crimes	88
Property crimes	557

Local School District

(school data 2007-08, except as noted)
Gardner
70 Waterford Street
Gardner, MA 01440
978-632-1000

Superintendent	Carol Daring
Grade plan	PK-12
Total enrollment '09-10	2,600
Grade 12 enrollment, '09-10	161
Graduation rate	63.8%
Dropout rate	19.2%
Per-pupil expenditure	$10,153
Avg teacher salary	$61,980
Student/teacher ratio '08-09	15.0 to 1
Highly-qualified teachers, '08-09	96.2%
Teachers licensed in assigned subject	97.4%
Students per computer	11.8

Massachusetts Competency Assessment System (MCAS), 2009 results

	English		Math	
	% Prof	CPI	% Prof	CPI
Gr 4	34%	69.9	32%	71.4
Gr 6	69%	87.3	56%	80.7
Gr 8	74%	88.6	43%	65.9
Gr 10	81%	91.3	72%	86.4

Other School Districts (see Appendix D for data)
Montachusett Vocational Tech

See Introduction for an explanation of all data sources.

Demographics & Socio-Economic Characteristics

Population

1990	6,384
2000	7,377
Male	3,663
Female	3,714
2008	8,629
2010 (projected)††	7,897
2020 (projected)††	8,125

Race & Hispanic Origin, 2000

Race	
White	7,268
Black/African American	11
American Indian/Alaska Native	10
Asian	31
Hawaiian Native/Pacific Islander	0
Other Race	23
Two or more races	34
Hispanic origin	47

Age & Nativity, 2000

Under 5 years	626
18 years and over	5,264
21 years and over	5,092
65 years and over	691
85 years and over	70
Median Age	37.4
Native-born	7,187
Foreign-born	190

Age, 2020 (projected)††

Under 5 years	537
5 to 19 years	1,698
20 to 39 years	1,751
40 to 64 years	2,820
65 years and over	1,319

Educational Attainment, 2000

Population 25 years and over	4,869
High School graduates or higher	90.3%
Bachelor's degree or higher	38.4%
Graduate degree	10.4%

Income & Poverty, 1999

Per capita income,	$28,846
Median household income	$76,260
Median family income	$79,649
Persons in poverty	309
H'holds receiving public assistance	6
H'holds receiving social security	594

Households, 2000

Total households	2,566
With persons under 18	1,113
With persons over 65	521
Family households	2,025
Single person households	434
Persons per household	2.9
Persons per family	3.3

Labor & Employment, 2000

Civilian labor force	3,934
Unemployment rate	1.9%
Civilian labor force, 2008†	4,212
Unemployment rate†	5.0%
Civilian labor force, 12/09†	4,229
Unemployment rate†	8.3%
Employed persons 16 years and over, by occupation:	
Managers & professionals	1,725
Service occupations	561
Sales & office occupations	925
Farming, fishing & forestry	0
Construction & maintenance	349
Production & transportation	301
Self-employed persons	292

Most demographic data is from the 2000 Decennial Census
† Massachusetts Department of Revenue
†† University of Massachusetts, MISER

General Information

Town of Georgetown
1 Library St
Georgetown, MA 01833
978-352-5755

Elevation	100 ft.
Land area (square miles)	12.9
Water area (square miles)	0.2
Population density, 2008 (est)	668.9
Year incorporated	1838
Website	www.georgetownma.gov

Voters & Government Information

Government type	Open Town Meeting
Number of Selectmen	5
US Congressional District(s)	6

Registered Voters, October 2008

Total	5,813
Democrats	1,394
Republicans	1,065
Unaffiliated/other	3,326

Local Officials, 2010

Chair, Bd. of Sel.	Philip Trapani
Town Admin	Michael Farrell (Int)
Clerk	Janice McGrane
Finance Director	Michael Farrell
Tax Collector	Jacqueline Cuomo
Tax Assessor	Thomas Berube
Attorney	Kopelman & Paige
Public Works	Peter Durkee
Building	John Q. Caldwell
Planning	Nicholas Cracknell
Police Chief	James Mulligan
Fire Chief	Albert Beardsley

Housing & Construction

New Privately Owned Housing Units Authorized by Building Permit

	Single Family	Total Bldgs	Total Units
2006	46	46	46
2007	36	36	36
2008	21	21	21

Parcel Count by Property Class, 2010

Total	3,047
Single family	2,398
Multiple units	60
Apartments	11
Condos	136
Vacant land	262
Open space	0
Commercial	57
Industrial	86
Misc. residential	10
Other use	27

Public Library

Peabody Library
Lincoln Park
Georgetown, MA 01833
(978)352-5728

Library Director	Ruth Eifert

Library Statistics, FY 2008

Population served, 2007	8,147
Registered users	4,458
Circulation	49,251
Reference transactons	0
Total program attendance	32,485
per capita:	
Holdings	5.68
Operating income	$34.84
Internet Access	
Internet computers available	20
Weekly users	117

Municipal Finance

Debt at year end 2008	$20,302,939
Moody's rating, July 2009	A1

Revenues, 2008

Total	$24,679,801
From all taxes	13,541,724
Federal aid	0
State aid	6,449,918
From other governments	0
Charges for services	14,947
Licenses, permits & fees	125,764
Fines & forfeits	110,813
Interfund transfers	2,818,279
Misc/other/special assessments	809,178

Expenditures, 2008

Total	$23,837,920
General government	959,649
Public safety	1,815,061
Other/fixed costs	3,366,030
Human services	228,013
Culture & recreation	320,591
Debt Service	5,184,027
Education	10,990,029
Public works	966,520
Intergovernmental	0

Taxation, 2010

Property type	Valuation	Rate
Total	$1,229,804,525	-
Residential	1,113,363,629	10.58
Open space	0	0.00
Commercial	44,438,321	10.58
Industrial	50,428,750	10.58
Personal	21,573,825	10.58

Average Single Family Tax Bill, 2010

Avg. assessed home value	$412,477
Avg. single fam. tax bill	$4,364
Hi-Lo ranking	110/301

Police & Crime, 2008

Number of police officers	12
Violent crimes	2
Property crimes	41

Local School District

(school data 2007-08, except as noted)

Georgetown
51 North Street
Georgetown, MA 01833
978-352-5777

Superintendent	Carol Jacobs
Grade plan	PK-12
Total enrollment '09-10	1,688
Grade 12 enrollment, '09-10	109
Graduation rate	90.9%
Dropout rate	7.1%
Per-pupil expenditure	$8,243
Avg teacher salary	$57,610
Student/teacher ratio '08-09	16.2 to 1
Highly-qualified teachers, '08-09	91.8%
Teachers licensed in assigned subject	94.2%
Students per computer	5.6

Massachusetts Competency Assessment System (MCAS), 2009 results

	English		Math	
	% Prof	CPI	% Prof	CPI
Gr 4	70%	87.6	53%	82.6
Gr 6	80%	93.1	71%	87.6
Gr 8	84%	94.4	63%	82
Gr 10	91%	97.5	89%	95.8

Other School Districts (see Appendix D for data)

Whittier Vocational Tech

©2010 Information Publications, Inc. All rights reserved. Photocopying prohibited. For additional copies, contact the publisher at www.informationpublications.com or (877)544-INFO (4636)

See Introduction for an explanation of all data sources.

Demographics & Socio-Economic Characteristics

Population

1990	1,583
2000	1,363
Male	665
Female	698
2008	1,388
2010 (projected)††	1,324
2020 (projected)††	1,281

Race & Hispanic Origin, 2000

Race	
White	1,328
Black/African American	4
American Indian/Alaska Native	1
Asian	11
Hawaiian Native/Pacific Islander	0
Other Race	5
Two or more races	14
Hispanic origin	10

Age & Nativity, 2000

Under 5 years	62
18 years and over	1,040
21 years and over	986
65 years and over	174
85 years and over	28
Median Age	42.0
Native-born	1,342
Foreign-born	21

Age, 2020 (projected)††

Under 5 years	72
5 to 19 years	214
20 to 39 years	287
40 to 64 years	463
65 years and over	245

Educational Attainment, 2000

Population 25 years and over	956
High School graduates or higher	90.4%
Bachelor's degree or higher	27.9%
Graduate degree	12.4%

Income & Poverty, 1999

Per capita income,	$23,381
Median household income	$50,750
Median family income	$61,339
Persons in poverty	60
H'holds receiving public assistance	4
H'holds receiving social security	154

Households, 2000

Total households	537
With persons under 18	183
With persons over 65	127
Family households	373
Single person households	124
Persons per household	2.5
Persons per family	3.0

Labor & Employment, 2000

Civilian labor force	786
Unemployment rate	3.2%
Civilian labor force, 2008†	785
Unemployment rate†	6.0%
Civilian labor force, 12/09†	801
Unemployment rate†	9.5%
Employed persons 16 years and over, by occupation:	
Managers & professionals	249
Service occupations	111
Sales & office occupations	208
Farming, fishing & forestry	3
Construction & maintenance	66
Production & transportation	124
Self-employed persons	83

Most demographic data is from the 2000 Decennial Census
† Massachusetts Department of Revenue
†† University of Massachusetts, MISER

General Information

Town of Gill
325 Main Rd
Gill, MA 01354
413-863-9347

Elevation	NA
Land area (square miles)	14.0
Water area (square miles)	0.8
Population density, 2008 (est)	99.1
Year incorporated	1793
Website	gillmass.org

Voters & Government Information

Government type	Open Town Meeting
Number of Selectmen	3
US Congressional District(s)	1

Registered Voters, October 2008

Total	1,118
Democrats	319
Republicans	99
Unaffiliated/other	694

Local Officials, 2010

Chair, Bd. of Sel.	Ann H. Banash
Manager/Admin	Raymond Purington
Town Clerk	Lynda Hodsdon Mayo
Finance Director	Veronica LaChance
Tax Collector	Veronica LaChance
Tax Assessor	Raymond Purington
Attorney	Donna MacNicol
Public Works	NA
Building	NA
Comm Dev/Planning	NA
Police Chief	David Hastings
Emerg/Fire Chief	Gene Beaubien

Housing & Construction

New Privately Owned Housing Units Authorized by Building Permit

	Single Family	Total Bldgs	Total Units
2006	6	6	6
2007	5	5	5
2008	1	1	1

Parcel Count by Property Class, 2010

Total	894
Single family	434
Multiple units	27
Apartments	2
Condos	16
Vacant land	155
Open space	0
Commercial	40
Industrial	41
Misc. residential	25
Other use	154

Public Library

Slate Memorial Library
332 Main Road
Gill, MA 01354
(413)863-2591

Librarian	Jocelyn Castro-Santos

Library Statistics, FY 2008

Population served, 2007	1,379
Registered users	678
Circulation	5,464
Reference transactons	0
Total program attendance	2,730
per capita:	
Holdings	3.61
Operating income	$16.28
Internet Access	
Internet computers available	1
Weekly users	15

Municipal Finance

Debt at year end 2008	$61,341
Moody's rating, July 2009	NA

Revenues, 2008

Total	$2,652,271
From all taxes	2,062,500
Federal aid	0
State aid	288,255
From other governments	17,442
Charges for services	44,723
Licenses, permits & fees	36,763
Fines & forfeits	0
Interfund transfers	114,882
Misc/other/special assessments	43,853

Expenditures, 2008

Total	$2,625,212
General government	283,391
Public safety	284,032
Other/fixed costs	149,772
Human services	30,672
Culture & recreation	21,693
Debt Service	55,705
Education	1,404,299
Public works	378,308
Intergovernmental	17,340

Taxation, 2010

Property type	Valuation	Rate
Total	$148,862,559	-
Residential	123,213,587	13.71
Open space	0	0.00
Commercial	11,533,772	13.71
Industrial	10,340,700	13.71
Personal	3,774,500	13.71

Average Single Family Tax Bill, 2010

Avg. assessed home value	$210,389
Avg. single fam. tax bill	$2,884
Hi-Lo ranking	246/301

Police & Crime, 2008

Number of police officers	3
Violent crimes	1
Property crimes	16

Local School District

(school data 2007-08, except as noted)

Gill (non-op)
35 Crocker Avenue
Turners Falls, MA 01376
413-863-9324

Superintendent	Carl Ladd

Non-operating district.
Resident students are sent to the Other School Districts listed below.

Grade plan	NA
Total enrollment '09-10	NA
Grade 12 enrollment, '09-10	NA
Graduation rate	NA
Dropout rate	NA
Per-pupil expenditure	NA
Avg teacher salary	NA
Student/teacher ratio '08-09	NA
Highly-qualified teachers, '08-09	NA
Teachers licensed in assigned subject	NA
Students per computer	NA

Other School Districts (see Appendix D for data)
Gill-Montague Regional, Franklin County Vocational Tech

©2010 Information Publications, Inc. All rights reserved. Photocopying prohibited. For additional copies, contact the publisher at www.informationpublications.com or (877)544-INFO (4636)

See Introduction for an explanation of all data sources.

Demographics & Socio-Economic Characteristics*

Population

1990	28,716
2000	30,273
Male	14,502
Female	15,771
2008	30,243
2010 (projected)††	30,877
2020 (projected)††	31,215

Race & Hispanic Origin, 2000

Race	
White	29,361
Black/African American	186
American Indian/Alaska Native	37
Asian	218
Hawaiian Native/Pacific Islander	7
Other Race	152
Two or more races	312
Hispanic origin	449

Age & Nativity, 2000

Under 5 years	1,757
18 years and over	23,614
21 years and over	22,762
65 years and over	4,713
85 years and over	620
Median Age	40.2
Native-born	28,665
Foreign-born	1,608

Age, 2020 (projected)††

Under 5 years	1,581
5 to 19 years	4,598
20 to 39 years	7,075
40 to 64 years	11,119
65 years and over	6,842

Educational Attainment, 2000

Population 25 years and over	21,598
High School graduates or higher	85.7%
Bachelor's degree or higher	27.5%
Graduate degree	10.2%

Income & Poverty, 1999

Per capita income,	$25,595
Median household income	$47,722
Median family income	$58,459
Persons in poverty	2,630
H'holds receiving public assistance	319
H'holds receiving social security	3,461

Households, 2000

Total households	12,592
With persons under 18	3,723
With persons over 65	3,379
Family households	7,896
Single person households	3,861
Persons per household	2.4
Persons per family	3.0

Labor & Employment, 2000

Civilian labor force	16,097
Unemployment rate	4.9%
Civilian labor force, 2008†	16,911
Unemployment rate†	8.7%
Civilian labor force, 12/09†	16,656
Unemployment rate†	10.7%
Employed persons 16 years and over, by occupation:	
Managers & professionals	5,529
Service occupations	2,305
Sales & office occupations	3,894
Farming, fishing & forestry	311
Construction & maintenance	1,222
Production & transportation	2,053
Self-employed persons	1,319

Most demographic data is from the 2000 Decennial Census
* see Appendix E for American Community Survey data
† Massachusetts Department of Revenue
†† University of Massachusetts, MISER

General Information

City of Gloucester
9 Dale Ave
Gloucester, MA 01930
978-281-9720

Elevation	50 ft.
Land area (square miles)	26.0
Water area (square miles)	15.5
Population density, 2008 (est)	1,163.2
Year incorporated	NA
Website	www.ci.gloucester.ma.us

Voters & Government Information

Government type	Mayor-Council
Number of Councilpersons	9
US Congressional District(s)	6

Registered Voters, October 2008

Total	20,976
Democrats	6,056
Republicans	2,208
Unaffiliated/other	12,563

Local Officials, 2010

Mayor	Carolyn Kirk
Chief Admin Off	Jim Duggan
City Clerk	Linda Lowe
Finance Director	Jeff Towne
Tax Collector	Jeff Towne
Tax Assessor	Nancy Papows (Chr)
Attorney	Linda Lowe
Public Works	Mike Hale Jr
Building	Bill Sanborn
Comm Dev/Planning	Gregg Cademartori
Police Chief	John Beaudette
Fire Chief	Barry McKay

Housing & Construction

New Privately Owned Housing Units Authorized by Building Permit

	Single Family	Total Bldgs	Total Units
2006	31	38	45
2007	53	54	57
2008	14	16	26

Parcel Count by Property Class, 2010

Total	13,232
Single family	7,162
Multiple units	1,613
Apartments	178
Condos	1,216
Vacant land	2,006
Open space	0
Commercial	428
Industrial	209
Misc. residential	229
Other use	191

Public Library

Gloucester Lyceum & Sawyer Free Library
2 Dale Ave.
Gloucester, MA 01930
(978)281-9763

Director	Carol Gray (Actg)

Library Statistics, FY 2008

Population served, 2007	30,308
Registered users	14,609
Circulation	171,280
Reference transactons	0
Total program attendance	154,301
per capita:	
Holdings	4.38
Operating income	$32.75
Internet Access	
Internet computers available	21
Weekly users	520

Municipal Finance

Debt at year end 2008	$100,509,842
Moody's rating, July 2009	A2

Revenues, 2008

Total	$80,450,402
From all taxes	56,156,634
Federal aid	0
State aid	13,193,714
From other governments	0
Charges for services	3,928,791
Licenses, permits & fees	1,101,855
Fines & forfeits	325,400
Interfund transfers	3,614,364
Misc/other/special assessments	1,064,822

Expenditures, 2008

Total	$79,065,198
General government	3,366,553
Public safety	11,147,817
Other/fixed costs	14,143,232
Human services	691,182
Culture & recreation	714,643
Debt Service	8,690,860
Education	30,649,121
Public works	5,568,082
Intergovernmental	3,463,771

Taxation, 2010

Property type	Valuation	Rate
Total	$5,381,431,000	-
Residential	4,823,470,706	10.49
Open space	0	0.00
Commercial	300,127,372	11.20
Industrial	167,286,322	11.20
Personal	90,546,600	11.20

Average Single Family Tax Bill, 2010

Avg. assessed home value	$475,858
Avg. single fam. tax bill	$4,992
Hi-Lo ranking	79/301

Police & Crime, 2008

Number of police officers	61
Violent crimes	26
Property crimes	624

Local School District

(school data 2007-08, except as noted)

Gloucester
6 School House Rd
Gloucester, MA 01930
978-281-9800

Superintendent	Christopher Farmer
Grade plan	PK-12
Total enrollment '09-10	3,372
Grade 12 enrollment, '09-10	258
Graduation rate	84.7%
Dropout rate	7.5%
Per-pupil expenditure	$12,044
Avg teacher salary	$65,392
Student/teacher ratio '08-09	13.6 to 1
Highly-qualified teachers, '08-09	96.4%
Teachers licensed in assigned subject	96.8%
Students per computer	4.9

Massachusetts Competency Assessment System (MCAS), 2009 results

	English		Math	
	% Prof	CPI	% Prof	CPI
Gr 4	52%	80.3	40%	75.4
Gr 6	61%	83.2	46%	71.5
Gr 8	69%	85.5	44%	67.3
Gr 10	81%	93.6	72%	87.9

Other School Districts (see Appendix D for data)
North Shore Vocational Tech

©2010 Information Publications, Inc. All rights reserved. Photocopying prohibited. For additional copies, contact the publisher at www.informationpublications.com or (877)544-INFO (4636)

©2010 Information Publications, Inc. All rights reserved. Photocopying prohibited. For additional copies, contact the publisher at www.informationpublications.com or (877)544-INFO (4636)

Demographics & Socio-Economic Characteristics

Population

1990	830
2000	921
Male	431
Female	490
2008	974
2010 (projected)††	994
2020 (projected)††	1,072

Race & Hispanic Origin, 2000

Race	
White	912
Black/African American	0
American Indian/Alaska Native	1
Asian	2
Hawaiian Native/Pacific Islander	0
Other Race	0
Two or more races	6
Hispanic origin	10

Age & Nativity, 2000

Under 5 years	42
18 years and over	719
21 years and over	693
65 years and over	98
85 years and over	10
Median Age	41.3
Native-born	891
Foreign-born	12

Age, 2020 (projected)††

Under 5 years	38
5 to 19 years	104
20 to 39 years	239
40 to 64 years	404
65 years and over	287

Educational Attainment, 2000

Population 25 years and over	681
High School graduates or higher	90.3%
Bachelor's degree or higher	30.1%
Graduate degree	11.0%

Income & Poverty, 1999

Per capita income,	$22,221
Median household income	$49,583
Median family income	$58,750
Persons in poverty	71
H'holds receiving public assistance	8
H'holds receiving social security	71

Households, 2000

Total households	365
With persons under 18	117
With persons over 65	77
Family households	247
Single person households	67
Persons per household	2.5
Persons per family	2.9

Labor & Employment, 2000

Civilian labor force	566
Unemployment rate	3.4%
Civilian labor force, 2008†	594
Unemployment rate†	5.4%
Civilian labor force, 12/09†	595
Unemployment rate†	7.2%
Employed persons 16 years and over, by occupation:	
Managers & professionals	204
Service occupations	91
Sales & office occupations	132
Farming, fishing & forestry	2
Construction & maintenance	55
Production & transportation	63
Self-employed persons	57

Most demographic data is from the 2000 Decennial Census
† Massachusetts Department of Revenue
†† University of Massachusetts, MISER

General Information

Town of Goshen
PO Box 106
Goshen, MA 01032
413-268-8236

Elevation	1,450 ft.
Land area (square miles)	17.4
Water area (square miles)	0.3
Population density, 2008 (est)	56.0
Year incorporated	1781
Website	www.egoshen.net

Voters & Government Information

Government type	Open Town Meeting
Number of Selectmen	3
US Congressional District(s)	1

Registered Voters, October 2008

Total	723
Democrats	195
Republicans	99
Unaffiliated/other	421

Local Officials, 2010

Chair, Bd. of Sel.	Edwin J. Brennan
Manager/Admin	NA
Clerk	Donna Polwrek
Treasurer	Kristine Bissell
Tax Collector	Lea Grippin
Tax Assessor	Cassandra Morrey
Attorney	Kopelman & Paige
Public Works	Joel Lagergren
Building	Paul Tacy
Planning	Roger Culver
Police Chief	Jeffrey Hewes
Emerg/Fire Chief	Susan Labrie

Housing & Construction

New Privately Owned Housing Units Authorized by Building Permit

	Single Family	Total Bldgs	Total Units
2006	4	4	4
2007	6	6	6
2008	2	2	2

Parcel Count by Property Class, 2010

Total	993
Single family	501
Multiple units	7
Apartments	3
Condos	12
Vacant land	307
Open space	0
Commercial	5
Industrial	9
Misc. residential	5
Other use	144

Public Library

Goshen Free Public Library
PO Box 320
Goshen, MA 01032
(413)268-7033

Library Director	Marcia Yudkin

Library Statistics, FY 2008

Population served, 2007	956
Registered users	307
Circulation	1,575
Reference transactons	0
Total program attendance	1,137
per capita:	
Holdings	7.65
Operating income	$6.00
Internet Access	
Internet computers available	2
Weekly users	3

Municipal Finance

Debt at year end 2008	$170,000
Moody's rating, July 2009	NA

Revenues, 2008

Total	$2,893,858
From all taxes	2,424,649
Federal aid	41,231
State aid	210,623
From other governments	347
Charges for services	67,635
Licenses, permits & fees	18,703
Fines & forfeits	10,795
Interfund transfers	59,593
Misc/other/special assessments	30,141

Expenditures, 2008

Total	$1,890,784
General government	265,004
Public safety	125,457
Other/fixed costs	78,479
Human services	13,613
Culture & recreation	9,599
Debt Service	52,634
Education	1,019,827
Public works	317,873
Intergovernmental	8,298

Taxation, 2010

Property type	Valuation	Rate
Total	$126,752,518	-
Residential	119,283,335	14.32
Open space	0	0.00
Commercial	2,450,766	14.32
Industrial	1,599,850	14.32
Personal	3,418,567	14.32

Average Single Family Tax Bill, 2010

Avg. assessed home value	$194,294
Avg. single fam. tax bill	$2,782
Hi-Lo ranking	255/301

Police & Crime, 2008

Number of police officers	2
Violent crimes	1
Property crimes	2

Local School District

(school data 2007-08, except as noted)

Goshen (non-op)
19 Stage Rd
Westhampton, MA 01027
413-527-7200

Superintendent	Craig Jurgensen

Non-operating district.
Resident students are sent to the Other School Districts listed below.

Grade plan	NA
Total enrollment '09-10	NA
Grade 12 enrollment, '09-10	NA
Graduation rate	NA
Dropout rate	NA
Per-pupil expenditure	NA
Avg teacher salary	NA
Student/teacher ratio '08-09	NA
Highly-qualified teachers, '08-09	NA
Teachers licensed in assigned subject	NA
Students per computer	NA

Other School Districts (see Appendix D for data)
Chesterfield-Goshen and Hampshire Regionals

See Introduction for an explanation of all data sources.

Demographics & Socio-Economic Characteristics

Population

1990	98
2000	86
Male	50
Female	36
2008	83
2010 (projected)††	110
2020 (projected)††	128

Race & Hispanic Origin, 2000

Race	
White	82
Black/African American	0
American Indian/Alaska Native	0
Asian	0
Hawaiian Native/Pacific Islander	0
Other Race	0
Two or more races	4
Hispanic origin	0

Age & Nativity, 2000

Under 5 years	5
18 years and over	71
21 years and over	69
65 years and over	11
85 years and over	1
Median Age	41.5
Native-born	81
Foreign-born	0

Age, 2020 (projected)††

Under 5 years	4
5 to 19 years	11
20 to 39 years	40
40 to 64 years	50
65 years and over	23

Educational Attainment, 2000

Population 25 years and over	58
High School graduates or higher	94.8%
Bachelor's degree or higher	20.7%
Graduate degree	5.2%

Income & Poverty, 1999

Per capita income,	$15,265
Median household income	$22,344
Median family income	$27,500
Persons in poverty	19
H'holds receiving public assistance	0
H'holds receiving social security	9

Households, 2000

Total households	46
With persons under 18	8
With persons over 65	9
Family households	21
Single person households	21
Persons per household	1.9
Persons per family	2.7

Labor & Employment, 2000

Civilian labor force	34
Unemployment rate	0.0%
Civilian labor force, 2008†	34
Unemployment rate†	2.9%
Civilian labor force, 12/09†	33
Unemployment rate†	3.0%
Employed persons 16 years and over, by occupation:	
Managers & professionals	9
Service occupations	7
Sales & office occupations	4
Farming, fishing & forestry	1
Construction & maintenance	5
Production & transportation	8
Self-employed persons	7

Most demographic data is from the 2000 Decennial Census
† Massachusetts Department of Revenue
†† University of Massachusetts, MISER

General Information

Town of Gosnold
PO Box 28
Cuttyhunk, MA 02713
508-990-7408

Elevation	NA
Land area (square miles)	13.3
Water area (square miles)	126.8
Population density, 2008 (est)	6.2
Year incorporated	1864
Email	gosnoldtownclerk@yahoo.com

Voters & Government Information

Government type	Open Town Meeting
Number of Selectmen	3
US Congressional District(s)	10

Registered Voters, October 2008

Total	129
Democrats	14
Republicans	17
Unaffiliated/other	98

Local Officials, 2010

Chair, Bd. of Sel.	Malcolm Davidson
Manager/Admin	Ray Pickles
Clerk	Elise Wright
Finance	Sarah Smith
Tax Collector	Frances Veeder
Tax Assessor	Kresenia Lombard
Attorney	Daniel Perry
Public Works	NA
Building	Andrew Bobola
Planning	Ray Pickles
Police Chief	George Isabel
Emerg/Fire Chief	Asa Lombard IV

Housing & Construction

New Privately Owned Housing Units Authorized by Building Permit

	Single Family	Total Bldgs	Total Units
2006	1	1	1
2007	1	1	1
2008	0	0	0

Parcel Count by Property Class, 2010

Total	NA
Single family	NA
Multiple units	NA
Apartments	NA
Condos	NA
Vacant land	NA
Open space	NA
Commercial	NA
Industrial	NA
Misc. residential	NA
Other use	NA

Public Library

Cuttyhunk Public Library
Cuttyhunk Post Office
Cuttyhunk, MA 02713

Director	Dorothy Garfield

Library Statistics, FY 2008

Population served, 2007	84
Registered users	538
Circulation	2,583
Reference transactons	118
Total program attendance	1,338
per capita:	
Holdings	120.50
Operating income	$84.01
Internet Access	
Internet computers available	0
Weekly users	0

Municipal Finance

Debt at year end 2008	$529,000
Moody's rating, July 2009	NA

Revenues, 2008

Total	$1,529,667
From all taxes	490,468
Federal aid	0
State aid	56,568
From other governments	0
Charges for services	646,441
Licenses, permits & fees	1,924
Fines & forfeits	0
Interfund transfers	0
Misc/other/special assessments	167,133

Expenditures, 2008

Total	$1,120,954
General government	136,183
Public safety	120,934
Other/fixed costs	82,588
Human services	0
Culture & recreation	4,434
Debt Service	90,670
Education	162,947
Public works	441,771
Intergovernmental	10,918

Taxation, 2010

Property type	Valuation	Rate
Total	NA	-
Residential	NA	NA
Open space	NA	NA
Commercial	NA	NA
Industrial	NA	NA
Personal	NA	NA

Average Single Family Tax Bill, 2010

Avg. assessed home value	NA
Avg. single fam. tax bill	NA
Hi-Lo ranking	NA

Police & Crime, 2008

Number of police officers	NA
Violent crimes	NA
Property crimes	NA

Local School District

(school data 2007-08, except as noted)

Gosnold
16 Williams Street
Rehoboth, MA 02769
508-252-4272

Superintendent	Russell Latham
Grade plan	PK-1
Total enrollment '09-10	4
Grade 12 enrollment, '09-10	0
Graduation rate	NA
Dropout rate	NA
Per-pupil expenditure	NA
Avg teacher salary	NA
Student/teacher ratio '08-09	4.0 to 1
Highly-qualified teachers, '08-09	100.0%
Teachers licensed in assigned subject	100.0%
Students per computer	NA

Massachusetts Competency Assessment System (MCAS), 2009 results

	English		Math	
	% Prof	CPI	% Prof	CPI
Gr 4	NA	NA	NA	NA
Gr 6	NA	NA	NA	NA
Gr 8	NA	NA	NA	NA
Gr 10	NA	NA	NA	NA

Other School Districts (see Appendix D for data)
None

©2010 Information Publications, Inc. All rights reserved. Photocopying prohibited. For additional copies, contact the publisher at www.informationpublications.com or (877)544-INFO (4636)

Demographics & Socio-Economic Characteristics

Population

1990	13,035
2000	14,894
Male	7,195
Female	7,699
2008	17,553
2010 (projected)††	16,347
2020 (projected)††	17,869

Race & Hispanic Origin, 2000

Race	
White	14,286
Black/African American	186
American Indian/Alaska Native	17
Asian	216
Hawaiian Native/Pacific Islander	0
Other Race	36
Two or more races	153
Hispanic origin	285

Age & Nativity, 2000

Under 5 years	1,086
18 years and over	11,058
21 years and over	10,563
65 years and over	1,671
85 years and over	147
Median Age	35.9
Native-born	14,248
Foreign-born	646

Age, 2020 (projected)††

Under 5 years	1,133
5 to 19 years	3,524
20 to 39 years	4,645
40 to 64 years	5,909
65 years and over	2,658

Educational Attainment, 2000

Population 25 years and over	10,040
High School graduates or higher	89.9%
Bachelor's degree or higher	34.8%
Graduate degree	11.8%

Income & Poverty, 1999

Per capita income,	$26,952
Median household income	$56,020
Median family income	$66,396
Persons in poverty	828
H'holds receiving public assistance	101
H'holds receiving social security	1,284

Households, 2000

Total households	5,694
With persons under 18	2,036
With persons over 65	1,191
Family households	3,952
Single person households	1,401
Persons per household	2.5
Persons per family	3.1

Labor & Employment, 2000

Civilian labor force	8,174
Unemployment rate	3.0%
Civilian labor force, 2008†	9,522
Unemployment rate†	6.0%
Civilian labor force, 12/09†	9,831
Unemployment rate†	8.7%
Employed persons 16 years and over, by occupation:	
Managers & professionals	3,580
Service occupations	790
Sales & office occupations	1,992
Farming, fishing & forestry	12
Construction & maintenance	700
Production & transportation	856
Self-employed persons	531

Most demographic data is from the 2000 Decennial Census
† Massachusetts Department of Revenue
†† University of Massachusetts, MISER

General Information

Town of Grafton
30 Providence Rd
Grafton, MA 01519
508-839-5335

Elevation	480 ft.
Land area (square miles)	22.7
Water area (square miles)	0.5
Population density, 2008 (est)	773.3
Year incorporated	1735
Website	www.grafton/ma.gov

Voters & Government Information

Government type	Open Town Meeting
Number of Selectmen	5
US Congressional District(s)	2

Registered Voters, October 2008

Total	11,740
Democrats	2,849
Republicans	1,821
Unaffiliated/other	6,996

Local Officials, 2010

Chair, Bd. of Sel.	Christopher LeMay
Town Administrator	Timothy McInerney
Clerk	Maureen Clark
Accountant	Timothy McInerney
Treas/Collector	Deborah Fox
Tax Assessor	Jennifer O'Neil
Attorney	Bowman & Penski
Public Works	(vacant)
Building	Robert Berger
Planning	Stephen Bishop
Police Chief	Norman A. Crepeau Jr
Fire Chief	Michael Gauthier

Housing & Construction

New Privately Owned Housing Units Authorized by Building Permit

	Single Family	Total Bldgs	Total Units
2006	142	142	142
2007	56	57	58
2008	30	31	32

Parcel Count by Property Class, 2010

Total	6,833
Single family	4,175
Multiple units	281
Apartments	92
Condos	1,224
Vacant land	664
Open space	0
Commercial	138
Industrial	74
Misc. residential	27
Other use	158

Public Library

Grafton Public Library
PO Box 387
Grafton, MA 01519
(508)839-4649

Director .... Hilding Hedberg

Library Statistics, FY 2008

Population served, 2007	17,525
Registered users	5,778
Circulation	92,709
Reference transactons	711
Total program attendance	77,012
per capita:	
Holdings	3.69
Operating income	$29.66
Internet Access	
Internet computers available	8
Weekly users	75

Municipal Finance

Debt at year end 2008	$9,489,666
Moody's rating, July 2009	A1

Revenues, 2008

Total	$38,906,653
From all taxes	26,078,686
Federal aid	93,675
State aid	9,970,790
From other governments	50
Charges for services	159,154
Licenses, permits & fees	250,979
Fines & forfeits	41,929
Interfund transfers	1,437,902
Misc/other/special assessments	436,744

Expenditures, 2008

Total	$36,347,258
General government	1,898,461
Public safety	2,375,161
Other/fixed costs	3,876,322
Human services	299,825
Culture & recreation	678,692
Debt Service	2,128,726
Education	22,005,664
Public works	2,824,243
Intergovernmental	260,164

Taxation, 2010

Property type	Valuation	Rate
Total	$2,154,670,006	-
Residential	1,952,034,246	12.43
Open space	0	0.00
Commercial	94,545,533	12.43
Industrial	55,667,847	12.43
Personal	52,422,380	12.43

Average Single Family Tax Bill, 2010

Avg. assessed home value	$344,408
Avg. single fam. tax bill	$4,281
Hi-Lo ranking	116/301

Police & Crime, 2008

Number of police officers	18
Violent crimes	7
Property crimes	136

Local School District

(school data 2007-08, except as noted)

Grafton
30 Providence Rd
Grafton, MA 01519
508-839-5421

Superintendent	Joseph Connors
Grade plan	PK-12
Total enrollment '09-10	2,902
Grade 12 enrollment, '09-10	141
Graduation rate	84.9%
Dropout rate	8.4%
Per-pupil expenditure	$9,180
Avg teacher salary	$61,073
Student/teacher ratio '08-09	15.1 to 1
Highly-qualified teachers, '08-09	98.5%
Teachers licensed in assigned subject	98.1%
Students per computer	3.3

Massachusetts Competency Assessment System (MCAS), 2009 results

	English		Math	
	% Prof	CPI	% Prof	CPI
Gr 4	59%	83.4	52%	78.5
Gr 6	75%	89.2	72%	85.5
Gr 8	85%	95.1	63%	83.3
Gr 10	81%	93.8	71%	88.8

Other School Districts (see Appendix D for data)
Blackstone Valley Vocational Tech

©2010 Information Publications, Inc. All rights reserved. Photocopying prohibited. For additional copies, contact the publisher at www.informationpublications.com or (877)544-INFO (4636)

See Introduction for an explanation of all data sources.

Demographics & Socio-Economic Characteristics

Population

1990	5,565
2000	6,132
Male	3,003
Female	3,129
2008	6,281
2010 (projected)††	6,212
2020 (projected)††	6,213

Race & Hispanic Origin, 2000

Race	
White	5,934
Black/African American	31
American Indian/Alaska Native	8
Asian	59
Hawaiian Native/Pacific Islander	1
Other Race	32
Two or more races	67
Hispanic origin	74

Age & Nativity, 2000

Under 5 years	345
18 years and over	4,568
21 years and over	4,367
65 years and over	716
85 years and over	63
Median Age	38.1
Native-born	5,985
Foreign-born	147

Age, 2020 (projected)††

Under 5 years	319
5 to 19 years	1,040
20 to 39 years	1,440
40 to 64 years	2,247
65 years and over	1,167

Educational Attainment, 2000

Population 25 years and over	4,143
High School graduates or higher	89.2%
Bachelor's degree or higher	23.0%
Graduate degree	9.8%

Income & Poverty, 1999

Per capita income,	$23,209
Median household income	$54,293
Median family income	$57,632
Persons in poverty	134
H'holds receiving public assistance	58
H'holds receiving social security	559

Households, 2000

Total households	2,247
With persons under 18	834
With persons over 65	514
Family households	1,662
Single person households	452
Persons per household	2.7
Persons per family	3.2

Labor & Employment, 2000

Civilian labor force	3,446
Unemployment rate	4.6%
Civilian labor force, 2008†	3,580
Unemployment rate†	6.3%
Civilian labor force, 12/09†	3,597
Unemployment rate†	9.0%
Employed persons 16 years and over, by occupation:	
Managers & professionals	1,079
Service occupations	528
Sales & office occupations	784
Farming, fishing & forestry	22
Construction & maintenance	344
Production & transportation	531
Self-employed persons	247

Most demographic data is from the 2000 Decennial Census
† Massachusetts Department of Revenue
†† University of Massachusetts, MISER

General Information

Town of Granby
250 State St
Granby, MA 01033
413-467-7177

Elevation	334 ft.
Land area (square miles)	27.9
Water area (square miles)	0.2
Population density, 2008 (est)	225.1
Year incorporated	1768
Website	www.granbyma.net

Voters & Government Information

Government type	Open Town Meeting
Number of Select Board	3
US Congressional District(s)	1

Registered Voters, October 2008

Total	4,500
Democrats	1,173
Republicans	685
Unaffiliated/other	2,613

Local Officials, 2010

Chair, Select Board	Mary A. McDowell
Town Administrator	Christopher Martin
Town Clerk	Katherine A. Kelly-Regan
Finance Committee	John Libera Jr (Chr)
Tax Collector	Karen M. Stellato
Tax Assessor	William D. Porter III (Chr)
Attorney	Edward Ryan Jr
Public Works	David Desrosiers
Building	Donald Demers
Planning Board	Emre Evren (Chr)
Police Chief	Louis Barry
Emerg/Fire Chief	Russel Anderson

Housing & Construction

New Privately Owned Housing Units Authorized by Building Permit

	Single Family	Total Bldgs	Total Units
2006	19	19	19
2007	11	12	14
2008	9	9	9

Parcel Count by Property Class, 2010

Total	3,031
Single family	2,035
Multiple units	46
Apartments	8
Condos	112
Vacant land	599
Open space	0
Commercial	64
Industrial	14
Misc. residential	21
Other use	132

Public Library

Granby Free Public Library
1 Library Lane
Granby, MA 01033
(413)467-3320

Director .... Jennifer Crosby

Library Statistics, FY 2008

Population served, 2007	6,285
Registered users	2,494
Circulation	55,311
Reference transactons	6,482
Total program attendance	32,840
per capita:	
Holdings	5.02
Operating income	$21.91
Internet Access	
Internet computers available	4
Weekly users	29

Municipal Finance

Debt at year end 2008	$1,651,609
Moody's rating, July 2009	NA

Revenues, 2008

Total	$16,927,782
From all taxes	8,669,234
Federal aid	56,628
State aid	5,413,030
From other governments	62,963
Charges for services	1,630,577
Licenses, permits & fees	62,354
Fines & forfeits	7,464
Interfund transfers	94,000
Misc/other/special assessments	465,766

Expenditures, 2008

Total	$13,240,684
General government	726,570
Public safety	992,148
Other/fixed costs	1,975,161
Human services	133,308
Culture & recreation	111,430
Debt Service	102,485
Education	8,269,395
Public works	301,538
Intergovernmental	628,649

Taxation, 2010

Property type	Valuation	Rate
Total	$580,888,581	-
Residential	540,673,670	14.51
Open space	0	0.00
Commercial	24,467,530	14.51
Industrial	3,630,800	14.51
Personal	12,116,581	14.51

Average Single Family Tax Bill, 2010

Avg. assessed home value	$232,096
Avg. single fam. tax bill	$3,368
Hi-Lo ranking	186/301

Police & Crime, 2008

Number of police officers	10
Violent crimes	7
Property crimes	102

Local School District

(school data 2007-08, except as noted)
Granby
387 East State Street
Granby, MA 01033
413-467-7193

Superintendent	Patricia Stevens
Grade plan	PK-12
Total enrollment '09-10	1,125
Grade 12 enrollment, '09-10	80
Graduation rate	94.1%
Dropout rate	2.4%
Per-pupil expenditure	$9,433
Avg teacher salary	$53,749
Student/teacher ratio '08-09	13.5 to 1
Highly-qualified teachers, '08-09	98.1%
Teachers licensed in assigned subject	99.4%
Students per computer	4

Massachusetts Competency Assessment System (MCAS), 2009 results

	English		Math	
	% Prof	CPI	% Prof	CPI
Gr 4	72%	88.1	67%	86.4
Gr 6	72%	88.8	70%	84.3
Gr 8	90%	96.4	54%	78.6
Gr 10	84%	95.3	84%	92.7

Other School Districts (see Appendix D for data)
Pathfinder Vocational Tech

©2010 Information Publications, Inc. All rights reserved. Photocopying prohibited. For additional copies, contact the publisher at www.informationpublications.com or (877)544-INFO (4636)

©2010 Information Publications, Inc. All rights reserved. Photocopying prohibited. For additional copies, contact the publisher at www.informationpublications.com or (877)544-INFO (4636)

Demographics & Socio-Economic Characteristics

Population

1990	1,403
2000	1,521
Male	786
Female	735
2008	1,686
2010 (projected)††	1,552
2020 (projected)††	1,601

Race & Hispanic Origin, 2000

Race	
White	1,501
Black/African American	4
American Indian/Alaska Native	0
Asian	3
Hawaiian Native/Pacific Islander	0
Other Race	6
Two or more races	7
Hispanic origin	10

Age & Nativity, 2000

Under 5 years	96
18 years and over	1,101
21 years and over	1,062
65 years and over	166
85 years and over	10
Median Age	39.0
Native-born	1,480
Foreign-born	41

Age, 2020 (projected)††

Under 5 years	90
5 to 19 years	267
20 to 39 years	386
40 to 64 years	568
65 years and over	290

Educational Attainment, 2000

Population 25 years and over	1,009
High School graduates or higher	92.3%
Bachelor's degree or higher	31.3%
Graduate degree	10.1%

Income & Poverty, 1999

Per capita income,	$22,315
Median household income	$53,148
Median family income	$59,219
Persons in poverty	51
H'holds receiving public assistance	0
H'holds receiving social security	145

Households, 2000

Total households	556
With persons under 18	227
With persons over 65	123
Family households	410
Single person households	116
Persons per household	2.7
Persons per family	3.2

Labor & Employment, 2000

Civilian labor force	873
Unemployment rate	5.6%
Civilian labor force, 2008†	951
Unemployment rate†	6.3%
Civilian labor force, 12/09†	970
Unemployment rate†	9.1%
Employed persons 16 years and over, by occupation:	
Managers & professionals	316
Service occupations	101
Sales & office occupations	176
Farming, fishing & forestry	13
Construction & maintenance	77
Production & transportation	141
Self-employed persons	102

Most demographic data is from the 2000 Decennial Census
† Massachusetts Department of Revenue
†† University of Massachusetts, MISER

General Information

Town of Granville
PO Box 247
Granville, MA 01034
413-357-8585

Elevation	1,040 ft.
Land area (square miles)	42.2
Water area (square miles)	0.7
Population density, 2008 (est)	40.0
Year incorporated	1754
Website	www.townofgranville.org

Voters & Government Information

Government type	Open Town Meeting
Number of Selectmen	3
US Congressional District(s)	1

Registered Voters, October 2008

Total	1,148
Democrats	177
Republicans	230
Unaffiliated/other	727

Local Officials, 2010

Chair, Bd. of Sel.	Robert Beckwith
Admin Assistant	Kathryn W. Martin
Clerk	Ann Sussmann
Finance Director	Linda Blakesley
Tax Collector	Mary Beth Sussmann
Tax Assessor	Leon Ripley
Attorney	Kopelman & Paige
Public Works	Doug Roberts
Building	Bob Sullivan
Planning	Rich Pierce
Police Chief	Jose A. Rivera
Emerg/Fire Chief	James Meadows Jr

Housing & Construction

New Privately Owned Housing Units Authorized by Building Permit

	Single Family	Total Bldgs	Total Units
2006	11	11	11
2007	9	9	9
2008	6	6	6

Parcel Count by Property Class, 2010

Total	928
Single family	567
Multiple units	24
Apartments	0
Condos	0
Vacant land	150
Open space	0
Commercial	28
Industrial	10
Misc. residential	6
Other use	143

Public Library

Granville Public Library
2 Granby Road
Granville, MA 01034
(413)357-8531

Librarian	Mary Short

Library Statistics, FY 2008

Population served, 2007	1,676
Registered users	890
Circulation	10,682
Reference transactons	0
Total program attendance	6,147
per capita:	
Holdings	5.68
Operating income	$22.05
Internet Access	
Internet computers available	3
Weekly users	16

Municipal Finance

Debt at year end 2008	$925,512
Moody's rating, July 2009	NA

Revenues, 2008

Total	$4,766,083
From all taxes	2,561,196
Federal aid	0
State aid	1,818,265
From other governments	11,263
Charges for services	91,201
Licenses, permits & fees	29,119
Fines & forfeits	0
Interfund transfers	82,477
Misc/other/special assessments	86,281

Expenditures, 2008

Total	$4,715,412
General government	209,482
Public safety	204,481
Other/fixed costs	440,434
Human services	12,829
Culture & recreation	34,644
Debt Service	403,164
Education	2,862,268
Public works	487,658
Intergovernmental	60,452

Taxation, 2010

Property type	Valuation	Rate
Total	$207,329,457	-
Residential	180,366,765	11.20
Open space	0	0.00
Commercial	9,764,717	11.20
Industrial	2,740,075	11.20
Personal	14,457,900	11.20

Average Single Family Tax Bill, 2010

Avg. assessed home value	$277,502
Avg. single fam. tax bill	$3,108
Hi-Lo ranking	225/301

Police & Crime, 2008

Number of police officers	1
Violent crimes	2
Property crimes	25

Local School District

(school data 2007-08, except as noted)

Granville
86 Powder Mill Road
Southwick, MA 01077
413-569-5391

Superintendent	John Barry
Grade plan	K-8
Total enrollment '09-10	163
Grade 12 enrollment, '09-10	0
Graduation rate	NA
Dropout rate	NA
Per-pupil expenditure	$13,128
Avg teacher salary	$50,544
Student/teacher ratio '08-09	8.9 to 1
Highly-qualified teachers, '08-09	100.0%
Teachers licensed in assigned subject	100.0%
Students per computer	3.2

Massachusetts Competency Assessment System (MCAS), 2009 results

	English		Math	
	% Prof	CPI	% Prof	CPI
Gr 4	47%	76.5	75%	89.1
Gr 6	58%	85.5	42%	69.7
Gr 8	70%	90	33%	57.1
Gr 10	NA	NA	NA	NA

Other School Districts (see Appendix D for data)
Southwick-Tolland Regional

See Introduction for an explanation of all data sources.

Demographics & Socio-Economic Characteristics

Population

1990	7,725
2000	7,527
Male	3,506
Female	4,021
2008	7,379
2010 (projected)††	7,493
2020 (projected)††	7,472

Race & Hispanic Origin, 2000

Race	
White	7,131
Black/African American	157
American Indian/Alaska Native	12
Asian	94
Hawaiian Native/Pacific Islander	2
Other Race	53
Two or more races	78
Hispanic origin	156

Age & Nativity, 2000

Under 5 years	328
18 years and over	5,828
21 years and over	5,462
65 years and over	1,413
85 years and over	260
Median Age	41.8
Native-born	7,081
Foreign-born	446

Age, 2020 (projected)††

Under 5 years	322
5 to 19 years	1,353
20 to 39 years	1,423
40 to 64 years	2,298
65 years and over	2,076

Educational Attainment, 2000

Population 25 years and over	5,141
High School graduates or higher	88.1%
Bachelor's degree or higher	33.3%
Graduate degree	16.3%

Income & Poverty, 1999

Per capita income,	$22,655
Median household income	$45,490
Median family income	$53,135
Persons in poverty	495
H'holds receiving public assistance	37
H'holds receiving social security	750

Households, 2000

Total households	3,008
With persons under 18	877
With persons over 65	854
Family households	1,826
Single person households	980
Persons per household	2.3
Persons per family	2.9

Labor & Employment, 2000

Civilian labor force	3,862
Unemployment rate	2.6%
Civilian labor force, 2008†	4,304
Unemployment rate†	6.4%
Civilian labor force, 12/09†	4,299
Unemployment rate†	7.6%
Employed persons 16 years and over, by occupation:	
Managers & professionals	1,368
Service occupations	779
Sales & office occupations	883
Farming, fishing & forestry	12
Construction & maintenance	263
Production & transportation	455
Self-employed persons	476

Most demographic data is from the 2000 Decennial Census
† Massachusetts Department of Revenue
†† University of Massachusetts, MISER

General Information

Town of Great Barrington
334 Main St
Great Barrington, MA 01230
413-528-1619

Elevation	721 ft.
Land area (square miles)	45.2
Water area (square miles)	0.5
Population density, 2008 (est)	163.3
Year incorporated	1761
Website	www.townofgb.org

Voters & Government Information

Government type	Open Town Meeting
Number of Selectmen	5
US Congressional District(s)	1

Registered Voters, October 2008

Total	4,753
Democrats	1,824
Republicans	439
Unaffiliated/other	2,439

Local Officials, 2010

Chair, Bd. of Sel.	Walter Atwood III
Manager	Kevin O'Donnell
Clerk	Marie Ryan
Finance Director	Lauren Sartori
Tax Collector	Sandra Larkin
Tax Assessor	Karen Avalle
Attorney	Kopelman & Paige
Public Works	Joe Sokul
Building	Edwin May
Planning	Donald Goranson
Police Chief	William R. Walsh Jr
Emerg/Fire Chief	Harry Jennings

Housing & Construction

New Privately Owned Housing Units Authorized by Building Permit

	Single Family	Total Bldgs	Total Units
2006	25	25	25
2007	10	10	10
2008	7	7	7

Parcel Count by Property Class, 2010

Total	3,811
Single family	2,096
Multiple units	229
Apartments	35
Condos	163
Vacant land	635
Open space	0
Commercial	277
Industrial	45
Misc. residential	66
Other use	265

Public Library

Mason Library
231 Main Street
Great Barrington, MA 01230
(413)528-2403

Director . . . . . Anne Just

Library Statistics, FY 2008

Population served, 2007	7,372
Registered users	3,114
Circulation	138,034
Reference transactons	22,880
Total program attendance	0
per capita:	
Holdings	8.85
Operating income	$58.93
Internet Access	
Internet computers available	24
Weekly users	450

Municipal Finance

Debt at year end 2008	$13,437,146
Moody's rating, July 2009	A1

Revenues, 2008

Total	$19,472,012
From all taxes	16,191,771
Federal aid	0
State aid	1,089,772
From other governments	0
Charges for services	468,045
Licenses, permits & fees	56,816
Fines & forfeits	0
Interfund transfers	414,524
Misc/other/special assessments	625,542

Expenditures, 2008

Total	$18,176,203
General government	1,398,954
Public safety	1,618,824
Other/fixed costs	1,324,780
Human services	224,192
Culture & recreation	456,505
Debt Service	1,612,508
Education	9,779,495
Public works	1,690,501
Intergovernmental	70,444

Taxation, 2010

Property type	Valuation	Rate
Total	$1,451,065,595	-
Residential	1,165,281,179	11.52
Open space	0	0.00
Commercial	236,697,931	11.52
Industrial	12,548,200	11.52
Personal	36,538,285	11.52

Average Single Family Tax Bill, 2010

Avg. assessed home value	$406,276
Avg. single fam. tax bill	$4,680
Hi-Lo ranking	92/301

Police & Crime, 2008

Number of police officers	14
Violent crimes	13
Property crimes	126

Local School District

(school data 2007-08, except as noted)

Great Barrington (non-op)
207 Pleasant Street, PO Box 596
Housatonic, MA 01236
413-274-6400

Superintendent . . . . . Peter Dillon

Non-operating district.
Resident students are sent to the Other School Districts listed below.

Grade plan	NA
Total enrollment '09-10	NA
Grade 12 enrollment, '09-10	NA
Graduation rate	NA
Dropout rate	NA
Per-pupil expenditure	NA
Avg teacher salary	NA
Student/teacher ratio '08-09	NA
Highly-qualified teachers, '08-09	NA
Teachers licensed in assigned subject	NA
Students per computer	NA

Other School Districts (see Appendix D for data)
Berkshire Hills Regional

©2010 Information Publications, Inc. All rights reserved. Photocopying prohibited. For additional copies, contact the publisher at www.informationpublications.com or (877)544-INFO (4636)

See Introduction for an explanation of all data sources.

Demographics & Socio-Economic Characteristics

Population

1990	18,666
2000	18,168
Male	8,548
Female	9,620
2008	17,828
2010 (projected)††	17,623
2020 (projected)††	17,119

Race & Hispanic Origin, 2000

Race	
White	16,967
Black/African American	244
American Indian/Alaska Native	58
Asian	199
Hawaiian Native/Pacific Islander	3
Other Race	256
Two or more races	441
Hispanic origin	644

Age & Nativity, 2000

Under 5 years	957
18 years and over	14,194
21 years and over	13,505
65 years and over	3,178
85 years and over	584
Median Age	39.5
Native-born	17,447
Foreign-born	721

Age, 2020 (projected)††

Under 5 years	869
5 to 19 years	2,627
20 to 39 years	4,124
40 to 64 years	5,484
65 years and over	4,015

Educational Attainment, 2000

Population 25 years and over	12,680
High School graduates or higher	86.0%
Bachelor's degree or higher	24.2%
Graduate degree	10.2%

Income & Poverty, 1999

Per capita income,	$18,830
Median household income	$33,110
Median family income	$46,412
Persons in poverty	2,435
H'holds receiving public assistance	427
H'holds receiving social security	2,344

Households, 2000

Total households	7,939
With persons under 18	2,215
With persons over 65	2,089
Family households	4,377
Single person households	2,929
Persons per household	2.2
Persons per family	2.9

Labor & Employment, 2000

Civilian labor force	9,325
Unemployment rate	4.9%
Civilian labor force, 2008†	8,878
Unemployment rate†	7.0%
Civilian labor force, 12/09†	8,953
Unemployment rate†	9.1%
Employed persons 16 years and over, by occupation:	
Managers & professionals	2,718
Service occupations	1,659
Sales & office occupations	2,227
Farming, fishing & forestry	11
Construction & maintenance	783
Production & transportation	1,468
Self-employed persons	688

Most demographic data is from the 2000 Decennial Census
† Massachusetts Department of Revenue
†† University of Massachusetts, MISER

General Information

Town of Greenfield
14 Court Sq
Greenfield, MA 01301
413-772-1580

Elevation	270 ft.
Land area (square miles)	21.7
Water area (square miles)	0.2
Population density, 2008 (est)	821.6
Year incorporated	1753
Website	www.greenfield-ma.gov

Voters & Government Information

Government type	Mayor-Council
Number of Councilpersons	13
US Congressional District(s)	1

Registered Voters, October 2008

Total	11,526
Democrats	3,831
Republicans	1,243
Unaffiliated/other	6,335

Local Officials, 2010

Mayor	William Martin
Manager/Admin	NA
Town Clerk	Maureen Winseck
Finance Director	Marjorie Lane Kelly
Tax Collector	NA
Tax Assessor	Audrey Murphy
Attorney	Richard Kos
Public Works	Sandra Shields
Building	Mark Snow
Comm Dev/Planning	Robert Pyers
Police Chief	David Guilbault
Emerg/Fire Chief	Michael Winn

Housing & Construction

New Privately Owned Housing Units Authorized by Building Permit

	Single Family	Total Bldgs	Total Units
2006	13	13	13
2007	8	10	12
2008	6	7	8

Parcel Count by Property Class, 2010

Total	6,575
Single family	3,853
Multiple units	783
Apartments	156
Condos	321
Vacant land	566
Open space	0
Commercial	475
Industrial	81
Misc. residential	41
Other use	299

Public Library

Greenfield Public Library
402 Main Street
Greenfield, MA 01301
(413)772-1544

Director	Sharon Sharry

Library Statistics, FY 2008

Population served, 2007	17,706
Registered users	10,710
Circulation	267,510
Reference transactons	7,883
Total program attendance	173,522
per capita:	
Holdings	4.30
Operating income	$38.54
Internet Access	
Internet computers available	17
Weekly users	397

Municipal Finance

Debt at year end 2008	$30,162,303
Moody's rating, July 2009	A3

Revenues, 2008

Total	$44,590,847
From all taxes	25,394,513
Federal aid	221,419
State aid	15,533,357
From other governments	151,430
Charges for services	581,510
Licenses, permits & fees	341,182
Fines & forfeits	115,750
Interfund transfers	1,510,600
Misc/other/special assessments	370,543

Expenditures, 2008

Total	$43,729,438
General government	1,804,515
Public safety	5,461,104
Other/fixed costs	9,470,176
Human services	621,311
Culture & recreation	1,017,785
Debt Service	3,736,457
Education	16,383,324
Public works	2,423,244
Intergovernmental	2,713,404

Taxation, 2010

Property type	Valuation	Rate
Total	$1,372,362,883	-
Residential	1,055,388,591	17.68
Open space	0	0.00
Commercial	243,076,431	17.68
Industrial	33,819,460	17.68
Personal	40,078,401	17.68

Average Single Family Tax Bill, 2010

Avg. assessed home value	$190,928
Avg. single fam. tax bill	$3,376
Hi-Lo ranking	185/301

Police & Crime, 2008

Number of police officers	34
Violent crimes	121
Property crimes	563

Local School District

(school data 2007-08, except as noted)

Greenfield
141 Davis Street
Greenfield, MA 01301
413-772-1311

Superintendent	Susan Hollins
Grade plan	PK-12
Total enrollment '09-10	1,496
Grade 12 enrollment, '09-10	93
Graduation rate	74.8%
Dropout rate	12.2%
Per-pupil expenditure	$13,135
Avg teacher salary	$57,888
Student/teacher ratio '08-09	14.8 to 1
Highly-qualified teachers, '08-09	86.8%
Teachers licensed in assigned subject	96.7%
Students per computer	2.6

Massachusetts Competency Assessment System (MCAS), 2009 results

	English		Math	
	% Prof	CPI	% Prof	CPI
Gr 4	40%	71.5	34%	70.7
Gr 6	64%	84.3	28%	57.8
Gr 8	76%	88.5	41%	68.7
Gr 10	71%	89	65%	84

Other School Districts (see Appendix D for data)
Franklin County Vocational Tech

©2010 Information Publications, Inc. All rights reserved. Photocopying prohibited. For additional copies, contact the publisher at www.informationpublications.com or (877)544-INFO (4636)

See Introduction for an explanation of all data sources.

Demographics & Socio-Economic Characteristics

Population

1990	7,511
2000	9,547
Male	4,731
Female	4,816
2008	10,632
2010 (projected)††	10,725
2020 (projected)††	11,751

Race & Hispanic Origin, 2000

Race	
White	9,282
Black/African American	33
American Indian/Alaska Native	12
Asian	93
Hawaiian Native/Pacific Islander	2
Other Race	26
Two or more races	99
Hispanic origin	109

Age & Nativity, 2000

Under 5 years	837
18 years and over	6,430
21 years and over	6,221
65 years and over	668
85 years and over	70
Median Age	36.5
Native-born	9,179
Foreign-born	368

Age, 2020 (projected)††

Under 5 years	877
5 to 19 years	2,674
20 to 39 years	2,913
40 to 64 years	3,832
65 years and over	1,455

Educational Attainment, 2000

Population 25 years and over	6,048
High School graduates or higher	96.4%
Bachelor's degree or higher	53.8%
Graduate degree	23.4%

Income & Poverty, 1999

Per capita income,	$33,877
Median household income	$82,869
Median family income	$92,014
Persons in poverty	376
H'holds receiving public assistance	27
H'holds receiving social security	527

Households, 2000

Total households	3,268
With persons under 18	1,582
With persons over 65	494
Family households	2,568
Single person households	558
Persons per household	2.9
Persons per family	3.3

Labor & Employment, 2000

Civilian labor force	4,978
Unemployment rate	2.3%
Civilian labor force, 2008†	5,664
Unemployment rate†	4.9%
Civilian labor force, 12/09†	5,637
Unemployment rate†	6.7%
Employed persons 16 years and over, by occupation:	
Managers & professionals	2,797
Service occupations	435
Sales & office occupations	1,070
Farming, fishing & forestry	11
Construction & maintenance	282
Production & transportation	267
Self-employed persons	252

Most demographic data is from the 2000 Decennial Census
† Massachusetts Department of Revenue
†† University of Massachusetts, MISER

General Information

Town of Groton
173 Main St
Groton, MA 01450
978-448-1100

Elevation	300 ft.
Land area (square miles)	32.8
Water area (square miles)	0.9
Population density, 2008 (est)	324.1
Year incorporated	1655
Website	www.townofgroton.org

Voters & Government Information

Government type	Open Town Meeting
Number of Selectmen	5
US Congressional District(s)	5

Registered Voters, October 2008

Total	7,239
Democrats	1,690
Republicans	1,285
Unaffiliated/other	4,227

Local Officials, 2010

Chair, Bd. of Sel.	Peter Cunningham
Admin	Mark Haddad
Town Clerk	Michael F. Bouchard
Accountant	Valerie Jenkins
Treas/Collector	Christine Collins
Tax Assessor	Rena Swezey (Chr)
Attorney	NA
Public Works	R. Thomas Delaney Jr
Building	Bentley Herget
Planning Board	Michelle Collette (Chr)
Police Chief	Donald L. Palma Jr
Fire Chief	Joseph Bosselait

Housing & Construction

New Privately Owned Housing Units Authorized by Building Permit

	Single Family	Total Bldgs	Total Units
2006	13	16	19
2007	16	16	16
2008	11	11	11

Parcel Count by Property Class, 2010

Total	4,307
Single family	3,065
Multiple units	157
Apartments	14
Condos	178
Vacant land	646
Open space	0
Commercial	92
Industrial	16
Misc. residential	40
Other use	99

Public Library

Groton Public Library
99 Main St.
Groton, MA 01450
(978)448-1167

Director	Owen Smith Shuman

Library Statistics, FY 2008

Population served, 2007	10,641
Registered users	12,574
Circulation	235,502
Reference transactons	5,259
Total program attendance	81,500
per capita:	
Holdings	6.91
Operating income	$75.84
Internet Access	
Internet computers available	25
Weekly users	175

Municipal Finance

Debt at year end 2008	$17,716,299
Moody's rating, July 2009	A2

Revenues, 2008

Total	$27,174,657
From all taxes	24,423,268
Federal aid	0
State aid	1,122,605
From other governments	97,806
Charges for services	796,601
Licenses, permits & fees	201,869
Fines & forfeits	22,433
Interfund transfers	364,475
Misc/other/special assessments	72,800

Expenditures, 2008

Total	$26,891,830
General government	1,510,756
Public safety	2,807,257
Other/fixed costs	2,389,649
Human services	210,747
Culture & recreation	797,048
Debt Service	1,631,314
Education	15,650,909
Public works	1,819,463
Intergovernmental	74,687

Taxation, 2010

Property type	Valuation	Rate
Total	$1,534,542,445	-
Residential	1,428,578,130	15.78
Open space	0	0.00
Commercial	64,851,210	15.78
Industrial	14,162,470	15.78
Personal	26,950,635	15.78

Average Single Family Tax Bill, 2010

Avg. assessed home value	$403,710
Avg. single fam. tax bill	$6,371
Hi-Lo ranking	43/301

Police & Crime, 2008

Number of police officers	16
Violent crimes	2
Property crimes	39

Local School District

(school data 2007-08, except as noted)

Groton (non-op)
P O Box 729
Groton, MA 01450
978-448-5505

Superintendent	Alan Genovese

Non-operating district.
Resident students are sent to the Other School Districts listed below.

Grade plan	NA
Total enrollment '09-10	NA
Grade 12 enrollment, '09-10	NA
Graduation rate	NA
Dropout rate	NA
Per-pupil expenditure	NA
Avg teacher salary	NA
Student/teacher ratio '08-09	NA
Highly-qualified teachers, '08-09	NA
Teachers licensed in assigned subject	NA
Students per computer	NA

Other School Districts (see Appendix D for data)
Groton-Dunstable Regional, Nashoba Valley Vocational Tech

©2010 Information Publications, Inc. All rights reserved. Photocopying prohibited. For additional copies, contact the publisher at www.informationpublications.com or (877)544-INFO (4636)

See Introduction for an explanation of all data sources.

Demographics & Socio-Economic Characteristics

Population

1990	5,214
2000	6,038
Male	2,992
Female	3,046
2008	7,198
2010 (projected)††	5,993
2020 (projected)††	5,927

Race & Hispanic Origin, 2000

Race	
White	5,941
Black/African American	21
American Indian/Alaska Native	8
Asian	36
Hawaiian Native/Pacific Islander	0
Other Race	5
Two or more races	27
Hispanic origin	28

Age & Nativity, 2000

Under 5 years	445
18 years and over	4,251
21 years and over	4,090
65 years and over	619
85 years and over	48
Median Age	37.6
Native-born	5,807
Foreign-born	231

Age, 2020 (projected)††

Under 5 years	386
5 to 19 years	1,160
20 to 39 years	1,380
40 to 64 years	1,986
65 years and over	1,015

Educational Attainment, 2000

Population 25 years and over	3,956
High School graduates or higher	92.3%
Bachelor's degree or higher	34.2%
Graduate degree	7.4%

Income & Poverty, 1999

Per capita income,	$25,430
Median household income	$69,167
Median family income	$73,996
Persons in poverty	269
H'holds receiving public assistance	16
H'holds receiving social security	479

Households, 2000

Total households	2,058
With persons under 18	944
With persons over 65	448
Family households	1,707
Single person households	289
Persons per household	2.9
Persons per family	3.3

Labor & Employment, 2000

Civilian labor force	3,217
Unemployment rate	1.2%
Civilian labor force, 2008†	3,519
Unemployment rate†	4.6%
Civilian labor force, 12/09†	3,610
Unemployment rate†	8.2%
Employed persons 16 years and over, by occupation:	
Managers & professionals	1,283
Service occupations	493
Sales & office occupations	706
Farming, fishing & forestry	8
Construction & maintenance	317
Production & transportation	370
Self-employed persons	161

Most demographic data is from the 2000 Decennial Census
† Massachusetts Department of Revenue
†† University of Massachusetts, MISER

General Information

Town of Groveland
183 Main St
Groveland, MA 01834
978-556-7200

Elevation	50 ft.
Land area (square miles)	8.9
Water area (square miles)	0.5
Population density, 2008 (est)	808.8
Year incorporated	1850
Website	www.grovelandma.com

Voters & Government Information

Government type	Open Town Meeting
Number of Selectmen	3
US Congressional District(s)	6

Registered Voters, October 2008

Total	4,774
Democrats	1,118
Republicans	788
Unaffiliated/other	2,813

Local Officials, 2010

Chair, Bd. of Sel.	William Darke
Manager/Admin	NA
Town Clerk	Anne Brodie
Finance Director	Gregg LeBrecque
Tax Collector	Patricia Rogers
Tax Assessor	Debbie Webster
Attorney	Kopelman & Paige
Public Works	NA
Building	Pat Schena
Comm Dev/Planning	Walter Sorenson
Police Chief	Robert Kirmelewicz
Emerg/Fire Chief	John Clement

Housing & Construction

New Privately Owned Housing Units Authorized by Building Permit

	Single Family	Total Bldgs	Total Units
2006	18	30	83
2007	15	26	75
2008	8	20	82

Parcel Count by Property Class, 2010

Total	2,482
Single family	1,838
Multiple units	84
Apartments	6
Condos	174
Vacant land	231
Open space	0
Commercial	43
Industrial	49
Misc. residential	3
Other use	54

Public Library

Langley Adams Library
185 Main Street
Groveland, MA 01834
(978)372-1732

Director	Deb Hoadley

Library Statistics, FY 2008

Population served, 2007	6,923
Registered users	3,934
Circulation	38,229
Reference transactons	2,106
Total program attendance	13,671
per capita:	
Holdings	4.76
Operating income	$28.11
Internet Access	
Internet computers available	2
Weekly users	60

Municipal Finance

Debt at year end 2008	$265,000
Moody's rating, July 2009	NA

Revenues, 2008

Total	$11,863,792
From all taxes	10,434,847
Federal aid	0
State aid	1,065,195
From other governments	0
Charges for services	0
Licenses, permits & fees	92,109
Fines & forfeits	15,211
Interfund transfers	20,000
Misc/other/special assessments	118,215

Expenditures, 2008

Total	$11,316,320
General government	827,044
Public safety	1,352,589
Other/fixed costs	551,450
Human services	199,931
Culture & recreation	240,076
Debt Service	274,540
Education	6,739,060
Public works	1,131,630
Intergovernmental	0

Taxation, 2010

Property type	Valuation	Rate
Total	$857,641,626	-
Residential	785,338,925	11.93
Open space	0	0.00
Commercial	24,763,701	11.93
Industrial	25,840,500	11.93
Personal	21,698,500	11.93

Average Single Family Tax Bill, 2010

Avg. assessed home value	$362,032
Avg. single fam. tax bill	$4,319
Hi-Lo ranking	113/301

Police & Crime, 2008

Number of police officers	9
Violent crimes	3
Property crimes	48

Local School District

(school data 2007-08, except as noted)

Groveland (non-op)
22 Main Street
West Newbury, MA 01985
617-363-2280

Superintendent	Paul Livingston

Non-operating district.
Resident students are sent to the Other School Districts listed below.

Grade plan	NA
Total enrollment '09-10	NA
Grade 12 enrollment, '09-10	NA
Graduation rate	NA
Dropout rate	NA
Per-pupil expenditure	NA
Avg teacher salary	NA
Student/teacher ratio '08-09	NA
Highly-qualified teachers, '08-09	NA
Teachers licensed in assigned subject	NA
Students per computer	NA

Other School Districts (see Appendix D for data)
Pentucket Regional, Whittier Vocational Tech

©2010 Information Publications, Inc. All rights reserved. Photocopying prohibited. For additional copies, contact the publisher at www.informationpublications.com or (877)544-INFO (4636)

See Introduction for an explanation of all data sources.

Demographics & Socio-Economic Characteristics

Population

1990	4,231
2000	4,793
Male	2,250
Female	2,543
2008	4,732
2010 (projected)††	4,925
2020 (projected)††	5,090

Race & Hispanic Origin, 2000

Race	
White	4,597
Black/African American	36
American Indian/Alaska Native	3
Asian	75
Hawaiian Native/Pacific Islander	0
Other Race	28
Two or more races	54
Hispanic origin	80

Age & Nativity, 2000

Under 5 years	222
18 years and over	3,834
21 years and over	3,694
65 years and over	937
85 years and over	160
Median Age	42.3
Native-born	4,583
Foreign-born	210

Age, 2020 (projected)††

Under 5 years	212
5 to 19 years	625
20 to 39 years	1,281
40 to 64 years	1,599
65 years and over	1,373

Educational Attainment, 2000

Population 25 years and over	3,486
High School graduates or higher	89.8%
Bachelor's degree or higher	40.2%
Graduate degree	17.0%

Income & Poverty, 1999

Per capita income,	$24,945
Median household income	$51,851
Median family income	$61,897
Persons in poverty	321
H'holds receiving public assistance	68
H'holds receiving social security	623

Households, 2000

Total households	1,895
With persons under 18	529
With persons over 65	583
Family households	1,249
Single person households	468
Persons per household	2.5
Persons per family	2.9

Labor & Employment, 2000

Civilian labor force	2,546
Unemployment rate	3.3%
Civilian labor force, 2008†	2,565
Unemployment rate†	5.0%
Civilian labor force, 12/09†	2,573
Unemployment rate†	7.2%
Employed persons 16 years and over, by occupation:	
Managers & professionals	1,124
Service occupations	325
Sales & office occupations	585
Farming, fishing & forestry	15
Construction & maintenance	170
Production & transportation	243
Self-employed persons	248

Most demographic data is from the 2000 Decennial Census
† Massachusetts Department of Revenue
†† University of Massachusetts, MISER

General Information

Town of Hadley
100 Middle St
Hadley, MA 01035
413-586-0221

Elevation	129 ft.
Land area (square miles)	23.3
Water area (square miles)	1.4
Population density, 2008 (est)	203.1
Year incorporated	1661
Website	www.hadleyma.org

Voters & Government Information

Government type	Open Town Meeting
Number of Selectmen	5
US Congressional District(s)	2

Registered Voters, October 2008

Total	3,839
Democrats	1,393
Republicans	383
Unaffiliated/other	2,033

Local Officials, 2010

Chair, Bd. of Sel.	Joyce Chunglo
Town Administrator	David Nixon
Clerk	Jessica Spanknebel
Finance Dir.	Constance Mieczkowski
Tax Collector	Susan Glowatsky
Tax Assessor	Daniel Omasta
Attorney	Joel Bard
Public Works	Gary Girouard
Building	Timothy Neyhart
Planning	James Maksimoski
Police Chief	Dennis Hukowicz
Emerg/Fire Chief	James Kicza

Housing & Construction

New Privately Owned Housing Units Authorized by Building Permit

	Single Family	Total Bldgs	Total Units
2006	9	9	9
2007	7	7	7
2008	9	9	9

Parcel Count by Property Class, 2010

Total	2,885
Single family	1,625
Multiple units	108
Apartments	4
Condos	0
Vacant land	402
Open space	0
Commercial	356
Industrial	14
Misc. residential	13
Other use	363

Public Library

Goodwin Memorial Library
50 Middle Street
Hadley, MA 01035
(413)584-7451

Director	Jane Babcock

Library Statistics, FY 2008

Population served, 2007	4,787
Registered users	1,674
Circulation	23,096
Reference transactons	1,827
Total program attendance	14,252
per capita:	
Holdings	3.85
Operating income	$22.31
Internet Access	
Internet computers available	6
Weekly users	30

Municipal Finance

Debt at year end 2008	$9,885,595
Moody's rating, July 2009	A2

Revenues, 2008

Total	$11,832,745
From all taxes	9,168,004
Federal aid	16,882
State aid	1,509,407
From other governments	65,456
Charges for services	244,362
Licenses, permits & fees	167,858
Fines & forfeits	4,210
Interfund transfers	341,762
Misc/other/special assessments	157,402

Expenditures, 2008

Total	$11,299,177
General government	808,406
Public safety	1,338,014
Other/fixed costs	1,458,539
Human services	122,758
Culture & recreation	129,471
Debt Service	947,707
Education	5,366,888
Public works	630,507
Intergovernmental	496,887

Taxation, 2010

Property type	Valuation	Rate
Total	$924,919,288	-
Residential	598,382,800	9.32
Open space	0	0.00
Commercial	281,310,000	9.32
Industrial	27,255,900	9.32
Personal	17,970,588	9.32

Average Single Family Tax Bill, 2010

Avg. assessed home value	$306,965
Avg. single fam. tax bill	$2,861
Hi-Lo ranking	247/301

Police & Crime, 2008

Number of police officers	11
Violent crimes	16
Property crimes	186

Local School District

(school data 2007-08, except as noted)

Hadley
125 Russell Street
Hadley, MA 01035
413-586-0822

Superintendent	Nicholas Young
Grade plan	PK-12
Total enrollment '09-10	714
Grade 12 enrollment, '09-10	46
Graduation rate	97.6%
Dropout rate	0.0%
Per-pupil expenditure	$9,698
Avg teacher salary	$51,423
Student/teacher ratio '08-09	13.7 to 1
Highly-qualified teachers, '08-09	99.6%
Teachers licensed in assigned subject	98.0%
Students per computer	2.7

Massachusetts Competency Assessment System (MCAS), 2009 results

	English		Math	
	% Prof	CPI	% Prof	CPI
Gr 4	82%	91.7	56%	83.3
Gr 6	70%	87.5	63%	81
Gr 8	96%	98	69%	85.2
Gr 10	95%	98.8	86%	95.2

Other School Districts (see Appendix D for data)
None

©2010 Information Publications, Inc. All rights reserved. Photocopying prohibited. For additional copies, contact the publisher at www.informationpublications.com or (877)544-INFO (4636)

©2010 Information Publications, Inc. All rights reserved. Photocopying prohibited. For additional copies, contact the publisher at www.informationpublications.com or (877)544-INFO (4636)

Demographics & Socio-Economic Characteristics

Population

1990	6,526
2000	7,500
Male	3,625
Female	3,875
2008	7,692
2010 (projected)††	8,493
2020 (projected)††	9,739

Race & Hispanic Origin, 2000

Race	
White	7,360
Black/African American	23
American Indian/Alaska Native	2
Asian	20
Hawaiian Native/Pacific Islander	0
Other Race	36
Two or more races	59
Hispanic origin	41

Age & Nativity, 2000

Under 5 years	518
18 years and over	5,594
21 years and over	5,360
65 years and over	959
85 years and over	93
Median Age	37.5
Native-born	7,346
Foreign-born	154

Age, 2020 (projected)††

Under 5 years	582
5 to 19 years	1,613
20 to 39 years	2,267
40 to 64 years	3,258
65 years and over	2,019

Educational Attainment, 2000

Population 25 years and over	5,109
High School graduates or higher	91.2%
Bachelor's degree or higher	21.2%
Graduate degree	6.2%

Income & Poverty, 1999

Per capita income,	$23,738
Median household income	$57,015
Median family income	$65,461
Persons in poverty	248
H'holds receiving public assistance	20
H'holds receiving social security	848

Households, 2000

Total households	2,758
With persons under 18	1,042
With persons over 65	722
Family households	2,055
Single person households	588
Persons per household	2.7
Persons per family	3.2

Labor & Employment, 2000

Civilian labor force	4,120
Unemployment rate	4.2%
Civilian labor force, 2008†	4,288
Unemployment rate†	6.8%
Civilian labor force, 12/09†	4,285
Unemployment rate†	10.4%
Employed persons 16 years and over, by occupation:	
Managers & professionals	1,361
Service occupations	544
Sales & office occupations	1,147
Farming, fishing & forestry	23
Construction & maintenance	394
Production & transportation	477
Self-employed persons	154

Most demographic data is from the 2000 Decennial Census
† Massachusetts Department of Revenue
†† University of Massachusetts, MISER

General Information

Town of Halifax
499 Plymouth St
Halifax, MA 02338
781-293-7970

Elevation	90 ft.
Land area (square miles)	16.1
Water area (square miles)	1.2
Population density, 2008 (est)	477.8
Year incorporated	1734
Website	www.town.halifax.ma.us

Voters & Government Information

Government type	Open Town Meeting
Number of Selectmen	3
US Congressional District(s)	4

Registered Voters, October 2008

Total	5,567
Democrats	1,322
Republicans	786
Unaffiliated/other	3,415

Local Officials, 2010

Chair, Bd. of Sel.	John H. Bruno
Administrator	Charles Seelig
Town Clerk	Barbara Gaynor
Town Accountant	Sandra Nolan
Tax Collector	Katherine Shiavone
Tax Assessor	Janyce Whitney
Attorney	John T. Spinale
Public Works	Robert Badore
Building	Thomas Millias
Comm Dev/Planning	Edward Whitney
Police Chief	Michael Manoogian
Fire Chief	William C. Carrico

Housing & Construction

New Privately Owned Housing Units Authorized by Building Permit

	Single Family	Total Bldgs	Total Units
2006	16	16	16
2007	12	12	12
2008	5	5	5

Parcel Count by Property Class, 2010

Total	3,041
Single family	2,104
Multiple units	12
Apartments	0
Condos	335
Vacant land	398
Open space	0
Commercial	60
Industrial	20
Misc. residential	12
Other use	100

Public Library

Holmes Public Library
470 Plymouth St.
Halifax, MA 02338
(781)293-2271

Director	Debra DeJonker-Berry

Library Statistics, FY 2008

Population served, 2007	7,700
Registered users	4,672
Circulation	67,585
Reference transactons	526
Total program attendance	66,609
per capita:	
Holdings	5.40
Operating income	$37.41
Internet Access	
Internet computers available	6
Weekly users	50

Municipal Finance

Debt at year end 2008	$4,405,401
Moody's rating, July 2009	A2

Revenues, 2008

Total	$17,876,540
From all taxes	12,661,882
Federal aid	0
State aid	4,084,178
From other governments	3,070
Charges for services	316,965
Licenses, permits & fees	220,360
Fines & forfeits	34,683
Interfund transfers	326,154
Misc/other/special assessments	114,624

Expenditures, 2008

Total	$17,449,243
General government	1,123,552
Public safety	2,093,121
Other/fixed costs	1,376,967
Human services	307,961
Culture & recreation	307,954
Debt Service	655,699
Education	10,438,296
Public works	905,726
Intergovernmental	157,288

Taxation, 2010

Property type	Valuation	Rate
Total	$892,766,000	-
Residential	808,020,300	13.99
Open space	0	0.00
Commercial	51,618,600	13.99
Industrial	13,429,700	13.99
Personal	19,697,400	13.99

Average Single Family Tax Bill, 2010

Avg. assessed home value	$321,409
Avg. single fam. tax bill	$4,497
Hi-Lo ranking	100/301

Police & Crime, 2008

Number of police officers	10
Violent crimes	20
Property crimes	70

Local School District

(school data 2007-08, except as noted)

Halifax
250 Pembroke Street
Kingston, MA 02364
781-585-4313

Superintendent	John Tuffy
Grade plan	K-6
Total enrollment '09-10	654
Grade 12 enrollment, '09-10	0
Graduation rate	NA
Dropout rate	NA
Per-pupil expenditure	$9,483
Avg teacher salary	$59,382
Student/teacher ratio '08-09	15.5 to 1
Highly-qualified teachers, '08-09	97.3%
Teachers licensed in assigned subject	100.0%
Students per computer	8.3

Massachusetts Competency Assessment System (MCAS), 2009 results

	English		Math	
	% Prof	CPI	% Prof	CPI
Gr 4	55%	78.4	55%	81.8
Gr 6	74%	86.4	75%	85.6
Gr 8	NA	NA	NA	NA
Gr 10	NA	NA	NA	NA

Other School Districts (see Appendix D for data)
Silver Lake Regional

See Introduction for an explanation of all data sources.

Demographics & Socio-Economic Characteristics

Population

1990	7,280
2000	8,315
Male	4,090
Female	4,225
2008	8,155
2010 (projected)††	8,209
2020 (projected)††	8,001

Race & Hispanic Origin, 2000

Race	
White	7,832
Black/African American	39
American Indian/Alaska Native	14
Asian	354
Hawaiian Native/Pacific Islander	4
Other Race	28
Two or more races	44
Hispanic origin	82

Age & Nativity, 2000

Under 5 years	571
18 years and over	6,035
21 years and over	5,870
65 years and over	867
85 years and over	79
Median Age	36.5
Native-born	7,996
Foreign-born	319

Age, 2020 (projected)††

Under 5 years	502
5 to 19 years	1,581
20 to 39 years	2,263
40 to 64 years	2,486
65 years and over	1,169

Educational Attainment, 2000

Population 25 years and over	5,524
High School graduates or higher	94.0%
Bachelor's degree or higher	52.5%
Graduate degree	20.5%

Income & Poverty, 1999

Per capita income,	$33,222
Median household income	$72,000
Median family income	$79,886
Persons in poverty	409
H'holds receiving public assistance	14
H'holds receiving social security	690

Households, 2000

Total households	2,668
With persons under 18	1,171
With persons over 65	603
Family households	2,143
Single person households	420
Persons per household	2.9
Persons per family	3.2

Labor & Employment, 2000

Civilian labor force	4,521
Unemployment rate	16.1%
Civilian labor force, 2008†	3,983
Unemployment rate†	5.4%
Civilian labor force, 12/09†	3,885
Unemployment rate†	6.7%
Employed persons 16 years and over, by occupation:	
Managers & professionals	2,047
Service occupations	455
Sales & office occupations	905
Farming, fishing & forestry	24
Construction & maintenance	165
Production & transportation	199
Self-employed persons	342

Most demographic data is from the 2000 Decennial Census
† Massachusetts Department of Revenue
†† University of Massachusetts, MISER

General Information

Town of Hamilton
577 Bay Road
PO Box 429
Hamilton, MA 01936
978-468-5570

Elevation	55 ft.
Land area (square miles)	14.6
Water area (square miles)	0.3
Population density, 2008 (est)	558.6
Year incorporated	1793
Website	www.hamiltonma.gov

Voters & Government Information

Government type	Open Town Meeting
Number of Selectmen	3
US Congressional District(s)	6

Registered Voters, October 2008

Total	5,885
Democrats	1,024
Republicans	1,358
Unaffiliated/other	3,469

Local Officials, 2010

Chair, Bd. of Sel.	David S. Carey
Administrator	Candace Wheeler
Town Clerk	Jane M. Wetson
Finance Director	Deborah Nippes-Mena
Treas/Collector	Cheryl Booth
Tax Assessor	Gelean Campbell (Chr)
Attorney	NA
Public Works	John Tomasz
Building	Deb Paskowski
Comm Dev/Planning	Marcella Ricker
Police Chief	Russell Stevens
Fire Chief	Philip Stevens

Housing & Construction

New Privately Owned Housing Units Authorized by Building Permit

	Single Family	Total Bldgs	Total Units
2006	2	2	2
2007	1	1	1
2008	2	2	2

Parcel Count by Property Class, 2010

Total	2,783
Single family	2,336
Multiple units	53
Apartments	1
Condos	43
Vacant land	186
Open space	0
Commercial	58
Industrial	1
Misc. residential	29
Other use	76

Public Library

Hamilton-Wenham Public Library
14 Union Street
Hamilton, MA 01982
(978)468-5577

Director	Jan Dempsey

Library Statistics, FY 2008

Population served, 2007	12,803
Registered users	11,245
Circulation	256,437
Reference transactons	16,940
Total program attendance	0
per capita:	
Holdings	8.72
Operating income	$57.56
Internet Access	
Internet computers available	18
Weekly users	716

Municipal Finance

Debt at year end 2008	$9,665,000
Moody's rating, July 2009	A1

Revenues, 2008

Total	$23,023,660
From all taxes	20,889,389
Federal aid	24,802
State aid	1,088,430
From other governments	254,116
Charges for services	288,455
Licenses, permits & fees	157,856
Fines & forfeits	0
Interfund transfers	169,418
Misc/other/special assessments	75,597

Expenditures, 2008

Total	$22,289,012
General government	1,148,914
Public safety	2,348,270
Other/fixed costs	1,335,094
Human services	164,206
Culture & recreation	721,276
Debt Service	957,878
Education	13,839,404
Public works	1,451,649
Intergovernmental	322,321

Taxation, 2010

Property type	Valuation	Rate
Total	$1,377,977,858	-
Residential	1,304,500,000	16.29
Open space	0	0.00
Commercial	56,885,000	16.29
Industrial	823,600	16.29
Personal	15,769,258	16.29

Average Single Family Tax Bill, 2010

Avg. assessed home value	$492,915
Avg. single fam. tax bill	$8,030
Hi-Lo ranking	22/301

Police & Crime, 2008

Number of police officers	15
Violent crimes	0
Property crimes	61

Local School District

(school data 2007-08, except as noted)

Hamilton (non-op)
5 School Street
Wenham, MA 01984
978-468-5310

Superintendent	Marinel McGrath

Non-operating district.
Resident students are sent to the Other School Districts listed below.

Grade plan	NA
Total enrollment '09-10	NA
Grade 12 enrollment, '09-10	NA
Graduation rate	NA
Dropout rate	NA
Per-pupil expenditure	NA
Avg teacher salary	NA
Student/teacher ratio '08-09	NA
Highly-qualified teachers, '08-09	NA
Teachers licensed in assigned subject	NA
Students per computer	NA

Other School Districts (see Appendix D for data)
Hamilton-Wenham Regional, North Shore Vocational Tech

©2010 Information Publications, Inc. All rights reserved. Photocopying prohibited. For additional copies, contact the publisher at www.informationpublications.com or (877)544-INFO (4636)

See Introduction for an explanation of all data sources.

Demographics & Socio-Economic Characteristics

Population

1990	4,709
2000	5,171
Male	2,499
Female	2,672
2008	5,400
2010 (projected)††	4,986
2020 (projected)††	4,702

Race & Hispanic Origin, 2000

Race	
White	5,084
Black/African American	9
American Indian/Alaska Native	10
Asian	22
Hawaiian Native/Pacific Islander	2
Other Race	14
Two or more races	30
Hispanic origin	33

Age & Nativity, 2000

Under 5 years	274
18 years and over	3,810
21 years and over	3,654
65 years and over	684
85 years and over	102
Median Age	41.1
Native-born	5,015
Foreign-born	156

Age, 2020 (projected)††

Under 5 years	204
5 to 19 years	718
20 to 39 years	942
40 to 64 years	1,585
65 years and over	1,253

Educational Attainment, 2000

Population 25 years and over	3,537
High School graduates or higher	89.7%
Bachelor's degree or higher	32.4%
Graduate degree	12.9%

Income & Poverty, 1999

Per capita income,	$26,690
Median household income	$65,662
Median family income	$75,407
Persons in poverty	112
H'holds receiving public assistance	6
H'holds receiving social security	465

Households, 2000

Total households	1,818
With persons under 18	719
With persons over 65	432
Family households	1,464
Single person households	295
Persons per household	2.8
Persons per family	3.2

Labor & Employment, 2000

Civilian labor force	2,729
Unemployment rate	2.0%
Civilian labor force, 2008†	2,874
Unemployment rate†	5.5%
Civilian labor force, 12/09†	2,890
Unemployment rate†	7.8%
Employed persons 16 years and over, by occupation:	
Managers & professionals	1,115
Service occupations	265
Sales & office occupations	695
Farming, fishing & forestry	10
Construction & maintenance	293
Production & transportation	296
Self-employed persons	201

Most demographic data is from the 2000 Decennial Census
† Massachusetts Department of Revenue
†† University of Massachusetts, MISER

General Information

Town of Hampden
625 Main St
Hampden, MA 01036
413-566-2151

Elevation	301 ft.
Land area (square miles)	19.6
Water area (square miles)	0.0
Population density, 2008 (est)	275.5
Year incorporated	1878
Website	hampden.org

Voters & Government Information

Government type	Open Town Meeting
Number of Selectmen	3
US Congressional District(s)	2

Registered Voters, October 2008

Total	3,679
Democrats	819
Republicans	749
Unaffiliated/other	2,086

Local Officials, 2010

Chair, Bd. of Sel.	Vincent J. Villamaino
Administrator	NA
Admin Asst.	Pamela Courtney
Treasurer	Tracy Sicbaldi
Tax Collector	Eva Wiseman
Tax Assessor	Norman Charest
Attorney	David Martel
Public Works	Dana Pixley
Building Inspector	Lance Trevallion
Planning Board	Cornelius R. Flynn (Chr)
Police Chief	Jeff Farnsworth
Emerg/Fire Chief	Michael Gorski

Housing & Construction

New Privately Owned Housing Units Authorized by Building Permit

	Single Family	Total Bldgs	Total Units
2006	14	14	14
2007	46	46	46
2008	4	4	4

Parcel Count by Property Class, 2010

Total	2,279
Single family	1,784
Multiple units	10
Apartments	2
Condos	52
Vacant land	317
Open space	0
Commercial	39
Industrial	9
Misc. residential	13
Other use	53

Public Library

Hampden Free Public Library
PO Box 129
Hampden, MA 01036
(413)566-3047

Director	Ellen Bump

Library Statistics, FY 2008

Population served, 2007	5,305
Registered users	2,207
Circulation	24,495
Reference transactons	0
Total program attendance	0
per capita:	
Holdings	5.59
Operating income	$17.58
Internet Access	
Internet computers available	6
Weekly users	40

Municipal Finance

Debt at year end 2008	$407,400
Moody's rating, July 2009	NA

Revenues, 2008

Total	$9,678,023
From all taxes	8,726,015
Federal aid	0
State aid	824,307
From other governments	17,360
Charges for services	34,001
Licenses, permits & fees	7,770
Fines & forfeits	0
Interfund transfers.	26,000
Misc/other/special assessments	21,285

Expenditures, 2008

Total	$9,090,651
General government	417,773
Public safety	970,248
Other/fixed costs	327,911
Human services	60,627
Culture & recreation	127,880
Debt Service	273,507
Education	6,339,447
Public works	550,289
Intergovernmental	22,969

Taxation, 2010

Property type	Valuation	Rate
Total	$562,040,110	-
Residential	526,173,900	15.84
Open space	0	0.00
Commercial	19,107,710	15.84
Industrial	1,954,300	15.84
Personal	14,804,200	15.84

Average Single Family Tax Bill, 2010

Avg. assessed home value	$273,753
Avg. single fam. tax bill	$4,336
Hi-Lo ranking	111/301

Police & Crime, 2008

Number of police officers	10
Violent crimes	9
Property crimes	45

Local School District

(school data 2007-08, except as noted)

Hampden (non-op)
621 Main Street
Wilbraham, MA 01095
413-596-3884

Superintendent	Maurice O'Shea

Non-operating district.
Resident students are sent to the Other School Districts listed below.

Grade plan	NA
Total enrollment '09-10	NA
Grade 12 enrollment, '09-10	NA
Graduation rate	NA
Dropout rate	NA
Per-pupil expenditure	NA
Avg teacher salary	NA
Student/teacher ratio '08-09	NA
Highly-qualified teachers, '08-09	NA
Teachers licensed in assigned subject	NA
Students per computer	NA

Other School Districts (see Appendix D for data)
Hampden-Wilbraham Regional

©2010 Information Publications, Inc. All rights reserved. Photocopying prohibited. For additional copies, contact the publisher at www.informationpublications.com or (877)544-INFO (4636)

See Introduction for an explanation of all data sources.

Demographics & Socio-Economic Characteristics

Population

1990	628
2000	721
Male	379
Female	342
2008	1,112
2010 (projected)††	724
2020 (projected)††	676

Race & Hispanic Origin, 2000

Race	
White	702
Black/African American	2
American Indian/Alaska Native	0
Asian	4
Hawaiian Native/Pacific Islander	0
Other Race	1
Two or more races	12
Hispanic origin	10

Age & Nativity, 2000

Under 5 years	49
18 years and over	547
21 years and over	534
65 years and over	92
85 years and over	10
Median Age	39.6
Native-born	719
Foreign-born	12

Age, 2020 (projected)††

Under 5 years	19
5 to 19 years	84
20 to 39 years	145
40 to 64 years	284
65 years and over	144

Educational Attainment, 2000

Population 25 years and over	519
High School graduates or higher	89.4%
Bachelor's degree or higher	29.5%
Graduate degree	11.9%

Income & Poverty, 1999

Per capita income,	$22,250
Median household income	$45,347
Median family income	$50,625
Persons in poverty	41
H'holds receiving public assistance	3
H'holds receiving social security	67

Households, 2000

Total households	296
With persons under 18	91
With persons over 65	66
Family households	210
Single person households	69
Persons per household	2.4
Persons per family	2.8

Labor & Employment, 2000

Civilian labor force	393
Unemployment rate	5.6%
Civilian labor force, 2008†	579
Unemployment rate†	3.3%
Civilian labor force, 12/09†	594
Unemployment rate†	3.0%
Employed persons 16 years and over, by occupation:	
Managers & professionals	146
Service occupations	70
Sales & office occupations	70
Farming, fishing & forestry	7
Construction & maintenance	25
Production & transportation	53
Self-employed persons	46

Most demographic data is from the 2000 Decennial Census
† Massachusetts Department of Revenue
†† University of Massachusetts, MISER

General Information

Town of Hancock
3650 Hancock Rd
PO Box 1064
Hancock, MA 01237
413-738-5225

Elevation	1,058 ft.
Land area (square miles)	35.7
Water area (square miles)	0.0
Population density, 2008 (est)	31.1
Year incorporated	1776
Email	bos@taconic.net

Voters & Government Information

Government type	Open Town Meeting
Number of Selectmen	3
US Congressional District(s)	1

Registered Voters, October 2008

Total	506
Democrats	116
Republicans	56
Unaffiliated/other	329

Local Officials, 2010

Chair, Bd. of Sel.	Sherman Derby Sr
Manager/Admin	NA
Town Clerk	Linda Burdick
Finance Director	Joan Burdick
Tax Collector	Julie Williams
Tax Assessor	Julie Bourassa
Attorney	Jeremia A. Pollard
Public Works	NA
Building	William Palmer
Comm Dev/Planning	Joan Burdick (Chr)
Police Chief	Sherman Derby Sr
Emerg/Fire Chief	David Rash

Housing & Construction

New Privately Owned Housing Units Authorized by Building Permit

	Single Family	Total Bldgs	Total Units
2006	3	3	3
2007	0	4	32
2008	4	16	120

Parcel Count by Property Class, 2010

Total	NA
Single family	NA
Multiple units	NA
Apartments	NA
Condos	NA
Vacant land	NA
Open space	NA
Commercial	NA
Industrial	NA
Misc. residential	NA
Other use	NA

Public Library

Taylor Memorial Library
PO Box 1155
Hancock, MA 01237
(413)738-5326

Librarian/Trustee	Patricia Herrick

Library Statistics, FY 2008

Population served, 2007	1,082
Registered users	0
Circulation	0
Reference transactons	0
Total program attendance	0
per capita:	
Holdings	0.00
Operating income	$0.00
Internet Access	
Internet computers available	0
Weekly users	0

Municipal Finance

Debt at year end 2008	$0
Moody's rating, July 2009	NA

Revenues, 2008

Total	$1,785,500
From all taxes	1,324,927
Federal aid	0
State aid	402,690
From other governments	8,095
Charges for services	2,006
Licenses, permits & fees	13,158
Fines & forfeits	0
Interfund transfers	0
Misc/other/special assessments	17,312

Expenditures, 2008

Total	$1,567,399
General government	119,883
Public safety	46,336
Other/fixed costs	30,972
Human services	15,491
Culture & recreation	4,354
Debt Service	2,039
Education	1,222,677
Public works	118,792
Intergovernmental	6,855

Taxation, 2010

Property type	Valuation	Rate
Total	NA	-
Residential	NA	NA
Open space	NA	NA
Commercial	NA	NA
Industrial	NA	NA
Personal	NA	NA

Average Single Family Tax Bill, 2010

Avg. assessed home value	NA
Avg. single fam. tax bill	NA
Hi-Lo ranking	NA

Police & Crime, 2008

Number of police officers	NA
Violent crimes	NA
Property crimes	NA

Local School District

(school data 2007-08, except as noted)

Hancock
1831 STATE ROAD
RICHMOND, MA 01254
413-698-4001

Superintendent	William Ballen
Grade plan	PK-6
Total enrollment '09-10	41
Grade 12 enrollment, '09-10	0
Graduation rate	NA
Dropout rate	NA
Per-pupil expenditure	$10,494
Avg teacher salary	$67,317
Student/teacher ratio '08-09	6.2 to 1
Highly-qualified teachers, '08-09	75.5%
Teachers licensed in assigned subject	85.7%
Students per computer	1.1

Massachusetts Competency Assessment System (MCAS), 2009 results

	English		Math	
	% Prof	CPI	% Prof	CPI
Gr 4	NA	NA	NA	NA
Gr 6	NA	NA	NA	NA
Gr 8	NA	NA	NA	NA
Gr 10	NA	NA	NA	NA

Other School Districts (see Appendix D for data)
None

©2010 Information Publications, Inc. All rights reserved. Photocopying prohibited. For additional copies, contact the publisher at www.informationpublications.com or (877)544-INFO (4636)

See Introduction for an explanation of all data sources.

Demographics & Socio-Economic Characteristics

Population

1990	11,912
2000	13,164
Male	6,445
Female	6,719
2008	13,995
2010 (projected)††	13,390
2020 (projected)††	13,194

Race & Hispanic Origin, 2000

Race	
White	12,858
Black/African American	73
American Indian/Alaska Native	10
Asian	101
Hawaiian Native/Pacific Islander	1
Other Race	36
Two or more races	85
Hispanic origin	90

Age & Nativity, 2000

Under 5 years	1,013
18 years and over	9,243
21 years and over	8,889
65 years and over	1,379
85 years and over	143
Median Age	37.5
Native-born	12,836
Foreign-born	328

Age, 2020 (projected)††

Under 5 years	767
5 to 19 years	2,553
20 to 39 years	2,919
40 to 64 years	4,314
65 years and over	2,641

Educational Attainment, 2000

Population 25 years and over	8,458
High School graduates or higher	93.8%
Bachelor's degree or higher	38.3%
Graduate degree	12.1%

Income & Poverty, 1999

Per capita income,	$30,268
Median household income	$73,838
Median family income	$86,835
Persons in poverty	308
H'holds receiving public assistance	17
H'holds receiving social security	1,066

Households, 2000

Total households	4,349
With persons under 18	2,002
With persons over 65	1,030
Family households	3,567
Single person households	662
Persons per household	3.0
Persons per family	3.4

Labor & Employment, 2000

Civilian labor force	7,013
Unemployment rate	2.9%
Civilian labor force, 2008†	7,705
Unemployment rate†	5.3%
Civilian labor force, 12/09†	7,578
Unemployment rate†	7.5%
Employed persons 16 years and over, by occupation:	
Managers & professionals	2,962
Service occupations	712
Sales & office occupations	1,963
Farming, fishing & forestry	20
Construction & maintenance	631
Production & transportation	524
Self-employed persons	526

Most demographic data is from the 2000 Decennial Census
† Massachusetts Department of Revenue
†† University of Massachusetts, MISER

General Information

Town of Hanover
550 Hanover St
Hanover, MA 02339
781-826-2691

Elevation	80 ft.
Land area (square miles)	15.6
Water area (square miles)	0.1
Population density, 2008 (est)	897.1
Year incorporated	1727
Website	www.hanover-ma.gov

Voters & Government Information

Government type	Open Town Meeting
Number of Selectmen	3
US Congressional District(s)	10

Registered Voters, October 2008

Total	9,463
Democrats	2,332
Republicans	1,422
Unaffiliated/other	5,697

Local Officials, 2010

Chair, Bd. of Sel.	R. Alan Rueman
Manager/Admin	Stephen Rollins
Town Clerk	Robert Shea
Finance Director	George Martin
Tax Collector	Joan Port-Farwell
Tax Assessor	Robert Brinkman
Attorney	James Toomey
Public Works	Victor Diniak
Building	Anthony Marino
Comm Dev/Planning	Andrew R. Port
Police Chief	W. Lawrence Sweeney Jr
Emerg/Fire Chief	Kenneth L. Blanchard

Housing & Construction

New Privately Owned Housing Units Authorized by Building Permit

	Single Family	Total Bldgs	Total Units
2006	24	24	24
2007	30	30	30
2008	13	13	13

Parcel Count by Property Class, 2010

Total	5,065
Single family	4,090
Multiple units	80
Apartments	7
Condos	153
Vacant land	315
Open space	0
Commercial	271
Industrial	95
Misc. residential	13
Other use	41

Public Library

John Curtis Free Library
534 Hanover St.
Hanover, MA 02339
(781)826-2972

Director	Lorraine Welsh

Library Statistics, FY 2008

Population served, 2007	13,966
Registered users	8,442
Circulation	154,790
Reference transactons	0
Total program attendance	0
per capita:	
Holdings	4.84
Operating income	$38.75
Internet Access	
Internet computers available	17
Weekly users	190

Municipal Finance

Debt at year end 2008	$25,968,049
Moody's rating, July 2009	Aa3

Revenues, 2008

Total	$42,861,925
From all taxes	30,262,910
Federal aid	0
State aid	9,791,662
From other governments	125,766
Charges for services	509,573
Licenses, permits & fees	490,292
Fines & forfeits	0
Interfund transfers	687,132
Misc/other/special assessments	497,295

Expenditures, 2008

Total	$41,843,863
General government	1,753,505
Public safety	5,350,435
Other/fixed costs	5,289,561
Human services	468,184
Culture & recreation	556,635
Debt Service	2,571,571
Education	22,844,452
Public works	2,557,942
Intergovernmental	451,578

Taxation, 2010

Property type	Valuation	Rate
Total	$2,369,061,032	-
Residential	1,910,225,359	13.41
Open space	0	0.00
Commercial	337,776,957	13.91
Industrial	68,512,496	13.91
Personal	52,546,220	13.91

Average Single Family Tax Bill, 2010

Avg. assessed home value	$428,538
Avg. single fam. tax bill	$5,747
Hi-Lo ranking	52/301

Police & Crime, 2008

Number of police officers	29
Violent crimes	4
Property crimes	368

Local School District

(school data 2007-08, except as noted)

Hanover
188 Broadway Street
Hanover, MA 02339
781-878-0786

Superintendent	Kristine Nash
Grade plan	PK-12
Total enrollment '09-10	2,698
Grade 12 enrollment, '09-10	156
Graduation rate	95.8%
Dropout rate	1.2%
Per-pupil expenditure	$10,121
Avg teacher salary	$59,162
Student/teacher ratio '08-09	13.1 to 1
Highly-qualified teachers, '08-09	98.6%
Teachers licensed in assigned subject	97.1%
Students per computer	5.9

Massachusetts Competency Assessment System (MCAS), 2009 results

	English		Math	
	% Prof	CPI	% Prof	CPI
Gr 4	66%	88.8	58%	86.5
Gr 6	85%	93.8	77%	89
Gr 8	95%	97.6	65%	84.3
Gr 10	94%	98.2	79%	92.1

Other School Districts (see Appendix D for data)

South Shore Vocational Tech

©2010 Information Publications, Inc. All rights reserved. Photocopying prohibited. For additional copies, contact the publisher at www.informationpublications.com or (877)544-INFO (4636)

See Introduction for an explanation of all data sources.

Demographics & Socio-Economic Characteristics

Population

1990	9,028
2000	9,495
Male	4,680
Female	4,815
2008	10,019
2010 (projected)††	9,578
2020 (projected)††	9,561

Race & Hispanic Origin, 2000

Race	
White	9,176
Black/African American	105
American Indian/Alaska Native	22
Asian	33
Hawaiian Native/Pacific Islander	0
Other Race	55
Two or more races	104
Hispanic origin	65

Age & Nativity, 2000

Under 5 years	678
18 years and over	6,813
21 years and over	6,498
65 years and over	818
85 years and over	59
Median Age	36.1
Native-born	9,242
Foreign-born	253

Age, 2020 (projected)††

Under 5 years	629
5 to 19 years	1,888
20 to 39 years	2,306
40 to 64 years	3,208
65 years and over	1,530

Educational Attainment, 2000

Population 25 years and over	6,157
High School graduates or higher	93.2%
Bachelor's degree or higher	24.6%
Graduate degree	8.2%

Income & Poverty, 1999

Per capita income,	$23,727
Median household income	$62,687
Median family income	$68,560
Persons in poverty	360
H'holds receiving public assistance	46
H'holds receiving social security	630

Households, 2000

Total households	3,123
With persons under 18	1,346
With persons over 65	615
Family households	2,544
Single person households	461
Persons per household	3.0
Persons per family	3.4

Labor & Employment, 2000

Civilian labor force	5,219
Unemployment rate	2.9%
Civilian labor force, 2008†	5,557
Unemployment rate†	6.4%
Civilian labor force, 12/09†	5,573
Unemployment rate†	9.6%
Employed persons 16 years and over, by occupation:	
Managers & professionals	1,819
Service occupations	584
Sales & office occupations	1,346
Farming, fishing & forestry	16
Construction & maintenance	761
Production & transportation	540
Self-employed persons	331

Most demographic data is from the 2000 Decennial Census
† Massachusetts Department of Revenue
†† University of Massachusetts, MISER

General Information

Town of Hanson
542 Liberty St
Hanson, MA 02341
781-293-2131

Elevation	100 ft.
Land area (square miles)	15.0
Water area (square miles)	0.7
Population density, 2008 (est)	667.9
Year incorporated	1820
Website	www.hanson-ma.gov

Voters & Government Information

Government type	Open Town Meeting
Number of Selectmen	5
US Congressional District(s)	9, 10

Registered Voters, October 2008

Total	6,807
Democrats	1,626
Republicans	1,015
Unaffiliated/other	4,127

Local Officials, 2010

Chair, Bd. of Sel.	James Egan
Manager/Exec.	Rene Read
Town Clerk	Sandra Harris
Finance Director	Jeanne Sullivan
Tax Collector	Jeanne Sullivan
Tax Assessor	Cynthia Long
Attorney	NA
Public Works	R. Harris/N. Merritt
Building	Robert Kirby
Comm Dev/Planning	Noreen O'Toole
Police Chief	Edward Savage III
Emerg/Fire Chief	Jerome Thompson Jr

Housing & Construction

New Privately Owned Housing Units Authorized by Building Permit

	Single Family	Total Bldgs	Total Units
2006	27	35	43
2007	27	31	35
2008	17	18	19

Parcel Count by Property Class, 2010

Total	3,963
Single family	3,099
Multiple units	74
Apartments	10
Condos	119
Vacant land	433
Open space	0
Commercial	83
Industrial	35
Misc. residential	32
Other use	78

Public Library

Hanson Public Library
132 Maquan St.
Hanson, MA 02341
(781)293-2151

Director . . . . . Nancy Cappellini

Library Statistics, FY 2008

Population served, 2007	9,956
Registered users	7,040
Circulation	77,281
Reference transactons	6,513
Total program attendance	61,880
per capita:	
Holdings	6.30
Operating income	$23.15
Internet Access	
Internet computers available	10
Weekly users	99

Municipal Finance

Debt at year end 2008	$4,170,766
Moody's rating, July 2009	A2

Revenues, 2008

Total	$17,648,378
From all taxes	14,023,555
Federal aid	0
State aid	2,002,951
From other governments	2,665
Charges for services	154,459
Licenses, permits & fees	126,831
Fines & forfeits	20,235
Interfund transfers	879,460
Misc/other/special assessments	219,111

Expenditures, 2008

Total	$16,793,436
General government	1,920,429
Public safety	3,471,028
Other/fixed costs	2,164,804
Human services	216,533
Culture & recreation	212,305
Debt Service	416,831
Education	7,249,679
Public works	1,015,529
Intergovernmental	126,298

Taxation, 2010

Property type	Valuation	Rate
Total	$1,207,853,770	-
Residential	1,115,605,718	11.98
Open space	0	0.00
Commercial	50,857,152	11.98
Industrial	22,409,800	11.98
Personal	18,981,100	11.98

Average Single Family Tax Bill, 2010

Avg. assessed home value	$324,316
Avg. single fam. tax bill	$3,885
Hi-Lo ranking	145/301

Police & Crime, 2008

Number of police officers	22
Violent crimes	NA
Property crimes	166

Local School District

(school data 2007-08, except as noted)

Hanson (non-op)
610 Franklin Street
Whitman, MA 02382
781-618-7412

Superintendent. . . . . Ruth Gilbert-Whitner

Non-operating district.
Resident students are sent to the Other School Districts listed below.

Grade plan	NA
Total enrollment '09-10	NA
Grade 12 enrollment, '09-10	NA
Graduation rate	NA
Dropout rate	NA
Per-pupil expenditure	NA
Avg teacher salary	NA
Student/teacher ratio '08-09	NA
Highly-qualified teachers, '08-09	NA
Teachers licensed in assigned subject	NA
Students per computer	NA

Other School Districts (see Appendix D for data)
Whitman-Hanson Regional, South Shore Vocational Tech

©2010 Information Publications, Inc. All rights reserved. Photocopying prohibited. For additional copies, contact the publisher at www.informationpublications.com or (877)544-INFO (4636)

See Introduction for an explanation of all data sources.

©2010 Information Publications, Inc. All rights reserved. Photocopying prohibited. For additional copies, contact the publisher at www.informationpublications.com or (877)544-INFO (4636)

Demographics & Socio-Economic Characteristics

Population

1990	2,385
2000	2,622
Male	1,277
Female	1,345
2008	2,649
2010 (projected)††	2,709
2020 (projected)††	2,879

Race & Hispanic Origin, 2000

Race	
White	2,564
Black/African American	14
American Indian/Alaska Native	4
Asian	3
Hawaiian Native/Pacific Islander	0
Other Race	5
Two or more races	32
Hispanic origin	23

Age & Nativity, 2000

Under 5 years	139
18 years and over	1,888
21 years and over	1,794
65 years and over	359
85 years and over	39
Median Age	37.5
Native-born	2,546
Foreign-born	76

Age, 2020 (projected)††

Under 5 years	186
5 to 19 years	557
20 to 39 years	701
40 to 64 years	867
65 years and over	568

Educational Attainment, 2000

Population 25 years and over	1,705
High School graduates or higher	84.1%
Bachelor's degree or higher	21.2%
Graduate degree	8.9%

Income & Poverty, 1999

Per capita income,	$20,824
Median household income	$45,742
Median family income	$54,667
Persons in poverty	195
H'holds receiving public assistance	21
H'holds receiving social security	290

Households, 2000

Total households	997
With persons under 18	370
With persons over 65	270
Family households	690
Single person households	257
Persons per household	2.6
Persons per family	3.1

Labor & Employment, 2000

Civilian labor force	1,281
Unemployment rate	2.7%
Civilian labor force, 2008†	1,340
Unemployment rate†	8.7%
Civilian labor force, 12/09†	1,365
Unemployment rate†	11.3%
Employed persons 16 years and over, by occupation:	
Managers & professionals	381
Service occupations	145
Sales & office occupations	290
Farming, fishing & forestry	0
Construction & maintenance	145
Production & transportation	285
Self-employed persons	110

Most demographic data is from the 2000 Decennial Census
† Massachusetts Department of Revenue
†† University of Massachusetts, MISER

General Information

Town of Hardwick
307 Main Street
PO Box 575
Gilbertville, MA 01031
413-477-6197

Elevation	880 ft.
Land area (square miles)	38.6
Water area (square miles)	2.2
Population density, 2008 (est)	68.6
Year incorporated	1739
Website	www.TownofHardwick.com

Voters & Government Information

Government type	Open Town Meeting
Number of Selectmen	3
US Congressional District(s)	1

Registered Voters, October 2008

Total	1,817
Democrats	459
Republicans	206
Unaffiliated/other	1,131

Local Officials, 2010

Chair, Bd. of Sel.	Eric Vollheim
Town Administrator	Sherry Patch
Town Clerk	Paula Roberts
Finance Director	James Shanahan
Tax Collector	Kristen Noel
Tax Assessor	Jennifer Kolenda
Attorney	Kopelman & Paige
Public Works	Michael Howe
Building	Ralph Brouillette
Comm Dev/Planning	Jeffrey Schaaf
Police Chief	James Owens
Fire Chief	Robert Goodfield

Housing & Construction

New Privately Owned Housing Units Authorized by Building Permit

	Single Family	Total Bldgs	Total Units
2006	8	8	8
2007	7	7	7
2008	1	1	1

Parcel Count by Property Class, 2010

Total	1,382
Single family	683
Multiple units	92
Apartments	41
Condos	8
Vacant land	307
Open space	0
Commercial	28
Industrial	12
Misc. residential	13
Other use	198

Public Library

Paige Memorial Library
PO Box 128
Hardwick, MA 01037
(413)477-6704

Director	Sonja Craig

Library Statistics, FY 2008

Population served, 2007	1,855
Registered users	432
Circulation	10,894
Reference transactons	3
Total program attendance	5,800
per capita:	
Holdings	6.14
Operating income	$37.36
Internet Access	
Internet computers available	3
Weekly users	22

Municipal Finance

Debt at year end 2008	$329,745
Moody's rating, July 2009	NA

Revenues, 2008

Total	$4,274,157
From all taxes	3,037,975
Federal aid	0
State aid	559,244
From other governments	9,520
Charges for services	129,224
Licenses, permits & fees	39,692
Fines & forfeits	0
Interfund transfers	333,544
Misc/other/special assessments	82,479

Expenditures, 2008

Total	$4,061,087
General government	402,874
Public safety	439,047
Other/fixed costs	310,268
Human services	170,091
Culture & recreation	77,997
Debt Service	92,142
Education	1,938,530
Public works	597,235
Intergovernmental	30,342

Taxation, 2010

Property type	Valuation	Rate
Total	$259,826,470	-
Residential	239,898,400	11.06
Open space	0	0.00
Commercial	12,603,373	11.06
Industrial	1,829,000	11.06
Personal	5,495,697	11.06

Average Single Family Tax Bill, 2010

Avg. assessed home value	$236,660
Avg. single fam. tax bill	$2,617
Hi-Lo ranking	275/301

Police & Crime, 2008

Number of police officers	3
Violent crimes	10
Property crimes	25

Local School District

(school data 2007-08, except as noted)

Hardwick (non-op)
PO Box 667
Barre, MA 01005
978-355-4668

Superintendent	Maureen Marshall

Non-operating district.
Resident students are sent to the Other School Districts listed below.

Grade plan	NA
Total enrollment '09-10	NA
Grade 12 enrollment, '09-10	NA
Graduation rate	NA
Dropout rate	NA
Per-pupil expenditure	NA
Avg teacher salary	NA
Student/teacher ratio '08-09	NA
Highly-qualified teachers, '08-09	NA
Teachers licensed in assigned subject	NA
Students per computer	NA

Other School Districts (see Appendix D for data)
Quabbin Regional, Pathfinder Vocational Tech

See Introduction for an explanation of all data sources.

Demographics & Socio-Economic Characteristics

Population

1990	4,662
2000	5,981
Male	3,319
Female	2,662
2008	6,006
2010 (projected)††	6,104
2020 (projected)††	6,286

Race & Hispanic Origin, 2000

Race	
White	5,484
Black/African American	269
American Indian/Alaska Native	10
Asian	118
Hawaiian Native/Pacific Islander	3
Other Race	30
Two or more races	67
Hispanic origin	364

Age & Nativity, 2000

Under 5 years	342
18 years and over	4,391
21 years and over	4,277
65 years and over	457
85 years and over	47
Median Age	40.6
Native-born	5,233
Foreign-born	748

Age, 2020 (projected)††

Under 5 years	339
5 to 19 years	843
20 to 39 years	2,107
40 to 64 years	1,566
65 years and over	1,431

Educational Attainment, 2000

Population 25 years and over	4,109
High School graduates or higher	91.3%
Bachelor's degree or higher	65.1%
Graduate degree	36.0%

Income & Poverty, 1999

Per capita income,	$40,867
Median household income	$107,934
Median family income	$119,352
Persons in poverty	106
H'holds receiving public assistance	0
H'holds receiving social security	338

Households, 2000

Total households	1,809
With persons under 18	828
With persons over 65	298
Family households	1,494
Single person households	259
Persons per household	2.9
Persons per family	3.2

Labor & Employment, 2000

Civilian labor force	2,872
Unemployment rate	3.2%
Civilian labor force, 2008†	2,924
Unemployment rate†	3.9%
Civilian labor force, 12/09†	2,894
Unemployment rate†	6.5%
Employed persons 16 years and over, by occupation:	
Managers & professionals	2,055
Service occupations	130
Sales & office occupations	424
Farming, fishing & forestry	10
Construction & maintenance	79
Production & transportation	83
Self-employed persons	341

Most demographic data is from the 2000 Decennial Census
† Massachusetts Department of Revenue
†† University of Massachusetts, MISER

General Information

Town of Harvard
13 Ayer Rd
Harvard, MA 01451
978-456-4100

Elevation	421 ft.
Land area (square miles)	26.4
Water area (square miles)	0.6
Population density, 2008 (est)	227.5
Year incorporated	1732
Website	www.harvard.ma.us

Voters & Government Information

Government type	Open Town Meeting
Number of Selectmen	5
US Congressional District(s)	5

Registered Voters, October 2008

Total	4,093
Democrats	1,019
Republicans	643
Unaffiliated/other	2,415

Local Officials, 2010

Chair, Bd. of Sel.	Ronald Ricci
Town Administrator	Timothy Bragan
Town Clerk	Janet Vellante
Finance Director	Lorraine Leonard
Treas/Collector	Victoria Smith
Tax Assessor	Celia Jornet (Asst)
Attorney	Mark Lanza
Public Works	Richard Nota
Building	Gabriel Vellante Jr
Comm Dev/Planning	Joseph Sudol Jr (Chr)
Police Chief	Edward Denmark
Fire Chief	Robert Mignard

Housing & Construction

New Privately Owned Housing Units Authorized by Building Permit

	Single Family	Total Bldgs	Total Units
2006	8	8	8
2007	7	9	15
2008	2	2	2

Parcel Count by Property Class, 2010

Total	2,351
Single family	1,655
Multiple units	30
Apartments	4
Condos	109
Vacant land	276
Open space	0
Commercial	62
Industrial	15
Misc. residential	28
Other use	172

Public Library

Harvard Public Library
4 Pond Road
Harvard, MA 01451
(978)456-4114

Director	Mary Wilson

Library Statistics, FY 2008

Population served, 2007	6,001
Registered users	4,613
Circulation	102,990
Reference transactons	10,898
Total program attendance	104,300
per capita:	
Holdings	12.38
Operating income	$89.94
Internet Access	
Internet computers available	12
Weekly users	424

Municipal Finance

Debt at year end 2008	$11,540,000
Moody's rating, July 2009	NA

Revenues, 2008

Total	$20,012,257
From all taxes	15,731,283
Federal aid	0
State aid	3,413,408
From other governments	66,011
Charges for services	397,908
Licenses, permits & fees	164,530
Fines & forfeits	0
Interfund transfers	122,789
Misc/other/special assessments	58,164

Expenditures, 2008

Total	$20,262,413
General government	1,369,031
Public safety	1,393,600
Other/fixed costs	2,583,215
Human services	117,648
Culture & recreation	559,617
Debt Service	1,286,166
Education	10,986,488
Public works	1,310,879
Intergovernmental	655,769

Taxation, 2010

Property type	Valuation	Rate
Total	$1,138,995,512	-
Residential	1,086,713,988	14.33
Open space	0	0.00
Commercial	34,767,212	14.33
Industrial	2,353,400	14.33
Personal	15,160,912	14.33

Average Single Family Tax Bill, 2010

Avg. assessed home value	$595,195
Avg. single fam. tax bill	$8,529
Hi-Lo ranking	17/301

Police & Crime, 2008

Number of police officers	NA
Violent crimes	2
Property crimes	49

Local School District

(school data 2007-08, except as noted)

Harvard
39 Massachusetts Avenue
Harvard, MA 01451
978-456-4140

Superintendent	Thomas Jefferson
Grade plan	PK-12
Total enrollment '09-10	1,277
Grade 12 enrollment, '09-10	97
Graduation rate	91.6%
Dropout rate	3.7%
Per-pupil expenditure	$12,429
Avg teacher salary	$69,246
Student/teacher ratio '08-09	15.3 to 1
Highly-qualified teachers, '08-09	99.3%
Teachers licensed in assigned subject	98.8%
Students per computer	4.4

Massachusetts Competency Assessment System (MCAS), 2009 results

	English		Math	
	% Prof	CPI	% Prof	CPI
Gr 4	77%	91.8	71%	89.8
Gr 6	86%	95	86%	94.6
Gr 8	96%	98.6	80%	91.9
Gr 10	92%	97.6	89%	95

Other School Districts (see Appendix D for data)
Montachusett Vocational Tech

©2010 Information Publications, Inc. All rights reserved. Photocopying prohibited. For additional copies, contact the publisher at www.informationpublications.com or (877)544-INFO (4636)

See Introduction for an explanation of all data sources.

Demographics & Socio-Economic Characteristics

Population

1990	10,275
2000	12,386
Male	5,672
Female	6,714
2008	12,298
2010 (projected)††	13,857
2020 (projected)††	15,771

Race & Hispanic Origin, 2000

Race	
White	11,817
Black/African American	88
American Indian/Alaska Native	23
Asian	27
Hawaiian Native/Pacific Islander	6
Other Race	252
Two or more races	173
Hispanic origin	119

Age & Nativity, 2000

Under 5 years	504
18 years and over	10,123
21 years and over	9,850
65 years and over	3,666
85 years and over	560
Median Age	48.8
Native-born	12,010
Foreign-born	376

Age, 2020 (projected)††

Under 5 years	582
5 to 19 years	1,853
20 to 39 years	2,388
40 to 64 years	5,210
65 years and over	5,738

Educational Attainment, 2000

Population 25 years and over	9,605
High School graduates or higher	93.7%
Bachelor's degree or higher	32.4%
Graduate degree	13.2%

Income & Poverty, 1999

Per capita income,	$23,063
Median household income	$41,552
Median family income	$51,070
Persons in poverty	668
H'holds receiving public assistance	68
H'holds receiving social security	2,443

Households, 2000

Total households	5,471
With persons under 18	1,260
With persons over 65	2,363
Family households	3,545
Single person households	1,631
Persons per household	2.2
Persons per family	2.7

Labor & Employment, 2000

Civilian labor force	5,505
Unemployment rate	4.3%
Civilian labor force, 2008†	6,109
Unemployment rate†	9.4%
Civilian labor force, 12/09†	6,049
Unemployment rate†	12.9%
Employed persons 16 years and over, by occupation:	
Managers & professionals	1,744
Service occupations	1,152
Sales & office occupations	1,393
Farming, fishing & forestry	45
Construction & maintenance	573
Production & transportation	363
Self-employed persons	747

Most demographic data is from the 2000 Decennial Census
† Massachusetts Department of Revenue
†† University of Massachusetts, MISER

©2010 Information Publications, Inc. All rights reserved. Photocopying prohibited. For additional copies, contact the publisher at www.informationpublications.com or (877)544-INFO (4636)

General Information

Town of Harwich
Harwich Center
732 Main St
Harwich, MA 02645
508-430-7514

Elevation	55 ft.
Land area (square miles)	21.0
Water area (square miles)	12.1
Population density, 2008 (est)	585.6
Year incorporated	1694
Website	harwichma.virtualtownhall.net

Voters & Government Information

Government type	Open Town Meeting
Number of Selectmen	5
US Congressional District(s)	10

Registered Voters, October 2008

Total	10,080
Democrats	2,561
Republicans	1,937
Unaffiliated/other	5,536

Local Officials, 2010

Chair, Bd. of Sel.	Edward McManus
Manager/Admin	James Merriam
Town Clerk	Anita Doucette
Town Accountant	David Ryan
Tax Collector	Dorothy Parkhurst
Tax Assessor	David Scannell
Attorney	Kopelman & Paige
Public Works	Lincoln Hooper
Building	Geoffrey Larsen
Comm Dev/Planning	David Spitz
Police Chief	William Mason
Emerg/Fire Chief	William Flynn Jr

Housing & Construction

New Privately Owned Housing Units Authorized by Building Permit

	Single Family	Total Bldgs	Total Units
2006	52	53	54
2007	42	43	55
2008	28	28	28

Parcel Count by Property Class, 2010

Total	11,380
Single family	8,340
Multiple units	180
Apartments	5
Condos	807
Vacant land	1,355
Open space	0
Commercial	322
Industrial	74
Misc. residential	145
Other use	152

Public Library

Brooks Free Library
739 Main Street
Harwich, MA 02645
(508)430-7562

Director	Virginia Hewitt

Library Statistics, FY 2008

Population served, 2007	12,387
Registered users	14,298
Circulation	193,024
Reference transactons	13,183
Total program attendance	0
per capita:	
Holdings	5.54
Operating income	$53.21
Internet Access	
Internet computers available	21
Weekly users	1,195

Municipal Finance

Debt at year end 2008	$32,764,755
Moody's rating, July 2009	A1

Revenues, 2008

Total	$46,847,413
From all taxes	33,635,232
Federal aid	0
State aid	3,940,145
From other governments	6,155
Charges for services	5,943,941
Licenses, permits & fees	459,389
Fines & forfeits	16,717
Interfund transfers	2,108,576
Misc/other/special assessments	368,629

Expenditures, 2008

Total	$38,910,899
General government	2,436,406
Public safety	6,271,215
Other/fixed costs	2,231,666
Human services	691,908
Culture & recreation	2,823,623
Debt Service	4,817,620
Education	14,246,500
Public works	3,342,516
Intergovernmental	2,049,445

Taxation, 2010

Property type	Valuation	Rate
Total	$4,944,911,740	-
Residential	4,586,390,128	7.03
Open space	0	0.00
Commercial	263,347,052	7.03
Industrial	32,410,500	7.03
Personal	62,764,060	7.03

Average Single Family Tax Bill, 2010

Avg. assessed home value	$477,993
Avg. single fam. tax bill	$3,360
Hi-Lo ranking	192/301

Police & Crime, 2008

Number of police officers	33
Violent crimes	32
Property crimes	273

Local School District

(school data 2007-08, except as noted)

Harwich
81 Oak Street
Harwich, MA 02645
508-430-7200

Superintendent	Carolyn Cragin
Grade plan	PK-12
Total enrollment '09-10	1,334
Grade 12 enrollment, '09-10	99
Graduation rate	84.6%
Dropout rate	6.8%
Per-pupil expenditure	$12,871
Avg teacher salary	$57,894
Student/teacher ratio '08-09	11.5 to 1
Highly-qualified teachers, '08-09	93.7%
Teachers licensed in assigned subject	98.3%
Students per computer	3.1

Massachusetts Competency Assessment System (MCAS), 2009 results

	English		Math	
	% Prof	CPI	% Prof	CPI
Gr 4	54%	82.9	48%	76.6
Gr 6	73%	88.9	57%	78.6
Gr 8	90%	97.4	43%	71.7
Gr 10	86%	95.5	86%	94.7

Other School Districts (see Appendix D for data)
Cape Cod Vocational Tech

See Introduction for an explanation of all data sources.

Demographics & Socio-Economic Characteristics

Population

1990	3,184
2000	3,249
Male	1,583
Female	1,666
2008	3,227
2010 (projected)††	3,106
2020 (projected)††	2,955

Race & Hispanic Origin, 2000

Race	
White	3,185
Black/African American	7
American Indian/Alaska Native	4
Asian	16
Hawaiian Native/Pacific Islander	2
Other Race	19
Two or more races	16
Hispanic origin	34

Age & Nativity, 2000

Under 5 years	154
18 years and over	2,575
21 years and over	2,483
65 years and over	544
85 years and over	52
Median Age	43.2
Native-born	3,182
Foreign-born	67

Age, 2020 (projected)††

Under 5 years	113
5 to 19 years	375
20 to 39 years	627
40 to 64 years	1,021
65 years and over	819

Educational Attainment, 2000

Population 25 years and over	2,401
High School graduates or higher	89.8%
Bachelor's degree or higher	28.9%
Graduate degree	9.7%

Income & Poverty, 1999

Per capita income,	$24,813
Median household income	$50,238
Median family income	$61,607
Persons in poverty	90
H'holds receiving public assistance	6
H'holds receiving social security	375

Households, 2000

Total households	1,381
With persons under 18	398
With persons over 65	404
Family households	871
Single person households	405
Persons per household	2.4
Persons per family	3.0

Labor & Employment, 2000

Civilian labor force	1,948
Unemployment rate	1.3%
Civilian labor force, 2008†	2,003
Unemployment rate†	5.1%
Civilian labor force, 12/09†	1,987
Unemployment rate†	5.8%
Employed persons 16 years and over, by occupation:	
Managers & professionals	791
Service occupations	280
Sales & office occupations	432
Farming, fishing & forestry	37
Construction & maintenance	184
Production & transportation	198
Self-employed persons	142

Most demographic data is from the 2000 Decennial Census
† Massachusetts Department of Revenue
†† University of Massachusetts, MISER

General Information

Town of Hatfield
59 Main St
Hatfield, MA 01038
413-247-9200

Elevation	129 ft.
Land area (square miles)	16.0
Water area (square miles)	0.8
Population density, 2008 (est)	201.7
Year incorporated	1670
Website	www.townofhatfield.org

Voters & Government Information

Government type	Open Town Meeting
Number of Selectmen	3
US Congressional District(s)	1

Registered Voters, October 2008

Total	2,599
Democrats	958
Republicans	212
Unaffiliated/other	1,421

Local Officials, 2010

Chair, Bd. of Sel.	Marcus J. Boyle
Manager/Admin	NA
Town Clerk	G. Louise Slysz
Treasurer	G. Louise Slysz
Tax Collector	Marie Chmura
Tax Assessor	Edward W. Lesko Jr
Attorney	William O'Neal
Public Works	Philip Genovese
Building	Stanley Sadowski
Comm Dev/Planning	J Michael Cahill
Police Chief	Thomas J. Osley
Fire Chief	William Belden

Housing & Construction

New Privately Owned Housing Units Authorized by Building Permit

	Single Family	Total Bldgs	Total Units
2006	14	14	14
2007	3	4	9
2008	9	9	9

Parcel Count by Property Class, 2010

Total	NA
Single family	NA
Multiple units	NA
Apartments	NA
Condos	NA
Vacant land	NA
Open space	NA
Commercial	NA
Industrial	NA
Misc. residential	NA
Other use	NA

Public Library

Hatfield Public Library
39 Main Street
Hatfield, MA 01038
(413)247-9097

Director	Eliza Langhans

Library Statistics, FY 2008

Population served, 2007	3,258
Registered users	2,837
Circulation	22,019
Reference transactons	398
Total program attendance	8,508
per capita:	
Holdings	8.21
Operating income	$28.34
Internet Access	
Internet computers available	2
Weekly users	30

Municipal Finance

Debt at year end 2008	$4,757,749
Moody's rating, July 2009	NA

Revenues, 2008

Total	$7,962,820
From all taxes	5,643,452
Federal aid	0
State aid	1,268,183
From other governments	63,918
Charges for services	102,210
Licenses, permits & fees	64,903
Fines & forfeits	0
Interfund transfers	0
Misc/other/special assessments	410,077

Expenditures, 2008

Total	$7,137,550
General government	443,258
Public safety	345,030
Other/fixed costs	615,710
Human services	91,019
Culture & recreation	97,628
Debt Service	620,110
Education	4,065,221
Public works	536,089
Intergovernmental	323,485

Taxation, 2010

Property type	Valuation	Rate
Total	NA	-
Residential	NA	NA
Open space	NA	NA
Commercial	NA	NA
Industrial	NA	NA
Personal	NA	NA

Average Single Family Tax Bill, 2010

Avg. assessed home value	NA
Avg. single fam. tax bill	NA
Hi-Lo ranking	NA

Police & Crime, 2008

Number of police officers	2
Violent crimes	2
Property crimes	4

Local School District

(school data 2007-08, except as noted)

Hatfield
34 School Street
Hatfield, MA 01038
413-247-5641

Superintendent	Francis Gougeon
Grade plan	PK-12
Total enrollment '09-10	456
Grade 12 enrollment, '09-10	39
Graduation rate	94.6%
Dropout rate	2.7%
Per-pupil expenditure	$11,144
Avg teacher salary	$51,208
Student/teacher ratio '08-09	11.5 to 1
Highly-qualified teachers, '08-09	99.4%
Teachers licensed in assigned subject	100.0%
Students per computer	2.8

Massachusetts Competency Assessment System (MCAS), 2009 results

	English		Math	
	% Prof	CPI	% Prof	CPI
Gr 4	63%	82.4	65%	86.5
Gr 6	70%	87.5	60%	81.3
Gr 8	92%	97.9	58%	81.3
Gr 10	91%	97.7	77%	92

Other School Districts (see Appendix D for data)
None

©2010 Information Publications, Inc. All rights reserved. Photocopying prohibited. For additional copies, contact the publisher at www.informationpublications.com or (877)544-INFO (4636)

Demographics & Socio-Economic Characteristics*

Population

1990	51,418
2000	58,969
Male	27,984
Female	30,985
2008	61,275
2010 (projected)††	65,798
2020 (projected)††	74,385

Race & Hispanic Origin, 2000

Race	
White	52,878
Black/African American	1,419
American Indian/Alaska Native	129
Asian	801
Hawaiian Native/Pacific Islander	18
Other Race	2,536
Two or more races	1,188
Hispanic origin	5,174

Age & Nativity, 2000

Under 5 years	4,338
18 years and over	43,817
21 years and over	41,856
65 years and over	7,547
85 years and over	1,189
Median Age	35.5
Native-born	54,884
Foreign-born	4,085

Age, 2020 (projected)††

Under 5 years	5,136
5 to 19 years	14,042
20 to 39 years	20,849
40 to 64 years	23,381
65 years and over	10,977

Educational Attainment, 2000

Population 25 years and over	39,354
High School graduates or higher	83.6%
Bachelor's degree or higher	23.4%
Graduate degree	7.3%

Income & Poverty, 1999

Per capita income,	$23,280
Median household income	$49,833
Median family income	$59,772
Persons in poverty	5,243
H'holds receiving public assistance	693
H'holds receiving social security	5,620

Households, 2000

Total households	22,976
With persons under 18	8,138
With persons over 65	5,175
Family households	14,858
Single person households	6,582
Persons per household	2.5
Persons per family	3.1

Labor & Employment, 2000

Civilian labor force	30,806
Unemployment rate	3.7%
Civilian labor force, 2008†	30,810
Unemployment rate†	7.4%
Civilian labor force, 12/09†	30,638
Unemployment rate†	10.5%
Employed persons 16 years and over, by occupation:	
Managers & professionals	10,170
Service occupations	4,149
Sales & office occupations	7,892
Farming, fishing & forestry	9
Construction & maintenance	2,414
Production & transportation	5,042
Self-employed persons	1,777

Most demographic data is from the 2000 Decennial Census
* see Appendix E for American Community Survey data
† Massachusetts Department of Revenue
†† University of Massachusetts, MISER

General Information

City of Haverhill
4 Summer St
Haverhill, MA 01830
978-374-2300

Elevation	50 ft.
Land area (square miles)	33.3
Water area (square miles)	2.3
Population density, 2008 (est)	1,840.1
Year incorporated	1641
Website	www.ci.haverhill.ma.us

Voters & Government Information

Government type	Mayor-Council
Number of Councilpersons	9
US Congressional District(s)	5

Registered Voters, October 2008

Total	40,980
Democrats	12,691
Republicans	4,830
Unaffiliated/other	23,097

Local Officials, 2010

Mayor	James J. Fiorentini
Council President	Michael Hart
City Clerk	Margaret A. Toomey
Finance Director	Charles Benevento
Treas/Collector	Mary E. Roy
Tax Assessor	Steven Gullo
Attorney	William Cox
Public Works	Michael Stankovich
Building	Richard Osborne
Comm Dev/Planning	William Pillsbury
Police Chief	Alan R. DeNaro
Fire Chief	Richard Borden

Housing & Construction

New Privately Owned Housing Units Authorized by Building Permit

	Single Family	Total Bldgs	Total Units
2006	95	123	163
2007	69	91	117
2008	47	51	55

Parcel Count by Property Class, 2010

Total	20,295
Single family	10,181
Multiple units	2,358
Apartments	354
Condos	4,810
Vacant land	1,232
Open space	0
Commercial	648
Industrial	225
Misc. residential	44
Other use	443

Public Library

Haverhill Public Library
99 Main St.
Haverhill, MA 01830
(978)373-1586

Director	Carol Vermy

Library Statistics, FY 2008

Population served, 2007	59,902
Registered users	61,786
Circulation	509,633
Reference transactons	56,954
Total program attendance	356,990
per capita:	
Holdings	3.48
Operating income	$29.85
Internet Access	
Internet computers available	46
Weekly users	1,963

Municipal Finance

Debt at year end 2008	$110,643,791
Moody's rating, July 2009	Baa1

Revenues, 2008

Total	$143,537,728
From all taxes	80,065,355
Federal aid	0
State aid	52,051,276
From other governments	211,582
Charges for services	1,375,770
Licenses, permits & fees	2,448,876
Fines & forfeits	110,692
Interfund transfers	3,954,697
Misc/other/special assessments	1,659,740

Expenditures, 2008

Total	$120,023,661
General government	3,596,235
Public safety	17,096,582
Other/fixed costs	11,986,125
Human services	2,156,007
Culture & recreation	1,235,822
Debt Service	10,026,844
Education	66,324,191
Public works	6,856,253
Intergovernmental	745,602

Taxation, 2010

Property type	Valuation	Rate
Total	$5,498,523,994	-
Residential	4,566,386,602	12.76
Open space	0	0.00
Commercial	464,942,316	21.31
Industrial	256,517,636	21.31
Personal	210,677,440	21.31

Average Single Family Tax Bill, 2010

Avg. assessed home value	$272,260
Avg. single fam. tax bill	$3,474
Hi-Lo ranking	175/301

Police & Crime, 2008

Number of police officers	93
Violent crimes	403
Property crimes	1,476

Local School District

(school data 2007-08, except as noted)

Haverhill
4 Summer Street
Haverhill, MA 01830
978-374-3405

Superintendent	Raleigh Buchanan
Grade plan	PK-12
Total enrollment '09-10	6,845
Grade 12 enrollment, '09-10	397
Graduation rate	68.5%
Dropout rate	15.6%
Per-pupil expenditure	$11,203
Avg teacher salary	$66,417
Student/teacher ratio '08-09	14.9 to 1
Highly-qualified teachers, '08-09	91.1%
Teachers licensed in assigned subject	93.9%
Students per computer	9.1

Massachusetts Competency Assessment System (MCAS), 2009 results

	English		Math	
	% Prof	CPI	% Prof	CPI
Gr 4	41%	73.1	39%	72.8
Gr 6	50%	78.2	41%	70.8
Gr 8	72%	89.3	37%	66.8
Gr 10	75%	90.2	64%	83.1

Other School Districts (see Appendix D for data)

Whittier Vocational Tech

See Introduction for an explanation of all data sources.

©2010 Information Publications, Inc. All rights reserved. Photocopying prohibited. For additional copies, contact the publisher at www.informationpublications.com or (877)544-INFO (4636)

Demographics & Socio-Economic Characteristics

Population

1990 317
2000 336
  Male 175
  Female 161
2008 337
2010 (projected)†† 341
2020 (projected)†† 339

Race & Hispanic Origin, 2000

Race
  White 327
  Black/African American 1
  American Indian/Alaska Native 0
  Asian 3
  Hawaiian Native/Pacific Islander 0
  Other Race 0
  Two or more races 5
Hispanic origin 1

Age & Nativity, 2000

Under 5 years 15
18 years and over 257
21 years and over 252
65 years and over 50
85 years and over 7
  Median Age 44.4
Native-born 326
Foreign-born 5

Age, 2020 (projected)††

Under 5 years 11
5 to 19 years 29
20 to 39 years 41
40 to 64 years 152
65 years and over 106

Educational Attainment, 2000

Population 25 years and over 241
  High School graduates or higher . . 82.6%
  Bachelor's degree or higher 23.2%
  Graduate degree 8.7%

Income & Poverty, 1999

Per capita income, ... $17,333
Median household income $38,125
Median family income $46,875
Persons in poverty 47
H'holds receiving public assistance 0
H'holds receiving social security 37

Households, 2000

Total households 137
  With persons under 18 45
  With persons over 65 34
  Family households 99
  Single person households 29
Persons per household 2.5
Persons per family 2.9

Labor & Employment, 2000

Civilian labor force 178
  Unemployment rate 7.9%
Civilian labor force, 2008† 166
  Unemployment rate† 3.6%
Civilian labor force, 12/09† 160
  Unemployment rate† 3.8%
Employed persons 16 years and over, by occupation:
  Managers & professionals 55
  Service occupations 14
  Sales & office occupations 38
  Farming, fishing & forestry 0
  Construction & maintenance 23
  Production & transportation 34
  Self-employed persons 33

Most demographic data is from the 2000 Decennial Census
† Massachusetts Department of Revenue
†† University of Massachusetts, MISER

General Information

Town of Hawley
8 Pudding Hollow Rd
Hawley, MA 01339
413-339-5518

Elevation . . . . NA
Land area (square miles) 30.9
Water area (square miles) 0.0
Population density, 2008 (est) 10.9
Year incorporated 1779
Website . . . . NA

Voters & Government Information

Government type . . . . Open Town Meeting
Number of Selectmen 3
US Congressional District(s) 1

Registered Voters, October 2008

Total 220
Democrats 32
Republicans 27
Unaffiliated/other 161

Local Officials, 2010

Chair, Bd. of Sel. . . . . Darwin Clark Jr
Manager/Admin . . . . NA
Clerk . . . . Cynthia L. Stetson
Finance . . . . Charles Stetson
Tax Collector . . . . Charles Stetson
Tax Assessor . . . . Richard Desmarais
Attorney . . . . NA
Public Works . . . . NA
Building . . . . NA
Comm Dev/Planning . . . . NA
Police Chief . . . . Steve Deane
Emerg/Fire Chief . . . . Greg Cox

Housing & Construction

New Privately Owned Housing Units Authorized by Building Permit

	Single Family	Total Bldgs	Total Units
2006	0	0	0
2007	3	3	3
2008	0	0	0

Parcel Count by Property Class, 2010

Total 285
Single family 135
Multiple units 2
Apartments 0
Condos 0
Vacant land 70
Open space 0
Commercial 2
Industrial 0
Misc. residential 24
Other use 52

Public Library

No Public Library

Library Statistics, FY 2008

Population served, 2007 . . . .
Registered users . . . .
Circulation . . . .
Reference transactons . . . .
Total program attendance . . . .
per capita:
Holdings . . . .
Operating income . . . .
Internet Access
Internet computers available . . . .
Weekly users . . . .

Municipal Finance

Debt at year end 2008 . . . . $0
Moody's rating, July 2009 . . . . NA

Revenues, 2008

Total $963,378
From all taxes 610,253
Federal aid 0
State aid 291,168
From other governments 0
Charges for services 3,092
Licenses, permits & fees 7,187
Fines & forfeits 0
Interfund transfers 25,532
Misc/other/special assessments 13,073

Expenditures, 2008

Total $814,460
General government 76,084
Public safety 19,671
Other/fixed costs 68,008
Human services 7,548
Culture & recreation 1,000
Debt Service 7,749
Education 328,381
Public works 296,254
Intergovernmental 9,534

Taxation, 2010

Property type	Valuation	Rate
Total	$47,090,641	-
Residential	43,288,294	14.65
Open space	0	0.00
Commercial	1,991,793	14.65
Industrial	0	0.00
Personal	1,810,554	14.65

Average Single Family Tax Bill, 2010

Avg. assessed home value $212,233
Avg. single fam. tax bill $3,109
Hi-Lo ranking 224/301

Police & Crime, 2008

Number of police officers . . . . NA
Violent crimes . . . . NA
Property crimes . . . . NA

Local School District

(school data 2007-08, except as noted)

Hawley (non-op)
24 Ashfield Rd
Shelburne Falls, MA 01370
413-625-0192
Superintendent . . . . Michael Buoniconti

Non-operating district.
Resident students are sent to the Other School Districts listed below.

Grade plan . . . . NA
Total enrollment '09-10 . . . . NA
Grade 12 enrollment, '09-10 . . . . NA
Graduation rate . . . . NA
Dropout rate . . . . NA
Per-pupil expenditure . . . . NA
Avg teacher salary . . . . NA
Student/teacher ratio '08-09 . . . . NA
Highly-qualified teachers, '08-09 . . . . NA
Teachers licensed in assigned subject . . . . NA
Students per computer . . . . NA

Other School Districts (see Appendix D for data)
Hawlemont and Mohawk Trail Regionals

©2010 Information Publications, Inc. All rights reserved. Photocopying prohibited. For additional copies, contact the publisher at www.informationpublications.com or (877)544-INFO (4636)

See Introduction for an explanation of all data sources.

Demographics & Socio-Economic Characteristics

Population

1990	716
2000	805
Male	405
Female	400
2008	798
2010 (projected)††	988
2020 (projected)††	1,194

Race & Hispanic Origin, 2000

Race	
White	787
Black/African American	0
American Indian/Alaska Native	0
Asian	4
Hawaiian Native/Pacific Islander	0
Other Race	3
Two or more races	11
Hispanic origin	5

Age & Nativity, 2000

Under 5 years	42
18 years and over	574
21 years and over	549
65 years and over	83
85 years and over	4
Median Age	39.3
Native-born	808
Foreign-born	11

Age, 2020 (projected)††

Under 5 years	65
5 to 19 years	208
20 to 39 years	260
40 to 64 years	394
65 years and over	267

Educational Attainment, 2000

Population 25 years and over	532
High School graduates or higher	85.7%
Bachelor's degree or higher	29.5%
Graduate degree	12.2%

Income & Poverty, 1999

Per capita income	$24,777
Median household income	$50,536
Median family income	$55,938
Persons in poverty	77
H'holds receiving public assistance	3
H'holds receiving social security	63

Households, 2000

Total households	292
With persons under 18	118
With persons over 65	54
Family households	213
Single person households	58
Persons per household	2.8
Persons per family	3.2

Labor & Employment, 2000

Civilian labor force	479
Unemployment rate	5.2%
Civilian labor force, 2008†	453
Unemployment rate†	4.4%
Civilian labor force, 12/09†	456
Unemployment rate†	7.2%
Employed persons 16 years and over, by occupation:	
Managers & professionals	153
Service occupations	70
Sales & office occupations	111
Farming, fishing & forestry	5
Construction & maintenance	59
Production & transportation	56
Self-employed persons	61

Most demographic data is from the 2000 Decennial Census
† Massachusetts Department of Revenue
†† University of Massachusetts, MISER

General Information

Town of Heath
1 E Main St
Heath, MA 01346
413-337-4934

Elevation	NA
Land area (square miles)	24.9
Water area (square miles)	0.0
Population density, 2008 (est)	32.0
Year incorporated	1785
Website	www.townofheath.org

Voters & Government Information

Government type	Open Town Meeting
Number of Selectmen	3
US Congressional District(s)	1

Registered Voters, October 2008

Total	525
Democrats	147
Republicans	50
Unaffiliated/other	328

Local Officials, 2010

Chair, Bd. of Sel.	Thomas Lively
Manager/Admin	Gloria Fisher
Town Clerk	Hilma Sumner
Finance	Kristi Nartowicz
Tax Collector	Elizabeth Nichols
Tax Assessor	Valerie Kaempfer (Chr)
Attorney	Kopelman & Paige
Public Works	Michael Smith
Building	NA
Comm Dev/Planning	Calvin Carr
Police Chief	Margo Newton
Emerg/Fire Chief	Michael Smith

Housing & Construction

New Privately Owned Housing Units Authorized by Building Permit

	Single Family	Total Bldgs	Total Units
2006	5	5	5
2007	2	2	2
2008	1	1	1

Parcel Count by Property Class, 2010

Total	913
Single family	365
Multiple units	3
Apartments	0
Condos	0
Vacant land	319
Open space	0
Commercial	1
Industrial	0
Misc. residential	172
Other use	53

Public Library

Heath Free Public Library
PO Box 38
Heath, MA 01346
(413)337-4934 x7

Librarian	Donald Purington

Library Statistics, FY 2008

Population served, 2007	797
Registered users	206
Circulation	11,129
Reference transactons	598
Total program attendance	5,467
per capita:	
Holdings	16.41
Operating income	$46.95
Internet Access	
Internet computers available	1
Weekly users	10

Municipal Finance

Debt at year end 2008	$1,727,848
Moody's rating, July 2009	NA

Revenues, 2008

Total	$2,339,612
From all taxes	1,562,840
Federal aid	17,839
State aid	297,057
From other governments	360
Charges for services	14,712
Licenses, permits & fees	12,789
Fines & forfeits	0
Interfund transfers	94,489
Misc/other/special assessments	169,763

Expenditures, 2008

Total	$2,014,817
General government	193,622
Public safety	53,543
Other/fixed costs	128,153
Human services	26,688
Culture & recreation	28,837
Debt Service	312,253
Education	785,392
Public works	477,525
Intergovernmental	866

Taxation, 2010

Property type	Valuation	Rate
Total	$94,223,444	-
Residential	90,452,396	16.98
Open space	0	0.00
Commercial	733,710	16.98
Industrial	73,100	16.98
Personal	2,964,238	16.98

Average Single Family Tax Bill, 2010

Avg. assessed home value	$198,307
Avg. single fam. tax bill	$3,367
Hi-Lo ranking	188/301

Police & Crime, 2008

Number of police officers	NA
Violent crimes	NA
Property crimes	NA

Local School District

(school data 2007-08, except as noted)

Heath (non-op)
24 Ashfield Rd
Shelburne Falls, MA 01370
413-625-0192

Superintendent	Michael Buoniconti

Non-operating district.
Resident students are sent to the Other School Districts listed below.

Grade plan	NA
Total enrollment '09-10	NA
Grade 12 enrollment, '09-10	NA
Graduation rate	NA
Dropout rate	NA
Per-pupil expenditure	NA
Avg teacher salary	NA
Student/teacher ratio '08-09	NA
Highly-qualified teachers, '08-09	NA
Teachers licensed in assigned subject	NA
Students per computer	NA

Other School Districts (see Appendix D for data)
Mohawk Trail Regional, Franklin County Vocational Tech

©2010 Information Publications, Inc. All rights reserved. Photocopying prohibited. For additional copies, contact the publisher at www.informationpublications.com or (877)544-INFO (4636)

See Introduction for an explanation of all data sources.

Demographics & Socio-Economic Characteristics

Population

1990	19,821
2000	19,882
Male	9,392
Female	10,490
2008	22,561
2010 (projected)††	18,751
2020 (projected)††	16,634

Race & Hispanic Origin, 2000

Race	
White	19,386
Black/African American	79
American Indian/Alaska Native	7
Asian	175
Hawaiian Native/Pacific Islander	3
Other Race	44
Two or more races	188
Hispanic origin	149

Age & Nativity, 2000

Under 5 years	1,487
18 years and over	14,367
21 years and over	13,955
65 years and over	2,803
85 years and over	394
Median Age	40.4
Native-born	19,101
Foreign-born	781

Age, 2020 (projected)††

Under 5 years	922
5 to 19 years	3,372
20 to 39 years	3,129
40 to 64 years	5,582
65 years and over	3,629

Educational Attainment, 2000

Population 25 years and over	13,581
High School graduates or higher	96.0%
Bachelor's degree or higher	57.5%
Graduate degree	23.0%

Income & Poverty, 1999

Per capita income,	$41,703
Median household income	$83,018
Median family income	$98,598
Persons in poverty	685
H'holds receiving public assistance	80
H'holds receiving social security	2,029

Households, 2000

Total households	7,189
With persons under 18	2,817
With persons over 65	1,897
Family households	5,479
Single person households	1,511
Persons per household	2.7
Persons per family	3.2

Labor & Employment, 2000

Civilian labor force	9,894
Unemployment rate	2.6%
Civilian labor force, 2008†	11,046
Unemployment rate†	4.6%
Civilian labor force, 12/09†	11,179
Unemployment rate†	5.8%
Employed persons 16 years and over, by occupation:	
Managers & professionals	5,521
Service occupations	701
Sales & office occupations	2,450
Farming, fishing & forestry	11
Construction & maintenance	644
Production & transportation	307
Self-employed persons	940

Most demographic data is from the 2000 Decennial Census
† Massachusetts Department of Revenue
†† University of Massachusetts, MISER

General Information

Town of Hingham
210 Central St
Hingham, MA 02043
781-741-1400

Elevation	50 ft.
Land area (square miles)	22.5
Water area (square miles)	2.6
Population density, 2008 (est)	1,002.7
Year incorporated	1635
Website	hingham-ma.com

Voters & Government Information

Government type	Open Town Meeting
Number of Selectmen	3
US Congressional District(s)	10

Registered Voters, October 2008

Total	16,003
Democrats	4,101
Republicans	2,976
Unaffiliated/other	8,870

Local Officials, 2010

Chair, Bd. of Sel.	Bruce Rabuffo
Manager/Admin	NA
Clerk	Eileen McCracken
Finance Director	Theodore Alexiades
Tax Collector	Jean M. Montgomery
Tax Assessor	Lane Partridge
Attorney	NA
Public Works	Randy Sylvester
Building	Mark Grylls
Planning	Katharine Lacy
Police Chief	Taylor A.B. Mills
Emerg/Fire Chief	Mark J. Duff

Housing & Construction

New Privately Owned Housing Units Authorized by Building Permit

	Single Family	Total Bldgs	Total Units
2006	34	37	374
2007	74	78	88
2008	22	47	274

Parcel Count by Property Class, 2010

Total	8,014
Single family	6,139
Multiple units	179
Apartments	12
Condos	758
Vacant land	458
Open space	0
Commercial	282
Industrial	120
Misc. residential	22
Other use	44

Public Library

Hingham Public Library
66 Leavitt St.
Hingham, MA 02043
(781)741-1405

Director	Dennis Corcoran

Library Statistics, FY 2008

Population served, 2007	22,394
Registered users	14,331
Circulation	500,557
Reference transactons	5,348
Total program attendance	284,000
per capita:	
Holdings	7.14
Operating income	$70.30
Internet Access	
Internet computers available	17
Weekly users	750

Municipal Finance

Debt at year end 2008	$38,561,734
Moody's rating, July 2009	Aaa

Revenues, 2008

Total	$75,635,686
From all taxes	57,069,127
Federal aid	0
State aid	9,277,414
From other governments	0
Charges for services	1,464,090
Licenses, permits & fees	1,606,901
Fines & forfeits	77,729
Interfund transfers	766,271
Misc/other/special assessments	2,687,077

Expenditures, 2008

Total	$67,416,985
General government	3,014,971
Public safety	9,620,216
Other/fixed costs	7,402,520
Human services	753,745
Culture & recreation	1,557,400
Debt Service	4,829,886
Education	33,390,577
Public works	4,159,921
Intergovernmental	2,677,907

Taxation, 2010

Property type	Valuation	Rate
Total	$5,636,105,233	-
Residential	4,883,302,232	10.77
Open space	0	0.00
Commercial	475,224,448	10.77
Industrial	182,626,233	10.77
Personal	94,952,320	10.77

Average Single Family Tax Bill, 2010

Avg. assessed home value	$659,994
Avg. single fam. tax bill	$7,108
Hi-Lo ranking	34/301

Police & Crime, 2008

Number of police officers	48
Violent crimes	7
Property crimes	358

Local School District

(school data 2007-08, except as noted)

Hingham
220 Central Street
Hingham, MA 02043
781-741-1500

Superintendent	Dorothy Galo
Grade plan	PK-12
Total enrollment '09-10	4,058
Grade 12 enrollment, '09-10	250
Graduation rate	97.1%
Dropout rate	2.2%
Per-pupil expenditure	$11,508
Avg teacher salary	$63,329
Student/teacher ratio '08-09	14.8 to 1
Highly-qualified teachers, '08-09	99.6%
Teachers licensed in assigned subject	99.8%
Students per computer	4.7

Massachusetts Competency Assessment System (MCAS), 2009 results

	English		Math	
	% Prof	CPI	% Prof	CPI
Gr 4	75%	91.3	72%	90
Gr 6	87%	95.2	71%	87
Gr 8	92%	97.6	69%	87.3
Gr 10	97%	99.3	92%	96.6

Other School Districts (see Appendix D for data)
None

©2010 Information Publications, Inc. All rights reserved. Photocopying prohibited. For additional copies, contact the publisher at www.informationpublications.com or (877)544-INFO (4636)

See Introduction for an explanation of all data sources.

Demographics & Socio-Economic Characteristics

Population

1990	1,959
2000	1,872
Male	950
Female	922
2008	1,913
2010 (projected)††	2,029
2020 (projected)††	2,160

Race & Hispanic Origin, 2000

Race	
White	1,831
Black/African American	10
American Indian/Alaska Native	0
Asian	5
Hawaiian Native/Pacific Islander	0
Other Race	0
Two or more races	26
Hispanic origin	6

Age & Nativity, 2000

Under 5 years	109
18 years and over	1,392
21 years and over	1,336
65 years and over	211
85 years and over	10
Median Age	38.0
Native-born	1,834
Foreign-born	38

Age, 2020 (projected)††

Under 5 years	116
5 to 19 years	349
20 to 39 years	481
40 to 64 years	783
65 years and over	431

Educational Attainment, 2000

Population 25 years and over	1,257
High School graduates or higher	89.1%
Bachelor's degree or higher	23.5%
Graduate degree	7.4%

Income & Poverty, 1999

Per capita income,	$19,797
Median household income	$42,500
Median family income	$51,118
Persons in poverty	154
H'holds receiving public assistance	16
H'holds receiving social security	190

Households, 2000

Total households	739
With persons under 18	247
With persons over 65	151
Family households	510
Single person households	190
Persons per household	2.5
Persons per family	3.0

Labor & Employment, 2000

Civilian labor force	996
Unemployment rate	4.1%
Civilian labor force, 2008†	1,041
Unemployment rate†	7.6%
Civilian labor force, 12/09†	1,153
Unemployment rate†	11.4%
Employed persons 16 years and over, by occupation:	
Managers & professionals	314
Service occupations	147
Sales & office occupations	227
Farming, fishing & forestry	2
Construction & maintenance	132
Production & transportation	133
Self-employed persons	72

Most demographic data is from the 2000 Decennial Census
† Massachusetts Department of Revenue
†† University of Massachusetts, MISER

General Information

Town of Hinsdale
39 South St
Hinsdale, MA 01235
413-655-2245

Elevation	1,440 ft.
Land area (square miles)	20.8
Water area (square miles)	0.9
Population density, 2008 (est)	92.0
Year incorporated	1804
Website	NA

Voters & Government Information

Government type	Open Town Meeting
Number of Selectmen	3
US Congressional District(s)	1

Registered Voters, October 2008

Total	1,487
Democrats	400
Republicans	161
Unaffiliated/other	919

Local Officials, 2010

Chair, Bd. of Sel.	Bruce Marshall
Manager/Admin	NA
Clerk	Dawn Frissell
Treasurer	Shaun F. Galliher
Tax Collector	Pauline Wheeler
Tax Assessor	Laura Galliher
Attorney	NA
Public Works	Peter Gallant
Building	Richard Haupt
Planning	Harold Stengl
Police Chief	Edward Reilly
Fire Chief	Larry Turner

Housing & Construction

New Privately Owned Housing Units Authorized by Building Permit

	Single Family	Total Bldgs	Total Units
2006	2	2	2
2007	2	2	2
2008	1	1	1

Parcel Count by Property Class, 2010

Total	1,467
Single family	832
Multiple units	28
Apartments	11
Condos	38
Vacant land	437
Open space	0
Commercial	29
Industrial	19
Misc. residential	29
Other use	44

Public Library

Hinsdale Public Library
PO Box 397
Hinsdale, MA 01235
(413)655-2303

Library Director....... Thomas A. Butler Jr

Library Statistics, FY 2008

Population served, 2007	1,937
Registered users	1,621
Circulation	6,869
Reference transactons	250
Total program attendance	0
per capita:	
Holdings	4.44
Operating income	$26.33
Internet Access	
Internet computers available	3
Weekly users	30

Municipal Finance

Debt at year end 2008	$5,016,688
Moody's rating, July 2009	NA

Revenues, 2008

Total	$3,768,927
From all taxes	3,010,436
Federal aid	0
State aid	448,551
From other governments	26,201
Charges for services	24,216
Licenses, permits & fees	6,964
Fines & forfeits	0
Interfund transfers	168,003
Misc/other/special assessments	42,278

Expenditures, 2008

Total	$3,281,869
General government	275,659
Public safety	238,135
Other/fixed costs	106,980
Human services	12,186
Culture & recreation	69,729
Debt Service	37,341
Education	2,062,089
Public works	435,841
Intergovernmental	36,409

Taxation, 2010

Property type	Valuation	Rate
Total	$276,071,052	-
Residential	237,078,507	11.13
Open space	0	0.00
Commercial	16,666,764	11.13
Industrial	2,195,970	11.13
Personal	20,129,811	11.13

Average Single Family Tax Bill, 2010

Avg. assessed home value	$224,301
Avg. single fam. tax bill	$2,496
Hi-Lo ranking	280/301

Police & Crime, 2008

Number of police officers	2
Violent crimes	6
Property crimes	5

Local School District

(school data 2007-08, except as noted)

Hinsdale (non-op)
PO Box 299
Dalton, MA 01227
413-684-0320

Superintendent......... James Stankiewicz

Non-operating district.
Resident students are sent to the Other School Districts listed below.

Grade plan	NA
Total enrollment '09-10	NA
Grade 12 enrollment, '09-10	NA
Graduation rate	NA
Dropout rate	NA
Per-pupil expenditure	NA
Avg teacher salary	NA
Student/teacher ratio '08-09	NA
Highly-qualified teachers, '08-09	NA
Teachers licensed in assigned subject	NA
Students per computer	NA

Other School Districts (see Appendix D for data)
Central Berkshire Regional

See Introduction for an explanation of all data sources.

©2010 Information Publications, Inc. All rights reserved. Photocopying prohibited. For additional copies, contact the publisher at www.informationpublications.com or (877)544-INFO (4636)

Demographics & Socio-Economic Characteristics

Population

1990	11,041
2000	10,785
Male	5,229
Female	5,556
2008	10,644
2010 (projected)††	10,326
2020 (projected)††	9,649

Race & Hispanic Origin, 2000

Race	
White	9,908
Black/African American	430
American Indian/Alaska Native	20
Asian	162
Hawaiian Native/Pacific Islander	1
Other Race	120
Two or more races	144
Hispanic origin	257

Age & Nativity, 2000

Under 5 years	643
18 years and over	8,305
21 years and over	7,974
65 years and over	1,739
85 years and over	145
Median Age	38.4
Native-born	10,175
Foreign-born	576

Age, 2020 (projected)††

Under 5 years	463
5 to 19 years	1,511
20 to 39 years	2,165
40 to 64 years	3,437
65 years and over	2,073

Educational Attainment, 2000

Population 25 years and over	7,548
High School graduates or higher	87.9%
Bachelor's degree or higher	18.2%
Graduate degree	6.1%

Income & Poverty, 1999

Per capita income,	$23,379
Median household income	$54,419
Median family income	$62,532
Persons in poverty	680
H'holds receiving public assistance	58
H'holds receiving social security	1,271

Households, 2000

Total households	4,076
With persons under 18	1,328
With persons over 65	1,250
Family households	2,854
Single person households	1,025
Persons per household	2.6
Persons per family	3.2

Labor & Employment, 2000

Civilian labor force	5,717
Unemployment rate	4.2%
Civilian labor force, 2008†	5,860
Unemployment rate†	7.1%
Civilian labor force, 12/09†	5,809
Unemployment rate†	9.5%
Employed persons 16 years and over, by occupation:	
Managers & professionals	1,672
Service occupations	665
Sales & office occupations	1,741
Farming, fishing & forestry	7
Construction & maintenance	619
Production & transportation	775
Self-employed persons	247

Most demographic data is from the 2000 Decennial Census
† Massachusetts Department of Revenue
†† University of Massachusetts, MISER

General Information

Town of Holbrook
50 N Franklin St
Holbrook, MA 02343
781-767-4312

Elevation	150 ft.
Land area (square miles)	7.4
Water area (square miles)	0.1
Population density, 2008 (est)	1,438.4
Year incorporated	1872
Email	town_clerk@holbrookmassachusetts.us

Voters & Government Information

Government type	Rep. Town Meeting
Number of Selectmen	5
US Congressional District(s)	9

Registered Voters, October 2008

Total	7,309
Democrats	2,521
Republicans	771
Unaffiliated/other	3,976

Local Officials, 2010

Chair, Bd. of Sel.	Robert A. Powilatis
Town Administrator	Michael D. Yunits
Town Clerk	M. Shirley Austin
Finance Director	Robert C. Haley
Tax Collector	Robert C. Haley
Tax Assessor	Robert A. Powilatis
Attorney	Arthur C. George
Public Works	Thomas R. Cummings
Building	Richard P. Monahan Jr
Planning	R. Wayne Crandlemere
Police Chief	William D. Marble, Jr.
Emerg/Fire Chief	Edward J. O'Brien

Housing & Construction

New Privately Owned Housing Units Authorized by Building Permit

	Single Family	Total Bldgs	Total Units
2006	9	9	9
2007	9	9	9
2008	14	14	14

Parcel Count by Property Class, 2010

Total	NA
Single family	NA
Multiple units	NA
Apartments	NA
Condos	NA
Vacant land	NA
Open space	NA
Commercial	NA
Industrial	NA
Misc. residential	NA
Other use	NA

Public Library

Holbrook Public Library
2 Plymouth St.
Holbrook, MA 02343
(781)767-3644

Director	Ruth Hathaway

Library Statistics, FY 2008

Population served, 2007	10,663
Registered users	5,338
Circulation	86,878
Reference transactons	0
Total program attendance	0
per capita:	
Holdings	4.17
Operating income	$38.24
Internet Access	
Internet computers available	8
Weekly users	215

Municipal Finance

Debt at year end 2008	$25,655,508
Moody's rating, July 2009	Baa2

Revenues, 2008

Total	$27,885,792
From all taxes	18,685,742
Federal aid	0
State aid	6,999,046
From other governments	10,755
Charges for services	0
Licenses, permits & fees	274,694
Fines & forfeits	5,970
Interfund transfers	124,939
Misc/other/special assessments	892,323

Expenditures, 2008

Total	$27,000,177
General government	987,264
Public safety	4,196,794
Other/fixed costs	4,180,580
Human services	174,248
Culture & recreation	363,551
Debt Service	2,159,699
Education	12,164,698
Public works	1,282,301
Intergovernmental	1,437,750

Taxation, 2010

Property type	Valuation	Rate
Total	NA	-
Residential	NA	NA
Open space	NA	NA
Commercial	NA	NA
Industrial	NA	NA
Personal	NA	NA

Average Single Family Tax Bill, 2010

Avg. assessed home value	NA
Avg. single fam. tax bill	NA
Hi-Lo ranking	NA

Police & Crime, 2008

Number of police officers	21
Violent crimes	NA
Property crimes	NA

Local School District

(school data 2007-08, except as noted)

Holbrook
245 So. Franklin Street
Holbrook, MA 02343
781-767-1226

Superintendent	Joseph Baeta
Grade plan	PK-12
Total enrollment '09-10	1,161
Grade 12 enrollment, '09-10	57
Graduation rate	75.9%
Dropout rate	18.4%
Per-pupil expenditure	$11,536
Avg teacher salary	$54,508
Student/teacher ratio '08-09	13.7 to 1
Highly-qualified teachers, '08-09	90.5%
Teachers licensed in assigned subject	96.5%
Students per computer	4.7

Massachusetts Competency Assessment System (MCAS), 2009 results

	English		Math	
	% Prof	CPI	% Prof	CPI
Gr 4	60%	80.6	43%	74.2
Gr 6	68%	87.6	55%	77.9
Gr 8	68%	86.3	23%	53.6
Gr 10	65%	85.4	49%	77.5

Other School Districts (see Appendix D for data)
Blue Hills Vocational Tech, Norfolk County Agricultural

©2010 Information Publications, Inc. All rights reserved. Photocopying prohibited. For additional copies, contact the publisher at www.informationpublications.com or (877)544-INFO (4636)

See Introduction for an explanation of all data sources.

Demographics & Socio-Economic Characteristics

Population

1990	14,628
2000	15,621
Male	7,542
Female	8,079
2008	16,608
2010 (projected)††	15,504
2020 (projected)††	15,453

Race & Hispanic Origin, 2000

Race	
White	15,214
Black/African American	76
American Indian/Alaska Native	15
Asian	154
Hawaiian Native/Pacific Islander	1
Other Race	37
Two or more races	124
Hispanic origin	150

Age & Nativity, 2000

Under 5 years	1,004
18 years and over	11,397
21 years and over	10,957
65 years and over	2,218
85 years and over	286
Median Age	40.1
Native-born	15,007
Foreign-born	614

Age, 2020 (projected)††

Under 5 years	894
5 to 19 years	2,838
20 to 39 years	3,406
40 to 64 years	5,162
65 years and over	3,153

Educational Attainment, 2000

Population 25 years and over	10,580
High School graduates or higher	94.0%
Bachelor's degree or higher	45.4%
Graduate degree	18.6%

Income & Poverty, 1999

Per capita income,	$27,971
Median household income	$64,297
Median family income	$73,614
Persons in poverty	479
H'holds receiving public assistance	82
H'holds receiving social security	1,601

Households, 2000

Total households	5,715
With persons under 18	2,222
With persons over 65	1,503
Family households	4,422
Single person households	1,112
Persons per household	2.7
Persons per family	3.1

Labor & Employment, 2000

Civilian labor force	8,180
Unemployment rate	2.9%
Civilian labor force, 2008†	8,676
Unemployment rate†	5.6%
Civilian labor force, 12/09†	8,804
Unemployment rate†	7.9%
Employed persons 16 years and over, by occupation:	
Managers & professionals	4,104
Service occupations	823
Sales & office occupations	1,927
Farming, fishing & forestry	0
Construction & maintenance	429
Production & transportation	657
Self-employed persons	451

Most demographic data is from the 2000 Decennial Census
† Massachusetts Department of Revenue
†† University of Massachusetts, MISER

General Information

Town of Holden
1204 Main St
Holden, MA 01520
508-829-0225

Elevation	818 ft.
Land area (square miles)	35.0
Water area (square miles)	1.2
Population density, 2008 (est)	474.5
Year incorporated	1741
Website	www.townofholden.net

Voters & Government Information

Government type	Open Town Meeting
Number of Selectmen	5
US Congressional District(s)	3

Registered Voters, October 2008

Total	12,525
Democrats	2,795
Republicans	2,101
Unaffiliated/other	7,571

Local Officials, 2010

Chair, Bd. of Sel.	Kimberly N. Ferguson
Manager	Nancy T. Galkowski
Town Clerk	Cheryl A. Jenkins
Treasurer	Jean Berg
Tax Collector	Jean Berg
Tax Assessor	Beverly Potvin
Attorney	NA
Public Works	James Shuris
Growth Mgmt Dir	Dennis Lipka
Comm Dev/Planning	Pamela Harding
Police Chief	George Sherrill
Emerg/Fire Chief	John Chandler III

Housing & Construction

New Privately Owned Housing Units Authorized by Building Permit

	Single Family	Total Bldgs	Total Units
2006	48	49	50
2007	49	49	49
2008	31	31	31

Parcel Count by Property Class, 2010

Total	7,917
Single family	5,470
Multiple units	106
Apartments	18
Condos	740
Vacant land	1,170
Open space	0
Commercial	142
Industrial	27
Misc. residential	110
Other use	134

Public Library

Gale Free Library
23 Highland St.
Holden, MA 01520
(508)829-0228

Director	Jane Dutton

Library Statistics, FY 2008

Population served, 2007	16,581
Registered users	10,014
Circulation	318,399
Reference transactons	13,800
Total program attendance	0
per capita:	
Holdings	4.51
Operating income	$48.27
Internet Access	
Internet computers available	8
Weekly users	290

Municipal Finance

Debt at year end 2008	$50,527,917
Moody's rating, July 2009	A2

Revenues, 2008

Total	$35,191,813
From all taxes	28,587,967
Federal aid	0
State aid	4,590,575
From other governments	88,370
Charges for services	399,350
Licenses, permits & fees	98,762
Fines & forfeits	5,718
Interfund transfers	813,541
Misc/other/special assessments	303,765

Expenditures, 2008

Total	$34,202,630
General government	1,586,951
Public safety	3,025,335
Other/fixed costs	1,831,344
Human services	200,572
Culture & recreation	683,154
Debt Service	3,847,473
Education	20,546,736
Public works	2,341,460
Intergovernmental	139,605

Taxation, 2010

Property type	Valuation	Rate
Total	$1,883,982,600	-
Residential	1,770,671,240	14.80
Open space	0	0.00
Commercial	61,807,660	14.80
Industrial	24,619,400	14.80
Personal	26,884,300	14.80

Average Single Family Tax Bill, 2010

Avg. assessed home value	$277,156
Avg. single fam. tax bill	$4,102
Hi-Lo ranking	127/301

Police & Crime, 2008

Number of police officers	24
Violent crimes	10
Property crimes	91

Local School District

(school data 2007-08, except as noted)

Holden (non-op)
Jefferson School, 1745 Main Street
Jefferson, MA 01522
508-829-1670
Superintendent........ Thomas Pandiscio

Non-operating district.
Resident students are sent to the Other School Districts listed below.

Grade plan	NA
Total enrollment '09-10	NA
Grade 12 enrollment, '09-10	NA
Graduation rate	NA
Dropout rate	NA
Per-pupil expenditure	NA
Avg teacher salary	NA
Student/teacher ratio '08-09	NA
Highly-qualified teachers, '08-09	NA
Teachers licensed in assigned subject	NA
Students per computer	NA

Other School Districts (see Appendix D for data)
Wachusett Regional, Montachusett Vocational Tech

©2010 Information Publications, Inc. All rights reserved. Photocopying prohibited. For additional copies, contact the publisher at www.informationpublications.com or (877)544-INFO (4636)

See Introduction for an explanation of all data sources.

Demographics & Socio-Economic Characteristics

Population

1990 2,185
2000 2,407
  Male 1,224
  Female 1,183
2008 2,529
2010 (projected)†† 2,725
2020 (projected)†† 3,223

Race & Hispanic Origin, 2000

Race
  White 2,334
  Black/African American 2
  American Indian/Alaska Native 20
  Asian 6
  Hawaiian Native/Pacific Islander 1
  Other Race 18
  Two or more races 26
Hispanic origin 34

Age & Nativity, 2000

Under 5 years 144
18 years and over 1,736
21 years and over 1,667
65 years and over 207
85 years and over 15
  Median Age 37.0
Native-born 2,348
Foreign-born 59

Age, 2020 (projected)††

Under 5 years 212
5 to 19 years 545
20 to 39 years 866
40 to 64 years 1,092
65 years and over 508

Educational Attainment, 2000

Population 25 years and over 1,602
  High School graduates or higher .. 83.0%
  Bachelor's degree or higher 19.8%
  Graduate degree 5.6%

Income & Poverty, 1999

Per capita income, ... $21,770
Median household income $52,073
Median family income $57,024
Persons in poverty 174
H'holds receiving public assistance 16
H'holds receiving social security 193

Households, 2000

Total households 898
  With persons under 18 358
  With persons over 65 146
  Family households 668
  Single person households 162
Persons per household 2.7
Persons per family 3.1

Labor & Employment, 2000

Civilian labor force 1,359
  Unemployment rate 3.3%
Civilian labor force, 2008† 1,441
  Unemployment rate† 7.1%
Civilian labor force, 12/09† 1,448
  Unemployment rate† 8.2%
Employed persons 16 years and over, by occupation:
  Managers & professionals 405
  Service occupations 205
  Sales & office occupations 292
  Farming, fishing & forestry 2
  Construction & maintenance 189
  Production & transportation 221
  Self-employed persons 120

Most demographic data is from the 2000 Decennial Census
† Massachusetts Department of Revenue
†† University of Massachusetts, MISER

General Information

Town of Holland
27 Sturbridge Rd
Holland, MA 01521
413-245-7108

Elevation .... 743 ft.
Land area (square miles) 12.4
Water area (square miles) 0.7
Population density, 2008 (est) 204.0
Year incorporated 1783
Website .... town.holland.ma.us

Voters & Government Information

Government type .... Open Town Meeting
Number of Selectmen 3
US Congressional District(s) 2

Registered Voters, October 2008

Total 1,814
Democrats 377
Republicans 274
Unaffiliated/other 1,135

Local Officials, 2010

Chair, Bd. of Sel. .... James Wettlaufer
Manager/Admin .... NA
Clerk .... Kristin LaPlante
Finance Director .... Linda A. Blodgett
Tax Collector .... Nancy Talbot
Tax Assessor .... JoAnne Higgins
Attorney .... Vincent McCaughey
Public Works .... Brian Johnson
Building .... Jack Keough
Planning .... Lynn Arnold (Chr)
Police Chief .... Bryan Haughey
Emerg/Fire Chief .... Paul Foster

Housing & Construction

New Privately Owned Housing Units Authorized by Building Permit

	Single Family	Total Bldgs	Total Units
2006	12	12	12
2007	8	8	8
2008	5	5	5

Parcel Count by Property Class, 2010

Total 2,200
Single family 1,358
Multiple units 16
Apartments 0
Condos 6
Vacant land 756
Open space 0
Commercial 14
Industrial 4
Misc. residential 17
Other use 29

Public Library

Holland Public Library
PO Box 9
Holland, MA 01521
(413)245-3607

Director .... Joan Markert

Library Statistics, FY 2008

Population served, 2007 2,532
Registered users 279
Circulation 4,479
Reference transactons 0
Total program attendance 2,674
per capita:
Holdings 4.23
Operating income $12.49
Internet Access
Internet computers available 1
Weekly users 6

Municipal Finance

Debt at year end 2008 .... $897,069
Moody's rating, July 2009 .... NA

Revenues, 2008

Total $6,142,047
From all taxes 4,843,968
Federal aid 1,092,716
State aid 0
From other governments 0
Charges for services 23,995
Licenses, permits & fees 11,113
Fines & forfeits 0
Interfund transfers 69,125
Misc/other/special assessments 50,565

Expenditures, 2008

Total $5,603,420
General government 313,603
Public safety 274,412
Other/fixed costs 538,556
Human services 34,680
Culture & recreation 46,712
Debt Service 214,827
Education 3,678,455
Public works 485,740
Intergovernmental 16,241

Taxation, 2010

Property type	Valuation	Rate
Total	$333,725,090	-
Residential	320,412,043	13.21
Open space	0	0.00
Commercial	5,139,457	13.21
Industrial	797,800	13.21
Personal	7,375,790	13.21

Average Single Family Tax Bill, 2010

Avg. assessed home value $210,996
Avg. single fam. tax bill $2,787
Hi-Lo ranking 254/301

Police & Crime, 2008

Number of police officers .... NA
Violent crimes .... NA
Property crimes .... NA

Local School District

(school data 2007-08, except as noted)

Holland
320 Brookfield Rd
Fiskdale, MA 01518
508-347-3077

Superintendent .... Daniel Durgin
Grade plan PK-6
Total enrollment '09-10 251
Grade 12 enrollment, '09-10 0
Graduation rate .... NA
Dropout rate .... NA
Per-pupil expenditure $10,500
Avg teacher salary $50,622
Student/teacher ratio '08-09 .... 13.9 to 1
Highly-qualified teachers, '08-09 .... 100.0%
Teachers licensed in assigned subject 100.0%
Students per computer 2.1

Massachusetts Competency Assessment System (MCAS), 2009 results

	English		Math	
	% Prof	CPI	% Prof	CPI
Gr 4	48%	75	45%	78.8
Gr 6	67%	88.3	61%	83.9
Gr 8	NA	NA	NA	NA
Gr 10	NA	NA	NA	NA

Other School Districts (see Appendix D for data)
Tantasqua Regional

©2010 Information Publications, Inc. All rights reserved. Photocopying prohibited. For additional copies, contact the publisher at www.informationpublications.com or (877)544-INFO (4636)

Demographics & Socio-Economic Characteristics

Population

1990 12,926
2000 13,801
Male 6,770
Female 7,031
2008 13,901
2010 (projected)†† 12,922
2020 (projected)†† 11,766

Race & Hispanic Origin, 2000

Race
White 13,346
Black/African American 123
American Indian/Alaska Native 18
Asian 165
Hawaiian Native/Pacific Islander 1
Other Race 43
Two or more races 105
Hispanic origin 190

Age & Nativity, 2000

Under 5 years 1,021
18 years and over 9,660
21 years and over 9,356
65 years and over 1,228
85 years and over 99
Median Age 38.2
Native-born 13,070
Foreign-born 731

Age, 2020 (projected)††

Under 5 years 681
5 to 19 years 2,171
20 to 39 years 2,741
40 to 64 years 3,946
65 years and over 2,227

Educational Attainment, 2000

Population 25 years and over 9,017
High School graduates or higher .. 96.9%
Bachelor's degree or higher 50.8%
Graduate degree 18.8%

Income & Poverty, 1999

Per capita income, ... $32,116
Median household income $78,092
Median family income $84,878
Persons in poverty 471
H'holds receiving public assistance 42
H'holds receiving social security 908

Households, 2000

Total households 4,795
With persons under 18 2,189
With persons over 65 874
Family households 3,842
Single person households 785
Persons per household 2.9
Persons per family 3.3

Labor & Employment, 2000

Civilian labor force 7,311
Unemployment rate 2.9%
Civilian labor force, 2008† 7,632
Unemployment rate† 4.7%
Civilian labor force, 12/09† 7,711
Unemployment rate† 6.8%
Employed persons 16 years and over, by occupation:
Managers & professionals 4,035
Service occupations 500
Sales & office occupations 1,679
Farming, fishing & forestry 6
Construction & maintenance 564
Production & transportation 317
Self-employed persons 579

Most demographic data is from the 2000 Decennial Census
† Massachusetts Department of Revenue
†† University of Massachusetts, MISER

General Information

Town of Holliston
703 Washington St
Holliston, MA 01746
508-429-0601

Elevation .... 188 ft.
Land area (square miles) 18.7
Water area (square miles) 0.3
Population density, 2008 (est) 743.4
Year incorporated 1724
Website .... www.townofholliston.us

Voters & Government Information

Government type .... Open Town Meeting
Number of Selectmen 3
US Congressional District(s) 3

Registered Voters, October 2008

Total 10,047
Democrats 2,850
Republicans 1,532
Unaffiliated/other 5,612

Local Officials, 2010

Chair, Bd. of Sel. .... Andrew Porter
Manager/Admin .... Paul LeBeau
Town Clerk .... Jacqueline Dellicker
Chief Financial Officer .... Paul LeBeau
Tax Collector .... Mary Bousquet
Tax Assessor .... Kathryn Peirce
Attorney .... NA
Public Works .... NA
Building .... Peter Tartakoff
Comm Dev/Planning .... Karen Sherman
Police Chief .... Thomas Lambert
Emerg/Fire Chief .... Michael Cassidy

Housing & Construction

New Privately Owned Housing Units Authorized by Building Permit

	Single Family	Total Bldgs	Total Units
2006	21	21	21
2007	19	19	19
2008	25	25	25

Parcel Count by Property Class, 2010

Total 5,579
Single family 4,249
Multiple units 76
Apartments 40
Condos 293
Vacant land 557
Open space 0
Commercial 112
Industrial 164
Misc. residential 21
Other use 67

Public Library

Holliston Public Library
752 Washington St.
Holliston, MA 01746
(508)429-0617

Director .... Leslie McDonnell

Library Statistics, FY 2008

Population served, 2007 13,941
Registered users 7,690
Circulation 183,791
Reference transactons 5,876
Total program attendance 147,000

per capita:

Holdings 4.95
Operating income $33.78

Internet Access

Internet computers available 13
Weekly users 395

Municipal Finance

Debt at year end 2008 .... $58,012,105
Moody's rating, July 2009 .... A1

Revenues, 2008

Total $47,142,658
From all taxes 32,768,166
Federal aid 0
State aid 11,070,296
From other governments 57,518
Charges for services 1,046,794
Licenses, permits & fees 326,004
Fines & forfeits 22,903
Interfund transfers 624,735
Misc/other/special assessments 613,121

Expenditures, 2008

Total $45,881,254
General government 1,477,608
Public safety 2,917,513
Other/fixed costs 4,947,349
Human services 431,305
Culture & recreation 514,559
Debt Service 5,355,090
Education 27,101,097
Public works 2,594,475
Intergovernmental 532,798

Taxation, 2010

Property type	Valuation	Rate
Total	$2,061,165,463	-
Residential	1,816,610,457	16.31
Open space	0	0.00
Commercial	63,448,622	16.31
Industrial	133,793,700	16.31
Personal	47,312,684	16.31

Average Single Family Tax Bill, 2010

Avg. assessed home value $394,464
Avg. single fam. tax bill $6,434
Hi-Lo ranking 41/301

Police & Crime, 2008

Number of police officers 22
Violent crimes 9
Property crimes 69

Local School District

(school data 2007-08, except as noted)

Holliston
370 Hollis Street
Holliston, MA 01746
508-429-0654

Superintendent .... Bradford Jackson
Grade plan PK-12
Total enrollment '09-10 2,864
Grade 12 enrollment, '09-10 207
Graduation rate 95.0%
Dropout rate 1.7%
Per-pupil expenditure $11,217
Avg teacher salary $64,271
Student/teacher ratio '08-09 .... 13.4 to 1
Highly-qualified teachers, '08-09 .... 97.5%
Teachers licensed in assigned subject .. 98.4%
Students per computer 2.9

Massachusetts Competency Assessment System (MCAS), 2009 results

	English		Math	
	% Prof	CPI	% Prof	CPI
Gr 4	60%	85.5	57%	85.2
Gr 6	76%	90.7	70%	86.5
Gr 8	92%	97.3	67%	84.6
Gr 10	94%	98	96%	98.1

Other School Districts (see Appendix D for data)
South Middlesex Vocational Tech

©2010 Information Publications, Inc. All rights reserved. Photocopying prohibited. For additional copies, contact the publisher at www.informationpublications.com or (877)544-INFO (4636)

See Introduction for an explanation of all data sources.

Demographics & Socio-Economic Characteristics*

Population

1990	43,704
2000	39,838
Male	18,664
Female	21,174
2008	39,947
2010 (projected)††	38,430
2020 (projected)††	37,431

Race & Hispanic Origin, 2000

Race	
White	26,197
Black/African American	1,476
American Indian/Alaska Native	151
Asian	324
Hawaiian Native/Pacific Islander	48
Other Race	10,521
Two or more races	1,121
Hispanic origin	16,485

Age & Nativity, 2000

Under 5 years	3,156
18 years and over	28,098
21 years and over	26,472
65 years and over	6,201
85 years and over	1,138
Median Age	34.0
Native-born	37,686
Foreign-born	2,152

Age, 2020 (projected)††

Under 5 years	2,947
5 to 19 years	8,440
20 to 39 years	9,791
40 to 64 years	10,285
65 years and over	5,968

Educational Attainment, 2000

Population 25 years and over	24,509
High School graduates or higher	70.0%
Bachelor's degree or higher	16.9%
Graduate degree	6.4%

Income & Poverty, 1999

Per capita income,	$15,913
Median household income	$30,441
Median family income	$36,130
Persons in poverty	10,082
H'holds receiving public assistance	1,678
H'holds receiving social security	4,886

Households, 2000

Total households	14,967
With persons under 18	5,523
With persons over 65	4,045
Family households	9,478
Single person households	4,631
Persons per household	2.6
Persons per family	3.2

Labor & Employment, 2000

Civilian labor force	15,919
Unemployment rate	6.7%
Civilian labor force, 2008†	16,132
Unemployment rate†	9.5%
Civilian labor force, 12/09†	16,380
Unemployment rate†	12.2%
Employed persons 16 years and over, by occupation:	
Managers & professionals	4,513
Service occupations	2,765
Sales & office occupations	3,782
Farming, fishing & forestry	16
Construction & maintenance	1,057
Production & transportation	2,715
Self-employed persons	584

Most demographic data is from the 2000 Decennial Census
* see Appendix E for American Community Survey data
† Massachusetts Department of Revenue
†† University of Massachusetts, MISER

General Information

City of Holyoke
536 Dwight St
Holyoke, MA 01040
413-322-5520

Elevation	152 ft.
Land area (square miles)	21.3
Water area (square miles)	1.5
Population density, 2008 (est)	1,875.4
Year incorporated	1850
Email	egans@ci.holyoke.ma.us

Voters & Government Information

Government type	Mayor-Council
Number of Councilpersons	15
US Congressional District(s)	1

Registered Voters, October 2008

Total	25,041
Democrats	11,486
Republicans	2,101
Unaffiliated/other	11,246

Local Officials, 2010

Mayor	Elaine A. Pluta
Manager/Admin	NA
City Clerk	Susan M. Egan
Finance	Jon Lumbra
Tax Collector	Robert F. Kane
Tax Assessor	Anthony Dulude
Attorney	Karen Betournay
Public Works	Bill Fuqua
Building	Paul Healy
Comm Dev/Planning	NA
Police Chief	Anthony Scott
Fire Chief	William Kane (Actg)

Housing & Construction

New Privately Owned Housing Units Authorized by Building Permit

	Single Family	Total Bldgs	Total Units
2006	13	17	29
2007	5	13	24
2008	7	10	13

Parcel Count by Property Class, 2010

Total	9,734
Single family	5,305
Multiple units	1,588
Apartments	312
Condos	454
Vacant land	862
Open space	0
Commercial	681
Industrial	268
Misc. residential	22
Other use	242

Public Library

Holyoke Public Library
335 Maple Street
Holyoke, MA 01040
(413)322-5640

Director	Maria Pagan

Library Statistics, FY 2008

Population served, 2007	39,737
Registered users	13,241
Circulation	81,963
Reference transactons	23,777
Total program attendance	84,473
per capita:	
Holdings	2.06
Operating income	$18.79
Internet Access	
Internet computers available	10
Weekly users	290

Municipal Finance

Debt at year end 2008	$52,766,601
Moody's rating, July 2009	Baa1

Revenues, 2008

Total	$135,835,055
From all taxes	46,047,986
Federal aid	0
State aid	85,446,234
From other governments	571,066
Charges for services	1,167,826
Licenses, permits & fees	487,669
Fines & forfeits	0
Interfund transfers	24,770
Misc/other/special assessments	1,044,752

Expenditures, 2008

Total	$135,013,702
General government	3,632,554
Public safety	21,192,903
Other/fixed costs	19,704,458
Human services	1,192,139
Culture & recreation	1,560,132
Debt Service	4,528,696
Education	66,417,805
Public works	5,449,244
Intergovernmental	11,332,559

Taxation, 2010

Property type	Valuation	Rate
Total	$2,166,901,252	-
Residential	1,524,866,172	14.98
Open space	0	0.00
Commercial	487,007,245	36.54
Industrial	86,164,005	36.54
Personal	68,863,830	36.54

Average Single Family Tax Bill, 2010

Avg. assessed home value	$184,495
Avg. single fam. tax bill	$2,764
Hi-Lo ranking	258/301

Police & Crime, 2008

Number of police officers	126
Violent crimes	451
Property crimes	2,347

Local School District

(school data 2007-08, except as noted)

Holyoke
57 Suffolk Street
Holyoke, MA 01040
413-534-2005

Superintendent	Eduardo Carballo
Grade plan	PK-12
Total enrollment '09-10	5,901
Grade 12 enrollment, '09-10	371
Graduation rate	49.8%
Dropout rate	32.9%
Per-pupil expenditure	$15,108
Avg teacher salary	$62,051
Student/teacher ratio '08-09	11.5 to 1
Highly-qualified teachers, '08-09	94.2%
Teachers licensed in assigned subject	95.8%
Students per computer	3.2

Massachusetts Competency Assessment System (MCAS), 2009 results

	English		Math	
	% Prof	CPI	% Prof	CPI
Gr 4	16%	52.1	13%	50.6
Gr 6	24%	60.3	23%	55.1
Gr 8	45%	71.8	14%	44.7
Gr 10	52%	77.8	42%	68.3

Other School Districts (see Appendix D for data)
None

©2010 Information Publications, Inc. All rights reserved. Photocopying prohibited. For additional copies, contact the publisher at www.informationpublications.com or (877)544-INFO (4636)

©2010 Information Publications, Inc. All rights reserved. Photocopying prohibited. For additional copies, contact the publisher at www.informationpublications.com or (877)544-INFO (4636)

Demographics & Socio-Economic Characteristics

Population

1990	5,666
2000	5,907
Male	2,812
Female	3,095
2008	6,142
2010 (projected)††	6,853
2020 (projected)††	8,146

Race & Hispanic Origin, 2000

Race	
White	5,761
Black/African American	33
American Indian/Alaska Native	1
Asian	42
Hawaiian Native/Pacific Islander	0
Other Race	30
Two or more races	40
Hispanic origin	69

Age & Nativity, 2000

Under 5 years	428
18 years and over	4,360
21 years and over	4,210
65 years and over	913
85 years and over	142
Median Age	38.7
Native-born	5,767
Foreign-born	140

Age, 2020 (projected)††

Under 5 years	518
5 to 19 years	1,513
20 to 39 years	2,161
40 to 64 years	2,567
65 years and over	1,387

Educational Attainment, 2000

Population 25 years and over	4,066
High School graduates or higher	92.2%
Bachelor's degree or higher	28.0%
Graduate degree	8.7%

Income & Poverty, 1999

Per capita income,	$24,791
Median household income	$60,176
Median family income	$68,571
Persons in poverty	232
H'holds receiving public assistance	27
H'holds receiving social security	601

Households, 2000

Total households	2,240
With persons under 18	843
With persons over 65	616
Family households	1,573
Single person households	580
Persons per household	2.6
Persons per family	3.1

Labor & Employment, 2000

Civilian labor force	3,106
Unemployment rate	1.9%
Civilian labor force, 2008†	3,463
Unemployment rate†	5.7%
Civilian labor force, 12/09†	3,426
Unemployment rate†	7.1%
Employed persons 16 years and over, by occupation:	
Managers & professionals	1,277
Service occupations	407
Sales & office occupations	859
Farming, fishing & forestry	7
Construction & maintenance	240
Production & transportation	256
Self-employed persons	246

Most demographic data is from the 2000 Decennial Census
† Massachusetts Department of Revenue
†† University of Massachusetts, MISER

General Information

Town of Hopedale
78 Hopedale St
PO Box 7
Hopedale, MA 01747
508-634-2203

Elevation	300 ft.
Land area (square miles)	5.2
Water area (square miles)	0.2
Population density, 2008 (est)	1,181.2
Year incorporated	1886
Website	www.hopedale-ma.gov

Voters & Government Information

Government type	Open Town Meeting
Number of Selectmen	3
US Congressional District(s)	2

Registered Voters, October 2008

Total	3,996
Democrats	895
Republicans	503
Unaffiliated/other	2,577

Local Officials, 2010

Chair, Bd. of Sel.	Alan J. Ryan
Manager/Town Coord	Eugene N. Phillips
Town Clerk	Janet Orff Jacaruso
Accountant	Linda Catanzariti
Tax Collector	Barbara Walls
Tax Assessor	Terri Gonsalves
Attorney	Kopelman & Paige
Public Works	Robert DePonte
Building	Michael Tusino
Comm Dev/Planning	Howard Maurer
Police Chief	Eugene Costanza Jr
Emerg/Fire Chief	Thomas Daige (Actg)

Housing & Construction

New Privately Owned Housing Units Authorized by Building Permit

	Single Family	Total Bldgs	Total Units
2006	8	8	8
2007	5	5	5
2008	0	0	0

Parcel Count by Property Class, 2010

Total	2,398
Single family	1,466
Multiple units	128
Apartments	3
Condos	427
Vacant land	188
Open space	0
Commercial	86
Industrial	71
Misc. residential	11
Other use	18

Public Library

Bancroft Memorial Library
50 Hopedale St.
Hopedale, MA 01747
(508)634-2209

Director ... Ann Fields

Library Statistics, FY 2008

Population served, 2007	6,165
Registered users	2,756
Circulation	29,451
Reference transactons	1,000
Total program attendance	24,733
per capita:	
Holdings	6.38
Operating income	$42.62
Internet Access	
Internet computers available	2
Weekly users	24

Municipal Finance

Debt at year end 2008	$17,538,675
Moody's rating, July 2009	A2

Revenues, 2008

Total	$19,295,925
From all taxes	10,227,807
Federal aid	0
State aid	8,133,979
From other governments	28,908
Charges for services	76,399
Licenses, permits & fees	73,443
Fines & forfeits	0
Interfund transfers	321,667
Misc/other/special assessments	216,861

Expenditures, 2008

Total	$16,720,446
General government	793,638
Public safety	1,742,703
Other/fixed costs	906,681
Human services	502,005
Culture & recreation	324,445
Debt Service	2,097,518
Education	9,397,037
Public works	569,673
Intergovernmental	385,391

Taxation, 2010

Property type	Valuation	Rate
Total	$707,054,706	-
Residential	629,073,717	13.52
Open space	0	0.00
Commercial	38,130,699	21.62
Industrial	27,687,820	21.62
Personal	12,162,470	21.62

Average Single Family Tax Bill, 2010

Avg. assessed home value	$326,085
Avg. single fam. tax bill	$4,409
Hi-Lo ranking	106/301

Police & Crime, 2008

Number of police officers	12
Violent crimes	8
Property crimes	47

Local School District

(school data 2007-08, except as noted)

Hopedale
25 Adin Street
Hopedale, MA 01747
508-634-2220

Superintendent	Patricia Ruane
Grade plan	PK-12
Total enrollment '09-10	1,308
Grade 12 enrollment, '09-10	87
Graduation rate	91.9%
Dropout rate	3.5%
Per-pupil expenditure	$9,613
Avg teacher salary	$57,832
Student/teacher ratio '08-09	15.4 to 1
Highly-qualified teachers, '08-09	98.1%
Teachers licensed in assigned subject	95.4%
Students per computer	3.7

Massachusetts Competency Assessment System (MCAS), 2009 results

	English		Math	
	% Prof	CPI	% Prof	CPI
Gr 4	63%	86.1	55%	82.9
Gr 6	83%	93.4	72%	85.9
Gr 8	86%	94.9	53%	73.3
Gr 10	92%	96.8	85%	93.3

Other School Districts (see Appendix D for data)
Blackstone Valley Vocational Tech

See Introduction for an explanation of all data sources.

Demographics & Socio-Economic Characteristics

Population

1990 . . . 9,191
2000 . . . 13,346
Male . . . 6,586
Female . . . 6,760
2008 . . . 14,338
2010 (projected)†† . . . 15,960
2020 (projected)†† . . . 18,744

Race & Hispanic Origin, 2000

Race
White . . . 12,856
Black/African American . . . 92
American Indian/Alaska Native . . . 20
Asian . . . 221
Hawaiian Native/Pacific Islander . . . 6
Other Race . . . 39
Two or more races . . . 112
Hispanic origin . . . 177

Age & Nativity, 2000

Under 5 years . . . 1,323
18 years and over . . . 8,929
21 years and over . . . 8,710
65 years and over . . . 917
85 years and over . . . 110
Median Age . . . 36.2
Native-born . . . 12,482
Foreign-born . . . 864

Age, 2020 (projected)††

Under 5 years . . . 1,438
5 to 19 years . . . 4,038
20 to 39 years . . . 4,843
40 to 64 years . . . 6,257
65 years and over . . . 2,168

Educational Attainment, 2000

Population 25 years and over . . . 8,401
High School graduates or higher . . 96.0%
Bachelor's degree or higher . . . 57.7%
Graduate degree . . . 22.2%

Income & Poverty, 1999

Per capita income, . . . $41,469
Median household income . . . $89,281
Median family income . . . $102,550
Persons in poverty . . . 220
H'holds receiving public assistance . . . 22
H'holds receiving social security . . . 720

Households, 2000

Total households . . . 4,444
With persons under 18 . . . 2,266
With persons over 65 . . . 638
Family households . . . 3,624
Single person households . . . 674
Persons per household . . . 3.0
Persons per family . . . 3.3

Labor & Employment, 2000

Civilian labor force . . . 6,724
Unemployment rate . . . 1.5%
Civilian labor force, 2008† . . . 7,492
Unemployment rate† . . . 4.5%
Civilian labor force, 12/09† . . . 7,576
Unemployment rate† . . . 6.1%
Employed persons 16 years and over, by occupation:
Managers & professionals . . . 3,908
Service occupations . . . 499
Sales & office occupations . . . 1,660
Farming, fishing & forestry . . . 17
Construction & maintenance . . . 275
Production & transportation . . . 266
Self-employed persons . . . 522

Most demographic data is from the 2000 Decennial Census
† Massachusetts Department of Revenue
†† University of Massachusetts, MISER

General Information

Town of Hopkinton
18 Main St
Hopkinton, MA 01748
508-497-9700

Elevation . . . 450 ft.
Land area (square miles) . . . 26.6
Water area (square miles) . . . 1.6
Population density, 2008 (est) . . . 539.0
Year incorporated . . . 1715
Website . . . www.hopkinton.org

Voters & Government Information

Government type . . . Open Town Meeting
Number of Selectmen . . . 5
US Congressional District(s) . . . 3

Registered Voters, October 2008

Total . . . 9,552
Democrats . . . 2,266
Republicans . . . 1,954
Unaffiliated/other . . . 5,305

Local Officials, 2010

Chair, Bd. of Sel. . . . Brian J. Herr
Town Manager . . . Norman Khumalo
Town Clerk . . . Ann M. Click
Finance Director . . . Heidi Kriger
Tax Collector . . . Maureen Dwinnell
Tax Assessor . . . Robert Bushway
Attorney . . . Miyares & Harrington
Public Works . . . John T. Gaucher
Building . . . Charles Kadlik
Planning Director . . . Elaine Lazarus
Police Chief . . . Thomas Irvin
Emerg/Fire Chief . . . Paul K. Clark

Housing & Construction

New Privately Owned Housing Units Authorized by Building Permit

	Single Family	Total Bldgs	Total Units
2006	51	51	51
2007	37	37	37
2008	29	29	29

Parcel Count by Property Class, 2010

Total . . . 6,008
Single family . . . 4,232
Multiple units . . . 84
Apartments . . . 19
Condos . . . 523
Vacant land . . . 761
Open space . . . 66
Commercial . . . 82
Industrial . . . 67
Misc. residential . . . 57
Other use . . . 117

Public Library

Hopkinton Public Library
13 Main St.
Hopkinton, MA 01748
(508)497-9777

Director . . . Rownak Hussain

Library Statistics, FY 2008

Population served, 2007 . . . 14,307
Registered users . . . 7,480
Circulation . . . 114,258
Reference transactons . . . 1,756
Total program attendance . . . 60,000

per capita:

Holdings . . . 3.00
Operating income . . . $26.17

Internet Access

Internet computers available . . . 6
Weekly users . . . 50

Municipal Finance

Debt at year end 2008 . . . $65,126,889
Moody's rating, July 2009 . . . Aa3

Revenues, 2008

Total . . . $56,839,694
From all taxes . . . 44,731,426
Federal aid . . . 0
State aid . . . 9,854,614
From other governments . . . 169,943
Charges for services . . . 153,614
Licenses, permits & fees . . . 279,738
Fines & forfeits . . . 10,999
Interfund transfers . . . 976,590
Misc/other/special assessments . . . 331,385

Expenditures, 2008

Total . . . $55,566,975
General government . . . 1,697,719
Public safety . . . 4,027,028
Other/fixed costs . . . 6,757,780
Human services . . . 414,599
Culture & recreation . . . 378,996
Debt Service . . . 7,091,408
Education . . . 31,508,092
Public works . . . 3,329,608
Intergovernmental . . . 361,745

Taxation, 2010

Property type	Valuation	Rate
Total	$2,814,895,029	-
Residential	2,343,952,130	15.76
Open space	368,300	15.76
Commercial	89,454,502	15.76
Industrial	291,956,027	15.76
Personal	89,164,070	15.76

Average Single Family Tax Bill, 2010

Avg. assessed home value . . . $487,768
Avg. single fam. tax bill . . . $7,687
Hi-Lo ranking . . . 25/301

Police & Crime, 2008

Number of police officers . . . 20
Violent crimes . . . 2
Property crimes . . . 84

Local School District

(school data 2007-08, except as noted)

Hopkinton
89 Hayden Rowe Street
Hopkinton, MA 01748
508-417-9360

Superintendent . . . John Phelan
Grade plan . . . PK-12
Total enrollment '09-10 . . . 3,453
Grade 12 enrollment, '09-10 . . . 260
Graduation rate . . . 94.8%
Dropout rate . . . 2.4%
Per-pupil expenditure . . . $11,338
Avg teacher salary . . . $67,600
Student/teacher ratio '08-09 . . . 14.9 to 1
Highly-qualified teachers, '08-09 . . . 98.4%
Teachers licensed in assigned subject . . 99.6%
Students per computer . . . 3

Massachusetts Competency Assessment System (MCAS), 2009 results

	English		Math	
	% Prof	CPI	% Prof	CPI
Gr 4	80%	92.5	68%	89.2
Gr 6	81%	93.6	81%	92
Gr 8	94%	98	65%	86.4
Gr 10	97%	99.1	94%	98.2

Other School Districts (see Appendix D for data)

South Middlesex Vocational Tech

©2010 Information Publications, Inc. All rights reserved. Photocopying prohibited. For additional copies, contact the publisher at www.informationpublications.com or (877)544-INFO (4636)

©2010 Information Publications, Inc. All rights reserved. Photocopying prohibited. For additional copies, contact the publisher at www.informationpublications.com or (877)544-INFO (4636)

Demographics & Socio-Economic Characteristics

Population

1990	2,797
2000	3,909
Male	1,977
Female	1,932
2008	4,482
2010 (projected)††	5,197
2020 (projected)††	7,196

Race & Hispanic Origin, 2000

Race	
White	3,846
Black/African American	6
American Indian/Alaska Native	3
Asian	19
Hawaiian Native/Pacific Islander	0
Other Race	11
Two or more races	24
Hispanic origin	52

Age & Nativity, 2000

Under 5 years	293
18 years and over	2,694
21 years and over	2,588
65 years and over	271
85 years and over	25
Median Age	35.9
Native-born	3,824
Foreign-born	85

Age, 2020 (projected)††

Under 5 years	599
5 to 19 years	1,582
20 to 39 years	1,876
40 to 64 years	2,279
65 years and over	860

Educational Attainment, 2000

Population 25 years and over	2,504
High School graduates or higher	92.6%
Bachelor's degree or higher	33.8%
Graduate degree	7.1%

Income & Poverty, 1999

Per capita income,	$23,072
Median household income	$61,462
Median family income	$66,058
Persons in poverty	143
H'holds receiving public assistance	17
H'holds receiving social security	252

Households, 2000

Total households	1,308
With persons under 18	606
With persons over 65	195
Family households	1,071
Single person households	179
Persons per household	3.0
Persons per family	3.3

Labor & Employment, 2000

Civilian labor force	2,162
Unemployment rate	2.7%
Civilian labor force, 2008†	2,479
Unemployment rate†	7.2%
Civilian labor force, 12/09†	2,550
Unemployment rate†	9.5%
Employed persons 16 years and over, by occupation:	
Managers & professionals	814
Service occupations	285
Sales & office occupations	446
Farming, fishing & forestry	6
Construction & maintenance	234
Production & transportation	319
Self-employed persons	149

Most demographic data is from the 2000 Decennial Census
† Massachusetts Department of Revenue
†† University of Massachusetts, MISER

General Information

Town of Hubbardston
7A Main St
PO Box 206
Hubbardston, MA 01452
978-928-5735

Elevation	993 ft.
Land area (square miles)	41.0
Water area (square miles)	0.9
Population density, 2008 (est)	109.3
Year incorporated	1767
Website	www.hubbardstonma.us

Voters & Government Information

Government type	Open Town Meeting
Number of Selectmen	3
US Congressional District(s)	1

Registered Voters, October 2008

Total	3,039
Democrats	524
Republicans	467
Unaffiliated/other	2,021

Local Officials, 2010

Chair, Bd. of Sel.	Matt Castriotta
Manager/Admin	Debra Roussel
Town Clerk	Joyce E. Green
Treasurer	James Dunbar
Tax Collector	C. Washburn-Doane
Tax Assessor	John Prentiss
Attorney	NA
Public Works	Lyn Gauthier
Building	Larry Brandt
Comm Dev/Planning	Vincent Ritchie
Police Chief	Dennis Perron
Fire Chief	Robert Hayes

Housing & Construction

New Privately Owned Housing Units Authorized by Building Permit

	Single Family	Total Bldgs	Total Units
2006	34	34	34
2007	18	18	18
2008	13	13	13

Parcel Count by Property Class, 2010

Total	NA
Single family	NA
Multiple units	NA
Apartments	NA
Condos	NA
Vacant land	NA
Open space	NA
Commercial	NA
Industrial	NA
Misc. residential	NA
Other use	NA

Public Library

Hubbardston Public Library
PO Box D
Hubbardston, MA 01452
(978)928-4775

Director	Jayne Arata

Library Statistics, FY 2008

Population served, 2007	4,461
Registered users	1,427
Circulation	17,415
Reference transactons	503
Total program attendance	0
per capita:	
Holdings	3.36
Operating income	$15.42
Internet Access	
Internet computers available	1
Weekly users	10

Municipal Finance

Debt at year end 2008	$711,723
Moody's rating, July 2009	NA

Revenues, 2008

Total	$7,330,209
From all taxes	5,939,338
Federal aid	0
State aid	584,027
From other governments	50,704
Charges for services	58,256
Licenses, permits & fees	58,400
Fines & forfeits	0
Interfund transfers	533,010
Misc/other/special assessments	53,237

Expenditures, 2008

Total	$6,778,928
General government	446,235
Public safety	1,186,112
Other/fixed costs	407,279
Human services	57,710
Culture & recreation	73,213
Debt Service	181,959
Education	3,570,407
Public works	834,224
Intergovernmental	21,789

Taxation, 2010

Property type	Valuation	Rate
Total	NA	-
Residential	NA	NA
Open space	NA	NA
Commercial	NA	NA
Industrial	NA	NA
Personal	NA	NA

Average Single Family Tax Bill, 2010

Avg. assessed home value	NA
Avg. single fam. tax bill	NA
Hi-Lo ranking	NA

Police & Crime, 2008

Number of police officers	5
Violent crimes	8
Property crimes	36

Local School District

(school data 2007-08, except as noted)

Hubbardston (non-op)
8 Elm Street
Hubbardston, MA 01452
978-928-4487

Superintendent	Maureen Marshall

Non-operating district.
Resident students are sent to the Other School Districts listed below.

Grade plan	NA
Total enrollment '09-10	NA
Grade 12 enrollment, '09-10	NA
Graduation rate	NA
Dropout rate	NA
Per-pupil expenditure	NA
Avg teacher salary	NA
Student/teacher ratio '08-09	NA
Highly-qualified teachers, '08-09	NA
Teachers licensed in assigned subject	NA
Students per computer	NA

Other School Districts (see Appendix D for data)
Quabbin Regional, Montachusett Vocational Tech

See Introduction for an explanation of all data sources.

Demographics & Socio-Economic Characteristics

Population

1990	17,233
2000	18,113
Male	8,956
Female	9,157
2008	19,597
2010 (projected)††	18,227
2020 (projected)††	18,079

Race & Hispanic Origin, 2000

Race	
White	17,048
Black/African American	165
American Indian/Alaska Native	23
Asian	254
Hawaiian Native/Pacific Islander	10
Other Race	254
Two or more races	359
Hispanic origin	554

Age & Nativity, 2000

Under 5 years	1,192
18 years and over	13,766
21 years and over	13,260
65 years and over	2,214
85 years and over	184
Median Age	37.3
Native-born	15,434
Foreign-born	2,679

Age, 2020 (projected)††

Under 5 years	997
5 to 19 years	2,997
20 to 39 years	4,426
40 to 64 years	6,352
65 years and over	3,307

Educational Attainment, 2000

Population 25 years and over	12,563
High School graduates or higher	85.0%
Bachelor's degree or higher	28.4%
Graduate degree	10.4%

Income & Poverty, 1999

Per capita income,	$26,679
Median household income	$58,549
Median family income	$70,145
Persons in poverty	805
H'holds receiving public assistance	180
H'holds receiving social security	1,721

Households, 2000

Total households	6,990
With persons under 18	2,394
With persons over 65	1,653
Family households	4,845
Single person households	1,761
Persons per household	2.6
Persons per family	3.1

Labor & Employment, 2000

Civilian labor force	10,334
Unemployment rate	2.8%
Civilian labor force, 2008†	11,747
Unemployment rate†	6.6%
Civilian labor force, 12/09†	11,854
Unemployment rate†	8.2%
Employed persons 16 years and over, by occupation:	
Managers & professionals	4,060
Service occupations	1,135
Sales & office occupations	2,486
Farming, fishing & forestry	8
Construction & maintenance	864
Production & transportation	1,495
Self-employed persons	494

Most demographic data is from the 2000 Decennial Census
† Massachusetts Department of Revenue
†† University of Massachusetts, MISER

General Information

Town of Hudson
78 Main St
Hudson, MA 01749
978-562-9963

Elevation	250 ft.
Land area (square miles)	11.5
Water area (square miles)	0.3
Population density, 2008 (est)	1,704.1
Year incorporated	1866
Website	www.townofhudson.org

Voters & Government Information

Government type	Open Town Meeting
Number of Selectmen	5
US Congressional District(s)	5

Registered Voters, October 2008

Total	12,603
Democrats	3,061
Republicans	1,501
Unaffiliated/other	7,936

Local Officials, 2010

Chair, Bd. of Sel.	Joseph Durant
Manager/Exec.	Paul Blazar
Town Clerk	Joan Wordell
Finance Director	Christopher Sandini
Tax Collector	Dianne Cush
Tax Assessor	Joanne McIntyre (Chr)
Attorney	NA
Public Works	Anthony Marques
Building	Jeffrey Wood
Comm Dev/Planning	Jennifer Burke
Police Chief	Richard Braga Jr
Fire Chief	John Blood

Housing & Construction

New Privately Owned Housing Units Authorized by Building Permit

	Single Family	Total Bldgs	Total Units
2006	64	64	64
2007	41	41	41
2008	27	27	27

Parcel Count by Property Class, 2010

Total	7,028
Single family	4,357
Multiple units	457
Apartments	78
Condos	1,309
Vacant land	366
Open space	0
Commercial	172
Industrial	167
Misc. residential	56
Other use	66

Public Library

Hudson Public Library
3 Washington Street at Wood Square
Hudson, MA 01749
(978)568-9644

Director: Patricia E. Desmond

Library Statistics, FY 2008

Population served, 2007	19,580
Registered users	12,022
Circulation	204,820
Reference transactons	5,340
Total program attendance	69,644
per capita:	
Holdings	3.76
Operating income	$34.19
Internet Access	
Internet computers available	8
Weekly users	157

Municipal Finance

Debt at year end 2008	$31,003,778
Moody's rating, July 2009	A1

Revenues, 2008

Total	$58,172,580
From all taxes	34,113,483
Federal aid	0
State aid	10,955,602
From other governments	114,772
Charges for services	5,192,470
Licenses, permits & fees	274,322
Fines & forfeits	0
Interfund transfers	4,511,275
Misc/other/special assessments	1,505,328

Expenditures, 2008

Total	$51,743,646
General government	1,860,323
Public safety	5,452,657
Other/fixed costs	3,931,631
Human services	368,891
Culture & recreation	870,435
Debt Service	3,569,318
Education	28,829,326
Public works	5,198,660
Intergovernmental	1,662,405

Taxation, 2010

Property type	Valuation	Rate
Total	$2,330,973,000	-
Residential	1,891,583,075	13.02
Open space	0	0.00
Commercial	175,006,525	25.30
Industrial	226,035,400	25.30
Personal	38,348,000	25.30

Average Single Family Tax Bill, 2010

Avg. assessed home value	$314,755
Avg. single fam. tax bill	$4,098
Hi-Lo ranking	128/301

Police & Crime, 2008

Number of police officers	31
Violent crimes	2
Property crimes	172

Local School District

(school data 2007-08, except as noted)

Hudson
155 Apsley Street
Hudson, MA 01749
978-567-6100

Superintendent	Kevin Lyons
Grade plan	PK-12
Total enrollment '09-10	3,071
Grade 12 enrollment, '09-10	239
Graduation rate	86.1%
Dropout rate	4.6%
Per-pupil expenditure	$11,490
Avg teacher salary	$65,727
Student/teacher ratio '08-09	13.1 to 1
Highly-qualified teachers, '08-09	98.7%
Teachers licensed in assigned subject	98.1%
Students per computer	2.4

Massachusetts Competency Assessment System (MCAS), 2009 results

	English		Math	
	% Prof	CPI	% Prof	CPI
Gr 4	57%	83.1	38%	75.9
Gr 6	75%	89.4	53%	77.3
Gr 8	76%	89.5	34%	64.1
Gr 10	87%	95.3	81%	92.6

Other School Districts (see Appendix D for data)
Assabet Valley Vocational Tech

©2010 Information Publications, Inc. All rights reserved. Photocopying prohibited. For additional copies, contact the publisher at www.informationpublications.com or (877)544-INFO (4636)

See Introduction for an explanation of all data sources.

©2010 Information Publications, Inc. All rights reserved. Photocopying prohibited. For additional copies, contact the publisher at www.informationpublications.com or (877)544-INFO (4636)

Demographics & Socio-Economic Characteristics

Population

1990 . . . 10,466
2000 . . . 11,050
Male . . . 5,332
Female . . . 5,718
2008 . . . 11,041
2010 (projected)†† . . . 11,491
2020 (projected)†† . . . 11,563

Race & Hispanic Origin, 2000

Race
White . . . 10,713
Black/African American . . . 51
American Indian/Alaska Native . . . 34
Asian . . . 98
Hawaiian Native/Pacific Islander . . . 5
Other Race . . . 51
Two or more races . . . 98
Hispanic origin . . . 120

Age & Nativity, 2000

Under 5 years . . . 628
18 years and over . . . 8,612
21 years and over . . . 8,324
65 years and over . . . 1,327
85 years and over . . . 108
Median Age . . . 40.2
Native-born . . . 10,527
Foreign-born . . . 523

Age, 2020 (projected)††

Under 5 years . . . 536
5 to 19 years . . . 1,663
20 to 39 years . . . 2,337
40 to 64 years . . . 4,542
65 years and over . . . 2,485

Educational Attainment, 2000

Population 25 years and over. . . 7,957
High School graduates or higher . . . 90.1%
Bachelor's degree or higher . . . 30.1%
Graduate degree . . . 10.6%

Income & Poverty, 1999

Per capita income, . . . $26,331
Median household income . . . $52,377
Median family income . . . $62,294
Persons in poverty . . . 918
H'holds receiving public assistance . . . 119
H'holds receiving social security . . . 1,198

Households, 2000

Total households . . . 4,522
With persons under 18 . . . 1,308
With persons over 65 . . . 1,013
Family households . . . 2,821
Single person households . . . 1,329
Persons per household . . . 2.4
Persons per family . . . 3.1

Labor & Employment, 2000

Civilian labor force . . . 6,123
Unemployment rate . . . 4.0%
Civilian labor force, 2008† . . . 6,392
Unemployment rate† . . . 6.6%
Civilian labor force, 12/09† . . . 6,327
Unemployment rate† . . . 9.7%
Employed persons 16 years and over, by occupation:
Managers & professionals . . . 2,311
Service occupations . . . 800
Sales & office occupations . . . 1,618
Farming, fishing & forestry . . . 11
Construction & maintenance . . . 561
Production & transportation . . . 579
Self-employed persons . . . 487

Most demographic data is from the 2000 Decennial Census
† Massachusetts Department of Revenue
†† University of Massachusetts, MISER

General Information

Town of Hull
253 Atlantic Ave
Hull, MA 02045
781-925-2000

Elevation . . . 50 ft.
Land area (square miles) . . . 3.0
Water area (square miles) . . . 25.2
Population density, 2008 (est) . . . 3,680.3
Year incorporated . . . 1647
Website . . . www.town.hull.ma.us

Voters & Government Information

Government type . . . Open Town Meeting
Number of Selectmen . . . 5
US Congressional District(s) . . . 10

Registered Voters, October 2008

Total . . . 7,763
Democrats . . . 2,801
Republicans . . . 841
Unaffiliated/other . . . 4,060

Local Officials, 2010

Chair, Bd. of Sel. . . . John D. Reilly Jr
Town Manager . . . Philip E. Lemnios
Clerk . . . Janet Bennett
Accountant . . . Marcia Bohinc
Treas/Collector . . . Joseph A. DiVito Jr
Tax Assessor . . . Elsa Miller
Attorney . . . James B. Lampke
Public Works . . . Joseph Stigliani
Building . . . Peter Lombardo
Comm Dev/Planning . . . Robert Fultz
Police Chief . . . Richard K. Billings
Fire Chief . . . Robert Hollingshead (Actg)

Housing & Construction

New Privately Owned Housing Units Authorized by Building Permit

	Single Family	Total Bldgs	Total Units
2006	10	10	10
2007	13	13	13
2008	8	8	8

Parcel Count by Property Class, 2010

Total . . . 5,344
Single family . . . 3,753
Multiple units . . . 193
Apartments . . . 46
Condos . . . 823
Vacant land . . . 362
Open space . . . 0
Commercial . . . 96
Industrial . . . 0
Misc. residential . . . 31
Other use . . . 40

Public Library

Hull Public Library
9 Main St.
Hull, MA 02045
(781)925-2295

Library Director . . . Daniel J. Johnson

Library Statistics, FY 2008

Population served, 2007 . . . 11,067
Registered users . . . 5,660
Circulation . . . 52,268
Reference transactons . . . 1,805
Total program attendance . . . 47,803

per capita:

Holdings . . . 2.56
Operating income . . . $27.51

Internet Access

Internet computers available . . . 9
Weekly users . . . 251

Municipal Finance

Debt at year end 2008 . . . $14,412,830
Moody's rating, July 2009 . . . NA

Revenues, 2008

Total . . . $31,604,501
From all taxes . . . 22,059,561
Federal aid . . . 214,492
State aid . . . 6,782,821
From other governments . . . 66,808
Charges for services . . . 487,133
Licenses, permits & fees . . . 223,408
Fines & forfeits . . . 81,180
Interfund transfers . . . 1,059,422
Misc/other/special assessments . . . 314,838

Expenditures, 2008

Total . . . $31,399,536
General government . . . 1,791,131
Public safety . . . 5,462,791
Other/fixed costs . . . 7,106,196
Human services . . . 502,213
Culture & recreation . . . 371,490
Debt Service . . . 1,006,794
Education . . . 12,618,725
Public works . . . 1,221,397
Intergovernmental . . . 1,307,399

Taxation, 2010

Property type	Valuation	Rate
Total	$1,950,842,140	-
Residential	1,869,906,827	11.47
Open space	0	0.00
Commercial	58,094,173	11.47
Industrial	0	0.00
Personal	22,841,140	11.47

Average Single Family Tax Bill, 2010

Avg. assessed home value . . . $390,280
Avg. single fam. tax bill . . . $4,477
Hi-Lo ranking . . . 101/301

Police & Crime, 2008

Number of police officers . . . 24
Violent crimes . . . 42
Property crimes . . . 150

Local School District

(school data 2007-08, except as noted)

Hull
180 Harborview Road
Hull, MA 02045
781-925-4400

Superintendent . . . Kathleen Tyrell
Grade plan . . . PK-12
Total enrollment '09-10 . . . 1,202
Grade 12 enrollment, '09-10 . . . 77
Graduation rate . . . 86.8%
Dropout rate . . . 8.3%
Per-pupil expenditure . . . $13,701
Avg teacher salary . . . $55,671
Student/teacher ratio '08-09 . . . 13.0 to 1
Highly-qualified teachers, '08-09 . . . 97.3%
Teachers licensed in assigned subject . . 95.7%
Students per computer . . . 2

Massachusetts Competency Assessment System (MCAS), 2009 results

	English		Math	
	% Prof	CPI	% Prof	CPI
Gr 4	40%	73.6	42%	77.2
Gr 6	62%	83	53%	74.4
Gr 8	83%	93.9	28%	65.2
Gr 10	89%	96.3	91%	96

Other School Districts (see Appendix D for data)
None

See Introduction for an explanation of all data sources.

Demographics & Socio-Economic Characteristics

Population

1990	1,987
2000	2,174
Male	1,079
Female	1,095
2008	2,219
2010 (projected)††	2,226
2020 (projected)††	2,304

Race & Hispanic Origin, 2000

Race	
White	2,121
Black/African American	9
American Indian/Alaska Native	4
Asian	9
Hawaiian Native/Pacific Islander	0
Other Race	6
Two or more races	25
Hispanic origin	40

Age & Nativity, 2000

Under 5 years	122
18 years and over	1,572
21 years and over	1,494
65 years and over	211
85 years and over	23
Median Age	37.0
Native-born	2,161
Foreign-born	31

Age, 2020 (projected)††

Under 5 years	128
5 to 19 years	384
20 to 39 years	532
40 to 64 years	785
65 years and over	475

Educational Attainment, 2000

Population 25 years and over	1,434
High School graduates or higher	89.7%
Bachelor's degree or higher	20.2%
Graduate degree	9.5%

Income & Poverty, 1999

Per capita income,	$19,385
Median household income	$48,958
Median family income	$52,308
Persons in poverty	126
H'holds receiving public assistance	26
H'holds receiving social security	177

Households, 2000

Total households	809
With persons under 18	308
With persons over 65	153
Family households	597
Single person households	155
Persons per household	2.7
Persons per family	3.1

Labor & Employment, 2000

Civilian labor force	1,228
Unemployment rate	3.7%
Civilian labor force, 2008†	1,287
Unemployment rate†	8.4%
Civilian labor force, 12/09†	1,297
Unemployment rate†	10.7%
Employed persons 16 years and over, by occupation:	
Managers & professionals	382
Service occupations	153
Sales & office occupations	289
Farming, fishing & forestry	15
Construction & maintenance	117
Production & transportation	226
Self-employed persons	92

Most demographic data is from the 2000 Decennial Census
† Massachusetts Department of Revenue
†† University of Massachusetts, MISER

General Information

Town of Huntington
PO Box 430
Huntington, MA 01050
413-667-3500

Elevation	382 ft.
Land area (square miles)	26.6
Water area (square miles)	0.3
Population density, 2008 (est)	83.4
Year incorporated	1855
Website	huntingtonma.org

Voters & Government Information

Government type	Open Town Meeting
Number of Selectmen	3
US Congressional District(s)	1

Registered Voters, October 2008

Total	1,405
Democrats	282
Republicans	178
Unaffiliated/other	927

Local Officials, 2010

Chair, Bd. of Sel.	Al LaFrance
Manager/Admin	Helen Speckels
Town Clerk	Pamela Donovan-Hall
Finance	Ann Marie Knox
Tax Collector	Ann Marie Knox
Tax Assessor	Neil Wheeler
Attorney	Kopelman & Paige
Public Works	Wayne McKinney
Building	Paul Tacy
Comm Dev/Planning	Paul Tacy
Police Chief	Robert Garriepy
Emerg/Fire Chief	Gary Dahill

Housing & Construction

New Privately Owned Housing Units Authorized by Building Permit

	Single Family	Total Bldgs	Total Units
2006	7	7	7
2007	7	7	7
2008	4	4	4

Parcel Count by Property Class, 2010

Total	1,378
Single family	733
Multiple units	47
Apartments	4
Condos	0
Vacant land	352
Open space	0
Commercial	17
Industrial	11
Misc. residential	49
Other use	165

Public Library

Huntington Public Library
PO Box 597
Huntington, MA 01050
(413)667-3506

Librarian	Margaret Nareau

Library Statistics, FY 2008

Population served, 2007	2,193
Registered users	1,821
Circulation	16,241
Reference transactons	1,247
Total program attendance	10,671
per capita:	
Holdings	7.84
Operating income	$29.87
Internet Access	
Internet computers available	5
Weekly users	90

Municipal Finance

Debt at year end 2008	$168,097
Moody's rating, July 2009	NA

Revenues, 2008

Total	$3,849,565
From all taxes	2,862,147
Federal aid	0
State aid	584,070
From other governments	8,751
Charges for services	56,966
Licenses, permits & fees	25,450
Fines & forfeits	0
Interfund transfers	203,765
Misc/other/special assessments	54,208

Expenditures, 2008

Total	$3,819,918
General government	263,134
Public safety	196,564
Other/fixed costs	150,243
Human services	41,185
Culture & recreation	82,161
Debt Service	96,729
Education	2,531,753
Public works	446,494
Intergovernmental	11,655

Taxation, 2010

Property type	Valuation	Rate
Total	$198,595,072	-
Residential	187,283,808	14.09
Open space	0	0.00
Commercial	5,326,373	14.09
Industrial	1,566,400	14.09
Personal	4,418,491	14.09

Average Single Family Tax Bill, 2010

Avg. assessed home value	$200,847
Avg. single fam. tax bill	$2,830
Hi-Lo ranking	250/301

Police & Crime, 2008

Number of police officers	NA
Violent crimes	NA
Property crimes	NA

Local School District

(school data 2007-08, except as noted)

Huntington (non-op)
12 Littleville Road
Huntington, MA 01050
413-685-1011

Superintendent	David Hopson

Non-operating district.
Resident students are sent to the Other School Districts listed below.

Grade plan	NA
Total enrollment '09-10	NA
Grade 12 enrollment, '09-10	NA
Graduation rate	NA
Dropout rate	NA
Per-pupil expenditure	NA
Avg teacher salary	NA
Student/teacher ratio '08-09	NA
Highly-qualified teachers, '08-09	NA
Teachers licensed in assigned subject	NA
Students per computer	NA

Other School Districts (see Appendix D for data)
Gateway Regional

©2010 Information Publications, Inc. All rights reserved. Photocopying prohibited. For additional copies, contact the publisher at www.informationpublications.com or (877)544-INFO (4636)

See Introduction for an explanation of all data sources.

Demographics & Socio-Economic Characteristics

Population

1990	11,873
2000	12,987
Male	6,145
Female	6,842
2008	13,219
2010 (projected)††	13,138
2020 (projected)††	13,221

Race & Hispanic Origin, 2000

Race	
White	12,675
Black/African American	51
American Indian/Alaska Native	11
Asian	104
Hawaiian Native/Pacific Islander	1
Other Race	43
Two or more races	102
Hispanic origin	135

Age & Nativity, 2000

Under 5 years	744
18 years and over	10,002
21 years and over	9,711
65 years and over	2,031
85 years and over	275
Median Age	41.7
Native-born	12,517
Foreign-born	470

Age, 2020 (projected)††

Under 5 years	655
5 to 19 years	1,968
20 to 39 years	2,775
40 to 64 years	4,513
65 years and over	3,310

Educational Attainment, 2000

Population 25 years and over	9,311
High School graduates or higher	92.2%
Bachelor's degree or higher	41.4%
Graduate degree	17.5%

Income & Poverty, 1999

Per capita income,	$32,516
Median household income	$57,284
Median family income	$74,931
Persons in poverty	921
H'holds receiving public assistance	66
H'holds receiving social security	1,573

Households, 2000

Total households	5,290
With persons under 18	1,658
With persons over 65	1,412
Family households	3,462
Single person households	1,496
Persons per household	2.4
Persons per family	3.0

Labor & Employment, 2000

Civilian labor force	7,076
Unemployment rate	2.5%
Civilian labor force, 2008†	7,421
Unemployment rate†	5.0%
Civilian labor force, 12/09†	7,391
Unemployment rate†	7.7%
Employed persons 16 years and over, by occupation:	
Managers & professionals	3,225
Service occupations	921
Sales & office occupations	1,637
Farming, fishing & forestry	49
Construction & maintenance	526
Production & transportation	539
Self-employed persons	747

Most demographic data is from the 2000 Decennial Census
† Massachusetts Department of Revenue
†† University of Massachusetts, MISER

General Information

Town of Ipswich
25 Green St
Ipswich, MA 01938
978-356-6600

Elevation	50 ft.
Land area (square miles)	32.6
Water area (square miles)	9.6
Population density, 2008 (est)	405.5
Year incorporated	1634
Website	www.town.ipswich.ma.us

Voters & Government Information

Government type	Open Town Meeting
Number of Selectmen	5
US Congressional District(s)	6

Registered Voters, October 2008

Total	10,168
Democrats	2,226
Republicans	1,589
Unaffiliated/other	6,331

Local Officials, 2010

Chair, Bd. of Sel.	Patrick J. McNally
Manager	Robert T. Markel
Clerk	Pamela Z. Carakatsane
Finance Director	Rita M. Negri
Tax Collector	Kevin A. Mertz
Tax Assessor	Frank J. Ragonese
Attorney	NA
Public Works	Robert C. Gravino
Building	James Sperber
Planning	Glenn C. Gibbs
Police Chief	Paul A. Nikas
Emerg/Fire Chief	Arthur Howe III

Housing & Construction

New Privately Owned Housing Units Authorized by Building Permit

	Single Family	Total Bldgs	Total Units
2006	21	24	45
2007	17	17	17
2008	13	15	25

Parcel Count by Property Class, 2010

Total	5,683
Single family	3,743
Multiple units	264
Apartments	42
Condos	714
Vacant land	406
Open space	0
Commercial	159
Industrial	116
Misc. residential	61
Other use	178

Public Library

Ipswich Public Library
25 North Main St.
Ipswich, MA 01938
(978)356-6648

Director	Victor Dyer

Library Statistics, FY 2008

Population served, 2007	13,245
Registered users	9,697
Circulation	154,270
Reference transactons	5,603
Total program attendance	103,000
per capita:	
Holdings	7.33
Operating income	$39.99
Internet Access	
Internet computers available	12
Weekly users	281

Municipal Finance

Debt at year end 2008	$41,890,100
Moody's rating, July 2009	A1

Revenues, 2008

Total	$36,095,974
From all taxes	27,118,544
Federal aid	17,445
State aid	6,315,705
From other governments	9,370
Charges for services	243,951
Licenses, permits & fees	508,856
Fines & forfeits	31,789
Interfund transfers	421,234
Misc/other/special assessments	714,540

Expenditures, 2008

Total	$35,389,000
General government	2,226,623
Public safety	4,129,637
Other/fixed costs	1,659,580
Human services	351,803
Culture & recreation	631,555
Debt Service	4,039,288
Education	19,014,363
Public works	2,957,454
Intergovernmental	240,187

Taxation, 2010

Property type	Valuation	Rate
Total	$2,446,150,549	-
Residential	2,175,491,225	11.54
Open space	0	0.00
Commercial	113,798,094	11.54
Industrial	128,337,360	11.54
Personal	28,523,870	11.54

Average Single Family Tax Bill, 2010

Avg. assessed home value	$456,271
Avg. single fam. tax bill	$5,265
Hi-Lo ranking	65/301

Police & Crime, 2008

Number of police officers	25
Violent crimes	NA
Property crimes	NA

Local School District

(school data 2007-08, except as noted)

Ipswich
1 Lord Square
Ipswich, MA 01938
978-356-2935

Superintendent	Richard Korb
Grade plan	PK-12
Total enrollment '09-10	2,137
Grade 12 enrollment, '09-10	151
Graduation rate	89.8%
Dropout rate	5.4%
Per-pupil expenditure	$10,186
Avg teacher salary	$59,829
Student/teacher ratio '08-09	14.2 to 1
Highly-qualified teachers, '08-09	98.4%
Teachers licensed in assigned subject	98.5%
Students per computer	4.1

Massachusetts Competency Assessment System (MCAS), 2009 results

	English		Math	
	% Prof	CPI	% Prof	CPI
Gr 4	68%	89	61%	86.1
Gr 6	83%	93.4	73%	90.3
Gr 8	91%	97.7	76%	90.1
Gr 10	92%	97.8	88%	95.8

Other School Districts (see Appendix D for data)
Whittier Vocational Tech

©2010 Information Publications, Inc. All rights reserved. Photocopying prohibited. For additional copies, contact the publisher at www.informationpublications.com or (877)544-INFO (4636)

See Introduction for an explanation of all data sources.

Demographics & Socio-Economic Characteristics

Population

1990	9,045
2000	11,780
Male	5,658
Female	6,122
2008	12,328
2010 (projected)††	14,158
2020 (projected)††	17,147

Race & Hispanic Origin, 2000

Race	
White	11,427
Black/African American	113
American Indian/Alaska Native	14
Asian	51
Hawaiian Native/Pacific Islander	1
Other Race	59
Two or more races	115
Hispanic origin	88

Age & Nativity, 2000

Under 5 years	986
18 years and over	8,544
21 years and over	8,254
65 years and over	1,601
85 years and over	261
Median Age	37.2
Native-born	11,411
Foreign-born	369

Age, 2020 (projected)††

Under 5 years	1,176
5 to 19 years	3,342
20 to 39 years	3,985
40 to 64 years	5,176
65 years and over	3,468

Educational Attainment, 2000

Population 25 years and over	7,943
High School graduates or higher	89.4%
Bachelor's degree or higher	31.7%
Graduate degree	9.2%

Income & Poverty, 1999

Per capita income,	$23,370
Median household income	$53,780
Median family income	$65,101
Persons in poverty	670
H'holds receiving public assistance	65
H'holds receiving social security	1,166

Households, 2000

Total households	4,248
With persons under 18	1,703
With persons over 65	1,062
Family households	3,138
Single person households	926
Persons per household	2.7
Persons per family	3.2

Labor & Employment, 2000

Civilian labor force	6,013
Unemployment rate	4.3%
Civilian labor force, 2008†	6,509
Unemployment rate†	6.4%
Civilian labor force, 12/09†	6,481
Unemployment rate†	9.7%
Employed persons 16 years and over, by occupation:	
Managers & professionals	2,087
Service occupations	922
Sales & office occupations	1,820
Farming, fishing & forestry	13
Construction & maintenance	444
Production & transportation	471
Self-employed persons	414

Most demographic data is from the 2000 Decennial Census
† Massachusetts Department of Revenue
†† University of Massachusetts, MISER

General Information

Town of Kingston
26 Evergreen St
Kingston, MA 02364
781-585-0500

Elevation	50 ft.
Land area (square miles)	18.5
Water area (square miles)	1.9
Population density, 2008 (est)	666.4
Year incorporated	1726
Website	www.kingstonmass.org

Voters & Government Information

Government type	Open Town Meeting
Number of Selectmen	5
US Congressional District(s)	10

Registered Voters, October 2008

Total	8,649
Democrats	2,188
Republicans	1,454
Unaffiliated/other	4,953

Local Officials, 2010

Chair, Bd. of Sel.	Sandra D. MacFarlane
Administrator	Jill R. Myers
Town Clerk	Mary Lou Murzyn
Treasurer	John S. LaBrache
Tax Collector	Priscilla L. Palombo
Tax Assessor	Anne Dunn
Attorney	Blatman, Bobrowski & Mead
Public Works	Paul F. Basler
Building	Paul L. Armstrong
Comm Dev/Planning	Thomas Bott
Police Chief	Joseph J. Rebello
Emerg/Fire Chief	Robert T. Heath

Housing & Construction

New Privately Owned Housing Units Authorized by Building Permit

	Single Family	Total Bldgs	Total Units
2006	24	24	24
2007	16	16	16
2008	22	24	28

Parcel Count by Property Class, 2010

Total	4,996
Single family	3,680
Multiple units	123
Apartments	20
Condos	186
Vacant land	613
Open space	0
Commercial	173
Industrial	84
Misc. residential	16
Other use	101

Public Library

Kingston Public Library
6 Green Street
Kingston, MA 02364
(781)585-0517

Director	Sia Stewart

Library Statistics, FY 2008

Population served, 2007	12,339
Registered users	7,199
Circulation	165,265
Reference transactons	6,765
Total program attendance	75,123
per capita:	
Holdings	5.76
Operating income	$52.30
Internet Access	
Internet computers available	17
Weekly users	233

Municipal Finance

Debt at year end 2008	$63,474,636
Moody's rating, July 2009	A2

Revenues, 2008

Total	$34,316,192
From all taxes	24,283,305
Federal aid	26,330
State aid	6,502,261
From other governments	0
Charges for services	520,604
Licenses, permits & fees	482,642
Fines & forfeits	51,196
Interfund transfers	598,220
Misc/other/special assessments	925,817

Expenditures, 2008

Total	$33,628,988
General government	1,870,962
Public safety	4,663,994
Other/fixed costs	3,270,931
Human services	423,711
Culture & recreation	825,987
Debt Service	3,013,353
Education	17,625,562
Public works	1,621,148
Intergovernmental	264,678

Taxation, 2010

Property type	Valuation	Rate
Total	$1,811,316,084	-
Residential	1,519,635,118	13.54
Open space	0	0.00
Commercial	236,800,557	13.54
Industrial	13,884,900	13.54
Personal	40,995,509	13.54

Average Single Family Tax Bill, 2010

Avg. assessed home value	$359,435
Avg. single fam. tax bill	$4,867
Hi-Lo ranking	84/301

Police & Crime, 2008

Number of police officers	23
Violent crimes	43
Property crimes	387

Local School District

(school data 2007-08, except as noted)

Kingston
250 Pembroke Street
Kingston, MA 02364
781-585-4313

Superintendent	John Tuffy
Grade plan	K-6
Total enrollment '09-10	1,180
Grade 12 enrollment, '09-10	0
Graduation rate	NA
Dropout rate	NA
Per-pupil expenditure	$10,146
Avg teacher salary	$62,505
Student/teacher ratio '08-09	16.4 to 1
Highly-qualified teachers, '08-09	100.0%
Teachers licensed in assigned subject	100.0%
Students per computer	10.5

Massachusetts Competency Assessment System (MCAS), 2009 results

	English		Math	
	% Prof	CPI	% Prof	CPI
Gr 4	63%	85.5	41%	77.8
Gr 6	75%	89.5	61%	82.6
Gr 8	NA	NA	NA	NA
Gr 10	NA	NA	NA	NA

Other School Districts (see Appendix D for data)
Silver Lake Regional

©2010 Information Publications, Inc. All rights reserved. Photocopying prohibited. For additional copies, contact the publisher at www.informationpublications.com or (877)544-INFO (4636)

Demographics & Socio-Economic Characteristics

Population

1990	7,785
2000	9,821
Male	4,756
Female	5,065
2008	10,515
2010 (projected)††	12,144
2020 (projected)††	14,809

Race & Hispanic Origin, 2000

Race	
White	9,555
Black/African American	30
American Indian/Alaska Native	14
Asian	58
Hawaiian Native/Pacific Islander	1
Other Race	49
Two or more races	114
Hispanic origin	104

Age & Nativity, 2000

Under 5 years	751
18 years and over	7,126
21 years and over	6,835
65 years and over	1,110
85 years and over	193
Median Age	37.8
Native-born	9,449
Foreign-born	372

Age, 2020 (projected)††

Under 5 years	959
5 to 19 years	2,998
20 to 39 years	3,501
40 to 64 years	4,913
65 years and over	2,438

Educational Attainment, 2000

Population 25 years and over	6,614
High School graduates or higher	87.2%
Bachelor's degree or higher	32.7%
Graduate degree	11.0%

Income & Poverty, 1999

Per capita income,	$26,046
Median household income	$70,495
Median family income	$75,838
Persons in poverty	284
H'holds receiving public assistance	38
H'holds receiving social security	736

Households, 2000

Total households	3,292
With persons under 18	1,412
With persons over 65	666
Family households	2,659
Single person households	483
Persons per household	2.9
Persons per family	3.2

Labor & Employment, 2000

Civilian labor force	5,306
Unemployment rate	2.6%
Civilian labor force, 2008†	6,109
Unemployment rate†	6.6%
Civilian labor force, 12/09†	6,060
Unemployment rate†	10.0%
Employed persons 16 years and over, by occupation:	
Managers & professionals	2,061
Service occupations	619
Sales & office occupations	1,434
Farming, fishing & forestry	45
Construction & maintenance	398
Production & transportation	611
Self-employed persons	380

Most demographic data is from the 2000 Decennial Census
† Massachusetts Department of Revenue
†† University of Massachusetts, MISER

General Information

Town of Lakeville
346 Bedford St
Lakeville, MA 02347
508-946-8800

Elevation	83 ft.
Land area (square miles)	29.9
Water area (square miles)	6.2
Population density, 2008 (est)	351.7
Year incorporated	1853
Website	www.lakevillema.org

Voters & Government Information

Government type	Open Town Meeting
Number of Selectmen	3
US Congressional District(s)	4

Registered Voters, October 2008

Total	7,327
Democrats	1,497
Republicans	1,245
Unaffiliated/other	4,506

Local Officials, 2010

Chair, Bd. of Sel.	Derek A. Maksy
Town Administrator	Rita Garbitt
Clerk	Janet L. Tracy
Finance Director	Cynthia McRae
Tax Collector	Debra Kenney
Tax Assessor	Janet Black
Attorney	Kopelman & Paige
Public Works	Christopher Peck
Building	Robert Iafrate
Planning	James Marot
Police Chief	Mark Sorel
Emerg/Fire Chief	Daniel Hopkins

Housing & Construction

New Privately Owned Housing Units Authorized by Building Permit

	Single Family	Total Bldgs	Total Units
2006	32	32	32
2007	44	44	44
2008	19	19	19

Parcel Count by Property Class, 2010

Total	4,809
Single family	3,733
Multiple units	16
Apartments	13
Condos	78
Vacant land	658
Open space	0
Commercial	97
Industrial	56
Misc. residential	42
Other use	116

Public Library

Lakeville Free Public Library
4 Precinct Street
Lakeville, MA 02347
(508)947-9028

Director	Olivia Melo

Library Statistics, FY 2008

Population served, 2007	10,587
Registered users	6,142
Circulation	142,796
Reference transactons	3,000
Total program attendance	85,975
per capita:	
Holdings	4.03
Operating income	$26.93
Internet Access	
Internet computers available	12
Weekly users	95

Municipal Finance

Debt at year end 2008	$4,392,427
Moody's rating, July 2009	NA

Revenues, 2008

Total	$21,465,706
From all taxes	15,899,752
Federal aid	11,622
State aid	3,938,922
From other governments	2,830
Charges for services	363,729
Licenses, permits & fees	390,345
Fines & forfeits	9,339
Interfund transfers	569,559
Misc/other/special assessments	139,804

Expenditures, 2008

Total	$21,613,947
General government	1,139,476
Public safety	2,576,797
Other/fixed costs	2,878,023
Human services	319,876
Culture & recreation	269,592
Debt Service	1,097,602
Education	12,465,554
Public works	683,946
Intergovernmental	153,982

Taxation, 2010

Property type	Valuation	Rate
Total	$1,549,658,450	-
Residential	1,311,866,900	10.22
Open space	0	0.00
Commercial	127,105,320	10.22
Industrial	82,498,900	10.22
Personal	28,187,330	10.22

Average Single Family Tax Bill, 2010

Avg. assessed home value	$324,041
Avg. single fam. tax bill	$3,312
Hi-Lo ranking	201/301

Police & Crime, 2008

Number of police officers	17
Violent crimes	4
Property crimes	184

Local School District

(school data 2007-08, except as noted)

Lakeville
98 Howland Rd
Lakeville, MA 02347
508-923-2000

Superintendent	John McCarthy
Grade plan	PK-4
Total enrollment '09-10	742
Grade 12 enrollment, '09-10	0
Graduation rate	NA
Dropout rate	NA
Per-pupil expenditure	$9,499
Avg teacher salary	$58,530
Student/teacher ratio '08-09	17.4 to 1
Highly-qualified teachers, '08-09	99.4%
Teachers licensed in assigned subject	99.2%
Students per computer	6

Massachusetts Competency Assessment System (MCAS), 2009 results

	English		Math	
	% Prof	CPI	% Prof	CPI
Gr 4	59%	83.7	55%	83
Gr 6	NA	NA	NA	NA
Gr 8	NA	NA	NA	NA
Gr 10	NA	NA	NA	NA

Other School Districts (see Appendix D for data)
Freetown-Lakeville Regional, Old Colony Vocational Tech

©2010 Information Publications, Inc. All rights reserved. Photocopying prohibited. For additional copies, contact the publisher at www.informationpublications.com or (877)544-INFO (4636)

See Introduction for an explanation of all data sources.

Demographics & Socio-Economic Characteristics

Population

1990	6,661
2000	7,380
Male	4,112
Female	3,268
2008	7,015
2010 (projected)††	6,068
2020 (projected)††	5,696

Race & Hispanic Origin, 2000

Race	
White	6,237
Black/African American	783
American Indian/Alaska Native	14
Asian	85
Hawaiian Native/Pacific Islander	0
Other Race	114
Two or more races	147
Hispanic origin	549

Age & Nativity, 2000

Under 5 years	367
18 years and over	5,775
21 years and over	5,421
65 years and over	733
85 years and over	122
Median Age	35.9
Native-born	6,925
Foreign-born	455

Age, 2020 (projected)††

Under 5 years	294
5 to 19 years	1,102
20 to 39 years	1,491
40 to 64 years	1,782
65 years and over	1,027

Educational Attainment, 2000

Population 25 years and over	4,989
High School graduates or higher	82.2%
Bachelor's degree or higher	30.9%
Graduate degree	12.0%

Income & Poverty, 1999

Per capita income,	$21,010
Median household income	$60,752
Median family income	$66,490
Persons in poverty	237
H'holds receiving public assistance	60
H'holds receiving social security	558

Households, 2000

Total households	2,049
With persons under 18	800
With persons over 65	479
Family households	1,552
Single person households	392
Persons per household	2.8
Persons per family	3.2

Labor & Employment, 2000

Civilian labor force	3,214
Unemployment rate	2.1%
Civilian labor force, 2008†	3,098
Unemployment rate†	7.3%
Civilian labor force, 12/09†	3,186
Unemployment rate†	9.3%
Employed persons 16 years and over, by occupation:	
Managers & professionals	1,518
Service occupations	357
Sales & office occupations	749
Farming, fishing & forestry	0
Construction & maintenance	262
Production & transportation	261
Self-employed persons	198

Most demographic data is from the 2000 Decennial Census
† Massachusetts Department of Revenue
†† University of Massachusetts, MISER

General Information

Town of Lancaster
695 Main St, Suite 1
Lancaster, MA 01523
978-365-3326

Elevation	300 ft.
Land area (square miles)	27.7
Water area (square miles)	0.5
Population density, 2008 (est)	253.2
Year incorporated	1653
Website	www.ci.lancaster.ma.us

Voters & Government Information

Government type	Open Town Meeting
Number of Selectmen	3
US Congressional District(s)	5

Registered Voters, October 2008

Total	4,704
Democrats	965
Republicans	748
Unaffiliated/other	2,957

Local Officials, 2010

Chair, Bd. of Sel.	Jennifer B. Leone
Town Administrator	Orlando Pacheco
Clerk	D. Susan Thompson
Finance Director	Cheryl Gariepy
Tax Collector	Charlotte LeBlanc
Tax Assessor	Cynthia K. Bradbury
Attorney	Kopelman & Paige
Public Works	John A. Foster
Building	Peter Munro
Planning	Noreen Piazza
Police Chief	Kevin D. Lamb
Emerg/Fire Chief	John Fleck

Housing & Construction

New Privately Owned Housing Units Authorized by Building Permit

	Single Family	Total Bldgs	Total Units
2006	63	63	63
2007	15	15	15
2008	11	11	11

Parcel Count by Property Class, 2010

Total	2,916
Single family	1,981
Multiple units	101
Apartments	19
Condos	143
Vacant land	436
Open space	0
Commercial	69
Industrial	50
Misc. residential	29
Other use	88

Public Library

Thayer Memorial Library
PO Box 5
Lancaster, MA 01523
(978)368-8928

Director	Joseph J. Mule

Library Statistics, FY 2008

Population served, 2007	7,047
Registered users	4,882
Circulation	103,136
Reference transactons	2,512
Total program attendance	0
per capita:	
Holdings	9.24
Operating income	$48.76
Internet Access	
Internet computers available	6
Weekly users	53

Municipal Finance

Debt at year end 2008	$17,626,466
Moody's rating, July 2009	A3

Revenues, 2008

Total	$15,548,512
From all taxes	12,885,679
Federal aid	0
State aid	1,192,348
From other governments	25,755
Charges for services	237,842
Licenses, permits & fees	160,415
Fines & forfeits	77,380
Interfund transfers	240,579
Misc/other/special assessments	364,257

Expenditures, 2008

Total	$14,880,131
General government	974,925
Public safety	1,536,742
Other/fixed costs	980,591
Human services	98,446
Culture & recreation	283,105
Debt Service	1,525,547
Education	8,774,728
Public works	706,047
Intergovernmental	0

Taxation, 2010

Property type	Valuation	Rate
Total	$826,026,350	-
Residential	728,730,268	16.07
Open space	0	0.00
Commercial	48,342,457	16.07
Industrial	29,707,100	16.07
Personal	19,246,525	16.07

Average Single Family Tax Bill, 2010

Avg. assessed home value	$309,536
Avg. single fam. tax bill	$4,974
Hi-Lo ranking	81/301

Police & Crime, 2008

Number of police officers	11
Violent crimes	9
Property crimes	50

Local School District

(school data 2007-08, except as noted)

Lancaster (non-op)
50 Mechanic Street
Bolton, MA 01740
978-779-0539

Superintendent.............Michael Wood

Non-operating district.
Resident students are sent to the Other School Districts listed below.

Grade plan	NA
Total enrollment '09-10	NA
Grade 12 enrollment, '09-10	NA
Graduation rate	NA
Dropout rate	NA
Per-pupil expenditure	NA
Avg teacher salary	NA
Student/teacher ratio '08-09	NA
Highly-qualified teachers, '08-09	NA
Teachers licensed in assigned subject	NA
Students per computer	NA

Other School Districts (see Appendix D for data)
Nashoba Regional, Minuteman Vocational Tech

©2010 Information Publications, Inc. All rights reserved. Photocopying prohibited. For additional copies, contact the publisher at www.informationpublications.com or (877)544-INFO (4636)

See Introduction for an explanation of all data sources.

Demographics & Socio-Economic Characteristics

Population

1990	3,032
2000	2,990
Male	1,470
Female	1,520
2008	2,866
2010 (projected)††	2,713
2020 (projected)††	2,435

Race & Hispanic Origin, 2000

Race	
White	2,911
Black/African American	21
American Indian/Alaska Native	1
Asian	24
Hawaiian Native/Pacific Islander	1
Other Race	5
Two or more races	27
Hispanic origin	20

Age & Nativity, 2000

Under 5 years	153
18 years and over	2,274
21 years and over	2,171
65 years and over	390
85 years and over	32
Median Age	40.2
Native-born	2,921
Foreign-born	69

Age, 2020 (projected)††

Under 5 years	112
5 to 19 years	403
20 to 39 years	533
40 to 64 years	885
65 years and over	502

Educational Attainment, 2000

Population 25 years and over	2,093
High School graduates or higher	90.3%
Bachelor's degree or higher	25.8%
Graduate degree	9.0%

Income & Poverty, 1999

Per capita income,	$21,106
Median household income	$46,496
Median family income	$51,887
Persons in poverty	170
H'holds receiving public assistance	20
H'holds receiving social security	283

Households, 2000

Total households	1,203
With persons under 18	425
With persons over 65	286
Family households	840
Single person households	287
Persons per household	2.5
Persons per family	3.0

Labor & Employment, 2000

Civilian labor force	1,754
Unemployment rate	7.5%
Civilian labor force, 2008†	1,788
Unemployment rate†	6.7%
Civilian labor force, 12/09†	1,778
Unemployment rate†	8.7%
Employed persons 16 years and over, by occupation:	
Managers & professionals	588
Service occupations	256
Sales & office occupations	404
Farming, fishing & forestry	5
Construction & maintenance	162
Production & transportation	208
Self-employed persons	125

Most demographic data is from the 2000 Decennial Census
† Massachusetts Department of Revenue
†† University of Massachusetts, MISER

©2010 Information Publications, Inc. All rights reserved. Photocopying prohibited. For additional copies, contact the publisher at www.informationpublications.com or (877)544-INFO (4636)

General Information

Town of Lanesborough
83 North Main St
PO Box 1492
Lanesborough, MA 01237
413-442-1167

Elevation	1,160 ft.
Land area (square miles)	29.0
Water area (square miles)	0.7
Population density, 2008 (est)	98.8
Year incorporated	1765
Website	www.lanesborough-ma.gov

Voters & Government Information

Government type	Open Town Meeting
Number of Selectmen	3
US Congressional District(s)	1

Registered Voters, October 2008

Total	2,182
Democrats	646
Republicans	221
Unaffiliated/other	1,303

Local Officials, 2010

Chair, Bd. of Sel.	John Boerlach
Town Administrator	Paul Boudreau
Town Clerk	Judith Gallant
Finance Director	Bruce Durwin
Treas/Collector	Nancy Giardina
Tax Assessor	Glen Bean
Attorney	Brackett & Lucas
Public Works	William Decelles
Building	Richard Haupt
Comm Dev/Planning	Aimee Thayer (Chr)
Police Chief	F. Mark Bashara
Fire Chief	Charles Durfee

Housing & Construction

New Privately Owned Housing Units Authorized by Building Permit

	Single Family	Total Bldgs	Total Units
2006	4	4	4
2007	4	4	4
2008	2	2	2

Parcel Count by Property Class, 2010

Total	1,998
Single family	1,197
Multiple units	42
Apartments	8
Condos	31
Vacant land	451
Open space	0
Commercial	62
Industrial	26
Misc. residential	13
Other use	168

Public Library

Lanesborough Public Library
PO Box 352
Lanesborough, MA 01237
(413)442-0222

Librarian	Kathy Adams

Library Statistics, FY 2008

Population served, 2007	2,891
Registered users	1,593
Circulation	17,064
Reference transactons	188
Total program attendance	5,392
per capita:	
Holdings	4.42
Operating income	$11.93
Internet Access	
Internet computers available	2
Weekly users	5

Municipal Finance

Debt at year end 2008	$6,554,600
Moody's rating, July 2009	A3

Revenues, 2008

Total	$8,932,246
From all taxes	6,571,066
Federal aid	0
State aid	1,776,309
From other governments	62,762
Charges for services	127,386
Licenses, permits & fees	76,972
Fines & forfeits	2,275
Interfund transfers	197,166
Misc/other/special assessments	59,155

Expenditures, 2008

Total	$8,663,929
General government	363,125
Public safety	701,538
Other/fixed costs	1,183,883
Human services	58,769
Culture & recreation	108,546
Debt Service	844,102
Education	4,758,035
Public works	478,763
Intergovernmental	167,168

Taxation, 2010

Property type	Valuation	Rate
Total	$409,212,467	-
Residential	310,974,180	16.30
Open space	0	0.00
Commercial	83,586,517	16.30
Industrial	4,320,430	16.30
Personal	10,331,340	16.30

Average Single Family Tax Bill, 2010

Avg. assessed home value	$213,094
Avg. single fam. tax bill	$3,473
Hi-Lo ranking	176/301

Police & Crime, 2008

Number of police officers	NA
Violent crimes	NA
Property crimes	NA

Local School District

(school data 2007-08, except as noted)

Lanesborough
188 Summer Street
Lanesborough, MA 01237
413-458-5840

Superintendent	Rose Ellis
Grade plan	PK-6
Total enrollment '09-10	270
Grade 12 enrollment, '09-10	0
Graduation rate	NA
Dropout rate	NA
Per-pupil expenditure	$11,460
Avg teacher salary	$59,817
Student/teacher ratio '08-09	13.4 to 1
Highly-qualified teachers, '08-09	100.0%
Teachers licensed in assigned subject	100.0%
Students per computer	4.5

Massachusetts Competency Assessment System (MCAS), 2009 results

	English		Math	
	% Prof	CPI	% Prof	CPI
Gr 4	51%	83.1	47%	77.9
Gr 6	85%	95.6	53%	75.6
Gr 8	NA	NA	NA	NA
Gr 10	NA	NA	NA	NA

Other School Districts (see Appendix D for data)

Receives students from New Ashford; sends to Mount Greylock Regional

See Introduction for an explanation of all data sources.

Demographics & Socio-Economic Characteristics*

Population

1990	70,207
2000	72,043
Male	34,439
Female	37,604
2008	70,014
2010 (projected)††	79,231
2020 (projected)††	88,483

Race & Hispanic Origin, 2000

Race	
White	35,044
Black/African American	3,516
American Indian/Alaska Native	583
Asian	1,910
Hawaiian Native/Pacific Islander	71
Other Race	26,418
Two or more races	4,501
Hispanic origin	43,019

Age & Nativity, 2000

Under 5 years	6,451
18 years and over	49,024
21 years and over	45,631
65 years and over	7,075
85 years and over	1,147
Median Age	29.5
Native-born	50,032
Foreign-born	22,011

Age, 2020 (projected)††

Under 5 years	8,156
5 to 19 years	22,264
20 to 39 years	27,575
40 to 64 years	22,565
65 years and over	7,923

Educational Attainment, 2000

Population 25 years and over	40,940
High School graduates or higher	58.2%
Bachelor's degree or higher	10.0%
Graduate degree	4.1%

Income & Poverty, 1999

Per capita income,	$13,360
Median household income	$27,983
Median family income	$31,809
Persons in poverty	17,217
H'holds receiving public assistance	2,204
H'holds receiving social security	5,992

Households, 2000

Total households	24,463
With persons under 18	11,263
With persons over 65	5,229
Family households	16,905
Single person households	6,233
Persons per household	2.9
Persons per family	3.5

Labor & Employment, 2000

Civilian labor force	28,148
Unemployment rate	8.4%
Civilian labor force, 2008†	29,553
Unemployment rate†	13.1%
Civilian labor force, 12/09†	30,007
Unemployment rate†	17.8%
Employed persons 16 years and over, by occupation:	
Managers & professionals	5,322
Service occupations	5,000
Sales & office occupations	6,225
Farming, fishing & forestry	115
Construction & maintenance	1,932
Production & transportation	7,178
Self-employed persons	946

Most demographic data is from the 2000 Decennial Census
* see Appendix D and E for American Community Survey data
† Massachusetts Department of Revenue
†† University of Massachusetts, MISER

General Information

City of Lawrence
200 Common St
Lawrence, MA 01840
978-794-5803

Elevation	50 ft.
Land area (square miles)	7.0
Water area (square miles)	0.5
Population density, 2008 (est)	10,002.0
Year incorporated	1847
Website	www.ci.lawrence.ma.us

Voters & Government Information

Government type	Mayor-Council
Number of Councilpersons	9
US Congressional District(s)	5

Registered Voters, October 2008

Total	39,911
Democrats	21,254
Republicans	2,980
Unaffiliated/other	15,380

Local Officials, 2010

Mayor	William Lantigua
Manager/Admin	NA
City Clerk	William Maloney
Finance	Patricia Cook
Tax Collector	Patricia Cook
Tax Assessor	Joseph Giuffrida
Attorney	Charles Boddy
Public Works	Frank McCann
Building	Luis Waldron
Comm Dev/Planning	James Barnes
Police Chief	John Romero
Emerg/Fire Chief	Peter Takvorian

Housing & Construction

New Privately Owned Housing Units Authorized by Building Permit

	Single Family	Total Bldgs	Total Units
2006	23	48	75
2007	5	22	39
2008	7	14	21

Parcel Count by Property Class, 2010

Total	NA
Single family	NA
Multiple units	NA
Apartments	NA
Condos	NA
Vacant land	NA
Open space	NA
Commercial	NA
Industrial	NA
Misc. residential	NA
Other use	NA

Public Library

Lawrence Public Library
51 Lawrence St.
Lawrence, MA 01841
(978)682-1727

Director	Maureen Nimmo

Library Statistics, FY 2008

Population served, 2007	70,066
Registered users	46,150
Circulation	141,508
Reference transactons	13,758
Total program attendance	193,881
per capita:	
Holdings	2.94
Operating income	$21.54
Internet Access	
Internet computers available	32
Weekly users	769

Municipal Finance

Debt at year end 2008	$139,282,392
Moody's rating, July 2009	Baa3

Revenues, 2008

Total	$225,840,438
From all taxes	45,980,828
Federal aid	3,154,559
State aid	163,930,525
From other governments	0
Charges for services	701,682
Licenses, permits & fees	860,542
Fines & forfeits	1,209,031
Interfund transfers	5,365,079
Misc/other/special assessments	2,319,096

Expenditures, 2008

Total	$210,255,126
General government	6,882,772
Public safety	25,150,579
Other/fixed costs	8,950,270
Human services	1,414,177
Culture & recreation	1,866,964
Debt Service	12,341,040
Education	140,724,781
Public works	7,573,642
Intergovernmental	4,618,362

Taxation, 2010

Property type	Valuation	Rate
Total	NA	-
Residential	NA	NA
Open space	NA	NA
Commercial	NA	NA
Industrial	NA	NA
Personal	NA	NA

Average Single Family Tax Bill, 2010

Avg. assessed home value	NA
Avg. single fam. tax bill	NA
Hi-Lo ranking	NA

Police & Crime, 2008

Number of police officers	151
Violent crimes	456
Property crimes	1,979

Local School District

(school data 2007-08, except as noted)

Lawrence
255 Essex Street
Lawrence, MA 01840
978-975-5900

Superintendent	Wilfredo Laboy
Grade plan	PK-12
Total enrollment '09-10	12,284
Grade 12 enrollment, '09-10	625
Graduation rate	35.8%
Dropout rate	36.5%
Per-pupil expenditure	$12,643
Avg teacher salary	$70,840
Student/teacher ratio '08-09	13.4 to 1
Highly-qualified teachers, '08-09	97.9%
Teachers licensed in assigned subject	97.3%
Students per computer	2.3

Massachusetts Competency Assessment System (MCAS), 2009 results

	English		Math	
	% Prof	CPI	% Prof	CPI
Gr 4	28%	66.9	29%	68.7
Gr 6	33%	68.4	19%	53.6
Gr 8	50%	78.1	14%	45.7
Gr 10	46%	74.3	30%	62.2

Other School Districts (see Appendix D for data)
Greater Lawrence Vocational Tech

©2010 Information Publications, Inc. All rights reserved. Photocopying prohibited. For additional copies, contact the publisher at www.informationpublications.com or (877)544-INFO (4636)

See Introduction for an explanation of all data sources.

Demographics & Socio-Economic Characteristics

Population

1990	5,849
2000	5,985
Male	2,900
Female	3,085
2008	5,763
2010 (projected)††	5,714
2020 (projected)††	5,414

Race & Hispanic Origin, 2000

Race	
White	5,801
Black/African American	37
American Indian/Alaska Native	9
Asian	57
Hawaiian Native/Pacific Islander	1
Other Race	44
Two or more races	36
Hispanic origin	149

Age & Nativity, 2000

Under 5 years	302
18 years and over	4,662
21 years and over	4,470
65 years and over	1,003
85 years and over	106
Median Age	40.4
Native-born	5,838
Foreign-born	147

Age, 2020 (projected)††

Under 5 years	221
5 to 19 years	705
20 to 39 years	1,174
40 to 64 years	1,953
65 years and over	1,361

Educational Attainment, 2000

Population 25 years and over	4,183
High School graduates or higher	88.8%
Bachelor's degree or higher	24.9%
Graduate degree	8.1%

Income & Poverty, 1999

Per capita income,	$19,799
Median household income	$41,556
Median family income	$49,630
Persons in poverty	390
H'holds receiving public assistance	49
H'holds receiving social security	726

Households, 2000

Total households	2,442
With persons under 18	742
With persons over 65	695
Family households	1,608
Single person households	688
Persons per household	2.4
Persons per family	2.9

Labor & Employment, 2000

Civilian labor force	3,334
Unemployment rate	3.4%
Civilian labor force, 2008†	3,660
Unemployment rate†	6.6%
Civilian labor force, 12/09†	3,638
Unemployment rate†	7.4%
Employed persons 16 years and over, by occupation:	
Managers & professionals	1,105
Service occupations	529
Sales & office occupations	949
Farming, fishing & forestry	28
Construction & maintenance	318
Production & transportation	292
Self-employed persons	248

Most demographic data is from the 2000 Decennial Census
† Massachusetts Department of Revenue
†† University of Massachusetts, MISER

General Information

Town of Lee
32 Main St
Lee, MA 01238
413-243-5500

Elevation	888 ft.
Land area (square miles)	26.4
Water area (square miles)	0.6
Population density, 2008 (est)	218.3
Year incorporated	1777
Website	www.lee.ma.us

Voters & Government Information

Government type	Rep. Town Meeting
Number of Selectmen	3
US Congressional District(s)	1

Registered Voters, October 2008

Total	3,978
Democrats	1,165
Republicans	348
Unaffiliated/other	2,438

Local Officials, 2010

Chair, Bd. of Sel.	Patricia Carlino
Town Administrator	Robert Nason
Town Clerk	Suzanne Scarpa
Chief Financial Officer	Robert Nason
Tax Collector	Janice Smith
Tax Assessor	William Derrick (Chr)
Attorney	Jeremia Pollard
Public Works	Christopher Pompi
Building	Donald Torrico
Planning Board	Anthony Caropreso (Chr)
Police Chief	Ronald Glidden
Fire Chief	Ronald Driscoll

Housing & Construction

New Privately Owned Housing Units Authorized by Building Permit

	Single Family	Total Bldgs	Total Units
2006	18	18	18
2007	15	15	15
2008	11	11	11

Parcel Count by Property Class, 2010

Total	2,868
Single family	1,812
Multiple units	153
Apartments	30
Condos	183
Vacant land	329
Open space	0
Commercial	137
Industrial	68
Misc. residential	42
Other use	114

Public Library

Lee Library Association
100 Main Street
Lee, MA 01238
(413)243-0385

Librarian	Georgia Massucco

Library Statistics, FY 2008

Population served, 2007	5,803
Registered users	2,595
Circulation	33,004
Reference transactons	1,908
Total program attendance	0
per capita:	
Holdings	7.92
Operating income	$43.98
Internet Access	
Internet computers available	1
Weekly users	77

Municipal Finance

Debt at year end 2008	$40,945,270
Moody's rating, July 2009	A2

Revenues, 2008

Total	$16,071,992
From all taxes	10,952,463
Federal aid	7,325
State aid	3,409,452
From other governments	35,044
Charges for services	710,037
Licenses, permits & fees	21,365
Fines & forfeits	0
Interfund transfers	45,904
Misc/other/special assessments	445,201

Expenditures, 2008

Total	$14,915,572
General government	676,138
Public safety	1,333,665
Other/fixed costs	2,751,844
Human services	149,618
Culture & recreation	296,335
Debt Service	1,284,608
Education	7,100,756
Public works	848,074
Intergovernmental	474,534

Taxation, 2010

Property type	Valuation	Rate
Total	$889,111,113	-
Residential	629,460,534	12.61
Open space	0	0.00
Commercial	160,081,074	12.61
Industrial	51,827,495	12.61
Personal	47,742,010	12.61

Average Single Family Tax Bill, 2010

Avg. assessed home value	$252,971
Avg. single fam. tax bill	$3,190
Hi-Lo ranking	214/301

Police & Crime, 2008

Number of police officers	11
Violent crimes	8
Property crimes	53

Local School District

(school data 2007-08, except as noted)

Lee
480 Pleasant Street, Suite 102
Lee, MA 01238
413-243-0276

Superintendent	Jason McCandless
Grade plan	PK-12
Total enrollment '09-10	839
Grade 12 enrollment, '09-10	74
Graduation rate	85.0%
Dropout rate	9.0%
Per-pupil expenditure	$12,335
Avg teacher salary	$55,901
Student/teacher ratio '08-09	11.2 to 1
Highly-qualified teachers, '08-09	83.8%
Teachers licensed in assigned subject	98.7%
Students per computer	2.4

Massachusetts Competency Assessment System (MCAS), 2009 results

	English		Math	
	% Prof	CPI	% Prof	CPI
Gr 4	31%	70.8	29%	67.8
Gr 6	82%	94.1	70%	87.9
Gr 8	76%	88.4	33%	63.4
Gr 10	84%	94.8	59%	82

Other School Districts (see Appendix D for data)
Receives students from Tyringham

©2010 Information Publications, Inc. All rights reserved. Photocopying prohibited. For additional copies, contact the publisher at www.informationpublications.com or (877)544-INFO (4636)

See Introduction for an explanation of all data sources.

Demographics & Socio-Economic Characteristics

Population

1990	10,191
2000	10,471
Male	5,094
Female	5,377
2008	10,990
2010 (projected)††	10,606
2020 (projected)††	10,727

Race & Hispanic Origin, 2000

Race	
White	10,083
Black/African American	134
American Indian/Alaska Native	32
Asian	78
Hawaiian Native/Pacific Islander	6
Other Race	32
Two or more races	106
Hispanic origin	183

Age & Nativity, 2000

Under 5 years	617
18 years and over	7,752
21 years and over	7,227
65 years and over	1,296
85 years and over	176
Median Age	36.4
Native-born	10,004
Foreign-born	467

Age, 2020 (projected)††

Under 5 years	602
5 to 19 years	2,002
20 to 39 years	2,761
40 to 64 years	3,550
65 years and over	1,812

Educational Attainment, 2000

Population 25 years and over	6,812
High School graduates or higher	84.5%
Bachelor's degree or higher	20.3%
Graduate degree	5.7%

Income & Poverty, 1999

Per capita income,	$20,822
Median household income	$55,039
Median family income	$64,202
Persons in poverty	433
H'holds receiving public assistance	68
H'holds receiving social security	1,049

Households, 2000

Total households	3,683
With persons under 18	1,414
With persons over 65	861
Family households	2,708
Single person households	805
Persons per household	2.7
Persons per family	3.2

Labor & Employment, 2000

Civilian labor force	5,717
Unemployment rate	2.8%
Civilian labor force, 2008†	5,999
Unemployment rate†	6.0%
Civilian labor force, 12/09†	6,202
Unemployment rate†	9.6%
Employed persons 16 years and over, by occupation:	
Managers & professionals	1,804
Service occupations	885
Sales & office occupations	1,489
Farming, fishing & forestry	9
Construction & maintenance	565
Production & transportation	804
Self-employed persons	292

Most demographic data is from the 2000 Decennial Census
† Massachusetts Department of Revenue
†† University of Massachusetts, MISER

General Information

Town of Leicester
3 Washburn Sq
Leicester, MA 01524
508-892-7000

Elevation	1,009 ft.
Land area (square miles)	23.4
Water area (square miles)	1.3
Population density, 2008 (est)	469.7
Year incorporated	1714
Website	www.leicesterma.org

Voters & Government Information

Government type	Open Town Meeting
Number of Selectmen	5
US Congressional District(s)	2

Registered Voters, October 2008

Total	7,439
Democrats	2,408
Republicans	825
Unaffiliated/other	4,157

Local Officials, 2010

Chair, Bd. of Sel.	Thomas V. Brennan
Manager/Admin	Robert Reed
Town Clerk	Deborah K. Davis
Finance Director	Deborah J. Kristoff
Tax Collector	Deborah J. Kristoff
Tax Assessor	John Prescott
Attorney	NA
Highway Supt	Thomas Wood
Building	Jeffrey Taylor
Comm Dev/Planning	Michelle Buck
Police Chief	James J. Hurley
Emerg/Fire Chief	Robert Wilson

Housing & Construction

New Privately Owned Housing Units Authorized by Building Permit

	Single Family	Total Bldgs	Total Units
2006	47	47	47
2007	22	22	22
2008	16	16	16

Parcel Count by Property Class, 2010

Total	4,983
Single family	3,107
Multiple units	215
Apartments	24
Condos	153
Vacant land	1,122
Open space	0
Commercial	114
Industrial	52
Misc. residential	12
Other use	184

Public Library

Leicester Public Library
1136 Main Street
Leicester, MA 01524
(508)892-7020

Director	Susan Dubois

Library Statistics, FY 2008

Population served, 2007	10,982
Registered users	6,538
Circulation	37,794
Reference transactons	6,461
Total program attendance	0
per capita:	
Holdings	3.45
Operating income	$15.61
Internet Access	
Internet computers available	7
Weekly users	81

Municipal Finance

Debt at year end 2008	$13,847,092
Moody's rating, July 2009	A3

Revenues, 2008

Total	$25,964,289
From all taxes	11,857,635
Federal aid	218,954
State aid	12,487,826
From other governments	100,438
Charges for services	22,009
Licenses, permits & fees	266,788
Fines & forfeits	8,656
Interfund transfers	536,705
Misc/other/special assessments	232,639

Expenditures, 2008

Total	$25,516,680
General government	985,146
Public safety	2,202,551
Other/fixed costs	2,901,715
Human services	237,820
Culture & recreation	152,194
Debt Service	1,876,452
Education	15,793,133
Public works	1,025,526
Intergovernmental	340,868

Taxation, 2010

Property type	Valuation	Rate
Total	$968,345,623	-
Residential	862,779,080	11.73
Open space	0	0.00
Commercial	57,884,781	11.73
Industrial	20,811,332	11.73
Personal	26,870,430	11.73

Average Single Family Tax Bill, 2010

Avg. assessed home value	$232,377
Avg. single fam. tax bill	$2,726
Hi-Lo ranking	260/301

Police & Crime, 2008

Number of police officers	18
Violent crimes	24
Property crimes	170

Local School District

(school data 2007-08, except as noted)

Leicester
1078 Main Street
Leicester, MA 01524
508-892-7040

Superintendent	Paul Soojian
Grade plan	PK-12
Total enrollment '09-10	1,881
Grade 12 enrollment, '09-10	122
Graduation rate	81.9%
Dropout rate	5.4%
Per-pupil expenditure	$10,195
Avg teacher salary	$62,875
Student/teacher ratio '08-09	14.7 to 1
Highly-qualified teachers, '08-09	99.4%
Teachers licensed in assigned subject	100.0%
Students per computer	4

Massachusetts Competency Assessment System (MCAS), 2009 results

	English		Math	
	% Prof	CPI	% Prof	CPI
Gr 4	42%	74.8	45%	76.9
Gr 6	74%	87.8	58%	77.2
Gr 8	85%	95.2	53%	75.5
Gr 10	78%	92.1	73%	90.4

Other School Districts (see Appendix D for data)
None

©2010 Information Publications, Inc. All rights reserved. Photocopying prohibited. For additional copies, contact the publisher at www.informationpublications.com or (877)544-INFO (4636)

©2010 Information Publications, Inc. All rights reserved. Photocopying prohibited. For additional copies, contact the publisher at www.informationpublications.com or (877)544-INFO (4636)

Demographics & Socio-Economic Characteristics

Population

1990	5,069
2000	5,077
Male	2,322
Female	2,755
2008	5,095
2010 (projected)††	4,601
2020 (projected)††	4,149

Race & Hispanic Origin, 2000

Race	
White	4,903
Black/African American	66
American Indian/Alaska Native	4
Asian	52
Hawaiian Native/Pacific Islander	2
Other Race	21
Two or more races	29
Hispanic origin	97

Age & Nativity, 2000

Under 5 years	176
18 years and over	4,019
21 years and over	3,900
65 years and over	1,237
85 years and over	281
Median Age	45.9
Native-born	4,676
Foreign-born	401

Age, 2020 (projected)††

Under 5 years	137
5 to 19 years	574
20 to 39 years	602
40 to 64 years	1,251
65 years and over	1,585

Educational Attainment, 2000

Population 25 years and over	3,751
High School graduates or higher	92.0%
Bachelor's degree or higher	47.5%
Graduate degree	21.9%

Income & Poverty, 1999

Per capita income,	$23,263
Median household income	$45,581
Median family income	$61,413
Persons in poverty	435
H'holds receiving public assistance	0
H'holds receiving social security	910

Households, 2000

Total households	2,212
With persons under 18	523
With persons over 65	871
Family households	1,292
Single person households	802
Persons per household	2.2
Persons per family	2.8

Labor & Employment, 2000

Civilian labor force	2,472
Unemployment rate	4.2%
Civilian labor force, 2008†	2,691
Unemployment rate†	5.9%
Civilian labor force, 12/09†	2,671
Unemployment rate†	7.8%
Employed persons 16 years and over, by occupation:	
Managers & professionals	1,147
Service occupations	317
Sales & office occupations	550
Farming, fishing & forestry	0
Construction & maintenance	124
Production & transportation	230
Self-employed persons	197

Most demographic data is from the 2000 Decennial Census
† Massachusetts Department of Revenue
†† University of Massachusetts, MISER

General Information

Town of Lenox
6 Walker St
Lenox, MA 01240
413-637-5500

Elevation	1,250 ft.
Land area (square miles)	21.2
Water area (square miles)	0.3
Population density, 2008 (est)	240.3
Year incorporated	1775
Website	www.townoflenox.com

Voters & Government Information

Government type	Open Town Meeting
Number of Selectmen	5
US Congressional District(s)	1

Registered Voters, October 2008

Total	3,774
Democrats	1,629
Republicans	492
Unaffiliated/other	1,628

Local Officials, 2010

Chair, Bd. of Sel.	Linda P. Messana
Manager	Greg T. Federspiel
Clerk	Marie C. Duby
Treasurer	Marie C. Duby
Tax Collector	Diana C. Kirby
Tax Assessor	Joseph A. Kellogg
Attorney	Jeremia Pollard
Public Works	Jeffrey T. Vincent
Building	William Thornton
Planning	Mary Albertson
Police Chief	Stephen E. O'Brien
Emerg/Fire Chief	Daniel W. Clifford

Housing & Construction

New Privately Owned Housing Units Authorized by Building Permit

	Single Family	Total Bldgs	Total Units
2006	15	15	15
2007	12	12	12
2008	11	11	11

Parcel Count by Property Class, 2010

Total	2,628
Single family	1,596
Multiple units	77
Apartments	17
Condos	414
Vacant land	252
Open space	0
Commercial	128
Industrial	20
Misc. residential	16
Other use	108

Public Library

Lenox Library Association
18 Main Street
Lenox, MA 01240
(413)637-0197

Executive Director	Denis Lesieur

Library Statistics, FY 2008

Population served, 2007	5,105
Registered users	3,497
Circulation	81,386
Reference transactons	24,949
Total program attendance	52,415
per capita:	
Holdings	20.17
Operating income	$109.18
Internet Access	
Internet computers available	8
Weekly users	140

Municipal Finance

Debt at year end 2008	$16,007,696
Moody's rating, July 2009	Aa3

Revenues, 2008

Total	$17,500,673
From all taxes	13,376,171
Federal aid	0
State aid	2,804,938
From other governments	0
Charges for services	95,554
Licenses, permits & fees	253,948
Fines & forfeits	40,106
Interfund transfers	295,306
Misc/other/special assessments	317,325

Expenditures, 2008

Total	$15,456,798
General government	756,477
Public safety	1,111,097
Other/fixed costs	2,805,490
Human services	116,432
Culture & recreation	487,037
Debt Service	1,598,525
Education	7,609,219
Public works	710,323
Intergovernmental	260,986

Taxation, 2010

Property type	Valuation	Rate
Total	$1,182,747,650	-
Residential	969,914,636	9.92
Open space	0	0.00
Commercial	174,289,524	13.50
Industrial	7,932,200	13.50
Personal	30,611,290	13.50

Average Single Family Tax Bill, 2010

Avg. assessed home value	$410,607
Avg. single fam. tax bill	$4,073
Hi-Lo ranking	131/301

Police & Crime, 2008

Number of police officers	9
Violent crimes	9
Property crimes	91

Local School District

(school data 2007-08, except as noted)

Lenox
6 Walker Street
Lenox, MA 01240
413-637-5550

Superintendent	Basan Nembirkow
Grade plan	PK-12
Total enrollment '09-10	829
Grade 12 enrollment, '09-10	76
Graduation rate	97.2%
Dropout rate	1.4%
Per-pupil expenditure	$13,680
Avg teacher salary	$65,541
Student/teacher ratio '08-09	11.6 to 1
Highly-qualified teachers, '08-09	90.8%
Teachers licensed in assigned subject	95.4%
Students per computer	3

Massachusetts Competency Assessment System (MCAS), 2009 results

	English		Math	
	% Prof	CPI	% Prof	CPI
Gr 4	47%	78	39%	74.6
Gr 6	77%	89.9	51%	74.6
Gr 8	87%	92.3	48%	69.8
Gr 10	91%	96.6	87%	95.1

Other School Districts (see Appendix D for data)

Receives students from Farmington River Regional

See Introduction for an explanation of all data sources.

Demographics & Socio-Economic Characteristics*

Population

1990	38,145
2000	41,303
Male	19,860
Female	21,443
2008	41,055
2010 (projected)††	44,072
2020 (projected)††	47,325

Race & Hispanic Origin, 2000

Race	
White	35,982
Black/African American	1,529
American Indian/Alaska Native	63
Asian	1,006
Hawaiian Native/Pacific Islander	24
Other Race	1,785
Two or more races	914
Hispanic origin	4,544

Age & Nativity, 2000

Under 5 years	2,929
18 years and over	30,762
21 years and over	29,538
65 years and over	5,633
85 years and over	702
Median Age	36.3
Native-born	36,995
Foreign-born	4,308

Age, 2020 (projected)††

Under 5 years	3,114
5 to 19 years	8,760
20 to 39 years	13,049
40 to 64 years	14,833
65 years and over	7,569

Educational Attainment, 2000

Population 25 years and over	27,797
High School graduates or higher	81.4%
Bachelor's degree or higher	21.9%
Graduate degree	7.9%

Income & Poverty, 1999

Per capita income,	$21,769
Median household income	$44,893
Median family income	$54,660
Persons in poverty	3,889
H'holds receiving public assistance	558
H'holds receiving social security	4,134

Households, 2000

Total households	16,491
With persons under 18	5,795
With persons over 65	4,013
Family households	10,902
Single person households	4,604
Persons per household	2.5
Persons per family	3.1

Labor & Employment, 2000

Civilian labor force	21,064
Unemployment rate	4.0%
Civilian labor force, 2008†	20,441
Unemployment rate†	7.7%
Civilian labor force, 12/09†	20,360
Unemployment rate†	11.8%
Employed persons 16 years and over, by occupation:	
Managers & professionals	6,641
Service occupations	2,924
Sales & office occupations	5,425
Farming, fishing & forestry	38
Construction & maintenance	1,619
Production & transportation	3,574
Self-employed persons	1,376

Most demographic data is from the 2000 Decennial Census
* see Appendix E for American Community Survey data
† Massachusetts Department of Revenue
†† University of Massachusetts, MISER

General Information

City of Leominster
25 West St
Leominster, MA 01453
978-534-7500

Elevation	400 ft.
Land area (square miles)	28.9
Water area (square miles)	0.9
Population density, 2008 (est)	1,420.6
Year incorporated	1740
Website	www.leominster-ma.gov

Voters & Government Information

Government type	Mayor-Council
Number of Councilpersons	9
US Congressional District(s)	1

Registered Voters, October 2008

Total	26,957
Democrats	8,126
Republicans	3,070
Unaffiliated/other	15,562

Local Officials, 2010

Mayor	Dean Mazzarella
Manager/Admin	NA
City Clerk	Lynn A. Bouchard
Finance Director	John Richard
Tax Collector	David Laplante
Tax Assessor	Walter Poirier
Attorney	NA
Public Works	Patrick LaPointe
Building	Edward Cataldo
Comm Dev/Planning	Kate Griffin-Brooks
Police Chief	Peter Roddy
Emerg/Fire Chief	Ronald Pierce

Housing & Construction

New Privately Owned Housing Units Authorized by Building Permit

	Single Family	Total Bldgs	Total Units
2006	50	50	50
2007	43	48	81
2008	12	14	44

Parcel Count by Property Class, 2010

Total	13,738
Single family	7,981
Multiple units	1,199
Apartments	327
Condos	1,872
Vacant land	1,151
Open space	19
Commercial	550
Industrial	350
Misc. residential	56
Other use	233

Public Library

Leominster Public Library
30 West St.
Leominster, MA 01453
(978)534-7522

Director	Susan T. Shelton

Library Statistics, FY 2008

Population served, 2007	41,128
Registered users	25,337
Circulation	392,051
Reference transactons	34,904
Total program attendance	0
per capita:	
Holdings	3.11
Operating income	$30.42
Internet Access	
Internet computers available	10
Weekly users	669

Municipal Finance

Debt at year end 2008	$23,944,039
Moody's rating, July 2009	A1

Revenues, 2008

Total	$102,087,620
From all taxes	48,172,021
Federal aid	1,367,044
State aid	45,411,809
From other governments	49,658
Charges for services	1,323,011
Licenses, permits & fees	704,158
Fines & forfeits	234,944
Interfund transfers	2,904,719
Misc/other/special assessments	960,128

Expenditures, 2008

Total	$85,058,649
General government	2,922,881
Public safety	13,742,999
Other/fixed costs	6,510,702
Human services	736,456
Culture & recreation	1,699,637
Debt Service	4,244,019
Education	45,818,257
Public works	6,930,263
Intergovernmental	2,362,278

Taxation, 2010

Property type	Valuation	Rate
Total	$3,510,329,703	-
Residential	2,747,259,075	13.82
Open space	450,700	13.82
Commercial	440,218,038	13.82
Industrial	227,963,690	13.82
Personal	94,438,200	13.82

Average Single Family Tax Bill, 2010

Avg. assessed home value	$238,471
Avg. single fam. tax bill	$3,296
Hi-Lo ranking	204/301

Police & Crime, 2008

Number of police officers	74
Violent crimes	224
Property crimes	1,246

Local School District

(school data 2007-08, except as noted)

Leominster
24 Church Street
Leominster, MA 01453
978-534-7700

Superintendent	Nadine Binkley
Grade plan	PK-12
Total enrollment '09-10	6,290
Grade 12 enrollment, '09-10	455
Graduation rate	82.4%
Dropout rate	8.6%
Per-pupil expenditure	$10,532
Avg teacher salary	$57,856
Student/teacher ratio '08-09	16.6 to 1
Highly-qualified teachers, '08-09	97.5%
Teachers licensed in assigned subject	96.5%
Students per computer	4.3

Massachusetts Competency Assessment System (MCAS), 2009 results

	English		Math	
	% Prof	CPI	% Prof	CPI
Gr 4	40%	72.8	38%	73.3
Gr 6	55%	78.6	58%	77.3
Gr 8	76%	90.9	38%	67.5
Gr 10	74%	88.5	68%	82.8

Other School Districts (see Appendix D for data)
None

©2010 Information Publications, Inc. All rights reserved. Photocopying prohibited. For additional copies, contact the publisher at www.informationpublications.com or (877)544-INFO (4636)

Demographics & Socio-Economic Characteristics

Population

1990 1,785
2000 1,663
Male 831
Female 832
2008 1,772
2010 (projected)†† 1,614
2020 (projected)†† 1,509

Race & Hispanic Origin, 2000

Race
White 1,585
Black/African American 4
American Indian/Alaska Native 9
Asian 23
Hawaiian Native/Pacific Islander 0
Other Race 27
Two or more races 15
Hispanic origin 24

Age & Nativity, 2000

Under 5 years 70
18 years and over 1,275
21 years and over 1,226
65 years and over 186
85 years and over 20
Median Age 43.3
Native-born 1,566
Foreign-born 97

Age, 2020 (projected)††

Under 5 years 62
5 to 19 years 205
20 to 39 years 363
40 to 64 years 436
65 years and over 443

Educational Attainment, 2000

Population 25 years and over 1,141
High School graduates or higher .. 94.4%
Bachelor's degree or higher 65.0%
Graduate degree 43.3%

Income & Poverty, 1999

Per capita income, ... $31,891
Median household income $63,203
Median family income $73,333
Persons in poverty 89
H'holds receiving public assistance 6
H'holds receiving social security 124

Households, 2000

Total households 632
With persons under 18 220
With persons over 65 125
Family households 449
Single person households 126
Persons per household 2.6
Persons per family 2.9

Labor & Employment, 2000

Civilian labor force 985
Unemployment rate 4.3%
Civilian labor force, 2008† 1,102
Unemployment rate† 4.6%
Civilian labor force, 12/09† 1,066
Unemployment rate† 5.1%
Employed persons 16 years and over, by occupation:
Managers & professionals 574
Service occupations 107
Sales & office occupations 138
Farming, fishing & forestry 4
Construction & maintenance 69
Production & transportation 51
Self-employed persons 143

Most demographic data is from the 2000 Decennial Census
† Massachusetts Department of Revenue
†† University of Massachusetts, MISER

General Information

Town of Leverett
9 Montague Rd
Box 300
Leverett, MA 01054
413-548-9150

Elevation .... NA
Land area (square miles) 22.8
Water area (square miles) 0.1
Population density, 2008 (est) 77.7
Year incorporated 1774
Website .... leverett.ma.us

Voters & Government Information

Government type .... Open Town Meeting
Number of Selectmen 3
US Congressional District(s) 1

Registered Voters, October 2008

Total 1,441
Democrats 691
Republicans 108
Unaffiliated/other 623

Local Officials, 2010

Chair, Bd. of Sel. .... Rich Brazeau
Manager .... Margie McGinnis
Town Clerk .... Lisa Stratford
Finance Director .... Dee Ann Civello
Tax Collector .... Dee Ann Civello
Tax Assessor .... Donald Robinson
Attorney .... Donna MacNicol
Public Works .... Will Stratford
Building .... Jim Hawkins
Comm Dev/Planning .... Jeff McQueen (Chr)
Police Chief .... Gary Billings
Emerg/Fire Chief .... John Moruzzi

Housing & Construction

New Privately Owned Housing Units Authorized by Building Permit

	Single Family	Total Bldgs	Total Units
2006	9	9	9
2007	6	6	6
2008	7	7	7

Parcel Count by Property Class, 2010

Total 1,149
Single family 640
Multiple units 35
Apartments 1
Condos 2
Vacant land 224
Open space 0
Commercial 4
Industrial 13
Misc. residential 24
Other use 206

Public Library

Leverett Library
PO Box 250
Leverett, MA 01054
(413)548-9220

Director .... Linda Wentworth

Library Statistics, FY 2008

Population served, 2007 1,746
Registered users 1,411
Circulation 37,773
Reference transactons 0
Total program attendance 0
per capita:
Holdings 10.92
Operating income $45.28
Internet Access
Internet computers available 6
Weekly users 74

Municipal Finance

Debt at year end 2008 .... $2,680,000
Moody's rating, July 2009 .... NA

Revenues, 2008

Total $4,948,543
From all taxes 4,065,274
Federal aid 17,526
State aid 500,612
From other governments 0
Charges for services 62,701
Licenses, permits & fees 42,268
Fines & forfeits 2,830
Interfund transfers 177,888
Misc/other/special assessments 39,722

Expenditures, 2008

Total $4,724,426
General government 266,185
Public safety 312,800
Other/fixed costs 192,510
Human services 13,742
Culture & recreation 69,197
Debt Service 238,752
Education 3,140,634
Public works 472,713
Intergovernmental 17,285

Taxation, 2010

Property type	Valuation	Rate
Total	$260,983,979	-
Residential	253,678,000	15.80
Open space	0	0.00
Commercial	1,992,179	15.80
Industrial	793,900	15.80
Personal	4,519,900	15.80

Average Single Family Tax Bill, 2010

Avg. assessed home value $319,344
Avg. single fam. tax bill $5,046
Hi-Lo ranking 73/301

Police & Crime, 2008

Number of police officers 2
Violent crimes 0
Property crimes 7

Local School District

(school data 2007-08, except as noted)

Leverett
18 Pleasant Street
Erving, MA 01344
413-423-3337

Superintendent .... Joan Wickman
Grade plan PK-6
Total enrollment '09-10 165
Grade 12 enrollment, '09-10 0
Graduation rate .... NA
Dropout rate .... NA
Per-pupil expenditure $14,522
Avg teacher salary $51,987
Student/teacher ratio '08-09 .... 9.7 to 1
Highly-qualified teachers, '08-09 .... 100.0%
Teachers licensed in assigned subject .. 99.4%
Students per computer 3.3

Massachusetts Competency Assessment System (MCAS), 2009 results

	English		Math	
	% Prof	CPI	% Prof	CPI
Gr 4	56%	87.5	56%	84.4
Gr 6	55%	81.8	55%	76.1
Gr 8	NA	NA	NA	NA
Gr 10	NA	NA	NA	NA

Other School Districts (see Appendix D for data)
Amherst-Pelham Regional

©2010 Information Publications, Inc. All rights reserved. Photocopying prohibited. For additional copies, contact the publisher at www.informationpublications.com or (877)544-INFO (4636)

See Introduction for an explanation of all data sources.

Demographics & Socio-Economic Characteristics*

Population

1990	28,974
2000	30,355
Male	14,265
Female	16,090
2008	30,272
2010 (projected)††	27,911
2020 (projected)††	23,712

Race & Hispanic Origin, 2000

Race	
White	26,146
Black/African American	343
American Indian/Alaska Native	23
Asian	3,310
Hawaiian Native/Pacific Islander	2
Other Race	102
Two or more races	429
Hispanic origin	428

Age & Nativity, 2000

Under 5 years	1,728
18 years and over	22,352
21 years and over	21,813
65 years and over	5,767
85 years and over	952
Median Age	43.7
Native-born	25,354
Foreign-born	5,001

Age, 2020 (projected)††

Under 5 years	935
5 to 19 years	3,828
20 to 39 years	4,373
40 to 64 years	7,735
65 years and over	6,841

Educational Attainment, 2000

Population 25 years and over	21,295
High School graduates or higher	96.3%
Bachelor's degree or higher	69.1%
Graduate degree	42.2%

Income & Poverty, 1999

Per capita income,	$46,119
Median household income	$96,825
Median family income	$111,899
Persons in poverty	1,007
H'holds receiving public assistance	85
H'holds receiving social security	3,373

Households, 2000

Total households	11,110
With persons under 18	4,344
With persons over 65	3,708
Family households	8,429
Single person households	2,312
Persons per household	2.7
Persons per family	3.1

Labor & Employment, 2000

Civilian labor force	15,020
Unemployment rate	2.5%
Civilian labor force, 2008†	15,186
Unemployment rate†	4.1%
Civilian labor force, 12/09†	15,093
Unemployment rate†	6.0%
Employed persons 16 years and over, by occupation:	
Managers & professionals	10,261
Service occupations	819
Sales & office occupations	2,678
Farming, fishing & forestry	8
Construction & maintenance	404
Production & transportation	467
Self-employed persons	1,385

Most demographic data is from the 2000 Decennial Census
* see Appendix E for American Community Survey data
† Massachusetts Department of Revenue
†† University of Massachusetts, MISER

General Information

Town of Lexington
1625 Massachusetts Ave
Lexington, MA 02420
781-862-0500

Elevation	200 ft.
Land area (square miles)	16.4
Water area (square miles)	0.1
Population density, 2008 (est)	1,845.9
Year incorporated	1713
Website	www.lexingtonma.gov

Voters & Government Information

Government type	Rep. Twn. Mtg. (198)
Number of Selectmen	5
US Congressional District(s)	7

Registered Voters, October 2008

Total	21,366
Democrats	8,534
Republicans	2,362
Unaffiliated/other	10,402

Local Officials, 2010

Chair, Bd. of Sel.	Norman P. Cohen
Town Manager	Carl F. Valente
Town Clerk	Donna M. Hooper
Finance Director	Robert Addelson
Treas/Collector	Arnold Lovering
Assessor	Joseph Nugent
Town Counsel	William L. Lahey
Public Works Dir	William P. Hadley
Building Commissioner	Garry Rhodes
Planning Director	Maryann McCall-Taylor
Police Chief	Mark J. Corr
Fire Chief	William Middlemiss

Housing & Construction

New Privately Owned Housing Units Authorized by Building Permit

	Single Family	Total Bldgs	Total Units
2006	55	55	55
2007	61	62	91
2008	52	53	60

Parcel Count by Property Class, 2010

Total	11,142
Single family	8,944
Multiple units	192
Apartments	14
Condos	878
Vacant land	588
Open space	0
Commercial	412
Industrial	41
Misc. residential	38
Other use	35

Public Library

Cary Memorial Library
1874 Massachusetts Ave.
Lexington, MA 02420
(781)862-6288

Director	Cornelia Rawson

Library Statistics, FY 2008

Population served, 2007	30,332
Registered users	23,039
Circulation	707,321
Reference transactons	43,298
Total program attendance	493,027
per capita:	
Holdings	8.43
Operating income	$79.01
Internet Access	
Internet computers available	14
Weekly users	779

Municipal Finance

Debt at year end 2008	$56,304,582
Moody's rating, July 2009	Aaa

Revenues, 2008

Total	$134,961,640
From all taxes	114,632,603
Federal aid	0
State aid	9,083,558
From other governments	13,282
Charges for services	2,789,932
Licenses, permits & fees	1,920,467
Fines & forfeits	357,086
Interfund transfers	2,412,942
Misc/other/special assessments	1,875,885

Expenditures, 2008

Total	$106,350,094
General government	5,069,020
Public safety	10,351,721
Other/fixed costs	4,436,800
Human services	731,546
Culture & recreation	2,728,948
Debt Service	8,207,917
Education	66,779,597
Public works	7,353,701
Intergovernmental	686,756

Taxation, 2010

Property type	Valuation	Rate
Total	$7,891,590,610	-
Residential	6,896,447,750	13.86
Open space	0	0.00
Commercial	634,105,250	26.21
Industrial	178,757,000	26.21
Personal	182,280,610	26.21

Average Single Family Tax Bill, 2010

Avg. assessed home value	$691,470
Avg. single fam. tax bill	$9,584
Hi-Lo ranking	10/301

Police & Crime, 2008

Number of police officers	47
Violent crimes	23
Property crimes	325

Local School District

(school data 2007-08, except as noted)

Lexington
146 Maple Street
Lexington, MA 02420
781-861-2550

Superintendent	Paul Ash
Grade plan	PK-12
Total enrollment '09-10	6,182
Grade 12 enrollment, '09-10	454
Graduation rate	94.0%
Dropout rate	0.6%
Per-pupil expenditure	$14,469
Avg teacher salary	$69,129
Student/teacher ratio '08-09	11.9 to 1
Highly-qualified teachers, '08-09	99.5%
Teachers licensed in assigned subject	99.8%
Students per computer	5.3

Massachusetts Competency Assessment System (MCAS), 2009 results

	English		Math	
	% Prof	CPI	% Prof	CPI
Gr 4	83%	93.2	77%	91.7
Gr 6	88%	95.9	83%	92.9
Gr 8	96%	98.6	88%	95
Gr 10	95%	98.5	94%	97.6

Other School Districts (see Appendix D for data)
Minuteman Vocational Tech

©2010 Information Publications, Inc. All rights reserved. Photocopying prohibited. For additional copies, contact the publisher at www.informationpublications.com or (877)544-INFO (4636)

Demographics & Socio-Economic Characteristics

Population

1990 662
2000 772
Male 390
Female 382
2008 801
2010 (projected)†† 859
2020 (projected)†† 961

Race & Hispanic Origin, 2000

Race
White 760
Black/African American 3
American Indian/Alaska Native 2
Asian 1
Hawaiian Native/Pacific Islander 0
Other Race 0
Two or more races 6
Hispanic origin 2

Age & Nativity, 2000

Under 5 years 39
18 years and over 564
21 years and over 540
65 years and over 60
85 years and over 8
Median Age 40.5
Native-born 765
Foreign-born 5

Age, 2020 (projected)††

Under 5 years 45
5 to 19 years 116
20 to 39 years 231
40 to 64 years 367
65 years and over 202

Educational Attainment, 2000

Population 25 years and over 530
High School graduates or higher 91.5%
Bachelor's degree or higher 26.4%
Graduate degree 10.8%

Income & Poverty, 1999

Per capita income, ... $26,076
Median household income $50,385
Median family income $53,750
Persons in poverty 36
H'holds receiving public assistance 4
H'holds receiving social security 71

Households, 2000

Total households 277
With persons under 18 111
With persons over 65 46
Family households 220
Single person households 45
Persons per household 2.8
Persons per family 3.1

Labor & Employment, 2000

Civilian labor force 466
Unemployment rate 3.0%
Civilian labor force, 2008† 487
Unemployment rate† 6.8%
Civilian labor force, 12/09† 475
Unemployment rate† 6.9%
Employed persons 16 years and over, by occupation:
Managers & professionals 157
Service occupations 64
Sales & office occupations 114
Farming, fishing & forestry 10
Construction & maintenance 42
Production & transportation 65
Self-employed persons 66

Most demographic data is from the 2000 Decennial Census
† Massachusetts Department of Revenue
†† University of Massachusetts, MISER

General Information

Town of Leyden
16 W Leyden Rd
Leyden, MA 01337
413-774-4111

Elevation .... NA
Land area (square miles) 18.0
Water area (square miles) 0.0
Population density, 2008 (est) 44.5
Year incorporated 1809
Email .... leydenselectboard@live.com

Voters & Government Information

Government type .... Open Town Meeting
Number of Selectmen 3
US Congressional District(s) 1

Registered Voters, October 2008

Total 569
Democrats 131
Republicans 89
Unaffiliated/other 344

Local Officials, 2010

Chair, Bd. of Sel. .... William Glabach
Manager/Admin .... Elizabeth Johnson
Town Clerk .... Robert Hardesty
Finance Com .... Michele Giarusso (Chr)
Tax Collector .... Roxanne Zimmerman
Tax Assessor .... Bruce Kaeppel
Attorney .... Kopelman & Paige
Public Works .... David Brooks
Building Inspector .... FCCIP
Comm Dev/Planning .... Jerry Lund
Police Chief .... Daniel Galvis
Emerg/Fire Chief .... Carey Barton

Housing & Construction

New Privately Owned Housing Units Authorized by Building Permit

	Single Family	Total Bldgs	Total Units
2006	0	0	0
2007	4	4	4
2008	4	4	4

Parcel Count by Property Class, 2010

Total 624
Single family 254
Multiple units 4
Apartments 0
Condos 0
Vacant land 207
Open space 0
Commercial 3
Industrial 1
Misc. residential 4
Other use 151

Public Library

Robertson Memorial Library
849 Greenfield Road
Leyden, MA 01301
(413)773-9334

Librarian .... Christine Johnston

Library Statistics, FY 2008

Population served, 2007 802
Registered users 286
Circulation 7,430
Reference transactons 600
Total program attendance 2,694

per capita:

Holdings 5.87
Operating income $29.44

Internet Access

Internet computers available 1
Weekly users 2

Municipal Finance

Debt at year end 2008 .... $125,700
Moody's rating, July 2009 .... NA

Revenues, 2008

Total $1,629,301
From all taxes 1,421,784
Federal aid 0
State aid 100,911
From other governments 5,483
Charges for services 0
Licenses, permits & fees 18,613
Fines & forfeits 0
Interfund transfers 59,300
Misc/other/special assessments 11,605

Expenditures, 2008

Total $1,518,603
General government 134,339
Public safety 73,521
Other/fixed costs 79,795
Human services 736
Culture & recreation 20,406
Debt Service 26,879
Education 853,288
Public works 320,873
Intergovernmental 8,766

Taxation, 2010

Property type	Valuation	Rate
Total	$84,064,720	-
Residential	79,721,700	16.60
Open space	0	0.00
Commercial	1,376,000	16.60
Industrial	240,400	16.60
Personal	2,726,620	16.60

Average Single Family Tax Bill, 2010

Avg. assessed home value $227,708
Avg. single fam. tax bill $3,780
Hi-Lo ranking 153/301

Police & Crime, 2008

Number of police officers .... NA
Violent crimes .... NA
Property crimes .... NA

Local School District

(school data 2007-08, except as noted)

Leyden (non-op)
97 F Sumner Turner Rd
Northfield, MA 01360
413-498-2911

Superintendent .... Dayle Doiron

Non-operating district.
Resident students are sent to the Other School Districts listed below.

Grade plan .... NA
Total enrollment '09-10 .... NA
Grade 12 enrollment, '09-10 .... NA
Graduation rate .... NA
Dropout rate .... NA
Per-pupil expenditure .... NA
Avg teacher salary .... NA
Student/teacher ratio '08-09 .... NA
Highly-qualified teachers, '08-09 .... NA
Teachers licensed in assigned subject .... NA
Students per computer .... NA

Other School Districts (see Appendix D for data)

Pioneer Valley Regional, Franklin County Vocational Tech

©2010 Information Publications, Inc. All rights reserved. Photocopying prohibited. For additional copies, contact the publisher at www.informationpublications.com or (877)544-INFO (4636)

See Introduction for an explanation of all data sources.

Demographics & Socio-Economic Characteristics

Population

1990	7,666
2000	8,056
Male	3,914
Female	4,142
2008	8,078
2010 (projected)††	7,569
2020 (projected)††	7,361

Race & Hispanic Origin, 2000

Race	
White	7,022
Black/African American	390
American Indian/Alaska Native	31
Asian	336
Hawaiian Native/Pacific Islander	2
Other Race	107
Two or more races	168
Hispanic origin	239

Age & Nativity, 2000

Under 5 years	768
18 years and over	5,582
21 years and over	5,438
65 years and over	888
85 years and over	67
Median Age	35.3
Native-born	7,504
Foreign-born	552

Age, 2020 (projected)††

Under 5 years	508
5 to 19 years	1,225
20 to 39 years	2,176
40 to 64 years	2,173
65 years and over	1,279

Educational Attainment, 2000

Population 25 years and over	5,148
High School graduates or higher	98.7%
Bachelor's degree or higher	69.2%
Graduate degree	40.7%

Income & Poverty, 1999

Per capita income,	$49,095
Median household income	$79,003
Median family income	$87,842
Persons in poverty	67
H'holds receiving public assistance	17
H'holds receiving social security	549

Households, 2000

Total households	2,790
With persons under 18	1,301
With persons over 65	629
Family households	2,255
Single person households	440
Persons per household	2.8
Persons per family	3.2

Labor & Employment, 2000

Civilian labor force	3,297
Unemployment rate	1.9%
Civilian labor force, 2008†	3,303
Unemployment rate†	3.5%
Civilian labor force, 12/09†	3,296
Unemployment rate†	5.5%
Employed persons 16 years and over, by occupation:	
Managers & professionals	2,118
Service occupations	290
Sales & office occupations	641
Farming, fishing & forestry	0
Construction & maintenance	90
Production & transportation	96
Self-employed persons	431

Most demographic data is from the 2000 Decennial Census
† Massachusetts Department of Revenue
†† University of Massachusetts, MISER

General Information

Town of Lincoln
16 Lincoln Road
PO Box 6353
Lincoln, MA 01773
781-259-2600

Elevation	250 ft.
Land area (square miles)	14.4
Water area (square miles)	0.6
Population density, 2008 (est)	561.0
Year incorporated	1754
Website	www.lincolntown.org

Voters & Government Information

Government type	Open Town Meeting
Number of Selectmen	3
US Congressional District(s)	7

Registered Voters, October 2008

Total	4,428
Democrats	1,535
Republicans	571
Unaffiliated/other	2,300

Local Officials, 2010

Chair, Bd. of Sel.	Sara Mattes
Manager/Exec.	Timothy Higgins
Town Clerk	Susan F. Brooks
Finance Director	Colleen Wilkins
Tax Collector	Mary Day
Tax Assessor	Harald Scheid
Attorney	Joel Bard
Public Works	Chris Bibbo
Building	Earl Midgley
Comm Dev/Planning	NA
Police Chief	Kevin Mooney
Emerg/Fire Chief	Arthur Cotoni

Housing & Construction

New Privately Owned Housing Units Authorized by Building Permit

	Single Family	Total Bldgs	Total Units
2006	20	20	20
2007	20	21	50
2008	4	4	4

Parcel Count by Property Class, 2010

Total	2,285
Single family	1,504
Multiple units	9
Apartments	2
Condos	400
Vacant land	293
Open space	0
Commercial	17
Industrial	3
Misc. residential	1
Other use	56

Public Library

Lincoln Public Library
3 Bedford Road
Lincoln, MA 01773
(781)259-8465

Director	Barbara Myles

Library Statistics, FY 2008

Population served, 2007	7,994
Registered users	3,952
Circulation	181,867
Reference transactons	3,873
Total program attendance	62,415
per capita:	
Holdings	12.07
Operating income	$98.06
Internet Access	
Internet computers available	10
Weekly users	410

Municipal Finance

Debt at year end 2008	$6,173,606
Moody's rating, July 2009	NA

Revenues, 2008

Total	$26,713,690
From all taxes	20,816,668
Federal aid	956,104
State aid	2,669,756
From other governments	0
Charges for services	675,057
Licenses, permits & fees	835,822
Fines & forfeits	52,690
Interfund transfers	140,957
Misc/other/special assessments	283,318

Expenditures, 2008

Total	$25,877,391
General government	1,862,110
Public safety	3,149,008
Other/fixed costs	3,926,886
Human services	156,900
Culture & recreation	1,284,650
Debt Service	1,256,726
Education	12,378,204
Public works	1,441,484
Intergovernmental	176,956

Taxation, 2010

Property type	Valuation	Rate
Total	$1,852,936,230	-
Residential	1,783,943,774	11.47
Open space	0	0.00
Commercial	42,094,676	15.09
Industrial	2,636,900	15.09
Personal	24,260,880	15.09

Average Single Family Tax Bill, 2010

Avg. assessed home value	$1,018,661
Avg. single fam. tax bill	$11,684
Hi-Lo ranking	4/301

Police & Crime, 2008

Number of police officers	13
Violent crimes	0
Property crimes	61

Local School District

(school data 2007-08, except as noted)

Lincoln
1 Ballfield Road
Lincoln, MA 01773
781-259-9409

Superintendent	Michael Brandmeyer
Grade plan	PK-8
Total enrollment '09-10	1,050
Grade 12 enrollment, '09-10	0
Graduation rate	NA
Dropout rate	NA
Per-pupil expenditure	$18,189
Avg teacher salary	$69,778
Student/teacher ratio '08-09	9.6 to 1
Highly-qualified teachers, '08-09	96.5%
Teachers licensed in assigned subject	97.9%
Students per computer	NA

Massachusetts Competency Assessment System (MCAS), 2009 results

	English		Math	
	% Prof	CPI	% Prof	CPI
Gr 4	51%	77.8	45%	75.5
Gr 6	75%	90.1	55%	78.4
Gr 8	87%	95.4	64%	80.8
Gr 10	NA	NA	NA	NA

Other School Districts (see Appendix D for data)
Lincoln-Sudbury Regional, Minuteman Vocational Tech

©2010 Information Publications, Inc. All rights reserved. Photocopying prohibited. For additional copies, contact the publisher at www.informationpublications.com or (877)544-INFO (4636)

©2010 Information Publications, Inc. All rights reserved. Photocopying prohibited. For additional copies, contact the publisher at www.informationpublications.com or (877)544-INFO (4636)

Demographics & Socio-Economic Characteristics

Population

1990 7,051
2000 8,184
Male 3,925
Female 4,259
2008 8,711
2010 (projected)†† 8,440
2020 (projected)†† 8,454

Race & Hispanic Origin, 2000

Race
White 7,897
Black/African American 28
American Indian/Alaska Native 6
Asian 140
Hawaiian Native/Pacific Islander 2
Other Race 27
Two or more races 84
Hispanic origin 79

Age & Nativity, 2000

Under 5 years 671
18 years and over 5,965
21 years and over 5,791
65 years and over 965
85 years and over 141
Median Age 37.9
Native-born 7,763
Foreign-born 421

Age, 2020 (projected)††

Under 5 years 496
5 to 19 years 1,521
20 to 39 years 1,872
40 to 64 years 2,916
65 years and over 1,649

Educational Attainment, 2000

Population 25 years and over 5,586
High School graduates or higher .. 92.6%
Bachelor's degree or higher 48.1%
Graduate degree 17.6%

Income & Poverty, 1999

Per capita income, ... $31,070
Median household income $71,384
Median family income $83,365
Persons in poverty 290
H'holds receiving public assistance 48
H'holds receiving social security 697

Households, 2000

Total households 2,960
With persons under 18 1,178
With persons over 65 643
Family households 2,217
Single person households 580
Persons per household 2.7
Persons per family 3.2

Labor & Employment, 2000

Civilian labor force 4,372
Unemployment rate 1.7%
Civilian labor force, 2008† 4,774
Unemployment rate† 5.0%
Civilian labor force, 12/09† 4,760
Unemployment rate† 6.7%
Employed persons 16 years and over, by occupation:
Managers & professionals 2,395
Service occupations 359
Sales & office occupations 947
Farming, fishing & forestry 0
Construction & maintenance 311
Production & transportation 285
Self-employed persons 261

Most demographic data is from the 2000 Decennial Census
† Massachusetts Department of Revenue
†† University of Massachusetts, MISER

General Information

Town of Littleton
37 Shattuck St
PO Box 1305
Littleton, MA 01460
978-540-2401

Elevation .... 229 ft.
Land area (square miles) 16.6
Water area (square miles) 0.9
Population density, 2008 (est) 524.8
Year incorporated 1715
Website .... www.littletonma.org

Voters & Government Information

Government type .... Open Town Meeting
Number of Selectmen 5
US Congressional District(s) 5

Registered Voters, October 2008

Total 6,104
Democrats 1,465
Republicans 874
Unaffiliated/other 3,741

Local Officials, 2010

Chair, Bd. of Sel. .... Alexander McCurdy
Town Administrator .... Keith Bergman
Clerk .... Diane Crory
Finance Director .... Bonnie Mae Holston
Tax Collector .... Rebecca J. Quinn
Tax Assessor .... Fred Freund
Attorney .... Miyares & Harrington
Public Works .... James Clyde
Building .... Roland J. Bernier
Planning .... Maren Toohill
Police Chief .... John Kelly
Fire Chief .... Steven Carter

Housing & Construction

New Privately Owned Housing Units Authorized by Building Permit

	Single Family	Total Bldgs	Total Units
2006	30	30	30
2007	21	21	21
2008	58	60	62

Parcel Count by Property Class, 2010

Total 3,945
Single family 2,808
Multiple units 55
Apartments 10
Condos 83
Vacant land 612
Open space 0
Commercial 92
Industrial 82
Misc. residential 19
Other use 184

Public Library

Reuben Hoar Library
41 Shattuck St.
Littleton, MA 01460
(978)540-2600

Director .... Marjorie Oakes

Library Statistics, FY 2008

Population served, 2007 8,714
Registered users 8,103
Circulation 197,441
Reference transactons 4,108
Total program attendance 61,427

per capita:

Holdings 10.02
Operating income $57.63

Internet Access

Internet computers available 11
Weekly users 91

Municipal Finance

Debt at year end 2008 .... $32,560,070
Moody's rating, July 2009 .... A1

Revenues, 2008

Total $29,807,206
From all taxes 22,503,083
Federal aid 1,099
State aid 4,620,579
From other governments 0
Charges for services 539,690
Licenses, permits & fees 325,187
Fines & forfeits 85,590
Interfund transfers 353,438
Misc/other/special assessments 689,270

Expenditures, 2008

Total $28,828,007
General government 1,559,290
Public safety 2,113,861
Other/fixed costs 3,499,988
Human services 136,008
Culture & recreation 514,617
Debt Service 3,934,245
Education 14,235,999
Public works 1,873,389
Intergovernmental 960,610

Taxation, 2010

Property type	Valuation	Rate
Total	$1,451,398,874	-
Residential	1,156,864,500	14.63
Open space	0	0.00
Commercial	77,753,444	23.11
Industrial	184,309,300	23.11
Personal	32,471,630	23.11

Average Single Family Tax Bill, 2010

Avg. assessed home value $370,111
Avg. single fam. tax bill $5,415
Hi-Lo ranking 58/301

Police & Crime, 2008

Number of police officers 16
Violent crimes 15
Property crimes 93

Local School District

(school data 2007-08, except as noted)

Littleton
PO Box 1486, 33 Shattuck St.
Littleton, MA 01460
978-486-8951

Superintendent .... Diane Bemis
Grade plan PK-12
Total enrollment '09-10 1,607
Grade 12 enrollment, '09-10 96
Graduation rate 92.9%
Dropout rate 3.0%
Per-pupil expenditure $11,357
Avg teacher salary $62,955
Student/teacher ratio '08-09 .... 17.9 to 1
Highly-qualified teachers, '08-09 .... 98.8%
Teachers licensed in assigned subject .. 98.7%
Students per computer 4.1

Massachusetts Competency Assessment System (MCAS), 2009 results

	English		Math	
	% Prof	CPI	% Prof	CPI
Gr 4	59%	83.6	51%	80.6
Gr 6	80%	92.3	62%	81.2
Gr 8	94%	98.1	65%	84
Gr 10	96%	98.5	96%	97.7

Other School Districts (see Appendix D for data)

Nashoba Valley Vocational Tech

See Introduction for an explanation of all data sources.

Demographics & Socio-Economic Characteristics

Population

1990	15,467
2000	15,633
Male	7,303
Female	8,330
2008	15,329
2010 (projected)††	14,395
2020 (projected)††	12,457

Race & Hispanic Origin, 2000

Race	
White	14,917
Black/African American	108
American Indian/Alaska Native	8
Asian	453
Hawaiian Native/Pacific Islander	9
Other Race	41
Two or more races	97
Hispanic origin	170

Age & Nativity, 2000

Under 5 years	966
18 years and over	11,444
21 years and over	11,010
65 years and over	2,785
85 years and over	502
Median Age	42.9
Native-born	14,547
Foreign-born	1,086

Age, 2020 (projected)††

Under 5 years	588
5 to 19 years	2,371
20 to 39 years	2,023
40 to 64 years	4,007
65 years and over	3,468

Educational Attainment, 2000

Population 25 years and over	10,766
High School graduates or higher	96.0%
Bachelor's degree or higher	60.7%
Graduate degree	30.2%

Income & Poverty, 1999

Per capita income,	$38,949
Median household income	$75,461
Median family income	$87,742
Persons in poverty	312
H'holds receiving public assistance	30
H'holds receiving social security	1,816

Households, 2000

Total households	5,734
With persons under 18	2,177
With persons over 65	1,897
Family households	4,435
Single person households	1,171
Persons per household	2.7
Persons per family	3.1

Labor & Employment, 2000

Civilian labor force	7,796
Unemployment rate	3.2%
Civilian labor force, 2008†	7,681
Unemployment rate†	4.1%
Civilian labor force, 12/09†	7,621
Unemployment rate†	5.8%
Employed persons 16 years and over, by occupation:	
Managers & professionals	4,391
Service occupations	578
Sales & office occupations	1,971
Farming, fishing & forestry	11
Construction & maintenance	235
Production & transportation	359
Self-employed persons	863

Most demographic data is from the 2000 Decennial Census
† Massachusetts Department of Revenue
†† University of Massachusetts, MISER

General Information

Town of Longmeadow
20 Williams St
Longmeadow, MA 01106
413-565-4103

Elevation	170 ft.
Land area (square miles)	9.0
Water area (square miles)	0.5
Population density, 2008 (est)	1,703.2
Year incorporated	1783
Website	www.longmeadow.org

Voters & Government Information

Government type	Open Town Meeting
Number of Select Board Member	5
US Congressional District(s)	2

Registered Voters, October 2008

Total	11,913
Democrats	3,975
Republicans	2,732
Unaffiliated/other	5,164

Local Officials, 2010

Chair, Bd. of Sel.	Robert Barkett
Manager/Admin	Robin Crosbie
Town Clerk	Katherine Ingram
Finance Director	Paul Pasterczyk
Tax Collector	Mary Pequignot
Tax Assessor	Robert LeClair
Attorney	David J. Martel
Public Works	Mike Wrabel
Building	Mark Denver
Planning	Walter Gunn
Police Chief	Robert Siano
Emerg/Fire Chief	Eric Madison

Housing & Construction

New Privately Owned Housing Units Authorized by Building Permit

	Single Family	Total Bldgs	Total Units
2006	4	4	4
2007	2	2	2
2008	5	5	5

Parcel Count by Property Class, 2010

Total	5,723
Single family	5,439
Multiple units	21
Apartments	5
Condos	53
Vacant land	163
Open space	0
Commercial	27
Industrial	7
Misc. residential	6
Other use	2

Public Library

Richard Salter Storrs Library
693 Longmeadow Street
Longmeadow, MA 01106
(413)565-4181

Director	Carl Sturgis

Library Statistics, FY 2008

Population served, 2007	15,315
Registered users	11,906
Circulation	185,219
Reference transactons	17,920
Total program attendance	100,199
per capita:	
Holdings	6.17
Operating income	$43.60
Internet Access	
Internet computers available	18
Weekly users	209

Municipal Finance

Debt at year end 2008	$15,520,855
Moody's rating, July 2009	Aa3

Revenues, 2008

Total	$49,626,627
From all taxes	38,215,685
Federal aid	0
State aid	6,140,532
From other governments	4,553
Charges for services	792,647
Licenses, permits & fees	340,240
Fines & forfeits	58,468
Interfund transfers	579,230
Misc/other/special assessments	1,747,636

Expenditures, 2008

Total	$45,654,422
General government	2,800,521
Public safety	4,238,578
Other/fixed costs	5,728,503
Human services	230,558
Culture & recreation	1,155,140
Debt Service	1,602,787
Education	27,079,991
Public works	2,291,401
Intergovernmental	149,529

Taxation, 2010

Property type	Valuation	Rate
Total	$2,084,466,814	-
Residential	1,984,497,200	18.28
Open space	0	0.00
Commercial	66,002,200	18.28
Industrial	2,995,400	18.28
Personal	30,972,014	18.28

Average Single Family Tax Bill, 2010

Avg. assessed home value	$349,758
Avg. single fam. tax bill	$6,394
Hi-Lo ranking	42/301

Police & Crime, 2008

Number of police officers	26
Violent crimes	6
Property crimes	297

Local School District

(school data 2007-08, except as noted)

Longmeadow
127 Grassy Gutter Rd
Longmeadow, MA 01106
413-565-4200

Superintendent	Elizabeth Hart
Grade plan	PK-12
Total enrollment '09-10	3,102
Grade 12 enrollment, '09-10	255
Graduation rate	98.5%
Dropout rate	0.4%
Per-pupil expenditure	$11,614
Avg teacher salary	$64,206
Student/teacher ratio '08-09	13.0 to 1
Highly-qualified teachers, '08-09	98.6%
Teachers licensed in assigned subject	99.1%
Students per computer	2.8

Massachusetts Competency Assessment System (MCAS), 2009 results

	English		Math	
	% Prof	CPI	% Prof	CPI
Gr 4	72%	90.4	61%	86.9
Gr 6	88%	95.7	75%	90.7
Gr 8	95%	98.5	81%	93.1
Gr 10	91%	96.8	88%	95.1

Other School Districts (see Appendix D for data)
None

©2010 Information Publications, Inc. All rights reserved. Photocopying prohibited. For additional copies, contact the publisher at www.informationpublications.com or (877)544-INFO (4636)

Demographics & Socio-Economic Characteristics*

Population

1990	103,439
2000	105,167
Male	51,807
Female	53,360
2008	103,615
2010 (projected)††	114,613
2020 (projected)††	124,710

Race & Hispanic Origin, 2000

Race	
White	72,145
Black/African American	4,423
American Indian/Alaska Native	256
Asian	17,371
Hawaiian Native/Pacific Islander	38
Other Race	6,813
Two or more races	4,121
Hispanic origin	14,734

Age & Nativity, 2000

Under 5 years	7,696
18 years and over	76,826
21 years and over	71,273
65 years and over	11,313
85 years and over	1,457
Median Age	31.4
Native-born	81,900
Foreign-born	23,267

Age, 2020 (projected)††

Under 5 years	8,921
5 to 19 years	25,819
20 to 39 years	39,289
40 to 64 years	36,295
65 years and over	14,386

Educational Attainment, 2000

Population 25 years and over	64,421
High School graduates or higher	71.2%
Bachelor's degree or higher	18.1%
Graduate degree	6.7%

Income & Poverty, 1999

Per capita income,	$17,557
Median household income	$39,192
Median family income	$45,901
Persons in poverty	17,066
H'holds receiving public assistance	2,194
H'holds receiving social security	8,801

Households, 2000

Total households	37,887
With persons under 18	14,166
With persons over 65	8,005
Family households	23,982
Single person households	10,969
Persons per household	2.7
Persons per family	3.4

Labor & Employment, 2000

Civilian labor force	51,084
Unemployment rate	6.6%
Civilian labor force, 2008†	50,633
Unemployment rate†	8.4%
Civilian labor force, 12/09†	50,757
Unemployment rate†	12.0%
Employed persons 16 years and over, by occupation:	
Managers & professionals	13,546
Service occupations	7,637
Sales & office occupations	11,626
Farming, fishing & forestry	34
Construction & maintenance	4,093
Production & transportation	10,799
Self-employed persons	1,607

Most demographic data is from the 2000 Decennial Census
* see Appendix D and E for American Community Survey data
† Massachusetts Department of Revenue
†† University of Massachusetts, MISER

General Information

City of Lowell
375 Merrimack St
Lowell, MA 01852
978-970-4000

Elevation	100 ft.
Land area (square miles)	13.8
Water area (square miles)	0.8
Population density, 2008 (est)	7,508.3
Year incorporated	1826
Website	www.lowellma.gov

Voters & Government Information

Government type	Council-Manager
Number of Councilpersons	9
US Congressional District(s)	5

Registered Voters, October 2008

Total	51,988
Democrats	21,505
Republicans	4,877
Unaffiliated/other	25,083

Local Officials, 2010

Mayor	James L. Milinezzo
Manager	Bernard Lynch
City Clerk	Richard C. Johnson
Auditor	Sheryl Wright
Treas/Collector	David P. McGurl
Tax Assessor	Susan LeMay (Chr)
Attorney	Christine O'Connor
Public Works	T.J. McCarthy
Building	Robert Camacho
Comm Dev/Planning	Adam Baacke
Police Chief	Kenneth Lavalle
Fire Chief	Edward Pitta

Housing & Construction

New Privately Owned Housing Units Authorized by Building Permit

	Single Family	Total Bldgs	Total Units
2006	143	151	168
2007	101	106	114
2008	92	95	141

Parcel Count by Property Class, 2010

Total	25,641
Single family	11,762
Multiple units	4,501
Apartments	905
Condos	5,288
Vacant land	1,014
Open space	0
Commercial	1,266
Industrial	455
Misc. residential	131
Other use	319

Public Library

Samuel S. Pollard Memorial Library
401 Merrimack St.
Lowell, MA 01852
(978)970-4120

Director . . . . Victoria Woodley

Library Statistics, FY 2008

Population served, 2007	103,512
Registered users	91,554
Circulation	227,100
Reference transactons	51,889
Total program attendance	0
per capita:	
Holdings	2.33
Operating income	$12.06
Internet Access	
Internet computers available	53
Weekly users	2,186

Municipal Finance

Debt at year end 2008	$199,212,477
Moody's rating, July 2009	A3

Revenues, 2008

Total	$300,856,304
From all taxes	99,753,818
Federal aid	3,046,414
State aid	167,690,730
From other governments	542,980
Charges for services	17,151,984
Licenses, permits & fees	1,715,123
Fines & forfeits	787,679
Interfund transfers	2,973,340
Misc/other/special assessments	3,597,118

Expenditures, 2008

Total	$273,347,312
General government	11,656,503
Public safety	36,591,489
Other/fixed costs	18,527,015
Human services	2,922,288
Culture & recreation	3,742,122
Debt Service	24,969,034
Education	141,251,009
Public works	21,104,234
Intergovernmental	12,237,768

Taxation, 2010

Property type	Valuation	Rate
Total	$6,390,673,111	-
Residential	5,300,037,070	13.27
Open space	0	0.00
Commercial	546,665,721	27.46
Industrial	370,326,700	27.46
Personal	173,643,620	27.46

Average Single Family Tax Bill, 2010

Avg. assessed home value	$231,515
Avg. single fam. tax bill	$3,072
Hi-Lo ranking	229/301

Police & Crime, 2008

Number of police officers	239
Violent crimes	1,167
Property crimes	3,750

Local School District

(school data 2007-08, except as noted)

Lowell
43 Highland Street
Lowell, MA 01852
978-674-4324

Superintendent	Chris Scott
Grade plan	PK-12
Total enrollment '09-10	13,331
Grade 12 enrollment, '09-10	775
Graduation rate	73.8%
Dropout rate	11.1%
Per-pupil expenditure	$12,907
Avg teacher salary	$69,387
Student/teacher ratio '08-09	13.1 to 1
Highly-qualified teachers, '08-09	98.2%
Teachers licensed in assigned subject	98.9%
Students per computer	5.5

Massachusetts Competency Assessment System (MCAS), 2009 results

	English		Math	
	% Prof	CPI	% Prof	CPI
Gr 4	28%	63.5	29%	64.8
Gr 6	46%	74.6	46%	69.2
Gr 8	63%	82.8	32%	59.3
Gr 10	66%	85.3	62%	80.4

Other School Districts (see Appendix D for data)
Greater Lowell Vocational Tech

See Introduction for an explanation of all data sources.

©2010 Information Publications, Inc. All rights reserved. Photocopying prohibited. For additional copies, contact the publisher at www.informationpublications.com or (877)544-INFO (4636)

Demographics & Socio-Economic Characteristics

Population

1990	18,820
2000	21,209
Male	10,904
Female	10,305
2008	22,410
2010 (projected)††	21,012
2020 (projected)††	20,563

Race & Hispanic Origin, 2000

Race	
White	20,315
Black/African American	432
American Indian/Alaska Native	20
Asian	125
Hawaiian Native/Pacific Islander	2
Other Race	65
Two or more races	250
Hispanic origin	1,372

Age & Nativity, 2000

Under 5 years	1,040
18 years and over	16,781
21 years and over	15,879
65 years and over	3,167
85 years and over	278
Median Age	38.5
Native-born	18,093
Foreign-born	3,116

Age, 2020 (projected)††

Under 5 years	857
5 to 19 years	3,064
20 to 39 years	5,699
40 to 64 years	7,077
65 years and over	3,866

Educational Attainment, 2000

Population 25 years and over	14,803
High School graduates or higher	75.2%
Bachelor's degree or higher	14.8%
Graduate degree	4.6%

Income & Poverty, 1999

Per capita income,	$20,105
Median household income	$47,002
Median family income	$55,717
Persons in poverty	1,238
H'holds receiving public assistance	134
H'holds receiving social security	2,555

Households, 2000

Total households	7,659
With persons under 18	2,511
With persons over 65	2,320
Family households	5,513
Single person households	1,852
Persons per household	2.6
Persons per family	3.0

Labor & Employment, 2000

Civilian labor force	10,449
Unemployment rate	3.6%
Civilian labor force, 2008†	11,235
Unemployment rate†	8.5%
Civilian labor force, 12/09†	11,386
Unemployment rate†	10.6%
Employed persons 16 years and over, by occupation:	
Managers & professionals	2,747
Service occupations	1,377
Sales & office occupations	2,740
Farming, fishing & forestry	51
Construction & maintenance	1,086
Production & transportation	2,075
Self-employed persons	507

Most demographic data is from the 2000 Decennial Census
† Massachusetts Department of Revenue
†† University of Massachusetts, MISER

General Information

Town of Ludlow
488 Chapin St
Ludlow, MA 01056
413-583-5600

Elevation	239 ft.
Land area (square miles)	27.1
Water area (square miles)	1.1
Population density, 2008 (est)	826.9
Year incorporated	1775
Website	www.ludlow.ma.us

Voters & Government Information

Government type	Rep. Town Meeting
Number of Selectmen	5
US Congressional District(s)	2

Registered Voters, October 2008

Total	13,897
Democrats	6,155
Republicans	1,643
Unaffiliated/other	5,997

Local Officials, 2010

Chair, Bd. of Sel.	Darlene Cincone
Town Administrator	Ellie Villeno
Town Clerk	Laurie Gibbons
Town Accountant	James W. Young
Tax Collector	Fred Pereira
Tax Assessor	Edward P. Mazur (Chr)
Attorney	David Martel
Public Works	Paul Dzubek
Building	Brien LaPorte
Comm Dev/Planning	Edgar Minnie (Chr)
Police Chief	James McGowan
Fire Chief	Charles Chaconas

Housing & Construction

New Privately Owned Housing Units Authorized by Building Permit

	Single Family	Total Bldgs	Total Units
2006	53	54	143
2007	50	51	61
2008	23	24	25

Parcel Count by Property Class, 2010

Total	8,650
Single family	5,875
Multiple units	493
Apartments	54
Condos	418
Vacant land	1,132
Open space	0
Commercial	275
Industrial	132
Misc. residential	43
Other use	228

Public Library

Hubbard Memorial Library
24 Center Street
Ludlow, MA 01056
(413)583-3408

Librarian	Judy Kelly

Library Statistics, FY 2008

Population served, 2007	22,062
Registered users	7,903
Circulation	145,465
Reference transactons	0
Total program attendance	0
per capita:	
Holdings	2.77
Operating income	$18.28
Internet Access	
Internet computers available	10
Weekly users	206

Municipal Finance

Debt at year end 2008	$25,990,255
Moody's rating, July 2009	A2

Revenues, 2008

Total	$48,621,162
From all taxes	28,417,455
Federal aid	0
State aid	17,692,410
From other governments	56,289
Charges for services	1,089,951
Licenses, permits & fees	499,591
Fines & forfeits	0
Interfund transfers	270,000
Misc/other/special assessments	297,733

Expenditures, 2008

Total	$48,637,769
General government	2,168,580
Public safety	5,434,454
Other/fixed costs	8,840,881
Human services	666,012
Culture & recreation	549,356
Debt Service	3,213,790
Education	23,809,143
Public works	3,652,037
Intergovernmental	303,516

Taxation, 2010

Property type	Valuation	Rate
Total	$1,801,425,170	-
Residential	1,550,378,145	14.82
Open space	0	0.00
Commercial	129,724,865	14.82
Industrial	52,798,620	14.82
Personal	68,523,540	14.82

Average Single Family Tax Bill, 2010

Avg. assessed home value	$218,477
Avg. single fam. tax bill	$3,238
Hi-Lo ranking	209/301

Police & Crime, 2008

Number of police officers	34
Violent crimes	15
Property crimes	306

Local School District

(school data 2007-08, except as noted)

Ludlow
63 Chestnut Street
Ludlow, MA 01056
413-583-8372

Superintendent	Theresa Kane
Grade plan	PK-12
Total enrollment '09-10	3,050
Grade 12 enrollment, '09-10	236
Graduation rate	89.4%
Dropout rate	3.9%
Per-pupil expenditure	$10,730
Avg teacher salary	$55,481
Student/teacher ratio '08-09	13.8 to 1
Highly-qualified teachers, '08-09	98.9%
Teachers licensed in assigned subject	99.5%
Students per computer	5.2

Massachusetts Competency Assessment System (MCAS), 2009 results

	English		Math	
	% Prof	CPI	% Prof	CPI
Gr 4	51%	79.2	46%	77.8
Gr 6	64%	86.5	63%	82.6
Gr 8	82%	93.2	49%	76.1
Gr 10	76%	90.9	65%	83.6

Other School Districts (see Appendix D for data)
None

©2010 Information Publications, Inc. All rights reserved. Photocopying prohibited. For additional copies, contact the publisher at www.informationpublications.com or (877)544-INFO (4636)

Demographics & Socio-Economic Characteristics

Population

1990	9,117
2000	9,401
Male	4,655
Female	4,746
2008	9,946
2010 (projected)††	9,189
2020 (projected)††	8,880

Race & Hispanic Origin, 2000

Race	
White	9,120
Black/African American	65
American Indian/Alaska Native	19
Asian	73
Hawaiian Native/Pacific Islander	2
Other Race	24
Two or more races	98
Hispanic origin	108

Age & Nativity, 2000

Under 5 years	554
18 years and over	6,974
21 years and over	6,702
65 years and over	1,129
85 years and over	107
Median Age	39.4
Native-born	9,001
Foreign-born	400

Age, 2020 (projected)††

Under 5 years	479
5 to 19 years	1,587
20 to 39 years	1,963
40 to 64 years	3,198
65 years and over	1,653

Educational Attainment, 2000

Population 25 years and over	6,467
High School graduates or higher	88.9%
Bachelor's degree or higher	31.5%
Graduate degree	12.1%

Income & Poverty, 1999

Per capita income,	$26,986
Median household income	$56,813
Median family income	$63,981
Persons in poverty	382
H'holds receiving public assistance	53
H'holds receiving social security	852

Households, 2000

Total households	3,535
With persons under 18	1,307
With persons over 65	817
Family households	2,668
Single person households	712
Persons per household	2.7
Persons per family	3.1

Labor & Employment, 2000

Civilian labor force	5,224
Unemployment rate	4.8%
Civilian labor force, 2008†	5,283
Unemployment rate†	7.0%
Civilian labor force, 12/09†	5,191
Unemployment rate†	9.6%
Employed persons 16 years and over, by occupation:	
Managers & professionals	2,131
Service occupations	503
Sales & office occupations	1,256
Farming, fishing & forestry	14
Construction & maintenance	492
Production & transportation	576
Self-employed persons	470

Most demographic data is from the 2000 Decennial Census
† Massachusetts Department of Revenue
†† University of Massachusetts, MISER

General Information

Town of Lunenburg
17 Main Street
PO Box 135
Lunenburg, MA 01462
978-582-4131

Elevation	570 ft.
Land area (square miles)	26.4
Water area (square miles)	1.3
Population density, 2008 (est)	376.7
Year incorporated	1728
Website	www.lunenburgonline.com

Voters & Government Information

Government type	Open Town Meeting
Number of Selectmen	5
US Congressional District(s)	1

Registered Voters, October 2008

Total	7,253
Democrats	1,523
Republicans	1,225
Unaffiliated/other	4,445

Local Officials, 2010

Chair, Bd. of Sel.	Tom Alonzo
Town Manager	Kerry Spiedel
Town Clerk	Kathryn Herrick
Finance Committee	Brian Laffond (Chr)
Tax Collector	Jeffrey Ugalde
Tax Assessor	Christopher Comeau
Attorney	Kopelman & Paige
Public Works Dir	John Rodriguenz
Building	Michael Sauvageau
Planning Director	Marion Benson
Police Chief	Daniel Bourgeois
Emerg/Fire Chief	Scott Glenny

Housing & Construction

New Privately Owned Housing Units Authorized by Building Permit

	Single Family	Total Bldgs	Total Units
2006	29	29	29
2007	16	19	24
2008	2	2	2

Parcel Count by Property Class, 2010

Total	4,540
Single family	3,418
Multiple units	93
Apartments	5
Condos	179
Vacant land	510
Open space	0
Commercial	139
Industrial	32
Misc. residential	38
Other use	126

Public Library

Lunenburg Public Library
1023 Massachusetts Ave.
Lunenburg, MA 01462
(978)582-4140

Director	Amy Sadkin

Library Statistics, FY 2008

Population served, 2007	9,948
Registered users	6,168
Circulation	116,126
Reference transactons	1,572
Total program attendance	104,104
per capita:	
Holdings	5.26
Operating income	$35.58
Internet Access	
Internet computers available	17
Weekly users	480

Municipal Finance

Debt at year end 2008	$29,127,893
Moody's rating, July 2009	A2

Revenues, 2008

Total	$25,771,238
From all taxes	17,314,050
Federal aid	0
State aid	6,354,506
From other governments	40,767
Charges for services	457,179
Licenses, permits & fees	154,601
Fines & forfeits	2,565
Interfund transfers	821,452
Misc/other/special assessments	313,059

Expenditures, 2008

Total	$25,642,812
General government	1,547,734
Public safety	2,116,040
Other/fixed costs	2,349,678
Human services	158,545
Culture & recreation	351,520
Debt Service	2,665,671
Education	14,716,120
Public works	1,003,040
Intergovernmental	734,464

Taxation, 2010

Property type	Valuation	Rate
Total	$1,227,274,404	-
Residential	1,110,439,200	14.20
Open space	0	0.00
Commercial	71,405,100	14.20
Industrial	22,444,600	14.20
Personal	22,985,504	14.20

Average Single Family Tax Bill, 2010

Avg. assessed home value	$281,062
Avg. single fam. tax bill	$3,991
Hi-Lo ranking	138/301

Police & Crime, 2008

Number of police officers	13
Violent crimes	24
Property crimes	174

Local School District

(school data 2007-08, except as noted)

Lunenburg
1033 Mass Avenue
Lunenburg, MA 01462
978-582-4100

Superintendent	Loxi Jo Calmes
Grade plan	PK-12
Total enrollment '09-10	1,702
Grade 12 enrollment, '09-10	127
Graduation rate	85.2%
Dropout rate	8.4%
Per-pupil expenditure	$9,740
Avg teacher salary	$59,180
Student/teacher ratio '08-09	14.5 to 1
Highly-qualified teachers, '08-09	98.5%
Teachers licensed in assigned subject	98.3%
Students per computer	NA

Massachusetts Competency Assessment System (MCAS), 2009 results

	English		Math	
	% Prof	CPI	% Prof	CPI
Gr 4	46%	77.7	45%	77
Gr 6	87%	95.8	76%	90.5
Gr 8	90%	96.1	64%	82
Gr 10	92%	97.4	88%	94.7

Other School Districts (see Appendix D for data)

Receives students from Shirley; sends to Montachusett Vocational Tech

©2010 Information Publications, Inc. All rights reserved. Photocopying prohibited. For additional copies, contact the publisher at www.informationpublications.com or (877)544-INFO (4636)

See Introduction for an explanation of all data sources.

Demographics & Socio-Economic Characteristics*

Population

1990	81,245
2000	89,050
Male	43,079
Female	45,971
2008	86,957
2010 (projected)††	97,330
2020 (projected)††	107,859

Race & Hispanic Origin, 2000

Race	
White	60,452
Black/African American	9,394
American Indian/Alaska Native	332
Asian	5,730
Hawaiian Native/Pacific Islander	79
Other Race	8,744
Two or more races	4,319
Hispanic origin	16,383

Age & Nativity, 2000

Under 5 years	6,505
18 years and over	64,999
21 years and over	61,451
65 years and over	11,368
85 years and over	1,486
Median Age	34.2
Native-born	68,774
Foreign-born	20,348

Age, 2020 (projected)††

Under 5 years	8,123
5 to 19 years	22,784
20 to 39 years	31,480
40 to 64 years	31,510
65 years and over	13,962

Educational Attainment, 2000

Population 25 years and over	57,093
High School graduates or higher	74.2%
Bachelor's degree or higher	16.4%
Graduate degree	4.8%

Income & Poverty, 1999

Per capita income,	$17,492
Median household income	$37,364
Median family income	$45,295
Persons in poverty	14,525
H'holds receiving public assistance	2,126
H'holds receiving social security	8,965

Households, 2000

Total households	33,511
With persons under 18	12,056
With persons over 65	8,446
Family households	21,033
Single person households	10,402
Persons per household	2.6
Persons per family	3.3

Labor & Employment, 2000

Civilian labor force	41,842
Unemployment rate	6.2%
Civilian labor force, 2008†	41,505
Unemployment rate†	7.6%
Civilian labor force, 12/09†	41,239
Unemployment rate†	10.3%
Employed persons 16 years and over, by occupation:	
Managers & professionals	10,112
Service occupations	7,796
Sales & office occupations	11,056
Farming, fishing & forestry	132
Construction & maintenance	3,414
Production & transportation	6,733
Self-employed persons	1,621

Most demographic data is from the 2000 Decennial Census
* see Appendix D and E for American Community Survey data
† Massachusetts Department of Revenue
†† University of Massachusetts, MISER

General Information

City of Lynn
3 City Hall Sq
Lynn, MA 01901
781-598-4000

Elevation	34 ft.
Land area (square miles)	10.8
Water area (square miles)	2.7
Population density, 2008 (est)	8,051.6
Year incorporated	1637
Website	www.ci.lynn.ma.us

Voters & Government Information

Government type	Mayor-Council
Number of Councilpersons	11
US Congressional District(s)	6

Registered Voters, October 2008

Total	48,676
Democrats	23,178
Republicans	3,217
Unaffiliated/other	21,942

Local Officials, 2010

Mayor	Judith Flanagan Kennedy
Manager/Admin	NA
City Clerk	Mary Audley
Finance Director	J. Pace/R. Pace
Tax Collector	Frederick Cronin
Tax Assessor	Peter Caron
Attorney	Michael J. Barry
Public Works	Jay Fink
Building	Michael Donovan
Comm Dev/Planning	Michael Donovan
Police Chief	Kevin Coppinger
Emerg/Fire Chief	Dennis Carmody

Housing & Construction

New Privately Owned Housing Units Authorized by Building Permit

	Single Family	Total Bldgs	Total Units
2006	31	35	56
2007	20	23	26
2008	20	21	22

Parcel Count by Property Class, 2010

Total	21,193
Single family	11,433
Multiple units	4,691
Apartments	504
Condos	2,623
Vacant land	623
Open space	0
Commercial	796
Industrial	137
Misc. residential	50
Other use	336

Public Library

Lynn Public Library
5 North Common St.
Lynn, MA 01902
(781)595-0567

Chief Librarian	Nadine Mitchell

Library Statistics, FY 2008

Population served, 2007	87,122
Registered users	39,070
Circulation	174,046
Reference transactons	6,879
Total program attendance	488,688
per capita:	
Holdings	1.49
Operating income	$13.28
Internet Access	
Internet computers available	17
Weekly users	4,084

Municipal Finance

Debt at year end 2008	$96,375,000
Moody's rating, July 2009	Baa1

Revenues, 2008

Total	$251,953,371
From all taxes	91,281,944
Federal aid	0
State aid	153,949,382
From other governments	412,699
Charges for services	2,035,124
Licenses, permits & fees	1,204,280
Fines & forfeits	1,014,536
Interfund transfers	101,496
Misc/other/special assessments	976,955

Expenditures, 2008

Total	$219,676,789
General government	6,057,597
Public safety	47,345,862
Other/fixed costs	23,239,216
Human services	976,320
Culture & recreation	1,457,516
Debt Service	13,149,981
Education	107,776,658
Public works	12,236,424
Intergovernmental	7,275,627

Taxation, 2010

Property type	Valuation	Rate
Total	$5,246,831,500	-
Residential	4,499,428,024	15.53
Open space	0	0.00
Commercial	464,501,216	31.05
Industrial	134,135,400	31.05
Personal	148,766,860	31.05

Average Single Family Tax Bill, 2010

Avg. assessed home value	$223,153
Avg. single fam. tax bill	$3,466
Hi-Lo ranking	177/301

Police & Crime, 2008

Number of police officers	178
Violent crimes	816
Property crimes	3,014

Local School District

(school data 2007-08, except as noted)

Lynn
90 Commercial Street
Lynn, MA 01905
781-593-1680

Superintendent	Catherine Latham
Grade plan	PK-12
Total enrollment '09-10	13,373
Grade 12 enrollment, '09-10	876
Graduation rate	70.5%
Dropout rate	15.4%
Per-pupil expenditure	$12,996
Avg teacher salary	$60,523
Student/teacher ratio '08-09	13.9 to 1
Highly-qualified teachers, '08-09	89.0%
Teachers licensed in assigned subject	98.4%
Students per computer	9.1

Massachusetts Competency Assessment System (MCAS), 2009 results

	English		Math	
	% Prof	CPI	% Prof	CPI
Gr 4	32%	68	30%	68.7
Gr 6	47%	75.7	37%	65.6
Gr 8	61%	82.3	28%	57.5
Gr 10	63%	83.9	56%	78

Other School Districts (see Appendix D for data)
None

©2010 Information Publications, Inc. All rights reserved. Photocopying prohibited. For additional copies, contact the publisher at www.informationpublications.com or (877)544-INFO (4636)

Demographics & Socio-Economic Characteristics

Population

1990	11,274
2000	11,542
Male	5,658
Female	5,884
2008	11,412
2010 (projected)††	10,881
2020 (projected)††	9,698

Race & Hispanic Origin, 2000

Race	
White	11,165
Black/African American	50
American Indian/Alaska Native	0
Asian	222
Hawaiian Native/Pacific Islander	4
Other Race	24
Two or more races	77
Hispanic origin	77

Age & Nativity, 2000

Under 5 years	735
18 years and over	8,676
21 years and over	8,398
65 years and over	1,987
85 years and over	196
Median Age	42.6
Native-born	10,961
Foreign-born	581

Age, 2020 (projected)††

Under 5 years	431
5 to 19 years	1,696
20 to 39 years	1,853
40 to 64 years	3,397
65 years and over	2,321

Educational Attainment, 2000

Population 25 years and over	8,093
High School graduates or higher	94.5%
Bachelor's degree or higher	49.3%
Graduate degree	21.3%

Income & Poverty, 1999

Per capita income,	$39,560
Median household income	$80,626
Median family income	$91,869
Persons in poverty	289
H'holds receiving public assistance	0
H'holds receiving social security	1,335

Households, 2000

Total households	4,186
With persons under 18	1,525
With persons over 65	1,401
Family households	3,350
Single person households	730
Persons per household	2.8
Persons per family	3.1

Labor & Employment, 2000

Civilian labor force	5,660
Unemployment rate	3.1%
Civilian labor force, 2008†	5,720
Unemployment rate†	5.1%
Civilian labor force, 12/09†	5,678
Unemployment rate†	7.6%
Employed persons 16 years and over, by occupation:	
Managers & professionals	2,934
Service occupations	526
Sales & office occupations	1,478
Farming, fishing & forestry	0
Construction & maintenance	283
Production & transportation	264
Self-employed persons	541

Most demographic data is from the 2000 Decennial Census
† Massachusetts Department of Revenue
†† University of Massachusetts, MISER

General Information

Town of Lynnfield
55 Summer St
Lynnfield, MA 01940
781-334-9400

Elevation	98 ft.
Land area (square miles)	10.1
Water area (square miles)	0.3
Population density, 2008 (est)	1,129.9
Year incorporated	1814
Website	www.town.lynnfield.ma.us

Voters & Government Information

Government type	Open Town Meeting
Number of Selectmen	3
US Congressional District(s)	6

Registered Voters, October 2008

Total	8,906
Democrats	2,005
Republicans	1,765
Unaffiliated/other	5,098

Local Officials, 2010

Chair, Bd. of Sel.	Robert MacKendrick
Manager/Admin	William Gustus
Town Clerk	Amy K. Summers
Accountant	Julie McCarthy
Tax Collector	Christine O'Sullivan
Tax Assessor	Richard Simmons
Attorney	Thomas Mullen
Public Works	Dennis R. Roy
Building	John Roberto
Planning	Richard O'Neil
Police Chief	Joseph Dunn
Emerg/Fire Chief	Francis Lennon

Housing & Construction

New Privately Owned Housing Units Authorized by Building Permit

	Single Family	Total Bldgs	Total Units
2006	11	14	25
2007	26	27	31
2008	17	20	217

Parcel Count by Property Class, 2010

Total	4,281
Single family	3,798
Multiple units	31
Apartments	8
Condos	84
Vacant land	195
Open space	0
Commercial	127
Industrial	6
Misc. residential	10
Other use	22

Public Library

Lynnfield Public Library
18 Summer St.
Lynnfield, MA 01940
(781)334-5411

Director	Nancy Ryan

Library Statistics, FY 2008

Population served, 2007	11,382
Registered users	8,964
Circulation	144,208
Reference transactons	26,129
Total program attendance	113,376
per capita:	
Holdings	8.07
Operating income	$67.02
Internet Access	
Internet computers available	11
Weekly users	2,468

Municipal Finance

Debt at year end 2008	$28,086,174
Moody's rating, July 2009	A1

Revenues, 2008

Total	$38,128,922
From all taxes	27,100,871
Federal aid	37
State aid	5,479,416
From other governments	0
Charges for services	369,095
Licenses, permits & fees	662,986
Fines & forfeits	98,503
Interfund transfers	3,130,064
Misc/other/special assessments	643,975

Expenditures, 2008

Total	$36,484,638
General government	1,555,734
Public safety	3,235,391
Other/fixed costs	6,150,426
Human services	235,783
Culture & recreation	616,074
Debt Service	2,861,352
Education	18,867,486
Public works	2,668,120
Intergovernmental	294,272

Taxation, 2010

Property type	Valuation	Rate
Total	$2,373,478,630	-
Residential	2,181,845,401	12.84
Open space	0	0.00
Commercial	143,990,369	13.72
Industrial	19,806,300	13.72
Personal	27,836,560	13.72

Average Single Family Tax Bill, 2010

Avg. assessed home value	$538,718
Avg. single fam. tax bill	$6,917
Hi-Lo ranking	36/301

Police & Crime, 2008

Number of police officers	18
Violent crimes	12
Property crimes	152

Local School District

(school data 2007-08, except as noted)

Lynnfield
55 Summer Street
Lynnfield, MA 01940
781-334-5800

Superintendent	Robert Hassett
Grade plan	PK-12
Total enrollment '09-10	2,353
Grade 12 enrollment, '09-10	167
Graduation rate	94.0%
Dropout rate	2.4%
Per-pupil expenditure	$10,276
Avg teacher salary	$65,940
Student/teacher ratio '08-09	15.8 to 1
Highly-qualified teachers, '08-09	99.9%
Teachers licensed in assigned subject	100.0%
Students per computer	2.3

Massachusetts Competency Assessment System (MCAS), 2009 results

	English		Math	
	% Prof	CPI	% Prof	CPI
Gr 4	88%	95.5	83%	94.6
Gr 6	79%	91.8	63%	81.6
Gr 8	89%	96.1	73%	87.4
Gr 10	94%	98	90%	96.2

Other School Districts (see Appendix D for data)
North Shore Vocational Tech

©2010 Information Publications, Inc. All rights reserved. Photocopying prohibited. For additional copies, contact the publisher at www.informationpublications.com or (877)544-INFO (4636)

See Introduction for an explanation of all data sources.

Demographics & Socio-Economic Characteristics*

Population

1990	53,884
2000	56,340
Male	27,122
Female	29,218
2008	55,597
2010 (projected)††	58,193
2020 (projected)††	60,383

Race & Hispanic Origin, 2000

Race	
White	40,618
Black/African American	4,592
American Indian/Alaska Native	80
Asian	7,882
Hawaiian Native/Pacific Islander	33
Other Race	1,184
Two or more races	1,951
Hispanic origin	2,696

Age & Nativity, 2000

Under 5 years	3,294
18 years and over	45,102
21 years and over	43,395
65 years and over	7,804
85 years and over	1,077
Median Age	35.7
Native-born	41,851
Foreign-born	14,489

Age, 2020 (projected)††

Under 5 years	3,352
5 to 19 years	9,745
20 to 39 years	17,838
40 to 64 years	20,380
65 years and over	9,068

Educational Attainment, 2000

Population 25 years and over	40,572
High School graduates or higher	83.4%
Bachelor's degree or higher	26.2%
Graduate degree	9.9%

Income & Poverty, 1999

Per capita income,	$22,004
Median household income	$45,654
Median family income	$55,557
Persons in poverty	5,118
H'holds receiving public assistance	542
H'holds receiving social security	5,806

Households, 2000

Total households	23,009
With persons under 18	6,377
With persons over 65	5,783
Family households	13,570
Single person households	7,410
Persons per household	2.4
Persons per family	3.1

Labor & Employment, 2000

Civilian labor force	31,147
Unemployment rate	4.0%
Civilian labor force, 2008†	31,419
Unemployment rate†	6.2%
Civilian labor force, 12/09†	31,412
Unemployment rate†	8.7%
Employed persons 16 years and over, by occupation:	
Managers & professionals	10,631
Service occupations	5,097
Sales & office occupations	8,703
Farming, fishing & forestry	14
Construction & maintenance	2,210
Production & transportation	3,248
Self-employed persons	1,499

Most demographic data is from the 2000 Decennial Census
* see Appendix E for American Community Survey data
† Massachusetts Department of Revenue
†† University of Massachusetts, MISER

General Information

City of Malden
200 Pleasant St
Malden, MA 02148
781-397-7116

Elevation	30 ft.
Land area (square miles)	5.1
Water area (square miles)	0.0
Population density, 2008 (est)	10,901.4
Year incorporated	1649
Website	www.ci.malden.ma.us

Voters & Government Information

Government type	Mayor-Council
Number of Councilpersons	11
US Congressional District(s)	7

Registered Voters, October 2008

Total	30,168
Democrats	13,819
Republicans	2,017
Unaffiliated/other	14,113

Local Officials, 2010

Mayor	Richard Howard
Manager/Admin	(vacant)
City Clerk	Karen Anderson
Finance Director	(vacant)
Tax Collector	(vacant)
Tax Assessor	Robert Donnelly
Attorney	Katherine Fallon
Public Works	Jeffrey Manship
Building	Chris Simonelli
Comm Dev/Planning	Michelle Romero
Police Chief	James Holland
Fire Chief	Michael Murphy

Housing & Construction

New Privately Owned Housing Units Authorized by Building Permit

	Single Family	Total Bldgs	Total Units
2006	16	22	87
2007	18	21	84
2008	2	2	2

Parcel Count by Property Class, 2010

Total	13,020
Single family	5,603
Multiple units	4,137
Apartments	303
Condos	2,015
Vacant land	293
Open space	0
Commercial	366
Industrial	130
Misc. residential	29
Other use	144

Public Library

Malden Public Library
36 Salem St.
Malden, MA 02148
(781)324-0218

Director	Dina G. Malgeri

Library Statistics, FY 2008

Population served, 2007	55,712
Registered users	29,847
Circulation	288,783
Reference transactons	14,066
Total program attendance	163,650
per capita:	
Holdings	4.16
Operating income	$27.21
Internet Access	
Internet computers available	17
Weekly users	1,291

Municipal Finance

Debt at year end 2008	$111,183,873
Moody's rating, July 2009	A3

Revenues, 2008

Total	$141,315,534
From all taxes	62,143,831
Federal aid	1,726,273
State aid	61,959,366
From other governments	235,702
Charges for services	3,574,220
Licenses, permits & fees	1,681,291
Fines & forfeits	1,046,793
Interfund transfers	5,384,308
Misc/other/special assessments	1,781,875

Expenditures, 2008

Total	$121,776,419
General government	11,749,811
Public safety	18,789,095
Other/fixed costs	9,234,273
Human services	989,956
Culture & recreation	2,097,180
Debt Service	11,932,476
Education	49,269,408
Public works	7,081,289
Intergovernmental	9,257,140

Taxation, 2010

Property type	Valuation	Rate
Total	$5,099,369,821	-
Residential	4,414,051,818	12.39
Open space	0	0.00
Commercial	412,991,823	21.38
Industrial	170,798,860	21.38
Personal	101,527,320	21.38

Average Single Family Tax Bill, 2010

Avg. assessed home value	NA
Avg. single fam. tax bill	NA
Hi-Lo ranking	NA

Police & Crime, 2008

Number of police officers	107
Violent crimes	NA
Property crimes	NA

Local School District

(school data 2007-08, except as noted)

Malden
200 Pleasant Street
Malden, MA 02148
781-397-7204

Superintendent	Sidney Smith
Grade plan	PK-12
Total enrollment '09-10	6,332
Grade 12 enrollment, '09-10	376
Graduation rate	72.3%
Dropout rate	13.5%
Per-pupil expenditure	$12,055
Avg teacher salary	$73,547
Student/teacher ratio '08-09	14.2 to 1
Highly-qualified teachers, '08-09	97.2%
Teachers licensed in assigned subject	98.8%
Students per computer	7.1

Massachusetts Competency Assessment System (MCAS), 2009 results

	English		Math	
	% Prof	CPI	% Prof	CPI
Gr 4	28%	67.1	30%	68.4
Gr 6	59%	82.5	49%	74.2
Gr 8	78%	90.6	37%	64.9
Gr 10	73%	89.3	65%	83.8

Other School Districts (see Appendix D for data)

Northeast Metro Vocational Tech

©2010 Information Publications, Inc. All rights reserved. Photocopying prohibited. For additional copies, contact the publisher at www.informationpublications.com or (877)544-INFO (4636)

See Introduction for an explanation of all data sources.

Demographics & Socio-Economic Characteristics

Population

1990	5,286
2000	5,228
Male	2,468
Female	2,760
2008	5,260
2010 (projected)††	4,759
2020 (projected)††	4,276

Race & Hispanic Origin, 2000

Race	
White	5,169
Black/African American	3
American Indian/Alaska Native	9
Asian	20
Hawaiian Native/Pacific Islander	0
Other Race	6
Two or more races	21
Hispanic origin	40

Age & Nativity, 2000

Under 5 years	255
18 years and over	3,978
21 years and over	3,876
65 years and over	859
85 years and over	102
Median Age	43.7
Native-born	4,965
Foreign-born	263

Age, 2020 (projected)††

Under 5 years	177
5 to 19 years	590
20 to 39 years	828
40 to 64 years	1,367
65 years and over	1,314

Educational Attainment, 2000

Population 25 years and over	3,704
High School graduates or higher	96.0%
Bachelor's degree or higher	56.0%
Graduate degree	22.1%

Income & Poverty, 1999

Per capita income,	$47,910
Median household income	$73,467
Median family income	$93,609
Persons in poverty	249
H'holds receiving public assistance	19
H'holds receiving social security	686

Households, 2000

Total households	2,168
With persons under 18	672
With persons over 65	626
Family households	1,436
Single person households	597
Persons per household	2.4
Persons per family	3.0

Labor & Employment, 2000

Civilian labor force	2,672
Unemployment rate	1.8%
Civilian labor force, 2008†	2,789
Unemployment rate†	4.9%
Civilian labor force, 12/09†	2,755
Unemployment rate†	7.0%
Employed persons 16 years and over, by occupation:	
Managers & professionals	1,363
Service occupations	234
Sales & office occupations	732
Farming, fishing & forestry	8
Construction & maintenance	99
Production & transportation	187
Self-employed persons	349

Most demographic data is from the 2000 Decennial Census
† Massachusetts Department of Revenue
†† University of Massachusetts, MISER

General Information

Town of Manchester-by-the-Sea
10 Central St
Manchester-by-the-Sea, MA 01944
978-526-2040

Elevation	57 ft.
Land area (square miles)	9.3
Water area (square miles)	9.0
Population density, 2008 (est)	565.6
Year incorporated	1645
Website	www.manchester.ma.us

Voters & Government Information

Government type	Open Town Meeting
Number of Selectmen	5
US Congressional District(s)	6

Registered Voters, October 2008

Total	3,878
Democrats	841
Republicans	841
Unaffiliated/other	2,180

Local Officials, 2010

Chair, Bd. of Sel.	Susan Thorne
Manager	Wayne Melville
Town Clerk	Denise Samolchuk
Finance Director	Charles Lane
Tax Collector	Caroline Johnson
Tax Assessor	Virginia Thompson
Attorney	NA
Public Works	Steven Kenney
Building	Elizabeth Heisey
Comm Dev/Planning	NA
Police Chief	Glenn McKiel
Emerg/Fire Chief	Andrew Paskalis

Housing & Construction

New Privately Owned Housing Units Authorized by Building Permit

	Single Family	Total Bldgs	Total Units
2006	17	17	17
2007	9	10	11
2008	9	9	9

Parcel Count by Property Class, 2010

Total	2,260
Single family	1,541
Multiple units	128
Apartments	13
Condos	183
Vacant land	185
Open space	0
Commercial	101
Industrial	14
Misc. residential	56
Other use	39

Public Library

Manchester-by-the-Sea Public Library
15 Union St.
Manchester-by-the-Sea, MA 01944
(978)526-7711

Director	Dorothy Sieradzki

Library Statistics, FY 2008

Population served, 2007	5,265
Registered users	5,365
Circulation	70,597
Reference transactons	3,512
Total program attendance	38,528
per capita:	
Holdings	10.08
Operating income	$71.44
Internet Access	
Internet computers available	6
Weekly users	75

Municipal Finance

Debt at year end 2008	$14,131,885
Moody's rating, July 2009	Aa2

Revenues, 2008

Total	$19,728,718
From all taxes	17,354,723
Federal aid	0
State aid	344,071
From other governments	32,225
Charges for services	420,980
Licenses, permits & fees	316,248
Fines & forfeits	57,366
Interfund transfers	990,921
Misc/other/special assessments	106,092

Expenditures, 2008

Total	$18,657,977
General government	995,753
Public safety	2,393,544
Other/fixed costs	2,013,345
Human services	217,482
Culture & recreation	516,381
Debt Service	1,650,639
Education	9,337,613
Public works	1,417,513
Intergovernmental	115,707

Taxation, 2010

Property type	Valuation	Rate
Total	$2,306,398,423	-
Residential	2,161,387,030	8.14
Open space	0	0.00
Commercial	88,761,973	8.14
Industrial	6,595,750	8.14
Personal	49,653,670	8.14

Average Single Family Tax Bill, 2010

Avg. assessed home value	$1,112,485
Avg. single fam. tax bill	$9,056
Hi-Lo ranking	13/301

Police & Crime, 2008

Number of police officers	14
Violent crimes	0
Property crimes	12

Local School District

(school data 2007-08, except as noted)

Manchester (non-op)
36 Lincoln Street
Manchester, MA 01944
978-526-4919

Superintendent	Marcia O'Neil

Non-operating district.
Resident students are sent to the Other School Districts listed below.

Grade plan	NA
Total enrollment '09-10	NA
Grade 12 enrollment, '09-10	NA
Graduation rate	NA
Dropout rate	NA
Per-pupil expenditure	NA
Avg teacher salary	NA
Student/teacher ratio '08-09	NA
Highly-qualified teachers, '08-09	NA
Teachers licensed in assigned subject	NA
Students per computer	NA

Other School Districts (see Appendix D for data)
Manchester Essex Regional, North Shore Vocational Tech

©2010 Information Publications, Inc. All rights reserved. Photocopying prohibited. For additional copies, contact the publisher at www.informationpublications.com or (877)544-INFO (4636)

See Introduction for an explanation of all data sources.

Demographics & Socio-Economic Characteristics

Population

1990	16,568
2000	22,414
Male	11,175
Female	11,239
2008	23,969
2010 (projected)††	26,523
2020 (projected)††	31,278

Race & Hispanic Origin, 2000

Race	
White	21,137
Black/African American	489
American Indian/Alaska Native	46
Asian	432
Hawaiian Native/Pacific Islander	4
Other Race	96
Two or more races	210
Hispanic origin	317

Age & Nativity, 2000

Under 5 years	2,154
18 years and over	15,386
21 years and over	14,893
65 years and over	1,426
85 years and over	161
Median Age	33.8
Native-born	21,520
Foreign-born	894

Age, 2020 (projected)††

Under 5 years	2,379
5 to 19 years	6,713
20 to 39 years	9,465
40 to 64 years	9,837
65 years and over	2,884

Educational Attainment, 2000

Population 25 years and over	14,306
High School graduates or higher	93.2%
Bachelor's degree or higher	42.1%
Graduate degree	13.4%

Income & Poverty, 1999

Per capita income,	$27,441
Median household income	$66,925
Median family income	$78,058
Persons in poverty	998
H'holds receiving public assistance	149
H'holds receiving social security	1,236

Households, 2000

Total households	7,942
With persons under 18	3,689
With persons over 65	1,108
Family households	5,859
Single person households	1,672
Persons per household	2.8
Persons per family	3.3

Labor & Employment, 2000

Civilian labor force	11,983
Unemployment rate	3.5%
Civilian labor force, 2008†	12,649
Unemployment rate†	5.9%
Civilian labor force, 12/09†	12,431
Unemployment rate†	7.4%
Employed persons 16 years and over, by occupation:	
Managers & professionals	5,691
Service occupations	1,175
Sales & office occupations	2,873
Farming, fishing & forestry	0
Construction & maintenance	822
Production & transportation	1,005
Self-employed persons	671

Most demographic data is from the 2000 Decennial Census
† Massachusetts Department of Revenue
†† University of Massachusetts, MISER

General Information

Town of Mansfield
6 Park Row
Mansfield, MA 02048
508-261-7370

Elevation	150 ft.
Land area (square miles)	20.5
Water area (square miles)	0.3
Population density, 2008 (est)	1,169.2
Year incorporated	1775
Email	hchristian@mansfieldma.com

Voters & Government Information

Government type	Open Town Meeting
Number of Selectmen	5
US Congressional District(s)	4

Registered Voters, October 2008

Total	14,399
Democrats	3,778
Republicans	2,275
Unaffiliated/other	8,260

Local Officials, 2010

Chair, Bd. of Sel.	Ann Baldwin
Manager	William Ross
Town Clerk	Helen Christian
Town Accountant	John Stanbrook Hart
Tax Collector	Roxanne Donovan
Tax Assessor	Nancy Hinote
Attorney	Robert S. Mangiaratti
Public Works	Lee Azinheria
Building	Nicholas Riccio
Comm Dev/Planning	Shaun Burke
Police Chief	Arthur O'Neill
Fire Chief	Neal Boldrighini

Housing & Construction

New Privately Owned Housing Units Authorized by Building Permit

	Single Family	Total Bldgs	Total Units
2006	18	22	43
2007	9	17	211
2008	5	9	14

Parcel Count by Property Class, 2010

Total	7,562
Single family	5,298
Multiple units	384
Apartments	56
Condos	943
Vacant land	423
Open space	0
Commercial	222
Industrial	118
Misc. residential	37
Other use	81

Public Library

Mansfield Public Library
255 Hope Street
Mansfield, MA 02048
(508)261-7380

Director	Janet Campbell

Library Statistics, FY 2008

Population served, 2007	22,993
Registered users	15,771
Circulation	246,782
Reference transactons	4,747
Total program attendance	0
per capita:	
Holdings	4.52
Operating income	$28.39
Internet Access	
Internet computers available	4
Weekly users	130

Municipal Finance

Debt at year end 2008	$43,139,943
Moody's rating, July 2009	A1

Revenues, 2008

Total	$72,739,229
From all taxes	44,927,904
Federal aid	0
State aid	20,821,700
From other governments	247,850
Charges for services	989,593
Licenses, permits & fees	707,135
Fines & forfeits	22,743
Interfund transfers	2,181,472
Misc/other/special assessments	1,420,416

Expenditures, 2008

Total	$70,335,870
General government	2,534,886
Public safety	7,265,569
Other/fixed costs	11,660,012
Human services	613,508
Culture & recreation	753,370
Debt Service	5,693,039
Education	36,150,522
Public works	3,990,155
Intergovernmental	1,674,809

Taxation, 2010

Property type	Valuation	Rate
Total	$3,274,781,510	-
Residential	2,487,620,328	13.33
Open space	0	0.00
Commercial	240,702,672	15.33
Industrial	427,691,700	15.33
Personal	118,766,810	15.33

Average Single Family Tax Bill, 2010

Avg. assessed home value	$374,519
Avg. single fam. tax bill	$4,992
Hi-Lo ranking	78/301

Police & Crime, 2008

Number of police officers	36
Violent crimes	NA
Property crimes	NA

Local School District

(school data 2007-08, except as noted)

Mansfield
2 Park Row
Mansfield, MA 02048
508-261-7500

Superintendent	Brenda Hodges
Grade plan	PK-12
Total enrollment '09-10	4,888
Grade 12 enrollment, '09-10	353
Graduation rate	94.0%
Dropout rate	2.3%
Per-pupil expenditure	$9,246
Avg teacher salary	$60,576
Student/teacher ratio '08-09	15.4 to 1
Highly-qualified teachers, '08-09	94.3%
Teachers licensed in assigned subject	92.6%
Students per computer	6.2

Massachusetts Competency Assessment System (MCAS), 2009 results

	English		Math	
	% Prof	CPI	% Prof	CPI
Gr 4	62%	86.3	57%	84.6
Gr 6	85%	94.1	73%	89.7
Gr 8	86%	95.7	56%	80.2
Gr 10	93%	97.6	89%	94.8

Other School Districts (see Appendix D for data)
Southeastern Vocational Tech, Bristol County Agricultural

©2010 Information Publications, Inc. All rights reserved. Photocopying prohibited. For additional copies, contact the publisher at www.informationpublications.com or (877)544-INFO (4636)

See Introduction for an explanation of all data sources.

Demographics & Socio-Economic Characteristics*

Population

1990	19,971
2000	20,377
Male	9,611
Female	10,766
2008	19,951
2010 (projected)††	19,027
2020 (projected)††	17,191

Race & Hispanic Origin, 2000

Race	
White	19,879
Black/African American	89
American Indian/Alaska Native	16
Asian	200
Hawaiian Native/Pacific Islander	6
Other Race	38
Two or more races	149
Hispanic origin	179

Age & Nativity, 2000

Under 5 years	1,368
18 years and over	15,507
21 years and over	15,149
65 years and over	3,177
85 years and over	396
Median Age	41.9
Native-born	19,014
Foreign-born	1,363

Age, 2020 (projected)††

Under 5 years	816
5 to 19 years	2,837
20 to 39 years	3,744
40 to 64 years	5,787
65 years and over	4,007

Educational Attainment, 2000

Population 25 years and over	14,724
High School graduates or higher	96.4%
Bachelor's degree or higher	61.5%
Graduate degree	25.7%

Income & Poverty, 1999

Per capita income,	$46,738
Median household income	$73,968
Median family income	$99,892
Persons in poverty	863
H'holds receiving public assistance	59
H'holds receiving social security	2,105

Households, 2000

Total households	8,541
With persons under 18	2,750
With persons over 65	2,257
Family households	5,683
Single person households	2,447
Persons per household	2.4
Persons per family	2.9

Labor & Employment, 2000

Civilian labor force	10,960
Unemployment rate	2.1%
Civilian labor force, 2008†	11,098
Unemployment rate†	5.1%
Civilian labor force, 12/09†	10,913
Unemployment rate†	6.9%
Employed persons 16 years and over, by occupation:	
Managers & professionals	6,115
Service occupations	839
Sales & office occupations	2,788
Farming, fishing & forestry	0
Construction & maintenance	478
Production & transportation	505
Self-employed persons	1,222

Most demographic data is from the 2000 Decennial Census
* see Appendix E for American Community Survey data
† Massachusetts Department of Revenue
†† University of Massachusetts, MISER

General Information

Town of Marblehead
188 Washington St
Marblehead, MA 01945
781-631-0528

Elevation	50 ft.
Land area (square miles)	4.5
Water area (square miles)	15.1
Population density, 2008 (est)	4,433.6
Year incorporated	1629
Website	marblehead.org

Voters & Government Information

Government type	Open Town Meeting
Number of Selectmen	5
US Congressional District(s)	6

Registered Voters, October 2008

Total	15,338
Democrats	4,108
Republicans	2,519
Unaffiliated/other	8,626

Local Officials, 2010

Chair, Bd. of Sel.	Jackie Belf-Becker
Manager/Admin	Anthony Sasso
Clerk	Robin Michaud
Finance Director	John McGinn
Treas/Collector	Patricia Murray
Tax Assessor	Michael Tumulty
Attorney	NA
Public Works	Dana Snow
Building	Robert Ives
Planning	Becky Curran
Police Chief	Robert Picariello
Emerg/Fire Chief	Gilliland Jason

Housing & Construction

New Privately Owned Housing Units Authorized by Building Permit

	Single Family	Total Bldgs	Total Units
2006	19	19	19
2007	10	10	10
2008	5	5	5

Parcel Count by Property Class, 2010

Total	8,482
Single family	6,155
Multiple units	412
Apartments	69
Condos	956
Vacant land	491
Open space	0
Commercial	256
Industrial	25
Misc. residential	28
Other use	90

Public Library

Abbot Public Library
235 Pleasant St.
Marblehead, MA 01945
(781)631-1481

Director	Patricia Rogers

Library Statistics, FY 2008

Population served, 2007	20,039
Registered users	17,388
Circulation	219,964
Reference transactons	19,019
Total program attendance	0
per capita:	
Holdings	6.13
Operating income	$47.88
Internet Access	
Internet computers available	22
Weekly users	450

Municipal Finance

Debt at year end 2008	$26,720,000
Moody's rating, July 2009	NA

Revenues, 2008

Total	$60,554,238
From all taxes	49,488,099
Federal aid	385,768
State aid	6,206,543
From other governments	24,730
Charges for services	770,824
Licenses, permits & fees	604,058
Fines & forfeits	171,462
Interfund transfers	799,718
Misc/other/special assessments	1,051,518

Expenditures, 2008

Total	$47,688,922
General government	1,838,204
Public safety	5,967,090
Other/fixed costs	2,975,784
Human services	428,665
Culture & recreation	1,631,220
Debt Service	4,239,169
Education	25,813,396
Public works	3,455,090
Intergovernmental	1,340,304

Taxation, 2010

Property type	Valuation	Rate
Total	$5,249,413,281	-
Residential	4,993,336,363	9.57
Open space	0	0.00
Commercial	192,606,528	9.57
Industrial	20,090,100	9.57
Personal	43,380,290	9.57

Average Single Family Tax Bill, 2010

Avg. assessed home value	$685,562
Avg. single fam. tax bill	$6,561
Hi-Lo ranking	40/301

Police & Crime, 2008

Number of police officers	32
Violent crimes	35
Property crimes	196

Local School District

(school data 2007-08, except as noted)

Marblehead
9 Widger Road
Marblehead, MA 01945
781-639-3141

Superintendent	Paul Dulac
Grade plan	PK-12
Total enrollment '09-10	3,232
Grade 12 enrollment, '09-10	236
Graduation rate	91.9%
Dropout rate	6.1%
Per-pupil expenditure	$11,133
Avg teacher salary	$57,477
Student/teacher ratio '08-09	13.7 to 1
Highly-qualified teachers, '08-09	88.5%
Teachers licensed in assigned subject	95.9%
Students per computer	3.5

Massachusetts Competency Assessment System (MCAS), 2009 results

	English		Math	
	% Prof	CPI	% Prof	CPI
Gr 4	70%	88.2	54%	82.6
Gr 6	84%	94.5	77%	89.3
Gr 8	96%	98.2	82%	92.7
Gr 10	95%	97.9	92%	97

Other School Districts (see Appendix D for data)
North Shore Vocational Tech

©2010 Information Publications, Inc. All rights reserved. Photocopying prohibited. For additional copies, contact the publisher at www.informationpublications.com or (877)544-INFO (4636)

See Introduction for an explanation of all data sources.

Demographics & Socio-Economic Characteristics

Population

1990	4,496
2000	5,123
Male	2,461
Female	2,662
2008	5,148
2010 (projected)††	5,502
2020 (projected)††	5,740

Race & Hispanic Origin, 2000

Race	
White	4,722
Black/African American	81
American Indian/Alaska Native	5
Asian	18
Hawaiian Native/Pacific Islander	4
Other Race	177
Two or more races	116
Hispanic origin	28

Age & Nativity, 2000

Under 5 years	297
18 years and over	3,838
21 years and over	3,730
65 years and over	907
85 years and over	132
Median Age	42.5
Native-born	4,951
Foreign-born	172

Age, 2020 (projected)††

Under 5 years	253
5 to 19 years	836
20 to 39 years	1,043
40 to 64 years	2,015
65 years and over	1,593

Educational Attainment, 2000

Population 25 years and over	3,632
High School graduates or higher	93.7%
Bachelor's degree or higher	49.3%
Graduate degree	23.8%

Income & Poverty, 1999

Per capita income,	$37,265
Median household income	$61,250
Median family income	$74,265
Persons in poverty	232
H'holds receiving public assistance	9
H'holds receiving social security	596

Households, 2000

Total households	1,996
With persons under 18	666
With persons over 65	601
Family households	1,442
Single person households	482
Persons per household	2.5
Persons per family	3.0

Labor & Employment, 2000

Civilian labor force	2,649
Unemployment rate	2.2%
Civilian labor force, 2008†	2,919
Unemployment rate†	4.9%
Civilian labor force, 12/09†	2,849
Unemployment rate†	7.3%
Employed persons 16 years and over, by occupation:	
Managers & professionals	1,363
Service occupations	240
Sales & office occupations	626
Farming, fishing & forestry	6
Construction & maintenance	193
Production & transportation	164
Self-employed persons	246

Most demographic data is from the 2000 Decennial Census
† Massachusetts Department of Revenue
†† University of Massachusetts, MISER

General Information

Town of Marion
2 Spring St
Marion, MA 02738
508-748-3500

Elevation	20 ft.
Land area (square miles)	14.6
Water area (square miles)	12.1
Population density, 2008 (est)	352.6
Year incorporated	1852
Website	www.marionma.gov

Voters & Government Information

Government type	Open Town Meeting
Number of Selectmen	3
US Congressional District(s)	4

Registered Voters, October 2008

Total	3,811
Democrats	896
Republicans	783
Unaffiliated/other	2,109

Local Officials, 2010

Chair, Bd. of Sel.	Jonathan Henry
Manager/Admin	Paul F. Dawson
Clerk	Ray Pickles
Finance Director	Judith Mooney
Tax Collector	Gary Carreiro
Tax Assessor	Catherine Gibbs
Attorney	Jonathan Witten
Public Works	Robert Zora
Building	Richard Marx
Comm Dev/Planning	Joseph Napoli (Chr)
Police Chief	Lincoln Miller
Emerg/Fire Chief	Thomas Joyce

Housing & Construction

New Privately Owned Housing Units Authorized by Building Permit

	Single Family	Total Bldgs	Total Units
2006	7	7	7
2007	2	2	2
2008	2	2	2

Parcel Count by Property Class, 2010

Total	3,123
Single family	2,185
Multiple units	27
Apartments	9
Condos	5
Vacant land	574
Open space	0
Commercial	121
Industrial	22
Misc. residential	74
Other use	106

Public Library

Elizabeth Taber Library
8 Spring St.
Marion, MA 02738
(508)748-1252

Director	Judith D. Kleven

Library Statistics, FY 2008

Population served, 2007	5,217
Registered users	4,150
Circulation	46,549
Reference transactons	13,500
Total program attendance	46,125
per capita:	
Holdings	7.75
Operating income	$38.52
Internet Access	
Internet computers available	7
Weekly users	90

Municipal Finance

Debt at year end 2008	$28,471,223
Moody's rating, July 2009	A1

Revenues, 2008

Total	$17,401,048
From all taxes	14,151,991
Federal aid	0
State aid	800,903
From other governments	1,700
Charges for services	235,688
Licenses, permits & fees	146,718
Fines & forfeits	0
Interfund transfers	478,514
Misc/other/special assessments	792,767

Expenditures, 2008

Total	$16,721,906
General government	1,309,516
Public safety	2,075,091
Other/fixed costs	1,716,322
Human services	139,357
Culture & recreation	207,519
Debt Service	765,083
Education	9,209,546
Public works	1,233,195
Intergovernmental	66,277

Taxation, 2010

Property type	Valuation	Rate
Total	$1,652,880,796	-
Residential	1,531,118,699	8.55
Open space	0	0.00
Commercial	79,596,801	8.55
Industrial	17,216,700	8.55
Personal	24,948,596	8.55

Average Single Family Tax Bill, 2010

Avg. assessed home value	$606,290
Avg. single fam. tax bill	$5,184
Hi-Lo ranking	69/301

Police & Crime, 2008

Number of police officers	14
Violent crimes	10
Property crimes	116

Local School District

(school data 2007-08, except as noted)

Marion
135 Marion Rd
Mattapoisett, MA 02739
508-758-2772

Superintendent	Douglas White
Grade plan	PK-6
Total enrollment '09-10	441
Grade 12 enrollment, '09-10	0
Graduation rate	NA
Dropout rate	NA
Per-pupil expenditure	$12,520
Avg teacher salary	$67,215
Student/teacher ratio '08-09	13.2 to 1
Highly-qualified teachers, '08-09	100.0%
Teachers licensed in assigned subject	100.0%
Students per computer	5.8

Massachusetts Competency Assessment System (MCAS), 2009 results

	English		Math	
	% Prof	CPI	% Prof	CPI
Gr 4	68%	90.5	51%	82.8
Gr 6	68%	89	62%	81.6
Gr 8	NA	NA	NA	NA
Gr 10	NA	NA	NA	NA

Other School Districts (see Appendix D for data)

Old Rochester Regional, Upper Cape Cod Vocational Tech

©2010 Information Publications, Inc. All rights reserved. Photocopying prohibited. For additional copies, contact the publisher at www.informationpublications.com or (877)544-INFO (4636)

See Introduction for an explanation of all data sources.

©2010 Information Publications, Inc. All rights reserved. Photocopying prohibited. For additional copies, contact the publisher at www.informationpublications.com or (877)544-INFO (4636)

Demographics & Socio-Economic Characteristics*

Population

1990	31,813
2000	36,255
Male	17,869
Female	18,386
2008	37,932
2010 (projected)††	38,699
2020 (projected)††	41,177

Race & Hispanic Origin, 2000

Race	
White	31,796
Black/African American	787
American Indian/Alaska Native	72
Asian	1,364
Hawaiian Native/Pacific Islander	13
Other Race	1,186
Two or more races	1,037
Hispanic origin	2,196

Age & Nativity, 2000

Under 5 years	2,554
18 years and over	27,824
21 years and over	26,893
65 years and over	4,190
85 years and over	629
Median Age	36.1
Native-born	30,398
Foreign-born	5,857

Age, 2020 (projected)††

Under 5 years	2,535
5 to 19 years	7,133
20 to 39 years	11,229
40 to 64 years	13,860
65 years and over	6,420

Educational Attainment, 2000

Population 25 years and over	25,512
High School graduates or higher	87.3%
Bachelor's degree or higher	35.6%
Graduate degree	13.1%

Income & Poverty, 1999

Per capita income,	$28,723
Median household income	$56,879
Median family income	$70,385
Persons in poverty	2,455
H'holds receiving public assistance	292
H'holds receiving social security	3,096

Households, 2000

Total households	14,501
With persons under 18	4,690
With persons over 65	2,887
Family households	9,285
Single person households	4,125
Persons per household	2.5
Persons per family	3.1

Labor & Employment, 2000

Civilian labor force	21,042
Unemployment rate	3.4%
Civilian labor force, 2008†	22,863
Unemployment rate†	5.1%
Civilian labor force, 12/09†	23,067
Unemployment rate†	7.4%
Employed persons 16 years and over, by occupation:	
Managers & professionals	8,693
Service occupations	3,066
Sales & office occupations	5,028
Farming, fishing & forestry	39
Construction & maintenance	1,359
Production & transportation	2,136
Self-employed persons	1,319

Most demographic data is from the 2000 Decennial Census
* see Appendix E for American Community Survey data
† Massachusetts Department of Revenue
†† University of Massachusetts, MISER

General Information

City of Marlborough
140 Main St
Marlborough, MA 01752
508-460-3700

Elevation	400 ft.
Land area (square miles)	21.1
Water area (square miles)	1.1
Population density, 2008 (est)	1,797.7
Year incorporated	1667
Email	cityclerk@marlborough-ma.gov

Voters & Government Information

Government type	Mayor-Council
Number of Councilpersons	11
US Congressional District(s)	3

Registered Voters, October 2008

Total	20,167
Democrats	6,350
Republicans	2,683
Unaffiliated/other	11,005

Local Officials, 2010

Mayor	Nancy E. Stevens
Comptroller	Thomas Abel
City Clerk	Lisa M. Thomas
Finance Director	Thomas Abel
Tax Collector	Deborah Puleo
Tax Assessor	Anthony Trodella
Attorney	Donald Rider
Public Works	Ronald A. LaFreniere
Building	Stephen Reid
Comm Dev/Planning	Nancy Savoie
Police Chief	Mark Leonard
Emerg/Fire Chief	David W. Adams

Housing & Construction

New Privately Owned Housing Units Authorized by Building Permit

	Single Family	Total Bldgs	Total Units
2006	15	16	17
2007	7	9	26
2008	10	11	17

Parcel Count by Property Class, 2010

Total	12,314
Single family	6,957
Multiple units	964
Apartments	159
Condos	2,291
Vacant land	945
Open space	0
Commercial	562
Industrial	268
Misc. residential	48
Other use	120

Public Library

Marlborough Public Library
35 West Main St.
Marlborough, MA 01752
(508)624-6900

Director	Salvatore Genovese

Library Statistics, FY 2008

Population served, 2007	38,065
Registered users	18,219
Circulation	214,076
Reference transactons	6,613
Total program attendance	0
per capita:	
Holdings	2.96
Operating income	$21.13
Internet Access	
Internet computers available	16
Weekly users	664

Municipal Finance

Debt at year end 2008	$46,850,794
Moody's rating, July 2009	Aa3

Revenues, 2008

Total	$115,333,064
From all taxes	85,360,309
Federal aid	0
State aid	19,508,167
From other governments	216,185
Charges for services	611,892
Licenses, permits & fees	1,302,569
Fines & forfeits	62,183
Interfund transfers	4,557,179
Misc/other/special assessments	1,857,290

Expenditures, 2008

Total	$94,659,668
General government	6,378,022
Public safety	13,216,570
Other/fixed costs	8,635,087
Human services	645,245
Culture & recreation	1,040,166
Debt Service	5,334,460
Education	50,955,436
Public works	6,391,656
Intergovernmental	2,063,026

Taxation, 2010

Property type	Valuation	Rate
Total	$4,716,118,822	-
Residential	3,159,637,559	13.41
Open space	0	0.00
Commercial	886,199,705	25.42
Industrial	451,382,078	25.42
Personal	218,899,480	25.42

Average Single Family Tax Bill, 2010

Avg. assessed home value	NA
Avg. single fam. tax bill	NA
Hi-Lo ranking	NA

Police & Crime, 2008

Number of police officers	64
Violent crimes	147
Property crimes	732

Local School District

(school data 2007-08, except as noted)

Marlborough
17 Washington Street
Marlborough, MA 01752
508-460-3509

Superintendent	Mary Carlson
Grade plan	PK-12
Total enrollment '09-10	4,539
Grade 12 enrollment, '09-10	304
Graduation rate	83.4%
Dropout rate	5.4%
Per-pupil expenditure	$13,444
Avg teacher salary	$59,902
Student/teacher ratio '08-09	12.4 to 1
Highly-qualified teachers, '08-09	99.2%
Teachers licensed in assigned subject	98.6%
Students per computer	NA

Massachusetts Competency Assessment System (MCAS), 2009 results

	English		Math	
	% Prof	CPI	% Prof	CPI
Gr 4	44%	75.8	48%	78.9
Gr 6	70%	88.9	54%	78.8
Gr 8	72%	88	48%	73.6
Gr 10	82%	92.1	74%	88.8

Other School Districts (see Appendix D for data)
Assabet Valley Vocational Tech

See Introduction for an explanation of all data sources.

Demographics & Socio-Economic Characteristics

Population

1990	21,531
2000	24,324
Male	11,869
Female	12,455
2008	24,735
2010 (projected)††	24,918
2020 (projected)††	24,882

Race & Hispanic Origin, 2000

Race	
White	23,761
Black/African American	131
American Indian/Alaska Native	26
Asian	91
Hawaiian Native/Pacific Islander	4
Other Race	126
Two or more races	185
Hispanic origin	163

Age & Nativity, 2000

Under 5 years	1,924
18 years and over	17,660
21 years and over	17,006
65 years and over	2,300
85 years and over	216
Median Age	37.4
Native-born	23,636
Foreign-born	688

Age, 2020 (projected)††

Under 5 years	1,552
5 to 19 years	4,753
20 to 39 years	5,646
40 to 64 years	8,352
65 years and over	4,579

Educational Attainment, 2000

Population 25 years and over	16,301
High School graduates or higher	94.1%
Bachelor's degree or higher	35.9%
Graduate degree	10.7%

Income & Poverty, 1999

Per capita income,	$28,768
Median household income	$66,508
Median family income	$76,541
Persons in poverty	1,307
H'holds receiving public assistance	151
H'holds receiving social security	2,098

Households, 2000

Total households	8,905
With persons under 18	3,523
With persons over 65	1,745
Family households	6,600
Single person households	1,861
Persons per household	2.7
Persons per family	3.2

Labor & Employment, 2000

Civilian labor force	13,202
Unemployment rate	2.7%
Civilian labor force, 2008†	13,965
Unemployment rate†	6.2%
Civilian labor force, 12/09†	13,745
Unemployment rate†	8.4%
Employed persons 16 years and over, by occupation:	
Managers & professionals	5,342
Service occupations	1,559
Sales & office occupations	3,630
Farming, fishing & forestry	29
Construction & maintenance	1,307
Production & transportation	981
Self-employed persons	831

Most demographic data is from the 2000 Decennial Census
† Massachusetts Department of Revenue
†† University of Massachusetts, MISER

General Information

Town of Marshfield
870 Moraine St
Marshfield, MA 02050
781-834-5563

Elevation	16 ft.
Land area (square miles)	28.5
Water area (square miles)	3.3
Population density, 2008 (est)	867.9
Year incorporated	1640
Website	www.townofmarshfield.org

Voters & Government Information

Government type	Open Town Meeting
Number of Selectmen	3
US Congressional District(s)	10

Registered Voters, October 2008

Total	17,752
Democrats	4,848
Republicans	2,509
Unaffiliated/other	10,338

Local Officials, 2010

Chair, Bd. of Sel.	Michael Maresco
Manager/Admin	Rocco Longo
Clerk	Patricia Picco
Accountant	Barbara Costa
Treas/Collector	Nancy Holt
Tax Assessor	James Haddad
Attorney	Robert Marzelli
Public Works	Dave Carriere
Building	Michael Clancy
Planning	Paul Halkiotis
Police Chief	William Sullivan
Fire Chief	Kevin Robinson

Housing & Construction

New Privately Owned Housing Units Authorized by Building Permit

	Single Family	Total Bldgs	Total Units
2006	53	53	53
2007	37	37	37
2008	19	20	21

Parcel Count by Property Class, 2010

Total	11,586
Single family	8,982
Multiple units	69
Apartments	25
Condos	762
Vacant land	1,171
Open space	0
Commercial	261
Industrial	136
Misc. residential	65
Other use	115

Public Library

Ventress Memorial Library
Library Plaza
Marshfield, MA 02050
(781)834-5535

Director	Ellen Riboldi

Library Statistics, FY 2008

Population served, 2007	24,576
Registered users	16,500
Circulation	298,166
Reference transactons	22,460
Total program attendance	0
per capita:	
Holdings	3.10
Operating income	$31.18
Internet Access	
Internet computers available	13
Weekly users	436

Municipal Finance

Debt at year end 2008	$40,898,130
Moody's rating, July 2009	Aa3

Revenues, 2008

Total	$70,813,840
From all taxes	45,395,923
Federal aid	328,791
State aid	18,798,377
From other governments	7,323
Charges for services	1,125,157
Licenses, permits & fees	677,733
Fines & forfeits	0
Interfund transfers	2,838,244
Misc/other/special assessments	821,146

Expenditures, 2008

Total	$70,260,058
General government	2,692,839
Public safety	7,969,986
Other/fixed costs	9,063,952
Human services	812,083
Culture & recreation	740,950
Debt Service	5,221,291
Education	39,616,804
Public works	3,092,103
Intergovernmental	643,063

Taxation, 2010

Property type	Valuation	Rate
Total	$4,288,104,785	-
Residential	3,967,268,613	10.75
Open space	0	0.00
Commercial	215,560,402	10.75
Industrial	41,011,300	10.75
Personal	64,264,470	10.75

Average Single Family Tax Bill, 2010

Avg. assessed home value	$392,400
Avg. single fam. tax bill	$4,218
Hi-Lo ranking	119/301

Police & Crime, 2008

Number of police officers	45
Violent crimes	47
Property crimes	306

Local School District

(school data 2007-08, except as noted)

Marshfield
76 South River Street
Marshfield, MA 02050
781-834-5000

Superintendent	Middleton McGoodwin
Grade plan	PK-12
Total enrollment '09-10	4,746
Grade 12 enrollment, '09-10	336
Graduation rate	93.0%
Dropout rate	5.1%
Per-pupil expenditure	$10,045
Avg teacher salary	$63,431
Student/teacher ratio '08-09	14.6 to 1
Highly-qualified teachers, '08-09	99.4%
Teachers licensed in assigned subject	99.1%
Students per computer	5.3

Massachusetts Competency Assessment System (MCAS), 2009 results

	English		Math	
	% Prof	CPI	% Prof	CPI
Gr 4	81%	92.5	63%	87.4
Gr 6	82%	93.7	64%	84.8
Gr 8	92%	97.1	65%	85.1
Gr 10	90%	96.3	82%	91.8

Other School Districts (see Appendix D for data)
None

©2010 Information Publications, Inc. All rights reserved. Photocopying prohibited. For additional copies, contact the publisher at www.informationpublications.com or (877)544-INFO (4636)

See Introduction for an explanation of all data sources.

Demographics & Socio-Economic Characteristics

Population

1990	7,884
2000	12,946
Male	6,091
Female	6,855
2008	14,227
2010 (projected)††	17,877
2020 (projected)††	23,440

Race & Hispanic Origin, 2000

Race	
White	11,683
Black/African American	365
American Indian/Alaska Native	377
Asian	74
Hawaiian Native/Pacific Islander	3
Other Race	142
Two or more races	302
Hispanic origin	212

Age & Nativity, 2000

Under 5 years	766
18 years and over	9,752
21 years and over	9,465
65 years and over	2,411
85 years and over	209
Median Age	40.6
Native-born	12,604
Foreign-born	342

Age, 2020 (projected)††

Under 5 years	1,380
5 to 19 years	3,710
20 to 39 years	5,615
40 to 64 years	7,256
65 years and over	5,479

Educational Attainment, 2000

Population 25 years and over	9,141
High School graduates or higher	92.8%
Bachelor's degree or higher	32.4%
Graduate degree	11.9%

Income & Poverty, 1999

Per capita income,	$25,215
Median household income	$50,871
Median family income	$56,702
Persons in poverty	697
H'holds receiving public assistance	112
H'holds receiving social security	1,647

Households, 2000

Total households	5,256
With persons under 18	1,722
With persons over 65	1,619
Family households	3,651
Single person households	1,312
Persons per household	2.4
Persons per family	2.9

Labor & Employment, 2000

Civilian labor force	6,347
Unemployment rate	3.6%
Civilian labor force, 2008†	7,636
Unemployment rate†	7.8%
Civilian labor force, 12/09†	7,488
Unemployment rate†	9.9%
Employed persons 16 years and over, by occupation:	
Managers & professionals	2,148
Service occupations	917
Sales & office occupations	1,685
Farming, fishing & forestry	12
Construction & maintenance	769
Production & transportation	590
Self-employed persons	582

Most demographic data is from the 2000 Decennial Census
† Massachusetts Department of Revenue
†† University of Massachusetts, MISER

General Information

Town of Mashpee
16 Great Neck Rd N
Mashpee, MA 02649
508-539-1400

Elevation	75 ft.
Land area (square miles)	23.5
Water area (square miles)	3.8
Population density, 2008 (est)	605.4
Year incorporated	1763
Website	www.ci.mashpee.ma.us

Voters & Government Information

Government type	Open Town Meeting
Number of Selectmen	5
US Congressional District(s)	10

Registered Voters, October 2008

Total	9,981
Democrats	2,715
Republicans	1,636
Unaffiliated/other	5,600

Local Officials, 2010

Chair, Bd. of Sel.	Don Myers
Manager/Admin	Joyce Mason
Town Clerk	Deborah Dami
Treasurer	David Leary
Tax Collector	David Leary
Tax Assessor	Jason Streeble
Attorney	Patrick Costello
Public Works	Catherine Laurent
Building	Richard Stevens
Comm Dev/Planning	F. Thomas Fudala
Police Chief	Rodney Collins
Emerg/Fire Chief	George Baker

Housing & Construction

New Privately Owned Housing Units Authorized by Building Permit

	Single Family	Total Bldgs	Total Units
2006	112	112	112
2007	85	85	85
2008	61	61	61

Parcel Count by Property Class, 2010

Total	11,165
Single family	6,813
Multiple units	63
Apartments	4
Condos	2,477
Vacant land	1,146
Open space	115
Commercial	379
Industrial	65
Misc. residential	76
Other use	27

Public Library

Mashpee Public Library
PO Box 657
Mashpee, MA 02649
(508)539-1435

Director	Helene B. DeFoe

Library Statistics, FY 2008

Population served, 2007	14,261
Registered users	10,728
Circulation	136,621
Reference transactons	0
Total program attendance	116,159
per capita:	
Holdings	2.32
Operating income	$23.14
Internet Access	
Internet computers available	6
Weekly users	137

Municipal Finance

Debt at year end 2008	$33,545,188
Moody's rating, July 2009	NA

Revenues, 2008

Total	$47,714,194
From all taxes	35,141,322
Federal aid	9,867
State aid	7,036,907
From other governments	18,782
Charges for services	835,579
Licenses, permits & fees	639,065
Fines & forfeits	29,430
Interfund transfers	2,015,190
Misc/other/special assessments	994,026

Expenditures, 2008

Total	$46,150,110
General government	2,845,404
Public safety	6,885,089
Other/fixed costs	6,717,351
Human services	585,545
Culture & recreation	613,903
Debt Service	4,631,064
Education	20,647,493
Public works	2,416,780
Intergovernmental	807,481

Taxation, 2010

Property type	Valuation	Rate
Total	$4,676,701,290	-
Residential	4,275,890,499	7.79
Open space	2,825,000	7.79
Commercial	318,773,551	7.79
Industrial	26,932,600	7.79
Personal	52,279,640	7.79

Average Single Family Tax Bill, 2010

Avg. assessed home value	$467,482
Avg. single fam. tax bill	$3,642
Hi-Lo ranking	161/301

Police & Crime, 2008

Number of police officers	37
Violent crimes	46
Property crimes	354

Local School District

(school data 2007-08, except as noted)

Mashpee
150-A Old Barnstable Road
Mashpee, MA 02649
508-539-1500

Superintendent	Ann Bradshaw
Grade plan	PK-12
Total enrollment '09-10	1,856
Grade 12 enrollment, '09-10	139
Graduation rate	80.0%
Dropout rate	17.1%
Per-pupil expenditure	$13,150
Avg teacher salary	$71,878
Student/teacher ratio '08-09	13.5 to 1
Highly-qualified teachers, '08-09	99.0%
Teachers licensed in assigned subject	98.5%
Students per computer	9.9

Massachusetts Competency Assessment System (MCAS), 2009 results

	English		Math	
	% Prof	CPI	% Prof	CPI
Gr 4	53%	81.1	45%	80.7
Gr 6	75%	89	59%	80.9
Gr 8	80%	92.2	33%	63.8
Gr 10	84%	93.8	83%	91.8

Other School Districts (see Appendix D for data)
Cape Cod Vocational Tech

©2010 Information Publications, Inc. All rights reserved. Photocopying prohibited. For additional copies, contact the publisher at www.informationpublications.com or (877)544-INFO (4636)

See Introduction for an explanation of all data sources.

Demographics & Socio-Economic Characteristics

Population

1990 . . . 5,850
2000 . . . 6,268
Male . . . 3,003
Female . . . 3,265
2008 . . . 6,463
2010 (projected)†† . . . 6,193
2020 (projected)†† . . . 5,979

Race & Hispanic Origin, 2000

Race
White . . . 6,049
Black/African American . . . 39
American Indian/Alaska Native . . . 8
Asian . . . 41
Hawaiian Native/Pacific Islander . . . 2
Other Race . . . 69
Two or more races . . . 60
Hispanic origin . . . 36

Age & Nativity, 2000

Under 5 years . . . 332
18 years and over . . . 4,772
21 years and over . . . 4,644
65 years and over . . . 1,043
85 years and over . . . 131
Median Age . . . 42.5
Native-born . . . 6,148
Foreign-born . . . 120

Age, 2020 (projected)††

Under 5 years . . . 254
5 to 19 years . . . 860
20 to 39 years . . . 1,113
40 to 64 years . . . 2,062
65 years and over . . . 1,690

Educational Attainment, 2000

Population 25 years and over . . . 4,518
High School graduates or higher . . 88.2%
Bachelor's degree or higher . . . 42.9%
Graduate degree . . . 15.6%

Income & Poverty, 1999

Per capita income, . . . $28,050
Median household income . . . $58,466
Median family income . . . $68,246
Persons in poverty . . . 223
H'holds receiving public assistance . . . 40
H'holds receiving social security . . . 760

Households, 2000

Total households . . . 2,532
With persons under 18 . . . 809
With persons over 65 . . . 754
Family households . . . 1,771
Single person households . . . 645
Persons per household . . . 2.5
Persons per family . . . 3.0

Labor & Employment, 2000

Civilian labor force . . . 3,217
Unemployment rate . . . 1.8%
Civilian labor force, 2008† . . . 3,383
Unemployment rate† . . . 5.1%
Civilian labor force, 12/09† . . . 3,418
Unemployment rate† . . . 8.1%
Employed persons 16 years and over, by occupation:
Managers & professionals . . . 1,545
Service occupations . . . 395
Sales & office occupations . . . 789
Farming, fishing & forestry . . . 27
Construction & maintenance . . . 223
Production & transportation . . . 179
Self-employed persons . . . 290

Most demographic data is from the 2000 Decennial Census
† Massachusetts Department of Revenue
†† University of Massachusetts, MISER

General Information

Town of Mattapoisett
16 Main St
Mattapoisett, MA 02739
508-758-4103

Elevation . . . NA
Land area (square miles) . . . 16.5
Water area (square miles) . . . 6.8
Population density, 2008 (est) . . . 391.7
Year incorporated . . . 1857
Website . . . www.mattapoisett.net

Voters & Government Information

Government type . . . Open Town Meeting
Number of Selectmen . . . 3
US Congressional District(s) . . . 4

Registered Voters, October 2008

Total . . . 4,963
Democrats . . . 1,180
Republicans . . . 744
Unaffiliated/other . . . 3,022

Local Officials, 2010

Chair, Bd. of Sel. . . . Jordan C. Collyer
Town Administrator . . . Michael Gagne'
Town Clerk . . . Barbara A. Sullivan
Town Accountant . . . Suzanne Szyndlar
Treas/Collector . . . Brenda Herbeck
Tax Assessor . . . Robert E. Cole
Attorney . . . Kopelman & Paige
Water & Sewer Dir. . . . William Nicholson
Building Inspector . . . Andrew J. Bobola
Planning Board . . . Thomas Tucker (Chr)
Police Chief . . . Mary Lyons
Fire Chief . . . Ronald Scott

Housing & Construction

New Privately Owned Housing Units Authorized by Building Permit

	Single Family	Total Bldgs	Total Units
2006	37	37	37
2007	20	20	20
2008	14	14	14

Parcel Count by Property Class, 2010

Total . . . 4,409
Single family . . . 2,842
Multiple units . . . 76
Apartments . . . 12
Condos . . . 60
Vacant land . . . 1,031
Open space . . . 0
Commercial . . . 170
Industrial . . . 42
Misc. residential . . . 54
Other use . . . 122

Public Library

Mattapoisett Free Public Library
PO Box 475
Mattapoisett, MA 02739
(508)758-4171

Director . . . Janice Bolton

Library Statistics, FY 2008

Population served, 2007 . . . 6,447
Registered users . . . 3,835
Circulation . . . 53,745
Reference transactons . . . 1,102
Total program attendance . . . 28,111

per capita:

Holdings . . . 6.01
Operating income . . . $42.21

Internet Access

Internet computers available . . . 9
Weekly users . . . 33

Municipal Finance

Debt at year end 2008 . . . $22,717,584
Moody's rating, July 2009 . . . A1

Revenues, 2008

Total . . . $20,123,807
From all taxes . . . 16,922,362
Federal aid . . . 0
State aid . . . 1,183,149
From other governments . . . 2,347
Charges for services . . . 57,269
Licenses, permits & fees . . . 247,104
Fines & forfeits . . . 4,717
Interfund transfers . . . 938,997
Misc/other/special assessments . . . 383,931

Expenditures, 2008

Total . . . $19,628,055
General government . . . 1,191,753
Public safety . . . 2,528,874
Other/fixed costs . . . 2,098,021
Human services . . . 351,120
Culture & recreation . . . 324,622
Debt Service . . . 1,077,006
Education . . . 11,005,929
Public works . . . 877,326
Intergovernmental . . . 74,791

Taxation, 2010

Property type	Valuation	Rate
Total	$1,690,184,238	-
Residential	1,573,065,178	10.34
Open space	0	0.00
Commercial	74,591,922	10.34
Industrial	16,145,100	10.34
Personal	26,382,038	10.34

Average Single Family Tax Bill, 2010

Avg. assessed home value . . . $478,815
Avg. single fam. tax bill . . . $4,951
Hi-Lo ranking . . . 82/301

Police & Crime, 2008

Number of police officers . . . 18
Violent crimes . . . 5
Property crimes . . . 100

Local School District

(school data 2007-08, except as noted)

Mattapoisett
135 Marion Rd
Mattapoisett, MA 02739
508-758-2772

Superintendent . . . Douglas White
Grade plan . . . PK-6
Total enrollment '09-10 . . . 514
Grade 12 enrollment, '09-10 . . . 0
Graduation rate . . . NA
Dropout rate . . . NA
Per-pupil expenditure . . . $13,105
Avg teacher salary . . . $60,598
Student/teacher ratio '08-09 . . . 13.7 to 1
Highly-qualified teachers, '08-09 . . . 100.0%
Teachers licensed in assigned subject . 100.0%
Students per computer . . . 2

Massachusetts Competency Assessment System (MCAS), 2009 results

	English		Math	
	% Prof	CPI	% Prof	CPI
Gr 4	68%	87.3	49%	80.4
Gr 6	85%	95.9	55%	79.1
Gr 8	NA	NA	NA	NA
Gr 10	NA	NA	NA	NA

Other School Districts (see Appendix D for data)
Old Rochester Regional, Old Colony Vocational Tech

©2010 Information Publications, Inc. All rights reserved. Photocopying prohibited. For additional copies, contact the publisher at www.informationpublications.com or (877)544-INFO (4636)

See Introduction for an explanation of all data sources.

Demographics & Socio-Economic Characteristics

Population

1990	10,325
2000	10,433
Male	4,988
Female	5,445
2008	10,182
2010 (projected)††	10,407
2020 (projected)††	10,369

Race & Hispanic Origin, 2000

Race	
White	9,874
Black/African American	108
American Indian/Alaska Native	28
Asian	169
Hawaiian Native/Pacific Islander	0
Other Race	123
Two or more races	131
Hispanic origin	290

Age & Nativity, 2000

Under 5 years	737
18 years and over	7,991
21 years and over	7,731
65 years and over	1,274
85 years and over	175
Median Age	37.7
Native-born	9,837
Foreign-born	596

Age, 2020 (projected)††

Under 5 years	594
5 to 19 years	1,703
20 to 39 years	2,549
40 to 64 years	3,709
65 years and over	1,814

Educational Attainment, 2000

Population 25 years and over	7,409
High School graduates or higher	90.2%
Bachelor's degree or higher	38.2%
Graduate degree	11.6%

Income & Poverty, 1999

Per capita income,	$27,016
Median household income	$60,812
Median family income	$71,875
Persons in poverty	582
H'holds receiving public assistance	97
H'holds receiving social security	1,035

Households, 2000

Total households	4,292
With persons under 18	1,308
With persons over 65	982
Family households	2,810
Single person households	1,222
Persons per household	2.4
Persons per family	3.0

Labor & Employment, 2000

Civilian labor force	6,147
Unemployment rate	3.5%
Civilian labor force, 2008†	6,108
Unemployment rate†	5.4%
Civilian labor force, 12/09†	6,041
Unemployment rate†	7.1%
Employed persons 16 years and over, by occupation:	
Managers & professionals	2,587
Service occupations	864
Sales & office occupations	1,592
Farming, fishing & forestry	0
Construction & maintenance	436
Production & transportation	451
Self-employed persons	461

Most demographic data is from the 2000 Decennial Census
† Massachusetts Department of Revenue
†† University of Massachusetts, MISER

General Information

Town of Maynard
195 Main St
Maynard, MA 01754
978-897-1301

Elevation	186 ft.
Land area (square miles)	5.2
Water area (square miles)	0.1
Population density, 2008 (est)	1,958.1
Year incorporated	1871
Website	www.townofmaynard-ma.gov

Voters & Government Information

Government type	Open Town Meeting
Number of Selectmen	5
US Congressional District(s)	5

Registered Voters, October 2008

Total	7,141
Democrats	2,311
Republicans	750
Unaffiliated/other	4,024

Local Officials, 2010

Chair, Bd. of Sel.	David D. Gavin
Manager/Admin	(vacant)
Town Clerk	Michelle L. Sokolowski
Town Accountant	Juli Colpoys
Tax Collector	Teresa Ambrosino
Tax Assessor	Angela Marrama
Attorney	Patricia Cantor
Public Works Supt	Gerard Flood (Actg)
Building Commissioner	Richard Asmann
Comm Dev/Planning	Marie Morando
Police Chief	James Corcoran
Fire Chief	Stephen Kulik

Housing & Construction

New Privately Owned Housing Units Authorized by Building Permit

	Single Family	Total Bldgs	Total Units
2006	4	4	4
2007	23	27	31
2008	5	8	38

Parcel Count by Property Class, 2010

Total	3,753
Single family	2,627
Multiple units	286
Apartments	47
Condos	476
Vacant land	106
Open space	0
Commercial	134
Industrial	19
Misc. residential	12
Other use	46

Public Library

Maynard Public Library
77 Nason Street
Maynard, MA 01754
(978)897-1010

Director	Stephen Weiner

Library Statistics, FY 2008

Population served, 2007	10,177
Registered users	5,343
Circulation	144,376
Reference transactons	0
Total program attendance	0
per capita:	
Holdings	5.49
Operating income	$39.75
Internet Access	
Internet computers available	14
Weekly users	303

Municipal Finance

Debt at year end 2008	$28,526,075
Moody's rating, July 2009	A2

Revenues, 2008

Total	$29,115,315
From all taxes	20,929,644
Federal aid	0
State aid	6,117,349
From other governments	10,826
Charges for services	842,701
Licenses, permits & fees	61,238
Fines & forfeits	100,183
Interfund transfers	770,228
Misc/other/special assessments	141,573

Expenditures, 2008

Total	$28,333,879
General government	1,358,126
Public safety	3,513,206
Other/fixed costs	5,269,738
Human services	211,438
Culture & recreation	387,566
Debt Service	2,137,962
Education	13,636,000
Public works	1,819,843
Intergovernmental	0

Taxation, 2010

Property type	Valuation	Rate
Total	$1,279,843,525	-
Residential	1,097,382,875	16.14
Open space	0	0.00
Commercial	69,263,456	25.71
Industrial	83,951,200	25.71
Personal	29,245,994	25.71

Average Single Family Tax Bill, 2010

Avg. assessed home value	$320,390
Avg. single fam. tax bill	$5,171
Hi-Lo ranking	70/301

Police & Crime, 2008

Number of police officers	NA
Violent crimes	13
Property crimes	16

Local School District

(school data 2007-08, except as noted)

Maynard
12 Bancroft Street
Maynard, MA 01754
978-897-2222

Superintendent	Mark Masterson
Grade plan	PK-12
Total enrollment '09-10	1,328
Grade 12 enrollment, '09-10	92
Graduation rate	78.0%
Dropout rate	12.0%
Per-pupil expenditure	$12,230
Avg teacher salary	$65,843
Student/teacher ratio '08-09	14.2 to 1
Highly-qualified teachers, '08-09	100.0%
Teachers licensed in assigned subject	98.5%
Students per computer	2.3

Massachusetts Competency Assessment System (MCAS), 2009 results

	English		Math	
	% Prof	CPI	% Prof	CPI
Gr 4	53%	81.5	53%	80.2
Gr 6	72%	86.3	55%	78.2
Gr 8	86%	94.6	47%	74.7
Gr 10	90%	97	86%	95.9

Other School Districts (see Appendix D for data)

Assabet Valley Vocational Tech

©2010 Information Publications, Inc. All rights reserved. Photocopying prohibited. For additional copies, contact the publisher at www.informationpublications.com or (877)544-INFO (4636)

See Introduction for an explanation of all data sources.

Demographics & Socio-Economic Characteristics

Population

1990	10,531
2000	12,273
Male	6,031
Female	6,242
2008	12,275
2010 (projected)††	11,739
2020 (projected)††	10,682

Race & Hispanic Origin, 2000

Race	
White	11,878
Black/African American	62
American Indian/Alaska Native	5
Asian	216
Hawaiian Native/Pacific Islander	1
Other Race	28
Two or more races	83
Hispanic origin	110

Age & Nativity, 2000

Under 5 years	1,042
18 years and over	8,151
21 years and over	7,924
65 years and over	1,137
85 years and over	117
Median Age	38.0
Native-born	11,619
Foreign-born	654

Age, 2020 (projected)††

Under 5 years	668
5 to 19 years	2,178
20 to 39 years	2,525
40 to 64 years	3,520
65 years and over	1,791

Educational Attainment, 2000

Population 25 years and over	7,702
High School graduates or higher	97.0%
Bachelor's degree or higher	62.1%
Graduate degree	27.7%

Income & Poverty, 1999

Per capita income,	$42,891
Median household income	$97,748
Median family income	$108,926
Persons in poverty	173
H'holds receiving public assistance	4
H'holds receiving social security	752

Households, 2000

Total households	4,002
With persons under 18	2,039
With persons over 65	793
Family households	3,268
Single person households	619
Persons per household	3.0
Persons per family	3.4

Labor & Employment, 2000

Civilian labor force	5,954
Unemployment rate	3.3%
Civilian labor force, 2008†	6,051
Unemployment rate†	4.8%
Civilian labor force, 12/09†	5,978
Unemployment rate†	6.6%
Employed persons 16 years and over, by occupation:	
Managers & professionals	3,342
Service occupations	365
Sales & office occupations	1,517
Farming, fishing & forestry	0
Construction & maintenance	295
Production & transportation	239
Self-employed persons	571

Most demographic data is from the 2000 Decennial Census
† Massachusetts Department of Revenue
†† University of Massachusetts, MISER

General Information

Town of Medfield
459 Main St
Medfield, MA 02052
508-359-8505

Elevation	180
Land area (square miles)	14.5
Water area (square miles)	0.1
Population density, 2008 (est)	846.6
Year incorporated	1651
Website	www.town.medfield.net

Voters & Government Information

Government type	Open Town Meeting
Number of Selectmen	3
US Congressional District(s)	9

Registered Voters, October 2008

Total	8,431
Democrats	1,749
Republicans	1,462
Unaffiliated/other	5,182

Local Officials, 2010

Chair, Bd. of Sel.	Ann Thompson
Manager/Admin	Michael Sullivan
Town Clerk	Carol Mayer
Finance Director	Georgia Colivas
Tax Collector	Georgia Colivas
Tax Assessor	R. Edward Beard
Attorney	Mark Cerel
Public Works	Kenneth Feeney
Building	Walter Tortorici
Comm Dev/Planning	Robert Sylvia
Police Chief	Robert Meaney
Emerg/Fire Chief	William Kingsbury

Housing & Construction

New Privately Owned Housing Units Authorized by Building Permit

	Single Family	Total Bldgs	Total Units
2006	22	22	22
2007	15	15	15
2008	9	9	9

Parcel Count by Property Class, 2010

Total	4,265
Single family	3,485
Multiple units	76
Apartments	17
Condos	263
Vacant land	230
Open space	0
Commercial	114
Industrial	43
Misc. residential	5
Other use	32

Public Library

Medfield Memorial Library
468 Main Street
Medfield, MA 02052
(508)359-4544

Director	Deborah Kelsey

Library Statistics, FY 2008

Population served, 2007	12,266
Registered users	9,049
Circulation	225,157
Reference transactons	0
Total program attendance	0
per capita:	
Holdings	6.73
Operating income	$50.09
Internet Access	
Internet computers available	10
Weekly users	0

Municipal Finance

Debt at year end 2008	$54,814,975
Moody's rating, July 2009	Aa2

Revenues, 2008

Total	$47,341,360
From all taxes	31,661,283
Federal aid	0
State aid	8,363,785
From other governments	4,318
Charges for services	587,010
Licenses, permits & fees	530,482
Fines & forfeits	14,961
Interfund transfers	1,417,137
Misc/other/special assessments	2,381,192

Expenditures, 2008

Total	$41,709,685
General government	1,516,130
Public safety	2,930,153
Other/fixed costs	1,636,071
Human services	339,212
Culture & recreation	904,247
Debt Service	6,681,840
Education	24,667,504
Public works	2,604,101
Intergovernmental	430,427

Taxation, 2010

Property type	Valuation	Rate
Total	$2,291,894,139	-
Residential	2,164,473,796	14.24
Open space	0	0.00
Commercial	68,487,743	14.24
Industrial	26,770,900	14.24
Personal	32,161,700	14.24

Average Single Family Tax Bill, 2010

Avg. assessed home value	$578,363
Avg. single fam. tax bill	$8,236
Hi-Lo ranking	21/301

Police & Crime, 2008

Number of police officers	15
Violent crimes	7
Property crimes	68

Local School District

(school data 2007-08, except as noted)

Medfield
459 Main St, 3rd Fl
Medfield, MA 02052
508-359-2302

Superintendent	Robert Maguire
Grade plan	PK-12
Total enrollment '09-10	3,020
Grade 12 enrollment, '09-10	212
Graduation rate	95.9%
Dropout rate	0.0%
Per-pupil expenditure	$9,957
Avg teacher salary	$65,346
Student/teacher ratio '08-09	15.0 to 1
Highly-qualified teachers, '08-09	99.1%
Teachers licensed in assigned subject	99.2%
Students per computer	2.5

Massachusetts Competency Assessment System (MCAS), 2009 results

	English		Math	
	% Prof	CPI	% Prof	CPI
Gr 4	65%	87.7	51%	83.5
Gr 6	85%	93.7	76%	88.1
Gr 8	96%	98.5	80%	91.7
Gr 10	97%	99.1	94%	97.5

Other School Districts (see Appendix D for data)
Tri County Vocational Tech, Norfolk County Agricultural

©2010 Information Publications, Inc. All rights reserved. Photocopying prohibited. For additional copies, contact the publisher at www.informationpublications.com or (877)544-INFO (4636)

Demographics & Socio-Economic Characteristics*

Population

1990	57,407
2000	55,765
Male	26,133
Female	29,632
2008	55,573
2010 (projected)††	54,063
2020 (projected)††	52,328

Race & Hispanic Origin, 2000

Race	
White	48,209
Black/African American	3,401
American Indian/Alaska Native	63
Asian	2,157
Hawaiian Native/Pacific Islander	17
Other Race	633
Two or more races	1,285
Hispanic origin	1,443

Age & Nativity, 2000

Under 5 years	2,718
18 years and over	45,756
21 years and over	43,088
65 years and over	9,666
85 years and over	1,367
Median Age	37.5
Native-born	46,728
Foreign-born	9,037

Age, 2020 (projected)††

Under 5 years	2,371
5 to 19 years	8,228
20 to 39 years	14,023
40 to 64 years	17,971
65 years and over	9,735

Educational Attainment, 2000

Population 25 years and over	39,762
High School graduates or higher	85.6%
Bachelor's degree or higher	31.7%
Graduate degree	11.8%

Income & Poverty, 1999

Per capita income,	$24,707
Median household income	$52,476
Median family income	$62,409
Persons in poverty	3,418
H'holds receiving public assistance	366
H'holds receiving social security	6,943

Households, 2000

Total households	22,067
With persons under 18	5,637
With persons over 65	6,765
Family households	13,494
Single person households	6,336
Persons per household	2.4
Persons per family	3.0

Labor & Employment, 2000

Civilian labor force	30,112
Unemployment rate	3.6%
Civilian labor force, 2008†	30,616
Unemployment rate†	5.5%
Civilian labor force, 12/09†	30,491
Unemployment rate†	8.0%
Employed persons 16 years and over, by occupation:	
Managers & professionals	12,230
Service occupations	4,032
Sales & office occupations	8,261
Farming, fishing & forestry	10
Construction & maintenance	2,030
Production & transportation	2,461
Self-employed persons	1,448

Most demographic data is from the 2000 Decennial Census
* see Appendix E for American Community Survey data
† Massachusetts Department of Revenue
†† University of Massachusetts, MISER

General Information

City of Medford
85 George P Hassett Dr
Medford, MA 02155
781-396-5500

Elevation	10 ft.
Land area (square miles)	8.1
Water area (square miles)	0.5
Population density, 2008 (est)	6,860.9
Year incorporated	1630
Website	www.medford.org

Voters & Government Information

Government type	Mayor-Council
Number of Councilpersons	7
US Congressional District(s)	7

Registered Voters, October 2008

Total	35,445
Democrats	16,588
Republicans	2,610
Unaffiliated/other	16,054

Local Officials, 2010

Mayor	Michael McGlynn
Manager/Admin	NA
Clerk	Edward Finn
Finance Director	Anne Baker
Treas/Collector	Alfred Pompeo Jr
Tax Assessor	Edward O'Neil
Attorney	Mark E. Rumley
Public Works	Paul Gere
Building	Paul Mochi
Planning	Lauren DiLorenzo
Police Chief	Leo A. Sacco Jr
Emerg/Fire Chief	Frank Giliberti Jr

Housing & Construction

New Privately Owned Housing Units Authorized by Building Permit

	Single Family	Total Bldgs	Total Units
2006	4	10	16
2007	3	8	13
2008	0	2	4

Parcel Count by Property Class, 2010

Total	16,873
Single family	7,843
Multiple units	4,584
Apartments	118
Condos	2,728
Vacant land	797
Open space	0
Commercial	614
Industrial	75
Misc. residential	21
Other use	93

Public Library

Medford Public Library
111 High St.
Medford, MA 02155
(781)395-7950

Director	Brian G. Boutilier

Library Statistics, FY 2008

Population served, 2007	55,565
Registered users	20,765
Circulation	323,303
Reference transactons	79,324
Total program attendance	0
per capita:	
Holdings	3.26
Operating income	$24.47
Internet Access	
Internet computers available	9
Weekly users	4,800

Municipal Finance

Debt at year end 2008	$61,454,293
Moody's rating, July 2009	A3

Revenues, 2008

Total	$121,973,426
From all taxes	81,057,642
Federal aid	1,181,794
State aid	30,875,096
From other governments	290,342
Charges for services	1,313,239
Licenses, permits & fees	1,845,934
Fines & forfeits	437,436
Interfund transfers	4,234,185
Misc/other/special assessments	368,879

Expenditures, 2008

Total	$106,774,413
General government	3,481,173
Public safety	21,107,806
Other/fixed costs	10,079,374
Human services	911,601
Culture & recreation	2,020,135
Debt Service	6,026,228
Education	45,309,162
Public works	8,514,072
Intergovernmental	9,324,862

Taxation, 2010

Property type	Valuation	Rate
Total	$6,581,472,630	-
Residential	5,711,770,075	10.98
Open space	0	0.00
Commercial	668,754,425	21.69
Industrial	93,601,500	21.69
Personal	107,346,630	21.69

Average Single Family Tax Bill, 2010

Avg. assessed home value	$358,006
Avg. single fam. tax bill	$3,931
Hi-Lo ranking	141/301

Police & Crime, 2008

Number of police officers	111
Violent crimes	89
Property crimes	1,466

Local School District

(school data 2007-08, except as noted)

Medford
489 Winthrop Street
Medford, MA 02155
781-393-2442

Superintendent	Roy Belson
Grade plan	PK-12
Total enrollment '09-10	4,854
Grade 12 enrollment, '09-10	361
Graduation rate	83.3%
Dropout rate	9.0%
Per-pupil expenditure	$13,376
Avg teacher salary	$66,627
Student/teacher ratio '08-09	14.3 to 1
Highly-qualified teachers, '08-09	97.4%
Teachers licensed in assigned subject	97.0%
Students per computer	2.2

Massachusetts Competency Assessment System (MCAS), 2009 results

	English		Math	
	% Prof	CPI	% Prof	CPI
Gr 4	51%	79.1	35%	72.2
Gr 6	61%	85	48%	77.3
Gr 8	77%	91.1	45%	70.5
Gr 10	77%	90.8	69%	85.7

Other School Districts (see Appendix D for data)
None

©2010 Information Publications, Inc. All rights reserved. Photocopying prohibited. For additional copies, contact the publisher at www.informationpublications.com or (877)544-INFO (4636)

See Introduction for an explanation of all data sources.

Demographics & Socio-Economic Characteristics

Population

1990	9,931
2000	12,448
Male	6,032
Female	6,416
2008	12,785
2010 (projected)††	13,829
2020 (projected)††	15,080

Race & Hispanic Origin, 2000

Race	
White	12,139
Black/African American	71
American Indian/Alaska Native	12
Asian	120
Hawaiian Native/Pacific Islander	2
Other Race	20
Two or more races	84
Hispanic origin	105

Age & Nativity, 2000

Under 5 years	1,067
18 years and over	8,483
21 years and over	8,231
65 years and over	1,137
85 years and over	143
Median Age	36.0
Native-born	11,859
Foreign-born	589

Age, 2020 (projected)††

Under 5 years	1,060
5 to 19 years	3,147
20 to 39 years	3,719
40 to 64 years	4,894
65 years and over	2,260

Educational Attainment, 2000

Population 25 years and over	7,960
High School graduates or higher	94.5%
Bachelor's degree or higher	43.5%
Graduate degree	13.2%

Income & Poverty, 1999

Per capita income,	$27,578
Median household income	$75,135
Median family income	$85,627
Persons in poverty	278
H'holds receiving public assistance	39
H'holds receiving social security	813

Households, 2000

Total households	4,182
With persons under 18	1,973
With persons over 65	773
Family households	3,336
Single person households	720
Persons per household	3.0
Persons per family	3.4

Labor & Employment, 2000

Civilian labor force	6,700
Unemployment rate	0.8%
Civilian labor force, 2008†	7,236
Unemployment rate†	5.5%
Civilian labor force, 12/09†	7,169
Unemployment rate†	7.9%
Employed persons 16 years and over, by occupation:	
Managers & professionals	3,281
Service occupations	753
Sales & office occupations	1,692
Farming, fishing & forestry	12
Construction & maintenance	460
Production & transportation	450
Self-employed persons	499

Most demographic data is from the 2000 Decennial Census
† Massachusetts Department of Revenue
†† University of Massachusetts, MISER

General Information

Town of Medway
155 Village St
Medway, MA 02053
508-533-3200

Elevation	200 ft.
Land area (square miles)	11.5
Water area (square miles)	0.1
Population density, 2008 (est)	1,111.7
Year incorporated	1713
Website	townofmedway.org

Voters & Government Information

Government type	Open Town Meeting
Number of Selectmen	5
US Congressional District(s)	3

Registered Voters, October 2008

Total	8,936
Democrats	2,101
Republicans	1,258
Unaffiliated/other	5,513

Local Officials, 2010

Chair, Bd. of Sel.	Andy Espinosa
Town Administrator	Suzanne Kennedy
Clerk	Maryjane White
Finance Director	Melanie Philips
Tax Collector	Melanie Philips
Tax Assessor	Pace Willisson
Attorney	NA
Public Works	Tom Holder
Building	Robert Speroni
Planning	Andy Rodenhiser
Police Chief	Allen Tingley
Emerg/Fire Chief	Paul Trufant

Housing & Construction

New Privately Owned Housing Units Authorized by Building Permit

	Single Family	Total Bldgs	Total Units
2006	11	11	11
2007	11	11	11
2008	8	8	8

Parcel Count by Property Class, 2010

Total	4,686
Single family	3,613
Multiple units	137
Apartments	25
Condos	252
Vacant land	374
Open space	0
Commercial	95
Industrial	116
Misc. residential	9
Other use	65

Public Library

Medway Public Library System
26 High St.
Medway, MA 02053
(508)533-3217

Director	Felicia Oti

Library Statistics, FY 2008

Population served, 2007	12,749
Registered users	6,193
Circulation	97,004
Reference transactons	1,833
Total program attendance	51,188
per capita:	
Holdings	5.15
Operating income	$32.53
Internet Access	
Internet computers available	6
Weekly users	46

Municipal Finance

Debt at year end 2008	$22,937,275
Moody's rating, July 2009	A3

Revenues, 2008

Total	$38,520,240
From all taxes	25,998,007
Federal aid	157,654
State aid	10,433,188
From other governments	0
Charges for services	387,336
Licenses, permits & fees	247,720
Fines & forfeits	34,193
Interfund transfers	48,750
Misc/other/special assessments	606,696

Expenditures, 2008

Total	$35,856,745
General government	1,547,106
Public safety	2,509,987
Other/fixed costs	5,143,462
Human services	170,153
Culture & recreation	252,495
Debt Service	2,922,233
Education	21,335,764
Public works	1,509,028
Intergovernmental	466,517

Taxation, 2010

Property type	Valuation	Rate
Total	$1,638,646,140	-
Residential	1,440,202,396	16.29
Open space	0	0.00
Commercial	69,724,264	16.29
Industrial	58,501,900	16.29
Personal	70,217,580	16.29

Average Single Family Tax Bill, 2010

Avg. assessed home value	$362,246
Avg. single fam. tax bill	$5,901
Hi-Lo ranking	49/301

Police & Crime, 2008

Number of police officers	19
Violent crimes	3
Property crimes	113

Local School District

(school data 2007-08, except as noted)
Medway
45 Holliston Street
Medway, MA 02053
508-533-3222

Superintendent	Judith Evans
Grade plan	PK-12
Total enrollment '09-10	2,693
Grade 12 enrollment, '09-10	211
Graduation rate	95.8%
Dropout rate	2.4%
Per-pupil expenditure	$9,714
Avg teacher salary	$60,164
Student/teacher ratio '08-09	15.1 to 1
Highly-qualified teachers, '08-09	96.9%
Teachers licensed in assigned subject	97.3%
Students per computer	4.7

Massachusetts Competency Assessment System (MCAS), 2009 results

	English		Math	
	% Prof	CPI	% Prof	CPI
Gr 4	68%	89	57%	86.7
Gr 6	83%	93.8	76%	90.7
Gr 8	87%	94.4	66%	84.3
Gr 10	97%	99	88%	95.1

Other School Districts (see Appendix D for data)
Tri County Vocational Tech, Norfolk County Agricultural

©2010 Information Publications, Inc. All rights reserved. Photocopying prohibited. For additional copies, contact the publisher at www.informationpublications.com or (877)544-INFO (4636)

See Introduction for an explanation of all data sources.

Demographics & Socio-Economic Characteristics*

Population

1990	28,150
2000	27,134
Male	12,757
Female	14,377
2008	26,708
2010 (projected)††	25,048
2020 (projected)††	22,635

Race & Hispanic Origin, 2000

Race	
White	25,820
Black/African American	255
American Indian/Alaska Native	26
Asian	546
Hawaiian Native/Pacific Islander	6
Other Race	109
Two or more races	372
Hispanic origin	283

Age & Nativity, 2000

Under 5 years	1,810
18 years and over	21,165
21 years and over	20,583
65 years and over	4,433
85 years and over	719
Median Age	39.4
Native-born	25,487
Foreign-born	1,647

Age, 2020 (projected)††

Under 5 years	1,067
5 to 19 years	3,531
20 to 39 years	5,010
40 to 64 years	8,003
65 years and over	5,024

Educational Attainment, 2000

Population 25 years and over	19,697
High School graduates or higher	91.6%
Bachelor's degree or higher	40.1%
Graduate degree	15.0%

Income & Poverty, 1999

Per capita income,	$30,347
Median household income	$62,811
Median family income	$78,144
Persons in poverty	897
H'holds receiving public assistance	179
H'holds receiving social security	3,313

Households, 2000

Total households	10,982
With persons under 18	3,336
With persons over 65	3,140
Family households	7,108
Single person households	3,260
Persons per household	2.4
Persons per family	3.1

Labor & Employment, 2000

Civilian labor force	14,999
Unemployment rate	2.0%
Civilian labor force, 2008†	15,169
Unemployment rate†	4.9%
Civilian labor force, 12/09†	15,191
Unemployment rate†	7.3%
Employed persons 16 years and over, by occupation:	
Managers & professionals	7,144
Service occupations	1,575
Sales & office occupations	3,973
Farming, fishing & forestry	6
Construction & maintenance	965
Production & transportation	1,037
Self-employed persons	898

Most demographic data is from the 2000 Decennial Census
* see Appendix E for American Community Survey data
† Massachusetts Department of Revenue
†† University of Massachusetts, MISER

General Information

City of Melrose
562 Main St
Melrose, MA 02176
781-979-4500

Elevation	50 ft.
Land area (square miles)	4.7
Water area (square miles)	0.1
Population density, 2008 (est)	5,682.6
Year incorporated	1899
Website	www.cityofmelrose.org

Voters & Government Information

Government type	Mayor-Alderman
Number of Aldermen	11
US Congressional District(s)	7

Registered Voters, October 2008

Total	19,729
Democrats	7,166
Republicans	2,447
Unaffiliated/other	10,016

Local Officials, 2010

Mayor	Robert Dolan
Manager/Admin	NA
City Clerk	Mary-Rita O'Shea
Finance Director	Arthur Flavin
Tax Collector	Arthur Flavin
Tax Assessor	Don Dragt
Attorney	Robert Van Campen
Public Works	Robert Beshara
Building	Paul Johnson
Comm Dev/Planning	Denise Gaffey
Police Chief	Michael Lyle
Emerg/Fire Chief	John O'Brien

Housing & Construction

New Privately Owned Housing Units Authorized by Building Permit

	Single Family	Total Bldgs	Total Units
2006	7	11	69
2007	6	10	39
2008	3	6	43

Parcel Count by Property Class, 2010

Total	8,948
Single family	6,301
Multiple units	924
Apartments	115
Condos	948
Vacant land	321
Open space	0
Commercial	234
Industrial	34
Misc. residential	6
Other use	65

Public Library

Melrose Public Library
69 West Emerson St.
Melrose, MA 02176
(781)665-2313

Director	Dennis J. Kelley

Library Statistics, FY 2008

Population served, 2007	26,782
Registered users	20,603
Circulation	265,470
Reference transactons	43,276
Total program attendance	249,787
per capita:	
Holdings	4.04
Operating income	$41.86
Internet Access	
Internet computers available	26
Weekly users	745

Municipal Finance

Debt at year end 2008	$25,147,686
Moody's rating, July 2009	A2

Revenues, 2008

Total	$66,244,142
From all taxes	42,707,047
Federal aid	0
State aid	13,970,107
From other governments	0
Charges for services	323,568
Licenses, permits & fees	3,333,832
Fines & forfeits	177,600
Interfund transfers	4,808,428
Misc/other/special assessments	461,780

Expenditures, 2008

Total	$55,681,120
General government	2,495,783
Public safety	7,816,256
Other/fixed costs	5,873,171
Human services	657,786
Culture & recreation	1,629,226
Debt Service	3,273,137
Education	26,707,876
Public works	3,866,377
Intergovernmental	2,895,401

Taxation, 2010

Property type	Valuation	Rate
Total	$3,518,831,885	-
Residential	3,309,199,082	12.07
Open space	0	0.00
Commercial	130,019,663	18.29
Industrial	17,494,550	18.29
Personal	62,118,590	18.29

Average Single Family Tax Bill, 2010

Avg. assessed home value	$395,233
Avg. single fam. tax bill	$4,770
Hi-Lo ranking	87/301

Police & Crime, 2008

Number of police officers	NA
Violent crimes	30
Property crimes	336

Local School District

(school data 2007-08, except as noted)

Melrose
360 Lynn Fells Pkwy
Melrose, MA 02176
781-662-2000

Superintendent	Joseph Casey
Grade plan	PK-12
Total enrollment '09-10	3,767
Grade 12 enrollment, '09-10	229
Graduation rate	89.9%
Dropout rate	4.2%
Per-pupil expenditure	$10,264
Avg teacher salary	$54,010
Student/teacher ratio '08-09	15.5 to 1
Highly-qualified teachers, '08-09	94.7%
Teachers licensed in assigned subject	98.1%
Students per computer	4.1

Massachusetts Competency Assessment System (MCAS), 2009 results

	English		Math	
	% Prof	CPI	% Prof	CPI
Gr 4	64%	84.4	57%	82.9
Gr 6	71%	87.9	60%	80.5
Gr 8	85%	93.7	52%	75.3
Gr 10	94%	97.6	80%	90.4

Other School Districts (see Appendix D for data)
Northeast Metro Vocational Tech

©2010 Information Publications, Inc. All rights reserved. Photocopying prohibited. For additional copies, contact the publisher at www.informationpublications.com or (877)544-INFO (4636)

See Introduction for an explanation of all data sources.

Demographics & Socio-Economic Characteristics

Population

1990	4,010
2000	5,286
Male	2,623
Female	2,663
2008	5,762
2010 (projected)††	6,343
2020 (projected)††	7,482

Race & Hispanic Origin, 2000

Race	
White	5,180
Black/African American	21
American Indian/Alaska Native	0
Asian	31
Hawaiian Native/Pacific Islander	0
Other Race	8
Two or more races	46
Hispanic origin	51

Age & Nativity, 2000

Under 5 years	416
18 years and over	3,725
21 years and over	3,600
65 years and over	443
85 years and over	54
Median Age	37.1
Native-born	5,150
Foreign-born	136

Age, 2020 (projected)††

Under 5 years	480
5 to 19 years	1,443
20 to 39 years	1,883
40 to 64 years	2,679
65 years and over	997

Educational Attainment, 2000

Population 25 years and over	3,472
High School graduates or higher	93.2%
Bachelor's degree or higher	35.9%
Graduate degree	10.8%

Income & Poverty, 1999

Per capita income,	$27,693
Median household income	$71,164
Median family income	$79,337
Persons in poverty	212
H'holds receiving public assistance	15
H'holds receiving social security	382

Households, 2000

Total households	1,815
With persons under 18	811
With persons over 65	332
Family households	1,451
Single person households	290
Persons per household	2.9
Persons per family	3.3

Labor & Employment, 2000

Civilian labor force	2,922
Unemployment rate	1.2%
Civilian labor force, 2008†	3,386
Unemployment rate†	5.4%
Civilian labor force, 12/09†	3,410
Unemployment rate†	7.4%
Employed persons 16 years and over, by occupation:	
Managers & professionals	1,242
Service occupations	288
Sales & office occupations	891
Farming, fishing & forestry	12
Construction & maintenance	252
Production & transportation	203
Self-employed persons	255

Most demographic data is from the 2000 Decennial Census
† Massachusetts Department of Revenue
†† University of Massachusetts, MISER

General Information

Town of Mendon
20 Main St
PO Box 2
Mendon, MA 01756
508-473-2312

Elevation	387 ft.
Land area (square miles)	18.1
Water area (square miles)	0.2
Population density, 2008 (est)	318.3
Year incorporated	1667
Website	www.mendonma.net

Voters & Government Information

Government type	Open Town Meeting
Number of Selectmen	3
US Congressional District(s)	2

Registered Voters, October 2008

Total	4,200
Democrats	825
Republicans	734
Unaffiliated/other	2,615

Local Officials, 2010

Chair, Bd. of Sel.	Michael Ammendolia
Manager/Admin	Dale Pleau
Town Clerk	Margaret Bonderenko
Finance Director	Claudia Cataldo
Tax Collector	Christine Kupstas
Tax Assessor	Bruce Tycks
Attorney	Robert S. Mangiaratti
Public Works	Alan D. Tetreault
Building	Thomas Hackenson
Planning/Dev.	William Ambrosino
Police Chief	Ernest Horn
Emerg/Fire Chief	Ernest Horn

Housing & Construction

New Privately Owned Housing Units Authorized by Building Permit

	Single Family	Total Bldgs	Total Units
2006	27	27	27
2007	10	10	10
2008	5	5	5

Parcel Count by Property Class, 2010

Total	2,652
Single family	1,815
Multiple units	62
Apartments	3
Condos	54
Vacant land	479
Open space	0
Commercial	102
Industrial	9
Misc. residential	17
Other use	111

Public Library

Taft Public Library
PO Box 35
Mendon, MA 01756
(508)473-3259

Director	Susan Hoar

Library Statistics, FY 2008

Population served, 2007	5,767
Registered users	1,946
Circulation	51,580
Reference transactons	3,898
Total program attendance	25,933
per capita:	
Holdings	5.47
Operating income	$36.96
Internet Access	
Internet computers available	4
Weekly users	25

Municipal Finance

Debt at year end 2008	$111,004
Moody's rating, July 2009	A2

Revenues, 2008

Total	$12,783,402
From all taxes	10,481,926
Federal aid	0
State aid	597,042
From other governments	19,184
Charges for services	651,479
Licenses, permits & fees	168,592
Fines & forfeits	39,580
Interfund transfers	344,771
Misc/other/special assessments	240,414

Expenditures, 2008

Total	$11,302,106
General government	788,202
Public safety	2,010,174
Other/fixed costs	805,416
Human services	126,312
Culture & recreation	294,830
Debt Service	460,160
Education	5,608,510
Public works	1,195,172
Intergovernmental	13,330

Taxation, 2010

Property type	Valuation	Rate
Total	$829,184,500	-
Residential	750,143,270	12.47
Open space	0	0.00
Commercial	47,676,190	12.47
Industrial	4,721,300	12.47
Personal	26,643,740	12.47

Average Single Family Tax Bill, 2010

Avg. assessed home value	$371,748
Avg. single fam. tax bill	$4,636
Hi-Lo ranking	93/301

Police & Crime, 2008

Number of police officers	13
Violent crimes	8
Property crimes	43

Local School District

(school data 2007-08, except as noted)

Mendon (non-op)
150 North Ave, POB 5
Mendon, MA 01756
508-634-1585

Superintendent	Antonio Fernandes

Non-operating district.
Resident students are sent to the Other School Districts listed below.

Grade plan	NA
Total enrollment '09-10	NA
Grade 12 enrollment, '09-10	NA
Graduation rate	NA
Dropout rate	NA
Per-pupil expenditure	NA
Avg teacher salary	NA
Student/teacher ratio '08-09	NA
Highly-qualified teachers, '08-09	NA
Teachers licensed in assigned subject	NA
Students per computer	NA

Other School Districts (see Appendix D for data)
Mendon-Upton Regional, Blackstone Valley Vocational Tech

©2010 Information Publications, Inc. All rights reserved. Photocopying prohibited. For additional copies, contact the publisher at www.informationpublications.com or (877)544-INFO (4636)

See Introduction for an explanation of all data sources.

Demographics & Socio-Economic Characteristics

Population

1990 . . . 5,166
2000 . . . 6,138
Male . . . 2,988
Female . . . 3,150
2008 . . . 6,504
2010 (projected)†† . . . 6,641
2020 (projected)†† . . . 7,193

Race & Hispanic Origin, 2000

Race
White . . . 6,032
Black/African American . . . 24
American Indian/Alaska Native . . . 7
Asian . . . 17
Hawaiian Native/Pacific Islander . . . 0
Other Race . . . 18
Two or more races . . . 40
Hispanic origin . . . 55

Age & Nativity, 2000

Under 5 years . . . 447
18 years and over . . . 4,359
21 years and over . . . 4,202
65 years and over . . . 675
85 years and over . . . 68
Median Age . . . 37.4
Native-born . . . 6,028
Foreign-born . . . 110

Age, 2020 (projected)††

Under 5 years . . . 467
5 to 19 years . . . 1,383
20 to 39 years . . . 1,641
40 to 64 years . . . 2,546
65 years and over . . . 1,156

Educational Attainment, 2000

Population 25 years and over . . . 4,048
High School graduates or higher . . 90.2%
Bachelor's degree or higher . . . 30.8%
Graduate degree . . . 11.3%

Income & Poverty, 1999

Per capita income, . . . $24,869
Median household income . . . $58,692
Median family income . . . $69,118
Persons in poverty . . . 165
H'holds receiving public assistance . . . 17
H'holds receiving social security . . . 582

Households, 2000

Total households . . . 2,233
With persons under 18 . . . 963
With persons over 65 . . . 501
Family households . . . 1,699
Single person households . . . 443
Persons per household . . . 2.7
Persons per family . . . 3.2

Labor & Employment, 2000

Civilian labor force . . . 3,436
Unemployment rate . . . 2.4%
Civilian labor force, 2008† . . . 3,502
Unemployment rate† . . . 6.1%
Civilian labor force, 12/09† . . . 3,466
Unemployment rate† . . . 7.9%
Employed persons 16 years and over, by occupation:
Managers & professionals . . . 1,249
Service occupations . . . 478
Sales & office occupations . . . 853
Farming, fishing & forestry . . . 6
Construction & maintenance . . . 367
Production & transportation . . . 400
Self-employed persons . . . 263

Most demographic data is from the 2000 Decennial Census
† Massachusetts Department of Revenue
†† University of Massachusetts, MISER

General Information

Town of Merrimac
Town Hall
2 School St
Merrimac, MA 01860
978-346-8862

Elevation . . . 107 ft.
Land area (square miles) . . . 8.5
Water area (square miles) . . . 0.3
Population density, 2008 (est) . . . 765.2
Year incorporated . . . 1876
Email . . . selectmen@townofmerrimac.com

Voters & Government Information

Government type . . . Open Town Meeting
Number of Selectmen . . . 3
US Congressional District(s) . . . 6

Registered Voters, October 2008

Total . . . 4,438
Democrats . . . 1,026
Republicans . . . 672
Unaffiliated/other . . . 2,711

Local Officials, 2010

Chair, Bd. of Sel. . . . W. Earl Baumgardner
Manager/Admin . . . NA
Town Clerk . . . Patricia E. True
Finance Director . . . Carol A. McLeod
Tax Collector . . . Geraldine Gozycki
Tax Assessor . . . Edward R. Davis
Attorney . . . Ashod N. Amirian
Public Works . . . Rick Spinale
Building . . . Philip J. Hagopian
Comm Dev/Planning . . . NA
Police Chief . . . James A. Flynn Jr
Emerg/Fire Chief . . . Ralph W. Spencer

Housing & Construction

New Privately Owned Housing Units Authorized by Building Permit

	Single Family	Total Bldgs	Total Units
2006	10	17	42
2007	10	16	37
2008	6	10	32

Parcel Count by Property Class, 2010

Total . . . 2,241
Single family . . . 1,575
Multiple units . . . 114
Apartments . . . 8
Condos . . . 217
Vacant land . . . 191
Open space . . . 0
Commercial . . . 51
Industrial . . . 21
Misc. residential . . . 8
Other use . . . 56

Public Library

Merrimac Public Library
86 West Main St.
Merrimac, MA 01860
(978)346-9441

Director . . . Martina Follansbee

Library Statistics, FY 2008

Population served, 2007 . . . 6,425
Registered users . . . 3,933
Circulation . . . 68,968
Reference transactons . . . 3,300
Total program attendance . . . 55,200
per capita:
Holdings . . . 6.70
Operating income . . . $39.17
Internet Access
Internet computers available . . . 13
Weekly users . . . 139

Municipal Finance

Debt at year end 2008 . . . $11,272,448
Moody's rating, July 2009 . . . A3

Revenues, 2008

Total . . . $11,609,031
From all taxes . . . 9,279,577
Federal aid . . . 0
State aid . . . 1,418,864
From other governments . . . 72,763
Charges for services . . . 299,812
Licenses, permits & fees . . . 93,939
Fines & forfeits . . . 2,710
Interfund transfers . . . 170,850
Misc/other/special assessments . . . 135,258

Expenditures, 2008

Total . . . $11,830,813
General government . . . 598,764
Public safety . . . 1,255,188
Other/fixed costs . . . 587,622
Human services . . . 240,654
Culture & recreation . . . 330,927
Debt Service . . . 1,819,521
Education . . . 6,016,936
Public works . . . 855,569
Intergovernmental . . . 123,643

Taxation, 2010

Property type	Valuation	Rate
Total	$720,721,568	-
Residential	686,583,334	13.08
Open space	0	0.00
Commercial	19,464,189	13.08
Industrial	7,954,140	13.08
Personal	6,719,905	13.08

Average Single Family Tax Bill, 2010

Avg. assessed home value . . . $351,972
Avg. single fam. tax bill . . . $4,604
Hi-Lo ranking . . . 95/301

Police & Crime, 2008

Number of police officers . . . 7
Violent crimes . . . 2
Property crimes . . . 32

Local School District

(school data 2007-08, except as noted)

Merrimac (non-op)
22 Main Street
West Newbury, MA 01985
978-363-2280
Superintendent . . . Paul Livingston

Non-operating district.
Resident students are sent to the Other School Districts listed below.

Grade plan . . . NA
Total enrollment '09-10 . . . NA
Grade 12 enrollment, '09-10 . . . NA
Graduation rate . . . NA
Dropout rate . . . NA
Per-pupil expenditure . . . NA
Avg teacher salary . . . NA
Student/teacher ratio '08-09 . . . NA
Highly-qualified teachers, '08-09 . . . NA
Teachers licensed in assigned subject . . . NA
Students per computer . . . NA

Other School Districts (see Appendix D for data)
Pentucket Regional, Whittier Vocational Tech

©2010 Information Publications, Inc. All rights reserved. Photocopying prohibited. For additional copies, contact the publisher at www.informationpublications.com or (877)544-INFO (4636)

See Introduction for an explanation of all data sources.

Demographics & Socio-Economic Characteristics*

Population

1990	39,990
2000	43,789
Male	20,967
Female	22,822
2008	44,055
2010 (projected)††	46,917
2020 (projected)††	50,529

Race & Hispanic Origin, 2000

Race	
White	39,126
Black/African American	591
American Indian/Alaska Native	97
Asian	1,040
Hawaiian Native/Pacific Islander	5
Other Race	2,131
Two or more races	799
Hispanic origin	4,221

Age & Nativity, 2000

Under 5 years	2,749
18 years and over	32,958
21 years and over	31,543
65 years and over	6,719
85 years and over	902
Median Age	37.5
Native-born	38,903
Foreign-born	4,886

Age, 2020 (projected)††

Under 5 years	3,055
5 to 19 years	9,338
20 to 39 years	12,875
40 to 64 years	16,628
65 years and over	8,633

Educational Attainment, 2000

Population 25 years and over	29,962
High School graduates or higher	81.8%
Bachelor's degree or higher	23.0%
Graduate degree	7.3%

Income & Poverty, 1999

Per capita income,	$22,305
Median household income	$49,627
Median family income	$59,831
Persons in poverty	3,201
H'holds receiving public assistance	464
H'holds receiving social security	5,143

Households, 2000

Total households	16,532
With persons under 18	5,885
With persons over 65	4,696
Family households	11,541
Single person households	4,181
Persons per household	2.6
Persons per family	3.2

Labor & Employment, 2000

Civilian labor force	21,743
Unemployment rate	4.3%
Civilian labor force, 2008†	23,197
Unemployment rate†	7.9%
Civilian labor force, 12/09†	23,331
Unemployment rate†	11.9%
Employed persons 16 years and over, by occupation:	
Managers & professionals	7,487
Service occupations	2,671
Sales & office occupations	5,649
Farming, fishing & forestry	18
Construction & maintenance	1,778
Production & transportation	3,207
Self-employed persons	1,119

Most demographic data is from the 2000 Decennial Census
* see Appendix E for American Community Survey data
† Massachusetts Department of Revenue
†† University of Massachusetts, MISER

General Information

City of Methuen
41 Pleasant St
Methuen, MA 01844
978-983-8595

Elevation	100 ft.
Land area (square miles)	22.4
Water area (square miles)	0.7
Population density, 2008 (est)	1,966.7
Year incorporated	1725
Website	www.ci.methuen.ma.us

Voters & Government Information

Government type	Mayor-Council
Number of Councilpersons	9
US Congressional District(s)	5

Registered Voters, October 2008

Total	30,259
Democrats	12,023
Republicans	4,022
Unaffiliated/other	13,987

Local Officials, 2010

Council Chair	William Manzi III
Mayor	Stephen Zanni
City Clerk	Christine Touma-Conway
Finance Director	Thomas J. Kelly
Tax Collector	Ann Guastaferro
Tax Assessor	John Cena
Attorney	Peter J. McQuillan
Public Works	Raymond DiFiore
Building	Gerald Deschene
Comm Dev/Planning	Karen Sawyer
Police Chief	Katherine Lavigne
Emerg/Fire Chief	Steven Buote

Housing & Construction

New Privately Owned Housing Units Authorized by Building Permit

	Single Family	Total Bldgs	Total Units
2006	75	78	81
2007	68	74	80
2008	47	53	59

Parcel Count by Property Class, 2010

Total	16,172
Single family	10,628
Multiple units	1,270
Apartments	125
Condos	2,007
Vacant land	1,363
Open space	0
Commercial	438
Industrial	145
Misc. residential	58
Other use	138

Public Library

Nevins Memorial Library
305 Broadway
Methuen, MA 01844
(978)686-4080

Director	Krista McLeod

Library Statistics, FY 2008

Population served, 2007	43,979
Registered users	44,742
Circulation	233,704
Reference transactons	22,992
Total program attendance	138,264
per capita:	
Holdings	3.21
Operating income	$29.57
Internet Access	
Internet computers available	22
Weekly users	487

Municipal Finance

Debt at year end 2008	$63,551,675
Moody's rating, July 2009	A3

Revenues, 2008

Total	$119,068,722
From all taxes	61,855,125
Federal aid	143,605
State aid	48,598,930
From other governments	0
Charges for services	1,751,933
Licenses, permits & fees	1,074,286
Fines & forfeits	318,059
Interfund transfers	1,730,466
Misc/other/special assessments	1,798,159

Expenditures, 2008

Total	$109,951,337
General government	3,853,996
Public safety	16,716,170
Other/fixed costs	7,245,012
Human services	1,041,005
Culture & recreation	1,078,373
Debt Service	8,592,406
Education	60,878,316
Public works	9,294,885
Intergovernmental	1,233,727

Taxation, 2010

Property type	Valuation	Rate
Total	$4,587,190,983	-
Residential	3,901,280,196	11.86
Open space	0	0.00
Commercial	379,345,556	21.91
Industrial	156,093,950	21.91
Personal	150,471,281	21.91

Average Single Family Tax Bill, 2010

Avg. assessed home value	$281,335
Avg. single fam. tax bill	$3,337
Hi-Lo ranking	195/301

Police & Crime, 2008

Number of police officers	88
Violent crimes	129
Property crimes	1,035

Local School District

(school data 2007-08, except as noted)

Methuen
10 Ditson Pl
Methuen, MA 01844
978-722-6001

Superintendent	Jeanne Whitten
Grade plan	PK-12
Total enrollment '09-10	7,230
Grade 12 enrollment, '09-10	453
Graduation rate	77.3%
Dropout rate	11.0%
Per-pupil expenditure	$10,267
Avg teacher salary	$64,061
Student/teacher ratio '08-09	14.7 to 1
Highly-qualified teachers, '08-09	96.8%
Teachers licensed in assigned subject	97.4%
Students per computer	5.8

Massachusetts Competency Assessment System (MCAS), 2009 results

	English		Math	
	% Prof	CPI	% Prof	CPI
Gr 4	43%	74.5	44%	76.5
Gr 6	62%	83.3	51%	76.4
Gr 8	72%	88.3	35%	64
Gr 10	75%	91.2	65%	83.9

Other School Districts (see Appendix D for data)
Greater Lawrence Vocational Tech

©2010 Information Publications, Inc. All rights reserved. Photocopying prohibited. For additional copies, contact the publisher at www.informationpublications.com or (877)544-INFO (4636)

See Introduction for an explanation of all data sources.

©2010 Information Publications, Inc. All rights reserved. Photocopying prohibited. For additional copies, contact the publisher at www.informationpublications.com or (877)544-INFO (4636)

Demographics & Socio-Economic Characteristics

Population

1990	17,867
2000	19,941
Male	9,784
Female	10,157
2008	21,117
2010 (projected)††	21,268
2020 (projected)††	22,644

Race & Hispanic Origin, 2000

Race	
White	19,168
Black/African American	252
American Indian/Alaska Native	51
Asian	87
Hawaiian Native/Pacific Islander	7
Other Race	114
Two or more races	262
Hispanic origin	156

Age & Nativity, 2000

Under 5 years	1,391
18 years and over	14,423
21 years and over	13,822
65 years and over	2,053
85 years and over	304
Median Age	35.6
Native-born	19,269
Foreign-born	672

Age, 2020 (projected)††

Under 5 years	1,417
5 to 19 years	4,193
20 to 39 years	5,689
40 to 64 years	7,631
65 years and over	3,714

Educational Attainment, 2000

Population 25 years and over	13,015
High School graduates or higher	86.0%
Bachelor's degree or higher	19.6%
Graduate degree	5.3%

Income & Poverty, 1999

Per capita income,	$20,246
Median household income	$52,755
Median family income	$59,173
Persons in poverty	1,066
H'holds receiving public assistance	148
H'holds receiving social security	1,472

Households, 2000

Total households	6,981
With persons under 18	2,944
With persons over 65	1,352
Family households	5,114
Single person households	1,423
Persons per household	2.8
Persons per family	3.2

Labor & Employment, 2000

Civilian labor force	10,796
Unemployment rate	3.8%
Civilian labor force, 2008†	11,768
Unemployment rate†	8.0%
Civilian labor force, 12/09†	11,788
Unemployment rate†	11.0%
Employed persons 16 years and over, by occupation:	
Managers & professionals	3,012
Service occupations	1,757
Sales & office occupations	2,951
Farming, fishing & forestry	29
Construction & maintenance	1,274
Production & transportation	1,359
Self-employed persons	451

Most demographic data is from the 2000 Decennial Census
† Massachusetts Department of Revenue
†† University of Massachusetts, MISER

General Information

Town of Middleborough
20 Centre St
Middleborough, MA 02346
508-946-2415

Elevation	100 ft.
Land area (square miles)	69.6
Water area (square miles)	2.7
Population density, 2008 (est)	303.4
Year incorporated	1669
Email	inforequest@middleborough.com

Voters & Government Information

Government type	Open Town Meeting
Number of Selectmen	5
US Congressional District(s)	4

Registered Voters, October 2008

Total	15,663
Democrats	3,472
Republicans	2,169
Unaffiliated/other	9,888

Local Officials, 2010

Chair, Bd. of Sel.	Marsha Brunelle
Manager	Charles Cristello
Town Clerk	Eileen S. Gates
Treasurer	Judy MacDonald
Tax Collector	Judy MacDonald
Tax Assessor	Anthony F. Freitas Jr
Attorney	Daniel F. Murray
Public Works	Andrew Bagas
Building	Robert Whalen
Comm Dev/Planning	Ruth Geoffrey
Police Chief	Bruce Gates
Emerg/Fire Chief	Lance Benjamino

Housing & Construction

New Privately Owned Housing Units Authorized by Building Permit

	Single Family	Total Bldgs	Total Units
2006	84	90	105
2007	69	73	83
2008	44	49	63

Parcel Count by Property Class, 2010

Total	9,122
Single family	5,376
Multiple units	421
Apartments	70
Condos	399
Vacant land	1,516
Open space	0
Commercial	551
Industrial	63
Misc. residential	114
Other use	612

Public Library

Middleborough Public Library
102 North Main St.
Middleborough, MA 02346
(508)946-2470

Director	Danielle Bowker

Library Statistics, FY 2008

Population served, 2007	21,245
Registered users	14,186
Circulation	153,116
Reference transactons	4,111
Total program attendance	98,836
per capita:	
Holdings	4.81
Operating income	$30.94
Internet Access	
Internet computers available	23
Weekly users	926

Municipal Finance

Debt at year end 2008	$35,902,207
Moody's rating, July 2009	A2

Revenues, 2008

Total	$66,184,154
From all taxes	29,811,097
Federal aid	0
State aid	21,788,346
From other governments	75,991
Charges for services	1,502,910
Licenses, permits & fees	878,911
Fines & forfeits	0
Interfund transfers	4,702,735
Misc/other/special assessments	3,712,082

Expenditures, 2008

Total	$59,809,220
General government	3,425,450
Public safety	6,543,267
Other/fixed costs	13,388,342
Human services	1,082,559
Culture & recreation	864,526
Debt Service	5,578,243
Education	26,838,574
Public works	1,607,313
Intergovernmental	462,319

Taxation, 2010

Property type	Valuation	Rate
Total	$2,481,105,459	-
Residential	2,046,850,213	11.83
Open space	0	0.00
Commercial	321,309,366	12.55
Industrial	58,978,100	12.55
Personal	53,967,780	12.55

Average Single Family Tax Bill, 2010

Avg. assessed home value	$294,751
Avg. single fam. tax bill	$3,487
Hi-Lo ranking	172/301

Police & Crime, 2008

Number of police officers	40
Violent crimes	92
Property crimes	509

Local School District

(school data 2007-08, except as noted)

Middleborough
30 Forest Street
Middleborough, MA 02346
508-946-2000

Superintendent	Robert Sullivan
Grade plan	PK-12
Total enrollment '09-10	3,506
Grade 12 enrollment, '09-10	176
Graduation rate	88.1%
Dropout rate	6.4%
Per-pupil expenditure	$10,530
Avg teacher salary	$60,510
Student/teacher ratio '08-09	15.5 to 1
Highly-qualified teachers, '08-09	97.4%
Teachers licensed in assigned subject	98.3%
Students per computer	8

Massachusetts Competency Assessment System (MCAS), 2009 results

	English		Math	
	% Prof	CPI	% Prof	CPI
Gr 4	47%	75.5	36%	71.4
Gr 6	62%	82.9	50%	76.4
Gr 8	79%	91.4	38%	64.6
Gr 10	76%	89.2	69%	87

Other School Districts (see Appendix D for data)

Bristol-Plymouth Vocational Tech

See Introduction for an explanation of all data sources.

Demographics & Socio-Economic Characteristics

Population

1990	392
2000	542
Male	276
Female	266
2008	557
2010 (projected)††	651
2020 (projected)††	768

Race & Hispanic Origin, 2000

Race	
White	536
Black/African American	1
American Indian/Alaska Native	1
Asian	0
Hawaiian Native/Pacific Islander	0
Other Race	1
Two or more races	3
Hispanic origin	3

Age & Nativity, 2000

Under 5 years	28
18 years and over	417
21 years and over	398
65 years and over	52
85 years and over	3
Median Age	40.3
Native-born	564
Foreign-born	16

Age, 2020 (projected)††

Under 5 years	49
5 to 19 years	138
20 to 39 years	174
40 to 64 years	295
65 years and over	112

Educational Attainment, 2000

Population 25 years and over	406
High School graduates or higher	88.4%
Bachelor's degree or higher	28.1%
Graduate degree	14.5%

Income & Poverty, 1999

Per capita income,	$24,137
Median household income	$50,938
Median family income	$53,889
Persons in poverty	50
H'holds receiving public assistance	3
H'holds receiving social security	44

Households, 2000

Total households	213
With persons under 18	65
With persons over 65	35
Family households	161
Single person households	37
Persons per household	2.5
Persons per family	2.9

Labor & Employment, 2000

Civilian labor force	319
Unemployment rate	4.4%
Civilian labor force, 2008†	311
Unemployment rate†	2.3%
Civilian labor force, 12/09†	323
Unemployment rate†	6.8%
Employed persons 16 years and over, by occupation:	
Managers & professionals	115
Service occupations	24
Sales & office occupations	66
Farming, fishing & forestry	0
Construction & maintenance	54
Production & transportation	46
Self-employed persons	37

Most demographic data is from the 2000 Decennial Census
† Massachusetts Department of Revenue
†† University of Massachusetts, MISER

General Information

Town of Middlefield
188 Skyline Trail
Middlefield, MA 01234
413-623-2079

Elevation	1,677 ft.
Land area (square miles)	24.2
Water area (square miles)	0.0
Population density, 2008 (est)	23.0
Year incorporated	1783
Website	www.middlefieldma.us

Voters & Government Information

Government type	Open Town Meeting
Number of Selectmen	3
US Congressional District(s)	1

Registered Voters, October 2008

Total	351
Democrats	94
Republicans	73
Unaffiliated/other	183

Local Officials, 2010

Chair, Bd. of Sel.	Larry Pease
Administrator	Terry Walker
Town Clerk	Marjorie Batorski
Finance Director	J. Kearns/P. Kearns
Tax Collector	Richard Wade
Tax Assessor	Gustel Progulski
Attorney	Kopelman & Paige
Public Works	Skip Savery
Building	Paul Tacy
Comm Dev/Planning	Maureen Sullivan
Police Chief	Thomas Austin
Emerg/Fire Chief	Larry Pease

Housing & Construction

New Privately Owned Housing Units Authorized by Building Permit

	Single Family	Total Bldgs	Total Units
2006	4	4	4
2007	3	3	3
2008	0	0	0

Parcel Count by Property Class, 2010

Total	491
Single family	192
Multiple units	3
Apartments	0
Condos	0
Vacant land	152
Open space	0
Commercial	3
Industrial	1
Misc. residential	1
Other use	139

Public Library

Middlefield Public Library
PO Box 128
Middlefield, MA 01243
(413)623-6421

Librarian	Cyndy Oligny

Library Statistics, FY 2008

Population served, 2007	551
Registered users	196
Circulation	2,133
Reference transactons	8
Total program attendance	970
per capita:	
Holdings	9.24
Operating income	$8.27
Internet Access	
Internet computers available	1
Weekly users	7

Municipal Finance

Debt at year end 2008	$15,390
Moody's rating, July 2009	NA

Revenues, 2008

Total	$1,117,682
From all taxes	857,540
Federal aid	0
State aid	188,407
From other governments	25
Charges for services	6,360
Licenses, permits & fees	25,266
Fines & forfeits	0
Interfund transfers	0
Misc/other/special assessments	20,042

Expenditures, 2008

Total	$1,297,091
General government	171,975
Public safety	38,469
Other/fixed costs	108,608
Human services	1,150
Culture & recreation	7,735
Debt Service	8,426
Education	674,119
Public works	279,627
Intergovernmental	682

Taxation, 2010

Property type	Valuation	Rate
Total	$64,177,382	-
Residential	58,836,000	16.53
Open space	0	0.00
Commercial	2,515,108	16.53
Industrial	25,800	16.53
Personal	2,800,474	16.53

Average Single Family Tax Bill, 2010

Avg. assessed home value	$189,868
Avg. single fam. tax bill	$3,139
Hi-Lo ranking	220/301

Police & Crime, 2008

Number of police officers	NA
Violent crimes	NA
Property crimes	NA

Local School District

(school data 2007-08, except as noted)

Middlefield (non-op)
12 Littleville Road
Huntington, MA 01050
413-685-1011

Superintendent	David Hopson

Non-operating district.
Resident students are sent to the Other School Districts listed below.

Grade plan	NA
Total enrollment '09-10	NA
Grade 12 enrollment, '09-10	NA
Graduation rate	NA
Dropout rate	NA
Per-pupil expenditure	NA
Avg teacher salary	NA
Student/teacher ratio '08-09	NA
Highly-qualified teachers, '08-09	NA
Teachers licensed in assigned subject	NA
Students per computer	NA

Other School Districts (see Appendix D for data)
Gateway Regional

©2010 Information Publications, Inc. All rights reserved. Photocopying prohibited. For additional copies, contact the publisher at www.informationpublications.com or (877)544-INFO (4636)

See Introduction for an explanation of all data sources.

Demographics & Socio-Economic Characteristics

Population

1990	4,921
2000	7,744
Male	4,503
Female	3,241
2008	9,634
2010 (projected)††	8,784
2020 (projected)††	9,903

Race & Hispanic Origin, 2000

Race	
White	7,390
Black/African American	128
American Indian/Alaska Native	4
Asian	86
Hawaiian Native/Pacific Islander	4
Other Race	21
Two or more races	111
Hispanic origin	485

Age & Nativity, 2000

Under 5 years	473
18 years and over	5,965
21 years and over	5,678
65 years and over	739
85 years and over	65
Median Age	36.3
Native-born	7,423
Foreign-born	321

Age, 2020 (projected)††

Under 5 years	506
5 to 19 years	1,587
20 to 39 years	3,042
40 to 64 years	3,304
65 years and over	1,464

Educational Attainment, 2000

Population 25 years and over	5,376
High School graduates or higher	80.5%
Bachelor's degree or higher	29.3%
Graduate degree	11.9%

Income & Poverty, 1999

Per capita income,	$29,031
Median household income	$81,395
Median family income	$87,605
Persons in poverty	235
H'holds receiving public assistance	43
H'holds receiving social security	594

Households, 2000

Total households	2,305
With persons under 18	922
With persons over 65	555
Family households	1,745
Single person households	462
Persons per household	2.8
Persons per family	3.2

Labor & Employment, 2000

Civilian labor force	3,460
Unemployment rate	2.4%
Civilian labor force, 2008†	4,291
Unemployment rate†	5.4%
Civilian labor force, 12/09†	4,343
Unemployment rate†	8.9%
Employed persons 16 years and over, by occupation:	
Managers & professionals	1,410
Service occupations	347
Sales & office occupations	1,012
Farming, fishing & forestry	0
Construction & maintenance	361
Production & transportation	248
Self-employed persons	293

Most demographic data is from the 2000 Decennial Census
† Massachusetts Department of Revenue
†† University of Massachusetts, MISER

General Information

Town of Middleton
48 S Main St
Middleton, MA 01949
978-774-3589

Elevation	95 ft.
Land area (square miles)	14.0
Water area (square miles)	0.5
Population density, 2008 (est)	688.1
Year incorporated	1728
Website	www.townofmiddleton.org

Voters & Government Information

Government type	Open Town Meeting
Number of Selectmen	5
US Congressional District(s)	6

Registered Voters, October 2008

Total	5,454
Democrats	1,249
Republicans	812
Unaffiliated/other	3,365

Local Officials, 2010

Chair, Bd. of Sel.	Nancy Jones
Manager/Admin	Ira Singer
Town Clerk	Sarah George
Finance Director	Andrew Vanni
Tax Collector	Kathleen McMahon
Tax Assessor	Bradford Swanson
Attorney	Thomas Fallon
Public Works	Robert LaBossiere
Building	NA
Comm Dev/Planning	NA
Police Chief	James DiGianvittorio
Emerg/Fire Chief	Frank Twiss

Housing & Construction

New Privately Owned Housing Units Authorized by Building Permit

	Single Family	Total Bldgs	Total Units
2006	43	43	43
2007	35	35	35
2008	25	27	29

Parcel Count by Property Class, 2010

Total	3,392
Single family	1,946
Multiple units	72
Apartments	11
Condos	737
Vacant land	333
Open space	0
Commercial	142
Industrial	63
Misc. residential	18
Other use	70

Public Library

Flint Public Library
1 South Main St., PO Box 98
Middleton, MA 01949
(978)774-8132

Director	Adela Carter

Library Statistics, FY 2008

Population served, 2007	9,347
Registered users	3,838
Circulation	66,092
Reference transactons	0
Total program attendance	20,215
per capita:	
Holdings	5.01
Operating income	$37.29
Internet Access	
Internet computers available	4
Weekly users	30

Municipal Finance

Debt at year end 2008	$5,507,200
Moody's rating, July 2009	Aa3

Revenues, 2008

Total	$23,237,736
From all taxes	18,684,477
Federal aid	0
State aid	2,635,412
From other governments	34,464
Charges for services	271,993
Licenses, permits & fees	84,302
Fines & forfeits	0
Interfund transfers	569,900
Misc/other/special assessments	478,594

Expenditures, 2008

Total	$21,857,914
General government	1,035,201
Public safety	2,684,339
Other/fixed costs	1,254,020
Human services	374,425
Culture & recreation	350,198
Debt Service	1,033,696
Education	13,626,616
Public works	1,236,945
Intergovernmental	262,474

Taxation, 2010

Property type	Valuation	Rate
Total	$1,575,444,537	-
Residential	1,268,424,640	11.84
Open space	0	0.00
Commercial	196,849,217	11.84
Industrial	59,579,100	11.84
Personal	50,591,580	11.84

Average Single Family Tax Bill, 2010

Avg. assessed home value	$479,050
Avg. single fam. tax bill	$5,672
Hi-Lo ranking	54/301

Police & Crime, 2008

Number of police officers	13
Violent crimes	NA
Property crimes	NA

Local School District

(school data 2007-08, except as noted)

Middleton
28 Middleton Road
Boxford, MA 01921
978-887-0771

Superintendent	Bernard Creeden
Grade plan	PK-6
Total enrollment '09-10	858
Grade 12 enrollment, '09-10	0
Graduation rate	NA
Dropout rate	NA
Per-pupil expenditure	$9,849
Avg teacher salary	$61,572
Student/teacher ratio '08-09	13.4 to 1
Highly-qualified teachers, '08-09	98.3%
Teachers licensed in assigned subject	98.5%
Students per computer	4.1

Massachusetts Competency Assessment System (MCAS), 2009 results

	English		Math	
	% Prof	CPI	% Prof	CPI
Gr 4	72%	89.8	58%	86.2
Gr 6	78%	93	73%	90.7
Gr 8	NA	NA	NA	NA
Gr 10	NA	NA	NA	NA

Other School Districts (see Appendix D for data)
Masconomet Regional, North Shore Vocational Tech

©2010 Information Publications, Inc. All rights reserved. Photocopying prohibited. For additional copies, contact the publisher at www.informationpublications.com or (877)544-INFO (4636)

See Introduction for an explanation of all data sources.

Demographics & Socio-Economic Characteristics*

Population

1990	25,355
2000	26,799
Male	13,006
Female	13,793
2008	27,246
2010 (projected)††	27,354
2020 (projected)††	27,921

Race & Hispanic Origin, 2000

Race	
White	24,909
Black/African American	362
American Indian/Alaska Native	29
Asian	473
Hawaiian Native/Pacific Islander	17
Other Race	534
Two or more races	475
Hispanic origin	1,168

Age & Nativity, 2000

Under 5 years	1,923
18 years and over	20,152
21 years and over	19,426
65 years and over	3,448
85 years and over	516
Median Age	36.6
Native-born	23,781
Foreign-born	3,018

Age, 2020 (projected)††

Under 5 years	1,612
5 to 19 years	4,673
20 to 39 years	7,411
40 to 64 years	9,258
65 years and over	4,967

Educational Attainment, 2000

Population 25 years and over	18,472
High School graduates or higher	83.9%
Bachelor's degree or higher	26.7%
Graduate degree	7.7%

Income & Poverty, 1999

Per capita income,	$23,742
Median household income	$50,856
Median family income	$61,029
Persons in poverty	1,908
H'holds receiving public assistance	307
H'holds receiving social security	2,603

Households, 2000

Total households	10,420
With persons under 18	3,678
With persons over 65	2,399
Family households	7,197
Single person households	2,670
Persons per household	2.5
Persons per family	3.1

Labor & Employment, 2000

Civilian labor force	14,462
Unemployment rate	3.7%
Civilian labor force, 2008†	15,542
Unemployment rate†	6.4%
Civilian labor force, 12/09†	15,516
Unemployment rate†	8.6%
Employed persons 16 years and over, by occupation:	
Managers & professionals	5,650
Service occupations	1,735
Sales & office occupations	3,823
Farming, fishing & forestry	26
Construction & maintenance	984
Production & transportation	1,706
Self-employed persons	628

Most demographic data is from the 2000 Decennial Census
* see Appendix E for American Community Survey data
† Massachusetts Department of Revenue
†† University of Massachusetts, MISER

General Information

Town of Milford
52 Main St
Milford, MA 01757
508-634-2303

Elevation	312 ft.
Land area (square miles)	14.6
Water area (square miles)	0.3
Population density, 2008 (est)	1,866.2
Year incorporated	1780
Website	www.milford.ma.us

Voters & Government Information

Government type	Rep. Town Meeting
Number of Selectmen	3
US Congressional District(s)	2

Registered Voters, October 2008

Total	15,984
Democrats	5,375
Republicans	1,747
Unaffiliated/other	8,768

Local Officials, 2010

Chair, Bd. of Sel.	Dino DeBartolomeis
Administrator	Louis Celozzi
Town Clerk	Amy Hennessy Neves
Treasurer	Barbara Auger
Tax Collector	Paula Fortin
Tax Assessor	Priscilla Hogan
Attorney	Gerald Moody
Public Works	Scott Crisafulli (Int)
Building	Anthony Deluca
Comm Dev/Planning	Larry Dunkin
Police Chief	Thomas O'Loughlin
Fire Chief	John Touhey

Housing & Construction

New Privately Owned Housing Units Authorized by Building Permit

	Single Family	Total Bldgs	Total Units
2006	41	41	41
2007	72	72	72
2008	24	24	24

Parcel Count by Property Class, 2010

Total	9,623
Single family	5,755
Multiple units	925
Apartments	148
Condos	1,459
Vacant land	583
Open space	0
Commercial	429
Industrial	177
Misc. residential	51
Other use	96

Public Library

Milford Town Library
80 Spruce St.
Milford, MA 01757
(508)473-2145

Director	Susan Edmonds

Library Statistics, FY 2008

Population served, 2007	27,263
Registered users	21,112
Circulation	201,367
Reference transactons	28,493
Total program attendance	145,587
per capita:	
Holdings	4.31
Operating income	$38.09
Internet Access	
Internet computers available	25
Weekly users	2,894

Municipal Finance

Debt at year end 2008	$43,267,000
Moody's rating, July 2009	A1

Revenues, 2008

Total	$75,563,769
From all taxes	49,965,813
Federal aid	0
State aid	21,969,665
From other governments	267,410
Charges for services	571,619
Licenses, permits & fees	806,869
Fines & forfeits	29,731
Interfund transfers	28,970
Misc/other/special assessments	961,846

Expenditures, 2008

Total	$64,241,877
General government	2,903,869
Public safety	7,815,123
Other/fixed costs	4,553,935
Human services	687,885
Culture & recreation	1,552,303
Debt Service	5,010,371
Education	36,126,653
Public works	4,847,348
Intergovernmental	744,390

Taxation, 2010

Property type	Valuation	Rate
Total	$3,074,937,774	-
Residential	2,423,094,792	14.08
Open space	0	0.00
Commercial	359,572,494	24.40
Industrial	195,391,988	24.40
Personal	96,878,500	24.40

Average Single Family Tax Bill, 2010

Avg. assessed home value	$299,354
Avg. single fam. tax bill	$4,215
Hi-Lo ranking	120/301

Police & Crime, 2008

Number of police officers	45
Violent crimes	NA
Property crimes	NA

Local School District

(school data 2007-08, except as noted)

Milford
31 West Fountain Street
Milford, MA 01757
508-478-1101

Superintendent	Robert Tremblay
Grade plan	PK-12
Total enrollment '09-10	4,122
Grade 12 enrollment, '09-10	260
Graduation rate	87.0%
Dropout rate	6.2%
Per-pupil expenditure	$10,872
Avg teacher salary	$61,961
Student/teacher ratio '08-09	13.0 to 1
Highly-qualified teachers, '08-09	97.1%
Teachers licensed in assigned subject	96.6%
Students per computer	4.6

Massachusetts Competency Assessment System (MCAS), 2009 results

	English		Math	
	% Prof	CPI	% Prof	CPI
Gr 4	54%	81.3	51%	81.2
Gr 6	68%	85.9	50%	76.9
Gr 8	86%	94.6	59%	80.9
Gr 10	82%	93	79%	90.3

Other School Districts (see Appendix D for data)
Blackstone Valley Vocational Tech

©2010 Information Publications, Inc. All rights reserved. Photocopying prohibited. For additional copies, contact the publisher at www.informationpublications.com or (877)544-INFO (4636)

See Introduction for an explanation of all data sources.

Demographics & Socio-Economic Characteristics

Population

1990	12,228
2000	12,784
Male	6,169
Female	6,615
2008	13,401
2010 (projected)††	12,845
2020 (projected)††	12,799

Race & Hispanic Origin, 2000

Race	
White	12,425
Black/African American	68
American Indian/Alaska Native	19
Asian	131
Hawaiian Native/Pacific Islander	4
Other Race	30
Two or more races	107
Hispanic origin	131

Age & Nativity, 2000

Under 5 years	750
18 years and over	9,835
21 years and over	9,459
65 years and over	2,049
85 years and over	316
Median Age	38.7
Native-born	12,404
Foreign-born	380

Age, 2020 (projected)††

Under 5 years	638
5 to 19 years	1,988
20 to 39 years	3,036
40 to 64 years	4,486
65 years and over	2,651

Educational Attainment, 2000

Population 25 years and over	9,005
High School graduates or higher	83.7%
Bachelor's degree or higher	17.8%
Graduate degree	5.8%

Income & Poverty, 1999

Per capita income,	$23,531
Median household income	$51,415
Median family income	$62,564
Persons in poverty	779
H'holds receiving public assistance	91
H'holds receiving social security	1,404

Households, 2000

Total households	4,927
With persons under 18	1,622
With persons over 65	1,303
Family households	3,442
Single person households	1,213
Persons per household	2.5
Persons per family	3.0

Labor & Employment, 2000

Civilian labor force	7,033
Unemployment rate	2.7%
Civilian labor force, 2008†	7,546
Unemployment rate†	6.7%
Civilian labor force, 12/09†	7,569
Unemployment rate†	8.4%
Employed persons 16 years and over, by occupation:	
Managers & professionals	1,977
Service occupations	960
Sales & office occupations	1,920
Farming, fishing & forestry	5
Construction & maintenance	744
Production & transportation	1,238
Self-employed persons	565

Most demographic data is from the 2000 Decennial Census
† Massachusetts Department of Revenue
†† University of Massachusetts, MISER

General Information

Town of Millbury
127 Elm St
Millbury, MA 01527
508-865-4710

Elevation	415 ft.
Land area (square miles)	15.7
Water area (square miles)	0.5
Population density, 2008 (est)	853.6
Year incorporated	1813
Email	dplante@townofmillbury.net

Voters & Government Information

Government type	Open Town Meeting
Number of Selectmen	5
US Congressional District(s)	2

Registered Voters, October 2008

Total	8,741
Democrats	2,718
Republicans	984
Unaffiliated/other	4,992

Local Officials, 2010

Chair, Bd. of Sel.	E. Bernard Plante
Manager	Robert Spain
Clerk	Kenneth Schold
Finance Director	Brian Turbitt
Tax Collector	Denise Marlborough
Tax Assessor	Dennis J. Piel
Attorney	Kopelman & Paige
Public Works	John McGarry
Building	Robert Blackman
Planning	Lori Connors
Police Chief	Richard Handfield
Emerg/Fire Chief	Matthew Belsito

Housing & Construction

New Privately Owned Housing Units Authorized by Building Permit

	Single Family	Total Bldgs	Total Units
2006	14	15	16
2007	16	18	21
2008	7	7	7

Parcel Count by Property Class, 2010

Total	5,307
Single family	3,419
Multiple units	422
Apartments	53
Condos	384
Vacant land	700
Open space	0
Commercial	140
Industrial	64
Misc. residential	38
Other use	87

Public Library

Millbury Public Library
128 Elm St.
Millbury, MA 01527
(508)865-1181

Director	Elizabeth Valero

Library Statistics, FY 2008

Population served, 2007	13,470
Registered users	4,040
Circulation	61,715
Reference transactons	0
Total program attendance	0
per capita:	
Holdings	3.45
Operating income	$28.65
Internet Access	
Internet computers available	4
Weekly users	135

Municipal Finance

Debt at year end 2008	$23,765,790
Moody's rating, July 2009	A2

Revenues, 2008

Total	$31,772,939
From all taxes	19,956,932
Federal aid	148,854
State aid	9,141,955
From other governments	438,959
Charges for services	375,517
Licenses, permits & fees	272,401
Fines & forfeits	75,822
Interfund transfers	430,875
Misc/other/special assessments	465,812

Expenditures, 2008

Total	$31,160,422
General government	1,552,937
Public safety	2,648,178
Other/fixed costs	4,906,205
Human services	350,841
Culture & recreation	461,454
Debt Service	2,219,111
Education	16,847,615
Public works	1,475,467
Intergovernmental	393,477

Taxation, 2010

Property type	Valuation	Rate
Total	$1,384,923,642	-
Residential	1,090,699,842	13.46
Open space	0	0.00
Commercial	158,212,358	13.46
Industrial	60,810,200	13.46
Personal	75,201,242	13.46

Average Single Family Tax Bill, 2010

Avg. assessed home value	$242,801
Avg. single fam. tax bill	$3,268
Hi-Lo ranking	207/301

Police & Crime, 2008

Number of police officers	20
Violent crimes	35
Property crimes	282

Local School District

(school data 2007-08, except as noted)

Millbury
12 Martin Street
Millbury, MA 01527
508-865-9501

Superintendent	Susan Hitchcock
Grade plan	PK-12
Total enrollment '09-10	1,893
Grade 12 enrollment, '09-10	154
Graduation rate	93.0%
Dropout rate	2.5%
Per-pupil expenditure	$11,015
Avg teacher salary	$63,771
Student/teacher ratio '08-09	14.1 to 1
Highly-qualified teachers, '08-09	95.7%
Teachers licensed in assigned subject	98.9%
Students per computer	3.7

Massachusetts Competency Assessment System (MCAS), 2009 results

	English		Math	
	% Prof	CPI	% Prof	CPI
Gr 4	43%	77.3	42%	76.2
Gr 6	54%	81	48%	74.7
Gr 8	73%	88.8	40%	67.4
Gr 10	83%	93.9	77%	90.4

Other School Districts (see Appendix D for data)
Blackstone Valley Vocational Tech

©2010 Information Publications, Inc. All rights reserved. Photocopying prohibited. For additional copies, contact the publisher at www.informationpublications.com or (877)544-INFO (4636)

See Introduction for an explanation of all data sources.

Demographics & Socio-Economic Characteristics

Population

1990	7,613
2000	7,902
Male	3,824
Female	4,078
2008	7,957
2010 (projected)††	7,926
2020 (projected)††	7,972

Race & Hispanic Origin, 2000

Race	
White	7,660
Black/African American	56
American Indian/Alaska Native	11
Asian	90
Hawaiian Native/Pacific Islander	0
Other Race	19
Two or more races	66
Hispanic origin	74

Age & Nativity, 2000

Under 5 years	657
18 years and over	5,774
21 years and over	5,612
65 years and over	743
85 years and over	59
Median Age	37.2
Native-born	7,455
Foreign-born	447

Age, 2020 (projected)††

Under 5 years	567
5 to 19 years	1,470
20 to 39 years	2,007
40 to 64 years	2,556
65 years and over	1,372

Educational Attainment, 2000

Population 25 years and over	5,407
High School graduates or higher	94.1%
Bachelor's degree or higher	37.5%
Graduate degree	11.0%

Income & Poverty, 1999

Per capita income,	$27,957
Median household income	$62,806
Median family income	$72,171
Persons in poverty	230
H'holds receiving public assistance	55
H'holds receiving social security	595

Households, 2000

Total households	3,004
With persons under 18	1,164
With persons over 65	551
Family households	2,164
Single person households	685
Persons per household	2.6
Persons per family	3.1

Labor & Employment, 2000

Civilian labor force	4,404
Unemployment rate	2.8%
Civilian labor force, 2008†	4,567
Unemployment rate†	5.6%
Civilian labor force, 12/09†	4,541
Unemployment rate†	8.3%
Employed persons 16 years and over, by occupation:	
Managers & professionals	1,890
Service occupations	433
Sales & office occupations	1,216
Farming, fishing & forestry	0
Construction & maintenance	431
Production & transportation	309
Self-employed persons	408

Most demographic data is from the 2000 Decennial Census
† Massachusetts Department of Revenue
†† University of Massachusetts, MISER

General Information

Town of Millis
900 Main St
Millis, MA 02054
508-376-7046

Elevation	163 ft.
Land area (square miles)	12.2
Water area (square miles)	0.1
Population density, 2008 (est)	652.2
Year incorporated	1885
Website	www.millis.net

Voters & Government Information

Government type	Open Town Meeting
Number of Selectmen	3
US Congressional District(s)	4

Registered Voters, October 2008

Total	5,328
Democrats	1,469
Republicans	815
Unaffiliated/other	3,008

Local Officials, 2010

Chair, Bd. of Sel.	Donald Hendon
Manager/Admin	Charles Aspinwall
Clerk	Lisa Jane Hardin
Accountant	Kathy LaPlant
Treas/Collector	Jeffrey Cannon
Tax Assessor	Lenard Johnson
Attorney	Kopelman & Paige
Public Works	Charles Aspinwall
Building	Michael Giampietro
Planning	Robert Cantoreggi
Police Chief	Peter McGowan
Emerg/Fire Chief	Warren Champagne

Housing & Construction

New Privately Owned Housing Units Authorized by Building Permit

	Single Family	Total Bldgs	Total Units
2006	5	6	7
2007	14	14	14
2008	2	4	6

Parcel Count by Property Class, 2010

Total	NA
Single family	NA
Multiple units	NA
Apartments	NA
Condos	NA
Vacant land	NA
Open space	NA
Commercial	NA
Industrial	NA
Misc. residential	NA
Other use	NA

Public Library

Millis Public Library
25 Auburn Road
Millis, MA 02054
(508)376-8282

Director	Tricia Perry

Library Statistics, FY 2008

Population served, 2007	7,927
Registered users	3,288
Circulation	84,857
Reference transactons	1,598
Total program attendance	32,944
per capita:	
Holdings	6.33
Operating income	$39.57
Internet Access	
Internet computers available	6
Weekly users	50

Municipal Finance

Debt at year end 2008	$17,070,000
Moody's rating, July 2009	A2

Revenues, 2008

Total	$21,818,484
From all taxes	14,652,026
Federal aid	0
State aid	4,804,040
From other governments	30,664
Charges for services	491,503
Licenses, permits & fees	175,326
Fines & forfeits	18,151
Interfund transfers	1,214,616
Misc/other/special assessments	216,079

Expenditures, 2008

Total	$21,848,238
General government	1,560,581
Public safety	2,550,627
Other/fixed costs	2,212,535
Human services	156,949
Culture & recreation	294,137
Debt Service	2,448,674
Education	10,615,820
Public works	1,020,633
Intergovernmental	988,282

Taxation, 2010

Property type	Valuation	Rate
Total	NA	-
Residential	NA	NA
Open space	NA	NA
Commercial	NA	NA
Industrial	NA	NA
Personal	NA	NA

Average Single Family Tax Bill, 2010

Avg. assessed home value	NA
Avg. single fam. tax bill	NA
Hi-Lo ranking	NA

Police & Crime, 2008

Number of police officers	15
Violent crimes	1
Property crimes	51

Local School District

(school data 2007-08, except as noted)

Millis
245 Plain Street, Central Office
Millis, MA 02054
508-376-7000

Superintendent	Nancy Gustafson
Grade plan	PK-12
Total enrollment '09-10	1,435
Grade 12 enrollment, '09-10	86
Graduation rate	85.3%
Dropout rate	7.4%
Per-pupil expenditure	$10,015
Avg teacher salary	$59,601
Student/teacher ratio '08-09	15.6 to 1
Highly-qualified teachers, '08-09	98.7%
Teachers licensed in assigned subject	98.9%
Students per computer	3.9

Massachusetts Competency Assessment System (MCAS), 2009 results

	English		Math	
	% Prof	CPI	% Prof	CPI
Gr 4	67%	88.6	54%	84.4
Gr 6	81%	91.5	63%	82
Gr 8	84%	95	58%	80.2
Gr 10	93%	97.3	79%	90.8

Other School Districts (see Appendix D for data)
Tri County Vocational Tech, Norfolk County Agricultural

©2010 Information Publications, Inc. All rights reserved. Photocopying prohibited. For additional copies, contact the publisher at www.informationpublications.com or (877)544-INFO (4636)

Demographics & Socio-Economic Characteristics

Population

1990	2,236
2000	2,724
Male	1,336
Female	1,388
2008	2,845
2010 (projected)††	3,308
2020 (projected)††	4,180

Race & Hispanic Origin, 2000

Race	
White	2,662
Black/African American	21
American Indian/Alaska Native	1
Asian	5
Hawaiian Native/Pacific Islander	0
Other Race	7
Two or more races	28
Hispanic origin	17

Age & Nativity, 2000

Under 5 years	222
18 years and over	1,875
21 years and over	1,786
65 years and over	221
85 years and over	15
Median Age	33.6
Native-born	2,660
Foreign-born	64

Age, 2020 (projected)††

Under 5 years	355
5 to 19 years	910
20 to 39 years	1,283
40 to 64 years	1,286
65 years and over	346

Educational Attainment, 2000

Population 25 years and over	1,712
High School graduates or higher	85.6%
Bachelor's degree or higher	20.4%
Graduate degree	5.0%

Income & Poverty, 1999

Per capita income,	$20,497
Median household income	$57,000
Median family income	$61,513
Persons in poverty	156
H'holds receiving public assistance	4
H'holds receiving social security	188

Households, 2000

Total households	923
With persons under 18	440
With persons over 65	165
Family households	720
Single person households	143
Persons per household	3.0
Persons per family	3.3

Labor & Employment, 2000

Civilian labor force	1,447
Unemployment rate	2.3%
Civilian labor force, 2008†	1,624
Unemployment rate†	7.4%
Civilian labor force, 12/09†	1,604
Unemployment rate†	12.5%
Employed persons 16 years and over, by occupation:	
Managers & professionals	500
Service occupations	192
Sales & office occupations	352
Farming, fishing & forestry	0
Construction & maintenance	152
Production & transportation	217
Self-employed persons	72

Most demographic data is from the 2000 Decennial Census
† Massachusetts Department of Revenue
†† University of Massachusetts, MISER

General Information

Town of Millville
8 Central Street
Millville, MA 01529
508-883-8433

Elevation	250 ft.
Land area (square miles)	4.9
Water area (square miles)	0.1
Population density, 2008 (est)	580.6
Year incorporated	1916
Website	www.millvillema.org

Voters & Government Information

Government type	Open Town Meeting
Number of Selectmen	5
US Congressional District(s)	2

Registered Voters, October 2008

Total	1,889
Democrats	408
Republicans	200
Unaffiliated/other	1,267

Local Officials, 2010

Chair, Bd. of Sel.	Jackie Lima
Executive Secretary	Helen Coffin
Town Clerk	Susan Gray-McNamara
Finance Director	Marilyn Mathieu
Tax Collector	Lisa A. Larue
Tax Assessor	Susan Gray-McNamara
Attorney	Brackett & Lucas
Public Works	John Dean
Building	Michael Giampietro
Comm Dev/Planning	Joe Laydon
Police Chief	Ronald Landry
Fire Chief	John Mullaly

Housing & Construction

New Privately Owned Housing Units Authorized by Building Permit

	Single Family	Total Bldgs	Total Units
2006	0	0	0
2007	4	5	10
2008	0	0	0

Parcel Count by Property Class, 2010

Total	1,264
Single family	808
Multiple units	83
Apartments	3
Condos	110
Vacant land	205
Open space	0
Commercial	18
Industrial	12
Misc. residential	3
Other use	22

Public Library

Millville Free Public Library
PO Box 726
Millville, MA 01529
(508)883-1887

Director — Lisa Cheever

Library Statistics, FY 2008

Population served, 2007	2,834
Registered users	2,576
Circulation	2,699
Reference transactons	0
Total program attendance	0
per capita:	
Holdings	4.18
Operating income	$15.20
Internet Access	
Internet computers available	4
Weekly users	20

Municipal Finance

Debt at year end 2008	$497,254
Moody's rating, July 2009	NA

Revenues, 2008

Total	$4,789,500
From all taxes	3,851,187
Federal aid	0
State aid	547,221
From other governments	10,656
Charges for services	22,229
Licenses, permits & fees	42,468
Fines & forfeits	3,885
Interfund transfers	157,900
Misc/other/special assessments	76,977

Expenditures, 2008

Total	$4,627,671
General government	444,383
Public safety	787,071
Other/fixed costs	239,545
Human services	102,746
Culture & recreation	38,010
Debt Service	31,702
Education	2,477,446
Public works	488,728
Intergovernmental	16,923

Taxation, 2010

Property type	Valuation	Rate
Total	$320,694,823	-
Residential	303,267,790	11.79
Open space	0	0.00
Commercial	4,261,783	11.79
Industrial	2,440,200	11.79
Personal	10,725,050	11.79

Average Single Family Tax Bill, 2010

Avg. assessed home value	$300,877
Avg. single fam. tax bill	$3,547
Hi-Lo ranking	168/301

Police & Crime, 2008

Number of police officers	4
Violent crimes	5
Property crimes	35

Local School District

(school data 2007-08, except as noted)

Millville (non-op)
175 Lincoln Street
Blackstone, MA 01504
508-883-4400

Superintendent — Kimberly Shaver-Hood

Non-operating district.
Resident students are sent to the Other School Districts listed below.

Grade plan	NA
Total enrollment '09-10	NA
Grade 12 enrollment, '09-10	NA
Graduation rate	NA
Dropout rate	NA
Per-pupil expenditure	NA
Avg teacher salary	NA
Student/teacher ratio '08-09	NA
Highly-qualified teachers, '08-09	NA
Teachers licensed in assigned subject	NA
Students per computer	NA

Other School Districts (see Appendix D for data)
Blackstone-Millville Regional, Blackstone Valley Vocational Tech

©2010 Information Publications, Inc. All rights reserved. Photocopying prohibited. For additional copies, contact the publisher at www.informationpublications.com or (877)544-INFO (4636)

See Introduction for an explanation of all data sources.

Demographics & Socio-Economic Characteristics*

Population

1990	25,725
2000	26,062
Male	12,321
Female	13,741
2008	26,187
2010 (projected)††	25,455
2020 (projected)††	24,471

Race & Hispanic Origin, 2000

Race	
White	22,252
Black/African American	2,666
American Indian/Alaska Native	17
Asian	531
Hawaiian Native/Pacific Islander	10
Other Race	164
Two or more races	422
Hispanic origin	450

Age & Nativity, 2000

Under 5 years	1,640
18 years and over	19,341
21 years and over	18,199
65 years and over	4,234
85 years and over	688
Median Age	39.3
Native-born	23,449
Foreign-born	2,613

Age, 2020 (projected)††

Under 5 years	1,363
5 to 19 years	5,028
20 to 39 years	5,833
40 to 64 years	7,764
65 years and over	4,483

Educational Attainment, 2000

Population 25 years and over	17,092
High School graduates or higher	94.6%
Bachelor's degree or higher	52.2%
Graduate degree	22.0%

Income & Poverty, 1999

Per capita income,	$37,138
Median household income	$78,985
Median family income	$94,359
Persons in poverty	697
H'holds receiving public assistance	65
H'holds receiving social security	2,959

Households, 2000

Total households	8,982
With persons under 18	3,529
With persons over 65	2,909
Family households	6,757
Single person households	1,905
Persons per household	2.8
Persons per family	3.3

Labor & Employment, 2000

Civilian labor force	13,382
Unemployment rate	2.6%
Civilian labor force, 2008†	13,627
Unemployment rate†	5.0%
Civilian labor force, 12/09†	13,454
Unemployment rate†	7.3%
Employed persons 16 years and over, by occupation:	
Managers & professionals	7,430
Service occupations	1,442
Sales & office occupations	2,926
Farming, fishing & forestry	0
Construction & maintenance	682
Production & transportation	559
Self-employed persons	1,017

Most demographic data is from the 2000 Decennial Census
* see Appendix E for American Community Survey data
† Massachusetts Department of Revenue
†† University of Massachusetts, MISER

General Information

Town of Milton
525 Canton Ave
Milton, MA 02186
617-898-4800

Elevation	110 ft.
Land area (square miles)	13.0
Water area (square miles)	0.2
Population density, 2008 (est)	2,014.4
Year incorporated	1662
Website	www.townofmilton.org

Voters & Government Information

Government type	Rep. Twn. Mtg. (279)
Number of Selectmen	3
US Congressional District(s)	9

Registered Voters, October 2008

Total	18,566
Democrats	8,795
Republicans	1,647
Unaffiliated/other	8,074

Local Officials, 2010

Chair, Bd. of Sel.	Kathryn A. Fagan
Manager/Admin	Kevin J. Mearn
Clerk	James G. Mullen Jr
Accountant	(vacant)
Treas/Collector	James D. McAuliffe
Tax Assessor	Jeffrey T. d'Ambly
Attorney	John P. Flynn
Public Works	Joseph Lynch
Building	Joseph F. Prondak
Planning	William B. Clark Jr
Police Chief	Richard G. Wells Jr
Fire Chief	John J. Grant Jr

Housing & Construction

New Privately Owned Housing Units Authorized by Building Permit

	Single Family	Total Bldgs	Total Units
2006	4	4	4
2007	5	5	5
2008	4	6	11

Parcel Count by Property Class, 2010

Total	8,396
Single family	7,113
Multiple units	640
Apartments	11
Condos	220
Vacant land	214
Open space	0
Commercial	116
Industrial	6
Misc. residential	38
Other use	38

Public Library

Milton Public Library
476 Canton Ave.
Milton, MA 02186
(617)698-5757

Director	Philip McNulty

Library Statistics, FY 2008

Population served, 2007	25,691
Registered users	13,591
Circulation	201,005
Reference transactons	6,310
Total program attendance	0
per capita:	
Holdings	4.51
Operating income	$36.40
Internet Access	
Internet computers available	14
Weekly users	244

Municipal Finance

Debt at year end 2008	$26,493,215
Moody's rating, July 2009	Aa3

Revenues, 2008

Total	$71,141,052
From all taxes	55,969,660
Federal aid	400,627
State aid	9,213,821
From other governments	44,905
Charges for services	1,692,640
Licenses, permits & fees	931,097
Fines & forfeits	0
Interfund transfers	914,236
Misc/other/special assessments	987,033

Expenditures, 2008

Total	$69,302,158
General government	2,042,242
Public safety	9,851,508
Other/fixed costs	12,556,521
Human services	380,680
Culture & recreation	1,186,284
Debt Service	2,765,414
Education	32,567,140
Public works	4,392,029
Intergovernmental	3,478,866

Taxation, 2010

Property type	Valuation	Rate
Total	$4,411,820,926	-
Residential	4,239,512,023	13.35
Open space	0	0.00
Commercial	103,526,103	20.44
Industrial	4,844,400	20.44
Personal	63,938,400	20.44

Average Single Family Tax Bill, 2010

Avg. assessed home value	$519,035
Avg. single fam. tax bill	$6,929
Hi-Lo ranking	35/301

Police & Crime, 2008

Number of police officers	52
Violent crimes	16
Property crimes	280

Local School District

(school data 2007-08, except as noted)

Milton
25 Gile Road
Milton, MA 02186
617-696-4808

Superintendent	Mary Gormley
Grade plan	PK-12
Total enrollment '09-10	3,952
Grade 12 enrollment, '09-10	268
Graduation rate	89.5%
Dropout rate	5.6%
Per-pupil expenditure	$11,340
Avg teacher salary	$72,221
Student/teacher ratio '08-09	15.1 to 1
Highly-qualified teachers, '08-09	98.7%
Teachers licensed in assigned subject	99.2%
Students per computer	3.5

Massachusetts Competency Assessment System (MCAS), 2009 results

	English		Math	
	% Prof	CPI	% Prof	CPI
Gr 4	65%	85.4	60%	83.7
Gr 6	79%	91.4	66%	85.8
Gr 8	87%	95.1	67%	85.4
Gr 10	89%	95.8	77%	90.9

Other School Districts (see Appendix D for data)
Blue Hills Vocational Tech, Norfolk County Agricultural

©2010 Information Publications, Inc. All rights reserved. Photocopying prohibited. For additional copies, contact the publisher at www.informationpublications.com or (877)544-INFO (4636)

Demographics & Socio-Economic Characteristics

Population

1990	115
2000	93
Male	43
Female	50
2008	96
2010 (projected)††	73
2020 (projected)††	53

Race & Hispanic Origin, 2000

Race	
White	93
Black/African American	0
American Indian/Alaska Native	0
Asian	0
Hawaiian Native/Pacific Islander	0
Other Race	0
Two or more races	0
Hispanic origin	0

Age & Nativity, 2000

Under 5 years	5
18 years and over	70
21 years and over	66
65 years and over	16
85 years and over	1
Median Age	40.8
Native-born	52
Foreign-born	3

Age, 2020 (projected)††

Under 5 years	2
5 to 19 years	9
20 to 39 years	15
40 to 64 years	16
65 years and over	11

Educational Attainment, 2000

Population 25 years and over	42
High School graduates or higher	76.2%
Bachelor's degree or higher	16.7%
Graduate degree	4.8%

Income & Poverty, 1999

Per capita income,	$12,400
Median household income	$25,500
Median family income	$21,250
Persons in poverty	12
H'holds receiving public assistance	0
H'holds receiving social security	14

Households, 2000

Total households	43
With persons under 18	14
With persons over 65	13
Family households	24
Single person households	16
Persons per household	2.2
Persons per family	2.8

Labor & Employment, 2000

Civilian labor force	23
Unemployment rate	8.7%
Civilian labor force, 2008†	24
Unemployment rate†	4.2%
Civilian labor force, 12/09†	25
Unemployment rate†	12.0%
Employed persons 16 years and over, by occupation:	
Managers & professionals	3
Service occupations	2
Sales & office occupations	13
Farming, fishing & forestry	0
Construction & maintenance	2
Production & transportation	1
Self-employed persons	3

Most demographic data is from the 2000 Decennial Census
† Massachusetts Department of Revenue
†† University of Massachusetts, MISER

General Information

Town of Monroe
3 C School St
Monroe Bridge, MA 01350
413-424-5272

Elevation	1,106 ft.
Land area (square miles)	10.7
Water area (square miles)	0.1
Population density, 2008 (est)	9.0
Year incorporated	1822
Website	NA

Voters & Government Information

Government type	Open Town Meeting
Number of Selectmen	3
US Congressional District(s)	1

Registered Voters, October 2008

Total	73
Democrats	9
Republicans	6
Unaffiliated/other	56

Local Officials, 2010

Chair, Bd. of Sel.	David Nash
Manager/Admin	NA
Clerk	Marcella Stafford-Gore
Finance	Jane Thoresen
Tax Collector	Marcella Stafford Gore
Tax Assessor	Russell Oaks
Attorney	Donna McNicol
Public Works	David Gagne
Building	David Gagne
Comm Dev/Planning	Select Board
Police Chief	NA
Emerg/Fire Chief	Larry Thoresen

Housing & Construction

New Privately Owned Housing Units Authorized by Building Permit

	Single Family	Total Bldgs	Total Units
2006	1	1	1
2007	0	0	0
2008	0	0	0

Parcel Count by Property Class, 2010

Total	NA
Single family	NA
Multiple units	NA
Apartments	NA
Condos	NA
Vacant land	NA
Open space	NA
Commercial	NA
Industrial	NA
Misc. residential	NA
Other use	NA

Public Library

Monroe Public Library
PO Box 35
Monroe Bridge, MA 01350
(413)424-7776

Librarian	Carla Davis-Little

Library Statistics, FY 2008

Population served, 2007	96
Registered users	0
Circulation	0
Reference transactons	0
Total program attendance	0
per capita:	
Holdings	0.00
Operating income	$0.00
Internet Access	
Internet computers available	0
Weekly users	0

Municipal Finance

Debt at year end 2008	$0
Moody's rating, July 2009	NA

Revenues, 2008

Total	$676,914
From all taxes	473,484
Federal aid	0
State aid	85,407
From other governments	360
Charges for services	23,854
Licenses, permits & fees	2,566
Fines & forfeits	0
Interfund transfers.	5,355
Misc/other/special assessments	42,944

Expenditures, 2008

Total	$593,668
General government	74,841
Public safety	14,883
Other/fixed costs	63,403
Human services	558
Culture & recreation	1,299
Debt Service	0
Education	198,328
Public works	216,085
Intergovernmental	24,271

Taxation, 2010

Property type	Valuation	Rate
Total	NA	-
Residential	NA	NA
Open space	NA	NA
Commercial	NA	NA
Industrial	NA	NA
Personal	NA	NA

Average Single Family Tax Bill, 2010

Avg. assessed home value	NA
Avg. single fam. tax bill	NA
Hi-Lo ranking	NA

Police & Crime, 2008

Number of police officers	NA
Violent crimes	NA
Property crimes	NA

Local School District

(school data 2007-08, except as noted)

Monroe (non-op)
98 Church Street
North Adams, MA 01247
413-664-9292

Superintendent	Jon Lev

Non-operating district.
Resident students are sent to the Other School Districts listed below.

Grade plan	NA
Total enrollment '09-10	NA
Grade 12 enrollment, '09-10	NA
Graduation rate	NA
Dropout rate	NA
Per-pupil expenditure	NA
Avg teacher salary	NA
Student/teacher ratio '08-09	NA
Highly-qualified teachers, '08-09	NA
Teachers licensed in assigned subject	NA
Students per computer	NA

Other School Districts (see Appendix D for data)

Sends grades P-8 to Florida; 9-12 to North Adams and Northern Berkshire Vocational Tech

©2010 Information Publications, Inc. All rights reserved. Photocopying prohibited. For additional copies, contact the publisher at www.informationpublications.com or (877)544-INFO (4636)

See Introduction for an explanation of all data sources.

Demographics & Socio-Economic Characteristics

Population

1990	7,776
2000	8,359
Male	4,125
Female	4,234
2008	8,952
2010 (projected)††	8,825
2020 (projected)††	9,313

Race & Hispanic Origin, 2000

Race	
White	8,166
Black/African American	56
American Indian/Alaska Native	19
Asian	26
Hawaiian Native/Pacific Islander	1
Other Race	19
Two or more races	72
Hispanic origin	98

Age & Nativity, 2000

Under 5 years	522
18 years and over	6,251
21 years and over	5,965
65 years and over	915
85 years and over	91
Median Age	38.5
Native-born	7,905
Foreign-born	454

Age, 2020 (projected)††

Under 5 years	508
5 to 19 years	1,575
20 to 39 years	2,209
40 to 64 years	3,326
65 years and over	1,695

Educational Attainment, 2000

Population 25 years and over	5,689
High School graduates or higher	83.3%
Bachelor's degree or higher	22.5%
Graduate degree	7.6%

Income & Poverty, 1999

Per capita income,	$22,519
Median household income	$52,030
Median family income	$58,607
Persons in poverty	450
H'holds receiving public assistance	45
H'holds receiving social security	687

Households, 2000

Total households	3,095
With persons under 18	1,131
With persons over 65	640
Family households	2,203
Single person households	705
Persons per household	2.6
Persons per family	3.1

Labor & Employment, 2000

Civilian labor force	4,383
Unemployment rate	3.9%
Civilian labor force, 2008†	4,689
Unemployment rate†	6.9%
Civilian labor force, 12/09†	4,805
Unemployment rate†	10.5%
Employed persons 16 years and over, by occupation:	
Managers & professionals	1,446
Service occupations	676
Sales & office occupations	831
Farming, fishing & forestry	20
Construction & maintenance	396
Production & transportation	844
Self-employed persons	270

Most demographic data is from the 2000 Decennial Census
† Massachusetts Department of Revenue
†† University of Massachusetts, MISER

General Information

Town of Monson
110 Main St
Monson, MA 01057
413-267-4100

Elevation	407 ft.
Land area (square miles)	44.3
Water area (square miles)	0.5
Population density, 2008 (est)	202.1
Year incorporated	1775
Website	www.monson-ma.gov

Voters & Government Information

Government type	Open Town Meeting
Number of Selectmen	3
US Congressional District(s)	2

Registered Voters, October 2008

Total	5,830
Democrats	1,737
Republicans	843
Unaffiliated/other	3,201

Local Officials, 2010

Chair, Bd. of Sel.	Edward S. Harrison
Manager/Admin	Gretchen Neggers
Clerk	Nancy C. Morrell
Finance Director	Deborah Mahar
Tax Collector	Dorothy Jenkins
Tax Assessor	Russell Bressette
Attorney	Kenneth Albano
Public Works	John R. Morrell
Building	Chip LaPointe
Planning	Craig Sweitzer (Chr)
Police Chief	Stephen Kozloski
Fire Chief	George Robichaud

Housing & Construction

New Privately Owned Housing Units Authorized by Building Permit

	Single Family	Total Bldgs	Total Units
2006	30	35	40
2007	33	33	33
2008	9	9	9

Parcel Count by Property Class, 2010

Total	3,859
Single family	2,617
Multiple units	130
Apartments	26
Condos	58
Vacant land	664
Open space	0
Commercial	77
Industrial	49
Misc. residential	71
Other use	167

Public Library

Monson Free Lib. and Reading Room Assn.
2 High Street
Monson, MA 01057
(413)267-3866

Director	Hope Bodwell

Library Statistics, FY 2008

Population served, 2007	8,788
Registered users	6,260
Circulation	55,183
Reference transactons	3,121
Total program attendance	0
per capita:	
Holdings	4.96
Operating income	$41.45
Internet Access	
Internet computers available	7
Weekly users	153

Municipal Finance

Debt at year end 2008	$31,002,457
Moody's rating, July 2009	A3

Revenues, 2008

Total	$23,880,737
From all taxes	10,388,990
Federal aid	48,032
State aid	11,928,852
From other governments	6,299
Charges for services	74,816
Licenses, permits & fees	72,244
Fines & forfeits	23,709
Interfund transfers	30,817
Misc/other/special assessments	653,489

Expenditures, 2008

Total	$23,357,804
General government	831,121
Public safety	1,647,801
Other/fixed costs	2,633,514
Human services	230,129
Culture & recreation	587,073
Debt Service	3,924,323
Education	11,786,287
Public works	1,145,277
Intergovernmental	572,279

Taxation, 2010

Property type	Valuation	Rate
Total	$771,116,435	-
Residential	711,895,660	13.45
Open space	0	0.00
Commercial	24,738,440	13.45
Industrial	9,277,635	13.45
Personal	25,204,700	13.45

Average Single Family Tax Bill, 2010

Avg. assessed home value	$235,781
Avg. single fam. tax bill	$3,171
Hi-Lo ranking	216/301

Police & Crime, 2008

Number of police officers	11
Violent crimes	28
Property crimes	133

Local School District

(school data 2007-08, except as noted)

Monson
P O Box 159
Monson, MA 01057
413-267-4150

Superintendent	Patrice Dardenne
Grade plan	PK-12
Total enrollment '09-10	1,419
Grade 12 enrollment, '09-10	78
Graduation rate	82.9%
Dropout rate	6.7%
Per-pupil expenditure	$9,901
Avg teacher salary	$51,256
Student/teacher ratio '08-09	15.0 to 1
Highly-qualified teachers, '08-09	100.0%
Teachers licensed in assigned subject	98.5%
Students per computer	2.7

Massachusetts Competency Assessment System (MCAS), 2009 results

	English		Math	
	% Prof	CPI	% Prof	CPI
Gr 4	42%	73.9	37%	72.2
Gr 6	63%	85	44%	72.7
Gr 8	74%	91.5	36%	67.1
Gr 10	90%	96.4	87%	94.3

Other School Districts (see Appendix D for data)
Pathfinder Vocational Tech

©2010 Information Publications, Inc. All rights reserved. Photocopying prohibited. For additional copies, contact the publisher at www.informationpublications.com or (877)544-INFO (4636)

Demographics & Socio-Economic Characteristics

Population

1990	8,316
2000	8,489
Male	4,031
Female	4,458
2008	8,316
2010 (projected)††	8,621
2020 (projected)††	8,882

Race & Hispanic Origin, 2000

Race	
White	8,076
Black/African American	71
American Indian/Alaska Native	33
Asian	79
Hawaiian Native/Pacific Islander	9
Other Race	58
Two or more races	163
Hispanic origin	217

Age & Nativity, 2000

Under 5 years	507
18 years and over	6,540
21 years and over	6,261
65 years and over	1,404
85 years and over	143
Median Age	39.0
Native-born	8,140
Foreign-born	349

Age, 2020 (projected)††

Under 5 years	511
5 to 19 years	1,456
20 to 39 years	2,241
40 to 64 years	2,886
65 years and over	1,788

Educational Attainment, 2000

Population 25 years and over	5,849
High School graduates or higher	84.0%
Bachelor's degree or higher	19.0%
Graduate degree	7.6%

Income & Poverty, 1999

Per capita income	$17,794
Median household income	$33,750
Median family income	$43,194
Persons in poverty	1,097
H'holds receiving public assistance	168
H'holds receiving social security	1,190

Households, 2000

Total households	3,616
With persons under 18	1,108
With persons over 65	1,008
Family households	2,170
Single person households	1,152
Persons per household	2.3
Persons per family	2.9

Labor & Employment, 2000

Civilian labor force	4,448
Unemployment rate	5.8%
Civilian labor force, 2008†	4,250
Unemployment rate†	7.1%
Civilian labor force, 12/09†	4,311
Unemployment rate†	10.2%
Employed persons 16 years and over, by occupation:	
Managers & professionals	1,262
Service occupations	733
Sales & office occupations	1,010
Farming, fishing & forestry	26
Construction & maintenance	457
Production & transportation	703
Self-employed persons	374

Most demographic data is from the 2000 Decennial Census
† Massachusetts Department of Revenue
†† University of Massachusetts, MISER

General Information

Town of Montague
1 Ave A
Turners Falls, MA 01376
413-863-3200

Elevation	235 ft.
Land area (square miles)	30.4
Water area (square miles)	1.0
Population density, 2008 (est)	273.6
Year incorporated	1754
Website	www.monague.net

Voters & Government Information

Government type	Rep. Twn. Mtg. (126)
Number of Selectmen	3
US Congressional District(s)	1

Registered Voters, October 2008

Total	5,863
Democrats	1,997
Republicans	466
Unaffiliated/other	3,332

Local Officials, 2010

Chair, Bd. of Sel.	Patricia Pruitt
Town Administrator	Frank Abbondonzio
Clerk	Debra Bourbeau
Finance Director	Carolyn Olsen
Tax Collector	Patricia Dion
Tax Assessor	Paul Emery
Attorney	Kopelman & Paige
Public Works	Thomas Bergeron
Building	David E. Jensen
Planning	Walter Ramsey (Int)
Police Chief	Raymond Zukowski
Emerg/Fire Chief	Raymond Godin

Housing & Construction

New Privately Owned Housing Units Authorized by Building Permit

	Single Family	Total Bldgs	Total Units
2006	11	11	11
2007	8	8	8
2008	5	5	5

Parcel Count by Property Class, 2010

Total	NA
Single family	NA
Multiple units	NA
Apartments	NA
Condos	NA
Vacant land	NA
Open space	NA
Commercial	NA
Industrial	NA
Misc. residential	NA
Other use	NA

Public Library

Carnegie Public Library
201 Avenue A
Turners Falls, MA 01376
(413)863-3214

Director	Susan SanSoucie

Library Statistics, FY 2008

Population served, 2007	8,334
Registered users	4,282
Circulation	107,226
Reference transactons	3,068
Total program attendance	37,310
per capita:	
Holdings	5.59
Operating income	$36.61
Internet Access	
Internet computers available	8
Weekly users	215

Municipal Finance

Debt at year end 2008	$4,551,559
Moody's rating, July 2009	A3

Revenues, 2008

Total	$14,547,736
From all taxes	11,145,545
Federal aid	562
State aid	1,787,552
From other governments	37,243
Charges for services	287,894
Licenses, permits & fees	114,605
Fines & forfeits	27,026
Interfund transfers	701,837
Misc/other/special assessments	222,736

Expenditures, 2008

Total	$14,343,035
General government	985,816
Public safety	1,364,875
Other/fixed costs	1,715,001
Human services	173,234
Culture & recreation	441,667
Debt Service	271,119
Education	7,960,308
Public works	1,277,926
Intergovernmental	153,089

Taxation, 2010

Property type	Valuation	Rate
Total	NA	-
Residential	NA	NA
Open space	NA	NA
Commercial	NA	NA
Industrial	NA	NA
Personal	NA	NA

Average Single Family Tax Bill, 2010

Avg. assessed home value	NA
Avg. single fam. tax bill	NA
Hi-Lo ranking	NA

Police & Crime, 2008

Number of police officers	15
Violent crimes	49
Property crimes	186

Local School District

(school data 2007-08, except as noted)

Montague (non-op)
35 Crocker Avenue
Turners Falls, MA 01376
413-863-9324

Superintendent	Carl Ladd

Non-operating district.
Resident students are sent to the Other School Districts listed below.

Grade plan	NA
Total enrollment '09-10	NA
Grade 12 enrollment, '09-10	NA
Graduation rate	NA
Dropout rate	NA
Per-pupil expenditure	NA
Avg teacher salary	NA
Student/teacher ratio '08-09	NA
Highly-qualified teachers, '08-09	NA
Teachers licensed in assigned subject	NA
Students per computer	NA

Other School Districts (see Appendix D for data)
Gill-Montague Regional, Franklin County Vocational Tech

©2010 Information Publications, Inc. All rights reserved. Photocopying prohibited. For additional copies, contact the publisher at www.informationpublications.com or (877)544-INFO (4636)

See Introduction for an explanation of all data sources.

Demographics & Socio-Economic Characteristics

Population

1990	805
2000	934
Male	445
Female	489
2008	950
2010 (projected)††	976
2020 (projected)††	1,009

Race & Hispanic Origin, 2000

Race	
White	905
Black/African American	5
American Indian/Alaska Native	2
Asian	3
Hawaiian Native/Pacific Islander	2
Other Race	7
Two or more races	10
Hispanic origin	14

Age & Nativity, 2000

Under 5 years	37
18 years and over	773
21 years and over	741
65 years and over	154
85 years and over	6
Median Age	44.5
Native-born	874
Foreign-born	58

Age, 2020 (projected)††

Under 5 years	50
5 to 19 years	138
20 to 39 years	181
40 to 64 years	344
65 years and over	296

Educational Attainment, 2000

Population 25 years and over	689
High School graduates or higher	95.1%
Bachelor's degree or higher	51.5%
Graduate degree	23.9%

Income & Poverty, 1999

Per capita income,	$30,992
Median household income	$49,750
Median family income	$59,643
Persons in poverty	83
H'holds receiving public assistance	4
H'holds receiving social security	105

Households, 2000

Total households	387
With persons under 18	94
With persons over 65	112
Family households	240
Single person households	108
Persons per household	2.2
Persons per family	2.7

Labor & Employment, 2000

Civilian labor force	567
Unemployment rate	12.3%
Civilian labor force, 2008†	578
Unemployment rate†	4.0%
Civilian labor force, 12/09†	573
Unemployment rate†	3.8%
Employed persons 16 years and over, by occupation:	
Managers & professionals	229
Service occupations	67
Sales & office occupations	99
Farming, fishing & forestry	9
Construction & maintenance	59
Production & transportation	34
Self-employed persons	85

Most demographic data is from the 2000 Decennial Census
† Massachusetts Department of Revenue
†† University of Massachusetts, MISER

General Information

Town of Monterey
PO Box 308
Monterey, MA 01245
413-528-1443

Elevation	1,244 ft.
Land area (square miles)	26.5
Water area (square miles)	0.8
Population density, 2008 (est)	35.8
Year incorporated	1847
Website	montereyma.gov

Voters & Government Information

Government type	Open Town Meeting
Number of Selectmen	3
US Congressional District(s)	1

Registered Voters, October 2008

Total	762
Democrats	309
Republicans	102
Unaffiliated/other	345

Local Officials, 2010

Chair, Bd. of Sel.	Scott Jensen
Manager/Admin	NA
Clerk	Linda Thorpe
Treasurer	Patricia Mielke
Tax Collector	Anne Marie Enoch
Tax Assessor	Donald Clawson (Asst)
Attorney	Jeremia Pollard
Public Works	Maynard Forbes
Building	Donald Torrico
Planning	Bridget Krans
Police Chief	Gareth Backhaus
Emerg/Fire Chief	Raymond W. Tryon

Housing & Construction

New Privately Owned Housing Units Authorized by Building Permit

	Single Family	Total Bldgs	Total Units
2006	12	12	12
2007	9	9	9
2008	3	3	3

Parcel Count by Property Class, 2010

Total	1,230
Single family	712
Multiple units	10
Apartments	0
Condos	15
Vacant land	339
Open space	0
Commercial	8
Industrial	2
Misc. residential	37
Other use	107

Public Library

Monterey Library
PO Box 172
Monterey, MA 01245
(413)528-3795

Director	Mark Makuc

Library Statistics, FY 2008

Population served, 2007	960
Registered users	1,013
Circulation	13,110
Reference transactons	273
Total program attendance	5,218
per capita:	
Holdings	9.09
Operating income	$53.08
Internet Access	
Internet computers available	2
Weekly users	22

Municipal Finance

Debt at year end 2008	$283,698
Moody's rating, July 2009	NA

Revenues, 2008

Total	$2,977,066
From all taxes	2,507,825
Federal aid	70,479
State aid	195,791
From other governments	28,545
Charges for services	27,216
Licenses, permits & fees	102,836
Fines & forfeits	0
Interfund transfers	5,000
Misc/other/special assessments	19,687

Expenditures, 2008

Total	$2,779,294
General government	264,924
Public safety	281,525
Other/fixed costs	205,216
Human services	33,202
Culture & recreation	90,680
Debt Service	112,628
Education	1,025,646
Public works	760,810
Intergovernmental	4,663

Taxation, 2010

Property type	Valuation	Rate
Total	$492,442,255	-
Residential	475,175,308	5.35
Open space	0	0.00
Commercial	9,997,202	5.35
Industrial	194,364	5.35
Personal	7,075,381	5.35

Average Single Family Tax Bill, 2010

Avg. assessed home value	$519,005
Avg. single fam. tax bill	$2,777
Hi-Lo ranking	257/301

Police & Crime, 2008

Number of police officers	1
Violent crimes	0
Property crimes	0

Local School District

(school data 2007-08, except as noted)

Monterey (non-op)
PO Box 339
Sheffield, MA 01257
413-229-8778

Superintendent . . . Michael Singleton

Non-operating district.
Resident students are sent to the Other School Districts listed below.

Grade plan	NA
Total enrollment '09-10	NA
Grade 12 enrollment, '09-10	NA
Graduation rate	NA
Dropout rate	NA
Per-pupil expenditure	NA
Avg teacher salary	NA
Student/teacher ratio '08-09	NA
Highly-qualified teachers, '08-09	NA
Teachers licensed in assigned subject	NA
Students per computer	NA

Other School Districts (see Appendix D for data)
Southern Berkshire Regional

©2010 Information Publications, Inc. All rights reserved. Photocopying prohibited. For additional copies, contact the publisher at www.informationpublications.com or (877)544-INFO (4636)

See Introduction for an explanation of all data sources.

Demographics & Socio-Economic Characteristics

Population

1990	759
2000	654
Male	334
Female	320
2008	720
2010 (projected)††	647
2020 (projected)††	634

Race & Hispanic Origin, 2000

Race	
White	641
Black/African American	0
American Indian/Alaska Native	2
Asian	2
Hawaiian Native/Pacific Islander	0
Other Race	2
Two or more races	7
Hispanic origin	5

Age & Nativity, 2000

Under 5 years	29
18 years and over	504
21 years and over	492
65 years and over	70
85 years and over	4
Median Age	42.5
Native-born	641
Foreign-born	15

Age, 2020 (projected)††

Under 5 years	30
5 to 19 years	85
20 to 39 years	103
40 to 64 years	231
65 years and over	185

Educational Attainment, 2000

Population 25 years and over	459
High School graduates or higher	93.0%
Bachelor's degree or higher	33.6%
Graduate degree	10.5%

Income & Poverty, 1999

Per capita income,	$25,942
Median household income	$59,063
Median family income	$66,250
Persons in poverty	19
H'holds receiving public assistance	4
H'holds receiving social security	43

Households, 2000

Total households	253
With persons under 18	81
With persons over 65	44
Family households	201
Single person households	40
Persons per household	2.6
Persons per family	2.8

Labor & Employment, 2000

Civilian labor force	378
Unemployment rate	2.1%
Civilian labor force, 2008†	437
Unemployment rate†	3.9%
Civilian labor force, 12/09†	458
Unemployment rate†	9.4%
Employed persons 16 years and over, by occupation:	
Managers & professionals	141
Service occupations	41
Sales & office occupations	85
Farming, fishing & forestry	6
Construction & maintenance	46
Production & transportation	51
Self-employed persons	29

Most demographic data is from the 2000 Decennial Census
† Massachusetts Department of Revenue
†† University of Massachusetts, MISER

General Information

Town of Montgomery
161 Main Rd
Montgomery, MA 01085
413-862-3386

Elevation	1,050 ft.
Land area (square miles)	15.1
Water area (square miles)	0.1
Population density, 2008 (est)	47.7
Year incorporated	1780
Email	montgomerymass@rcn.com

Voters & Government Information

Government type	Open Town Meeting
Number of Selectmen	3
US Congressional District(s)	1

Registered Voters, October 2008

Total	587
Democrats	91
Republicans	91
Unaffiliated/other	400

Local Officials, 2010

Chair, Bd. of Sel.	Daniel Jacques
Manager/Admin	Jane R. Thielen
Town Clerk	Judith L. Murphy
Finance	Philip Shaw
Tax Collector	Jane Thielen
Tax Assessor	Charles Darling
Attorney	Kopelman & Paige
Public Works	Curtis Bush Jr
Building	Elwin Clark
Comm Dev/Planning	NA
Police Chief	James Stevens
Emerg/Fire Chief	Stephen Frye

Housing & Construction

New Privately Owned Housing Units Authorized by Building Permit

	Single Family	Total Bldgs	Total Units
2006	4	4	4
2007	3	3	3
2008	2	2	2

Parcel Count by Property Class, 2010

Total	NA
Single family	NA
Multiple units	NA
Apartments	NA
Condos	NA
Vacant land	NA
Open space	NA
Commercial	NA
Industrial	NA
Misc. residential	NA
Other use	NA

Public Library

Grace Hall Memorial Library
161 Main Road
Montgomery, MA 01085
(413)862-3894

Librarian	Paula Long

Library Statistics, FY 2008

Population served, 2007	754
Registered users	545
Circulation	5,063
Reference transactons	890
Total program attendance	3,190
per capita:	
Holdings	9.08
Operating income	$29.69
Internet Access	
Internet computers available	2
Weekly users	2

Municipal Finance

Debt at year end 2008	$102,416
Moody's rating, July 2009	NA

Revenues, 2008

Total	$1,574,386
From all taxes	1,342,037
Federal aid	0
State aid	134,226
From other governments	1,280
Charges for services	61,066
Licenses, permits & fees	4,997
Fines & forfeits	0
Interfund transfers	454
Misc/other/special assessments	15,163

Expenditures, 2008

Total	$1,511,828
General government	197,811
Public safety	29,381
Other/fixed costs	77,340
Human services	2,403
Culture & recreation	16,208
Debt Service	37,335
Education	946,577
Public works	202,772
Intergovernmental	811

Taxation, 2010

Property type	Valuation	Rate
Total	NA	-
Residential	NA	NA
Open space	NA	NA
Commercial	NA	NA
Industrial	NA	NA
Personal	NA	NA

Average Single Family Tax Bill, 2010

Avg. assessed home value	NA
Avg. single fam. tax bill	NA
Hi-Lo ranking	NA

Police & Crime, 2008

Number of police officers	NA
Violent crimes	NA
Property crimes	NA

Local School District

(school data 2007-08, except as noted)

Montgomery (non-op)
12 Littleville Road
Huntington, MA 01050
413-685-1011

Superintendent	David Hopson

Non-operating district.
Resident students are sent to the Other School Districts listed below.

Grade plan	NA
Total enrollment '09-10	NA
Grade 12 enrollment, '09-10	NA
Graduation rate	NA
Dropout rate	NA
Per-pupil expenditure	NA
Avg teacher salary	NA
Student/teacher ratio '08-09	NA
Highly-qualified teachers, '08-09	NA
Teachers licensed in assigned subject	NA
Students per computer	NA

Other School Districts (see Appendix D for data)
Gateway Regional

See Introduction for an explanation of all data sources.

©2010 Information Publications, Inc. All rights reserved. Photocopying prohibited. For additional copies, contact the publisher at www.informationpublications.com or (877)544-INFO (4636)

Demographics & Socio-Economic Characteristics

Population

1990	135
2000	130
Male	68
Female	62
2008	136
2010 (projected)††	149
2020 (projected)††	171

Race & Hispanic Origin, 2000

Race	
White	130
Black/African American	0
American Indian/Alaska Native	0
Asian	0
Hawaiian Native/Pacific Islander	0
Other Race	0
Two or more races	0
Hispanic origin	0

Age & Nativity, 2000

Under 5 years	8
18 years and over	108
21 years and over	107
65 years and over	20
85 years and over	3
Median Age	51.5
Native-born	134
Foreign-born	0

Age, 2020 (projected)††

Under 5 years	6
5 to 19 years	23
20 to 39 years	36
40 to 64 years	47
65 years and over	59

Educational Attainment, 2000

Population 25 years and over	114
High School graduates or higher	87.7%
Bachelor's degree or higher	42.1%
Graduate degree	21.9%

Income & Poverty, 1999

Per capita income,	$50,149
Median household income	$53,125
Median family income	$55,750
Persons in poverty	11
H'holds receiving public assistance	0
H'holds receiving social security	15

Households, 2000

Total households	64
With persons under 18	11
With persons over 65	15
Family households	37
Single person households	24
Persons per household	2.0
Persons per family	2.7

Labor & Employment, 2000

Civilian labor force	86
Unemployment rate	5.8%
Civilian labor force, 2008†	96
Unemployment rate†	3.1%
Civilian labor force, 12/09†	98
Unemployment rate†	5.1%
Employed persons 16 years and over, by occupation:	
Managers & professionals	44
Service occupations	10
Sales & office occupations	12
Farming, fishing & forestry	0
Construction & maintenance	10
Production & transportation	5
Self-employed persons	14

Most demographic data is from the 2000 Decennial Census
† Massachusetts Department of Revenue
†† University of Massachusetts, MISER

General Information

Town of Mount Washington
118 East St
Mount Washington, MA 01258
413-528-2839

Elevation	1,661 ft.
Land area (square miles)	22.2
Water area (square miles)	0.1
Population density, 2008 (est)	6.1
Year incorporated	1779
Email	mtwashington01258@peoplepc.com

Voters & Government Information

Government type	Open Town Meeting
Number of Selectmen	3
US Congressional District(s)	1

Registered Voters, October 2008

Total	127
Democrats	45
Republicans	12
Unaffiliated/other	66

Local Officials, 2010

Chair, Bd. of Sel.	James Lovejoy
Manager/Admin	NA
Town Clerk	Thomas Furcht
Treasurer	Patricia Verones
Tax Collector	James Lovejoy
Tax Assessor	Carolyn Romano
Attorney	Kopelman & Paige
Highway Foreman	James Beckwith
Building	Bengt Granskog
Comm Dev/Planning	Marie Cane
Police Chief	(vacant)
Emerg/Fire Chief	William Turner

Housing & Construction

New Privately Owned Housing Units Authorized by Building Permit

	Single Family	Total Bldgs	Total Units
2006	2	2	2
2007	0	0	0
2008	0	0	0

Parcel Count by Property Class, 2010

Total	260
Single family	146
Multiple units	0
Apartments	0
Condos	0
Vacant land	107
Open space	0
Commercial	0
Industrial	2
Misc. residential	4
Other use	1

Public Library

Mount Washington Library
118 East Street
Mount Washington, MA 01258
(413)528-2839

Librarian	Eleanor Lovejoy

Library Statistics, FY 2008

Population served, 2007	138
Registered users	0
Circulation	1,429
Reference transactons	0
Total program attendance	246
per capita:	
Holdings	10.58
Operating income	$21.05
Internet Access	
Internet computers available	1
Weekly users	2

Municipal Finance

Debt at year end 2008	$0
Moody's rating, July 2009	NA

Revenues, 2008

Total	$741,281
From all taxes	456,835
Federal aid	0
State aid	235,517
From other governments	50
Charges for services	24,235
Licenses, permits & fees	7,584
Fines & forfeits	0
Interfund transfers	0
Misc/other/special assessments	8,530

Expenditures, 2008

Total	$528,521
General government	78,374
Public safety	8,365
Other/fixed costs	71,465
Human services	7,542
Culture & recreation	1,314
Debt Service	0
Education	158,889
Public works	202,572
Intergovernmental	0

Taxation, 2010

Property type	Valuation	Rate
Total	$67,584,570	-
Residential	65,571,000	6.63
Open space	0	0.00
Commercial	35,590	6.63
Industrial	616,500	6.63
Personal	1,361,480	6.63

Average Single Family Tax Bill, 2010

Avg. assessed home value	$321,116
Avg. single fam. tax bill	$2,129
Hi-Lo ranking	292/301

Police & Crime, 2008

Number of police officers	NA
Violent crimes	NA
Property crimes	NA

Local School District

(school data 2007-08, except as noted)

Mount Washington (non-op)
118 East Street
Mt Washington, MA 01258
413-528-2839

Superintendent	Leslieann Furcht

Non-operating district.
Resident students are sent to the Other School Districts listed below.

Grade plan	NA
Total enrollment '09-10	NA
Grade 12 enrollment, '09-10	NA
Graduation rate	NA
Dropout rate	NA
Per-pupil expenditure	NA
Avg teacher salary	NA
Student/teacher ratio '08-09	NA
Highly-qualified teachers, '08-09	NA
Teachers licensed in assigned subject	NA
Students per computer	NA

Other School Districts (see Appendix D for data)
Southern Berkshire Regional

©2010 Information Publications, Inc. All rights reserved. Photocopying prohibited. For additional copies, contact the publisher at www.informationpublications.com or (877)544-INFO (4636)

See Introduction for an explanation of all data sources.

Demographics & Socio-Economic Characteristics

Population

1990	3,828
2000	3,632
Male	1,732
Female	1,900
2008	3,498
2010 (projected)††	3,344
2020 (projected)††	3,027

Race & Hispanic Origin, 2000

Race	
White	3,527
Black/African American	14
American Indian/Alaska Native	3
Asian	39
Hawaiian Native/Pacific Islander	2
Other Race	17
Two or more races	30
Hispanic origin	39

Age & Nativity, 2000

Under 5 years	164
18 years and over	2,956
21 years and over	2,893
65 years and over	706
85 years and over	112
Median Age	44.6
Native-born	3,375
Foreign-born	257

Age, 2020 (projected)††

Under 5 years	104
5 to 19 years	333
20 to 39 years	558
40 to 64 years	1,046
65 years and over	986

Educational Attainment, 2000

Population 25 years and over	2,810
High School graduates or higher	94.6%
Bachelor's degree or higher	47.5%
Graduate degree	22.1%

Income & Poverty, 1999

Per capita income,	$41,807
Median household income	$64,052
Median family income	$76,926
Persons in poverty	92
H'holds receiving public assistance	14
H'holds receiving social security	463

Households, 2000

Total households	1,629
With persons under 18	387
With persons over 65	479
Family households	971
Single person households	551
Persons per household	2.2
Persons per family	2.9

Labor & Employment, 2000

Civilian labor force	1,957
Unemployment rate	1.5%
Civilian labor force, 2008†	1,977
Unemployment rate†	5.6%
Civilian labor force, 12/09†	1,928
Unemployment rate†	6.7%
Employed persons 16 years and over, by occupation:	
Managers & professionals	1,016
Service occupations	226
Sales & office occupations	418
Farming, fishing & forestry	0
Construction & maintenance	128
Production & transportation	140
Self-employed persons	223

Most demographic data is from the 2000 Decennial Census
† Massachusetts Department of Revenue
†† University of Massachusetts, MISER

General Information

Town of Nahant
334 Nahant Rd
Nahant, MA 01908
781-581-0088

Elevation	95 ft.
Land area (square miles)	1.2
Water area (square miles)	14.2
Population density, 2008 (est)	2,915.0
Year incorporated	1853
Website	nahant.org

Voters & Government Information

Government type	Open Town Meeting
Number of Selectmen	3
US Congressional District(s)	6

Registered Voters, October 2008

Total	2,620
Democrats	1,012
Republicans	264
Unaffiliated/other	1,341

Local Officials, 2010

Chair, Bd. of Sel.	Michael P. Manning
Town Administrator	Mark P. Cullinan
Clerk	Margaret R. Barile
Accountant	Deborah Waters
Treas/Collector	Joan Bingham
Tax Assessor	Perry C. Barrasso
Attorney	Charles H. Riley Jr
Public Works	Robert Ward
Building	Wayne Wilson
Comm Dev/Planning	NA
Police Chief	Robert C. Dwyer
Emerg/Fire Chief	Kevin Howard

Housing & Construction

New Privately Owned Housing Units Authorized by Building Permit

	Single Family	Total Bldgs	Total Units
2006	3	3	3
2007	1	1	1
2008	2	2	2

Parcel Count by Property Class, 2010

Total	1,372
Single family	1,125
Multiple units	75
Apartments	5
Condos	78
Vacant land	32
Open space	0
Commercial	8
Industrial	2
Misc. residential	32
Other use	15

Public Library

Nahant Public Library
15 Pleasant St., PO Box 76
Nahant, MA 01908
(781)581-0306

Director .... Daniel A. deStefano

Library Statistics, FY 2008

Population served, 2007	3,519
Registered users	2,276
Circulation	23,865
Reference transactons	3,903
Total program attendance	11,828
per capita:	
Holdings	19.86
Operating income	$53.73
Internet Access	
Internet computers available	0
Weekly users	0

Municipal Finance

Debt at year end 2008	$8,767,299
Moody's rating, July 2009	A2

Revenues, 2008

Total	$9,848,972
From all taxes	7,552,524
Federal aid	0
State aid	1,060,413
From other governments	22,910
Charges for services	832,691
Licenses, permits & fees	69,621
Fines & forfeits	26,170
Interfund transfers	157,341
Misc/other/special assessments	63,651

Expenditures, 2008

Total	$9,406,927
General government	751,744
Public safety	1,912,114
Other/fixed costs	1,234,937
Human services	93,362
Culture & recreation	189,498
Debt Service	988,742
Education	3,255,819
Public works	795,546
Intergovernmental	185,165

Taxation, 2010

Property type	Valuation	Rate
Total	$778,519,185	-
Residential	747,105,295	9.42
Open space	0	0.00
Commercial	14,550,340	9.42
Industrial	274,300	9.42
Personal	16,589,250	9.42

Average Single Family Tax Bill, 2010

Avg. assessed home value	$560,265
Avg. single fam. tax bill	$5,278
Hi-Lo ranking	63/301

Police & Crime, 2008

Number of police officers	12
Violent crimes	9
Property crimes	30

Local School District

(school data 2007-08, except as noted)

Nahant
290 Castle Road
Nahant, MA 01908
781-581-1600

Superintendent	Philip Devaux
Grade plan	PK-6
Total enrollment '09-10	239
Grade 12 enrollment, '09-10	0
Graduation rate	NA
Dropout rate	NA
Per-pupil expenditure	$9,783
Avg teacher salary	$45,752
Student/teacher ratio '08-09	15.4 to 1
Highly-qualified teachers, '08-09	86.1%
Teachers licensed in assigned subject	100.0%
Students per computer	NA

Massachusetts Competency Assessment System (MCAS), 2009 results

	English		Math	
	% Prof	CPI	% Prof	CPI
Gr 4	51%	78.2	53%	80.6
Gr 6	84%	95	40%	70
Gr 8	NA	NA	NA	NA
Gr 10	NA	NA	NA	NA

Other School Districts (see Appendix D for data)
Sends grades 7-12 to Swampscott, 9-12 to North Shore Vocational Tech

See Introduction for an explanation of all data sources.

©2010 Information Publications, Inc. All rights reserved. Photocopying prohibited. For additional copies, contact the publisher at www.informationpublications.com or (877)544-INFO (4636)

Demographics & Socio-Economic Characteristics

Population

1990	6,012
2000	9,520
Male	4,884
Female	4,636
2008	11,215
2010 (projected)††	11,939
2020 (projected)††	14,426

Race & Hispanic Origin, 2000

Race	
White	8,363
Black/African American	789
American Indian/Alaska Native	1
Asian	61
Hawaiian Native/Pacific Islander	4
Other Race	152
Two or more races	150
Hispanic origin	212

Age & Nativity, 2000

Under 5 years	525
18 years and over	7,692
21 years and over	7,465
65 years and over	1,000
85 years and over	113
Median Age	36.7
Native-born	8,761
Foreign-born	759

Age, 2020 (projected)††

Under 5 years	766
5 to 19 years	2,237
20 to 39 years	4,259
40 to 64 years	5,126
65 years and over	2,038

Educational Attainment, 2000

Population 25 years and over	6,976
High School graduates or higher	91.6%
Bachelor's degree or higher	38.4%
Graduate degree	11.4%

Income & Poverty, 1999

Per capita income,	$31,314
Median household income	$55,522
Median family income	$66,786
Persons in poverty	712
H'holds receiving public assistance	22
H'holds receiving social security	751

Households, 2000

Total households	3,699
With persons under 18	1,045
With persons over 65	721
Family households	2,106
Single person households	1,104
Persons per household	2.4
Persons per family	2.9

Labor & Employment, 2000

Civilian labor force	5,695
Unemployment rate	4.3%
Civilian labor force, 2008†	6,997
Unemployment rate†	6.3%
Civilian labor force, 12/09†	6,774
Unemployment rate†	10.7%
Employed persons 16 years and over, by occupation:	
Managers & professionals	1,638
Service occupations	919
Sales & office occupations	1,300
Farming, fishing & forestry	35
Construction & maintenance	1,214
Production & transportation	345
Self-employed persons	1,387

Most demographic data is from the 2000 Decennial Census
† Massachusetts Department of Revenue
†† University of Massachusetts, MISER

General Information

Town of Nantucket
16 Broad St
Nantucket, MA 02554
508-228-7216

Elevation	10 ft.
Land area (square miles)	47.8
Water area (square miles)	57.5
Population density, 2008 (est)	234.6
Year incorporated	1671
Website	www.nantucket-ma.gov

Voters & Government Information

Government type	Open Town Meeting
Number of Selectmen	5
US Congressional District(s)	10

Registered Voters, October 2008

Total	8,164
Democrats	2,293
Republicans	1,360
Unaffiliated/other	4,434

Local Officials, 2010

Chair, Bd. of Sel.	Michael O'Brien Kopko
Town Manager	C. Elizabeth Gibson
Town Clerk	Catherine Flanagan Stover
Finance Director	Constance Voges
Tax Collector	Elizabeth Brown
Tax Assessor	Deborah Dilworth
Attorney	Paul DeRensis
Public Works	Jeff Willett
Building	Bernie Bartlett
Comm Dev/Planning	Andrew Vorce
Police Chief	William Pittman
Emerg/Fire Chief	Mark McDougall

Housing & Construction

New Privately Owned Housing Units Authorized by Building Permit

	Single Family	Total Bldgs	Total Units
2006	168	168	168
2007	139	139	139
2008	76	82	88

Parcel Count by Property Class, 2010

Total	NA
Single family	NA
Multiple units	NA
Apartments	NA
Condos	NA
Vacant land	NA
Open space	NA
Commercial	NA
Industrial	NA
Misc. residential	NA
Other use	NA

Public Library

Nantucket Atheneum
PO Box 808
Nantucket, MA 02554
(508)228-1110

Director ... Molly C. Anderson

Library Statistics, FY 2008

Population served, 2007	10,531
Registered users	21,272
Circulation	167,062
Reference transactons	8,050
Total program attendance	130,000
per capita:	
Holdings	5.31
Operating income	$60.45
Internet Access	
Internet computers available	14
Weekly users	375

Municipal Finance

Debt at year end 2008	$82,633,113
Moody's rating, July 2009	Aa3

Revenues, 2008

Total	$70,763,740
From all taxes	59,284,109
Federal aid	0
State aid	1,755,154
From other governments	1,725
Charges for services	4,896,335
Licenses, permits & fees	1,321,793
Fines & forfeits	301,084
Interfund transfers	642,464
Misc/other/special assessments	1,280,538

Expenditures, 2008

Total	$56,286,034
General government	4,968,994
Public safety	7,585,569
Other/fixed costs	4,627,331
Human services	6,045,246
Culture & recreation	1,945,383
Debt Service	7,123,958
Education	20,902,564
Public works	2,624,857
Intergovernmental	462,130

Taxation, 2010

Property type	Valuation	Rate
Total	NA	-
Residential	NA	NA
Open space	NA	NA
Commercial	NA	NA
Industrial	NA	NA
Personal	NA	NA

Average Single Family Tax Bill, 2010

Avg. assessed home value	NA
Avg. single fam. tax bill	NA
Hi-Lo ranking	NA

Police & Crime, 2008

Number of police officers	34
Violent crimes	NA
Property crimes	NA

Local School District

(school data 2007-08, except as noted)

Nantucket
10 Surfside Road
Nantucket, MA 02554
508-228-7285

Superintendent	Robert Pellicone
Grade plan	PK-12
Total enrollment '09-10	1,234
Grade 12 enrollment, '09-10	83
Graduation rate	87.6%
Dropout rate	7.6%
Per-pupil expenditure	$20,760
Avg teacher salary	$78,627
Student/teacher ratio '08-09	10.5 to 1
Highly-qualified teachers, '08-09	93.2%
Teachers licensed in assigned subject	96.7%
Students per computer	2.1

Massachusetts Competency Assessment System (MCAS), 2009 results

	English		Math	
	% Prof	CPI	% Prof	CPI
Gr 4	38%	69.3	15%	53.8
Gr 6	60%	82.1	47%	71.2
Gr 8	77%	91.7	31%	60.4
Gr 10	86%	93.6	85%	93.5

Other School Districts (see Appendix D for data)
None

©2010 Information Publications, Inc. All rights reserved. Photocopying prohibited. For additional copies, contact the publisher at www.informationpublications.com or (877)544-INFO (4636)

Demographics & Socio-Economic Characteristics

Population

1990	30,510
2000	32,170
Male	15,216
Female	16,954
2008	31,880
2010 (projected)††	32,254
2020 (projected)††	31,921

Race & Hispanic Origin, 2000

Race	
White	29,602
Black/African American	525
American Indian/Alaska Native	34
Asian	1,242
Hawaiian Native/Pacific Islander	17
Other Race	247
Two or more races	503
Hispanic origin	635

Age & Nativity, 2000

Under 5 years	2,370
18 years and over	24,769
21 years and over	24,166
65 years and over	4,608
85 years and over	608
Median Age	38.2
Native-born	29,002
Foreign-born	3,168

Age, 2020 (projected)††

Under 5 years	1,744
5 to 19 years	5,389
20 to 39 years	8,034
40 to 64 years	10,953
65 years and over	5,801

Educational Attainment, 2000

Population 25 years and over	23,262
High School graduates or higher	94.0%
Bachelor's degree or higher	52.5%
Graduate degree	23.0%

Income & Poverty, 1999

Per capita income,	$36,358
Median household income	$69,755
Median family income	$85,715
Persons in poverty	879
H'holds receiving public assistance	118
H'holds receiving social security	3,271

Households, 2000

Total households	13,080
With persons under 18	4,144
With persons over 65	3,141
Family households	8,532
Single person households	3,697
Persons per household	2.4
Persons per family	3.0

Labor & Employment, 2000

Civilian labor force	18,235
Unemployment rate	2.1%
Civilian labor force, 2008†	18,781
Unemployment rate†	4.2%
Civilian labor force, 12/09†	18,919
Unemployment rate†	6.1%
Employed persons 16 years and over, by occupation:	
Managers & professionals	10,072
Service occupations	1,731
Sales & office occupations	4,220
Farming, fishing & forestry	8
Construction & maintenance	959
Production & transportation	861
Self-employed persons	1,241

Most demographic data is from the 2000 Decennial Census
† Massachusetts Department of Revenue
†† University of Massachusetts, MISER

General Information

Town of Natick
13 East Central St
Natick, MA 01760
508-647-6400

Elevation	100 ft.
Land area (square miles)	15.1
Water area (square miles)	1.0
Population density, 2008 (est)	2,111.3
Year incorporated	1781
Website	natickma.org

Voters & Government Information

Government type	Rep. Twn. Mtg. (180)
Number of Selectmen	5
US Congressional District(s)	7

Registered Voters, October 2008

Total	22,457
Democrats	7,811
Republicans	2,786
Unaffiliated/other	11,761

Local Officials, 2010

Chair, Bd. of Sel.	Joshua Ostroff
Manager/Admin	Martha L. White
Clerk	Diane Packer
Finance Director	Robert Palmer
Tax Collector	Robert Palmer
Tax Assessor	Janice DeAngelo
Attorney	John Flynn
Public Works	Thomas C. Collins (Int)
Building	NA
Planning	Patrick Reffett
Police Chief	Nicholas S. Mabardy
Fire Chief	James Sheridan

Housing & Construction

New Privately Owned Housing Units Authorized by Building Permit

	Single Family	Total Bldgs	Total Units
2006	56	56	56
2007	47	47	47
2008	33	33	33

Parcel Count by Property Class, 2010

Total	13,135
Single family	8,459
Multiple units	660
Apartments	56
Condos	2,326
Vacant land	877
Open space	0
Commercial	555
Industrial	69
Misc. residential	40
Other use	93

Public Library

Morse Institute Library
14 East Central Street
Natick, MA 01760
(508)647-6521

Director .... Linda Stetson

Library Statistics, FY 2008

Population served, 2007	9,593
Registered users	0
Circulation	27,648
Reference transactons	400
Total program attendance	0
per capita:	
Holdings	1.66
Operating income	$13.21
Internet Access	
Internet computers available	1
Weekly users	0

Municipal Finance

Debt at year end 2008	$65,657,383
Moody's rating, July 2009	Aa2

Revenues, 2008

Total	$94,682,728
From all taxes	70,707,942
Federal aid	0
State aid	12,248,722
From other governments	140,547
Charges for services	3,149,469
Licenses, permits & fees	2,366,758
Fines & forfeits	91,353
Interfund transfers	3,806,085
Misc/other/special assessments	1,085,926

Expenditures, 2008

Total	$97,641,748
General government	6,192,533
Public safety	11,406,376
Other/fixed costs	17,904,645
Human services	1,040,594
Culture & recreation	2,378,405
Debt Service	12,211,328
Education	41,435,716
Public works	5,072,151
Intergovernmental	0

Taxation, 2010

Property type	Valuation	Rate
Total	$6,595,636,170	-
Residential	5,025,308,180	11.67
Open space	0	0.00
Commercial	1,391,446,520	11.67
Industrial	64,945,700	11.67
Personal	113,935,770	11.67

Average Single Family Tax Bill, 2010

Avg. assessed home value	$452,621
Avg. single fam. tax bill	$5,282
Hi-Lo ranking	62/301

Police & Crime, 2008

Number of police officers	54
Violent crimes	60
Property crimes	817

Local School District

(school data 2007-08, except as noted)

Natick
13 East Central Street
Natick, MA 01760
508-647-6500

Superintendent	Peter Sanchioni
Grade plan	PK-12
Total enrollment '09-10	4,734
Grade 12 enrollment, '09-10	326
Graduation rate	92.9%
Dropout rate	1.8%
Per-pupil expenditure	$12,279
Avg teacher salary	$62,757
Student/teacher ratio '08-09	14.2 to 1
Highly-qualified teachers, '08-09	95.0%
Teachers licensed in assigned subject	98.7%
Students per computer	8

Massachusetts Competency Assessment System (MCAS), 2009 results

	English		Math	
	% Prof	CPI	% Prof	CPI
Gr 4	78%	93	78%	93.4
Gr 6	79%	92.4	76%	88.9
Gr 8	91%	96.9	64%	82.4
Gr 10	94%	98	87%	95

Other School Districts (see Appendix D for data)
South Middlesex Vocational Tech

©2010 Information Publications, Inc. All rights reserved. Photocopying prohibited. For additional copies, contact the publisher at www.informationpublications.com or (877)544-INFO (4636)

See Introduction for an explanation of all data sources.

Demographics & Socio-Economic Characteristics*

Population

1990	27,557
2000	28,911
Male	13,702
Female	15,209
2008	28,560
2010 (projected)††	27,226
2020 (projected)††	24,654

Race & Hispanic Origin, 2000

Race	
White	27,412
Black/African American	201
American Indian/Alaska Native	8
Asian	1,024
Hawaiian Native/Pacific Islander	0
Other Race	73
Two or more races	193
Hispanic origin	341

Age & Nativity, 2000

Under 5 years	2,153
18 years and over	21,335
21 years and over	20,510
65 years and over	5,190
85 years and over	1,040
Median Age	40.8
Native-born	26,146
Foreign-born	2,765

Age, 2020 (projected)††

Under 5 years	1,361
5 to 19 years	4,752
20 to 39 years	5,118
40 to 64 years	7,656
65 years and over	5,767

Educational Attainment, 2000

Population 25 years and over	19,730
High School graduates or higher	96.4%
Bachelor's degree or higher	64.9%
Graduate degree	33.5%

Income & Poverty, 1999

Per capita income,	$44,549
Median household income	$88,079
Median family income	$107,570
Persons in poverty	705
H'holds receiving public assistance	110
H'holds receiving social security	3,224

Households, 2000

Total households	10,612
With persons under 18	4,013
With persons over 65	3,419
Family households	7,782
Single person households	2,479
Persons per household	2.6
Persons per family	3.2

Labor & Employment, 2000

Civilian labor force	14,282
Unemployment rate	2.9%
Civilian labor force, 2008†	14,203
Unemployment rate†	4.3%
Civilian labor force, 12/09†	13,970
Unemployment rate†	5.8%
Employed persons 16 years and over, by occupation:	
Managers & professionals	8,856
Service occupations	898
Sales & office occupations	3,122
Farming, fishing & forestry	9
Construction & maintenance	522
Production & transportation	465
Self-employed persons	1,432

Most demographic data is from the 2000 Decennial Census
* see Appendix E for American Community Survey data
† Massachusetts Department of Revenue
†† University of Massachusetts, MISER

General Information

Town of Needham
1471 Highland Ave
Needham, MA 02492
781-455-7500

Elevation	160 ft.
Land area (square miles)	12.6
Water area (square miles)	0.1
Population density, 2008 (est)	2,266.7
Year incorporated	1711
Website	www.needhamma.gov

Voters & Government Information

Government type	Rep. Town Meeting
Number of Selectmen	5
US Congressional District(s)	9

Registered Voters, October 2008

Total	21,011
Democrats	7,321
Republicans	2,907
Unaffiliated/other	10,728

Local Officials, 2010

Chair, Bd. of Sel.	Daniel P. Matthews
Town Manager	Kate Fitzpatrick
Town Clerk	Theodora K. Eaton
Finance Director	David Davison
Tax Collector	Evelyn M. Poness
Tax Assessor	Hoyt B. Davis Jr
Attorney	David S. Tobin
Public Works	Richard P. Merson
Building	Daniel Walsh
Comm Dev/Planning	Lee Newman
Police Chief	Thomas Leary
Fire Chief	Paul Buckley

Housing & Construction

New Privately Owned Housing Units Authorized by Building Permit

	Single Family	Total Bldgs	Total Units
2006	53	53	53
2007	88	88	88
2008	64	64	64

Parcel Count by Property Class, 2010

Total	10,059
Single family	8,334
Multiple units	297
Apartments	27
Condos	755
Vacant land	187
Open space	0
Commercial	373
Industrial	45
Misc. residential	4
Other use	37

Public Library

Needham Free Public Library
1139 Highland Ave.
Needham, MA 02494
(781)455-7559

Director	Ann C. MacFate

Library Statistics, FY 2008

Population served, 2007	28,263
Registered users	17,843
Circulation	529,632
Reference transactons	35,660
Total program attendance	307,890
per capita:	
Holdings	5.71
Operating income	$46.96
Internet Access	
Internet computers available	29
Weekly users	677

Municipal Finance

Debt at year end 2008	$60,598,343
Moody's rating, July 2009	NA

Revenues, 2008

Total	$100,243,156
From all taxes	82,198,981
Federal aid	0
State aid	8,272,525
From other governments	141,783
Charges for services	1,867,712
Licenses, permits & fees	2,086,461
Fines & forfeits	116,382
Interfund transfers	1,717,696
Misc/other/special assessments	1,920,808

Expenditures, 2008

Total	$92,351,823
General government	4,657,341
Public safety	11,432,075
Other/fixed costs	15,058,692
Human services	853,475
Culture & recreation	1,757,408
Debt Service	7,272,655
Education	45,374,026
Public works	4,404,013
Intergovernmental	1,044,511

Taxation, 2010

Property type	Valuation	Rate
Total	$7,431,763,903	-
Residential	6,488,349,842	10.53
Open space	0	0.00
Commercial	663,613,511	20.68
Industrial	130,298,600	20.68
Personal	149,501,950	20.68

Average Single Family Tax Bill, 2010

Avg. assessed home value	$700,739
Avg. single fam. tax bill	$7,379
Hi-Lo ranking	29/301

Police & Crime, 2008

Number of police officers	46
Violent crimes	5
Property crimes	237

Local School District

(school data 2007-08, except as noted)

Needham
1330 Highland Avenue
Needham, MA 02492
781-455-0400

Superintendent	Daniel Gutekanst
Grade plan	PK-12
Total enrollment '09-10	5,311
Grade 12 enrollment, '09-10	367
Graduation rate	94.8%
Dropout rate	1.1%
Per-pupil expenditure	$12,552
Avg teacher salary	$67,977
Student/teacher ratio '08-09	15.1 to 1
Highly-qualified teachers, '08-09	97.9%
Teachers licensed in assigned subject	98.0%
Students per computer	3.2

Massachusetts Competency Assessment System (MCAS), 2009 results

	English		Math	
	% Prof	CPI	% Prof	CPI
Gr 4	70%	89.3	65%	87.4
Gr 6	86%	94.4	78%	90.6
Gr 8	95%	98.2	82%	92
Gr 10	96%	98	93%	97.1

Other School Districts (see Appendix D for data)
Minuteman Vocational Tech, Norfolk County Agricultural

©2010 Information Publications, Inc. All rights reserved. Photocopying prohibited. For additional copies, contact the publisher at www.informationpublications.com or (877)544-INFO (4636)

Demographics & Socio-Economic Characteristics

Population

1990	192
2000	247
Male	124
Female	123
2008	247
2010 (projected)††	284
2020 (projected)††	320

Race & Hispanic Origin, 2000

Race	
White	236
Black/African American	2
American Indian/Alaska Native	0
Asian	8
Hawaiian Native/Pacific Islander	0
Other Race	0
Two or more races	1
Hispanic origin	0

Age & Nativity, 2000

Under 5 years	15
18 years and over	185
21 years and over	179
65 years and over	23
85 years and over	1
Median Age	37.5
Native-born	224
Foreign-born	8

Age, 2020 (projected)††

Under 5 years	14
5 to 19 years	44
20 to 39 years	96
40 to 64 years	113
65 years and over	53

Educational Attainment, 2000

Population 25 years and over	169
High School graduates or higher	91.1%
Bachelor's degree or higher	41.4%
Graduate degree	11.2%

Income & Poverty, 1999

Per capita income,	$28,323
Median household income	$51,250
Median family income	$58,125
Persons in poverty	5
H'holds receiving public assistance	4
H'holds receiving social security	23

Households, 2000

Total households	94
With persons under 18	37
With persons over 65	18
Family households	72
Single person households	15
Persons per household	2.6
Persons per family	3.0

Labor & Employment, 2000

Civilian labor force	145
Unemployment rate	3.4%
Civilian labor force, 2008†	157
Unemployment rate†	5.7%
Civilian labor force, 12/09†	151
Unemployment rate†	3.3%
Employed persons 16 years and over, by occupation:	
Managers & professionals	62
Service occupations	20
Sales & office occupations	34
Farming, fishing & forestry	1
Construction & maintenance	15
Production & transportation	8
Self-employed persons	14

Most demographic data is from the 2000 Decennial Census
† **Massachusetts Department of Revenue**
†† **University of Massachusetts, MISER**

General Information

Town of New Ashford
188 Mallery Rd
New Ashford, MA 01237
413-458-5461

Elevation	1,256 ft.
Land area (square miles)	13.5
Water area (square miles)	0.0
Population density, 2008 (est)	18.3
Year incorporated	1781
Website	NA

Voters & Government Information

Government type	Open Town Meeting
Number of Selectmen	3
US Congressional District(s)	1

Registered Voters, October 2008

Total	167
Democrats	33
Republicans	9
Unaffiliated/other	120

Local Officials, 2010

Chair, Bd. of Sel.	Ben Glick
Manager/Admin	NA
Clerk	Dick DeMyer
Finance Director	NA
Tax Collector	NA
Tax Assessor	Everett Martin
Attorney	NA
Public Works	NA
Building	Ben Lively
Planning	Diane Glick
Police Chief	Richard Clermont
Emerg/Fire Chief	Frank McAlister

Housing & Construction

New Privately Owned Housing Units Authorized by Building Permit

	Single Family	Total Bldgs	Total Units
2006	2	2	2
2007	1	1	1
2008	1	1	1

Parcel Count by Property Class, 2010

Total	204
Single family	84
Multiple units	4
Apartments	0
Condos	0
Vacant land	76
Open space	13
Commercial	13
Industrial	0
Misc. residential	3
Other use	11

Public Library

No Public Library

Library Statistics, FY 2008

Population served, 2007	
Registered users	
Circulation	
Reference transactons	
Total program attendance	
per capita:	
Holdings	
Operating income	
Internet Access	
Internet computers available	
Weekly users	

Municipal Finance

Debt at year end 2008	$42,120
Moody's rating, July 2009	NA

Revenues, 2008

Total	$531,072
From all taxes	309,822
Federal aid	0
State aid	198,411
From other governments	2,740
Charges for services	0
Licenses, permits & fees	2,660
Fines & forfeits	0
Interfund transfers	2,219
Misc/other/special assessments	7,610

Expenditures, 2008

Total	$503,132
General government	45,373
Public safety	19,153
Other/fixed costs	683
Human services	228
Culture & recreation	0
Debt Service	6,575
Education	339,984
Public works	85,131
Intergovernmental	6,005

Taxation, 2010

Property type	Valuation	Rate
Total	$45,535,300	-
Residential	34,029,100	6.84
Open space	609,400	6.84
Commercial	8,507,000	11.53
Industrial	292,500	11.53
Personal	2,097,300	11.38

Average Single Family Tax Bill, 2010

Avg. assessed home value	$259,425
Avg. single fam. tax bill	$1,774
Hi-Lo ranking	296/301

Police & Crime, 2008

Number of police officers	NA
Violent crimes	NA
Property crimes	NA

Local School District

(school data 2007-08, except as noted)

New Ashford (non-op)
1831 STATE ROAD
RICHMOND, MA 01254
413-698-4001

Superintendent............ William Ballen

Non-operating district.
Resident students are sent to the Other School Districts listed below.

Grade plan	NA
Total enrollment '09-10	NA
Grade 12 enrollment, '09-10	NA
Graduation rate	NA
Dropout rate	NA
Per-pupil expenditure	NA
Avg teacher salary	NA
Student/teacher ratio '08-09	NA
Highly-qualified teachers, '08-09	NA
Teachers licensed in assigned subject	NA
Students per computer	NA

Other School Districts (see Appendix D for data)
Sends grades P-6 to Lanesborough, 7-12 to Mount Greylock Regional

©2010 Information Publications, Inc. All rights reserved. Photocopying prohibited. For additional copies, contact the publisher at www.informationpublications.com or (877)544-INFO (4636)

See Introduction for an explanation of all data sources.

Demographics & Socio-Economic Characteristics*

Population

1990	99,922
2000	93,768
Male	44,173
Female	49,595
2008	91,365
2010 (projected)††	91,108
2020 (projected)††	89,257

Race & Hispanic Origin, 2000

Race	
White	73,950
Black/African American	4,112
American Indian/Alaska Native	579
Asian	614
Hawaiian Native/Pacific Islander	44
Other Race	8,915
Two or more races	5,554
Hispanic origin	9,576

Age & Nativity, 2000

Under 5 years	6,272
18 years and over	70,441
21 years and over	66,779
65 years and over	15,648
85 years and over	2,239
Median Age	35.9
Native-born	75,376
Foreign-born	18,392

Age, 2020 (projected)††

Under 5 years	5,509
5 to 19 years	16,250
20 to 39 years	24,041
40 to 64 years	28,091
65 years and over	15,366

Educational Attainment, 2000

Population 25 years and over	61,709
High School graduates or higher	57.6%
Bachelor's degree or higher	10.7%
Graduate degree	3.2%

Income & Poverty, 1999

Per capita income,	$15,602
Median household income	$27,569
Median family income	$35,708
Persons in poverty	18,553
H'holds receiving public assistance	2,703
H'holds receiving social security	12,133

Households, 2000

Total households	38,178
With persons under 18	13,036
With persons over 65	11,060
Family households	24,083
Single person households	12,057
Persons per household	2.4
Persons per family	3.0

Labor & Employment, 2000

Civilian labor force	42,169
Unemployment rate	8.7%
Civilian labor force, 2008†	42,432
Unemployment rate†	11.8%
Civilian labor force, 12/09†	43,271
Unemployment rate†	15.8%
Employed persons 16 years and over, by occupation:	
Managers & professionals	7,995
Service occupations	7,610
Sales & office occupations	9,067
Farming, fishing & forestry	379
Construction & maintenance	3,778
Production & transportation	9,653
Self-employed persons	1,485

Most demographic data is from the 2000 Decennial Census
* see Appendix D and E for American Community Survey data
† Massachusetts Department of Revenue
†† University of Massachusetts, MISER

General Information

City of New Bedford
133 William St
New Bedford, MA 02740
508-979-1400

Elevation	50 ft.
Land area (square miles)	20.1
Water area (square miles)	3.9
Population density, 2008 (est)	4,545.5
Year incorporated	1787
Website	www.newbedford.ma.gov

Voters & Government Information

Government type	Mayor-Council
Number of Councilpersons	11
US Congressional District(s)	4

Registered Voters, October 2008

Total	55,246
Democrats	28,625
Republicans	3,482
Unaffiliated/other	22,640

Local Officials, 2010

Mayor	Scott W. Lang
Manager/Admin	NA
City Clerk	Rita D. Arruda
Treasurer	(vacant)
Tax Collector	R. Renee Fernandes-Abbott
Tax Assessor	Marty Treadup (Chr)
Attorney	Irene B. Schall
Public Works	Lawrence Worden
Building Commissioner	Ronald Durgin
Comm Dev/Planning	David Kennedy
Police Chief	Thomas Hodgson
Fire Chief	Mark McGraw (Actg)

Housing & Construction

New Privately Owned Housing Units Authorized by Building Permit

	Single Family	Total Bldgs	Total Units
2006	51	57	127
2007	93	97	103
2008	33	34	35

Parcel Count by Property Class, 2010

Total	NA
Single family	NA
Multiple units	NA
Apartments	NA
Condos	NA
Vacant land	NA
Open space	NA
Commercial	NA
Industrial	NA
Misc. residential	NA
Other use	NA

Public Library

New Bedford Free Public Library
613 Pleasant Street
New Bedford, MA 02740
(508)991-6275

Director	Stephen A. Fulchino

Library Statistics, FY 2008

Population served, 2007	91,849
Registered users	41,038
Circulation	295,571
Reference transactons	17,958
Total program attendance	260,291
per capita:	
Holdings	4.78
Operating income	$22.90
Internet Access	
Internet computers available	43
Weekly users	767

Municipal Finance

Debt at year end 2008	$220,347,882
Moody's rating, July 2009	A3

Revenues, 2008

Total	$265,427,157
From all taxes	89,665,824
Federal aid	25,903
State aid	144,612,565
From other governments	299,881
Charges for services	10,457,664
Licenses, permits & fees	1,745,296
Fines & forfeits	15,451
Interfund transfers	3,254,809
Misc/other/special assessments	7,674,882

Expenditures, 2008

Total	$225,867,741
General government	20,918,563
Public safety	42,830,658
Other/fixed costs	19,316,008
Human services	3,657,660
Culture & recreation	3,152,771
Debt Service	10,033,999
Education	112,836,198
Public works	7,331,568
Intergovernmental	5,790,316

Taxation, 2010

Property type	Valuation	Rate
Total	NA	-
Residential	NA	NA
Open space	NA	NA
Commercial	NA	NA
Industrial	NA	NA
Personal	NA	NA

Average Single Family Tax Bill, 2010

Avg. assessed home value	NA
Avg. single fam. tax bill	NA
Hi-Lo ranking	NA

Police & Crime, 2008

Number of police officers	288
Violent crimes	1,191
Property crimes	3,353

Local School District

(school data 2007-08, except as noted)

New Bedford
455 County Street, C/O Paul Rodrigues
Administration Bldg.
New Bedford, MA 02740
508-997-4511

Superintendent	Portia Bonner
Grade plan	PK-12
Total enrollment '09-10	12,636
Grade 12 enrollment, '09-10	554
Graduation rate	56.1%
Dropout rate	26.8%
Per-pupil expenditure	$12,682
Avg teacher salary	$71,638
Student/teacher ratio '08-09	14.6 to 1
Highly-qualified teachers, '08-09	91.4%
Teachers licensed in assigned subject	94.7%
Students per computer	2.9

Massachusetts Competency Assessment System (MCAS), 2009 results

	English		Math	
	% Prof	CPI	% Prof	CPI
Gr 4	33%	68.3	33%	71.5
Gr 6	37%	69.6	40%	68.4
Gr 8	54%	78.1	22%	52.8
Gr 10	55%	81.5	44%	71.6

Other School Districts (see Appendix D for data)

Receives students from Acushnet; sends to Bristol County Agricultural, Greater New Bedford Vocational Tech

©2010 Information Publications, Inc. All rights reserved. Photocopying prohibited. For additional copies, contact the publisher at www.informationpublications.com or (877)544-INFO (4636)

Demographics & Socio-Economic Characteristics

Population

1990	881
2000	927
Male	470
Female	457
2008	1,116
2010 (projected)††	947
2020 (projected)††	1,007

Race & Hispanic Origin, 2000

Race	
White	919
Black/African American	2
American Indian/Alaska Native	1
Asian	1
Hawaiian Native/Pacific Islander	0
Other Race	0
Two or more races	4
Hispanic origin	3

Age & Nativity, 2000

Under 5 years	57
18 years and over	655
21 years and over	624
65 years and over	79
85 years and over	5
Median Age	37.5
Native-born	909
Foreign-born	18

Age, 2020 (projected)††

Under 5 years	60
5 to 19 years	172
20 to 39 years	285
40 to 64 years	326
65 years and over	164

Educational Attainment, 2000

Population 25 years and over	589
High School graduates or higher	90.0%
Bachelor's degree or higher	21.4%
Graduate degree	8.0%

Income & Poverty, 1999

Per capita income,	$21,072
Median household income	$54,844
Median family income	$60,417
Persons in poverty	42
H'holds receiving public assistance	6
H'holds receiving social security	65

Households, 2000

Total households	318
With persons under 18	142
With persons over 65	57
Family households	267
Single person households	42
Persons per household	2.9
Persons per family	3.1

Labor & Employment, 2000

Civilian labor force	527
Unemployment rate	3.4%
Civilian labor force, 2008†	633
Unemployment rate†	7.6%
Civilian labor force, 12/09†	666
Unemployment rate†	11.7%
Employed persons 16 years and over, by occupation:	
Managers & professionals	176
Service occupations	93
Sales & office occupations	86
Farming, fishing & forestry	10
Construction & maintenance	64
Production & transportation	80
Self-employed persons	70

Most demographic data is from the 2000 Decennial Census
† Massachusetts Department of Revenue
†† University of Massachusetts, MISER

General Information

Town of New Braintree
20 Memorial Dr
New Braintree, MA 01531
508-867-2071

Elevation	945 ft.
Land area (square miles)	20.7
Water area (square miles)	0.2
Population density, 2008 (est)	53.9
Year incorporated	1751
Website	www.newbraintree.org

Voters & Government Information

Government type	Open Town Meeting
Number of Selectmen	3
US Congressional District(s)	1

Registered Voters, October 2008

Total	679
Democrats	137
Republicans	78
Unaffiliated/other	459

Local Officials, 2010

Chair, Bd. of Sel.	Robert Hunt
Manager/Exec.	Katharine Tyler
Town Clerk	Jessica Bennett
Finance Director	Janet Pierce
Tax Collector	Janet Pierce
Tax Assessor	Timothy Jones
Attorney	Kopelman & Paige
Public Works	Richard Ayer
Building	Ralph Brouilette
Comm Dev/Planning	Joseph Chenevert
Police Chief	Bert DuVernay
Emerg/Fire Chief	Dennis Letendre Jr

Housing & Construction

New Privately Owned Housing Units Authorized by Building Permit

	Single Family	Total Bldgs	Total Units
2006	9	9	9
2007	4	4	4
2008	2	2	2

Parcel Count by Property Class, 2010

Total	675
Single family	302
Multiple units	10
Apartments	0
Condos	0
Vacant land	171
Open space	0
Commercial	23
Industrial	0
Misc. residential	6
Other use	163

Public Library

Leroy Pollard Memorial Library
45 Memorial Dr.
New Braintree, MA 01531
(508)867-7650

Director . . . . . Alice G. Webb

Library Statistics, FY 2008

Population served, 2007	1,112
Registered users	685
Circulation	8,622
Reference transactons	0
Total program attendance	3,591
per capita:	
Holdings	9.68
Operating income	$14.41
Internet Access	
Internet computers available	2
Weekly users	2

Municipal Finance

Debt at year end 2008	$36,000
Moody's rating, July 2009	NA

Revenues, 2008

Total	$1,909,386
From all taxes	1,591,543
Federal aid	0
State aid	208,631
From other governments	4,273
Charges for services	5,541
Licenses, permits & fees	4,930
Fines & forfeits	0
Interfund transfers	0
Misc/other/special assessments	47,234

Expenditures, 2008

Total	$1,829,522
General government	144,393
Public safety	124,790
Other/fixed costs	83,486
Human services	12,759
Culture & recreation	16,448
Debt Service	57,014
Education	1,064,981
Public works	322,874
Intergovernmental	2,777

Taxation, 2010

Property type	Valuation	Rate
Total	$113,918,130	-
Residential	107,152,491	13.98
Open space	0	0.00
Commercial	4,248,427	13.98
Industrial	43,124	13.98
Personal	2,474,088	13.98

Average Single Family Tax Bill, 2010

Avg. assessed home value	$268,794
Avg. single fam. tax bill	$3,758
Hi-Lo ranking	154/301

Police & Crime, 2008

Number of police officers	1
Violent crimes	NA
Property crimes	NA

Local School District

(school data 2007-08, except as noted)

New Braintree (non-op)
15 Memorial Drive
New Braintree, MA 01531
978-355-4668

Superintendent . . . . . Maureen Marshall

Non-operating district.
Resident students are sent to the Other School Districts listed below.

Grade plan	NA
Total enrollment '09-10	NA
Grade 12 enrollment, '09-10	NA
Graduation rate	NA
Dropout rate	NA
Per-pupil expenditure	NA
Avg teacher salary	NA
Student/teacher ratio '08-09	NA
Highly-qualified teachers, '08-09	NA
Teachers licensed in assigned subject	NA
Students per computer	NA

Other School Districts (see Appendix D for data)
Quabbin Regional, Pathfinder Vocational Tech

©2010 Information Publications, Inc. All rights reserved. Photocopying prohibited. For additional copies, contact the publisher at www.informationpublications.com or (877)544-INFO (4636)

See Introduction for an explanation of all data sources.

Demographics & Socio-Economic Characteristics

Population

1990	1,240
2000	1,494
Male	770
Female	724
2008	1,508
2010 (projected)††	1,613
2020 (projected)††	1,729

Race & Hispanic Origin, 2000

Race	
White	1,457
Black/African American	25
American Indian/Alaska Native	0
Asian	2
Hawaiian Native/Pacific Islander	0
Other Race	2
Two or more races	8
Hispanic origin	17

Age & Nativity, 2000

Under 5 years	86
18 years and over	1,125
21 years and over	1,068
65 years and over	216
85 years and over	21
Median Age	41.2
Native-born	1,438
Foreign-born	56

Age, 2020 (projected)††

Under 5 years	89
5 to 19 years	335
20 to 39 years	298
40 to 64 years	603
65 years and over	404

Educational Attainment, 2000

Population 25 years and over	1,020
High School graduates or higher	87.0%
Bachelor's degree or higher	33.0%
Graduate degree	16.9%

Income & Poverty, 1999

Per capita income,	$25,658
Median household income	$46,875
Median family income	$56,944
Persons in poverty	90
H'holds receiving public assistance	5
H'holds receiving social security	166

Households, 2000

Total households	582
With persons under 18	173
With persons over 65	159
Family households	404
Single person households	146
Persons per household	2.4
Persons per family	2.9

Labor & Employment, 2000

Civilian labor force	789
Unemployment rate	3.9%
Civilian labor force, 2008†	898
Unemployment rate†	6.0%
Civilian labor force, 12/09†	895
Unemployment rate†	6.9%
Employed persons 16 years and over, by occupation:	
Managers & professionals	276
Service occupations	101
Sales & office occupations	132
Farming, fishing & forestry	7
Construction & maintenance	109
Production & transportation	133
Self-employed persons	120

Most demographic data is from the 2000 Decennial Census
† Massachusetts Department of Revenue
†† University of Massachusetts, MISER

General Information

Town of New Marlborough
PO Box 99
Mill River, MA 01244
413-229-8116

Elevation	1,351 ft.
Land area (square miles)	47.2
Water area (square miles)	0.7
Population density, 2008 (est)	31.9
Year incorporated	1775
Email	nmbdselectmen@aol.com

Voters & Government Information

Government type	Open Town Meeting
Number of Selectmen	3
US Congressional District(s)	1

Registered Voters, October 2008

Total	1,108
Democrats	297
Republicans	147
Unaffiliated/other	653

Local Officials, 2010

Chair, Bd. of Sel.	Lawrence H. Davis III
Admin Assistant	Michael Skorput
Town Clerk	Katherine M. Chretien
Treasurer	Patricia Mielke
Tax Collector	Caren Adams
Tax Assessor	Marsha Pshenishny (Chr)
Attorney	Jeramia Pollard
Highway Supt	Peter Marks
Building Inspector	Thomas Carmody
Planning Board	James Mullens (Chr)
Police Chief	Scott Farrell
Fire Chief	Peter Scala

Housing & Construction

New Privately Owned Housing Units Authorized by Building Permit

	Single Family	Total Bldgs	Total Units
2006	8	8	8
2007	4	4	4
2008	6	6	6

Parcel Count by Property Class, 2010

Total	NA
Single family	NA
Multiple units	NA
Apartments	NA
Condos	NA
Vacant land	NA
Open space	NA
Commercial	NA
Industrial	NA
Misc. residential	NA
Other use	NA

Public Library

New Marlborough Town Library
PO Box 239
Mill River, MA 01244
(413)229-6668

Librarian . . . . . Debora O' Brien

Library Statistics, FY 2008

Population served, 2007	1,521
Registered users	400
Circulation	21,078
Reference transactons	0
Total program attendance	8,292
per capita:	
Holdings	9.10
Operating income	$59.17
Internet Access	
Internet computers available	5
Weekly users	52

Municipal Finance

Debt at year end 2008	$647,600
Moody's rating, July 2009	NA

Revenues, 2008

Total	$3,896,199
From all taxes	3,540,773
Federal aid	0
State aid	173,860
From other governments	1,930
Charges for services	26,165
Licenses, permits & fees	30,636
Fines & forfeits	352
Interfund transfers	56,381
Misc/other/special assessments	33,051

Expenditures, 2008

Total	$3,681,961
General government	240,193
Public safety	168,520
Other/fixed costs	202,910
Human services	14,238
Culture & recreation	80,730
Debt Service	165,685
Education	1,810,157
Public works	976,767
Intergovernmental	22,761

Taxation, 2010

Property type	Valuation	Rate
Total	NA	-
Residential	NA	NA
Open space	NA	NA
Commercial	NA	NA
Industrial	NA	NA
Personal	NA	NA

Average Single Family Tax Bill, 2010

Avg. assessed home value	NA
Avg. single fam. tax bill	NA
Hi-Lo ranking	NA

Police & Crime, 2008

Number of police officers	NA
Violent crimes	NA
Property crimes	NA

Local School District

(school data 2007-08, except as noted)

New Marlborough (non-op)
PO Box 339
Sheffield, MA 01257
413-229-8778

Superintendent. . . . . Michael Singleton

Non-operating district.
Resident students are sent to the Other School Districts listed below.

Grade plan	NA
Total enrollment '09-10	NA
Grade 12 enrollment, '09-10	NA
Graduation rate	NA
Dropout rate	NA
Per-pupil expenditure	NA
Avg teacher salary	NA
Student/teacher ratio '08-09	NA
Highly-qualified teachers, '08-09	NA
Teachers licensed in assigned subject	NA
Students per computer	NA

Other School Districts (see Appendix D for data)
Southern Berkshire Regional

©2010 Information Publications, Inc. All rights reserved. Photocopying prohibited. For additional copies, contact the publisher at www.informationpublications.com or (877)544-INFO (4636)

See Introduction for an explanation of all data sources.

Demographics & Socio-Economic Characteristics

Population

1990	802
2000	929
Male	475
Female	454
2008	990
2010 (projected)††	992
2020 (projected)††	1,030

Race & Hispanic Origin, 2000

Race	
White	887
Black/African American	7
American Indian/Alaska Native	5
Asian	7
Hawaiian Native/Pacific Islander	0
Other Race	3
Two or more races	20
Hispanic origin	8

Age & Nativity, 2000

Under 5 years	48
18 years and over	704
21 years and over	685
65 years and over	92
85 years and over	14
Median Age	42.0
Native-born	909
Foreign-born	20

Age, 2020 (projected)††

Under 5 years	41
5 to 19 years	145
20 to 39 years	180
40 to 64 years	406
65 years and over	258

Educational Attainment, 2000

Population 25 years and over	673
High School graduates or higher	92.0%
Bachelor's degree or higher	39.5%
Graduate degree	15.0%

Income & Poverty, 1999

Per capita income,	$23,234
Median household income	$48,688
Median family income	$54,500
Persons in poverty	58
H'holds receiving public assistance	0
H'holds receiving social security	81

Households, 2000

Total households	379
With persons under 18	121
With persons over 65	70
Family households	264
Single person households	82
Persons per household	2.5
Persons per family	2.9

Labor & Employment, 2000

Civilian labor force	553
Unemployment rate	4.0%
Civilian labor force, 2008†	547
Unemployment rate†	7.7%
Civilian labor force, 12/09†	561
Unemployment rate†	9.3%
Employed persons 16 years and over, by occupation:	
Managers & professionals	224
Service occupations	50
Sales & office occupations	106
Farming, fishing & forestry	6
Construction & maintenance	58
Production & transportation	87
Self-employed persons	68

Most demographic data is from the 2000 Decennial Census
† Massachusetts Department of Revenue
†† University of Massachusetts, MISER

General Information

Town of New Salem
15 S Main St
New Salem, MA 01355
978-544-6437

Elevation	1,048 ft.
Land area (square miles)	45.0
Water area (square miles)	13.8
Population density, 2008 (est)	22.0
Year incorporated	1755
Website	NA

Voters & Government Information

Government type	Open Town Meeting
Number of Selectmen	3
US Congressional District(s)	1

Registered Voters, October 2008

Total	781
Democrats	185
Republicans	114
Unaffiliated/other	469

Local Officials, 2010

Chair, Bd. of Sel.	Jennifer Sandova
Manager/Admin	Nancy Albrich
Town Clerk	Stacy Senflug
Finance	Gabriele Voelker
Tax Collector	Kathryn Soule-Regine
Tax Assessor	Wayne Hachey
Attorney	Kopelman & Paige
Public Works	Tom Swan
Building	Chip Lapointe
Comm Dev/Planning	Liz Wiley (Chr)
Police Chief	Joseph Camden
Emerg/Fire Chief	Joseph Cuneo

Housing & Construction

New Privately Owned Housing Units Authorized by Building Permit

	Single Family	Total Bldgs	Total Units
2006	9	9	9
2007	2	2	2
2008	1	1	1

Parcel Count by Property Class, 2010

Total	699
Single family	431
Multiple units	7
Apartments	0
Condos	0
Vacant land	197
Open space	0
Commercial	9
Industrial	3
Misc. residential	6
Other use	46

Public Library

New Salem Public Library
23 South Main Street
New Salem, MA 01355
(978)544-6334

Director ... Diana Smith

Library Statistics, FY 2008

Population served, 2007	990
Registered users	314
Circulation	10,340
Reference transactons	194
Total program attendance	3,993
per capita:	
Holdings	11.82
Operating income	$41.68
Internet Access	
Internet computers available	2
Weekly users	9

Municipal Finance

Debt at year end 2008	$386,057
Moody's rating, July 2009	NA

Revenues, 2008

Total	$2,164,286
From all taxes	1,833,670
Federal aid	0
State aid	213,631
From other governments	14,276
Charges for services	29,279
Licenses, permits & fees	5,039
Fines & forfeits	0
Interfund transfers	40,985
Misc/other/special assessments	13,703

Expenditures, 2008

Total	$1,981,812
General government	150,647
Public safety	133,567
Other/fixed costs	110,475
Human services	9,401
Culture & recreation	37,260
Debt Service	73,451
Education	1,201,137
Public works	241,099
Intergovernmental	24,775

Taxation, 2010

Property type	Valuation	Rate
Total	$119,678,521	-
Residential	114,422,000	12.30
Open space	263,800	12.30
Commercial	1,603,000	14.24
Industrial	408,400	14.24
Personal	2,981,321	14.24

Average Single Family Tax Bill, 2010

Avg. assessed home value	$239,314
Avg. single fam. tax bill	$2,944
Hi-Lo ranking	239/301

Police & Crime, 2008

Number of police officers	NA
Violent crimes	0
Property crimes	1

Local School District

(school data 2007-08, except as noted)

New Salem (non-op)
18 Pleasant Street
Erving, MA 01344
413-423-3337

Superintendent ... Joan Wickman

Non-operating district.
Resident students are sent to the Other School Districts listed below.

Grade plan	NA
Total enrollment '09-10	NA
Grade 12 enrollment, '09-10	NA
Graduation rate	NA
Dropout rate	NA
Per-pupil expenditure	NA
Avg teacher salary	NA
Student/teacher ratio '08-09	NA
Highly-qualified teachers, '08-09	NA
Teachers licensed in assigned subject	NA
Students per computer	NA

Other School Districts (see Appendix D for data)

New Salem-Wendell and Ralph C. Mahar Regionals, Franklin County Vocational Tech

©2010 Information Publications, Inc. All rights reserved. Photocopying prohibited. For additional copies, contact the publisher at www.informationpublications.com or (877)544-INFO (4636)

See Introduction for an explanation of all data sources.

Demographics & Socio-Economic Characteristics

Population

1990 5,623
2000 6,717
Male 3,254
Female 3,463
2008 6,934
2010 (projected)†† 7,406
2020 (projected)†† 8,177

Race & Hispanic Origin, 2000

Race
White 6,604
Black/African American 25
American Indian/Alaska Native 9
Asian 30
Hawaiian Native/Pacific Islander 1
Other Race 19
Two or more races 29
Hispanic origin 61

Age & Nativity, 2000

Under 5 years 450
18 years and over 4,897
21 years and over 4,744
65 years and over 721
85 years and over 74
Median Age 39.5
Native-born 6,431
Foreign-born 286

Age, 2020 (projected)††

Under 5 years 462
5 to 19 years 1,391
20 to 39 years 1,778
40 to 64 years 2,916
65 years and over 1,630

Educational Attainment, 2000

Population 25 years and over 4,633
High School graduates or higher 95.6%
Bachelor's degree or higher 43.9%
Graduate degree 16.2%

Income & Poverty, 1999

Per capita income, ... $34,640
Median household income $74,836
Median family income $83,428
Persons in poverty 208
H'holds receiving public assistance 30
H'holds receiving social security 586

Households, 2000

Total households 2,514
With persons under 18 955
With persons over 65 549
Family households 1,815
Single person households 569
Persons per household 2.7
Persons per family 3.2

Labor & Employment, 2000

Civilian labor force 3,604
Unemployment rate 1.6%
Civilian labor force, 2008† 3,891
Unemployment rate† 5.8%
Civilian labor force, 12/09† 3,824
Unemployment rate† 7.2%
Employed persons 16 years and over, by occupation:
Managers & professionals 1,692
Service occupations 349
Sales & office occupations 863
Farming, fishing & forestry 16
Construction & maintenance 331
Production & transportation 296
Self-employed persons 382

Most demographic data is from the 2000 Decennial Census
† Massachusetts Department of Revenue
†† University of Massachusetts, MISER

General Information

Town of Newbury
25 High Rd
Newbury, MA 01951
978-465-0862

Elevation .... 37 ft.
Land area (square miles) 24.2
Water area (square miles) 2.2
Population density, 2008 (est) 286.5
Year incorporated 1635
Website .... www.townofnewbury.org

Voters & Government Information

Government type .... Open Town Meeting
Number of Selectmen 5
US Congressional District(s) 6

Registered Voters, October 2008

Total 5,128
Democrats 1,136
Republicans 838
Unaffiliated/other 3,137

Local Officials, 2010

Chair, Bd. of Sel. .... Joseph Story II
Manager/Admin .... Charles E. Kostro
Clerk .... Anne Hatheway
Finance Director .... Charles E. Kostro
Tax Collector .... Charles E. Kostro
Tax Assessor .... Frank N. Kelley III
Attorney .... Anthony E. Penski
Public Works .... Timothy Leonard
Building .... Sam Joslin
Planning .... Martha L. Taylor
Police Chief .... Michael Reilly
Emerg/Fire Chief .... William Pearson

Housing & Construction

New Privately Owned Housing Units Authorized by Building Permit

	Single Family	Total Bldgs	Total Units
2006	19	20	21
2007	18	18	18
2008	18	18	18

Parcel Count by Property Class, 2010

Total 3,248
Single family 2,313
Multiple units 141
Apartments 3
Condos 120
Vacant land 387
Open space 0
Commercial 53
Industrial 16
Misc. residential 67
Other use 148

Public Library

Newbury Town Library
0 Lunt Street
Byfield, MA 01922
(978)465-0539

Director .... Jennifer Brown

Library Statistics, FY 2008

Population served, 2007 6,926
Registered users 5,400
Circulation 84,214
Reference transactons 0
Total program attendance 55,637

per capita:

Holdings 7.54
Operating income $41.36

Internet Access

Internet computers available 16
Weekly users 120

Municipal Finance

Debt at year end 2008 .... $23,462,934
Moody's rating, July 2009 .... A1

Revenues, 2008

Total $17,324,653
From all taxes 13,380,458
Federal aid 0
State aid 1,497,231
From other governments 21,811
Charges for services 0
Licenses, permits & fees 462,102
Fines & forfeits 112,648
Interfund transfers 333,389
Misc/other/special assessments 758,507

Expenditures, 2008

Total $16,384,362
General government 948,795
Public safety 1,932,975
Other/fixed costs 1,081,813
Human services 377,852
Culture & recreation 355,717
Debt Service 2,439,130
Education 8,183,002
Public works 905,534
Intergovernmental 159,544

Taxation, 2010

Property type	Valuation	Rate
Total	$1,367,542,555	-
Residential	1,307,266,786	9.52
Open space	0	0.00
Commercial	39,725,215	9.52
Industrial	3,040,775	9.52
Personal	17,509,779	9.52

Average Single Family Tax Bill, 2010

Avg. assessed home value $461,116
Avg. single fam. tax bill $4,390
Hi-Lo ranking 107/301

Police & Crime, 2008

Number of police officers 12
Violent crimes 3
Property crimes 49

Local School District

(school data 2007-08, except as noted)

Newbury (non-op)
112 Elm Street
Byfield, MA 01922
978-465-2397

Superintendent .... Sandra Halloran

Non-operating district.
Resident students are sent to the Other School Districts listed below.

Grade plan .... NA
Total enrollment '09-10 .... NA
Grade 12 enrollment, '09-10 .... NA
Graduation rate .... NA
Dropout rate .... NA
Per-pupil expenditure .... NA
Avg teacher salary .... NA
Student/teacher ratio '08-09 .... NA
Highly-qualified teachers, '08-09 .... NA
Teachers licensed in assigned subject .... NA
Students per computer .... NA

Other School Districts (see Appendix D for data)
Triton Regional, Whittier Vocational Tech

©2010 Information Publications, Inc. All rights reserved. Photocopying prohibited. For additional copies, contact the publisher at www.informationpublications.com or (877)544-INFO (4636)

See Introduction for an explanation of all data sources.

Demographics & Socio-Economic Characteristics

Population

1990	16,317
2000	17,189
Male	7,982
Female	9,207
2008	17,542
2010 (projected)††	17,484
2020 (projected)††	17,430

Race & Hispanic Origin, 2000

Race	
White	16,864
Black/African American	73
American Indian/Alaska Native	21
Asian	105
Hawaiian Native/Pacific Islander	2
Other Race	27
Two or more races	97
Hispanic origin	151

Age & Nativity, 2000

Under 5 years	972
18 years and over	13,638
21 years and over	13,299
65 years and over	2,414
85 years and over	379
Median Age	40.9
Native-born	16,533
Foreign-born	709

Age, 2020 (projected)††

Under 5 years	774
5 to 19 years	2,510
20 to 39 years	3,383
40 to 64 years	6,335
65 years and over	4,428

Educational Attainment, 2000

Population 25 years and over	12,844
High School graduates or higher	90.3%
Bachelor's degree or higher	42.3%
Graduate degree	17.1%

Income & Poverty, 1999

Per capita income,	$34,187
Median household income	$58,557
Median family income	$73,306
Persons in poverty	877
H'holds receiving public assistance	156
H'holds receiving social security	1,810

Households, 2000

Total households	7,519
With persons under 18	2,046
With persons over 65	1,619
Family households	4,429
Single person households	2,492
Persons per household	2.2
Persons per family	2.9

Labor & Employment, 2000

Civilian labor force	9,619
Unemployment rate	2.9%
Civilian labor force, 2008†	9,897
Unemployment rate†	5.1%
Civilian labor force, 12/09†	9,749
Unemployment rate†	7.3%
Employed persons 16 years and over, by occupation:	
Managers & professionals	4,710
Service occupations	1,055
Sales & office occupations	2,167
Farming, fishing & forestry	15
Construction & maintenance	576
Production & transportation	816
Self-employed persons	912

Most demographic data is from the 2000 Decennial Census
† Massachusetts Department of Revenue
†† University of Massachusetts, MISER

General Information

City of Newburyport
60 Pleasant St
Newburyport, MA 01950
978-465-4411

Elevation	37 ft.
Land area (square miles)	8.4
Water area (square miles)	2.2
Population density, 2008 (est)	2,088.3
Year incorporated	1764
Website	www.cityofnewburyport.com

Voters & Government Information

Government type	Mayor-Council
Number of Councilpersons	11
US Congressional District(s)	6

Registered Voters, October 2008

Total	12,914
Democrats	4,058
Republicans	1,700
Unaffiliated/other	7,095

Local Officials, 2010

Mayor	Donna D. Holaday
Manager/Admin	NA
City Clerk	Richard B. Jones
Auditor	William Squillace
Treas/Collector	Cheryl Robertson
Tax Assessor	Daniel Raycroft
Attorney	Kopelman & Paige
Public Works	Brendan O'Regan
Building	Gary Calderwood
Comm Dev/Planning	(vacant)
Police Chief	Thomas Howard
Emerg/Fire Chief	Stephen Cutter

Housing & Construction

New Privately Owned Housing Units Authorized by Building Permit

	Single Family	Total Bldgs	Total Units
2006	17	17	17
2007	11	13	37
2008	18	18	18

Parcel Count by Property Class, 2010

Total	7,973
Single family	4,271
Multiple units	436
Apartments	103
Condos	1,999
Vacant land	390
Open space	8
Commercial	386
Industrial	246
Misc. residential	24
Other use	110

Public Library

Newburyport Public Library
94 State St.
Newburyport, MA 01950
(978)465-4428

Director	Cynthia Diminture

Library Statistics, FY 2008

Population served, 2007	17,144
Registered users	19,593
Circulation	340,368
Reference transactons	21,796
Total program attendance	282,967
per capita:	
Holdings	6.98
Operating income	$72.85
Internet Access	
Internet computers available	20
Weekly users	809

Municipal Finance

Debt at year end 2008	$41,367,462
Moody's rating, July 2009	A1

Revenues, 2008

Total	$48,103,820
From all taxes	38,780,369
Federal aid	0
State aid	7,535,272
From other governments	19,897
Charges for services	21,763
Licenses, permits & fees	718,396
Fines & forfeits	85,715
Interfund transfers	265,194
Misc/other/special assessments	338,607

Expenditures, 2008

Total	$47,865,490
General government	2,506,978
Public safety	6,300,823
Other/fixed costs	9,314,077
Human services	1,688,486
Culture & recreation	1,187,516
Debt Service	2,048,617
Education	20,565,551
Public works	2,044,156
Intergovernmental	2,209,286

Taxation, 2010

Property type	Valuation	Rate
Total	$3,369,691,485	-
Residential	2,868,495,595	11.66
Open space	335,400	11.66
Commercial	277,150,605	11.66
Industrial	165,911,200	11.66
Personal	57,798,685	11.66

Average Single Family Tax Bill, 2010

Avg. assessed home value	$451,108
Avg. single fam. tax bill	$5,260
Hi-Lo ranking	66/301

Police & Crime, 2008

Number of police officers	24
Violent crimes	19
Property crimes	249

Local School District

(school data 2007-08, except as noted)

Newburyport
70 Low Street
Newburyport, MA 01950
978-465-4457

Superintendent	Deirdre Farrell
Grade plan	PK-12
Total enrollment '09-10	2,251
Grade 12 enrollment, '09-10	171
Graduation rate	90.3%
Dropout rate	3.4%
Per-pupil expenditure	$12,199
Avg teacher salary	$67,884
Student/teacher ratio '08-09	13.5 to 1
Highly-qualified teachers, '08-09	96.2%
Teachers licensed in assigned subject	97.6%
Students per computer	2.6

Massachusetts Competency Assessment System (MCAS), 2009 results

	English		Math	
	% Prof	CPI	% Prof	CPI
Gr 4	55%	83.2	50%	82
Gr 6	81%	92.4	61%	83.1
Gr 8	89%	95.2	59%	79.9
Gr 10	94%	97.7	91%	95.4

Other School Districts (see Appendix D for data)
Whittier Vocational Tech

©2010 Information Publications, Inc. All rights reserved. Photocopying prohibited. For additional copies, contact the publisher at www.informationpublications.com or (877)544-INFO (4636)

See Introduction for an explanation of all data sources.

Demographics & Socio-Economic Characteristics*

Population

1990	82,585
2000	83,829
Male	38,951
Female	44,878
2008	82,139
2010 (projected)††	79,965
2020 (projected)††	75,982

Race & Hispanic Origin, 2000

Race	
White	73,831
Black/African American	1,653
American Indian/Alaska Native	61
Asian	6,434
Hawaiian Native/Pacific Islander	29
Other Race	598
Two or more races	1,223
Hispanic origin	2,111

Age & Nativity, 2000

Under 5 years	4,401
18 years and over	66,018
21 years and over	61,286
65 years and over	12,640
85 years and over	2,055
Median Age	38.7
Native-born	68,713
Foreign-born	15,116

Age, 2020 (projected)††

Under 5 years	3,536
5 to 19 years	13,989
20 to 39 years	20,784
40 to 64 years	22,797
65 years and over	14,876

Educational Attainment, 2000

Population 25 years and over	57,687
High School graduates or higher	94.5%
Bachelor's degree or higher	68.0%
Graduate degree	38.9%

Income & Poverty, 1999

Per capita income,	$45,708
Median household income	$86,052
Median family income	$105,289
Persons in poverty	3,382
H'holds receiving public assistance	425
H'holds receiving social security	8,091

Households, 2000

Total households	31,201
With persons under 18	10,076
With persons over 65	8,748
Family households	20,485
Single person households	7,958
Persons per household	2.5
Persons per family	3.0

Labor & Employment, 2000

Civilian labor force	46,368
Unemployment rate	2.9%
Civilian labor force, 2008†	46,321
Unemployment rate†	4.1%
Civilian labor force, 12/09†	46,076
Unemployment rate†	5.8%
Employed persons 16 years and over, by occupation:	
Managers & professionals	29,419
Service occupations	3,531
Sales & office occupations	9,468
Farming, fishing & forestry	24
Construction & maintenance	1,111
Production & transportation	1,465
Self-employed persons	4,659

Most demographic data is from the 2000 Decennial Census
* see Appendix D and E for American Community Survey data
† Massachusetts Department of Revenue
†† University of Massachusetts, MISER

General Information

City of Newton
1000 Commonwealth Ave
Newton, MA 02459
617-796-1000

Elevation	50 ft.
Land area (square miles)	18.1
Water area (square miles)	0.1
Population density, 2008 (est)	4,538.1
Year incorporated	1688
Website	www.ci.newton.ma.us

Voters & Government Information

Government type	Mayor-Board
Number of Aldermen	24
US Congressional District(s)	4

Registered Voters, October 2008

Total	55,353
Democrats	25,873
Republicans	4,642
Unaffiliated/other	24,574

Local Officials, 2010

Mayor	Setti Warren
Chief Operating Officer	Robert Rooney
Clerk	David A. Olson
Comptroller	David Wilkinson
Treas/Collector	James Reardon (Actg)
Tax Assessor	Elizabeth Dromey
Attorney	Donnalyn Kahn (Int)
Public Works	Thomas Daley
Building	(vacant)
Planning	Candace Havens (Int)
Police Chief	Matthew Cummings
Emerg/Fire Chief	Joseph E. LaCroix

Housing & Construction

New Privately Owned Housing Units Authorized by Building Permit

	Single Family	Total Bldgs	Total Units
2006	66	67	246
2007	67	70	115
2008	40	55	70

Parcel Count by Property Class, 2010

Total	26,898
Single family	16,929
Multiple units	3,241
Apartments	160
Condos	4,391
Vacant land	874
Open space	0
Commercial	756
Industrial	76
Misc. residential	170
Other use	301

Public Library

Newton Free Public Library
330 Homer Street
Newton Centre, MA 02459
(617)796-1360

Director	Nancy Perlow

Library Statistics, FY 2008

Population served, 2007	83,271
Registered users	52,365
Circulation	1,955,025
Reference transactons	155,259
Total program attendance	656,214
per capita:	
Holdings	7.50
Operating income	$69.75
Internet Access	
Internet computers available	52
Weekly users	2,700

Municipal Finance

Debt at year end 2008	$74,552,864
Moody's rating, July 2009	Aaa

Revenues, 2008

Total	$281,140,508
From all taxes	228,766,011
Federal aid	1,353,734
State aid	28,255,273
From other governments	171,255
Charges for services	1,684,059
Licenses, permits & fees	4,897,247
Fines & forfeits	1,706,928
Interfund transfers	3,614,125
Misc/other/special assessments	5,345,938

Expenditures, 2008

Total	$229,204,947
General government	11,257,920
Public safety	26,626,954
Other/fixed costs	16,748,957
Human services	3,071,647
Culture & recreation	9,537,113
Debt Service	7,426,543
Education	130,841,435
Public works	18,085,097
Intergovernmental	5,512,027

Taxation, 2010

Property type	Valuation	Rate
Total	$20,487,831,700	-
Residential	18,384,685,100	10.41
Open space	0	0.00
Commercial	1,670,748,000	19.93
Industrial	149,224,600	19.93
Personal	283,174,000	19.93

Average Single Family Tax Bill, 2010

Avg. assessed home value	$799,218
Avg. single fam. tax bill	$8,320
Hi-Lo ranking	20/301

Police & Crime, 2008

Number of police officers	139
Violent crimes	117
Property crimes	1,111

Local School District

(school data 2007-08, except as noted)

Newton
100 Walnut Street
Newtonville, MA 02460
617-559-6100

Superintendent	V. Marini
Grade plan	PK-12
Total enrollment '09-10	11,765
Grade 12 enrollment, '09-10	894
Graduation rate	94.2%
Dropout rate	1.7%
Per-pupil expenditure	$15,498
Avg teacher salary	$70,961
Student/teacher ratio '08-09	13.3 to 1
Highly-qualified teachers, '08-09	96.9%
Teachers licensed in assigned subject	97.5%
Students per computer	4.9

Massachusetts Competency Assessment System (MCAS), 2009 results

	English		Math	
	% Prof	CPI	% Prof	CPI
Gr 4	76%	91.5	75%	90.8
Gr 6	84%	94	79%	90.5
Gr 8	89%	96.3	77%	90
Gr 10	91%	96.9	89%	95.1

Other School Districts (see Appendix D for data)
None

©2010 Information Publications, Inc. All rights reserved. Photocopying prohibited. For additional copies, contact the publisher at www.informationpublications.com or (877)544-INFO (4636)

See Introduction for an explanation of all data sources.

Demographics & Socio-Economic Characteristics

Population

1990	9,270
2000	10,460
Male	6,149
Female	4,311
2008	11,029
2010 (projected)††	11,298
2020 (projected)††	12,355

Race & Hispanic Origin, 2000

Race	
White	9,306
Black/African American	513
American Indian/Alaska Native	32
Asian	123
Hawaiian Native/Pacific Islander	2
Other Race	359
Two or more races	125
Hispanic origin	510

Age & Nativity, 2000

Under 5 years	764
18 years and over	7,611
21 years and over	7,379
65 years and over	577
85 years and over	47
Median Age	37.4
Native-born	9,608
Foreign-born	852

Age, 2020 (projected)††

Under 5 years	839
5 to 19 years	2,297
20 to 39 years	3,467
40 to 64 years	4,153
65 years and over	1,599

Educational Attainment, 2000

Population 25 years and over	7,106
High School graduates or higher	86.4%
Bachelor's degree or higher	37.9%
Graduate degree	14.1%

Income & Poverty, 1999

Per capita income,	$32,454
Median household income	$86,153
Median family income	$92,001
Persons in poverty	95
H'holds receiving public assistance	28
H'holds receiving social security	484

Households, 2000

Total households	2,818
With persons under 18	1,461
With persons over 65	378
Family households	2,413
Single person households	304
Persons per household	3.1
Persons per family	3.4

Labor & Employment, 2000

Civilian labor force	4,530
Unemployment rate	2.2%
Civilian labor force, 2008†	4,758
Unemployment rate†	5.8%
Civilian labor force, 12/09†	4,784
Unemployment rate†	8.5%
Employed persons 16 years and over, by occupation:	
Managers & professionals	2,295
Service occupations	408
Sales & office occupations	1,123
Farming, fishing & forestry	0
Construction & maintenance	367
Production & transportation	238
Self-employed persons	265

Most demographic data is from the 2000 Decennial Census
† Massachusetts Department of Revenue
†† University of Massachusetts, MISER

General Information

Town of Norfolk
One Liberty Ln
Norfolk, MA 02056
508-528-1400

Elevation	200 ft.
Land area (square miles)	14.8
Water area (square miles)	0.4
Population density, 2008 (est)	745.2
Year incorporated	1870
Website	www.virtualnorfolk.org

Voters & Government Information

Government type	Open Town Meeting
Number of Selectmen	3
US Congressional District(s)	4

Registered Voters, October 2008

Total	6,293
Democrats	1,307
Republicans	1,255
Unaffiliated/other	3,708

Local Officials, 2010

Chair, Bd. of Sel.	NA
Manager/Admin	Jack Hathaway
Clerk	Gail Bernardo
Finance Director	NA
Treas/Collector	Cheryl Kelley
Tax Assessor	John Neas
Attorney	George Hall
Public Works	Remo Vito
Building	Robert Bullock
Comm Dev/Planning	NA
Police Chief	Charles Stone
Emerg/Fire Chief	Coleman Bushnell

Housing & Construction

New Privately Owned Housing Units Authorized by Building Permit

	Single Family	Total Bldgs	Total Units
2006	40	40	40
2007	33	33	33
2008	10	10	10

Parcel Count by Property Class, 2010

Total	3,730
Single family	2,879
Multiple units	27
Apartments	2
Condos	131
Vacant land	453
Open space	3
Commercial	96
Industrial	63
Misc. residential	18
Other use	58

Public Library

Norfolk Public Library
139 Main St.
Norfolk, MA 02056
(508)528-3380

Director	Robin Glasser

Library Statistics, FY 2008

Population served, 2007	10,646
Registered users	6,671
Circulation	141,764
Reference transactons	2,080
Total program attendance	74,734
per capita:	
Holdings	6.29
Operating income	$56.87
Internet Access	
Internet computers available	16
Weekly users	191

Municipal Finance

Debt at year end 2008	$11,449,771
Moody's rating, July 2009	A1

Revenues, 2008

Total	$30,306,357
From all taxes	20,988,657
Federal aid	0
State aid	5,867,726
From other governments	1,400
Charges for services	445,969
Licenses, permits & fees	321,046
Fines & forfeits	20,394
Interfund transfers	411,605
Misc/other/special assessments	1,124,780

Expenditures, 2008

Total	$28,956,560
General government	1,742,966
Public safety	3,208,044
Other/fixed costs	2,640,085
Human services	208,800
Culture & recreation	529,471
Debt Service	2,377,706
Education	15,893,347
Public works	1,855,219
Intergovernmental	323,961

Taxation, 2010

Property type	Valuation	Rate
Total	$1,501,202,458	-
Residential	1,401,251,920	14.07
Open space	386,400	14.07
Commercial	59,358,980	14.07
Industrial	12,173,900	14.07
Personal	28,031,258	14.07

Average Single Family Tax Bill, 2010

Avg. assessed home value	$444,962
Avg. single fam. tax bill	$6,261
Hi-Lo ranking	45/301

Police & Crime, 2008

Number of police officers	17
Violent crimes	11
Property crimes	87

Local School District

(school data 2007-08, except as noted)

Norfolk
70 Boardman Street
Norfolk, MA 02056
508-528-1225

Superintendent	Don Leclerc
Grade plan	PK-6
Total enrollment '09-10	1,071
Grade 12 enrollment, '09-10	0
Graduation rate	NA
Dropout rate	NA
Per-pupil expenditure	$11,437
Avg teacher salary	$62,178
Student/teacher ratio '08-09	13.7 to 1
Highly-qualified teachers, '08-09	98.2%
Teachers licensed in assigned subject	98.7%
Students per computer	5.8

Massachusetts Competency Assessment System (MCAS), 2009 results

	English		Math	
	% Prof	CPI	% Prof	CPI
Gr 4	70%	89.8	65%	87.8
Gr 6	92%	96.9	85%	93.6
Gr 8	NA	NA	NA	NA
Gr 10	NA	NA	NA	NA

Other School Districts (see Appendix D for data)
King Philip Regional, Tri County Vocational Tech, Norfolk County Agricultural

©2010 Information Publications, Inc. All rights reserved. Photocopying prohibited. For additional copies, contact the publisher at www.informationpublications.com or (877)544-INFO (4636)

See Introduction for an explanation of all data sources.

Demographics & Socio-Economic Characteristics

Population

1990	16,797
2000	14,681
Male	6,794
Female	7,887
2008	13,711
2010 (projected)††	13,379
2020 (projected)††	12,182

Race & Hispanic Origin, 2000

Race	
White	13,946
Black/African American	245
American Indian/Alaska Native	39
Asian	117
Hawaiian Native/Pacific Islander	5
Other Race	117
Two or more races	212
Hispanic origin	298

Age & Nativity, 2000

Under 5 years	802
18 years and over	11,399
21 years and over	10,544
65 years and over	2,703
85 years and over	394
Median Age	38.0
Native-born	14,346
Foreign-born	331

Age, 2020 (projected)††

Under 5 years	616
5 to 19 years	2,095
20 to 39 years	3,153
40 to 64 years	3,785
65 years and over	2,533

Educational Attainment, 2000

Population 25 years and over	9,717
High School graduates or higher	73.2%
Bachelor's degree or higher	14.0%
Graduate degree	4.4%

Income & Poverty, 1999

Per capita income,	$16,381
Median household income	$27,601
Median family income	$37,635
Persons in poverty	2,531
H'holds receiving public assistance	362
H'holds receiving social security	2,437

Households, 2000

Total households	6,311
With persons under 18	1,789
With persons over 65	1,986
Family households	3,634
Single person households	2,286
Persons per household	2.2
Persons per family	2.9

Labor & Employment, 2000

Civilian labor force	7,150
Unemployment rate	5.7%
Civilian labor force, 2008†	7,131
Unemployment rate†	9.1%
Civilian labor force, 12/09†	7,143
Unemployment rate†	10.8%
Employed persons 16 years and over, by occupation:	
Managers & professionals	1,824
Service occupations	1,656
Sales & office occupations	1,590
Farming, fishing & forestry	0
Construction & maintenance	601
Production & transportation	1,074
Self-employed persons	418

Most demographic data is from the 2000 Decennial Census
† Massachusetts Department of Revenue
†† University of Massachusetts, MISER

General Information

City of North Adams
10 Main St
North Adams, MA 01247
413-662-3000

Elevation	1,000 ft.
Land area (square miles)	20.4
Water area (square miles)	0.1
Population density, 2008 (est)	672.1
Year incorporated	1878
Website	www.northadams-ma.gov

Voters & Government Information

Government type	Mayor-Council
Number of Councilpersons	9
US Congressional District(s)	1

Registered Voters, October 2008

Total	9,055
Democrats	3,168
Republicans	696
Unaffiliated/other	5,091

Local Officials, 2010

Mayor	Richard J. Alcombright
Manager/Admin	Jay Green
Clerk	Marilyn Gomeau
Finance Director	Nancy Ziter
Tax Collector	Audrey Dumas
Tax Assessor	Christopher Lamarre
Attorney	John DeRosa
Public Works	Paul Markland
Building	William Miranti
Comm Dev/Planning	Michael Nuvaille
Police Chief	Michael Cozzaglio
Emerg/Fire Chief	Steve Miranti

Housing & Construction

New Privately Owned Housing Units Authorized by Building Permit

	Single Family	Total Bldgs	Total Units
2006	4	4	4
2007	5	5	5
2008	2	2	2

Parcel Count by Property Class, 2010

Total	5,010
Single family	2,629
Multiple units	825
Apartments	185
Condos	49
Vacant land	814
Open space	0
Commercial	269
Industrial	80
Misc. residential	49
Other use	110

Public Library

North Adams Public Library
74 Church Street
North Adams, MA 01247
(413)662-3133

Director . . . Richard Moon (Int)

Library Statistics, FY 2008

Population served, 2007	13,617
Registered users	7,441
Circulation	142,211
Reference transactons	5,021
Total program attendance	93,580
per capita:	
Holdings	4.22
Operating income	$29.53
Internet Access	
Internet computers available	9
Weekly users	289

Municipal Finance

Debt at year end 2008	$15,287,539
Moody's rating, July 2009	A3

Revenues, 2008

Total	$40,162,235
From all taxes	11,875,023
Federal aid	8,855
State aid	21,956,205
From other governments	0
Charges for services	4,145,035
Licenses, permits & fees	237,638
Fines & forfeits	112,477
Interfund transfers	1,358,600
Misc/other/special assessments	234,201

Expenditures, 2008

Total	$35,895,283
General government	1,371,843
Public safety	3,523,073
Other/fixed costs	2,691,277
Human services	452,808
Culture & recreation	668,624
Debt Service	2,112,221
Education	16,795,545
Public works	4,538,506
Intergovernmental	2,864,346

Taxation, 2010

Property type	Valuation	Rate
Total	$727,183,465	-
Residential	562,104,232	12.44
Open space	0	0.00
Commercial	105,965,641	27.92
Industrial	25,940,412	27.92
Personal	33,173,180	27.92

Average Single Family Tax Bill, 2010

Avg. assessed home value	$138,963
Avg. single fam. tax bill	$1,729
Hi-Lo ranking	297/301

Police & Crime, 2008

Number of police officers	25
Violent crimes	85
Property crimes	634

Local School District

(school data 2007-08, except as noted)

North Adams
191 East Main Street, Ste 1
North Adams, MA 01247
413-662-3225

Superintendent	James Montepare
Grade plan	PK-12
Total enrollment '09-10	1,612
Grade 12 enrollment, '09-10	128
Graduation rate	78.4%
Dropout rate	14.4%
Per-pupil expenditure	$15,248
Avg teacher salary	$58,475
Student/teacher ratio '08-09	11.0 to 1
Highly-qualified teachers, '08-09	95.8%
Teachers licensed in assigned subject	97.7%
Students per computer	1.7

Massachusetts Competency Assessment System (MCAS), 2009 results

	English		Math	
	% Prof	CPI	% Prof	CPI
Gr 4	46%	81.9	38%	75.8
Gr 6	46%	78	42%	72
Gr 8	51%	78.4	22%	57.3
Gr 10	72%	88.6	59%	80.1

Other School Districts (see Appendix D for data)

Receives students from Clarksburg, Florida, and Monroe; sends to Northern Berkshire Vocational Tech

©2010 Information Publications, Inc. All rights reserved. Photocopying prohibited. For additional copies, contact the publisher at www.informationpublications.com or (877)544-INFO (4636)

©2010 Information Publications, Inc. All rights reserved. Photocopying prohibited. For additional copies, contact the publisher at www.informationpublications.com or (877)544-INFO (4636)

Demographics & Socio-Economic Characteristics

Population

1990	22,792
2000	27,202
Male	13,099
Female	14,103
2008	27,522
2010 (projected)††	30,082
2020 (projected)††	32,153

Race & Hispanic Origin, 2000

Race	
White	25,481
Black/African American	196
American Indian/Alaska Native	14
Asian	1,078
Hawaiian Native/Pacific Islander	2
Other Race	201
Two or more races	230
Hispanic origin	541

Age & Nativity, 2000

Under 5 years	1,915
18 years and over	20,276
21 years and over	18,768
65 years and over	3,644
85 years and over	705
Median Age	37.2
Native-born	25,011
Foreign-born	2,191

Age, 2020 (projected)††

Under 5 years	1,904
5 to 19 years	7,111
20 to 39 years	7,711
40 to 64 years	10,158
65 years and over	5,269

Educational Attainment, 2000

Population 25 years and over	17,672
High School graduates or higher	93.1%
Bachelor's degree or higher	50.3%
Graduate degree	20.9%

Income & Poverty, 1999

Per capita income,	$34,335
Median household income	$72,728
Median family income	$91,105
Persons in poverty	739
H'holds receiving public assistance	132
H'holds receiving social security	2,494

Households, 2000

Total households	9,724
With persons under 18	3,725
With persons over 65	2,424
Family households	6,904
Single person households	2,440
Persons per household	2.6
Persons per family	3.2

Labor & Employment, 2000

Civilian labor force	13,591
Unemployment rate	2.3%
Civilian labor force, 2008†	13,231
Unemployment rate†	5.5%
Civilian labor force, 12/09†	13,335
Unemployment rate†	8.0%
Employed persons 16 years and over, by occupation:	
Managers & professionals	6,881
Service occupations	1,368
Sales & office occupations	3,642
Farming, fishing & forestry	24
Construction & maintenance	604
Production & transportation	754
Self-employed persons	986

Most demographic data is from the 2000 Decennial Census
† Massachusetts Department of Revenue
†† University of Massachusetts, MISER

General Information

Town of North Andover
120 Main St
North Andover, MA 01845
978-688-9500

Elevation	100 ft.
Land area (square miles)	26.7
Water area (square miles)	1.2
Population density, 2008 (est)	1,030.8
Year incorporated	1855
Website	www.townofnorthandover.com

Voters & Government Information

Government type	Open Town Meeting
Number of Selectmen	5
US Congressional District(s)	6

Registered Voters, October 2008

Total	18,141
Democrats	4,545
Republicans	3,090
Unaffiliated/other	10,414

Local Officials, 2010

Chair, Bd. of Sel.	Tracy M. Watson
Town Manager	Mark H. Rees
Clerk	Joyce A. Bradshaw
Finance Director	NA
Tax Collector	Jennifer Yarid
Tax Assessor	Garrett Boles
Attorney	Thomas J. Urbelis
Public Works	Bruce Thibodeau
Building	Gerald Brown
Planning	Curt Bellavance
Police Chief	Richard M. Stanley
Emerg/Fire Chief	William Martineau

Housing & Construction

New Privately Owned Housing Units Authorized by Building Permit

	Single Family	Total Bldgs	Total Units
2006	24	54	294
2007	19	19	19
2008	20	21	29

Parcel Count by Property Class, 2010

Total	9,895
Single family	6,173
Multiple units	466
Apartments	48
Condos	1,915
Vacant land	492
Open space	0
Commercial	490
Industrial	84
Misc. residential	28
Other use	199

Public Library

Stevens Memorial Library
345 Main Street, PO Box 8
North Andover, MA 01845
(978)688-9505

Director	Mary Rose Quinn

Library Statistics, FY 2008

Population served, 2007	27,637
Registered users	28,568
Circulation	218,273
Reference transactons	24,549
Total program attendance	161,070
per capita:	
Holdings	4.33
Operating income	$29.11
Internet Access	
Internet computers available	8
Weekly users	804

Municipal Finance

Debt at year end 2008	$79,798,875
Moody's rating, July 2009	A1

Revenues, 2008

Total	$75,456,859
From all taxes	56,961,931
Federal aid	0
State aid	10,595,282
From other governments	116,479
Charges for services	2,724,425
Licenses, permits & fees	1,426,954
Fines & forfeits	53,047
Interfund transfers	931,091
Misc/other/special assessments	1,323,825

Expenditures, 2008

Total	$66,707,578
General government	2,430,440
Public safety	8,458,281
Other/fixed costs	3,414,558
Human services	808,842
Culture & recreation	772,115
Debt Service	8,258,471
Education	35,602,791
Public works	4,287,584
Intergovernmental	2,200,498

Taxation, 2010

Property type	Valuation	Rate
Total	$4,233,059,057	-
Residential	3,670,178,348	12.74
Open space	0	0.00
Commercial	286,494,949	17.69
Industrial	168,247,500	17.69
Personal	108,138,260	17.69

Average Single Family Tax Bill, 2010

Avg. assessed home value	$469,012
Avg. single fam. tax bill	$5,975
Hi-Lo ranking	47/301

Police & Crime, 2008

Number of police officers	39
Violent crimes	13
Property crimes	222

Local School District

(school data 2007-08, except as noted)

North Andover
1600 Osgood Street, Suite 3-59
North Andover, MA 01845
978-794-1503

Superintendent	Christopher Hottel
Grade plan	PK-12
Total enrollment '09-10	4,614
Grade 12 enrollment, '09-10	335
Graduation rate	91.9%
Dropout rate	2.3%
Per-pupil expenditure	$10,479
Avg teacher salary	$72,277
Student/teacher ratio '08-09	19.5 to 1
Highly-qualified teachers, '08-09	99.1%
Teachers licensed in assigned subject	97.9%
Students per computer	3

Massachusetts Competency Assessment System (MCAS), 2009 results

	English		Math	
	% Prof	CPI	% Prof	CPI
Gr 4	63%	85	52%	81.2
Gr 6	77%	90	70%	86.8
Gr 8	88%	95.9	60%	80.3
Gr 10	89%	95.5	84%	92.3

Other School Districts (see Appendix D for data)

Greater Lawrence Vocational Tech

See Introduction for an explanation of all data sources.

Demographics & Socio-Economic Characteristics

Population

1990	25,038
2000	27,143
Male	13,192
Female	13,951
2008	27,794
2010 (projected)††	29,561
2020 (projected)††	32,168

Race & Hispanic Origin, 2000

Race	
White	26,048
Black/African American	251
American Indian/Alaska Native	33
Asian	463
Hawaiian Native/Pacific Islander	5
Other Race	122
Two or more races	221
Hispanic origin	358

Age & Nativity, 2000

Under 5 years	1,957
18 years and over	19,852
21 years and over	19,076
65 years and over	2,622
85 years and over	317
Median Age	35.6
Native-born	25,960
Foreign-born	1,183

Age, 2020 (projected)††

Under 5 years	2,092
5 to 19 years	6,021
20 to 39 years	9,002
40 to 64 years	10,600
65 years and over	4,453

Educational Attainment, 2000

Population 25 years and over	18,041
High School graduates or higher	88.6%
Bachelor's degree or higher	33.5%
Graduate degree	10.3%

Income & Poverty, 1999

Per capita income,	$25,974
Median household income	$59,371
Median family income	$69,461
Persons in poverty	1,037
H'holds receiving public assistance	186
H'holds receiving social security	2,177

Households, 2000

Total households	10,391
With persons under 18	3,941
With persons over 65	1,871
Family households	7,227
Single person households	2,568
Persons per household	2.6
Persons per family	3.2

Labor & Employment, 2000

Civilian labor force	15,495
Unemployment rate	3.9%
Civilian labor force, 2008†	16,227
Unemployment rate†	7.3%
Civilian labor force, 12/09†	16,405
Unemployment rate†	11.0%
Employed persons 16 years and over, by occupation:	
Managers & professionals	5,884
Service occupations	1,776
Sales & office occupations	4,224
Farming, fishing & forestry	0
Construction & maintenance	1,252
Production & transportation	1,747
Self-employed persons	737

Most demographic data is from the 2000 Decennial Census
† Massachusetts Department of Revenue
†† University of Massachusetts, MISER

General Information

Town of North Attleborough
43 S Washington St
North Attleborough, MA 02760
508-699-0100

Elevation	185 ft.
Land area (square miles)	18.6
Water area (square miles)	0.4
Population density, 2008 (est)	1,494.3
Year incorporated	1887
Email	mfisher@nattleboro.com

Voters & Government Information

Government type	Rep. Twn. Mtg. (162)
Number of Selectmen	5
US Congressional District(s)	3

Registered Voters, October 2008

Total	18,884
Democrats	4,262
Republicans	3,313
Unaffiliated/other	11,164

Local Officials, 2010

Chair, Bd. of Sel.	Paul Belham
Manager/Admin	Mark Fisher
Clerk	Maxwell G. Gould
Finance Director	NA
Tax Collector	Diana Asanza
Tax Assessor	John Kraskouskas
Attorney	Roger Ferris
Public Works	Mark Hollowell
Building	Rodman Palmer
Comm Dev/Planning	NA
Police Chief	Michael Gould Sr
Emerg/Fire Chief	Peter Lamb

Housing & Construction

New Privately Owned Housing Units Authorized by Building Permit

	Single Family	Total Bldgs	Total Units
2006	43	45	99
2007	26	27	30
2008	16	17	18

Parcel Count by Property Class, 2010

Total	10,278
Single family	6,710
Multiple units	579
Apartments	160
Condos	1,191
Vacant land	1,026
Open space	0
Commercial	313
Industrial	148
Misc. residential	52
Other use	99

Public Library

Richards Memorial Library
118 North Washington Street
North Attleborough, MA 02760
(508)699-0198

Director	Francis Ward

Library Statistics, FY 2008

Population served, 2007	27,907
Registered users	13,126
Circulation	153,828
Reference transactons	4,000
Total program attendance	156,000
per capita:	
Holdings	1.98
Operating income	$22.63
Internet Access	
Internet computers available	3
Weekly users	160

Municipal Finance

Debt at year end 2008	$57,670,857
Moody's rating, July 2009	A1

Revenues, 2008

Total	$74,836,183
From all taxes	39,028,266
Federal aid	205,985
State aid	25,916,980
From other governments	0
Charges for services	308,249
Licenses, permits & fees	406,679
Fines & forfeits	45,540
Interfund transfers	6,012,408
Misc/other/special assessments	1,456,038

Expenditures, 2008

Total	$73,961,409
General government	2,808,323
Public safety	9,744,469
Other/fixed costs	9,583,667
Human services	620,360
Culture & recreation	1,153,002
Debt Service	8,211,015
Education	37,194,018
Public works	1,815,361
Intergovernmental	2,831,194

Taxation, 2010

Property type	Valuation	Rate
Total	$3,749,081,100	-
Residential	2,913,608,466	10.44
Open space	0	0.00
Commercial	668,142,014	10.44
Industrial	107,821,520	10.44
Personal	59,509,100	10.44

Average Single Family Tax Bill, 2010

Avg. assessed home value	$341,432
Avg. single fam. tax bill	$3,565
Hi-Lo ranking	165/301

Police & Crime, 2008

Number of police officers	47
Violent crimes	30
Property crimes	635

Local School District

(school data 2007-08, except as noted)
North Attleborough
6 Morse Street
No. Attleborough, MA 02760
508-643-2100

Superintendent	Suzan Cullen
Grade plan	PK-12
Total enrollment '09-10	4,750
Grade 12 enrollment, '09-10	299
Graduation rate	83.7%
Dropout rate	7.6%
Per-pupil expenditure	$9,787
Avg teacher salary	$63,155
Student/teacher ratio '08-09	15.6 to 1
Highly-qualified teachers, '08-09	96.9%
Teachers licensed in assigned subject	97.9%
Students per computer	10.1

Massachusetts Competency Assessment System (MCAS), 2009 results

	English		Math	
	% Prof	CPI	% Prof	CPI
Gr 4	71%	89.8	60%	87.3
Gr 6	77%	92.9	68%	87.5
Gr 8	88%	96.8	57%	80.9
Gr 10	89%	95.8	83%	93.8

Other School Districts (see Appendix D for data)
Tri County Vocational Tech, Bristol County Agricultural

©2010 Information Publications, Inc. All rights reserved. Photocopying prohibited. For additional copies, contact the publisher at www.informationpublications.com or (877)544-INFO (4636)

See Introduction for an explanation of all data sources.

Demographics & Socio-Economic Characteristics

Population

1990 4,708
2000 4,683
Male 2,299
Female 2,384
2008 4,833
2010 (projected)†† 4,615
2020 (projected)†† 4,604

Race & Hispanic Origin, 2000

Race
White 4,573
Black/African American 16
American Indian/Alaska Native 12
Asian 10
Hawaiian Native/Pacific Islander 0
Other Race 17
Two or more races 55
Hispanic origin 51

Age & Nativity, 2000

Under 5 years 260
18 years and over 3,407
21 years and over 3,268
65 years and over 605
85 years and over 58
Median Age 36.9
Native-born 4,598
Foreign-born 85

Age, 2020 (projected)††

Under 5 years 245
5 to 19 years 766
20 to 39 years 1,167
40 to 64 years 1,565
65 years and over 861

Educational Attainment, 2000

Population 25 years and over 3,100
High School graduates or higher .. 80.4%
Bachelor's degree or higher 17.6%
Graduate degree 5.8%

Income & Poverty, 1999

Per capita income, ... $20,205
Median household income $44,286
Median family income $51,750
Persons in poverty 250
H'holds receiving public assistance 48
H'holds receiving social security 540

Households, 2000

Total households 1,811
With persons under 18 652
With persons over 65 459
Family households 1,236
Single person households 467
Persons per household 2.6
Persons per family 3.1

Labor & Employment, 2000

Civilian labor force 2,440
Unemployment rate 4.6%
Civilian labor force, 2008† 2,481
Unemployment rate† 6.5%
Civilian labor force, 12/09† 2,569
Unemployment rate† 10.3%
Employed persons 16 years and over, by occupation:
Managers & professionals 783
Service occupations 316
Sales & office occupations 512
Farming, fishing & forestry 5
Construction & maintenance 280
Production & transportation 432
Self-employed persons 184

Most demographic data is from the 2000 Decennial Census
† Massachusetts Department of Revenue
†† University of Massachusetts, MISER

General Information

Town of North Brookfield
215 North Main Street
North Brookfield, MA 01535
508-867-0200

Elevation .... 915 ft.
Land area (square miles) 21.1
Water area (square miles) 0.7
Population density, 2008 (est) 229.1
Year incorporated 1812
Website .... www.northbrookfield.net

Voters & Government Information

Government type .... Open Town Meeting
Number of Selectmen 3
US Congressional District(s) 2

Registered Voters, October 2008

Total 3,262
Democrats 749
Republicans 477
Unaffiliated/other 2,000

Local Officials, 2010

Chair, Bd. of Sel. .... Jason M. Petraitis
Manager/Admin .... NA
Town Clerk .... Sheila A. Buzzell
Finance Director .... Anne B. Jannette
Tax Collector .... Donna M. Gauthier
Tax Assessor .... Sheila A. Buzzell
Attorney .... Kopelman & Paige
Public Works .... Gary Jean
Building .... John Couture
Comm Dev/Planning .... Stephen Cummings
Police Chief .... Aram Thomasian Jr
Emerg/Fire Chief .... James F. Black

Housing & Construction

New Privately Owned Housing Units Authorized by Building Permit

	Single Family	Total Bldgs	Total Units
2006	23	23	23
2007	19	19	19
2008	0	0	0

Parcel Count by Property Class, 2010

Total 2,202
Single family 1,293
Multiple units 151
Apartments 41
Condos 40
Vacant land 447
Open space 0
Commercial 34
Industrial 21
Misc. residential 14
Other use 161

Public Library

Haston Free Public Library
161 Main St.
North Brookfield, MA 01535
(508)867-0208

Director .... Ann L. Kidd

Library Statistics, FY 2008

Population served, 2007 4,819
Registered users 2,510
Circulation 28,962
Reference transactons 0
Total program attendance 0

per capita:

Holdings 5.17
Operating income $22.16

Internet Access

Internet computers available 7
Weekly users 27

Municipal Finance

Debt at year end 2008 .... $11,835,071
Moody's rating, July 2009 .... NA

Revenues, 2008

Total $11,053,502
From all taxes 4,942,989
Federal aid 0
State aid 5,462,726
From other governments 8,270
Charges for services 208,708
Licenses, permits & fees 43,620
Fines & forfeits 0
Interfund transfers 216,583
Misc/other/special assessments 85,303

Expenditures, 2008

Total $11,116,435
General government 408,501
Public safety 563,675
Other/fixed costs 2,095,843
Human services 101,907
Culture & recreation 106,590
Debt Service 699,977
Education 5,878,214
Public works 636,552
Intergovernmental 624,726

Taxation, 2010

Property type	Valuation	Rate
Total	$393,045,412	-
Residential	361,525,200	12.56
Open space	0	0.00
Commercial	13,735,223	12.56
Industrial	9,832,251	12.56
Personal	7,952,738	12.56

Average Single Family Tax Bill, 2010

Avg. assessed home value $211,013
Avg. single fam. tax bill $2,650
Hi-Lo ranking 272/301

Police & Crime, 2008

Number of police officers 6
Violent crimes .... NA
Property crimes 38

Local School District

(school data 2007-08, except as noted)

North Brookfield
10 New School Drive
North Brookfield, MA 01535
508-867-9821

Superintendent .... Erin Nosek
Grade plan K-12
Total enrollment '09-10 627
Grade 12 enrollment, '09-10 39
Graduation rate 89.8%
Dropout rate 6.8%
Per-pupil expenditure $10,911
Avg teacher salary $58,774
Student/teacher ratio '08-09 .... 12.0 to 1
Highly-qualified teachers, '08-09 .... 94.6%
Teachers licensed in assigned subject .. 98.2%
Students per computer 1.8

Massachusetts Competency Assessment System (MCAS), 2009 results

	English		Math	
	% Prof	CPI	% Prof	CPI
Gr 4	39%	73	37%	73.5
Gr 6	72%	88.4	61%	80.1
Gr 8	88%	95.8	37%	70.3
Gr 10	80%	93.4	75%	88.2

Other School Districts (see Appendix D for data)

Southern Worchester County Vocational Tech

©2010 Information Publications, Inc. All rights reserved. Photocopying prohibited. For additional copies, contact the publisher at www.informationpublications.com or (877)544-INFO (4636)

See Introduction for an explanation of all data sources.

Demographics & Socio-Economic Characteristics

Population

1990	12,002
2000	13,837
Male	6,818
Female	7,019
2008	17,272
2010 (projected)††	14,112
2020 (projected)††	14,013

Race & Hispanic Origin, 2000

Race	
White	13,495
Black/African American	55
American Indian/Alaska Native	6
Asian	180
Hawaiian Native/Pacific Islander	1
Other Race	33
Two or more races	67
Hispanic origin	102

Age & Nativity, 2000

Under 5 years	1,068
18 years and over	10,026
21 years and over	9,669
65 years and over	1,444
85 years and over	137
Median Age	37.8
Native-born	13,055
Foreign-born	782

Age, 2020 (projected)††

Under 5 years	835
5 to 19 years	2,524
20 to 39 years	3,338
40 to 64 years	4,891
65 years and over	2,425

Educational Attainment, 2000

Population 25 years and over	9,282
High School graduates or higher	92.2%
Bachelor's degree or higher	41.0%
Graduate degree	13.3%

Income & Poverty, 1999

Per capita income,	$30,902
Median household income	$76,962
Median family income	$86,341
Persons in poverty	204
H'holds receiving public assistance	22
H'holds receiving social security	1,073

Households, 2000

Total households	4,795
With persons under 18	2,017
With persons over 65	964
Family households	3,755
Single person households	858
Persons per household	2.9
Persons per family	3.3

Labor & Employment, 2000

Civilian labor force	7,535
Unemployment rate	0.9%
Civilian labor force, 2008†	7,994
Unemployment rate†	5.9%
Civilian labor force, 12/09†	7,983
Unemployment rate†	8.0%
Employed persons 16 years and over, by occupation:	
Managers & professionals	3,624
Service occupations	718
Sales & office occupations	1,832
Farming, fishing & forestry	17
Construction & maintenance	638
Production & transportation	640
Self-employed persons	512

Most demographic data is from the 2000 Decennial Census
† Massachusetts Department of Revenue
†† University of Massachusetts, MISER

General Information

Town of North Reading
235 North St
North Reading, MA 01864
978-664-6000

Elevation	100 ft.
Land area (square miles)	13.3
Water area (square miles)	0.3
Population density, 2008 (est)	1,298.6
Year incorporated	1853
Website	www.northreadingma.gov

Voters & Government Information

Government type	Open Town Meeting
Number of Selectmen	5
US Congressional District(s)	6

Registered Voters, October 2008

Total	10,282
Democrats	2,804
Republicans	1,687
Unaffiliated/other	5,738

Local Officials, 2010

Chair, Bd. of Sel.	Robert J. Mauceri
Manager/Admin	Greg L. Balukonis
Town Clerk	Barbara Stats
Finance Director	Joseph Tassone
Tax Collector	Maryann MacKay
Tax Assessor	Faye Ingraham
Attorney	Kopelman & Paige
Public Works	Richard Carnavale
Building	James DeCola
Comm Dev/Planning	Heidi Griffin
Police Chief	Edward Nolan
Fire Chief	Richard Harris

Housing & Construction

New Privately Owned Housing Units Authorized by Building Permit

	Single Family	Total Bldgs	Total Units
2006	31	31	31
2007	31	64	1249
2008	18	18	18

Parcel Count by Property Class, 2010

Total	5,616
Single family	4,190
Multiple units	45
Apartments	4
Condos	741
Vacant land	274
Open space	0
Commercial	221
Industrial	85
Misc. residential	25
Other use	31

Public Library

Flint Memorial Library
147 Park St.
North Reading, MA 01864
(978)664-4942

Director	Helena Minton

Library Statistics, FY 2008

Population served, 2007	14,021
Registered users	11,536
Circulation	105,802
Reference transactons	5,889
Total program attendance	42,120
per capita:	
Holdings	5.58
Operating income	$31.28
Internet Access	
Internet computers available	11
Weekly users	220

Municipal Finance

Debt at year end 2008	$37,015,689
Moody's rating, July 2009	A1

Revenues, 2008

Total	$47,930,179
From all taxes	33,351,365
Federal aid	0
State aid	8,527,917
From other governments	0
Charges for services	803,474
Licenses, permits & fees	648,504
Fines & forfeits	15,423
Interfund transfers	427,526
Misc/other/special assessments	2,077,985

Expenditures, 2008

Total	$43,977,642
General government	1,575,290
Public safety	5,583,247
Other/fixed costs	6,261,856
Human services	459,566
Culture & recreation	618,709
Debt Service	4,263,125
Education	21,022,970
Public works	3,519,998
Intergovernmental	313,062

Taxation, 2010

Property type	Valuation	Rate
Total	$2,504,171,881	-
Residential	2,165,114,653	13.47
Open space	0	0.00
Commercial	172,127,878	13.47
Industrial	110,943,700	13.47
Personal	55,985,650	13.47

Average Single Family Tax Bill, 2010

Avg. assessed home value	$446,021
Avg. single fam. tax bill	$6,008
Hi-Lo ranking	46/301

Police & Crime, 2008

Number of police officers	29
Violent crimes	11
Property crimes	122

Local School District

(school data 2007-08, except as noted)

North Reading
19 Sherman Road
North Reading, MA 01864
978-664-7810

Superintendent	Keith Manville
Grade plan	PK-12
Total enrollment '09-10	2,735
Grade 12 enrollment, '09-10	192
Graduation rate	92.8%
Dropout rate	5.0%
Per-pupil expenditure	$9,908
Avg teacher salary	$61,324
Student/teacher ratio '08-09	14.5 to 1
Highly-qualified teachers, '08-09	96.6%
Teachers licensed in assigned subject	96.3%
Students per computer	3.5

Massachusetts Competency Assessment System (MCAS), 2009 results

	English		Math	
	% Prof	CPI	% Prof	CPI
Gr 4	71%	90.4	65%	88.5
Gr 6	78%	92.5	73%	88.3
Gr 8	95%	98.2	70%	88.1
Gr 10	89%	96.4	88%	94.1

Other School Districts (see Appendix D for data)
Northeast Metro Vocational Tech

©2010 Information Publications, Inc. All rights reserved. Photocopying prohibited. For additional copies, contact the publisher at www.informationpublications.com or (877)544-INFO (4636)

See Introduction for an explanation of all data sources.

©2010 Information Publications, Inc. All rights reserved. Photocopying prohibited. For additional copies, contact the publisher at www.informationpublications.com or (877)544-INFO (4636)

Demographics & Socio-Economic Characteristics*

Population

1990	29,289
2000	28,978
Male	12,480
Female	16,498
2008	28,379
2010 (projected)††	29,118
2020 (projected)††	29,136

Race & Hispanic Origin, 2000

Race	
White	26,083
Black/African American	602
American Indian/Alaska Native	86
Asian	906
Hawaiian Native/Pacific Islander	15
Other Race	697
Two or more races	589
Hispanic origin	1,518

Age & Nativity, 2000

Under 5 years	1,189
18 years and over	24,061
21 years and over	21,810
65 years and over	3,993
85 years and over	682
Median Age	37.3
Native-born	27,108
Foreign-born	1,870

Age, 2020 (projected)††

Under 5 years	1,212
5 to 19 years	4,821
20 to 39 years	8,140
40 to 64 years	9,170
65 years and over	5,793

Educational Attainment, 2000

Population 25 years and over	19,714
High School graduates or higher	88.7%
Bachelor's degree or higher	46.1%
Graduate degree	25.0%

Income & Poverty, 1999

Per capita income,	$24,022
Median household income	$41,808
Median family income	$56,844
Persons in poverty	2,508
H'holds receiving public assistance	245
H'holds receiving social security	2,821

Households, 2000

Total households	11,880
With persons under 18	2,884
With persons over 65	2,570
Family households	5,878
Single person households	4,431
Persons per household	2.1
Persons per family	2.9

Labor & Employment, 2000

Civilian labor force	16,989
Unemployment rate	4.1%
Civilian labor force, 2008†	16,581
Unemployment rate†	4.5%
Civilian labor force, 12/09†	16,491
Unemployment rate†	5.9%
Employed persons 16 years and over, by occupation:	
Managers & professionals	8,170
Service occupations	2,411
Sales & office occupations	3,521
Farming, fishing & forestry	25
Construction & maintenance	841
Production & transportation	1,323
Self-employed persons	1,430

Most demographic data is from the 2000 Decennial Census
* see Appendix E for American Community Survey data
† Massachusetts Department of Revenue
†† University of Massachusetts, MISER

General Information

City of Northampton
210 Main St
Northampton, MA 01060
413-586-6950

Elevation	130 ft.
Land area (square miles)	34.5
Water area (square miles)	1.1
Population density, 2008 (est)	822.6
Year incorporated	1883
Website	www.northamptonma.gov

Voters & Government Information

Government type	Mayor-Council
Number of Councilpersons	9
US Congressional District(s)	2

Registered Voters, October 2008

Total	20,338
Democrats	10,066
Republicans	994
Unaffiliated/other	8,998

Local Officials, 2010

Mayor	Mary Clare Higgins
Manager/Admin	NA
City Clerk	Wendy Mazza
Finance Director	Chris Pile
Tax Collector	Melissa Lampron
Tax Assessor	Joan Sarafin
Attorney	Elaine Reall
Public Works	Ned Huntley
Building	Louis Hasbrouck (Actg)
Comm Dev/Planning	Wayne Feiden
Police Chief	Russell Sienkiewicz
Fire Chief	Brian Duggan

Housing & Construction

New Privately Owned Housing Units Authorized by Building Permit

	Single Family	Total Bldgs	Total Units
2006	22	25	35
2007	22	29	45
2008	19	25	59

Parcel Count by Property Class, 2010

Total	10,598
Single family	5,531
Multiple units	1,066
Apartments	216
Condos	1,415
Vacant land	1,009
Open space	0
Commercial	761
Industrial	159
Misc. residential	63
Other use	378

Public Library

Forbes Library
20 West Street
Northampton, MA 01060
(413)587-1011

Director	Janet Moulding

Library Statistics, FY 2008

Population served, 2007	25,570
Registered users	18,535
Circulation	344,844
Reference transactons	37,559
Total program attendance	163,391
per capita:	
Holdings	7.79
Operating income	$51.75
Internet Access	
Internet computers available	28
Weekly users	873

Municipal Finance

Debt at year end 2008	$53,450,555
Moody's rating, July 2009	A1

Revenues, 2008

Total	$70,610,999
From all taxes	38,148,825
Federal aid	484,232
State aid	17,474,321
From other governments	25,848
Charges for services	6,127,102
Licenses, permits & fees	852,538
Fines & forfeits	975,781
Interfund transfers	5,134,540
Misc/other/special assessments	693,906

Expenditures, 2008

Total	$69,667,920
General government	3,768,075
Public safety	9,557,572
Other/fixed costs	14,093,416
Human services	708,416
Culture & recreation	1,525,101
Debt Service	5,854,618
Education	28,407,876
Public works	3,545,556
Intergovernmental	2,207,290

Taxation, 2010

Property type	Valuation	Rate
Total	$3,193,555,130	-
Residential	2,570,772,410	12.64
Open space	0	0.00
Commercial	451,555,850	12.64
Industrial	84,013,220	12.64
Personal	87,213,650	12.64

Average Single Family Tax Bill, 2010

Avg. assessed home value	$302,155
Avg. single fam. tax bill	$3,819
Hi-Lo ranking	148/301

Police & Crime, 2008

Number of police officers	58
Violent crimes	97
Property crimes	813

Local School District

(school data 2007-08, except as noted)

Northampton
212 Main Street
Northampton, MA 01060
413-587-1327

Superintendent	Isabelina Rodriguez
Grade plan	PK-12
Total enrollment '09-10	2,692
Grade 12 enrollment, '09-10	212
Graduation rate	91.8%
Dropout rate	2.6%
Per-pupil expenditure	$11,614
Avg teacher salary	$54,002
Student/teacher ratio '08-09	12.7 to 1
Highly-qualified teachers, '08-09	99.3%
Teachers licensed in assigned subject	99.5%
Students per computer	4.2

Massachusetts Competency Assessment System (MCAS), 2009 results

	English		Math	
	% Prof	CPI	% Prof	CPI
Gr 4	48%	76.8	30%	68.5
Gr 6	75%	90	52%	74.6
Gr 8	81%	91.6	44%	67.6
Gr 10	89%	95.5	79%	91.1

Other School Districts (see Appendix D for data)
Northampton-Smith Independent Vocational

See Introduction for an explanation of all data sources.

Demographics & Socio-Economic Characteristics

Population

1990	11,929
2000	14,013
Male	6,893
Female	7,120
2008	14,646
2010 (projected)††	14,680
2020 (projected)††	14,978

Race & Hispanic Origin, 2000

Race	
White	13,033
Black/African American	91
American Indian/Alaska Native	11
Asian	708
Hawaiian Native/Pacific Islander	10
Other Race	51
Two or more races	109
Hispanic origin	179

Age & Nativity, 2000

Under 5 years	1,028
18 years and over	9,881
21 years and over	9,593
65 years and over	1,370
85 years and over	137
Median Age	37.4
Native-born	13,026
Foreign-born	987

Age, 2020 (projected)††

Under 5 years	902
5 to 19 years	2,799
20 to 39 years	3,515
40 to 64 years	5,043
65 years and over	2,719

Educational Attainment, 2000

Population 25 years and over	9,221
High School graduates or higher	93.4%
Bachelor's degree or higher	51.0%
Graduate degree	20.2%

Income & Poverty, 1999

Per capita income,	$32,889
Median household income	$79,781
Median family income	$90,480
Persons in poverty	386
H'holds receiving public assistance	63
H'holds receiving social security	1,034

Households, 2000

Total households	4,906
With persons under 18	2,217
With persons over 65	915
Family households	3,866
Single person households	841
Persons per household	2.8
Persons per family	3.2

Labor & Employment, 2000

Civilian labor force	7,657
Unemployment rate	1.8%
Civilian labor force, 2008†	8,020
Unemployment rate†	5.1%
Civilian labor force, 12/09†	8,184
Unemployment rate†	7.9%
Employed persons 16 years and over, by occupation:	
Managers & professionals	4,169
Service occupations	737
Sales & office occupations	1,821
Farming, fishing & forestry	20
Construction & maintenance	334
Production & transportation	436
Self-employed persons	537

Most demographic data is from the 2000 Decennial Census
† Massachusetts Department of Revenue
†† University of Massachusetts, MISER

General Information

Town of Northborough
63 Main St
Northborough, MA 01532
508-393-5001

Elevation	300 ft.
Land area (square miles)	18.5
Water area (square miles)	0.2
Population density, 2008 (est)	791.7
Year incorporated	1776
Website	www.town.northborough.ma.us

Voters & Government Information

Government type	Open Town Meeting
Number of Selectmen	5
US Congressional District(s)	3

Registered Voters, October 2008

Total	9,789
Democrats	2,268
Republicans	1,582
Unaffiliated/other	5,898

Local Officials, 2010

Chair, Bd. of Sel.	Frances Bakstran
Manager/Admin	John W. Coderre
Clerk	Andrew T. Dowd
Finance Director	Jason Little
Tax Collector	June Hubbard-Ward
Tax Assessor	Diane O'Connor
Attorney	Kopelman & Paige
Public Works	Kara Buzanoski
Building	William Farnsworth
Planning	Kathy Joubert
Police Chief	Mark Leahy
Emerg/Fire Chief	David Durgin

Housing & Construction

New Privately Owned Housing Units Authorized by Building Permit

	Single Family	Total Bldgs	Total Units
2006	40	41	43
2007	43	43	43
2008	17	18	49

Parcel Count by Property Class, 2010

Total	NA
Single family	NA
Multiple units	NA
Apartments	NA
Condos	NA
Vacant land	NA
Open space	NA
Commercial	NA
Industrial	NA
Misc. residential	NA
Other use	NA

Public Library

Northborough Free Library
34 Main St.
Northborough, MA 01532
(508)393-5025

Director .... Jean M. Langley

Library Statistics, FY 2008

Population served, 2007	14,611
Registered users	10,137
Circulation	138,379
Reference transactons	6,712
Total program attendance	26,935
per capita:	
Holdings	5.98
Operating income	$50.61
Internet Access	
Internet computers available	4
Weekly users	62

Municipal Finance

Debt at year end 2008	$15,034,295
Moody's rating, July 2009	Aa3

Revenues, 2008

Total	$43,133,905
From all taxes	35,035,918
Federal aid	0
State aid	5,361,927
From other governments	0
Charges for services	623,817
Licenses, permits & fees	607,295
Fines & forfeits	0
Interfund transfers	0
Misc/other/special assessments	752,474

Expenditures, 2008

Total	$42,025,656
General government	1,834,675
Public safety	3,372,243
Other/fixed costs	5,138,542
Human services	445,301
Culture & recreation	867,505
Debt Service	1,405,402
Education	26,582,659
Public works	2,148,661
Intergovernmental	230,668

Taxation, 2010

Property type	Valuation	Rate
Total	NA	-
Residential	NA	NA
Open space	NA	NA
Commercial	NA	NA
Industrial	NA	NA
Personal	NA	NA

Average Single Family Tax Bill, 2010

Avg. assessed home value	NA
Avg. single fam. tax bill	NA
Hi-Lo ranking	NA

Police & Crime, 2008

Number of police officers	20
Violent crimes	8
Property crimes	101

Local School District

(school data 2007-08, except as noted)

Northborough
53 Parkerville Road
Southborough, MA 01772
508-486-5115

Superintendent	Charles Gobron
Grade plan	PK-8
Total enrollment '09-10	1,883
Grade 12 enrollment, '09-10	0
Graduation rate	NA
Dropout rate	NA
Per-pupil expenditure	$11,266
Avg teacher salary	$70,190
Student/teacher ratio '08-09	13.9 to 1
Highly-qualified teachers, '08-09	100.0%
Teachers licensed in assigned subject	100.0%
Students per computer	3.2

Massachusetts Competency Assessment System (MCAS), 2009 results

	English		Math	
	% Prof	CPI	% Prof	CPI
Gr 4	69%	87.7	63%	87.4
Gr 6	87%	94.9	68%	85.9
Gr 8	94%	97.3	70%	84.7
Gr 10	NA	NA	NA	NA

Other School Districts (see Appendix D for data)

Northboro-Southboro Regional, Assabet Valley Vocational Tech

©2010 Information Publications, Inc. All rights reserved. Photocopying prohibited. For additional copies, contact the publisher at www.informationpublications.com or (877)544-INFO (4636)

Demographics & Socio-Economic Characteristics

Population

1990	13,371
2000	13,182
Male	6,274
Female	6,908
2008	14,383
2010 (projected)††	13,258
2020 (projected)††	13,467

Race & Hispanic Origin, 2000

Race	
White	12,688
Black/African American	79
American Indian/Alaska Native	22
Asian	42
Hawaiian Native/Pacific Islander	4
Other Race	131
Two or more races	216
Hispanic origin	241

Age & Nativity, 2000

Under 5 years	975
18 years and over	9,558
21 years and over	9,199
65 years and over	1,821
85 years and over	359
Median Age	36.5
Native-born	12,808
Foreign-born	394

Age, 2020 (projected)††

Under 5 years	922
5 to 19 years	2,623
20 to 39 years	3,355
40 to 64 years	4,171
65 years and over	2,396

Educational Attainment, 2000

Population 25 years and over	8,821
High School graduates or higher	84.6%
Bachelor's degree or higher	23.7%
Graduate degree	6.9%

Income & Poverty, 1999

Per capita income,	$22,515
Median household income	$50,457
Median family income	$62,095
Persons in poverty	676
H'holds receiving public assistance	117
H'holds receiving social security	1,312

Households, 2000

Total households	4,800
With persons under 18	1,889
With persons over 65	1,090
Family households	3,501
Single person households	1,080
Persons per household	2.7
Persons per family	3.2

Labor & Employment, 2000

Civilian labor force	6,675
Unemployment rate	2.9%
Civilian labor force, 2008†	7,432
Unemployment rate†	7.8%
Civilian labor force, 12/09†	7,591
Unemployment rate†	10.4%
Employed persons 16 years and over, by occupation:	
Managers & professionals	2,187
Service occupations	921
Sales & office occupations	1,657
Farming, fishing & forestry	5
Construction & maintenance	677
Production & transportation	1,034
Self-employed persons	465

Most demographic data is from the 2000 Decennial Census
† Massachusetts Department of Revenue
†† University of Massachusetts, MISER

General Information

Town of Northbridge
7 Main St
Whitinsville, MA 01588
508-234-2095

Elevation	300 ft.
Land area (square miles)	17.2
Water area (square miles)	0.9
Population density, 2008 (est)	836.2
Year incorporated	1775
Website	www.northbridgemass.org

Voters & Government Information

Government type	Open Town Meeting
Number of Selectmen	5
US Congressional District(s)	2

Registered Voters, October 2008

Total	10,651
Democrats	2,448
Republicans	1,844
Unaffiliated/other	6,280

Local Officials, 2010

Chair, Bd. of Sel.	Joseph Montecalvo
Town Manager	Theodore Kozak
Town Clerk	Doreen A. Cedrone
Town Accountant	Neil Vaidya
Tax Collector	Kimberly Yarseau
Tax Assessor	Robert Fitzgerald
Attorney	Kopelman & Paige
Public Works	Richard Sasseville
Building	James Sheehan
Comm Dev/Planning	Gary Bechtholdt
Police Chief	Walter Warchol
Emerg/Fire Chief	Gary Nestor

Housing & Construction

New Privately Owned Housing Units Authorized by Building Permit

	Single Family	Total Bldgs	Total Units
2006	54	54	54
2007	37	37	37
2008	22	22	22

Parcel Count by Property Class, 2010

Total	5,567
Single family	3,326
Multiple units	448
Apartments	146
Condos	741
Vacant land	633
Open space	0
Commercial	164
Industrial	41
Misc. residential	25
Other use	43

Public Library

Whitinsville Social Library
17 Church St
Whitinsville, MA 01588
(508)234-2151 x4

Director .... Marcia Nichols (Actg)

Library Statistics, FY 2008

Population served, 2007	
Registered users	
Circulation	
Reference transactons	
Total program attendance	
per capita:	
Holdings	
Operating income	
Internet Access	
Internet computers available	
Weekly users	

Municipal Finance

Debt at year end 2008	$30,477,504
Moody's rating, July 2009	A2

Revenues, 2008

Total	$37,686,548
From all taxes	16,518,031
Federal aid	0
State aid	18,826,837
From other governments	26,059
Charges for services	363,788
Licenses, permits & fees	240,063
Fines & forfeits	0
Interfund transfers	622,748
Misc/other/special assessments	544,511

Expenditures, 2008

Total	$35,513,058
General government	1,281,593
Public safety	3,275,874
Other/fixed costs	5,916,730
Human services	225,997
Culture & recreation	1,668
Debt Service	2,815,040
Education	20,578,487
Public works	1,253,508
Intergovernmental	162,479

Taxation, 2010

Property type	Valuation	Rate
Total	$1,535,937,499	-
Residential	1,321,733,360	10.40
Open space	0	0.00
Commercial	126,612,830	10.40
Industrial	40,346,700	10.40
Personal	47,244,609	10.40

Average Single Family Tax Bill, 2010

Avg. assessed home value	$288,555
Avg. single fam. tax bill	$3,001
Hi-Lo ranking	235/301

Police & Crime, 2008

Number of police officers	18
Violent crimes	33
Property crimes	237

Local School District

(school data 2007-08, except as noted)

Northbridge
87 Linwood Avenue
Whitinsville, MA 01588
508-234-8156

Superintendent	Susan Gorky
Grade plan	PK-12
Total enrollment '09-10	2,539
Grade 12 enrollment, '09-10	172
Graduation rate	77.9%
Dropout rate	10.8%
Per-pupil expenditure	$9,935
Avg teacher salary	$70,056
Student/teacher ratio '08-09	16.0 to 1
Highly-qualified teachers, '08-09	100.0%
Teachers licensed in assigned subject	100.0%
Students per computer	7.7

Massachusetts Competency Assessment System (MCAS), 2009 results

	English		Math	
	% Prof	CPI	% Prof	CPI
Gr 4	53%	79.1	46%	78.3
Gr 6	72%	87	60%	81.3
Gr 8	87%	95.1	52%	75.4
Gr 10	70%	87.4	60%	81.3

Other School Districts (see Appendix D for data)
Blackstone Valley Vocational Tech

See Introduction for an explanation of all data sources.

©2010 Information Publications, Inc. All rights reserved. Photocopying prohibited. For additional copies, contact the publisher at www.informationpublications.com or (877)544-INFO (4636)

Demographics & Socio-Economic Characteristics

Population

1990 ... 2,838
2000 ... 2,951
  Male ... 1,416
  Female ... 1,535
2008 ... 3,026
2010 (projected)†† ... 3,032
2020 (projected)†† ... 3,196

Race & Hispanic Origin, 2000

Race
  White ... 2,907
  Black/African American ... 3
  American Indian/Alaska Native ... 6
  Asian ... 6
  Hawaiian Native/Pacific Islander ... 0
  Other Race ... 1
  Two or more races ... 28
Hispanic origin ... 17

Age & Nativity, 2000

Under 5 years ... 166
18 years and over ... 2,175
21 years and over ... 2,071
65 years and over ... 397
85 years and over ... 47
  Median Age ... 40.0
Native-born ... 2,812
Foreign-born ... 139

Age, 2020 (projected)††

Under 5 years ... 186
5 to 19 years ... 601
20 to 39 years ... 749
40 to 64 years ... 1,054
65 years and over ... 606

Educational Attainment, 2000

Population 25 years and over ... 1,992
  High School graduates or higher .. 93.3%
  Bachelor's degree or higher ... 30.8%
  Graduate degree ... 15.0%

Income & Poverty, 1999

Per capita income, ... $21,517
Median household income ... $49,141
Median family income ... $56,816
Persons in poverty ... 148
H'holds receiving public assistance ... 29
H'holds receiving social security ... 309

Households, 2000

Total households ... 1,158
  With persons under 18 ... 419
  With persons over 65 ... 288
  Family households ... 815
  Single person households ... 292
Persons per household ... 2.5
Persons per family ... 3.0

Labor & Employment, 2000

Civilian labor force ... 1,690
  Unemployment rate ... 1.8%
Civilian labor force, 2008† ... 1,851
  Unemployment rate† ... 4.9%
Civilian labor force, 12/09† ... 1,735
  Unemployment rate† ... 8.9%
Employed persons 16 years and over, by occupation:
  Managers & professionals ... 615
  Service occupations ... 195
  Sales & office occupations ... 400
  Farming, fishing & forestry ... 34
  Construction & maintenance ... 191
  Production & transportation ... 224
  Self-employed persons ... 146

Most demographic data is from the 2000 Decennial Census
† Massachusetts Department of Revenue
†† University of Massachusetts, MISER

General Information

Town of Northfield
69 Main St
Northfield, MA 01360
413-498-2901

Elevation ... NA
Land area (square miles) ... 34.4
Water area (square miles) ... 0.9
Population density, 2008 (est) ... 88.0
Year incorporated ... NA
Website ... town.northfield.ma.us

Voters & Government Information

Government type ... Open Town Meeting
Number of Selectmen ... 3
US Congressional District(s) ... 1

Registered Voters, October 2008

Total ... 2,104
Democrats ... 505
Republicans ... 231
Unaffiliated/other ... 1,357

Local Officials, 2010

Chair, Bd. of Sel. ... Kathleen Wright
Admin Assistant ... Tracy Rogers
Town Clerk ... Gail V. Zukowski
Accountant ... Deb Mero
Tax Collector ... Barbara Brassor
Tax Assessor ... Alice Lord (Chr)
Attorney ... Joel Bard
Highway Supt ... Thomas Walker
Building ... James Hawkins
Comm Dev/Planning ... NA
Police Chief ... Leonard Crossman Jr
Emerg/Fire Chief ... Floyd M. Dunnell III

Housing & Construction

New Privately Owned Housing Units Authorized by Building Permit

	Single Family	Total Bldgs	Total Units
2006	31	31	31
2007	26	26	26
2008	19	19	19

Parcel Count by Property Class, 2010

Total ... 2,280
Single family ... 1,071
Multiple units ... 65
Apartments ... 4
Condos ... 0
Vacant land ... 580
Open space ... 0
Commercial ... 38
Industrial ... 154
Misc. residential ... 13
Other use ... 355

Public Library

Dickinson Memorial Library
115 Main Street
Northfield, MA 01360
(413)498-2455

Director ... Deb Kern

Library Statistics, FY 2008

Population served, 2007 ... 2,985
Registered users ... 2,104
Circulation ... 55,088
Reference transactons ... 525
Total program attendance ... 23,092

per capita:

Holdings ... 7.25
Operating income ... $44.36

Internet Access

Internet computers available ... 5
Weekly users ... 0

Municipal Finance

Debt at year end 2008 ... $865,034
Moody's rating, July 2009 ... NA

Revenues, 2008

Total ... $6,401,751
From all taxes ... 5,322,865
Federal aid ... 0
State aid ... 643,877
From other governments ... 20,942
Charges for services ... 277,757
Licenses, permits & fees ... 38,493
Fines & forfeits ... 3,495
Interfund transfers ... 5,800
Misc/other/special assessments ... 44,261

Expenditures, 2008

Total ... $6,422,120
General government ... 359,993
Public safety ... 376,520
Other/fixed costs ... 354,881
Human services ... 52,269
Culture & recreation ... 139,589
Debt Service ... 276,320
Education ... 4,027,947
Public works ... 802,361
Intergovernmental ... 32,240

Taxation, 2010

Property type	Valuation	Rate
Total	$394,118,313	-
Residential	291,039,327	13.91
Open space	0	0.00
Commercial	14,093,999	13.91
Industrial	72,105,977	13.91
Personal	16,879,010	13.91

Average Single Family Tax Bill, 2010

Avg. assessed home value ... $216,645
Avg. single fam. tax bill ... $3,014
Hi-Lo ranking ... 232/301

Police & Crime, 2008

Number of police officers ... 2
Violent crimes ... 11
Property crimes ... 70

Local School District

(school data 2007-08, except as noted)

Northfield (non-op)
97 F Sumner Turner Rd
Northfield, MA 01360
413-498-2911

Superintendent ... Dayle Doiron

Non-operating district.
Resident students are sent to the Other School Districts listed below.

Grade plan ... NA
Total enrollment '09-10 ... NA
Grade 12 enrollment, '09-10 ... NA
Graduation rate ... NA
Dropout rate ... NA
Per-pupil expenditure ... NA
Avg teacher salary ... NA
Student/teacher ratio '08-09 ... NA
Highly-qualified teachers, '08-09 ... NA
Teachers licensed in assigned subject ... NA
Students per computer ... NA

Other School Districts (see Appendix D for data)

Pioneer Valley Regional, Franklin County Vocational Tech

©2010 Information Publications, Inc. All rights reserved. Photocopying prohibited. For additional copies, contact the publisher at www.informationpublications.com or (877)544-INFO (4636)

See Introduction for an explanation of all data sources.

Demographics & Socio-Economic Characteristics

Population

1990	14,265
2000	18,036
Male	8,578
Female	9,458
2008	19,186
2010 (projected)††	20,676
2020 (projected)††	23,678

Race & Hispanic Origin, 2000

Race	
White	16,621
Black/African American	209
American Indian/Alaska Native	24
Asian	180
Hawaiian Native/Pacific Islander	1
Other Race	806
Two or more races	195
Hispanic origin	206

Age & Nativity, 2000

Under 5 years	1,444
18 years and over	13,175
21 years and over	11,869
65 years and over	1,399
85 years and over	201
Median Age	33.4
Native-born	17,394
Foreign-born	642

Age, 2020 (projected)††

Under 5 years	1,746
5 to 19 years	5,466
20 to 39 years	6,464
40 to 64 years	6,856
65 years and over	3,146

Educational Attainment, 2000

Population 25 years and over	10,869
High School graduates or higher	89.2%
Bachelor's degree or higher	30.8%
Graduate degree	9.4%

Income & Poverty, 1999

Per capita income,	$23,876
Median household income	$64,818
Median family income	$71,848
Persons in poverty	663
H'holds receiving public assistance	42
H'holds receiving social security	1,042

Households, 2000

Total households	5,872
With persons under 18	2,610
With persons over 65	1,001
Family households	4,472
Single person households	1,132
Persons per household	2.8
Persons per family	3.2

Labor & Employment, 2000

Civilian labor force	10,367
Unemployment rate	12.2%
Civilian labor force, 2008†	10,595
Unemployment rate†	6.5%
Civilian labor force, 12/09†	10,522
Unemployment rate†	9.7%
Employed persons 16 years and over, by occupation:	
Managers & professionals	3,620
Service occupations	1,209
Sales & office occupations	2,362
Farming, fishing & forestry	23
Construction & maintenance	807
Production & transportation	1,083
Self-employed persons	429

Most demographic data is from the 2000 Decennial Census
† Massachusetts Department of Revenue
†† University of Massachusetts, MISER

General Information

Town of Norton
70 East Main St
Norton, MA 02766
508-285-0200

Elevation	100 ft.
Land area (square miles)	28.7
Water area (square miles)	1.1
Population density, 2008 (est)	668.5
Year incorporated	1711
Website	nortonma.org

Voters & Government Information

Government type	Open Town Meeting
Number of Selectmen/Manager	5
US Congressional District(s)	4

Registered Voters, October 2008

Total	11,564
Democrats	2,687
Republicans	1,636
Unaffiliated/other	7,161

Local Officials, 2010

Chair, Bd. of Sel.	Timothy R. Giblin
Town Manager	James Purcell
Town Clerk	Janet Linehan
Accountant	James Puello
Treas/Collector	Jacqueline Boudreau
Tax Assessor	Joan DeCosta
Attorney	Kopelman & Paige
Public Works	NA
Building	Brian Butler
Comm Dev/Planning	Charles Gabriel
Police Chief	Brian Clark
Emerg/Fire Chief	Richard Gomes

Housing & Construction

New Privately Owned Housing Units Authorized by Building Permit

	Single Family	Total Bldgs	Total Units
2006	57	57	57
2007	57	57	57
2008	34	34	34

Parcel Count by Property Class, 2010

Total	6,658
Single family	4,370
Multiple units	117
Apartments	75
Condos	1,090
Vacant land	628
Open space	0
Commercial	158
Industrial	45
Misc. residential	50
Other use	125

Public Library

Norton Public Library
68 E. Main Street
Norton, MA 02766
(508)285-0265

Director	Elaine Jackson

Library Statistics, FY 2008

Population served, 2007	19,222
Registered users	13,342
Circulation	129,179
Reference transactons	9,854
Total program attendance	88,466
per capita:	
Holdings	3.14
Operating income	$28.12
Internet Access	
Internet computers available	4
Weekly users	550

Municipal Finance

Debt at year end 2008	$22,249,893
Moody's rating, July 2009	A2

Revenues, 2008

Total	$48,208,944
From all taxes	26,258,893
Federal aid	0
State aid	17,284,147
From other governments	21,085
Charges for services	912,319
Licenses, permits & fees	672,185
Fines & forfeits	43,594
Interfund transfers	1,239,051
Misc/other/special assessments	888,835

Expenditures, 2008

Total	$46,198,300
General government	1,553,201
Public safety	5,616,845
Other/fixed costs	8,223,732
Human services	468,887
Culture & recreation	518,206
Debt Service	2,427,388
Education	23,302,847
Public works	1,475,684
Intergovernmental	2,210,443

Taxation, 2010

Property type	Valuation	Rate
Total	$2,207,532,780	-
Residential	1,855,653,803	11.58
Open space	0	0.00
Commercial	157,807,957	11.58
Industrial	123,533,350	11.58
Personal	70,537,670	11.58

Average Single Family Tax Bill, 2010

Avg. assessed home value	$320,469
Avg. single fam. tax bill	$3,711
Hi-Lo ranking	158/301

Police & Crime, 2008

Number of police officers	26
Violent crimes	12
Property crimes	104

Local School District

(school data 2007-08, except as noted)

Norton
64 West Main Street
Norton, MA 02766
508-285-0100

Superintendent	Patricia Ansay
Grade plan	PK-12
Total enrollment '09-10	2,829
Grade 12 enrollment, '09-10	174
Graduation rate	85.9%
Dropout rate	10.6%
Per-pupil expenditure	$10,781
Avg teacher salary	$61,899
Student/teacher ratio '08-09	15.4 to 1
Highly-qualified teachers, '08-09	96.6%
Teachers licensed in assigned subject	96.7%
Students per computer	4.2

Massachusetts Competency Assessment System (MCAS), 2009 results

	English		Math	
	% Prof	CPI	% Prof	CPI
Gr 4	66%	88.4	63%	88.5
Gr 6	73%	91	59%	82.5
Gr 8	79%	94	46%	75.7
Gr 10	90%	95.9	82%	92

Other School Districts (see Appendix D for data)
Southeastern Vocational Tech, Bristol County Agricultural

See Introduction for an explanation of all data sources.

©2010 Information Publications, Inc. All rights reserved. Photocopying prohibited. For additional copies, contact the publisher at www.informationpublications.com or (877)544-INFO (4636)

Demographics & Socio-Economic Characteristics

Population

1990	9,279
2000	9,765
Male	4,770
Female	4,995
2008	10,293
2010 (projected)††	9,503
2020 (projected)††	8,685

Race & Hispanic Origin, 2000

Race	
White	9,529
Black/African American	36
American Indian/Alaska Native	5
Asian	113
Hawaiian Native/Pacific Islander	0
Other Race	16
Two or more races	66
Hispanic origin	62

Age & Nativity, 2000

Under 5 years	705
18 years and over	6,973
21 years and over	6,756
65 years and over	1,227
85 years and over	228
Median Age	40.1
Native-born	9,433
Foreign-born	332

Age, 2020 (projected)††

Under 5 years	448
5 to 19 years	1,657
20 to 39 years	1,677
40 to 64 years	2,867
65 years and over	2,036

Educational Attainment, 2000

Population 25 years and over	6,564
High School graduates or higher	96.3%
Bachelor's degree or higher	51.9%
Graduate degree	20.2%

Income & Poverty, 1999

Per capita income,	$37,222
Median household income	$87,397
Median family income	$96,771
Persons in poverty	179
H'holds receiving public assistance	25
H'holds receiving social security	801

Households, 2000

Total households	3,250
With persons under 18	1,424
With persons over 65	752
Family households	2,709
Single person households	462
Persons per household	2.9
Persons per family	3.3

Labor & Employment, 2000

Civilian labor force	4,961
Unemployment rate	1.9%
Civilian labor force, 2008†	5,440
Unemployment rate†	5.1%
Civilian labor force, 12/09†	5,346
Unemployment rate†	7.1%
Employed persons 16 years and over, by occupation:	
Managers & professionals	2,548
Service occupations	324
Sales & office occupations	1,426
Farming, fishing & forestry	7
Construction & maintenance	331
Production & transportation	233
Self-employed persons	451

Most demographic data is from the 2000 Decennial Census
† Massachusetts Department of Revenue
†† University of Massachusetts, MISER

General Information

Town of Norwell
PO Box 295
Norwell, MA 02061
781-659-8000

Elevation	81 ft.
Land area (square miles)	20.9
Water area (square miles)	0.3
Population density, 2008 (est)	492.5
Year incorporated	1888
Website	www.townofnorwell.net

Voters & Government Information

Government type	Open Town Meeting
Number of Selectmen	3
US Congressional District(s)	10

Registered Voters, October 2008

Total	7,656
Democrats	1,829
Republicans	1,543
Unaffiliated/other	4,263

Local Officials, 2010

Chair, Bd. of Sel.	Richard A. Merritt
Manager/Admin	James Boudreau
Town Clerk	Patricia M. Anderson
Finance Director	James Boudreau
Tax Collector	Angela Parks
Tax Assessor	Edward Dunford
Attorney	Robert E. Galvin
Public Works	Paul M. Foulsham
Building	Timothy J. Fitzgerald
Comm Dev/Planning	Todd Thomas
Police Chief	Theodore Ross
Emerg/Fire Chief	T. Andrew Reardon

Housing & Construction

New Privately Owned Housing Units Authorized by Building Permit

	Single Family	Total Bldgs	Total Units
2006	22	22	22
2007	17	17	17
2008	10	10	10

Parcel Count by Property Class, 2010

Total	4,234
Single family	3,280
Multiple units	7
Apartments	1
Condos	136
Vacant land	431
Open space	0
Commercial	260
Industrial	32
Misc. residential	20
Other use	67

Public Library

Norwell Public Library
64 South St.
Norwell, MA 02061
(781)659-2015

Director	Rebecca Freer

Library Statistics, FY 2008

Population served, 2007	10,271
Registered users	5,739
Circulation	164,619
Reference transactons	5,084
Total program attendance	67,400
per capita:	
Holdings	6.32
Operating income	$57.45
Internet Access	
Internet computers available	11
Weekly users	0

Municipal Finance

Debt at year end 2008	$28,394,292
Moody's rating, July 2009	NA

Revenues, 2008

Total	$38,107,031
From all taxes	29,485,345
Federal aid	18,383
State aid	4,616,392
From other governments	53,468
Charges for services	840,473
Licenses, permits & fees	390,472
Fines & forfeits	14,014
Interfund transfers	1,156,348
Misc/other/special assessments	766,068

Expenditures, 2008

Total	$36,265,325
General government	1,569,351
Public safety	4,117,581
Other/fixed costs	5,257,998
Human services	380,988
Culture & recreation	703,403
Debt Service	3,410,089
Education	17,786,023
Public works	1,960,044
Intergovernmental	1,075,848

Taxation, 2010

Property type	Valuation	Rate
Total	$2,370,357,847	-
Residential	2,004,523,008	12.75
Open space	0	0.00
Commercial	274,162,179	12.75
Industrial	58,114,100	12.75
Personal	33,558,560	12.75

Average Single Family Tax Bill, 2010

Avg. assessed home value	$569,881
Avg. single fam. tax bill	$7,266
Hi-Lo ranking	30/301

Police & Crime, 2008

Number of police officers	23
Violent crimes	10
Property crimes	107

Local School District

(school data 2007-08, except as noted)

Norwell
322 Main Street
Norwell, MA 02061
781-659-8800

Superintendent	Donald Beaudette
Grade plan	PK-12
Total enrollment '09-10	2,345
Grade 12 enrollment, '09-10	171
Graduation rate	96.6%
Dropout rate	1.4%
Per-pupil expenditure	$10,812
Avg teacher salary	$65,999
Student/teacher ratio '08-09	16.4 to 1
Highly-qualified teachers, '08-09	98.5%
Teachers licensed in assigned subject	99.0%
Students per computer	2.6

Massachusetts Competency Assessment System (MCAS), 2009 results

	English		Math	
	% Prof	CPI	% Prof	CPI
Gr 4	82%	93.5	72%	90.3
Gr 6	90%	96.8	88%	95.1
Gr 8	96%	98.4	64%	83.1
Gr 10	98%	99.4	96%	98.3

Other School Districts (see Appendix D for data)
South Shore Vocational Tech

©2010 Information Publications, Inc. All rights reserved. Photocopying prohibited. For additional copies, contact the publisher at www.informationpublications.com or (877)544-INFO (4636)

Demographics & Socio-Economic Characteristics*

Population

1990	28,700
2000	28,587
Male	13,517
Female	15,070
2008	28,211
2010 (projected)††	27,340
2020 (projected)††	26,037

Race & Hispanic Origin, 2000

Race	
White	25,873
Black/African American	659
American Indian/Alaska Native	27
Asian	1,446
Hawaiian Native/Pacific Islander	4
Other Race	221
Two or more races	357
Hispanic origin	473

Age & Nativity, 2000

Under 5 years	1,693
18 years and over	22,652
21 years and over	22,003
65 years and over	5,022
85 years and over	746
Median Age	38.6
Native-born	25,226
Foreign-born	3,361

Age, 2020 (projected)††

Under 5 years	1,187
5 to 19 years	3,908
20 to 39 years	6,674
40 to 64 years	9,091
65 years and over	5,177

Educational Attainment, 2000

Population 25 years and over	20,788
High School graduates or higher	91.8%
Bachelor's degree or higher	39.2%
Graduate degree	14.5%

Income & Poverty, 1999

Per capita income,	$27,720
Median household income	$58,421
Median family income	$70,164
Persons in poverty	1,227
H'holds receiving public assistance	207
H'holds receiving social security	3,399

Households, 2000

Total households	11,623
With persons under 18	3,314
With persons over 65	3,357
Family households	7,382
Single person households	3,413
Persons per household	2.4
Persons per family	3.1

Labor & Employment, 2000

Civilian labor force	15,511
Unemployment rate	2.7%
Civilian labor force, 2008†	15,857
Unemployment rate†	5.7%
Civilian labor force, 12/09†	15,636
Unemployment rate†	7.7%
Employed persons 16 years and over, by occupation:	
Managers & professionals	7,070
Service occupations	1,746
Sales & office occupations	4,265
Farming, fishing & forestry	0
Construction & maintenance	1,097
Production & transportation	917
Self-employed persons	783

Most demographic data is from the 2000 Decennial Census
* see Appendix E for American Community Survey data
† Massachusetts Department of Revenue
†† University of Massachusetts, MISER

General Information

Town of Norwood
566 Washington St
Norwood, MA 02062
781-762-1240

Elevation	100 ft.
Land area (square miles)	10.5
Water area (square miles)	0.1
Population density, 2008 (est)	2,686.8
Year incorporated	1872
Website	www.norwoodma.gov

Voters & Government Information

Government type	Rep. Town Meeting
Number of Selectmen	5
US Congressional District(s)	9

Registered Voters, October 2008

Total	19,424
Democrats	7,029
Republicans	2,040
Unaffiliated/other	10,239

Local Officials, 2010

Chair, Bd. of Sel.	William J. Plasko
Manager	John Carroll
Town Clerk	Robert Thornton
Treasurer	Robert McGuire
Treas/Collector	Robert McGuire
Tax Assessor	Paul Wanecek (Chr)
Attorney	Michael Lehane
Public Works	Mark Ryan
Building	Mark Chubet
Comm Dev/Planning	Stephen Costello
Police Chief	Bartley King Jr
Fire Chief	Michael Howard

Housing & Construction

New Privately Owned Housing Units Authorized by Building Permit

	Single Family	Total Bldgs	Total Units
2006	13	15	17
2007	16	21	65
2008	8	9	10

Parcel Count by Property Class, 2010

Total	8,744
Single family	5,812
Multiple units	971
Apartments	92
Condos	930
Vacant land	157
Open space	0
Commercial	511
Industrial	151
Misc. residential	19
Other use	101

Public Library

Morrill Memorial Library
PO Box 220
Norwood, MA 02062
(781)769-0200

Director	Charlotte Canelli

Library Statistics, FY 2008

Population served, 2007	28,172
Registered users	17,273
Circulation	310,216
Reference transactons	19,779
Total program attendance	203,361
per capita:	
Holdings	3.98
Operating income	$51.83
Internet Access	
Internet computers available	15
Weekly users	730

Municipal Finance

Debt at year end 2008	$38,931,356
Moody's rating, July 2009	NA

Revenues, 2008

Total	$107,560,847
From all taxes	49,471,466
Federal aid	0
State aid	20,974,023
From other governments	0
Charges for services	17,177,362
Licenses, permits & fees	1,779,064
Fines & forfeits	0
Interfund transfers	8,183,318
Misc/other/special assessments	4,987,807

Expenditures, 2008

Total	$98,630,789
General government	4,117,328
Public safety	12,727,814
Other/fixed costs	12,513,654
Human services	787,130
Culture & recreation	2,267,394
Debt Service	4,531,894
Education	41,152,465
Public works	19,584,202
Intergovernmental	948,908

Taxation, 2010

Property type	Valuation	Rate
Total	$4,368,997,490	-
Residential	3,055,932,461	9.33
Open space	0	0.00
Commercial	893,929,084	17.40
Industrial	299,614,955	17.40
Personal	119,520,990	17.40

Average Single Family Tax Bill, 2010

Avg. assessed home value	$368,872
Avg. single fam. tax bill	$3,442
Hi-Lo ranking	181/301

Police & Crime, 2008

Number of police officers	59
Violent crimes	35
Property crimes	594

Local School District

(school data 2007-08, except as noted)

Norwood
275 Prospect Street, PO BOX 67
Norwood, MA 02062
781-762-6804

Superintendent	Jeffrey Granatino
Grade plan	PK-12
Total enrollment '09-10	3,437
Grade 12 enrollment, '09-10	281
Graduation rate	82.1%
Dropout rate	10.9%
Per-pupil expenditure	$12,226
Avg teacher salary	$57,974
Student/teacher ratio '08-09	13.0 to 1
Highly-qualified teachers, '08-09	98.8%
Teachers licensed in assigned subject	98.9%
Students per computer	6.7

Massachusetts Competency Assessment System (MCAS), 2009 results

	English		Math	
	% Prof	CPI	% Prof	CPI
Gr 4	58%	83.6	47%	81.3
Gr 6	65%	85.4	45%	72.7
Gr 8	84%	94.3	50%	75
Gr 10	87%	95.1	74%	87.4

Other School Districts (see Appendix D for data)
Blue Hills Vocational Tech, Norfolk County Agricultural

See Introduction for an explanation of all data sources.

©2010 Information Publications, Inc. All rights reserved. Photocopying prohibited. For additional copies, contact the publisher at www.informationpublications.com or (877)544-INFO (4636)

Demographics & Socio-Economic Characteristics

Population

1990	2,804
2000	3,713
Male	1,802
Female	1,911
2008	3,735
2010 (projected)††	4,832
2020 (projected)††	6,061

Race & Hispanic Origin, 2000

Race	
White	3,220
Black/African American	160
American Indian/Alaska Native	56
Asian	25
Hawaiian Native/Pacific Islander	0
Other Race	93
Two or more races	159
Hispanic origin	44

Age & Nativity, 2000

Under 5 years	219
18 years and over	2,875
21 years and over	2,766
65 years and over	549
85 years and over	54
Median Age	39.4
Native-born	3,488
Foreign-born	225

Age, 2020 (projected)††

Under 5 years	337
5 to 19 years	963
20 to 39 years	1,461
40 to 64 years	2,100
65 years and over	1,200

Educational Attainment, 2000

Population 25 years and over	2,593
High School graduates or higher	86.8%
Bachelor's degree or higher	32.3%
Graduate degree	12.9%

Income & Poverty, 1999

Per capita income,	$23,829
Median household income	$42,044
Median family income	$53,841
Persons in poverty	313
H'holds receiving public assistance	24
H'holds receiving social security	490

Households, 2000

Total households	1,590
With persons under 18	472
With persons over 65	421
Family households	915
Single person households	519
Persons per household	2.3
Persons per family	2.9

Labor & Employment, 2000

Civilian labor force	1,949
Unemployment rate	3.0%
Civilian labor force, 2008†	2,166
Unemployment rate†	7.8%
Civilian labor force, 12/09†	2,267
Unemployment rate†	11.7%
Employed persons 16 years and over, by occupation:	
Managers & professionals	525
Service occupations	301
Sales & office occupations	581
Farming, fishing & forestry	0
Construction & maintenance	351
Production & transportation	132
Self-employed persons	398

Most demographic data is from the 2000 Decennial Census
† Massachusetts Department of Revenue
†† University of Massachusetts, MISER

General Information

Town of Oak Bluffs
56 School Street
PO Box 1327
Oak Bluffs, MA 02557
508-693-3554

Elevation	NA
Land area (square miles)	7.4
Water area (square miles)	18.6
Population density, 2008 (est)	504.7
Year incorporated	1880
Website	www.ci.oak-bluffs.ma.us

Voters & Government Information

Government type	Open Town Meeting
Number of Selectmen	5
US Congressional District(s)	10

Registered Voters, October 2008

Total	3,247
Democrats	1,120
Republicans	359
Unaffiliated/other	1,755

Local Officials, 2010

Chair, Bd. of Sel.	Ronald DiOrio
Manager/Admin	Michael Dutton
Town Clerk	Deborah Ratcliff
Finance Director	Paul Manzi
Tax Collector	Cheryll Shasin
Tax Assessor	Jesse B. Law III
Attorney	Ronald Rappaport
Public Works	NA
Building	Jerry Weiner
Comm Dev/Planning	John Bradford
Police Chief	Erik Blake
Fire Chief	Gilbert Forend

Housing & Construction

New Privately Owned Housing Units Authorized by Building Permit

	Single Family	Total Bldgs	Total Units
2006	20	20	20
2007	40	40	40
2008	21	21	21

Parcel Count by Property Class, 2010

Total	4,791
Single family	3,290
Multiple units	102
Apartments	4
Condos	80
Vacant land	756
Open space	39
Commercial	183
Industrial	4
Misc. residential	221
Other use	112

Public Library

Oak Bluffs Public Library
PO Box 2039
Oak Bluffs, MA 02557
(508)693-9433

Director	Danguole Budris

Library Statistics, FY 2008

Population served, 2007	3,731
Registered users	8,181
Circulation	110,934
Reference transactons	7,930
Total program attendance	74,747
per capita:	
Holdings	8.81
Operating income	$116.40
Internet Access	
Internet computers available	23
Weekly users	486

Municipal Finance

Debt at year end 2008	$22,745,035
Moody's rating, July 2009	NA

Revenues, 2008

Total	$23,459,533
From all taxes	17,353,052
Federal aid	0
State aid	1,658,891
From other governments	633,778
Charges for services	503,588
Licenses, permits & fees	364,418
Fines & forfeits	0
Interfund transfers	815,204
Misc/other/special assessments	1,065,301

Expenditures, 2008

Total	$21,792,111
General government	1,874,835
Public safety	2,793,387
Other/fixed costs	2,925,067
Human services	382,797
Culture & recreation	610,020
Debt Service	2,981,565
Education	7,946,648
Public works	1,335,088
Intergovernmental	942,704

Taxation, 2010

Property type	Valuation	Rate
Total	$2,873,709,066	-
Residential	2,656,393,324	6.30
Open space	1,997,400	6.30
Commercial	155,179,816	6.30
Industrial	4,512,300	6.30
Personal	55,626,226	6.30

Average Single Family Tax Bill, 2010

Avg. assessed home value	$640,870
Avg. single fam. tax bill	$4,037
Hi-Lo ranking	134/301

Police & Crime, 2008

Number of police officers	15
Violent crimes	6
Property crimes	110

Local School District

(school data 2007-08, except as noted)
Oak Bluffs
4 Pine Street, RR2 Box 261
Vineyard Haven, MA 02568
508-693-2007

Superintendent	James Weiss
Grade plan	PK-8
Total enrollment '09-10	406
Grade 12 enrollment, '09-10	0
Graduation rate	NA
Dropout rate	NA
Per-pupil expenditure	$16,318
Avg teacher salary	$63,665
Student/teacher ratio '08-09	9.3 to 1
Highly-qualified teachers, '08-09	94.4%
Teachers licensed in assigned subject	97.1%
Students per computer	4.6

Massachusetts Competency Assessment System (MCAS), 2009 results

	English		Math	
	% Prof	CPI	% Prof	CPI
Gr 4	82%	93.8	63%	86.2
Gr 6	85%	94.2	74%	90.1
Gr 8	88%	98	68%	88.5
Gr 10	NA	NA	NA	NA

Other School Districts (see Appendix D for data)
Marthas Vineyard Regional

©2010 Information Publications, Inc. All rights reserved. Photocopying prohibited. For additional copies, contact the publisher at www.informationpublications.com or (877)544-INFO (4636)

See Introduction for an explanation of all data sources.

Demographics & Socio-Economic Characteristics

Population

1990	1,503
2000	1,673
Male	838
Female	835
2008	1,914
2010 (projected)††	1,969
2020 (projected)††	2,553

Race & Hispanic Origin, 2000

Race	
White	1,645
Black/African American	6
American Indian/Alaska Native	2
Asian	10
Hawaiian Native/Pacific Islander	0
Other Race	4
Two or more races	6
Hispanic origin	17

Age & Nativity, 2000

Under 5 years	91
18 years and over	1,177
21 years and over	1,121
65 years and over	130
85 years and over	12
Median Age	38.1
Native-born	1,626
Foreign-born	47

Age, 2020 (projected)††

Under 5 years	190
5 to 19 years	464
20 to 39 years	751
40 to 64 years	751
65 years and over	397

Educational Attainment, 2000

Population 25 years and over	1,072
High School graduates or higher	91.2%
Bachelor's degree or higher	30.7%
Graduate degree	11.9%

Income & Poverty, 1999

Per capita income,	$23,175
Median household income	$60,729
Median family income	$63,487
Persons in poverty	32
H'holds receiving public assistance	6
H'holds receiving social security	105

Households, 2000

Total households	578
With persons under 18	253
With persons over 65	95
Family households	467
Single person households	85
Persons per household	2.9
Persons per family	3.2

Labor & Employment, 2000

Civilian labor force	923
Unemployment rate	3.0%
Civilian labor force, 2008†	1,051
Unemployment rate†	6.1%
Civilian labor force, 12/09†	1,092
Unemployment rate†	10.2%
Employed persons 16 years and over, by occupation:	
Managers & professionals	405
Service occupations	86
Sales & office occupations	158
Farming, fishing & forestry	9
Construction & maintenance	96
Production & transportation	141
Self-employed persons	72

Most demographic data is from the 2000 Decennial Census
† Massachusetts Department of Revenue
†† University of Massachusetts, MISER

General Information

Town of Oakham
PO Box 118
Oakham, MA 01068
508-882-5549

Elevation	1,050 ft.
Land area (square miles)	21.1
Water area (square miles)	0.4
Population density, 2008 (est)	90.7
Year incorporated	1762
Email	cathyamidio@oakham-ma.gov

Voters & Government Information

Government type	Open Town Meeting
Number of Selectmen	3
US Congressional District(s)	1

Registered Voters, October 2008

Total	1,332
Democrats	216
Republicans	180
Unaffiliated/other	928

Local Officials, 2010

Chair, Bd. of Sel.	Dennis Bergin
Town Administrator	Cathy Amidio
Clerk	Christine Mardirosian
Finance Director	Donna Sands
Tax Collector	Susan Carpenter
Tax Assessor	Peter Joyce
Attorney	Kopelman & Paige
Highway Dir	Kevin Currier
Building	Louis Pepi
Planning	Phillip Warbasse
Police Chief	Donald Haapakoski
Emerg/Fire Chief	Thomas McCaffrey

Housing & Construction

New Privately Owned Housing Units Authorized by Building Permit

	Single Family	Total Bldgs	Total Units
2006	6	7	8
2007	7	7	7
2008	4	4	4

Parcel Count by Property Class, 2010

Total	952
Single family	645
Multiple units	18
Apartments	0
Condos	2
Vacant land	215
Open space	0
Commercial	7
Industrial	7
Misc. residential	9
Other use	49

Public Library

Fobes Memorial Library
PO Box 338
Oakham, MA 01068
(508)882-3372

Director	Sharon Loricco

Library Statistics, FY 2008

Population served, 2007	1,906
Registered users	800
Circulation	5,378
Reference transactons	250
Total program attendance	3,900
per capita:	
Holdings	7.46
Operating income	$27.40
Internet Access	
Internet computers available	2
Weekly users	15

Municipal Finance

Debt at year end 2008	$580,000
Moody's rating, July 2009	NA

Revenues, 2008

Total	$3,070,102
From all taxes	2,189,963
Federal aid	0
State aid	389,071
From other governments	19,825
Charges for services	2,790
Licenses, permits & fees	4,263
Fines & forfeits	0
Interfund transfers	83,000
Misc/other/special assessments	190,595

Expenditures, 2008

Total	$2,782,506
General government	224,397
Public safety	448,276
Other/fixed costs	132,110
Human services	8,703
Culture & recreation	54,356
Debt Service	52,269
Education	1,546,130
Public works	308,446
Intergovernmental	6,374

Taxation, 2010

Property type	Valuation	Rate
Total	$203,372,895	-
Residential	192,040,145	10.32
Open space	0	0.00
Commercial	5,998,635	10.32
Industrial	803,600	10.32
Personal	4,530,515	10.32

Average Single Family Tax Bill, 2010

Avg. assessed home value	$262,292
Avg. single fam. tax bill	$2,707
Hi-Lo ranking	263/301

Police & Crime, 2008

Number of police officers	3
Violent crimes	NA
Property crimes	NA

Local School District

(school data 2007-08, except as noted)

Oakham (non-op)
1 Deacon Allen Drive, PO Box 99
Oakham, MA 01068
978-355-4668

Superintendent........ Maureen Marshall

Non-operating district.
Resident students are sent to the Other School Districts listed below.

Grade plan	NA
Total enrollment '09-10	NA
Grade 12 enrollment, '09-10	NA
Graduation rate	NA
Dropout rate	NA
Per-pupil expenditure	NA
Avg teacher salary	NA
Student/teacher ratio '08-09	NA
Highly-qualified teachers, '08-09	NA
Teachers licensed in assigned subject	NA
Students per computer	NA

Other School Districts (see Appendix D for data)
Quabbin Regional

See Introduction for an explanation of all data sources.

©2010 Information Publications, Inc. All rights reserved. Photocopying prohibited. For additional copies, contact the publisher at www.informationpublications.com or (877)544-INFO (4636)

Demographics & Socio-Economic Characteristics

Population

1990	7,312
2000	7,518
Male	3,619
Female	3,899
2008	7,688
2010 (projected)††	7,521
2020 (projected)††	7,610

Race & Hispanic Origin, 2000

Race	
White	7,239
Black/African American	80
American Indian/Alaska Native	17
Asian	36
Hawaiian Native/Pacific Islander	1
Other Race	44
Two or more races	101
Hispanic origin	124

Age & Nativity, 2000

Under 5 years	414
18 years and over	5,514
21 years and over	5,247
65 years and over	1,081
85 years and over	110
Median Age	38.0
Native-born	7,381
Foreign-born	137

Age, 2020 (projected)††

Under 5 years	400
5 to 19 years	1,205
20 to 39 years	1,759
40 to 64 years	2,629
65 years and over	1,617

Educational Attainment, 2000

Population 25 years and over	4,984
High School graduates or higher	79.6%
Bachelor's degree or higher	15.9%
Graduate degree	6.0%

Income & Poverty, 1999

Per capita income,	$17,361
Median household income	$36,849
Median family income	$44,128
Persons in poverty	583
H'holds receiving public assistance	111
H'holds receiving social security	1,032

Households, 2000

Total households	3,045
With persons under 18	1,044
With persons over 65	832
Family households	1,979
Single person households	873
Persons per household	2.5
Persons per family	3.0

Labor & Employment, 2000

Civilian labor force	3,803
Unemployment rate	4.8%
Civilian labor force, 2008†	3,662
Unemployment rate†	8.4%
Civilian labor force, 12/09†	3,846
Unemployment rate†	12.2%
Employed persons 16 years and over, by occupation:	
Managers & professionals	815
Service occupations	616
Sales & office occupations	767
Farming, fishing & forestry	0
Construction & maintenance	321
Production & transportation	1,100
Self-employed persons	205

Most demographic data is from the 2000 Decennial Census
† Massachusetts Department of Revenue
†† University of Massachusetts, MISER

General Information

Town of Orange
6 Prospect St
Orange, MA 01364
978-544-1100

Elevation	512 ft.
Land area (square miles)	35.4
Water area (square miles)	0.6
Population density, 2008 (est)	217.2
Year incorporated	1810
Website	townoforange.org

Voters & Government Information

Government type	Open Town Meeting
Number of Selectmen	3
US Congressional District(s)	1

Registered Voters, October 2008

Total	4,886
Democrats	1,113
Republicans	642
Unaffiliated/other	3,065

Local Officials, 2010

Chair, Bd. of Sel.	Steven Adam
Administrator	Richard Kwiatkowski
Town Clerk	Nancy Blackmer
Treasurer	Leigh Deveneau-Martinelli
Tax Collector	Jerilynn Deyo
Tax Assessor	Jay Closser
Attorney	NA
Public Works	NA
Building	Brian Gale
Comm Dev/Planning	Bruce Scharer (Chr)
Police Chief	Brian Spear
Fire Chief	Dennis Annear

Housing & Construction

New Privately Owned Housing Units Authorized by Building Permit

	Single Family	Total Bldgs	Total Units
2006	33	40	47
2007	15	16	17
2008	11	11	11

Parcel Count by Property Class, 2010

Total	3,444
Single family	2,067
Multiple units	186
Apartments	39
Condos	50
Vacant land	529
Open space	0
Commercial	162
Industrial	43
Misc. residential	146
Other use	222

Public Library

Wheeler Memorial Library
49 East Main Street
Orange, MA 01364
(978)544-2495

Director	Walt Owens

Library Statistics, FY 2008

Population served, 2007	7,796
Registered users	4,310
Circulation	71,606
Reference transactons	3,331
Total program attendance	46,953
per capita:	
Holdings	6.70
Operating income	$35.23
Internet Access	
Internet computers available	13
Weekly users	191

Municipal Finance

Debt at year end 2008	$1,835,649
Moody's rating, July 2009	Baa2

Revenues, 2008

Total	$17,486,642
From all taxes	7,770,591
Federal aid	0
State aid	7,629,216
From other governments	5,243
Charges for services	745,677
Licenses, permits & fees	94,745
Fines & forfeits	18,628
Interfund transfers	326,890
Misc/other/special assessments	447,826

Expenditures, 2008

Total	$15,541,972
General government	653,722
Public safety	1,810,285
Other/fixed costs	994,501
Human services	93,732
Culture & recreation	274,864
Debt Service	568,891
Education	9,396,655
Public works	1,296,225
Intergovernmental	453,097

Taxation, 2010

Property type	Valuation	Rate
Total	$530,615,533	-
Residential	454,499,700	13.87
Open space	0	0.00
Commercial	42,572,988	13.87
Industrial	19,986,495	13.87
Personal	13,556,350	13.87

Average Single Family Tax Bill, 2010

Avg. assessed home value	$164,677
Avg. single fam. tax bill	$2,284
Hi-Lo ranking	286/301

Police & Crime, 2008

Number of police officers	13
Violent crimes	24
Property crimes	194

Local School District

(school data 2007-08, except as noted)

Orange
131 West Main Street
Orange, MA 01364
978-544-6763

Superintendent	Paul Burnim
Grade plan	PK-6
Total enrollment '09-10	840
Grade 12 enrollment, '09-10	0
Graduation rate	NA
Dropout rate	NA
Per-pupil expenditure	$10,785
Avg teacher salary	$52,825
Student/teacher ratio '08-09	14.9 to 1
Highly-qualified teachers, '08-09	100.0%
Teachers licensed in assigned subject	100.0%
Students per computer	2.6

Massachusetts Competency Assessment System (MCAS), 2009 results

	English		Math	
	% Prof	CPI	% Prof	CPI
Gr 4	37%	77.3	46%	78.5
Gr 6	50%	77.2	41%	68.3
Gr 8	NA	NA	NA	NA
Gr 10	NA	NA	NA	NA

Other School Districts (see Appendix D for data)
Ralph C. Mahar Regional, Franklin County Vocational Tech

©2010 Information Publications, Inc. All rights reserved. Photocopying prohibited. For additional copies, contact the publisher at www.informationpublications.com or (877)544-INFO (4636)

Demographics & Socio-Economic Characteristics

Population

1990 . . . 5,838
2000 . . . 6,341
Male . . . 2,958
Female . . . 3,383
2008 . . . 6,269
2010 (projected)†† . . . 6,585
2020 (projected)†† . . . 7,017

Race & Hispanic Origin, 2000

Race
White . . . 6,187
Black/African American . . . 37
American Indian/Alaska Native . . . 11
Asian . . . 34
Hawaiian Native/Pacific Islander . . . 0
Other Race . . . 9
Two or more races . . . 63
Hispanic origin . . . 49

Age & Nativity, 2000

Under 5 years . . . 159
18 years and over . . . 5,468
21 years and over . . . 5,361
65 years and over . . . 2,284
85 years and over . . . 299
Median Age . . . 55.5
Native-born . . . 6,013
Foreign-born . . . 273

Age, 2020 (projected)††

Under 5 years . . . 125
5 to 19 years . . . 465
20 to 39 years . . . 739
40 to 64 years . . . 2,285
65 years and over . . . 3,403

Educational Attainment, 2000

Population 25 years and over . . . 5,242
High School graduates or higher . . 94.5%
Bachelor's degree or higher . . . 45.1%
Graduate degree . . . 17.8%

Income & Poverty, 1999

Per capita income, . . . $29,553
Median household income . . . $42,594
Median family income . . . $62,909
Persons in poverty . . . 397
H'holds receiving public assistance . . . 28
H'holds receiving social security . . . 1,610

Households, 2000

Total households . . . 3,087
With persons under 18 . . . 493
With persons over 65 . . . 1,557
Family households . . . 1,772
Single person households . . . 1,147
Persons per household . . . 2.0
Persons per family . . . 2.6

Labor & Employment, 2000

Civilian labor force . . . 2,609
Unemployment rate . . . 2.1%
Civilian labor force, 2008† . . . 2,892
Unemployment rate† . . . 7.5%
Civilian labor force, 12/09† . . . 2,809
Unemployment rate† . . . 9.4%
Employed persons 16 years and over, by occupation:
Managers & professionals . . . 873
Service occupations . . . 358
Sales & office occupations . . . 817
Farming, fishing & forestry . . . 22
Construction & maintenance . . . 328
Production & transportation . . . 157
Self-employed persons . . . 481

Most demographic data is from the 2000 Decennial Census
† Massachusetts Department of Revenue
†† University of Massachusetts, MISER

General Information

Town of Orleans
19 School Rd
Orleans, MA 02653
508-240-3700

Elevation . . . 60 ft.
Land area (square miles) . . . 14.2
Water area (square miles) . . . 6.9
Population density, 2008 (est) . . . 441.5
Year incorporated . . . 1797
Website . . . www.town.orleans.ma.us

Voters & Government Information

Government type . . . Open Town Meeting
Number of Selectmen . . . 5
US Congressional District(s) . . . 10

Registered Voters, October 2008

Total . . . 5,574
Democrats . . . 1,323
Republicans . . . 1,313
Unaffiliated/other . . . 2,916

Local Officials, 2010

Chair, Bd. of Sel. . . . David Dunford
Town Administrator . . . John Kelly
Clerk . . . Cynthia May
Finance Director . . . David Withrow
Treas/Collector . . . Christine Lorge
Tax Assessor . . . Kenneth Hull
Attorney . . . Michael Ford
Public Works . . . NA
Building . . . Brian Harrison
Planning . . . George Meservey
Police Chief . . . Jeffrey Roy
Fire Chief . . . William Quinn

Housing & Construction

New Privately Owned Housing Units Authorized by Building Permit

	Single Family	Total Bldgs	Total Units
2006	23	23	23
2007	21	21	21
2008	41	41	41

Parcel Count by Property Class, 2010

Total . . . 5,892
Single family . . . 3,720
Multiple units . . . 53
Apartments . . . 4
Condos . . . 716
Vacant land . . . 571
Open space . . . 0
Commercial . . . 466
Industrial . . . 25
Misc. residential . . . 226
Other use . . . 111

Public Library

Snow Library
67 Main St.
Orleans, MA 02653
(508)240-3761

Director . . . Mary S. Reuland

Library Statistics, FY 2008

Population served, 2007 . . . 6,315
Registered users . . . 10,471
Circulation . . . 181,832
Reference transactons . . . 6,240
Total program attendance . . . 166,520

per capita:

Holdings . . . 10.75
Operating income . . . $87.27

Internet Access

Internet computers available . . . 6
Weekly users . . . 350

Municipal Finance

Debt at year end 2008 . . . $23,269,000
Moody's rating, July 2009 . . . NA

Revenues, 2008

Total . . . $25,525,340
From all taxes . . . 19,122,020
Federal aid . . . 0
State aid . . . 821,002
From other governments . . . 2,051
Charges for services . . . 1,569,640
Licenses, permits & fees . . . 608,684
Fines & forfeits . . . 32,438
Interfund transfers . . . 1,506,973
Misc/other/special assessments . . . 931,266

Expenditures, 2008

Total . . . $23,057,992
General government . . . 1,933,665
Public safety . . . 4,899,916
Other/fixed costs . . . 2,786,977
Human services . . . 795,003
Culture & recreation . . . 1,653,214
Debt Service . . . 2,215,712
Education . . . 7,109,461
Public works . . . 1,213,117
Intergovernmental . . . 450,927

Taxation, 2010

Property type	Valuation	Rate
Total	$3,783,860,990	-
Residential	3,493,272,772	5.15
Open space	0	0.00
Commercial	238,607,708	5.15
Industrial	8,201,500	5.15
Personal	43,779,010	5.15

Average Single Family Tax Bill, 2010

Avg. assessed home value . . . $751,795
Avg. single fam. tax bill . . . $3,872
Hi-Lo ranking . . . 146/301

Police & Crime, 2008

Number of police officers . . . 22
Violent crimes . . . 7
Property crimes . . . 196

Local School District

(school data 2007-08, except as noted)

Orleans
78 Eldredge Pkwy
Orleans, MA 02653
508-255-8800

Superintendent . . . Richard Hoffmann
Grade plan . . . PK-5
Total enrollment '09-10 . . . 189
Grade 12 enrollment, '09-10 . . . 0
Graduation rate . . . NA
Dropout rate . . . NA
Per-pupil expenditure . . . $19,343
Avg teacher salary . . . $60,979
Student/teacher ratio '08-09 . . . 7.9 to 1
Highly-qualified teachers, '08-09 . . . 100.0%
Teachers licensed in assigned subject . 100.0%
Students per computer . . . 3.4

Massachusetts Competency Assessment System (MCAS), 2009 results

	English		Math	
	% Prof	CPI	% Prof	CPI
Gr 4	74%	88	70%	89.8
Gr 6	NA	NA	NA	NA
Gr 8	NA	NA	NA	NA
Gr 10	NA	NA	NA	NA

Other School Districts (see Appendix D for data)
Nauset Regional, Cape Cod Vocational Tech

See Introduction for an explanation of all data sources.

©2010 Information Publications, Inc. All rights reserved. Photocopying prohibited. For additional copies, contact the publisher at www.informationpublications.com or (877)544-INFO (4636)

Demographics & Socio-Economic Characteristics

Population

1990	1,073
2000	1,365
Male	720
Female	645
2008	1,396
2010 (projected)††	1,520
2020 (projected)††	1,740

Race & Hispanic Origin, 2000

Race	
White	1,318
Black/African American	8
American Indian/Alaska Native	4
Asian	12
Hawaiian Native/Pacific Islander	0
Other Race	5
Two or more races	18
Hispanic origin	4

Age & Nativity, 2000

Under 5 years	54
18 years and over	1,068
21 years and over	1,028
65 years and over	193
85 years and over	13
Median Age	42.3
Native-born	1,323
Foreign-born	31

Age, 2020 (projected)††

Under 5 years	68
5 to 19 years	188
20 to 39 years	317
40 to 64 years	653
65 years and over	514

Educational Attainment, 2000

Population 25 years and over	966
High School graduates or higher	88.7%
Bachelor's degree or higher	25.1%
Graduate degree	9.3%

Income & Poverty, 1999

Per capita income,	$25,029
Median household income	$51,488
Median family income	$55,455
Persons in poverty	100
H'holds receiving public assistance	8
H'holds receiving social security	149

Households, 2000

Total households	567
With persons under 18	161
With persons over 65	133
Family households	386
Single person households	138
Persons per household	2.4
Persons per family	2.9

Labor & Employment, 2000

Civilian labor force	738
Unemployment rate	4.9%
Civilian labor force, 2008†	842
Unemployment rate†	7.7%
Civilian labor force, 12/09†	851
Unemployment rate†	9.0%
Employed persons 16 years and over, by occupation:	
Managers & professionals	227
Service occupations	100
Sales & office occupations	154
Farming, fishing & forestry	8
Construction & maintenance	120
Production & transportation	93
Self-employed persons	108

Most demographic data is from the 2000 Decennial Census
† Massachusetts Department of Revenue
†† University of Massachusetts, MISER

General Information

Town of Otis
PO Box 237
Otis, MA 01253
413-269-0100

Elevation	1,220 ft.
Land area (square miles)	35.8
Water area (square miles)	2.2
Population density, 2008 (est)	39.0
Year incorporated	1810
Website	townofotisma.com

Voters & Government Information

Government type	Open Town Meeting
Number of Selectmen	3
US Congressional District(s)	1, 2

Registered Voters, October 2008

Total	1,085
Democrats	280
Republicans	154
Unaffiliated/other	644

Local Officials, 2010

Chair, Bd. of Sel.	Donald Hawley
Town Administrator	Chris Morris
Town Clerk	Lyn Minery
Finance Director	Linda O'Neil
Tax Collector	Ann Pyenson
Tax Assessor	Lee Marcella
Attorney	Jeremia Pollard
Public Works	Christopher Bouchard
Building	Larry Gould
Comm Dev/Planning	Howard Levin (Chr)
Police Chief	Roberta Sarnacki
Emerg/Fire Chief	Sandy Pinkham

Housing & Construction

New Privately Owned Housing Units Authorized by Building Permit

	Single Family	Total Bldgs	Total Units
2006	31	31	31
2007	24	24	24
2008	12	12	12

Parcel Count by Property Class, 2010

Total	2,856
Single family	1,518
Multiple units	10
Apartments	1
Condos	0
Vacant land	1,176
Open space	0
Commercial	26
Industrial	10
Misc. residential	66
Other use	49

Public Library

Otis Library and Museum
PO Box 126
Otis, MA 01253
(413)269-0109

Librarian	Kathy Bort

Library Statistics, FY 2008

Population served, 2007	1,394
Registered users	490
Circulation	10,800
Reference transactons	600
Total program attendance	7,584
per capita:	
Holdings	5.93
Operating income	$33.29
Internet Access	
Internet computers available	2
Weekly users	30

Municipal Finance

Debt at year end 2008	$0
Moody's rating, July 2009	NA

Revenues, 2008

Total	$4,127,830
From all taxes	3,652,829
Federal aid	0
State aid	129,216
From other governments	6,743
Charges for services	185,102
Licenses, permits & fees	43,660
Fines & forfeits	0
Interfund transfers	0
Misc/other/special assessments	55,140

Expenditures, 2008

Total	$3,477,759
General government	586,842
Public safety	243,252
Other/fixed costs	257,091
Human services	21,798
Culture & recreation	100,147
Debt Service	0
Education	1,624,233
Public works	603,266
Intergovernmental	28,715

Taxation, 2010

Property type	Valuation	Rate
Total	$606,048,721	-
Residential	571,795,140	6.33
Open space	0	0.00
Commercial	15,865,360	6.33
Industrial	3,100,500	6.33
Personal	15,287,721	6.33

Average Single Family Tax Bill, 2010

Avg. assessed home value	$319,539
Avg. single fam. tax bill	$2,023
Hi-Lo ranking	294/301

Police & Crime, 2008

Number of police officers	NA
Violent crimes	NA
Property crimes	NA

Local School District

(school data 2007-08, except as noted)

Otis (non-op)
555 N Main, POB 679
Otis, MA 01253
413-269-4466

Superintendent: Joanne Austin

Non-operating district.
Resident students are sent to the Other School Districts listed below.

Grade plan	NA
Total enrollment '09-10	NA
Grade 12 enrollment, '09-10	NA
Graduation rate	NA
Dropout rate	NA
Per-pupil expenditure	NA
Avg teacher salary	NA
Student/teacher ratio '08-09	NA
Highly-qualified teachers, '08-09	NA
Teachers licensed in assigned subject	NA
Students per computer	NA

Other School Districts (see Appendix D for data)
Farmington River Regional

©2010 Information Publications, Inc. All rights reserved. Photocopying prohibited. For additional copies, contact the publisher at www.informationpublications.com or (877)544-INFO (4636)

See Introduction for an explanation of all data sources.

Demographics & Socio-Economic Characteristics

Population

1990	12,588
2000	13,352
Male	6,453
Female	6,899
2008	13,615
2010 (projected)††	13,614
2020 (projected)††	13,818

Race & Hispanic Origin, 2000

Race	
White	12,901
Black/African American	116
American Indian/Alaska Native	34
Asian	112
Hawaiian Native/Pacific Islander	3
Other Race	43
Two or more races	143
Hispanic origin	263

Age & Nativity, 2000

Under 5 years	845
18 years and over	9,872
21 years and over	9,401
65 years and over	1,496
85 years and over	144
Median Age	36.6
Native-born	13,061
Foreign-born	291

Age, 2020 (projected)††

Under 5 years	800
5 to 19 years	2,436
20 to 39 years	3,313
40 to 64 years	4,819
65 years and over	2,450

Educational Attainment, 2000

Population 25 years and over	8,859
High School graduates or higher	85.3%
Bachelor's degree or higher	17.7%
Graduate degree	6.9%

Income & Poverty, 1999

Per capita income,	$21,828
Median household income	$52,233
Median family income	$58,973
Persons in poverty	1,026
H'holds receiving public assistance	96
H'holds receiving social security	1,363

Households, 2000

Total households	5,058
With persons under 18	1,887
With persons over 65	1,068
Family households	3,598
Single person households	1,195
Persons per household	2.6
Persons per family	3.1

Labor & Employment, 2000

Civilian labor force	7,424
Unemployment rate	3.5%
Civilian labor force, 2008†	7,595
Unemployment rate†	6.4%
Civilian labor force, 12/09†	7,746
Unemployment rate†	9.1%
Employed persons 16 years and over, by occupation:	
Managers & professionals	2,276
Service occupations	939
Sales & office occupations	1,927
Farming, fishing & forestry	27
Construction & maintenance	875
Production & transportation	1,119
Self-employed persons	388

Most demographic data is from the 2000 Decennial Census
† Massachusetts Department of Revenue
†† University of Massachusetts, MISER

General Information

Town of Oxford
325 Main St
Oxford, MA 01540
508-987-6032

Elevation	510 ft.
Land area (square miles)	26.6
Water area (square miles)	0.9
Population density, 2008 (est)	511.8
Year incorporated	1693
Website	www.town.oxford.ma.us

Voters & Government Information

Government type	Open Town Meeting
Number of Selectmen	5
US Congressional District(s)	2

Registered Voters, October 2008

Total	8,924
Democrats	2,538
Republicans	1,070
Unaffiliated/other	5,239

Local Officials, 2010

Chair, Bd. of Sel.	Jennie L. Caissie
Manager	Joseph M. Zeneski
Clerk	Lori A. Kelley
Finance Director	Donald F. Kaminski
Tax Collector	Donald F. Kaminski
Tax Assessor	Christopher T. Pupka
Attorney	Kopelman & Paige
Public Works	Sean M. Divoll
Building	Adelle Reynolds
Planning	David M. Manugian
Police Chief	Michael J. Boss
Emerg/Fire Chief	Sheri R. Bemis (Actg)

Housing & Construction

New Privately Owned Housing Units Authorized by Building Permit

	Single Family	Total Bldgs	Total Units
2006	39	41	43
2007	22	22	22
2008	9	9	9

Parcel Count by Property Class, 2010

Total	5,694
Single family	3,630
Multiple units	234
Apartments	45
Condos	532
Vacant land	624
Open space	0
Commercial	196
Industrial	165
Misc. residential	27
Other use	241

Public Library

Oxford Free Public Library
339 Main St.
Oxford, MA 01540
(508)987-6003

Director . . . . . Timothy Kelley

Library Statistics, FY 2008

Population served, 2007	13,641
Registered users	8,439
Circulation	125,396
Reference transactons	0
Total program attendance	0
per capita:	
Holdings	3.90
Operating income	$32.22
Internet Access	
Internet computers available	16
Weekly users	248

Municipal Finance

Debt at year end 2008	$15,880,000
Moody's rating, July 2009	A2

Revenues, 2008

Total	$31,937,304
From all taxes	16,328,394
Federal aid	1,214
State aid	13,094,485
From other governments	72,780
Charges for services	90,965
Licenses, permits & fees	27,015
Fines & forfeits	8,550
Interfund transfers	1,458,157
Misc/other/special assessments	427,872

Expenditures, 2008

Total	$31,185,147
General government	2,655,399
Public safety	2,554,148
Other/fixed costs	5,020,047
Human services	138,540
Culture & recreation	474,894
Debt Service	1,945,991
Education	15,202,533
Public works	2,260,143
Intergovernmental	690,204

Taxation, 2010

Property type	Valuation	Rate
Total	$1,344,836,010	-
Residential	1,104,871,103	12.30
Open space	0	0.00
Commercial	93,973,707	12.30
Industrial	90,637,800	12.30
Personal	55,353,400	12.30

Average Single Family Tax Bill, 2010

Avg. assessed home value	$236,496
Avg. single fam. tax bill	$2,909
Hi-Lo ranking	245/301

Police & Crime, 2008

Number of police officers	20
Violent crimes	44
Property crimes	169

Local School District

(school data 2007-08, except as noted)

Oxford
5 Sigourney Street
Oxford, MA 01540
508-987-6050

Superintendent	Allen Himmelberger
Grade plan	PK-12
Total enrollment '09-10	2,042
Grade 12 enrollment, '09-10	139
Graduation rate	76.3%
Dropout rate	11.5%
Per-pupil expenditure	$10,568
Avg teacher salary	$58,200
Student/teacher ratio '08-09	14.3 to 1
Highly-qualified teachers, '08-09	98.7%
Teachers licensed in assigned subject	96.5%
Students per computer	4.5

Massachusetts Competency Assessment System (MCAS), 2009 results

	English		Math	
	% Prof	CPI	% Prof	CPI
Gr 4	44%	78.5	41%	77.8
Gr 6	67%	85.5	55%	77.3
Gr 8	71%	87.8	44%	69.4
Gr 10	71%	89.1	68%	82.6

Other School Districts (see Appendix D for data)

Southern Worcester County Vocational Tech

©2010 Information Publications, Inc. All rights reserved. Photocopying prohibited. For additional copies, contact the publisher at www.informationpublications.com or (877)544-INFO (4636)

See Introduction for an explanation of all data sources.

Demographics & Socio-Economic Characteristics

Population

1990	12,054
2000	12,497
Male	6,039
Female	6,458
2008	12,933
2010 (projected)††	12,675
2020 (projected)††	12,986

Race & Hispanic Origin, 2000

Race	
White	12,100
Black/African American	94
American Indian/Alaska Native	29
Asian	70
Hawaiian Native/Pacific Islander	0
Other Race	55
Two or more races	149
Hispanic origin	154

Age & Nativity, 2000

Under 5 years	693
18 years and over	9,349
21 years and over	8,931
65 years and over	1,940
85 years and over	249
Median Age	38.1
Native-born	12,138
Foreign-born	359

Age, 2020 (projected)††

Under 5 years	725
5 to 19 years	2,204
20 to 39 years	3,440
40 to 64 years	4,312
65 years and over	2,305

Educational Attainment, 2000

Population 25 years and over	8,510
High School graduates or higher	79.9%
Bachelor's degree or higher	13.5%
Graduate degree	3.4%

Income & Poverty, 1999

Per capita income,	$18,664
Median household income	$41,443
Median family income	$49,358
Persons in poverty	975
H'holds receiving public assistance	172
H'holds receiving social security	1,573

Households, 2000

Total households	5,078
With persons under 18	1,722
With persons over 65	1,419
Family households	3,329
Single person households	1,456
Persons per household	2.5
Persons per family	3.0

Labor & Employment, 2000

Civilian labor force	6,633
Unemployment rate	4.1%
Civilian labor force, 2008†	6,973
Unemployment rate†	7.0%
Civilian labor force, 12/09†	7,124
Unemployment rate†	10.8%
Employed persons 16 years and over, by occupation:	
Managers & professionals	1,687
Service occupations	1,062
Sales & office occupations	1,659
Farming, fishing & forestry	12
Construction & maintenance	503
Production & transportation	1,440
Self-employed persons	426

Most demographic data is from the 2000 Decennial Census
† Massachusetts Department of Revenue
†† University of Massachusetts, MISER

General Information

Town of Palmer
4417 Main St
Palmer, MA 01069
413-283-2603

Elevation	332 ft.
Land area (square miles)	31.5
Water area (square miles)	0.5
Population density, 2008 (est)	410.6
Year incorporated	1775
Website	townofpalmer.com

Voters & Government Information

Government type	Manager-Town Council
Number of Councilpersons	9
US Congressional District(s)	2

Registered Voters, October 2008

Total	8,367
Democrats	2,580
Republicans	1,033
Unaffiliated/other	4,689

Local Officials, 2010

Mayor	NA
Town Manager	Matthew Streeter
Town Clerk	Patricia Donovan
Finance Director	Valerie Bernier
Tax Collector	Melissa Zawadski
Tax Assessor	Bev Morin
Attorney	Charles Ksieniewicz
Public Works	Richard Kaczmarczyk
Building	Richard Rollet
Comm Dev/Planning	Alice Davey
Police Chief	Robert Frydryk
Emerg/Fire Chief	Alan Roy

Housing & Construction

New Privately Owned Housing Units Authorized by Building Permit

	Single Family	Total Bldgs	Total Units
2006	36	36	36
2007	29	29	29
2008	21	21	21

Parcel Count by Property Class, 2010

Total	5,630
Single family	3,176
Multiple units	464
Apartments	106
Condos	201
Vacant land	1,057
Open space	0
Commercial	235
Industrial	138
Misc. residential	153
Other use	100

Public Library

Palmer Public Library
1455 North Main Street
Palmer, MA 01069
(413)283-3330

Director	Nancy Menard

Library Statistics, FY 2008

Population served, 2007	12,849
Registered users	10,512
Circulation	139,883
Reference transactons	18,967
Total program attendance	135,429
per capita:	
Holdings	5.75
Operating income	$56.75
Internet Access	
Internet computers available	46
Weekly users	773

Municipal Finance

Debt at year end 2008	$18,509,624
Moody's rating, July 2009	Baa1

Revenues, 2008

Total	$32,391,085
From all taxes	14,746,628
Federal aid	0
State aid	16,043,742
From other governments	8,483
Charges for services	202,767
Licenses, permits & fees	127,015
Fines & forfeits	0
Interfund transfers	902,414
Misc/other/special assessments	180,018

Expenditures, 2008

Total	$32,718,742
General government	1,176,431
Public safety	1,819,827
Other/fixed costs	6,625,503
Human services	190,702
Culture & recreation	942,356
Debt Service	3,832,681
Education	16,761,508
Public works	1,065,097
Intergovernmental	304,637

Taxation, 2010

Property type	Valuation	Rate
Total	$974,776,965	-
Residential	812,119,460	15.01
Open space	0	0.00
Commercial	71,528,945	15.01
Industrial	48,429,400	15.01
Personal	42,699,160	15.01

Average Single Family Tax Bill, 2010

Avg. assessed home value	$188,955
Avg. single fam. tax bill	$2,836
Hi-Lo ranking	249/301

Police & Crime, 2008

Number of police officers	20
Violent crimes	37
Property crimes	182

Local School District

(school data 2007-08, except as noted)

Palmer
24 Converse Street, c/o Suite 1
Palmer, MA 01069
413-283-2650

Superintendent	Gerald Fournier
Grade plan	PK-12
Total enrollment '09-10	1,748
Grade 12 enrollment, '09-10	116
Graduation rate	72.8%
Dropout rate	15.2%
Per-pupil expenditure	$11,064
Avg teacher salary	$54,736
Student/teacher ratio '08-09	13.0 to 1
Highly-qualified teachers, '08-09	92.8%
Teachers licensed in assigned subject	100.0%
Students per computer	3.8

Massachusetts Competency Assessment System (MCAS), 2009 results

	English		Math	
	% Prof	CPI	% Prof	CPI
Gr 4	41%	73.4	40%	75.6
Gr 6	64%	86.6	48%	76.3
Gr 8	77%	91.4	37%	66.6
Gr 10	75%	89.3	69%	84.1

Other School Districts (see Appendix D for data)
Pathfinder Vocational Tech

©2010 Information Publications, Inc. All rights reserved. Photocopying prohibited. For additional copies, contact the publisher at www.informationpublications.com or (877)544-INFO (4636)

©2010 Information Publications, Inc. All rights reserved. Photocopying prohibited. For additional copies, contact the publisher at www.informationpublications.com or (877)544-INFO (4636)

Demographics & Socio-Economic Characteristics

Population

1990	4,047
2000	4,386
Male	2,096
Female	2,290
2008	4,632
2010 (projected)††	4,342
2020 (projected)††	4,255

Race & Hispanic Origin, 2000

Race	
White	4,241
Black/African American	30
American Indian/Alaska Native	4
Asian	47
Hawaiian Native/Pacific Islander	0
Other Race	25
Two or more races	39
Hispanic origin	68

Age & Nativity, 2000

Under 5 years	219
18 years and over	3,338
21 years and over	2,937
65 years and over	640
85 years and over	55
Median Age	38.1
Native-born	4,046
Foreign-born	340

Age, 2020 (projected)††

Under 5 years	243
5 to 19 years	972
20 to 39 years	1,013
40 to 64 years	1,308
65 years and over	719

Educational Attainment, 2000

Population 25 years and over	2,739
High School graduates or higher	93.9%
Bachelor's degree or higher	44.2%
Graduate degree	20.0%

Income & Poverty, 1999

Per capita income,	$29,573
Median household income	$72,039
Median family income	$80,498
Persons in poverty	74
H'holds receiving public assistance	26
H'holds receiving social security	408

Households, 2000

Total households	1,428
With persons under 18	537
With persons over 65	426
Family households	1,154
Single person households	224
Persons per household	2.8
Persons per family	3.1

Labor & Employment, 2000

Civilian labor force	2,289
Unemployment rate	2.9%
Civilian labor force, 2008†	2,338
Unemployment rate†	4.4%
Civilian labor force, 12/09†	2,424
Unemployment rate†	8.9%
Employed persons 16 years and over, by occupation:	
Managers & professionals	1,202
Service occupations	255
Sales & office occupations	544
Farming, fishing & forestry	0
Construction & maintenance	95
Production & transportation	127
Self-employed persons	229

Most demographic data is from the 2000 Decennial Census
† Massachusetts Department of Revenue
†† University of Massachusetts, MISER

General Information

Town of Paxton
697 Pleasant St
Paxton, MA 01612
508-753-2803

Elevation	1,134 ft.
Land area (square miles)	14.7
Water area (square miles)	0.7
Population density, 2008 (est)	315.1
Year incorporated	1765
Website	www.townofpaxton.net

Voters & Government Information

Government type	Open Town Meeting
Number of Selectmen	3
US Congressional District(s)	3

Registered Voters, October 2008

Total	3,162
Democrats	821
Republicans	453
Unaffiliated/other	1,880

Local Officials, 2010

Chair, Bd. of Sel.	Frederick Goodrich
Manager/Admin	Charles Blanchard
Town Clerk	Susan Stone
Finance Director	Donna Couture
Tax Collector	Deirdre L. Malone
Tax Assessor	Donna Graf-Parsons
Attorney	Peter Dawson
Public Works	Michael Putnam
Building	NA
Comm Dev/Planning	NA
Police Chief	Robert Desrosiers
Emerg/Fire Chief	Jay Conte

Housing & Construction

New Privately Owned Housing Units Authorized by Building Permit

	Single Family	Total Bldgs	Total Units
2006	7	7	7
2007	7	7	7
2008	1	1	1

Parcel Count by Property Class, 2010

Total	1,831
Single family	1,501
Multiple units	29
Apartments	0
Condos	19
Vacant land	221
Open space	0
Commercial	22
Industrial	8
Misc. residential	3
Other use	28

Public Library

Richards Memorial Library
44 Richards Ave.
Paxton, MA 01612
(508)754-0793

Director	Deborah Bailey

Library Statistics, FY 2008

Population served, 2007	4,530
Registered users	4,646
Circulation	62,992
Reference transactons	416
Total program attendance	0
per capita:	
Holdings	6.13
Operating income	$40.80
Internet Access	
Internet computers available	6
Weekly users	80

Municipal Finance

Debt at year end 2008	$4,497,614
Moody's rating, July 2009	A2

Revenues, 2008

Total	$9,545,613
From all taxes	7,517,512
Federal aid	0
State aid	707,109
From other governments	11,955
Charges for services	249,772
Licenses, permits & fees	58,245
Fines & forfeits	0
Interfund transfers	44,000
Misc/other/special assessments	478,510

Expenditures, 2008

Total	$9,343,728
General government	594,794
Public safety	1,334,615
Other/fixed costs	599,747
Human services	69,298
Culture & recreation	241,896
Debt Service	664,064
Education	4,915,875
Public works	855,655
Intergovernmental	40,607

Taxation, 2010

Property type	Valuation	Rate
Total	$502,477,792	-
Residential	482,408,890	16.30
Open space	0	0.00
Commercial	10,985,160	16.30
Industrial	4,417,150	16.30
Personal	4,666,592	16.30

Average Single Family Tax Bill, 2010

Avg. assessed home value	$301,283
Avg. single fam. tax bill	$4,911
Hi-Lo ranking	83/301

Police & Crime, 2008

Number of police officers	9
Violent crimes	3
Property crimes	27

Local School District

(school data 2007-08, except as noted)

Paxton (non-op)
Jefferson School, 1745 Main Street
Jefferson, MA 01522
508-829-1670

Superintendent........ Thomas Pandiscio

Non-operating district.
Resident students are sent to the Other School Districts listed below.

Grade plan	NA
Total enrollment '09-10	NA
Grade 12 enrollment, '09-10	NA
Graduation rate	NA
Dropout rate	NA
Per-pupil expenditure	NA
Avg teacher salary	NA
Student/teacher ratio '08-09	NA
Highly-qualified teachers, '08-09	NA
Teachers licensed in assigned subject	NA
Students per computer	NA

Other School Districts (see Appendix D for data)
Wachusett Regional, Southern Worchester County Vocational Tech

See Introduction for an explanation of all data sources.

Demographics & Socio-Economic Characteristics*

Population

1990	47,039
2000	48,129
Male	23,047
Female	25,082
2008	51,331
2010 (projected)††	46,776
2020 (projected)††	45,004

Race & Hispanic Origin, 2000

Race	
White	45,204
Black/African American	466
American Indian/Alaska Native	57
Asian	667
Hawaiian Native/Pacific Islander	7
Other Race	883
Two or more races	845
Hispanic origin	1,651

Age & Nativity, 2000

Under 5 years	2,805
18 years and over	37,413
21 years and over	36,129
65 years and over	8,398
85 years and over	980
Median Age	40.3
Native-born	42,718
Foreign-born	5,411

Age, 2020 (projected)††

Under 5 years	2,246
5 to 19 years	6,932
20 to 39 years	10,314
40 to 64 years	15,420
65 years and over	10,092

Educational Attainment, 2000

Population 25 years and over	34,274
High School graduates or higher	85.1%
Bachelor's degree or higher	23.1%
Graduate degree	7.3%

Income & Poverty, 1999

Per capita income,	$24,827
Median household income	$54,829
Median family income	$65,483
Persons in poverty	2,531
H'holds receiving public assistance	274
H'holds receiving social security	5,977

Households, 2000

Total households	18,581
With persons under 18	5,974
With persons over 65	5,824
Family households	12,981
Single person households	4,722
Persons per household	2.6
Persons per family	3.1

Labor & Employment, 2000

Civilian labor force	25,299
Unemployment rate	3.8%
Civilian labor force, 2008†	27,544
Unemployment rate†	6.0%
Civilian labor force, 12/09†	27,416
Unemployment rate†	8.6%
Employed persons 16 years and over, by occupation:	
Managers & professionals	8,871
Service occupations	3,346
Sales & office occupations	7,352
Farming, fishing & forestry	28
Construction & maintenance	1,967
Production & transportation	2,777
Self-employed persons	1,231

Most demographic data is from the 2000 Decennial Census
* see Appendix E for American Community Survey data
† Massachusetts Department of Revenue
†† University of Massachusetts, MISER

General Information

City of Peabody
24 Lowell St
Peabody, MA 01960
978-538-5900

Elevation	50 ft.
Land area (square miles)	16.4
Water area (square miles)	0.5
Population density, 2008 (est)	3,129.9
Year incorporated	1868
Website	www.peabody-ma.gov

Voters & Government Information

Government type	Mayor-Council
Number of Councilpersons	11
US Congressional District(s)	6

Registered Voters, October 2008

Total	33,224
Democrats	11,750
Republicans	2,950
Unaffiliated/other	18,398

Local Officials, 2010

Mayor	Michael J. Bonfanti
Manager/Admin	NA
Clerk	Timothy E. Spanos
Finance Director	Patricia Davis Schaffer
Tax Collector	Soterios Yokas
Tax Assessor	Frederick Martini
Attorney	John Christopher
Public Works	Robert Langley (Actg)
Building	Kevin Groggin
Planning	Karen Sawyer Delios
Police Chief	Robert Champagne
Emerg/Fire Chief	Stephen Pasdon

Housing & Construction

New Privately Owned Housing Units Authorized by Building Permit

	Single Family	Total Bldgs	Total Units
2006	48	55	119
2007	20	24	31
2008	18	26	41

Parcel Count by Property Class, 2010

Total	15,827
Single family	10,843
Multiple units	1,155
Apartments	132
Condos	2,233
Vacant land	511
Open space	0
Commercial	578
Industrial	188
Misc. residential	55
Other use	132

Public Library

Peabody Institute Library
82 Main Street
Peabody, MA 01960
(978)531-0100

Director	Martha Holden

Library Statistics, FY 2008

Population served, 2007	51,441
Registered users	30,204
Circulation	297,817
Reference transactons	30,596
Total program attendance	296,047
per capita:	
Holdings	3.24
Operating income	$31.31
Internet Access	
Internet computers available	30
Weekly users	847

Municipal Finance

Debt at year end 2008	$43,209,085
Moody's rating, July 2009	Aa2

Revenues, 2008

Total	$138,763,567
From all taxes	83,350,078
Federal aid	702,162
State aid	30,339,272
From other governments	0
Charges for services	17,459,963
Licenses, permits & fees	4,696,332
Fines & forfeits	258,176
Interfund transfers	4,000
Misc/other/special assessments	976,792

Expenditures, 2008

Total	$113,704,047
General government	3,918,155
Public safety	15,097,972
Other/fixed costs	8,315,037
Human services	1,737,405
Culture & recreation	2,938,605
Debt Service	5,336,955
Education	49,935,190
Public works	20,364,619
Intergovernmental	5,639,566

Taxation, 2010

Property type	Valuation	Rate
Total	$6,391,562,930	-
Residential	4,844,387,102	10.50
Open space	0	0.00
Commercial	1,096,240,398	20.57
Industrial	336,744,700	20.57
Personal	114,190,730	20.57

Average Single Family Tax Bill, 2010

Avg. assessed home value	$311,748
Avg. single fam. tax bill	$3,273
Hi-Lo ranking	206/301

Police & Crime, 2008

Number of police officers	97
Violent crimes	144
Property crimes	1,318

Local School District

(school data 2007-08, except as noted)

Peabody
21 Johnson Street
Peabody, MA 01960
978-536-6500

Superintendent	Charles Burnett
Grade plan	PK-12
Total enrollment '09-10	6,093
Grade 12 enrollment, '09-10	436
Graduation rate	79.7%
Dropout rate	9.2%
Per-pupil expenditure	$11,947
Avg teacher salary	$60,227
Student/teacher ratio '08-09	14.2 to 1
Highly-qualified teachers, '08-09	96.4%
Teachers licensed in assigned subject	98.2%
Students per computer	4.4

Massachusetts Competency Assessment System (MCAS), 2009 results

	English		Math	
	% Prof	CPI	% Prof	CPI
Gr 4	60%	84.6	45%	77.9
Gr 6	72%	88.6	56%	78
Gr 8	79%	91.9	43%	69.9
Gr 10	73%	87.8	69%	85.8

Other School Districts (see Appendix D for data)
None

©2010 Information Publications, Inc. All rights reserved. Photocopying prohibited. For additional copies, contact the publisher at www.informationpublications.com or (877)544-INFO (4636)

See Introduction for an explanation of all data sources.

Demographics & Socio-Economic Characteristics

Population

1990	1,373
2000	1,403
Male	701
Female	702
2008	1,386
2010 (projected)††	1,412
2020 (projected)††	1,414

Race & Hispanic Origin, 2000

Race	
White	1,334
Black/African American	20
American Indian/Alaska Native	0
Asian	15
Hawaiian Native/Pacific Islander	0
Other Race	9
Two or more races	25
Hispanic origin	26

Age & Nativity, 2000

Under 5 years	55
18 years and over	1,077
21 years and over	1,040
65 years and over	175
85 years and over	9
Median Age	42.4
Native-born	1,332
Foreign-born	71

Age, 2020 (projected)††

Under 5 years	55
5 to 19 years	180
20 to 39 years	358
40 to 64 years	460
65 years and over	361

Educational Attainment, 2000

Population 25 years and over	965
High School graduates or higher	94.5%
Bachelor's degree or higher	60.8%
Graduate degree	38.3%

Income & Poverty, 1999

Per capita income,	$29,821
Median household income	$61,339
Median family income	$71,667
Persons in poverty	68
H'holds receiving public assistance	6
H'holds receiving social security	119

Households, 2000

Total households	545
With persons under 18	188
With persons over 65	121
Family households	382
Single person households	108
Persons per household	2.6
Persons per family	3.0

Labor & Employment, 2000

Civilian labor force	829
Unemployment rate	3.1%
Civilian labor force, 2008†	864
Unemployment rate†	3.0%
Civilian labor force, 12/09†	843
Unemployment rate†	2.5%
Employed persons 16 years and over, by occupation:	
Managers & professionals	468
Service occupations	88
Sales & office occupations	144
Farming, fishing & forestry	1
Construction & maintenance	56
Production & transportation	46
Self-employed persons	89

Most demographic data is from the 2000 Decennial Census
† Massachusetts Department of Revenue
†† University of Massachusetts, MISER

General Information

Town of Pelham
351 Amherst Rd
Pelham, MA 01002
413-253-7129

Elevation	1,146 ft.
Land area (square miles)	25.1
Water area (square miles)	1.4
Population density, 2008 (est)	55.2
Year incorporated	1743
Website	townofpelham.org

Voters & Government Information

Government type	Open Town Meeting
Number of Selectmen	3
US Congressional District(s)	1

Registered Voters, October 2008

Total	1,118
Democrats	538
Republicans	52
Unaffiliated/other	515

Local Officials, 2010

Chair, Bd. of Sel.	Edward Martin
Manager/Admin	NA
Town Clerk	Kathy Martell
Finance Director	John Trickey
Tax Collector	Edna Holloway
Tax Assessor	Robert Rowell
Attorney	NA
Public Works	Richard Adamcek
Building	Chip LaPointe
Comm Dev/Planning	NA
Police Chief	Gary Thomann
Emerg/Fire Chief	Raymond Murphy

Housing & Construction

New Privately Owned Housing Units Authorized by Building Permit

	Single Family	Total Bldgs	Total Units
2006	2	2	2
2007	1	1	1
2008	1	1	1

Parcel Count by Property Class, 2010

Total	669
Single family	466
Multiple units	28
Apartments	0
Condos	0
Vacant land	98
Open space	0
Commercial	2
Industrial	6
Misc. residential	11
Other use	58

Public Library

Pelham Library
2 South Valley Road
Pelham, MA 01002
(413)253-0657

Director	Adam Novitt

Library Statistics, FY 2008

Population served, 2007	1,404
Registered users	1,614
Circulation	37,819
Reference transactons	2,500
Total program attendance	15,000
per capita:	
Holdings	23.42
Operating income	$39.12
Internet Access	
Internet computers available	8
Weekly users	80

Municipal Finance

Debt at year end 2008	$1,765,000
Moody's rating, July 2009	Baa2

Revenues, 2008

Total	$4,000,961
From all taxes	3,239,862
Federal aid	0
State aid	454,637
From other governments	13,468
Charges for services	18
Licenses, permits & fees	11,246
Fines & forfeits	0
Interfund transfers	232,652
Misc/other/special assessments	24,539

Expenditures, 2008

Total	$3,922,354
General government	257,875
Public safety	223,703
Other/fixed costs	301,940
Human services	25,189
Culture & recreation	36,720
Debt Service	222,208
Education	2,475,881
Public works	320,979
Intergovernmental	19,056

Taxation, 2010

Property type	Valuation	Rate
Total	$177,889,700	-
Residential	170,991,370	18.34
Open space	0	0.00
Commercial	1,346,830	18.34
Industrial	839,500	18.34
Personal	4,712,000	18.34

Average Single Family Tax Bill, 2010

Avg. assessed home value	$321,727
Avg. single fam. tax bill	$5,900
Hi-Lo ranking	50/301

Police & Crime, 2008

Number of police officers	2
Violent crimes	NA
Property crimes	NA

Local School District

(school data 2007-08, except as noted)

Pelham
170 Chestnut Street, Business Office
Amherst, MA 01002
413-362-1805

Superintendent	Maria Geryk
Grade plan	K-6
Total enrollment '09-10	125
Grade 12 enrollment, '09-10	0
Graduation rate	NA
Dropout rate	NA
Per-pupil expenditure	$14,037
Avg teacher salary	$59,722
Student/teacher ratio '08-09	9.9 to 1
Highly-qualified teachers, '08-09	100.0%
Teachers licensed in assigned subject	100.0%
Students per computer	1.6

Massachusetts Competency Assessment System (MCAS), 2009 results

	English		Math	
	% Prof	CPI	% Prof	CPI
Gr 4	45%	76.3	55%	81.3
Gr 6	95%	97.4	100%	100
Gr 8	NA	NA	NA	NA
Gr 10	NA	NA	NA	NA

Other School Districts (see Appendix D for data)
Amherst-Pelham Regional

©2010 Information Publications, Inc. All rights reserved. Photocopying prohibited. For additional copies, contact the publisher at www.informationpublications.com or (877)544-INFO (4636)

See Introduction for an explanation of all data sources.

Demographics & Socio-Economic Characteristics

Population

1990	14,544
2000	16,927
Male	8,373
Female	8,554
2008	18,714
2010 (projected)††	18,109
2020 (projected)††	19,047

Race & Hispanic Origin, 2000

Race	
White	16,569
Black/African American	85
American Indian/Alaska Native	12
Asian	86
Hawaiian Native/Pacific Islander	2
Other Race	48
Two or more races	125
Hispanic origin	90

Age & Nativity, 2000

Under 5 years	1,342
18 years and over	12,081
21 years and over	11,573
65 years and over	1,412
85 years and over	130
Median Age	36.0
Native-born	16,587
Foreign-born	340

Age, 2020 (projected)††

Under 5 years	1,323
5 to 19 years	3,969
20 to 39 years	4,371
40 to 64 years	6,274
65 years and over	3,110

Educational Attainment, 2000

Population 25 years and over	11,081
High School graduates or higher	92.9%
Bachelor's degree or higher	28.5%
Graduate degree	6.7%

Income & Poverty, 1999

Per capita income,	$27,066
Median household income	$65,050
Median family income	$74,985
Persons in poverty	810
H'holds receiving public assistance	48
H'holds receiving social security	1,240

Households, 2000

Total households	5,750
With persons under 18	2,511
With persons over 65	1,058
Family households	4,556
Single person households	961
Persons per household	2.9
Persons per family	3.3

Labor & Employment, 2000

Civilian labor force	9,195
Unemployment rate	3.1%
Civilian labor force, 2008†	10,525
Unemployment rate†	6.4%
Civilian labor force, 12/09†	10,432
Unemployment rate†	9.0%
Employed persons 16 years and over, by occupation:	
Managers & professionals	3,399
Service occupations	1,140
Sales & office occupations	2,483
Farming, fishing & forestry	24
Construction & maintenance	1,058
Production & transportation	806
Self-employed persons	382

Most demographic data is from the 2000 Decennial Census
† Massachusetts Department of Revenue
†† University of Massachusetts, MISER

General Information

Town of Pembroke
100 Center St
Pembroke, MA 02359
781-293-3844

Elevation	50 ft.
Land area (square miles)	21.8
Water area (square miles)	1.6
Population density, 2008 (est)	858.4
Year incorporated	1712
Website	www.townofpembrokemass.org

Voters & Government Information

Government type	Open Town Meeting
Number of Selectmen	5
US Congressional District(s)	10

Registered Voters, October 2008

Total	12,311
Democrats	3,169
Republicans	1,761
Unaffiliated/other	7,323

Local Officials, 2010

Chair, Bd. of Sel.	Arthur P. Boyle, Jr.
Manager/Admin	Edwin J. Thorne
Town Clerk	Mary Ann Smith (Asst)
Town Treasurer	Deborah Mulrain
Tax Collector	Deborah Mulrain
Tax Assessor	Catherine Salmon
Attorney	Kopelman & Paige
Public Works	Eugene Fulmine
Building	George Verry
Comm Dev/Planning	NA
Police Chief	Michael Ohrenberger
Emerg/Fire Chief	James Neenan

Housing & Construction

New Privately Owned Housing Units Authorized by Building Permit

	Single Family	Total Bldgs	Total Units
2006	52	52	52
2007	69	69	69
2008	23	23	23

Parcel Count by Property Class, 2010

Total	6,648
Single family	5,159
Multiple units	238
Apartments	8
Condos	463
Vacant land	374
Open space	0
Commercial	179
Industrial	60
Misc. residential	39
Other use	128

Public Library

Pembroke Public Library
142 Center St.
Pembroke, MA 02359
(781)293-6771

Director	Deborah Wall

Library Statistics, FY 2008

Population served, 2007	18,595
Registered users	12,954
Circulation	173,509
Reference transactons	11,830
Total program attendance	125,200
per capita:	
Holdings	4.52
Operating income	$31.48
Internet Access	
Internet computers available	11
Weekly users	365

Municipal Finance

Debt at year end 2008	$36,566,028
Moody's rating, July 2009	A2

Revenues, 2008

Total	$46,804,463
From all taxes	30,608,401
Federal aid	0
State aid	14,233,005
From other governments	1,274
Charges for services	422,336
Licenses, permits & fees	301,351
Fines & forfeits	24,019
Interfund transfers	580,095
Misc/other/special assessments	316,991

Expenditures, 2008

Total	$46,276,061
General government	1,521,489
Public safety	5,303,723
Other/fixed costs	7,594,102
Human services	428,704
Culture & recreation	690,602
Debt Service	3,666,459
Education	25,110,326
Public works	1,553,790
Intergovernmental	388,209

Taxation, 2010

Property type	Valuation	Rate
Total	$2,344,020,669	-
Residential	2,044,957,026	12.89
Open space	0	0.00
Commercial	200,958,261	12.89
Industrial	64,211,352	12.89
Personal	33,894,030	12.89

Average Single Family Tax Bill, 2010

Avg. assessed home value	$333,182
Avg. single fam. tax bill	$4,295
Hi-Lo ranking	115/301

Police & Crime, 2008

Number of police officers	26
Violent crimes	41
Property crimes	252

Local School District

(school data 2007-08, except as noted)

Pembroke
72 Pilgrim Road, Office of the Superintendent
Pembroke, MA 02359
781-829-1178

Superintendent	Frank Hackett
Grade plan	PK-12
Total enrollment '09-10	3,441
Grade 12 enrollment, '09-10	226
Graduation rate	88.8%
Dropout rate	5.2%
Per-pupil expenditure	$9,440
Avg teacher salary	$60,213
Student/teacher ratio '08-09	16.7 to 1
Highly-qualified teachers, '08-09	99.7%
Teachers licensed in assigned subject	98.6%
Students per computer	4.5

Massachusetts Competency Assessment System (MCAS), 2009 results

	English		Math	
	% Prof	CPI	% Prof	CPI
Gr 4	62%	85.9	48%	80.1
Gr 6	79%	91.8	72%	87.8
Gr 8	86%	95.3	65%	84.7
Gr 10	86%	95.4	81%	92

Other School Districts (see Appendix D for data)
None

©2010 Information Publications, Inc. All rights reserved. Photocopying prohibited. For additional copies, contact the publisher at www.informationpublications.com or (877)544-INFO (4636)

Demographics & Socio-Economic Characteristics

Population

1990	10,098
2000	11,142
Male	5,481
Female	5,661
2008	11,382
2010 (projected)††	11,904
2020 (projected)††	13,028

Race & Hispanic Origin, 2000

Race	
White	10,826
Black/African American	52
American Indian/Alaska Native	14
Asian	80
Hawaiian Native/Pacific Islander	0
Other Race	37
Two or more races	133
Hispanic origin	114

Age & Nativity, 2000

Under 5 years	867
18 years and over	7,728
21 years and over	7,366
65 years and over	832
85 years and over	85
Median Age	35.3
Native-born	10,716
Foreign-born	426

Age, 2020 (projected)††

Under 5 years	955
5 to 19 years	2,572
20 to 39 years	3,554
40 to 64 years	3,989
65 years and over	1,958

Educational Attainment, 2000

Population 25 years and over	6,975
High School graduates or higher	93.1%
Bachelor's degree or higher	32.8%
Graduate degree	10.6%

Income & Poverty, 1999

Per capita income,	$25,722
Median household income	$65,163
Median family income	$73,967
Persons in poverty	411
H'holds receiving public assistance	34
H'holds receiving social security	667

Households, 2000

Total households	3,847
With persons under 18	1,802
With persons over 65	615
Family households	3,016
Single person households	670
Persons per household	2.9
Persons per family	3.3

Labor & Employment, 2000

Civilian labor force	6,069
Unemployment rate	2.6%
Civilian labor force, 2008†	6,505
Unemployment rate†	4.9%
Civilian labor force, 12/09†	6,512
Unemployment rate†	8.4%
Employed persons 16 years and over, by occupation:	
Managers & professionals	2,477
Service occupations	604
Sales & office occupations	1,417
Farming, fishing & forestry	0
Construction & maintenance	609
Production & transportation	803
Self-employed persons	329

Most demographic data is from the 2000 Decennial Census
† Massachusetts Department of Revenue
†† University of Massachusetts, MISER

General Information

Town of Pepperell
1 Main St
Pepperell, MA 01463
978-433-0333

Elevation	244 ft.
Land area (square miles)	22.6
Water area (square miles)	0.6
Population density, 2008 (est)	503.6
Year incorporated	1753
Website	www.town.pepperell.ma.us

Voters & Government Information

Government type	Open Town Meeting
Number of Selectmen	3
US Congressional District(s)	1

Registered Voters, October 2008

Total	8,106
Democrats	1,791
Republicans	1,476
Unaffiliated/other	4,791

Local Officials, 2010

Chair, Bd. of Sel.	Joseph A. Sergi
Administrator	John B. Moak
Town Clerk	Lois A. Libby
Finance	Christopher F. DeSimone (Chr)
Tax Collector	Michael Hartnett
Tax Assessor	Michael Coffey
Attorney	Edward J. Richardson
Public Works	Robert E. Lee
Building	Harry Cullinan
Comm Dev/Planning	Susan Snyder
Police Chief	Alan Davis
Emerg/Fire Chief	Toby Tyler

Housing & Construction

New Privately Owned Housing Units Authorized by Building Permit

	Single Family	Total Bldgs	Total Units
2006	7	7	7
2007	13	14	15
2008	9	9	9

Parcel Count by Property Class, 2010

Total	4,363
Single family	3,030
Multiple units	195
Apartments	35
Condos	267
Vacant land	457
Open space	0
Commercial	59
Industrial	123
Misc. residential	55
Other use	142

Public Library

Lawrence Library
15 Main St.
Pepperell, MA 01463
(978)433-0330

Director	Debra Spratt

Library Statistics, FY 2008

Population served, 2007	11,409
Registered users	7,136
Circulation	134,565
Reference transactons	2,415
Total program attendance	0
per capita:	
Holdings	4.87
Operating income	$40.82
Internet Access	
Internet computers available	7
Weekly users	87

Municipal Finance

Debt at year end 2008	$9,303,352
Moody's rating, July 2009	A1

Revenues, 2008

Total	$17,623,704
From all taxes	14,536,746
Federal aid	0
State aid	1,669,867
From other governments	13,913
Charges for services	150,165
Licenses, permits & fees	162,965
Fines & forfeits	0
Interfund transfers	755,606
Misc/other/special assessments	167,221

Expenditures, 2008

Total	$17,439,738
General government	1,038,279
Public safety	2,281,858
Other/fixed costs	1,316,329
Human services	300,788
Culture & recreation	563,994
Debt Service	243,318
Education	10,626,717
Public works	1,041,599
Intergovernmental	24,979

Taxation, 2010

Property type	Valuation	Rate
Total	$1,177,137,008	-
Residential	1,102,088,896	12.58
Open space	0	0.00
Commercial	29,707,012	12.58
Industrial	26,758,800	12.58
Personal	18,582,300	12.58

Average Single Family Tax Bill, 2010

Avg. assessed home value	$301,105
Avg. single fam. tax bill	$3,788
Hi-Lo ranking	152/301

Police & Crime, 2008

Number of police officers	18
Violent crimes	27
Property crimes	172

Local School District

(school data 2007-08, except as noted)

Pepperell (non-op)
23 Main Street
Townsend, MA 01469
978-597-8713

Superintendent	Maureen Marshall

Non-operating district.
Resident students are sent to the Other School Districts listed below.

Grade plan	NA
Total enrollment '09-10	NA
Grade 12 enrollment, '09-10	NA
Graduation rate	NA
Dropout rate	NA
Per-pupil expenditure	NA
Avg teacher salary	NA
Student/teacher ratio '08-09	NA
Highly-qualified teachers, '08-09	NA
Teachers licensed in assigned subject	NA
Students per computer	NA

Other School Districts (see Appendix D for data)
North Middlesex Regional, Nashoba Valley Vocational Tech

©2010 Information Publications, Inc. All rights reserved. Photocopying prohibited. For additional copies, contact the publisher at www.informationpublications.com or (877)544-INFO (4636)

See Introduction for an explanation of all data sources.

Demographics & Socio-Economic Characteristics

Population

1990	779
2000	821
Male	425
Female	396
2008	832
2010 (projected)††	859
2020 (projected)††	961

Race & Hispanic Origin, 2000

Race	
White	804
Black/African American	2
American Indian/Alaska Native	1
Asian	4
Hawaiian Native/Pacific Islander	0
Other Race	1
Two or more races	9
Hispanic origin	1

Age & Nativity, 2000

Under 5 years	32
18 years and over	593
21 years and over	566
65 years and over	64
85 years and over	11
Median Age	37.2
Native-born	793
Foreign-born	8

Age, 2020 (projected)††

Under 5 years	47
5 to 19 years	120
20 to 39 years	266
40 to 64 years	312
65 years and over	216

Educational Attainment, 2000

Population 25 years and over	528
High School graduates or higher	87.1%
Bachelor's degree or higher	18.9%
Graduate degree	8.9%

Income & Poverty, 1999

Per capita income,	$18,636
Median household income	$44,531
Median family income	$51,071
Persons in poverty	39
H'holds receiving public assistance	13
H'holds receiving social security	65

Households, 2000

Total households	295
With persons under 18	121
With persons over 65	48
Family households	228
Single person households	48
Persons per household	2.8
Persons per family	3.1

Labor & Employment, 2000

Civilian labor force	437
Unemployment rate	2.3%
Civilian labor force, 2008†	487
Unemployment rate†	4.9%
Civilian labor force, 12/09†	472
Unemployment rate†	4.4%
Employed persons 16 years and over, by occupation:	
Managers & professionals	98
Service occupations	73
Sales & office occupations	111
Farming, fishing & forestry	4
Construction & maintenance	61
Production & transportation	80
Self-employed persons	36

Most demographic data is from the 2000 Decennial Census
† Massachusetts Department of Revenue
†† University of Massachusetts, MISER

General Information

Town of Peru
PO Box 1175
Peru, MA 01235
413-655-8312

Elevation	2,064 ft.
Land area (square miles)	25.9
Water area (square miles)	0.1
Population density, 2008 (est)	32.1
Year incorporated	1771
Email	townclerk@townofperuma.com

Voters & Government Information

Government type	Open Town Meeting
Number of Selectmen	3
US Congressional District(s)	1

Registered Voters, October 2008

Total	585
Democrats	139
Republicans	69
Unaffiliated/other	372

Local Officials, 2010

Chair, Bd. of Sel.	Douglas Haskins
Manager/Admin	NA
Town Clerk	S. Christine Richards
Finance Director	Douglas Haskins
Tax Collector	Caryn Wendling
Tax Assessor	Sara Adams
Attorney	Kopelman & Paige
Public Works	Ronald Radwich
Building	Joseph Mendoca
Comm Dev/Planning	Samual Haupt
Police Chief	Scott Vega
Emerg/Fire Chief	Eric Autenreith

Housing & Construction

New Privately Owned Housing Units Authorized by Building Permit

	Single Family	Total Bldgs	Total Units
2006	3	3	3
2007	3	3	3
2008	3	3	3

Parcel Count by Property Class, 2010

Total	751
Single family	338
Multiple units	2
Apartments	0
Condos	0
Vacant land	309
Open space	0
Commercial	1
Industrial	2
Misc. residential	53
Other use	46

Public Library

Peru Library
c/o Kimberly Wetherell, PO Box 1190
Hinsdale, MA 01235
(413)655-8650

Librarian	Kimberly Wetherell

Library Statistics, FY 2008

Population served, 2007	838
Registered users	276
Circulation	1,793
Reference transactons	0
Total program attendance	0
per capita:	
Holdings	5.45
Operating income	$13.44
Internet Access	
Internet computers available	1
Weekly users	4

Municipal Finance

Debt at year end 2008	$242,525
Moody's rating, July 2009	NA

Revenues, 2008

Total	$1,740,231
From all taxes	1,374,559
Federal aid	0
State aid	269,591
From other governments	2,283
Charges for services	7,251
Licenses, permits & fees	575
Fines & forfeits	40
Interfund transfers	9,530
Misc/other/special assessments	38,201

Expenditures, 2008

Total	$1,730,325
General government	220,041
Public safety	51,213
Other/fixed costs	73,203
Human services	990
Culture & recreation	6,846
Debt Service	23,596
Education	953,228
Public works	400,743
Intergovernmental	465

Taxation, 2010

Property type	Valuation	Rate
Total	$85,669,458	-
Residential	78,740,409	15.33
Open space	0	0.00
Commercial	4,026,892	15.33
Industrial	393,500	15.33
Personal	2,508,657	15.33

Average Single Family Tax Bill, 2010

Avg. assessed home value	$177,624
Avg. single fam. tax bill	$2,723
Hi-Lo ranking	261/301

Police & Crime, 2008

Number of police officers	NA
Violent crimes	NA
Property crimes	NA

Local School District

(school data 2007-08, except as noted)

Peru (non-op)
PO Box 299
Dalton, MA 01227
413-684-0320

Superintendent	James Stankiewicz

Non-operating district.
Resident students are sent to the Other School Districts listed below.

Grade plan	NA
Total enrollment '09-10	NA
Grade 12 enrollment, '09-10	NA
Graduation rate	NA
Dropout rate	NA
Per-pupil expenditure	NA
Avg teacher salary	NA
Student/teacher ratio '08-09	NA
Highly-qualified teachers, '08-09	NA
Teachers licensed in assigned subject	NA
Students per computer	NA

Other School Districts (see Appendix D for data)
Central Berkshire Regional

©2010 Information Publications, Inc. All rights reserved. Photocopying prohibited. For additional copies, contact the publisher at www.informationpublications.com or (877)544-INFO (4636)

See Introduction for an explanation of all data sources.

Demographics & Socio-Economic Characteristics

Population

1990	1,131
2000	1,180
Male	594
Female	586
2008	1,288
2010 (projected)††	1,191
2020 (projected)††	1,209

Race & Hispanic Origin, 2000

Race	
White	1,147
Black/African American	8
American Indian/Alaska Native	9
Asian	3
Hawaiian Native/Pacific Islander	0
Other Race	1
Two or more races	12
Hispanic origin	13

Age & Nativity, 2000

Under 5 years	60
18 years and over	916
21 years and over	897
65 years and over	207
85 years and over	28
Median Age	43.2
Native-born	1,118
Foreign-born	62

Age, 2020 (projected)††

Under 5 years	57
5 to 19 years	183
20 to 39 years	227
40 to 64 years	389
65 years and over	353

Educational Attainment, 2000

Population 25 years and over	861
High School graduates or higher	94.7%
Bachelor's degree or higher	46.0%
Graduate degree	23.7%

Income & Poverty, 1999

Per capita income,	$24,222
Median household income	$47,833
Median family income	$58,125
Persons in poverty	66
H'holds receiving public assistance	7
H'holds receiving social security	156

Households, 2000

Total households	438
With persons under 18	137
With persons over 65	118
Family households	299
Single person households	119
Persons per household	2.5
Persons per family	3.0

Labor & Employment, 2000

Civilian labor force	639
Unemployment rate	6.6%
Civilian labor force, 2008†	666
Unemployment rate†	5.6%
Civilian labor force, 12/09†	687
Unemployment rate†	9.2%
Employed persons 16 years and over, by occupation:	
Managers & professionals	328
Service occupations	59
Sales & office occupations	117
Farming, fishing & forestry	2
Construction & maintenance	41
Production & transportation	50
Self-employed persons	78

Most demographic data is from the 2000 Decennial Census
† Massachusetts Department of Revenue
†† University of Massachusetts, MISER

General Information

Town of Petersham
3 South Main Street
PO Box 486
Petersham, MA 01366
978-724-3353

Elevation	1,070 ft.
Land area (square miles)	54.2
Water area (square miles)	14.1
Population density, 2008 (est)	23.8
Year incorporated	1754
Website	NA

Voters & Government Information

Government type	Open Town Meeting
Number of Selectmen	3
US Congressional District(s)	1

Registered Voters, October 2008

Total	946
Democrats	201
Republicans	144
Unaffiliated/other	595

Local Officials, 2010

Chair, Bd. of Sel.	Frederik Marsh
Admin Coordinator	Dale Bull
Town Clerk	Diana L. Cooley
Finance Director	Ross France
Tax Collector	Virginia Newman
Tax Assessor	Dana W. Kennan
Attorney	Kopelman & Paige
Public Works	Timothy Graves
Building	Brianna Skowyra
Planning	Fred Day
Police Chief	Denis N. Legare
Emerg/Fire Chief	Dana C. Robinson

Housing & Construction

New Privately Owned Housing Units Authorized by Building Permit

	Single Family	Total Bldgs	Total Units
2006	6	6	6
2007	6	6	6
2008	3	3	3

Parcel Count by Property Class, 2010

Total	850
Single family	461
Multiple units	16
Apartments	1
Condos	0
Vacant land	253
Open space	0
Commercial	10
Industrial	3
Misc. residential	15
Other use	91

Public Library

Petersham Memorial Library
23 Common St.
Petersham, MA 01366
(978)724-3405

Director	Jayne Arata

Library Statistics, FY 2008

Population served, 2007	1,283
Registered users	561
Circulation	9,957
Reference transactons	377
Total program attendance	6,704
per capita:	
Holdings	12.22
Operating income	$59.68
Internet Access	
Internet computers available	2
Weekly users	12

Municipal Finance

Debt at year end 2008	$1,255,000
Moody's rating, July 2009	NA

Revenues, 2008

Total	$3,131,120
From all taxes	2,332,625
Federal aid	0
State aid	651,806
From other governments	1,125
Charges for services	2,065
Licenses, permits & fees	3,650
Fines & forfeits	9,647
Interfund transfers	107,834
Misc/other/special assessments	11,184

Expenditures, 2008

Total	$3,114,638
General government	271,631
Public safety	249,825
Other/fixed costs	193,100
Human services	13,882
Culture & recreation	19,377
Debt Service	103,169
Education	1,881,261
Public works	282,192
Intergovernmental	92,077

Taxation, 2010

Property type	Valuation	Rate
Total	$154,027,076	-
Residential	144,819,130	13.30
Open space	0	0.00
Commercial	4,277,370	13.30
Industrial	160,200	13.30
Personal	4,770,376	13.30

Average Single Family Tax Bill, 2010

Avg. assessed home value	$261,832
Avg. single fam. tax bill	$3,482
Hi-Lo ranking	173/301

Police & Crime, 2008

Number of police officers	2
Violent crimes	NA
Property crimes	NA

Local School District

(school data 2007-08, except as noted)

Petersham
P O Box 148
Petersham, MA 01366
978-724-3363

Superintendent	Patricia Martin
Grade plan	K-6
Total enrollment '09-10	107
Grade 12 enrollment, '09-10	0
Graduation rate	NA
Dropout rate	NA
Per-pupil expenditure	$10,920
Avg teacher salary	$52,183
Student/teacher ratio '08-09	11.2 to 1
Highly-qualified teachers, '08-09	100.0%
Teachers licensed in assigned subject	96.1%
Students per computer	NA

Massachusetts Competency Assessment System (MCAS), 2009 results

	English		Math	
	% Prof	CPI	% Prof	CPI
Gr 4	50%	87.5	57%	83.9
Gr 6	82%	91.2	47%	79.4
Gr 8	NA	NA	NA	NA
Gr 10	NA	NA	NA	NA

Other School Districts (see Appendix D for data)

Ralph C. Mahar Regional, Montachusett Vocational Tech

©2010 Information Publications, Inc. All rights reserved. Photocopying prohibited. For additional copies, contact the publisher at www.informationpublications.com or (877)544-INFO (4636)

See Introduction for an explanation of all data sources.

Demographics & Socio-Economic Characteristics

Population

1990	1,485
2000	1,621
Male	815
Female	806
2008	1,787
2010 (projected)††	1,901
2020 (projected)††	2,304

Race & Hispanic Origin, 2000

Race	
White	1,584
Black/African American	6
American Indian/Alaska Native	2
Asian	6
Hawaiian Native/Pacific Islander	0
Other Race	0
Two or more races	23
Hispanic origin	7

Age & Nativity, 2000

Under 5 years	96
18 years and over	1,147
21 years and over	1,103
65 years and over	122
85 years and over	19
Median Age	36.6
Native-born	1,603
Foreign-born	18

Age, 2020 (projected)††

Under 5 years	125
5 to 19 years	355
20 to 39 years	630
40 to 64 years	868
65 years and over	326

Educational Attainment, 2000

Population 25 years and over	1,056
High School graduates or higher	90.1%
Bachelor's degree or higher	16.2%
Graduate degree	6.1%

Income & Poverty, 1999

Per capita income,	$18,706
Median household income	$46,845
Median family income	$52,011
Persons in poverty	93
H'holds receiving public assistance	12
H'holds receiving social security	116

Households, 2000

Total households	580
With persons under 18	244
With persons over 65	94
Family households	443
Single person households	102
Persons per household	2.8
Persons per family	3.2

Labor & Employment, 2000

Civilian labor force	887
Unemployment rate	3.0%
Civilian labor force, 2008†	943
Unemployment rate†	7.1%
Civilian labor force, 12/09†	937
Unemployment rate†	9.8%
Employed persons 16 years and over, by occupation:	
Managers & professionals	244
Service occupations	121
Sales & office occupations	209
Farming, fishing & forestry	14
Construction & maintenance	109
Production & transportation	163
Self-employed persons	90

Most demographic data is from the 2000 Decennial Census
† Massachusetts Department of Revenue
†† University of Massachusetts, MISER

General Information

Town of Phillipston
50 The Common
Phillipston, MA 01331
978-249-6828

Elevation	1,166 ft.
Land area (square miles)	24.3
Water area (square miles)	0.4
Population density, 2008 (est)	73.5
Year incorporated	1814
Website	phillipston-ma.gov

Voters & Government Information

Government type	Open Town Meeting
Number of Selectmen	3
US Congressional District(s)	1

Registered Voters, October 2008

Total	1,192
Democrats	204
Republicans	131
Unaffiliated/other	847

Local Officials, 2010

Chair, Bd. of Sel.	Bernard Malouin
Manager/Admin	Susan Varney
Town Clerk	Karin Foley
Finance Director	R. French/T. French
Tax Collector	Sally Kastberg
Tax Assessor	Reginald Haughton Jr
Attorney	Kopelman & Paige
Public Works	James Mackie
Building	Geoffrey Newton
Comm Dev/Planning	Geoffrey Newton
Police Chief	Richard Valcourt
Fire Chief	Richard Stevens

Housing & Construction

New Privately Owned Housing Units Authorized by Building Permit

	Single Family	Total Bldgs	Total Units
2006	13	13	13
2007	5	5	5
2008	1	1	1

Parcel Count by Property Class, 2010

Total	NA
Single family	NA
Multiple units	NA
Apartments	NA
Condos	NA
Vacant land	NA
Open space	NA
Commercial	NA
Industrial	NA
Misc. residential	NA
Other use	NA

Public Library

Phillips Free Public Library
25 Templeton Rd.
Phillipston, MA 01331
(978)249-1734

Director: Jennifer Mosher (Int)

Library Statistics, FY 2008

Population served, 2007	1,787
Registered users	0
Circulation	5,680
Reference transactons	6
Total program attendance	2,500
per capita:	
Holdings	7.45
Operating income	$30.54
Internet Access	
Internet computers available	1
Weekly users	3

Municipal Finance

Debt at year end 2008	$174,023
Moody's rating, July 2009	NA

Revenues, 2008

Total	$3,272,730
From all taxes	2,617,947
Federal aid	0
State aid	435,595
From other governments	0
Charges for services	40,887
Licenses, permits & fees	11,600
Fines & forfeits	22,685
Interfund transfers	92,280
Misc/other/special assessments	25,868

Expenditures, 2008

Total	$2,893,238
General government	349,084
Public safety	386,495
Other/fixed costs	122,219
Human services	59,705
Culture & recreation	35,905
Debt Service	71,792
Education	1,558,741
Public works	304,398
Intergovernmental	4,899

Taxation, 2010

Property type	Valuation	Rate
Total	NA	-
Residential	NA	NA
Open space	NA	NA
Commercial	NA	NA
Industrial	NA	NA
Personal	NA	NA

Average Single Family Tax Bill, 2010

Avg. assessed home value	NA
Avg. single fam. tax bill	NA
Hi-Lo ranking	NA

Police & Crime, 2008

Number of police officers	2
Violent crimes	NA
Property crimes	NA

Local School District

(school data 2007-08, except as noted)

Phillipston (non-op)
4 Elm Street
Baldwinville, MA 01436
978-939-5661

Superintendent: Stephen Hemman

Non-operating district.
Resident students are sent to the Other School Districts listed below.

Grade plan	NA
Total enrollment '09-10	NA
Grade 12 enrollment, '09-10	NA
Graduation rate	NA
Dropout rate	NA
Per-pupil expenditure	NA
Avg teacher salary	NA
Student/teacher ratio '08-09	NA
Highly-qualified teachers, '08-09	NA
Teachers licensed in assigned subject	NA
Students per computer	NA

Other School Districts (see Appendix D for data)
Narragansett Regional, Montachusett Vocational Tech

©2010 Information Publications, Inc. All rights reserved. Photocopying prohibited. For additional copies, contact the publisher at www.informationpublications.com or (877)544-INFO (4636)

Demographics & Socio-Economic Characteristics*

Population

1990	48,622
2000	45,793
Male	21,765
Female	24,028
2008	42,652
2010 (projected)††	41,203
2020 (projected)††	37,146

Race & Hispanic Origin, 2000

Race	
White	42,395
Black/African American	1,674
American Indian/Alaska Native	65
Asian	533
Hawaiian Native/Pacific Islander	20
Other Race	354
Two or more races	752
Hispanic origin	934

Age & Nativity, 2000

Under 5 years	2,719
18 years and over	35,190
21 years and over	33,787
65 years and over	8,538
85 years and over	1,231
Median Age	39.6
Native-born	44,020
Foreign-born	1,773

Age, 2020 (projected)††

Under 5 years	1,868
5 to 19 years	5,625
20 to 39 years	8,807
40 to 64 years	12,320
65 years and over	8,526

Educational Attainment, 2000

Population 25 years and over	32,063
High School graduates or higher	84.4%
Bachelor's degree or higher	20.5%
Graduate degree	8.1%

Income & Poverty, 1999

Per capita income,	$20,549
Median household income	$35,655
Median family income	$46,228
Persons in poverty	5,075
H'holds receiving public assistance	702
H'holds receiving social security	6,601

Households, 2000

Total households	19,704
With persons under 18	5,793
With persons over 65	5,913
Family households	11,822
Single person households	6,694
Persons per household	2.3
Persons per family	2.9

Labor & Employment, 2000

Civilian labor force	22,626
Unemployment rate	6.0%
Civilian labor force, 2008†	22,813
Unemployment rate†	6.8%
Civilian labor force, 12/09†	22,708
Unemployment rate†	9.2%
Employed persons 16 years and over, by occupation:	
Managers & professionals	6,890
Service occupations	4,375
Sales & office occupations	5,883
Farming, fishing & forestry	109
Construction & maintenance	1,674
Production & transportation	2,335
Self-employed persons	1,209

Most demographic data is from the 2000 Decennial Census
* see Appendix E for American Community Survey data
† Massachusetts Department of Revenue
†† University of Massachusetts, MISER

General Information

City of Pittsfield
70 Allen St
Pittsfield, MA 01201

Elevation	1,000 ft.
Land area (square miles)	40.7
Water area (square miles)	1.6
Population density, 2008 (est)	1,048.0
Year incorporated	1761
Website	www.pittsfield.com

Voters & Government Information

Government type	Mayor-Council
Number of Councilors	11
US Congressional District(s)	1

Registered Voters, October 2008

Total	30,080
Democrats	13,468
Republicans	3,173
Unaffiliated/other	13,168

Local Officials, 2010

Mayor	James M. Ruberto
Manager/Admin	NA
Clerk	Linda M. Tyer
Finance Director	Susan Carmel
Tax Collector	Marilyn Sheehan
Tax Assessor	William Marsele Sr
Attorney	NA
Public Works	Bruce Collingwood
Building	Gerald Garner
Planning	Deanna Ruffer
Police Chief	Michael Wynn (Actg)
Fire Chief	Robert Czerwinski (Actg)

Housing & Construction

New Privately Owned Housing Units Authorized by Building Permit

	Single Family	Total Bldgs	Total Units
2006	88	88	88
2007	73	73	73
2008	20	25	63

Parcel Count by Property Class, 2010

Total	17,773
Single family	11,265
Multiple units	2,060
Apartments	450
Condos	576
Vacant land	1,921
Open space	82
Commercial	745
Industrial	247
Misc. residential	71
Other use	356

Public Library

Berkshire Athenaeum
1 Wendell Avenue
Pittsfield, MA 01201
(413)499-9480

Director	Ronald Latham

Library Statistics, FY 2008

Population served, 2007	42,931
Registered users	32,735
Circulation	257,938
Reference transactons	36,266
Total program attendance	0
per capita:	
Holdings	4.22
Operating income	$25.42
Internet Access	
Internet computers available	12
Weekly users	678

Municipal Finance

Debt at year end 2008	$51,310,000
Moody's rating, July 2009	A3

Revenues, 2008

Total	$117,335,161
From all taxes	60,111,983
Federal aid	0
State aid	48,747,614
From other governments	0
Charges for services	1,562,650
Licenses, permits & fees	452,642
Fines & forfeits	218,453
Interfund transfers	151,373
Misc/other/special assessments	3,045,223

Expenditures, 2008

Total	$113,984,795
General government	6,899,519
Public safety	13,065,737
Other/fixed costs	27,963,255
Human services	1,435,507
Culture & recreation	1,482,768
Debt Service	6,478,422
Education	48,255,595
Public works	7,165,252
Intergovernmental	2,338,303

Taxation, 2010

Property type	Valuation	Rate
Total	$3,472,586,080	-
Residential	2,729,423,890	14.20
Open space	23,354,900	14.20
Commercial	423,360,590	29.41
Industrial	128,942,170	29.41
Personal	167,504,530	29.41

Average Single Family Tax Bill, 2010

Avg. assessed home value	$187,519
Avg. single fam. tax bill	$2,663
Hi-Lo ranking	268/301

Police & Crime, 2008

Number of police officers	88
Violent crimes	298
Property crimes	1,105

Local School District

(school data 2007-08, except as noted)

Pittsfield
269 First Street
Pittsfield, MA 01201
413-499-9512

Superintendent	Howard Eberwein
Grade plan	PK-12
Total enrollment '09-10	6,072
Grade 12 enrollment, '09-10	410
Graduation rate	74.0%
Dropout rate	12.5%
Per-pupil expenditure	$11,930
Avg teacher salary	$51,351
Student/teacher ratio '08-09	11.8 to 1
Highly-qualified teachers, '08-09	94.8%
Teachers licensed in assigned subject	95.4%
Students per computer	2.3

Massachusetts Competency Assessment System (MCAS), 2009 results

	English		Math	
	% Prof	CPI	% Prof	CPI
Gr 4	43%	77.4	46%	78.8
Gr 6	57%	82.2	51%	75.8
Gr 8	73%	88.6	40%	69.7
Gr 10	64%	86.4	60%	81.1

Other School Districts (see Appendix D for data)
Receives students from Richmond

©2010 Information Publications, Inc. All rights reserved. Photocopying prohibited. For additional copies, contact the publisher at www.informationpublications.com or (877)544-INFO (4636)

See Introduction for an explanation of all data sources.

Demographics & Socio-Economic Characteristics

Population

1990	571
2000	589
Male	286
Female	303
2008	591
2010 (projected)††	689
2020 (projected)††	762

Race & Hispanic Origin, 2000

Race	
White	578
Black/African American	0
American Indian/Alaska Native	2
Asian	1
Hawaiian Native/Pacific Islander	0
Other Race	0
Two or more races	8
Hispanic origin	4

Age & Nativity, 2000

Under 5 years	28
18 years and over	443
21 years and over	427
65 years and over	76
85 years and over	6
Median Age	42.3
Native-born	553
Foreign-born	23

Age, 2020 (projected)††

Under 5 years	26
5 to 19 years	79
20 to 39 years	114
40 to 64 years	336
65 years and over	207

Educational Attainment, 2000

Population 25 years and over	415
High School graduates or higher	88.7%
Bachelor's degree or higher	30.8%
Graduate degree	16.6%

Income & Poverty, 1999

Per capita income,	$20,785
Median household income	$37,250
Median family income	$46,042
Persons in poverty	46
H'holds receiving public assistance	7
H'holds receiving social security	69

Households, 2000

Total households	243
With persons under 18	78
With persons over 65	58
Family households	167
Single person households	63
Persons per household	2.4
Persons per family	2.9

Labor & Employment, 2000

Civilian labor force	285
Unemployment rate	1.4%
Civilian labor force, 2008†	309
Unemployment rate†	8.4%
Civilian labor force, 12/09†	306
Unemployment rate†	9.2%
Employed persons 16 years and over, by occupation:	
Managers & professionals	135
Service occupations	21
Sales & office occupations	41
Farming, fishing & forestry	4
Construction & maintenance	33
Production & transportation	47
Self-employed persons	61

Most demographic data is from the 2000 Decennial Census
† Massachusetts Department of Revenue
†† University of Massachusetts, MISER

General Information

Town of Plainfield
304 Main St
Plainfield, MA 01070
413-634-5420

Elevation	1,600 ft.
Land area (square miles)	21.1
Water area (square miles)	0.2
Population density, 2008 (est)	28.0
Year incorporated	1785
Website	plainfieldmass.us

Voters & Government Information

Government type	Open Town Meeting
Number of Selectmen	3
US Congressional District(s)	1

Registered Voters, October 2008

Total	430
Democrats	114
Republicans	38
Unaffiliated/other	273

Local Officials, 2010

Chair, Bd. of Sel.	Phillip Lococo
Manager/Admin	NA
Clerk	Theresa Thatcher
Treasurer	Linda Alvord
Tax Collector	Mary Lynn Sabourin
Tax Assessor	Wayne Phillips
Attorney	Ronald Berenson
Public Works	Claude Dupont
Building	Claude Dupont
Planning	Robert L. Pershing
Police Chief	David Wood
Fire Chief	Dennis A. Thatcher

Housing & Construction

New Privately Owned Housing Units Authorized by Building Permit

	Single Family	Total Bldgs	Total Units
2006	3	3	3
2007	2	2	2
2008	0	0	0

Parcel Count by Property Class, 2010

Total	608
Single family	247
Multiple units	9
Apartments	0
Condos	0
Vacant land	178
Open space	0
Commercial	4
Industrial	23
Misc. residential	21
Other use	126

Public Library

Shaw Memorial Library
312 Main Street
Plainfield, MA 01070
(413)634-5406

Librarian	Denise Sessions

Library Statistics, FY 2008

Population served, 2007	600
Registered users	0
Circulation	9,552
Reference transactons	0
Total program attendance	0
per capita:	
Holdings	21.95
Operating income	$25.95
Internet Access	
Internet computers available	2
Weekly users	0

Municipal Finance

Debt at year end 2008	$0
Moody's rating, July 2009	NA

Revenues, 2008

Total	$1,584,988
From all taxes	1,158,128
Federal aid	0
State aid	169,187
From other governments	6,084
Charges for services	10,114
Licenses, permits & fees	10,359
Fines & forfeits	0
Interfund transfers	200,000
Misc/other/special assessments	15,558

Expenditures, 2008

Total	$1,348,843
General government	150,280
Public safety	56,798
Other/fixed costs	114,194
Human services	2,232
Culture & recreation	15,719
Debt Service	633
Education	733,864
Public works	269,140
Intergovernmental	2,975

Taxation, 2010

Property type	Valuation	Rate
Total	$84,464,941	-
Residential	72,623,185	14.54
Open space	0	0.00
Commercial	8,256,684	14.54
Industrial	1,035,200	14.54
Personal	2,549,872	14.54

Average Single Family Tax Bill, 2010

Avg. assessed home value	$201,150
Avg. single fam. tax bill	$2,925
Hi-Lo ranking	244/301

Police & Crime, 2008

Number of police officers	NA
Violent crimes	NA
Property crimes	NA

Local School District

(school data 2007-08, except as noted)

Plainfield (non-op)
24 Ashfield Rd
Shelburne Falls, MA 01370
413-625-0192

Superintendent. . . . . Michael Buoniconti

Non-operating district.
Resident students are sent to the Other School Districts listed below.

Grade plan	NA
Total enrollment '09-10	NA
Grade 12 enrollment, '09-10	NA
Graduation rate	NA
Dropout rate	NA
Per-pupil expenditure	NA
Avg teacher salary	NA
Student/teacher ratio '08-09	NA
Highly-qualified teachers, '08-09	NA
Teachers licensed in assigned subject	NA
Students per computer	NA

Other School Districts (see Appendix D for data)
Mohawk Trail Regional

©2010 Information Publications, Inc. All rights reserved. Photocopying prohibited. For additional copies, contact the publisher at www.informationpublications.com or (877)544-INFO (4636)

See Introduction for an explanation of all data sources.

Demographics & Socio-Economic Characteristics

Population

1990 . . . 6,871
2000 . . . 7,683
Male . . . 3,795
Female . . . 3,888
2008 . . . 8,204
2010 (projected)†† . . . 8,297
2020 (projected)†† . . . 9,057

Race & Hispanic Origin, 2000

Race
White . . . 7,435
Black/African American . . . 54
American Indian/Alaska Native . . . 0
Asian . . . 125
Hawaiian Native/Pacific Islander . . . 0
Other Race . . . 19
Two or more races . . . 50
Hispanic origin . . . 73

Age & Nativity, 2000

Under 5 years . . . 523
18 years and over . . . 5,721
21 years and over . . . 5,498
65 years and over . . . 928
85 years and over . . . 83
Median Age . . . 36.9
Native-born . . . 7,321
Foreign-born . . . 362

Age, 2020 (projected)††

Under 5 years . . . 534
5 to 19 years . . . 1,479
20 to 39 years . . . 2,592
40 to 64 years . . . 2,968
65 years and over . . . 1,484

Educational Attainment, 2000

Population 25 years and over . . . 5,226
High School graduates or higher . . . 87.3%
Bachelor's degree or higher . . . 28.3%
Graduate degree . . . 7.2%

Income & Poverty, 1999

Per capita income, . . . $25,816
Median household income . . . $57,155
Median family income . . . $68,640
Persons in poverty . . . 309
H'holds receiving public assistance . . . 71
H'holds receiving social security . . . 690

Households, 2000

Total households . . . 3,009
With persons under 18 . . . 1,055
With persons over 65 . . . 674
Family households . . . 2,040
Single person households . . . 788
Persons per household . . . 2.5
Persons per family . . . 3.1

Labor & Employment, 2000

Civilian labor force . . . 4,423
Unemployment rate . . . 3.6%
Civilian labor force, 2008† . . . 4,779
Unemployment rate† . . . 7.6%
Civilian labor force, 12/09† . . . 4,960
Unemployment rate† . . . 11.3%
Employed persons 16 years and over, by occupation:
Managers & professionals . . . 1,452
Service occupations . . . 643
Sales & office occupations . . . 1,198
Farming, fishing & forestry . . . 6
Construction & maintenance . . . 417
Production & transportation . . . 547
Self-employed persons . . . 187

Most demographic data is from the 2000 Decennial Census
† Massachusetts Department of Revenue
†† University of Massachusetts, MISER

General Information

Town of Plainville
142 South St
PO Box 1717
Plainville, MA 02762
508-695-3142

Elevation . . . 250 ft.
Land area (square miles) . . . 11.1
Water area (square miles) . . . 0.5
Population density, 2008 (est) . . . 739.1
Year incorporated . . . 1905
Website . . . plainville.ma.us

Voters & Government Information

Government type . . . Open Town Meeting
Number of Selectmen . . . 3
US Congressional District(s) . . . 3

Registered Voters, October 2008

Total . . . 5,645
Democrats . . . 1,282
Republicans . . . 890
Unaffiliated/other . . . 3,434

Local Officials, 2010

Chair, Bd. of Sel. . . . Andrea Soucy
Manager/Admin . . . Joseph Fernandes
Town Clerk . . . Ellen Robertson
Finance . . . Kathleen Parker
Tax Collector . . . Kathleen Parker
Tax Assessor . . . Patricia Stewart
Attorney . . . NA
Public Works . . . NA
Building . . . NA
Comm Dev/Planning . . . NA
Police Chief . . . James Alfred Jr
Emerg/Fire Chief . . . Theodore Joubert

Housing & Construction

New Privately Owned Housing Units Authorized by Building Permit

	Single Family	Total Bldgs	Total Units
2006	31	34	37
2007	9	13	41
2008	7	8	13

Parcel Count by Property Class, 2010

Total . . . 3,061
Single family . . . 1,887
Multiple units . . . 121
Apartments . . . 24
Condos . . . 380
Vacant land . . . 328
Open space . . . 0
Commercial . . . 170
Industrial . . . 75
Misc. residential . . . 20
Other use . . . 56

Public Library

Plainville Public Library
198 South St.
Plainville, MA 02762
(508)695-1784

Director . . . Melissa Campbell

Library Statistics, FY 2008

Population served, 2007 . . . 8,311
Registered users . . . 5,140
Circulation . . . 103,628
Reference transactons . . . 0
Total program attendance . . . 0

per capita:

Holdings . . . 5.32
Operating income . . . $26.86

Internet Access

Internet computers available . . . 6
Weekly users . . . 51

Municipal Finance

Debt at year end 2008 . . . $21,278,854
Moody's rating, July 2009 . . . A2

Revenues, 2008

Total . . . $21,522,810
From all taxes . . . 13,914,582
Federal aid . . . 0
State aid . . . 5,200,745
From other governments . . . 9,822
Charges for services . . . 1,193,234
Licenses, permits & fees . . . 66,610
Fines & forfeits . . . 45,410
Interfund transfers . . . 799,155
Misc/other/special assessments . . . 146,626

Expenditures, 2008

Total . . . $22,025,301
General government . . . 1,269,636
Public safety . . . 3,034,281
Other/fixed costs . . . 2,047,625
Human services . . . 296,251
Culture & recreation . . . 253,549
Debt Service . . . 2,441,023
Education . . . 10,870,323
Public works . . . 1,368,894
Intergovernmental . . . 433,329

Taxation, 2010

Property type	Valuation	Rate
Total	$1,178,214,572	-
Residential	914,835,112	12.57
Open space	0	0.00
Commercial	180,597,560	12.57
Industrial	56,231,100	12.57
Personal	26,550,800	12.57

Average Single Family Tax Bill, 2010

Avg. assessed home value . . . $351,007
Avg. single fam. tax bill . . . $4,412
Hi-Lo ranking . . . 105/301

Police & Crime, 2008

Number of police officers . . . 15
Violent crimes . . . 9
Property crimes . . . 118

Local School District

(school data 2007-08, except as noted)

Plainville
68 Messenger Street
Plainville, MA 02762
508-699-1300

Superintendent . . . David Raiche
Grade plan . . . PK-6
Total enrollment '09-10 . . . 823
Grade 12 enrollment, '09-10 . . . 0
Graduation rate . . . NA
Dropout rate . . . NA
Per-pupil expenditure . . . $10,406
Avg teacher salary . . . $56,164
Student/teacher ratio '08-09 . . . 15.4 to 1
Highly-qualified teachers, '08-09 . . . 100.0%
Teachers licensed in assigned subject . 100.0%
Students per computer . . . 2

Massachusetts Competency Assessment System (MCAS), 2009 results

	English		Math	
	% Prof	CPI	% Prof	CPI
Gr 4	49%	79.5	43%	78.7
Gr 6	81%	91	72%	88.6
Gr 8	NA	NA	NA	NA
Gr 10	NA	NA	NA	NA

Other School Districts (see Appendix D for data)

King Philip Regional, Tri County Vocational Tech, Norfolk County Agricultural

©2010 Information Publications, Inc. All rights reserved. Photocopying prohibited. For additional copies, contact the publisher at www.informationpublications.com or (877)544-INFO (4636)

See Introduction for an explanation of all data sources.

Demographics & Socio-Economic Characteristics

Population

1990	45,608
2000	51,701
Male	25,691
Female	26,010
2008	55,705
2010 (projected)††	59,041
2020 (projected)††	68,024

Race & Hispanic Origin, 2000

Race	
White	49,022
Black/African American	988
American Indian/Alaska Native	131
Asian	295
Hawaiian Native/Pacific Islander	20
Other Race	481
Two or more races	764
Hispanic origin	870

Age & Nativity, 2000

Under 5 years	3,478
18 years and over	38,358
21 years and over	36,686
65 years and over	5,812
85 years and over	970
Median Age	36.5
Native-born	49,873
Foreign-born	1,828

Age, 2020 (projected)††

Under 5 years	4,238
5 to 19 years	11,980
20 to 39 years	17,586
40 to 64 years	21,468
65 years and over	12,752

Educational Attainment, 2000

Population 25 years and over	34,729
High School graduates or higher	89.4%
Bachelor's degree or higher	26.4%
Graduate degree	8.5%

Income & Poverty, 1999

Per capita income,	$23,732
Median household income	$54,677
Median family income	$63,266
Persons in poverty	2,640
H'holds receiving public assistance	313
H'holds receiving social security	4,445

Households, 2000

Total households	18,423
With persons under 18	7,099
With persons over 65	3,917
Family households	13,268
Single person households	4,006
Persons per household	2.7
Persons per family	3.2

Labor & Employment, 2000

Civilian labor force	27,061
Unemployment rate	4.5%
Civilian labor force, 2008†	29,954
Unemployment rate†	7.4%
Civilian labor force, 12/09†	29,841
Unemployment rate†	10.3%
Employed persons 16 years and over, by occupation:	
Managers & professionals	9,081
Service occupations	3,853
Sales & office occupations	7,357
Farming, fishing & forestry	97
Construction & maintenance	2,999
Production & transportation	2,467
Self-employed persons	1,593

Most demographic data is from the 2000 Decennial Census
† Massachusetts Department of Revenue
†† University of Massachusetts, MISER

General Information

Town of Plymouth
11 Lincoln St
Plymouth, MA 02360
508-747-1620

Elevation	50 ft.
Land area (square miles)	96.5
Water area (square miles)	37.5
Population density, 2008 (est)	577.3
Year incorporated	1620
Website	www.plymouth-ma.gov

Voters & Government Information

Government type	Rep. Town Meeting
Number of Selectmen/Manager	5
US Congressional District(s)	10

Registered Voters, October 2008

Total	37,824
Democrats	9,593
Republicans	5,457
Unaffiliated/other	22,471

Local Officials, 2010

Chair, Bd. of Sel.	Richard J. Quintal Jr
Manager	Mark Stankiewicz
Town Clerk	Laurence Pizer
Finance Director	Lynne Barrett
Tax Collector	Edward Maccaferri Jr
Tax Assessor	Anne Dunn
Attorney	Kopelman & Paige
Public Works	Hector Castro
Building	Paul McAuliffe
Comm Dev/Planning	Lee Hartmann
Police Chief	Michael Botieri
Emerg/Fire Chief	G. Edward Bradley

Housing & Construction

New Privately Owned Housing Units Authorized by Building Permit

	Single Family	Total Bldgs	Total Units
2006	182	200	225
2007	164	177	191
2008	141	142	176

Parcel Count by Property Class, 2010

Total	25,696
Single family	17,700
Multiple units	607
Apartments	135
Condos	2,439
Vacant land	2,991
Open space	0
Commercial	727
Industrial	297
Misc. residential	167
Other use	633

Public Library

Plymouth Public Library
132 South Street
Plymouth, MA 02360
(508)830-4250

Director	Dinah O'Brien

Library Statistics, FY 2008

Population served, 2007	55,188
Registered users	28,982
Circulation	424,685
Reference transactons	49,795
Total program attendance	232,835
per capita:	
Holdings	4.95
Operating income	$28.77
Internet Access	
Internet computers available	26
Weekly users	1,728

Municipal Finance

Debt at year end 2008	$68,072,744
Moody's rating, July 2009	Aa2

Revenues, 2008

Total	$152,733,973
From all taxes	107,776,608
Federal aid	1,817,673
State aid	28,262,971
From other governments	569,132
Charges for services	1,306,817
Licenses, permits & fees	1,825,375
Fines & forfeits	276,355
Interfund transfers	7,675,134
Misc/other/special assessments	1,611,954

Expenditures, 2008

Total	$122,914,308
General government	6,087,366
Public safety	17,720,301
Other/fixed costs	8,703,679
Human services	1,055,093
Culture & recreation	1,943,653
Debt Service	5,469,543
Education	72,667,799
Public works	5,271,626
Intergovernmental	3,943,617

Taxation, 2010

Property type	Valuation	Rate
Total	$8,987,624,130	-
Residential	6,924,808,248	12.42
Open space	0	0.00
Commercial	818,911,854	12.42
Industrial	982,084,000	12.42
Personal	261,820,028	12.42

Average Single Family Tax Bill, 2010

Avg. assessed home value	$314,154
Avg. single fam. tax bill	$3,902
Hi-Lo ranking	144/301

Police & Crime, 2008

Number of police officers	101
Violent crimes	87
Property crimes	995

Local School District

(school data 2007-08, except as noted)
Plymouth
253 South Meadow Rd
Plymouth, MA 02360
508-830-4300

Superintendent	Gary Maestas
Grade plan	PK-12
Total enrollment '09-10	8,240
Grade 12 enrollment, '09-10	554
Graduation rate	83.8%
Dropout rate	9.1%
Per-pupil expenditure	$12,061
Avg teacher salary	$60,283
Student/teacher ratio '08-09	13.9 to 1
Highly-qualified teachers, '08-09	99.4%
Teachers licensed in assigned subject	99.0%
Students per computer	4.9

Massachusetts Competency Assessment System (MCAS), 2009 results

	English		Math	
	% Prof	CPI	% Prof	CPI
Gr 4	63%	85.5	51%	81.6
Gr 6	70%	87.5	57%	77.8
Gr 8	87%	95.4	50%	76.4
Gr 10	85%	94.2	73%	88.3

Other School Districts (see Appendix D for data)
None

©2010 Information Publications, Inc. All rights reserved. Photocopying prohibited. For additional copies, contact the publisher at www.informationpublications.com or (877)544-INFO (4636)

©2010 Information Publications, Inc. All rights reserved. Photocopying prohibited. For additional copies, contact the publisher at www.informationpublications.com or (877)544-INFO (4636)

Demographics & Socio-Economic Characteristics

Population

1990	2,384
2000	2,637
Male	1,296
Female	1,341
2008	2,785
2010 (projected)††	2,783
2020 (projected)††	2,936

Race & Hispanic Origin, 2000

Race	
White	2,554
Black/African American	26
American Indian/Alaska Native	16
Asian	9
Hawaiian Native/Pacific Islander	0
Other Race	14
Two or more races	18
Hispanic origin	11

Age & Nativity, 2000

Under 5 years	161
18 years and over	1,884
21 years and over	1,797
65 years and over	173
85 years and over	18
Median Age	37.7
Native-born	2,583
Foreign-born	54

Age, 2020 (projected)††

Under 5 years	192
5 to 19 years	594
20 to 39 years	693
40 to 64 years	1,011
65 years and over	446

Educational Attainment, 2000

Population 25 years and over	1,706
High School graduates or higher	92.7%
Bachelor's degree or higher	27.3%
Graduate degree	12.1%

Income & Poverty, 1999

Per capita income,	$24,344
Median household income	$70,045
Median family income	$75,000
Persons in poverty	54
H'holds receiving public assistance	20
H'holds receiving social security	157

Households, 2000

Total households	854
With persons under 18	404
With persons over 65	130
Family households	737
Single person households	90
Persons per household	3.1
Persons per family	3.3

Labor & Employment, 2000

Civilian labor force	1,537
Unemployment rate	4.0%
Civilian labor force, 2008†	1,636
Unemployment rate†	7.8%
Civilian labor force, 12/09†	1,612
Unemployment rate†	8.7%
Employed persons 16 years and over, by occupation:	
Managers & professionals	510
Service occupations	217
Sales & office occupations	391
Farming, fishing & forestry	0
Construction & maintenance	231
Production & transportation	127
Self-employed persons	115

Most demographic data is from the 2000 Decennial Census
† Massachusetts Department of Revenue
†† University of Massachusetts, MISER

General Information

Town of Plympton
5 Palmer Road
Plympton, MA 02367
781-585-3220

Elevation	105 ft.
Land area (square miles)	14.8
Water area (square miles)	0.4
Population density, 2008 (est)	188.2
Year incorporated	1707
Website	www.town.plympton.ma.us

Voters & Government Information

Government type	Open Town Meeting
Number of Selectmen	3
US Congressional District(s)	10

Registered Voters, October 2008

Total	2,015
Democrats	353
Republicans	297
Unaffiliated/other	1,355

Local Officials, 2010

Chair, Bd. of Sel.	Joseph A. Freitas
Manager/Admin	NA
Town Clerk	Nancy J. Butler
Finance Director	Carolyn A. Northon
Tax Collector	Carolyn A. Northon
Tax Assessor	George I. Thompson
Attorney	Kopelman & Paige
Public Works	James Mulcahy
Building	Robert Jacobson
Comm Dev/Planning	John D. O'Leary
Police Chief	Matthew M. Clancy
Emerg/Fire Chief	David Rich

Housing & Construction

New Privately Owned Housing Units Authorized by Building Permit

	Single Family	Total Bldgs	Total Units
2006	17	17	17
2007	6	7	8
2008	5	5	5

Parcel Count by Property Class, 2010

Total	1,279
Single family	891
Multiple units	10
Apartments	2
Condos	14
Vacant land	211
Open space	0
Commercial	23
Industrial	23
Misc. residential	7
Other use	98

Public Library

Plympton Public Library
248 Main St.
Plympton, MA 02367
(781)585-4551

Director	Debra Batson

Library Statistics, FY 2008

Population served, 2007	2,772
Registered users	1,200
Circulation	24,898
Reference transactons	624
Total program attendance	7,141
per capita:	
Holdings	9.55
Operating income	$37.01
Internet Access	
Internet computers available	3
Weekly users	33

Municipal Finance

Debt at year end 2008	$1,362,852
Moody's rating, July 2009	NA

Revenues, 2008

Total	$6,885,757
From all taxes	5,658,000
Federal aid	0
State aid	847,401
From other governments	0
Charges for services	156,979
Licenses, permits & fees	87,873
Fines & forfeits	0
Interfund transfers	77,790
Misc/other/special assessments	28,857

Expenditures, 2008

Total	$6,853,610
General government	360,773
Public safety	780,188
Other/fixed costs	529,975
Human services	55,353
Culture & recreation	107,571
Debt Service	138,250
Education	4,359,510
Public works	475,729
Intergovernmental	44,261

Taxation, 2010

Property type	Valuation	Rate
Total	$379,236,180	-
Residential	338,339,739	15.01
Open space	0	0.00
Commercial	12,351,874	15.01
Industrial	13,122,687	15.01
Personal	15,421,880	15.01

Average Single Family Tax Bill, 2010

Avg. assessed home value	$332,675
Avg. single fam. tax bill	$4,993
Hi-Lo ranking	76/301

Police & Crime, 2008

Number of police officers	7
Violent crimes	NA
Property crimes	NA

Local School District

(school data 2007-08, except as noted)

Plympton
250 Pembroke Street
Kingston, MA 02364
781-585-4313

Superintendent	John Tuffy
Grade plan	K-6
Total enrollment '09-10	245
Grade 12 enrollment, '09-10	0
Graduation rate	NA
Dropout rate	NA
Per-pupil expenditure	$10,080
Avg teacher salary	$63,816
Student/teacher ratio '08-09	14.1 to 1
Highly-qualified teachers, '08-09	100.0%
Teachers licensed in assigned subject	100.0%
Students per computer	3.5

Massachusetts Competency Assessment System (MCAS), 2009 results

	English		Math	
	% Prof	CPI	% Prof	CPI
Gr 4	48%	75	31%	74.1
Gr 6	81%	93.8	75%	91.4
Gr 8	NA	NA	NA	NA
Gr 10	NA	NA	NA	NA

Other School Districts (see Appendix D for data)
Silver Lake Regional

See Introduction for an explanation of all data sources.

Demographics & Socio-Economic Characteristics

Population

1990	3,189
2000	3,353
Male	1,693
Female	1,660
2008	3,475
2010 (projected)††	3,313
2020 (projected)††	3,384

Race & Hispanic Origin, 2000

Race	
White	3,244
Black/African American	10
American Indian/Alaska Native	11
Asian	32
Hawaiian Native/Pacific Islander	0
Other Race	21
Two or more races	35
Hispanic origin	49

Age & Nativity, 2000

Under 5 years	191
18 years and over	2,383
21 years and over	2,285
65 years and over	286
85 years and over	28
Median Age	40.1
Native-born	3,189
Foreign-born	164

Age, 2020 (projected)††

Under 5 years	194
5 to 19 years	550
20 to 39 years	800
40 to 64 years	1,120
65 years and over	720

Educational Attainment, 2000

Population 25 years and over	2,218
High School graduates or higher	97.7%
Bachelor's degree or higher	54.8%
Graduate degree	23.9%

Income & Poverty, 1999

Per capita income,	$32,232
Median household income	$80,993
Median family income	$84,300
Persons in poverty	148
H'holds receiving public assistance	16
H'holds receiving social security	216

Households, 2000

Total households	1,166
With persons under 18	509
With persons over 65	204
Family households	960
Single person households	157
Persons per household	2.9
Persons per family	3.2

Labor & Employment, 2000

Civilian labor force	1,865
Unemployment rate	2.7%
Civilian labor force, 2008†	1,937
Unemployment rate†	5.0%
Civilian labor force, 12/09†	1,945
Unemployment rate†	6.5%
Employed persons 16 years and over, by occupation:	
Managers & professionals	1,032
Service occupations	228
Sales & office occupations	355
Farming, fishing & forestry	0
Construction & maintenance	92
Production & transportation	107
Self-employed persons	146

Most demographic data is from the 2000 Decennial Census
† Massachusetts Department of Revenue
†† University of Massachusetts, MISER

General Information

Town of Princeton
6 Town Hall Dr
Princeton, MA 01541
978-464-2100

Elevation	1,175 ft.
Land area (square miles)	35.4
Water area (square miles)	0.4
Population density, 2008 (est)	98.2
Year incorporated	1771
Website	www.town.princeton.ma.us

Voters & Government Information

Government type	Open Town Meeting
Number of Selectmen	3
US Congressional District(s)	3

Registered Voters, October 2008

Total	2,721
Democrats	492
Republicans	457
Unaffiliated/other	1,759

Local Officials, 2010

Chair, Bd. of Sel.	Alan Sentkowski
Manager	John Lebeaux
Town Clerk	Lynne Grettum
Treasurer	Wendy Graves
Tax Collector	Bonnie Schmohl
Tax Assessor	Gary MacLeod
Attorney	Brackett & Lucas
Public Works	Glen Lyons
Building	John Wilson
Comm Dev/Planning	NA
Police Chief	Michele Powers
Emerg/Fire Chief	Ray LaPorte

Housing & Construction

New Privately Owned Housing Units Authorized by Building Permit

	Single Family	Total Bldgs	Total Units
2006	6	6	6
2007	5	5	5
2008	3	3	3

Parcel Count by Property Class, 2010

Total	1,641
Single family	1,205
Multiple units	20
Apartments	1
Condos	7
Vacant land	250
Open space	0
Commercial	10
Industrial	5
Misc. residential	1
Other use	142

Public Library

Princeton Public Library
2 Town Hall Dr.
Princeton, MA 01541
(978)464-2115

Director	Wendy F. Pape

Library Statistics, FY 2008

Population served, 2007	3,494
Registered users	2,098
Circulation	39,392
Reference transactons	260
Total program attendance	0
per capita:	
Holdings	6.05
Operating income	$48.22
Internet Access	
Internet computers available	6
Weekly users	26

Municipal Finance

Debt at year end 2008	$2,035,000
Moody's rating, July 2009	A3

Revenues, 2008

Total	$8,383,172
From all taxes	7,257,004
Federal aid	0
State aid	920,322
From other governments	30,880
Charges for services	0
Licenses, permits & fees	78,418
Fines & forfeits	1,360
Interfund transfers	5,000
Misc/other/special assessments	45,094

Expenditures, 2008

Total	$8,088,213
General government	474,187
Public safety	817,494
Other/fixed costs	458,924
Human services	21,785
Culture & recreation	143,088
Debt Service	723,279
Education	4,619,509
Public works	768,952
Intergovernmental	31,995

Taxation, 2010

Property type	Valuation	Rate
Total	$472,906,740	-
Residential	456,793,677	15.38
Open space	0	0.00
Commercial	5,925,818	15.38
Industrial	1,792,000	15.38
Personal	8,395,245	15.38

Average Single Family Tax Bill, 2010

Avg. assessed home value	$332,168
Avg. single fam. tax bill	$5,109
Hi-Lo ranking	72/301

Police & Crime, 2008

Number of police officers	5
Violent crimes	0
Property crimes	32

Local School District

(school data 2007-08, except as noted)

Princeton (non-op)
Jefferson School, 1745 Main Street
Jefferson, MA 01522
508-829-1670

Superintendent	Thomas Pandiscio

Non-operating district.
Resident students are sent to the Other School Districts listed below.

Grade plan	NA
Total enrollment '09-10	NA
Grade 12 enrollment, '09-10	NA
Graduation rate	NA
Dropout rate	NA
Per-pupil expenditure	NA
Avg teacher salary	NA
Student/teacher ratio '08-09	NA
Highly-qualified teachers, '08-09	NA
Teachers licensed in assigned subject	NA
Students per computer	NA

Other School Districts (see Appendix D for data)
Wachusett Regional, Montachusett Vocational Tech

©2010 Information Publications, Inc. All rights reserved. Photocopying prohibited. For additional copies, contact the publisher at www.informationpublications.com or (877)544-INFO (4636)

See Introduction for an explanation of all data sources.

Demographics & Socio-Economic Characteristics

Population

1990	3,561
2000	3,431
Male	1,839
Female	1,592
2008	3,376
2010 (projected)††	3,254
2020 (projected)††	3,029

Race & Hispanic Origin, 2000

Race	
White	3,004
Black/African American	258
American Indian/Alaska Native	11
Asian	17
Hawaiian Native/Pacific Islander	0
Other Race	37
Two or more races	104
Hispanic origin	74

Age & Nativity, 2000

Under 5 years	60
18 years and over	3,158
21 years and over	3,082
65 years and over	610
85 years and over	103
Median Age	45.4
Native-born	3,150
Foreign-born	281

Age, 2020 (projected)††

Under 5 years	49
5 to 19 years	168
20 to 39 years	586
40 to 64 years	1,218
65 years and over	1,008

Educational Attainment, 2000

Population 25 years and over	2,999
High School graduates or higher	85.6%
Bachelor's degree or higher	37.9%
Graduate degree	15.1%

Income & Poverty, 1999

Per capita income,	$26,109
Median household income	$32,716
Median family income	$39,679
Persons in poverty	527
H'holds receiving public assistance	46
H'holds receiving social security	475

Households, 2000

Total households	1,837
With persons under 18	175
With persons over 65	463
Family households	465
Single person households	977
Persons per household	1.7
Persons per family	2.7

Labor & Employment, 2000

Civilian labor force	2,020
Unemployment rate	20.0%
Civilian labor force, 2008†	2,333
Unemployment rate†	28.5%
Civilian labor force, 12/09†	2,508
Unemployment rate†	36.3%
Employed persons 16 years and over, by occupation:	
Managers & professionals	491
Service occupations	375
Sales & office occupations	464
Farming, fishing & forestry	15
Construction & maintenance	175
Production & transportation	96
Self-employed persons	251

Most demographic data is from the 2000 Decennial Census
† Massachusetts Department of Revenue
†† University of Massachusetts, MISER

General Information

Town of Provincetown
260 Commercial St
Provincetown, MA 02657
508-487-7000

Elevation	13 ft.
Land area (square miles)	9.7
Water area (square miles)	7.8
Population density, 2008 (est)	348.0
Year incorporated	1727
Website	www.provincetown-ma.gov

Voters & Government Information

Government type	Open Town Meeting
Number of Selectmen	5
US Congressional District(s)	10

Registered Voters, October 2008

Total	2,958
Democrats	1,699
Republicans	102
Unaffiliated/other	1,133

Local Officials, 2010

Chair, Bd. of Sel.	Michele Couture
Manager	Sharon Lynn
Town Clerk	Doug Johnstone
Finance Director	Alix Heilala
Tax Collector	Barry Stephen
Tax Assessor	Paul Gavin
Attorney	NA
Public Works	David Guertin
Building	Russell Braun
Comm Dev/Planning	NA
Police Chief	Jeff Jaran (Actg)
Emerg/Fire Chief	Michael Trovato

Housing & Construction

New Privately Owned Housing Units Authorized by Building Permit

	Single Family	Total Bldgs	Total Units
2006	22	25	44
2007	18	22	46
2008	14	16	41

Parcel Count by Property Class, 2010

Total	NA
Single family	NA
Multiple units	NA
Apartments	NA
Condos	NA
Vacant land	NA
Open space	NA
Commercial	NA
Industrial	NA
Misc. residential	NA
Other use	NA

Public Library

Provincetown Public Library
356 Commercial St.
Provincetown, MA 02657
(508)487-7094

Director	Jan Voogd

Library Statistics, FY 2008

Population served, 2007	3,390
Registered users	5,611
Circulation	64,042
Reference transactons	11,699
Total program attendance	317,110
per capita:	
Holdings	10.20
Operating income	$104.35
Internet Access	
Internet computers available	14
Weekly users	476

Municipal Finance

Debt at year end 2008	$34,358,731
Moody's rating, July 2009	A2

Revenues, 2008

Total	$20,017,111
From all taxes	14,181,749
Federal aid	123,648
State aid	558,233
From other governments	13,155
Charges for services	1,885,613
Licenses, permits & fees	589,547
Fines & forfeits	179,277
Interfund transfers	708,663
Misc/other/special assessments	888,613

Expenditures, 2008

Total	$18,445,130
General government	2,194,558
Public safety	3,113,466
Other/fixed costs	3,821,545
Human services	500,015
Culture & recreation	514,020
Debt Service	1,759,992
Education	3,946,685
Public works	1,989,879
Intergovernmental	604,970

Taxation, 2010

Property type	Valuation	Rate
Total	NA	-
Residential	NA	NA
Open space	NA	NA
Commercial	NA	NA
Industrial	NA	NA
Personal	NA	NA

Average Single Family Tax Bill, 2010

Avg. assessed home value	NA
Avg. single fam. tax bill	NA
Hi-Lo ranking	NA

Police & Crime, 2008

Number of police officers	17
Violent crimes	17
Property crimes	189

Local School District

(school data 2007-08, except as noted)

Provincetown
2 Mayflower Lane
Provincetown, MA 02657
508-487-5000

Superintendent	Beth Singer
Grade plan	PK-12
Total enrollment '09-10	152
Grade 12 enrollment, '09-10	16
Graduation rate	92.3%
Dropout rate	0.0%
Per-pupil expenditure	$24,002
Avg teacher salary	$57,497
Student/teacher ratio '08-09	5.8 to 1
Highly-qualified teachers, '08-09	94.6%
Teachers licensed in assigned subject	94.6%
Students per computer	1

Massachusetts Competency Assessment System (MCAS), 2009 results

	English		Math	
	% Prof	CPI	% Prof	CPI
Gr 4	58%	87.5	17%	62.5
Gr 6	NA	NA	NA	NA
Gr 8	85%	95	45%	67.5
Gr 10	93%	98.3	88%	93.8

Other School Districts (see Appendix D for data)
Receives students from Truro; sends to Cape Cod Vocational Tech

©2010 Information Publications, Inc. All rights reserved. Photocopying prohibited. For additional copies, contact the publisher at www.informationpublications.com or (877)544-INFO (4636)

See Introduction for an explanation of all data sources.

Demographics & Socio-Economic Characteristics*

Population

1990	84,985
2000	88,025
Male	41,944
Female	46,081
2008	92,339
2010 (projected)††	89,428
2020 (projected)††	91,742

Race & Hispanic Origin, 2000

Race	
White	70,066
Black/African American	1,947
American Indian/Alaska Native	142
Asian	13,546
Hawaiian Native/Pacific Islander	20
Other Race	751
Two or more races	1,553
Hispanic origin	1,835

Age & Nativity, 2000

Under 5 years	4,492
18 years and over	72,644
21 years and over	70,174
65 years and over	14,348
85 years and over	1,999
Median Age	37.6
Native-born	70,383
Foreign-born	17,642

Age, 2020 (projected)††

Under 5 years	4,165
5 to 19 years	13,338
20 to 39 years	24,928
40 to 64 years	32,914
65 years and over	16,397

Educational Attainment, 2000

Population 25 years and over	65,520
High School graduates or higher	85.2%
Bachelor's degree or higher	31.8%
Graduate degree	10.1%

Income & Poverty, 1999

Per capita income,	$26,001
Median household income	$47,121
Median family income	$59,735
Persons in poverty	6,286
H'holds receiving public assistance	812
H'holds receiving social security	11,146

Households, 2000

Total households	38,883
With persons under 18	8,777
With persons over 65	10,717
Family households	20,534
Single person households	14,618
Persons per household	2.2
Persons per family	3.0

Labor & Employment, 2000

Civilian labor force	49,585
Unemployment rate	3.4%
Civilian labor force, 2008†	52,758
Unemployment rate†	6.2%
Civilian labor force, 12/09†	53,073
Unemployment rate†	8.8%
Employed persons 16 years and over, by occupation:	
Managers & professionals	19,236
Service occupations	7,197
Sales & office occupations	14,249
Farming, fishing & forestry	38
Construction & maintenance	3,428
Production & transportation	3,763
Self-employed persons	1,905

Most demographic data is from the 2000 Decennial Census
* see Appendix D and E for American Community Survey data
† Massachusetts Department of Revenue
†† University of Massachusetts, MISER

General Information

City of Quincy
1305 Hancock St
Quincy, MA 02169
617-376-1000

Elevation	44 ft.
Land area (square miles)	16.8
Water area (square miles)	10.1
Population density, 2008 (est)	5,496.4
Year incorporated	1888
Website	www.quincyma.gov

Voters & Government Information

Government type	Mayor-Council
Number of Councilpersons	9
US Congressional District(s)	10

Registered Voters, October 2008

Total	63,219
Democrats	27,789
Republicans	6,812
Unaffiliated/other	28,092

Local Officials, 2010

Mayor	Thomas Koch
Manager/Admin	NA
Clerk	Joseph Shea
Auditor	Nick Puled
Treas/Collector	Deborah Coughlin
Tax Assessor	Marion Fantucchio
Attorney	Jim Timmons
Public Works	Larry Prendeville
Building	Jay Duca
Planning	Dennis Harrington
Police Chief	Paul Kennan
Fire Chief	Joseph Barron

Housing & Construction

New Privately Owned Housing Units Authorized by Building Permit

	Single Family	Total Bldgs	Total Units
2006	37	69	641
2007	21	39	419
2008	12	30	381

Parcel Count by Property Class, 2010

Total	26,027
Single family	13,635
Multiple units	3,790
Apartments	911
Condos	5,850
Vacant land	425
Open space	0
Commercial	998
Industrial	103
Misc. residential	117
Other use	198

Public Library

Thomas Crane Public Library
40 Washington Street
Quincy, MA 02169
(617)376-1301

Director of Libraries . . . Ann E. McLaughlin

Library Statistics, FY 2008

Population served, 2007	91,622
Registered users	42,491
Circulation	750,656
Reference transactons	52,447
Total program attendance	838,508
per capita:	
Holdings	6.71
Operating income	$31.52
Internet Access	
Internet computers available	95
Weekly users	9,044

Municipal Finance

Debt at year end 2008	$74,553,453
Moody's rating, July 2009	A1

Revenues, 2008

Total	$231,943,606
From all taxes	155,292,284
Federal aid	768,676
State aid	43,108,209
From other governments	295,072
Charges for services	1,551,513
Licenses, permits & fees	1,754,527
Fines & forfeits	142,244
Interfund transfers	17,802,127
Misc/other/special assessments	5,614,477

Expenditures, 2008

Total	$190,540,543
General government	10,241,755
Public safety	40,192,585
Other/fixed costs	22,344,633
Human services	2,229,181
Culture & recreation	5,610,492
Debt Service	11,342,924
Education	78,316,436
Public works	14,828,531
Intergovernmental	2,744,488

Taxation, 2010

Property type	Valuation	Rate
Total	$10,850,166,720	-
Residential	8,969,822,436	13.22
Open space	0	0.00
Commercial	1,488,558,464	27.45
Industrial	100,892,500	27.45
Personal	290,893,320	27.45

Average Single Family Tax Bill, 2010

Avg. assessed home value	$330,755
Avg. single fam. tax bill	$4,373
Hi-Lo ranking	108/301

Police & Crime, 2008

Number of police officers	198
Violent crimes	347
Property crimes	1,872

Local School District

(school data 2007-08, except as noted)

Quincy
159 Burgin Parkway
Quincy, MA 02169
617-984-8700

Superintendent	Richard Decristofaro
Grade plan	PK-12
Total enrollment '09-10	8,969
Grade 12 enrollment, '09-10	640
Graduation rate	83.9%
Dropout rate	7.2%
Per-pupil expenditure	$12,945
Avg teacher salary	$64,825
Student/teacher ratio '08-09	13.1 to 1
Highly-qualified teachers, '08-09	95.4%
Teachers licensed in assigned subject	94.6%
Students per computer	5.3

Massachusetts Competency Assessment System (MCAS), 2009 results

	English		Math	
	% Prof	CPI	% Prof	CPI
Gr 4	46%	75.7	38%	73.6
Gr 6	65%	84.9	54%	76.9
Gr 8	84%	93.5	51%	74.4
Gr 10	76%	90.1	73%	88.5

Other School Districts (see Appendix D for data)
Norfolk County Agricultural

©2010 Information Publications, Inc. All rights reserved. Photocopying prohibited. For additional copies, contact the publisher at www.informationpublications.com or (877)544-INFO (4636)

Demographics & Socio-Economic Characteristics*

Population

1990	30,093
2000	30,963
Male	14,808
Female	16,155
2008	30,082
2010 (projected)††	32,201
2020 (projected)††	33,356

Race & Hispanic Origin, 2000

Race	
White	19,455
Black/African American	6,456
American Indian/Alaska Native	70
Asian	3,151
Hawaiian Native/Pacific Islander	11
Other Race	782
Two or more races	1,038
Hispanic origin	1,006

Age & Nativity, 2000

Under 5 years	1,868
18 years and over	23,748
21 years and over	22,818
65 years and over	4,427
85 years and over	559
Median Age	38.3
Native-born	24,313
Foreign-born	6,684

Age, 2020 (projected)††

Under 5 years	1,941
5 to 19 years	6,029
20 to 39 years	8,658
40 to 64 years	11,002
65 years and over	5,726

Educational Attainment, 2000

Population 25 years and over	21,622
High School graduates or higher	87.3%
Bachelor's degree or higher	26.6%
Graduate degree	9.0%

Income & Poverty, 1999

Per capita income,	$23,413
Median household income	$55,255
Median family income	$61,942
Persons in poverty	1,245
H'holds receiving public assistance	240
H'holds receiving social security	3,263

Households, 2000

Total households	11,313
With persons under 18	3,983
With persons over 65	3,200
Family households	7,982
Single person households	2,675
Persons per household	2.7
Persons per family	3.3

Labor & Employment, 2000

Civilian labor force	16,765
Unemployment rate	3.7%
Civilian labor force, 2008†	16,845
Unemployment rate†	6.3%
Civilian labor force, 12/09†	16,844
Unemployment rate†	9.4%
Employed persons 16 years and over, by occupation:	
Managers & professionals	6,035
Service occupations	2,199
Sales & office occupations	4,801
Farming, fishing & forestry	0
Construction & maintenance	1,219
Production & transportation	1,885
Self-employed persons	713

Most demographic data is from the 2000 Decennial Census
* see Appendix E for American Community Survey data
† Massachusetts Department of Revenue
†† University of Massachusetts, MISER

General Information

Town of Randolph
41 South Main St
Randolph, MA 02368
781-961-0900

Elevation	190 ft.
Land area (square miles)	10.1
Water area (square miles)	0.4
Population density, 2008 (est)	2,978.4
Year incorporated	1793
Website	www.townofrandolph.com

Voters & Government Information

Government type	Rep. Twn. Mtg. (240)
Number of Selectmen	5
US Congressional District(s)	9

Registered Voters, October 2008

Total	19,570
Democrats	9,632
Republicans	1,277
Unaffiliated/other	8,561

Local Officials, 2010

Chair, Bd. of Sel.	NA
Manager	David Murphy
Clerk/Registrar	Brian Howard
Treasurer	Loretta Owens
Tax Collector	Loretta Owens
Tax Assessor	Jolanta Briffett Jr
Attorney	Robert Sullivan
Public Works	David Zecchini
Building	Mary McNeil
Planning	Richard McCarthy
Police Chief	Paul Porter
Emerg/Fire Chief	Charles Foley

Housing & Construction

New Privately Owned Housing Units Authorized by Building Permit

	Single Family	Total Bldgs	Total Units
2006	32	32	32
2007	9	9	9
2008	8	17	284

Parcel Count by Property Class, 2010

Total	10,018
Single family	7,080
Multiple units	513
Apartments	69
Condos	1,528
Vacant land	444
Open space	0
Commercial	223
Industrial	104
Misc. residential	19
Other use	38

Public Library

Turner Free Library
Crawford Square, 2 North Main Street
Randolph, MA 02368
(781)961-0931

Director	Charles Michaud

Library Statistics, FY 2008

Population served, 2007	30,168
Registered users	16,073
Circulation	216,221
Reference transactons	13,000
Total program attendance	84,644
per capita:	
Holdings	2.23
Operating income	$23.58
Internet Access	
Internet computers available	10
Weekly users	560

Municipal Finance

Debt at year end 2008	$25,547,125
Moody's rating, July 2009	A3

Revenues, 2008

Total	$74,537,920
From all taxes	41,293,872
Federal aid	0
State aid	20,705,501
From other governments	57,639
Charges for services	10,277,500
Licenses, permits & fees	737,095
Fines & forfeits	28,885
Interfund transfers	1,050,000
Misc/other/special assessments	193,714

Expenditures, 2008

Total	$72,310,248
General government	2,611,230
Public safety	8,791,371
Other/fixed costs	8,114,199
Human services	2,498,024
Culture & recreation	935,949
Debt Service	3,421,429
Education	33,079,813
Public works	7,880,642
Intergovernmental	4,977,591

Taxation, 2010

Property type	Valuation	Rate
Total	$3,010,194,972	-
Residential	2,600,494,373	13.94
Open space	0	0.00
Commercial	251,626,609	25.23
Industrial	95,594,710	25.23
Personal	62,479,280	25.23

Average Single Family Tax Bill, 2010

Avg. assessed home value	$267,015
Avg. single fam. tax bill	$3,722
Hi-Lo ranking	157/301

Police & Crime, 2008

Number of police officers	NA
Violent crimes	150
Property crimes	756

Local School District

(school data 2007-08, except as noted)

Randolph
40 Highland Avenue
Randolph, MA 02368
781-961-6205

Superintendent	Richard Silverman
Grade plan	PK-12
Total enrollment '09-10	2,851
Grade 12 enrollment, '09-10	184
Graduation rate	73.9%
Dropout rate	9.7%
Per-pupil expenditure	$11,858
Avg teacher salary	$59,137
Student/teacher ratio '08-09	12.5 to 1
Highly-qualified teachers, '08-09	92.4%
Teachers licensed in assigned subject	94.2%
Students per computer	6

Massachusetts Competency Assessment System (MCAS), 2009 results

	English		Math	
	% Prof	CPI	% Prof	CPI
Gr 4	27%	66.7	21%	64.5
Gr 6	50%	77.1	36%	64.3
Gr 8	71%	89.1	40%	68.3
Gr 10	68%	88.9	62%	81.5

Other School Districts (see Appendix D for data)
Blue Hills Vocational Tech, Norfolk County Agricultural

©2010 Information Publications, Inc. All rights reserved. Photocopying prohibited. For additional copies, contact the publisher at www.informationpublications.com or (877)544-INFO (4636)

See Introduction for an explanation of all data sources.

Demographics & Socio-Economic Characteristics

Population

1990	9,867
2000	11,739
Male	5,618
Female	6,121
2008	13,566
2010 (projected)††	12,998
2020 (projected)††	14,008

Race & Hispanic Origin, 2000

Race	
White	11,333
Black/African American	122
American Indian/Alaska Native	7
Asian	81
Hawaiian Native/Pacific Islander	3
Other Race	83
Two or more races	110
Hispanic origin	97

Age & Nativity, 2000

Under 5 years	789
18 years and over	8,723
21 years and over	8,361
65 years and over	1,521
85 years and over	176
Median Age	37.8
Native-born	11,075
Foreign-born	664

Age, 2020 (projected)††

Under 5 years	779
5 to 19 years	2,667
20 to 39 years	3,067
40 to 64 years	4,631
65 years and over	2,864

Educational Attainment, 2000

Population 25 years and over	8,045
High School graduates or higher	85.3%
Bachelor's degree or higher	23.3%
Graduate degree	8.9%

Income & Poverty, 1999

Per capita income,	$24,476
Median household income	$60,449
Median family income	$68,354
Persons in poverty	478
H'holds receiving public assistance	65
H'holds receiving social security	1,063

Households, 2000

Total households	4,143
With persons under 18	1,650
With persons over 65	1,004
Family households	3,232
Single person households	742
Persons per household	2.8
Persons per family	3.2

Labor & Employment, 2000

Civilian labor force	6,583
Unemployment rate	3.2%
Civilian labor force, 2008†	8,044
Unemployment rate†	6.0%
Civilian labor force, 12/09†	7,944
Unemployment rate†	8.7%
Employed persons 16 years and over, by occupation:	
Managers & professionals	2,196
Service occupations	914
Sales & office occupations	1,960
Farming, fishing & forestry	3
Construction & maintenance	586
Production & transportation	711
Self-employed persons	459

Most demographic data is from the 2000 Decennial Census
† Massachusetts Department of Revenue
†† University of Massachusetts, MISER

General Information

Town of Raynham
558 South Main St
Raynham, MA 02767
508-824-2700

Elevation	82 ft.
Land area (square miles)	20.5
Water area (square miles)	0.4
Population density, 2008 (est)	661.8
Year incorporated	1731
Website	www.town.raynham.ma.us

Voters & Government Information

Government type	Open Town Meeting
Number of Selectmen	3
US Congressional District(s)	4

Registered Voters, October 2008

Total	9,283
Democrats	2,345
Republicans	1,301
Unaffiliated/other	5,591

Local Officials, 2010

Chair, Bd. of Sel.	Joseph Pacheco
Manager/Admin	Randall Buckner
Town Clerk	Helen B. Lounsbury
Finance Director	Dwayne Wheeler
Tax Collector	Linda King
Tax Assessor	Gordon Luciano
Attorney	NA
Public Works	Roger Stolte
Building	Rod Palmer
Comm Dev/Planning	Marilyn Whalley
Police Chief	Louis Pacheco
Emerg/Fire Chief	James Januse

Housing & Construction

New Privately Owned Housing Units Authorized by Building Permit

	Single Family	Total Bldgs	Total Units
2006	43	43	43
2007	29	29	29
2008	20	20	20

Parcel Count by Property Class, 2010

Total	5,138
Single family	3,532
Multiple units	66
Apartments	24
Condos	397
Vacant land	714
Open space	0
Commercial	262
Industrial	69
Misc. residential	15
Other use	59

Public Library

Raynham Public Library
760 South Main St.
Raynham, MA 02767
(508)823-1344

Director	Eden Fergusson

Library Statistics, FY 2008

Population served, 2007	13,641
Registered users	4,906
Circulation	95,253
Reference transactons	750
Total program attendance	31,000
per capita:	
Holdings	3.07
Operating income	$22.48
Internet Access	
Internet computers available	5
Weekly users	115

Municipal Finance

Debt at year end 2008	$17,722,654
Moody's rating, July 2009	A3

Revenues, 2008

Total	$30,871,489
From all taxes	24,915,195
Federal aid	0
State aid	2,016,395
From other governments	133,050
Charges for services	314,390
Licenses, permits & fees	330,701
Fines & forfeits	30,812
Interfund transfers	1,723,884
Misc/other/special assessments	703,531

Expenditures, 2008

Total	$28,803,555
General government	1,530,697
Public safety	6,341,174
Other/fixed costs	2,652,997
Human services	249,363
Culture & recreation	424,222
Debt Service	298,842
Education	14,978,534
Public works	2,006,645
Intergovernmental	321,081

Taxation, 2010

Property type	Valuation	Rate
Total	$1,876,908,930	-
Residential	1,370,551,650	12.09
Open space	0	0.00
Commercial	336,957,440	16.85
Industrial	123,581,600	16.85
Personal	45,818,240	16.85

Average Single Family Tax Bill, 2010

Avg. assessed home value	$326,393
Avg. single fam. tax bill	$3,946
Hi-Lo ranking	140/301

Police & Crime, 2008

Number of police officers	26
Violent crimes	21
Property crimes	455

Local School District

(school data 2007-08, except as noted)

Raynham (non-op)
687 Pleasant Street
Raynham, MA 02767
508-824-2730

Superintendent	Jacqueline Forbes

Non-operating district.
Resident students are sent to the Other School Districts listed below.

Grade plan	NA
Total enrollment '09-10	NA
Grade 12 enrollment, '09-10	NA
Graduation rate	NA
Dropout rate	NA
Per-pupil expenditure	NA
Avg teacher salary	NA
Student/teacher ratio '08-09	NA
Highly-qualified teachers, '08-09	NA
Teachers licensed in assigned subject	NA
Students per computer	NA

Other School Districts (see Appendix D for data)
Bridgewater-Raynham Regional, Bristol-Plymouth Vocational Tech, Bristol County Agricultural

©2010 Information Publications, Inc. All rights reserved. Photocopying prohibited. For additional copies, contact the publisher at www.informationpublications.com or (877)544-INFO (4636)

See Introduction for an explanation of all data sources.

Demographics & Socio-Economic Characteristics*

Population

1990	22,539
2000	23,708
Male	11,436
Female	12,272
2008	23,052
2010 (projected)††	22,985
2020 (projected)††	21,475

Race & Hispanic Origin, 2000

Race	
White	22,871
Black/African American	86
American Indian/Alaska Native	15
Asian	525
Hawaiian Native/Pacific Islander	6
Other Race	50
Two or more races	155
Hispanic origin	200

Age & Nativity, 2000

Under 5 years	1,701
18 years and over	17,476
21 years and over	16,954
65 years and over	3,369
85 years and over	423
Median Age	39.1
Native-born	22,688
Foreign-born	1,020

Age, 2020 (projected)††

Under 5 years	1,161
5 to 19 years	3,953
20 to 39 years	4,882
40 to 64 years	7,247
65 years and over	4,232

Educational Attainment, 2000

Population 25 years and over	16,304
High School graduates or higher	94.5%
Bachelor's degree or higher	47.8%
Graduate degree	19.7%

Income & Poverty, 1999

Per capita income,	$32,888
Median household income	$77,059
Median family income	$89,076
Persons in poverty	616
H'holds receiving public assistance	69
H'holds receiving social security	2,332

Households, 2000

Total households	8,688
With persons under 18	3,326
With persons over 65	2,326
Family households	6,437
Single person households	1,942
Persons per household	2.7
Persons per family	3.2

Labor & Employment, 2000

Civilian labor force	12,742
Unemployment rate	1.9%
Civilian labor force, 2008†	12,778
Unemployment rate†	4.8%
Civilian labor force, 12/09†	12,773
Unemployment rate†	7.3%
Employed persons 16 years and over, by occupation:	
Managers & professionals	6,590
Service occupations	1,124
Sales & office occupations	3,242
Farming, fishing & forestry	4
Construction & maintenance	769
Production & transportation	774
Self-employed persons	939

Most demographic data is from the 2000 Decennial Census
* see Appendix E for American Community Survey data
† Massachusetts Department of Revenue
†† University of Massachusetts, MISER

General Information

Town of Reading
16 Lowell St
Reading, MA 01867
781-942-9001

Elevation	133 ft.
Land area (square miles)	9.9
Water area (square miles)	0.0
Population density, 2008 (est)	2,328.5
Year incorporated	1644
Website	www.ci.reading.ma.us

Voters & Government Information

Government type	Rep. Twn. Mtg. (192)
Number of Selectmen	5
US Congressional District(s)	6

Registered Voters, October 2008

Total	16,904
Democrats	5,640
Republicans	2,777
Unaffiliated/other	8,395

Local Officials, 2010

Chair, Bd. of Sel.	Ben Tafoya
Town Manager	Peter Hechenbleikner
Town Clerk	Laura A. Gemme
Finance Director	Robert LeLacheur
Tax Collector	Nancy Heffernan
Tax Assessor	NA
Attorney	NA
Public Works	Jeff Zager
Building	Glen Redmond
Comm Dev and Planning	Jean Delios
Police Chief	James W. Cormier
Fire Chief	Gregory Burns

Housing & Construction

New Privately Owned Housing Units Authorized by Building Permit

	Single Family	Total Bldgs	Total Units
2006	22	25	28
2007	18	20	22
2008	12	13	14

Parcel Count by Property Class, 2010

Total	8,276
Single family	6,505
Multiple units	362
Apartments	31
Condos	859
Vacant land	251
Open space	0
Commercial	205
Industrial	19
Misc. residential	11
Other use	33

Public Library

Reading Public Library
64 Middlesex Ave.
Reading, MA 01867
(781)944-0840

Director	Ruth Urell

Library Statistics, FY 2008

Population served, 2007	23,129
Registered users	19,912
Circulation	413,048
Reference transactons	61,934
Total program attendance	0
per capita:	
Holdings	5.52
Operating income	$51.99
Internet Access	
Internet computers available	24
Weekly users	0

Municipal Finance

Debt at year end 2008	$65,587,320
Moody's rating, July 2009	Aa3

Revenues, 2008

Total	$93,137,699
From all taxes	50,699,908
Federal aid	0
State aid	14,751,717
From other governments	164,022
Charges for services	1,478,783
Licenses, permits & fees	137,957
Fines & forfeits	0
Interfund transfers	2,680,840
Misc/other/special assessments	11,612,236

Expenditures, 2008

Total	$74,150,587
General government	2,653,270
Public safety	7,224,441
Other/fixed costs	10,322,411
Human services	492,417
Culture & recreation	1,292,186
Debt Service	11,717,588
Education	34,775,817
Public works	5,064,543
Intergovernmental	583,408

Taxation, 2010

Property type	Valuation	Rate
Total	$3,645,760,801	-
Residential	3,308,115,508	13.75
Open space	0	0.00
Commercial	270,816,033	13.75
Industrial	21,050,500	13.75
Personal	45,778,760	13.75

Average Single Family Tax Bill, 2010

Avg. assessed home value	$432,939
Avg. single fam. tax bill	$5,953
Hi-Lo ranking	48/301

Police & Crime, 2008

Number of police officers	37
Violent crimes	13
Property crimes	265

Local School District

(school data 2007-08, except as noted)

Reading
82 Oakland Road
Reading, MA 01867
781-944-5800

Superintendent	John Doherty
Grade plan	PK-12
Total enrollment '09-10	4,392
Grade 12 enrollment, '09-10	312
Graduation rate	94.2%
Dropout rate	1.8%
Per-pupil expenditure	$10,407
Avg teacher salary	$61,212
Student/teacher ratio '08-09	14.6 to 1
Highly-qualified teachers, '08-09	99.1%
Teachers licensed in assigned subject	98.7%
Students per computer	4.2

Massachusetts Competency Assessment System (MCAS), 2009 results

	English		Math	
	% Prof	CPI	% Prof	CPI
Gr 4	67%	88	63%	88
Gr 6	85%	94	83%	91.6
Gr 8	93%	97.7	77%	90.6
Gr 10	94%	98.2	89%	95.2

Other School Districts (see Appendix D for data)
Northeast Metro Vocational Tech

©2010 Information Publications, Inc. All rights reserved. Photocopying prohibited. For additional copies, contact the publisher at www.informationpublications.com or (877)544-INFO (4636)

See Introduction for an explanation of all data sources.

Demographics & Socio-Economic Characteristics

Population

1990	8,656
2000	10,172
Male	5,040
Female	5,132
2008	11,474
2010 (projected)††	10,825
2020 (projected)††	11,314

Race & Hispanic Origin, 2000

Race	
White	9,938
Black/African American	36
American Indian/Alaska Native	31
Asian	53
Hawaiian Native/Pacific Islander	1
Other Race	26
Two or more races	87
Hispanic origin	51

Age & Nativity, 2000

Under 5 years	602
18 years and over	7,502
21 years and over	7,172
65 years and over	1,013
85 years and over	99
Median Age	39.1
Native-born	9,710
Foreign-born	462

Age, 2020 (projected)††

Under 5 years	596
5 to 19 years	2,029
20 to 39 years	2,511
40 to 64 years	4,115
65 years and over	2,063

Educational Attainment, 2000

Population 25 years and over	6,875
High School graduates or higher	86.8%
Bachelor's degree or higher	32.1%
Graduate degree	10.1%

Income & Poverty, 1999

Per capita income,	$26,467
Median household income	$65,373
Median family income	$71,992
Persons in poverty	313
H'holds receiving public assistance	39
H'holds receiving social security	787

Households, 2000

Total households	3,523
With persons under 18	1,443
With persons over 65	721
Family households	2,872
Single person households	495
Persons per household	2.9
Persons per family	3.2

Labor & Employment, 2000

Civilian labor force	5,813
Unemployment rate	3.3%
Civilian labor force, 2008†	6,674
Unemployment rate†	7.6%
Civilian labor force, 12/09†	6,769
Unemployment rate†	10.6%
Employed persons 16 years and over, by occupation:	
Managers & professionals	2,187
Service occupations	683
Sales & office occupations	1,452
Farming, fishing & forestry	20
Construction & maintenance	588
Production & transportation	689
Self-employed persons	473

Most demographic data is from the 2000 Decennial Census
† Massachusetts Department of Revenue
†† University of Massachusetts, MISER

General Information

Town of Rehoboth
148 Peck St
Rehoboth, MA 02769
508-252-3758

Elevation	50 ft.
Land area (square miles)	46.5
Water area (square miles)	0.3
Population density, 2008 (est)	246.8
Year incorporated	1645
Website	www.town.rehoboth.ma.us

Voters & Government Information

Government type	Open Town Meeting
Number of Selectmen	3
US Congressional District(s)	3

Registered Voters, October 2008

Total	8,173
Democrats	1,547
Republicans	1,381
Unaffiliated/other	5,190

Local Officials, 2010

Chair, Bd. of Sel.	Frederick E. Vadnais Jr
Manager/Exec.	David Marciello
Town Clerk	Kathleen J. Conti
Accountant	Cathy Doane
Treas/Collector	Cheryl Gouveia
Tax Assessor	Eugene Campbell
Attorney	Kopelman & Paige
Public Works	Peter B. Richmond
Building	Michael J. O'Hern
Comm Dev/Planning	LeeAnn Bradley
Police Chief	Stephen J. Enos
Fire Chief	Robert Pray

Housing & Construction

New Privately Owned Housing Units Authorized by Building Permit

	Single Family	Total Bldgs	Total Units
2006	81	81	81
2007	46	46	46
2008	21	21	21

Parcel Count by Property Class, 2010

Total	NA
Single family	NA
Multiple units	NA
Apartments	NA
Condos	NA
Vacant land	NA
Open space	NA
Commercial	NA
Industrial	NA
Misc. residential	NA
Other use	NA

Public Library

Blanding Free Public Library
124 Bay State Rd.
Rehoboth, MA 02769
(508)252-4236

Director	Laura Bennett

Library Statistics, FY 2008

Population served, 2007	11,484
Registered users	3,352
Circulation	67,470
Reference transactons	0
Total program attendance	0
per capita:	
Holdings	3.15
Operating income	$19.00
Internet Access	
Internet computers available	4
Weekly users	0

Municipal Finance

Debt at year end 2008	$1,650,000
Moody's rating, July 2009	A2

Revenues, 2008

Total	$19,063,525
From all taxes	16,855,031
Federal aid	4,823
State aid	1,402,029
From other governments	79,415
Charges for services	244,677
Licenses, permits & fees	244,697
Fines & forfeits	1,267
Interfund transfers	89,224
Misc/other/special assessments	71,181

Expenditures, 2008

Total	$19,110,646
General government	1,216,893
Public safety	2,669,411
Other/fixed costs	1,497,576
Human services	413,945
Culture & recreation	189,639
Debt Service	306,133
Education	11,303,223
Public works	1,209,778
Intergovernmental	304,048

Taxation, 2010

Property type	Valuation	Rate
Total	NA	-
Residential	NA	NA
Open space	NA	NA
Commercial	NA	NA
Industrial	NA	NA
Personal	NA	NA

Average Single Family Tax Bill, 2010

Avg. assessed home value	NA
Avg. single fam. tax bill	NA
Hi-Lo ranking	NA

Police & Crime, 2008

Number of police officers	23
Violent crimes	10
Property crimes	163

Local School District

(school data 2007-08, except as noted)

Rehoboth (non-op)
2700 Regional Road
North Dighton, MA 02764
508-252-5000
Superintendent....... Kathleen Montagano

Non-operating district.
Resident students are sent to the Other School Districts listed below.

Grade plan	NA
Total enrollment '09-10	NA
Grade 12 enrollment, '09-10	NA
Graduation rate	NA
Dropout rate	NA
Per-pupil expenditure	NA
Avg teacher salary	NA
Student/teacher ratio '08-09	NA
Highly-qualified teachers, '08-09	NA
Teachers licensed in assigned subject	NA
Students per computer	NA

Other School Districts (see Appendix D for data)
Dighton-Rehoboth Regional, Bristol County Agricultural

©2010 Information Publications, Inc. All rights reserved. Photocopying prohibited. For additional copies, contact the publisher at www.informationpublications.com or (877)544-INFO (4636)

Demographics & Socio-Economic Characteristics*

Population

1990 . . . 42,786
2000 . . . 47,283
Male . . . 22,862
Female . . . 24,421
2008 . . . 60,204
2010 (projected)†† . . . 50,268
2020 (projected)†† . . . 53,908

Race & Hispanic Origin, 2000

Race
White . . . 39,884
Black/African American . . . 1,364
American Indian/Alaska Native . . . 124
Asian . . . 2,146
Hawaiian Native/Pacific Islander . . . 35
Other Race . . . 1,942
Two or more races . . . 1,788
Hispanic origin . . . 4,465

Age & Nativity, 2000

Under 5 years . . . 2,741
18 years and over . . . 37,363
21 years and over . . . 35,853
65 years and over . . . 7,870
85 years and over . . . 1,011
Median Age . . . 37.6
Native-born . . . 37,347
Foreign-born . . . 9,936

Age, 2020 (projected)††

Under 5 years . . . 3,028
5 to 19 years . . . 9,170
20 to 39 years . . . 15,224
40 to 64 years . . . 17,568
65 years and over . . . 8,918

Educational Attainment, 2000

Population 25 years and over . . . 33,723
High School graduates or higher . . . 76.7%
Bachelor's degree or higher . . . 13.5%
Graduate degree . . . 4.3%

Income & Poverty, 1999

Per capita income, . . . $19,698
Median household income . . . $37,067
Median family income . . . $45,865
Persons in poverty . . . 6,873
H'holds receiving public assistance . . . 598
H'holds receiving social security . . . 5,979

Households, 2000

Total households . . . 19,463
With persons under 18 . . . 5,506
With persons over 65 . . . 5,766
Family households . . . 11,865
Single person households . . . 6,359
Persons per household . . . 2.4
Persons per family . . . 3.1

Labor & Employment, 2000

Civilian labor force . . . 22,506
Unemployment rate . . . 5.9%
Civilian labor force, 2008† . . . 22,680
Unemployment rate† . . . 7.6%
Civilian labor force, 12/09† . . . 26,542
Unemployment rate† . . . 9.4%
Employed persons 16 years and over, by occupation:
Managers & professionals . . . 5,411
Service occupations . . . 3,976
Sales & office occupations . . . 6,979
Farming, fishing & forestry . . . 45
Construction & maintenance . . . 1,951
Production & transportation . . . 2,822
Self-employed persons . . . 1,074

Most demographic data is from the 2000 Decennial Census
* see Appendix E for American Community Survey data
† Massachusetts Department of Revenue
†† University of Massachusetts, MISER

General Information

City of Revere
281 Broadway
Revere, MA 02151
781-286-8100

Elevation . . . 20 ft.
Land area (square miles) . . . 5.9
Water area (square miles) . . . 4.1
Population density, 2008 (est) . . . 10,204.1
Year incorporated . . . 1871
Website . . . www.revere.org

Voters & Government Information

Government type . . . Mayor-Council
Number of City Council . . . 11
US Congressional District(s) . . . 7

Registered Voters, October 2008

Total . . . 24,738
Democrats . . . 12,513
Republicans . . . 1,837
Unaffiliated/other . . . 10,236

Local Officials, 2010

Mayor . . . Thomas Ambrosino
Manager/Admin . . . NA
City Clerk . . . Ashley Melnik
Finance . . . George Anzuoni
Tax Collector . . . George Anzuoni
Tax Assessor . . . Andrew Iovanna
Attorney . . . Paul Capizzi
Public Works . . . Donald Goodwin
Building . . . Benjamin DeChristoforo
Comm Dev/Planning . . . Frank Stringi
Police Chief . . . Terance Reardon
Emerg/Fire Chief . . . Gene Doherty

Housing & Construction

New Privately Owned Housing Units Authorized by Building Permit

	Single Family	Total Bldgs	Total Units
2006	9	23	299
2007	14	20	26
2008	13	15	17

Parcel Count by Property Class, 2010

Total . . . 14,182
Single family . . . 4,441
Multiple units . . . 4,362
Apartments . . . 357
Condos . . . 2,615
Vacant land . . . 1,535
Open space . . . 0
Commercial . . . 608
Industrial . . . 76
Misc. residential . . . 61
Other use . . . 127

Public Library

Revere Public Library
179 Beach St.
Revere, MA 02151
(781)286-8380

Director . . . Mark Ferrante (Actg)

Library Statistics, FY 2008

Population served, 2007 . . . 55,341
Registered users . . . 19,773
Circulation . . . 56,758
Reference transactons . . . 0
Total program attendance . . . 32,890

per capita:

Holdings . . . 1.14
Operating income . . . $9.68

Internet Access

Internet computers available . . . 36
Weekly users . . . 0

Municipal Finance

Debt at year end 2008 . . . $19,218,082
Moody's rating, July 2009 . . . A3

Revenues, 2008

Total . . . $116,562,940
From all taxes . . . 63,108,774
Federal aid . . . 0
State aid . . . 45,858,648
From other governments . . . 0
Charges for services . . . 1,861,087
Licenses, permits & fees . . . 857,647
Fines & forfeits . . . 1,051,717
Interfund transfers . . . 2,640,195
Misc/other/special assessments . . . 592,436

Expenditures, 2008

Total . . . $101,964,468
General government . . . 5,422,416
Public safety . . . 15,313,529
Other/fixed costs . . . 9,544,441
Human services . . . 1,268,062
Culture & recreation . . . 663,391
Debt Service . . . 3,819,275
Education . . . 52,034,008
Public works . . . 7,028,173
Intergovernmental . . . 6,706,619

Taxation, 2010

Property type	Valuation	Rate
Total	$4,036,076,629	-
Residential	3,447,300,073	13.37
Open space	0	0.00
Commercial	441,902,327	26.84
Industrial	84,948,600	26.84
Personal	61,925,629	26.84

Average Single Family Tax Bill, 2010

Avg. assessed home value . . . $250,334
Avg. single fam. tax bill . . . $3,347
Hi-Lo ranking . . . 194/301

Police & Crime, 2008

Number of police officers . . . 92
Violent crimes . . . 237
Property crimes . . . 1,594

Local School District

(school data 2007-08, except as noted)

Revere
101 School Street
Revere, MA 02151
781-286-8226

Superintendent . . . Paul Dakin
Grade plan . . . PK-12
Total enrollment '09-10 . . . 6,145
Grade 12 enrollment, '09-10 . . . 365
Graduation rate . . . 67.5%
Dropout rate . . . 18.7%
Per-pupil expenditure . . . $11,653
Avg teacher salary . . . $65,306
Student/teacher ratio '08-09 . . . 13.9 to 1
Highly-qualified teachers, '08-09 . . . 98.2%
Teachers licensed in assigned subject . . . 98.2%
Students per computer . . . 3.3

Massachusetts Competency Assessment System (MCAS), 2009 results

	English		Math	
	% Prof	CPI	% Prof	CPI
Gr 4	47%	77.8	46%	79.2
Gr 6	51%	79.7	43%	70
Gr 8	78%	90.4	35%	65.8
Gr 10	71%	86	71%	85.6

Other School Districts (see Appendix D for data)
Northeast Metro Vocational Tech

©2010 Information Publications, Inc. All rights reserved. Photocopying prohibited. For additional copies, contact the publisher at www.informationpublications.com or (877)544-INFO (4636)

See Introduction for an explanation of all data sources.

Demographics & Socio-Economic Characteristics

Population

1990	1,677
2000	1,604
Male	789
Female	815
2008	1,572
2010 (projected)††	1,423
2020 (projected)††	1,233

Race & Hispanic Origin, 2000

Race	
White	1,566
Black/African American	16
American Indian/Alaska Native	8
Asian	7
Hawaiian Native/Pacific Islander	1
Other Race	6
Two or more races	0
Hispanic origin	9

Age & Nativity, 2000

Under 5 years	66
18 years and over	1,259
21 years and over	1,219
65 years and over	252
85 years and over	23
Median Age	45.3
Native-born	1,555
Foreign-born	54

Age, 2020 (projected)††

Under 5 years	43
5 to 19 years	174
20 to 39 years	189
40 to 64 years	442
65 years and over	385

Educational Attainment, 2000

Population 25 years and over	1,185
High School graduates or higher	92.7%
Bachelor's degree or higher	38.6%
Graduate degree	18.1%

Income & Poverty, 1999

Per capita income,	$35,568
Median household income	$60,917
Median family income	$72,500
Persons in poverty	49
H'holds receiving public assistance	7
H'holds receiving social security	212

Households, 2000

Total households	643
With persons under 18	188
With persons over 65	188
Family households	481
Single person households	134
Persons per household	2.5
Persons per family	2.9

Labor & Employment, 2000

Civilian labor force	907
Unemployment rate	3.2%
Civilian labor force, 2008†	962
Unemployment rate†	4.0%
Civilian labor force, 12/09†	942
Unemployment rate†	4.4%
Employed persons 16 years and over, by occupation:	
Managers & professionals	458
Service occupations	113
Sales & office occupations	173
Farming, fishing & forestry	3
Construction & maintenance	69
Production & transportation	62
Self-employed persons	121

Most demographic data is from the 2000 Decennial Census
† Massachusetts Department of Revenue
†† University of Massachusetts, MISER

General Information

Town of Richmond
1529 State Rd
PO Box 81
Richmond, MA 01254
413-698-3355

Elevation	1,057 ft.
Land area (square miles)	19.0
Water area (square miles)	0.3
Population density, 2008 (est)	82.7
Year incorporated	1785
Website	www.richmondma.org

Voters & Government Information

Government type	Open Town Meeting
Number of Selectmen	3
US Congressional District(s)	1

Registered Voters, October 2008

Total	1,142
Democrats	369
Republicans	137
Unaffiliated/other	625

Local Officials, 2010

Chair, Bd. of Sel.	Alan Hanson
Town Administrator	Matthew Kerwood
Clerk	David Morrison
Treasurer	Anna Schubert
Tax Collector	Frederick Schubert
Tax Assessor	Raymond Supranowicz
Attorney	Sarah H. Bell
Public Works	Gerald Coppola
Building	Walt Potash
Planning	Craig Swinson
Police Chief	William Bullett
Fire Chief	Paul Sintoni

Housing & Construction

New Privately Owned Housing Units Authorized by Building Permit

	Single Family	Total Bldgs	Total Units
2006	1	1	1
2007	0	0	0
2008	4	4	4

Parcel Count by Property Class, 2010

Total	1,187
Single family	737
Multiple units	13
Apartments	0
Condos	12
Vacant land	261
Open space	0
Commercial	7
Industrial	4
Misc. residential	27
Other use	126

Public Library

Richmond Free Public Library
2821 State Road
Richmond, MA 01254
(413)698-3834

Director	Kristin Smith

Library Statistics, FY 2008

Population served, 2007	1,591
Registered users	899
Circulation	14,931
Reference transactons	151
Total program attendance	6,604
per capita:	
Holdings	10.93
Operating income	$34.44
Internet Access	
Internet computers available	3
Weekly users	9

Municipal Finance

Debt at year end 2008	$8,198,160
Moody's rating, July 2009	Baa1

Revenues, 2008

Total	$4,147,734
From all taxes	2,626,607
Federal aid	0
State aid	1,084,160
From other governments	8,098
Charges for services	52,475
Licenses, permits & fees	1,260
Fines & forfeits	0
Interfund transfers	286,504
Misc/other/special assessments	44,315

Expenditures, 2008

Total	$4,738,333
General government	264,097
Public safety	137,513
Other/fixed costs	514,536
Human services	71,208
Culture & recreation	79,787
Debt Service	474,491
Education	2,498,873
Public works	581,413
Intergovernmental	116,415

Taxation, 2010

Property type	Valuation	Rate
Total	$438,395,389	-
Residential	418,734,001	8.92
Open space	0	0.00
Commercial	5,372,907	8.92
Industrial	865,900	8.92
Personal	13,422,581	8.92

Average Single Family Tax Bill, 2010

Avg. assessed home value	$439,569
Avg. single fam. tax bill	$3,921
Hi-Lo ranking	142/301

Police & Crime, 2008

Number of police officers	NA
Violent crimes	NA
Property crimes	NA

Local School District

(school data 2007-08, except as noted)

Richmond
188 Summer Street
Lanesborough, MA 01237
413-442-2229

Superintendent	William Ballen
Grade plan	PK-8
Total enrollment '09-10	172
Grade 12 enrollment, '09-10	0
Graduation rate	NA
Dropout rate	NA
Per-pupil expenditure	$12,032
Avg teacher salary	$68,645
Student/teacher ratio '08-09	10.5 to 1
Highly-qualified teachers, '08-09	100.0%
Teachers licensed in assigned subject	100.0%
Students per computer	2.5

Massachusetts Competency Assessment System (MCAS), 2009 results

	English		Math	
	% Prof	CPI	% Prof	CPI
Gr 4	83%	90.2	41%	78.4
Gr 6	76%	89.7	65%	82.4
Gr 8	95%	96.1	63%	85.5
Gr 10	NA	NA	NA	NA

Other School Districts (see Appendix D for data)
Sends grades 9-12 to Pittsfield.

©2010 Information Publications, Inc. All rights reserved. Photocopying prohibited. For additional copies, contact the publisher at www.informationpublications.com or (877)544-INFO (4636)

Demographics & Socio-Economic Characteristics

Population

1990	3,921
2000	4,581
Male	2,297
Female	2,284
2008	5,268
2010 (projected)††	5,057
2020 (projected)††	5,551

Race & Hispanic Origin, 2000

Race	
White	4,427
Black/African American	29
American Indian/Alaska Native	9
Asian	16
Hawaiian Native/Pacific Islander	0
Other Race	53
Two or more races	47
Hispanic origin	17

Age & Nativity, 2000

Under 5 years	278
18 years and over	3,353
21 years and over	3,203
65 years and over	379
85 years and over	38
Median Age	38.1
Native-born	4,466
Foreign-born	115

Age, 2020 (projected)††

Under 5 years	284
5 to 19 years	909
20 to 39 years	1,242
40 to 64 years	2,027
65 years and over	1,089

Educational Attainment, 2000

Population 25 years and over	3,060
High School graduates or higher	88.6%
Bachelor's degree or higher	27.7%
Graduate degree	8.0%

Income & Poverty, 1999

Per capita income,	$24,630
Median household income	$63,289
Median family income	$67,031
Persons in poverty	141
H'holds receiving public assistance	30
H'holds receiving social security	326

Households, 2000

Total households	1,575
With persons under 18	667
With persons over 65	282
Family households	1,294
Single person households	216
Persons per household	2.9
Persons per family	3.2

Labor & Employment, 2000

Civilian labor force	2,583
Unemployment rate	4.6%
Civilian labor force, 2008†	3,045
Unemployment rate†	5.9%
Civilian labor force, 12/09†	2,945
Unemployment rate†	7.8%
Employed persons 16 years and over, by occupation:	
Managers & professionals	936
Service occupations	322
Sales & office occupations	583
Farming, fishing & forestry	40
Construction & maintenance	255
Production & transportation	328
Self-employed persons	246

Most demographic data is from the 2000 Decennial Census
† Massachusetts Department of Revenue
†† University of Massachusetts, MISER

General Information

Town of Rochester
One Constitution Way
Rochester, MA 02770
508-763-3871

Elevation	29 ft.
Land area (square miles)	33.9
Water area (square miles)	2.5
Population density, 2008 (est)	155.4
Year incorporated	1686
Website	www.townofrochestermass.com

Voters & Government Information

Government type	Open Town Meeting
Number of Selectmen	3
US Congressional District(s)	4

Registered Voters, October 2008

Total	3,887
Democrats	766
Republicans	700
Unaffiliated/other	2,391

Local Officials, 2010

Chair, Bd. of Sel.	Richard D. Nunes
Town Administrator	Richard LaCamera
Clerk	Naida L. Parker
Treasurer	Cynthia L. Mello
Tax Collector	Thomas Gayoski Jr
Tax Assessor	John Mello
Attorney	Blair S. Bailey
Public Works	Jeffrey G. Eldridge
Building	James Buckles
Planning	Randall Kunz
Police Chief	Paul Magee
Fire Chief	Scott A. Ashworth

Housing & Construction

New Privately Owned Housing Units Authorized by Building Permit

	Single Family	Total Bldgs	Total Units
2006	15	18	21
2007	13	13	13
2008	6	6	6

Parcel Count by Property Class, 2010

Total	2,694
Single family	1,676
Multiple units	61
Apartments	0
Condos	69
Vacant land	476
Open space	0
Commercial	50
Industrial	28
Misc. residential	12
Other use	322

Public Library

Joseph H. Plumb Memorial Library
PO Box 69
Rochester, MA 02770
(508)763-8600

Director	Gail Roberts

Library Statistics, FY 2008

Population served, 2007	5,218
Registered users	2,361
Circulation	63,688
Reference transactons	1,500
Total program attendance	33,600
per capita:	
Holdings	4.65
Operating income	$40.26
Internet Access	
Internet computers available	6
Weekly users	84

Municipal Finance

Debt at year end 2008	$4,112,790
Moody's rating, July 2009	A2

Revenues, 2008

Total	$15,858,777
From all taxes	12,188,098
Federal aid	0
State aid	2,604,501
From other governments	743
Charges for services	146,826
Licenses, permits & fees	99,836
Fines & forfeits	12,795
Interfund transfers	20,000
Misc/other/special assessments	392,989

Expenditures, 2008

Total	$15,187,808
General government	1,093,475
Public safety	1,577,344
Other/fixed costs	1,025,335
Human services	281,986
Culture & recreation	197,142
Debt Service	723,687
Education	9,484,351
Public works	726,917
Intergovernmental	75,427

Taxation, 2010

Property type	Valuation	Rate
Total	$823,739,500	-
Residential	714,547,460	10.79
Open space	0	0.00
Commercial	39,644,240	10.79
Industrial	35,818,400	10.79
Personal	33,729,400	10.79

Average Single Family Tax Bill, 2010

Avg. assessed home value	$355,504
Avg. single fam. tax bill	$3,836
Hi-Lo ranking	147/301

Police & Crime, 2008

Number of police officers	10
Violent crimes	11
Property crimes	77

Local School District

(school data 2007-08, except as noted)

Rochester
135 Marion Rd
Mattapoisett, MA 02739
508-758-2772

Superintendent	Douglas White
Grade plan	PK-6
Total enrollment '09-10	599
Grade 12 enrollment, '09-10	0
Graduation rate	NA
Dropout rate	NA
Per-pupil expenditure	$10,037
Avg teacher salary	$62,143
Student/teacher ratio '08-09	14.2 to 1
Highly-qualified teachers, '08-09	100.0%
Teachers licensed in assigned subject	99.5%
Students per computer	2.8

Massachusetts Competency Assessment System (MCAS), 2009 results

	English		Math	
	% Prof	CPI	% Prof	CPI
Gr 4	70%	88.1	46%	82.5
Gr 6	86%	94.2	84%	94
Gr 8	NA	NA	NA	NA
Gr 10	NA	NA	NA	NA

Other School Districts (see Appendix D for data)
Old Rochester Regional, Old Colony Vocational Tech

©2010 Information Publications, Inc. All rights reserved. Photocopying prohibited. For additional copies, contact the publisher at www.informationpublications.com or (877)544-INFO (4636)

See Introduction for an explanation of all data sources.

Demographics & Socio-Economic Characteristics

Population

1990	16,123
2000	17,670
Male	8,458
Female	9,212
2008	17,883
2010 (projected)††	18,159
2020 (projected)††	18,510

Race & Hispanic Origin, 2000

Race	
White	16,753
Black/African American	302
American Indian/Alaska Native	26
Asian	190
Hawaiian Native/Pacific Islander	0
Other Race	139
Two or more races	260
Hispanic origin	180

Age & Nativity, 2000

Under 5 years	1,290
18 years and over	12,996
21 years and over	12,442
65 years and over	2,275
85 years and over	256
Median Age	36.3
Native-born	17,244
Foreign-born	426

Age, 2020 (projected)††

Under 5 years	1,057
5 to 19 years	3,112
20 to 39 years	4,493
40 to 64 years	6,206
65 years and over	3,642

Educational Attainment, 2000

Population 25 years and over	11,813
High School graduates or higher	88.6%
Bachelor's degree or higher	18.2%
Graduate degree	4.7%

Income & Poverty, 1999

Per capita income,	$23,068
Median household income	$50,613
Median family income	$60,088
Persons in poverty	1,188
H'holds receiving public assistance	178
H'holds receiving social security	1,736

Households, 2000

Total households	6,539
With persons under 18	2,436
With persons over 65	1,616
Family households	4,584
Single person households	1,628
Persons per household	2.7
Persons per family	3.2

Labor & Employment, 2000

Civilian labor force	9,637
Unemployment rate	2.9%
Civilian labor force, 2008†	10,168
Unemployment rate†	6.9%
Civilian labor force, 12/09†	10,063
Unemployment rate†	9.2%
Employed persons 16 years and over, by occupation:	
Managers & professionals	3,014
Service occupations	1,592
Sales & office occupations	2,666
Farming, fishing & forestry	8
Construction & maintenance	1,019
Production & transportation	1,059
Self-employed persons	484

Most demographic data is from the 2000 Decennial Census
† Massachusetts Department of Revenue
†† University of Massachusetts, MISER

General Information

Town of Rockland
242 Union St
Rockland, MA 02370
781-871-1874

Elevation	130 ft.
Land area (square miles)	10.0
Water area (square miles)	0.1
Population density, 2008 (est)	1,788.3
Year incorporated	1874
Email	clerk@rockland-ma.gov

Voters & Government Information

Government type	Open Town Meeting
Number of Selectmen	5
US Congressional District(s)	10

Registered Voters, October 2008

Total	11,692
Democrats	3,349
Republicans	1,231
Unaffiliated/other	7,033

Local Officials, 2010

Chair, Bd. of Sel.	James F. Simpson
Town Administrator	Allan R. Chiocca
Clerk	Mary Pat Kaszanek
Treasurer	Karen M. Sepeck
Tax Collector	Judith A. Hartigan
Appraiser	III
Attorney	John J. Clifford
Public Works	Robert Corvi
Building	Thomas E. Ruble
Planning	Thomas J. Henderson
Police Chief	John R. Llewellyn
Emerg/Fire Chief	Robert A. Dipoli

Housing & Construction

New Privately Owned Housing Units Authorized by Building Permit

	Single Family	Total Bldgs	Total Units
2006	67	68	69
2007	57	57	57
2008	35	35	35

Parcel Count by Property Class, 2010

Total	5,959
Single family	3,712
Multiple units	432
Apartments	62
Condos	944
Vacant land	328
Open space	0
Commercial	217
Industrial	181
Misc. residential	28
Other use	55

Public Library

Rockland Memorial Library
20 Belmont St.
Rockland, MA 02370
(781)878-1236

Director	Beverly Cyr Brown

Library Statistics, FY 2008

Population served, 2007	17,780
Registered users	8,460
Circulation	93,721
Reference transactons	4,640
Total program attendance	62,804
per capita:	
Holdings	2.95
Operating income	$23.80
Internet Access	
Internet computers available	9
Weekly users	234

Municipal Finance

Debt at year end 2008	$5,727,694
Moody's rating, July 2009	Baa1

Revenues, 2008

Total	$39,864,591
From all taxes	22,411,706
Federal aid	0
State aid	13,569,944
From other governments	0
Charges for services	2,017,761
Licenses, permits & fees	706,001
Fines & forfeits	38,966
Interfund transfers	26,687
Misc/other/special assessments	546,763

Expenditures, 2008

Total	$39,262,199
General government	1,276,473
Public safety	5,674,017
Other/fixed costs	7,859,274
Human services	360,206
Culture & recreation	823,101
Debt Service	330,850
Education	18,803,881
Public works	2,076,425
Intergovernmental	2,057,972

Taxation, 2010

Property type	Valuation	Rate
Total	$1,697,533,230	-
Residential	1,340,845,157	14.39
Open space	0	0.00
Commercial	187,831,283	14.39
Industrial	125,557,000	14.39
Personal	43,299,790	14.39

Average Single Family Tax Bill, 2010

Avg. assessed home value	$254,027
Avg. single fam. tax bill	$3,655
Hi-Lo ranking	160/301

Police & Crime, 2008

Number of police officers	32
Violent crimes	19
Property crimes	302

Local School District

(school data 2007-08, except as noted)

Rockland
34 MacKinlay Way
Rockland, MA 02370
781-878-3893

Superintendent	John Retchless
Grade plan	PK-12
Total enrollment '09-10	2,278
Grade 12 enrollment, '09-10	136
Graduation rate	80.0%
Dropout rate	16.5%
Per-pupil expenditure	$10,747
Avg teacher salary	$60,769
Student/teacher ratio '08-09	16.2 to 1
Highly-qualified teachers, '08-09	98.8%
Teachers licensed in assigned subject	98.3%
Students per computer	9.7

Massachusetts Competency Assessment System (MCAS), 2009 results

	English		Math	
	% Prof	CPI	% Prof	CPI
Gr 4	46%	80.8	34%	76.9
Gr 6	51%	80.6	38%	68.5
Gr 8	71%	89.7	39%	68
Gr 10	84%	93.3	72%	88.5

Other School Districts (see Appendix D for data)
South Shore Vocational Tech

©2010 Information Publications, Inc. All rights reserved. Photocopying prohibited. For additional copies, contact the publisher at www.informationpublications.com or (877)544-INFO (4636)

See Introduction for an explanation of all data sources.

Demographics & Socio-Economic Characteristics

Population

1990	7,482
2000	7,767
Male	3,576
Female	4,191
2008	7,612
2010 (projected)††	8,257
2020 (projected)††	8,909

Race & Hispanic Origin, 2000

Race	
White	7,591
Black/African American	21
American Indian/Alaska Native	17
Asian	35
Hawaiian Native/Pacific Islander	2
Other Race	40
Two or more races	61
Hispanic origin	83

Age & Nativity, 2000

Under 5 years	365
18 years and over	6,113
21 years and over	5,947
65 years and over	1,571
85 years and over	261
Median Age	44.9
Native-born	7,312
Foreign-born	455

Age, 2020 (projected)††

Under 5 years	383
5 to 19 years	1,157
20 to 39 years	1,843
40 to 64 years	2,898
65 years and over	2,628

Educational Attainment, 2000

Population 25 years and over	5,716
High School graduates or higher	95.1%
Bachelor's degree or higher	44.4%
Graduate degree	17.8%

Income & Poverty, 1999

Per capita income,	$29,294
Median household income	$50,661
Median family income	$69,263
Persons in poverty	286
H'holds receiving public assistance	46
H'holds receiving social security	1,209

Households, 2000

Total households	3,490
With persons under 18	895
With persons over 65	1,155
Family households	2,029
Single person households	1,266
Persons per household	2.2
Persons per family	2.9

Labor & Employment, 2000

Civilian labor force	4,107
Unemployment rate	3.6%
Civilian labor force, 2008†	4,208
Unemployment rate†	7.0%
Civilian labor force, 12/09†	4,105
Unemployment rate†	8.0%
Employed persons 16 years and over, by occupation:	
Managers & professionals	1,972
Service occupations	616
Sales & office occupations	909
Farming, fishing & forestry	37
Construction & maintenance	174
Production & transportation	252
Self-employed persons	425

Most demographic data is from the 2000 Decennial Census
† Massachusetts Department of Revenue
†† University of Massachusetts, MISER

General Information

Town of Rockport
34 Broadway
Rockport, MA 01966
978-546-6786

Elevation	171 ft.
Land area (square miles)	7.1
Water area (square miles)	10.5
Population density, 2008 (est)	1,072.1
Year incorporated	1840
Website	www.town.rockport.ma.us

Voters & Government Information

Government type	Open Town Meeting
Number of Selectmen	5
US Congressional District(s)	6

Registered Voters, October 2008

Total	5,559
Democrats	1,363
Republicans	614
Unaffiliated/other	3,551

Local Officials, 2010

Chair, Bd. of Sel.	Sarah Wilkinson
Manager/Admin	Linda Sanders
Town Clerk	Frederick Frithsen
Finance Director	Bernard Halupowski
Tax Collector	Roberta Josephson
Tax Assessor	Paul Fuhs Jr (Chr)
Attorney	Darren Klein
Public Works	Joseph Parisi
Building	Paul Orlando
Comm Dev/Planning	Carolyn Britt
Police Chief	Thomas McCarthy
Emerg/Fire Chief	James Doyle

Housing & Construction

New Privately Owned Housing Units Authorized by Building Permit

	Single Family	Total Bldgs	Total Units
2006	19	19	19
2007	10	11	12
2008	8	9	10

Parcel Count by Property Class, 2010

Total	4,124
Single family	2,336
Multiple units	302
Apartments	31
Condos	485
Vacant land	550
Open space	0
Commercial	144
Industrial	15
Misc. residential	154
Other use	107

Public Library

Rockport Public Library
17 School Street
Rockport, MA 01966
(978)546-6934

Director	M. Hope Coffman

Library Statistics, FY 2008

Population served, 2007	7,633
Registered users	9,774
Circulation	91,034
Reference transactons	12,975
Total program attendance	102,600
per capita:	
Holdings	7.63
Operating income	$62.68
Internet Access	
Internet computers available	12
Weekly users	291

Municipal Finance

Debt at year end 2008	$14,566,962
Moody's rating, July 2009	Aa3

Revenues, 2008

Total	$24,886,069
From all taxes	17,291,219
Federal aid	0
State aid	3,108,256
From other governments	3,440
Charges for services	1,100,828
Licenses, permits & fees	268,691
Fines & forfeits	113,810
Interfund transfers	970,281
Misc/other/special assessments	1,014,772

Expenditures, 2008

Total	$23,028,469
General government	1,507,963
Public safety	1,896,324
Other/fixed costs	4,248,791
Human services	151,982
Culture & recreation	456,449
Debt Service	3,485,776
Education	9,034,118
Public works	1,603,941
Intergovernmental	643,125

Taxation, 2010

Property type	Valuation	Rate
Total	$1,861,619,639	-
Residential	1,728,525,907	8.96
Open space	0	0.00
Commercial	113,107,193	8.96
Industrial	5,537,600	8.96
Personal	14,448,939	8.96

Average Single Family Tax Bill, 2010

Avg. assessed home value	$526,739
Avg. single fam. tax bill	$4,720
Hi-Lo ranking	91/301

Police & Crime, 2008

Number of police officers	16
Violent crimes	10
Property crimes	23

Local School District

(school data 2007-08, except as noted)

Rockport
24 Jerdens Lane, c/o Rockport Public Schools
Rockport, MA 01966
978-546-1200

Superintendent	Susan King
Grade plan	PK-12
Total enrollment '09-10	977
Grade 12 enrollment, '09-10	87
Graduation rate	87.7%
Dropout rate	7.4%
Per-pupil expenditure	$11,436
Avg teacher salary	$60,967
Student/teacher ratio '08-09	12.2 to 1
Highly-qualified teachers, '08-09	96.9%
Teachers licensed in assigned subject	99.4%
Students per computer	3.8

Massachusetts Competency Assessment System (MCAS), 2009 results

	English		Math	
	% Prof	CPI	% Prof	CPI
Gr 4	59%	86.8	61%	88.2
Gr 6	72%	88	79%	90.2
Gr 8	87%	95.9	75%	85.7
Gr 10	86%	93.7	76%	88.9

Other School Districts (see Appendix D for data)
North Shore Vocational Tech

©2010 Information Publications, Inc. All rights reserved. Photocopying prohibited. For additional copies, contact the publisher at www.informationpublications.com or (877)544-INFO (4636)

See Introduction for an explanation of all data sources.

Demographics & Socio-Economic Characteristics

Population

1990 . . . 378
2000 . . . 351
Male . . . 167
Female . . . 184
2008 . . . 348
2010 (projected)†† . . . 374
2020 (projected)†† . . . 391

Race & Hispanic Origin, 2000

Race
White . . . 350
Black/African American . . . 0
American Indian/Alaska Native . . . 0
Asian . . . 0
Hawaiian Native/Pacific Islander . . . 0
Other Race . . . 1
Two or more races . . . 0
Hispanic origin . . . 4

Age & Nativity, 2000

Under 5 years . . . 19
18 years and over . . . 282
21 years and over . . . 274
65 years and over . . . 66
85 years and over . . . 8
Median Age . . . 48.4
Native-born . . . 349
Foreign-born . . . 12

Age, 2020 (projected)††

Under 5 years . . . 22
5 to 19 years . . . 67
20 to 39 years . . . 52
40 to 64 years . . . 116
65 years and over . . . 134

Educational Attainment, 2000

Population 25 years and over . . . 259
High School graduates or higher . . . 93.4%
Bachelor's degree or higher . . . 30.1%
Graduate degree . . . 9.7%

Income & Poverty, 1999

Per capita income, . . . $28,134
Median household income . . . $41,944
Median family income . . . $53,750
Persons in poverty . . . 10
H'holds receiving public assistance . . . 5
H'holds receiving social security . . . 47

Households, 2000

Total households . . . 154
With persons under 18 . . . 39
With persons over 65 . . . 49
Family households . . . 105
Single person households . . . 40
Persons per household . . . 2.3
Persons per family . . . 2.8

Labor & Employment, 2000

Civilian labor force . . . 184
Unemployment rate . . . 2.7%
Civilian labor force, 2008† . . . 180
Unemployment rate† . . . 4.4%
Civilian labor force, 12/09† . . . 188
Unemployment rate† . . . 11.2%
Employed persons 16 years and over, by occupation:
Managers & professionals . . . 71
Service occupations . . . 14
Sales & office occupations . . . 39
Farming, fishing & forestry . . . 2
Construction & maintenance . . . 29
Production & transportation . . . 24
Self-employed persons . . . 24

Most demographic data is from the 2000 Decennial Census
† Massachusetts Department of Revenue
†† University of Massachusetts, MISER

General Information

Town of Rowe
PO Box 308
Rowe, MA 01367
413-339-5520

Elevation . . . NA
Land area (square miles) . . . 23.5
Water area (square miles) . . . 0.5
Population density, 2008 (est) . . . 14.8
Year incorporated . . . 1785
Website . . . www.rowe-ma.gov

Voters & Government Information

Government type . . . Open Town Meeting
Number of Selectmen . . . 3
US Congressional District(s) . . . 1

Registered Voters, October 2008

Total . . . 300
Democrats . . . 72
Republicans . . . 39
Unaffiliated/other . . . 188

Local Officials, 2010

Chair, Bd. of Sel. . . . William A. Loomis
Town Coordinator . . . Ellen Babcock
Town Clerk . . . Carrie Silva
Treasurer . . . Heidi Cousineau
Tax Collector . . . Sandra Daviau
Tax Assessor . . . Frederick Williams
Attorney . . . Janet H. Pumphrey
Public Works . . . James Taylor
Building . . . William Foster
Comm Dev/Planning . . . David Roberson
Police Chief . . . Henry Dandeneau
Emerg/Fire Chief . . . Edwin May

Housing & Construction

New Privately Owned Housing Units Authorized by Building Permit

	Single Family	Total Bldgs	Total Units
2006	1	1	1
2007	1	1	1
2008	0	0	0

Parcel Count by Property Class, 2010

Total . . . 579
Single family . . . 208
Multiple units . . . 1
Apartments . . . 0
Condos . . . 0
Vacant land . . . 257
Open space . . . 0
Commercial . . . 5
Industrial . . . 78
Misc. residential . . . 3
Other use . . . 27

Public Library

Rowe Town Library
PO Box 457
Rowe, MA 01367
(413)339-4761

Director . . . Susan Gleason

Library Statistics, FY 2008

Population served, 2007 . . . 347
Registered users . . . 407
Circulation . . . 8,743
Reference transactons . . . 157
Total program attendance . . . 3,195

per capita:

Holdings . . . 39.47
Operating income . . . $165.99

Internet Access

Internet computers available . . . 3
Weekly users . . . 9

Municipal Finance

Debt at year end 2008 . . . $0
Moody's rating, July 2009 . . . NA

Revenues, 2008

Total . . . $3,108,780
From all taxes . . . 2,788,772
Federal aid . . . 0
State aid . . . 105,409
From other governments . . . 155
Charges for services . . . 1,100
Licenses, permits & fees . . . 1,050
Fines & forfeits . . . 0
Interfund transfers . . . 145,400
Misc/other/special assessments . . . 33,447

Expenditures, 2008

Total . . . $2,729,073
General government . . . 326,598
Public safety . . . 94,215
Other/fixed costs . . . 460,032
Human services . . . 45,364
Culture & recreation . . . 159,182
Debt Service . . . 0
Education . . . 1,075,778
Public works . . . 542,667
Intergovernmental . . . 25,237

Taxation, 2010

Property type	Valuation	Rate
Total	$283,502,093	-
Residential	49,338,871	5.22
Open space	0	0.00
Commercial	340,654	11.29
Industrial	132,156,698	11.29
Personal	101,665,870	11.29

Average Single Family Tax Bill, 2010

Avg. assessed home value . . . $200,845
Avg. single fam. tax bill . . . $1,048
Hi-Lo ranking . . . 301/301

Police & Crime, 2008

Number of police officers . . . NA
Violent crimes . . . NA
Property crimes . . . NA

Local School District

(school data 2007-08, except as noted)

Rowe
24 Ashfield Rd
Shelburne Falls, MA 01370
413-625-0192

Superintendent . . . Michael Buoniconti
Grade plan . . . PK-6
Total enrollment '09-10 . . . 65
Grade 12 enrollment, '09-10 . . . 0
Graduation rate . . . NA
Dropout rate . . . NA
Per-pupil expenditure . . . $18,826
Avg teacher salary . . . $47,290
Student/teacher ratio '08-09 . . . 8.0 to 1
Highly-qualified teachers, '08-09 . . . 100.0%
Teachers licensed in assigned subject . 100.0%
Students per computer . . . 1.7

Massachusetts Competency Assessment System (MCAS), 2009 results

	English		Math	
	% Prof	CPI	% Prof	CPI
Gr 4	NA	NA	NA	NA
Gr 6	NA	NA	NA	NA
Gr 8	NA	NA	NA	NA
Gr 10	NA	NA	NA	NA

Other School Districts (see Appendix D for data)

Mohawk Trail Regional, Franklin County Vocational Tech

©2010 Information Publications, Inc. All rights reserved. Photocopying prohibited. For additional copies, contact the publisher at www.informationpublications.com or (877)544-INFO (4636)

Demographics & Socio-Economic Characteristics

Population

1990	4,452
2000	5,500
Male	2,720
Female	2,780
2008	5,738
2010 (projected)††	5,947
2020 (projected)††	6,489

Race & Hispanic Origin, 2000

Race	
White	5,411
Black/African American	13
American Indian/Alaska Native	14
Asian	25
Hawaiian Native/Pacific Islander	0
Other Race	15
Two or more races	22
Hispanic origin	47

Age & Nativity, 2000

Under 5 years	393
18 years and over	3,961
21 years and over	3,802
65 years and over	515
85 years and over	89
Median Age	37.7
Native-born	5,364
Foreign-born	136

Age, 2020 (projected)††

Under 5 years	413
5 to 19 years	1,158
20 to 39 years	1,672
40 to 64 years	2,115
65 years and over	1,131

Educational Attainment, 2000

Population 25 years and over	3,619
High School graduates or higher	89.7%
Bachelor's degree or higher	36.1%
Graduate degree	12.4%

Income & Poverty, 1999

Per capita income,	$27,413
Median household income	$62,130
Median family income	$75,527
Persons in poverty	224
H'holds receiving public assistance	7
H'holds receiving social security	374

Households, 2000

Total households	1,958
With persons under 18	792
With persons over 65	352
Family households	1,468
Single person households	393
Persons per household	2.8
Persons per family	3.2

Labor & Employment, 2000

Civilian labor force	3,088
Unemployment rate	1.7%
Civilian labor force, 2008†	3,431
Unemployment rate†	5.7%
Civilian labor force, 12/09†	3,392
Unemployment rate†	7.9%
Employed persons 16 years and over, by occupation:	
Managers & professionals	1,348
Service occupations	306
Sales & office occupations	714
Farming, fishing & forestry	32
Construction & maintenance	277
Production & transportation	357
Self-employed persons	213

Most demographic data is from the 2000 Decennial Census
† Massachusetts Department of Revenue
†† University of Massachusetts, MISER

General Information

Town of Rowley
139 Main St
Rowley, MA 01969
978-948-2705

Elevation	50 ft.
Land area (square miles)	18.7
Water area (square miles)	1.9
Population density, 2008 (est)	306.8
Year incorporated	1639
Email	townclerk@townofrowley.org

Voters & Government Information

Government type	Open Town Meeting
Number of Selectmen	5
US Congressional District(s)	6

Registered Voters, October 2008

Total	4,350
Democrats	816
Republicans	722
Unaffiliated/other	2,798

Local Officials, 2010

Chair, Bd. of Sel.	David C. Peterson
Administrator	Deborah Eagan
Town Clerk	Susan G. Hazen
Finance Director	NA
Tax Collector	Jacqueline Vigeant
Tax Assessor	William DiMento
Attorney	Brackett & Lucas
Public Works	Scott Leavitt
Building	David Lovering
Comm Dev/Planning	NA
Police Chief	Kevin Barry
Emerg/Fire Chief	James Broderick

Housing & Construction

New Privately Owned Housing Units Authorized by Building Permit

	Single Family	Total Bldgs	Total Units
2006	10	10	10
2007	5	5	5
2008	15	18	23

Parcel Count by Property Class, 2010

Total	2,567
Single family	1,621
Multiple units	53
Apartments	14
Condos	175
Vacant land	374
Open space	55
Commercial	88
Industrial	33
Misc. residential	14
Other use	140

Public Library

Rowley Public Library
141 Main St., PO Box 276
Rowley, MA 01969
(978)948-2850

Library Director .... Pamela Jacobson

Library Statistics, FY 2008

Population served, 2007	5,839
Registered users	1,399
Circulation	34,384
Reference transactons	7,865
Total program attendance	29,407
per capita:	
Holdings	6.29
Operating income	$35.23
Internet Access	
Internet computers available	14
Weekly users	107

Municipal Finance

Debt at year end 2008	$5,449,649
Moody's rating, July 2009	A1

Revenues, 2008

Total	$12,767,836
From all taxes	10,874,824
Federal aid	0
State aid	1,140,910
From other governments	0
Charges for services	156,281
Licenses, permits & fees	232,112
Fines & forfeits	63,268
Interfund transfers	151,853
Misc/other/special assessments	74,294

Expenditures, 2008

Total	$12,456,344
General government	803,592
Public safety	1,961,029
Other/fixed costs	693,949
Human services	207,982
Culture & recreation	235,929
Debt Service	721,715
Education	7,133,098
Public works	567,179
Intergovernmental	131,871

Taxation, 2010

Property type	Valuation	Rate
Total	$878,114,050	-
Residential	747,827,072	12.50
Open space	138,400	12.50
Commercial	70,910,488	12.50
Industrial	41,499,040	12.50
Personal	17,739,050	12.50

Average Single Family Tax Bill, 2010

Avg. assessed home value	$387,562
Avg. single fam. tax bill	$4,845
Hi-Lo ranking	85/301

Police & Crime, 2008

Number of police officers	13
Violent crimes	5
Property crimes	29

Local School District

(school data 2007-08, except as noted)

Rowley (non-op)
112 Elm Street
Byfield, MA 01922
978-465-2397

Superintendent .... Sandra Halloran

Non-operating district.
Resident students are sent to the Other School Districts listed below.

Grade plan	NA
Total enrollment '09-10	NA
Grade 12 enrollment, '09-10	NA
Graduation rate	NA
Dropout rate	NA
Per-pupil expenditure	NA
Avg teacher salary	NA
Student/teacher ratio '08-09	NA
Highly-qualified teachers, '08-09	NA
Teachers licensed in assigned subject	NA
Students per computer	NA

Other School Districts (see Appendix D for data)
Triton Regional, Whittier Vocational Tech

©2010 Information Publications, Inc. All rights reserved. Photocopying prohibited. For additional copies, contact the publisher at www.informationpublications.com or (877)544-INFO (4636)

See Introduction for an explanation of all data sources.

Demographics & Socio-Economic Characteristics

Population

1990	1,147
2000	1,254
Male	649
Female	605
2008	1,376
2010 (projected)††	1,240
2020 (projected)††	1,273

Race & Hispanic Origin, 2000

Race	
White	1,237
Black/African American	1
American Indian/Alaska Native	0
Asian	7
Hawaiian Native/Pacific Islander	0
Other Race	2
Two or more races	7
Hispanic origin	14

Age & Nativity, 2000

Under 5 years	71
18 years and over	889
21 years and over	849
65 years and over	123
85 years and over	18
Median Age	38.0
Native-born	1,224
Foreign-born	29

Age, 2020 (projected)††

Under 5 years	47
5 to 19 years	145
20 to 39 years	332
40 to 64 years	472
65 years and over	277

Educational Attainment, 2000

Population 25 years and over	786
High School graduates or higher	82.8%
Bachelor's degree or higher	17.2%
Graduate degree	7.6%

Income & Poverty, 1999

Per capita income,	$18,297
Median household income	$44,444
Median family income	$51,818
Persons in poverty	109
H'holds receiving public assistance	15
H'holds receiving social security	107

Households, 2000

Total households	449
With persons under 18	173
With persons over 65	94
Family households	330
Single person households	92
Persons per household	2.8
Persons per family	3.3

Labor & Employment, 2000

Civilian labor force	628
Unemployment rate	4.5%
Civilian labor force, 2008†	670
Unemployment rate†	8.7%
Civilian labor force, 12/09†	650
Unemployment rate†	9.4%
Employed persons 16 years and over, by occupation:	
Managers & professionals	175
Service occupations	104
Sales & office occupations	121
Farming, fishing & forestry	7
Construction & maintenance	77
Production & transportation	116
Self-employed persons	86

Most demographic data is from the 2000 Decennial Census
† Massachusetts Department of Revenue
†† University of Massachusetts, MISER

General Information

Town of Royalston
13 On The Common
PO Box 125
Royalston, MA 01368
978-249-9641

Elevation	1,000 ft.
Land area (square miles)	41.9
Water area (square miles)	0.6
Population density, 2008 (est)	32.8
Year incorporated	1765
Website	www.royalston-ma.gov

Voters & Government Information

Government type	Open Town Meeting
Number of Selectmen	3
US Congressional District(s)	1

Registered Voters, October 2008

Total	915
Democrats	141
Republicans	112
Unaffiliated/other	647

Local Officials, 2010

Chair, Bd. of Sel.	Andrew J. West
Admin Assistant	Helen E. Divoll
Town Clerk	Melanie Mangum
Town Accountant	Eddie W. Wheeler
Tax Collector	Rebecca Krause-Hardie
Tax Assessor	Michael LaJoie (Chr)
Attorney	Kopelman & Paige
Public Works	Keith R. Newton
Building	Geoffrey L. Newton
Planning Board	Vyto Andreliunas (Chr)
Police Chief	Curtis A. Deveneau
Emerg/Fire Chief	Keith R. Newton

Housing & Construction

New Privately Owned Housing Units Authorized by Building Permit

	Single Family	Total Bldgs	Total Units
2006	8	8	8
2007	2	2	2
2008	1	1	1

Parcel Count by Property Class, 2010

Total	NA
Single family	NA
Multiple units	NA
Apartments	NA
Condos	NA
Vacant land	NA
Open space	NA
Commercial	NA
Industrial	NA
Misc. residential	NA
Other use	NA

Public Library

Phinehas S. Newton Library
PO Box 133
Royalston, MA 01368
(978)249-3572

Director	Katherine Morris

Library Statistics, FY 2008

Population served, 2007	1,380
Registered users	1,121
Circulation	14,037
Reference transactons	856
Total program attendance	9,971
per capita:	
Holdings	10.25
Operating income	$43.32
Internet Access	
Internet computers available	2
Weekly users	18

Municipal Finance

Debt at year end 2008	$0
Moody's rating, July 2009	NA

Revenues, 2008

Total	$2,023,535
From all taxes	1,238,551
Federal aid	0
State aid	280,713
From other governments	4,900
Charges for services	88,055
Licenses, permits & fees	8,414
Fines & forfeits	0
Interfund transfers	337,498
Misc/other/special assessments	32,702

Expenditures, 2008

Total	$1,839,056
General government	165,121
Public safety	173,992
Other/fixed costs	140,404
Human services	97,127
Culture & recreation	57,423
Debt Service	4,351
Education	608,128
Public works	588,759
Intergovernmental	3,751

Taxation, 2010

Property type	Valuation	Rate
Total	NA	-
Residential	NA	NA
Open space	NA	NA
Commercial	NA	NA
Industrial	NA	NA
Personal	NA	NA

Average Single Family Tax Bill, 2010

Avg. assessed home value	NA
Avg. single fam. tax bill	NA
Hi-Lo ranking	NA

Police & Crime, 2008

Number of police officers	1
Violent crimes	2
Property crimes	12

Local School District

(school data 2007-08, except as noted)

Royalston (non-op)
250 South Main Street
Athol, MA 01331
978-249-2400

Superintendent	Anthony Polito

Non-operating district.
Resident students are sent to the Other School Districts listed below.

Grade plan	NA
Total enrollment '09-10	NA
Grade 12 enrollment, '09-10	NA
Graduation rate	NA
Dropout rate	NA
Per-pupil expenditure	NA
Avg teacher salary	NA
Student/teacher ratio '08-09	NA
Highly-qualified teachers, '08-09	NA
Teachers licensed in assigned subject	NA
Students per computer	NA

Other School Districts (see Appendix D for data)
Athol-Royalston Regional, Montachusett Vocational Tech

©2010 Information Publications, Inc. All rights reserved. Photocopying prohibited. For additional copies, contact the publisher at www.informationpublications.com or (877)544-INFO (4636)

See Introduction for an explanation of all data sources.

Demographics & Socio-Economic Characteristics

Population
1990 1,594
2000 1,657
Male 828
Female 829
2008 1,719
2010 (projected)†† 1,622
2020 (projected)†† 1,590

Race & Hispanic Origin, 2000
Race
White 1,615
Black/African American 7
American Indian/Alaska Native 5
Asian 5
Hawaiian Native/Pacific Islander 0
Other Race 10
Two or more races 15
Hispanic origin 25

Age & Nativity, 2000
Under 5 years 104
18 years and over 1,224
21 years and over 1,147
65 years and over 168
85 years and over 12
Median Age 36.9
Native-born 1,586
Foreign-born 69

Age, 2020 (projected)††
Under 5 years 98
5 to 19 years 307
20 to 39 years 383
40 to 64 years 536
65 years and over 266

Educational Attainment, 2000
Population 25 years and over 1,118
High School graduates or higher 83.5%
Bachelor's degree or higher 17.3%
Graduate degree 5.7%

Income & Poverty, 1999
Per capita income, ... $21,318
Median household income $46,600
Median family income $48,641
Persons in poverty 149
H'holds receiving public assistance 26
H'holds receiving social security 142

Households, 2000
Total households 611
With persons under 18 236
With persons over 65 127
Family households 482
Single person households 106
Persons per household 2.7
Persons per family 3.0

Labor & Employment, 2000
Civilian labor force 919
Unemployment rate 4.0%
Civilian labor force, 2008† 966
Unemployment rate† 5.6%
Civilian labor force, 12/09† 986
Unemployment rate† 9.2%
Employed persons 16 years and over, by occupation:
Managers & professionals 224
Service occupations 131
Sales & office occupations 228
Farming, fishing & forestry 2
Construction & maintenance 108
Production & transportation 189
Self-employed persons 43

Most demographic data is from the 2000 Decennial Census
† Massachusetts Department of Revenue
†† University of Massachusetts, MISER

General Information

Town of Russell
65 Main St
Russell, MA 01071
413-862-3265

Elevation .... 339 ft.
Land area (square miles) 17.6
Water area (square miles) 0.3
Population density, 2008 (est) 97.7
Year incorporated 1792
Email .... pbrooks@townofrussell.us

Voters & Government Information

Government type .... Open Town Meeting
Number of Selectmen 3
US Congressional District(s) 1

Registered Voters, October 2008
Total 1,029
Democrats 216
Republicans 210
Unaffiliated/other 598

Local Officials, 2010
Chair, Bd. of Sel. .... Dennis Moran
Manager/Admin .... Nancy Boersi
Town Clerk .... Virginia Hardie
Finance Director .... Philip Wintersen
Tax Collector .... Wendy Thompson
Tax Assessor .... Susan Maxwell
Attorney .... Paul Maleck
Public Works .... Lyle G. Maxwell
Building .... Thomas Lagodich
Comm Dev/Planning .... Thomas Lagodich
Police Chief .... Thomas Mulligan
Emerg/Fire Chief .... Mike Morrissey

Housing & Construction

New Privately Owned Housing Units Authorized by Building Permit

	Single Family	Total Bldgs	Total Units
2006	4	4	4
2007	4	4	4
2008	3	3	3

Parcel Count by Property Class, 2010
Total .... NA
Single family .... NA
Multiple units .... NA
Apartments .... NA
Condos .... NA
Vacant land .... NA
Open space .... NA
Commercial .... NA
Industrial .... NA
Misc. residential .... NA
Other use .... NA

Public Library

Russell Public Library
PO Box 438
Russell, MA 01071
(413)862-6221

Librarian .... Gail Duso

Library Statistics, FY 2008
Population served, 2007 1,730
Registered users 1,209
Circulation 4,459
Reference transactons 0
Total program attendance 0
per capita:
Holdings 3.65
Operating income $33.81
Internet Access
Internet computers available 4
Weekly users 0

Municipal Finance

Debt at year end 2008 .... $2,761,395
Moody's rating, July 2009 .... NA

Revenues, 2008
Total $3,139,354
From all taxes 2,400,889
Federal aid 0
State aid 556,720
From other governments 16,545
Charges for services 42,504
Licenses, permits & fees 14,692
Fines & forfeits 0
Interfund transfers 0
Misc/other/special assessments 54,002

Expenditures, 2008
Total $2,914,195
General government 293,683
Public safety 171,974
Other/fixed costs 165,379
Human services 28,407
Culture & recreation 42,534
Debt Service 30,625
Education 1,883,500
Public works 287,310
Intergovernmental 3,702

Taxation, 2010

Property type	Valuation	Rate
Total	NA	-
Residential	NA	NA
Open space	NA	NA
Commercial	NA	NA
Industrial	NA	NA
Personal	NA	NA

Average Single Family Tax Bill, 2010
Avg. assessed home value .... NA
Avg. single fam. tax bill .... NA
Hi-Lo ranking .... NA

Police & Crime, 2008

Number of police officers .... NA
Violent crimes .... NA
Property crimes .... NA

Local School District

(school data 2007-08, except as noted)

Russell (non-op)
12 Littleville Road
Huntington, MA 01050
413-685-1011
Superintendent .... David Hopson

Non-operating district.
Resident students are sent to the Other School Districts listed below.

Grade plan .... NA
Total enrollment '09-10 .... NA
Grade 12 enrollment, '09-10 .... NA
Graduation rate .... NA
Dropout rate .... NA
Per-pupil expenditure .... NA
Avg teacher salary .... NA
Student/teacher ratio '08-09 .... NA
Highly-qualified teachers, '08-09 .... NA
Teachers licensed in assigned subject .... NA
Students per computer .... NA

Other School Districts (see Appendix D for data)
Gateway Regional

©2010 Information Publications, Inc. All rights reserved. Photocopying prohibited. For additional copies, contact the publisher at www.informationpublications.com or (877)544-INFO (4636)

See Introduction for an explanation of all data sources.

Demographics & Socio-Economic Characteristics

Population

1990	4,936
2000	6,353
Male	3,209
Female	3,144
2008	7,899
2010 (projected)††	7,408
2020 (projected)††	8,696

Race & Hispanic Origin, 2000

Race	
White	6,136
Black/African American	66
American Indian/Alaska Native	9
Asian	29
Hawaiian Native/Pacific Islander	0
Other Race	28
Two or more races	85
Hispanic origin	84

Age & Nativity, 2000

Under 5 years	506
18 years and over	4,399
21 years and over	4,208
65 years and over	487
85 years and over	65
Median Age	34.6
Native-born	6,183
Foreign-born	170

Age, 2020 (projected)††

Under 5 years	620
5 to 19 years	1,904
20 to 39 years	2,371
40 to 64 years	2,750
65 years and over	1,051

Educational Attainment, 2000

Population 25 years and over	3,996
High School graduates or higher	92.6%
Bachelor's degree or higher	29.5%
Graduate degree	8.8%

Income & Poverty, 1999

Per capita income,	$23,311
Median household income	$62,846
Median family income	$70,689
Persons in poverty	206
H'holds receiving public assistance	18
H'holds receiving social security	405

Households, 2000

Total households	2,253
With persons under 18	998
With persons over 65	365
Family households	1,694
Single person households	449
Persons per household	2.8
Persons per family	3.2

Labor & Employment, 2000

Civilian labor force	3,550
Unemployment rate	4.2%
Civilian labor force, 2008†	4,175
Unemployment rate†	5.7%
Civilian labor force, 12/09†	4,385
Unemployment rate†	7.9%
Employed persons 16 years and over, by occupation:	
Managers & professionals	1,233
Service occupations	450
Sales & office occupations	937
Farming, fishing & forestry	6
Construction & maintenance	262
Production & transportation	512
Self-employed persons	198

Most demographic data is from the 2000 Decennial Census
† Massachusetts Department of Revenue
†† University of Massachusetts, MISER

General Information

Town of Rutland
250 Main St
Rutland, MA 01543
508-886-4100

Elevation	1,205 ft.
Land area (square miles)	35.3
Water area (square miles)	1.1
Population density, 2008 (est)	223.8
Year incorporated	1713
Website	www.townofrutland.org

Voters & Government Information

Government type	Open Town Meeting
Number of Selectmen	5
US Congressional District(s)	3

Registered Voters, October 2008

Total	5,221
Democrats	1,159
Republicans	873
Unaffiliated/other	3,169

Local Officials, 2010

Chair, Bd. of Sel.	Leroy Clark
Manager/Admin	NA
Town Clerk	Sally Hayden
Finance Director	Lyndon Nichols
Tax Collector	Sally Hayden
Tax Assessor	Joyce McGuinness
Attorney	NA
Public Works	Gary Kellaher Jr
Building	Harry Johnson Jr
Comm Dev/Planning	Norman Anderson
Police Chief	Joseph Baril
Emerg/Fire Chief	Thomas Ruchala

Housing & Construction

New Privately Owned Housing Units Authorized by Building Permit

	Single Family	Total Bldgs	Total Units
2006	97	102	133
2007	44	44	44
2008	29	30	33

Parcel Count by Property Class, 2010

Total	3,978
Single family	2,394
Multiple units	47
Apartments	13
Condos	249
Vacant land	1,104
Open space	0
Commercial	25
Industrial	8
Misc. residential	33
Other use	105

Public Library

Rutland Free Public Library
280 Main St.
Rutland, MA 01543
(508)886-4108

Director .... Kerry Remington

Library Statistics, FY 2008

Population served, 2007	7,846
Registered users	6,290
Circulation	78,632
Reference transactons	4,620
Total program attendance	0
per capita:	
Holdings	5.72
Operating income	$21.75
Internet Access	
Internet computers available	9
Weekly users	94

Municipal Finance

Debt at year end 2008	$29,784,548
Moody's rating, July 2009	Baa1

Revenues, 2008

Total	$13,647,244
From all taxes	10,498,270
Federal aid	0
State aid	2,147,340
From other governments	48,818
Charges for services	560,997
Licenses, permits & fees	162,575
Fines & forfeits	0
Interfund transfers	66,500
Misc/other/special assessments	81,372

Expenditures, 2008

Total	$13,753,060
General government	634,069
Public safety	1,428,034
Other/fixed costs	560,418
Human services	68,201
Culture & recreation	243,239
Debt Service	2,727,203
Education	6,742,612
Public works	1,095,015
Intergovernmental	254,269

Taxation, 2010

Property type	Valuation	Rate
Total	$788,047,200	-
Residential	754,815,246	12.92
Open space	0	0.00
Commercial	16,338,954	12.92
Industrial	3,083,200	12.92
Personal	13,809,800	12.92

Average Single Family Tax Bill, 2010

Avg. assessed home value	$267,982
Avg. single fam. tax bill	$3,462
Hi-Lo ranking	179/301

Police & Crime, 2008

Number of police officers	8
Violent crimes	16
Property crimes	47

Local School District

(school data 2007-08, except as noted)

Rutland (non-op)
Jefferson School, 1745 Main Street
Jefferson, MA 01522
508-829-1670

Superintendent......... Thomas Pandiscio

Non-operating district.
Resident students are sent to the Other School Districts listed below.

Grade plan	NA
Total enrollment '09-10	NA
Grade 12 enrollment, '09-10	NA
Graduation rate	NA
Dropout rate	NA
Per-pupil expenditure	NA
Avg teacher salary	NA
Student/teacher ratio '08-09	NA
Highly-qualified teachers, '08-09	NA
Teachers licensed in assigned subject	NA
Students per computer	NA

Other School Districts (see Appendix D for data)
Wachusett Regional, Southern Worcester County Vocational Tech

©2010 Information Publications, Inc. All rights reserved. Photocopying prohibited. For additional copies, contact the publisher at www.informationpublications.com or (877)544-INFO (4636)

Demographics & Socio-Economic Characteristics*

Population

1990	38,091
2000	40,407
Male	18,745
Female	21,662
2008	41,256
2010 (projected)††	41,764
2020 (projected)††	43,630

Race & Hispanic Origin, 2000

Race	
White	34,497
Black/African American	1,274
American Indian/Alaska Native	87
Asian	807
Hawaiian Native/Pacific Islander	19
Other Race	2,724
Two or more races	999
Hispanic origin	4,541

Age & Nativity, 2000

Under 5 years	2,264
18 years and over	32,250
21 years and over	30,429
65 years and over	5,716
85 years and over	745
Median Age	36.4
Native-born	35,598
Foreign-born	4,809

Age, 2020 (projected)††

Under 5 years	2,372
5 to 19 years	7,142
20 to 39 years	12,850
40 to 64 years	14,110
65 years and over	7,156

Educational Attainment, 2000

Population 25 years and over	28,169
High School graduates or higher	85.2%
Bachelor's degree or higher	31.1%
Graduate degree	10.2%

Income & Poverty, 1999

Per capita income,	$23,857
Median household income	$44,033
Median family income	$55,635
Persons in poverty	3,787
H'holds receiving public assistance	508
H'holds receiving social security	4,712

Households, 2000

Total households	17,492
With persons under 18	4,584
With persons over 65	4,281
Family households	9,707
Single person households	6,105
Persons per household	2.2
Persons per family	3.0

Labor & Employment, 2000

Civilian labor force	22,920
Unemployment rate	5.4%
Civilian labor force, 2008†	23,452
Unemployment rate†	6.4%
Civilian labor force, 12/09†	23,363
Unemployment rate†	9.5%
Employed persons 16 years and over, by occupation:	
Managers & professionals	8,104
Service occupations	3,269
Sales & office occupations	6,394
Farming, fishing & forestry	38
Construction & maintenance	1,292
Production & transportation	2,587
Self-employed persons	1,320

Most demographic data is from the 2000 Decennial Census
* see Appendix E for American Community Survey data
† Massachusetts Department of Revenue
†† University of Massachusetts, MISER

General Information

City of Salem
93 Washington St
Salem, MA 01970
978-745-9595

Elevation	13 ft.
Land area (square miles)	8.1
Water area (square miles)	10.0
Population density, 2008 (est)	5,093.3
Year incorporated	1626
Email	clapointe@salem.com

Voters & Government Information

Government type	Mayor-Council
Number of Councilpersons	11
US Congressional District(s)	6

Registered Voters, October 2008

Total	26,253
Democrats	10,717
Republicans	2,074
Unaffiliated/other	13,236

Local Officials, 2010

Mayor	Kimberley Driscoll
Manager/Admin	NA
Clerk	Cheryl A. LaPointe
Finance Director	Richard Viscay
Tax Collector	Bonnie Celi
Tax Assessor	Frank Kulik
Attorney	NA
Public Works	David Knowton
Building	Thomas St. Pierre
Planning	Lynn Duncan
Police Chief	Robert St. Pierre
Emerg/Fire Chief	David Cody

Housing & Construction

New Privately Owned Housing Units Authorized by Building Permit

	Single Family	Total Bldgs	Total Units
2006	2	4	21
2007	16	16	16
2008	6	8	10

Parcel Count by Property Class, 2010

Total	12,760
Single family	4,805
Multiple units	2,189
Apartments	354
Condos	3,909
Vacant land	403
Open space	0
Commercial	760
Industrial	126
Misc. residential	48
Other use	166

Public Library

Salem Public Library
370 Essex St.
Salem, MA 01970
(978)744-0860

Director	Lorraine Jackson

Library Statistics, FY 2008

Population served, 2007	40,922
Registered users	30,502
Circulation	546,002
Reference transactons	44,551
Total program attendance	239,262
per capita:	
Holdings	3.57
Operating income	$30.61
Internet Access	
Internet computers available	13
Weekly users	519

Municipal Finance

Debt at year end 2008	$53,645,656
Moody's rating, July 2009	A2

Revenues, 2008

Total	$114,361,731
From all taxes	68,956,651
Federal aid	0
State aid	28,082,311
From other governments	274,330
Charges for services	3,270,931
Licenses, permits & fees	510,120
Fines & forfeits	947,840
Interfund transfers.	1,250,068
Misc/other/special assessments	5,534,740

Expenditures, 2008

Total	$106,202,012
General government	4,128,587
Public safety	15,425,463
Other/fixed costs	19,529,120
Human services	811,837
Culture & recreation	2,039,513
Debt Service	6,988,434
Education	47,874,121
Public works	3,471,267
Intergovernmental	5,933,670

Taxation, 2010

Property type	Valuation	Rate
Total	$4,294,563,427	-
Residential	3,527,110,563	14.01
Open space	0	0.00
Commercial	432,747,534	26.93
Industrial	127,061,700	26.93
Personal	207,643,630	26.93

Average Single Family Tax Bill, 2010

Avg. assessed home value	$311,918
Avg. single fam. tax bill	$4,370
Hi-Lo ranking	109/301

Police & Crime, 2008

Number of police officers	79
Violent crimes	86
Property crimes	846

Local School District

(school data 2007-08, except as noted)

Salem
29 Highland Avenue
Salem, MA 01970
978-740-1212

Superintendent	William Cameron
Grade plan	PK-12
Total enrollment '09-10	4,496
Grade 12 enrollment, '09-10	258
Graduation rate	67.5%
Dropout rate	18.7%
Per-pupil expenditure	$13,774
Avg teacher salary	$57,731
Student/teacher ratio '08-09	11.1 to 1
Highly-qualified teachers, '08-09	96.7%
Teachers licensed in assigned subject	96.8%
Students per computer	6.1

Massachusetts Competency Assessment System (MCAS), 2009 results

	English		Math	
	% Prof	CPI	% Prof	CPI
Gr 4	42%	73.7	33%	69
Gr 6	53%	80.3	42%	69
Gr 8	65%	86.3	34%	62.2
Gr 10	68%	86.4	61%	80.1

Other School Districts (see Appendix D for data)
North Shore Vocational Tech

©2010 Information Publications, Inc. All rights reserved. Photocopying prohibited. For additional copies, contact the publisher at www.informationpublications.com or (877)544-INFO (4636)

See Introduction for an explanation of all data sources.

Demographics & Socio-Economic Characteristics

Population

1990	6,882
2000	7,827
Male	3,863
Female	3,964
2008	8,417
2010 (projected)††	8,807
2020 (projected)††	9,737

Race & Hispanic Origin, 2000

Race	
White	7,635
Black/African American	32
American Indian/Alaska Native	24
Asian	27
Hawaiian Native/Pacific Islander	7
Other Race	20
Two or more races	82
Hispanic origin	92

Age & Nativity, 2000

Under 5 years	483
18 years and over	5,980
21 years and over	5,761
65 years and over	931
85 years and over	84
Median Age	38.8
Native-born	7,503
Foreign-born	324

Age, 2020 (projected)††

Under 5 years	527
5 to 19 years	1,633
20 to 39 years	2,121
40 to 64 years	3,588
65 years and over	1,868

Educational Attainment, 2000

Population 25 years and over	5,493
High School graduates or higher	84.0%
Bachelor's degree or higher	17.1%
Graduate degree	5.2%

Income & Poverty, 1999

Per capita income,	$21,608
Median household income	$49,310
Median family income	$56,327
Persons in poverty	526
H'holds receiving public assistance	75
H'holds receiving social security	846

Households, 2000

Total households	3,082
With persons under 18	1,025
With persons over 65	701
Family households	1,991
Single person households	819
Persons per household	2.5
Persons per family	3.1

Labor & Employment, 2000

Civilian labor force	4,217
Unemployment rate	3.6%
Civilian labor force, 2008†	4,455
Unemployment rate†	7.3%
Civilian labor force, 12/09†	4,510
Unemployment rate†	10.8%
Employed persons 16 years and over, by occupation:	
Managers & professionals	1,009
Service occupations	606
Sales & office occupations	1,061
Farming, fishing & forestry	22
Construction & maintenance	504
Production & transportation	862
Self-employed persons	363

Most demographic data is from the 2000 Decennial Census
† Massachusetts Department of Revenue
†† University of Massachusetts, MISER

General Information

Town of Salisbury
5 Beach Rd
Salisbury, MA 01952
978-465-2310

Elevation	20 ft.
Land area (square miles)	15.4
Water area (square miles)	2.4
Population density, 2008 (est)	546.6
Year incorporated	1638
Website	www.salisburyma.gov

Voters & Government Information

Government type	Open Town Meeting
Number of Selectmen	5
US Congressional District(s)	6

Registered Voters, October 2008

Total	5,947
Democrats	1,582
Republicans	758
Unaffiliated/other	3,574

Local Officials, 2010

Chair, Bd. of Sel.	Donald W. Beaulieu
Manager	Neil Harrington
Clerk	Wilma McDonald
Finance Director	Andrew Gould
Treas/Collector	Christine Caron
Tax Assessor	Cheryl Gillespie
Attorney	Kopelman & Paige
Public Works	Donald Levesque
Building	David Lovering
Planning	Lisa Pearson
Police Chief	David L'Esperance
Fire Chief	Richard Souliotis

Housing & Construction

New Privately Owned Housing Units Authorized by Building Permit

	Single Family	Total Bldgs	Total Units
2006	98	99	100
2007	25	29	49
2008	13	13	13

Parcel Count by Property Class, 2010

Total	4,643
Single family	2,016
Multiple units	357
Apartments	67
Condos	674
Vacant land	568
Open space	0
Commercial	351
Industrial	35
Misc. residential	365
Other use	210

Public Library

Salisbury Public Library
17 Elm Street
Salisbury, MA 01952
(978)465-5071

Director	Terry Kyrios

Library Statistics, FY 2008

Population served, 2007	8,521
Registered users	5,096
Circulation	39,670
Reference transactons	2,964
Total program attendance	0
per capita:	
Holdings	3.89
Operating income	$20.74
Internet Access	
Internet computers available	2
Weekly users	60

Municipal Finance

Debt at year end 2008	$16,816,923
Moody's rating, July 2009	A2

Revenues, 2008

Total	$17,561,880
From all taxes	14,466,174
Federal aid	0
State aid	1,154,656
From other governments	0
Charges for services	278,585
Licenses, permits & fees	278,820
Fines & forfeits	66,789
Interfund transfers	567,688
Misc/other/special assessments	374,584

Expenditures, 2008

Total	$17,688,883
General government	1,623,108
Public safety	3,290,821
Other/fixed costs	1,600,377
Human services	346,835
Culture & recreation	250,994
Debt Service	785,164
Education	8,671,285
Public works	813,080
Intergovernmental	215,243

Taxation, 2010

Property type	Valuation	Rate
Total	$1,501,760,433	-
Residential	1,218,189,620	9.86
Open space	0	0.00
Commercial	226,431,193	9.86
Industrial	30,713,870	9.86
Personal	26,425,750	9.86

Average Single Family Tax Bill, 2010

Avg. assessed home value	$328,169
Avg. single fam. tax bill	$3,236
Hi-Lo ranking	210/301

Police & Crime, 2008

Number of police officers	20
Violent crimes	46
Property crimes	191

Local School District

(school data 2007-08, except as noted)

Salisbury (non-op)
112 Elm Street
Byfield, MA 01922
978-465-2397

Superintendent	Sandra Halloran

Non-operating district.
Resident students are sent to the Other School Districts listed below.

Grade plan	NA
Total enrollment '09-10	NA
Grade 12 enrollment, '09-10	NA
Graduation rate	NA
Dropout rate	NA
Per-pupil expenditure	NA
Avg teacher salary	NA
Student/teacher ratio '08-09	NA
Highly-qualified teachers, '08-09	NA
Teachers licensed in assigned subject	NA
Students per computer	NA

Other School Districts (see Appendix D for data)
Triton Regional, Whittier Vocational Tech

©2010 Information Publications, Inc. All rights reserved. Photocopying prohibited. For additional copies, contact the publisher at www.informationpublications.com or (877)544-INFO (4636)

©2010 Information Publications, Inc. All rights reserved. Photocopying prohibited. For additional copies, contact the publisher at www.informationpublications.com or (877)544-INFO (4636)

Demographics & Socio-Economic Characteristics

Population

1990 .667
2000 .824
Male .442
Female .382
2008 .848
2010 (projected)†† .913
2020 (projected)†† 1,032

Race & Hispanic Origin, 2000

Race
White .798
Black/African American .4
American Indian/Alaska Native .1
Asian .1
Hawaiian Native/Pacific Islander .0
Other Race .3
Two or more races .17
Hispanic origin .8

Age & Nativity, 2000

Under 5 years .39
18 years and over .658
21 years and over .641
65 years and over .148
85 years and over .9
Median Age 44.7
Native-born .814
Foreign-born .21

Age, 2020 (projected)††

Under 5 years .49
5 to 19 years .144
20 to 39 years .189
40 to 64 years .359
65 years and over .291

Educational Attainment, 2000

Population 25 years and over .647
High School graduates or higher 83.3%
Bachelor's degree or higher 24.7%
Graduate degree .13.9%

Income & Poverty, 1999

Per capita income, $27,628
Median household income $45,972
Median family income $57,083
Persons in poverty .19
H'holds receiving public assistance .3
H'holds receiving social security .116

Households, 2000

Total households .327
With persons under 18 .93
With persons over 65 .88
Family households .213
Single person households .98
Persons per household 2.4
Persons per family 3.0

Labor & Employment, 2000

Civilian labor force .418
Unemployment rate .1.7%
Civilian labor force, 2008† .484
Unemployment rate† 6.2%
Civilian labor force, 12/09† .498
Unemployment rate† .9.6%
Employed persons 16 years and over, by occupation:
Managers & professionals .129
Service occupations .68
Sales & office occupations .77
Farming, fishing & forestry .0
Construction & maintenance .73
Production & transportation .64
Self-employed persons .76

Most demographic data is from the 2000 Decennial Census
† Massachusetts Department of Revenue
†† University of Massachusetts, MISER

General Information

Town of Sandisfield
66 Sandisfield Rd
Sandisfield, MA 01255
413-258-4711

Elevation 250 ft.
Land area (square miles) 52.3
Water area (square miles) 0.7
Population density, 2008 (est) 16.2
Year incorporated 1762
Website NA

Voters & Government Information

Government type Open Town Meeting
Number of Selectmen .3
US Congressional District(s) .1

Registered Voters, October 2008

Total .568
Democrats .192
Republicans .70
Unaffiliated/other .301

Local Officials, 2010

Chair, Bd. of Sel. Richard Campetti
Manager/Admin NA
Town Clerk Dolores Harasyko
Finance Kathleen Jacobs
Tax Collector Edna Leavenworth
Tax Assessor Bethany Perry
Attorney Hannon Learner
Public Works NA
Building Eric Munson Jr
Comm Dev/Planning Barbara Cormier
Police Chief Michael D. Morrison
Emerg/Fire Chief Ralph E. Morrison

Housing & Construction

New Privately Owned Housing Units Authorized by Building Permit

	Single Family	Total Bldgs	Total Units
2006	8	8	8
2007	7	7	7
2008	10	10	10

Parcel Count by Property Class, 2010

Total 1,293
Single family .591
Multiple units .3
Apartments .0
Condos .0
Vacant land .470
Open space .0
Commercial .9
Industrial .4
Misc. residential .17
Other use .199

Public Library

Sandisfield Free Public Library
PO Box 183
Sandisfield, MA 01255
(413)258-4966

Librarian Sadie O'Rourke

Library Statistics, FY 2008

Population served, 2007 .837
Registered users .386
Circulation 2,252
Reference transactons .0
Total program attendance 1,726

per capita:

Holdings 5.73
Operating income $13.45

Internet Access

Internet computers available .1
Weekly users .4

Municipal Finance

Debt at year end 2008 $0
Moody's rating, July 2009 NA

Revenues, 2008

Total $2,473,127
From all taxes 2,013,688
Federal aid .0
State aid 91,335
From other governments 6,025
Charges for services 27,698
Licenses, permits & fees 3,455
Fines & forfeits .0
Interfund transfers 216,688
Misc/other/special assessments 57,119

Expenditures, 2008

Total $2,066,886
General government 242,675
Public safety 105,698
Other/fixed costs 150,549
Human services 15,620
Culture & recreation 16,514
Debt Service .0
Education 962,450
Public works 566,893
Intergovernmental 1,321

Taxation, 2010

Property type	Valuation	Rate
Total	$242,030,621	-
Residential	223,196,930	8.63
Open space	0	0.00
Commercial	5,853,028	8.63
Industrial	621,700	8.63
Personal	12,358,963	8.63

Average Single Family Tax Bill, 2010

Avg. assessed home value $278,230
Avg. single fam. tax bill $2,401
Hi-Lo ranking 283/301

Police & Crime, 2008

Number of police officers NA
Violent crimes NA
Property crimes NA

Local School District

(school data 2007-08, except as noted)

Sandisfield (non-op)
555 N Main, POB 679
Otis, MA 01253
413-269-4466

Superintendent Joanne Austin

Non-operating district.
Resident students are sent to the Other School Districts listed below.

Grade plan NA
Total enrollment '09-10 NA
Grade 12 enrollment, '09-10 NA
Graduation rate NA
Dropout rate NA
Per-pupil expenditure NA
Avg teacher salary NA
Student/teacher ratio '08-09 NA
Highly-qualified teachers, '08-09 NA
Teachers licensed in assigned subject NA
Students per computer NA

Other School Districts (see Appendix D for data)

Farmington River Regional

See Introduction for an explanation of all data sources.

Demographics & Socio-Economic Characteristics

Population

1990	15,489
2000	20,136
Male	9,783
Female	10,353
2008	20,129
2010 (projected)††	25,987
2020 (projected)††	32,646

Race & Hispanic Origin, 2000

Race	
White	19,683
Black/African American	77
American Indian/Alaska Native	62
Asian	109
Hawaiian Native/Pacific Islander	2
Other Race	65
Two or more races	138
Hispanic origin	161

Age & Nativity, 2000

Under 5 years	1,329
18 years and over	14,423
21 years and over	13,885
65 years and over	2,757
85 years and over	311
Median Age	39.5
Native-born	19,523
Foreign-born	622

Age, 2020 (projected)††

Under 5 years	2,034
5 to 19 years	6,009
20 to 39 years	7,665
40 to 64 years	10,456
65 years and over	6,482

Educational Attainment, 2000

Population 25 years and over	13,315
High School graduates or higher	94.7%
Bachelor's degree or higher	38.3%
Graduate degree	14.6%

Income & Poverty, 1999

Per capita income,	$26,895
Median household income	$61,250
Median family income	$66,553
Persons in poverty	611
H'holds receiving public assistance	102
H'holds receiving social security	2,055

Households, 2000

Total households	7,335
With persons under 18	2,932
With persons over 65	1,887
Family households	5,515
Single person households	1,468
Persons per household	2.7
Persons per family	3.2

Labor & Employment, 2000

Civilian labor force	9,988
Unemployment rate	3.3%
Civilian labor force, 2008†	10,970
Unemployment rate†	6.9%
Civilian labor force, 12/09†	10,662
Unemployment rate†	8.9%
Employed persons 16 years and over, by occupation:	
Managers & professionals	4,051
Service occupations	1,290
Sales & office occupations	2,665
Farming, fishing & forestry	35
Construction & maintenance	926
Production & transportation	690
Self-employed persons	1,028

Most demographic data is from the 2000 Decennial Census
† Massachusetts Department of Revenue
†† University of Massachusetts, MISER

General Information

Town of Sandwich
130 Main Street
Sandwich, MA 02563
508-888-4910

Elevation	50 ft.
Land area (square miles)	43.0
Water area (square miles)	1.3
Population density, 2008 (est)	468.1
Year incorporated	1638
Website	www.sandwichmass.org

Voters & Government Information

Government type	Open Town Meeting
Number of Selectmen	5
US Congressional District(s)	10

Registered Voters, October 2008

Total	15,649
Democrats	3,582
Republicans	3,080
Unaffiliated/other	8,923

Local Officials, 2010

Chair, Bd. of Sel.	John Kennan
Administrator	George H. Dunham
Town Clerk	Taylor D. White
Treasurer	Craig Mayen
Tax Collector	E. Susan Flynn
Tax Assessor	Edward Childs
Attorney	Kopelman & Paige
Public Works	Paul Tilton
Building	Pete Sherwin
Comm Dev/Planning	Greg Smith
Police Chief	Michael Miller
Emerg/Fire Chief	George P. Russell Jr

Housing & Construction

New Privately Owned Housing Units Authorized by Building Permit

	Single Family	Total Bldgs	Total Units
2006	45	45	45
2007	43	45	49
2008	25	25	25

Parcel Count by Property Class, 2010

Total	10,563
Single family	8,346
Multiple units	69
Apartments	4
Condos	476
Vacant land	995
Open space	0
Commercial	305
Industrial	154
Misc. residential	90
Other use	124

Public Library

Sandwich Free Public Library
142 Main Street
Sandwich, MA 02563
(508)888-0625

Director	Richard J. Connor

Library Statistics, FY 2008

Population served, 2007	20,255
Registered users	12,839
Circulation	293,164
Reference transactons	3,240
Total program attendance	174,558
per capita:	
Holdings	3.46
Operating income	$42.86
Internet Access	
Internet computers available	29
Weekly users	0

Municipal Finance

Debt at year end 2008	$43,307,884
Moody's rating, July 2009	A1

Revenues, 2008

Total	$63,738,333
From all taxes	47,957,118
Federal aid	301,144
State aid	10,640,517
From other governments	3,344
Charges for services	1,039,812
Licenses, permits & fees	473,841
Fines & forfeits	0
Interfund transfers	2,013,309
Misc/other/special assessments	654,624

Expenditures, 2008

Total	$60,453,965
General government	2,990,152
Public safety	6,749,800
Other/fixed costs	8,954,424
Human services	420,924
Culture & recreation	1,071,128
Debt Service	6,218,032
Education	30,426,766
Public works	2,479,026
Intergovernmental	1,143,713

Taxation, 2010

Property type	Valuation	Rate
Total	$4,030,844,600	-
Residential	3,486,941,405	11.24
Open space	0	0.00
Commercial	199,808,495	11.24
Industrial	68,915,900	11.24
Personal	275,178,800	11.24

Average Single Family Tax Bill, 2010

Avg. assessed home value	$376,765
Avg. single fam. tax bill	$4,235
Hi-Lo ranking	118/301

Police & Crime, 2008

Number of police officers	34
Violent crimes	26
Property crimes	351

Local School District

(school data 2007-08, except as noted)

Sandwich
365 Quaker Meetinghouse Road, Suite A
East Sandwich, MA 02537
508-888-1054

Superintendent	Mary Johnson
Grade plan	PK-12
Total enrollment '09-10	3,579
Grade 12 enrollment, '09-10	244
Graduation rate	89.8%
Dropout rate	4.1%
Per-pupil expenditure	$10,809
Avg teacher salary	$62,297
Student/teacher ratio '08-09	15.1 to 1
Highly-qualified teachers, '08-09	72.7%
Teachers licensed in assigned subject	98.9%
Students per computer	9.2

Massachusetts Competency Assessment System (MCAS), 2009 results

	English		Math	
	% Prof	CPI	% Prof	CPI
Gr 4	63%	85.1	51%	81.5
Gr 6	83%	94.2	66%	87.2
Gr 8	84%	95	61%	82.4
Gr 10	90%	96.5	93%	96.8

Other School Districts (see Appendix D for data)
Upper Cape Cod Vocational Tech

©2010 Information Publications, Inc. All rights reserved. Photocopying prohibited. For additional copies, contact the publisher at www.informationpublications.com or (877)544-INFO (4636)

See Introduction for an explanation of all data sources.

Demographics & Socio-Economic Characteristics*

Population

1990	25,549
2000	26,078
Male	12,476
Female	13,602
2008	27,478
2010 (projected)††	25,852
2020 (projected)††	25,125

Race & Hispanic Origin, 2000

Race	
White	25,379
Black/African American	114
American Indian/Alaska Native	14
Asian	314
Hawaiian Native/Pacific Islander	10
Other Race	70
Two or more races	177
Hispanic origin	254

Age & Nativity, 2000

Under 5 years	1,304
18 years and over	20,728
21 years and over	19,971
65 years and over	4,594
85 years and over	520
Median Age	41.3
Native-born	24,686
Foreign-born	1,320

Age, 2020 (projected)††

Under 5 years	1,059
5 to 19 years	3,598
20 to 39 years	5,297
40 to 64 years	9,072
65 years and over	6,099

Educational Attainment, 2000

Population 25 years and over	19,021
High School graduates or higher	87.6%
Bachelor's degree or higher	19.2%
Graduate degree	6.7%

Income & Poverty, 1999

Per capita income,	$25,524
Median household income	$55,301
Median family income	$65,782
Persons in poverty	1,097
H'holds receiving public assistance	141
H'holds receiving social security	3,551

Households, 2000

Total households	9,975
With persons under 18	3,008
With persons over 65	3,253
Family households	7,144
Single person households	2,422
Persons per household	2.6
Persons per family	3.1

Labor & Employment, 2000

Civilian labor force	13,903
Unemployment rate	3.2%
Civilian labor force, 2008†	14,911
Unemployment rate†	6.3%
Civilian labor force, 12/09†	14,996
Unemployment rate†	9.2%
Employed persons 16 years and over, by occupation:	
Managers & professionals	4,276
Service occupations	1,501
Sales & office occupations	4,845
Farming, fishing & forestry	40
Construction & maintenance	1,344
Production & transportation	1,456
Self-employed persons	664

Most demographic data is from the 2000 Decennial Census
* see Appendix E for American Community Survey data
† Massachusetts Department of Revenue
†† University of Massachusetts, MISER

General Information

Town of Saugus
298 Central St
Saugus, MA 01906
781-231-4111

Elevation	27 ft.
Land area (square miles)	11.0
Water area (square miles)	0.8
Population density, 2008 (est)	2,498.0
Year incorporated	1815
Website	www.saugas-ma.gov

Voters & Government Information

Government type	Rep. Twn. Mtg. (50)
Number of Selectmen	5
US Congressional District(s)	6

Registered Voters, October 2008

Total	17,037
Democrats	6,203
Republicans	1,641
Unaffiliated/other	9,107

Local Officials, 2010

Chair, Bd. of Sel.	Donald H. Wong
Manager	Andrew Bisignani
Clerk	Joanne D. Rappa
Accountant	Joan Regan
Treas/Collector	Wendy Hatch
Tax Assessor	Ronald Keohan
Attorney	John J. Vasapolli
Public Works	Joseph Attubato
Building	Fred Varone
Planning	Mary Carfagna
Police Chief	Domenic J. DiMella
Fire Chief	James L. Blanchard

Housing & Construction

New Privately Owned Housing Units Authorized by Building Permit

	Single Family	Total Bldgs	Total Units
2006	23	37	159
2007	20	33	177
2008	13	27	171

Parcel Count by Property Class, 2010

Total	10,017
Single family	7,114
Multiple units	643
Apartments	35
Condos	822
Vacant land	833
Open space	0
Commercial	378
Industrial	94
Misc. residential	18
Other use	80

Public Library

Saugus Public Library
295 Central St.
Saugus, MA 01906
(781)231-4168

Director .... Ewa Jankowska (Int)

Library Statistics, FY 2008

Population served, 2007	27,192
Registered users	14,586
Circulation	76,229
Reference transactons	5,467
Total program attendance	142,047
per capita:	
Holdings	3.02
Operating income	$0.00
Internet Access	
Internet computers available	18
Weekly users	670

Municipal Finance

Debt at year end 2008	$33,409,076
Moody's rating, July 2009	Baa1

Revenues, 2008

Total	$62,557,862
From all taxes	47,682,000
Federal aid	0
State aid	9,955,607
From other governments	0
Charges for services	201,741
Licenses, permits & fees	1,696,014
Fines & forfeits	201,835
Interfund transfers	996,517
Misc/other/special assessments	912,074

Expenditures, 2008

Total	$59,417,256
General government	2,321,245
Public safety	9,207,304
Other/fixed costs	13,042,176
Human services	226,701
Culture & recreation	502,928
Debt Service	3,207,108
Education	23,180,435
Public works	5,218,941
Intergovernmental	2,440,346

Taxation, 2010

Property type	Valuation	Rate
Total	$3,962,136,947	-
Residential	3,119,032,860	9.68
Open space	0	0.00
Commercial	615,637,827	21.24
Industrial	146,336,900	21.24
Personal	81,129,360	21.24

Average Single Family Tax Bill, 2010

Avg. assessed home value	$343,052
Avg. single fam. tax bill	$3,321
Hi-Lo ranking	200/301

Police & Crime, 2008

Number of police officers	54
Violent crimes	101
Property crimes	1,115

Local School District

(school data 2007-08, except as noted)

Saugus
23 Main Street
Saugus, MA 01906
781-231-5000

Superintendent	Richard Langlois
Grade plan	PK-12
Total enrollment '09-10	2,866
Grade 12 enrollment, '09-10	206
Graduation rate	79.8%
Dropout rate	9.1%
Per-pupil expenditure	$10,608
Avg teacher salary	$59,299
Student/teacher ratio '08-09	15.1 to 1
Highly-qualified teachers, '08-09	97.9%
Teachers licensed in assigned subject	96.9%
Students per computer	10

Massachusetts Competency Assessment System (MCAS), 2009 results

	English		Math	
	% Prof	CPI	% Prof	CPI
Gr 4	46%	80.2	38%	77.2
Gr 6	51%	77.7	45%	72.7
Gr 8	71%	86.8	34%	63.3
Gr 10	74%	89.6	69%	86.1

Other School Districts (see Appendix D for data)
Northeast Metro Vocational Tech

©2010 Information Publications, Inc. All rights reserved. Photocopying prohibited. For additional copies, contact the publisher at www.informationpublications.com or (877)544-INFO (4636)

See Introduction for an explanation of all data sources.

Demographics & Socio-Economic Characteristics

Population

1990	634
2000	705
Male	378
Female	327
2008	722
2010 (projected)††	697
2020 (projected)††	653

Race & Hispanic Origin, 2000

Race	
White	687
Black/African American	5
American Indian/Alaska Native	3
Asian	0
Hawaiian Native/Pacific Islander	0
Other Race	2
Two or more races	8
Hispanic origin	5

Age & Nativity, 2000

Under 5 years	43
18 years and over	533
21 years and over	519
65 years and over	72
85 years and over	8
Median Age	39.6
Native-born	685
Foreign-born	7

Age, 2020 (projected)††

Under 5 years	25
5 to 19 years	94
20 to 39 years	152
40 to 64 years	254
65 years and over	128

Educational Attainment, 2000

Population 25 years and over	509
High School graduates or higher	84.3%
Bachelor's degree or higher	15.1%
Graduate degree	6.3%

Income & Poverty, 1999

Per capita income,	$20,223
Median household income	$41,477
Median family income	$50,114
Persons in poverty	37
H'holds receiving public assistance	9
H'holds receiving social security	86

Households, 2000

Total households	287
With persons under 18	94
With persons over 65	52
Family households	202
Single person households	67
Persons per household	2.5
Persons per family	2.9

Labor & Employment, 2000

Civilian labor force	374
Unemployment rate	4.8%
Civilian labor force, 2008†	426
Unemployment rate†	9.2%
Civilian labor force, 12/09†	428
Unemployment rate†	12.1%
Employed persons 16 years and over, by occupation:	
Managers & professionals	107
Service occupations	56
Sales & office occupations	49
Farming, fishing & forestry	6
Construction & maintenance	66
Production & transportation	72
Self-employed persons	32

Most demographic data is from the 2000 Decennial Census
† Massachusetts Department of Revenue
†† University of Massachusetts, MISER

General Information

Town of Savoy
720 Main Rd
Savoy, MA 01256
413-743-4290

Elevation	1,720 ft.
Land area (square miles)	35.9
Water area (square miles)	0.1
Population density, 2008 (est)	20.1
Year incorporated	1797
Email	townofsavoy@verizon.net

Voters & Government Information

Government type	Open Town Meeting
Number of Selectmen	3
US Congressional District(s)	1

Registered Voters, October 2008

Total	537
Democrats	95
Republicans	42
Unaffiliated/other	395

Local Officials, 2010

Chair, Bd. of Sel.	Scott Koczela
Manager/Admin	NA
Town Clerk	Brenda Smith
Finance	Beverly Cooper
Tax Collector	Susan J. McGrath
Tax Assessor	Sam Davis
Attorney	NA
Public Works	Sean Frank
Building	Gerald Garner
Comm Dev/Planning	Karen Dobe-Costa
Police Chief	Stephen Deane
Emerg/Fire Chief	Lawrence Orayna

Housing & Construction

New Privately Owned Housing Units Authorized by Building Permit

	Single Family	Total Bldgs	Total Units
2006	7	7	7
2007	6	6	6
2008	1	1	1

Parcel Count by Property Class, 2010

Total	NA
Single family	NA
Multiple units	NA
Apartments	NA
Condos	NA
Vacant land	NA
Open space	NA
Commercial	NA
Industrial	NA
Misc. residential	NA
Other use	NA

Public Library

Savoy Hollow Library
720 Main Road
Savoy, MA 01256
(413)743-3759

Director	James Groves

Library Statistics, FY 2008

Population served, 2007	720
Registered users	0
Circulation	0
Reference transactons	0
Total program attendance	0
per capita:	
Holdings	0.00
Operating income	$0.00
Internet Access	
Internet computers available	0
Weekly users	0

Municipal Finance

Debt at year end 2008	$104,282
Moody's rating, July 2009	NA

Revenues, 2008

Total	$1,789,292
From all taxes	859,253
Federal aid	0
State aid	784,467
From other governments	6,913
Charges for services	12,594
Licenses, permits & fees	7,145
Fines & forfeits	50
Interfund transfers	97,000
Misc/other/special assessments	10,935

Expenditures, 2008

Total	$1,839,765
General government	94,311
Public safety	43,263
Other/fixed costs	111,341
Human services	6,313
Culture & recreation	2,016
Debt Service	23,501
Education	1,002,835
Public works	420,439
Intergovernmental	135,746

Taxation, 2010

Property type	Valuation	Rate
Total	NA	-
Residential	NA	NA
Open space	NA	NA
Commercial	NA	NA
Industrial	NA	NA
Personal	NA	NA

Average Single Family Tax Bill, 2010

Avg. assessed home value	NA
Avg. single fam. tax bill	NA
Hi-Lo ranking	NA

Police & Crime, 2008

Number of police officers	NA
Violent crimes	1
Property crimes	3

Local School District

(school data 2007-08, except as noted)

Savoy
26 Chapel Road
Savoy, MA 01256
413-743-1992

Superintendent	Jon Lev
Grade plan	PK-5
Total enrollment '09-10	42
Grade 12 enrollment, '09-10	0
Graduation rate	NA
Dropout rate	NA
Per-pupil expenditure	$10,177
Avg teacher salary	$36,261
Student/teacher ratio '08-09	11.3 to 1
Highly-qualified teachers, '08-09	100.0%
Teachers licensed in assigned subject	97.9%
Students per computer	1.6

Massachusetts Competency Assessment System (MCAS), 2009 results

	English		Math	
	% Prof	CPI	% Prof	CPI
Gr 4	91%	97.7	55%	84.1
Gr 6	NA	NA	NA	NA
Gr 8	NA	NA	NA	NA
Gr 10	NA	NA	NA	NA

Other School Districts (see Appendix D for data)
Adams-Cheshire Regional, Northern Berkshire Vocational Tech

©2010 Information Publications, Inc. All rights reserved. Photocopying prohibited. For additional copies, contact the publisher at www.informationpublications.com or (877)544-INFO (4636)

Demographics & Socio-Economic Characteristics

Population

1990	16,786
2000	17,863
Male	8,523
Female	9,340
2008	17,926
2010 (projected)††	17,155
2020 (projected)††	15,710

Race & Hispanic Origin, 2000

Race	
White	17,276
Black/African American	88
American Indian/Alaska Native	6
Asian	80
Hawaiian Native/Pacific Islander	2
Other Race	231
Two or more races	180
Hispanic origin	148

Age & Nativity, 2000

Under 5 years	1,235
18 years and over	13,203
21 years and over	12,817
65 years and over	2,726
85 years and over	311
Median Age	40.7
Native-born	17,179
Foreign-born	684

Age, 2020 (projected)††

Under 5 years	749
5 to 19 years	2,604
20 to 39 years	2,965
40 to 64 years	5,467
65 years and over	3,925

Educational Attainment, 2000

Population 25 years and over	12,486
High School graduates or higher	95.8%
Bachelor's degree or higher	47.6%
Graduate degree	15.4%

Income & Poverty, 1999

Per capita income,	$33,940
Median household income	$70,868
Median family income	$86,058
Persons in poverty	451
H'holds receiving public assistance	71
H'holds receiving social security	2,019

Households, 2000

Total households	6,694
With persons under 18	2,437
With persons over 65	1,887
Family households	4,921
Single person households	1,488
Persons per household	2.6
Persons per family	3.1

Labor & Employment, 2000

Civilian labor force	9,218
Unemployment rate	2.3%
Civilian labor force, 2008†	9,592
Unemployment rate†	5.1%
Civilian labor force, 12/09†	9,466
Unemployment rate†	7.6%
Employed persons 16 years and over, by occupation:	
Managers & professionals	4,557
Service occupations	1,060
Sales & office occupations	2,177
Farming, fishing & forestry	80
Construction & maintenance	638
Production & transportation	492
Self-employed persons	837

Most demographic data is from the 2000 Decennial Census
† Massachusetts Department of Revenue
†† University of Massachusetts, MISER

General Information

Town of Scituate
600 Chief Just. Cushing Hwy
Scituate, MA 02066
781-545-8743

Elevation	50 ft.
Land area (square miles)	17.2
Water area (square miles)	14.6
Population density, 2008 (est)	1,042.2
Year incorporated	1633
Website	www.town.scituate.ma.us

Voters & Government Information

Government type	Open Town Meeting
Number of Selectmen	5
US Congressional District(s)	10

Registered Voters, October 2008

Total	13,340
Democrats	3,689
Republicans	2,282
Unaffiliated/other	7,314

Local Officials, 2010

Chair, Bd. of Sel.	Joseph P. Norton
Administrator	Patricia Vinchesi
Clerk	Bernice R. Brown
Accountant	Marry Gallagher
Tax Collector	Jane Lepardo
Tax Assessor	Steven Jarzembowski
Attorney	NA
Public Works	Albert Paul Bangert
Building	Neil Duggan
Planning	Laura Harbottle
Police Chief	Brian Stewart
Emerg/Fire Chief	Richard Judge

Housing & Construction

New Privately Owned Housing Units Authorized by Building Permit

	Single Family	Total Bldgs	Total Units
2006	36	37	38
2007	55	55	55
2008	14	14	14

Parcel Count by Property Class, 2010

Total	8,791
Single family	6,622
Multiple units	152
Apartments	11
Condos	491
Vacant land	1,184
Open space	0
Commercial	146
Industrial	11
Misc. residential	82
Other use	92

Public Library

Scituate Town Library
85 Branch St.
Scituate, MA 02066
(781)545-8727

Director	Kathleen P. Meeker

Library Statistics, FY 2008

Population served, 2007	17,881
Registered users	10,936
Circulation	256,930
Reference transactons	13,536
Total program attendance	115,411
per capita:	
Holdings	5.44
Operating income	$52.00
Internet Access	
Internet computers available	7
Weekly users	400

Municipal Finance

Debt at year end 2008	$43,975,631
Moody's rating, July 2009	Aa3

Revenues, 2008

Total	$52,317,522
From all taxes	41,324,094
Federal aid	0
State aid	7,396,003
From other governments	3,203
Charges for services	995,375
Licenses, permits & fees	697,481
Fines & forfeits	64,293
Interfund transfers	545,699
Misc/other/special assessments	645,687

Expenditures, 2008

Total	$50,543,318
General government	2,166,143
Public safety	7,202,247
Other/fixed costs	7,239,618
Human services	436,446
Culture & recreation	1,095,794
Debt Service	1,588,019
Education	27,583,680
Public works	2,790,801
Intergovernmental	440,570

Taxation, 2010

Property type	Valuation	Rate
Total	$3,982,377,590	-
Residential	3,804,980,088	10.56
Open space	0	0.00
Commercial	130,039,832	10.56
Industrial	5,585,400	10.56
Personal	41,772,270	10.56

Average Single Family Tax Bill, 2010

Avg. assessed home value	$505,815
Avg. single fam. tax bill	$5,341
Hi-Lo ranking	59/301

Police & Crime, 2008

Number of police officers	30
Violent crimes	19
Property crimes	196

Local School District

(school data 2007-08, except as noted)

Scituate
606 C J Cushing Hwy
Scituate, MA 02066
781-545-8759

Superintendent	Susan Martin
Grade plan	PK-12
Total enrollment '09-10	3,278
Grade 12 enrollment, '09-10	188
Graduation rate	93.5%
Dropout rate	0.0%
Per-pupil expenditure	$10,792
Avg teacher salary	$59,709
Student/teacher ratio '08-09	13.2 to 1
Highly-qualified teachers, '08-09	99.2%
Teachers licensed in assigned subject	99.2%
Students per computer	3.7

Massachusetts Competency Assessment System (MCAS), 2009 results

	English		Math	
	% Prof	CPI	% Prof	CPI
Gr 4	78%	92.6	76%	91.3
Gr 6	91%	96.5	79%	90.9
Gr 8	92%	97.2	66%	83.9
Gr 10	93%	97.3	88%	93.8

Other School Districts (see Appendix D for data)

South Shore Vocational Tech

©2010 Information Publications, Inc. All rights reserved. Photocopying prohibited. For additional copies, contact the publisher at www.informationpublications.com or (877)544-INFO (4636)

See Introduction for an explanation of all data sources.

Demographics & Socio-Economic Characteristics

Population

1990	13,046
2000	13,425
Male	6,517
Female	6,908
2008	13,575
2010 (projected)††	13,045
2020 (projected)††	12,505

Race & Hispanic Origin, 2000

Race	
White	12,964
Black/African American	70
American Indian/Alaska Native	38
Asian	127
Hawaiian Native/Pacific Islander	0
Other Race	68
Two or more races	158
Hispanic origin	99

Age & Nativity, 2000

Under 5 years	751
18 years and over	10,033
21 years and over	9,612
65 years and over	1,810
85 years and over	159
Median Age	39.7
Native-born	12,410
Foreign-born	1,015

Age, 2020 (projected)††

Under 5 years	611
5 to 19 years	2,058
20 to 39 years	2,805
40 to 64 years	4,581
65 years and over	2,450

Educational Attainment, 2000

Population 25 years and over	9,213
High School graduates or higher	83.0%
Bachelor's degree or higher	26.2%
Graduate degree	8.3%

Income & Poverty, 1999

Per capita income,	$24,058
Median household income	$56,364
Median family income	$62,361
Persons in poverty	324
H'holds receiving public assistance	50
H'holds receiving social security	1,383

Households, 2000

Total households	4,843
With persons under 18	1,860
With persons over 65	1,311
Family households	3,874
Single person households	815
Persons per household	2.8
Persons per family	3.1

Labor & Employment, 2000

Civilian labor force	7,110
Unemployment rate	3.3%
Civilian labor force, 2008†	7,450
Unemployment rate†	7.9%
Civilian labor force, 12/09†	7,495
Unemployment rate†	11.4%
Employed persons 16 years and over, by occupation:	
Managers & professionals	2,419
Service occupations	931
Sales & office occupations	2,023
Farming, fishing & forestry	0
Construction & maintenance	605
Production & transportation	896
Self-employed persons	375

Most demographic data is from the 2000 Decennial Census
† Massachusetts Department of Revenue
†† University of Massachusetts, MISER

General Information

Town of Seekonk
100 Peck St
Seekonk, MA 02771
508-336-2900

Elevation	50 ft.
Land area (square miles)	18.3
Water area (square miles)	0.1
Population density, 2008 (est)	741.8
Year incorporated	1812
Website	www.seekonk.info

Voters & Government Information

Government type	Open Town Meeting
Number of Selectmen	5
US Congressional District(s)	3

Registered Voters, October 2008

Total	9,480
Democrats	2,137
Republicans	968
Unaffiliated/other	6,318

Local Officials, 2010

Chair, Bd. of Sel.	Frances Cavaco
Manager/Admin	Michael Carroll
Town Clerk	Jan Parker
Finance Director	Bruce Alexander
Tax Collector	Christine DeFontes
Tax Assessor	Theodora Gabriel
Attorney	Kopelman & Paige
Public Works	Robert Lamoureux
Building	Mary McNeil
Comm Dev/Planning	John Hanson
Police Chief	Ronald Charron
Emerg/Fire Chief	Alan Jack

Housing & Construction

New Privately Owned Housing Units Authorized by Building Permit

	Single Family	Total Bldgs	Total Units
2006	31	31	31
2007	58	58	58
2008	56	56	56

Parcel Count by Property Class, 2010

Total	6,128
Single family	4,662
Multiple units	130
Apartments	5
Condos	42
Vacant land	695
Open space	0
Commercial	327
Industrial	99
Misc. residential	35
Other use	133

Public Library

Seekonk Public Library
410 Newman Ave.
Seekonk, MA 02771
(508)336-8230

Library Director..... Sharon E. St. Hilaire

Library Statistics, FY 2008

Population served, 2007	13,593
Registered users	10,516
Circulation	249,100
Reference transactons	8,680
Total program attendance	131,328
per capita:	
Holdings	6.90
Operating income	$55.04
Internet Access	
Internet computers available	34
Weekly users	0

Municipal Finance

Debt at year end 2008	$38,066,026
Moody's rating, July 2009	A2

Revenues, 2008

Total	$39,282,725
From all taxes	29,061,561
Federal aid	246,919
State aid	8,189,410
From other governments	102,911
Charges for services	260,871
Licenses, permits & fees	395,847
Fines & forfeits	0
Interfund transfers	395,152
Misc/other/special assessments	315,027

Expenditures, 2008

Total	$36,940,776
General government	1,583,329
Public safety	4,860,636
Other/fixed costs	5,830,664
Human services	466,207
Culture & recreation	759,348
Debt Service	3,906,778
Education	18,008,167
Public works	968,295
Intergovernmental	310,945

Taxation, 2010

Property type	Valuation	Rate
Total	$2,200,512,840	-
Residential	1,643,105,133	10.57
Open space	0	0.00
Commercial	440,549,767	21.57
Industrial	40,728,600	21.57
Personal	76,129,340	21.46

Average Single Family Tax Bill, 2010

Avg. assessed home value	$318,320
Avg. single fam. tax bill	$3,365
Hi-Lo ranking	191/301

Police & Crime, 2008

Number of police officers	33
Violent crimes	36
Property crimes	512

Local School District

(school data 2007-08, except as noted)

Seekonk
25 Water Lane
Seekonk, MA 02771
508-399-5106

Superintendent	Madeline Meyer
Grade plan	PK-12
Total enrollment '09-10	2,154
Grade 12 enrollment, '09-10	165
Graduation rate	87.3%
Dropout rate	6.6%
Per-pupil expenditure	$10,596
Avg teacher salary	$62,000
Student/teacher ratio '08-09	15.1 to 1
Highly-qualified teachers, '08-09	98.4%
Teachers licensed in assigned subject	99.3%
Students per computer	2.6

Massachusetts Competency Assessment System (MCAS), 2009 results

	English		Math	
	% Prof	CPI	% Prof	CPI
Gr 4	68%	85.4	41%	76.7
Gr 6	80%	92.4	60%	80.5
Gr 8	87%	95.4	48%	73.4
Gr 10	86%	94.6	66%	83.7

Other School Districts (see Appendix D for data)
Tri County Vocational Tech, Bristol County Agricultural

©2010 Information Publications, Inc. All rights reserved. Photocopying prohibited. For additional copies, contact the publisher at www.informationpublications.com or (877)544-INFO (4636)

Demographics & Socio-Economic Characteristics

Population

1990 ... 15,517
2000 ... 17,408
Male ... 8,404
Female ... 9,004
2008 ... 17,373
2010 (projected)†† ... 16,908
2020 (projected)†† ... 16,534

Race & Hispanic Origin, 2000

Race
White ... 15,659
Black/African American ... 591
American Indian/Alaska Native ... 23
Asian ... 846
Hawaiian Native/Pacific Islander ... 1
Other Race ... 74
Two or more races ... 214
Hispanic origin ... 194

Age & Nativity, 2000

Under 5 years ... 1,218
18 years and over ... 12,152
21 years and over ... 11,769
65 years and over ... 1,897
85 years and over ... 219
Median Age ... 39.9
Native-born ... 15,297
Foreign-born ... 2,111

Age, 2020 (projected)††

Under 5 years ... 1,091
5 to 19 years ... 3,180
20 to 39 years ... 3,585
40 to 64 years ... 5,240
65 years and over ... 3,438

Educational Attainment, 2000

Population 25 years and over ... 11,476
High School graduates or higher ... 96.8%
Bachelor's degree or higher ... 63.1%
Graduate degree ... 31.9%

Income & Poverty, 1999

Per capita income, ... $41,323
Median household income ... $89,256
Median family income ... $99,015
Persons in poverty ... 527
H'holds receiving public assistance ... 46
H'holds receiving social security ... 1,453

Households, 2000

Total households ... 5,934
With persons under 18 ... 2,773
With persons over 65 ... 1,331
Family households ... 4,930
Single person households ... 867
Persons per household ... 2.9
Persons per family ... 3.3

Labor & Employment, 2000

Civilian labor force ... 9,130
Unemployment rate ... 2.4%
Civilian labor force, 2008† ... 9,217
Unemployment rate† ... 4.9%
Civilian labor force, 12/09† ... 9,073
Unemployment rate† ... 6.7%
Employed persons 16 years and over, by occupation:
Managers & professionals ... 5,596
Service occupations ... 645
Sales & office occupations ... 2,120
Farming, fishing & forestry ... 5
Construction & maintenance ... 243
Production & transportation ... 306
Self-employed persons ... 724

Most demographic data is from the 2000 Decennial Census
† Massachusetts Department of Revenue
†† University of Massachusetts, MISER

General Information

Town of Sharon
90 South Main St
Sharon, MA 02067
781-784-1505

Elevation ... 302 ft.
Land area (square miles) ... 23.3
Water area (square miles) ... 0.9
Population density, 2008 (est) ... 745.6
Year incorporated ... 1765
Website ... townofsharon.net

Voters & Government Information

Government type ... Open Town Meeting
Number of Selectmen ... 3
US Congressional District(s) ... 4

Registered Voters, October 2008

Total ... 12,342
Democrats ... 4,237
Republicans ... 1,020
Unaffiliated/other ... 7,045

Local Officials, 2010

Chair, Bd. of Sel. ... William A. Heitin
Manager/Exec. ... Benjamin E. Puritz
Town Clerk ... Marlene B. Chused
Finance Director ... William Fowler
Tax Collector ... NA
Tax Assessor ... Richard B. Gorden
Attorney ... NA
Public Works ... Eric Hooper
Building ... Joseph Kent
Comm Dev/Planning ... NA
Police Chief ... Joseph S. Bernstein
Emerg/Fire Chief ... Dennis Mann

Housing & Construction

New Privately Owned Housing Units Authorized by Building Permit

	Single Family	Total Bldgs	Total Units
2006	9	9	9
2007	15	20	139
2008	5	8	29

Parcel Count by Property Class, 2010

Total ... NA
Single family ... NA
Multiple units ... NA
Apartments ... NA
Condos ... NA
Vacant land ... NA
Open space ... NA
Commercial ... NA
Industrial ... NA
Misc. residential ... NA
Other use ... NA

Public Library

Sharon Public Library
11 North Main Street
Sharon, MA 02067
(781)784-1578

Director ... Barbra Nadler

Library Statistics, FY 2008

Population served, 2007 ... 17,033
Registered users ... 11,559
Circulation ... 237,935
Reference transactons ... 0
Total program attendance ... 0

per capita:

Holdings ... 4.89
Operating income ... $47.14

Internet Access

Internet computers available ... 8
Weekly users ... 786

Municipal Finance

Debt at year end 2008 ... $50,047,124
Moody's rating, July 2009 ... Aa3

Revenues, 2008

Total ... $72,461,775
From all taxes ... 49,448,630
Federal aid ... 0
State aid ... 12,550,621
From other governments ... 0
Charges for services ... 312,990
Licenses, permits & fees ... 422,755
Fines & forfeits ... 117,966
Interfund transfers ... 558,125
Misc/other/special assessments ... 4,525,344

Expenditures, 2008

Total ... $62,412,987
General government ... 1,749,274
Public safety ... 4,835,713
Other/fixed costs ... 10,323,736
Human services ... 415,298
Culture & recreation ... 964,920
Debt Service ... 7,931,647
Education ... 32,790,671
Public works ... 2,694,802
Intergovernmental ... 706,926

Taxation, 2010

Property type	Valuation	Rate
Total	NA	-
Residential	NA	NA
Open space	NA	NA
Commercial	NA	NA
Industrial	NA	NA
Personal	NA	NA

Average Single Family Tax Bill, 2010

Avg. assessed home value ... NA
Avg. single fam. tax bill ... NA
Hi-Lo ranking ... NA

Police & Crime, 2008

Number of police officers ... 30
Violent crimes ... 5
Property crimes ... 114

Local School District

(school data 2007-08, except as noted)

Sharon
1 School Street
Sharon, MA 02067
781-784-1570

Superintendent ... Barbara Dunham
Grade plan ... PK-12
Total enrollment '09-10 ... 3,426
Grade 12 enrollment, '09-10 ... 282
Graduation rate ... 94.9%
Dropout rate ... 1.4%
Per-pupil expenditure ... $13,217
Avg teacher salary ... $61,611
Student/teacher ratio '08-09 ... 13.3 to 1
Highly-qualified teachers, '08-09 ... 98.8%
Teachers licensed in assigned subject ... 98.6%
Students per computer ... 3.6

Massachusetts Competency Assessment System (MCAS), 2009 results

	English		Math	
	% Prof	CPI	% Prof	CPI
Gr 4	74%	90.5	58%	85.2
Gr 6	90%	96.3	82%	92.1
Gr 8	95%	98.3	77%	90.7
Gr 10	96%	98.7	94%	97.7

Other School Districts (see Appendix D for data)

Southeastern Vocational Tech, Norfolk County Agricultural

See Introduction for an explanation of all data sources.

©2010 Information Publications, Inc. All rights reserved. Photocopying prohibited. For additional copies, contact the publisher at www.informationpublications.com or (877)544-INFO (4636)

Demographics & Socio-Economic Characteristics

Population

1990	2,910
2000	3,335
Male	1,623
Female	1,712
2008	3,309
2010 (projected)††	3,491
2020 (projected)††	3,615

Race & Hispanic Origin, 2000

Race	
White	3,247
Black/African American	35
American Indian/Alaska Native	10
Asian	8
Hawaiian Native/Pacific Islander	0
Other Race	18
Two or more races	17
Hispanic origin	44

Age & Nativity, 2000

Under 5 years	178
18 years and over	2,541
21 years and over	2,458
65 years and over	527
85 years and over	46
Median Age	41.0
Native-born	3,248
Foreign-born	87

Age, 2020 (projected)††

Under 5 years	178
5 to 19 years	572
20 to 39 years	731
40 to 64 years	1,309
65 years and over	825

Educational Attainment, 2000

Population 25 years and over	2,347
High School graduates or higher	88.1%
Bachelor's degree or higher	28.3%
Graduate degree	10.0%

Income & Poverty, 1999

Per capita income,	$25,492
Median household income	$45,082
Median family income	$50,944
Persons in poverty	174
H'holds receiving public assistance	7
H'holds receiving social security	423

Households, 2000

Total households	1,369
With persons under 18	414
With persons over 65	388
Family households	912
Single person households	364
Persons per household	2.4
Persons per family	2.9

Labor & Employment, 2000

Civilian labor force	1,786
Unemployment rate	2.5%
Civilian labor force, 2008†	2,009
Unemployment rate†	5.1%
Civilian labor force, 12/09†	2,040
Unemployment rate†	8.0%
Employed persons 16 years and over, by occupation:	
Managers & professionals	495
Service occupations	334
Sales & office occupations	402
Farming, fishing & forestry	35
Construction & maintenance	260
Production & transportation	215
Self-employed persons	284

Most demographic data is from the 2000 Decennial Census
† Massachusetts Department of Revenue
†† University of Massachusetts, MISER

General Information

Town of Sheffield
PO Box 325
Sheffield, MA 01257
413-229-7000

Elevation	675 ft.
Land area (square miles)	48.1
Water area (square miles)	0.4
Population density, 2008 (est)	68.8
Year incorporated	1733
Website	sheffieldma.gov

Voters & Government Information

Government type	Open Town Meeting
Number of Selectmen	3
US Congressional District(s)	1

Registered Voters, October 2008

Total	2,272
Democrats	644
Republicans	365
Unaffiliated/other	1,244

Local Officials, 2010

Chair, Bd. of Sel.	David D. Macy
Manager/Admin	Joseph A. Kellog
Clerk	Felecie O. Joyce
Finance Director	Michael C. Ovitt
Tax Collector	Michael C. Ovitt
Tax Assessor	Tammy H. Blackwell (Chr)
Attorney	NA
Public Works	NA
Building	Thomas M. Carmody
Planning	Christopher Tomich (Chr)
Police Chief	James M. McGarry
Emerg/Fire Chief	Richard A. Boardman

Housing & Construction

New Privately Owned Housing Units Authorized by Building Permit

	Single Family	Total Bldgs	Total Units
2006	11	11	11
2007	9	9	9
2008	4	4	4

Parcel Count by Property Class, 2010

Total	NA
Single family	NA
Multiple units	NA
Apartments	NA
Condos	NA
Vacant land	NA
Open space	NA
Commercial	NA
Industrial	NA
Misc. residential	NA
Other use	NA

Public Library

Bushnell-Sage Memorial Library
PO Box 487
Sheffield, MA 01257
(413)229-7004

Librarian	Nancy Hahn

Library Statistics, FY 2008

Population served, 2007	3,334
Registered users	1,540
Circulation	64,783
Reference transactons	0
Total program attendance	0
per capita:	
Holdings	13.31
Operating income	$48.10
Internet Access	
Internet computers available	4
Weekly users	0

Municipal Finance

Debt at year end 2008	$210,525
Moody's rating, July 2009	NA

Revenues, 2008

Total	$8,375,656
From all taxes	7,044,013
Federal aid	0
State aid	369,421
From other governments	16,315
Charges for services	2,015
Licenses, permits & fees	130,330
Fines & forfeits	0
Interfund transfers	22,190
Misc/other/special assessments	395,686

Expenditures, 2008

Total	$7,523,357
General government	590,817
Public safety	510,673
Other/fixed costs	473,987
Human services	89,963
Culture & recreation	146,233
Debt Service	31,053
Education	5,025,301
Public works	611,133
Intergovernmental	44,197

Taxation, 2010

Property type	Valuation	Rate
Total	NA	-
Residential	NA	NA
Open space	NA	NA
Commercial	NA	NA
Industrial	NA	NA
Personal	NA	NA

Average Single Family Tax Bill, 2010

Avg. assessed home value	NA
Avg. single fam. tax bill	NA
Hi-Lo ranking	NA

Police & Crime, 2008

Number of police officers	6
Violent crimes	NA
Property crimes	NA

Local School District

(school data 2007-08, except as noted)

Sheffield (non-op)
491 Berkshire School Road, P. O. Box 339
Sheffield, MA 01257
413-229-8778

Superintendent	Michael Singleton

Non-operating district.
Resident students are sent to the Other School Districts listed below.

Grade plan	NA
Total enrollment '09-10	NA
Grade 12 enrollment, '09-10	NA
Graduation rate	NA
Dropout rate	NA
Per-pupil expenditure	NA
Avg teacher salary	NA
Student/teacher ratio '08-09	NA
Highly-qualified teachers, '08-09	NA
Teachers licensed in assigned subject	NA
Students per computer	NA

Other School Districts (see Appendix D for data)
Southern Berkshire Regional

©2010 Information Publications, Inc. All rights reserved. Photocopying prohibited. For additional copies, contact the publisher at www.informationpublications.com or (877)544-INFO (4636)

Demographics & Socio-Economic Characteristics

Population

1990 2,012
2000 2,058
Male 974
Female 1,084
2008 2,035
2010 (projected)†† 2,028
2020 (projected)†† 2,068

Race & Hispanic Origin, 2000

Race
White 2,002
Black/African American 10
American Indian/Alaska Native 9
Asian 5
Hawaiian Native/Pacific Islander 1
Other Race 8
Two or more races 23
Hispanic origin 12

Age & Nativity, 2000

Under 5 years 75
18 years and over 1,623
21 years and over 1,559
65 years and over 421
85 years and over 72
Median Age 44.8
Native-born 1,965
Foreign-born 85

Age, 2020 (projected)††

Under 5 years 94
5 to 19 years 299
20 to 39 years 373
40 to 64 years 574
65 years and over 728

Educational Attainment, 2000

Population 25 years and over 1,454
High School graduates or higher .. 93.3%
Bachelor's degree or higher 37.0%
Graduate degree 14.7%

Income & Poverty, 1999

Per capita income, ... $20,329
Median household income $42,054
Median family income $51,364
Persons in poverty 188
H'holds receiving public assistance 25
H'holds receiving social security 221

Households, 2000

Total households 834
With persons under 18 242
With persons over 65 243
Family households 518
Single person households 253
Persons per household 2.3
Persons per family 2.9

Labor & Employment, 2000

Civilian labor force 1,098
Unemployment rate 4.6%
Civilian labor force, 2008† 1,089
Unemployment rate† 8.6%
Civilian labor force, 12/09† 1,109
Unemployment rate† 12.1%
Employed persons 16 years and over, by occupation:
Managers & professionals 401
Service occupations 127
Sales & office occupations 249
Farming, fishing & forestry 9
Construction & maintenance 133
Production & transportation 128
Self-employed persons 149

Most demographic data is from the 2000 Decennial Census
† Massachusetts Department of Revenue
†† University of Massachusetts, MISER

General Information

Town of Shelburne
51 Bridge St
Shelburne, MA 01370
413-625-0300

Elevation .... 420 ft.
Land area (square miles) 23.3
Water area (square miles) 0.2
Population density, 2008 (est) 87.3
Year incorporated 1768
Website .... www.townofshelburne.com

Voters & Government Information

Government type .... Open Town Meeting
Number of Selectmen 3
US Congressional District(s) 1

Registered Voters, October 2008

Total 1,413
Democrats 414
Republicans 141
Unaffiliated/other 843

Local Officials, 2010

Chair, Bd. of Sel. .... John A. Payne
Manager/Exec. .... Terry Mosher
Town Clerk .... Beverly Neeley
Treasurer .... Virginia Peck
Tax Collector .... Maureen E. Pike
Tax Assessor .... Joseph P. Mattei (Chr)
Attorney .... NA
Public Works .... NA
Building .... NA
Comm Dev/Planning .... NA
Police Chief .... Steven Walker
Emerg/Fire Chief .... Greg Bardwell

Housing & Construction

New Privately Owned Housing Units Authorized by Building Permit

	Single Family	Total Bldgs	Total Units
2006	3	3	3
2007	2	2	2
2008	1	1	1

Parcel Count by Property Class, 2010

Total 1,030
Single family 471
Multiple units 81
Apartments 18
Condos 20
Vacant land 151
Open space 0
Commercial 61
Industrial 26
Misc. residential 15
Other use 187

Public Library

Shelburne Free Public Library
233 Shelburne Center Road
Shelburne, MA 01370
(413)625-0307

Librarian .... Elizabeth Burnham

Library Statistics, FY 2008

Population served, 2007 1,018
Registered users 850
Circulation 14,883
Reference transactons 0
Total program attendance 0
per capita:
Holdings 15.54
Operating income $35.84
Internet Access
Internet computers available 1
Weekly users 0

Municipal Finance

Debt at year end 2008 .... $160,000
Moody's rating, July 2009 .... NA

Revenues, 2008

Total $3,494,052
From all taxes 2,825,754
Federal aid 0
State aid 333,154
From other governments 0
Charges for services 57,365
Licenses, permits & fees 38,481
Fines & forfeits 19,025
Interfund transfers 108,359
Misc/other/special assessments 55,957

Expenditures, 2008

Total $3,354,158
General government 265,735
Public safety 185,386
Other/fixed costs 242,374
Human services 54,686
Culture & recreation 63,292
Debt Service 2,961
Education 1,983,163
Public works 530,178
Intergovernmental 26,383

Taxation, 2010

Property type	Valuation	Rate
Total	$224,428,815	-
Residential	179,720,200	12.68
Open space	0	0.00
Commercial	24,812,400	12.68
Industrial	6,844,200	12.68
Personal	13,052,015	12.68

Average Single Family Tax Bill, 2010

Avg. assessed home value $241,154
Avg. single fam. tax bill $3,058
Hi-Lo ranking 230/301

Police & Crime, 2008

Number of police officers 2
Violent crimes 0
Property crimes 15

Local School District

(school data 2007-08, except as noted)

Shelburne (non-op)
24 Ashfield Rd
Shelburne Falls, MA 01370
413-625-0192

Superintendent .... Michael Buoniconti

Non-operating district.
Resident students are sent to the Other School Districts listed below.

Grade plan .... NA
Total enrollment '09-10 .... NA
Grade 12 enrollment, '09-10 .... NA
Graduation rate .... NA
Dropout rate .... NA
Per-pupil expenditure .... NA
Avg teacher salary .... NA
Student/teacher ratio '08-09 .... NA
Highly-qualified teachers, '08-09 .... NA
Teachers licensed in assigned subject .... NA
Students per computer .... NA

Other School Districts (see Appendix D for data)
Mohawk Trail Regional, Franklin County Vocational Tech

©2010 Information Publications, Inc. All rights reserved. Photocopying prohibited. For additional copies, contact the publisher at www.informationpublications.com or (877)544-INFO (4636)

See Introduction for an explanation of all data sources.

Demographics & Socio-Economic Characteristics

Population

1990	3,989
2000	4,200
Male	2,028
Female	2,172
2008	4,204
2010 (projected)††	3,815
2020 (projected)††	3,085

Race & Hispanic Origin, 2000

Race	
White	4,053
Black/African American	16
American Indian/Alaska Native	2
Asian	101
Hawaiian Native/Pacific Islander	0
Other Race	11
Two or more races	17
Hispanic origin	47

Age & Nativity, 2000

Under 5 years	317
18 years and over	2,861
21 years and over	2,780
65 years and over	474
85 years and over	50
Median Age	41.1
Native-born	3,951
Foreign-born	249

Age, 2020 (projected)††

Under 5 years	166
5 to 19 years	684
20 to 39 years	538
40 to 64 years	1,031
65 years and over	666

Educational Attainment, 2000

Population 25 years and over	2,728
High School graduates or higher	98.5%
Bachelor's degree or higher	75.6%
Graduate degree	36.7%

Income & Poverty, 1999

Per capita income,	$58,055
Median household income	$121,693
Median family income	$136,211
Persons in poverty	98
H'holds receiving public assistance	7
H'holds receiving social security	276

Households, 2000

Total households	1,423
With persons under 18	677
With persons over 65	337
Family households	1,223
Single person households	176
Persons per household	3.0
Persons per family	3.2

Labor & Employment, 2000

Civilian labor force	1,960
Unemployment rate	4.5%
Civilian labor force, 2008†	1,947
Unemployment rate†	3.7%
Civilian labor force, 12/09†	1,941
Unemployment rate†	6.0%
Employed persons 16 years and over, by occupation:	
Managers & professionals	1,228
Service occupations	101
Sales & office occupations	452
Farming, fishing & forestry	0
Construction & maintenance	42
Production & transportation	49
Self-employed persons	172

Most demographic data is from the 2000 Decennial Census
† Massachusetts Department of Revenue
†† University of Massachusetts, MISER

General Information

Town of Sherborn
19 Washington St
Sherborn, MA 01770
508-651-7850

Elevation	175 ft.
Land area (square miles)	16.0
Water area (square miles)	0.2
Population density, 2008 (est)	262.8
Year incorporated	1674
Website	www.sherbornma.org

Voters & Government Information

Government type	Open Town Meeting
Number of Selectmen	3
US Congressional District(s)	4

Registered Voters, October 2008

Total	3,087
Democrats	769
Republicans	648
Unaffiliated/other	1,655

Local Officials, 2010

Chair, Bd. of Sel.	Ronald J. Fernandes
Manager/Admin	Daniel M. Keyes
Clerk	Carole B. Marple
Finance Dir	Descom D. Hoagland III
Tax Collector	Nancy E. Hess
Tax Assessor	Jean Rosseau
Attorney	Petrinni & Assoc
Public Works	Ed Wagner
Building	Walter A. Avalone
Planning	Gino D. Carlucci
Police Chief	Richard Thompson
Fire Chief	Neil W. McPherson

Housing & Construction

New Privately Owned Housing Units Authorized by Building Permit

	Single Family	Total Bldgs	Total Units
2006	3	3	3
2007	4	4	4
2008	6	6	6

Parcel Count by Property Class, 2010

Total	1,769
Single family	1,326
Multiple units	15
Apartments	0
Condos	41
Vacant land	209
Open space	0
Commercial	20
Industrial	7
Misc. residential	18
Other use	133

Public Library

Sherborn Library
4 Sanger St.
Sherborn, MA 01770
(508)653-0770

Library Director........Elizabeth Johnston

Library Statistics, FY 2008

Population served, 2007	4,217
Registered users	4,277
Circulation	89,583
Reference transactons	4,040
Total program attendance	0
per capita:	
Holdings	12.21
Operating income	$89.64
Internet Access	
Internet computers available	4
Weekly users	0

Municipal Finance

Debt at year end 2008	$11,388,000
Moody's rating, July 2009	Aa2

Revenues, 2008

Total	$22,116,317
From all taxes	19,118,011
Federal aid	0
State aid	1,084,073
From other governments	31,500
Charges for services	317,696
Licenses, permits & fees	127,385
Fines & forfeits	23,481
Interfund transfers	561,195
Misc/other/special assessments	426,488

Expenditures, 2008

Total	$20,985,912
General government	1,195,137
Public safety	1,681,295
Other/fixed costs	1,626,306
Human services	211,450
Culture & recreation	601,210
Debt Service	1,502,388
Education	12,811,602
Public works	1,292,286
Intergovernmental	64,238

Taxation, 2010

Property type	Valuation	Rate
Total	$1,114,417,642	-
Residential	1,064,520,747	17.44
Open space	0	0.00
Commercial	22,715,355	17.44
Industrial	2,331,100	17.44
Personal	24,850,440	17.44

Average Single Family Tax Bill, 2010

Avg. assessed home value	$723,985
Avg. single fam. tax bill	$12,626
Hi-Lo ranking	2/301

Police & Crime, 2008

Number of police officers	NA
Violent crimes	0
Property crimes	22

Local School District

(school data 2007-08, except as noted)

Sherborn
157 Farm Street
Dover, MA 02030
508-785-0036

Superintendent	Valerie Spriggs
Grade plan	PK-5
Total enrollment '09-10	450
Grade 12 enrollment, '09-10	0
Graduation rate	NA
Dropout rate	NA
Per-pupil expenditure	$12,700
Avg teacher salary	$75,260
Student/teacher ratio '08-09	13.9 to 1
Highly-qualified teachers, '08-09	100.0%
Teachers licensed in assigned subject	100.0%
Students per computer	2.7

Massachusetts Competency Assessment System (MCAS), 2009 results

	English		Math	
	% Prof	CPI	% Prof	CPI
Gr 4	82%	93.7	67%	90.2
Gr 6	NA	NA	NA	NA
Gr 8	NA	NA	NA	NA
Gr 10	NA	NA	NA	NA

Other School Districts (see Appendix D for data)
Dover-Sherborn Regional, Tri County Vocational Tech

©2010 Information Publications, Inc. All rights reserved. Photocopying prohibited. For additional copies, contact the publisher at www.informationpublications.com or (877)544-INFO (4636)

Demographics & Socio-Economic Characteristics

Population

1990	6,118
2000	6,373
Male	3,693
Female	2,680
2008	7,904
2010 (projected)††	7,335
2020 (projected)††	7,056

Race & Hispanic Origin, 2000

Race	
White	5,347
Black/African American	428
American Indian/Alaska Native	30
Asian	134
Hawaiian Native/Pacific Islander	5
Other Race	326
Two or more races	103
Hispanic origin	437

Age & Nativity, 2000

Under 5 years	379
18 years and over	4,991
21 years and over	4,818
65 years and over	586
85 years and over	49
Median Age	36.6
Native-born	5,914
Foreign-born	454

Age, 2020 (projected)††

Under 5 years	265
5 to 19 years	781
20 to 39 years	2,793
40 to 64 years	2,295
65 years and over	922

Educational Attainment, 2000

Population 25 years and over	4,516
High School graduates or higher	81.2%
Bachelor's degree or higher	19.6%
Graduate degree	6.4%

Income & Poverty, 1999

Per capita income,	$20,556
Median household income	$53,344
Median family income	$66,250
Persons in poverty	172
H'holds receiving public assistance	30
H'holds receiving social security	518

Households, 2000

Total households	2,067
With persons under 18	748
With persons over 65	427
Family households	1,426
Single person households	524
Persons per household	2.6
Persons per family	3.1

Labor & Employment, 2000

Civilian labor force	2,952
Unemployment rate	3.6%
Civilian labor force, 2008†	3,664
Unemployment rate†	6.7%
Civilian labor force, 12/09†	3,664
Unemployment rate†	8.6%
Employed persons 16 years and over, by occupation:	
Managers & professionals	1,011
Service occupations	365
Sales & office occupations	720
Farming, fishing & forestry	6
Construction & maintenance	354
Production & transportation	391
Self-employed persons	215

Most demographic data is from the 2000 Decennial Census
† Massachusetts Department of Revenue
†† University of Massachusetts, MISER

General Information

Town of Shirley
7 Keady Way
Shirley, MA 01464
978-425-2600

Elevation	300 ft.
Land area (square miles)	15.8
Water area (square miles)	0.1
Population density, 2008 (est)	500.3
Year incorporated	1775
Website	www.shirley-ma.gov

Voters & Government Information

Government type	Open Town Meeting
Number of Selectmen	3
US Congressional District(s)	5

Registered Voters, October 2008

Total	3,887
Democrats	879
Republicans	494
Unaffiliated/other	2,492

Local Officials, 2010

Chair, Bd. of Sel.	Armand Deveau
Town Administrator	Kyle J. Keady
Clerk	Amy McDougall
Treasurer	Kevin Johnston
Tax Collector	Holly Haase
Tax Assessor	Joseph Saball
Attorney	Kopelman & Paige
Public Works	Joseph Lynch
Building	Donald Farrar
Planning	NA
Police Chief	Paul Thibodeau
Fire Chief	Dennis Levesque

Housing & Construction

New Privately Owned Housing Units Authorized by Building Permit

	Single Family	Total Bldgs	Total Units
2006	31	31	31
2007	22	22	22
2008	7	7	7

Parcel Count by Property Class, 2010

Total	2,570
Single family	1,410
Multiple units	103
Apartments	24
Condos	273
Vacant land	468
Open space	0
Commercial	52
Industrial	45
Misc. residential	86
Other use	109

Public Library

Hazen Memorial Library
3 Keady Way
Shirley, MA 01464
(978)425-2620

Director	Debra Roy

Library Statistics, FY 2008

Population served, 2007	7,726
Registered users	3,188
Circulation	114,648
Reference transactons	0
Total program attendance	66,556
per capita:	
Holdings	6.33
Operating income	$28.13
Internet Access	
Internet computers available	8
Weekly users	288

Municipal Finance

Debt at year end 2008	$20,050,373
Moody's rating, July 2009	A3

Revenues, 2008

Total	$14,657,631
From all taxes	7,629,272
Federal aid	0
State aid	6,498,201
From other governments	4,450
Charges for services	45,566
Licenses, permits & fees	105,092
Fines & forfeits	8,833
Interfund transfers	236,529
Misc/other/special assessments	64,844

Expenditures, 2008

Total	$15,080,320
General government	861,322
Public safety	1,643,677
Other/fixed costs	2,281,302
Human services	68,988
Culture & recreation	202,638
Debt Service	775,147
Education	7,052,378
Public works	1,060,023
Intergovernmental	1,132,770

Taxation, 2010

Property type	Valuation	Rate
Total	$626,018,758	-
Residential	560,486,235	12.31
Open space	0	0.00
Commercial	21,013,352	12.31
Industrial	25,423,300	12.31
Personal	19,095,871	12.31

Average Single Family Tax Bill, 2010

Avg. assessed home value	$290,234
Avg. single fam. tax bill	$3,573
Hi-Lo ranking	164/301

Police & Crime, 2008

Number of police officers	10
Violent crimes	7
Property crimes	58

Local School District

(school data 2007-08, except as noted)

Shirley
34 Lancaster Rd
Shirley, MA 01464
978-425-2630

Superintendent	Malcolm Reid
Grade plan	PK-8
Total enrollment '09-10	533
Grade 12 enrollment, '09-10	0
Graduation rate	NA
Dropout rate	NA
Per-pupil expenditure	$11,758
Avg teacher salary	$57,341
Student/teacher ratio '08-09	12.5 to 1
Highly-qualified teachers, '08-09	99.1%
Teachers licensed in assigned subject	95.6%
Students per computer	3.3

Massachusetts Competency Assessment System (MCAS), 2009 results

	English		Math	
	% Prof	CPI	% Prof	CPI
Gr 4	30%	68.7	39%	79.7
Gr 6	55%	84.9	43%	71.8
Gr 8	83%	92.9	71%	89.6
Gr 10	NA	NA	NA	NA

Other School Districts (see Appendix D for data)
Sends grades 9-12 to Ayer, Lunenburg and Nashoba Valley Vocational Tech

©2010 Information Publications, Inc. All rights reserved. Photocopying prohibited. For additional copies, contact the publisher at www.informationpublications.com or (877)544-INFO (4636)

See Introduction for an explanation of all data sources.

Demographics & Socio-Economic Characteristics

Population

1990	24,146
2000	31,640
Male	15,380
Female	16,260
2008	33,435
2010 (projected)††	36,141
2020 (projected)††	40,381

Race & Hispanic Origin, 2000

Race	
White	28,199
Black/African American	459
American Indian/Alaska Native	37
Asian	2,408
Hawaiian Native/Pacific Islander	4
Other Race	218
Two or more races	315
Hispanic origin	504

Age & Nativity, 2000

Under 5 years	2,483
18 years and over	23,529
21 years and over	22,891
65 years and over	4,274
85 years and over	547
Median Age	37.6
Native-born	28,233
Foreign-born	3,407

Age, 2020 (projected)††

Under 5 years	2,361
5 to 19 years	7,508
20 to 39 years	10,146
40 to 64 years	14,024
65 years and over	6,342

Educational Attainment, 2000

Population 25 years and over	21,876
High School graduates or higher	91.8%
Bachelor's degree or higher	46.1%
Graduate degree	19.6%

Income & Poverty, 1999

Per capita income,	$31,570
Median household income	$64,237
Median family income	$77,674
Persons in poverty	1,498
H'holds receiving public assistance	184
H'holds receiving social security	3,143

Households, 2000

Total households	12,366
With persons under 18	4,438
With persons over 65	3,090
Family households	8,689
Single person households	3,125
Persons per household	2.5
Persons per family	3.1

Labor & Employment, 2000

Civilian labor force	16,424
Unemployment rate	2.9%
Civilian labor force, 2008†	17,067
Unemployment rate†	5.1%
Civilian labor force, 12/09†	17,510
Unemployment rate†	7.3%
Employed persons 16 years and over, by occupation:	
Managers & professionals	8,579
Service occupations	1,507
Sales & office occupations	3,910
Farming, fishing & forestry	9
Construction & maintenance	797
Production & transportation	1,140
Self-employed persons	710

Most demographic data is from the 2000 Decennial Census
† Massachusetts Department of Revenue
†† University of Massachusetts, MISER

General Information

Town of Shrewsbury
100 Maple Ave
Shrewsbury, MA 01545
508-841-8508

Elevation	668 ft.
Land area (square miles)	20.7
Water area (square miles)	0.9
Population density, 2008 (est)	1,615.2
Year incorporated	1727
Website	www.shrewsbury-ma.gov

Voters & Government Information

Government type	Rep. Town Meeting
Number of Selectmen	5
US Congressional District(s)	3

Registered Voters, October 2008

Total	22,468
Democrats	6,559
Republicans	3,646
Unaffiliated/other	12,162

Local Officials, 2010

Chair, Bd. of Sel.	Moira Miller
Manager	Daniel J. Morgado
Town Clerk	Sandra E. Wright
Finance Director	Daniel J. Morgado
Tax Collector	Carolyn J. Marcotte
Tax Assessor	Christopher R. Reidy
Attorney	NA
Water & Sewer Dir.	Robert A. Tozeski
Building	Ronald S. Alarie
Comm Dev/Planning	Eric Denoncourt
Police Chief	James J. Hester Jr
Emerg/Fire Chief	James Vuona (Actg)

Housing & Construction

New Privately Owned Housing Units Authorized by Building Permit

	Single Family	Total Bldgs	Total Units
2006	57	77	272
2007	50	52	57
2008	34	34	34

Parcel Count by Property Class, 2010

Total	NA
Single family	NA
Multiple units	NA
Apartments	NA
Condos	NA
Vacant land	NA
Open space	NA
Commercial	NA
Industrial	NA
Misc. residential	NA
Other use	NA

Public Library

Shrewsbury Free Public Library
609 Main St.
Shrewsbury, MA 01545
(508)842-0081

Director	Ellen Dolan

Library Statistics, FY 2008

Population served, 2007	33,489
Registered users	24,124
Circulation	402,057
Reference transactons	31,902
Total program attendance	238,134
per capita:	
Holdings	8.76
Operating income	$44.26
Internet Access	
Internet computers available	13
Weekly users	345

Municipal Finance

Debt at year end 2008	$67,604,905
Moody's rating, July 2009	Aa3

Revenues, 2008

Total	$90,526,682
From all taxes	50,468,851
Federal aid	0
State aid	25,431,195
From other governments	308,415
Charges for services	4,731,489
Licenses, permits & fees	737,415
Fines & forfeits	0
Interfund transfers	2,829,467
Misc/other/special assessments	3,009,925

Expenditures, 2008

Total	$83,435,429
General government	5,044,160
Public safety	7,253,674
Other/fixed costs	10,495,744
Human services	2,213,064
Culture & recreation	1,671,817
Debt Service	8,784,616
Education	42,124,450
Public works	4,105,528
Intergovernmental	1,191,230

Taxation, 2010

Property type	Valuation	Rate
Total	NA	-
Residential	NA	NA
Open space	NA	NA
Commercial	NA	NA
Industrial	NA	NA
Personal	NA	NA

Average Single Family Tax Bill, 2010

Avg. assessed home value	NA
Avg. single fam. tax bill	NA
Hi-Lo ranking	NA

Police & Crime, 2008

Number of police officers	45
Violent crimes	7
Property crimes	439

Local School District

(school data 2007-08, except as noted)
Shrewsbury
100 Maple Avenue
Shrewsbury, MA 01545
508-841-8400

Superintendent	Joseph Sawyer
Grade plan	PK-12
Total enrollment '09-10	5,841
Grade 12 enrollment, '09-10	390
Graduation rate	91.2%
Dropout rate	2.8%
Per-pupil expenditure	$9,859
Avg teacher salary	$60,915
Student/teacher ratio '08-09	16.0 to 1
Highly-qualified teachers, '08-09	99.7%
Teachers licensed in assigned subject	98.5%
Students per computer	4.7

Massachusetts Competency Assessment System (MCAS), 2009 results

	English		Math	
	% Prof	CPI	% Prof	CPI
Gr 4	80%	93.2	74%	90.6
Gr 6	86%	95.2	82%	92.1
Gr 8	91%	97.3	69%	85.3
Gr 10	90%	96.5	88%	94.8

Other School Districts (see Appendix D for data)
None

©2010 Information Publications, Inc. All rights reserved. Photocopying prohibited. For additional copies, contact the publisher at www.informationpublications.com or (877)544-INFO (4636)

©2010 Information Publications, Inc. All rights reserved. Photocopying prohibited. For additional copies, contact the publisher at www.informationpublications.com or (877)544-INFO (4636)

Demographics & Socio-Economic Characteristics

Population

1990	1,561
2000	1,810
Male	871
Female	939
2008	1,847
2010 (projected)††	2,027
2020 (projected)††	2,392

Race & Hispanic Origin, 2000

Race	
White	1,696
Black/African American	19
American Indian/Alaska Native	10
Asian	23
Hawaiian Native/Pacific Islander	0
Other Race	8
Two or more races	54
Hispanic origin	39

Age & Nativity, 2000

Under 5 years	94
18 years and over	1,293
21 years and over	1,244
65 years and over	104
85 years and over	9
Median Age	38.9
Native-born	1,760
Foreign-born	50

Age, 2020 (projected)††

Under 5 years	149
5 to 19 years	382
20 to 39 years	755
40 to 64 years	678
65 years and over	428

Educational Attainment, 2000

Population 25 years and over	1,184
High School graduates or higher	97.5%
Bachelor's degree or higher	62.7%
Graduate degree	38.1%

Income & Poverty, 1999

Per capita income,	$26,260
Median household income	$60,438
Median family income	$65,521
Persons in poverty	69
H'holds receiving public assistance	11
H'holds receiving social security	86

Households, 2000

Total households	662
With persons under 18	296
With persons over 65	78
Family households	480
Single person households	116
Persons per household	2.7
Persons per family	3.1

Labor & Employment, 2000

Civilian labor force	1,105
Unemployment rate	2.7%
Civilian labor force, 2008†	1,195
Unemployment rate†	4.2%
Civilian labor force, 12/09†	1,171
Unemployment rate†	4.9%
Employed persons 16 years and over, by occupation:	
Managers & professionals	637
Service occupations	132
Sales & office occupations	182
Farming, fishing & forestry	5
Construction & maintenance	60
Production & transportation	59
Self-employed persons	178

Most demographic data is from the 2000 Decennial Census
† Massachusetts Department of Revenue
†† University of Massachusetts, MISER

General Information

Town of Shutesbury
PO Box 276
1 Cooleyville Road
Shutesbury, MA 01072
413-259-1214

Elevation	1,225 ft.
Land area (square miles)	26.6
Water area (square miles)	0.6
Population density, 2008 (est)	69.4
Year incorporated	1761
Website	www.shutesbury.org

Voters & Government Information

Government type	Open Town Meeting
Number of Selectmen	3
US Congressional District(s)	1

Registered Voters, October 2008

Total	1,461
Democrats	653
Republicans	93
Unaffiliated/other	691

Local Officials, 2010

Chair, Bd. of Sel.	Elaine Puleo
Town Administrator	Rebecca Torres
Town Clerk	Leslie Bracebridge
Finance Director	Gabriele Voelker
Tax Collector	F. Ellen McKay
Tax Assessor	Kenneth Holmberg
Attorney	NA
Public Works	Timothy Hunting
Building	FCCIP
Comm Dev/Planning	Deacon Bonnar
Police Chief	Thomas Harding
Emerg/Fire Chief	Walter Tibbetts

Housing & Construction

New Privately Owned Housing Units Authorized by Building Permit

	Single Family	Total Bldgs	Total Units
2006	11	11	11
2007	5	5	5
2008	2	2	2

Parcel Count by Property Class, 2010

Total	1,239
Single family	781
Multiple units	27
Apartments	2
Condos	2
Vacant land	238
Open space	0
Commercial	3
Industrial	4
Misc. residential	5
Other use	177

Public Library

M.N. Spear Memorial Library
PO Box 256
Shutesbury, MA 01072
(413)259-1213

Librarian .... Mary Anne Antonellis

Library Statistics, FY 2008

Population served, 2007	1,834
Registered users	967
Circulation	20,246
Reference transactons	100
Total program attendance	9,405
per capita:	
Holdings	6.97
Operating income	$27.22
Internet Access	
Internet computers available	2
Weekly users	40

Municipal Finance

Debt at year end 2008	$1,930,122
Moody's rating, July 2009	NA

Revenues, 2008

Total	$5,174,566
From all taxes	4,019,037
Federal aid	19,438
State aid	969,933
From other governments	7,750
Charges for services	24,754
Licenses, permits & fees	0
Fines & forfeits	0
Interfund transfers	33,348
Misc/other/special assessments	50,153

Expenditures, 2008

Total	$5,065,306
General government	326,514
Public safety	278,622
Other/fixed costs	515,124
Human services	29,901
Culture & recreation	31,602
Debt Service	361,963
Education	3,065,441
Public works	397,281
Intergovernmental	58,858

Taxation, 2010

Property type	Valuation	Rate
Total	$212,939,100	-
Residential	206,970,146	18.76
Open space	0	0.00
Commercial	1,703,554	18.76
Industrial	564,700	18.76
Personal	3,700,700	18.76

Average Single Family Tax Bill, 2010

Avg. assessed home value	$243,814
Avg. single fam. tax bill	$4,574
Hi-Lo ranking	97/301

Police & Crime, 2008

Number of police officers	NA
Violent crimes	NA
Property crimes	NA

Local School District

(school data 2007-08, except as noted)

Shutesbury
18 Pleasant Street
Erving, MA 01344
413-423-3337

Superintendent	Joan Wickman
Grade plan	PK-6
Total enrollment '09-10	154
Grade 12 enrollment, '09-10	0
Graduation rate	NA
Dropout rate	NA
Per-pupil expenditure	$12,365
Avg teacher salary	$53,579
Student/teacher ratio '08-09	11.8 to 1
Highly-qualified teachers, '08-09	100.0%
Teachers licensed in assigned subject	100.0%
Students per computer	3.8

Massachusetts Competency Assessment System (MCAS), 2009 results

	English		Math	
	% Prof	CPI	% Prof	CPI
Gr 4	92%	98.1	77%	94.2
Gr 6	77%	95.5	64%	86.4
Gr 8	NA	NA	NA	NA
Gr 10	NA	NA	NA	NA

Other School Districts (see Appendix D for data)
Amherst-Pelham Regional

See Introduction for an explanation of all data sources.

Demographics & Socio-Economic Characteristics

Population

1990	17,655
2000	18,234
Male	8,635
Female	9,599
2008	18,055
2010 (projected)††	16,969
2020 (projected)††	15,353

Race & Hispanic Origin, 2000

Race	
White	17,909
Black/African American	30
American Indian/Alaska Native	22
Asian	97
Hawaiian Native/Pacific Islander	4
Other Race	28
Two or more races	144
Hispanic origin	90

Age & Nativity, 2000

Under 5 years	791
18 years and over	14,516
21 years and over	13,958
65 years and over	3,835
85 years and over	467
Median Age	43.0
Native-born	16,794
Foreign-born	1,440

Age, 2020 (projected)††

Under 5 years	510
5 to 19 years	1,979
20 to 39 years	2,956
40 to 64 years	5,615
65 years and over	4,293

Educational Attainment, 2000

Population 25 years and over	13,345
High School graduates or higher	76.0%
Bachelor's degree or higher	19.7%
Graduate degree	7.2%

Income & Poverty, 1999

Per capita income,	$22,420
Median household income	$51,770
Median family income	$60,067
Persons in poverty	716
H'holds receiving public assistance	131
H'holds receiving social security	2,746

Households, 2000

Total households	6,987
With persons under 18	2,177
With persons over 65	2,557
Family households	5,260
Single person households	1,501
Persons per household	2.6
Persons per family	3.0

Labor & Employment, 2000

Civilian labor force	9,416
Unemployment rate	4.6%
Civilian labor force, 2008†	9,728
Unemployment rate†	8.4%
Civilian labor force, 12/09†	9,709
Unemployment rate†	11.6%
Employed persons 16 years and over, by occupation:	
Managers & professionals	2,931
Service occupations	1,158
Sales & office occupations	2,615
Farming, fishing & forestry	10
Construction & maintenance	927
Production & transportation	1,342
Self-employed persons	427

Most demographic data is from the 2000 Decennial Census
† Massachusetts Department of Revenue
†† University of Massachusetts, MISER

General Information

Town of Somerset
140 Wood St
Somerset, MA 02726
508-646-2818

Elevation	60 ft.
Land area (square miles)	8.1
Water area (square miles)	3.9
Population density, 2008 (est)	2,229.0
Year incorporated	1790
Website	www.townofsomerset.org

Voters & Government Information

Government type	Open Town Meeting
Number of Selectmen	3
US Congressional District(s)	3

Registered Voters, October 2008

Total	13,465
Democrats	5,556
Republicans	1,176
Unaffiliated/other	6,667

Local Officials, 2010

Chair, Bd. of Sel.	William P. Meehan
Manager/Town Admin	Dennis Luttrell
Clerk	Patricia A. Hart
Finance Director	NA
Tax Collector	Lisa M. Viana
Tax Assessor	Donald P. Setters Jr (Chr)
Attorney	Clement P. Brown
Public Works	Thomas Fitzgerald
Building	Joseph Lawrence
Planning	NA
Police Chief	Joseph C. Ferreira
Emerg/Fire Chief	Scott Jepson

Housing & Construction

New Privately Owned Housing Units Authorized by Building Permit

	Single Family	Total Bldgs	Total Units
2006	9	9	9
2007	7	7	7
2008	7	7	7

Parcel Count by Property Class, 2010

Total	NA
Single family	NA
Multiple units	NA
Apartments	NA
Condos	NA
Vacant land	NA
Open space	NA
Commercial	NA
Industrial	NA
Misc. residential	NA
Other use	NA

Public Library

Somerset Public Library
1464 County St.
Somerset, MA 02726
(508)646-2830

Director	Bonnie Mendes

Library Statistics, FY 2008

Population served, 2007	18,268
Registered users	10,633
Circulation	122,176
Reference transactons	3,903
Total program attendance	151,115
per capita:	
Holdings	4.98
Operating income	$31.30
Internet Access	
Internet computers available	13
Weekly users	1,297

Municipal Finance

Debt at year end 2008	$16,514,801
Moody's rating, July 2009	Aa3

Revenues, 2008

Total	$50,716,519
From all taxes	38,988,174
Federal aid	0
State aid	6,787,686
From other governments	83,452
Charges for services	1,878,162
Licenses, permits & fees	299,368
Fines & forfeits	0
Interfund transfers	675,579
Misc/other/special assessments	1,002,049

Expenditures, 2008

Total	$40,179,611
General government	1,416,380
Public safety	4,445,783
Other/fixed costs	2,616,859
Human services	338,255
Culture & recreation	618,998
Debt Service	1,275,365
Education	25,939,771
Public works	3,124,123
Intergovernmental	404,077

Taxation, 2010

Property type	Valuation	Rate
Total	NA	-
Residential	NA	NA
Open space	NA	NA
Commercial	NA	NA
Industrial	NA	NA
Personal	NA	NA

Average Single Family Tax Bill, 2010

Avg. assessed home value	NA
Avg. single fam. tax bill	NA
Hi-Lo ranking	NA

Police & Crime, 2008

Number of police officers	32
Violent crimes	49
Property crimes	307

Local School District

(school data 2007-08, except as noted)

Somerset
580 Whetstone Hill Road
Somerset, MA 02726
508-324-3100

Superintendent	Richard Medeiros
Grade plan	PK-12
Total enrollment '09-10	2,729
Grade 12 enrollment, '09-10	221
Graduation rate	93.4%
Dropout rate	2.7%
Per-pupil expenditure	$11,515
Avg teacher salary	$55,016
Student/teacher ratio '08-09	12.7 to 1
Highly-qualified teachers, '08-09	98.4%
Teachers licensed in assigned subject	98.6%
Students per computer	3.1

Massachusetts Competency Assessment System (MCAS), 2009 results

	English		Math	
	% Prof	CPI	% Prof	CPI
Gr 4	64%	86.3	55%	84.6
Gr 6	71%	89.3	59%	81.2
Gr 8	83%	93.9	56%	79.6
Gr 10	86%	93.7	80%	91.1

Other School Districts (see Appendix D for data)

Receives students from Berkley; sends to Greater Fall River Vocational Tech, Bristol County Agricultural

©2010 Information Publications, Inc. All rights reserved. Photocopying prohibited. For additional copies, contact the publisher at www.informationpublications.com or (877)544-INFO (4636)

Demographics & Socio-Economic Characteristics*

Population

1990	76,210
2000	77,478
Male	37,730
Female	39,748
2008	75,662
2010 (projected)††	76,340
2020 (projected)††	74,816

Race & Hispanic Origin, 2000

Race	
White	59,635
Black/African American	5,035
American Indian/Alaska Native	171
Asian	4,990
Hawaiian Native/Pacific Islander	50
Other Race	3,840
Two or more races	3,757
Hispanic origin	6,786

Age & Nativity, 2000

Under 5 years	3,500
18 years and over	65,983
21 years and over	62,285
65 years and over	8,099
85 years and over	1,106
Median Age	31.1
Native-born	54,751
Foreign-born	22,727

Age, 2020 (projected)††

Under 5 years	3,591
5 to 19 years	11,643
20 to 39 years	27,616
40 to 64 years	24,312
65 years and over	7,654

Educational Attainment, 2000

Population 25 years and over	53,693
High School graduates or higher	80.6%
Bachelor's degree or higher	40.6%
Graduate degree	17.7%

Income & Poverty, 1999

Per capita income,	$23,628
Median household income	$46,315
Median family income	$51,243
Persons in poverty	9,395
H'holds receiving public assistance	705
H'holds receiving social security	6,106

Households, 2000

Total households	31,555
With persons under 18	6,603
With persons over 65	6,099
Family households	14,668
Single person households	9,797
Persons per household	2.4
Persons per family	3.1

Labor & Employment, 2000

Civilian labor force	47,628
Unemployment rate	3.5%
Civilian labor force, 2008†	46,246
Unemployment rate†	4.5%
Civilian labor force, 12/09†	45,927
Unemployment rate†	6.7%
Employed persons 16 years and over, by occupation:	
Managers & professionals	21,997
Service occupations	7,514
Sales & office occupations	10,216
Farming, fishing & forestry	13
Construction & maintenance	2,312
Production & transportation	3,915
Self-employed persons	2,377

Most demographic data is from the 2000 Decennial Census
* see Appendix D and E for American Community Survey data
† Massachusetts Department of Revenue
†† University of Massachusetts, MISER

General Information

City of Somerville
93 Highland Ave
Somerville, MA 02143
617-625-6600

Elevation	50 ft.
Land area (square miles)	4.1
Water area (square miles)	0.1
Population density, 2008 (est)	18,454.1
Year incorporated	1630
Website	www.somervillema.gov

Voters & Government Information

Government type	Mayor-Council
Number of Aldermen	11
US Congressional District(s)	8

Registered Voters, October 2008

Total	44,673
Democrats	24,456
Republicans	2,128
Unaffiliated/other	17,636

Local Officials, 2010

Mayor	Joseph A. Curtatone
Manager/Admin	NA
City Clerk	John J. Long
Finance Director	Edward Bean
Tax Collector	Elizabeth Craveiro
Tax Assessor	Marc Levye (Actg)
Attorney	John Gannon
Public Works	Stanley Koty
Building	George Landers
Comm Dev/Planning	Monica Lamboy
Police Chief	Anthony Holloway
Emerg/Fire Chief	Kevin Kelleher

Housing & Construction

New Privately Owned Housing Units Authorized by Building Permit

	Single Family	Total Bldgs	Total Units
2006	6	9	12
2007	4	4	4
2008	3	3	3

Parcel Count by Property Class, 2010

Total	15,984
Single family	2,360
Multiple units	7,768
Apartments	663
Condos	3,928
Vacant land	210
Open space	0
Commercial	604
Industrial	125
Misc. residential	70
Other use	256

Public Library

Somerville Public Library
79 Highland Avenue
Somerville, MA 02143
(617)623-5000

Library Director: Nancy Milnor

Library Statistics, FY 2008

Population served, 2007	74,405
Registered users	27,447
Circulation	425,743
Reference transactons	32,917
Total program attendance	0
per capita:	
Holdings	2.50
Operating income	$28.53
Internet Access	
Internet computers available	36
Weekly users	1,145

Municipal Finance

Debt at year end 2008	$74,431,100
Moody's rating, July 2009	Aa3

Revenues, 2008

Total	$171,394,862
From all taxes	92,252,638
Federal aid	390,004
State aid	58,599,391
From other governments	317,334
Charges for services	1,609,388
Licenses, permits & fees	2,758,670
Fines & forfeits	7,703,782
Interfund transfers	2,582,783
Misc/other/special assessments	2,590,436

Expenditures, 2008

Total	$140,391,958
General government	15,979,342
Public safety	32,426,837
Other/fixed costs	13,561,844
Human services	2,067,149
Culture & recreation	2,697,289
Debt Service	7,443,577
Education	45,952,250
Public works	10,977,889
Intergovernmental	9,083,059

Taxation, 2010

Property type	Valuation	Rate
Total	$8,261,279,820	-
Residential	7,017,857,230	12.30
Open space	0	0.00
Commercial	820,005,970	20.44
Industrial	274,302,300	20.44
Personal	149,114,320	20.44

Average Single Family Tax Bill, 2010

Avg. assessed home value	NA
Avg. single fam. tax bill	NA
Hi-Lo ranking	NA

Police & Crime, 2008

Number of police officers	128
Violent crimes	304
Property crimes	2,313

Local School District

(school data 2007-08, except as noted)

Somerville
181 Washington Street
Somerville, MA 02143
617-625-6600

Superintendent	Anthony Pierantozzi
Grade plan	PK-12
Total enrollment '09-10	4,842
Grade 12 enrollment, '09-10	303
Graduation rate	76.0%
Dropout rate	9.2%
Per-pupil expenditure	$15,972
Avg teacher salary	$66,942
Student/teacher ratio '08-09	12.4 to 1
Highly-qualified teachers, '08-09	97.0%
Teachers licensed in assigned subject	98.0%
Students per computer	2.3

Massachusetts Competency Assessment System (MCAS), 2009 results

	English		Math	
	% Prof	CPI	% Prof	CPI
Gr 4	32%	66.6	37%	71.6
Gr 6	52%	77.8	48%	72.6
Gr 8	65%	83	31%	59.7
Gr 10	70%	88.9	60%	80.3

Other School Districts (see Appendix D for data)
None

©2010 Information Publications, Inc. All rights reserved. Photocopying prohibited. For additional copies, contact the publisher at www.informationpublications.com or (877)544-INFO (4636)

See Introduction for an explanation of all data sources.

Demographics & Socio-Economic Characteristics

Population

1990	16,685
2000	17,196
Male	7,205
Female	9,991
2008	17,241
2010 (projected)††	17,636
2020 (projected)††	18,108

Race & Hispanic Origin, 2000

Race	
White	16,172
Black/African American	207
American Indian/Alaska Native	20
Asian	435
Hawaiian Native/Pacific Islander	10
Other Race	132
Two or more races	220
Hispanic origin	405

Age & Nativity, 2000

Under 5 years	783
18 years and over	13,817
21 years and over	12,365
65 years and over	2,991
85 years and over	368
Median Age	38.4
Native-born	16,026
Foreign-born	1,170

Age, 2020 (projected)††

Under 5 years	998
5 to 19 years	3,972
20 to 39 years	4,370
40 to 64 years	5,226
65 years and over	3,542

Educational Attainment, 2000

Population 25 years and over	11,297
High School graduates or higher	89.4%
Bachelor's degree or higher	32.9%
Graduate degree	13.6%

Income & Poverty, 1999

Per capita income,	$22,732
Median household income	$46,678
Median family income	$58,693
Persons in poverty	901
H'holds receiving public assistance	102
H'holds receiving social security	2,201

Households, 2000

Total households	6,586
With persons under 18	1,875
With persons over 65	2,102
Family households	4,208
Single person households	2,004
Persons per household	2.3
Persons per family	2.9

Labor & Employment, 2000

Civilian labor force	9,582
Unemployment rate	5.2%
Civilian labor force, 2008†	9,370
Unemployment rate†	5.4%
Civilian labor force, 12/09†	9,378
Unemployment rate†	7.2%
Employed persons 16 years and over, by occupation:	
Managers & professionals	4,036
Service occupations	1,133
Sales & office occupations	2,257
Farming, fishing & forestry	13
Construction & maintenance	611
Production & transportation	1,035
Self-employed persons	637

Most demographic data is from the 2000 Decennial Census
† Massachusetts Department of Revenue
†† University of Massachusetts, MISER

General Information

Town of South Hadley
116 Main St
South Hadley, MA 01075
413-538-5017

Elevation	257 ft.
Land area (square miles)	17.7
Water area (square miles)	0.7
Population density, 2008 (est)	974.1
Year incorporated	1753
Website	www.southhadley.org

Voters & Government Information

Government type	Rep. Town Meeting
Number of Selectmen	5
US Congressional District(s)	2

Registered Voters, October 2008

Total	11,264
Democrats	3,721
Republicans	1,333
Unaffiliated/other	6,147

Local Officials, 2010

Chair, Bd. of Sel.	John R. Hine
Manager/Admin	Paul Beeder
Town Clerk	Carlene C. Hamlin
Treasurer	Carlene C. Hamlin
Tax Collector	Deborah Baldini
Tax Assessor	Francis Conti
Attorney	Edward J. Ryan Jr
Public Works Dir.	Jim Reidy
Building	Steven Reno
Comm Dev/Planning	Richard Harris
Police Chief	David Labrie
Emerg/Fire Chief	William Judd

Housing & Construction

New Privately Owned Housing Units Authorized by Building Permit

	Single Family	Total Bldgs	Total Units
2006	32	32	32
2007	23	23	23
2008	18	18	18

Parcel Count by Property Class, 2010

Total	7,059
Single family	4,276
Multiple units	376
Apartments	53
Condos	978
Vacant land	1,023
Open space	17
Commercial	145
Industrial	71
Misc. residential	23
Other use	97

Public Library

South Hadley Public Library
27 Bardwell Street
South Hadley, MA 01075
(413)538-5045

Director	Joseph Rodio

Library Statistics, FY 2008

Population served, 2007	15,257
Registered users	8,931
Circulation	155,740
Reference transactons	1,430
Total program attendance	0
per capita:	
Holdings	3.13
Operating income	$36.13
Internet Access	
Internet computers available	14
Weekly users	251

Municipal Finance

Debt at year end 2008	$34,977,790
Moody's rating, July 2009	A1

Revenues, 2008

Total	$36,548,919
From all taxes	21,357,521
Federal aid	62,635
State aid	11,529,345
From other governments	43,815
Charges for services	168,991
Licenses, permits & fees	231,965
Fines & forfeits	12,152
Interfund transfers	1,582,819
Misc/other/special assessments	779,838

Expenditures, 2008

Total	$34,473,593
General government	1,583,459
Public safety	2,478,518
Other/fixed costs	5,565,280
Human services	404,647
Culture & recreation	1,059,424
Debt Service	4,050,234
Education	17,543,354
Public works	1,029,163
Intergovernmental	759,514

Taxation, 2010

Property type	Valuation	Rate
Total	$1,463,159,363	-
Residential	1,322,522,955	13.99
Open space	394,800	13.99
Commercial	72,916,470	13.99
Industrial	39,220,375	13.99
Personal	28,104,763	13.99

Average Single Family Tax Bill, 2010

Avg. assessed home value	$232,576
Avg. single fam. tax bill	$3,254
Hi-Lo ranking	208/301

Police & Crime, 2008

Number of police officers	28
Violent crimes	33
Property crimes	257

Local School District

(school data 2007-08, except as noted)

South Hadley
116 Main Street
South Hadley, MA 01075
413-538-5060

Superintendent	Gus Sayer
Grade plan	PK-12
Total enrollment '09-10	2,132
Grade 12 enrollment, '09-10	161
Graduation rate	86.5%
Dropout rate	9.7%
Per-pupil expenditure	$10,631
Avg teacher salary	$58,071
Student/teacher ratio '08-09	13.1 to 1
Highly-qualified teachers, '08-09	94.8%
Teachers licensed in assigned subject	98.6%
Students per computer	4.6

Massachusetts Competency Assessment System (MCAS), 2009 results

	English		Math	
	% Prof	CPI	% Prof	CPI
Gr 4	54%	81.3	51%	81.3
Gr 6	56%	80.2	44%	70.9
Gr 8	79%	91.4	54%	74.4
Gr 10	86%	94.6	81%	90.9

Other School Districts (see Appendix D for data)
None

©2010 Information Publications, Inc. All rights reserved. Photocopying prohibited. For additional copies, contact the publisher at www.informationpublications.com or (877)544-INFO (4636)

Demographics & Socio-Economic Characteristics

Population

1990	4,478
2000	5,387
Male	2,614
Female	2,773
2008	5,970
2010 (projected)††	5,657
2020 (projected)††	5,875

Race & Hispanic Origin, 2000

Race	
White	5,295
Black/African American	11
American Indian/Alaska Native	7
Asian	34
Hawaiian Native/Pacific Islander	0
Other Race	11
Two or more races	29
Hispanic origin	47

Age & Nativity, 2000

Under 5 years	297
18 years and over	4,012
21 years and over	3,836
65 years and over	536
85 years and over	64
Median Age	39.1
Native-born	5,172
Foreign-born	215

Age, 2020 (projected)††

Under 5 years	317
5 to 19 years	977
20 to 39 years	1,268
40 to 64 years	2,080
65 years and over	1,233

Educational Attainment, 2000

Population 25 years and over	3,669
High School graduates or higher	90.9%
Bachelor's degree or higher	31.3%
Graduate degree	11.4%

Income & Poverty, 1999

Per capita income,	$26,205
Median household income	$61,831
Median family income	$64,960
Persons in poverty	127
H'holds receiving public assistance	46
H'holds receiving social security	481

Households, 2000

Total households	1,985
With persons under 18	756
With persons over 65	393
Family households	1,556
Single person households	334
Persons per household	2.7
Persons per family	3.1

Labor & Employment, 2000

Civilian labor force	3,191
Unemployment rate	4.2%
Civilian labor force, 2008†	3,500
Unemployment rate†	5.2%
Civilian labor force, 12/09†	3,508
Unemployment rate†	6.3%
Employed persons 16 years and over, by occupation:	
Managers & professionals	1,363
Service occupations	373
Sales & office occupations	715
Farming, fishing & forestry	0
Construction & maintenance	202
Production & transportation	404
Self-employed persons	216

Most demographic data is from the 2000 Decennial Census
† Massachusetts Department of Revenue
†† University of Massachusetts, MISER

General Information

Town of Southampton
8 East St
Southampton, MA 01073
413-529-0106

Elevation	230 ft.
Land area (square miles)	28.1
Water area (square miles)	0.9
Population density, 2008 (est)	212.5
Year incorporated	1775
Website	town.southampton.ma.us

Voters & Government Information

Government type	Open Town Meeting
Number of Selectmen	5
US Congressional District(s)	1

Registered Voters, October 2008

Total	4,058
Democrats	1,002
Republicans	556
Unaffiliated/other	2,478

Local Officials, 2010

Chair, Bd. of Sel.	David McDougall
Town Administrator	Diana Schindler
Clerk	Eileen Couture
Accountant	David Kielson
Treas/Collector	Kristi-Ann Shea
Tax Assessor	Barbara Laflam (Chr)
Attorney	Kopelman & Paige
Public Works	Edward Cauley
Building	Richard Oleksak
Planning	Mark Girard
Police Chief	David Silvernail
Fire Chief	Steve Hyde

Housing & Construction

New Privately Owned Housing Units Authorized by Building Permit

	Single Family	Total Bldgs	Total Units
2006	33	33	33
2007	37	37	37
2008	29	29	29

Parcel Count by Property Class, 2010

Total	2,764
Single family	1,994
Multiple units	17
Apartments	5
Condos	78
Vacant land	418
Open space	0
Commercial	45
Industrial	11
Misc. residential	22
Other use	174

Public Library

Edwards Public Library
30 East Street
Southampton, MA 01073
(413)527-9480

Director . . . Karen Kappenman

Library Statistics, FY 2008

Population served, 2007	5,962
Registered users	2,689
Circulation	42,107
Reference transactons	0
Total program attendance	0
per capita:	
Holdings	6.04
Operating income	$18.47
Internet Access	
Internet computers available	5
Weekly users	50

Municipal Finance

Debt at year end 2008	$6,466,840
Moody's rating, July 2009	NA

Revenues, 2008

Total	$12,363,062
From all taxes	8,196,888
Federal aid	5,927
State aid	3,742,437
From other governments	12,784
Charges for services	77,053
Licenses, permits & fees	19,085
Fines & forfeits	0
Interfund transfers	171,148
Misc/other/special assessments	68,870

Expenditures, 2008

Total	$12,396,935
General government	568,010
Public safety	969,010
Other/fixed costs	1,340,349
Human services	66,164
Culture & recreation	99,629
Debt Service	672,912
Education	8,032,993
Public works	633,422
Intergovernmental	14,446

Taxation, 2010

Property type	Valuation	Rate
Total	$660,442,418	-
Residential	618,144,180	12.36
Open space	0	0.00
Commercial	25,325,620	12.36
Industrial	6,217,700	12.36
Personal	10,754,918	12.36

Average Single Family Tax Bill, 2010

Avg. assessed home value	$280,205
Avg. single fam. tax bill	$3,463
Hi-Lo ranking	178/301

Police & Crime, 2008

Number of police officers	8
Violent crimes	NA
Property crimes	53

Local School District

(school data 2007-08, except as noted)

Southampton
19 Stage Rd
Westhampton, MA 01027
413-527-7200

Superintendent	Craig Jurgensen
Grade plan	PK-6
Total enrollment '09-10	559
Grade 12 enrollment, '09-10	0
Graduation rate	NA
Dropout rate	NA
Per-pupil expenditure	$9,555
Avg teacher salary	$57,871
Student/teacher ratio '08-09	15.1 to 1
Highly-qualified teachers, '08-09	100.0%
Teachers licensed in assigned subject	97.3%
Students per computer	4.4

Massachusetts Competency Assessment System (MCAS), 2009 results

	English		Math	
	% Prof	CPI	% Prof	CPI
Gr 4	62%	85.4	60%	85.7
Gr 6	74%	88.5	58%	79.9
Gr 8	NA	NA	NA	NA
Gr 10	NA	NA	NA	NA

Other School Districts (see Appendix D for data)
Hampshire Regional

©2010 Information Publications, Inc. All rights reserved. Photocopying prohibited. For additional copies, contact the publisher at www.informationpublications.com or (877)544-INFO (4636)

See Introduction for an explanation of all data sources.

Demographics & Socio-Economic Characteristics

Population

1990	6,628
2000	8,781
Male	4,389
Female	4,392
2008	9,583
2010 (projected)††	9,746
2020 (projected)††	9,754

Race & Hispanic Origin, 2000

Race	
White	8,295
Black/African American	47
American Indian/Alaska Native	6
Asian	309
Hawaiian Native/Pacific Islander	4
Other Race	44
Two or more races	76
Hispanic origin	132

Age & Nativity, 2000

Under 5 years	872
18 years and over	5,963
21 years and over	5,803
65 years and over	708
85 years and over	63
Median Age	36.9
Native-born	8,003
Foreign-born	778

Age, 2020 (projected)††

Under 5 years	626
5 to 19 years	2,283
20 to 39 years	2,237
40 to 64 years	3,362
65 years and over	1,246

Educational Attainment, 2000

Population 25 years and over	5,628
High School graduates or higher	96.4%
Bachelor's degree or higher	63.1%
Graduate degree	26.0%

Income & Poverty, 1999

Per capita income,	$44,310
Median household income	$102,986
Median family income	$119,454
Persons in poverty	139
H'holds receiving public assistance	13
H'holds receiving social security	581

Households, 2000

Total households	2,952
With persons under 18	1,450
With persons over 65	517
Family households	2,427
Single person households	412
Persons per household	3.0
Persons per family	3.3

Labor & Employment, 2000

Civilian labor force	4,369
Unemployment rate	1.8%
Civilian labor force, 2008†	4,934
Unemployment rate†	3.8%
Civilian labor force, 12/09†	4,967
Unemployment rate†	6.5%
Employed persons 16 years and over, by occupation:	
Managers & professionals	2,612
Service occupations	270
Sales & office occupations	978
Farming, fishing & forestry	0
Construction & maintenance	233
Production & transportation	198
Self-employed persons	336

Most demographic data is from the 2000 Decennial Census
† Massachusetts Department of Revenue
†† University of Massachusetts, MISER

General Information

Town of Southborough
17 Common St
Southborough, MA 01772
508-485-0710

Elevation	550 ft.
Land area (square miles)	14.1
Water area (square miles)	1.5
Population density, 2008 (est)	679.6
Year incorporated	1727
Website	www.southboroughtown.com

Voters & Government Information

Government type	Open Town Meeting
Number of Selectmen	3
US Congressional District(s)	3

Registered Voters, October 2008

Total	6,704
Democrats	1,617
Republicans	1,252
Unaffiliated/other	3,822

Local Officials, 2010

Chair, Bd. of Sel.	William Boland
Administrator	Jean Kitchen
Town Clerk	Paul Berry
Finance Director	Brian Ballantine
Tax Collector	Brian Ballantine
Tax Assessor	Paul Cibelli
Attorney	Aldo A. Cipriano
Public Works	Karen M. Galligan
Building	Peter Johnson
Comm Dev/Planning	Vera Kolias
Police Chief	Jane Moran
Emerg/Fire Chief	John Mauro Jr

Housing & Construction

New Privately Owned Housing Units Authorized by Building Permit

	Single Family	Total Bldgs	Total Units
2006	19	19	19
2007	29	29	29
2008	10	10	10

Parcel Count by Property Class, 2010

Total	3,686
Single family	2,774
Multiple units	93
Apartments	5
Condos	274
Vacant land	279
Open space	0
Commercial	123
Industrial	55
Misc. residential	26
Other use	57

Public Library

Southborough Public Library
25 Main St.
Southborough, MA 01772
(508)485-5031

Director	Jain Cain

Library Statistics, FY 2008

Population served, 2007	9,484
Registered users	6,413
Circulation	149,021
Reference transactons	14,248
Total program attendance	77,324
per capita:	
Holdings	6.80
Operating income	$41.31
Internet Access	
Internet computers available	4
Weekly users	85

Municipal Finance

Debt at year end 2008	$41,106,362
Moody's rating, July 2009	Aa2

Revenues, 2008

Total	$39,322,993
From all taxes	30,441,882
Federal aid	0
State aid	5,359,173
From other governments	16,482
Charges for services	653,862
Licenses, permits & fees	341,854
Fines & forfeits	62,642
Interfund transfers	832,044
Misc/other/special assessments	807,527

Expenditures, 2008

Total	$38,894,892
General government	2,147,566
Public safety	3,184,665
Other/fixed costs	4,707,251
Human services	441,079
Culture & recreation	489,358
Debt Service	4,747,887
Education	21,031,962
Public works	1,916,522
Intergovernmental	228,602

Taxation, 2010

Property type	Valuation	Rate
Total	$2,200,552,897	-
Residential	1,764,192,507	14.06
Open space	0	0.00
Commercial	235,709,090	14.06
Industrial	113,195,400	14.06
Personal	87,455,900	14.06

Average Single Family Tax Bill, 2010

Avg. assessed home value	$548,620
Avg. single fam. tax bill	$7,714
Hi-Lo ranking	24/301

Police & Crime, 2008

Number of police officers	16
Violent crimes	0
Property crimes	55

Local School District

(school data 2007-08, except as noted)

Southborough
53 Parkerville Road
Southborough, MA 01772
508-486-5115

Superintendent	Charles Gobron
Grade plan	PK-8
Total enrollment '09-10	1,556
Grade 12 enrollment, '09-10	0
Graduation rate	NA
Dropout rate	NA
Per-pupil expenditure	$11,768
Avg teacher salary	$62,802
Student/teacher ratio '08-09	14.2 to 1
Highly-qualified teachers, '08-09	99.0%
Teachers licensed in assigned subject	99.1%
Students per computer	2.9

Massachusetts Competency Assessment System (MCAS), 2009 results

	English		Math	
	% Prof	CPI	% Prof	CPI
Gr 4	77%	92.1	62%	86.4
Gr 6	83%	94.1	66%	84.4
Gr 8	92%	96.4	62%	83.6
Gr 10	NA	NA	NA	NA

Other School Districts (see Appendix D for data)
Northboro-Southboro Regional, Assabet Valley Vocational Tech

©2010 Information Publications, Inc. All rights reserved. Photocopying prohibited. For additional copies, contact the publisher at www.informationpublications.com or (877)544-INFO (4636)

See Introduction for an explanation of all data sources.

Demographics & Socio-Economic Characteristics

Population

1990	17,816
2000	17,214
Male	8,287
Female	8,927
2008	16,852
2010 (projected)††	17,409
2020 (projected)††	17,669

Race & Hispanic Origin, 2000

Race	
White	14,672
Black/African American	246
American Indian/Alaska Native	73
Asian	261
Hawaiian Native/Pacific Islander	11
Other Race	1,498
Two or more races	453
Hispanic origin	3,472

Age & Nativity, 2000

Under 5 years	1,138
18 years and over	12,847
21 years and over	12,246
65 years and over	2,600
85 years and over	396
Median Age	35.8
Native-born	16,283
Foreign-born	931

Age, 2020 (projected)††

Under 5 years	1,114
5 to 19 years	3,280
20 to 39 years	4,721
40 to 64 years	5,547
65 years and over	3,007

Educational Attainment, 2000

Population 25 years and over	11,291
High School graduates or higher	71.4%
Bachelor's degree or higher	12.5%
Graduate degree	3.8%

Income & Poverty, 1999

Per capita income,	$18,514
Median household income	$33,913
Median family income	$41,863
Persons in poverty	2,616
H'holds receiving public assistance	484
H'holds receiving social security	2,164

Households, 2000

Total households	7,077
With persons under 18	2,358
With persons over 65	1,850
Family households	4,520
Single person households	2,103
Persons per household	2.4
Persons per family	3.0

Labor & Employment, 2000

Civilian labor force	8,113
Unemployment rate	5.4%
Civilian labor force, 2008†	8,337
Unemployment rate†	11.5%
Civilian labor force, 12/09†	8,214
Unemployment rate†	11.6%
Employed persons 16 years and over, by occupation:	
Managers & professionals	1,935
Service occupations	1,177
Sales & office occupations	2,029
Farming, fishing & forestry	7
Construction & maintenance	734
Production & transportation	1,795
Self-employed persons	364

Most demographic data is from the 2000 Decennial Census
† Massachusetts Department of Revenue
†† University of Massachusetts, MISER

General Information

Town of Southbridge
41 Elm St
Southbridge, MA 01550
508-764-5405

Elevation	500 ft.
Land area (square miles)	20.4
Water area (square miles)	0.5
Population density, 2008 (est)	826.1
Year incorporated	1816
Email	Mdaoust@southbridgemass.org

Voters & Government Information

Government type	Council-Manager
Number of Councilpersons	9
US Congressional District(s)	2

Registered Voters, October 2008

Total	11,927
Democrats	4,590
Republicans	1,132
Unaffiliated/other	6,096

Local Officials, 2010

Council Chair	Steven S. Lazo
Manager	Christopher Clark
Town Clerk	Madaline I. Daoust
Finance Director	Karen Harnois
Tax Collector	Melinda R. Ernst-Fournier
Tax Assessor	Wilfrid Cournoyer
Attorney	Robert Caprera
Public Works	Kenneth Kalinowski
Building	Nicola Tortis
Comm Dev/Planning	Cassandra Acly
Police Chief	Daniel R. Charette
Fire Chief	Richard J. Ciesla Jr

Housing & Construction

New Privately Owned Housing Units Authorized by Building Permit

	Single Family	Total Bldgs	Total Units
2006	18	18	18
2007	15	15	15
2008	14	15	16

Parcel Count by Property Class, 2010

Total	5,530
Single family	2,665
Multiple units	989
Apartments	239
Condos	173
Vacant land	989
Open space	0
Commercial	205
Industrial	78
Misc. residential	40
Other use	152

Public Library

Jacob Edwards Memorial Library
236 Main St.
Southbridge, MA 01550
(508)764-5426

Director	Margaret Morrissey

Library Statistics, FY 2008

Population served, 2007	16,926
Registered users	9,726
Circulation	79,570
Reference transactons	0
Total program attendance	109,725
per capita:	
Holdings	5.57
Operating income	$30.23
Internet Access	
Internet computers available	12
Weekly users	292

Municipal Finance

Debt at year end 2008	$34,448,303
Moody's rating, July 2009	A3

Revenues, 2008

Total	$50,199,506
From all taxes	14,744,839
Federal aid	0
State aid	21,919,111
From other governments	66,950
Charges for services	1,021,978
Licenses, permits & fees	425,125
Fines & forfeits	0
Interfund transfers	10,312,267
Misc/other/special assessments	854,618

Expenditures, 2008

Total	$41,558,266
General government	2,126,139
Public safety	4,928,271
Other/fixed costs	4,920,940
Human services	110,992
Culture & recreation	445,139
Debt Service	2,422,478
Education	23,789,707
Public works	1,966,237
Intergovernmental	841,797

Taxation, 2010

Property type	Valuation	Rate
Total	$975,430,512	-
Residential	774,855,381	15.16
Open space	0	0.00
Commercial	115,930,651	15.16
Industrial	40,914,800	15.16
Personal	43,729,680	15.16

Average Single Family Tax Bill, 2010

Avg. assessed home value	$183,421
Avg. single fam. tax bill	$2,781
Hi-Lo ranking	256/301

Police & Crime, 2008

Number of police officers	36
Violent crimes	80
Property crimes	401

Local School District

(school data 2007-08, except as noted)

Southbridge
41 Elm Street
Southbridge, MA 01550
508-764-5414

Superintendent	Dale Hanley
Grade plan	PK-12
Total enrollment '09-10	2,166
Grade 12 enrollment, '09-10	70
Graduation rate	64.7%
Dropout rate	26.1%
Per-pupil expenditure	$13,104
Avg teacher salary	$67,483
Student/teacher ratio '08-09	11.7 to 1
Highly-qualified teachers, '08-09	94.6%
Teachers licensed in assigned subject	92.9%
Students per computer	1.9

Massachusetts Competency Assessment System (MCAS), 2009 results

	English		Math	
	% Prof	CPI	% Prof	CPI
Gr 4	29%	66.6	35%	68.3
Gr 6	36%	65.5	25%	56.1
Gr 8	63%	83.3	25%	53.1
Gr 10	68%	90.1	53%	79.5

Other School Districts (see Appendix D for data)
Southern Worcester County Vocational Tech

©2010 Information Publications, Inc. All rights reserved. Photocopying prohibited. For additional copies, contact the publisher at www.informationpublications.com or (877)544-INFO (4636)

See Introduction for an explanation of all data sources.

Demographics & Socio-Economic Characteristics

Population

1990	7,667
2000	8,835
Male	4,427
Female	4,408
2008	9,571
2010 (projected)††	8,944
2020 (projected)††	9,017

Race & Hispanic Origin, 2000

Race	
White	8,606
Black/African American	45
American Indian/Alaska Native	18
Asian	33
Hawaiian Native/Pacific Islander	1
Other Race	30
Two or more races	102
Hispanic origin	152

Age & Nativity, 2000

Under 5 years	558
18 years and over	6,490
21 years and over	6,223
65 years and over	1,031
85 years and over	112
Median Age	37.9
Native-born	8,608
Foreign-born	227

Age, 2020 (projected)††

Under 5 years	496
5 to 19 years	1,502
20 to 39 years	2,093
40 to 64 years	3,176
65 years and over	1,750

Educational Attainment, 2000

Population 25 years and over	5,950
High School graduates or higher	84.7%
Bachelor's degree or higher	21.4%
Graduate degree	7.0%

Income & Poverty, 1999

Per capita income,	$21,756
Median household income	$52,296
Median family income	$64,456
Persons in poverty	537
H'holds receiving public assistance	75
H'holds receiving social security	840

Households, 2000

Total households	3,318
With persons under 18	1,300
With persons over 65	764
Family households	2,419
Single person households	726
Persons per household	2.7
Persons per family	3.1

Labor & Employment, 2000

Civilian labor force	4,818
Unemployment rate	5.3%
Civilian labor force, 2008†	5,257
Unemployment rate†	7.1%
Civilian labor force, 12/09†	5,235
Unemployment rate†	9.7%
Employed persons 16 years and over, by occupation:	
Managers & professionals	1,456
Service occupations	604
Sales & office occupations	1,190
Farming, fishing & forestry	19
Construction & maintenance	563
Production & transportation	729
Self-employed persons	354

Most demographic data is from the 2000 Decennial Census
† Massachusetts Department of Revenue
†† University of Massachusetts, MISER

General Information

Town of Southwick
454 College Hwy
Southwick, MA 01077
413-569-5995

Elevation	244 ft.
Land area (square miles)	31.0
Water area (square miles)	0.7
Population density, 2008 (est)	308.7
Year incorporated	1770
Website	www.southwickma.org

Voters & Government Information

Government type	Open Town Meeting
Number of Selectmen	3
US Congressional District(s)	1

Registered Voters, October 2008

Total	6,801
Democrats	1,642
Republicans	1,540
Unaffiliated/other	3,563

Local Officials, 2010

Chair, Bd. of Sel.	Arthur Pinell
Manager/Admin	Karl Stinehart
Town Clerk	Michelle L. Hill
Accountant	Linda Carr
Treas/Collector	Michelle L. Hill
Tax Assessor	Sure Gore
Attorney	Bacon & Wilson
Public Works	Jeffrey Neece
Building	Denis Gaido
Comm Dev/Planning	Marcus Phelps
Police Chief	Mark Krynicki
Emerg/Fire Chief	Don Morris

Housing & Construction

New Privately Owned Housing Units Authorized by Building Permit

	Single Family	Total Bldgs	Total Units
2006	20	20	20
2007	19	19	19
2008	10	10	10

Parcel Count by Property Class, 2010

Total	4,272
Single family	2,982
Multiple units	83
Apartments	109
Condos	199
Vacant land	515
Open space	0
Commercial	107
Industrial	49
Misc. residential	24
Other use	204

Public Library

Southwick Public Library
95 Feeding Hills Road
Southwick, MA 01077
(413)569-1221

Librarian	Anne M. Murray

Library Statistics, FY 2008

Population served, 2007	9,431
Registered users	11,406
Circulation	82,075
Reference transactons	3,334
Total program attendance	57,434
per capita:	
Holdings	5.42
Operating income	$37.74
Internet Access	
Internet computers available	7
Weekly users	82

Municipal Finance

Debt at year end 2008	$16,359,262
Moody's rating, July 2009	A1

Revenues, 2008

Total	$17,341,177
From all taxes	14,214,509
Federal aid	0
State aid	1,535,847
From other governments	40,784
Charges for services	261,814
Licenses, permits & fees	277,779
Fines & forfeits	0
Interfund transfers	216,256
Misc/other/special assessments	397,094

Expenditures, 2008

Total	$15,560,144
General government	1,794,216
Public safety	2,246,587
Other/fixed costs	1,228,533
Human services	207,660
Culture & recreation	389,795
Debt Service	779,846
Education	7,593,266
Public works	1,292,970
Intergovernmental	27,271

Taxation, 2010

Property type	Valuation	Rate
Total	$1,005,864,517	-
Residential	905,030,095	13.44
Open space	0	0.00
Commercial	54,346,376	13.44
Industrial	21,025,250	13.44
Personal	25,462,796	13.44

Average Single Family Tax Bill, 2010

Avg. assessed home value	$254,771
Avg. single fam. tax bill	$3,424
Hi-Lo ranking	182/301

Police & Crime, 2008

Number of police officers	16
Violent crimes	11
Property crimes	132

Local School District

(school data 2007-08, except as noted)

Southwick (non-op)
86 Powder Mill Road
Southwick, MA 01077
413-569-5391

Superintendent	John Barry

Non-operating district.
Resident students are sent to the Other School Districts listed below.

Grade plan	NA
Total enrollment '09-10	NA
Grade 12 enrollment, '09-10	NA
Graduation rate	NA
Dropout rate	NA
Per-pupil expenditure	NA
Avg teacher salary	NA
Student/teacher ratio '08-09	NA
Highly-qualified teachers, '08-09	NA
Teachers licensed in assigned subject	NA
Students per computer	NA

Other School Districts (see Appendix D for data)
Southwick-Tolland Regional

©2010 Information Publications, Inc. All rights reserved. Photocopying prohibited. For additional copies, contact the publisher at www.informationpublications.com or (877)544-INFO (4636)

See Introduction for an explanation of all data sources.

Demographics & Socio-Economic Characteristics

Population

1990	11,645
2000	11,691
Male	5,785
Female	5,906
2008	11,922
2010 (projected)††	11,836
2020 (projected)††	11,897

Race & Hispanic Origin, 2000

Race	
White	11,449
Black/African American	69
American Indian/Alaska Native	28
Asian	38
Hawaiian Native/Pacific Islander	2
Other Race	30
Two or more races	75
Hispanic origin	156

Age & Nativity, 2000

Under 5 years	743
18 years and over	8,819
21 years and over	8,379
65 years and over	1,448
85 years and over	134
Median Age	37.0
Native-born	11,470
Foreign-born	221

Age, 2020 (projected)††

Under 5 years	641
5 to 19 years	1,891
20 to 39 years	2,979
40 to 64 years	4,048
65 years and over	2,338

Educational Attainment, 2000

Population 25 years and over	7,798
High School graduates or higher	81.8%
Bachelor's degree or higher	17.7%
Graduate degree	5.9%

Income & Poverty, 1999

Per capita income,	$21,017
Median household income	$46,598
Median family income	$56,763
Persons in poverty	1,001
H'holds receiving public assistance	100
H'holds receiving social security	1,317

Households, 2000

Total households	4,583
With persons under 18	1,575
With persons over 65	1,040
Family households	3,094
Single person households	1,187
Persons per household	2.5
Persons per family	3.1

Labor & Employment, 2000

Civilian labor force	6,450
Unemployment rate	3.7%
Civilian labor force, 2008†	6,709
Unemployment rate†	7.5%
Civilian labor force, 12/09†	6,907
Unemployment rate†	11.2%
Employed persons 16 years and over, by occupation:	
Managers & professionals	1,935
Service occupations	882
Sales & office occupations	1,736
Farming, fishing & forestry	30
Construction & maintenance	692
Production & transportation	935
Self-employed persons	418

Most demographic data is from the 2000 Decennial Census
† Massachusetts Department of Revenue
†† University of Massachusetts, MISER

General Information

Town of Spencer
157 Main Street
Town Hall
Spencer, MA 01562
508-885-7500

Elevation	925 ft.
Land area (square miles)	32.8
Water area (square miles)	1.2
Population density, 2008 (est)	363.5
Year incorporated	1753
Website	www.spencerma.gov

Voters & Government Information

Government type	Open Town Meeting
Number of Selectmen	5
US Congressional District(s)	2

Registered Voters, October 2008

Total	7,861
Democrats	2,235
Republicans	978
Unaffiliated/other	4,583

Local Officials, 2010

Chair, Bd. of Sel.	Donald R. Berthiaume, Jr.
Manager/Town Admin.	Paul J. Guida
Town Clerk	Jean M. Mulhall
Finance Director	Mary C. Barrell
Tax Collector	Mary C. Barrell
Tax Assessor	Mary C. Williams
Attorney	Stanley L. Weinberg
Public Works	Robert McNeil
Building	William A. Klansek
Comm Dev/Planning	Adam Gaudette
Police Chief	David Darrin
Emerg/Fire Chief	Robert Parsons

Housing & Construction

New Privately Owned Housing Units Authorized by Building Permit

	Single Family	Total Bldgs	Total Units
2006	28	29	31
2007	2	2	2
2008	17	17	17

Parcel Count by Property Class, 2010

Total	4,993
Single family	3,015
Multiple units	450
Apartments	90
Condos	73
Vacant land	957
Open space	0
Commercial	99
Industrial	40
Misc. residential	62
Other use	207

Public Library

Richard Sugden Public Library
8 Pleasant St.
Spencer, MA 01562
(508)885-7513

Director	Mary Baker-Wood

Library Statistics, FY 2008

Population served, 2007	12,006
Registered users	11,465
Circulation	69,045
Reference transactons	4,958
Total program attendance	0
per capita:	
Holdings	4.66
Operating income	$27.37
Internet Access	
Internet computers available	9
Weekly users	423

Municipal Finance

Debt at year end 2008	$3,149,129
Moody's rating, July 2009	NA

Revenues, 2008

Total	$14,891,510
From all taxes	10,605,205
Federal aid	0
State aid	2,841,891
From other governments	0
Charges for services	379,228
Licenses, permits & fees	405,265
Fines & forfeits	57,777
Interfund transfers	329,472
Misc/other/special assessments	136,336

Expenditures, 2008

Total	$13,780,377
General government	904,834
Public safety	2,137,827
Other/fixed costs	1,402,466
Human services	125,982
Culture & recreation	382,251
Debt Service	351,818
Education	6,930,652
Public works	1,401,964
Intergovernmental	107,417

Taxation, 2010

Property type	Valuation	Rate
Total	$1,051,403,083	-
Residential	932,824,436	9.82
Open space	0	0.00
Commercial	63,983,838	9.82
Industrial	32,903,540	9.82
Personal	21,691,269	9.82

Average Single Family Tax Bill, 2010

Avg. assessed home value	$236,431
Avg. single fam. tax bill	$2,322
Hi-Lo ranking	284/301

Police & Crime, 2008

Number of police officers	17
Violent crimes	NA
Property crimes	NA

Local School District

(school data 2007-08, except as noted)

Spencer (non-op)
306 Main Street
Spencer, MA 01562
508-885-8500

Superintendent	Ralph Hicks

Non-operating district.
Resident students are sent to the Other School Districts listed below.

Grade plan	NA
Total enrollment '09-10	NA
Grade 12 enrollment, '09-10	NA
Graduation rate	NA
Dropout rate	NA
Per-pupil expenditure	NA
Avg teacher salary	NA
Student/teacher ratio '08-09	NA
Highly-qualified teachers, '08-09	NA
Teachers licensed in assigned subject	NA
Students per computer	NA

Other School Districts (see Appendix D for data)
Spencer-East Brookfield Regional, Southern Worchester County Vocational Tech

©2010 Information Publications, Inc. All rights reserved. Photocopying prohibited. For additional copies, contact the publisher at www.informationpublications.com or (877)544-INFO (4636)

See Introduction for an explanation of all data sources.

Demographics & Socio-Economic Characteristics*

Population

1990	156,983
2000	152,082
Male	71,802
Female	80,280
2008	150,640
2010 (projected)††	153,245
2020 (projected)††	156,476

Race & Hispanic Origin, 2000

Race	
White	85,329
Black/African American	31,960
American Indian/Alaska Native	569
Asian	2,916
Hawaiian Native/Pacific Islander	143
Other Race	25,016
Two or more races	6,149
Hispanic origin	41,343

Age & Nativity, 2000

Under 5 years	11,606
18 years and over	108,055
21 years and over	99,852
65 years and over	18,906
85 years and over	2,346
Median Age	31.9
Native-born	139,923
Foreign-born	12,159

Age, 2020 (projected)††

Under 5 years	11,874
5 to 19 years	35,014
20 to 39 years	46,820
40 to 64 years	41,876
65 years and over	20,892

Educational Attainment, 2000

Population 25 years and over	90,800
High School graduates or higher	73.4%
Bachelor's degree or higher	15.4%
Graduate degree	5.9%

Income & Poverty, 1999

Per capita income,	$15,232
Median household income	$30,417
Median family income	$36,285
Persons in poverty	33,772
H'holds receiving public assistance	4,910
H'holds receiving social security	16,161

Households, 2000

Total households	57,130
With persons under 18	21,643
With persons over 65	13,973
Family households	36,394
Single person households	17,236
Persons per household	2.6
Persons per family	3.2

Labor & Employment, 2000

Civilian labor force	66,262
Unemployment rate	8.5%
Civilian labor force, 2008†	65,780
Unemployment rate†	9.7%
Civilian labor force, 12/09†	66,871
Unemployment rate†	13.2%
Employed persons 16 years and over, by occupation:	
Managers & professionals	16,441
Service occupations	13,075
Sales & office occupations	15,905
Farming, fishing & forestry	177
Construction & maintenance	4,277
Production & transportation	10,776
Self-employed persons	2,439

Most demographic data is from the 2000 Decennial Census
* see Appendix D and E for American Community Survey data
† Massachusetts Department of Revenue
†† University of Massachusetts, MISER

General Information

City of Springfield
36 Court St
Springfield, MA 01103
413-787-6000

Elevation	100 ft.
Land area (square miles)	32.1
Water area (square miles)	1.1
Population density, 2008 (est)	4,692.8
Year incorporated	1636
Website	www.cityofspringfieldmass.com

Voters & Government Information

Government type	Mayor-Council
Number of Councilpersons	13
US Congressional District(s)	2

Registered Voters, October 2008

Total	84,565
Democrats	44,148
Republicans	7,734
Unaffiliated/other	32,035

Local Officials, 2010

Mayor	Domenic J. Sarno
Manager/Admin	NA
City Clerk	Wayman Lee
Finance Dir	Timothy J. Plante (Actg)
Treas/Collector	Ehsanul Bhuiya (Actg)
Tax Assessor	Stephen P. O'Malley
Attorney	Edward M. Pikula
Public Works	Allan R. Chawlek
Building	Steve Desilets
Comm Dev/Planning	John Judge
Police Chief	William J. Fitchet
Emerg/Fire Chief	Gary G. Cassanelli

Housing & Construction

New Privately Owned Housing Units Authorized by Building Permit

	Single Family	Total Bldgs	Total Units
2006	135	179	223
2007	94	112	130
2008	54	65	76

Parcel Count by Property Class, 2010

Total	42,554
Single family	25,986
Multiple units	7,648
Apartments	705
Condos	1,985
Vacant land	3,170
Open space	0
Commercial	2,281
Industrial	403
Misc. residential	101
Other use	275

Public Library

Springfield City Library
220 State Street
Springfield, MA 01103
(413)263-6828

Director	Lee Fogarty (Int)

Library Statistics, FY 2008

Population served, 2007	149,938
Registered users	74,175
Circulation	647,913
Reference transactons	113,695
Total program attendance	1,561,446
per capita:	
Holdings	5.34
Operating income	$43.18
Internet Access	
Internet computers available	125
Weekly users	0

Municipal Finance

Debt at year end 2008	$347,890,883
Moody's rating, July 2009	Baa2

Revenues, 2008

Total	$530,548,784
From all taxes	156,012,860
Federal aid	0
State aid	341,095,573
From other governments	0
Charges for services	5,180,144
Licenses, permits & fees	3,515,844
Fines & forfeits	1,632,457
Interfund transfers	0
Misc/other/special assessments	11,555,953

Expenditures, 2008

Total	$472,938,159
General government	22,022,715
Public safety	59,438,695
Other/fixed costs	24,994,866
Human services	2,826,868
Culture & recreation	13,976,990
Debt Service	39,522,411
Education	293,908,412
Public works	13,012,642
Intergovernmental	2,591,642

Taxation, 2010

Property type	Valuation	Rate
Total	$6,994,818,900	-
Residential	5,252,153,800	19.50
Open space	0	0.00
Commercial	1,052,016,750	39.25
Industrial	229,288,700	39.25
Personal	461,359,650	39.25

Average Single Family Tax Bill, 2010

Avg. assessed home value	$137,709
Avg. single fam. tax bill	$2,685
Hi-Lo ranking	265/301

Police & Crime, 2008

Number of police officers	467
Violent crimes	1,898
Property crimes	7,336

Local School District

(school data 2007-08, except as noted)

Springfield
195 State Street, PO Box 1410
Springfield, MA 01102
413-787-7000

Superintendent	Alan Ingram
Grade plan	PK-12
Total enrollment '09-10	25,141
Grade 12 enrollment, '09-10	1,302
Graduation rate	54.4%
Dropout rate	28.4%
Per-pupil expenditure	$12,911
Avg teacher salary	$55,505
Student/teacher ratio '08-09	13.5 to 1
Highly-qualified teachers, '08-09	90.4%
Teachers licensed in assigned subject	90.7%
Students per computer	3

Massachusetts Competency Assessment System (MCAS), 2009 results

	English		Math	
	% Prof	CPI	% Prof	CPI
Gr 4	28%	64.4	27%	64.8
Gr 6	31%	65.7	21%	52.7
Gr 8	48%	74.9	12%	41.1
Gr 10	50%	77.9	36%	66.3

Other School Districts (see Appendix D for data)
None

©2010 Information Publications, Inc. All rights reserved. Photocopying prohibited. For additional copies, contact the publisher at www.informationpublications.com or (877)544-INFO (4636)

Demographics & Socio-Economic Characteristics

Population

1990	6,481
2000	7,257
Male	3,612
Female	3,645
2008	7,865
2010 (projected)††	7,656
2020 (projected)††	7,967

Race & Hispanic Origin, 2000

Race	
White	7,116
Black/African American	42
American Indian/Alaska Native	7
Asian	29
Hawaiian Native/Pacific Islander	1
Other Race	20
Two or more races	42
Hispanic origin	59

Age & Nativity, 2000

Under 5 years	483
18 years and over	5,260
21 years and over	5,060
65 years and over	655
85 years and over	56
Median Age	38.1
Native-born	7,127
Foreign-born	130

Age, 2020 (projected)††

Under 5 years	472
5 to 19 years	1,443
20 to 39 years	1,830
40 to 64 years	2,791
65 years and over	1,431

Educational Attainment, 2000

Population 25 years and over	4,884
High School graduates or higher	91.7%
Bachelor's degree or higher	35.9%
Graduate degree	12.2%

Income & Poverty, 1999

Per capita income,	$28,844
Median household income	$67,188
Median family income	$76,943
Persons in poverty	213
H'holds receiving public assistance	40
H'holds receiving social security	638

Households, 2000

Total households	2,573
With persons under 18	1,079
With persons over 65	484
Family households	2,069
Single person households	394
Persons per household	2.8
Persons per family	3.2

Labor & Employment, 2000

Civilian labor force	4,068
Unemployment rate	1.7%
Civilian labor force, 2008†	4,446
Unemployment rate†	6.0%
Civilian labor force, 12/09†	4,512
Unemployment rate†	7.5%
Employed persons 16 years and over, by occupation:	
Managers & professionals	1,785
Service occupations	500
Sales & office occupations	881
Farming, fishing & forestry	0
Construction & maintenance	325
Production & transportation	507
Self-employed persons	297

Most demographic data is from the 2000 Decennial Census
† Massachusetts Department of Revenue
†† University of Massachusetts, MISER

General Information

Town of Sterling
1 Park St
Sterling, MA 01564
978-422-8111

Elevation	505 ft.
Land area (square miles)	30.5
Water area (square miles)	1.1
Population density, 2008 (est)	257.9
Year incorporated	1781
Website	www.sterling-ma.gov

Voters & Government Information

Government type	Open Town Meeting
Number of Selectmen	3
US Congressional District(s)	1

Registered Voters, October 2008

Total	5,670
Democrats	1,122
Republicans	1,000
Unaffiliated/other	3,500

Local Officials, 2010

Chair, Bd. of Sel.	Paul M. Sushchyk
Town Administrator	Terri Ackerman
Clerk	Dawn Michanavicz
Treasurer	NA
Tax Collector	Donna Erickson
Tax Assessor	Michael Olson
Attorney	Collins & Weinberg
Public Works	William Tuttle
Building	Mark Brodeur
Comm Dev/Planning	NA
Police Chief	Gary Chamberlain
Fire Chief	David Hurlbut

Housing & Construction

New Privately Owned Housing Units Authorized by Building Permit

	Single Family	Total Bldgs	Total Units
2006	48	48	48
2007	13	13	13
2008	8	8	8

Parcel Count by Property Class, 2010

Total	3,549
Single family	2,505
Multiple units	111
Apartments	9
Condos	127
Vacant land	431
Open space	0
Commercial	73
Industrial	113
Misc. residential	19
Other use	161

Public Library

Conant Public Library
4 Meetinghouse Hill Rd.
Sterling, MA 01564
(978)422-6409

Director	Patricia Campbell

Library Statistics, FY 2008

Population served, 2007	7,874
Registered users	4,541
Circulation	86,653
Reference transactons	551
Total program attendance	49,400
per capita:	
Holdings	3.92
Operating income	$40.77
Internet Access	
Internet computers available	13
Weekly users	167

Municipal Finance

Debt at year end 2008	$20,442,884
Moody's rating, July 2009	A1

Revenues, 2008

Total	$22,428,034
From all taxes	15,488,241
Federal aid	0
State aid	942,325
From other governments	0
Charges for services	125,434
Licenses, permits & fees	179,738
Fines & forfeits	90,902
Interfund transfers	1,253,796
Misc/other/special assessments	2,173,799

Expenditures, 2008

Total	$18,189,649
General government	934,870
Public safety	2,083,961
Other/fixed costs	1,257,385
Human services	162,717
Culture & recreation	368,873
Debt Service	2,199,944
Education	9,417,704
Public works	1,696,667
Intergovernmental	67,528

Taxation, 2010

Property type	Valuation	Rate
Total	$1,017,236,101	-
Residential	880,724,285	14.29
Open space	0	0.00
Commercial	44,790,115	14.29
Industrial	59,833,000	14.29
Personal	31,888,701	14.29

Average Single Family Tax Bill, 2010

Avg. assessed home value	$311,328
Avg. single fam. tax bill	$4,449
Hi-Lo ranking	102/301

Police & Crime, 2008

Number of police officers	13
Violent crimes	NA
Property crimes	NA

Local School District

(school data 2007-08, except as noted)

Sterling (non-op)
Jefferson School, 1745 Main Street
Jefferson, MA 01522
508-829-1670

Superintendent........ Thomas Pandiscio

Non-operating district.
Resident students are sent to the Other School Districts listed below.

Grade plan	NA
Total enrollment '09-10	NA
Grade 12 enrollment, '09-10	NA
Graduation rate	NA
Dropout rate	NA
Per-pupil expenditure	NA
Avg teacher salary	NA
Student/teacher ratio '08-09	NA
Highly-qualified teachers, '08-09	NA
Teachers licensed in assigned subject	NA
Students per computer	NA

Other School Districts (see Appendix D for data)
Wachusett Regional, Montachusett

See Introduction for an explanation of all data sources.

©2010 Information Publications, Inc. All rights reserved. Photocopying prohibited. For additional copies, contact the publisher at www.informationpublications.com or (877)544-INFO (4636)

Demographics & Socio-Economic Characteristics

Population

1990	2,408
2000	2,276
Male	1,086
Female	1,190
2008	2,217
2010 (projected)††	2,077
2020 (projected)††	1,860

Race & Hispanic Origin, 2000

Race	
White	2,206
Black/African American	28
American Indian/Alaska Native	1
Asian	10
Hawaiian Native/Pacific Islander	1
Other Race	22
Two or more races	8
Hispanic origin	66

Age & Nativity, 2000

Under 5 years	75
18 years and over	1,929
21 years and over	1,841
65 years and over	512
85 years and over	54
Median Age	48.6
Native-born	2,089
Foreign-born	191

Age, 2020 (projected)††

Under 5 years	47
5 to 19 years	195
20 to 39 years	290
40 to 64 years	574
65 years and over	754

Educational Attainment, 2000

Population 25 years and over	1,741
High School graduates or higher	90.4%
Bachelor's degree or higher	50.2%
Graduate degree	23.1%

Income & Poverty, 1999

Per capita income	$32,499
Median household income	$48,571
Median family income	$59,556
Persons in poverty	188
H'holds receiving public assistance	15
H'holds receiving social security	292

Households, 2000

Total households	991
With persons under 18	199
With persons over 65	359
Family households	568
Single person households	364
Persons per household	2.1
Persons per family	2.7

Labor & Employment, 2000

Civilian labor force	1,239
Unemployment rate	4.1%
Civilian labor force, 2008†	1,345
Unemployment rate†	4.9%
Civilian labor force, 12/09†	1,328
Unemployment rate†	5.3%
Employed persons 16 years and over, by occupation:	
Managers & professionals	583
Service occupations	150
Sales & office occupations	285
Farming, fishing & forestry	0
Construction & maintenance	83
Production & transportation	87
Self-employed persons	151

Most demographic data is from the 2000 Decennial Census
† Massachusetts Department of Revenue
†† University of Massachusetts, MISER

General Information

Town of Stockbridge
50 Main St
PO Box 417
Stockbridge, MA 01262
413-298-4170

Elevation	840 ft.
Land area (square miles)	22.9
Water area (square miles)	0.8
Population density, 2008 (est)	96.8
Year incorporated	1739
Website	www.townofstockbridge.com

Voters & Government Information

Government type	Open Town Meeting
Number of Selectmen	3
US Congressional District(s)	1

Registered Voters, October 2008

Total	1,519
Democrats	655
Republicans	188
Unaffiliated/other	662

Local Officials, 2010

Chair, Bd. of Sel.	Robert L. Flower
Town Admin	Jorja-Ann P. Marsden
Town Clerk	Linda Hunt
Treasurer	Karen Williams
Tax Collector	Nancy Socha
Tax Assessor	John Miller
Attorney	J. Raymond Miyares
Public Works	Clinton Schneyer
Building Inspector	Edward Baldwin
Comm Dev/Planning	NA
Police Chief	Richard B. Wilcox
Fire Chief	Louis J. Peyron

Housing & Construction

New Privately Owned Housing Units Authorized by Building Permit

	Single Family	Total Bldgs	Total Units
2006	9	9	9
2007	4	4	4
2008	5	5	5

Parcel Count by Property Class, 2010

Total	1,767
Single family	1,092
Multiple units	33
Apartments	6
Condos	150
Vacant land	281
Open space	0
Commercial	38
Industrial	9
Misc. residential	88
Other use	70

Public Library

Stockbridge Library Association
PO Box 119
Stockbridge, MA 01262
(413)298-5501

Librarian	Rosemary Schneyer

Library Statistics, FY 2008

Population served, 2007	2,232
Registered users	3,863
Circulation	46,342
Reference transactons	780
Total program attendance	27,641
per capita:	
Holdings	15.08
Operating income	$131.67
Internet Access	
Internet computers available	4
Weekly users	330

Municipal Finance

Debt at year end 2008	$13,556,706
Moody's rating, July 2009	NA

Revenues, 2008

Total	$8,546,531
From all taxes	6,688,804
Federal aid	0
State aid	184,785
From other governments	11,762
Charges for services	65,960
Licenses, permits & fees	237,809
Fines & forfeits	9,568
Interfund transfers	340,221
Misc/other/special assessments	503,811

Expenditures, 2008

Total	$6,489,546
General government	779,247
Public safety	688,764
Other/fixed costs	593,783
Human services	97,218
Culture & recreation	121,264
Debt Service	1,148,252
Education	2,276,105
Public works	696,172
Intergovernmental	87,329

Taxation, 2010

Property type	Valuation	Rate
Total	$862,756,391	-
Residential	776,766,100	6.99
Open space	0	0.00
Commercial	48,199,000	6.99
Industrial	3,846,800	6.99
Personal	33,944,491	6.99

Average Single Family Tax Bill, 2010

Avg. assessed home value	$514,281
Avg. single fam. tax bill	$3,595
Hi-Lo ranking	162/301

Police & Crime, 2008

Number of police officers	6
Violent crimes	2
Property crimes	121

Local School District

(school data 2007-08, except as noted)

Stockbridge (non-op)
207 Pleasant Street, PO Box 596
Housatonic, MA 01236
413-274-6400

Superintendent . . . . . Peter Dillon

Non-operating district.
Resident students are sent to the Other School Districts listed below.

Grade plan	NA
Total enrollment '09-10	NA
Grade 12 enrollment, '09-10	NA
Graduation rate	NA
Dropout rate	NA
Per-pupil expenditure	NA
Avg teacher salary	NA
Student/teacher ratio '08-09	NA
Highly-qualified teachers, '08-09	NA
Teachers licensed in assigned subject	NA
Students per computer	NA

Other School Districts (see Appendix D for data)
Berkshire Hills Regional

©2010 Information Publications, Inc. All rights reserved. Photocopying prohibited. For additional copies, contact the publisher at www.informationpublications.com or (877)544-INFO (4636)

See Introduction for an explanation of all data sources.

Demographics & Socio-Economic Characteristics*

Population

1990	22,203
2000	22,219
Male	10,462
Female	11,757
2008	21,471
2010 (projected)††	21,661
2020 (projected)††	20,842

Race & Hispanic Origin, 2000

Race	
White	21,110
Black/African American	197
American Indian/Alaska Native	12
Asian	558
Hawaiian Native/Pacific Islander	9
Other Race	132
Two or more races	201
Hispanic origin	397

Age & Nativity, 2000

Under 5 years	1,287
18 years and over	17,562
21 years and over	17,040
65 years and over	4,108
85 years and over	611
Median Age	40.6
Native-born	20,426
Foreign-born	1,793

Age, 2020 (projected)††

Under 5 years	916
5 to 19 years	2,993
20 to 39 years	4,668
40 to 64 years	7,268
65 years and over	4,997

Educational Attainment, 2000

Population 25 years and over	16,310
High School graduates or higher	90.8%
Bachelor's degree or higher	31.6%
Graduate degree	11.7%

Income & Poverty, 1999

Per capita income,	$27,599
Median household income	$56,605
Median family income	$71,334
Persons in poverty	892
H'holds receiving public assistance	174
H'holds receiving social security	2,994

Households, 2000

Total households	9,050
With persons under 18	2,571
With persons over 65	2,841
Family households	5,871
Single person households	2,721
Persons per household	2.4
Persons per family	3.1

Labor & Employment, 2000

Civilian labor force	11,883
Unemployment rate	2.1%
Civilian labor force, 2008†	11,899
Unemployment rate†	5.7%
Civilian labor force, 12/09†	11,794
Unemployment rate†	7.4%
Employed persons 16 years and over, by occupation:	
Managers & professionals	5,030
Service occupations	1,363
Sales & office occupations	3,529
Farming, fishing & forestry	0
Construction & maintenance	816
Production & transportation	892
Self-employed persons	697

Most demographic data is from the 2000 Decennial Census
* see Appendix E for American Community Survey data
† Massachusetts Department of Revenue
†† University of Massachusetts, MISER

General Information

Town of Stoneham
35 Central St
Stoneham, MA 02180
781-279-2650

Elevation	109 ft.
Land area (square miles)	6.1
Water area (square miles)	0.6
Population density, 2008 (est)	3,519.8
Year incorporated	1725
Website	www.ci.stoneham.ma.us

Voters & Government Information

Government type	Open Town Meeting
Number of Selectmen	5
US Congressional District(s)	7

Registered Voters, October 2008

Total	15,363
Democrats	5,445
Republicans	1,711
Unaffiliated/other	8,132

Local Officials, 2010

Chair, Bd. of Sel.	John DePinto
Manager/Admin	David Ragucci
Clerk	John Hanright
Finance Director	Diane Murphy
Tax Collector	Diane Murphy
Tax Assessor	William Jordan
Attorney	William Solomon
Public Works	Robert Grover
Building	Cheryl Glover
Planning	Ronald Forino
Police Chief	Richard Bongiorno
Emerg/Fire Chief	Joseph Rolli

Housing & Construction

New Privately Owned Housing Units Authorized by Building Permit

	Single Family	Total Bldgs	Total Units
2006	13	14	27
2007	6	7	11
2008	3	4	5

Parcel Count by Property Class, 2010

Total	7,599
Single family	5,039
Multiple units	523
Apartments	45
Condos	1,424
Vacant land	198
Open space	0
Commercial	278
Industrial	20
Misc. residential	17
Other use	55

Public Library

Stoneham Public Library
431 Main St.
Stoneham, MA 02180
(781)438-1324

Director	Mary Todd

Library Statistics, FY 2008

Population served, 2007	21,508
Registered users	14,180
Circulation	99,207
Reference transactons	24,334
Total program attendance	99,681
per capita:	
Holdings	3.80
Operating income	$37.45
Internet Access	
Internet computers available	14
Weekly users	401

Municipal Finance

Debt at year end 2008	$42,906,999
Moody's rating, July 2009	A1

Revenues, 2008

Total	$54,243,442
From all taxes	38,352,862
Federal aid	0
State aid	10,300,794
From other governments	86,765
Charges for services	2,935,868
Licenses, permits & fees	552,160
Fines & forfeits	43,132
Interfund transfers	900,677
Misc/other/special assessments	535,592

Expenditures, 2008

Total	$52,691,118
General government	1,820,909
Public safety	5,879,798
Other/fixed costs	11,319,823
Human services	333,486
Culture & recreation	1,660,905
Debt Service	4,883,680
Education	21,595,048
Public works	3,116,140
Intergovernmental	2,045,264

Taxation, 2010

Property type	Valuation	Rate
Total	$3,067,844,785	-
Residential	2,719,699,682	11.49
Open space	0	0.00
Commercial	278,835,841	18.87
Industrial	25,444,300	18.87
Personal	43,864,962	18.87

Average Single Family Tax Bill, 2010

Avg. assessed home value	$401,628
Avg. single fam. tax bill	$4,615
Hi-Lo ranking	94/301

Police & Crime, 2008

Number of police officers	32
Violent crimes	NA
Property crimes	NA

Local School District

(school data 2007-08, except as noted)

Stoneham
149 Franklin Street
Stoneham, MA 02180
781-279-3802

Superintendent	Les Olson
Grade plan	PK-12
Total enrollment '09-10	2,650
Grade 12 enrollment, '09-10	178
Graduation rate	92.0%
Dropout rate	3.5%
Per-pupil expenditure	$10,827
Avg teacher salary	$57,795
Student/teacher ratio '08-09	14.3 to 1
Highly-qualified teachers, '08-09	98.5%
Teachers licensed in assigned subject	98.4%
Students per computer	7.2

Massachusetts Competency Assessment System (MCAS), 2009 results

	English		Math	
	% Prof	CPI	% Prof	CPI
Gr 4	63%	84.9	57%	83.5
Gr 6	66%	84.7	58%	77
Gr 8	77%	89.6	43%	71.1
Gr 10	92%	97.3	86%	93.3

Other School Districts (see Appendix D for data)
Northeast Metro Vocational Tech

©2010 Information Publications, Inc. All rights reserved. Photocopying prohibited. For additional copies, contact the publisher at www.informationpublications.com or (877)544-INFO (4636)

See Introduction for an explanation of all data sources.

Demographics & Socio-Economic Characteristics

Population

1990	26,777
2000	27,149
Male	13,027
Female	14,122
2008	26,927
2010 (projected)††	26,243
2020 (projected)††	24,946

Race & Hispanic Origin, 2000

Race	
White	24,017
Black/African American	1,548
American Indian/Alaska Native	28
Asian	580
Hawaiian Native/Pacific Islander	13
Other Race	344
Two or more races	619
Hispanic origin	419

Age & Nativity, 2000

Under 5 years	1,522
18 years and over	21,057
21 years and over	20,246
65 years and over	4,103
85 years and over	493
Median Age	39.2
Native-born	23,439
Foreign-born	3,710

Age, 2020 (projected)††

Under 5 years	1,173
5 to 19 years	3,822
20 to 39 years	5,758
40 to 64 years	8,826
65 years and over	5,367

Educational Attainment, 2000

Population 25 years and over	19,209
High School graduates or higher	86.3%
Bachelor's degree or higher	28.4%
Graduate degree	9.4%

Income & Poverty, 1999

Per capita income,	$25,480
Median household income	$57,838
Median family income	$69,942
Persons in poverty	1,219
H'holds receiving public assistance	143
H'holds receiving social security	2,842

Households, 2000

Total households	10,254
With persons under 18	3,426
With persons over 65	2,778
Family households	7,267
Single person households	2,505
Persons per household	2.6
Persons per family	3.1

Labor & Employment, 2000

Civilian labor force	14,896
Unemployment rate	2.7%
Civilian labor force, 2008†	15,331
Unemployment rate†	6.4%
Civilian labor force, 12/09†	15,205
Unemployment rate†	8.2%
Employed persons 16 years and over, by occupation:	
Managers & professionals	5,255
Service occupations	1,838
Sales & office occupations	4,416
Farming, fishing & forestry	7
Construction & maintenance	1,168
Production & transportation	1,809
Self-employed persons	652

Most demographic data is from the 2000 Decennial Census
† Massachusetts Department of Revenue
†† University of Massachusetts, MISER

General Information

Town of Stoughton
10 Pearl St
Stoughton, MA 02072
781-341-1300

Elevation	232 ft.
Land area (square miles)	16.0
Water area (square miles)	0.2
Population density, 2008 (est)	1,682.9
Year incorporated	1726
Website	www.stoughton-ma.gov

Voters & Government Information

Government type	Rep. Town Meeting
Number of Selectmen	5
US Congressional District(s)	9

Registered Voters, October 2008

Total	17,598
Democrats	6,423
Republicans	1,601
Unaffiliated/other	9,447

Local Officials, 2010

Chair, Bd. of Sel.	Lawrence Gray
Manager	Francis Crimmins Jr
Town Clerk	Cheryl Mooney
Accountant	Bill Rowe
Treas/Collector	Thomas Rorrie
Tax Assessor	Paula Keefe
Attorney	Kopelman & Paige
Public Works	John Batchelder
Building	David Tonis
Comm Dev/Planning	Joseph Laydon
Police Chief	NA
Fire Chief	David Jardin

Housing & Construction

New Privately Owned Housing Units Authorized by Building Permit

	Single Family	Total Bldgs	Total Units
2006	26	31	108
2007	21	23	32
2008	6	6	6

Parcel Count by Property Class, 2010

Total	10,430
Single family	6,505
Multiple units	368
Apartments	80
Condos	1,639
Vacant land	971
Open space	0
Commercial	485
Industrial	266
Misc. residential	26
Other use	90

Public Library

Stoughton Public Library
84 Park St.
Stoughton, MA 02072
(781)344-2711

Director	Patricia Basler

Library Statistics, FY 2008

Population served, 2007	26,951
Registered users	10,537
Circulation	174,387
Reference transactons	2,485
Total program attendance	151,197
per capita:	
Holdings	3.78
Operating income	$37.60
Internet Access	
Internet computers available	5
Weekly users	321

Municipal Finance

Debt at year end 2008	$33,107,441
Moody's rating, July 2009	A3

Revenues, 2008

Total	$67,272,409
From all taxes	46,380,819
Federal aid	386,401
State aid	16,370,151
From other governments	126,539
Charges for services	1,583,144
Licenses, permits & fees	479,701
Fines & forfeits	29,771
Interfund transfers	1,200,571
Misc/other/special assessments	357,656

Expenditures, 2008

Total	$60,169,747
General government	2,445,436
Public safety	8,134,234
Other/fixed costs	4,062,899
Human services	975,632
Culture & recreation	1,147,947
Debt Service	3,249,986
Education	34,245,030
Public works	3,290,697
Intergovernmental	2,609,988

Taxation, 2010

Property type	Valuation	Rate
Total	$3,280,858,847	-
Residential	2,572,143,074	12.46
Open space	0	0.00
Commercial	433,495,118	21.68
Industrial	174,986,695	21.68
Personal	100,233,960	21.68

Average Single Family Tax Bill, 2010

Avg. assessed home value	$300,498
Avg. single fam. tax bill	$3,744
Hi-Lo ranking	155/301

Police & Crime, 2008

Number of police officers	52
Violent crimes	88
Property crimes	500

Local School District

(school data 2007-08, except as noted)

Stoughton
232 Pearl Street
Stoughton, MA 02072
781-344-4000

Superintendent	Marguerite Rizzi
Grade plan	PK-12
Total enrollment '09-10	3,776
Grade 12 enrollment, '09-10	260
Graduation rate	87.0%
Dropout rate	6.1%
Per-pupil expenditure	$10,652
Avg teacher salary	$62,235
Student/teacher ratio '08-09	13.0 to 1
Highly-qualified teachers, '08-09	99.0%
Teachers licensed in assigned subject	98.3%
Students per computer	2.5

Massachusetts Competency Assessment System (MCAS), 2009 results

	English		Math	
	% Prof	CPI	% Prof	CPI
Gr 4	43%	75.6	49%	77.9
Gr 6	76%	90.5	66%	85.8
Gr 8	82%	93.5	55%	77.9
Gr 10	84%	94.5	75%	89.3

Other School Districts (see Appendix D for data)
Southeastern Vocational Tech, Norfolk County Agricultural

©2010 Information Publications, Inc. All rights reserved. Photocopying prohibited. For additional copies, contact the publisher at www.informationpublications.com or (877)544-INFO (4636)

See Introduction for an explanation of all data sources.

Demographics & Socio-Economic Characteristics

Population

1990	5,328
2000	5,902
Male	2,948
Female	2,954
2008	6,446
2010 (projected)††	5,837
2020 (projected)††	5,433

Race & Hispanic Origin, 2000

Race	
White	5,635
Black/African American	21
American Indian/Alaska Native	11
Asian	120
Hawaiian Native/Pacific Islander	0
Other Race	20
Two or more races	95
Hispanic origin	84

Age & Nativity, 2000

Under 5 years	510
18 years and over	4,235
21 years and over	4,109
65 years and over	485
85 years and over	48
Median Age	38.8
Native-born	5,451
Foreign-born	451

Age, 2020 (projected)††

Under 5 years	340
5 to 19 years	1,113
20 to 39 years	1,085
40 to 64 years	1,927
65 years and over	968

Educational Attainment, 2000

Population 25 years and over	3,962
High School graduates or higher	96.5%
Bachelor's degree or higher	61.9%
Graduate degree	28.0%

Income & Poverty, 1999

Per capita income,	$38,260
Median household income	$96,290
Median family income	$102,530
Persons in poverty	157
H'holds receiving public assistance	11
H'holds receiving social security	366

Households, 2000

Total households	2,082
With persons under 18	896
With persons over 65	345
Family households	1,678
Single person households	308
Persons per household	2.8
Persons per family	3.2

Labor & Employment, 2000

Civilian labor force	3,229
Unemployment rate	2.5%
Civilian labor force, 2008†	3,482
Unemployment rate†	4.9%
Civilian labor force, 12/09†	3,512
Unemployment rate†	6.8%
Employed persons 16 years and over, by occupation:	
Managers & professionals	1,952
Service occupations	277
Sales & office occupations	633
Farming, fishing & forestry	1
Construction & maintenance	133
Production & transportation	151
Self-employed persons	349

Most demographic data is from the 2000 Decennial Census
† Massachusetts Department of Revenue
†† University of Massachusetts, MISER

General Information

Town of Stow
380 Great Road
Stow, MA 01775
978-897-4514

Elevation	231 ft.
Land area (square miles)	17.6
Water area (square miles)	0.5
Population density, 2008 (est)	366.3
Year incorporated	1683
Website	www.stow-ma.gov

Voters & Government Information

Government type	Open Town Meeting
Number of Selectmen	5
US Congressional District(s)	5

Registered Voters, October 2008

Total	4,667
Democrats	1,123
Republicans	744
Unaffiliated/other	2,781

Local Officials, 2010

Chair, Bd. of Sel.	Stephen M. Dungan
Town Administrator	William J. Wrigley
Town Clerk	Linda E. Hathaway
Treasurer/Collector	Pamela Landry
Treas/Collector	Pamela Landry
Tax Assessor	Dorothy K. Wilbur
Attorney	NA
Streets Superint	Michael Clayton
Building/Zoning	Craig Martin
Planning Coordinator.	Karen Kelleher
Police Chief	Mark H. Trefry
Fire Chief	Michael McLaughlin

Housing & Construction

New Privately Owned Housing Units Authorized by Building Permit

	Single Family	Total Bldgs	Total Units
2006	43	43	43
2007	55	55	55
2008	45	45	45

Parcel Count by Property Class, 2010

Total	2,769
Single family	2,047
Multiple units	53
Apartments	5
Condos	230
Vacant land	233
Open space	0
Commercial	42
Industrial	14
Misc. residential	21
Other use	124

Public Library

Randall Library
19 Crescent Street
Stow, MA 01775
(978)897-8572

Director	Susan C. Wysk

Library Statistics, FY 2008

Population served, 2007	6,327
Registered users	4,082
Circulation	110,049
Reference transactons	0
Total program attendance	0
per capita:	
Holdings	7.64
Operating income	$34.40
Internet Access	
Internet computers available	4
Weekly users	0

Municipal Finance

Debt at year end 2008	$9,375,000
Moody's rating, July 2009	A1

Revenues, 2008

Total	$20,381,801
From all taxes	18,760,536
Federal aid	0
State aid	1,090,479
From other governments	14,033
Charges for services	222,896
Licenses, permits & fees	138,912
Fines & forfeits	8,597
Interfund transfers	20,620
Misc/other/special assessments	62,864

Expenditures, 2008

Total	$19,436,753
General government	952,238
Public safety	1,784,453
Other/fixed costs	1,087,699
Human services	244,366
Culture & recreation	255,734
Debt Service	1,065,457
Education	12,952,386
Public works	983,276
Intergovernmental	82,424

Taxation, 2010

Property type	Valuation	Rate
Total	$1,170,108,445	-
Residential	1,067,468,095	16.58
Open space	0	0.00
Commercial	55,462,300	16.58
Industrial	25,181,200	16.58
Personal	21,996,850	16.58

Average Single Family Tax Bill, 2010

Avg. assessed home value	$445,062
Avg. single fam. tax bill	$7,379
Hi-Lo ranking	28/301

Police & Crime, 2008

Number of police officers	10
Violent crimes	4
Property crimes	46

Local School District

(school data 2007-08, except as noted)

Stow (non-op)
50 Mechanic Street
Bolton, MA 01740
978-779-0539

Superintendent	Michael Wood

Non-operating district.
Resident students are sent to the Other School Districts listed below.

Grade plan	NA
Total enrollment '09-10	NA
Grade 12 enrollment, '09-10	NA
Graduation rate	NA
Dropout rate	NA
Per-pupil expenditure	NA
Avg teacher salary	NA
Student/teacher ratio '08-09	NA
Highly-qualified teachers, '08-09	NA
Teachers licensed in assigned subject	NA
Students per computer	NA

Other School Districts (see Appendix D for data)
Nashoba Regional, Minuteman Vocational Tech

©2010 Information Publications, Inc. All rights reserved. Photocopying prohibited. For additional copies, contact the publisher at www.informationpublications.com or (877)544-INFO (4636)

See Introduction for an explanation of all data sources.

Demographics & Socio-Economic Characteristics

Population

1990	7,775
2000	7,837
Male	3,857
Female	3,980
2008	9,103
2010 (projected)††	8,323
2020 (projected)††	8,847

Race & Hispanic Origin, 2000

Race	
White	7,613
Black/African American	28
American Indian/Alaska Native	21
Asian	89
Hawaiian Native/Pacific Islander	7
Other Race	24
Two or more races	55
Hispanic origin	102

Age & Nativity, 2000

Under 5 years	468
18 years and over	5,841
21 years and over	5,629
65 years and over	1,052
85 years and over	103
Median Age	39.3
Native-born	7,564
Foreign-born	273

Age, 2020 (projected)††

Under 5 years	443
5 to 19 years	1,431
20 to 39 years	1,951
40 to 64 years	3,038
65 years and over	1,984

Educational Attainment, 2000

Population 25 years and over	5,442
High School graduates or higher	87.0%
Bachelor's degree or higher	34.2%
Graduate degree	12.1%

Income & Poverty, 1999

Per capita income,	$25,559
Median household income	$56,519
Median family income	$64,455
Persons in poverty	474
H'holds receiving public assistance	40
H'holds receiving social security	798

Households, 2000

Total households	3,066
With persons under 18	1,102
With persons over 65	759
Family households	2,213
Single person households	718
Persons per household	2.6
Persons per family	3.0

Labor & Employment, 2000

Civilian labor force	4,315
Unemployment rate	2.4%
Civilian labor force, 2008†	4,966
Unemployment rate†	6.2%
Civilian labor force, 12/09†	5,169
Unemployment rate†	9.0%
Employed persons 16 years and over, by occupation:	
Managers & professionals	1,827
Service occupations	476
Sales & office occupations	1,148
Farming, fishing & forestry	0
Construction & maintenance	354
Production & transportation	408
Self-employed persons	179

Most demographic data is from the 2000 Decennial Census
† Massachusetts Department of Revenue
†† University of Massachusetts, MISER

General Information

Town of Sturbridge
308 Main St
Sturbridge, MA 01566
508-347-2510

Elevation	620 ft.
Land area (square miles)	37.4
Water area (square miles)	1.5
Population density, 2008 (est)	243.4
Year incorporated	1738
Website	www.town.sturbridge.ma.us

Voters & Government Information

Government type	Open Town Meeting
Number of Selectmen	5
US Congressional District(s)	2

Registered Voters, October 2008

Total	6,448
Democrats	1,712
Republicans	1,139
Unaffiliated/other	3,570

Local Officials, 2010

Chair, Bd. of Sel.	Mary Blanchard
Administrator	Michael Racicot (Int)
Town Clerk	Lorraine Murawski
Finance Director	Barbara Barry
Tax Collector	NA
Tax Assessor	William Mitchell
Attorney	NA
Public Works	Greg Morse
Building	Eric Wight
Comm Dev/Planning	Jean Bubon
Police Chief	Thomas Ford III
Emerg/Fire Chief	Leonard Senecal

Housing & Construction

New Privately Owned Housing Units Authorized by Building Permit

	Single Family	Total Bldgs	Total Units
2006	52	54	111
2007	26	26	26
2008	10	10	10

Parcel Count by Property Class, 2010

Total	4,456
Single family	2,968
Multiple units	86
Apartments	27
Condos	248
Vacant land	793
Open space	0
Commercial	189
Industrial	24
Misc. residential	27
Other use	94

Public Library

Joshua Hyde Public Library
306 Main St.
Sturbridge, MA 01566
(508)347-2512

Director	Ellie Chesebrough

Library Statistics, FY 2008

Population served, 2007	9,102
Registered users	4,578
Circulation	129,327
Reference transactons	0
Total program attendance	0
per capita:	
Holdings	5.89
Operating income	$45.85
Internet Access	
Internet computers available	10
Weekly users	164

Municipal Finance

Debt at year end 2008	$14,059,660
Moody's rating, July 2009	A2

Revenues, 2008

Total	$22,681,090
From all taxes	18,018,824
Federal aid	0
State aid	3,073,076
From other governments	310,539
Charges for services	313,495
Licenses, permits & fees	297,869
Fines & forfeits	19,218
Interfund transfers	1,501
Misc/other/special assessments	323,284

Expenditures, 2008

Total	$21,984,404
General government	1,184,165
Public safety	2,525,618
Other/fixed costs	1,775,639
Human services	390,546
Culture & recreation	384,103
Debt Service	268,179
Education	14,073,977
Public works	958,459
Intergovernmental	166,514

Taxation, 2010

Property type	Valuation	Rate
Total	$1,205,578,619	-
Residential	979,346,271	14.55
Open space	642,700	14.55
Commercial	148,557,249	14.55
Industrial	29,011,799	14.55
Personal	48,020,600	14.55

Average Single Family Tax Bill, 2010

Avg. assessed home value	$277,918
Avg. single fam. tax bill	$4,044
Hi-Lo ranking	133/301

Police & Crime, 2008

Number of police officers	18
Violent crimes	20
Property crimes	163

Local School District

(school data 2007-08, except as noted)

Sturbridge
320 Brookfield Rd
Fiskdale, MA 01518
508-347-3077

Superintendent	Daniel Durgin
Grade plan	PK-6
Total enrollment '09-10	920
Grade 12 enrollment, '09-10	0
Graduation rate	NA
Dropout rate	NA
Per-pupil expenditure	$12,260
Avg teacher salary	$63,142
Student/teacher ratio '08-09	13.1 to 1
Highly-qualified teachers, '08-09	100.0%
Teachers licensed in assigned subject	100.0%
Students per computer	5.1

Massachusetts Competency Assessment System (MCAS), 2009 results

	English		Math	
	% Prof	CPI	% Prof	CPI
Gr 4	62%	83.9	64%	87.9
Gr 6	79%	91.5	76%	88.6
Gr 8	NA	NA	NA	NA
Gr 10	NA	NA	NA	NA

Other School Districts (see Appendix D for data)
Tantasqua Regional

©2010 Information Publications, Inc. All rights reserved. Photocopying prohibited. For additional copies, contact the publisher at www.informationpublications.com or (877)544-INFO (4636)

See Introduction for an explanation of all data sources.

Demographics & Socio-Economic Characteristics

Population

1990	14,358
2000	16,841
Male	8,223
Female	8,618
2008	17,207
2010 (projected)††	16,753
2020 (projected)††	15,050

Race & Hispanic Origin, 2000

Race	
White	15,870
Black/African American	134
American Indian/Alaska Native	5
Asian	626
Hawaiian Native/Pacific Islander	5
Other Race	39
Two or more races	162
Hispanic origin	208

Age & Nativity, 2000

Under 5 years	1,489
18 years and over	11,365
21 years and over	11,070
65 years and over	1,653
85 years and over	214
Median Age	38.8
Native-born	15,376
Foreign-born	1,465

Age, 2020 (projected)††

Under 5 years	965
5 to 19 years	3,565
20 to 39 years	2,894
40 to 64 years	4,980
65 years and over	2,646

Educational Attainment, 2000

Population 25 years and over	10,824
High School graduates or higher	96.3%
Bachelor's degree or higher	71.9%
Graduate degree	37.5%

Income & Poverty, 1999

Per capita income,	$53,285
Median household income	$118,579
Median family income	$130,399
Persons in poverty	466
H'holds receiving public assistance	34
H'holds receiving social security	997

Households, 2000

Total households	5,504
With persons under 18	2,875
With persons over 65	1,023
Family households	4,751
Single person households	608
Persons per household	3.0
Persons per family	3.3

Labor & Employment, 2000

Civilian labor force	8,176
Unemployment rate	1.9%
Civilian labor force, 2008†	8,471
Unemployment rate†	4.4%
Civilian labor force, 12/09†	8,477
Unemployment rate†	6.5%
Employed persons 16 years and over, by occupation:	
Managers & professionals	5,592
Service occupations	457
Sales & office occupations	1,480
Farming, fishing & forestry	6
Construction & maintenance	226
Production & transportation	257
Self-employed persons	735

Most demographic data is from the 2000 Decennial Census
† Massachusetts Department of Revenue
†† University of Massachusetts, MISER

General Information

Town of Sudbury
278 Old Sudbury Rd
Sudbury, MA 01776
978-639-3381

Elevation	200 ft.
Land area (square miles)	24.4
Water area (square miles)	0.3
Population density, 2008 (est)	705.2
Year incorporated	1639
Website	www.town.sudbury.ma.us

Voters & Government Information

Government type	Open Town Meeting
Number of Selectmen	3
US Congressional District(s)	5

Registered Voters, October 2008

Total	12,045
Democrats	3,403
Republicans	2,113
Unaffiliated/other	6,485

Local Officials, 2010

Chair, Bd. of Sel.	William J. Keller Jr
Town Manager	Maureen Valente
Town Clerk	Rosemary B. Harvell
Accountant	Barbara Chisholm
Treas/Collector	Andrea Terkelsen
Tax Assessor	Maureen Hafner
Attorney	Paul Kenny
Public Works	William Place
Building	Jim Kelly
Comm Dev/Planning	Jody Kablack
Police Chief	Peter F. Fadgen
Fire Chief	Kenneth J. MacLean

Housing & Construction

New Privately Owned Housing Units Authorized by Building Permit

	Single Family	Total Bldgs	Total Units
2006	50	50	50
2007	79	79	79
2008	55	55	55

Parcel Count by Property Class, 2010

Total	NA
Single family	NA
Multiple units	NA
Apartments	NA
Condos	NA
Vacant land	NA
Open space	NA
Commercial	NA
Industrial	NA
Misc. residential	NA
Other use	NA

Public Library

Goodnow Public Library
21 Concord Rd.
Sudbury, MA 01776
(978)443-1035

Director	William R. Talentino

Library Statistics, FY 2008

Population served, 2007	17,159
Registered users	12,139
Circulation	354,754
Reference transactons	21,000
Total program attendance	0
per capita:	
Holdings	6.57
Operating income	$58.77
Internet Access	
Internet computers available	16
Weekly users	600

Municipal Finance

Debt at year end 2008	$42,040,000
Moody's rating, July 2009	Aa1

Revenues, 2008

Total	$74,750,010
From all taxes	63,431,170
Federal aid	0
State aid	8,829,339
From other governments	0
Charges for services	338,829
Licenses, permits & fees	641,210
Fines & forfeits	93,900
Interfund transfers	286,254
Misc/other/special assessments	564,654

Expenditures, 2008

Total	$67,622,854
General government	2,252,637
Public safety	6,196,032
Other/fixed costs	2,986,049
Human services	581,493
Culture & recreation	1,371,243
Debt Service	4,472,354
Education	46,295,265
Public works	3,208,727
Intergovernmental	169,420

Taxation, 2010

Property type	Valuation	Rate
Total	NA	-
Residential	NA	NA
Open space	NA	NA
Commercial	NA	NA
Industrial	NA	NA
Personal	NA	NA

Average Single Family Tax Bill, 2010

Avg. assessed home value	NA
Avg. single fam. tax bill	NA
Hi-Lo ranking	NA

Police & Crime, 2008

Number of police officers	29
Violent crimes	4
Property crimes	112

Local School District

(school data 2007-08, except as noted)

Sudbury
40 Fairbank Rd
Sudbury, MA 01776
978-639-3211

Superintendent	John Brackett
Grade plan	PK-8
Total enrollment '09-10	3,164
Grade 12 enrollment, '09-10	0
Graduation rate	NA
Dropout rate	NA
Per-pupil expenditure	$11,158
Avg teacher salary	$58,395
Student/teacher ratio '08-09	15.1 to 1
Highly-qualified teachers, '08-09	94.0%
Teachers licensed in assigned subject	99.5%
Students per computer	11

Massachusetts Competency Assessment System (MCAS), 2009 results

	English		Math	
	% Prof	CPI	% Prof	CPI
Gr 4	82%	93.8	81%	93.3
Gr 6	90%	96	85%	93.4
Gr 8	95%	98.6	75%	89.4
Gr 10	NA	NA	NA	NA

Other School Districts (see Appendix D for data)

Lincoln-Sudbury Regional, Minuteman Vocational Tech

©2010 Information Publications, Inc. All rights reserved. Photocopying prohibited. For additional copies, contact the publisher at www.informationpublications.com or (877)544-INFO (4636)

See Introduction for an explanation of all data sources.

Demographics & Socio-Economic Characteristics

Population

1990	3,399
2000	3,777
Male	1,845
Female	1,932
2008	3,710
2010 (projected)††	4,250
2020 (projected)††	4,684

Race & Hispanic Origin, 2000

Race	
White	3,353
Black/African American	89
American Indian/Alaska Native	10
Asian	243
Hawaiian Native/Pacific Islander	3
Other Race	40
Two or more races	39
Hispanic origin	89

Age & Nativity, 2000

Under 5 years	189
18 years and over	3,091
21 years and over	2,894
65 years and over	318
85 years and over	41
Median Age	29.7
Native-born	3,385
Foreign-born	402

Age, 2020 (projected)††

Under 5 years	211
5 to 19 years	558
20 to 39 years	2,033
40 to 64 years	1,242
65 years and over	640

Educational Attainment, 2000

Population 25 years and over	2,291
High School graduates or higher	94.4%
Bachelor's degree or higher	50.5%
Graduate degree	23.2%

Income & Poverty, 1999

Per capita income,	$20,024
Median household income	$37,147
Median family income	$53,021
Persons in poverty	520
H'holds receiving public assistance	26
H'holds receiving social security	233

Households, 2000

Total households	1,633
With persons under 18	383
With persons over 65	203
Family households	766
Single person households	456
Persons per household	2.3
Persons per family	2.9

Labor & Employment, 2000

Civilian labor force	2,371
Unemployment rate	4.7%
Civilian labor force, 2008†	2,455
Unemployment rate†	4.1%
Civilian labor force, 12/09†	2,377
Unemployment rate†	4.2%
Employed persons 16 years and over, by occupation:	
Managers & professionals	1,040
Service occupations	374
Sales & office occupations	506
Farming, fishing & forestry	14
Construction & maintenance	162
Production & transportation	164
Self-employed persons	159

Most demographic data is from the 2000 Decennial Census
† Massachusetts Department of Revenue
†† University of Massachusetts, MISER

General Information

Town of Sunderland
12 School St
Sunderland, MA 01375
413-665-1441

Elevation	142 ft.
Land area (square miles)	14.4
Water area (square miles)	0.4
Population density, 2008 (est)	257.6
Year incorporated	1718
Website	www.townofsunderland.us

Voters & Government Information

Government type	Open Town Meeting
Number of Selectmen	3
US Congressional District(s)	1

Registered Voters, October 2008

Total	2,526
Democrats	940
Republicans	211
Unaffiliated/other	1,340

Local Officials, 2010

Chair, Bd. of Sel.	Scott Bergeron
Manager/Admin	Margaret Nartowicz
Town Clerk	Wendy Houle
Finance Committee	Sean Randall (Chr)
Tax Collector	Herbert Sanderson Jr
Tax Assessor	James Kowaleck
Attorney	Kopelman & Paige
Public Works	George Emery
Building	Erik Wight
Comm Dev/Planning	Dana Roscoe
Police Chief	Jeffrey Gilbert
Emerg/Fire Chief	Robert Ahearn

Housing & Construction

New Privately Owned Housing Units Authorized by Building Permit

	Single Family	Total Bldgs	Total Units
2006	5	5	5
2007	5	5	5
2008	4	4	4

Parcel Count by Property Class, 2010

Total	1,434
Single family	749
Multiple units	63
Apartments	14
Condos	49
Vacant land	233
Open space	0
Commercial	55
Industrial	20
Misc. residential	1
Other use	250

Public Library

Sunderland Public Library
20 School Street
Sunderland, MA 01375
(413)665-2642

Director	Sheila McCormick

Library Statistics, FY 2008

Population served, 2007	3,721
Registered users	2,350
Circulation	60,754
Reference transactons	465
Total program attendance	49,674
per capita:	
Holdings	9.51
Operating income	$35.35
Internet Access	
Internet computers available	17
Weekly users	0

Municipal Finance

Debt at year end 2008	$6,770,150
Moody's rating, July 2009	NA

Revenues, 2008

Total	$6,836,414
From all taxes	4,578,241
Federal aid	20,632
State aid	1,713,411
From other governments	6,299
Charges for services	31,472
Licenses, permits & fees	44,972
Fines & forfeits	27,598
Interfund transfers	292,787
Misc/other/special assessments	60,501

Expenditures, 2008

Total	$6,786,721
General government	533,028
Public safety	534,059
Other/fixed costs	487,147
Human services	12,597
Culture & recreation	124,989
Debt Service	740,568
Education	3,704,314
Public works	527,684
Intergovernmental	122,335

Taxation, 2010

Property type	Valuation	Rate
Total	$341,610,453	-
Residential	304,465,519	12.66
Open space	0	0.00
Commercial	24,343,484	12.66
Industrial	5,063,800	12.66
Personal	7,737,650	12.66

Average Single Family Tax Bill, 2010

Avg. assessed home value	$276,988
Avg. single fam. tax bill	$3,507
Hi-Lo ranking	171/301

Police & Crime, 2008

Number of police officers	5
Violent crimes	14
Property crimes	43

Local School District

(school data 2007-08, except as noted)
Sunderland
219 Christian Ln RFD1
South Deerfield, MA 01373
413-665-1155

Superintendent	Regina Nash
Grade plan	PK-6
Total enrollment '09-10	186
Grade 12 enrollment, '09-10	0
Graduation rate	NA
Dropout rate	NA
Per-pupil expenditure	$12,414
Avg teacher salary	$51,643
Student/teacher ratio '08-09	10.9 to 1
Highly-qualified teachers, '08-09	100.0%
Teachers licensed in assigned subject	100.0%
Students per computer	3.3

Massachusetts Competency Assessment System (MCAS), 2009 results

	English		Math	
	% Prof	CPI	% Prof	CPI
Gr 4	55%	78.8	75%	90
Gr 6	74%	91.1	58%	79.8
Gr 8	NA	NA	NA	NA
Gr 10	NA	NA	NA	NA

Other School Districts (see Appendix D for data)
Frontier Regional, Franklin County Vocational Tech

©2010 Information Publications, Inc. All rights reserved. Photocopying prohibited. For additional copies, contact the publisher at www.informationpublications.com or (877)544-INFO (4636)

Demographics & Socio-Economic Characteristics

Population

1990	6,824
2000	8,250
Male	4,111
Female	4,139
2008	9,028
2010 (projected)††	9,067
2020 (projected)††	9,836

Race & Hispanic Origin, 2000

Race	
White	8,100
Black/African American	23
American Indian/Alaska Native	11
Asian	49
Hawaiian Native/Pacific Islander	0
Other Race	22
Two or more races	45
Hispanic origin	58

Age & Nativity, 2000

Under 5 years	629
18 years and over	5,821
21 years and over	5,595
65 years and over	670
85 years and over	63
Median Age	36.5
Native-born	8,045
Foreign-born	205

Age, 2020 (projected)††

Under 5 years	640
5 to 19 years	1,928
20 to 39 years	2,414
40 to 64 years	3,419
65 years and over	1,435

Educational Attainment, 2000

Population 25 years and over	5,356
High School graduates or higher	90.4%
Bachelor's degree or higher	36.0%
Graduate degree	13.3%

Income & Poverty, 1999

Per capita income,	$27,490
Median household income	$75,141
Median family income	$81,000
Persons in poverty	360
H'holds receiving public assistance	41
H'holds receiving social security	602

Households, 2000

Total households	2,811
With persons under 18	1,260
With persons over 65	503
Family households	2,283
Single person households	421
Persons per household	2.9
Persons per family	3.3

Labor & Employment, 2000

Civilian labor force	4,472
Unemployment rate	3.1%
Civilian labor force, 2008†	4,877
Unemployment rate†	6.0%
Civilian labor force, 12/09†	4,969
Unemployment rate†	8.4%
Employed persons 16 years and over, by occupation:	
Managers & professionals	2,026
Service occupations	474
Sales & office occupations	1,059
Farming, fishing & forestry	0
Construction & maintenance	305
Production & transportation	468
Self-employed persons	303

Most demographic data is from the 2000 Decennial Census
† Massachusetts Department of Revenue
†† University of Massachusetts, MISER

General Information

Town of Sutton
4 Uxbridge Rd
Sutton, MA 01590
508-865-8727

Elevation	706 ft.
Land area (square miles)	32.4
Water area (square miles)	1.6
Population density, 2008 (est)	278.6
Year incorporated	1714
Website	www.suttonma.org

Voters & Government Information

Government type	Open Town Meeting
Number of Selectmen	5
US Congressional District(s)	2

Registered Voters, October 2008

Total	6,724
Democrats	1,279
Republicans	937
Unaffiliated/other	4,479

Local Officials, 2010

Chair, Bd. of Sel.	John L. Hebert
Manager/Admin	James Smith
Clerk	Laura Rodgers
Finance Director	Cheryl Ouillette
Tax Collector	Cheryl Ouillette
Tax Assessor	Joyce Sardagnola
Attorney	NA
Public Works	Mark Brigham
Building	John Couture
Planning	Jennifer Hager
Police Chief	Dennis Towle
Emerg/Fire Chief	Paul Maynard

Housing & Construction

New Privately Owned Housing Units Authorized by Building Permit

	Single Family	Total Bldgs	Total Units
2006	34	34	34
2007	24	24	24
2008	15	15	15

Parcel Count by Property Class, 2010

Total	4,413
Single family	2,818
Multiple units	94
Apartments	12
Condos	291
Vacant land	784
Open space	0
Commercial	106
Industrial	95
Misc. residential	30
Other use	183

Public Library

Sutton Free Public Library
4 Uxbridge Rd.
Sutton, MA 01590
(508)865-8752

Director ... Roberta Rothwell

Library Statistics, FY 2008

Population served, 2007	9,015
Registered users	3,008
Circulation	54,324
Reference transactons	832
Total program attendance	26,310
per capita:	
Holdings	3.43
Operating income	$20.86
Internet Access	
Internet computers available	4
Weekly users	70

Municipal Finance

Debt at year end 2008	$23,850,561
Moody's rating, July 2009	A2

Revenues, 2008

Total	$26,970,565
From all taxes	15,695,250
Federal aid	0
State aid	7,656,689
From other governments	0
Charges for services	235,368
Licenses, permits & fees	77,560
Fines & forfeits	0
Interfund transfers	207,640
Misc/other/special assessments	1,549,029

Expenditures, 2008

Total	$23,855,918
General government	1,148,993
Public safety	1,919,256
Other/fixed costs	2,385,883
Human services	261,729
Culture & recreation	172,543
Debt Service	3,377,151
Education	13,698,224
Public works	803,981
Intergovernmental	71,266

Taxation, 2010

Property type	Valuation	Rate
Total	$1,268,737,786	-
Residential	1,138,367,051	12.32
Open space	0	0.00
Commercial	60,269,239	12.32
Industrial	36,163,200	12.32
Personal	33,938,296	12.32

Average Single Family Tax Bill, 2010

Avg. assessed home value	$340,638
Avg. single fam. tax bill	$4,197
Hi-Lo ranking	121/301

Police & Crime, 2008

Number of police officers	15
Violent crimes	11
Property crimes	82

Local School District

(school data 2007-08, except as noted)

Sutton
383 Boston Rd
Sutton, MA 01590
508-581-1600

Superintendent	Cecilia Di Bella
Grade plan	PK-12
Total enrollment '09-10	1,643
Grade 12 enrollment, '09-10	99
Graduation rate	87.2%
Dropout rate	6.4%
Per-pupil expenditure	$9,739
Avg teacher salary	$63,251
Student/teacher ratio '08-09	14.7 to 1
Highly-qualified teachers, '08-09	93.5%
Teachers licensed in assigned subject	96.5%
Students per computer	2.2

Massachusetts Competency Assessment System (MCAS), 2009 results

	English		Math	
	% Prof	CPI	% Prof	CPI
Gr 4	59%	84.7	54%	81.9
Gr 6	68%	87.1	72%	86.9
Gr 8	88%	95.6	67%	84.6
Gr 10	94%	98	87%	94.4

Other School Districts (see Appendix D for data)
Blackstone Valley Vocational Tech

©2010 Information Publications, Inc. All rights reserved. Photocopying prohibited. For additional copies, contact the publisher at www.informationpublications.com or (877)544-INFO (4636)

See Introduction for an explanation of all data sources.

Demographics & Socio-Economic Characteristics

Population

1990	13,650
2000	14,412
Male	6,685
Female	7,727
2008	13,944
2010 (projected)††	14,087
2020 (projected)††	13,463

Race & Hispanic Origin, 2000

Race	
White	14,047
Black/African American	106
American Indian/Alaska Native	9
Asian	98
Hawaiian Native/Pacific Islander	3
Other Race	41
Two or more races	108
Hispanic origin	183

Age & Nativity, 2000

Under 5 years	920
18 years and over	10,959
21 years and over	10,651
65 years and over	2,549
85 years and over	510
Median Age	41.5
Native-born	13,239
Foreign-born	1,173

Age, 2020 (projected)††

Under 5 years	670
5 to 19 years	2,299
20 to 39 years	2,991
40 to 64 years	4,528
65 years and over	2,975

Educational Attainment, 2000

Population 25 years and over	10,214
High School graduates or higher	94.8%
Bachelor's degree or higher	50.2%
Graduate degree	21.2%

Income & Poverty, 1999

Per capita income,	$35,487
Median household income	$71,089
Median family income	$82,795
Persons in poverty	517
H'holds receiving public assistance	72
H'holds receiving social security	1,674

Households, 2000

Total households	5,719
With persons under 18	1,981
With persons over 65	1,718
Family households	3,989
Single person households	1,484
Persons per household	2.5
Persons per family	3.0

Labor & Employment, 2000

Civilian labor force	7,634
Unemployment rate	2.0%
Civilian labor force, 2008†	7,679
Unemployment rate†	5.4%
Civilian labor force, 12/09†	7,606
Unemployment rate†	8.0%
Employed persons 16 years and over, by occupation:	
Managers & professionals	3,914
Service occupations	694
Sales & office occupations	2,060
Farming, fishing & forestry	37
Construction & maintenance	354
Production & transportation	426
Self-employed persons	665

Most demographic data is from the 2000 Decennial Census
† Massachusetts Department of Revenue
†† University of Massachusetts, MISER

General Information

Town of Swampscott
22 Monument Ave
Swampscott, MA 01907
781-596-8850

Elevation	50 ft.
Land area (square miles)	3.0
Water area (square miles)	3.7
Population density, 2008 (est)	4,648.0
Year incorporated	1852
Website	www.town.swampscott.ma.us

Voters & Government Information

Government type	Rep. Town Meeting
Number of Selectmen	5
US Congressional District(s)	6

Registered Voters, October 2008

Total	10,247
Democrats	3,538
Republicans	1,136
Unaffiliated/other	5,549

Local Officials, 2010

Chair, Bd. of Sel.	Jill G. Sullivan
Town Administrator	Andrew Maylor
Town Clerk	Susan J. Duplin
Accountant	Dave Castellarin
Treas/Collector	Denise Dembkoski
Tax Assessor	Donna Champagne O'Keefe
Attorney	Thomas McEnaney
Public Works	Gino Cresta
Building	Alan Hezekiah
Comm Dev/Planning	NA
Police Chief	Ronald Madigan
Fire Chief	Michael Champion

Housing & Construction

New Privately Owned Housing Units Authorized by Building Permit

	Single Family	Total Bldgs	Total Units
2006	3	3	3
2007	5	7	10
2008	3	3	3

Parcel Count by Property Class, 2010

Total	5,448
Single family	3,421
Multiple units	510
Apartments	14
Condos	985
Vacant land	343
Open space	0
Commercial	91
Industrial	26
Misc. residential	11
Other use	47

Public Library

Swampscott Public Library
61 Burrill St.
Swampscott, MA 01907
(781)596-8867

Director	Alyce Deveau

Library Statistics, FY 2008

Population served, 2007	13,994
Registered users	10,386
Circulation	176,725
Reference transactons	6,565
Total program attendance	70,772
per capita:	
Holdings	6.61
Operating income	$43.03
Internet Access	
Internet computers available	16
Weekly users	338

Municipal Finance

Debt at year end 2008	$51,332,517
Moody's rating, July 2009	Aa3

Revenues, 2008

Total	$47,097,246
From all taxes	39,008,812
Federal aid	0
State aid	4,622,667
From other governments	1,285,120
Charges for services	574,747
Licenses, permits & fees	176,160
Fines & forfeits	91,634
Interfund transfers	650,000
Misc/other/special assessments	344,053

Expenditures, 2008

Total	$47,046,826
General government	1,773,718
Public safety	5,854,727
Other/fixed costs	7,462,800
Human services	1,307,624
Culture & recreation	580,922
Debt Service	6,580,748
Education	21,573,700
Public works	1,066,946
Intergovernmental	845,641

Taxation, 2010

Property type	Valuation	Rate
Total	$2,298,779,232	-
Residential	2,137,083,093	16.48
Open space	0	0.00
Commercial	117,564,459	30.58
Industrial	13,000,300	30.58
Personal	31,131,380	30.58

Average Single Family Tax Bill, 2010

Avg. assessed home value	$475,930
Avg. single fam. tax bill	$7,843
Hi-Lo ranking	23/301

Police & Crime, 2008

Number of police officers	33
Violent crimes	14
Property crimes	245

Local School District

(school data 2007-08, except as noted)

Swampscott
207 Forest Avenue
Swampscott, MA 01907
781-596-8800

Superintendent	Maureen Bingham
Grade plan	PK-12
Total enrollment '09-10	2,256
Grade 12 enrollment, '09-10	211
Graduation rate	93.8%
Dropout rate	2.2%
Per-pupil expenditure	$11,802
Avg teacher salary	$65,007
Student/teacher ratio '08-09	13.2 to 1
Highly-qualified teachers, '08-09	96.6%
Teachers licensed in assigned subject	96.9%
Students per computer	2.9

Massachusetts Competency Assessment System (MCAS), 2009 results

	English		Math	
	% Prof	CPI	% Prof	CPI
Gr 4	73%	90.1	54%	84
Gr 6	78%	91	69%	83.6
Gr 8	90%	96.5	55%	76.9
Gr 10	92%	96.6	84%	93.7

Other School Districts (see Appendix D for data)
Receives students from Nahant; sends to North Shore Vocational Tech

©2010 Information Publications, Inc. All rights reserved. Photocopying prohibited. For additional copies, contact the publisher at www.informationpublications.com or (877)544-INFO (4636)

See Introduction for an explanation of all data sources.

©2010 Information Publications, Inc. All rights reserved. Photocopying prohibited. For additional copies, contact the publisher at www.informationpublications.com or (877)544-INFO (4636)

Demographics & Socio-Economic Characteristics

Population

1990 ... 15,411
2000 ... 15,901
  Male ... 7,825
  Female ... 8,076
2008 ... 16,155
2010 (projected)†† ... 15,286
2020 (projected)†† ... 14,454

Race & Hispanic Origin, 2000

Race
  White ... 15,569
  Black/African American ... 60
  American Indian/Alaska Native ... 12
  Asian ... 57
  Hawaiian Native/Pacific Islander ... 1
  Other Race ... 43
  Two or more races ... 159
Hispanic origin ... 96

Age & Nativity, 2000

Under 5 years ... 750
18 years and over ... 12,371
21 years and over ... 11,839
65 years and over ... 2,499
85 years and over ... 281
  Median Age ... 40.5
Native-born ... 14,607
Foreign-born ... 1,294

Age, 2020 (projected)††

Under 5 years ... 570
5 to 19 years ... 2,115
20 to 39 years ... 2,987
40 to 64 years ... 5,217
65 years and over ... 3,565

Educational Attainment, 2000

Population 25 years and over ... 11,306
  High School graduates or higher ... 76.4%
  Bachelor's degree or higher ... 17.6%
  Graduate degree ... 5.5%

Income & Poverty, 1999

Per capita income, ... $21,776
Median household income ... $52,524
Median family income ... $60,567
Persons in poverty ... 774
H'holds receiving public assistance ... 169
H'holds receiving social security ... 2,033

Households, 2000

Total households ... 5,888
  With persons under 18 ... 2,013
  With persons over 65 ... 1,715
  Family households ... 4,540
  Single person households ... 1,155
Persons per household ... 2.7
Persons per family ... 3.1

Labor & Employment, 2000

Civilian labor force ... 8,699
  Unemployment rate ... 3.4%
Civilian labor force, 2008† ... 9,263
  Unemployment rate† ... 9.2%
Civilian labor force, 12/09† ... 9,341
  Unemployment rate† ... 12.4%
Employed persons 16 years and over, by occupation:
  Managers & professionals ... 2,676
  Service occupations ... 1,253
  Sales & office occupations ... 2,227
  Farming, fishing & forestry ... 14
  Construction & maintenance ... 966
  Production & transportation ... 1,265
  Self-employed persons ... 396

Most demographic data is from the 2000 Decennial Census
† Massachusetts Department of Revenue
†† University of Massachusetts, MISER

General Information

Town of Swansea
81 Main St
Swansea, MA 02777
508-678-2981

Elevation ... 42 ft.
Land area (square miles) ... 23.1
Water area (square miles) ... 2.5
Population density, 2008 (est) ... 699.4
Year incorporated ... 1667
Website ... NA

Voters & Government Information

Government type ... Open Town Meeting
Number of Selectmen ... 3
US Congressional District(s) ... 3

Registered Voters, October 2008

Total ... 11,994
Democrats ... 4,103
Republicans ... 1,194
Unaffiliated/other ... 6,642

Local Officials, 2010

Chair, Bd. of Sel. ... Kenneth D. Furtado
Manager/Admin ... James Kern
Town Clerk ... Susan E. Taveira
Finance Director ... Elizabeth B. Leonardo
Tax Collector ... Elizabeth B. Leonardo
Tax Assessor ... Madlon Jenkins-Rudziak
Attorney ... Arthur Frank
Public Works ... Moe Pukulis
Building ... David Betts
Comm Dev/Planning ... Steve Antinelli
Police Chief ... George Arruda
Emerg/Fire Chief ... Peter Burke

Housing & Construction

New Privately Owned Housing Units Authorized by Building Permit

	Single Family	Total Bldgs	Total Units
2006	47	51	71
2007	32	32	32
2008	23	23	23

Parcel Count by Property Class, 2010

Total ... 7,247
Single family ... 5,562
Multiple units ... 160
Apartments ... 11
Condos ... 28
Vacant land ... 981
Open space ... 0
Commercial ... 241
Industrial ... 28
Misc. residential ... 82
Other use ... 154

Public Library

Swansea Free Public Library
69 Main St.
Swansea, MA 02777
(508)674-9609

Director ... J. Kevin Lawton

Library Statistics, FY 2008

Population served, 2007 ... 16,237
Registered users ... 5,504
Circulation ... 81,180
Reference transactons ... 0
Total program attendance ... 0

per capita:

Holdings ... 3.99
Operating income ... $15.48

Internet Access

Internet computers available ... 10
Weekly users ... 90

Municipal Finance

Debt at year end 2008 ... $4,112,676
Moody's rating, July 2009 ... A3

Revenues, 2008

Total ... $31,495,387
From all taxes ... 22,065,704
Federal aid ... 63,561
State aid ... 8,214,688
From other governments ... 90,835
Charges for services ... 138,984
Licenses, permits & fees ... 319,517
Fines & forfeits ... 0
Interfund transfers ... 124,468
Misc/other/special assessments ... 238,815

Expenditures, 2008

Total ... $30,684,577
General government ... 1,244,456
Public safety ... 3,270,095
Other/fixed costs ... 5,721,032
Human services ... 478,801
Culture & recreation ... 285,421
Debt Service ... 744,961
Education ... 17,328,036
Public works ... 1,235,351
Intergovernmental ... 376,424

Taxation, 2010

Property type	Valuation	Rate
Total	$2,076,942,527	-
Residential	1,756,920,399	9.48
Open space	0	0.00
Commercial	251,293,588	19.21
Industrial	13,774,800	19.21
Personal	54,953,740	19.21

Average Single Family Tax Bill, 2010

Avg. assessed home value ... $280,209
Avg. single fam. tax bill ... $2,656
Hi-Lo ranking ... 271/301

Police & Crime, 2008

Number of police officers ... 31
Violent crimes ... 49
Property crimes ... 306

Local School District

(school data 2007-08, except as noted)

Swansea
1 Gardners Neck Road
Swansea, MA 02777
508-675-1195

Superintendent ... Christine Stanton
Grade plan ... PK-12
Total enrollment '09-10 ... 2,078
Grade 12 enrollment, '09-10 ... 135
Graduation rate ... 89.2%
Dropout rate ... 3.8%
Per-pupil expenditure ... $10,562
Avg teacher salary ... $55,820
Student/teacher ratio '08-09 ... 14.3 to 1
Highly-qualified teachers, '08-09 ... 100.0%
Teachers licensed in assigned subject ... 100.0%
Students per computer ... 4

Massachusetts Competency Assessment System (MCAS), 2009 results

	English		Math	
	% Prof	CPI	% Prof	CPI
Gr 4	48%	80.1	41%	81
Gr 6	60%	85.6	52%	76.8
Gr 8	75%	90.3	38%	69.4
Gr 10	87%	95.5	83%	92.4

Other School Districts (see Appendix D for data)

Greater Fall River Vocational Tech, Bristol County Agricultural

See Introduction for an explanation of all data sources.

Demographics & Socio-Economic Characteristics*

Population

1990	49,832
2000	55,976
Male	26,904
Female	29,072
2008	55,702
2010 (projected)††	62,222
2020 (projected)††	69,493

Race & Hispanic Origin, 2000

Race	
White	51,315
Black/African American	1,534
American Indian/Alaska Native	92
Asian	334
Hawaiian Native/Pacific Islander	18
Other Race	1,448
Two or more races	1,235
Hispanic origin	2,198

Age & Nativity, 2000

Under 5 years	3,977
18 years and over	42,057
21 years and over	40,195
65 years and over	7,217
85 years and over	913
Median Age	35.7
Native-born	50,337
Foreign-born	5,639

Age, 2020 (projected)††

Under 5 years	4,453
5 to 19 years	12,666
20 to 39 years	18,891
40 to 64 years	23,139
65 years and over	10,344

Educational Attainment, 2000

Population 25 years and over	37,856
High School graduates or higher	74.8%
Bachelor's degree or higher	15.1%
Graduate degree	4.4%

Income & Poverty, 1999

Per capita income,	$19,899
Median household income	$42,932
Median family income	$52,433
Persons in poverty	5,552
H'holds receiving public assistance	826
H'holds receiving social security	5,674

Households, 2000

Total households	22,045
With persons under 18	7,736
With persons over 65	5,168
Family households	14,476
Single person households	6,208
Persons per household	2.5
Persons per family	3.1

Labor & Employment, 2000

Civilian labor force	29,655
Unemployment rate	4.3%
Civilian labor force, 2008†	31,397
Unemployment rate†	7.7%
Civilian labor force, 12/09†	30,875
Unemployment rate†	10.3%
Employed persons 16 years and over, by occupation:	
Managers & professionals	7,458
Service occupations	4,680
Sales & office occupations	7,815
Farming, fishing & forestry	48
Construction & maintenance	2,778
Production & transportation	5,612
Self-employed persons	1,225

Most demographic data is from the 2000 Decennial Census
* see Appendix E for American Community Survey data
† Massachusetts Department of Revenue
†† University of Massachusetts, MISER

General Information

City of Taunton
15 Summer St
Taunton, MA 02780
508-821-1024

Elevation	43 ft.
Land area (square miles)	46.6
Water area (square miles)	1.4
Population density, 2008 (est)	1,195.3
Year incorporated	1639
Website	www.ci.taunton.ma.us

Voters & Government Information

Government type	Mayor-Council
Number of Councilpersons	9
US Congressional District(s)	4

Registered Voters, October 2008

Total	33,316
Democrats	11,856
Republicans	2,746
Unaffiliated/other	18,471

Local Officials, 2010

Mayor	Charles Crowley
Manager/Admin	NA
City Clerk	Rose Marie Blackwell
Auditor	Ann Hebert
Treas/Collector	Jayne Ross
Tax Assessor	Barry Cooperstein
Attorney	Jane Estey
Public Works	Fred Cornaglia
Building	Wayne Walkden
Comm Dev/Planning	Kevin Shea
Police Chief	John Reardon (Actg)
Fire Chief	Ronald Nastri (Int)

Housing & Construction

New Privately Owned Housing Units Authorized by Building Permit

	Single Family	Total Bldgs	Total Units
2006	89	102	119
2007	68	82	100
2008	43	47	51

Parcel Count by Property Class, 2010

Total	NA
Single family	NA
Multiple units	NA
Apartments	NA
Condos	NA
Vacant land	NA
Open space	NA
Commercial	NA
Industrial	NA
Misc. residential	NA
Other use	NA

Public Library

Taunton Public Library
12 Pleasant Street
Taunton, MA 02780
(508)821-1410

Director	Susanne C. Duquette

Library Statistics, FY 2008

Population served, 2007	55,783
Registered users	26,358
Circulation	201,652
Reference transactons	62,515
Total program attendance	0
per capita:	
Holdings	4.01
Operating income	$21.46
Internet Access	
Internet computers available	22
Weekly users	1,719

Municipal Finance

Debt at year end 2008	$78,596,766
Moody's rating, July 2009	A3

Revenues, 2008

Total	$156,918,154
From all taxes	68,939,748
Federal aid	0
State aid	58,868,590
From other governments	155,620
Charges for services	9,926,387
Licenses, permits & fees	1,118,711
Fines & forfeits	121,305
Interfund transfers	12,782,441
Misc/other/special assessments	2,502,676

Expenditures, 2008

Total	$134,535,100
General government	5,465,474
Public safety	21,011,578
Other/fixed costs	21,673,149
Human services	2,081,585
Culture & recreation	2,224,724
Debt Service	7,155,760
Education	63,618,768
Public works	9,802,010
Intergovernmental	1,420,230

Taxation, 2010

Property type	Valuation	Rate
Total	NA	-
Residential	NA	NA
Open space	NA	NA
Commercial	NA	NA
Industrial	NA	NA
Personal	NA	NA

Average Single Family Tax Bill, 2010

Avg. assessed home value	NA
Avg. single fam. tax bill	NA
Hi-Lo ranking	NA

Police & Crime, 2008

Number of police officers	113
Violent crimes	305
Property crimes	1,267

Local School District

(school data 2007-08, except as noted)

Taunton
110 County Street
Taunton, MA 02780
508-821-1201

Superintendent	Julie Hackett
Grade plan	PK-12
Total enrollment '09-10	7,920
Grade 12 enrollment, '09-10	377
Graduation rate	73.1%
Dropout rate	17.2%
Per-pupil expenditure	$10,474
Avg teacher salary	$63,800
Student/teacher ratio '08-09	15.5 to 1
Highly-qualified teachers, '08-09	98.0%
Teachers licensed in assigned subject	97.6%
Students per computer	3.3

Massachusetts Competency Assessment System (MCAS), 2009 results

	English		Math	
	% Prof	CPI	% Prof	CPI
Gr 4	55%	85.7	54%	84.9
Gr 6	66%	87.3	50%	77.5
Gr 8	74%	90.5	38%	68.5
Gr 10	79%	91.7	70%	87.4

Other School Districts (see Appendix D for data)
Bristol-Plymouth Vocational Tech, Bristol County Agricultural

©2010 Information Publications, Inc. All rights reserved. Photocopying prohibited. For additional copies, contact the publisher at www.informationpublications.com or (877)544-INFO (4636)

See Introduction for an explanation of all data sources.

Demographics & Socio-Economic Characteristics

Population

1990	6,438
2000	6,799
Male	3,417
Female	3,382
2008	7,831
2010 (projected)††	7,096
2020 (projected)††	7,362

Race & Hispanic Origin, 2000

Race	
White	6,673
Black/African American	24
American Indian/Alaska Native	15
Asian	19
Hawaiian Native/Pacific Islander	0
Other Race	29
Two or more races	39
Hispanic origin	98

Age & Nativity, 2000

Under 5 years	457
18 years and over	5,022
21 years and over	4,843
65 years and over	875
85 years and over	105
Median Age	38.0
Native-born	6,697
Foreign-born	102

Age, 2020 (projected)††

Under 5 years	427
5 to 19 years	1,342
20 to 39 years	1,656
40 to 64 years	2,641
65 years and over	1,296

Educational Attainment, 2000

Population 25 years and over	4,575
High School graduates or higher	79.4%
Bachelor's degree or higher	13.6%
Graduate degree	4.5%

Income & Poverty, 1999

Per capita income,	$21,994
Median household income	$48,482
Median family income	$52,936
Persons in poverty	588
H'holds receiving public assistance	42
H'holds receiving social security	639

Households, 2000

Total households	2,411
With persons under 18	928
With persons over 65	567
Family households	1,809
Single person households	474
Persons per household	2.7
Persons per family	3.1

Labor & Employment, 2000

Civilian labor force	3,454
Unemployment rate	4.9%
Civilian labor force, 2008†	3,810
Unemployment rate†	9.4%
Civilian labor force, 12/09†	3,822
Unemployment rate†	12.2%
Employed persons 16 years and over, by occupation:	
Managers & professionals	975
Service occupations	451
Sales & office occupations	1,000
Farming, fishing & forestry	10
Construction & maintenance	416
Production & transportation	434
Self-employed persons	237

Most demographic data is from the 2000 Decennial Census
† Massachusetts Department of Revenue
†† University of Massachusetts, MISER

General Information

Town of Templeton
690 Patriots Rd
Templeton, MA 01468
978-939-8801

Elevation	1,141 ft.
Land area (square miles)	32.0
Water area (square miles)	0.4
Population density, 2008 (est)	244.7
Year incorporated	1785
Website	templeton1.org

Voters & Government Information

Government type	Open Town Meeting
Number of Selectmen	5
US Congressional District(s)	1

Registered Voters, October 2008

Total	5,028
Democrats	1,180
Republicans	600
Unaffiliated/other	3,205

Local Officials, 2010

Chair, Bd. of Sel.	Gerald Skelton
Town Coordinator	Carol Skelton
Town Clerk	Carol A. Harris
Finance Director	Tammy Coller
Tax Collector	Carolee Eaton
Tax Assessor	Fred Henshaw
Attorney	Kopelman & Paige
Public Works	NA
Building	Larry Brandt
Comm Dev/Planning	NA
Police Chief	David Whitaker
Emerg/Fire Chief	Thomas Smith

Housing & Construction

New Privately Owned Housing Units Authorized by Building Permit

	Single Family	Total Bldgs	Total Units
2006	57	64	77
2007	33	35	39
2008	14	15	17

Parcel Count by Property Class, 2010

Total	3,948
Single family	2,387
Multiple units	117
Apartments	15
Condos	126
Vacant land	842
Open space	0
Commercial	226
Industrial	80
Misc. residential	60
Other use	95

Public Library

Boynton Public Library
PO Box 296
Templeton, MA 01468
(978)939-5582

Director	Jacqueline Prime

Library Statistics, FY 2008

Population served, 2007	7,783
Registered users	1,800
Circulation	24,150
Reference transactons	350
Total program attendance	0
per capita:	
Holdings	3.01
Operating income	$8.38
Internet Access	
Internet computers available	3
Weekly users	25

Municipal Finance

Debt at year end 2008	$15,971,486
Moody's rating, July 2009	A3

Revenues, 2008

Total	$11,694,033
From all taxes	8,071,377
Federal aid	0
State aid	1,700,614
From other governments	170,562
Charges for services	377,094
Licenses, permits & fees	203,827
Fines & forfeits	0
Interfund transfers	1,170,559
Misc/other/special assessments	0

Expenditures, 2008

Total	$10,977,371
General government	989,241
Public safety	1,417,043
Other/fixed costs	930,093
Human services	169,552
Culture & recreation	75,207
Debt Service	1,446,973
Education	4,785,171
Public works	1,120,660
Intergovernmental	43,431

Taxation, 2010

Property type	Valuation	Rate
Total	$616,456,474	-
Residential	550,021,477	11.75
Open space	0	0.00
Commercial	36,887,365	11.75
Industrial	19,263,300	11.75
Personal	10,284,332	11.75

Average Single Family Tax Bill, 2010

Avg. assessed home value	$189,512
Avg. single fam. tax bill	$2,227
Hi-Lo ranking	289/301

Police & Crime, 2008

Number of police officers	10
Violent crimes	14
Property crimes	100

Local School District

(school data 2007-08, except as noted)

Templeton (non-op)
4 Elm Street
Baldwinville, MA 01436
978-939-5661

Superintendent	Stephen Hemman

Non-operating district.
Resident students are sent to the Other School Districts listed below.

Grade plan	NA
Total enrollment '09-10	NA
Grade 12 enrollment, '09-10	NA
Graduation rate	NA
Dropout rate	NA
Per-pupil expenditure	NA
Avg teacher salary	NA
Student/teacher ratio '08-09	NA
Highly-qualified teachers, '08-09	NA
Teachers licensed in assigned subject	NA
Students per computer	NA

Other School Districts (see Appendix D for data)
Narragansett Regional, Montachusett Vocational Tech

©2010 Information Publications, Inc. All rights reserved. Photocopying prohibited. For additional copies, contact the publisher at www.informationpublications.com or (877)544-INFO (4636)

See Introduction for an explanation of all data sources.

Demographics & Socio-Economic Characteristics

Population

1990	27,266
2000	28,851
Male	14,141
Female	14,710
2008	29,543
2010 (projected)††	29,641
2020 (projected)††	30,002

Race & Hispanic Origin, 2000

Race	
White	27,824
Black/African American	194
American Indian/Alaska Native	36
Asian	460
Hawaiian Native/Pacific Islander	2
Other Race	118
Two or more races	217
Hispanic origin	352

Age & Nativity, 2000

Under 5 years	2,020
18 years and over	21,638
21 years and over	20,812
65 years and over	3,311
85 years and over	316
Median Age	37.6
Native-born	27,212
Foreign-born	1,675

Age, 2020 (projected)††

Under 5 years	1,658
5 to 19 years	4,955
20 to 39 years	7,081
40 to 64 years	10,374
65 years and over	5,934

Educational Attainment, 2000

Population 25 years and over	19,882
High School graduates or higher	87.9%
Bachelor's degree or higher	25.2%
Graduate degree	8.4%

Income & Poverty, 1999

Per capita income,	$27,031
Median household income	$68,800
Median family income	$76,443
Persons in poverty	1,074
H'holds receiving public assistance	162
H'holds receiving social security	2,446

Households, 2000

Total households	9,964
With persons under 18	3,896
With persons over 65	2,204
Family households	7,695
Single person households	1,880
Persons per household	2.8
Persons per family	3.2

Labor & Employment, 2000

Civilian labor force	15,923
Unemployment rate	2.0%
Civilian labor force, 2008†	16,779
Unemployment rate†	6.1%
Civilian labor force, 12/09†	16,640
Unemployment rate†	8.5%
Employed persons 16 years and over, by occupation:	
Managers & professionals	6,101
Service occupations	1,666
Sales & office occupations	4,355
Farming, fishing & forestry	22
Construction & maintenance	1,770
Production & transportation	1,697
Self-employed persons	753

Most demographic data is from the 2000 Decennial Census
† Massachusetts Department of Revenue
†† University of Massachusetts, MISER

General Information

Town of Tewksbury
1009 Main St
Tewksbury, MA 01876
978-640-4300

Elevation	120 ft.
Land area (square miles)	20.7
Water area (square miles)	0.3
Population density, 2008 (est)	1,427.2
Year incorporated	1734
Website	tewksburyma.virtualtownhall.net

Voters & Government Information

Government type	Open Town Meeting
Number of Selectmen	5
US Congressional District(s)	5

Registered Voters, October 2008

Total	19,986
Democrats	6,234
Republicans	2,315
Unaffiliated/other	11,341

Local Officials, 2010

Chair, Bd. of Sel.	Todd Johnson
Manager	John J. Kelley Jr (Int)
Town Clerk	Mary-Ann O'Brien Nichols
Finance Director	Donna Walsh
Tax Collector	Lorraine Langlois
Tax Assessor	John J. Kelley Jr
Attorney	Charles Zaroulis
Public Works	Brian Gilbert
Building	Edward Johnson
Comm Dev/Planning	Steven Sadwick
Police Chief	Timothy Sheehan
Fire Chief	Richard Mackey

Housing & Construction

New Privately Owned Housing Units Authorized by Building Permit

	Single Family	Total Bldgs	Total Units
2006	40	45	79
2007	43	44	48
2008	51	65	417

Parcel Count by Property Class, 2010

Total	NA
Single family	NA
Multiple units	NA
Apartments	NA
Condos	NA
Vacant land	NA
Open space	NA
Commercial	NA
Industrial	NA
Misc. residential	NA
Other use	NA

Public Library

Tewksbury Public Library
300 Chandler Street
Tewksbury, MA 01876
(978)640-4490

Director	Jennifer Hinderer

Library Statistics, FY 2008

Population served, 2007	29,607
Registered users	18,683
Circulation	274,796
Reference transactons	8,281
Total program attendance	187,771
per capita:	
Holdings	3.02
Operating income	$38.17
Internet Access	
Internet computers available	24
Weekly users	477

Municipal Finance

Debt at year end 2008	$82,932,595
Moody's rating, July 2009	A2

Revenues, 2008

Total	$75,996,632
From all taxes	53,839,006
Federal aid	537,946
State aid	17,886,569
From other governments	52,950
Charges for services	1,671,663
Licenses, permits & fees	1,008,024
Fines & forfeits	21,544
Interfund transfers	39,400
Misc/other/special assessments	469,765

Expenditures, 2008

Total	$65,603,015
General government	2,442,758
Public safety	10,188,042
Other/fixed costs	5,851,829
Human services	659,827
Culture & recreation	1,340,358
Debt Service	3,495,004
Education	36,711,623
Public works	4,326,999
Intergovernmental	586,575

Taxation, 2010

Property type	Valuation	Rate
Total	NA	-
Residential	NA	NA
Open space	NA	NA
Commercial	NA	NA
Industrial	NA	NA
Personal	NA	NA

Average Single Family Tax Bill, 2010

Avg. assessed home value	NA
Avg. single fam. tax bill	NA
Hi-Lo ranking	NA

Police & Crime, 2008

Number of police officers	54
Violent crimes	59
Property crimes	501

Local School District

(school data 2007-08, except as noted)

Tewksbury
139 Pleasant Street
Tewksbury, MA 01876
978-640-7800

Superintendent	Christine McGrath
Grade plan	PK-12
Total enrollment '09-10	4,217
Grade 12 enrollment, '09-10	257
Graduation rate	85.6%
Dropout rate	6.6%
Per-pupil expenditure	$10,084
Avg teacher salary	$62,972
Student/teacher ratio '08-09	17.8 to 1
Highly-qualified teachers, '08-09	100.0%
Teachers licensed in assigned subject	100.0%
Students per computer	4.8

Massachusetts Competency Assessment System (MCAS), 2009 results

	English		Math	
	% Prof	CPI	% Prof	CPI
Gr 4	44%	77.2	42%	78
Gr 6	76%	89.6	56%	78.6
Gr 8	85%	94	43%	70.5
Gr 10	79%	91.6	78%	90.3

Other School Districts (see Appendix D for data)
Shawsheen Valley Vocational Tech

©2010 Information Publications, Inc. All rights reserved. Photocopying prohibited. For additional copies, contact the publisher at www.informationpublications.com or (877)544-INFO (4636)

See Introduction for an explanation of all data sources.

Demographics & Socio-Economic Characteristics

Population

1990	3,120
2000	3,755
Male	1,758
Female	1,997
2008	3,811
2010 (projected)††	4,084
2020 (projected)††	4,501

Race & Hispanic Origin, 2000

Race	
White	3,381
Black/African American	111
American Indian/Alaska Native	51
Asian	12
Hawaiian Native/Pacific Islander	2
Other Race	50
Two or more races	148
Hispanic origin	39

Age & Nativity, 2000

Under 5 years	187
18 years and over	2,948
21 years and over	2,859
65 years and over	673
85 years and over	97
Median Age	42.0
Native-born	3,501
Foreign-born	254

Age, 2020 (projected)††

Under 5 years	194
5 to 19 years	614
20 to 39 years	966
40 to 64 years	1,568
65 years and over	1,159

Educational Attainment, 2000

Population 25 years and over	2,723
High School graduates or higher	89.0%
Bachelor's degree or higher	33.2%
Graduate degree	11.5%

Income & Poverty, 1999

Per capita income,	$26,783
Median household income	$37,041
Median family income	$53,051
Persons in poverty	444
H'holds receiving public assistance	26
H'holds receiving social security	494

Households, 2000

Total households	1,646
With persons under 18	457
With persons over 65	454
Family households	902
Single person households	604
Persons per household	2.2
Persons per family	2.9

Labor & Employment, 2000

Civilian labor force	1,992
Unemployment rate	1.6%
Civilian labor force, 2008†	2,268
Unemployment rate†	8.7%
Civilian labor force, 12/09†	2,373
Unemployment rate†	11.7%
Employed persons 16 years and over, by occupation:	
Managers & professionals	615
Service occupations	291
Sales & office occupations	448
Farming, fishing & forestry	8
Construction & maintenance	451
Production & transportation	148
Self-employed persons	466

Most demographic data is from the 2000 Decennial Census
† Massachusetts Department of Revenue
†† University of Massachusetts, MISER

©2010 Information Publications, Inc. All rights reserved. Photocopying prohibited. For additional copies, contact the publisher at www.informationpublications.com or (877)544-INFO (4636)

General Information

Town of Tisbury
51 Spring St
PO Box 1239
Tisbury, MA 02568
508-696-4200

Elevation	NA
Land area (square miles)	6.6
Water area (square miles)	12.6
Population density, 2008 (est)	577.4
Year incorporated	1671
Website	www.tisburygov.org

Voters & Government Information

Government type	Open Town Meeting
Number of Selectmen	3
US Congressional District(s)	10

Registered Voters, October 2008

Total	3,080
Democrats	1,108
Republicans	335
Unaffiliated/other	1,617

Local Officials, 2010

Chair, Bd. of Sel.	Tristan R. Israel
Manager/Admin	John R. Bugbee
Clerk	Marion A. Mudge
Finance Director	Timothy W. McLean
Tax Collector	Timothy W. McLean
Tax Assessor	Annmarie Cywinski
Attorney	Kopelman & Paige
Public Works	Fred LaPiana
Building	Kenneth A. Barwick
Planning	L. Anthony Peak
Police Chief	Daniel Hanavan
Fire Chief	John Schilling

Housing & Construction

New Privately Owned Housing Units Authorized by Building Permit

	Single Family	Total Bldgs	Total Units
2006	41	41	41
2007	31	31	31
2008	22	22	22

Parcel Count by Property Class, 2010

Total	3,252
Single family	1,858
Multiple units	157
Apartments	14
Condos	118
Vacant land	410
Open space	0
Commercial	290
Industrial	16
Misc. residential	241
Other use	148

Public Library

Vineyard Haven Public Library
RFD 139A Main Street
Vineyard Haven, MA 02568
(508)696-4210

Director	Amy Ryan

Library Statistics, FY 2008

Population served, 2007	3,805
Registered users	8,654
Circulation	114,288
Reference transactons	0
Total program attendance	91,904
per capita:	
Holdings	11.15
Operating income	$136.82
Internet Access	
Internet computers available	17
Weekly users	250

Municipal Finance

Debt at year end 2008	$10,355,771
Moody's rating, July 2009	NA

Revenues, 2008

Total	$21,015,008
From all taxes	16,526,787
Federal aid	0
State aid	928,613
From other governments	18,660
Charges for services	496,490
Licenses, permits & fees	230,831
Fines & forfeits	86,079
Interfund transfers	146,842
Misc/other/special assessments	1,290,353

Expenditures, 2008

Total	$18,464,911
General government	1,310,767
Public safety	2,007,185
Other/fixed costs	2,869,997
Human services	393,237
Culture & recreation	437,086
Debt Service	1,363,186
Education	8,218,311
Public works	1,323,762
Intergovernmental	541,380

Taxation, 2010

Property type	Valuation	Rate
Total	$2,717,459,531	-
Residential	2,402,939,893	6.57
Open space	0	0.00
Commercial	261,986,607	8.27
Industrial	4,695,700	8.27
Personal	47,837,331	8.27

Average Single Family Tax Bill, 2010

Avg. assessed home value	NA
Avg. single fam. tax bill	NA
Hi-Lo ranking	NA

Police & Crime, 2008

Number of police officers	13
Violent crimes	7
Property crimes	121

Local School District

(school data 2007-08, except as noted)

Tisbury
4 Pine Street, RR2 Box 261
Vineyard Haven, MA 02568
508-693-2007

Superintendent	James Weiss
Grade plan	PK-8
Total enrollment '09-10	305
Grade 12 enrollment, '09-10	0
Graduation rate	NA
Dropout rate	NA
Per-pupil expenditure	$17,608
Avg teacher salary	$65,873
Student/teacher ratio '08-09	8.3 to 1
Highly-qualified teachers, '08-09	98.7%
Teachers licensed in assigned subject	99.4%
Students per computer	2.6

Massachusetts Competency Assessment System (MCAS), 2009 results

	English		Math	
	% Prof	CPI	% Prof	CPI
Gr 4	86%	94.4	78%	91.9
Gr 6	82%	93.8	57%	79.5
Gr 8	95%	98.2	73%	88.4
Gr 10	NA	NA	NA	NA

Other School Districts (see Appendix D for data)
Marthas Vineyard Regional

See Introduction for an explanation of all data sources.

Demographics & Socio-Economic Characteristics

Population

1990	289
2000	426
Male	227
Female	199
2008	457
2010 (projected)††	518
2020 (projected)††	616

Race & Hispanic Origin, 2000

Race	
White	415
Black/African American	4
American Indian/Alaska Native	5
Asian	1
Hawaiian Native/Pacific Islander	0
Other Race	0
Two or more races	1
Hispanic origin	5

Age & Nativity, 2000

Under 5 years	27
18 years and over	324
21 years and over	317
65 years and over	55
85 years and over	4
Median Age	41.4
Native-born	425
Foreign-born	3

Age, 2020 (projected)††

Under 5 years	33
5 to 19 years	96
20 to 39 years	121
40 to 64 years	245
65 years and over	121

Educational Attainment, 2000

Population 25 years and over	328
High School graduates or higher	87.2%
Bachelor's degree or higher	29.9%
Graduate degree	13.1%

Income & Poverty, 1999

Per capita income,	$30,126
Median household income	$53,125
Median family income	$65,417
Persons in poverty	18
H'holds receiving public assistance	2
H'holds receiving social security	57

Households, 2000

Total households	169
With persons under 18	51
With persons over 65	45
Family households	115
Single person households	48
Persons per household	2.5
Persons per family	3.1

Labor & Employment, 2000

Civilian labor force	237
Unemployment rate	3.8%
Civilian labor force, 2008†	248
Unemployment rate†	4.4%
Civilian labor force, 12/09†	252
Unemployment rate†	7.1%
Employed persons 16 years and over, by occupation:	
Managers & professionals	106
Service occupations	24
Sales & office occupations	49
Farming, fishing & forestry	0
Construction & maintenance	20
Production & transportation	29
Self-employed persons	30

Most demographic data is from the 2000 Decennial Census
† Massachusetts Department of Revenue
†† University of Massachusetts, MISER

General Information

Town of Tolland
241 W Granville Rd
Tolland, MA 01034
413-258-4794

Elevation	1,520 ft.
Land area (square miles)	31.6
Water area (square miles)	1.1
Population density, 2008 (est)	14.5
Year incorporated	1810
Website	www.tolland-ma.gov

Voters & Government Information

Government type	Open Town Meeting
Number of Selectmen	3
US Congressional District(s)	1

Registered Voters, October 2008

Total	328
Democrats	67
Republicans	78
Unaffiliated/other	183

Local Officials, 2010

Chair, Bd. of Sel.	Eric R. Munson Jr
Manager/Admin	NA
Town Clerk	Susan Voudren
Treasurer	Margaret McClellan
Tax Collector	Margaret McClellan
Tax Assessor	Susan Voudren (Chr)
Attorney	Jerry Pollard
Public Works	Wayne Carr
Building Inspector	Eric R. Munson Jr
Planning & Zoning	James Deming (Chr)
Police Chief	Eric Munson III
Fire Chief	Robert Littlefield

Housing & Construction

New Privately Owned Housing Units Authorized by Building Permit

	Single Family	Total Bldgs	Total Units
2006	8	8	8
2007	4	4	4
2008	4	4	4

Parcel Count by Property Class, 2010

Total	997
Single family	491
Multiple units	2
Apartments	0
Condos	0
Vacant land	475
Open space	0
Commercial	12
Industrial	3
Misc. residential	6
Other use	8

Public Library

Tolland Public Library
22 Club House Road
Tolland, MA 01034
(413)258-4201

Director . . . Jessica Kelmelis

Library Statistics, FY 2008

Population served, 2007	451
Registered users	326
Circulation	2,742
Reference transactons	0
Total program attendance	1,793
per capita:	
Holdings	12.33
Operating income	$38.15
Internet Access	
Internet computers available	3
Weekly users	12

Municipal Finance

Debt at year end 2008	$290,703
Moody's rating, July 2009	NA

Revenues, 2008

Total	$1,599,909
From all taxes	987,299
Federal aid	0
State aid	149,486
From other governments	1,850
Charges for services	1,730
Licenses, permits & fees	1,895
Fines & forfeits	0
Interfund transfers	47,317
Misc/other/special assessments	205,166

Expenditures, 2008

Total	$1,062,767
General government	195,331
Public safety	78,395
Other/fixed costs	74,319
Human services	4,869
Culture & recreation	10,388
Debt Service	91,639
Education	311,330
Public works	293,205
Intergovernmental	335

Taxation, 2010

Property type	Valuation	Rate
Total	$194,845,562	-
Residential	183,180,780	4.76
Open space	0	0.00
Commercial	4,215,220	4.76
Industrial	372,700	4.76
Personal	7,076,862	4.76

Average Single Family Tax Bill, 2010

Avg. assessed home value	$317,043
Avg. single fam. tax bill	$1,509
Hi-Lo ranking	298/301

Police & Crime, 2008

Number of police officers	NA
Violent crimes	NA
Property crimes	NA

Local School District

(school data 2007-08, except as noted)

Tolland (non-op)
86 Powder Mill Road
Southwick, MA 01077
413-569-5391

Superintendent . . . John Barry

Non-operating district.
Resident students are sent to the Other School Districts listed below.

Grade plan	NA
Total enrollment '09-10	NA
Grade 12 enrollment, '09-10	NA
Graduation rate	NA
Dropout rate	NA
Per-pupil expenditure	NA
Avg teacher salary	NA
Student/teacher ratio '08-09	NA
Highly-qualified teachers, '08-09	NA
Teachers licensed in assigned subject	NA
Students per computer	NA

Other School Districts (see Appendix D for data)
Southwick-Tolland Regional

©2010 Information Publications, Inc. All rights reserved. Photocopying prohibited. For additional copies, contact the publisher at www.informationpublications.com or (877)544-INFO (4636)

See Introduction for an explanation of all data sources.

Demographics & Socio-Economic Characteristics

Population

1990	5,754
2000	6,141
Male	2,979
Female	3,162
2008	6,051
2010 (projected)††	5,788
2020 (projected)††	5,097

Race & Hispanic Origin, 2000

Race	
White	6,003
Black/African American	23
American Indian/Alaska Native	2
Asian	52
Hawaiian Native/Pacific Islander	0
Other Race	21
Two or more races	40
Hispanic origin	51

Age & Nativity, 2000

Under 5 years	395
18 years and over	4,407
21 years and over	4,259
65 years and over	947
85 years and over	101
Median Age	41.0
Native-born	5,725
Foreign-born	416

Age, 2020 (projected)††

Under 5 years	243
5 to 19 years	882
20 to 39 years	899
40 to 64 years	1,645
65 years and over	1,428

Educational Attainment, 2000

Population 25 years and over	4,135
High School graduates or higher	96.8%
Bachelor's degree or higher	52.0%
Graduate degree	21.0%

Income & Poverty, 1999

Per capita income,	$37,770
Median household income	$96,430
Median family income	$104,475
Persons in poverty	104
H'holds receiving public assistance	8
H'holds receiving social security	582

Households, 2000

Total households	2,099
With persons under 18	875
With persons over 65	593
Family households	1,713
Single person households	335
Persons per household	2.9
Persons per family	3.2

Labor & Employment, 2000

Civilian labor force	3,001
Unemployment rate	3.5%
Civilian labor force, 2008†	3,030
Unemployment rate†	4.7%
Civilian labor force, 12/09†	2,994
Unemployment rate†	7.3%
Employed persons 16 years and over, by occupation:	
Managers & professionals	1,618
Service occupations	185
Sales & office occupations	741
Farming, fishing & forestry	0
Construction & maintenance	224
Production & transportation	128
Self-employed persons	301

Most demographic data is from the 2000 Decennial Census
† Massachusetts Department of Revenue
†† University of Massachusetts, MISER

General Information

Town of Topsfield
8 West Common St
Topsfield, MA 01983
978-887-1500

Elevation	63 ft.
Land area (square miles)	12.7
Water area (square miles)	0.1
Population density, 2008 (est)	476.5
Year incorporated	1650
Website	www.topsfield-ma.gov

Voters & Government Information

Government type	Open Town Meeting
Number of Selectmen	5
US Congressional District(s)	6

Registered Voters, October 2008

Total	4,316
Democrats	809
Republicans	905
Unaffiliated/other	2,596

Local Officials, 2010

Chair, Bd. of Sel.	Martha Morrison
Town Administrator	Virginia Wilder
Town Clerk	Beverly Ann Guarino
Town Accountant	Pamela Wood
Treas/Collector	Barbara Michalowski
Tax Assessor	Pauline Evans
Attorney	Kopelman & Paige
Public Works	G. Krom/D. Krom
Building Inspector	Glenn Clohecy
Comm Dev Coordinator	Roberta Knight
Police Chief	Evan Haglund
Fire Chief	Ronald Giovannacci

Housing & Construction

New Privately Owned Housing Units Authorized by Building Permit

	Single Family	Total Bldgs	Total Units
2006	1	1	1
2007	4	4	4
2008	2	2	2

Parcel Count by Property Class, 2010

Total	2,313
Single family	1,836
Multiple units	32
Apartments	4
Condos	36
Vacant land	153
Open space	0
Commercial	116
Industrial	58
Misc. residential	19
Other use	59

Public Library

Topsfield Town Library
1 South Common Street
Topsfield, MA 01983
(978)887-1528

Director	Jaclyn White

Library Statistics, FY 2008

Population served, 2007	6,067
Registered users	6,495
Circulation	180,059
Reference transactons	3,961
Total program attendance	124,440
per capita:	
Holdings	10.51
Operating income	$94.25
Internet Access	
Internet computers available	19
Weekly users	215

Municipal Finance

Debt at year end 2008	$10,965,000
Moody's rating, July 2009	Aa3

Revenues, 2008

Total	$20,181,967
From all taxes	16,535,041
Federal aid	0
State aid	2,552,387
From other governments	11,890
Charges for services	79,584
Licenses, permits & fees	316,162
Fines & forfeits	42,595
Interfund transfers	196,670
Misc/other/special assessments	223,819

Expenditures, 2008

Total	$19,870,116
General government	1,000,881
Public safety	2,021,436
Other/fixed costs	2,127,679
Human services	191,555
Culture & recreation	671,626
Debt Service	1,072,939
Education	11,394,432
Public works	1,207,772
Intergovernmental	181,796

Taxation, 2010

Property type	Valuation	Rate
Total	$1,199,414,915	-
Residential	1,099,109,837	13.87
Open space	0	0.00
Commercial	61,687,913	13.87
Industrial	18,888,500	13.87
Personal	19,728,665	13.87

Average Single Family Tax Bill, 2010

Avg. assessed home value	$532,305
Avg. single fam. tax bill	$7,383
Hi-Lo ranking	27/301

Police & Crime, 2008

Number of police officers	10
Violent crimes	1
Property crimes	67

Local School District

(school data 2007-08, except as noted)

Topsfield
28 Middleton Road
Boxford, MA 01921
978-887-0771

Superintendent	Bernard Creeden
Grade plan	PK-6
Total enrollment '09-10	660
Grade 12 enrollment, '09-10	0
Graduation rate	NA
Dropout rate	NA
Per-pupil expenditure	$10,852
Avg teacher salary	$60,755
Student/teacher ratio '08-09	12.9 to 1
Highly-qualified teachers, '08-09	100.0%
Teachers licensed in assigned subject	100.0%
Students per computer	4.1

Massachusetts Competency Assessment System (MCAS), 2009 results

	English		Math	
	% Prof	CPI	% Prof	CPI
Gr 4	71%	91.3	70%	90.8
Gr 6	90%	95.8	81%	91.2
Gr 8	NA	NA	NA	NA
Gr 10	NA	NA	NA	NA

Other School Districts (see Appendix D for data)
Masconomet Regional, North Shore Vocational Tech

©2010 Information Publications, Inc. All rights reserved. Photocopying prohibited. For additional copies, contact the publisher at www.informationpublications.com or (877)544-INFO (4636)

See Introduction for an explanation of all data sources.

Demographics & Socio-Economic Characteristics

Population

1990	8,496
2000	9,198
Male	4,561
Female	4,637
2008	9,400
2010 (projected)††	9,507
2020 (projected)††	10,123

Race & Hispanic Origin, 2000

Race	
White	8,972
Black/African American	67
American Indian/Alaska Native	21
Asian	21
Hawaiian Native/Pacific Islander	2
Other Race	36
Two or more races	79
Hispanic origin	108

Age & Nativity, 2000

Under 5 years	647
18 years and over	6,399
21 years and over	6,027
65 years and over	622
85 years and over	62
Median Age	35.4
Native-born	8,865
Foreign-born	338

Age, 2020 (projected)††

Under 5 years	719
5 to 19 years	1,977
20 to 39 years	2,794
40 to 64 years	3,094
65 years and over	1,539

Educational Attainment, 2000

Population 25 years and over	5,701
High School graduates or higher	91.5%
Bachelor's degree or higher	28.2%
Graduate degree	7.7%

Income & Poverty, 1999

Per capita income,	$22,658
Median household income	$61,745
Median family income	$67,173
Persons in poverty	464
H'holds receiving public assistance	74
H'holds receiving social security	472

Households, 2000

Total households	3,110
With persons under 18	1,460
With persons over 65	462
Family households	2,476
Single person households	501
Persons per household	3.0
Persons per family	3.3

Labor & Employment, 2000

Civilian labor force	5,064
Unemployment rate	4.0%
Civilian labor force, 2008†	5,307
Unemployment rate†	5.1%
Civilian labor force, 12/09†	5,329
Unemployment rate†	8.4%
Employed persons 16 years and over, by occupation:	
Managers & professionals	1,898
Service occupations	675
Sales & office occupations	1,092
Farming, fishing & forestry	0
Construction & maintenance	593
Production & transportation	604
Self-employed persons	418

Most demographic data is from the 2000 Decennial Census
† Massachusetts Department of Revenue
†† University of Massachusetts, MISER

General Information

Town of Townsend
272 Main St
Townsend, MA 01469
978-597-1704

Elevation	310 ft.
Land area (square miles)	32.9
Water area (square miles)	0.2
Population density, 2008 (est)	285.7
Year incorporated	1732
Website	townsend.ma.us

Voters & Government Information

Government type	Open Town Meeting
Number of Selectmen	3
US Congressional District(s)	1

Registered Voters, October 2008

Total	6,344
Democrats	1,116
Republicans	1,046
Unaffiliated/other	4,124

Local Officials, 2010

Chair, Bd. of Sel.	David Chenelle
Manager/Superint	Gregory W. Barnes
Town Clerk	Susan A. Funaiole
Town Accountant	Kim Fales
Tax Collector	Kathleen Rossbach
Tax Assessor	Niles Busler (Chr)
Attorney	Leonard Kopelman
Public Works	NA
Building Commissioner	Richard Hanks
Comm Dev/Planning	Jeanne Hollows
Police Chief	Erving Marshall Jr
Emerg/Fire Chief	Donald Klein

Housing & Construction

New Privately Owned Housing Units Authorized by Building Permit

	Single Family	Total Bldgs	Total Units
2006	19	19	19
2007	23	25	29
2008	14	14	14

Parcel Count by Property Class, 2010

Total	3,894
Single family	2,776
Multiple units	55
Apartments	7
Condos	272
Vacant land	443
Open space	0
Commercial	79
Industrial	18
Misc. residential	18
Other use	226

Public Library

Townsend Public Library
PO Box 526
Townsend, MA 01469
(978)597-1714

Director	Heidi Fowler

Library Statistics, FY 2008

Population served, 2007	9,374
Registered users	4,924
Circulation	66,963
Reference transactons	0
Total program attendance	24,751
per capita:	
Holdings	3.52
Operating income	$20.05
Internet Access	
Internet computers available	3
Weekly users	25

Municipal Finance

Debt at year end 2008	$6,877,720
Moody's rating, July 2009	A2

Revenues, 2008

Total	$16,109,751
From all taxes	13,354,201
Federal aid	0
State aid	1,870,653
From other governments	20,770
Charges for services	117,698
Licenses, permits & fees	125,517
Fines & forfeits	0
Interfund transfers	417,308
Misc/other/special assessments	101,802

Expenditures, 2008

Total	$15,943,115
General government	794,775
Public safety	2,445,352
Other/fixed costs	1,191,990
Human services	173,493
Culture & recreation	190,199
Debt Service	669,946
Education	8,773,233
Public works	1,592,796
Intergovernmental	68,597

Taxation, 2010

Property type	Valuation	Rate
Total	$863,440,319	-
Residential	788,673,345	15.31
Open space	0	0.00
Commercial	36,564,264	15.31
Industrial	18,975,700	15.31
Personal	19,227,010	15.31

Average Single Family Tax Bill, 2010

Avg. assessed home value	$248,492
Avg. single fam. tax bill	$3,804
Hi-Lo ranking	151/301

Police & Crime, 2008

Number of police officers	15
Violent crimes	5
Property crimes	149

Local School District

(school data 2007-08, except as noted)

Townsend (non-op)
23 Main Street
Townsend, MA 01469
978-597-8713

Superintendent	Maureen Marshall

Non-operating district.
Resident students are sent to the Other School Districts listed below.

Grade plan	NA
Total enrollment '09-10	NA
Grade 12 enrollment, '09-10	NA
Graduation rate	NA
Dropout rate	NA
Per-pupil expenditure	NA
Avg teacher salary	NA
Student/teacher ratio '08-09	NA
Highly-qualified teachers, '08-09	NA
Teachers licensed in assigned subject	NA
Students per computer	NA

Other School Districts (see Appendix D for data)
North Middlesex Regional, Nashoba Valley Vocational Tech

©2010 Information Publications, Inc. All rights reserved. Photocopying prohibited. For additional copies, contact the publisher at www.informationpublications.com or (877)544-INFO (4636)

©2010 Information Publications, Inc. All rights reserved. Photocopying prohibited. For additional copies, contact the publisher at www.informationpublications.com or (877)544-INFO (4636)

Demographics & Socio-Economic Characteristics

Population

1990 1,573
2000 2,087
Male 968
Female 1,119
2008 2,125
2010 (projected)†† 2,349
2020 (projected)†† 2,603

Race & Hispanic Origin, 2000

Race
White 1,985
Black/African American 39
American Indian/Alaska Native 9
Asian 8
Hawaiian Native/Pacific Islander 2
Other Race 16
Two or more races 28
Hispanic origin 24

Age & Nativity, 2000

Under 5 years 72
18 years and over 1,723
21 years and over 1,681
65 years and over 354
85 years and over 35
Median Age 45.7
Native-born 2,015
Foreign-born 70

Age, 2020 (projected)††

Under 5 years 76
5 to 19 years 222
20 to 39 years 495
40 to 64 years 1,042
65 years and over 768

Educational Attainment, 2000

Population 25 years and over 1,626
High School graduates or higher .. 92.8%
Bachelor's degree or higher 40.5%
Graduate degree 13.2%

Income & Poverty, 1999

Per capita income, ... $22,608
Median household income $42,981
Median family income $51,389
Persons in poverty 234
H'holds receiving public assistance 16
H'holds receiving social security 308

Households, 2000

Total households 907
With persons under 18 208
With persons over 65 263
Family households 515
Single person households 290
Persons per household 2.2
Persons per family 2.8

Labor & Employment, 2000

Civilian labor force 1,117
Unemployment rate 13.9%
Civilian labor force, 2008† 1,243
Unemployment rate† 17.1%
Civilian labor force, 12/09† 1,284
Unemployment rate† 23.4%
Employed persons 16 years and over, by occupation:
Managers & professionals 373
Service occupations 156
Sales & office occupations 213
Farming, fishing & forestry 10
Construction & maintenance 158
Production & transportation 52
Self-employed persons 180

Most demographic data is from the 2000 Decennial Census
† Massachusetts Department of Revenue
†† University of Massachusetts, MISER

General Information

Town of Truro
PO Box 2030
Truro, MA 02666
508-349-7004

Elevation .... 22 ft.
Land area (square miles) 21.1
Water area (square miles) 5.3
Population density, 2008 (est) 100.7
Year incorporated 1709
Website .... truro-ma.gov

Voters & Government Information

Government type .... Open Town Meeting
Number of Selectmen 5
US Congressional District(s) 10

Registered Voters, October 2008

Total 1,724
Democrats 631
Republicans 142
Unaffiliated/other 941

Local Officials, 2010

Chair, Bd. of Sel. .... Gary D. Palmer
Manager/Admin .... Pamela T. Nolan
Town Clerk .... Cynthia A. Slade
Treasurer .... Cynthia A. Slade
Tax Collector .... Cynthia A. Slade
Tax Assessor .... Linda V. Maloney-Tarvers
Attorney .... NA
Public Works Dir .... Paul A. Morris
Building .... Thomas J. Wingard
Comm Dev/Planning .... NA
Police Chief .... John J. Thomas
Emerg/Fire Chief .... Brian G. Davis

Housing & Construction

New Privately Owned Housing Units Authorized by Building Permit

	Single Family	Total Bldgs	Total Units
2006	25	25	25
2007	24	24	24
2008	10	11	12

Parcel Count by Property Class, 2010

Total 3,317
Single family 2,006
Multiple units 52
Apartments 8
Condos 433
Vacant land 532
Open space 0
Commercial 85
Industrial 4
Misc. residential 146
Other use 51

Public Library

Truro Public Library
5 Library Lane, PO Box 357
North Truro, MA 02652
(508)487-1125

Director .... Margaret Royka

Library Statistics, FY 2008

Population served, 2007 2,134
Registered users 5,109
Circulation 39,699
Reference transactons 4,826
Total program attendance 0

per capita:

Holdings 16.23
Operating income $122.95

Internet Access

Internet computers available 5
Weekly users 108

Municipal Finance

Debt at year end 2008 .... $5,620,402
Moody's rating, July 2009 .... NA

Revenues, 2008

Total $13,532,853
From all taxes 10,609,362
Federal aid 7,080
State aid 524,758
From other governments 2,591
Charges for services 270,232
Licenses, permits & fees 264,537
Fines & forfeits 43,174
Interfund transfers 1,060,809
Misc/other/special assessments 375,155

Expenditures, 2008

Total $12,453,553
General government 1,568,604
Public safety 1,938,393
Other/fixed costs 1,748,718
Human services 300,742
Culture & recreation 1,162,409
Debt Service 852,343
Education 3,635,945
Public works 843,880
Intergovernmental 402,519

Taxation, 2010

Property type	Valuation	Rate
Total	$2,144,817,310	-
Residential	2,015,473,602	5.39
Open space	0	0.00
Commercial	103,854,678	5.39
Industrial	1,782,600	5.39
Personal	23,706,430	5.39

Average Single Family Tax Bill, 2010

Avg. assessed home value $771,042
Avg. single fam. tax bill $4,156
Hi-Lo ranking 124/301

Police & Crime, 2008

Number of police officers 10
Violent crimes 2
Property crimes 23

Local School District

(school data 2007-08, except as noted)

Truro
P O Box 2029
Truro, MA 02666
508-487-1558

Superintendent .... Brian Davis
Grade plan PK-6
Total enrollment '09-10 146
Grade 12 enrollment, '09-10 0
Graduation rate .... NA
Dropout rate .... NA
Per-pupil expenditure $18,582
Avg teacher salary $54,160
Student/teacher ratio '08-09 .... 10.1 to 1
Highly-qualified teachers, '08-09 .... 100.0%
Teachers licensed in assigned subject 100.0%
Students per computer 1.8

Massachusetts Competency Assessment System (MCAS), 2009 results

	English		Math	
	% Prof	CPI	% Prof	CPI
Gr 4	62%	85.7	52%	86.9
Gr 6	83%	91.7	92%	100
Gr 8	NA	NA	NA	NA
Gr 10	NA	NA	NA	NA

Other School Districts (see Appendix D for data)

Sends grades 7-12 to Provincetown; member Nauset Reg, Cape Cod Voc Tech

See Introduction for an explanation of all data sources.

Demographics & Socio-Economic Characteristics

Population

1990	8,642
2000	11,081
Male	5,470
Female	5,611
2008	12,019
2010 (projected)††	14,338
2020 (projected)††	18,810

Race & Hispanic Origin, 2000

Race	
White	10,597
Black/African American	55
American Indian/Alaska Native	25
Asian	275
Hawaiian Native/Pacific Islander	4
Other Race	15
Two or more races	110
Hispanic origin	123

Age & Nativity, 2000

Under 5 years	987
18 years and over	7,721
21 years and over	7,427
65 years and over	732
85 years and over	58
Median Age	34.7
Native-born	10,545
Foreign-born	536

Age, 2020 (projected)††

Under 5 years	1,474
5 to 19 years	4,058
20 to 39 years	5,344
40 to 64 years	5,867
65 years and over	2,067

Educational Attainment, 2000

Population 25 years and over	7,139
High School graduates or higher	90.0%
Bachelor's degree or higher	30.6%
Graduate degree	10.0%

Income & Poverty, 1999

Per capita income,	$27,249
Median household income	$69,818
Median family income	$78,680
Persons in poverty	519
H'holds receiving public assistance	70
H'holds receiving social security	584

Households, 2000

Total households	3,731
With persons under 18	1,755
With persons over 65	565
Family households	2,949
Single person households	602
Persons per household	3.0
Persons per family	3.4

Labor & Employment, 2000

Civilian labor force	6,126
Unemployment rate	3.2%
Civilian labor force, 2008†	6,467
Unemployment rate†	5.4%
Civilian labor force, 12/09†	6,608
Unemployment rate†	8.7%
Employed persons 16 years and over, by occupation:	
Managers & professionals	2,685
Service occupations	622
Sales & office occupations	1,328
Farming, fishing & forestry	0
Construction & maintenance	656
Production & transportation	641
Self-employed persons	414

Most demographic data is from the 2000 Decennial Census
† Massachusetts Department of Revenue
†† University of Massachusetts, MISER

General Information

Town of Tyngsborough
25 Bryants Ln
Tyngsborough, MA 01879
978-649-2300

Elevation	112 ft.
Land area (square miles)	16.9
Water area (square miles)	1.2
Population density, 2008 (est)	711.2
Year incorporated	1809
Website	www.tyngsboroughma.gov

Voters & Government Information

Government type	Open Town Meeting
Number of Selectmen	5
US Congressional District(s)	5

Registered Voters, October 2008

Total	7,929
Democrats	1,964
Republicans	1,077
Unaffiliated/other	4,844

Local Officials, 2010

Chair, Bd. of Sel.	Richard Lemoine
Town Administrator	open
Town Clerk	Joanne Shifres
Treasurer	Kerry Colburn-Dion
Tax Collector	Gene Spickler
Tax Assessor	Phillip O'Brien (Chr)
Attorney	NA
Public Works	NA
Building	Mark Dupell
Comm Dev/Planning	NA
Police Chief	William Mulligan
Fire Chief	Timothy Madden

Housing & Construction

New Privately Owned Housing Units Authorized by Building Permit

	Single Family	Total Bldgs	Total Units
2006	116	116	116
2007	80	80	80
2008	16	16	16

Parcel Count by Property Class, 2010

Total	4,686
Single family	3,091
Multiple units	113
Apartments	7
Condos	625
Vacant land	393
Open space	0
Commercial	202
Industrial	126
Misc. residential	37
Other use	92

Public Library

Tyngsborough Public Library
25 Bryants Lane
Tyngsborough, MA 01879
(978)649-7361

Director	Carol Sides (Actg)

Library Statistics, FY 2008

Population served, 2007	11,860
Registered users	7,331
Circulation	127,706
Reference transactons	1,512
Total program attendance	70,043
per capita:	
Holdings	4.62
Operating income	$25.71
Internet Access	
Internet computers available	11
Weekly users	229

Municipal Finance

Debt at year end 2008	$9,791,248
Moody's rating, July 2009	A2

Revenues, 2008

Total	$30,870,342
From all taxes	19,473,448
Federal aid	0
State aid	9,591,094
From other governments	37,342
Charges for services	287,608
Licenses, permits & fees	358,198
Fines & forfeits	0
Interfund transfers	554,500
Misc/other/special assessments	284,076

Expenditures, 2008

Total	$30,576,158
General government	1,169,212
Public safety	3,079,720
Other/fixed costs	4,399,274
Human services	339,530
Culture & recreation	329,749
Debt Service	1,420,826
Education	17,330,710
Public works	2,214,648
Intergovernmental	292,489

Taxation, 2010

Property type	Valuation	Rate
Total	$1,387,380,323	-
Residential	1,187,023,145	13.95
Open space	0	0.00
Commercial	102,379,560	13.95
Industrial	55,968,305	13.95
Personal	42,009,313	13.95

Average Single Family Tax Bill, 2010

Avg. assessed home value	$324,403
Avg. single fam. tax bill	$4,525
Hi-Lo ranking	99/301

Police & Crime, 2008

Number of police officers	22
Violent crimes	13
Property crimes	195

Local School District

(school data 2007-08, except as noted)

Tyngsborough
50 Norris Rd
Tyngsborough, MA 01879
978-649-7488

Superintendent	Darrell Lockwood
Grade plan	PK-12
Total enrollment '09-10	2,031
Grade 12 enrollment, '09-10	136
Graduation rate	95.1%
Dropout rate	3.7%
Per-pupil expenditure	$10,185
Avg teacher salary	$59,591
Student/teacher ratio '08-09	14.3 to 1
Highly-qualified teachers, '08-09	97.2%
Teachers licensed in assigned subject	99.3%
Students per computer	9.3

Massachusetts Competency Assessment System (MCAS), 2009 results

	English		Math	
	% Prof	CPI	% Prof	CPI
Gr 4	56%	81.4	51%	81.4
Gr 6	71%	87.4	62%	80.1
Gr 8	87%	95.9	66%	84.4
Gr 10	91%	96.8	85%	94.2

Other School Districts (see Appendix D for data)
Greater Lowell Vocational Tech

©2010 Information Publications, Inc. All rights reserved. Photocopying prohibited. For additional copies, contact the publisher at www.informationpublications.com or (877)544-INFO (4636)

See Introduction for an explanation of all data sources.

Demographics & Socio-Economic Characteristics

Population

1990	369
2000	350
Male	176
Female	174
2008	339
2010 (projected)††	331
2020 (projected)††	302

Race & Hispanic Origin, 2000

Race	
White	334
Black/African American	1
American Indian/Alaska Native	1
Asian	9
Hawaiian Native/Pacific Islander	0
Other Race	0
Two or more races	5
Hispanic origin	1

Age & Nativity, 2000

Under 5 years	12
18 years and over	285
21 years and over	274
65 years and over	54
85 years and over	12
Median Age	47.5
Native-born	340
Foreign-born	12

Age, 2020 (projected)††

Under 5 years	8
5 to 19 years	25
20 to 39 years	46
40 to 64 years	115
65 years and over	108

Educational Attainment, 2000

Population 25 years and over	256
High School graduates or higher	94.5%
Bachelor's degree or higher	46.5%
Graduate degree	24.6%

Income & Poverty, 1999

Per capita income,	$35,503
Median household income	$60,250
Median family income	$67,679
Persons in poverty	12
H'holds receiving public assistance	0
H'holds receiving social security	40

Households, 2000

Total households	133
With persons under 18	37
With persons over 65	37
Family households	99
Single person households	27
Persons per household	2.6
Persons per family	2.9

Labor & Employment, 2000

Civilian labor force	227
Unemployment rate	1.8%
Civilian labor force, 2008†	253
Unemployment rate†	4.7%
Civilian labor force, 12/09†	252
Unemployment rate†	6.3%
Employed persons 16 years and over, by occupation:	
Managers & professionals	102
Service occupations	35
Sales & office occupations	50
Farming, fishing & forestry	0
Construction & maintenance	17
Production & transportation	19
Self-employed persons	24

Most demographic data is from the 2000 Decennial Census
† Massachusetts Department of Revenue
†† University of Massachusetts, MISER

General Information

Town of Tyringham
PO Box 442
Tyringham, MA 01264
413-243-1749

Elevation	901 ft.
Land area (square miles)	18.7
Water area (square miles)	0.2
Population density, 2008 (est)	18.1
Year incorporated	1762
Website	www.tyringham-ma.gov

Voters & Government Information

Government type	Open Town Meeting
Number of Selectmen	3
US Congressional District(s)	1

Registered Voters, October 2008

Total	313
Democrats	90
Republicans	37
Unaffiliated/other	185

Local Officials, 2010

Chair, Bd. of Sel.	Alan Wilcox Sr
Manager/Admin	Molly Curtin-Schaefer
Clerk	John Curtin Jr
Finance Dir	Suzanne Hale Delmolino
Tax Collector	Margaret DeSantis
Tax Assessor	Terry Clark
Attorney	NA
Public Works	Les Beebe
Building	Larry Gould
Comm Dev/Planning	NA
Police Chief	Peter Curtin Sr
Emerg/Fire Chief	James Curtin

Housing & Construction

New Privately Owned Housing Units Authorized by Building Permit

	Single Family	Total Bldgs	Total Units
2006	0	0	0
2007	4	4	4
2008	2	2	2

Parcel Count by Property Class, 2010

Total	523
Single family	255
Multiple units	10
Apartments	0
Condos	0
Vacant land	173
Open space	0
Commercial	0
Industrial	0
Misc. residential	17
Other use	68

Public Library

Tyringham Free Public Library
PO Box 440
Tyringham, MA 01264

Librarian/Trustee Chr	Mary Garner

Library Statistics, FY 2008

Population served, 2007	343
Registered users	0
Circulation	1,201
Reference transactons	0
Total program attendance	1,401
per capita:	
Holdings	19.93
Operating income	$0.00
Internet Access	
Internet computers available	2
Weekly users	4

Municipal Finance

Debt at year end 2008	$33,333
Moody's rating, July 2009	NA

Revenues, 2008

Total	$1,243,829
From all taxes	1,079,042
Federal aid	0
State aid	69,564
From other governments	2,991
Charges for services	11,246
Licenses, permits & fees	4,905
Fines & forfeits	0
Interfund transfers	20,085
Misc/other/special assessments	27,998

Expenditures, 2008

Total	$1,108,017
General government	222,260
Public safety	83,742
Other/fixed costs	204,898
Human services	13,087
Culture & recreation	6,520
Debt Service	17,679
Education	289,041
Public works	257,812
Intergovernmental	12,978

Taxation, 2010

Property type	Valuation	Rate
Total	$186,519,790	-
Residential	176,718,970	5.72
Open space	0	0.00
Commercial	1,445,010	5.72
Industrial	0	0.00
Personal	8,355,810	5.72

Average Single Family Tax Bill, 2010

Avg. assessed home value	$513,092
Avg. single fam. tax bill	$2,935
Hi-Lo ranking	242/301

Police & Crime, 2008

Number of police officers	NA
Violent crimes	NA
Property crimes	NA

Local School District

(school data 2007-08, except as noted)

Tyringham (non-op)
480 Pleasant Street, Suite 102
Lee, MA 01238
413-243-0276

Superintendent	Jason McCandless

Non-operating district.
Resident students are sent to the Other School Districts listed below.

Grade plan	NA
Total enrollment '09-10	NA
Grade 12 enrollment, '09-10	NA
Graduation rate	NA
Dropout rate	NA
Per-pupil expenditure	NA
Avg teacher salary	NA
Student/teacher ratio '08-09	NA
Highly-qualified teachers, '08-09	NA
Teachers licensed in assigned subject	NA
Students per computer	NA

Other School Districts (see Appendix D for data)
Sends grades PK-12 to Lee

©2010 Information Publications, Inc. All rights reserved. Photocopying prohibited. For additional copies, contact the publisher at www.informationpublications.com or (877)544-INFO (4636)

See Introduction for an explanation of all data sources.

Demographics & Socio-Economic Characteristics

Population

1990	4,677
2000	5,642
Male	2,757
Female	2,885
2008	6,584
2010 (projected)††	6,421
2020 (projected)††	7,185

Race & Hispanic Origin, 2000

Race	
White	5,492
Black/African American	27
American Indian/Alaska Native	4
Asian	55
Hawaiian Native/Pacific Islander	0
Other Race	17
Two or more races	47
Hispanic origin	41

Age & Nativity, 2000

Under 5 years	558
18 years and over	4,001
21 years and over	3,876
65 years and over	535
85 years and over	70
Median Age	37.0
Native-born	5,463
Foreign-born	179

Age, 2020 (projected)††

Under 5 years	559
5 to 19 years	1,592
20 to 39 years	1,667
40 to 64 years	2,376
65 years and over	991

Educational Attainment, 2000

Population 25 years and over	3,775
High School graduates or higher	90.4%
Bachelor's degree or higher	44.9%
Graduate degree	11.9%

Income & Poverty, 1999

Per capita income,	$34,924
Median household income	$78,595
Median family income	$89,251
Persons in poverty	197
H'holds receiving public assistance	21
H'holds receiving social security	442

Households, 2000

Total households	2,042
With persons under 18	878
With persons over 65	384
Family households	1,562
Single person households	387
Persons per household	2.7
Persons per family	3.2

Labor & Employment, 2000

Civilian labor force	2,878
Unemployment rate	3.3%
Civilian labor force, 2008†	3,458
Unemployment rate†	6.0%
Civilian labor force, 12/09†	3,531
Unemployment rate†	8.7%
Employed persons 16 years and over, by occupation:	
Managers & professionals	1,470
Service occupations	243
Sales & office occupations	532
Farming, fishing & forestry	0
Construction & maintenance	305
Production & transportation	233
Self-employed persons	201

Most demographic data is from the 2000 Decennial Census
† Massachusetts Department of Revenue
†† University of Massachusetts, MISER

General Information

Town of Upton
1 Main St
PO Box 479
Upton, MA 01568
508-529-6901

Elevation	301 ft.
Land area (square miles)	21.5
Water area (square miles)	0.2
Population density, 2008 (est)	306.2
Year incorporated	1735
Website	www.upton.ma.us

Voters & Government Information

Government type	Open Town Meeting
Number of Selectmen	3
US Congressional District(s)	2

Registered Voters, October 2008

Total	4,995
Democrats	1,037
Republicans	821
Unaffiliated/other	3,113

Local Officials, 2010

Chair, Bd. of Sel.	Ken Picard
Manager/Admin	James Bates
Town Clerk	Kelly McElreath
Finance Director	Kenneth Glowacki
Tax Collector	Kenneth Glowacki
Tax Assessor	Charles Marsden
Attorney	NA
Public Works	John Johnson (Actg)
Building	Patrick Roche
Comm Dev/Planning	Gary Bohan
Police Chief	Michael Bradley
Emerg/Fire Chief	Michael Bradford Sr

Housing & Construction

New Privately Owned Housing Units Authorized by Building Permit

	Single Family	Total Bldgs	Total Units
2006	48	48	48
2007	37	37	37
2008	23	23	23

Parcel Count by Property Class, 2010

Total	2,950
Single family	2,157
Multiple units	87
Apartments	19
Condos	105
Vacant land	399
Open space	0
Commercial	42
Industrial	38
Misc. residential	19
Other use	84

Public Library

Upton Town Library
PO Box 1196
Upton, MA 01568
(508)529-6272

Director	Matthew Bachtold

Library Statistics, FY 2008

Population served, 2007	6,526
Registered users	4,536
Circulation	72,955
Reference transactons	3,588
Total program attendance	31,954
per capita:	
Holdings	5.07
Operating income	$30.68
Internet Access	
Internet computers available	3
Weekly users	32

Municipal Finance

Debt at year end 2008	$8,535,264
Moody's rating, July 2009	A2

Revenues, 2008

Total	$16,181,755
From all taxes	13,239,054
Federal aid	0
State aid	798,842
From other governments	33,827
Charges for services	891,401
Licenses, permits & fees	276,298
Fines & forfeits	1,235
Interfund transfers	130,890
Misc/other/special assessments	405,104

Expenditures, 2008

Total	$15,269,505
General government	699,069
Public safety	2,243,600
Other/fixed costs	1,067,051
Human services	353,351
Culture & recreation	313,419
Debt Service	794,116
Education	7,559,510
Public works	2,180,804
Intergovernmental	57,943

Taxation, 2010

Property type	Valuation	Rate
Total	$1,053,358,370	-
Residential	994,087,381	12.77
Open space	0	0.00
Commercial	23,520,019	12.77
Industrial	8,890,800	12.77
Personal	26,860,170	12.77

Average Single Family Tax Bill, 2010

Avg. assessed home value	$394,661
Avg. single fam. tax bill	$5,040
Hi-Lo ranking	74/301

Police & Crime, 2008

Number of police officers	12
Violent crimes	5
Property crimes	53

Local School District

(school data 2007-08, except as noted)

Upton (non-op)
150 North Ave, POB 5
Mendon, MA 01756
508-634-1585

Superintendent	Antonio Fernandes

Non-operating district.
Resident students are sent to the Other School Districts listed below.

Grade plan	NA
Total enrollment '09-10	NA
Grade 12 enrollment, '09-10	NA
Graduation rate	NA
Dropout rate	NA
Per-pupil expenditure	NA
Avg teacher salary	NA
Student/teacher ratio '08-09	NA
Highly-qualified teachers, '08-09	NA
Teachers licensed in assigned subject	NA
Students per computer	NA

Other School Districts (see Appendix D for data)
Mendon-Upton Regional, Blackstone Valley Vocational Tech

©2010 Information Publications, Inc. All rights reserved. Photocopying prohibited. For additional copies, contact the publisher at www.informationpublications.com or (877)544-INFO (4636)

See Introduction for an explanation of all data sources.

©2010 Information Publications, Inc. All rights reserved. Photocopying prohibited. For additional copies, contact the publisher at www.informationpublications.com or (877)544-INFO (4636)

Demographics & Socio-Economic Characteristics

Population

1990	10,415
2000	11,156
Male	5,479
Female	5,677
2008	12,672
2010 (projected)††	12,566
2020 (projected)††	14,277

Race & Hispanic Origin, 2000

Race	
White	10,937
Black/African American	17
American Indian/Alaska Native	15
Asian	68
Hawaiian Native/Pacific Islander	8
Other Race	33
Two or more races	78
Hispanic origin	106

Age & Nativity, 2000

Under 5 years	889
18 years and over	7,899
21 years and over	7,603
65 years and over	1,105
85 years and over	121
Median Age	35.3
Native-born	10,783
Foreign-born	353

Age, 2020 (projected)††

Under 5 years	1,066
5 to 19 years	2,997
20 to 39 years	3,914
40 to 64 years	4,739
65 years and over	1,561

Educational Attainment, 2000

Population 25 years and over	7,232
High School graduates or higher	87.2%
Bachelor's degree or higher	26.9%
Graduate degree	8.0%

Income & Poverty, 1999

Per capita income,	$24,540
Median household income	$61,855
Median family income	$70,068
Persons in poverty	520
H'holds receiving public assistance	59
H'holds receiving social security	924

Households, 2000

Total households	3,988
With persons under 18	1,731
With persons over 65	832
Family households	3,036
Single person households	767
Persons per household	2.8
Persons per family	3.2

Labor & Employment, 2000

Civilian labor force	6,068
Unemployment rate	3.0%
Civilian labor force, 2008†	6,939
Unemployment rate†	7.4%
Civilian labor force, 12/09†	7,081
Unemployment rate†	9.5%
Employed persons 16 years and over, by occupation:	
Managers & professionals	2,247
Service occupations	688
Sales & office occupations	1,462
Farming, fishing & forestry	19
Construction & maintenance	613
Production & transportation	854
Self-employed persons	328

Most demographic data is from the 2000 Decennial Census
† Massachusetts Department of Revenue
†† University of Massachusetts, MISER

General Information

Town of Uxbridge
21 S Main St
Uxbridge, MA 01569
508-278-8600

Elevation	270 ft.
Land area (square miles)	29.5
Water area (square miles)	0.8
Population density, 2008 (est)	429.6
Year incorporated	1727
Website	www.uxbridge-ma.gov

Voters & Government Information

Government type	Open Town Meeting
Number of Selectmen	5
US Congressional District(s)	2

Registered Voters, October 2008

Total	9,530
Democrats	2,300
Republicans	1,428
Unaffiliated/other	5,721

Local Officials, 2010

Chair, Bd. of Sel.	Michael Potaski
Town Manager	Michael A. Szlosek
Town Clerk	Kelly J. Poulin
Finance Director	David Genereux
Tax Collector	David Genereux
Tax Assessor	Paula Dumont
Attorney	Merrick, Louison & Costello
Public Works	Benn Sherman (Actg)
Building	NA
Comm Dev/Planning	NA
Police Chief	Scott Freitas
Emerg/Fire Chief	Peter Ostroskey

Housing & Construction

New Privately Owned Housing Units Authorized by Building Permit

	Single Family	Total Bldgs	Total Units
2006	70	70	70
2007	45	45	45
2008	28	28	28

Parcel Count by Property Class, 2010

Total	5,610
Single family	3,288
Multiple units	318
Apartments	39
Condos	894
Vacant land	614
Open space	0
Commercial	151
Industrial	98
Misc. residential	40
Other use	168

Public Library

Uxbridge Free Public Library
15 N. Main St.
Uxbridge, MA 01569
(508)278-8624

Director	Jane Granatino

Library Statistics, FY 2008

Population served, 2007	12,634
Registered users	5,994
Circulation	84,707
Reference transactons	1,026
Total program attendance	36,959
per capita:	
Holdings	3.77
Operating income	$28.67
Internet Access	
Internet computers available	3
Weekly users	41

Municipal Finance

Debt at year end 2008	$18,685,000
Moody's rating, July 2009	A2

Revenues, 2008

Total	$38,544,987
From all taxes	19,491,565
Federal aid	164,904
State aid	13,098,026
From other governments	30,952
Charges for services	93,026
Licenses, permits & fees	219,953
Fines & forfeits	121,671
Interfund transfers	946,684
Misc/other/special assessments	2,189,103

Expenditures, 2008

Total	$36,319,281
General government	1,533,775
Public safety	2,176,569
Other/fixed costs	5,403,779
Human services	252,175
Culture & recreation	422,362
Debt Service	2,652,247
Education	20,847,009
Public works	1,435,517
Intergovernmental	1,281,734

Taxation, 2010

Property type	Valuation	Rate
Total	$1,589,056,020	-
Residential	1,379,953,527	12.55
Open space	0	0.00
Commercial	79,370,913	12.55
Industrial	76,798,100	12.55
Personal	52,933,480	12.55

Average Single Family Tax Bill, 2010

Avg. assessed home value	$311,507
Avg. single fam. tax bill	$3,909
Hi-Lo ranking	143/301

Police & Crime, 2008

Number of police officers	18
Violent crimes	20
Property crimes	142

Local School District

(school data 2007-08, except as noted)

Uxbridge
21 South Main Street
Uxbridge, MA 01569
508-278-8648

Superintendent	George Zini
Grade plan	PK-12
Total enrollment '09-10	2,002
Grade 12 enrollment, '09-10	114
Graduation rate	79.7%
Dropout rate	10.9%
Per-pupil expenditure	$11,146
Avg teacher salary	$65,658
Student/teacher ratio '08-09	13.6 to 1
Highly-qualified teachers, '08-09	99.6%
Teachers licensed in assigned subject	98.7%
Students per computer	NA

Massachusetts Competency Assessment System (MCAS), 2009 results

	English		Math	
	% Prof	CPI	% Prof	CPI
Gr 4	57%	82.2	52%	82.2
Gr 6	71%	87.5	58%	81.2
Gr 8	83%	93.3	53%	79.8
Gr 10	79%	92.4	80%	92.7

Other School Districts (see Appendix D for data)
Blackstone Valley Vocational Tech

See Introduction for an explanation of all data sources.

Demographics & Socio-Economic Characteristics*

Population

1990 . . . 24,825
2000 . . . 24,804
Male . . . 11,762
Female . . . 13,042
2008 . . . 24,717
2010 (projected)†† . . . 23,972
2020 (projected)†† . . . 23,006

Race & Hispanic Origin, 2000

Race
White . . . 24,045
Black/African American . . . 111
American Indian/Alaska Native . . . 19
Asian . . . 354
Hawaiian Native/Pacific Islander . . . 2
Other Race . . . 49
Two or more races . . . 224
Hispanic origin . . . 204

Age & Nativity, 2000

Under 5 years . . . 1,593
18 years and over . . . 19,197
21 years and over . . . 18,578
65 years and over . . . 3,749
85 years and over . . . 532
Median Age . . . 38.9
Native-born . . . 23,566
Foreign-born . . . 1,238

Age, 2020 (projected)††

Under 5 years . . . 1,216
5 to 19 years . . . 3,801
20 to 39 years . . . 5,550
40 to 64 years . . . 8,124
65 years and over . . . 4,315

Educational Attainment, 2000

Population 25 years and over . . . 17,788
High School graduates or higher . . 90.6%
Bachelor's degree or higher . . . 39.7%
Graduate degree . . . 14.6%

Income & Poverty, 1999

Per capita income, . . . $30,369
Median household income . . . $66,117
Median family income . . . $77,834
Persons in poverty . . . 759
H'holds receiving public assistance . . . 133
H'holds receiving social security . . . 2,756

Households, 2000

Total households . . . 9,747
With persons under 18 . . . 3,103
With persons over 65 . . . 2,623
Family households . . . 6,604
Single person households . . . 2,575
Persons per household . . . 2.5
Persons per family . . . 3.1

Labor & Employment, 2000

Civilian labor force . . . 13,644
Unemployment rate . . . 3.1%
Civilian labor force, 2008† . . . 13,915
Unemployment rate† . . . 6.0%
Civilian labor force, 12/09† . . . 13,847
Unemployment rate† . . . 7.8%
Employed persons 16 years and over, by occupation:
Managers & professionals . . . 6,292
Service occupations . . . 1,303
Sales & office occupations . . . 3,622
Farming, fishing & forestry . . . 10
Construction & maintenance . . . 979
Production & transportation . . . 1,011
Self-employed persons . . . 922

Most demographic data is from the 2000 Decennial Census
* see Appendix E for American Community Survey data
† Massachusetts Department of Revenue
†† University of Massachusetts, MISER

General Information

Town of Wakefield
One Lafayette St
Wakefield, MA 01880
781-246-6300

Elevation . . . 100 ft.
Land area (square miles) . . . 7.5
Water area (square miles) . . . 0.4
Population density, 2008 (est) . . . 3,295.6
Year incorporated . . . 1868
Website . . . www.wakefield.ma.us

Voters & Government Information

Government type . . . Open Town Meeting
Number of Selectmen . . . 7
US Congressional District(s) . . . 6

Registered Voters, October 2008

Total . . . 17,103
Democrats . . . 5,674
Republicans . . . 2,139
Unaffiliated/other . . . 9,194

Local Officials, 2010

Chair, Bd. of Sel. . . . Betsy Sheeran
Town Administrator . . . Stephen P. Maio
Town Clerk . . . Mary K. Galvin
Acct/Treas . . . Kevin M. Gill
Tax Collector . . . Kathleen M. Kelly
Tax Assessor . . . Victor Santaniello
Attorney . . . Thomas A. Mullen
Public Works . . . Richard F. Stinson
Building . . . John J. Roberto
Comm Dev/Planning . . . Paul Reavis
Police Chief . . . Richard E. Smith
Emerg/Fire Chief . . . Michael J. Sullivan (Actg)

Housing & Construction

New Privately Owned Housing Units Authorized by Building Permit

	Single Family	Total Bldgs	Total Units
2006	66	66	66
2007	57	57	57
2008	39	41	69

Parcel Count by Property Class, 2010

Total . . . 9,026
Single family . . . 6,196
Multiple units . . . 864
Apartments . . . 91
Condos . . . 1,077
Vacant land . . . 299
Open space . . . 0
Commercial . . . 319
Industrial . . . 96
Misc. residential . . . 1
Other use . . . 83

Public Library

Lucius Beebe Memorial Library
345 Main Street
Wakefield, MA 01880
(781)246-6334

Director . . . Sharon A. Gilley

Library Statistics, FY 2008

Population served, 2007 . . . 24,706
Registered users . . . 18,808
Circulation . . . 307,389
Reference transactons . . . 30,116
Total program attendance . . . 318,842

per capita:

Holdings . . . 5.03
Operating income . . . $50.45

Internet Access

Internet computers available . . . 24
Weekly users . . . 1,354

Municipal Finance

Debt at year end 2008 . . . $33,615,814
Moody's rating, July 2009 . . . Aa3

Revenues, 2008

Total . . . $61,423,130
From all taxes . . . 47,647,650
Federal aid . . . 0
State aid . . . 11,052,878
From other governments . . . 23,336
Charges for services . . . 696,793
Licenses, permits & fees . . . 554,998
Fines & forfeits . . . 122,265
Interfund transfers . . . 97,944
Misc/other/special assessments . . . 613,633

Expenditures, 2008

Total . . . $57,018,473
General government . . . 1,761,458
Public safety . . . 7,265,628
Other/fixed costs . . . 12,618,350
Human services . . . 380,980
Culture & recreation . . . 1,128,566
Debt Service . . . 0
Education . . . 26,729,782
Public works . . . 5,954,876
Intergovernmental . . . 1,114,502

Taxation, 2010

Property type	Valuation	Rate
Total	$3,785,082,150	-
Residential	3,213,453,608	10.88
Open space	0	0.00
Commercial	434,929,359	21.97
Industrial	91,946,400	21.97
Personal	44,752,783	21.97

Average Single Family Tax Bill, 2010

Avg. assessed home value . . . $395,826
Avg. single fam. tax bill . . . $4,307
Hi-Lo ranking . . . 114/301

Police & Crime, 2008

Number of police officers . . . 41
Violent crimes . . . NA
Property crimes . . . NA

Local School District

(school data 2007-08, except as noted)

Wakefield
60 Farm Street
Wakefield, MA 01880
781-246-6400

Superintendent . . . Joan Landers
Grade plan . . . PK-12
Total enrollment '09-10 . . . 3,360
Grade 12 enrollment, '09-10 . . . 238
Graduation rate . . . 91.0%
Dropout rate . . . 5.6%
Per-pupil expenditure . . . $11,014
Avg teacher salary . . . $60,347
Student/teacher ratio '08-09 . . . 14.0 to 1
Highly-qualified teachers, '08-09 . . . 98.7%
Teachers licensed in assigned subject . . 98.6%
Students per computer . . . 4.1

Massachusetts Competency Assessment System (MCAS), 2009 results

	English		Math	
	% Prof	CPI	% Prof	CPI
Gr 4	70%	90	66%	88.5
Gr 6	79%	93	66%	86.6
Gr 8	81%	92.1	53%	77.3
Gr 10	91%	97.1	85%	92.5

Other School Districts (see Appendix D for data)

Northeast Metro Vocational Tech

©2010 Information Publications, Inc. All rights reserved. Photocopying prohibited. For additional copies, contact the publisher at www.informationpublications.com or (877)544-INFO (4636)

See Introduction for an explanation of all data sources.

Demographics & Socio-Economic Characteristics

Population

1990	1,566
2000	1,737
Male	865
Female	872
2008	1,881
2010 (projected)††	2,028
2020 (projected)††	2,288

Race & Hispanic Origin, 2000

Race	
White	1,698
Black/African American	9
American Indian/Alaska Native	5
Asian	3
Hawaiian Native/Pacific Islander	0
Other Race	6
Two or more races	16
Hispanic origin	11

Age & Nativity, 2000

Under 5 years	104
18 years and over	1,302
21 years and over	1,243
65 years and over	127
85 years and over	13
Median Age	38.0
Native-born	1,713
Foreign-born	24

Age, 2020 (projected)††

Under 5 years	123
5 to 19 years	413
20 to 39 years	513
40 to 64 years	800
65 years and over	439

Educational Attainment, 2000

Population 25 years and over	1,194
High School graduates or higher	85.3%
Bachelor's degree or higher	14.8%
Graduate degree	5.6%

Income & Poverty, 1999

Per capita income,	$21,267
Median household income	$48,906
Median family income	$51,629
Persons in poverty	60
H'holds receiving public assistance	20
H'holds receiving social security	124

Households, 2000

Total households	660
With persons under 18	242
With persons over 65	103
Family households	481
Single person households	134
Persons per household	2.6
Persons per family	3.0

Labor & Employment, 2000

Civilian labor force	1,010
Unemployment rate	6.1%
Civilian labor force, 2008†	1,067
Unemployment rate†	7.3%
Civilian labor force, 12/09†	1,086
Unemployment rate†	10.0%
Employed persons 16 years and over, by occupation:	
Managers & professionals	263
Service occupations	157
Sales & office occupations	169
Farming, fishing & forestry	6
Construction & maintenance	150
Production & transportation	203
Self-employed persons	70

Most demographic data is from the 2000 Decennial Census
† Massachusetts Department of Revenue
†† University of Massachusetts, MISER

General Information

Town of Wales
3 Hollow Road
PO Box 834
Wales, MA 01081
413-245-7571

Elevation	949 ft.
Land area (square miles)	15.7
Water area (square miles)	0.2
Population density, 2008 (est)	119.8
Year incorporated	1775
Email	select@townofwales.net

Voters & Government Information

Government type	Open Town Meeting
Number of Selectmen	3
US Congressional District(s)	2

Registered Voters, October 2008

Total	1,323
Democrats	278
Republicans	171
Unaffiliated/other	860

Local Officials, 2010

Chair, Bd. of Sel.	Michael Valanzola
Manager/Admin	Kaye Rose Worth
Clerk	Lynn S. Greene
Finance Director	Candis Cook
Tax Collector	Rebecca Smith
Tax Assessor	Beverly Poirier
Attorney	Kopelman & Paige
Public Works	Michael Wasiluk
Building	Harold Leaming
Planning	David McClain
Police Chief	Dawn Charette
Emerg/Fire Chief	Paul Morin

Housing & Construction

New Privately Owned Housing Units Authorized by Building Permit

	Single Family	Total Bldgs	Total Units
2006	13	13	13
2007	9	9	9
2008	7	7	7

Parcel Count by Property Class, 2010

Total	1,124
Single family	704
Multiple units	38
Apartments	0
Condos	2
Vacant land	308
Open space	0
Commercial	7
Industrial	3
Misc. residential	17
Other use	45

Public Library

Wales Public Library
PO Box 243
Wales, MA 01081
(413)245-9072

Director	Nancy Baer

Library Statistics, FY 2008

Population served, 2007	1,844
Registered users	1,431
Circulation	8,474
Reference transactons	348
Total program attendance	4,198
per capita:	
Holdings	5.93
Operating income	$24.42
Internet Access	
Internet computers available	3
Weekly users	20

Municipal Finance

Debt at year end 2008	$180,000
Moody's rating, July 2009	NA

Revenues, 2008

Total	$3,695,846
From all taxes	2,490,785
Federal aid	0
State aid	1,027,162
From other governments	555
Charges for services	13,832
Licenses, permits & fees	11,417
Fines & forfeits	10,248
Interfund transfers	92,401
Misc/other/special assessments	24,723

Expenditures, 2008

Total	$3,555,444
General government	243,722
Public safety	102,533
Other/fixed costs	397,684
Human services	45,356
Culture & recreation	53,684
Debt Service	30,493
Education	2,312,935
Public works	242,303
Intergovernmental	126,734

Taxation, 2010

Property type	Valuation	Rate
Total	$169,360,618	-
Residential	157,896,465	14.50
Open space	0	0.00
Commercial	2,840,035	14.50
Industrial	890,900	14.50
Personal	7,733,218	14.50

Average Single Family Tax Bill, 2010

Avg. assessed home value	$190,073
Avg. single fam. tax bill	$2,756
Hi-Lo ranking	259/301

Police & Crime, 2008

Number of police officers	NA
Violent crimes	1
Property crimes	3

Local School District

(school data 2007-08, except as noted)

Wales
320 Brookfield Rd
Fiskdale, MA 01518
508-347-3077

Superintendent	Daniel Durgin
Grade plan	PK-6
Total enrollment '09-10	169
Grade 12 enrollment, '09-10	0
Graduation rate	NA
Dropout rate	NA
Per-pupil expenditure	$13,663
Avg teacher salary	$49,668
Student/teacher ratio '08-09	14.3 to 1
Highly-qualified teachers, '08-09	100.0%
Teachers licensed in assigned subject	100.0%
Students per computer	2.2

Massachusetts Competency Assessment System (MCAS), 2009 results

	English		Math	
	% Prof	CPI	% Prof	CPI
Gr 4	71%	89.6	48%	85
Gr 6	67%	87.5	63%	82.3
Gr 8	NA	NA	NA	NA
Gr 10	NA	NA	NA	NA

Other School Districts (see Appendix D for data)
Tantasqua Regional

©2010 Information Publications, Inc. All rights reserved. Photocopying prohibited. For additional copies, contact the publisher at www.informationpublications.com or (877)544-INFO (4636)

See Introduction for an explanation of all data sources.

Demographics & Socio-Economic Characteristics

Population

1990	20,212
2000	22,824
Male	11,412
Female	11,412
2008	23,133
2010 (projected)††	23,436
2020 (projected)††	23,417

Race & Hispanic Origin, 2000

Race	
White	21,777
Black/African American	363
American Indian/Alaska Native	24
Asian	257
Hawaiian Native/Pacific Islander	2
Other Race	256
Two or more races	145
Hispanic origin	461

Age & Nativity, 2000

Under 5 years	1,543
18 years and over	16,925
21 years and over	16,401
65 years and over	3,293
85 years and over	477
Median Age	38.8
Native-born	21,564
Foreign-born	1,260

Age, 2020 (projected)††

Under 5 years	1,255
5 to 19 years	4,086
20 to 39 years	5,603
40 to 64 years	7,830
65 years and over	4,643

Educational Attainment, 2000

Population 25 years and over	15,909
High School graduates or higher	93.0%
Bachelor's degree or higher	39.8%
Graduate degree	13.1%

Income & Poverty, 1999

Per capita income,	$32,117
Median household income	$74,757
Median family income	$84,458
Persons in poverty	472
H'holds receiving public assistance	32
H'holds receiving social security	2,319

Households, 2000

Total households	8,060
With persons under 18	2,966
With persons over 65	2,357
Family households	5,972
Single person households	1,817
Persons per household	2.7
Persons per family	3.2

Labor & Employment, 2000

Civilian labor force	11,932
Unemployment rate	3.2%
Civilian labor force, 2008†	12,345
Unemployment rate†	5.2%
Civilian labor force, 12/09†	12,227
Unemployment rate†	7.3%
Employed persons 16 years and over, by occupation:	
Managers & professionals	5,134
Service occupations	1,560
Sales & office occupations	3,126
Farming, fishing & forestry	0
Construction & maintenance	883
Production & transportation	842
Self-employed persons	807

Most demographic data is from the 2000 Decennial Census
† Massachusetts Department of Revenue
†† University of Massachusetts, MISER

General Information

Town of Walpole
135 School St
Walpole, MA 02081
508-660-7300

Elevation	166 ft.
Land area (square miles)	20.5
Water area (square miles)	0.5
Population density, 2008 (est)	1,128.4
Year incorporated	1724
Website	www.walpole-ma.gov

Voters & Government Information

Government type	Rep. Town Meeting
Number of Selectmen	5
US Congressional District(s)	9

Registered Voters, October 2008

Total	16,494
Democrats	4,381
Republicans	2,294
Unaffiliated/other	9,768

Local Officials, 2010

Chair, Bd. of Sel.	Christopher G. Timson
Manager/Admin	Michael Boynton
Town Clerk	Ronald Fucile
Finance Director	Mark Good
Tax Collector	Mark Good
Tax Assessor	Dennis Flis
Attorney	Kopelman & Paige
Public Works	Robert O'Brien
Building Inspector	Jack Mee
Comm Dev/Planning	Don Johnson
Police Chief	Richard Stillman
Emerg/Fire Chief	Timothy Bailey

Housing & Construction

New Privately Owned Housing Units Authorized by Building Permit

	Single Family	Total Bldgs	Total Units
2006	38	38	38
2007	22	23	24
2008	34	36	39

Parcel Count by Property Class, 2010

Total	8,914
Single family	6,272
Multiple units	247
Apartments	37
Condos	1,063
Vacant land	615
Open space	0
Commercial	249
Industrial	272
Misc. residential	35
Other use	124

Public Library

Walpole Public Library
65 Common St.
Walpole, MA 02081
(508)660-7340

Director	Jerry Romelczyk

Library Statistics, FY 2008

Population served, 2007	23,086
Registered users	13,552
Circulation	218,509
Reference transactons	5,107
Total program attendance	0
per capita:	
Holdings	5.03
Operating income	$31.98
Internet Access	
Internet computers available	15
Weekly users	190

Municipal Finance

Debt at year end 2008	$34,110,567
Moody's rating, July 2009	Aa3

Revenues, 2008

Total	$63,479,027
From all taxes	47,682,581
Federal aid	531,411
State aid	11,175,094
From other governments	0
Charges for services	225,820
Licenses, permits & fees	906,153
Fines & forfeits	62,805
Interfund transfers	1,646,457
Misc/other/special assessments	624,353

Expenditures, 2008

Total	$62,384,740
General government	3,853,396
Public safety	7,218,937
Other/fixed costs	10,624,600
Human services	422,970
Culture & recreation	1,407,933
Debt Service	2,491,921
Education	31,675,641
Public works	3,958,462
Intergovernmental	730,880

Taxation, 2010

Property type	Valuation	Rate
Total	$3,679,198,820	-
Residential	3,164,957,070	12.64
Open space	0	0.00
Commercial	235,666,065	16.47
Industrial	173,018,065	16.47
Personal	105,557,620	16.47

Average Single Family Tax Bill, 2010

Avg. assessed home value	$417,956
Avg. single fam. tax bill	$5,283
Hi-Lo ranking	61/301

Police & Crime, 2008

Number of police officers	38
Violent crimes	25
Property crimes	356

Local School District

(school data 2007-08, except as noted)

Walpole
135 School Street
Walpole, MA 02081
508-660-7200

Superintendent	Lincoln Lynch
Grade plan	PK-12
Total enrollment '09-10	3,954
Grade 12 enrollment, '09-10	287
Graduation rate	87.3%
Dropout rate	4.9%
Per-pupil expenditure	$11,232
Avg teacher salary	$58,908
Student/teacher ratio '08-09	14.0 to 1
Highly-qualified teachers, '08-09	91.5%
Teachers licensed in assigned subject	96.9%
Students per computer	3.8

Massachusetts Competency Assessment System (MCAS), 2009 results

	English		Math	
	% Prof	CPI	% Prof	CPI
Gr 4	74%	91.5	66%	89.5
Gr 6	78%	91.9	70%	86.1
Gr 8	92%	96.8	60%	81
Gr 10	94%	98.2	86%	94.2

Other School Districts (see Appendix D for data)
Tri County Vocational Tech, Norfolk County Agricultural

©2010 Information Publications, Inc. All rights reserved. Photocopying prohibited. For additional copies, contact the publisher at www.informationpublications.com or (877)544-INFO (4636)

See Introduction for an explanation of all data sources.

Demographics & Socio-Economic Characteristics*

Population

1990	57,878
2000	59,226
Male	29,194
Female	30,032
2008	60,236
2010 (projected)††	59,715
2020 (projected)††	60,153

Race & Hispanic Origin, 2000

Race	
White	49,145
Black/African American	2,614
American Indian/Alaska Native	95
Asian	4,318
Hawaiian Native/Pacific Islander	38
Other Race	1,896
Two or more races	1,120
Hispanic origin	5,031

Age & Nativity, 2000

Under 5 years	2,795
18 years and over	50,053
21 years and over	45,234
65 years and over	7,775
85 years and over	1,023
Median Age	34.2
Native-born	47,251
Foreign-born	11,975

Age, 2020 (projected)††

Under 5 years	2,871
5 to 19 years	10,810
20 to 39 years	18,217
40 to 64 years	19,029
65 years and over	9,226

Educational Attainment, 2000

Population 25 years and over	39,912
High School graduates or higher	85.4%
Bachelor's degree or higher	38.4%
Graduate degree	15.7%

Income & Poverty, 1999

Per capita income,	$26,364
Median household income	$54,010
Median family income	$64,595
Persons in poverty	3,752
H'holds receiving public assistance	444
H'holds receiving social security	5,697

Households, 2000

Total households	23,207
With persons under 18	5,112
With persons over 65	5,470
Family households	12,455
Single person households	7,943
Persons per household	2.3
Persons per family	3.0

Labor & Employment, 2000

Civilian labor force	35,195
Unemployment rate	5.4%
Civilian labor force, 2008†	35,101
Unemployment rate†	5.1%
Civilian labor force, 12/09†	35,016
Unemployment rate†	6.9%
Employed persons 16 years and over, by occupation:	
Managers & professionals	15,072
Service occupations	4,290
Sales & office occupations	9,063
Farming, fishing & forestry	17
Construction & maintenance	1,927
Production & transportation	2,921
Self-employed persons	1,746

Most demographic data is from the 2000 Decennial Census
* see Appendix E for American Community Survey data
† Massachusetts Department of Revenue
†† University of Massachusetts, MISER

General Information

City of Waltham
610 Main St
Waltham, MA 02452
781-314-3000

Elevation	67 ft.
Land area (square miles)	12.7
Water area (square miles)	0.9
Population density, 2008 (est)	4,743.0
Year incorporated	NA
Website	www.city.waltham.ma.us

Voters & Government Information

Government type	Mayor-Council
Number of Councilpersons	15
US Congressional District(s)	7

Registered Voters, October 2008

Total	35,348
Democrats	12,770
Republicans	3,490
Unaffiliated/other	18,820

Local Officials, 2010

Mayor	Jeannette A. McCarthy
Manager/Admin	NA
City Clerk	Rosario C. Malone
Auditor	Dennis Quinn
Treas/Collector	Thomas Magno
Tax Assessor	Joseph Goode (Chr)
Attorney	John Cervone
Public Works	John Tashjian
Building	Ralph Gaudet
Comm Dev/Planning	Ronald Vokey
Police Chief	Thomas Lacroix
Fire Chief	Richard Cardillo

Housing & Construction

New Privately Owned Housing Units Authorized by Building Permit

	Single Family	Total Bldgs	Total Units
2006	57	78	219
2007	21	32	113
2008	22	25	76

Parcel Count by Property Class, 2010

Total	15,417
Single family	8,642
Multiple units	1,712
Apartments	759
Condos	2,842
Vacant land	344
Open space	0
Commercial	730
Industrial	196
Misc. residential	41
Other use	151

Public Library

Waltham Public Library
735 Main St.
Waltham, MA 02451
(781)314-3425

Director	Kate Tranquada

Library Statistics, FY 2008

Population served, 2007	59,758
Registered users	30,268
Circulation	654,628
Reference transactons	30,451
Total program attendance	0
per capita:	
Holdings	3.46
Operating income	$35.69
Internet Access	
Internet computers available	23
Weekly users	2,016

Municipal Finance

Debt at year end 2008	$68,827,569
Moody's rating, July 2009	Aa1

Revenues, 2008

Total	$164,781,227
From all taxes	127,169,623
Federal aid	583,677
State aid	20,957,425
From other governments	228,549
Charges for services	1,296,423
Licenses, permits & fees	4,986,611
Fines & forfeits	393,992
Interfund transfers	3,740,585
Misc/other/special assessments	2,712,171

Expenditures, 2008

Total	$135,426,861
General government	9,196,247
Public safety	27,853,105
Other/fixed costs	15,713,300
Human services	1,779,996
Culture & recreation	2,986,841
Debt Service	7,830,354
Education	55,957,827
Public works	12,592,754
Intergovernmental	1,438,294

Taxation, 2010

Property type	Valuation	Rate
Total	$8,542,640,122	-
Residential	5,795,080,312	12.54
Open space	0	0.00
Commercial	2,026,368,766	28.67
Industrial	464,727,284	28.67
Personal	256,463,760	28.67

Average Single Family Tax Bill, 2010

Avg. assessed home value	NA
Avg. single fam. tax bill	NA
Hi-Lo ranking	NA

Police & Crime, 2008

Number of police officers	146
Violent crimes	89
Property crimes	848

Local School District

(school data 2007-08, except as noted)

Waltham
617 Lexington Street
Waltham, MA 02452
781-314-5440

Superintendent	Peter Azar
Grade plan	PK-12
Total enrollment '09-10	4,763
Grade 12 enrollment, '09-10	364
Graduation rate	81.0%
Dropout rate	11.5%
Per-pupil expenditure	$17,681
Avg teacher salary	$65,017
Student/teacher ratio '08-09	10.7 to 1
Highly-qualified teachers, '08-09	99.8%
Teachers licensed in assigned subject	99.1%
Students per computer	3

Massachusetts Competency Assessment System (MCAS), 2009 results

	English		Math	
	% Prof	CPI	% Prof	CPI
Gr 4	49%	79.4	38%	74.6
Gr 6	69%	86.8	53%	77.2
Gr 8	79%	92.2	46%	72.1
Gr 10	84%	93.3	69%	85.4

Other School Districts (see Appendix D for data)
None

©2010 Information Publications, Inc. All rights reserved. Photocopying prohibited. For additional copies, contact the publisher at www.informationpublications.com or (877)544-INFO (4636)

See Introduction for an explanation of all data sources.

Demographics & Socio-Economic Characteristics

Population

1990	9,808
2000	9,707
Male	4,727
Female	4,980
2008	9,824
2010 (projected)††	9,798
2020 (projected)††	9,989

Race & Hispanic Origin, 2000

Race	
White	9,366
Black/African American	53
American Indian/Alaska Native	22
Asian	58
Hawaiian Native/Pacific Islander	6
Other Race	74
Two or more races	128
Hispanic origin	202

Age & Nativity, 2000

Under 5 years	590
18 years and over	7,307
21 years and over	6,938
65 years and over	1,465
85 years and over	190
Median Age	37.7
Native-born	9,387
Foreign-born	321

Age, 2020 (projected)††

Under 5 years	553
5 to 19 years	1,655
20 to 39 years	2,690
40 to 64 years	3,314
65 years and over	1,777

Educational Attainment, 2000

Population 25 years and over	6,519
High School graduates or higher	80.5%
Bachelor's degree or higher	13.6%
Graduate degree	3.9%

Income & Poverty, 1999

Per capita income,	$18,908
Median household income	$36,875
Median family income	$45,505
Persons in poverty	1,082
H'holds receiving public assistance	190
H'holds receiving social security	1,203

Households, 2000

Total households	4,027
With persons under 18	1,282
With persons over 65	1,104
Family households	2,598
Single person households	1,172
Persons per household	2.4
Persons per family	3.0

Labor & Employment, 2000

Civilian labor force	5,100
Unemployment rate	4.6%
Civilian labor force, 2008†	5,314
Unemployment rate†	7.2%
Civilian labor force, 12/09†	5,416
Unemployment rate†	10.7%
Employed persons 16 years and over, by occupation:	
Managers & professionals	1,059
Service occupations	956
Sales & office occupations	1,274
Farming, fishing & forestry	18
Construction & maintenance	574
Production & transportation	986
Self-employed persons	292

Most demographic data is from the 2000 Decennial Census
† Massachusetts Department of Revenue
†† University of Massachusetts, MISER

General Information

Town of Ware
126 Main St
Ware, MA 01082
413-967-9648

Elevation	488 ft.
Land area (square miles)	34.4
Water area (square miles)	5.6
Population density, 2008 (est)	285.6
Year incorporated	1761
Website	www.townofware.com

Voters & Government Information

Government type	Open Town Meeting
Number of Selectmen	5
US Congressional District(s)	1

Registered Voters, October 2008

Total	6,286
Democrats	2,151
Republicans	722
Unaffiliated/other	3,376

Local Officials, 2010

Chair, Bd. of Sel.	Nancy J. Talbot
Town Manager	Mary T. Tzambazakis
Clerk	Nancy J. Talbot
Treasurer	Paul Nowicki
Tax Collector	Paul Nowicki
Tax Assessor	Peter Harder
Attorney	Christopher, Hays, Wojcik, Mavricos
Public Works	Gilbert St. George-Sorel
Building	Michael Agnew
Planning	Christopher Dimarzio
Police Chief	Dennis A. Healey
Fire Chief	Thomas Coulombe

Housing & Construction

New Privately Owned Housing Units Authorized by Building Permit

	Single Family	Total Bldgs	Total Units
2006	25	25	25
2007	21	21	21
2008	11	11	11

Parcel Count by Property Class, 2010

Total	4,501
Single family	2,523
Multiple units	378
Apartments	86
Condos	19
Vacant land	866
Open space	0
Commercial	131
Industrial	61
Misc. residential	169
Other use	268

Public Library

Young Men's Library Association
37 Main Street
Ware, MA 01082
(413)967-5491

Director	Heidi Reed

Library Statistics, FY 2008

Population served, 2007	9,933
Registered users	4,370
Circulation	36,957
Reference transactons	995
Total program attendance	20,835
per capita:	
Holdings	5.06
Operating income	$30.92
Internet Access	
Internet computers available	5
Weekly users	90

Municipal Finance

Debt at year end 2008	$13,375,812
Moody's rating, July 2009	A3

Revenues, 2008

Total	$25,887,093
From all taxes	11,398,886
Federal aid	0
State aid	11,960,268
From other governments	81,784
Charges for services	1,383,194
Licenses, permits & fees	245,160
Fines & forfeits	7,515
Interfund transfers	528,726
Misc/other/special assessments	140,780

Expenditures, 2008

Total	$26,249,901
General government	1,182,970
Public safety	2,781,140
Other/fixed costs	3,940,540
Human services	369,874
Culture & recreation	467,034
Debt Service	2,017,485
Education	12,600,685
Public works	2,257,854
Intergovernmental	632,319

Taxation, 2010

Property type	Valuation	Rate
Total	$781,320,211	-
Residential	668,418,044	14.45
Open space	0	0.00
Commercial	60,440,547	14.45
Industrial	25,313,960	14.45
Personal	27,147,660	14.45

Average Single Family Tax Bill, 2010

Avg. assessed home value	$194,218
Avg. single fam. tax bill	$2,806
Hi-Lo ranking	253/301

Police & Crime, 2008

Number of police officers	18
Violent crimes	43
Property crimes	186

Local School District

(school data 2007-08, except as noted)

Ware
P O Box 240
Ware, MA 01082
413-967-4271

Superintendent	Mary Elizabeth Beach
Grade plan	PK-12
Total enrollment '09-10	1,309
Grade 12 enrollment, '09-10	86
Graduation rate	66.3%
Dropout rate	17.5%
Per-pupil expenditure	$11,950
Avg teacher salary	$55,328
Student/teacher ratio '08-09	14.2 to 1
Highly-qualified teachers, '08-09	96.1%
Teachers licensed in assigned subject	98.9%
Students per computer	3.7

Massachusetts Competency Assessment System (MCAS), 2009 results

	English		Math	
	% Prof	CPI	% Prof	CPI
Gr 4	29%	67.8	35%	70.7
Gr 6	47%	75.9	48%	73.6
Gr 8	70%	84.5	44%	69.5
Gr 10	73%	90.3	78%	91.1

Other School Districts (see Appendix D for data)
Pathfinder Vocational Tech

©2010 Information Publications, Inc. All rights reserved. Photocopying prohibited. For additional copies, contact the publisher at www.informationpublications.com or (877)544-INFO (4636)

See Introduction for an explanation of all data sources.

©2010 Information Publications, Inc. All rights reserved. Photocopying prohibited. For additional copies, contact the publisher at www.informationpublications.com or (877)544-INFO (4636)

Demographics & Socio-Economic Characteristics

Population

1990	19,232
2000	20,335
Male	9,716
Female	10,619
2008	21,221
2010 (projected)††	21,048
2020 (projected)††	22,022

Race & Hispanic Origin, 2000

Race	
White	17,776
Black/African American	594
American Indian/Alaska Native	109
Asian	90
Hawaiian Native/Pacific Islander	10
Other Race	1,058
Two or more races	698
Hispanic origin	292

Age & Nativity, 2000

Under 5 years	1,201
18 years and over	15,346
21 years and over	14,734
65 years and over	3,290
85 years and over	384
Median Age	39.3
Native-born	19,628
Foreign-born	707

Age, 2020 (projected)††

Under 5 years	1,173
5 to 19 years	3,371
20 to 39 years	4,837
40 to 64 years	7,463
65 years and over	5,178

Educational Attainment, 2000

Population 25 years and over	14,090
High School graduates or higher	82.5%
Bachelor's degree or higher	16.3%
Graduate degree	5.4%

Income & Poverty, 1999

Per capita income,	$21,312
Median household income	$40,422
Median family income	$45,750
Persons in poverty	2,131
H'holds receiving public assistance	338
H'holds receiving social security	2,606

Households, 2000

Total households	8,200
With persons under 18	2,690
With persons over 65	2,342
Family households	5,337
Single person households	2,396
Persons per household	2.4
Persons per family	3.0

Labor & Employment, 2000

Civilian labor force	10,228
Unemployment rate	5.4%
Civilian labor force, 2008†	11,453
Unemployment rate†	8.1%
Civilian labor force, 12/09†	11,253
Unemployment rate†	10.5%
Employed persons 16 years and over, by occupation:	
Managers & professionals	2,486
Service occupations	1,820
Sales & office occupations	2,538
Farming, fishing & forestry	89
Construction & maintenance	1,167
Production & transportation	1,574
Self-employed persons	444

Most demographic data is from the 2000 Decennial Census
† Massachusetts Department of Revenue
†† University of Massachusetts, MISER

General Information

Town of Wareham
54 Marion Rd
Wareham, MA 02571
508-291-3100

Elevation	24 ft.
Land area (square miles)	35.8
Water area (square miles)	10.5
Population density, 2008 (est)	592.8
Year incorporated	1739
Website	www.wareham.ma.us

Voters & Government Information

Government type	Open Town Meeting
Number of Selectmen	5
US Congressional District(s)	4

Registered Voters, October 2008

Total	14,783
Democrats	4,190
Republicans	1,752
Unaffiliated/other	8,712

Local Officials, 2010

Chair, Bd. of Sel.	Bruce D. Sauvageau
Administrator	Mark J. Andrews
Town Clerk	Mary Ann Silva
Accountant	Elizabeth Zaleski
Treas/Collector	John Foster
Tax Assessor	Richard Gonsolves
Attorney	Kopelman & Paige
Public Works	Mark Gifford
Building	Theodore Misiaszek
Comm Dev/Planning	(vacant)
Police Chief	Richard A. Stanley
Emerg/Fire Chief	Robert McDuffy Jr

Housing & Construction

New Privately Owned Housing Units Authorized by Building Permit

	Single Family	Total Bldgs	Total Units
2006	87	91	97
2007	71	83	97
2008	27	27	27

Parcel Count by Property Class, 2010

Total	13,968
Single family	9,231
Multiple units	221
Apartments	45
Condos	516
Vacant land	2,565
Open space	0
Commercial	552
Industrial	107
Misc. residential	217
Other use	514

Public Library

Wareham Free Library
59 Marion Road
Wareham, MA 02571
(508)295-2343

Director	Marcia Griswold

Library Statistics, FY 2008

Population served, 2007	21,154
Registered users	16,937
Circulation	178,684
Reference transactons	7,000
Total program attendance	0
per capita:	
Holdings	4.99
Operating income	$31.26
Internet Access	
Internet computers available	27
Weekly users	575

Municipal Finance

Debt at year end 2008	$50,216,572
Moody's rating, July 2009	Baa1

Revenues, 2008

Total	$49,693,217
From all taxes	29,515,392
Federal aid	526,234
State aid	15,980,225
From other governments	8,890
Charges for services	494,206
Licenses, permits & fees	1,016,602
Fines & forfeits	27,857
Interfund transfers	1,333,675
Misc/other/special assessments	395,068

Expenditures, 2008

Total	$44,874,584
General government	2,818,797
Public safety	4,746,731
Other/fixed costs	3,335,015
Human services	566,390
Culture & recreation	540,742
Debt Service	2,834,640
Education	26,694,181
Public works	1,596,206
Intergovernmental	1,681,052

Taxation, 2010

Property type	Valuation	Rate
Total	$3,664,105,690	-
Residential	3,083,877,503	8.11
Open space	0	0.00
Commercial	404,166,197	8.11
Industrial	67,324,310	8.11
Personal	108,737,680	8.11

Average Single Family Tax Bill, 2010

Avg. assessed home value	$282,306
Avg. single fam. tax bill	$2,290
Hi-Lo ranking	285/301

Police & Crime, 2008

Number of police officers	50
Violent crimes	NA
Property crimes	NA

Local School District

(school data 2007-08, except as noted)

Wareham
54 Marion Road
Wareham, MA 02571
508-291-3500

Superintendent	Barry Rabinovitch
Grade plan	PK-12
Total enrollment '09-10	3,142
Grade 12 enrollment, '09-10	205
Graduation rate	79.5%
Dropout rate	12.4%
Per-pupil expenditure	$11,211
Avg teacher salary	$67,448
Student/teacher ratio '08-09	14.2 to 1
Highly-qualified teachers, '08-09	99.2%
Teachers licensed in assigned subject	99.6%
Students per computer	4.2

Massachusetts Competency Assessment System (MCAS), 2009 results

	English		Math	
	% Prof	CPI	% Prof	CPI
Gr 4	43%	76.7	36%	76.2
Gr 6	57%	83.8	47%	74.4
Gr 8	77%	90.5	21%	58
Gr 10	78%	91.8	56%	81

Other School Districts (see Appendix D for data)
Upper Cape Cod Vocational Tech

See Introduction for an explanation of all data sources.

Demographics & Socio-Economic Characteristics

Population

1990	4,437
2000	4,776
Male	2,342
Female	2,434
2008	5,068
2010 (projected)††	5,136
2020 (projected)††	5,640

Race & Hispanic Origin, 2000

Race	
White	4,653
Black/African American	20
American Indian/Alaska Native	14
Asian	13
Hawaiian Native/Pacific Islander	0
Other Race	10
Two or more races	66
Hispanic origin	42

Age & Nativity, 2000

Under 5 years	279
18 years and over	3,494
21 years and over	3,329
65 years and over	630
85 years and over	70
Median Age	36.9
Native-born	4,579
Foreign-born	197

Age, 2020 (projected)††

Under 5 years	335
5 to 19 years	974
20 to 39 years	1,434
40 to 64 years	1,975
65 years and over	922

Educational Attainment, 2000

Population 25 years and over	3,171
High School graduates or higher	79.4%
Bachelor's degree or higher	9.8%
Graduate degree	3.3%

Income & Poverty, 1999

Per capita income,	$17,192
Median household income	$34,583
Median family income	$39,598
Persons in poverty	287
H'holds receiving public assistance	31
H'holds receiving social security	572

Households, 2000

Total households	1,889
With persons under 18	668
With persons over 65	477
Family households	1,287
Single person households	491
Persons per household	2.5
Persons per family	3.0

Labor & Employment, 2000

Civilian labor force	2,330
Unemployment rate	5.2%
Civilian labor force, 2008†	2,455
Unemployment rate†	7.1%
Civilian labor force, 12/09†	2,531
Unemployment rate†	10.8%
Employed persons 16 years and over, by occupation:	
Managers & professionals	521
Service occupations	377
Sales & office occupations	493
Farming, fishing & forestry	7
Construction & maintenance	304
Production & transportation	508
Self-employed persons	118

Most demographic data is from the 2000 Decennial Census
† Massachusetts Department of Revenue
†† University of Massachusetts, MISER

General Information

Town of Warren
48 High St
PO Box 609
Warren, MA 01083
413-436-5701

Elevation	605 ft.
Land area (square miles)	27.5
Water area (square miles)	0.1
Population density, 2008 (est)	184.3
Year incorporated	1834
Website	www.warren-ma.gov

Voters & Government Information

Government type	Open Town Meeting
Number of Selectmen	3
US Congressional District(s)	2

Registered Voters, October 2008

Total	3,091
Democrats	875
Republicans	401
Unaffiliated/other	1,781

Local Officials, 2010

Chair, Bd. of Sel.	Robert W. Souza Jr
Manager/Admin	NA
Town Clerk	Nancy J. Lowell
Treasurer	William F. Schlosstein
Tax Collector	Deborah Leger
Tax Assessor	Seth H. Blackwell
Attorney	NA
Public Works	NA
Building	Jack Keough
Comm Dev/Planning	H. William Ramsey
Police Chief	Bruce D. Spiewakowski
Emerg/Fire Chief	James W. Dolan

Housing & Construction

New Privately Owned Housing Units Authorized by Building Permit

	Single Family	Total Bldgs	Total Units
2006	20	20	20
2007	14	14	14
2008	5	7	10

Parcel Count by Property Class, 2010

Total	2,490
Single family	1,255
Multiple units	175
Apartments	31
Condos	30
Vacant land	566
Open space	0
Commercial	37
Industrial	33
Misc. residential	43
Other use	320

Public Library

Warren Public Library
PO Box 937
Warren, MA 01083
(413)436-7690

Director . . . Sylvia G. Buck

Library Statistics, FY 2008

Population served, 2007	4,108
Registered users	4,120
Circulation	17,451
Reference transactons	153
Total program attendance	0
per capita:	
Holdings	7.30
Operating income	$30.24
Internet Access	
Internet computers available	1
Weekly users	14

Municipal Finance

Debt at year end 2008	$1,142,478
Moody's rating, July 2009	A3

Revenues, 2008

Total	$7,259,398
From all taxes	5,406,250
Federal aid	0
State aid	1,158,796
From other governments	20,348
Charges for services	122,069
Licenses, permits & fees	37,912
Fines & forfeits	0
Interfund transfers	265,625
Misc/other/special assessments	124,199

Expenditures, 2008

Total	$6,809,440
General government	568,593
Public safety	1,106,663
Other/fixed costs	574,355
Human services	121,676
Culture & recreation	226,322
Debt Service	187,307
Education	3,372,530
Public works	611,298
Intergovernmental	17,714

Taxation, 2010

Property type	Valuation	Rate
Total	$369,175,444	-
Residential	329,671,575	15.53
Open space	0	0.00
Commercial	10,494,379	15.53
Industrial	9,095,400	15.53
Personal	19,914,090	15.53

Average Single Family Tax Bill, 2010

Avg. assessed home value	$193,569
Avg. single fam. tax bill	$3,006
Hi-Lo ranking	234/301

Police & Crime, 2008

Number of police officers	NA
Violent crimes	25
Property crimes	59

Local School District

(school data 2007-08, except as noted)

Warren (non-op)
48 High Street, PO Box 1538
Warren, MA 01083
413-436-9256

Superintendent . . . Brett Kustigian

Non-operating district.
Resident students are sent to the Other School Districts listed below.

Grade plan	NA
Total enrollment '09-10	NA
Grade 12 enrollment, '09-10	NA
Graduation rate	NA
Dropout rate	NA
Per-pupil expenditure	NA
Avg teacher salary	NA
Student/teacher ratio '08-09	NA
Highly-qualified teachers, '08-09	NA
Teachers licensed in assigned subject	NA
Students per computer	NA

Other School Districts (see Appendix D for data)
Quaboag Regional

©2010 Information Publications, Inc. All rights reserved. Photocopying prohibited. For additional copies, contact the publisher at www.informationpublications.com or (877)544-INFO (4636)

See Introduction for an explanation of all data sources.

Demographics & Socio-Economic Characteristics

Population

1990	740
2000	750
Male	380
Female	370
2008	749
2010 (projected)††	857
2020 (projected)††	974

Race & Hispanic Origin, 2000

Race	
White	727
Black/African American	0
American Indian/Alaska Native	2
Asian	2
Hawaiian Native/Pacific Islander	0
Other Race	8
Two or more races	11
Hispanic origin	7

Age & Nativity, 2000

Under 5 years	46
18 years and over	565
21 years and over	546
65 years and over	83
85 years and over	4
Median Age	40.6
Native-born	749
Foreign-born	4

Age, 2020 (projected)††

Under 5 years	57
5 to 19 years	168
20 to 39 years	225
40 to 64 years	350
65 years and over	174

Educational Attainment, 2000

Population 25 years and over	496
High School graduates or higher	93.5%
Bachelor's degree or higher	25.0%
Graduate degree	8.9%

Income & Poverty, 1999

Per capita income,	$19,989
Median household income	$42,083
Median family income	$45,795
Persons in poverty	60
H'holds receiving public assistance	2
H'holds receiving social security	75

Households, 2000

Total households	293
With persons under 18	100
With persons over 65	58
Family households	211
Single person households	60
Persons per household	2.6
Persons per family	3.0

Labor & Employment, 2000

Civilian labor force	373
Unemployment rate	5.1%
Civilian labor force, 2008†	342
Unemployment rate†	5.0%
Civilian labor force, 12/09†	361
Unemployment rate†	11.6%
Employed persons 16 years and over, by occupation:	
Managers & professionals	98
Service occupations	40
Sales & office occupations	90
Farming, fishing & forestry	4
Construction & maintenance	49
Production & transportation	73
Self-employed persons	55

Most demographic data is from the 2000 Decennial Census
† Massachusetts Department of Revenue
†† University of Massachusetts, MISER

General Information

Town of Warwick
12 Athol Rd
Warwick, MA 01378
978-544-6315

Elevation	937 ft.
Land area (square miles)	37.3
Water area (square miles)	0.3
Population density, 2008 (est)	20.1
Year incorporated	1763
Website	www.warwickma.org

Voters & Government Information

Government type	Open Town Meeting
Number of Selectmen	3
US Congressional District(s)	1

Registered Voters, October 2008

Total	539
Democrats	138
Republicans	67
Unaffiliated/other	332

Local Officials, 2010

Chair, Bd. of Sel.	Nicholas C. Arguimbau
Town Coordinator	James David Young
Town Clerk	Jeannette H. Fellows
Treasurer	Terry L. Kemerer
Tax Collector	Terry L. Kemerer
Tax Assessor	Christopher Ryan (Chr)
Attorney	Fernand Dupre
Highway Supt	Timothy Kilhart
Building Inspector	Phillip Delorey
Planning Board	Edwin P. Cady (Chr)
Police Chief	Brian Peters
Fire Chief	Gunnar Lambert

Housing & Construction

New Privately Owned Housing Units Authorized by Building Permit

	Single Family	Total Bldgs	Total Units
2006	2	2	2
2007	1	1	1
2008	0	0	0

Parcel Count by Property Class, 2010

Total	695
Single family	338
Multiple units	2
Apartments	1
Condos	0
Vacant land	208
Open space	0
Commercial	1
Industrial	0
Misc. residential	21
Other use	124

Public Library

Warwick Free Public Library
4 Hotel Road
Warwick, MA 01378
(978)544-7866

Librarian	Nancy E. Hickler

Library Statistics, FY 2008

Population served, 2007	750
Registered users	572
Circulation	8,392
Reference transactons	341
Total program attendance	4,570
per capita:	
Holdings	16.15
Operating income	$37.35
Internet Access	
Internet computers available	4
Weekly users	60

Municipal Finance

Debt at year end 2008	$0
Moody's rating, July 2009	NA

Revenues, 2008

Total	$1,780,580
From all taxes	1,450,727
Federal aid	0
State aid	265,950
From other governments	3,212
Charges for services	6,032
Licenses, permits & fees	5,339
Fines & forfeits	0
Interfund transfers	15,000
Misc/other/special assessments	17,160

Expenditures, 2008

Total	$1,491,308
General government	132,691
Public safety	56,304
Other/fixed costs	134,969
Human services	12,880
Culture & recreation	25,092
Debt Service	0
Education	723,523
Public works	404,599
Intergovernmental	1,250

Taxation, 2010

Property type	Valuation	Rate
Total	$82,169,190	-
Residential	78,278,383	16.16
Open space	0	0.00
Commercial	1,588,828	16.16
Industrial	119,009	16.16
Personal	2,182,970	16.16

Average Single Family Tax Bill, 2010

Avg. assessed home value	$181,706
Avg. single fam. tax bill	$2,936
Hi-Lo ranking	240/301

Police & Crime, 2008

Number of police officers	NA
Violent crimes	NA
Property crimes	NA

Local School District

(school data 2007-08, except as noted)

Warwick (non-op)
97 F Sumner Turner Rd
Northfield, MA 01360
413-498-2911

Superintendent	Dayle Doiron

Non-operating district.
Resident students are sent to the Other School Districts listed below.

Grade plan	NA
Total enrollment '09-10	NA
Grade 12 enrollment, '09-10	NA
Graduation rate	NA
Dropout rate	NA
Per-pupil expenditure	NA
Avg teacher salary	NA
Student/teacher ratio '08-09	NA
Highly-qualified teachers, '08-09	NA
Teachers licensed in assigned subject	NA
Students per computer	NA

Other School Districts (see Appendix D for data)
Pioneer Valley Regional, Franklin County Vocational Tech

©2010 Information Publications, Inc. All rights reserved. Photocopying prohibited. For additional copies, contact the publisher at www.informationpublications.com or (877)544-INFO (4636)

See Introduction for an explanation of all data sources.

Demographics & Socio-Economic Characteristics

Population

1990	615
2000	544
Male	280
Female	264
2008	542
2010 (projected)††	501
2020 (projected)††	471

Race & Hispanic Origin, 2000

Race	
White	541
Black/African American	2
American Indian/Alaska Native	0
Asian	0
Hawaiian Native/Pacific Islander	0
Other Race	0
Two or more races	1
Hispanic origin	4

Age & Nativity, 2000

Under 5 years	27
18 years and over	400
21 years and over	380
65 years and over	54
85 years and over	4
Median Age	40.7
Native-born	540
Foreign-born	8

Age, 2020 (projected)††

Under 5 years	17
5 to 19 years	53
20 to 39 years	104
40 to 64 years	161
65 years and over	136

Educational Attainment, 2000

Population 25 years and over	378
High School graduates or higher	88.4%
Bachelor's degree or higher	25.4%
Graduate degree	7.9%

Income & Poverty, 1999

Per capita income,	$23,610
Median household income	$54,583
Median family income	$55,357
Persons in poverty	38
H'holds receiving public assistance	2
H'holds receiving social security	66

Households, 2000

Total households	203
With persons under 18	78
With persons over 65	42
Family households	163
Single person households	30
Persons per household	2.7
Persons per family	3.0

Labor & Employment, 2000

Civilian labor force	301
Unemployment rate	4.7%
Civilian labor force, 2008†	320
Unemployment rate†	5.0%
Civilian labor force, 12/09†	321
Unemployment rate†	6.9%
Employed persons 16 years and over, by occupation:	
Managers & professionals	79
Service occupations	55
Sales & office occupations	82
Farming, fishing & forestry	2
Construction & maintenance	34
Production & transportation	35
Self-employed persons	29

Most demographic data is from the 2000 Decennial Census
† Massachusetts Department of Revenue
†† University of Massachusetts, MISER

General Information

Town of Washington
8 Summit Hill Rd
Washington, MA 01223
413-623-8878

Elevation	1,420 ft.
Land area (square miles)	37.8
Water area (square miles)	0.9
Population density, 2008 (est)	14.3
Year incorporated	1777
Website	www.washington-ma.com

Voters & Government Information

Government type	Open Town Meeting
Number of Selectmen	3
US Congressional District(s)	1

Registered Voters, October 2008

Total	422
Democrats	141
Republicans	32
Unaffiliated/other	248

Local Officials, 2010

Chair, Bd. of Sel.	Rose Borgnis
Manager/Admin	NA
Clerk	Allison Mikaniewicz
Treasurer	Sandra Brazee
Tax Collector	Belinda Phillips
Tax Assessor	Kimbery Denault
Attorney	Sarah Bell
Public Works	David Fish
Building	Gary Danko
Comm Dev/Planning	NA
Police Chief	Victor Breen
Emerg/Fire Chief	Paul Mikaniewicz

Housing & Construction

New Privately Owned Housing Units Authorized by Building Permit

	Single Family	Total Bldgs	Total Units
2006	4	4	4
2007	3	3	3
2008	1	1	1

Parcel Count by Property Class, 2010

Total	516
Single family	243
Multiple units	0
Apartments	0
Condos	0
Vacant land	225
Open space	0
Commercial	7
Industrial	3
Misc. residential	5
Other use	33

Public Library

No Public Library

Library Statistics, FY 2008

Population served, 2007	
Registered users	
Circulation	
Reference transactons	
Total program attendance	
per capita:	
Holdings	
Operating income	
Internet Access	
Internet computers available	
Weekly users	

Municipal Finance

Debt at year end 2008	$151,770
Moody's rating, July 2009	NA

Revenues, 2008

Total	$1,165,378
From all taxes	831,407
Federal aid	0
State aid	194,030
From other governments	8,255
Charges for services	5,322
Licenses, permits & fees	2,461
Fines & forfeits	0
Interfund transfers	121,115
Misc/other/special assessments	1,394

Expenditures, 2008

Total	$1,183,496
General government	116,134
Public safety	27,614
Other/fixed costs	74,505
Human services	5,607
Culture & recreation	5,230
Debt Service	50,799
Education	574,015
Public works	320,356
Intergovernmental	6,272

Taxation, 2010

Property type	Valuation	Rate
Total	$70,666,890	-
Residential	65,916,914	12.42
Open space	0	0.00
Commercial	2,147,594	12.42
Industrial	229,100	12.42
Personal	2,373,282	12.42

Average Single Family Tax Bill, 2010

Avg. assessed home value	$209,413
Avg. single fam. tax bill	$2,601
Hi-Lo ranking	276/301

Police & Crime, 2008

Number of police officers	NA
Violent crimes	NA
Property crimes	NA

Local School District

(school data 2007-08, except as noted)

Washington (non-op)
PO Box 299
Dalton, MA 01227
413-684-0320

Superintendent .... James Stankiewicz

Non-operating district.
Resident students are sent to the Other School Districts listed below.

Grade plan	NA
Total enrollment '09-10	NA
Grade 12 enrollment, '09-10	NA
Graduation rate	NA
Dropout rate	NA
Per-pupil expenditure	NA
Avg teacher salary	NA
Student/teacher ratio '08-09	NA
Highly-qualified teachers, '08-09	NA
Teachers licensed in assigned subject	NA
Students per computer	NA

Other School Districts (see Appendix D for data)
Central Berkshire Regional

©2010 Information Publications, Inc. All rights reserved. Photocopying prohibited. For additional copies, contact the publisher at www.informationpublications.com or (877)544-INFO (4636)

Demographics & Socio-Economic Characteristics*

Population

1990	33,284
2000	32,986
Male	15,265
Female	17,721
2008	32,365
2010 (projected)††	30,984
2020 (projected)††	29,454

Race & Hispanic Origin, 2000

Race	
White	30,155
Black/African American	572
American Indian/Alaska Native	54
Asian	1,276
Hawaiian Native/Pacific Islander	6
Other Race	281
Two or more races	642
Hispanic origin	883

Age & Nativity, 2000

Under 5 years	1,535
18 years and over	28,327
21 years and over	27,096
65 years and over	5,505
85 years and over	807
Median Age	36.7
Native-born	26,279
Foreign-born	6,707

Age, 2020 (projected)††

Under 5 years	1,182
5 to 19 years	3,826
20 to 39 years	8,980
40 to 64 years	10,132
65 years and over	5,334

Educational Attainment, 2000

Population 25 years and over	25,300
High School graduates or higher	87.4%
Bachelor's degree or higher	47.2%
Graduate degree	21.1%

Income & Poverty, 1999

Per capita income,	$33,262
Median household income	$59,764
Median family income	$67,441
Persons in poverty	2,000
H'holds receiving public assistance	245
H'holds receiving social security	3,779

Households, 2000

Total households	14,629
With persons under 18	2,782
With persons over 65	3,913
Family households	7,325
Single person households	4,993
Persons per household	2.2
Persons per family	2.9

Labor & Employment, 2000

Civilian labor force	19,794
Unemployment rate	2.4%
Civilian labor force, 2008†	19,707
Unemployment rate†	4.5%
Civilian labor force, 12/09†	19,784
Unemployment rate†	6.6%
Employed persons 16 years and over, by occupation:	
Managers & professionals	10,703
Service occupations	1,861
Sales & office occupations	4,541
Farming, fishing & forestry	18
Construction & maintenance	894
Production & transportation	1,302
Self-employed persons	1,389

Most demographic data is from the 2000 Decennial Census
* see Appendix E for American Community Survey data
† Massachusetts Department of Revenue
†† University of Massachusetts, MISER

General Information

City of Watertown
149 Main St
Watertown, MA 02472
617-972-6465

Elevation	30 ft.
Land area (square miles)	4.1
Water area (square miles)	0.1
Population density, 2008 (est)	7,893.9
Year incorporated	1630
Website	www.watertown-ma.gov

Voters & Government Information

Government type	Council-Manager
Number of Councilpersons	9
US Congressional District(s)	7

Registered Voters, October 2008

Total	22,272
Democrats	10,292
Republicans	1,839
Unaffiliated/other	9,974

Local Officials, 2010

Council President	Mark Sideris
Manager	Michael J. Driscoll
City Clerk	John E. Flynn
Finance Director	Phyllis Marshall
Tax Collector	Phyllis Marshall
Tax Assessor	Daniel A. Loughlin
Attorney	Kopelman & Paige
Public Works	Gerald S. Mee Jr
Building	Steven Magoon
Comm Dev/Planning	Steven Magoon
Police Chief	Edward Deveau
Emerg/Fire Chief	Mario Orangio

Housing & Construction

New Privately Owned Housing Units Authorized by Building Permit

	Single Family	Total Bldgs	Total Units
2006	2	10	199
2007	2	7	15
2008	0	1	2

Parcel Count by Property Class, 2010

Total	NA
Single family	NA
Multiple units	NA
Apartments	NA
Condos	NA
Vacant land	NA
Open space	NA
Commercial	NA
Industrial	NA
Misc. residential	NA
Other use	NA

Public Library

Watertown Free Public Library
123 Main Street
Watertown, MA 02472
(617)972-6436

Director .... Leone E. Cole

Library Statistics, FY 2008

Population served, 2007	32,521
Registered users	18,114
Circulation	583,516
Reference transactons	35,784
Total program attendance	360,039
per capita:	
Holdings	4.23
Operating income	$68.48
Internet Access	
Internet computers available	60
Weekly users	1,674

Municipal Finance

Debt at year end 2008	$39,698,019
Moody's rating, July 2009	Aa3

Revenues, 2008

Total	$91,996,602
From all taxes	69,989,657
Federal aid	0
State aid	12,651,353
From other governments	35,643
Charges for services	2,586,356
Licenses, permits & fees	207,629
Fines & forfeits	935,137
Interfund transfers	3,210,447
Misc/other/special assessments	1,190,190

Expenditures, 2008

Total	$88,238,787
General government	3,918,485
Public safety	14,103,664
Other/fixed costs	18,090,445
Human services	774,318
Culture & recreation	2,614,001
Debt Service	6,075,457
Education	30,345,050
Public works	8,201,467
Intergovernmental	3,760,776

Taxation, 2010

Property type	Valuation	Rate
Total	NA	-
Residential	NA	NA
Open space	NA	NA
Commercial	NA	NA
Industrial	NA	NA
Personal	NA	NA

Average Single Family Tax Bill, 2010

Avg. assessed home value	NA
Avg. single fam. tax bill	NA
Hi-Lo ranking	NA

Police & Crime, 2008

Number of police officers	70
Violent crimes	52
Property crimes	563

Local School District

(school data 2007-08, except as noted)

Watertown
30 Common Street
Watertown, MA 02472
617-926-7700

Superintendent	Ann Koufman-Frederick
Grade plan	PK-12
Total enrollment '09-10	2,613
Grade 12 enrollment, '09-10	181
Graduation rate	90.4%
Dropout rate	3.8%
Per-pupil expenditure	$15,974
Avg teacher salary	$63,801
Student/teacher ratio '08-09	11.5 to 1
Highly-qualified teachers, '08-09	98.6%
Teachers licensed in assigned subject	98.2%
Students per computer	3.2

Massachusetts Competency Assessment System (MCAS), 2009 results

	English		Math	
	% Prof	CPI	% Prof	CPI
Gr 4	49%	79.4	43%	77.2
Gr 6	76%	90.1	62%	81.6
Gr 8	81%	91.9	46%	71.4
Gr 10	83%	93.5	76%	88.8

Other School Districts (see Appendix D for data)
None

©2010 Information Publications, Inc. All rights reserved. Photocopying prohibited. For additional copies, contact the publisher at www.informationpublications.com or (877)544-INFO (4636)

See Introduction for an explanation of all data sources.

Demographics & Socio-Economic Characteristics

Population

1990	11,874
2000	13,100
Male	6,312
Female	6,788
2008	12,996
2010 (projected)††	12,333
2020 (projected)††	10,789

Race & Hispanic Origin, 2000

Race	
White	12,080
Black/African American	98
American Indian/Alaska Native	13
Asian	699
Hawaiian Native/Pacific Islander	4
Other Race	35
Two or more races	171
Hispanic origin	151

Age & Nativity, 2000

Under 5 years	937
18 years and over	9,341
21 years and over	9,088
65 years and over	1,868
85 years and over	213
Median Age	41.4
Native-born	11,939
Foreign-born	1,161

Age, 2020 (projected)††

Under 5 years	593
5 to 19 years	2,176
20 to 39 years	1,944
40 to 64 years	3,578
65 years and over	2,498

Educational Attainment, 2000

Population 25 years and over	8,968
High School graduates or higher	96.5%
Bachelor's degree or higher	68.3%
Graduate degree	37.9%

Income & Poverty, 1999

Per capita income,	$52,717
Median household income	$101,036
Median family income	$113,671
Persons in poverty	322
H'holds receiving public assistance	31
H'holds receiving social security	1,089

Households, 2000

Total households	4,625
With persons under 18	1,969
With persons over 65	1,194
Family households	3,722
Single person households	743
Persons per household	2.8
Persons per family	3.2

Labor & Employment, 2000

Civilian labor force	6,630
Unemployment rate	2.0%
Civilian labor force, 2008†	6,720
Unemployment rate†	4.4%
Civilian labor force, 12/09†	6,725
Unemployment rate†	6.8%
Employed persons 16 years and over, by occupation:	
Managers & professionals	4,232
Service occupations	483
Sales & office occupations	1,304
Farming, fishing & forestry	0
Construction & maintenance	270
Production & transportation	210
Self-employed persons	748

Most demographic data is from the 2000 Decennial Census
† Massachusetts Department of Revenue
†† University of Massachusetts, MISER

General Information

Town of Wayland
41 Cochituate Rd
Wayland, MA 01778
508-358-7701

Elevation	127 ft.
Land area (square miles)	15.2
Water area (square miles)	0.7
Population density, 2008 (est)	855.0
Year incorporated	1835
Website	www.wayland.ma.us

Voters & Government Information

Government type	Open Town Meeting
Number of Selectmen	5
US Congressional District(s)	5, 7

Registered Voters, October 2008

Total	10,029
Democrats	2,952
Republicans	1,412
Unaffiliated/other	5,639

Local Officials, 2010

Chair, Bd. of Sel.	Joseph Nolan
Manager/Exec.	Fred Turkington
Town Clerk	Lois M. Toombs
Finance Director	Michael DiPietro
Treas/Collector	Paul Keating
Tax Assessor	Ellen Brideau (Chr)
Attorney	Mark J. Lanza
Public Works	Don Ouellette
Building	Daniel Bennett
Comm Dev/Planning	Sarkis Sarkisian
Police Chief	Robert Irving
Fire Chief	Robert Loomer

Housing & Construction

New Privately Owned Housing Units Authorized by Building Permit

	Single Family	Total Bldgs	Total Units
2006	23	23	23
2007	17	17	17
2008	5	5	5

Parcel Count by Property Class, 2010

Total	5,041
Single family	4,030
Multiple units	55
Apartments	6
Condos	514
Vacant land	258
Open space	0
Commercial	101
Industrial	8
Misc. residential	34
Other use	35

Public Library

Wayland Free Public Library
5 Concord Rd.
Wayland, MA 01778
(508)358-2311

Director .... Ann F. Knight

Library Statistics, FY 2008

Population served, 2007	13,017
Registered users	7,893
Circulation	273,823
Reference transactons	20,200
Total program attendance	120,597
per capita:	
Holdings	7.42
Operating income	$78.14
Internet Access	
Internet computers available	11
Weekly users	423

Municipal Finance

Debt at year end 2008	$26,841,054
Moody's rating, July 2009	Aaa

Revenues, 2008

Total	$58,169,718
From all taxes	49,386,146
Federal aid	0
State aid	4,788,989
From other governments	54,336
Charges for services	845,849
Licenses, permits & fees	548,530
Fines & forfeits	16,931
Interfund transfers	634,851
Misc/other/special assessments	947,043

Expenditures, 2008

Total	$55,195,321
General government	2,750,446
Public safety	5,102,717
Other/fixed costs	9,204,712
Human services	970,779
Culture & recreation	1,636,271
Debt Service	3,805,967
Education	29,307,676
Public works	2,241,149
Intergovernmental	161,873

Taxation, 2010

Property type	Valuation	Rate
Total	$3,020,718,290	-
Residential	2,871,312,611	17.78
Open space	0	0.00
Commercial	89,028,689	17.78
Industrial	28,549,000	17.78
Personal	31,827,990	17.78

Average Single Family Tax Bill, 2010

Avg. assessed home value	$617,648
Avg. single fam. tax bill	$10,982
Hi-Lo ranking	6/301

Police & Crime, 2008

Number of police officers	22
Violent crimes	NA
Property crimes	NA

Local School District

(school data 2007-08, except as noted)

Wayland
41 Cochituate Rd
Wayland, MA 01778
508-358-3774

Superintendent	Gary Burton
Grade plan	PK-12
Total enrollment '09-10	2,738
Grade 12 enrollment, '09-10	217
Graduation rate	98.7%
Dropout rate	0.0%
Per-pupil expenditure	$14,033
Avg teacher salary	$73,015
Student/teacher ratio '08-09	13.7 to 1
Highly-qualified teachers, '08-09	98.7%
Teachers licensed in assigned subject	99.4%
Students per computer	2.3

Massachusetts Competency Assessment System (MCAS), 2009 results

	English		Math	
	% Prof	CPI	% Prof	CPI
Gr 4	74%	90.1	64%	87.1
Gr 6	89%	95.7	75%	89.1
Gr 8	96%	98.9	75%	89.2
Gr 10	93%	97.6	95%	97.6

Other School Districts (see Appendix D for data)
Minuteman Vocational Tech

©2010 Information Publications, Inc. All rights reserved. Photocopying prohibited. For additional copies, contact the publisher at www.informationpublications.com or (877)544-INFO (4636)

See Introduction for an explanation of all data sources.

Demographics & Socio-Economic Characteristics

Population

1990	16,196
2000	16,415
Male	7,901
Female	8,514
2008	16,655
2010 (projected)††	17,287
2020 (projected)††	18,306

Race & Hispanic Origin, 2000

Race	
White	15,564
Black/African American	183
American Indian/Alaska Native	56
Asian	156
Hawaiian Native/Pacific Islander	0
Other Race	245
Two or more races	211
Hispanic origin	649

Age & Nativity, 2000

Under 5 years	1,081
18 years and over	12,599
21 years and over	12,148
65 years and over	2,734
85 years and over	430
Median Age	38.0
Native-born	15,606
Foreign-born	809

Age, 2020 (projected)††

Under 5 years	1,014
5 to 19 years	2,883
20 to 39 years	4,640
40 to 64 years	6,272
65 years and over	3,497

Educational Attainment, 2000

Population 25 years and over	11,302
High School graduates or higher	76.6%
Bachelor's degree or higher	15.9%
Graduate degree	5.8%

Income & Poverty, 1999

Per capita income,	$20,410
Median household income	$38,169
Median family income	$48,898
Persons in poverty	1,767
H'holds receiving public assistance	310
H'holds receiving social security	2,119

Households, 2000

Total households	6,905
With persons under 18	2,096
With persons over 65	1,895
Family households	4,271
Single person households	2,186
Persons per household	2.3
Persons per family	2.9

Labor & Employment, 2000

Civilian labor force	8,127
Unemployment rate	4.6%
Civilian labor force, 2008†	8,379
Unemployment rate†	8.4%
Civilian labor force, 12/09†	8,541
Unemployment rate†	11.2%
Employed persons 16 years and over, by occupation:	
Managers & professionals	2,062
Service occupations	1,150
Sales & office occupations	2,211
Farming, fishing & forestry	14
Construction & maintenance	781
Production & transportation	1,534
Self-employed persons	438

Most demographic data is from the 2000 Decennial Census
† Massachusetts Department of Revenue
†† University of Massachusetts, MISER

General Information

Town of Webster
350 Main St
Webster, MA 01570
508-949-3800

Elevation	450 ft.
Land area (square miles)	12.5
Water area (square miles)	2.0
Population density, 2008 (est)	1,332.4
Year incorporated	1832
Website	webster-ma.gov

Voters & Government Information

Government type	Open Town Meeting
Number of Selectmen	5
US Congressional District(s)	2

Registered Voters, October 2008

Total	11,413
Democrats	3,633
Republicans	1,256
Unaffiliated/other	6,400

Local Officials, 2010

Chair, Bd. of Sel.	Robert Miller
Manager/Town Admin.	John F. McAuliffe
Clerk	Robert T. Craver
Finance Director	Pamela A. Regis
Tax Collector	Maryann McGeary
Tax Assessor	Marc Becker
Attorney	NA
Public Works	NA
Building	Wesley Mrocka
Planning	Paul LaFramboise
Police Chief	Timothy Bent
Emerg/Fire Chief	Gordon Forrester

Housing & Construction

New Privately Owned Housing Units Authorized by Building Permit

	Single Family	Total Bldgs	Total Units
2006	38	43	50
2007	20	20	20
2008	13	14	15

Parcel Count by Property Class, 2010

Total	6,632
Single family	3,747
Multiple units	795
Apartments	226
Condos	356
Vacant land	950
Open space	0
Commercial	328
Industrial	64
Misc. residential	61
Other use	105

Public Library

Chester C. Corbin Public Library
2 Lake St.
Webster, MA 01570
(508)949-3880

Director	Carrie Grimshaw

Library Statistics, FY 2008

Population served, 2007	16,705
Registered users	7,613
Circulation	50,744
Reference transactons	7,003
Total program attendance	32,120
per capita:	
Holdings	2.44
Operating income	$27.78
Internet Access	
Internet computers available	7
Weekly users	504

Municipal Finance

Debt at year end 2008	$24,258,116
Moody's rating, July 2009	A3

Revenues, 2008

Total	$31,469,066
From all taxes	17,032,733
Federal aid	299,565
State aid	12,305,150
From other governments	59,125
Charges for services	282,628
Licenses, permits & fees	309,063
Fines & forfeits	25,256
Interfund transfers	678,726
Misc/other/special assessments	238,410

Expenditures, 2008

Total	$27,921,905
General government	1,599,709
Public safety	2,790,522
Other/fixed costs	2,461,737
Human services	236,573
Culture & recreation	322,249
Debt Service	705,319
Education	17,580,386
Public works	1,618,756
Intergovernmental	606,654

Taxation, 2010

Property type	Valuation	Rate
Total	$1,552,795,850	-
Residential	1,321,093,796	9.77
Open space	0	0.00
Commercial	176,268,984	15.65
Industrial	24,994,070	15.65
Personal	30,439,000	15.65

Average Single Family Tax Bill, 2010

Avg. assessed home value	$248,626
Avg. single fam. tax bill	$2,429
Hi-Lo ranking	282/301

Police & Crime, 2008

Number of police officers	28
Violent crimes	NA
Property crimes	NA

Local School District

(school data 2007-08, except as noted)

Webster
P.O. Box 430
Webster, MA 01570
508-943-0104

Superintendent	Gregory Ciardi
Grade plan	PK-12
Total enrollment '09-10	1,942
Grade 12 enrollment, '09-10	140
Graduation rate	70.6%
Dropout rate	20.6%
Per-pupil expenditure	$11,409
Avg teacher salary	$60,260
Student/teacher ratio '08-09	14.7 to 1
Highly-qualified teachers, '08-09	94.6%
Teachers licensed in assigned subject	99.1%
Students per computer	4.1

Massachusetts Competency Assessment System (MCAS), 2009 results

	English		Math	
	% Prof	CPI	% Prof	CPI
Gr 4	42%	73.5	28%	69.7
Gr 6	60%	81.5	33%	65.8
Gr 8	51%	78.5	23%	52.6
Gr 10	74%	88.9	67%	84.3

Other School Districts (see Appendix D for data)
Southern Worcester County Vocational Tech

©2010 Information Publications, Inc. All rights reserved. Photocopying prohibited. For additional copies, contact the publisher at www.informationpublications.com or (877)544-INFO (4636)

See Introduction for an explanation of all data sources.

Demographics & Socio-Economic Characteristics*

Population

1990	26,615
2000	26,613
Male	11,651
Female	14,962
2008	27,244
2010 (projected)††	26,002
2020 (projected)††	24,291

Race & Hispanic Origin, 2000

Race	
White	23,947
Black/African American	426
American Indian/Alaska Native	22
Asian	1,691
Hawaiian Native/Pacific Islander	3
Other Race	141
Two or more races	383
Hispanic origin	617

Age & Nativity, 2000

Under 5 years	1,954
18 years and over	19,938
21 years and over	17,589
65 years and over	3,710
85 years and over	533
Median Age	37.6
Native-born	23,723
Foreign-born	2,890

Age, 2020 (projected)††

Under 5 years	1,806
5 to 19 years	7,150
20 to 39 years	5,249
40 to 64 years	5,984
65 years and over	4,102

Educational Attainment, 2000

Population 25 years and over	16,228
High School graduates or higher	97.6%
Bachelor's degree or higher	75.9%
Graduate degree	41.2%

Income & Poverty, 1999

Per capita income,	$52,866
Median household income	$113,686
Median family income	$134,769
Persons in poverty	885
H'holds receiving public assistance	92
H'holds receiving social security	2,308

Households, 2000

Total households	8,594
With persons under 18	3,480
With persons over 65	2,436
Family households	6,537
Single person households	1,775
Persons per household	2.7
Persons per family	3.1

Labor & Employment, 2000

Civilian labor force	12,945
Unemployment rate	3.5%
Civilian labor force, 2008†	13,131
Unemployment rate†	3.6%
Civilian labor force, 12/09†	12,999
Unemployment rate†	5.4%
Employed persons 16 years and over, by occupation:	
Managers & professionals	8,313
Service occupations	893
Sales & office occupations	2,840
Farming, fishing & forestry	0
Construction & maintenance	205
Production & transportation	243
Self-employed persons	1,362

Most demographic data is from the 2000 Decennial Census
* see Appendix E for American Community Survey data
† Massachusetts Department of Revenue
†† University of Massachusetts, MISER

General Information

Town of Wellesley
525 Washington St
Wellesley, MA 02482
781-431-1019

Elevation	145 ft.
Land area (square miles)	10.2
Water area (square miles)	0.3
Population density, 2008 (est)	2,671.0
Year incorporated	1881
Website	www.wellesleyma.gov

Voters & Government Information

Government type	Rep. Twn. Mtg. (240)
Number of Selectmen	5
US Congressional District(s)	4

Registered Voters, October 2008

Total	18,878
Democrats	5,672
Republicans	3,716
Unaffiliated/other	9,421

Local Officials, 2010

Chair, Bd. of Sel.	Barbara Searle
Manager/Exec.	Hans Larsen
Clerk	Kathleen F. Nagle
Finance Director	Sheryl Strother
Tax Collector	Marc Waldman
Tax Assessor	Donna McCabe
Attorney	Albert S. Robinson
Public Works	Michael Pakstis
Building	Michael Grant
Planning	Meghan Jop
Police Chief	Terrence Cunningham
Emerg/Fire Chief	Rick Delorie

Housing & Construction

New Privately Owned Housing Units Authorized by Building Permit

	Single Family	Total Bldgs	Total Units
2006	53	54	81
2007	69	69	69
2008	51	51	51

Parcel Count by Property Class, 2010

Total	8,416
Single family	7,283
Multiple units	149
Apartments	32
Condos	425
Vacant land	266
Open space	0
Commercial	208
Industrial	3
Misc. residential	27
Other use	23

Public Library

Wellesley Free Library
530 Washington Street
Wellesley, MA 02482
(781)235-1610

Director	Janice Coduri

Library Statistics, FY 2008

Population served, 2007	26,985
Registered users	23,973
Circulation	669,844
Reference transactons	29,941
Total program attendance	409,555
per capita:	
Holdings	9.68
Operating income	$93.65
Internet Access	
Internet computers available	50
Weekly users	2,268

Municipal Finance

Debt at year end 2008	$55,306,792
Moody's rating, July 2009	Aaa

Revenues, 2008

Total	$105,494,695
From all taxes	89,030,401
Federal aid	0
State aid	7,259,251
From other governments	180,047
Charges for services	1,480,809
Licenses, permits & fees	1,846,562
Fines & forfeits	0
Interfund transfers	555,151
Misc/other/special assessments	2,571,237

Expenditures, 2008

Total	$94,348,576
General government	3,716,211
Public safety	9,425,166
Other/fixed costs	14,014,361
Human services	828,845
Culture & recreation	2,720,845
Debt Service	8,068,646
Education	48,102,609
Public works	6,618,656
Intergovernmental	1,009,686

Taxation, 2010

Property type	Valuation	Rate
Total	$8,981,931,000	-
Residential	7,936,624,000	10.48
Open space	0	0.00
Commercial	947,998,000	10.48
Industrial	6,622,000	10.48
Personal	90,687,000	10.48

Average Single Family Tax Bill, 2010

Avg. assessed home value	$1,009,640
Avg. single fam. tax bill	$10,581
Hi-Lo ranking	8/301

Police & Crime, 2008

Number of police officers	39
Violent crimes	14
Property crimes	215

Local School District

(school data 2007-08, except as noted)

Wellesley
40 Kingsbury Street
Wellesley, MA 02481
781-446-6210

Superintendent	Bella Wong
Grade plan	PK-12
Total enrollment '09-10	4,868
Grade 12 enrollment, '09-10	290
Graduation rate	96.2%
Dropout rate	0.3%
Per-pupil expenditure	$13,916
Avg teacher salary	$71,128
Student/teacher ratio '08-09	13.7 to 1
Highly-qualified teachers, '08-09	95.4%
Teachers licensed in assigned subject	97.4%
Students per computer	3.2

Massachusetts Competency Assessment System (MCAS), 2009 results

	English		Math	
	% Prof	CPI	% Prof	CPI
Gr 4	83%	93.1	66%	87.5
Gr 6	92%	96.8	79%	91.2
Gr 8	96%	99	73%	89.1
Gr 10	97%	98.7	96%	98.1

Other School Districts (see Appendix D for data)
Norfolk County Agricultural

©2010 Information Publications, Inc. All rights reserved. Photocopying prohibited. For additional copies, contact the publisher at www.informationpublications.com or (877)544-INFO (4636)

©2010 Information Publications, Inc. All rights reserved. Photocopying prohibited. For additional copies, contact the publisher at www.informationpublications.com or (877)544-INFO (4636)

Demographics & Socio-Economic Characteristics

Population

1990	2,493
2000	2,749
Male	1,296
Female	1,453
2008	2,724
2010 (projected)††	3,056
2020 (projected)††	3,388

Race & Hispanic Origin, 2000

Race	
White	2,655
Black/African American	26
American Indian/Alaska Native	8
Asian	10
Hawaiian Native/Pacific Islander	1
Other Race	16
Two or more races	33
Hispanic origin	19

Age & Nativity, 2000

Under 5 years	118
18 years and over	2,259
21 years and over	2,199
65 years and over	597
85 years and over	68
Median Age	47.0
Native-born	2,656
Foreign-born	95

Age, 2020 (projected)††

Under 5 years	113
5 to 19 years	302
20 to 39 years	555
40 to 64 years	1,203
65 years and over	1,215

Educational Attainment, 2000

Population 25 years and over	2,135
High School graduates or higher	92.7%
Bachelor's degree or higher	40.3%
Graduate degree	19.0%

Income & Poverty, 1999

Per capita income,	$25,712
Median household income	$43,558
Median family income	$50,990
Persons in poverty	205
H'holds receiving public assistance	16
H'holds receiving social security	474

Households, 2000

Total households	1,301
With persons under 18	279
With persons over 65	433
Family households	725
Single person households	453
Persons per household	2.1
Persons per family	2.8

Labor & Employment, 2000

Civilian labor force	1,452
Unemployment rate	7.6%
Civilian labor force, 2008†	1,642
Unemployment rate†	13.9%
Civilian labor force, 12/09†	1,707
Unemployment rate†	21.4%
Employed persons 16 years and over, by occupation:	
Managers & professionals	422
Service occupations	254
Sales & office occupations	291
Farming, fishing & forestry	47
Construction & maintenance	242
Production & transportation	86
Self-employed persons	312

Most demographic data is from the 2000 Decennial Census
† Massachusetts Department of Revenue
†† University of Massachusetts, MISER

General Information

Town of Wellfleet
300 Main St
Wellfleet, MA 02667
508-349-0300

Elevation	25 ft.
Land area (square miles)	19.8
Water area (square miles)	15.5
Population density, 2008 (est)	137.6
Year incorporated	1763
Website	www.wellfleet-ma.gov

Voters & Government Information

Government type	Open Town Meeting
Number of Selectmen	5
US Congressional District(s)	10

Registered Voters, October 2008

Total	2,625
Democrats	998
Republicans	299
Unaffiliated/other	1,307

Local Officials, 2010

Chair, Bd. of Sel.	Dale Donovan
Town Administrator	Paul Sieloff
Town Clerk	Dawn E. Rickman
Treasurer	Dawn E. Rickman
Tax Collector	Marianne L. Nickerson
Tax Assessor	Nancy Vail
Attorney	Kopelman & Paige
Public Works	Mark Vincent
Building Inspector	Paul Murphy
Planning	NA
Police Chief	Richard Rosenthal
Fire Chief	Daniel Silverman

Housing & Construction

New Privately Owned Housing Units Authorized by Building Permit

	Single Family	Total Bldgs	Total Units
2006	15	15	15
2007	16	16	16
2008	13	13	13

Parcel Count by Property Class, 2010

Total	4,360
Single family	3,018
Multiple units	73
Apartments	10
Condos	313
Vacant land	605
Open space	0
Commercial	94
Industrial	5
Misc. residential	171
Other use	71

Public Library

Wellfleet Public Library
55 West Main Street
Wellfleet, MA 02667
(508)349-0310

Director	Elaine R. McIlroy

Library Statistics, FY 2008

Population served, 2007	2,748
Registered users	9,550
Circulation	110,073
Reference transactons	6,357
Total program attendance	87,255
per capita:	
Holdings	17.93
Operating income	$140.51
Internet Access	
Internet computers available	18
Weekly users	540

Municipal Finance

Debt at year end 2008	$7,839,641
Moody's rating, July 2009	NA

Revenues, 2008

Total	$14,965,649
From all taxes	12,188,283
Federal aid	0
State aid	520,570
From other governments	2,380
Charges for services	168,912
Licenses, permits & fees	196,294
Fines & forfeits	39,672
Interfund transfers	1,608,888
Misc/other/special assessments	120,325

Expenditures, 2008

Total	$13,928,898
General government	1,271,805
Public safety	2,659,519
Other/fixed costs	1,864,517
Human services	363,979
Culture & recreation	742,527
Debt Service	1,205,775
Education	3,890,947
Public works	1,625,868
Intergovernmental	302,427

Taxation, 2010

Property type	Valuation	Rate
Total	$2,189,898,760	-
Residential	2,081,989,976	6.09
Open space	0	0.00
Commercial	80,885,424	6.09
Industrial	1,146,600	6.09
Personal	25,876,760	6.09

Average Single Family Tax Bill, 2010

Avg. assessed home value	$567,314
Avg. single fam. tax bill	$3,455
Hi-Lo ranking	180/301

Police & Crime, 2008

Number of police officers	13
Violent crimes	10
Property crimes	66

Local School District

(school data 2007-08, except as noted)

Wellfleet
78 Eldredge Pkwy
Orleans, MA 02653
508-255-8800

Superintendent	Richard Hoffmann
Grade plan	PK-5
Total enrollment '09-10	147
Grade 12 enrollment, '09-10	0
Graduation rate	NA
Dropout rate	NA
Per-pupil expenditure	$18,052
Avg teacher salary	$52,231
Student/teacher ratio '08-09	7.1 to 1
Highly-qualified teachers, '08-09	100.0%
Teachers licensed in assigned subject	100.0%
Students per computer	2.1

Massachusetts Competency Assessment System (MCAS), 2009 results

	English		Math	
	% Prof	CPI	% Prof	CPI
Gr 4	57%	82.6	57%	83.7
Gr 6	NA	NA	NA	NA
Gr 8	NA	NA	NA	NA
Gr 10	NA	NA	NA	NA

Other School Districts (see Appendix D for data)
Nauset Regional, Cape Cod Vocational Tech

See Introduction for an explanation of all data sources.

Demographics & Socio-Economic Characteristics

Population

1990	899
2000	986
Male	509
Female	477
2008	1,000
2010 (projected)††	1,079
2020 (projected)††	1,122

Race & Hispanic Origin, 2000

Race	
White	912
Black/African American	34
American Indian/Alaska Native	0
Asian	4
Hawaiian Native/Pacific Islander	0
Other Race	13
Two or more races	23
Hispanic origin	14

Age & Nativity, 2000

Under 5 years	42
18 years and over	733
21 years and over	695
65 years and over	45
85 years and over	12
Median Age	38.1
Native-born	971
Foreign-born	15

Age, 2020 (projected)††

Under 5 years	54
5 to 19 years	202
20 to 39 years	265
40 to 64 years	435
65 years and over	166

Educational Attainment, 2000

Population 25 years and over	642
High School graduates or higher	92.1%
Bachelor's degree or higher	41.1%
Graduate degree	17.3%

Income & Poverty, 1999

Per capita income,	$19,701
Median household income	$43,846
Median family income	$60,147
Persons in poverty	91
H'holds receiving public assistance	8
H'holds receiving social security	48

Households, 2000

Total households	378
With persons under 18	112
With persons over 65	33
Family households	225
Single person households	108
Persons per household	2.4
Persons per family	2.9

Labor & Employment, 2000

Civilian labor force	614
Unemployment rate	4.7%
Civilian labor force, 2008†	592
Unemployment rate†	5.9%
Civilian labor force, 12/09†	585
Unemployment rate†	8.4%
Employed persons 16 years and over, by occupation:	
Managers & professionals	221
Service occupations	85
Sales & office occupations	115
Farming, fishing & forestry	11
Construction & maintenance	83
Production & transportation	70
Self-employed persons	106

Most demographic data is from the 2000 Decennial Census
† Massachusetts Department of Revenue
†† University of Massachusetts, MISER

General Information

Town of Wendell
PO Box 41
Wendell, MA 01379
978-544-3395

Elevation	1,164 ft.
Land area (square miles)	32.0
Water area (square miles)	0.2
Population density, 2008 (est)	31.3
Year incorporated	1781
Website	www.wendellmass.us

Voters & Government Information

Government type	Open Town Meeting
Number of Selectmen	3
US Congressional District(s)	1

Registered Voters, October 2008

Total	702
Democrats	225
Republicans	33
Unaffiliated/other	433

Local Officials, 2010

Chair, Bd. of Sel.	Theodore Lewis
Town Coordinator	Nancy Aldrich
Clerk	Anny Hartjens
Treasurer	Carolyn Manley
Tax Collector	Penny Delorey
Tax Assessor	Paul Sullivan
Attorney	NA
Public Works	NA
Building	Phil Delorey
Planning	Deirdre Cabral
Police Chief	Edward Chase
Fire Chief	Everett Ricketts Sr

Housing & Construction

New Privately Owned Housing Units Authorized by Building Permit

	Single Family	Total Bldgs	Total Units
2006	6	6	6
2007	5	5	5
2008	4	4	4

Parcel Count by Property Class, 2010

Total	NA
Single family	NA
Multiple units	NA
Apartments	NA
Condos	NA
Vacant land	NA
Open space	NA
Commercial	NA
Industrial	NA
Misc. residential	NA
Other use	NA

Public Library

Wendell Free Library
PO Box 236
Wendell, MA 01379
(978)544-3559

Librarian	Rosie Heidkamp

Library Statistics, FY 2008

Population served, 2007	1,003
Registered users	1,018
Circulation	11,879
Reference transactons	0
Total program attendance	7,964
per capita:	
Holdings	14.63
Operating income	$43.44
Internet Access	
Internet computers available	6
Weekly users	35

Municipal Finance

Debt at year end 2008	$388,460
Moody's rating, July 2009	NA

Revenues, 2008

Total	$2,076,847
From all taxes	1,497,633
Federal aid	0
State aid	435,793
From other governments	477
Charges for services	31,472
Licenses, permits & fees	4,915
Fines & forfeits	0
Interfund transfers	35,745
Misc/other/special assessments	35,406

Expenditures, 2008

Total	$1,819,720
General government	228,173
Public safety	55,248
Other/fixed costs	111,000
Human services	16,588
Culture & recreation	21,082
Debt Service	109,835
Education	916,363
Public works	354,452
Intergovernmental	6,979

Taxation, 2010

Property type	Valuation	Rate
Total	NA	-
Residential	NA	NA
Open space	NA	NA
Commercial	NA	NA
Industrial	NA	NA
Personal	NA	NA

Average Single Family Tax Bill, 2010

Avg. assessed home value	NA
Avg. single fam. tax bill	NA
Hi-Lo ranking	NA

Police & Crime, 2008

Number of police officers	NA
Violent crimes	NA
Property crimes	NA

Local School District

(school data 2007-08, except as noted)

Wendell (non-op)
18 Pleasant Street
Erving, MA 01344
413-423-3337

Superintendent........... Joan Wickman

Non-operating district.
Resident students are sent to the Other School Districts listed below.

Grade plan	NA
Total enrollment '09-10	NA
Grade 12 enrollment, '09-10	NA
Graduation rate	NA
Dropout rate	NA
Per-pupil expenditure	NA
Avg teacher salary	NA
Student/teacher ratio '08-09	NA
Highly-qualified teachers, '08-09	NA
Teachers licensed in assigned subject	NA
Students per computer	NA

Other School Districts (see Appendix D for data)
New Salem-Wendell and Ralph C. Mahar Regionals, Franklin County Vocational Tech

©2010 Information Publications, Inc. All rights reserved. Photocopying prohibited. For additional copies, contact the publisher at www.informationpublications.com or (877)544-INFO (4636)

See Introduction for an explanation of all data sources.

Demographics & Socio-Economic Characteristics

Population

1990	4,212
2000	4,440
Male	2,006
Female	2,434
2008	4,788
2010 (projected)††	4,586
2020 (projected)††	4,561

Race & Hispanic Origin, 2000

Race	
White	4,344
Black/African American	19
American Indian/Alaska Native	1
Asian	60
Hawaiian Native/Pacific Islander	0
Other Race	3
Two or more races	13
Hispanic origin	26

Age & Nativity, 2000

Under 5 years	231
18 years and over	3,464
21 years and over	2,717
65 years and over	624
85 years and over	65
Median Age	33.6
Native-born	4,263
Foreign-born	177

Age, 2020 (projected)††

Under 5 years	277
5 to 19 years	1,466
20 to 39 years	1,081
40 to 64 years	1,017
65 years and over	720

Educational Attainment, 2000

Population 25 years and over	2,403
High School graduates or higher	94.3%
Bachelor's degree or higher	50.6%
Graduate degree	19.7%

Income & Poverty, 1999

Per capita income,	$36,812
Median household income	$90,524
Median family income	$98,004
Persons in poverty	115
H'holds receiving public assistance	30
H'holds receiving social security	508

Households, 2000

Total households	1,285
With persons under 18	505
With persons over 65	455
Family households	957
Single person households	289
Persons per household	2.7
Persons per family	3.2

Labor & Employment, 2000

Civilian labor force	2,352
Unemployment rate	30.7%
Civilian labor force, 2008†	1,798
Unemployment rate†	5.8%
Civilian labor force, 12/09†	1,806
Unemployment rate†	9.0%
Employed persons 16 years and over, by occupation:	
Managers & professionals	942
Service occupations	108
Sales & office occupations	401
Farming, fishing & forestry	0
Construction & maintenance	115
Production & transportation	64
Self-employed persons	182

Most demographic data is from the 2000 Decennial Census
† Massachusetts Department of Revenue
†† University of Massachusetts, MISER

General Information

Town of Wenham
138 Main St
Wenham, MA 01984
978-468-5520

Elevation	67 ft.
Land area (square miles)	7.7
Water area (square miles)	0.4
Population density, 2008 (est)	621.8
Year incorporated	1643
Website	www.wenhamma.gov

Voters & Government Information

Government type	Open Town Meeting
Number of Selectmen	3
US Congressional District(s)	6

Registered Voters, October 2008

Total	2,843
Democrats	552
Republicans	771
Unaffiliated/other	1,509

Local Officials, 2010

Chair, Bd. of Sel.	Lawrence Swartz
Manager/Admin	Jeff Chelgren
Town Clerk	Elizabeth Carey (Int)
Finance Director	Sarah Johnson
Tax Collector	Sarah Johnson
Tax Assessor	Stephen Gasperoni
Attorney	NA
Public Works	William Tyack
Building	NA
Comm Dev/Planning	NA
Police Chief	Kenneth Walsh
Emerg/Fire Chief	Robert Blanchard

Housing & Construction

New Privately Owned Housing Units Authorized by Building Permit

	Single Family	Total Bldgs	Total Units
2006	15	15	15
2007	18	18	18
2008	1	1	1

Parcel Count by Property Class, 2010

Total	1,373
Single family	1,082
Multiple units	50
Apartments	1
Condos	38
Vacant land	135
Open space	0
Commercial	12
Industrial	3
Misc. residential	24
Other use	28

Public Library

Hamilton-Wenham Public Library
14 Union Street
Hamilton, MA 01982
(978)468-5577

Director . . . . Jan Dempsey

Library Statistics, FY 2008

Population served, 2007	12,803
Registered users	11,245
Circulation	256,437
Reference transactons	16,940
Total program attendance	0
per capita:	
Holdings	8.72
Operating income	$57.56
Internet Access	
Internet computers available	18
Weekly users	716

Municipal Finance

Debt at year end 2008	$9,263,000
Moody's rating, July 2009	Aa3

Revenues, 2008

Total	$13,691,728
From all taxes	11,264,108
Federal aid	4,168
State aid	579,704
From other governments	16,970
Charges for services	147,440
Licenses, permits & fees	107,036
Fines & forfeits	26,760
Interfund transfers	15,000
Misc/other/special assessments	765,271

Expenditures, 2008

Total	$12,939,265
General government	773,174
Public safety	1,765,049
Other/fixed costs	1,031,222
Human services	91,849
Culture & recreation	715,947
Debt Service	753,274
Education	6,603,286
Public works	1,084,717
Intergovernmental	120,747

Taxation, 2010

Property type	Valuation	Rate
Total	$770,250,958	-
Residential	738,873,464	15.56
Open space	0	0.00
Commercial	22,774,859	15.56
Industrial	708,800	15.56
Personal	7,893,835	15.56

Average Single Family Tax Bill, 2010

Avg. assessed home value	$585,126
Avg. single fam. tax bill	$9,105
Hi-Lo ranking	12/301

Police & Crime, 2008

Number of police officers	10
Violent crimes	7
Property crimes	30

Local School District

(school data 2007-08, except as noted)

Wenham (non-op)
5 School Street
Wenham, MA 01984
978-468-5310

Superintendent . . . . Marinel McGrath

Non-operating district.
Resident students are sent to the Other School Districts listed below.

Grade plan	NA
Total enrollment '09-10	NA
Grade 12 enrollment, '09-10	NA
Graduation rate	NA
Dropout rate	NA
Per-pupil expenditure	NA
Avg teacher salary	NA
Student/teacher ratio '08-09	NA
Highly-qualified teachers, '08-09	NA
Teachers licensed in assigned subject	NA
Students per computer	NA

Other School Districts (see Appendix D for data)
Hamilton-Wenham Regional, North Shore Vocational Tech

©2010 Information Publications, Inc. All rights reserved. Photocopying prohibited. For additional copies, contact the publisher at www.informationpublications.com or (877)544-INFO (4636)

See Introduction for an explanation of all data sources.

Demographics & Socio-Economic Characteristics

Population

1990	6,611
2000	7,481
Male	4,232
Female	3,249
2008	8,277
2010 (projected)††	7,302
2020 (projected)††	7,056

Race & Hispanic Origin, 2000

Race	
White	6,855
Black/African American	399
American Indian/Alaska Native	12
Asian	64
Hawaiian Native/Pacific Islander	1
Other Race	47
Two or more races	103
Hispanic origin	357

Age & Nativity, 2000

Under 5 years	325
18 years and over	5,883
21 years and over	5,593
65 years and over	1,101
85 years and over	139
Median Age	38.4
Native-born	7,310
Foreign-born	171

Age, 2020 (projected)††

Under 5 years	307
5 to 19 years	1,091
20 to 39 years	2,119
40 to 64 years	2,227
65 years and over	1,312

Educational Attainment, 2000

Population 25 years and over	5,181
High School graduates or higher	89.4%
Bachelor's degree or higher	29.6%
Graduate degree	10.3%

Income & Poverty, 1999

Per capita income,	$22,899
Median household income	$53,777
Median family income	$69,100
Persons in poverty	196
H'holds receiving public assistance	21
H'holds receiving social security	836

Households, 2000

Total households	2,413
With persons under 18	843
With persons over 65	719
Family households	1,746
Single person households	574
Persons per household	2.6
Persons per family	3.0

Labor & Employment, 2000

Civilian labor force	3,193
Unemployment rate	2.9%
Civilian labor force, 2008†	3,331
Unemployment rate†	6.5%
Civilian labor force, 12/09†	3,443
Unemployment rate†	10.0%
Employed persons 16 years and over, by occupation:	
Managers & professionals	1,486
Service occupations	362
Sales & office occupations	794
Farming, fishing & forestry	9
Construction & maintenance	194
Production & transportation	254
Self-employed persons	210

Most demographic data is from the 2000 Decennial Census
† Massachusetts Department of Revenue
†† University of Massachusetts, MISER

General Information

Town of West Boylston
127 Hartwell Street, Suite 100
West Boylston, MA 01583
508-835-6240

Elevation	481 ft.
Land area (square miles)	12.9
Water area (square miles)	0.9
Population density, 2008 (est)	641.6
Year incorporated	1808
Website	www.westboylston-ma.gov

Voters & Government Information

Government type	Open Town Meeting
Number of Selectmen	5
US Congressional District(s)	3

Registered Voters, October 2008

Total	4,868
Democrats	1,054
Republicans	664
Unaffiliated/other	3,121

Local Officials, 2010

Chair, Bd. of Sel.	NA
Town Administrator	Leon Gaumond Jr
Clerk	Kim Donna Hopewell
Finance	Michael Daley
Treas/Collector	Bonnie Yasick
Tax Assessor	Harald Scheid
Attorney	Kopelman & Paige
Public Works	John Westerling
Building	Mark Brodeur
Planning	Lawrence Salate
Police Chief	Dennis Minnich Sr
Fire Chief	Richard Pauley Jr

Housing & Construction

New Privately Owned Housing Units Authorized by Building Permit

	Single Family	Total Bldgs	Total Units
2006	36	36	36
2007	45	45	45
2008	14	14	14

Parcel Count by Property Class, 2010

Total	2,866
Single family	1,934
Multiple units	65
Apartments	23
Condos	353
Vacant land	284
Open space	0
Commercial	80
Industrial	48
Misc. residential	11
Other use	68

Public Library

Beaman Memorial Public Library
8 Newton St.
West Boylston, MA 01583
(508)835-3711

Director	Louise Howland

Library Statistics, FY 2008

Population served, 2007	7,779
Registered users	6,896
Circulation	71,839
Reference transactons	7,943
Total program attendance	52,093
per capita:	
Holdings	7.73
Operating income	$45.06
Internet Access	
Internet computers available	11
Weekly users	74

Municipal Finance

Debt at year end 2008	$19,445,328
Moody's rating, July 2009	A3

Revenues, 2008

Total	$19,055,347
From all taxes	13,188,410
Federal aid	14,825
State aid	4,755,947
From other governments	44,848
Charges for services	65,060
Licenses, permits & fees	188,276
Fines & forfeits	8,490
Interfund transfers	589,477
Misc/other/special assessments	100,007

Expenditures, 2008

Total	$19,298,650
General government	1,085,247
Public safety	2,041,107
Other/fixed costs	3,529,292
Human services	89,060
Culture & recreation	328,552
Debt Service	1,685,803
Education	8,914,246
Public works	1,336,399
Intergovernmental	288,944

Taxation, 2010

Property type	Valuation	Rate
Total	$858,112,273	-
Residential	681,715,446	15.17
Open space	0	0.00
Commercial	67,907,254	15.17
Industrial	51,232,400	15.17
Personal	57,257,173	15.17

Average Single Family Tax Bill, 2010

Avg. assessed home value	$276,357
Avg. single fam. tax bill	$4,192
Hi-Lo ranking	122/301

Police & Crime, 2008

Number of police officers	13
Violent crimes	15
Property crimes	177

Local School District

(school data 2007-08, except as noted)

West Boylston
125 Crescent Street
West Boylston, MA 01583
508-835-2917

Superintendent	Thomas Kane
Grade plan	PK-12
Total enrollment '09-10	1,013
Grade 12 enrollment, '09-10	84
Graduation rate	91.9%
Dropout rate	4.7%
Per-pupil expenditure	$11,077
Avg teacher salary	$64,308
Student/teacher ratio '08-09	13.1 to 1
Highly-qualified teachers, '08-09	96.4%
Teachers licensed in assigned subject	99.0%
Students per computer	1.8

Massachusetts Competency Assessment System (MCAS), 2009 results

	English		Math	
	% Prof	CPI	% Prof	CPI
Gr 4	65%	85.8	54%	81.9
Gr 6	74%	88.7	55%	76.7
Gr 8	86%	93.5	36%	70.1
Gr 10	86%	93.8	88%	94.8

Other School Districts (see Appendix D for data)
None

©2010 Information Publications, Inc. All rights reserved. Photocopying prohibited. For additional copies, contact the publisher at www.informationpublications.com or (877)544-INFO (4636)

©2010 Information Publications, Inc. All rights reserved. Photocopying prohibited. For additional copies, contact the publisher at www.informationpublications.com or (877)544-INFO (4636)

Demographics & Socio-Economic Characteristics

Population

1990	6,389
2000	6,634
Male	3,244
Female	3,390
2008	6,674
2010 (projected)††	6,491
2020 (projected)††	6,239

Race & Hispanic Origin, 2000

Race	
White	6,395
Black/African American	63
American Indian/Alaska Native	17
Asian	45
Hawaiian Native/Pacific Islander	0
Other Race	30
Two or more races	84
Hispanic origin	67

Age & Nativity, 2000

Under 5 years	392
18 years and over	5,125
21 years and over	4,916
65 years and over	1,181
85 years and over	183
Median Age	40.1
Native-born	6,414
Foreign-born	238

Age, 2020 (projected)††

Under 5 years	290
5 to 19 years	1,002
20 to 39 years	1,282
40 to 64 years	2,123
65 years and over	1,542

Educational Attainment, 2000

Population 25 years and over	4,645
High School graduates or higher	88.0%
Bachelor's degree or higher	20.2%
Graduate degree	5.4%

Income & Poverty, 1999

Per capita income,	$23,701
Median household income	$55,958
Median family income	$64,815
Persons in poverty	235
H'holds receiving public assistance	35
H'holds receiving social security	740

Households, 2000

Total households	2,444
With persons under 18	833
With persons over 65	760
Family households	1,796
Single person households	531
Persons per household	2.7
Persons per family	3.1

Labor & Employment, 2000

Civilian labor force	3,422
Unemployment rate	3.1%
Civilian labor force, 2008†	3,545
Unemployment rate†	6.9%
Civilian labor force, 12/09†	3,502
Unemployment rate†	9.7%
Employed persons 16 years and over, by occupation:	
Managers & professionals	1,107
Service occupations	504
Sales & office occupations	952
Farming, fishing & forestry	7
Construction & maintenance	338
Production & transportation	407
Self-employed persons	160

Most demographic data is from the 2000 Decennial Census
† Massachusetts Department of Revenue
†† University of Massachusetts, MISER

General Information

Town of West Bridgewater
65 N Main St
West Bridgewater, MA 02379
508-894-1200

Elevation	50 ft.
Land area (square miles)	15.7
Water area (square miles)	0.1
Population density, 2008 (est)	425.1
Year incorporated	1822
Website	www.town.west-bridgewater.ma.us

Voters & Government Information

Government type	Open Town Meeting
Number of Selectmen	3
US Congressional District(s)	9

Registered Voters, October 2008

Total	5,063
Democrats	1,156
Republicans	865
Unaffiliated/other	3,007

Local Officials, 2010

Chair, Bd. of Sel.	Matthew P. Albanese
Administrator	Elizabeth Faricy
Town Clerk	Nancy L. Morrison
Finance Director	John Duggan
Tax Collector	John Duggan
Tax Assessor	Stephen McCarthy
Attorney	David Gay
Public Works	William Kovatis
Building	Paul Stringham
Comm Dev/Planning	Hugh Hurley
Police Chief	Donald Clark
Emerg/Fire Chief	Leonard Hunt

Housing & Construction

New Privately Owned Housing Units Authorized by Building Permit

	Single Family	Total Bldgs	Total Units
2006	6	7	8
2007	11	11	11
2008	5	5	5

Parcel Count by Property Class, 2010

Total	2,993
Single family	1,982
Multiple units	99
Apartments	3
Condos	79
Vacant land	350
Open space	0
Commercial	166
Industrial	95
Misc. residential	27
Other use	192

Public Library

West Bridgewater Public Library
80 Howard Street
West Bridgewater, MA 02379
(508)894-1255

Director	Beth Roll Smith

Library Statistics, FY 2008

Population served, 2007	6,679
Registered users	4,985
Circulation	80,308
Reference transactons	8,424
Total program attendance	43,538
per capita:	
Holdings	10.55
Operating income	$55.41
Internet Access	
Internet computers available	10
Weekly users	114

Municipal Finance

Debt at year end 2008	$7,851,872
Moody's rating, July 2009	A3

Revenues, 2008

Total	$24,891,116
From all taxes	15,744,452
Federal aid	0
State aid	3,275,454
From other governments	59,426
Charges for services	701,219
Licenses, permits & fees	200,328
Fines & forfeits	11,211
Interfund transfers	16,500
Misc/other/special assessments	2,441,263

Expenditures, 2008

Total	$22,412,681
General government	1,057,643
Public safety	3,383,936
Other/fixed costs	2,631,474
Human services	314,832
Culture & recreation	535,271
Debt Service	3,529,829
Education	9,274,367
Public works	983,016
Intergovernmental	678,450

Taxation, 2010

Property type	Valuation	Rate
Total	$1,048,518,431	-
Residential	737,200,271	13.00
Open space	0	0.00
Commercial	155,109,575	22.99
Industrial	122,444,035	22.99
Personal	33,764,550	22.99

Average Single Family Tax Bill, 2010

Avg. assessed home value	$311,359
Avg. single fam. tax bill	$4,048
Hi-Lo ranking	132/301

Police & Crime, 2008

Number of police officers	20
Violent crimes	7
Property crimes	133

Local School District

(school data 2007-08, except as noted)

West Bridgewater
2 Spring Street
West Bridgewater, MA 02379
508-894-1230

Superintendent	Patricia Oakley
Grade plan	PK-12
Total enrollment '09-10	1,292
Grade 12 enrollment, '09-10	93
Graduation rate	93.6%
Dropout rate	3.8%
Per-pupil expenditure	$9,808
Avg teacher salary	$59,631
Student/teacher ratio '08-09	15.8 to 1
Highly-qualified teachers, '08-09	100.0%
Teachers licensed in assigned subject	100.0%
Students per computer	5.1

Massachusetts Competency Assessment System (MCAS), 2009 results

	English		Math	
	% Prof	CPI	% Prof	CPI
Gr 4	65%	87.4	61%	88.1
Gr 6	69%	89.7	58%	82.5
Gr 8	81%	92.8	52%	76.1
Gr 10	93%	97.6	95%	97.9

Other School Districts (see Appendix D for data)
Southeastern Vocational Tech

See Introduction for an explanation of all data sources.

Demographics & Socio-Economic Characteristics

Population

1990	3,532
2000	3,804
Male	1,710
Female	2,094
2008	3,806
2010 (projected)††	3,936
2020 (projected)††	4,167

Race & Hispanic Origin, 2000

Race	
White	3,734
Black/African American	12
American Indian/Alaska Native	9
Asian	9
Hawaiian Native/Pacific Islander	2
Other Race	6
Two or more races	32
Hispanic origin	40

Age & Nativity, 2000

Under 5 years	193
18 years and over	2,932
21 years and over	2,823
65 years and over	795
85 years and over	246
Median Age	42.6
Native-born	3,732
Foreign-born	72

Age, 2020 (projected)††

Under 5 years	217
5 to 19 years	665
20 to 39 years	792
40 to 64 years	1,277
65 years and over	1,216

Educational Attainment, 2000

Population 25 years and over	2,721
High School graduates or higher	81.1%
Bachelor's degree or higher	21.5%
Graduate degree	9.2%

Income & Poverty, 1999

Per capita income,	$21,501
Median household income	$49,722
Median family income	$58,750
Persons in poverty	233
H'holds receiving public assistance	35
H'holds receiving social security	425

Households, 2000

Total households	1,362
With persons under 18	489
With persons over 65	336
Family households	965
Single person households	321
Persons per household	2.5
Persons per family	3.0

Labor & Employment, 2000

Civilian labor force	1,816
Unemployment rate	2.2%
Civilian labor force, 2008†	1,885
Unemployment rate†	7.5%
Civilian labor force, 12/09†	1,911
Unemployment rate†	10.1%
Employed persons 16 years and over, by occupation:	
Managers & professionals	584
Service occupations	285
Sales & office occupations	435
Farming, fishing & forestry	0
Construction & maintenance	187
Production & transportation	285
Self-employed persons	166

Most demographic data is from the 2000 Decennial Census
† Massachusetts Department of Revenue
†† University of Massachusetts, MISER

General Information

Town of West Brookfield
PO Box 372
West Brookfield, MA 01585
508-867-1421

Elevation	633 ft.
Land area (square miles)	20.5
Water area (square miles)	0.6
Population density, 2008 (est)	185.7
Year incorporated	1848
Email	tclerk@wbrookfield.com

Voters & Government Information

Government type	Open Town Meeting
Number of Selectmen	3
US Congressional District(s)	1

Registered Voters, October 2008

Total	2,627
Democrats	605
Republicans	397
Unaffiliated/other	1,604

Local Officials, 2010

Chair, Bd. of Sel.	Tom Long Jr
Manager/Admin	Johanna Barry
Clerk	Sarah Allen
Finance Director	Keith Arsenault
Tax Collector	Teresa Barrett
Tax Assessor	Peggy Walker
Attorney	NA
Public Works	Jason Benoit
Building	Jeffrey Taylor
Comm Dev/Planning	Tim Morrell
Police Chief	C. Thomas O'Donnell
Emerg/Fire Chief	Tim Batchelor

Housing & Construction

New Privately Owned Housing Units Authorized by Building Permit

	Single Family	Total Bldgs	Total Units
2006	9	9	9
2007	7	7	7
2008	6	6	6

Parcel Count by Property Class, 2010

Total	2,356
Single family	1,268
Multiple units	62
Apartments	10
Condos	23
Vacant land	792
Open space	0
Commercial	51
Industrial	17
Misc. residential	17
Other use	116

Public Library

Merriam-Gilbert Public Library
PO Box 364
West Brookfield, MA 01585
(508)867-1410

Director	Lisa Careau

Library Statistics, FY 2008

Population served, 2007	3,826
Registered users	2,385
Circulation	30,772
Reference transactons	0
Total program attendance	0
per capita:	
Holdings	4.49
Operating income	$51.44
Internet Access	
Internet computers available	3
Weekly users	85

Municipal Finance

Debt at year end 2008	$209,705
Moody's rating, July 2009	NA

Revenues, 2008

Total	$5,882,792
From all taxes	4,424,104
Federal aid	0
State aid	912,264
From other governments	10,642
Charges for services	33,031
Licenses, permits & fees	56,687
Fines & forfeits	0
Interfund transfers	208,446
Misc/other/special assessments	118,809

Expenditures, 2008

Total	$5,388,031
General government	519,750
Public safety	597,641
Other/fixed costs	455,522
Human services	118,058
Culture & recreation	239,082
Debt Service	0
Education	2,952,009
Public works	475,838
Intergovernmental	30,131

Taxation, 2010

Property type	Valuation	Rate
Total	$379,475,856	-
Residential	353,091,037	11.28
Open space	0	0.00
Commercial	13,730,042	11.28
Industrial	6,452,580	11.28
Personal	6,202,197	11.28

Average Single Family Tax Bill, 2010

Avg. assessed home value	$234,453
Avg. single fam. tax bill	$2,645
Hi-Lo ranking	273/301

Police & Crime, 2008

Number of police officers	6
Violent crimes	8
Property crimes	55

Local School District

(school data 2007-08, except as noted)

West Brookfield (non-op)
P.O. Box 1538, 48 High Street
Warren, MA 01083
413-436-9256

Superintendent	Brett Kustigian

Non-operating district.
Resident students are sent to the Other School Districts listed below.

Grade plan	NA
Total enrollment '09-10	NA
Grade 12 enrollment, '09-10	NA
Graduation rate	NA
Dropout rate	NA
Per-pupil expenditure	NA
Avg teacher salary	NA
Student/teacher ratio '08-09	NA
Highly-qualified teachers, '08-09	NA
Teachers licensed in assigned subject	NA
Students per computer	NA

Other School Districts (see Appendix D for data)
Quaboag Regional

©2010 Information Publications, Inc. All rights reserved. Photocopying prohibited. For additional copies, contact the publisher at www.informationpublications.com or (877)544-INFO (4636)

©2010 Information Publications, Inc. All rights reserved. Photocopying prohibited. For additional copies, contact the publisher at www.informationpublications.com or (877)544-INFO (4636)

Demographics & Socio-Economic Characteristics

Population

1990	3,421
2000	4,149
Male	2,069
Female	2,080
2008	4,269
2010 (projected)††	4,566
2020 (projected)††	5,001

Race & Hispanic Origin, 2000

Race	
White	4,086
Black/African American	8
American Indian/Alaska Native	1
Asian	22
Hawaiian Native/Pacific Islander	0
Other Race	15
Two or more races	17
Hispanic origin	27

Age & Nativity, 2000

Under 5 years	312
18 years and over	2,903
21 years and over	2,808
65 years and over	365
85 years and over	41
Median Age	39.6
Native-born	4,031
Foreign-born	118

Age, 2020 (projected)††

Under 5 years	388
5 to 19 years	1,203
20 to 39 years	963
40 to 64 years	1,603
65 years and over	844

Educational Attainment, 2000

Population 25 years and over	2,787
High School graduates or higher	96.6%
Bachelor's degree or higher	57.2%
Graduate degree	23.6%

Income & Poverty, 1999

Per capita income,	$35,323
Median household income	$92,828
Median family income	$99,050
Persons in poverty	156
H'holds receiving public assistance	11
H'holds receiving social security	303

Households, 2000

Total households	1,392
With persons under 18	676
With persons over 65	261
Family households	1,183
Single person households	165
Persons per household	3.0
Persons per family	3.3

Labor & Employment, 2000

Civilian labor force	2,240
Unemployment rate	1.7%
Civilian labor force, 2008†	2,234
Unemployment rate†	4.1%
Civilian labor force, 12/09†	2,229
Unemployment rate†	7.6%
Employed persons 16 years and over, by occupation:	
Managers & professionals	1,142
Service occupations	217
Sales & office occupations	598
Farming, fishing & forestry	8
Construction & maintenance	90
Production & transportation	146
Self-employed persons	160

Most demographic data is from the 2000 Decennial Census
† Massachusetts Department of Revenue
†† University of Massachusetts, MISER

General Information

Town of West Newbury
381 Main St
West Newbury, MA 01985
978-363-1100

Elevation	100 ft.
Land area (square miles)	13.5
Water area (square miles)	1.1
Population density, 2008 (est)	316.2
Year incorporated	1819
Website	www.wnewbury.org

Voters & Government Information

Government type	Open Town Meeting
Number of Selectmen	3
US Congressional District(s)	6

Registered Voters, October 2008

Total	3,281
Democrats	821
Republicans	696
Unaffiliated/other	1,744

Local Officials, 2010

Chair, Bd. of Sel.	Glenn A. Kemper
Manager/Admin	Kristine A. Pyle
Town Clerk	Lawrence J. Murphy
Finance Director	Tracy Blais
Tax Collector	Jennifer Yaskell
Tax Assessor	Karen Rassias
Attorney	Lawrence J. Murphy
Public Works	Gary Bill
Building	NA
Comm Dev/Planning	NA
Police Chief	Lisa Holmes
Emerg/Fire Chief	Scott Berkenbush

Housing & Construction

New Privately Owned Housing Units Authorized by Building Permit

	Single Family	Total Bldgs	Total Units
2006	10	10	10
2007	12	12	12
2008	15	15	15

Parcel Count by Property Class, 2010

Total	1,746
Single family	1,318
Multiple units	67
Apartments	0
Condos	30
Vacant land	183
Open space	0
Commercial	13
Industrial	17
Misc. residential	10
Other use	108

Public Library

G.A.R. Memorial Library
490 Main St.
West Newbury, MA 01985
(978)363-1105

Director . . . Katharine M. Gove

Library Statistics, FY 2008

Population served, 2007	4,269
Registered users	3,706
Circulation	112,985
Reference transactons	1,820
Total program attendance	43,983
per capita:	
Holdings	13.18
Operating income	$77.06
Internet Access	
Internet computers available	7
Weekly users	152

Municipal Finance

Debt at year end 2008	$9,763,652
Moody's rating, July 2009	Aa3

Revenues, 2008

Total	$12,066,459
From all taxes	9,757,403
Federal aid	0
State aid	457,677
From other governments	30,568
Charges for services	35,420
Licenses, permits & fees	149,613
Fines & forfeits	0
Interfund transfers	388,410
Misc/other/special assessments	623,684

Expenditures, 2008

Total	$10,680,314
General government	763,396
Public safety	1,465,547
Other/fixed costs	683,164
Human services	181,488
Culture & recreation	284,187
Debt Service	1,075,719
Education	4,535,459
Public works	1,598,669
Intergovernmental	92,685

Taxation, 2010

Property type	Valuation	Rate
Total	$763,954,702	-
Residential	743,921,633	12.92
Open space	0	0.00
Commercial	6,338,049	12.92
Industrial	1,965,900	12.92
Personal	11,729,120	12.92

Average Single Family Tax Bill, 2010

Avg. assessed home value	$491,224
Avg. single fam. tax bill	$6,347
Hi-Lo ranking	44/301

Police & Crime, 2008

Number of police officers	7
Violent crimes	6
Property crimes	25

Local School District

(school data 2007-08, except as noted)

West Newbury (non-op)
22 Main Street
West Newbury, MA 01985
978-363-2280

Superintendent . . . Paul Livingston

Non-operating district.
Resident students are sent to the Other School Districts listed below.

Grade plan	NA
Total enrollment '09-10	NA
Grade 12 enrollment, '09-10	NA
Graduation rate	NA
Dropout rate	NA
Per-pupil expenditure	NA
Avg teacher salary	NA
Student/teacher ratio '08-09	NA
Highly-qualified teachers, '08-09	NA
Teachers licensed in assigned subject	NA
Students per computer	NA

Other School Districts (see Appendix D for data)

Pentucket Regional, Whittier Vocational Tech

See Introduction for an explanation of all data sources.

Demographics & Socio-Economic Characteristics*

Population

1990	27,537
2000	27,899
Male	13,604
Female	14,295
2008	27,459
2010 (projected)††	27,870
2020 (projected)††	27,791

Race & Hispanic Origin, 2000

Race	
White	25,300
Black/African American	572
American Indian/Alaska Native	61
Asian	551
Hawaiian Native/Pacific Islander	10
Other Race	819
Two or more races	586
Hispanic origin	1,605

Age & Nativity, 2000

Under 5 years	1,631
18 years and over	21,360
21 years and over	20,452
65 years and over	4,447
85 years and over	533
Median Age	38.2
Native-born	24,865
Foreign-born	3,034

Age, 2020 (projected)††

Under 5 years	1,487
5 to 19 years	4,677
20 to 39 years	7,528
40 to 64 years	8,873
65 years and over	5,226

Educational Attainment, 2000

Population 25 years and over	19,168
High School graduates or higher	83.7%
Bachelor's degree or higher	21.6%
Graduate degree	8.5%

Income & Poverty, 1999

Per capita income,	$20,982
Median household income	$40,266
Median family income	$50,282
Persons in poverty	3,278
H'holds receiving public assistance	552
H'holds receiving social security	3,736

Households, 2000

Total households	11,823
With persons under 18	3,451
With persons over 65	3,146
Family households	7,113
Single person households	4,025
Persons per household	2.3
Persons per family	3.0

Labor & Employment, 2000

Civilian labor force	14,255
Unemployment rate	4.1%
Civilian labor force, 2008†	14,578
Unemployment rate†	7.8%
Civilian labor force, 12/09†	14,550
Unemployment rate†	9.8%
Employed persons 16 years and over, by occupation:	
Managers & professionals	4,214
Service occupations	2,034
Sales & office occupations	3,935
Farming, fishing & forestry	39
Construction & maintenance	1,077
Production & transportation	2,365
Self-employed persons	619

Most demographic data is from the 2000 Decennial Census
* see Appendix E for American Community Survey data
† Massachusetts Department of Revenue
†† University of Massachusetts, MISER

General Information

Town of West Springfield
26 Central St
West Springfield, MA 01089
413-263-3000

Elevation	204 ft.
Land area (square miles)	16.7
Water area (square miles)	0.8
Population density, 2008 (est)	1,644.3
Year incorporated	1774
Website	www.west-springfield.ma.us

Voters & Government Information

Government type	Mayor-Council
Number of Councilpersons	9
US Congressional District(s)	1

Registered Voters, October 2008

Total	17,438
Democrats	5,716
Republicans	2,587
Unaffiliated/other	8,986

Local Officials, 2010

Mayor	Edward Gibson
Manager/Admin	NA
Town Clerk	Diane F. Foley
CFO	Sharon A. Wilcox
Tax Collector	Kathleen O'Brien-Moore
Tax Assessor	christopher Keefe
Attorney	James T. Donahue
Public Works	Jack Dowd
Building	Patrick Moore
Comm Dev/Planning	Richard Werbiskis
Police Chief	Thomas Burke
Fire Chief	David R. Barkman

Housing & Construction

New Privately Owned Housing Units Authorized by Building Permit

	Single Family	Total Bldgs	Total Units
2006	36	36	36
2007	45	46	47
2008	26	26	26

Parcel Count by Property Class, 2010

Total	9,448
Single family	6,447
Multiple units	793
Apartments	140
Condos	662
Vacant land	439
Open space	0
Commercial	690
Industrial	170
Misc. residential	25
Other use	82

Public Library

West Springfield Public Library
200 Park Street
West Springfield, MA 01089
(413)736-4561

Director	Antonia Golinski-Foisy

Library Statistics, FY 2008

Population served, 2007	27,603
Registered users	18,069
Circulation	249,601
Reference transactons	55,695
Total program attendance	162,952
per capita:	
Holdings	4.13
Operating income	$33.94
Internet Access	
Internet computers available	17
Weekly users	416

Municipal Finance

Debt at year end 2008	$19,965,000
Moody's rating, July 2009	A2

Revenues, 2008

Total	$111,749,020
From all taxes	53,571,801
Federal aid	452,557
State aid	22,726,665
From other governments	125,762
Charges for services	5,617,140
Licenses, permits & fees	365,870
Fines & forfeits	0
Interfund transfers	104,743
Misc/other/special assessments	14,392,241

Expenditures, 2008

Total	$84,568,007
General government	2,984,942
Public safety	11,039,949
Other/fixed costs	5,687,222
Human services	883,915
Culture & recreation	1,234,372
Debt Service	16,979,297
Education	33,944,777
Public works	9,600,025
Intergovernmental	2,128,485

Taxation, 2010

Property type	Valuation	Rate
Total	$2,574,503,922	-
Residential	1,841,202,100	16.00
Open space	0	0.00
Commercial	501,703,900	34.69
Industrial	145,734,700	34.69
Personal	85,863,222	34.69

Average Single Family Tax Bill, 2010

Avg. assessed home value	$223,945
Avg. single fam. tax bill	$3,583
Hi-Lo ranking	163/301

Police & Crime, 2008

Number of police officers	82
Violent crimes	NA
Property crimes	NA

Local School District

(school data 2007-08, except as noted)

West Springfield
26 Central Street
West Springfield, MA 01089
413-263-3290

Superintendent	Suzanne Marotta
Grade plan	PK-12
Total enrollment '09-10	3,954
Grade 12 enrollment, '09-10	289
Graduation rate	66.3%
Dropout rate	20.4%
Per-pupil expenditure	$11,661
Avg teacher salary	$55,990
Student/teacher ratio '08-09	13.2 to 1
Highly-qualified teachers, '08-09	95.1%
Teachers licensed in assigned subject	99.4%
Students per computer	4.8

Massachusetts Competency Assessment System (MCAS), 2009 results

	English		Math	
	% Prof	CPI	% Prof	CPI
Gr 4	58%	81.8	57%	82.1
Gr 6	50%	77.7	52%	76.9
Gr 8	75%	89.2	53%	76.2
Gr 10	71%	87.4	64%	82.3

Other School Districts (see Appendix D for data)
None

©2010 Information Publications, Inc. All rights reserved. Photocopying prohibited. For additional copies, contact the publisher at www.informationpublications.com or (877)544-INFO (4636)

See Introduction for an explanation of all data sources.

Demographics & Socio-Economic Characteristics

Population

1990	1,483
2000	1,416
Male	694
Female	722
2008	1,432
2010 (projected)††	1,344
2020 (projected)††	1,271

Race & Hispanic Origin, 2000

Race	
White	1,389
Black/African American	4
American Indian/Alaska Native	1
Asian	13
Hawaiian Native/Pacific Islander	0
Other Race	1
Two or more races	8
Hispanic origin	12

Age & Nativity, 2000

Under 5 years	57
18 years and over	1,107
21 years and over	1,071
65 years and over	239
85 years and over	26
Median Age	44.3
Native-born	1,346
Foreign-born	70

Age, 2020 (projected)††

Under 5 years	43
5 to 19 years	142
20 to 39 years	234
40 to 64 years	476
65 years and over	376

Educational Attainment, 2000

Population 25 years and over	1,040
High School graduates or higher	92.9%
Bachelor's degree or higher	43.8%
Graduate degree	21.4%

Income & Poverty, 1999

Per capita income,	$31,425
Median household income	$51,000
Median family income	$64,464
Persons in poverty	61
H'holds receiving public assistance	6
H'holds receiving social security	183

Households, 2000

Total households	601
With persons under 18	178
With persons over 65	179
Family households	406
Single person households	162
Persons per household	2.4
Persons per family	2.9

Labor & Employment, 2000

Civilian labor force	761
Unemployment rate	3.8%
Civilian labor force, 2008†	860
Unemployment rate†	4.9%
Civilian labor force, 12/09†	874
Unemployment rate†	7.7%
Employed persons 16 years and over, by occupation:	
Managers & professionals	354
Service occupations	101
Sales & office occupations	157
Farming, fishing & forestry	3
Construction & maintenance	58
Production & transportation	59
Self-employed persons	95

Most demographic data is from the 2000 Decennial Census
† Massachusetts Department of Revenue
†† University of Massachusetts, MISER

General Information

Town of West Stockbridge
21 State Line Rd
PO Box 163
West Stockbridge, MA 01266
413-232-0300

Elevation	1,140 ft.
Land area (square miles)	18.5
Water area (square miles)	0.2
Population density, 2008 (est)	77.4
Year incorporated	1774
Website	www.weststockbridge-ma.gov

Voters & Government Information

Government type	Open Town Meeting
Number of Selectmen	3
US Congressional District(s)	1

Registered Voters, October 2008

Total	1,157
Democrats	394
Republicans	92
Unaffiliated/other	664

Local Officials, 2010

Chair, Bd. of Sel.	Tina Skorput Cooper
Manager/Admin	NA
Town Clerk	Tina Skorput Cooper
Finance Director	Karen Williams
Tax Collector	June Biggs
Tax Assessor	Amy Butterworth
Attorney	Kopelman & Paige
Public Works	Curt G. Wilton
Building	Donald Fitzgerald
Comm Dev/Planning	Dana Bixby
Police Chief	Michael Stanton Jr
Fire Chief	Peter A. Skorput

Housing & Construction

New Privately Owned Housing Units Authorized by Building Permit

	Single Family	Total Bldgs	Total Units
2006	7	7	7
2007	2	2	2
2008	1	1	1

Parcel Count by Property Class, 2010

Total	1,066
Single family	683
Multiple units	20
Apartments	2
Condos	0
Vacant land	232
Open space	0
Commercial	44
Industrial	6
Misc. residential	38
Other use	41

Public Library

West Stockbridge Public Library
PO Box 60
West Stockbridge, MA 01266
(413)232-0308 x308

Library Director........Danielle Chretien

Library Statistics, FY 2008

Population served, 2007	1,447
Registered users	909
Circulation	3,293
Reference transactons	0
Total program attendance	3,452
per capita:	
Holdings	4.61
Operating income	$13.76
Internet Access	
Internet computers available	4
Weekly users	14

Municipal Finance

Debt at year end 2008	$3,615,087
Moody's rating, July 2009	NA

Revenues, 2008

Total	$4,631,794
From all taxes	3,996,709
Federal aid	0
State aid	72,626
From other governments	7,143
Charges for services	61,388
Licenses, permits & fees	14,978
Fines & forfeits	0
Interfund transfers	366,600
Misc/other/special assessments	56,175

Expenditures, 2008

Total	$4,366,719
General government	307,367
Public safety	193,792
Other/fixed costs	148,865
Human services	45,375
Culture & recreation	22,271
Debt Service	570,600
Education	2,591,271
Public works	482,797
Intergovernmental	1,881

Taxation, 2010

Property type	Valuation	Rate
Total	$419,268,697	-
Residential	391,450,587	9.40
Open space	0	0.00
Commercial	14,588,186	9.40
Industrial	2,026,000	9.40
Personal	11,203,924	9.40

Average Single Family Tax Bill, 2010

Avg. assessed home value	$469,540
Avg. single fam. tax bill	$4,414
Hi-Lo ranking	104/301

Police & Crime, 2008

Number of police officers	NA
Violent crimes	NA
Property crimes	NA

Local School District

(school data 2007-08, except as noted)

West Stockbridge (non-op)
207 Pleasant Street, PO Box 596
Housatonic, MA 01236
413-274-6400

Superintendent...............Peter Dillon

Non-operating district.
Resident students are sent to the Other School Districts listed below.

Grade plan	NA
Total enrollment '09-10	NA
Grade 12 enrollment, '09-10	NA
Graduation rate	NA
Dropout rate	NA
Per-pupil expenditure	NA
Avg teacher salary	NA
Student/teacher ratio '08-09	NA
Highly-qualified teachers, '08-09	NA
Teachers licensed in assigned subject	NA
Students per computer	NA

Other School Districts (see Appendix D for data)
Berkshire Hills Regional

©2010 Information Publications, Inc. All rights reserved. Photocopying prohibited. For additional copies, contact the publisher at www.informationpublications.com or (877)544-INFO (4636)

See Introduction for an explanation of all data sources.

Demographics & Socio-Economic Characteristics

Population

1990	1,704
2000	2,467
Male	1,219
Female	1,248
2008	2,638
2010 (projected)††	3,160
2020 (projected)††	3,883

Race & Hispanic Origin, 2000

Race	
White	2,374
Black/African American	17
American Indian/Alaska Native	5
Asian	9
Hawaiian Native/Pacific Islander	7
Other Race	12
Two or more races	43
Hispanic origin	17

Age & Nativity, 2000

Under 5 years	127
18 years and over	1,834
21 years and over	1,778
65 years and over	250
85 years and over	22
Median Age	41.1
Native-born	2,377
Foreign-born	90

Age, 2020 (projected)††

Under 5 years	194
5 to 19 years	563
20 to 39 years	927
40 to 64 years	1,367
65 years and over	832

Educational Attainment, 2000

Population 25 years and over	1,728
High School graduates or higher	96.5%
Bachelor's degree or higher	53.0%
Graduate degree	17.1%

Income & Poverty, 1999

Per capita income,	$31,021
Median household income	$54,077
Median family income	$59,514
Persons in poverty	60
H'holds receiving public assistance	4
H'holds receiving social security	212

Households, 2000

Total households	1,034
With persons under 18	377
With persons over 65	189
Family households	669
Single person households	278
Persons per household	2.4
Persons per family	2.9

Labor & Employment, 2000

Civilian labor force	1,441
Unemployment rate	2.0%
Civilian labor force, 2008†	1,642
Unemployment rate†	3.9%
Civilian labor force, 12/09†	1,691
Unemployment rate†	6.3%
Employed persons 16 years and over, by occupation:	
Managers & professionals	547
Service occupations	187
Sales & office occupations	308
Farming, fishing & forestry	6
Construction & maintenance	251
Production & transportation	113
Self-employed persons	369

Most demographic data is from the 2000 Decennial Census
† Massachusetts Department of Revenue
†† University of Massachusetts, MISER

General Information

Town of West Tisbury
1059 State Rd
PO Box 278
West Tisbury, MA 02575
508-696-0101

Elevation	NA
Land area (square miles)	25.0
Water area (square miles)	16.7
Population density, 2008 (est)	105.5
Year incorporated	1892
Website	www.westtisbury-ma.gov

Voters & Government Information

Government type	Open Town Meeting
Number of Selectmen	3
US Congressional District(s)	10

Registered Voters, October 2008

Total	2,258
Democrats	881
Republicans	164
Unaffiliated/other	1,198

Local Officials, 2010

Chair, Bd. of Sel.	Richard Knable
Manager/Admin	Jennifer Rand
Town Clerk	Tara J. Whiting
Finance	Kathy Logue
Tax Collector	Brent B. Taylor
Tax Assessor	Kristina West
Attorney	Ronald Rappaport
Public Works	Richard Olsen
Building	Ernest Mendenhall
Comm Dev/Planning	Simone DeSorcy
Police Chief	Beth Toomey
Emerg/Fire Chief	Manuel Estrella III

Housing & Construction

New Privately Owned Housing Units Authorized by Building Permit

	Single Family	Total Bldgs	Total Units
2006	14	14	14
2007	25	25	25
2008	18	18	18

Parcel Count by Property Class, 2010

Total	2,554
Single family	1,428
Multiple units	21
Apartments	4
Condos	4
Vacant land	641
Open space	0
Commercial	59
Industrial	7
Misc. residential	275
Other use	115

Public Library

West Tisbury Free Public Library
1042 State Rd.
Vineyard Haven, MA 02568
(508)693-3366

Director ... Beth Kramer

Library Statistics, FY 2008

Population served, 2007	2,628
Registered users	7,521
Circulation	118,144
Reference transactons	17,940
Total program attendance	110,208
per capita:	
Holdings	18.24
Operating income	$164.99
Internet Access	
Internet computers available	9
Weekly users	215

Municipal Finance

Debt at year end 2008	$4,845,000
Moody's rating, July 2009	A1

Revenues, 2008

Total	$13,225,944
From all taxes	11,425,979
Federal aid	0
State aid	1,073,432
From other governments	109,382
Charges for services	301,323
Licenses, permits & fees	75,629
Fines & forfeits	5,825
Interfund transfers	54,300
Misc/other/special assessments	90,037

Expenditures, 2008

Total	$12,908,405
General government	1,075,424
Public safety	1,352,608
Other/fixed costs	575,732
Human services	295,301
Culture & recreation	426,885
Debt Service	1,034,408
Education	7,576,400
Public works	330,199
Intergovernmental	216,117

Taxation, 2010

Property type	Valuation	Rate
Total	$2,542,553,601	-
Residential	2,443,116,150	4.46
Open space	0	0.00
Commercial	65,375,950	4.46
Industrial	4,130,500	4.46
Personal	29,931,001	4.46

Average Single Family Tax Bill, 2010

Avg. assessed home value	$1,066,313
Avg. single fam. tax bill	$4,756
Hi-Lo ranking	88/301

Police & Crime, 2008

Number of police officers	9
Violent crimes	0
Property crimes	15

Local School District

(school data 2007-08, except as noted)

West Tisbury (non-op)
RR2, Box 261, 4 Pine Street
Vineyard Haven, MA 02568
508-693-2007

Superintendent ... James Weiss

Non-operating district.
Resident students are sent to the Other School Districts listed below.

Grade plan	NA
Total enrollment '09-10	NA
Grade 12 enrollment, '09-10	NA
Graduation rate	NA
Dropout rate	NA
Per-pupil expenditure	NA
Avg teacher salary	NA
Student/teacher ratio '08-09	NA
Highly-qualified teachers, '08-09	NA
Teachers licensed in assigned subject	NA
Students per computer	NA

Other School Districts (see Appendix D for data)
Marthas Vineyard and Up-Island Regionals

©2010 Information Publications, Inc. All rights reserved. Photocopying prohibited. For additional copies, contact the publisher at www.informationpublications.com or (877)544-INFO (4636)

Demographics & Socio-Economic Characteristics

Population

1990	14,133
2000	17,997
Male	8,946
Female	9,051
2008	18,467
2010 (projected)††	19,730
2020 (projected)††	21,170

Race & Hispanic Origin, 2000

Race	
White	15,869
Black/African American	259
American Indian/Alaska Native	24
Asian	1,456
Hawaiian Native/Pacific Islander	4
Other Race	142
Two or more races	243
Hispanic origin	587

Age & Nativity, 2000

Under 5 years	1,303
18 years and over	12,885
21 years and over	12,490
65 years and over	2,085
85 years and over	453
Median Age	36.9
Native-born	15,453
Foreign-born	2,544

Age, 2020 (projected)††

Under 5 years	1,210
5 to 19 years	4,174
20 to 39 years	5,958
40 to 64 years	6,498
65 years and over	3,330

Educational Attainment, 2000

Population 25 years and over	11,948
High School graduates or higher	93.4%
Bachelor's degree or higher	53.2%
Graduate degree	23.9%

Income & Poverty, 1999

Per capita income,	$35,063
Median household income	$73,418
Median family income	$94,610
Persons in poverty	805
H'holds receiving public assistance	28
H'holds receiving social security	1,352

Households, 2000

Total households	6,534
With persons under 18	2,616
With persons over 65	1,337
Family households	4,520
Single person households	1,643
Persons per household	2.6
Persons per family	3.2

Labor & Employment, 2000

Civilian labor force	8,974
Unemployment rate	3.4%
Civilian labor force, 2008†	9,113
Unemployment rate†	4.8%
Civilian labor force, 12/09†	9,138
Unemployment rate†	6.4%
Employed persons 16 years and over, by occupation:	
Managers & professionals	4,998
Service occupations	801
Sales & office occupations	1,973
Farming, fishing & forestry	0
Construction & maintenance	360
Production & transportation	539
Self-employed persons	597

Most demographic data is from the 2000 Decennial Census
† Massachusetts Department of Revenue
†† University of Massachusetts, MISER

General Information

Town of Westborough
34 West Main St
Westborough, MA 01581
508-366-3030

Elevation	300 ft.
Land area (square miles)	20.5
Water area (square miles)	1.1
Population density, 2008 (est)	900.8
Year incorporated	1717
Website	www.town.westborough.ma.us

Voters & Government Information

Government type	Open Town Meeting
Number of Selectmen	5
US Congressional District(s)	3

Registered Voters, October 2008

Total	11,966
Democrats	3,135
Republicans	2,127
Unaffiliated/other	6,650

Local Officials, 2010

Chair, Bd. of Sel.	NA
Town Coordinator	James J. Malloy
Town Clerk	Nancy Yendriga
Treasurer/Collector	Joanne Savignac
Tax Collector	Joanne Savignac
Tax Assessor	Linda Swadel
Town Counsel	Gregory Franks
Public Works	John Walden
Building	Joseph Inman
Planning	James Robbins
Police Chief	Alan Gordon
Emerg/Fire Chief	Walter Perron Jr

Housing & Construction

New Privately Owned Housing Units Authorized by Building Permit

	Single Family	Total Bldgs	Total Units
2006	21	21	21
2007	35	36	49
2008	10	11	12

Parcel Count by Property Class, 2010

Total	5,603
Single family	3,829
Multiple units	213
Apartments	40
Condos	698
Vacant land	250
Open space	0
Commercial	258
Industrial	187
Misc. residential	36
Other use	92

Public Library

Westborough Public Library
55 West Main St.
Westborough, MA 01581
(508)366-3050

Director	Carolyn Delude

Library Statistics, FY 2008

Population served, 2007	18,459
Registered users	17,673
Circulation	205,756
Reference transactons	13,204
Total program attendance	0
per capita:	
Holdings	4.90
Operating income	$46.22
Internet Access	
Internet computers available	9
Weekly users	0

Municipal Finance

Debt at year end 2008	$91,637,240
Moody's rating, July 2009	Aa3

Revenues, 2008

Total	$70,339,071
From all taxes	56,645,037
Federal aid	0
State aid	9,567,740
From other governments	269,212
Charges for services	1,331,692
Licenses, permits & fees	764,082
Fines & forfeits	16,626
Interfund transfers	572,212
Misc/other/special assessments	586,235

Expenditures, 2008

Total	$68,214,020
General government	2,344,309
Public safety	5,930,003
Other/fixed costs	10,030,620
Human services	691,262
Culture & recreation	1,088,489
Debt Service	8,575,788
Education	35,761,228
Public works	3,510,144
Intergovernmental	282,177

Taxation, 2010

Property type	Valuation	Rate
Total	$3,392,442,851	-
Residential	2,055,747,190	16.98
Open space	0	0.00
Commercial	581,387,321	16.98
Industrial	480,236,120	16.98
Personal	275,072,220	16.98

Average Single Family Tax Bill, 2010

Avg. assessed home value	$422,996
Avg. single fam. tax bill	$7,182
Hi-Lo ranking	33/301

Police & Crime, 2008

Number of police officers	29
Violent crimes	13
Property crimes	278

Local School District

(school data 2007-08, except as noted)

Westborough
45 West Main Street, P O Box 1152
Westborough, MA 01581
508-836-7700

Superintendent	Anne Towle
Grade plan	PK-12
Total enrollment '09-10	3,581
Grade 12 enrollment, '09-10	285
Graduation rate	93.6%
Dropout rate	2.5%
Per-pupil expenditure	$12,890
Avg teacher salary	$74,375
Student/teacher ratio '08-09	13.3 to 1
Highly-qualified teachers, '08-09	98.1%
Teachers licensed in assigned subject	97.0%
Students per computer	3.1

Massachusetts Competency Assessment System (MCAS), 2009 results

	English		Math	
	% Prof	CPI	% Prof	CPI
Gr 4	67%	87.9	61%	86.1
Gr 6	88%	95.1	79%	90.8
Gr 8	94%	98.5	72%	87.7
Gr 10	96%	98.6	95%	97.8

Other School Districts (see Appendix D for data)

Assabet Valley Vocational Tech

See Introduction for an explanation of all data sources.

©2010 Information Publications, Inc. All rights reserved. Photocopying prohibited. For additional copies, contact the publisher at www.informationpublications.com or (877)544-INFO (4636)

Demographics & Socio-Economic Characteristics*

Population

1990	38,372
2000	40,072
Male	19,385
Female	20,687
2008	40,608
2010 (projected)††	40,599
2020 (projected)††	41,253

Race & Hispanic Origin, 2000

Race	
White	37,881
Black/African American	365
American Indian/Alaska Native	90
Asian	329
Hawaiian Native/Pacific Islander	19
Other Race	850
Two or more races	538
Hispanic origin	2,008

Age & Nativity, 2000

Under 5 years	2,366
18 years and over	30,534
21 years and over	27,774
65 years and over	5,474
85 years and over	738
Median Age	35.8
Native-born	37,222
Foreign-born	2,850

Age, 2020 (projected)††

Under 5 years	2,325
5 to 19 years	7,874
20 to 39 years	11,123
40 to 64 years	12,538
65 years and over	7,393

Educational Attainment, 2000

Population 25 years and over	25,439
High School graduates or higher	84.9%
Bachelor's degree or higher	24.2%
Graduate degree	8.0%

Income & Poverty, 1999

Per capita income,	$20,600
Median household income	$45,240
Median family income	$55,327
Persons in poverty	4,234
H'holds receiving public assistance	548
H'holds receiving social security	4,086

Households, 2000

Total households	14,797
With persons under 18	4,987
With persons over 65	3,739
Family households	10,012
Single person households	3,826
Persons per household	2.5
Persons per family	3.1

Labor & Employment, 2000

Civilian labor force	20,868
Unemployment rate	4.9%
Civilian labor force, 2008†	21,081
Unemployment rate†	6.3%
Civilian labor force, 12/09†	21,157
Unemployment rate†	8.7%
Employed persons 16 years and over, by occupation:	
Managers & professionals	6,440
Service occupations	2,989
Sales & office occupations	5,551
Farming, fishing & forestry	30
Construction & maintenance	1,770
Production & transportation	3,063
Self-employed persons	1,077

Most demographic data is from the 2000 Decennial Census
* see Appendix E for American Community Survey data
† Massachusetts Department of Revenue
†† University of Massachusetts, MISER

General Information

City of Westfield
59 Court St
Westfield, MA 01085
413-572-6200

Elevation	144 ft.
Land area (square miles)	46.6
Water area (square miles)	0.7
Population density, 2008 (est)	871.4
Year incorporated	1669
Website	cityofwestfield.org

Voters & Government Information

Government type	Mayor-Council
Number of Councilpersons	13
US Congressional District(s)	1

Registered Voters, October 2008

Total	24,291
Democrats	7,390
Republicans	4,675
Unaffiliated/other	12,023

Local Officials, 2010

Mayor	Daniel Knapik
Manager/Admin	NA
Clerk	Karen Fanion
Finance Director	Gregory Kallfa
Tax Collector	Michael McMahon
Tax Assessor	James Pettengill
Attorney	Susan Phillips
Public Works	James Mulvenna (Actg)
Building	Donald York
Comm Dev Dir.	Larry Smith
Police Chief	John Camerota
Emerg/Fire Chief	William Phelon

Housing & Construction

New Privately Owned Housing Units Authorized by Building Permit

	Single Family	Total Bldgs	Total Units
2006	47	53	63
2007	35	40	45
2008	19	26	41

Parcel Count by Property Class, 2010

Total	13,380
Single family	9,300
Multiple units	1,125
Apartments	147
Condos	741
Vacant land	902
Open space	0
Commercial	552
Industrial	190
Misc. residential	80
Other use	343

Public Library

Westfield Athenaeum
6 Elm Street
Westfield, MA 01085
(413)568-7833

Director	Christopher Lindquist

Library Statistics, FY 2008

Population served, 2007	40,160
Registered users	22,255
Circulation	297,610
Reference transactons	22,254
Total program attendance	207,554
per capita:	
Holdings	2.87
Operating income	$28.05
Internet Access	
Internet computers available	20
Weekly users	1,000

Municipal Finance

Debt at year end 2008	$74,999,016
Moody's rating, July 2009	A3

Revenues, 2008

Total	$114,302,284
From all taxes	54,160,155
Federal aid	655,158
State aid	47,152,683
From other governments	241,707
Charges for services	1,610,602
Licenses, permits & fees	468,970
Fines & forfeits	79,657
Interfund transfers	604,112
Misc/other/special assessments	4,664,620

Expenditures, 2008

Total	$92,718,866
General government	4,442,486
Public safety	11,456,125
Other/fixed costs	7,411,488
Human services	1,197,190
Culture & recreation	1,148,605
Debt Service	7,186,208
Education	51,129,501
Public works	5,488,442
Intergovernmental	3,233,481

Taxation, 2010

Property type	Valuation	Rate
Total	$3,211,965,484	-
Residential	2,694,474,908	14.68
Open space	0	0.00
Commercial	334,191,063	28.60
Industrial	117,163,000	28.60
Personal	66,136,513	28.60

Average Single Family Tax Bill, 2010

Avg. assessed home value	$236,945
Avg. single fam. tax bill	$3,478
Hi-Lo ranking	174/301

Police & Crime, 2008

Number of police officers	79
Violent crimes	106
Property crimes	648

Local School District

(school data 2007-08, except as noted)

Westfield
22 Ashley Street
Westfield, MA 01085
413-572-6403

Superintendent	Shirley Alvira
Grade plan	PK-12
Total enrollment '09-10	6,100
Grade 12 enrollment, '09-10	490
Graduation rate	81.6%
Dropout rate	11.3%
Per-pupil expenditure	$10,888
Avg teacher salary	$54,058
Student/teacher ratio '08-09	12.2 to 1
Highly-qualified teachers, '08-09	98.9%
Teachers licensed in assigned subject	97.9%
Students per computer	17

Massachusetts Competency Assessment System (MCAS), 2009 results

	English		Math	
	% Prof	CPI	% Prof	CPI
Gr 4	49%	78.9	46%	78.2
Gr 6	63%	84.4	41%	70.6
Gr 8	73%	88.4	36%	64.7
Gr 10	78%	90.5	68%	84.9

Other School Districts (see Appendix D for data)
None

©2010 Information Publications, Inc. All rights reserved. Photocopying prohibited. For additional copies, contact the publisher at www.informationpublications.com or (877)544-INFO (4636)

See Introduction for an explanation of all data sources.

Demographics & Socio-Economic Characteristics

Population

1990	16,392
2000	20,754
Male	10,324
Female	10,430
2008	22,066
2010 (projected)††	22,984
2020 (projected)††	24,197

Race & Hispanic Origin, 2000

Race	
White	19,444
Black/African American	62
American Indian/Alaska Native	13
Asian	994
Hawaiian Native/Pacific Islander	3
Other Race	62
Two or more races	176
Hispanic origin	229

Age & Nativity, 2000

Under 5 years	1,842
18 years and over	14,153
21 years and over	13,664
65 years and over	1,501
85 years and over	184
Median Age	36.9
Native-born	19,442
Foreign-born	1,312

Age, 2020 (projected)††

Under 5 years	1,562
5 to 19 years	5,097
20 to 39 years	5,627
40 to 64 years	8,410
65 years and over	3,501

Educational Attainment, 2000

Population 25 years and over	13,275
High School graduates or higher	94.1%
Bachelor's degree or higher	56.8%
Graduate degree	24.9%

Income & Poverty, 1999

Per capita income,	$37,979
Median household income	$98,272
Median family income	$104,029
Persons in poverty	345
H'holds receiving public assistance	36
H'holds receiving social security	1,055

Households, 2000

Total households	6,808
With persons under 18	3,426
With persons over 65	1,036
Family households	5,806
Single person households	796
Persons per household	3.0
Persons per family	3.3

Labor & Employment, 2000

Civilian labor force	11,087
Unemployment rate	1.8%
Civilian labor force, 2008†	11,728
Unemployment rate†	4.8%
Civilian labor force, 12/09†	11,756
Unemployment rate†	7.6%
Employed persons 16 years and over, by occupation:	
Managers & professionals	6,573
Service occupations	840
Sales & office occupations	2,184
Farming, fishing & forestry	8
Construction & maintenance	561
Production & transportation	719
Self-employed persons	740

Most demographic data is from the 2000 Decennial Census
† Massachusetts Department of Revenue
†† University of Massachusetts, MISER

General Information

Town of Westford
55 Main St
Westford, MA 01886
978-692-5500

Elevation	160 ft.
Land area (square miles)	30.6
Water area (square miles)	0.7
Population density, 2008 (est)	721.1
Year incorporated	1729
Website	westfordma.gov

Voters & Government Information

Government type	Open Town Meeting
Number of Selectmen	5
US Congressional District(s)	5

Registered Voters, October 2008

Total	15,262
Democrats	3,548
Republicans	2,352
Unaffiliated/other	9,288

Local Officials, 2010

Chair, Bd. of Sel.	Kelly Ross
Manager	Jodi Ross
Clerk	Kaari Mai Tari
Finance Director	Suzanne Marchand
Tax Collector	Cheryl Accardi
Tax Assessor	Jean-Paul Plouffe
Attorney	NA
Public Works	Richard Barrett
Building	Mathew Hakala
Planning	Ross Altobelli
Police Chief	Thomas McEnaney
Fire Chief	Richard Rochon

Housing & Construction

New Privately Owned Housing Units Authorized by Building Permit

	Single Family	Total Bldgs	Total Units
2006	105	105	105
2007	99	101	140
2008	50	50	50

Parcel Count by Property Class, 2010

Total	8,491
Single family	6,269
Multiple units	108
Apartments	17
Condos	992
Vacant land	523
Open space	0
Commercial	263
Industrial	127
Misc. residential	36
Other use	156

Public Library

J.V. Fletcher Library
50 Main St.
Westford, MA 01886
(978)692-5557

Director	Ellen D. Rainville

Library Statistics, FY 2008

Population served, 2007	21,790
Registered users	21,310
Circulation	354,845
Reference transactons	121,654
Total program attendance	264,177
per capita:	
Holdings	7.21
Operating income	$66.68
Internet Access	
Internet computers available	12
Weekly users	1,416

Municipal Finance

Debt at year end 2008	$97,298,089
Moody's rating, July 2009	Aa3

Revenues, 2008

Total	$82,099,067
From all taxes	55,496,523
Federal aid	2,973
State aid	19,500,713
From other governments	0
Charges for services	535,683
Licenses, permits & fees	964,023
Fines & forfeits	22,945
Interfund transfers	459,603
Misc/other/special assessments	2,558,302

Expenditures, 2008

Total	$78,079,262
General government	3,477,279
Public safety	6,680,435
Other/fixed costs	8,660,667
Human services	806,725
Culture & recreation	1,805,051
Debt Service	9,821,933
Education	41,514,188
Public works	4,964,216
Intergovernmental	348,768

Taxation, 2010

Property type	Valuation	Rate
Total	$3,822,820,412	-
Residential	3,276,832,758	14.63
Open space	0	0.00
Commercial	228,564,394	14.82
Industrial	244,148,160	14.82
Personal	73,275,100	14.63

Average Single Family Tax Bill, 2010

Avg. assessed home value	$450,723
Avg. single fam. tax bill	$6,594
Hi-Lo ranking	39/301

Police & Crime, 2008

Number of police officers	40
Violent crimes	5
Property crimes	133

Local School District

(school data 2007-08, except as noted)

Westford
23 Depot Street
Westford, MA 01886
978-692-5560

Superintendent	Everett Olsen
Grade plan	PK-12
Total enrollment '09-10	5,273
Grade 12 enrollment, '09-10	390
Graduation rate	96.4%
Dropout rate	0.8%
Per-pupil expenditure	$9,796
Avg teacher salary	$60,708
Student/teacher ratio '08-09	15.0 to 1
Highly-qualified teachers, '08-09	98.4%
Teachers licensed in assigned subject	98.6%
Students per computer	4.6

Massachusetts Competency Assessment System (MCAS), 2009 results

	English		Math	
	% Prof	CPI	% Prof	CPI
Gr 4	81%	93.3	75%	91.9
Gr 6	92%	97	86%	94.2
Gr 8	97%	99.1	83%	93.9
Gr 10	97%	98.4	94%	97

Other School Districts (see Appendix D for data)
Nashoba Valley Vocational Tech

©2010 Information Publications, Inc. All rights reserved. Photocopying prohibited. For additional copies, contact the publisher at www.informationpublications.com or (877)544-INFO (4636)

See Introduction for an explanation of all data sources.

Demographics & Socio-Economic Characteristics

Population

1990	1,327
2000	1,468
Male	728
Female	740
2008	1,576
2010 (projected)††	1,455
2020 (projected)††	1,452

Race & Hispanic Origin, 2000

Race	
White	1,446
Black/African American	0
American Indian/Alaska Native	5
Asian	2
Hawaiian Native/Pacific Islander	0
Other Race	4
Two or more races	11
Hispanic origin	8

Age & Nativity, 2000

Under 5 years	76
18 years and over	1,095
21 years and over	1,054
65 years and over	135
85 years and over	14
Median Age	40.2
Native-born	1,448
Foreign-born	20

Age, 2020 (projected)††

Under 5 years	69
5 to 19 years	199
20 to 39 years	309
40 to 64 years	549
65 years and over	326

Educational Attainment, 2000

Population 25 years and over	1,033
High School graduates or higher	92.6%
Bachelor's degree or higher	34.9%
Graduate degree	14.5%

Income & Poverty, 1999

Per capita income,	$25,360
Median household income	$60,089
Median family income	$66,625
Persons in poverty	52
H'holds receiving public assistance	0
H'holds receiving social security	123

Households, 2000

Total households	542
With persons under 18	198
With persons over 65	98
Family households	422
Single person households	86
Persons per household	2.7
Persons per family	3.1

Labor & Employment, 2000

Civilian labor force	860
Unemployment rate	1.3%
Civilian labor force, 2008†	956
Unemployment rate†	5.4%
Civilian labor force, 12/09†	962
Unemployment rate†	7.4%
Employed persons 16 years and over, by occupation:	
Managers & professionals	372
Service occupations	81
Sales & office occupations	204
Farming, fishing & forestry	8
Construction & maintenance	120
Production & transportation	64
Self-employed persons	102

Most demographic data is from the 2000 Decennial Census
† Massachusetts Department of Revenue
†† University of Massachusetts, MISER

General Information

Town of Westhampton
1 South Rd
Westhampton, MA 01027
413-527-0463

Elevation	618 ft.
Land area (square miles)	27.1
Water area (square miles)	0.2
Population density, 2008 (est)	58.2
Year incorporated	1778
Email	westhamptontownhall@comcast.net

Voters & Government Information

Government type	Open Town Meeting
Number of Selectmen	3
US Congressional District(s)	1

Registered Voters, October 2008

Total	1,292
Democrats	240
Republicans	141
Unaffiliated/other	902

Local Officials, 2010

Chair, Bd. of Sel.	Brian Mulvehill
Manager/Admin	NA
Town Clerk	Catherine Shaw
Finance Director	Margaret A. Parsons
Tax Collector	Laura Blakesley
Tax Assessor	Dolores Thornhill
Attorney	Kopelman & Paige
Public Works	David Blakesley
Building Inspector	Charles Miller
Comm Dev/Planning	Board of Selectmen
Police Chief	David White
Emerg/Fire Chief	Christopher Norris

Housing & Construction

New Privately Owned Housing Units Authorized by Building Permit

	Single Family	Total Bldgs	Total Units
2006	7	7	7
2007	6	6	6
2008	5	5	5

Parcel Count by Property Class, 2010

Total	1,219
Single family	640
Multiple units	19
Apartments	0
Condos	0
Vacant land	304
Open space	0
Commercial	13
Industrial	6
Misc. residential	18
Other use	219

Public Library

Westhampton Memorial Library
3 South Road
Westhampton, MA 01027
(413)527-5386

Librarian	Lyn Keating

Library Statistics, FY 2008

Population served, 2007	1,586
Registered users	972
Circulation	24,419
Reference transactons	0
Total program attendance	0
per capita:	
Holdings	9.61
Operating income	$45.01
Internet Access	
Internet computers available	2
Weekly users	0

Municipal Finance

Debt at year end 2008	$1,535,000
Moody's rating, July 2009	Baa1

Revenues, 2008

Total	$3,998,750
From all taxes	3,223,987
Federal aid	15,067
State aid	620,980
From other governments	2,970
Charges for services	78,189
Licenses, permits & fees	3,974
Fines & forfeits	0
Interfund transfers	14,451
Misc/other/special assessments	19,566

Expenditures, 2008

Total	$3,814,232
General government	113,506
Public safety	102,796
Other/fixed costs	433,555
Human services	5,805
Culture & recreation	65,910
Debt Service	248,330
Education	2,345,393
Public works	495,002
Intergovernmental	3,935

Taxation, 2010

Property type	Valuation	Rate
Total	$231,249,164	-
Residential	219,515,746	14.64
Open space	0	0.00
Commercial	5,610,256	14.64
Industrial	1,176,700	14.64
Personal	4,946,462	14.64

Average Single Family Tax Bill, 2010

Avg. assessed home value	$291,668
Avg. single fam. tax bill	$4,270
Hi-Lo ranking	117/301

Police & Crime, 2008

Number of police officers	NA
Violent crimes	1
Property crimes	5

Local School District

(school data 2007-08, except as noted)

Westhampton
19 Stage Rd
Westhampton, MA 01027
413-527-7200

Superintendent	Craig Jurgensen
Grade plan	PK-6
Total enrollment '09-10	140
Grade 12 enrollment, '09-10	0
Graduation rate	NA
Dropout rate	NA
Per-pupil expenditure	$10,648
Avg teacher salary	$52,172
Student/teacher ratio '08-09	10.7 to 1
Highly-qualified teachers, '08-09	100.0%
Teachers licensed in assigned subject	100.0%
Students per computer	5.4

Massachusetts Competency Assessment System (MCAS), 2009 results

	English		Math	
	% Prof	CPI	% Prof	CPI
Gr 4	83%	95.8	83%	97.2
Gr 6	53%	85.5	58%	90.8
Gr 8	NA	NA	NA	NA
Gr 10	NA	NA	NA	NA

Other School Districts (see Appendix D for data)
Hampshire Regional

©2010 Information Publications, Inc. All rights reserved. Photocopying prohibited. For additional copies, contact the publisher at www.informationpublications.com or (877)544-INFO (4636)

See Introduction for an explanation of all data sources.

Demographics & Socio-Economic Characteristics

Population

1990	6,191
2000	6,907
Male	3,445
Female	3,462
2008	7,391
2010 (projected)††	7,395
2020 (projected)††	7,953

Race & Hispanic Origin, 2000

Race	
White	6,734
Black/African American	32
American Indian/Alaska Native	10
Asian	79
Hawaiian Native/Pacific Islander	0
Other Race	10
Two or more races	42
Hispanic origin	77

Age & Nativity, 2000

Under 5 years	415
18 years and over	5,057
21 years and over	4,836
65 years and over	753
85 years and over	72
Median Age	38.6
Native-born	6,678
Foreign-born	229

Age, 2020 (projected)††

Under 5 years	447
5 to 19 years	1,441
20 to 39 years	1,895
40 to 64 years	2,671
65 years and over	1,499

Educational Attainment, 2000

Population 25 years and over	4,639
High School graduates or higher	88.4%
Bachelor's degree or higher	28.5%
Graduate degree	9.3%

Income & Poverty, 1999

Per capita income,	$24,913
Median household income	$57,755
Median family income	$61,835
Persons in poverty	212
H'holds receiving public assistance	14
H'holds receiving social security	559

Households, 2000

Total households	2,529
With persons under 18	991
With persons over 65	527
Family households	1,954
Single person households	447
Persons per household	2.7
Persons per family	3.1

Labor & Employment, 2000

Civilian labor force	3,657
Unemployment rate	2.4%
Civilian labor force, 2008†	3,825
Unemployment rate†	7.0%
Civilian labor force, 12/09†	3,851
Unemployment rate†	11.6%
Employed persons 16 years and over, by occupation:	
Managers & professionals	1,367
Service occupations	406
Sales & office occupations	875
Farming, fishing & forestry	19
Construction & maintenance	344
Production & transportation	557
Self-employed persons	327

Most demographic data is from the 2000 Decennial Census
† Massachusetts Department of Revenue
†† University of Massachusetts, MISER

General Information

Town of Westminster
11 South St
Westminster, MA 01473
978-874-7400

Elevation	1,064 ft.
Land area (square miles)	35.5
Water area (square miles)	1.8
Population density, 2008 (est)	208.2
Year incorporated	1759
Website	westminster-ma.gov

Voters & Government Information

Government type	Open Town Meeting
Number of Selectmen	3
US Congressional District(s)	1

Registered Voters, October 2008

Total	5,467
Democrats	1,134
Republicans	899
Unaffiliated/other	3,383

Local Officials, 2010

Chair, Bd. of Sel.	John F. Fairbanks
Manager/Town Coord	Karen Murphy
Town Clerk	Denise L. MacAloney
Finance Director	Donna Allard
Tax Collector	Melody Gallant
Tax Assessor	Robin Holm
Attorney	Kopelman
Public Works	Joshua Hall
Building	Peter Munro
Comm Dev/Planning	Domenica Tatasciore
Police Chief	Salvatore Albert
Emerg/Fire Chief	Brenton MacAloney

Housing & Construction

New Privately Owned Housing Units Authorized by Building Permit

	Single Family	Total Bldgs	Total Units
2006	21	23	25
2007	20	20	20
2008	10	10	10

Parcel Count by Property Class, 2010

Total	NA
Single family	NA
Multiple units	NA
Apartments	NA
Condos	NA
Vacant land	NA
Open space	NA
Commercial	NA
Industrial	NA
Misc. residential	NA
Other use	NA

Public Library

Forbush Memorial Library
118 Main St., PO Box 468
Westminster, MA 01473
(978)874-7416

Director .... Margaret Howe-Soper

Library Statistics, FY 2008

Population served, 2007	7,388
Registered users	4,415
Circulation	66,821
Reference transactons	6,110
Total program attendance	0
per capita:	
Holdings	6.02
Operating income	$44.31
Internet Access	
Internet computers available	9
Weekly users	65

Municipal Finance

Debt at year end 2008	$8,299,123
Moody's rating, July 2009	A2

Revenues, 2008

Total	$17,753,367
From all taxes	12,687,416
Federal aid	0
State aid	1,148,518
From other governments	13,946
Charges for services	2,142,328
Licenses, permits & fees	168,525
Fines & forfeits	125,784
Interfund transfers	1,222,898
Misc/other/special assessments	121,976

Expenditures, 2008

Total	$17,447,749
General government	1,199,594
Public safety	2,635,609
Other/fixed costs	1,124,364
Human services	220,028
Culture & recreation	561,917
Debt Service	930,091
Education	8,411,349
Public works	2,279,159
Intergovernmental	85,638

Taxation, 2010

Property type	Valuation	Rate
Total	NA	-
Residential	NA	NA
Open space	NA	NA
Commercial	NA	NA
Industrial	NA	NA
Personal	NA	NA

Average Single Family Tax Bill, 2010

Avg. assessed home value	NA
Avg. single fam. tax bill	NA
Hi-Lo ranking	NA

Police & Crime, 2008

Number of police officers	13
Violent crimes	7
Property crimes	144

Local School District

(school data 2007-08, except as noted)

Westminster (non-op)
2 Narrows Rd / Suite 101
Westminster, MA 01473
978-874-1501

Superintendent .... Michael Zapantis

Non-operating district.
Resident students are sent to the Other School Districts listed below.

Grade plan	NA
Total enrollment '09-10	NA
Grade 12 enrollment, '09-10	NA
Graduation rate	NA
Dropout rate	NA
Per-pupil expenditure	NA
Avg teacher salary	NA
Student/teacher ratio '08-09	NA
Highly-qualified teachers, '08-09	NA
Teachers licensed in assigned subject	NA
Students per computer	NA

Other School Districts (see Appendix D for data)
Ashburnham-Westminster Regional, Montachusett Vocational Tech

©2010 Information Publications, Inc. All rights reserved. Photocopying prohibited. For additional copies, contact the publisher at www.informationpublications.com or (877)544-INFO (4636)

See Introduction for an explanation of all data sources.

Demographics & Socio-Economic Characteristics

Population

1990	10,200
2000	11,469
Male	5,323
Female	6,146
2008	11,711
2010 (projected)††	11,373
2020 (projected)††	10,132

Race & Hispanic Origin, 2000

Race	
White	10,352
Black/African American	135
American Indian/Alaska Native	6
Asian	782
Hawaiian Native/Pacific Islander	6
Other Race	49
Two or more races	139
Hispanic origin	218

Age & Nativity, 2000

Under 5 years	794
18 years and over	8,254
21 years and over	7,733
65 years and over	1,892
85 years and over	360
Median Age	41.9
Native-born	10,020
Foreign-born	1,449

Age, 2020 (projected)††

Under 5 years	559
5 to 19 years	2,548
20 to 39 years	1,820
40 to 64 years	2,900
65 years and over	2,305

Educational Attainment, 2000

Population 25 years and over	7,373
High School graduates or higher	96.1%
Bachelor's degree or higher	75.1%
Graduate degree	45.0%

Income & Poverty, 1999

Per capita income,	$79,640
Median household income	$153,918
Median family income	$181,041
Persons in poverty	314
H'holds receiving public assistance	5
H'holds receiving social security	973

Households, 2000

Total households	3,718
With persons under 18	1,608
With persons over 65	1,143
Family households	2,993
Single person households	638
Persons per household	2.9
Persons per family	3.2

Labor & Employment, 2000

Civilian labor force	5,232
Unemployment rate	1.7%
Civilian labor force, 2008†	5,413
Unemployment rate†	3.6%
Civilian labor force, 12/09†	5,346
Unemployment rate†	4.8%
Employed persons 16 years and over, by occupation:	
Managers & professionals	3,573
Service occupations	360
Sales & office occupations	1,026
Farming, fishing & forestry	0
Construction & maintenance	70
Production & transportation	115
Self-employed persons	654

Most demographic data is from the 2000 Decennial Census
† Massachusetts Department of Revenue
†† University of Massachusetts, MISER

General Information

Town of Weston
11 Town House Road
PO Box 378
Weston, MA 02493
781-893-7320

Elevation	203 ft.
Land area (square miles)	17.0
Water area (square miles)	0.3
Population density, 2008 (est)	688.9
Year incorporated	1713
Website	www.weston.org

Voters & Government Information

Government type	Open Town Meeting
Number of Selectmen	3
US Congressional District(s)	7

Registered Voters, October 2008

Total	7,961
Democrats	2,018
Republicans	1,620
Unaffiliated/other	4,303

Local Officials, 2010

Chair, Bd. of Sel.	Michael H. Harrity
Manager	Donna S. VanderClock
Town Clerk	Deborah M. Davenport
Finance Director	David R. Williams
Tax Collector	David Okun
Tax Assessor	Eric Josephson
Attorney	NA
Public Works	Robert L. Hoffman
Building	Rob Morra
Planning	Susan S. Haber
Police Chief	Steven Shaw
Emerg/Fire Chief	David Soar

Housing & Construction

New Privately Owned Housing Units Authorized by Building Permit

	Single Family	Total Bldgs	Total Units
2006	24	24	24
2007	39	39	39
2008	33	33	33

Parcel Count by Property Class, 2010

Total	3,881
Single family	3,343
Multiple units	22
Apartments	3
Condos	178
Vacant land	199
Open space	0
Commercial	48
Industrial	2
Misc. residential	46
Other use	40

Public Library

Weston Public Library
87 School Street
Weston, MA 02493
(781)893-3312

Director .... Susan Brennan

Library Statistics, FY 2008

Population served, 2007	11,698
Registered users	7,806
Circulation	351,697
Reference transactons	24,381
Total program attendance	160,788
per capita:	
Holdings	10.35
Operating income	$116.40
Internet Access	
Internet computers available	15
Weekly users	249

Municipal Finance

Debt at year end 2008	$67,291,665
Moody's rating, July 2009	Aaa

Revenues, 2008

Total	$66,332,500
From all taxes	56,807,475
Federal aid	0
State aid	4,136,510
From other governments	117,334
Charges for services	977,915
Licenses, permits & fees	990,514
Fines & forfeits	0
Interfund transfers	1,048,910
Misc/other/special assessments	1,126,921

Expenditures, 2008

Total	$54,509,839
General government	3,296,880
Public safety	5,306,725
Other/fixed costs	3,888,579
Human services	472,812
Culture & recreation	893,305
Debt Service	8,347,345
Education	28,714,490
Public works	3,165,482
Intergovernmental	257,901

Taxation, 2010

Property type	Valuation	Rate
Total	$5,232,011,700	-
Residential	5,035,905,790	11.10
Open space	0	0.00
Commercial	152,826,610	11.10
Industrial	8,494,700	11.10
Personal	34,784,600	11.10

Average Single Family Tax Bill, 2010

Avg. assessed home value	$1,400,149
Avg. single fam. tax bill	$15,542
Hi-Lo ranking	1/301

Police & Crime, 2008

Number of police officers	27
Violent crimes	NA
Property crimes	NA

Local School District

(school data 2007-08, except as noted)

Weston
89 Wellesley Street
Weston, MA 02493
781-529-8080

Superintendent	Cheryl Maloney
Grade plan	PK-12
Total enrollment '09-10	2,388
Grade 12 enrollment, '09-10	175
Graduation rate	97.3%
Dropout rate	0.5%
Per-pupil expenditure	$17,017
Avg teacher salary	$73,338
Student/teacher ratio '08-09	12.5 to 1
Highly-qualified teachers, '08-09	99.0%
Teachers licensed in assigned subject	98.9%
Students per computer	2.4

Massachusetts Competency Assessment System (MCAS), 2009 results

	English		Math	
	% Prof	CPI	% Prof	CPI
Gr 4	85%	94.5	83%	93.5
Gr 6	96%	98.7	83%	94
Gr 8	93%	96.3	77%	88.4
Gr 10	97%	98.8	95%	98.5

Other School Districts (see Appendix D for data)
Minuteman Vocational Tech

©2010 Information Publications, Inc. All rights reserved. Photocopying prohibited. For additional copies, contact the publisher at www.informationpublications.com or (877)544-INFO (4636)

See Introduction for an explanation of all data sources.

Demographics & Socio-Economic Characteristics

Population

1990 13,852
2000 14,183
Male 6,947
Female 7,236
2008 15,417
2010 (projected)†† 13,780
2020 (projected)†† 13,028

Race & Hispanic Origin, 2000

Race
White 13,901
Black/African American 24
American Indian/Alaska Native 20
Asian 70
Hawaiian Native/Pacific Islander 3
Other Race 53
Two or more races 112
Hispanic origin 98

Age & Nativity, 2000

Under 5 years 652
18 years and over 11,113
21 years and over 10,694
65 years and over 2,074
85 years and over 205
Median Age 41.0
Native-born 13,036
Foreign-born 1,147

Age, 2020 (projected)††

Under 5 years 492
5 to 19 years 1,811
20 to 39 years 2,560
40 to 64 years 4,819
65 years and over 3,346

Educational Attainment, 2000

Population 25 years and over 10,156
High School graduates or higher .. 78.5%
Bachelor's degree or higher 25.3%
Graduate degree 11.8%

Income & Poverty, 1999

Per capita income, ... $25,281
Median household income $55,436
Median family income $64,568
Persons in poverty 695
H'holds receiving public assistance 68
H'holds receiving social security 1,551

Households, 2000

Total households 5,386
With persons under 18 1,722
With persons over 65 1,508
Family households 4,080
Single person households 1,063
Persons per household 2.6
Persons per family 3.0

Labor & Employment, 2000

Civilian labor force 7,519
Unemployment rate 3.7%
Civilian labor force, 2008† 8,381
Unemployment rate† 9.5%
Civilian labor force, 12/09† 8,481
Unemployment rate† 13.0%
Employed persons 16 years and over, by occupation:
Managers & professionals 2,675
Service occupations 924
Sales & office occupations 1,780
Farming, fishing & forestry 55
Construction & maintenance 772
Production & transportation 1,037
Self-employed persons 457

Most demographic data is from the 2000 Decennial Census
† Massachusetts Department of Revenue
†† University of Massachusetts, MISER

General Information

Town of Westport
816 Main Rd
Westport, MA 02790
508-636-1003

Elevation .... 7 ft.
Land area (square miles) 50.0
Water area (square miles) 14.3
Population density, 2008 (est) 308.3
Year incorporated 1787
Website .... NA

Voters & Government Information

Government type ..... Open Town Meeting
Number of Selectmen 5
US Congressional District(s) 4

Registered Voters, October 2008

Total 11,475
Democrats 4,674
Republicans 1,385
Unaffiliated/other 5,350

Local Officials, 2010

Chair, Bd. of Sel. .... Steven J. Ouellette
Manager/Admin ...... Michael J. Coughlin
Town Clerk .... Marlene Samson
Finance Director .... George Foster
Tax Collector .... Carol A. Borden
Tax Assessor .... John J. McDermott
Attorney .... NA
Public Works .... Harold Jack Sisson Jr
Building .... Ralph Souza (Actg)
Comm Dev/Planning .... NA
Police Chief .... Keith Pelletier
Emerg/Fire Chief .... Brian Legendre

Housing & Construction

New Privately Owned Housing Units Authorized by Building Permit

	Single Family	Total Bldgs	Total Units
2006	67	67	67
2007	53	53	53
2008	34	34	34

Parcel Count by Property Class, 2010

Total 8,518
Single family 5,640
Multiple units 383
Apartments 29
Condos 145
Vacant land 1,382
Open space 0
Commercial 266
Industrial 18
Misc. residential 160
Other use 495

Public Library

Westport Free Public Library
PO Box N-157
Westport, MA 02790
(508)636-1100

Director .... Susan Branco

Library Statistics, FY 2008

Population served, 2007 15,136
Registered users 6,674
Circulation 70,459
Reference transactons 0
Total program attendance 0
per capita:
Holdings 2.99
Operating income $15.52
Internet Access
Internet computers available 8
Weekly users 0

Municipal Finance

Debt at year end 2008 .... $2,560,000
Moody's rating, July 2009 .... A2

Revenues, 2008

Total $29,589,964
From all taxes 20,443,047
Federal aid 0
State aid 6,456,539
From other governments 6,015
Charges for services 924,090
Licenses, permits & fees 434,430
Fines & forfeits 106,286
Interfund transfers 52,857
Misc/other/special assessments 583,350

Expenditures, 2008

Total $28,328,157
General government 1,630,982
Public safety 4,804,789
Other/fixed costs 3,918,282
Human services 548,363
Culture & recreation 233,794
Debt Service 498,101
Education 14,835,785
Public works 1,395,499
Intergovernmental 462,562

Taxation, 2010

Property type	Valuation	Rate
Total	$3,115,662,470	-
Residential	2,823,173,785	6.27
Open space	0	0.00
Commercial	232,689,045	6.27
Industrial	8,619,500	6.27
Personal	51,180,140	6.27

Average Single Family Tax Bill, 2010

Avg. assessed home value $405,747
Avg. single fam. tax bill $2,544
Hi-Lo ranking 278/301

Police & Crime, 2008

Number of police officers 29
Violent crimes 55
Property crimes 183

Local School District

(school data 2007-08, except as noted)

Westport
17 Main Rd
Westport, MA 02790
508-636-1137

Superintendent .... Carlos Colley
Grade plan PK-12
Total enrollment '09-10 1,895
Grade 12 enrollment, '09-10 121
Graduation rate 79.5%
Dropout rate 11.5%
Per-pupil expenditure $9,530
Avg teacher salary $56,829
Student/teacher ratio '08-09 .... 14.6 to 1
Highly-qualified teachers, '08-09 .... 98.6%
Teachers licensed in assigned subject .. 99.2%
Students per computer 5.9

Massachusetts Competency Assessment System (MCAS), 2009 results

	English		Math	
	% Prof	CPI	% Prof	CPI
Gr 4	74%	90.9	56%	84.8
Gr 6	66%	88.3	58%	80.5
Gr 8	86%	94.3	54%	77.5
Gr 10	80%	92.8	73%	88.2

Other School Districts (see Appendix D for data)
Greater Fall River Vocational Tech, Bristol County Agricultural

See Introduction for an explanation of all data sources.

©2010 Information Publications, Inc. All rights reserved. Photocopying prohibited. For additional copies, contact the publisher at www.informationpublications.com or (877)544-INFO (4636)

Demographics & Socio-Economic Characteristics

Population

1990	12,557
2000	14,117
Male	6,714
Female	7,403
2008	14,189
2010 (projected)††	13,828
2020 (projected)††	12,448

Race & Hispanic Origin, 2000

Race	
White	13,549
Black/African American	70
American Indian/Alaska Native	6
Asian	350
Hawaiian Native/Pacific Islander	0
Other Race	30
Two or more races	112
Hispanic origin	132

Age & Nativity, 2000

Under 5 years	1,105
18 years and over	10,190
21 years and over	9,955
65 years and over	2,701
85 years and over	496
Median Age	41.0
Native-born	12,861
Foreign-born	1,256

Age, 2020 (projected)††

Under 5 years	614
5 to 19 years	2,381
20 to 39 years	2,443
40 to 64 years	4,022
65 years and over	2,988

Educational Attainment, 2000

Population 25 years and over	9,724
High School graduates or higher	94.5%
Bachelor's degree or higher	57.4%
Graduate degree	23.9%

Income & Poverty, 1999

Per capita income,	$41,553
Median household income	$87,394
Median family income	$103,242
Persons in poverty	352
H'holds receiving public assistance	33
H'holds receiving social security	1,803

Households, 2000

Total households	5,122
With persons under 18	1,942
With persons over 65	1,926
Family households	3,866
Single person households	1,150
Persons per household	2.7
Persons per family	3.2

Labor & Employment, 2000

Civilian labor force	6,711
Unemployment rate	2.5%
Civilian labor force, 2008†	6,681
Unemployment rate†	4.2%
Civilian labor force, 12/09†	6,741
Unemployment rate†	6.6%
Employed persons 16 years and over, by occupation:	
Managers & professionals	3,832
Service occupations	521
Sales & office occupations	1,571
Farming, fishing & forestry	6
Construction & maintenance	319
Production & transportation	291
Self-employed persons	582

Most demographic data is from the 2000 Decennial Census
† Massachusetts Department of Revenue
†† University of Massachusetts, MISER

General Information

Town of Westwood
580 High St
Westwood, MA 02090
781-326-6450

Elevation	262 ft.
Land area (square miles)	11.0
Water area (square miles)	0.1
Population density, 2008 (est)	1,289.9
Year incorporated	1897
Website	www.townhall.westwood.ma.us

Voters & Government Information

Government type	Open Town Meeting
Number of Selectmen	3
US Congressional District(s)	9

Registered Voters, October 2008

Total	10,154
Democrats	2,810
Republicans	1,731
Unaffiliated/other	5,587

Local Officials, 2010

Chair, Bd. of Sel.	Philip N. Shapiro
Town Administrator	Michael A. Jaillet
Town Clerk	Dorothy A. Powers
Finance Dir/Treas	Pamela M. Dukeman
Tax Collector	Albert F. Wisialko
Tax Assessor	Louis A. Rizoli (Chr)
Attorney	Thomas P. McCusker
Public Works	J. Timothy Walsh
Building	Joseph J. Doyle Jr
Comm Dev/Planning	Nora W. Loughnane
Police Chief	William G. Chase
Emerg/Fire Chief	William Scoble

Housing & Construction

New Privately Owned Housing Units Authorized by Building Permit

	Single Family	Total Bldgs	Total Units
2006	12	14	114
2007	9	18	88
2008	13	13	13

Parcel Count by Property Class, 2010

Total	4,924
Single family	4,470
Multiple units	48
Apartments	7
Condos	4
Vacant land	211
Open space	0
Commercial	99
Industrial	43
Misc. residential	16
Other use	26

Public Library

Westwood Public Library
668 High St.
Westwood, MA 02090
(781)326-7562

Library Director .... Thomas P. Viti

Library Statistics, FY 2008

Population served, 2007	14,010
Registered users	9,556
Circulation	277,226
Reference transactons	11,994
Total program attendance	112,653
per capita:	
Holdings	8.22
Operating income	$65.54
Internet Access	
Internet computers available	15
Weekly users	0

Municipal Finance

Debt at year end 2008	$44,947,828
Moody's rating, July 2009	Aa1

Revenues, 2008

Total	$61,122,130
From all taxes	50,632,468
Federal aid	0
State aid	7,389,198
From other governments	5,082
Charges for services	799,796
Licenses, permits & fees	536,552
Fines & forfeits	16,825
Interfund transfers	510,221
Misc/other/special assessments	615,994

Expenditures, 2008

Total	$58,215,726
General government	2,587,666
Public safety	5,688,151
Other/fixed costs	6,509,240
Human services	623,508
Culture & recreation	1,177,119
Debt Service	6,124,070
Education	30,530,258
Public works	3,905,999
Intergovernmental	1,069,715

Taxation, 2010

Property type	Valuation	Rate
Total	$3,566,682,921	-
Residential	3,088,616,907	13.07
Open space	0	0.00
Commercial	313,502,764	23.98
Industrial	116,181,450	23.98
Personal	48,381,800	23.98

Average Single Family Tax Bill, 2010

Avg. assessed home value	$636,918
Avg. single fam. tax bill	$8,325
Hi-Lo ranking	19/301

Police & Crime, 2008

Number of police officers	28
Violent crimes	12
Property crimes	156

Local School District

(school data 2007-08, except as noted)

Westwood
220 Nahatan Street
Westwood, MA 02090
781-326-7500

Superintendent	John Antonucci
Grade plan	PK-12
Total enrollment '09-10	3,100
Grade 12 enrollment, '09-10	194
Graduation rate	95.2%
Dropout rate	1.4%
Per-pupil expenditure	$13,305
Avg teacher salary	$66,504
Student/teacher ratio '08-09	13.5 to 1
Highly-qualified teachers, '08-09	98.1%
Teachers licensed in assigned subject	98.4%
Students per computer	2.6

Massachusetts Competency Assessment System (MCAS), 2009 results

	English		Math	
	% Prof	CPI	% Prof	CPI
Gr 4	84%	94.7	76%	92.1
Gr 6	90%	96.4	82%	92.1
Gr 8	94%	98.4	66%	86.3
Gr 10	95%	98.2	94%	97.6

Other School Districts (see Appendix D for data)

Blue Hills Vocational Tech, Norfolk County Agricultural

©2010 Information Publications, Inc. All rights reserved. Photocopying prohibited. For additional copies, contact the publisher at www.informationpublications.com or (877)544-INFO (4636)

See Introduction for an explanation of all data sources.

Demographics & Socio-Economic Characteristics*

Population

1990 ... 54,063
2000 ... 53,988
  Male ... 25,640
  Female ... 28,348
2008 ... 53,261
2010 (projected)†† ... 52,205
2020 (projected)†† ... 50,011

Race & Hispanic Origin, 2000

Race
  White ... 51,229
  Black/African American ... 779
  American Indian/Alaska Native ... 102
  Asian ... 843
  Hawaiian Native/Pacific Islander ... 28
  Other Race ... 344
  Two or more races ... 663
Hispanic origin ... 721

Age & Nativity, 2000

Under 5 years ... 3,436
18 years and over ... 42,132
21 years and over ... 40,724
65 years and over ... 8,313
85 years and over ... 952
  Median Age ... 38.4
Native-born ... 51,075
Foreign-born ... 2,913

Age, 2020 (projected)††

Under 5 years ... 2,584
5 to 19 years ... 8,015
20 to 39 years ... 12,234
40 to 64 years ... 17,300
65 years and over ... 9,878

Educational Attainment, 2000

Population 25 years and over ... 38,442
  High School graduates or higher ... 90.5%
  Bachelor's degree or higher ... 26.0%
  Graduate degree ... 7.7%

Income & Poverty, 1999

Per capita income, ... $24,976
Median household income ... $51,665
Median family income ... $64,083
Persons in poverty ... 3,092
H'holds receiving public assistance ... 348
H'holds receiving social security ... 6,093

Households, 2000

Total households ... 22,028
  With persons under 18 ... 6,496
  With persons over 65 ... 5,880
  Family households ... 13,928
  Single person households ... 6,746
Persons per household ... 2.4
Persons per family ... 3.1

Labor & Employment, 2000

Civilian labor force ... 29,590
  Unemployment rate ... 4.0%
Civilian labor force, 2008† ... 30,127
  Unemployment rate† ... 6.5%
Civilian labor force, 12/09† ... 29,984
  Unemployment rate† ... 9.3%
Employed persons 16 years and over, by occupation:
  Managers & professionals ... 10,377
  Service occupations ... 3,572
  Sales & office occupations ... 8,942
  Farming, fishing & forestry ... 14
  Construction & maintenance ... 3,053
  Production & transportation ... 2,443
  Self-employed persons ... 1,326

Most demographic data is from the 2000 Decennial Census
* see Appendix E for American Community Survey data
† Massachusetts Department of Revenue
†† University of Massachusetts, MISER

General Information

Town of Weymouth
75 Middle St
Weymouth, MA 02189
781-335-2000

Elevation ... 100 ft.
Land area (square miles) ... 17.0
Water area (square miles) ... 4.6
Population density, 2008 (est) ... 3,133.0
Year incorporated ... 1622
Website ... www.weymouth.ma.us

Voters & Government Information

Government type ... Mayor-Council
Number of Councilpersons ... 11
US Congressional District(s) ... 10

Registered Voters, October 2008

Total ... 34,564
Democrats ... 12,254
Republicans ... 3,690
Unaffiliated/other ... 18,497

Local Officials, 2010

Mayor ... Susan M. Kay
Manager/Admin ... Michael Gallagher
Town Clerk ... Franklin Fryer
Finance ... James Wilson
Tax Collector ... NA
Tax Assessor ... Pam Berrigan
Attorney ... George Lane Jr
Public Works ... Robert O'Connor
Building ... Jeffrey Richards
Comm Dev/Planning ... James F. Clarke
Police Chief ... Richard Grimes
Emerg/Fire Chief ... Robert Leary

Housing & Construction

New Privately Owned Housing Units Authorized by Building Permit

	Single Family	Total Bldgs	Total Units
2006	23	27	48
2007	23	27	63
2008	16	18	36

Parcel Count by Property Class, 2010

Total ... 18,784
Single family ... 13,074
Multiple units ... 787
Apartments ... 139
Condos ... 2,967
Vacant land ... 799
Open space ... 0
Commercial ... 704
Industrial ... 113
Misc. residential ... 55
Other use ... 146

Public Library

Weymouth Public Libraries
46 Broad St.
Weymouth, MA 02188
(781)337-1402

Director ... Joanne Lamothe

Library Statistics, FY 2008

Population served, 2007 ... 53,272
Registered users ... 21,767
Circulation ... 322,103
Reference transactons ... 17,431
Total program attendance ... 0

per capita:

Holdings ... 2.62
Operating income ... $26.90

Internet Access

Internet computers available ... 28
Weekly users ... 587

Municipal Finance

Debt at year end 2008 ... $62,276,757
Moody's rating, July 2009 ... A2

Revenues, 2008

Total ... $125,822,982
From all taxes ... 76,759,173
Federal aid ... 821,486
State aid ... 34,218,044
From other governments ... 1,049
Charges for services ... 1,061,810
Licenses, permits & fees ... 2,033,974
Fines & forfeits ... 348,036
Interfund transfers ... 8,491,114
Misc/other/special assessments ... 1,044,148

Expenditures, 2008

Total ... $113,853,939
General government ... 4,327,623
Public safety ... 18,373,967
Other/fixed costs ... 9,835,039
Human services ... 864,411
Culture & recreation ... 1,859,721
Debt Service ... 8,060,694
Education ... 55,626,594
Public works ... 9,256,257
Intergovernmental ... 5,614,650

Taxation, 2010

Property type	Valuation	Rate
Total	$6,151,439,700	-
Residential	5,168,002,206	11.09
Open space	0	0.00
Commercial	557,506,174	18.38
Industrial	301,531,600	18.38
Personal	124,399,720	18.38

Average Single Family Tax Bill, 2010

Avg. assessed home value ... $299,544
Avg. single fam. tax bill ... $3,322
Hi-Lo ranking ... 199/301

Police & Crime, 2008

Number of police officers ... 93
Violent crimes ... 106
Property crimes ... 859

Local School District

(school data 2007-08, except as noted)

Weymouth
111 Middle Street
Weymouth, MA 02189
781-335-1460

Superintendent ... Mary Livingstone
Grade plan ... PK-12
Total enrollment '09-10 ... 6,919
Grade 12 enrollment, '09-10 ... 536
Graduation rate ... 82.6%
Dropout rate ... 10.1%
Per-pupil expenditure ... $12,034
Avg teacher salary ... $61,526
Student/teacher ratio '08-09 ... 15.4 to 1
Highly-qualified teachers, '08-09 ... 96.6%
Teachers licensed in assigned subject ... 98.4%
Students per computer ... 4.3

Massachusetts Competency Assessment System (MCAS), 2009 results

	English		Math	
	% Prof	CPI	% Prof	CPI
Gr 4	62%	85.7	54%	82.6
Gr 6	64%	84.4	49%	72.8
Gr 8	81%	92	44%	70.7
Gr 10	82%	93.1	74%	89.6

Other School Districts (see Appendix D for data)
Norfolk County Agricultural

©2010 Information Publications, Inc. All rights reserved. Photocopying prohibited. For additional copies, contact the publisher at www.informationpublications.com or (877)544-INFO (4636)

See Introduction for an explanation of all data sources.

Demographics & Socio-Economic Characteristics

Population

1990	1,375
2000	1,573
Male	790
Female	783
2008	1,566
2010 (projected)††	1,558
2020 (projected)††	1,560

Race & Hispanic Origin, 2000

Race	
White	1,541
Black/African American	8
American Indian/Alaska Native	2
Asian	8
Hawaiian Native/Pacific Islander	0
Other Race	5
Two or more races	9
Hispanic origin	18

Age & Nativity, 2000

Under 5 years	70
18 years and over	1,230
21 years and over	1,175
65 years and over	194
85 years and over	24
Median Age	41.2
Native-born	1,514
Foreign-born	49

Age, 2020 (projected)††

Under 5 years	70
5 to 19 years	201
20 to 39 years	362
40 to 64 years	588
65 years and over	339

Educational Attainment, 2000

Population 25 years and over	1,116
High School graduates or higher	89.9%
Bachelor's degree or higher	37.6%
Graduate degree	16.4%

Income & Poverty, 1999

Per capita income,	$27,826
Median household income	$58,929
Median family income	$66,488
Persons in poverty	46
H'holds receiving public assistance	4
H'holds receiving social security	183

Households, 2000

Total households	629
With persons under 18	192
With persons over 65	140
Family households	425
Single person households	148
Persons per household	2.5
Persons per family	3.0

Labor & Employment, 2000

Civilian labor force	980
Unemployment rate	4.7%
Civilian labor force, 2008†	958
Unemployment rate†	3.9%
Civilian labor force, 12/09†	936
Unemployment rate†	4.3%
Employed persons 16 years and over, by occupation:	
Managers & professionals	403
Service occupations	136
Sales & office occupations	191
Farming, fishing & forestry	20
Construction & maintenance	107
Production & transportation	77
Self-employed persons	134

Most demographic data is from the 2000 Decennial Census
† Massachusetts Department of Revenue
†† University of Massachusetts, MISER

General Information

Town of Whately
218 Chestnut Plain Road
PO Box 181
Whately, MA 01093
413-665-4400

Elevation	290 ft.
Land area (square miles)	20.2
Water area (square miles)	0.5
Population density, 2008 (est)	77.5
Year incorporated	1771
Website	www.whately.org

Voters & Government Information

Government type	Open Town Meeting
Number of Selectmen	3
US Congressional District(s)	1

Registered Voters, October 2008

Total	1,157
Democrats	355
Republicans	154
Unaffiliated/other	640

Local Officials, 2010

Chair, Bd. of Sel.	Jonathan S. Edwards
Town Administrator	Lynn M. Sibley
Clerk	Lynn M. Sibley
Town Accountant	Joyce Muka
Tax Collector	Susan Warriner
Tax Assessor	Katherine Fleuriel
Attorney	Patricia Cantor
Public Works	Keith Bardwell
Building	James Hawkins
Planning	Donald Sluter
Police Chief	James Sevigne Jr
Emerg/Fire Chief	John Hannum

Housing & Construction

New Privately Owned Housing Units Authorized by Building Permit

	Single Family	Total Bldgs	Total Units
2006	4	4	4
2007	3	3	3
2008	4	4	4

Parcel Count by Property Class, 2010

Total	1,097
Single family	501
Multiple units	30
Apartments	1
Condos	0
Vacant land	259
Open space	0
Commercial	51
Industrial	10
Misc. residential	7
Other use	238

Public Library

S. White Dickinson Memorial Library
PO Box 187
Whately, MA 01093
(413)665-2170

Librarian	Tiffany Hilton

Library Statistics, FY 2008

Population served, 2007	1,555
Registered users	901
Circulation	8,738
Reference transactons	241
Total program attendance	0
per capita:	
Holdings	10.09
Operating income	$32.35
Internet Access	
Internet computers available	2
Weekly users	0

Municipal Finance

Debt at year end 2008	$730,000
Moody's rating, July 2009	Baa2

Revenues, 2008

Total	$4,519,926
From all taxes	3,476,968
Federal aid	0
State aid	615,894
From other governments	6,245
Charges for services	183,235
Licenses, permits & fees	40,087
Fines & forfeits	46,755
Interfund transfers	0
Misc/other/special assessments	75,371

Expenditures, 2008

Total	$4,162,717
General government	314,226
Public safety	175,829
Other/fixed costs	377,378
Human services	21,484
Culture & recreation	46,412
Debt Service	396,840
Education	2,316,669
Public works	366,845
Intergovernmental	90,217

Taxation, 2010

Property type	Valuation	Rate
Total	$228,098,535	-
Residential	182,757,899	14.51
Open space	0	0.00
Commercial	20,211,459	14.51
Industrial	18,778,300	14.51
Personal	6,350,877	14.51

Average Single Family Tax Bill, 2010

Avg. assessed home value	$276,231
Avg. single fam. tax bill	$4,008
Hi-Lo ranking	136/301

Police & Crime, 2008

Number of police officers	2
Violent crimes	NA
Property crimes	NA

Local School District

(school data 2007-08, except as noted)
Whately
219 Christian Ln RFD1
South Deerfield, MA 01373
413-665-1155

Superintendent	Regina Nash
Grade plan	PK-6
Total enrollment '09-10	132
Grade 12 enrollment, '09-10	0
Graduation rate	NA
Dropout rate	NA
Per-pupil expenditure	$13,495
Avg teacher salary	$51,653
Student/teacher ratio '08-09	12.2 to 1
Highly-qualified teachers, '08-09	100.0%
Teachers licensed in assigned subject	100.0%
Students per computer	3.3

Massachusetts Competency Assessment System (MCAS), 2009 results

	English		Math	
	% Prof	CPI	% Prof	CPI
Gr 4	50%	82.8	56%	89.1
Gr 6	71%	88.2	59%	76.5
Gr 8	NA	NA	NA	NA
Gr 10	NA	NA	NA	NA

Other School Districts (see Appendix D for data)
Frontier Regional, Franklin County Vocational Tech

©2010 Information Publications, Inc. All rights reserved. Photocopying prohibited. For additional copies, contact the publisher at www.informationpublications.com or (877)544-INFO (4636)

See Introduction for an explanation of all data sources.

©2010 Information Publications, Inc. All rights reserved. Photocopying prohibited. For additional copies, contact the publisher at www.informationpublications.com or (877)544-INFO (4636)

Demographics & Socio-Economic Characteristics

Population

1990	13,240
2000	13,882
Male	6,812
Female	7,070
2008	14,447
2010 (projected)††	13,565
2020 (projected)††	13,145

Race & Hispanic Origin, 2000

Race	
White	13,487
Black/African American	90
American Indian/Alaska Native	22
Asian	59
Hawaiian Native/Pacific Islander	2
Other Race	66
Two or more races	156
Hispanic origin	122

Age & Nativity, 2000

Under 5 years	950
18 years and over	10,169
21 years and over	9,623
65 years and over	1,318
85 years and over	142
Median Age	34.7
Native-born	13,574
Foreign-born	308

Age, 2020 (projected)††

Under 5 years	795
5 to 19 years	2,390
20 to 39 years	3,527
40 to 64 years	4,480
65 years and over	1,953

Educational Attainment, 2000

Population 25 years and over	9,037
High School graduates or higher	90.2%
Bachelor's degree or higher	21.7%
Graduate degree	5.3%

Income & Poverty, 1999

Per capita income,	$23,002
Median household income	$55,303
Median family income	$63,706
Persons in poverty	462
H'holds receiving public assistance	133
H'holds receiving social security	1,124

Households, 2000

Total households	4,999
With persons under 18	1,978
With persons over 65	991
Family households	3,604
Single person households	1,119
Persons per household	2.8
Persons per family	3.3

Labor & Employment, 2000

Civilian labor force	7,844
Unemployment rate	3.4%
Civilian labor force, 2008†	8,256
Unemployment rate†	6.8%
Civilian labor force, 12/09†	8,310
Unemployment rate†	10.5%
Employed persons 16 years and over, by occupation:	
Managers & professionals	2,481
Service occupations	996
Sales & office occupations	2,193
Farming, fishing & forestry	10
Construction & maintenance	925
Production & transportation	969
Self-employed persons	344

Most demographic data is from the 2000 Decennial Census
† Massachusetts Department of Revenue
†† University of Massachusetts, MISER

General Information

Town of Whitman
PO Box 426
Whitman, MA 02382
781-618-9701

Elevation	119 ft.
Land area (square miles)	7.0
Water area (square miles)	0.0
Population density, 2008 (est)	2,063.9
Year incorporated	1875
Email	fjlynam@whitman-ma.gov

Voters & Government Information

Government type	Open Town Meeting
Number of Selectmen	5
US Congressional District(s)	9

Registered Voters, October 2008

Total	9,285
Democrats	2,546
Republicans	1,090
Unaffiliated/other	5,595

Local Officials, 2010

Chair, Bd. of Sel.	Carl Kowalski
Manager	Frank Lynam
Town Clerk	Pamela Martin
Treasurer	Mary Beth Carter
Tax Collector	Mary Beth Carter
Tax Assessor	Kathleen Keefe
Attorney	NA
Public Works	Donnie Westhaver
Building	Robert Curran
Comm Dev/Planning	Joseph Foscaldo
Police Chief	Christine May-Stafford
Emerg/Fire Chief	Timothy Grenno

Housing & Construction

New Privately Owned Housing Units Authorized by Building Permit

	Single Family	Total Bldgs	Total Units
2006	61	61	61
2007	48	48	48
2008	31	31	31

Parcel Count by Property Class, 2010

Total	4,871
Single family	3,274
Multiple units	539
Apartments	56
Condos	419
Vacant land	238
Open space	0
Commercial	165
Industrial	91
Misc. residential	19
Other use	70

Public Library

Whitman Public Library
100 Webster Street
Whitman, MA 02382
(781)447-7613

Director	Jennifer Inglis

Library Statistics, FY 2008

Population served, 2007	14,385
Registered users	7,766
Circulation	99,188
Reference transactons	3,000
Total program attendance	90,883
per capita:	
Holdings	3.65
Operating income	$26.73
Internet Access	
Internet computers available	12
Weekly users	680

Municipal Finance

Debt at year end 2008	$10,783,034
Moody's rating, July 2009	A2

Revenues, 2008

Total	$25,908,355
From all taxes	18,267,768
Federal aid	11,645
State aid	2,928,382
From other governments	0
Charges for services	1,346,835
Licenses, permits & fees	153,799
Fines & forfeits	0
Interfund transfers	2,193,370
Misc/other/special assessments	503,278

Expenditures, 2008

Total	$23,070,262
General government	1,587,392
Public safety	4,980,386
Other/fixed costs	2,552,520
Human services	408,722
Culture & recreation	382,305
Debt Service	303,545
Education	10,516,729
Public works	2,166,705
Intergovernmental	171,624

Taxation, 2010

Property type	Valuation	Rate
Total	$1,403,422,684	-
Residential	1,265,029,928	12.40
Open space	0	0.00
Commercial	86,974,556	12.40
Industrial	22,925,892	12.40
Personal	28,492,308	12.40

Average Single Family Tax Bill, 2010

Avg. assessed home value	$287,022
Avg. single fam. tax bill	$3,559
Hi-Lo ranking	166/301

Police & Crime, 2008

Number of police officers	26
Violent crimes	NA
Property crimes	NA

Local School District

(school data 2007-08, except as noted)

Whitman (non-op)
610 Franklin Street
Whitman, MA 02382
781-618-7412

Superintendent...... Ruth Gilbert-Whitner

Non-operating district.
Resident students are sent to the Other School Districts listed below.

Grade plan	NA
Total enrollment '09-10	NA
Grade 12 enrollment, '09-10	NA
Graduation rate	NA
Dropout rate	NA
Per-pupil expenditure	NA
Avg teacher salary	NA
Student/teacher ratio '08-09	NA
Highly-qualified teachers, '08-09	NA
Teachers licensed in assigned subject	NA
Students per computer	NA

Other School Districts (see Appendix D for data)
Whitman-Hanson Regional, South Shore Vocational Tech

See Introduction for an explanation of all data sources.

Demographics & Socio-Economic Characteristics

Population

1990	12,635
2000	13,473
Male	6,473
Female	7,000
2008	13,970
2010 (projected)††	12,896
2020 (projected)††	11,913

Race & Hispanic Origin, 2000

Race	
White	12,988
Black/African American	161
American Indian/Alaska Native	8
Asian	170
Hawaiian Native/Pacific Islander	8
Other Race	34
Two or more races	104
Hispanic origin	189

Age & Nativity, 2000

Under 5 years	754
18 years and over	9,854
21 years and over	9,530
65 years and over	2,279
85 years and over	312
Median Age	42.1
Native-born	12,909
Foreign-born	564

Age, 2020 (projected)††

Under 5 years	522
5 to 19 years	1,903
20 to 39 years	2,271
40 to 64 years	4,007
65 years and over	3,210

Educational Attainment, 2000

Population 25 years and over	9,320
High School graduates or higher	92.6%
Bachelor's degree or higher	44.4%
Graduate degree	18.5%

Income & Poverty, 1999

Per capita income,	$29,854
Median household income	$65,014
Median family income	$73,825
Persons in poverty	679
H'holds receiving public assistance	34
H'holds receiving social security	1,623

Households, 2000

Total households	4,891
With persons under 18	1,887
With persons over 65	1,446
Family households	3,872
Single person households	876
Persons per household	2.7
Persons per family	3.1

Labor & Employment, 2000

Civilian labor force	6,564
Unemployment rate	3.3%
Civilian labor force, 2008†	6,897
Unemployment rate†	5.4%
Civilian labor force, 12/09†	6,918
Unemployment rate†	7.2%
Employed persons 16 years and over, by occupation:	
Managers & professionals	3,183
Service occupations	710
Sales & office occupations	1,614
Farming, fishing & forestry	0
Construction & maintenance	255
Production & transportation	588
Self-employed persons	431

Most demographic data is from the 2000 Decennial Census
† Massachusetts Department of Revenue
†† University of Massachusetts, MISER

General Information

Town of Wilbraham
240 Springfield St
Wilbraham, MA 01095
413-596-2800

Elevation	290 ft.
Land area (square miles)	22.2
Water area (square miles)	0.2
Population density, 2008 (est)	629.3
Year incorporated	1763
Website	www.wilbraham-ma.gov

Voters & Government Information

Government type	Open Town Meeting
Number of Selectmen	3
US Congressional District(s)	2

Registered Voters, October 2008

Total	10,451
Democrats	3,125
Republicans	2,302
Unaffiliated/other	4,985

Local Officials, 2010

Chair, Bd. of Sel.	David W. Barry
Town Administrator	Robert Weitz
Town Clerk	Beverly Litchfield
Treasurer	Thomas Sullivan
Tax Collector	Thomas Sullivan
Tax Assessor	Lawrence G. LaBarbera
Attorney	Michael Hassett
Public Works	Edmond Miga
Building	Lance Trevallion
Comm Dev/Planning	John Pearsall
Police Chief	Allen Stratton
Emerg/Fire Chief	Francis Nothe

Housing & Construction

New Privately Owned Housing Units Authorized by Building Permit

	Single Family	Total Bldgs	Total Units
2006	57	57	57
2007	20	20	20
2008	12	12	12

Parcel Count by Property Class, 2010

Total	5,687
Single family	4,594
Multiple units	66
Apartments	7
Condos	369
Vacant land	380
Open space	0
Commercial	161
Industrial	64
Misc. residential	17
Other use	29

Public Library

Wilbraham Public Library
25 Crane Park Drive
Wilbraham, MA 01095
(413)596-6141

Director	Christine Bergquist

Library Statistics, FY 2008

Population served, 2007	14,032
Registered users	10,065
Circulation	212,287
Reference transactons	14,149
Total program attendance	142,844
per capita:	
Holdings	4.73
Operating income	$52.49
Internet Access	
Internet computers available	13
Weekly users	367

Municipal Finance

Debt at year end 2008	$3,313,000
Moody's rating, July 2009	A1

Revenues, 2008

Total	$29,700,620
From all taxes	27,271,766
Federal aid	0
State aid	1,836,650
From other governments	38,522
Charges for services	103,802
Licenses, permits & fees	166,418
Fines & forfeits	10,249
Interfund transfers	76,065
Misc/other/special assessments	98,574

Expenditures, 2008

Total	$29,200,203
General government	1,772,990
Public safety	3,944,669
Other/fixed costs	2,463,371
Human services	197,924
Culture & recreation	904,486
Debt Service	729,855
Education	17,514,546
Public works	1,387,410
Intergovernmental	284,952

Taxation, 2010

Property type	Valuation	Rate
Total	$1,693,563,000	-
Residential	1,514,745,810	16.19
Open space	0	0.00
Commercial	119,040,590	16.19
Industrial	27,762,900	16.19
Personal	32,013,700	16.19

Average Single Family Tax Bill, 2010

Avg. assessed home value	$295,952
Avg. single fam. tax bill	$4,791
Hi-Lo ranking	86/301

Police & Crime, 2008

Number of police officers	28
Violent crimes	12
Property crimes	187

Local School District

(school data 2007-08, except as noted)

Wilbraham (non-op)
621 Main Street
Wilbraham, MA 01095
413-596-3884

Superintendent	Maurice O'Shea

Non-operating district.
Resident students are sent to the Other School Districts listed below.

Grade plan	NA
Total enrollment '09-10	NA
Grade 12 enrollment, '09-10	NA
Graduation rate	NA
Dropout rate	NA
Per-pupil expenditure	NA
Avg teacher salary	NA
Student/teacher ratio '08-09	NA
Highly-qualified teachers, '08-09	NA
Teachers licensed in assigned subject	NA
Students per computer	NA

Other School Districts (see Appendix D for data)
Hampden-Wilbraham Regional

©2010 Information Publications, Inc. All rights reserved. Photocopying prohibited. For additional copies, contact the publisher at www.informationpublications.com or (877)544-INFO (4636)

Demographics & Socio-Economic Characteristics

Population

1990	2,515
2000	2,427
Male	1,145
Female	1,282
2008	2,509
2010 (projected)††	2,314
2020 (projected)††	2,231

Race & Hispanic Origin, 2000

Race	
White	2,377
Black/African American	6
American Indian/Alaska Native	2
Asian	12
Hawaiian Native/Pacific Islander	0
Other Race	4
Two or more races	26
Hispanic origin	16

Age & Nativity, 2000

Under 5 years	108
18 years and over	1,909
21 years and over	1,847
65 years and over	313
85 years and over	35
Median Age	41.5
Native-born	2,380
Foreign-born	47

Age, 2020 (projected)††

Under 5 years	98
5 to 19 years	288
20 to 39 years	481
40 to 64 years	793
65 years and over	571

Educational Attainment, 2000

Population 25 years and over	1,771
High School graduates or higher	92.3%
Bachelor's degree or higher	39.4%
Graduate degree	18.7%

Income & Poverty, 1999

Per capita income,	$25,813
Median household income	$47,250
Median family income	$55,833
Persons in poverty	133
H'holds receiving public assistance	34
H'holds receiving social security	248

Households, 2000

Total households	1,027
With persons under 18	313
With persons over 65	239
Family households	658
Single person households	258
Persons per household	2.4
Persons per family	2.9

Labor & Employment, 2000

Civilian labor force	1,480
Unemployment rate	3.8%
Civilian labor force, 2008†	1,508
Unemployment rate†	6.5%
Civilian labor force, 12/09†	1,548
Unemployment rate†	10.1%
Employed persons 16 years and over, by occupation:	
Managers & professionals	589
Service occupations	247
Sales & office occupations	286
Farming, fishing & forestry	6
Construction & maintenance	93
Production & transportation	203
Self-employed persons	191

Most demographic data is from the 2000 Decennial Census
† Massachusetts Department of Revenue
†† University of Massachusetts, MISER

General Information

Town of Williamsburg
141 Main St
PO Box 447
Haydenville, MA 01039
413-268-8400

Elevation	530 ft.
Land area (square miles)	25.6
Water area (square miles)	0.1
Population density, 2008 (est)	98.0
Year incorporated	1775
Website	www.burgy.org

Voters & Government Information

Government type	Open Town Meeting
Number of Selectmen	3
US Congressional District(s)	1

Registered Voters, October 2008

Total	1,967
Democrats	710
Republicans	170
Unaffiliated/other	1,063

Local Officials, 2010

Chair, Bd. of Sel.	David Mathers
Town Administrator	Steve Herzberg
Clerk	Brenda Lessard
Finance Director	Peter Mahieu
Tax Collector	Bonnie Roberge
Tax Assessor	Marjorie Dunphy
Attorney	Kopelman & Paige
Public Works	William Turner
Building	Paul Tacy
Planning	Roger Bisbee
Police Chief	Denise Wickland
Emerg/Fire Chief	Donald Lawton

Housing & Construction

New Privately Owned Housing Units Authorized by Building Permit

	Single Family	Total Bldgs	Total Units
2006	10	11	12
2007	18	19	21
2008	3	3	3

Parcel Count by Property Class, 2010

Total	1,276
Single family	716
Multiple units	115
Apartments	9
Condos	46
Vacant land	203
Open space	0
Commercial	38
Industrial	7
Misc. residential	18
Other use	124

Public Library

Meekins Public Library
PO Box 772
Williamsburg, MA 01096
(413)268-7472

Director of Library Services .. Lisa Wenner

Library Statistics, FY 2008

Population served, 2007	2,440
Registered users	2,081
Circulation	87,501
Reference transactons	4,500
Total program attendance	40,000
per capita:	
Holdings	20.19
Operating income	$62.96
Internet Access	
Internet computers available	10
Weekly users	80

Municipal Finance

Debt at year end 2008	$1,600,000
Moody's rating, July 2009	NA

Revenues, 2008

Total	$5,738,812
From all taxes	4,590,594
Federal aid	0
State aid	844,883
From other governments	4,700
Charges for services	64,321
Licenses, permits & fees	37,948
Fines & forfeits	0
Interfund transfers	51,700
Misc/other/special assessments	72,333

Expenditures, 2008

Total	$5,285,214
General government	330,357
Public safety	310,573
Other/fixed costs	500,307
Human services	81,498
Culture & recreation	110,685
Debt Service	201,144
Education	3,066,269
Public works	487,279
Intergovernmental	191,525

Taxation, 2010

Property type	Valuation	Rate
Total	$312,297,611	-
Residential	286,173,648	14.43
Open space	0	0.00
Commercial	18,619,047	14.43
Industrial	1,896,733	14.43
Personal	5,608,183	14.43

Average Single Family Tax Bill, 2010

Avg. assessed home value	$277,290
Avg. single fam. tax bill	$4,001
Hi-Lo ranking	137/301

Police & Crime, 2008

Number of police officers	1
Violent crimes	3
Property crimes	48

Local School District

(school data 2007-08, except as noted)

Williamsburg
19 Stage Rd
Westhampton, MA 01027
413-527-7200

Superintendent	Craig Jurgensen
Grade plan	PK-6
Total enrollment '09-10	165
Grade 12 enrollment, '09-10	0
Graduation rate	NA
Dropout rate	NA
Per-pupil expenditure	$13,006
Avg teacher salary	$57,815
Student/teacher ratio '08-09	10.7 to 1
Highly-qualified teachers, '08-09	100.0%
Teachers licensed in assigned subject	100.0%
Students per computer	3.2

Massachusetts Competency Assessment System (MCAS), 2009 results

	English		Math	
	% Prof	CPI	% Prof	CPI
Gr 4	47%	77.6	37%	80.3
Gr 6	84%	93	68%	87
Gr 8	NA	NA	NA	NA
Gr 10	NA	NA	NA	NA

Other School Districts (see Appendix D for data)

Hampshire Regional

©2010 Information Publications, Inc. All rights reserved. Photocopying prohibited. For additional copies, contact the publisher at www.informationpublications.com or (877)544-INFO (4636)

See Introduction for an explanation of all data sources.

Demographics & Socio-Economic Characteristics

Population

1990	8,220
2000	8,424
Male	3,939
Female	4,485
2008	7,968
2010 (projected)††	7,921
2020 (projected)††	7,503

Race & Hispanic Origin, 2000

Race	
White	7,648
Black/African American	229
American Indian/Alaska Native	9
Asian	263
Hawaiian Native/Pacific Islander	10
Other Race	65
Two or more races	200
Hispanic origin	233

Age & Nativity, 2000

Under 5 years	275
18 years and over	7,131
21 years and over	5,721
65 years and over	1,647
85 years and over	350
Median Age	35.6
Native-born	7,791
Foreign-born	633

Age, 2020 (projected)††

Under 5 years	296
5 to 19 years	1,732
20 to 39 years	2,076
40 to 64 years	1,538
65 years and over	1,861

Educational Attainment, 2000

Population 25 years and over	4,856
High School graduates or higher	88.8%
Bachelor's degree or higher	53.6%
Graduate degree	29.1%

Income & Poverty, 1999

Per capita income,	$26,039
Median household income	$51,875
Median family income	$67,589
Persons in poverty	335
H'holds receiving public assistance	38
H'holds receiving social security	938

Households, 2000

Total households	2,753
With persons under 18	705
With persons over 65	969
Family households	1,694
Single person households	901
Persons per household	2.2
Persons per family	2.8

Labor & Employment, 2000

Civilian labor force	3,990
Unemployment rate	6.3%
Civilian labor force, 2008†	3,891
Unemployment rate†	4.8%
Civilian labor force, 12/09†	3,937
Unemployment rate†	7.0%
Employed persons 16 years and over, by occupation:	
Managers & professionals	2,036
Service occupations	691
Sales & office occupations	698
Farming, fishing & forestry	8
Construction & maintenance	140
Production & transportation	165
Self-employed persons	295

Most demographic data is from the 2000 Decennial Census
† Massachusetts Department of Revenue
†† University of Massachusetts, MISER

General Information

Town of Williamstown
31 North St
Williamstown, MA 01267
413-458-3500

Elevation	700 ft.
Land area (square miles)	46.9
Water area (square miles)	0.0
Population density, 2008 (est)	169.9
Year incorporated	1765
Website	www.williamstown.net

Voters & Government Information

Government type	Open Town Meeting
Number of Selectmen	5
US Congressional District(s)	1

Registered Voters, October 2008

Total	4,747
Democrats	2,060
Republicans	444
Unaffiliated/other	2,224

Local Officials, 2010

Chair, Bd. of Sel.	Tom Costley
Manager	Peter Fohlin
Town Clerk	Mary Kennedy
Finance Director	Charles St. John
Tax Collector	Janet Saddler
Tax Assessor	William Barkin
Attorney	NA
Public Works	Timothy A. Kaiser
Building	Michael J. Card
Comm Dev/Planning	Michael J. Card
Police Chief	Kyle Johnson
Emerg/Fire Chief	Craig Pedercini

Housing & Construction

New Privately Owned Housing Units Authorized by Building Permit

	Single Family	Total Bldgs	Total Units
2006	11	11	11
2007	8	8	8
2008	6	6	6

Parcel Count by Property Class, 2010

Total	2,807
Single family	1,843
Multiple units	133
Apartments	18
Condos	187
Vacant land	300
Open space	0
Commercial	118
Industrial	15
Misc. residential	35
Other use	158

Public Library

David and Joyce Milne Public Library
1095 Main Street
Williamstown, MA 01267
(413)458-5369

Director	Patricia McLeod

Library Statistics, FY 2008

Population served, 2007	8,108
Registered users	5,707
Circulation	170,460
Reference transactons	10,955
Total program attendance	75,801
per capita:	
Holdings	8.59
Operating income	$67.18
Internet Access	
Internet computers available	13
Weekly users	230

Municipal Finance

Debt at year end 2008	$7,250,000
Moody's rating, July 2009	Aa3

Revenues, 2008

Total	$17,155,160
From all taxes	13,357,986
Federal aid	0
State aid	2,299,696
From other governments	22,290
Charges for services	163,686
Licenses, permits & fees	206,520
Fines & forfeits	32,795
Interfund transfers	340,747
Misc/other/special assessments	365,720

Expenditures, 2008

Total	$16,100,292
General government	870,540
Public safety	1,248,095
Other/fixed costs	2,470,335
Human services	252,833
Culture & recreation	669,405
Debt Service	566,048
Education	8,665,455
Public works	1,309,715
Intergovernmental	46,041

Taxation, 2010

Property type	Valuation	Rate
Total	$1,071,641,458	-
Residential	944,692,162	12.30
Open space	0	0.00
Commercial	95,536,432	12.30
Industrial	12,468,503	12.30
Personal	18,944,361	12.30

Average Single Family Tax Bill, 2010

Avg. assessed home value	$385,009
Avg. single fam. tax bill	$4,736
Hi-Lo ranking	89/301

Police & Crime, 2008

Number of police officers	12
Violent crimes	13
Property crimes	146

Local School District

(school data 2007-08, except as noted)
Williamstown
115 Church Street
Williamstown, MA 01267
413-458-5707

Superintendent	Rose Ellis
Grade plan	PK-6
Total enrollment '09-10	426
Grade 12 enrollment, '09-10	0
Graduation rate	NA
Dropout rate	NA
Per-pupil expenditure	$13,143
Avg teacher salary	$64,242
Student/teacher ratio '08-09	12.6 to 1
Highly-qualified teachers, '08-09	93.0%
Teachers licensed in assigned subject	100.0%
Students per computer	2.8

Massachusetts Competency Assessment System (MCAS), 2009 results

	English		Math	
	% Prof	CPI	% Prof	CPI
Gr 4	73%	90.7	61%	83.3
Gr 6	75%	92.3	66%	84.9
Gr 8	NA	NA	NA	NA
Gr 10	NA	NA	NA	NA

Other School Districts (see Appendix D for data)
Mount Greylock Regional, Northern Berkshire Vocational Tech

©2010 Information Publications, Inc. All rights reserved. Photocopying prohibited. For additional copies, contact the publisher at www.informationpublications.com or (877)544-INFO (4636)

See Introduction for an explanation of all data sources.

Demographics & Socio-Economic Characteristics*

Population

1990	17,651
2000	21,363
Male	10,580
Female	10,783
2008	21,649
2010 (projected)††	22,798
2020 (projected)††	23,472

Race & Hispanic Origin, 2000

Race	
White	20,575
Black/African American	88
American Indian/Alaska Native	17
Asian	434
Hawaiian Native/Pacific Islander	1
Other Race	90
Two or more races	158
Hispanic origin	203

Age & Nativity, 2000

Under 5 years	1,715
18 years and over	15,463
21 years and over	14,909
65 years and over	2,311
85 years and over	282
Median Age	36.3
Native-born	20,296
Foreign-born	1,067

Age, 2020 (projected)††

Under 5 years	1,436
5 to 19 years	4,614
20 to 39 years	5,656
40 to 64 years	8,132
65 years and over	3,634

Educational Attainment, 2000

Population 25 years and over	14,160
High School graduates or higher	92.4%
Bachelor's degree or higher	31.4%
Graduate degree	9.1%

Income & Poverty, 1999

Per capita income,	$25,835
Median household income	$70,652
Median family income	$76,760
Persons in poverty	410
H'holds receiving public assistance	92
H'holds receiving social security	1,716

Households, 2000

Total households	7,027
With persons under 18	3,127
With persons over 65	1,519
Family households	5,777
Single person households	985
Persons per household	3.0
Persons per family	3.3

Labor & Employment, 2000

Civilian labor force	11,668
Unemployment rate	1.5%
Civilian labor force, 2008†	12,230
Unemployment rate†	5.4%
Civilian labor force, 12/09†	12,288
Unemployment rate†	7.9%
Employed persons 16 years and over, by occupation:	
Managers & professionals	4,879
Service occupations	1,216
Sales & office occupations	3,256
Farming, fishing & forestry	5
Construction & maintenance	1,068
Production & transportation	1,069
Self-employed persons	632

Most demographic data is from the 2000 Decennial Census
* see Appendix E for American Community Survey data
† Massachusetts Department of Revenue
†† University of Massachusetts, MISER

General Information

Town of Wilmington
121 Glen Rd
Wilmington, MA 01887
978-658-3311

Elevation	96 ft.
Land area (square miles)	17.1
Water area (square miles)	0.1
Population density, 2008 (est)	1,266.0
Year incorporated	1730
Website	www.town.wilmington.ma.us

Voters & Government Information

Government type	Open Town Meeting
Number of Selectmen	5
US Congressional District(s)	6

Registered Voters, October 2008

Total	15,823
Democrats	4,531
Republicans	1,959
Unaffiliated/other	9,257

Local Officials, 2010

Chair, Bd. of Sel.	Michael Newhouse
Manager	Michael Caira
Clerk	Sharon George
Accountant	Michael Morris
Treas/Collector	Pamela MacKenzie
Tax Assessor	Humphrey Moynihan
Attorney	Paul R. DeRensis
Public Works	Donald Onusseit
Building	Al Spaulding
Planning	Carole Hamilton
Police Chief	Michael Begonis
Fire Chief	Edward Bradbury

Housing & Construction

New Privately Owned Housing Units Authorized by Building Permit

	Single Family	Total Bldgs	Total Units
2006	60	60	60
2007	32	32	32
2008	22	23	25

Parcel Count by Property Class, 2010

Total	8,287
Single family	6,860
Multiple units	87
Apartments	5
Condos	168
Vacant land	663
Open space	0
Commercial	203
Industrial	251
Misc. residential	15
Other use	35

Public Library

Wilmington Memorial Library
175 Middlesex Ave.
Wilmington, MA 01887
(978)658-2967

Director	Christina Stewart

Library Statistics, FY 2008

Population served, 2007	21,679
Registered users	15,384
Circulation	235,744
Reference transactons	8,427
Total program attendance	133,915
per capita:	
Holdings	3.46
Operating income	$42.02
Internet Access	
Internet computers available	18
Weekly users	321

Municipal Finance

Debt at year end 2008	$14,442,704
Moody's rating, July 2009	NA

Revenues, 2008

Total	$73,158,861
From all taxes	53,707,157
Federal aid	0
State aid	12,423,381
From other governments	123,203
Charges for services	2,526,571
Licenses, permits & fees	878,442
Fines & forfeits	21,332
Interfund transfers	818,869
Misc/other/special assessments	1,329,953

Expenditures, 2008

Total	$62,303,687
General government	3,052,050
Public safety	7,550,244
Other/fixed costs	4,273,578
Human services	804,344
Culture & recreation	1,395,473
Debt Service	4,246,215
Education	33,472,848
Public works	5,120,973
Intergovernmental	2,372,890

Taxation, 2010

Property type	Valuation	Rate
Total	$3,497,381,090	-
Residential	2,604,043,007	11.53
Open space	0	0.00
Commercial	139,654,845	27.17
Industrial	675,131,828	27.17
Personal	78,551,410	27.17

Average Single Family Tax Bill, 2010

Avg. assessed home value	$356,075
Avg. single fam. tax bill	$4,106
Hi-Lo ranking	126/301

Police & Crime, 2008

Number of police officers	48
Violent crimes	46
Property crimes	395

Local School District

(school data 2007-08, except as noted)

Wilmington
161 Church Street
Wilmington, MA 01887
978-694-6000

Superintendent	Joanne Benton
Grade plan	PK-12
Total enrollment '09-10	3,783
Grade 12 enrollment, '09-10	233
Graduation rate	91.5%
Dropout rate	2.7%
Per-pupil expenditure	$10,340
Avg teacher salary	$61,603
Student/teacher ratio '08-09	13.5 to 1
Highly-qualified teachers, '08-09	99.9%
Teachers licensed in assigned subject	98.9%
Students per computer	3.6

Massachusetts Competency Assessment System (MCAS), 2009 results

	English		Math	
	% Prof	CPI	% Prof	CPI
Gr 4	69%	87.6	57%	83.6
Gr 6	74%	90.3	65%	83.3
Gr 8	88%	95.7	58%	81.6
Gr 10	90%	96.6	86%	94.5

Other School Districts (see Appendix D for data)
Shawsheen Valley Vocational Tech

See Introduction for an explanation of all data sources.

©2010 Information Publications, Inc. All rights reserved. Photocopying prohibited. For additional copies, contact the publisher at www.informationpublications.com or (877)544-INFO (4636)

Demographics & Socio-Economic Characteristics

Population

1990	8,805
2000	9,611
Male	4,766
Female	4,845
2008	10,164
2010 (projected)††	10,768
2020 (projected)††	12,404

Race & Hispanic Origin, 2000

Race	
White	9,223
Black/African American	77
American Indian/Alaska Native	29
Asian	60
Hawaiian Native/Pacific Islander	7
Other Race	91
Two or more races	124
Hispanic origin	195

Age & Nativity, 2000

Under 5 years	690
18 years and over	6,704
21 years and over	6,361
65 years and over	1,007
85 years and over	112
Median Age	35.0
Native-born	9,333
Foreign-born	279

Age, 2020 (projected)††

Under 5 years	872
5 to 19 years	2,374
20 to 39 years	3,487
40 to 64 years	3,927
65 years and over	1,744

Educational Attainment, 2000

Population 25 years and over	6,056
High School graduates or higher	82.1%
Bachelor's degree or higher	14.0%
Graduate degree	4.3%

Income & Poverty, 1999

Per capita income,	$18,798
Median household income	$43,750
Median family income	$50,086
Persons in poverty	953
H'holds receiving public assistance	122
H'holds receiving social security	938

Households, 2000

Total households	3,447
With persons under 18	1,459
With persons over 65	738
Family households	2,477
Single person households	767
Persons per household	2.8
Persons per family	3.2

Labor & Employment, 2000

Civilian labor force	4,791
Unemployment rate	5.6%
Civilian labor force, 2008†	4,905
Unemployment rate†	9.7%
Civilian labor force, 12/09†	4,848
Unemployment rate†	12.3%
Employed persons 16 years and over, by occupation:	
Managers & professionals	1,235
Service occupations	644
Sales & office occupations	952
Farming, fishing & forestry	20
Construction & maintenance	583
Production & transportation	1,089
Self-employed persons	262

Most demographic data is from the 2000 Decennial Census
† Massachusetts Department of Revenue
†† University of Massachusetts, MISER

General Information

Town of Winchendon
109 Front St
Winchendon, MA 01475
978-297-0085

Elevation	1,000 ft.
Land area (square miles)	43.3
Water area (square miles)	0.8
Population density, 2008 (est)	234.7
Year incorporated	1764
Website	townofwinchendon.com

Voters & Government Information

Government type	Open Town Meeting
Number of Selectmen	5
US Congressional District(s)	1

Registered Voters, October 2008

Total	6,787
Democrats	1,571
Republicans	955
Unaffiliated/other	4,182

Local Officials, 2010

Chair, Bd. of Sel.	Keith Barrows
Manager	James Kreidler Jr
Town Clerk	Lois Abare
Finance Director	Joan Bousquet
Tax Collector	NA
Tax Assessor	Linda Bevan
Attorney	NA
Public Works	Michael Murphy
Building	Paul Blanchard
Planning Agent	Ellen Decoteau
Police Chief	Scott Livingston
Emerg/Fire Chief	Allen Lafrennie III

Housing & Construction

New Privately Owned Housing Units Authorized by Building Permit

	Single Family	Total Bldgs	Total Units
2006	43	45	47
2007	35	37	39
2008	26	27	28

Parcel Count by Property Class, 2010

Total	4,757
Single family	2,776
Multiple units	262
Apartments	50
Condos	62
Vacant land	1,079
Open space	0
Commercial	169
Industrial	70
Misc. residential	24
Other use	265

Public Library

Beals Memorial Library
50 Pleasant St.
Winchendon, MA 01475
(978)297-0300

Director	Julia White Cardinal

Library Statistics, FY 2008

Population served, 2007	10,130
Registered users	2,467
Circulation	34,326
Reference transactons	3,627
Total program attendance	0
per capita:	
Holdings	4.64
Operating income	$18.20
Internet Access	
Internet computers available	5
Weekly users	75

Municipal Finance

Debt at year end 2008	$24,326,806
Moody's rating, July 2009	Baa1

Revenues, 2008

Total	$28,174,122
From all taxes	9,887,051
Federal aid	291,641
State aid	13,800,575
From other governments	42,583
Charges for services	578,399
Licenses, permits & fees	167,817
Fines & forfeits	4,275
Interfund transfers	536,973
Misc/other/special assessments	1,432,404

Expenditures, 2008

Total	$23,970,389
General government	1,276,912
Public safety	2,025,549
Other/fixed costs	1,020,432
Human services	375,001
Culture & recreation	153,424
Debt Service	2,484,671
Education	14,158,788
Public works	1,364,063
Intergovernmental	914,821

Taxation, 2010

Property type	Valuation	Rate
Total	$727,384,406	-
Residential	665,384,954	13.20
Open space	0	0.00
Commercial	33,410,962	13.20
Industrial	11,597,100	13.20
Personal	16,991,390	13.20

Average Single Family Tax Bill, 2010

Avg. assessed home value	$194,280
Avg. single fam. tax bill	$2,564
Hi-Lo ranking	277/301

Police & Crime, 2008

Number of police officers	12
Violent crimes	50
Property crimes	242

Local School District

(school data 2007-08, except as noted)

Winchendon
175 Grove Street
Winchendon, MA 01475
978-297-0031

Superintendent	Brooke Clenchy
Grade plan	PK-12
Total enrollment '09-10	1,626
Grade 12 enrollment, '09-10	105
Graduation rate	77.9%
Dropout rate	14.7%
Per-pupil expenditure	$11,062
Avg teacher salary	$57,689
Student/teacher ratio '08-09	15.3 to 1
Highly-qualified teachers, '08-09	90.7%
Teachers licensed in assigned subject	98.7%
Students per computer	3.7

Massachusetts Competency Assessment System (MCAS), 2009 results

	English		Math	
	% Prof	CPI	% Prof	CPI
Gr 4	21%	61.3	30%	65.7
Gr 6	44%	74.2	36%	63.4
Gr 8	65%	84.4	41%	68.8
Gr 10	72%	87.6	57%	81.1

Other School Districts (see Appendix D for data)
Montachusett Vocational Tech

©2010 Information Publications, Inc. All rights reserved. Photocopying prohibited. For additional copies, contact the publisher at www.informationpublications.com or (877)544-INFO (4636)

See Introduction for an explanation of all data sources.

Demographics & Socio-Economic Characteristics*

Population

1990	20,267
2000	20,810
Male	9,792
Female	11,018
2008	21,090
2010 (projected)††	19,612
2020 (projected)††	17,513

Race & Hispanic Origin, 2000

Race	
White	19,375
Black/African American	142
American Indian/Alaska Native	29
Asian	961
Hawaiian Native/Pacific Islander	3
Other Race	57
Two or more races	243
Hispanic origin	211

Age & Nativity, 2000

Under 5 years	1,529
18 years and over	15,468
21 years and over	15,118
65 years and over	3,556
85 years and over	654
Median Age	41.1
Native-born	18,569
Foreign-born	2,241

Age, 2020 (projected)††

Under 5 years	828
5 to 19 years	3,021
20 to 39 years	3,622
40 to 64 years	5,939
65 years and over	4,103

Educational Attainment, 2000

Population 25 years and over	14,800
High School graduates or higher	94.5%
Bachelor's degree or higher	64.9%
Graduate degree	32.7%

Income & Poverty, 1999

Per capita income,	$50,414
Median household income	$94,049
Median family income	$110,226
Persons in poverty	531
H'holds receiving public assistance	67
H'holds receiving social security	2,179

Households, 2000

Total households	7,715
With persons under 18	2,845
With persons over 65	2,278
Family households	5,721
Single person households	1,693
Persons per household	2.7
Persons per family	3.1

Labor & Employment, 2000

Civilian labor force	10,463
Unemployment rate	2.4%
Civilian labor force, 2008†	10,789
Unemployment rate†	4.2%
Civilian labor force, 12/09†	10,678
Unemployment rate†	5.7%
Employed persons 16 years and over, by occupation:	
Managers & professionals	6,711
Service occupations	581
Sales & office occupations	2,167
Farming, fishing & forestry	6
Construction & maintenance	364
Production & transportation	387
Self-employed persons	990

Most demographic data is from the 2000 Decennial Census
* see Appendix E for American Community Survey data
† Massachusetts Department of Revenue
†† University of Massachusetts, MISER

General Information

Town of Winchester
71 Mt Vernon St
Winchester, MA 01890
781-721-7133

Elevation	50 ft.
Land area (square miles)	6.0
Water area (square miles)	0.3
Population density, 2008 (est)	3,515.0
Year incorporated	1850
Website	www.winchester.us

Voters & Government Information

Government type	Rep. Town Meeting
Number of Selectmen	5
US Congressional District(s)	7

Registered Voters, October 2008

Total	15,201
Democrats	4,692
Republicans	2,388
Unaffiliated/other	8,060

Local Officials, 2010

Chair, Bd. of Sel.	Brian O'Connor
Manager	Melvin Kleckner
Town Clerk	Mary Ellen Lannon
Finance Director	Sheila Tracy
Tax Collector	Sheila Tracy
Tax Assessor	Daniel McGurl
Attorney	Wade Welch
Public Works	Edward Grant
Building	Ronald Haverty
Comm Dev/Planning	Betsy Ware
Police Chief	Kenneth Albertelli
Emerg/Fire Chief	John Nash

Housing & Construction

New Privately Owned Housing Units Authorized by Building Permit

	Single Family	Total Bldgs	Total Units
2006	19	21	32
2007	16	19	31
2008	13	15	24

Parcel Count by Property Class, 2010

Total	7,730
Single family	5,594
Multiple units	406
Apartments	12
Condos	1,220
Vacant land	243
Open space	0
Commercial	205
Industrial	17
Misc. residential	4
Other use	29

Public Library

Winchester Public Library
80 Washington St.
Winchester, MA 01890
(781)721-7171

Director . . . Ann C. Wirtanen

Library Statistics, FY 2008

Population served, 2007	21,137
Registered users	16,093
Circulation	573,709
Reference transactons	53,250
Total program attendance	297,655
per capita:	
Holdings	5.62
Operating income	$74.60
Internet Access	
Internet computers available	14
Weekly users	725

Municipal Finance

Debt at year end 2008	$50,450,751
Moody's rating, July 2009	Aaa

Revenues, 2008

Total	$76,985,248
From all taxes	60,211,687
Federal aid	0
State aid	7,315,376
From other governments	0
Charges for services	2,431,603
Licenses, permits & fees	1,086,754
Fines & forfeits	0
Interfund transfers	2,916,028
Misc/other/special assessments	1,511,900

Expenditures, 2008

Total	$69,561,552
General government	7,836,693
Public safety	7,194,891
Other/fixed costs	11,041,488
Human services	171,446
Culture & recreation	1,502,372
Debt Service	5,952,687
Education	29,715,307
Public works	5,686,718
Intergovernmental	459,950

Taxation, 2010

Property type	Valuation	Rate
Total	$5,382,360,300	-
Residential	5,081,279,530	11.51
Open space	0	0.00
Commercial	220,862,340	10.82
Industrial	25,976,500	10.82
Personal	54,241,930	10.82

Average Single Family Tax Bill, 2010

Avg. assessed home value	$762,067
Avg. single fam. tax bill	$8,771
Hi-Lo ranking	14/301

Police & Crime, 2008

Number of police officers	38
Violent crimes	5
Property crimes	295

Local School District

(school data 2007-08, except as noted)

Winchester
154 Horn Pond Brk Rd
Winchester, MA 01890
781-721-7004

Superintendent	William McAlduff
Grade plan	PK-12
Total enrollment '09-10	4,198
Grade 12 enrollment, '09-10	266
Graduation rate	93.4%
Dropout rate	4.2%
Per-pupil expenditure	$10,865
Avg teacher salary	$71,681
Student/teacher ratio '08-09	14.7 to 1
Highly-qualified teachers, '08-09	98.2%
Teachers licensed in assigned subject	97.9%
Students per computer	5.3

Massachusetts Competency Assessment System (MCAS), 2009 results

	English		Math	
	% Prof	CPI	% Prof	CPI
Gr 4	87%	95.7	78%	93.5
Gr 6	89%	96.4	87%	94.5
Gr 8	91%	96.9	76%	90.2
Gr 10	95%	98	92%	97.2

Other School Districts (see Appendix D for data)
Northeast Metro Vocational Tech

©2010 Information Publications, Inc. All rights reserved. Photocopying prohibited. For additional copies, contact the publisher at www.informationpublications.com or (877)544-INFO (4636)

See Introduction for an explanation of all data sources.

Demographics & Socio-Economic Characteristics

Population

1990	770
2000	875
Male	441
Female	434
2008	846
2010 (projected)††	956
2020 (projected)††	1,055

Race & Hispanic Origin, 2000

Race	
White	865
Black/African American	0
American Indian/Alaska Native	0
Asian	0
Hawaiian Native/Pacific Islander	0
Other Race	3
Two or more races	7
Hispanic origin	1

Age & Nativity, 2000

Under 5 years	56
18 years and over	642
21 years and over	622
65 years and over	90
85 years and over	8
Median Age	40.9
Native-born	873
Foreign-born	22

Age, 2020 (projected)††

Under 5 years	70
5 to 19 years	196
20 to 39 years	202
40 to 64 years	347
65 years and over	240

Educational Attainment, 2000

Population 25 years and over	608
High School graduates or higher	91.0%
Bachelor's degree or higher	30.9%
Graduate degree	9.2%

Income & Poverty, 1999

Per capita income,	$21,794
Median household income	$51,389
Median family income	$57,500
Persons in poverty	45
H'holds receiving public assistance	4
H'holds receiving social security	80

Households, 2000

Total households	328
With persons under 18	125
With persons over 65	67
Family households	249
Single person households	63
Persons per household	2.7
Persons per family	3.1

Labor & Employment, 2000

Civilian labor force	462
Unemployment rate	0.6%
Civilian labor force, 2008†	499
Unemployment rate†	5.4%
Civilian labor force, 12/09†	509
Unemployment rate†	8.8%
Employed persons 16 years and over, by occupation:	
Managers & professionals	179
Service occupations	68
Sales & office occupations	112
Farming, fishing & forestry	2
Construction & maintenance	39
Production & transportation	59
Self-employed persons	54

Most demographic data is from the 2000 Decennial Census
† Massachusetts Department of Revenue
†† University of Massachusetts, MISER

General Information

Town of Windsor
1890 Route 9
Windsor, MA 01270
413-684-3811

Elevation	2,291 ft.
Land area (square miles)	35.0
Water area (square miles)	0.1
Population density, 2008 (est)	24.2
Year incorporated	1771
Email	windsor_townclerk@yahoo.com

Voters & Government Information

Government type	Open Town Meeting
Number of Selectmen	3
US Congressional District(s)	1

Registered Voters, October 2008

Total	661
Democrats	157
Republicans	66
Unaffiliated/other	433

Local Officials, 2010

Chair, Bd. of Sel.	Stephen L. Bird Sr
Manager/Admin	NA
Clerk	Evelyn Bird
Treasurer	Rebecca Herzog
Tax Collector	Rebecca Herzog
Tax Assessor	Robin Wadsworth
Attorney	NA
Public Works	NA
Building	NA
Comm Dev/Planning	NA
Police Chief	Peter Pyskaty
Fire Chief	Michael Tirrell

Housing & Construction

New Privately Owned Housing Units Authorized by Building Permit

	Single Family	Total Bldgs	Total Units
2006	4	4	4
2007	3	3	3
2008	3	3	3

Parcel Count by Property Class, 2010

Total	806
Single family	443
Multiple units	4
Apartments	0
Condos	0
Vacant land	264
Open space	0
Commercial	2
Industrial	17
Misc. residential	9
Other use	67

Public Library

Windsor Free Public Library
PO Box 118
Windsor, MA 01270
(413)684-3811

Director	Margaret Birchfield

Library Statistics, FY 2008

Population served, 2007	856
Registered users	410
Circulation	4,169
Reference transactons	83
Total program attendance	1,700
per capita:	
Holdings	5.52
Operating income	$5.70
Internet Access	
Internet computers available	1
Weekly users	5

Municipal Finance

Debt at year end 2008	$51,999
Moody's rating, July 2009	NA

Revenues, 2008

Total	$1,834,577
From all taxes	1,358,083
Federal aid	7,961
State aid	256,540
From other governments	0
Charges for services	42,404
Licenses, permits & fees	9,078
Fines & forfeits	6,270
Interfund transfers	30,555
Misc/other/special assessments	61,843

Expenditures, 2008

Total	$1,617,722
General government	101,985
Public safety	47,387
Other/fixed costs	97,996
Human services	3,750
Culture & recreation	3,812
Debt Service	27,794
Education	1,001,063
Public works	316,550
Intergovernmental	0

Taxation, 2010

Property type	Valuation	Rate
Total	$115,325,230	-
Residential	109,898,778	11.12
Open space	0	0.00
Commercial	1,353,718	11.12
Industrial	995,500	11.12
Personal	3,077,234	11.12

Average Single Family Tax Bill, 2010

Avg. assessed home value	$203,453
Avg. single fam. tax bill	$2,262
Hi-Lo ranking	287/301

Police & Crime, 2008

Number of police officers	NA
Violent crimes	NA
Property crimes	NA

Local School District

(school data 2007-08, except as noted)

Windsor (non-op)
PO Box 299
Dalton, MA 01227
413-684-0320

Superintendent	James Stankiewicz

Non-operating district.
Resident students are sent to the Other School Districts listed below.

Grade plan	NA
Total enrollment '09-10	NA
Grade 12 enrollment, '09-10	NA
Graduation rate	NA
Dropout rate	NA
Per-pupil expenditure	NA
Avg teacher salary	NA
Student/teacher ratio '08-09	NA
Highly-qualified teachers, '08-09	NA
Teachers licensed in assigned subject	NA
Students per computer	NA

Other School Districts (see Appendix D for data)
Central Berkshire Regional

©2010 Information Publications, Inc. All rights reserved. Photocopying prohibited. For additional copies, contact the publisher at www.informationpublications.com or (877)544-INFO (4636)

See Introduction for an explanation of all data sources.

©2010 Information Publications, Inc. All rights reserved. Photocopying prohibited. For additional copies, contact the publisher at www.informationpublications.com or (877)544-INFO (4636)

Demographics & Socio-Economic Characteristics*

Population

1990	18,127
2000	18,303
Male	8,608
Female	9,695
2008	21,880
2010 (projected)††	17,834
2020 (projected)††	17,431

Race & Hispanic Origin, 2000

Race	
White	17,286
Black/African American	308
American Indian/Alaska Native	30
Asian	210
Hawaiian Native/Pacific Islander	8
Other Race	249
Two or more races	212
Hispanic origin	493

Age & Nativity, 2000

Under 5 years	906
18 years and over	14,890
21 years and over	14,374
65 years and over	3,024
85 years and over	441
Median Age	39.9
Native-born	16,718
Foreign-born	1,585

Age, 2020 (projected)††

Under 5 years	729
5 to 19 years	2,354
20 to 39 years	4,618
40 to 64 years	6,043
65 years and over	3,687

Educational Attainment, 2000

Population 25 years and over	13,610
High School graduates or higher	90.0%
Bachelor's degree or higher	29.0%
Graduate degree	8.8%

Income & Poverty, 1999

Per capita income,	$27,374
Median household income	$53,122
Median family income	$65,696
Persons in poverty	996
H'holds receiving public assistance	183
H'holds receiving social security	2,227

Households, 2000

Total households	7,843
With persons under 18	1,988
With persons over 65	2,145
Family households	4,584
Single person households	2,550
Persons per household	2.3
Persons per family	3.0

Labor & Employment, 2000

Civilian labor force	9,983
Unemployment rate	4.1%
Civilian labor force, 2008†	9,556
Unemployment rate†	5.8%
Civilian labor force, 12/09†	11,089
Unemployment rate†	7.8%
Employed persons 16 years and over, by occupation:	
Managers & professionals	3,694
Service occupations	1,348
Sales & office occupations	2,911
Farming, fishing & forestry	16
Construction & maintenance	693
Production & transportation	913
Self-employed persons	456

Most demographic data is from the 2000 Decennial Census
* see Appendix E for American Community Survey data
† Massachusetts Department of Revenue
†† University of Massachusetts, MISER

General Information

Town of Winthrop
1 Metcalf Sq
Winthrop, MA 02152
617-846-1077

Elevation	10 ft.
Land area (square miles)	2.0
Water area (square miles)	6.3
Population density, 2008 (est)	10,940.0
Year incorporated	1852
Website	www.town.winthrop.ma.us

Voters & Government Information

Government type	Town Manager
Number of Councilors	8
US Congressional District(s)	7

Registered Voters, October 2008

Total	12,020
Democrats	5,167
Republicans	1,086
Unaffiliated/other	5,686

Local Officials, 2010

Council President	Jeffrey Rosario Turco
Manager/Exec.	James McKenna
Town Clerk	Carla Vitale
Finance Director	Michael Bertino
Tax Collector	Monica Ford
Tax Assessor	Allen E. Maruzzi
Attorney	NA
Public Works	David Hickey
Building	Jim Soper
Comm Dev/Planning	NA
Police Chief	Terrance Delehanty
Emerg/Fire Chief	Paul Flanagan

Housing & Construction

New Privately Owned Housing Units Authorized by Building Permit

	Single Family	Total Bldgs	Total Units
2006	2	4	48
2007	0	0	0
2008	1	2	6

Parcel Count by Property Class, 2010

Total	5,442
Single family	2,269
Multiple units	1,473
Apartments	96
Condos	1,145
Vacant land	159
Open space	2
Commercial	193
Industrial	16
Misc. residential	36
Other use	53

Public Library

Winthrop Public Library
2 Metcalf Square
Winthrop, MA 02152
(617)846-1703

Director	Alan Thibeault

Library Statistics, FY 2008

Population served, 2007	20,154
Registered users	10,609
Circulation	88,076
Reference transactons	0
Total program attendance	0
per capita:	
Holdings	4.70
Operating income	$27.28
Internet Access	
Internet computers available	11
Weekly users	280

Municipal Finance

Debt at year end 2008	$16,187,000
Moody's rating, July 2009	A2

Revenues, 2008

Total	$36,537,927
From all taxes	20,285,425
Federal aid	0
State aid	10,612,602
From other governments	0
Charges for services	1,352,581
Licenses, permits & fees	148,577
Fines & forfeits	0
Interfund transfers	2,690,744
Misc/other/special assessments	723,999

Expenditures, 2008

Total	$38,151,388
General government	1,683,624
Public safety	5,105,608
Other/fixed costs	6,913,244
Human services	463,957
Culture & recreation	620,245
Debt Service	1,769,356
Education	17,292,641
Public works	2,854,229
Intergovernmental	1,391,348

Taxation, 2010

Property type	Valuation	Rate
Total	$1,815,523,870	-
Residential	1,696,718,745	12.70
Open space	67,200	12.70
Commercial	93,371,755	12.70
Industrial	3,643,600	12.70
Personal	21,722,570	12.70

Average Single Family Tax Bill, 2010

Avg. assessed home value	$324,714
Avg. single fam. tax bill	$4,124
Hi-Lo ranking	125/301

Police & Crime, 2008

Number of police officers	33
Violent crimes	70
Property crimes	279

Local School District

(school data 2007-08, except as noted)

Winthrop
45 Pauline Street
Winthrop, MA 02152
617-846-5500

Superintendent	Steven Jenkins
Grade plan	PK-12
Total enrollment '09-10	1,970
Grade 12 enrollment, '09-10	124
Graduation rate	72.5%
Dropout rate	13.0%
Per-pupil expenditure	$11,349
Avg teacher salary	$68,447
Student/teacher ratio '08-09	14.6 to 1
Highly-qualified teachers, '08-09	94.2%
Teachers licensed in assigned subject	97.8%
Students per computer	NA

Massachusetts Competency Assessment System (MCAS), 2009 results

	English		Math	
	% Prof	CPI	% Prof	CPI
Gr 4	51%	78	34%	70.7
Gr 6	70%	89.8	46%	73.2
Gr 8	75%	91	43%	68.4
Gr 10	86%	95.8	80%	91.5

Other School Districts (see Appendix D for data)
Northeast Metro Vocational Tech

See Introduction for an explanation of all data sources.

Demographics & Socio-Economic Characteristics*

Population

1990	35,943
2000	37,258
Male	18,212
Female	19,046
2008	36,871
2010 (projected)††	36,238
2020 (projected)††	35,070

Race & Hispanic Origin, 2000

Race	
White	33,744
Black/African American	697
American Indian/Alaska Native	36
Asian	1,806
Hawaiian Native/Pacific Islander	19
Other Race	535
Two or more races	421
Hispanic origin	1,152

Age & Nativity, 2000

Under 5 years	2,148
18 years and over	29,396
21 years and over	28,419
65 years and over	5,730
85 years and over	608
Median Age	37.7
Native-born	33,669
Foreign-born	3,589

Age, 2020 (projected)††

Under 5 years	1,657
5 to 19 years	5,076
20 to 39 years	9,106
40 to 64 years	12,585
65 years and over	6,646

Educational Attainment, 2000

Population 25 years and over	26,829
High School graduates or higher	88.1%
Bachelor's degree or higher	29.5%
Graduate degree	10.5%

Income & Poverty, 1999

Per capita income,	$26,207
Median household income	$54,897
Median family income	$66,364
Persons in poverty	2,269
H'holds receiving public assistance	263
H'holds receiving social security	4,301

Households, 2000

Total households	14,997
With persons under 18	4,346
With persons over 65	4,110
Family households	9,652
Single person households	4,304
Persons per household	2.5
Persons per family	3.1

Labor & Employment, 2000

Civilian labor force	20,913
Unemployment rate	3.0%
Civilian labor force, 2008†	21,367
Unemployment rate†	5.8%
Civilian labor force, 12/09†	21,471
Unemployment rate†	8.9%
Employed persons 16 years and over, by occupation:	
Managers & professionals	7,793
Service occupations	2,615
Sales & office occupations	5,938
Farming, fishing & forestry	26
Construction & maintenance	1,694
Production & transportation	2,221
Self-employed persons	1,030

Most demographic data is from the 2000 Decennial Census
* see Appendix E for American Community Survey data
† Massachusetts Department of Revenue
†† University of Massachusetts, MISER

General Information

City of Woburn
10 Common St
Woburn, MA 01801
781-897-5800

Elevation	107 ft.
Land area (square miles)	12.7
Water area (square miles)	0.2
Population density, 2008 (est)	2,903.2
Year incorporated	1642
Website	www.cityofwoburn.com

Voters & Government Information

Government type	Mayor-Council
Number of Aldermen	9
US Congressional District(s)	7

Registered Voters, October 2008

Total	24,963
Democrats	9,686
Republicans	2,668
Unaffiliated/other	12,453

Local Officials, 2010

Mayor	Scott D. Galvin
Manager/Admin	NA
Clerk	William Campbell
Treasurer	Donald Jensen
Tax Collector	Donald Jensen
Tax Assessor	Robert Maguire Jr
City Solicitor	John D. McElhiney
Public Works	Vincent Ferlisi
Building Commissioner	Steven Paris
Planning Director	Edmund Tarallo
Police Chief	Philip Mahoney
Emerg/Fire Chief	Paul Tortolano

Housing & Construction

New Privately Owned Housing Units Authorized by Building Permit

	Single Family	Total Bldgs	Total Units
2006	20	24	28
2007	22	23	24
2008	6	7	10

Parcel Count by Property Class, 2010

Total	12,422
Single family	7,924
Multiple units	1,239
Apartments	121
Condos	1,542
Vacant land	516
Open space	0
Commercial	437
Industrial	447
Misc. residential	55
Other use	141

Public Library

Woburn Public Library
45 Pleasant St., PO Box 298
Woburn, MA 01801
(781)933-0148

Director	Kathleen O'Doherty

Library Statistics, FY 2008

Population served, 2007	37,042
Registered users	13,446
Circulation	220,966
Reference transactons	7,340
Total program attendance	281,366
per capita:	
Holdings	2.45
Operating income	$30.99
Internet Access	
Internet computers available	12
Weekly users	1,450

Municipal Finance

Debt at year end 2008	$57,252,595
Moody's rating, July 2009	Aa3

Revenues, 2008

Total	$105,003,535
From all taxes	81,539,853
Federal aid	586,868
State aid	13,946,934
From other governments	244,072
Charges for services	579,320
Licenses, permits & fees	928,077
Fines & forfeits	59,805
Interfund transfers	5,103,764
Misc/other/special assessments	1,007,421

Expenditures, 2008

Total	$100,435,838
General government	3,207,340
Public safety	14,764,817
Other/fixed costs	18,840,379
Human services	758,259
Culture & recreation	1,673,996
Debt Service	5,139,311
Education	43,769,133
Public works	8,464,686
Intergovernmental	3,817,917

Taxation, 2010

Property type	Valuation	Rate
Total	$5,560,894,260	-
Residential	3,942,319,569	10.32
Open space	0	0.00
Commercial	721,086,531	26.10
Industrial	723,454,000	26.10
Personal	174,034,160	26.10

Average Single Family Tax Bill, 2010

Avg. assessed home value	$341,718
Avg. single fam. tax bill	$3,527
Hi-Lo ranking	170/301

Police & Crime, 2008

Number of police officers	NA
Violent crimes	74
Property crimes	888

Local School District

(school data 2007-08, except as noted)

Woburn
55 Locust Street
Woburn, MA 01801
781-937-8233

Superintendent	Mark Donovan
Grade plan	PK-12
Total enrollment '09-10	4,769
Grade 12 enrollment, '09-10	332
Graduation rate	84.7%
Dropout rate	8.7%
Per-pupil expenditure	$13,422
Avg teacher salary	$61,640
Student/teacher ratio '08-09	13.0 to 1
Highly-qualified teachers, '08-09	98.3%
Teachers licensed in assigned subject	98.6%
Students per computer	2.5

Massachusetts Competency Assessment System (MCAS), 2009 results

	English		Math	
	% Prof	CPI	% Prof	CPI
Gr 4	64%	87.6	53%	84.1
Gr 6	70%	88.4	53%	77.5
Gr 8	83%	94	43%	70.7
Gr 10	82%	93.3	73%	88.7

Other School Districts (see Appendix D for data)
Northeast Metro Vocational Tech

©2010 Information Publications, Inc. All rights reserved. Photocopying prohibited. For additional copies, contact the publisher at www.informationpublications.com or (877)544-INFO (4636)

See Introduction for an explanation of all data sources.

Demographics & Socio-Economic Characteristics*

Population

1990	169,759
2000	172,648
Male	82,914
Female	89,734
2008	175,011
2010 (projected)††	182,635
2020 (projected)††	194,869

Race & Hispanic Origin, 2000

Race	
White	133,124
Black/African American	11,892
American Indian/Alaska Native	769
Asian	8,402
Hawaiian Native/Pacific Islander	96
Other Race	12,504
Two or more races	5,861
Hispanic origin	26,155

Age & Nativity, 2000

Under 5 years	11,142
18 years and over	131,921
21 years and over	120,586
65 years and over	24,389
85 years and over	3,851
Median Age	33.4
Native-born	147,551
Foreign-born	25,097

Age, 2020 (projected)††

Under 5 years	12,589
5 to 19 years	39,321
20 to 39 years	58,280
40 to 64 years	57,337
65 years and over	27,342

Educational Attainment, 2000

Population 25 years and over	108,769
High School graduates or higher	76.7%
Bachelor's degree or higher	23.3%
Graduate degree	9.8%

Income & Poverty, 1999

Per capita income,	$18,614
Median household income	$35,623
Median family income	$42,988
Persons in poverty	29,115
H'holds receiving public assistance	4,049
H'holds receiving social security	18,294

Households, 2000

Total households	67,028
With persons under 18	21,199
With persons over 65	16,818
Family households	39,228
Single person households	22,128
Persons per household	2.4
Persons per family	3.1

Labor & Employment, 2000

Civilian labor force	82,666
Unemployment rate	6.3%
Civilian labor force, 2008†	82,029
Unemployment rate†	7.2%
Civilian labor force, 12/09†	83,438
Unemployment rate†	10.0%
Employed persons 16 years and over, by occupation:	
Managers & professionals	25,694
Service occupations	13,831
Sales & office occupations	20,378
Farming, fishing & forestry	50
Construction & maintenance	4,927
Production & transportation	12,595
Self-employed persons	3,150

Most demographic data is from the 2000 Decennial Census
* see Appendix D and E for American Community Survey data
† Massachusetts Department of Revenue
†† University of Massachusetts, MISER

©2010 Information Publications, Inc. All rights reserved. Photocopying prohibited. For additional copies, contact the publisher at www.informationpublications.com or (877)544-INFO (4636)

General Information

City of Worcester
455 Main St
Worcester, MA 01608
508-799-1000

Elevation	400 ft.
Land area (square miles)	37.6
Water area (square miles)	1.0
Population density, 2008 (est)	4,654.5
Year incorporated	1684
Website	www.ci.worcester.ma.us

Voters & Government Information

Government type	Council-Manager
Number of Councilpersons	10
US Congressional District(s)	3

Registered Voters, October 2008

Total	103,115
Democrats	46,395
Republicans	9,980
Unaffiliated/other	45,704

Local Officials, 2010

Mayor	Konstantina Lukes
Manager	Michael O'Brien
City Clerk	David Rushford
CFO	Thomas Zidelis
Treas/Collector	Michael Conrad (Actg)
Tax Assessor	Robert J. Allard Jr
Attorney	David M. Moore
Public Works	Robert Moylan Jr
Building	John R. Kelly (Actg)
Planning/Dev.	J. Fontane Jr/D. Hennessy
Police Chief	Gary Gemme
Fire Chief	Gerard A. Dio

Housing & Construction

New Privately Owned Housing Units Authorized by Building Permit

	Single Family	Total Bldgs	Total Units
2006	292	303	332
2007	214	218	239
2008	61	67	73

Parcel Count by Property Class, 2010

Total	45,941
Single family	24,709
Multiple units	8,481
Apartments	1,217
Condos	4,989
Vacant land	2,649
Open space	0
Commercial	2,332
Industrial	611
Misc. residential	282
Other use	671

Public Library

Worcester Public Library
3 Salem Square
Worcester, MA 01608
(508)799-1655

Head Librarian	Lucy Gangone

Library Statistics, FY 2008

Population served, 2007	173,966
Registered users	112,052
Circulation	661,402
Reference transactons	101,650
Total program attendance	824,449
per capita:	
Holdings	4.80
Operating income	$28.42
Internet Access	
Internet computers available	120
Weekly users	10,467

Municipal Finance

Debt at year end 2008	$609,513,123
Moody's rating, July 2009	A3

Revenues, 2008

Total	$496,386,368
From all taxes	207,071,873
Federal aid	7,734,836
State aid	254,937,606
From other governments	1,367,332
Charges for services	6,231,913
Licenses, permits & fees	4,725,903
Fines & forfeits	1,940,576
Interfund transfers	6,260,065
Misc/other/special assessments	3,058,132

Expenditures, 2008

Total	$413,576,868
General government	13,344,770
Public safety	78,545,710
Other/fixed costs	22,819,318
Human services	3,776,314
Culture & recreation	8,400,203
Debt Service	45,328,289
Education	196,975,672
Public works	20,120,850
Intergovernmental	23,913,921

Taxation, 2010

Property type	Valuation	Rate
Total	$10,911,942,365	-
Residential	8,585,028,213	15.15
Open space	0	0.00
Commercial	1,482,946,949	33.28
Industrial	433,955,303	33.28
Personal	410,011,900	33.28

Average Single Family Tax Bill, 2010

Avg. assessed home value	$206,517
Avg. single fam. tax bill	$3,129
Hi-Lo ranking	221/301

Police & Crime, 2008

Number of police officers	449
Violent crimes	1,718
Property crimes	6,356

Local School District

(school data 2007-08, except as noted)

Worcester
20 Irving Street
Worcester, MA 01609
508-799-3115

Superintendent	Melinda Boone
Grade plan	PK-12
Total enrollment '09-10	23,988
Grade 12 enrollment, '09-10	1,527
Graduation rate	69.2%
Dropout rate	14.8%
Per-pupil expenditure	$12,838
Avg teacher salary	$70,106
Student/teacher ratio '08-09	14.1 to 1
Highly-qualified teachers, '08-09	98.6%
Teachers licensed in assigned subject	98.4%
Students per computer	2.9

Massachusetts Competency Assessment System (MCAS), 2009 results

	English		Math	
	% Prof	CPI	% Prof	CPI
Gr 4	31%	65.6	31%	66.6
Gr 6	48%	75.1	43%	69.1
Gr 8	60%	82.3	28%	56.3
Gr 10	67%	86.2	57%	78.8

Other School Districts (see Appendix D for data)
None

See Introduction for an explanation of all data sources.

Demographics & Socio-Economic Characteristics

Population

1990	1,156
2000	1,270
Male	629
Female	641
2008	1,272
2010 (projected)††	1,328
2020 (projected)††	1,440

Race & Hispanic Origin, 2000

Race	
White	1,248
Black/African American	4
American Indian/Alaska Native	1
Asian	3
Hawaiian Native/Pacific Islander	0
Other Race	0
Two or more races	14
Hispanic origin	13

Age & Nativity, 2000

Under 5 years	59
18 years and over	959
21 years and over	913
65 years and over	140
85 years and over	14
Median Age	41.7
Native-born	1,200
Foreign-born	19

Age, 2020 (projected)††

Under 5 years	72
5 to 19 years	215
20 to 39 years	302
40 to 64 years	479
65 years and over	372

Educational Attainment, 2000

Population 25 years and over	834
High School graduates or higher	93.5%
Bachelor's degree or higher	36.3%
Graduate degree	16.2%

Income & Poverty, 1999

Per capita income,	$24,190
Median household income	$53,047
Median family income	$60,132
Persons in poverty	42
H'holds receiving public assistance	5
H'holds receiving social security	131

Households, 2000

Total households	503
With persons under 18	168
With persons over 65	106
Family households	363
Single person households	107
Persons per household	2.5
Persons per family	3.0

Labor & Employment, 2000

Civilian labor force	667
Unemployment rate	3.0%
Civilian labor force, 2008†	689
Unemployment rate†	6.5%
Civilian labor force, 12/09†	685
Unemployment rate†	8.2%
Employed persons 16 years and over, by occupation:	
Managers & professionals	273
Service occupations	84
Sales & office occupations	128
Farming, fishing & forestry	7
Construction & maintenance	55
Production & transportation	100
Self-employed persons	109

Most demographic data is from the 2000 Decennial Census
† Massachusetts Department of Revenue
†† University of Massachusetts, MISER

General Information

Town of Worthington
160 Huntington Road
PO Box 247
Worthington, MA 01098
413-238-5577

Elevation	1,433 ft.
Land area (square miles)	32.1
Water area (square miles)	0.0
Population density, 2008 (est)	39.6
Year incorporated	1769
Website	www.worthington-ma.us

Voters & Government Information

Government type	Open Town Meeting
Number of Selectmen	3
US Congressional District(s)	1

Registered Voters, October 2008

Total	926
Democrats	253
Republicans	112
Unaffiliated/other	557

Local Officials, 2010

Chair, Bd. of Sel.	Evan Johnson
Manager/Admin	Sylvia Howes
Clerk	Katrin Kaminsky
Treasurer	Barbara Miller
Tax Collector	Kirsten Henshaw
Tax Assessor	Jean Boudreau
Attorney	John FitzGibbon
Public Works	NA
Building	Joseph Fydenkevez Jr
Planning	David Veleta (Chr)
Police Chief	Jeffrey Johnson
Emerg/Fire Chief	Richard Granger

Housing & Construction

New Privately Owned Housing Units Authorized by Building Permit

	Single Family	Total Bldgs	Total Units
2006	4	4	4
2007	3	3	3
2008	3	3	3

Parcel Count by Property Class, 2010

Total	856
Single family	474
Multiple units	9
Apartments	0
Condos	0
Vacant land	151
Open space	0
Commercial	3
Industrial	4
Misc. residential	28
Other use	187

Public Library

Worthington Library
PO Box 598
Worthington, MA 01098
(413)238-5565

Library Director........... Leona Arthen

Library Statistics, FY 2008

Population served, 2007	1,272
Registered users	550
Circulation	7,179
Reference transactons	0
Total program attendance	5,478
per capita:	
Holdings	9.57
Operating income	$24.90
Internet Access	
Internet computers available	3
Weekly users	12

Municipal Finance

Debt at year end 2008	$148,666
Moody's rating, July 2009	NA

Revenues, 2008

Total	$2,729,931
From all taxes	2,203,451
Federal aid	12,910
State aid	274,938
From other governments	2,508
Charges for services	54,997
Licenses, permits & fees	23,285
Fines & forfeits	0
Interfund transfers	117,134
Misc/other/special assessments	20,354

Expenditures, 2008

Total	$2,515,814
General government	158,915
Public safety	97,524
Other/fixed costs	127,057
Human services	3,750
Culture & recreation	12,328
Debt Service	63,737
Education	1,521,783
Public works	528,557
Intergovernmental	2,163

Taxation, 2010

Property type	Valuation	Rate
Total	$175,492,339	-
Residential	164,757,890	12.24
Open space	0	0.00
Commercial	5,936,439	12.24
Industrial	520,000	12.24
Personal	4,278,010	12.24

Average Single Family Tax Bill, 2010

Avg. assessed home value	$255,408
Avg. single fam. tax bill	$3,126
Hi-Lo ranking	223/301

Police & Crime, 2008

Number of police officers	NA
Violent crimes	NA
Property crimes	NA

Local School District

(school data 2007-08, except as noted)

Worthington (non-op)
12 Littleville Road
Huntington, MA 01050
413-685-1011

Superintendent............. David Hopson

Non-operating district.
Resident students are sent to the Other School Districts listed below.

Grade plan	NA
Total enrollment '09-10	NA
Grade 12 enrollment, '09-10	NA
Graduation rate	NA
Dropout rate	NA
Per-pupil expenditure	NA
Avg teacher salary	NA
Student/teacher ratio '08-09	NA
Highly-qualified teachers, '08-09	NA
Teachers licensed in assigned subject	NA
Students per computer	NA

Other School Districts (see Appendix D for data)
Gateway Regional

©2010 Information Publications, Inc. All rights reserved. Photocopying prohibited. For additional copies, contact the publisher at www.informationpublications.com or (877)544-INFO (4636)

See Introduction for an explanation of all data sources.

Demographics & Socio-Economic Characteristics

Population

1990	9,006
2000	10,554
Male	5,160
Female	5,394
2008	11,133
2010 (projected)††	11,984
2020 (projected)††	13,838

Race & Hispanic Origin, 2000

Race	
White	10,305
Black/African American	64
American Indian/Alaska Native	13
Asian	84
Hawaiian Native/Pacific Islander	1
Other Race	34
Two or more races	53
Hispanic origin	83

Age & Nativity, 2000

Under 5 years	791
18 years and over	7,619
21 years and over	7,363
65 years and over	1,228
85 years and over	257
Median Age	38.6
Native-born	10,161
Foreign-born	393

Age, 2020 (projected)††

Under 5 years	959
5 to 19 years	2,668
20 to 39 years	3,206
40 to 64 years	4,400
65 years and over	2,605

Educational Attainment, 2000

Population 25 years and over	7,133
High School graduates or higher	87.9%
Bachelor's degree or higher	39.1%
Graduate degree	11.7%

Income & Poverty, 1999

Per capita income,	$30,792
Median household income	$78,043
Median family income	$89,058
Persons in poverty	389
H'holds receiving public assistance	58
H'holds receiving social security	655

Households, 2000

Total households	3,402
With persons under 18	1,522
With persons over 65	613
Family households	2,653
Single person households	579
Persons per household	2.9
Persons per family	3.3

Labor & Employment, 2000

Civilian labor force	5,400
Unemployment rate	2.5%
Civilian labor force, 2008†	5,883
Unemployment rate†	5.7%
Civilian labor force, 12/09†	5,829
Unemployment rate†	7.7%
Employed persons 16 years and over, by occupation:	
Managers & professionals	2,401
Service occupations	493
Sales & office occupations	1,313
Farming, fishing & forestry	0
Construction & maintenance	605
Production & transportation	453
Self-employed persons	334

Most demographic data is from the 2000 Decennial Census
† Massachusetts Department of Revenue
†† University of Massachusetts, MISER

General Information

Town of Wrentham
79 South St
Wrentham, MA 02093
508-384-5400

Elevation	253 ft.
Land area (square miles)	22.2
Water area (square miles)	0.7
Population density, 2008 (est)	501.5
Year incorporated	1673
Website	www.wrentham.ma.us

Voters & Government Information

Government type	Open Town Meeting
Number of Selectmen	5
US Congressional District(s)	3

Registered Voters, October 2008

Total	7,569
Democrats	1,664
Republicans	1,454
Unaffiliated/other	4,404

Local Officials, 2010

Chair, Bd. of Sel.	Edward J. Goddard
Manager/Admin	Jack McFeeley
Clerk	Carol A. Mollica
Finance Director	Karen Jelloe
Tax Collector	NA
Tax Assessor	Joan Dooley
Attorney	Anderson Kreiger
Public Works	Irving Priest
Building Inspector	Nicholas Tobichuk
Planner	Paige Duncan
Police Chief	James Anderson (Int)
Emerg/Fire Chief	Mark Pare (Int)

Housing & Construction

New Privately Owned Housing Units Authorized by Building Permit

	Single Family	Total Bldgs	Total Units
2006	21	22	23
2007	17	17	17
2008	17	17	17

Parcel Count by Property Class, 2010

Total	4,304
Single family	3,220
Multiple units	76
Apartments	16
Condos	220
Vacant land	462
Open space	0
Commercial	120
Industrial	66
Misc. residential	22
Other use	102

Public Library

Fiske Public Library
PO Box 340
Wrentham, MA 02093
(508)384-5440

Director . . . Mary Tobichuk

Library Statistics, FY 2008

Population served, 2007	11,116
Registered users	7,391
Circulation	124,308
Reference transactons	3,000
Total program attendance	0
per capita:	
Holdings	5.80
Operating income	$30.38
Internet Access	
Internet computers available	13
Weekly users	60

Municipal Finance

Debt at year end 2008	$23,982,367
Moody's rating, July 2009	A1

Revenues, 2008

Total	$30,631,636
From all taxes	23,090,939
Federal aid	0
State aid	5,481,587
From other governments	72,503
Charges for services	212,867
Licenses, permits & fees	295,114
Fines & forfeits	12,127
Interfund transfers	771,183
Misc/other/special assessments	347,658

Expenditures, 2008

Total	$27,413,136
General government	1,217,537
Public safety	3,534,534
Other/fixed costs	1,394,313
Human services	416,578
Culture & recreation	416,761
Debt Service	2,720,306
Education	15,002,341
Public works	2,293,780
Intergovernmental	416,986

Taxation, 2010

Property type	Valuation	Rate
Total	$1,764,415,790	-
Residential	1,440,753,977	13.12
Open space	0	0.00
Commercial	235,004,463	14.98
Industrial	41,350,900	14.98
Personal	47,306,450	14.93

Average Single Family Tax Bill, 2010

Avg. assessed home value	$397,285
Avg. single fam. tax bill	$5,212
Hi-Lo ranking	68/301

Police & Crime, 2008

Number of police officers	15
Violent crimes	2
Property crimes	43

Local School District

(school data 2007-08, except as noted)
Wrentham
120 Taunton Street
Wrentham, MA 02093
508-384-5439

Superintendent	Jeffrey Marsden
Grade plan	PK-6
Total enrollment '09-10	1,274
Grade 12 enrollment, '09-10	0
Graduation rate	81.2%
Dropout rate	9.9%
Per-pupil expenditure	$9,272
Avg teacher salary	$62,075
Student/teacher ratio '08-09	17.4 to 1
Highly-qualified teachers, '08-09	97.6%
Teachers licensed in assigned subject	98.7%
Students per computer	2

Massachusetts Competency Assessment System (MCAS), 2009 results

	English		Math	
	% Prof	CPI	% Prof	CPI
Gr 4	73%	91.4	62%	88
Gr 6	82%	94.1	73%	89.3
Gr 8	NA	NA	NA	NA
Gr 10	NA	NA	NA	NA

Other School Districts (see Appendix D for data)
King Philip Regional, Tri County Vocational Tech, Norfolk County Agricultural

©2010 Information Publications, Inc. All rights reserved. Photocopying prohibited. For additional copies, contact the publisher at www.informationpublications.com or (877)544-INFO (4636)

See Introduction for an explanation of all data sources.

Demographics & Socio-Economic Characteristics

Population

1990	21,174
2000	24,807
Male	11,438
Female	13,369
2008	23,778
2010 (projected)††	27,651
2020 (projected)††	31,315

Race & Hispanic Origin, 2000

Race	
White	23,623
Black/African American	333
American Indian/Alaska Native	81
Asian	132
Hawaiian Native/Pacific Islander	10
Other Race	233
Two or more races	395
Hispanic origin	358

Age & Nativity, 2000

Under 5 years	1,084
18 years and over	20,537
21 years and over	20,007
65 years and over	7,469
85 years and over	1,153
Median Age	48.7
Native-born	23,387
Foreign-born	1,420

Age, 2020 (projected)††

Under 5 years	1,126
5 to 19 years	3,518
20 to 39 years	5,246
40 to 64 years	10,159
65 years and over	11,266

Educational Attainment, 2000

Population 25 years and over	19,292
High School graduates or higher	90.8%
Bachelor's degree or higher	26.2%
Graduate degree	9.5%

Income & Poverty, 1999

Per capita income,	$22,731
Median household income	$39,808
Median family income	$48,148
Persons in poverty	1,842
H'holds receiving public assistance	311
H'holds receiving social security	5,544

Households, 2000

Total households	11,520
With persons under 18	2,385
With persons over 65	5,196
Family households	6,902
Single person households	3,916
Persons per household	2.1
Persons per family	2.7

Labor & Employment, 2000

Civilian labor force	11,004
Unemployment rate	5.9%
Civilian labor force, 2008†	11,804
Unemployment rate†	10.6%
Civilian labor force, 12/09†	11,585
Unemployment rate†	13.4%
Employed persons 16 years and over, by occupation:	
Managers & professionals	2,942
Service occupations	2,136
Sales & office occupations	3,342
Farming, fishing & forestry	35
Construction & maintenance	1,104
Production & transportation	800
Self-employed persons	892

Most demographic data is from the 2000 Decennial Census
† Massachusetts Department of Revenue
†† University of Massachusetts, MISER

General Information

Town of Yarmouth
1146 Rte 28
South Yarmouth, MA 02664
508-398-2231

Elevation	16 ft.
Land area (square miles)	24.2
Water area (square miles)	4.0
Population density, 2008 (est)	982.6
Year incorporated	1639
Website	www.yarmouth.ma.us

Voters & Government Information

Government type	Open Town Meeting
Number of Selectmen	5
US Congressional District(s)	10

Registered Voters, October 2008

Total	18,364
Democrats	4,889
Republicans	3,397
Unaffiliated/other	9,967

Local Officials, 2010

Chair, Bd. of Sel.	James Hoben
Town Administrator	Robert C. Lawton Jr
Clerk	Jane E. Hibbert
Finance Director	Sue Milne
Tax Collector	Shirley Sprague
Tax Assessor	Matthew Zurowick
Attorney	Bruce Gilmore
Public Works	George Allaire
Building	James Brandolini
Planning	Terry Sylva
Police Chief	Michael Almonte
Fire Chief	Michael Walker (Int)

Housing & Construction

New Privately Owned Housing Units Authorized by Building Permit

	Single Family	Total Bldgs	Total Units
2006	54	54	54
2007	27	27	27
2008	33	33	33

Parcel Count by Property Class, 2010

Total	17,338
Single family	12,719
Multiple units	570
Apartments	23
Condos	1,597
Vacant land	843
Open space	0
Commercial	1,258
Industrial	117
Misc. residential	132
Other use	79

Public Library

Yarmouth Town Libraries
312 Old Main Street
South Yarmouth, MA 02664
(508)760-4822

Director	Jacqueline Adams

Library Statistics, FY 2008

Population served, 2007	24,010
Registered users	15,156
Circulation	263,776
Reference transactons	5,200
Total program attendance	173,256
per capita:	
Holdings	4.11
Operating income	$33.48
Internet Access	
Internet computers available	23
Weekly users	700

Municipal Finance

Debt at year end 2008	$34,132,747
Moody's rating, July 2009	A2

Revenues, 2008

Total	$54,425,315
From all taxes	44,770,421
Federal aid	0
State aid	2,197,250
From other governments	101,507
Charges for services	2,517,423
Licenses, permits & fees	713,736
Fines & forfeits	3,880
Interfund transfers	2,875,006
Misc/other/special assessments	623,046

Expenditures, 2008

Total	$52,198,535
General government	3,756,508
Public safety	12,490,681
Other/fixed costs	4,977,231
Human services	718,940
Culture & recreation	1,767,421
Debt Service	3,195,219
Education	21,851,014
Public works	2,763,211
Intergovernmental	678,310

Taxation, 2010

Property type	Valuation	Rate
Total	$5,766,802,400	-
Residential	5,162,288,421	7.72
Open space	0	0.00
Commercial	467,611,379	7.72
Industrial	38,132,500	7.72
Personal	98,770,100	7.72

Average Single Family Tax Bill, 2010

Avg. assessed home value	$339,537
Avg. single fam. tax bill	$2,621
Hi-Lo ranking	274/301

Police & Crime, 2008

Number of police officers	54
Violent crimes	166
Property crimes	949

Local School District

(school data 2007-08, except as noted)

Yarmouth (non-op)
296 Station Avenue
South Yarmouth, MA 02664
508-398-7605

Superintendent	Carol Woodbury

Non-operating district.
Resident students are sent to the Other School Districts listed below.

Grade plan	NA
Total enrollment '09-10	NA
Grade 12 enrollment, '09-10	NA
Graduation rate	NA
Dropout rate	NA
Per-pupil expenditure	NA
Avg teacher salary	NA
Student/teacher ratio '08-09	NA
Highly-qualified teachers, '08-09	NA
Teachers licensed in assigned subject	NA
Students per computer	NA

Other School Districts (see Appendix D for data)
Dennis-Yarmouth Regional, Cape Cod Vocational Tech

©2010 Information Publications, Inc. All rights reserved. Photocopying prohibited. For additional copies, contact the publisher at www.informationpublications.com or (877)544-INFO (4636)

See Introduction for an explanation of all data sources.

Massachusetts Municipal Profiles

2010

Note to the reader:

These pages are extracted from the 2010 edition of the *Almanac of the 50 States*, also published by Information Publications. Please refer to that volume for similar information on each of the 50 States, the District of Columbia and the United States in general. (ISBN: 978-0-929960-62-3, paper; 978-0-929960-63-0, hardcover.)

Massachusetts 1

State Summary

Capital city .... Boston
Governor .... Deval Patrick

State House
Office of the Governor, Room 360
Boston, MA 02133
(617) 725-4005

Admitted as a state 1788
Area (square miles) 10,555
Population, 2009 (estimate) 6,593,587
Largest city .... Boston
  Population, 2008 609,023
Personal income per capita, 2008
  (in current dollars) $50,735
Gross domestic product, 2008 ($ mil) $364,988

Leading industries by payroll, 2007

Health care/Social assistance, Professional/Scientific/Technical, Finance & Insurance

Leading agricultural commodities by receipts, 2008

Greenhouse/nursery, Cranberries, Dairy products, Sweet corn, Apples

Geography & Environment

Total area (square miles) 10,555
  land 7,840
  water 2,715
Highest point .... Mt. Greylock
  elevation (feet) 3,491
Lowest point .... Atlantic Ocean
  elevation (feet) .... sea level
General coastline (miles) 192
Tidal shoreline (miles) 1,519
Capital city .... Boston
  Population 2000 589,141
  Population 2008 609,023
Largest city .... Boston
  Population 2000 589,141
  Population 2008 609,023

Number of cities with over 100,000 population

1990 3
2000 5
2008 5

State park and recreation areas, 2007

Area (x 1,000 acres) 341
Number of visitors (x 1,000) 31,635
Revenues ($1,000) 11,299
  percent of operating expenditures 14.6%

National Park Service Areas, 2008

Total area (x 1,000 acres) 57.9
  Federal land 34.0
  Nonfederal land 23.9
Recreation visits (x 1,000) 10,281.7

National forest system land, 2009

Acres 0

Demographics & Population Characteristics

Population

1980 5,737,037
1990 6,016,425
2000 6,349,113
2008 6,497,967
  Male 3,153,176
  Female 3,344,791
Living in group quarters, 2008 243,596
  percent of total 3.7%
2009 (estimate) 6,593,587
  persons per square mile of land 841.0
2020 (projected) 6,855,546
2030 (projected) 7,012,009

Population of Core-Based Statistical Areas (formerly Metropolitan Areas), x 1,000

	CBSA	Non-CBSA
1990	5,999	18
2000	6,325	25
2008	6,471	27

Change in population, 2000-2009

Number 244,474
  percent 3.9%
Natural increase (births minus deaths) 220,701
Net internal migration .... -276,768
Net international migration 245,145

Persons by age, 2008

Under 5 years 383,568
5 to 17 years 1,043,465
18 years and over 5,070,934
65 years and over 871,098
85 years and over 143,097
  Median age 38.6

Race, 2008

One Race
  White 5,601,486
  Black or African American 455,880
  Asian 321,130
  American Indian/Alaska Native 20,361
  Hawaiian Native/Pacific Islander 5,507
Two or more races 93,603

Persons of Asian origin, 2008

Total Asian 322,218
  Asian Indian 66,429
  Chinese 116,784
  Filipino 10,884
  Japanese 10,289
  Korean 21,320
  Vietnamese 37,496

Persons of Hispanic origin, 2008

Total Hispanic or Latino 556,898
  Mexican 38,223
  Puerto Rican 232,293
  Cuban 9,107

©2010 Information Publications, Inc. All rights reserved. Photocopying prohibited. For additional copies, contact the publisher at www.informationpublications.com or (877)544-INFO (4636)

©2010 Information Publications, Inc. All rights reserved. Photocopying prohibited. For additional copies, contact the publisher at www.informationpublications.com or (877)544-INFO (4636)

2 Massachusetts

Marital status, 2008

Population 15 years & over	5,328,765
Never married	1,881,689
Married	2,631,841
Separated	102,077
Widowed	332,075
Divorced	483,160

Language spoken at home, 2008

Population 5 years and older	6,116,518
English only	4,832,030
Spanish	447,466
French	124,545
German	24,187
Chinese	91,157

Households & families, 2008

Households	2,467,323
with persons under 18 years	788,823
with persons over 65 years	602,891
persons per household	2.53
Families	1,568,641
persons per family	3.17
Married couples	1,168,273
Unmarried couples	149,432
Same-sex	19,550
Male couple	7,241
Female couple	12,309
Female householder, no husband present	301,283
One-person households	726,235
Grandparents living with grandkids	73,669
Financially responsible for children	22,423
Not financially responsible	51,246

Nativity, 2008

Number of residents born in state	4,125,489
percent of population	63.5%

Immigration & Naturalization, 2008

Legal permanent residents admitted	30,369
Persons naturalized	28,728
Non-immigrant admissions	847,608

Vital Statistics and Health

Marriages

2006	37,993
2007	37,895
2008	33,996

Divorces

2006	14,621
2007	14,644
2008	12,992

Physicians, 2007

Total	30,335
rate per 100,000 persons	469

Health care expenditures, 2004

Total expenditures ($ mil)	$43,009
per capita	$6,683

Births, 2006

Total	77,676
Birth rate (per 1,000)	12.1
Teen birth rate (per 1,000)	21.3
White, non-Hispanic	53,644
Black, non-Hispanic	7,104
Hispanic	10,749
Asian/Pacific Islander	5,712
American Indian/Alaska Native	172
Low birth weight (2,500g or less)	7.9%
Cesarian births	33.2%
Preterm births	11.3%
To unmarried mothers	32.2%
2008 (provisional)	76,526

Deaths, 2006

All causes	53,450
rate per 100,000	719.7
Heart disease	12,947
rate per 100,000	205.6
Malignant neoplasms	13,407
rate per 100,000	186.7
Cerebrovascular disease	2,880
rate per 100,000	37.6
Chronic lower respiratory disease	2,535
rate per 100,000	34.5
Diabetes	1,132
rate per 100,000	15.4
2007 (preliminary)	52,936
rate per 100,000	707.7
2008 (provisional)	52,892

Infant deaths

2005	396
rate per 1,000	5.15
2006	370
rate per 1,000	4.76

HIV and AIDS, 2007

HIV (non-AIDS) cases	777
estimated living with HIV	NA
AIDS cases	612
estimated living with AIDS	9,181

Abortions, 2006

Total performed in state	24,246
rate per 1,000 women age 15-44	17.7
% obtained by out-of-state residents	4.1%

Health risks for adults, 2007

Cigarette smokers	16.4%
Binge drinkers	17.6%
Overweight (BMI > 25)	58.9%
Obese (BMI > 30)	21.7%
No exercise	21.1%
Recommended level of exercise	51.4%
Eat 5 fruit & vegetable servings per day	27.5%

Disability status of population, 2008

Under 18 years	4.5%
18 to 64 years	9.3%
65 years and over	34.7%

Massachusetts 3

Education

Educational attainment, 2007

Population over 25 years 4,373,025
Less than 9th grade. 4.9%
High school graduate or more 88.4%
College graduate or more. 37.7%
Graduate or professional degree. 16.0%

Public school enrollment, 2007-08

Total. 962,958
Pre-kindergarten through grade 8. . . . 666,276
Grades 9 through 12 296,032

Graduates and dropouts, 2006-07

Graduation rate 80.8%
Dropout rate. 3.8%

SAT scores, 2009

Average critical reading score. 514
Average writing score 510
Average math score 526
Percent of graduates taking test 84%

Public school teachers, 2009-10 (estimate)

Total (x 1,000) 70.3
Elementary. 46.2
Secondary. 24.1
Average salary $68,000

State receipts & expenditures for public schools, 2009-10 (estimate)

Total receipts ($ mil). $14,623
Revenue receipts $14,622
Total expenditures ($ mil) $14,144
for public day schools. $13,120
per capita $1,115
per pupil $14,604

NAEP proficiency scores, 2007

	Reading		Math	
	Basic	Proficient	Basic	Proficient
Grade 4	81.1%	49.2%	93.2%	57.6%
Grade 8	83.9%	43.0%	85.0%	50.7%

Higher education enrollment, fall 2007

Total. 463,366
Full-time men 144,749
Full-time women. 174,317
Part-time men 52,884
Part-time women. 91,416

Minority enrollment in institutions of higher education, 2007

Black, non-Hispanic 37,817
Hispanic 31,383
Asian/Pacific Islander 34,210
American Indian/Alaska Native. 1,947

Institutions of higher education, 2007-08

Total. 122
Public. 31
Private 91

Earned degrees conferred, 2006-07

Associate's. 10,691
Bachelor's 47,885
Master's. 27,802
First-professional. 4,503
Doctor's. 3,325

Public Libraries, FY 2007

Number of libraries. 370
Number of outlets 480
Annual visits per capita 6.1
Circulation per capita. 8.1
Print holdings per capita 5.0

State & local financial support for higher education, FY 2008

Full-time equivalent enrollment (x 1,000) 144.6
Appropriations per FTE. $7,381

Social Insurance & Welfare Programs

Social Security benefits & beneficiaries, 2008

Beneficiaries (x 1,000) 1,081
Retired & dependents. 750
Survivors. 120
Disabled & dependents. 211
Annual benefit payments ($ mil) $12,849
Retired & dependents. $8,644
Survivors. $1,898
Disabled & dependents. $2,307
Median monthly benefit
Retired & dependents. $1,083.40
Disabled & dependents. $911.70
Widowed. $1,085.40

Medicare, 2008

Enrollment (x 1,000). 1,019
Payment per enrollee $9,115

Medicaid, 2005

Beneficiaries (x 1,000). 1,110
Payments ($ mil) $8,308

Children's Health Insurance Program, 2008

Enrollment (x 1,000). 201.0
Expenditures ($ mil). $259.3

Federal and state public aid

State unemployment insurance, 2007
Recipients, first payments (x 1,000). 219
Total payments ($ mil) $1,357
Average weekly benefit $379
Temporary Assistance for Needy Families, 2008
Recipients (x 1,000). 1,093.8
Families (x 1,000) 550.0
Supplemental Security Income, 2008
Recipients (x 1,000). 178.9
Payments ($ mil) $1,014.2
Supplemental Nutritional Asst. Program, 2008
Avg monthly participants (x 1,000) 505.8
Total benefits ($ mil). $586.6

©2010 Information Publications, Inc. All rights reserved. Photocopying prohibited. For additional copies, contact the publisher at www.informationpublications.com or (877)544-INFO (4636)

©2010 Information Publications, Inc. All rights reserved. Photocopying prohibited. For additional copies, contact the publisher at www.informationpublications.com or (877)544-INFO (4636)

4 Massachusetts

Persons without health insurance, 2008

Number (x 1,000)	352
percent	5.5%
Number of children (x 1,000)	49
percent of children	3.4%

Type of health insurance coverage, 2008

Some coverage	94.5%
Private	76.3%
Government	31.1%
Medicaid	17.2%
Medicare	15.1%

Housing & Construction

Housing units

Total 2007 (estimate)	2,726,175
Total 2008 (estimate)	2,735,443
Single-family home	1,447,629
Multifamily dwelling	1,264,055
Mobile home or trailer	23,542
Seasonal or recreational use, 2008	107,151
Owner-occupied, 2008	1,592,324
Median home value	$353,600
Homeowner vacancy rate	1.6%
Renter-occupied, 2008	874,999
Median rent	$991
Rental vacancy rate	6.5%
Home ownership rate, 2007	64.3%
Home ownership rate, 2008	65.7%

New privately-owned housing units

Number authorized, 2008 (x 1,000)	9.2
Value ($ mil)	$1,734.5
Started 2007 (x 1,000, estimate)	15.4
Started 2008 (x 1,000, estimate)	9.9

Existing home sales

2007 (x 1,000)	122.4
2008 (x 1,000)	103.8

Government & Elections

State officials 2010

Governor	Deval Patrick Democratic, term expires 1/11
Lieutenant Governor	Tim Murray
Secretary of State	William Galvin
Attorney General	Martha Coakley
Chief Justice	Margaret Marshall

Governorship

Minimum age	not specified
Length of term	4 years
Consecutive terms permitted	not specified
Who succeeds	Lieutenant Governor

State government employment, 2008

Full-time equivalent employees	97,601
Payroll ($ mil)	$462.2

Local government employment, 2008

Full-time equivalent employees	245,378
Payroll ($ mil)	$1,068.0

State legislature

Name	General Court
Upper chamber	Senate
Number of members	40
Length of term	2 years
Party in majority, 2010	Democratic
Lower chamber	House of Representatives
Number of members	160
Length of term	2 years
Party in majority, 2010	Democratic

Federal representation, 2010 (112th Congress)

Senator	John Kerry
Party	Democratic
Year term expires	2015
Senator	Scott Brown
Party	Republican
Year term expires	2013
Representatives, total	10
Democrats	10
Republicans	0

Presidential election, 2008

Total popular vote	3,080,985
Barack Obama	1,904,097
John McCain	1,108,854
Total electoral votes	12

Votes cast for US Senators

2006

Total vote (x 1,000)	2,244
Leading party	Democratic
Percent for leading party	66.9%

2008

Total vote (x 1,000)	3,103
Leading party	Democratic
Percent for leading party	63.6%

Votes cast for US Representatives

2006

Total vote (x 1,000)	2,244
Democratic	1,632
Republican	199
Leading party	Democratic
Percent for leading party	72.7%

2008

Total vote (x 1,000)	3,103
Democratic	2,246
Republican	318
Leading party	Democratic
Percent for leading party	72.4%

Voters in Nov. 2008 election (est. in thousands)

Total	3,044
Male	1,458
Female	1,586
White	2,787
Black	145
Hispanic	77
Asian	76

Massachusetts 5

Local governments by type, 2007

Total	861
County	5
Municipal	45
Township	306
School District	423
Special District	82

Women holding public office, 2010

US Congress	1
Statewide elected office	1
State legislature	52

Black public officials, 2002

Total	79
US and state legislatures	6
City/county/regional offices	60
Judicial/law enforcement	2
Education/school boards	11

Hispanic public officials, 2008

Total	20
State executives & legislators	4
City/county/regional offices	9
Judicial/law enforcement	0
Education/school boards	7

Governmental Finance

State government revenues, 2008

Total revenue (x $1,000)	$51,759,773
per capita	$7,965.53
General revenue (x $1,000)	$41,607,421
per capita, total	$6,403.14
Intergovernmental	1,546.27
Taxes	3,371.61
Sales taxes	932.05
General sales tax	630.67
Selective sales taxes	301.38
Individual income tax	1,923.08
Corporate income tax	335.48
License fees	105.42
Current charges	571.21
Miscellaneous	914.06

State government expenditure, 2008

Total expenditure (x $1,000)	$45,634,948
per capita	$7,022.96
General expenditure (x $1,000)	$40,398,126
per capita, total	*$6,217.04*
Education	1,648.82
Public welfare	1,951.81
Health	164.40
Hospitals	71.85
Highways	345.60
Police protection	87.69
Corrections	205.13
Natural resources	52.02
Parks & recreation	36.66
Governmental administration	256.54
Interest on general debt	558.19

State debt & cash, 2008 ($ per capita)

Debt	$11,063.81
Cash/security holdings	$15,972.91

Federal government grants to state & local government, 2008 (x $1,000)

Total	$20,427,439
by Federal agency	
Defense	200,803
Education	752,232
Energy	143,564
Environmental Protection Agency	95,639
Health & Human Services	15,566,816
Homeland Security	134,149
Housing & Urban Development	1,130,084
Justice	56,360
Labor	183,400
Transportation	1,025,753

Crime & Law Enforcement

Crime, 2008 (rates per 100,000 residents)

Property crimes	155,959
Burglary	36,094
Larceny	107,128
Motor vehicle theft	12,737
Property crime rate	2,400.1
Violent crimes	29,174
Murder	167
Forcible rape	1,736
Robbery	7,069
Aggravated assault	20,202
Violent crime rate	449.0
Hate crimes	386

Child abuse and neglect cases, 2007

Number of reports	39,801
Children subject of investigation	80,752
Number of child victims	37,690

Law enforcement agencies, 2008

Total agencies	331
Total employees	20,173
Officers	16,609
Civilians	3,564

Prisoners, probation, and parole, 2008

Total prisoners, 12/31/2008	11,408
percent change from 2007	-0.2%
in private facilities	0%
in local jails	1.6%
Sentenced to more than one year	10,166
rate per 100,000 residents	218
Male	434
Female	13
Adults on probation	184,308
Adults on parole	3,185

Prisoner demographics, June 30, 2005 (rate per 100,000 residents)

White	201
Black	1,635
Hispanic	1,229

©2010 Information Publications, Inc. All rights reserved. Photocopying prohibited. For additional copies, contact the publisher at www.informationpublications.com or (877)544-INFO (4636)

©2010 Information Publications, Inc. All rights reserved. Photocopying prohibited. For additional copies, contact the publisher at www.informationpublications.com or (877)544-INFO (4636)

6 Massachusetts

Arrests, 2008

Total	149,582
Persons under 18 years of age	17,974

Persons under sentence of death, 1/1/09

Total	0
White	0
Black	0
Hispanic	0

Fraud and identity theft, 2008

Fraud complaints	15,515
rate per 100,000 residents	238.8
Identity theft complaints	5,408
rate per 100,000 residents	83.2

State's highest court

Name	Supreme Judicial Court
Number of members	7
Length of term	to age 70
Intermediate appeals court?	yes

Labor & Income

Civilian labor force, 2008 (x 1,000)

Total	3,421
Men	1,777
Women	1,644
Persons 16-19 years	154
White	2,985
Black	211
Hispanic	196

Civilian labor force as a percent of civilian non-institutional population, 2008

Total	66.6%
Men	72.3%
Women	61.4%
Persons 16-19 years	43.5%
White	66.8%
Black	64.7%
Hispanic	63.9%

Employment, 2008 (x 1,000)

Total	3,238
Men	1,673
Women	1,565
Persons 16-19 years	131
White	2,830
Black	195
Hispanic	177

Unemployment rate, 2008

Total	5.3%
Men	5.9%
Women	4.8%
Persons 16-19 years	14.9%
White	5.2%
Black	7.6%
Hispanic	10.0%

Hourly wages, 2008

Mean hourly wage	$24.52
Median hourly wage	$19.09

Average annual and weekly wages, 2008

Average annual wages	$56,746
increase from 2006	2.7%
Average weekly wage	$1,091

Experienced civilian labor force by private industry, 2008

Total	2,831,525
Natural resources & mining	7,760
Construction	132,550
Manufacturing	286,470
Trade, transportation & utilities	565,536
Information	89,230
Finance	221,568
Professional & business	487,384
Education & health	606,436
Leisure & hospitality	305,888
Other	128,703

Experienced civilian labor force by occupation, May 2008

Management	185,940
Business & financial	171,590
Legal	25,550
Sales	334,150
Office & admin. support	547,620
Computers & math	121,680
Architecture & engineering	77,030
Arts & entertainment	51,830
Education	215,880
Social services	65,800
Health care practitioner & technical	208,500
Health care support	100,040
Maintenance & repair	103,220
Construction	108,160
Transportation & moving	161,800
Production	173,110
Farming, fishing & forestry	2,700

Income and poverty, 2008

Median household income	$65,401
Median family income	$81,569
Personal income, per capita (current $)	$50,735
in constant (2000) dollars	$41,724
Disposable income (current $)	$43,134
in constant (2000) dollars	$35,473
Persons below poverty level	10.0%

Labor unions, 2008

Members of unions (x 1,000)	458
percent of employed	15.7%
Represented by unions (x 1,000)	491
percent of employed	16.9%

Federal individual income tax returns, 2007

Returns filed	3,461,517
Adjusted gross income ($1,000)	$243,829,482
Total tax liability ($1,000)	$37,709,755
Charitable contributions (x 1,000)	1,101.0
Total amount ($1,000)	$4,680,168

Massachusetts 7

Economy, Business, Industry & Agriculture

Bankruptcy cases filed, FY 2008	15,636
Business	340
Non-business	15,296
Patents awarded, 2009	3,880
Trademarks awarded, 2009	2,364

Business firm ownership, 2002

Women-owned	161,918
Sales ($ mil)	$23,134
Black-owned	12,819
Sales ($ mil)	$1,239
Hispanic-owned	15,933
Sales ($ mil)	$2,068
Asian-owned	18,081
Sales ($ mil)	$5,020
Amer. Indian/Alaska Native-owned	2,220
Sales ($ mil)	$340
Hawaiian/Pacific Islander-owned	208
Sales ($ mil)	$24

Gross domestic product, 2008 ($ mil)

Total gross domestic product	$364,988
Agriculture, forestry, fishing and hunting	892
Mining	211
Utilities	5,517
Construction	13,267
Manufacturing, durable goods	23,646
Manufacturing, non-durable goods	11,160
Wholesale trade	20,666
Retail trade	17,710
Transportation & warehousing	5,998
Information	17,565
Finance & insurance	35,487
Real estate, rental & leasing	51,799
Professional and technical services	44,532
Educational services	9,387
Health care and social assistance	34,623
Accommodation/food services	9,573
Other services, except government	7,648
Government	33,134

Establishments, payroll, employees & receipts, by major industry group, 2007

Total	176,701
Annual payroll ($1,000)	$157,235,733
Paid employees	3,073,941
Forestry, fishing & agriculture	398
Annual payroll ($1,000)	$32,708
Paid employees	1,085
Mining	90
Annual payroll ($1,000)	$66,757
Paid employees	1,464
Receipts, 2002 ($1,000)	*$297,738*
Utilities	251
Annual payroll ($1,000)	$1,109,068
Paid employees	12,711
Receipts, 2002 ($1,000)	*NA*
Construction	19,574
Annual payroll ($1,000)	$7,685,989
Paid employees	129,529
Receipts, 2002 ($1,000)	*$31,547,604*
Manufacturing	7,656
Annual payroll ($1,000)	$15,958,926
Paid employees	271,519
Receipts, 2002 ($1,000)	*$77,996,586*
Wholesale trade	8,720
Annual payroll ($1,000)	$10,021,073
Paid employees	143,053
Receipts, 2002 ($1,000)	*$127,129,789*
Retail trade	25,666
Annual payroll ($1,000)	$9,290,750
Paid employees	367,059
Receipts, 2002 ($1,000)	*$73,903,837*
Transportation & warehousing	3,737
Annual payroll ($1,000)	$2,989,098
Paid employees	78,686
Receipts, 2002 ($1,000)	*$5,919,533*
Information	3,808
Annual payroll ($1,000)	$8,556,816
Paid employees	108,037
Receipts, 2002 ($1,000)	*NA*
Finance & insurance	10,073
Annual payroll ($1,000)	$21,715,598
Paid employees	214,822
Receipts, 2002 ($1,000)	*NA*
Professional, scientific & technical	22,421
Annual payroll ($1,000)	$21,944,257
Paid employees	259,056
Receipts, 2002 ($1,000)	*$37,329,788*
Education	2,565
Annual payroll ($1,000)	$6,724,208
Paid employees	185,466
Receipts, 2002 ($1,000)	*$1,130,911*
Health care & social assistance	17,797
Annual payroll ($1,000)	$22,519,765
Paid employees	507,615
Receipts, 2002 ($1,000)	*$37,307,723*
Arts and entertainment	3,136
Annual payroll ($1,000)	$1,645,621
Paid employees	50,763
Receipts, 2002 ($1,000)	*$3,310,135*
Real estate	6,963
Annual payroll ($1,000)	$2,478,247
Paid employees	50,213
Receipts, 2002 ($1,000)	*$8,440,569*
Accommodation & food service	15,954
Annual payroll ($1,000)	$4,490,343
Paid employees	253,535
Receipts, 2002 ($1,000)	*$11,789,582*

©2010 Information Publications, Inc. All rights reserved. Photocopying prohibited. For additional copies, contact the publisher at www.informationpublications.com or (877)544-INFO (4636)

©2010 Information Publications, Inc. All rights reserved. Photocopying prohibited. For additional copies, contact the publisher at www.informationpublications.com or (877)544-INFO (4636)

8 Massachusetts

Exports, 2008

Value of exported goods ($ mil) $28,293
Manufactured $23,339
Non-manufactured..................$2,131

Foreign direct investment in US affiliates, 2006

Property, plants & equipment ($ mil) ... $23,951
Employment (x 1,000)...................173.0

Agriculture, 2008

Number of farms.......................7,700
Farm acreage (x 1,000) 510
Acres per farm......................... 66

Farm marketings and income ($ mil)

Total................................ $569.8
Crops.............................. $454.3
Livestock...........................$115.5
Net farm income $178.6

Principal agricultural commodities, in order by marketing receipts, 2008

Greenhouse/nursery, Cranberries, Dairy products, Sweet corn, Apples

Federal economic activity in state

Expenditures, 2008 ($ mil)

Total..............................$72,115
Per capita $11,098.08
Defense $12,430
Non-defense...................... $59,685

Defense department, 2008 ($ mil)

Payroll............................$1,170
Contract awards $11,283
Grants $202

Homeland security grants ($1,000)

2008............................. $32,303
2009............................. $40,151

FDIC-insured financial institutions, 2007

Number of institutions................... 175
Assets ($ billion) $268.6
Number of offices...................... 2,228
Deposits ($ billion) $185.3

Communication, Energy & Transportation

Communication

Households with internet access, 2007 .... 66.4%
using broadband 61.1%
using dialup 5.2%
High-speed internet providers, 12/2007...... 46
Total high-speed internet lines........3,140,383
Residential 1,852,275
Business.........................1,288,108
Cable modem....................1,135,807
DSL .... NA
Wireless phone customers, 12/2007 5,469,503

FCC-licensed stations (as of January 6, 2010)

TV stations............................. 20
FM radio stations....................... 124
AM radio stations 75

Energy

Energy consumption, 2007

Total (trillion Btu)................... 1,514.6
Energy balance (trillion Btu) 192.5

By source of production (trillion Btu)

Coal 120.1
Natural gas..........................417.3
Petroleum........................... 684.6
Nuclear electric power 53.7
Hydroelectric power.....................7.9
Biomass & other renewable.............35.1

By end-use sector (trillion Btu)

Residential 443.1
Commercial 384.0
Industrial 195.6
Transportation 491.7

Energy spending, 2007 ($ mil) $25,862
price per million Btu $23.89

Electric energy, 2007

Primary source of electricity............. Gas
Net generation (billion kWh) 47.1
percent from renewable sources....... 4.3%
Net summer capability (million kW) 13.6
Retail sales (billion kWh) 57.1
price per kWh ....15.16¢

Natural gas utilities, 2007

Customers (x 1,000) 1,485
Sales (trillion Btu)..................... 175
Revenues ($ mil) $2,771

Nuclear power plants, 2009 1
CO_2 emitted, 2005 (mil. metric tons) 80.1

Transportation, 2008

Public road & street mileage 36,105
Urban.............................. 28,127
Rural 7,978
Interstate............................. 573

Vehicle miles of travel (millions) 54,505
per capita 8,388

Total motor vehicle registrations.......5,328,349
Automobiles.....................3,236,056
Trucks..........................2,081,052
Motorcycles 153,444

Licensed drivers 4,674,058
19 years & under 184,196

Deaths from motor vehicle accidents 363
involving alcohol......................42%
driver with blood alcohol level over .08 ...34%

Gasoline consumed (x 1,000 gallons) 2,807,736
per capita 432.1

Commuting Statistics, 2008

Average commute time (min) 27.3
Drove to work alone 72.3%
Carpooled........................... 8.6%
Public transit 8.9%
Walk to work 4.6%
Work from home...................... 3.9%

Barnstable County
Barnstable Town
Bourne
Brewster
Chatham
Dennis
Eastham
Falmouth
Harwich
Mashpee
Orleans
Provincetown
Sandwich
Truro
Wellfleet
Yarmouth

Berkshire County
Adams
Alford
Becket
Cheshire
Clarksburg
Dalton
Egremont
Florida
Great Barrington
Hancock
Hinsdale
Lanesborough
Lee
Lenox
Monterey
Mount Washington
New Ashford
New Marlborough
North Adams
Otis
Peru
Pittsfield
Richmond
Sandisfield
Savoy
Sheffield
Stockbridge
Tyringham
Washington
West Stockbridge
Williamstown
Windsor

Bristol County
Acushnet
Attleboro
Berkley
Dartmouth
Dighton
Easton
Fairhaven
Fall River
Freetown
Mansfield
New Bedford
North Attleborough
Norton
Raynham
Rehoboth
Seekonk
Somerset
Swansea
Taunton
Westport

Dukes County
Aquinnah
Chilmark
Edgartown
Gosnold
Oak Bluffs
Tisbury
West Tisbury
Essex County
Amesbury
Andover
Beverly
Boxford
Danvers

Essex
Georgetown
Gloucester
Groveland
Hamilton
Haverhill
Ipswich
Lawrence
Lynn
Lynnfield
Manchester-by-the-Sea

Essex County, cont.
Marblehead
Merrimac
Methuen
Middleton Nahant
Newbury
Newburyport
North Andover
Peabody
Rockport
Rowley
Salem
Salisbury
Saugus
Swampscott
Topsfield
Wenham
West Newbury

Franklin County
Ashfield
Bernardston
Buckland
Charlemont
Colrain
Conway
Deerfield
Erving
Gill
Greenfield
Hawley
Heath
Leverett
Leyden
Monroe
Montague
New Salem
Northfield
Orange
Rowe
Shelburne
Shutesbury
Sunderland
Warwick
Wendell
Whately

Hampden County
Agawam
Blandford
Brimfield
Chester
Chicopee
East Longmeadow
Granville
Hampden
Holland
Holyoke
Longmeadow
Ludlow
Monson
Montgomery
Palmer
Russell
Southwick
Springfield
Tolland
Wales
West Springfield
Westfield
Wilbraham

Hampshire County
Amherst
Belchertown
Chesterfield
Cummington
Easthampton
Goshen
Granby
Hadley
Hatfield
Huntington
Middlefield
Northampton
Pelham
Plainfield
South Hadley
Southampton
Ware
Westhampton
Williamsburg
Worthington

©2010 Information Publications, Inc. All rights reserved. Photocopying prohibited. For additional copies, contact the publisher at www.informationpublications.com or (877)544-INFO (4636)

Middlesex County
Acton
Arlington
Ashby
Ashland
Ayer
Bedford
Belmont
Billerica
Boxborough
Burlington
Cambridge
Carlisle
Chelmsford
Concord
Dracut
Dunstable
Everett
Framingham
Groton
Holliston
Hopkinton
Hudson
Lexington
Lincoln
Littleton
Lowell
Malden
Marlborough
Maynard
Medford
Melrose
Natick
Newton
North Reading
Pepperell
Reading
Sherborn
Shirley
Somerville
Stoneham
Stow
Sudbury
Tewksbury
Townsend
Tyngsborough

Middlesex County (con't)
Wakefield
Waltham
Watertown
Wayland
Westford
Weston
Wilmington
Winchester
Woburn

Nantucket County
Nantucket

Norfolk County
Avon
Bellingham
Braintree
Brookline
Canton
Cohasset
Dedham
Dover
Foxborough
Franklin
Holbrook
Medfield
Medway
Millis
Milton
Needham
Norfolk
Norwood
Plainville
Quincy
Randolph
Sharon
Stoughton
Walpole
Wellesley
Westwood
Weymouth
Wrentham

Plymouth County
Abington
Bridgewater
Brockton
Carver
Duxbury
East Bridgewater
Halifax
Hanover
Hanson
Hingham
Hull
Kingston
Lakeville
Marion
Marshfield
Mattapoisett
Middleborough
Norwell
Pembroke
Plymouth
Plympton
Rochester
Rockland
Scituate
Wareham
West Bridgewater
Whitman

Suffolk County
Boston
Chelsea
Revere
Winthrop

Worcester County
Ashburnham
Athol
Auburn
Barre
Berlin
Blackstone
Bolton
Boylston
Brookfield
Charlton
Clinton
Douglas
Dudley
East Brookfield

Worcester County (con't)
Fitchburg
Gardner
Grafton
Hardwick
Harvard
Holden
Hopedale
Hubbardston
Lancaster
Leicester
Leominster
Lunenburg
Mendon
Milford
Millbury
Millville
New Braintree
North Brookfield
Northborough
Northbridge
Oakham
Oxford
Paxton
Petersham
Phillipston
Princeton
Royalston
Rutland
Shrewsbury
Southborough
Southbridge
Spencer
Sterling
Sturbridge
Sutton
Templeton
Upton
Uxbridge
Warren
Webster
West Boylston
West Brookfield
Westborough
Westminster
Winchendon
Worcester

©2010 Information Publications, Inc. All rights reserved. Photocopying prohibited. For additional copies, contact the publisher at www.informationpublications.com or (877)544-INFO (4636)

Barnstable County

Land area (square miles)	396
Water area (square miles)	910
Population	
2000	222,230
2008 (estimate)	221,049
Male	104,559
Female	116,490
Persons per square mile, 2008	558.2
2010 (projected)†	257,844
2020 (projected)†	299,035
Race & Hispanic Origin, 2008	
Race	
White	209,811
Black/African American	4,920
American Indian/Alaska Native	1,394
Asian	2,164
Hawaiian Native/Pacific Islander	92
Two or more races	2,668
Hispanic origin	4,057
Age, 2008	
Under 5 years	9,544
5 to 13 years	18,839
15 to 44 years	74,703
45 to 64 years	62,581
18 years and over	182,440
65 years and over	53,032
85 years and over	9,218
Median Age	46.6
Educational Attainment, 2008*	
Population 25 years and over	165,670
High School graduates or higher	96.1%
Bachelor's degree or higher	41.1%
Graduate degree	16.2%
Nativity, 2008*	
Native-born	208,385
Foreign-born	12,664
Income & Poverty, 2008*	
Median household income	$57,314
Median family income	$73,608
Per capita family income	$34,481
Persons in poverty	7.5%
Households & Housing Units, 2008*	
Total households	93,027
Family households	58,237
Average household size	2.33
Average family size	2.96
Total housing units	156,141
Owner-occupied	75,556
Median SF home value	$393,300
Renter-occupied	17,471
Median rent	$1,031
Labor & Employment	
Civilian labor force, 2008††	122,097
Unemployment rate	5.8%
Civilian labor force, Dec. 2009††	119,071
Unemployment rate	10.8%
Employed persons 16 years and over by occupation, 2008*	
Managers & professionals	39,049
Service occupations	20,110
Sales & office occupations	29,326
Farming, fishing & forestry	584
Construction & maintenance	12,286
Production & transportation	7,332
Self-employed persons	13,685

Most demographic data is from the Census Bureau's Population Estimates Division
* 2008 American Community Survey
† University of Massachusetts, MISER
†† Massachusetts Department of Revenue

Berkshire County

Land area (square miles)	931
Water area (square miles)	15
Population	
2000	134,953
2008 (estimate)	129,395
Male	62,248
Female	67,147
Persons per square mile, 2008	139.0
2010 (projected)†	126,255
2020 (projected)†	118,452
Race & Hispanic Origin, 2008	
Race	
White	122,043
Black/African American	3,404
American Indian/Alaska Native	232
Asian	1,827
Hawaiian Native/Pacific Islander	56
Two or more races	1,833
Hispanic origin	3,357
Age, 2008	
Under 5 years	6,196
5 to 13 years	11,736
15 to 44 years	48,864
45 to 64 years	37,332
18 years and over	104,579
65 years and over	23,662
85 years and over	4,220
Median Age	43.0
Educational Attainment, 2008*	
Population 25 years and over	92,003
High School graduates or higher	92.0%
Bachelor's degree or higher	28.6%
Graduate degree	11.9%
Nativity, 2008*	
Native-born	124,076
Foreign-born	5,319
Income & Poverty, 2008*	
Median household income	$44,797
Median family income	$59,275
Per capita family income	$28,279
Persons in poverty	12.6%
Households & Housing Units, 2008*	
Total households	57,455
Family households	34,038
Average household size	2.14
Average family size	2.76
Total housing units	68,242
Owner-occupied	38,576
Median SF home value	$208,900
Renter-occupied	18,879
Median rent	$703
Labor & Employment	
Civilian labor force, 2008††	73,102
Unemployment rate	5.1%
Civilian labor force, Dec. 2009††	72,160
Unemployment rate	8.8%
Employed persons 16 years and over by occupation, 2008*	
Managers & professionals	21,563
Service occupations	15,336
Sales & office occupations	16,102
Farming, fishing & forestry	221
Construction & maintenance	5,956
Production & transportation	6,277
Self-employed persons	5,438

Most demographic data is from the Census Bureau's Population Estimates Division
* 2008 American Community Survey
† University of Massachusetts, MISER
†† Massachusetts Department of Revenue

Bristol County

Land area (square miles)	556
Water area (square miles)	135
Population	
2000	534,678
2008 (estimate)	545,823
Male	263,656
Female	282,167
Persons per square mile, 2008	981.7
2010 (projected)†	554,124
2020 (projected)†	576,868
Race & Hispanic Origin, 2008	
Race	
White	505,759
Black/African American	20,252
American Indian/Alaska Native	1,972
Asian	9,668
Hawaiian Native/Pacific Islander	304
Two or more races	7,868
Hispanic origin	28,107
Age, 2008	
Under 5 years	32,054
5 to 13 years	60,659
15 to 44 years	225,770
45 to 64 years	145,317
18 years and over	422,985
65 years and over	74,700
85 years and over	12,816
Median Age	38.6
Educational Attainment, 2008*	
Population 25 years and over	371,302
High School graduates or higher	79.7%
Bachelor's degree or higher	24.0%
Graduate degree	7.4%
Nativity, 2008*	
Native-born	481,555
Foreign-born	64,268
Income & Poverty, 2008*	
Median household income	$56,241
Median family income	$69,920
Per capita family income	$28,034
Persons in poverty	11.7%
Households & Housing Units, 2008*	
Total households	204,454
Family households	139,413
Average household size	2.58
Average family size	3.12
Total housing units	225,201
Owner-occupied	131,295
Median SF home value	$319,800
Renter-occupied	73,159
Median rent	$783
Labor & Employment	
Civilian labor force, 2008††	291,678
Unemployment rate	7.0%
Civilian labor force, Dec. 2009††	293,356
Unemployment rate	12.0%
Employed persons 16 years and over by occupation, 2008*	
Managers & professionals	88,677
Service occupations	54,482
Sales & office occupations	75,042
Farming, fishing & forestry	785
Construction & maintenance	27,579
Production & transportation	35,154
Self-employed persons	14,583

Most demographic data is from the Census Bureau's Population Estimates Division
* 2008 American Community Survey
† University of Massachusetts, MISER
†† Massachusetts Department of Revenue

©2010 Information Publications, Inc. All rights reserved. Photocopying prohibited. For additional copies, contact the publisher at www.informationpublications.com or (877)544-INFO (4636)

See Introduction for an explanation of all data sources.

©2010 Information Publications, Inc. All rights reserved. Photocopying prohibited. For additional copies, contact the publisher at www.informationpublications.com or (877)544-INFO (4636)

Dukes County

Land area (square miles)	104
Water area (square miles)	387

Population

2000	14,987
2008 (estimate)	15,527
Male	7,579
Female	7,948
Persons per square mile, 2008	149.3
2010 (projected)†	18,271
2020 (projected)†	21,822

Race & Hispanic Origin, 2008

Race	
White	14,315
Black/African American	426
American Indian/Alaska Native	356
Asian	121
Hawaiian Native/Pacific Islander	17
Two or more races	292
Hispanic origin	275

Age, 2008

Under 5 years	855
5 to 13 years	1,385
15 to 44 years	5,659
45 to 64 years	5,111
18 years and over	12,591
65 years and over	2,360
85 years and over	340
Median Age	43.9

Educational Attainment, 2000**

Population 25 years and over	10,693
High School graduates or higher	90.4%
Bachelor's degree or higher	38.4%
Graduate degree	13.0%

Nativity, 2000**

Native-born	14,042
Foreign-born	945

Income & Poverty, 1999**

Median household income	$45,559
Median family income	$55,018
Per capita income	$26,472
Persons in poverty	7.2%

Households & Housing Units, 2000**

Total households	6,421
Family households	3,791
Average household size	2.30
Average family size	2.91
Total housing units	14,836
Owner-occupied	4,577
Median SF home value	$304,000
Renter-occupied	1,844
Median rent	$741

Labor & Employment

Civilian labor force, 2008††	11,232
Unemployment rate	4.1%
Civilian labor force, Dec. 2009††	10,004
Unemployment rate	10.0%
Employed persons 16 years and over by occupation, 2000**	
Managers & professionals	2,519
Service occupations	1,268
Sales & office occupations	1,997
Farming, fishing & forestry	51
Construction & maintenance	1,502
Production & transportation	592
Self-employed persons	1,745

Most demographic data is from the Census Bureau's Population Estimates Division
** 2000 Decennial Census
† University of Massachusetts, MISER
†† Massachusetts Department of Revenue

Essex County

Land area (square miles)	501
Water area (square miles)	328

Population

2000	723,419
2008 (estimate)	736,457
Male	355,892
Female	380,565
Persons per square mile, 2008	1470.0
2010 (projected)†	754,724
2020 (projected)†	787,032

Race & Hispanic Origin, 2008

Race	
White	658,863
Black/African American	39,188
American Indian/Alaska Native	2,523
Asian	22,509
Hawaiian Native/Pacific Islander	792
Two or more races	12,582
Hispanic origin	107,809

Age, 2008

Under 5 years	45,183
5 to 13 years	85,107
15 to 44 years	286,666
45 to 64 years	208,083
18 years and over	564,192
65 years and over	101,390
85 years and over	16,860
Median Age	39.7

Educational Attainment, 2008*

Population 25 years and over	496,487
High School graduates or higher	88.0%
Bachelor's degree or higher	36.5%
Graduate degree	14.0%

Nativity, 2008*

Native-born	629,840
Foreign-born	106,617

Income & Poverty, 2008*

Median household income	$65,562
Median family income	$83,348
Per capita family income	$34,354
Persons in poverty	9.2%

Households & Housing Units, 2008*

Total households	277,380
Family households	182,571
Average household size	2.59
Average family size	3.24
Total housing units	298,888
Owner-occupied	181,967
Median SF home value	$374,500
Renter-occupied	95,413
Median rent	$964

Labor & Employment

Civilian labor force, 2008††	379,407
Unemployment rate	5.6%
Civilian labor force, Dec. 2009††	382,541
Unemployment rate	9.6%
Employed persons 16 years and over by occupation, 2008*	
Managers & professionals	154,575
Service occupations	61,290
Sales & office occupations	94,734
Farming, fishing & forestry	1,111
Construction & maintenance	25,578
Production & transportation	39,746
Self-employed persons	25,844

Most demographic data is from the Census Bureau's Population Estimates Division
* 2008 American Community Survey
† University of Massachusetts, MISER
†† Massachusetts Department of Revenue

Franklin County

Land area (square miles)	702
Water area (square miles)	23

Population

2000	71,535
2008 (estimate)	71,735
Male	35,038
Female	36,697
Persons per square mile, 2008	102.2
2010 (projected)†	72,375
2020 (projected)†	73,806

Race & Hispanic Origin, 2008

Race	
White	68,342
Black/African American	924
American Indian/Alaska Native	241
Asian	1,074
Hawaiian Native/Pacific Islander	18
Two or more races	1,136
Hispanic origin	1,934

Age, 2008

Under 5 years	3,379
5 to 13 years	6,545
15 to 44 years	28,187
45 to 64 years	22,439
18 years and over	58,167
65 years and over	10,324
85 years and over	1,912
Median Age	41.9

Educational Attainment, 2008*

Population 25 years and over	51,836
High School graduates or higher	90.0%
Bachelor's degree or higher	30.8%
Graduate degree	13.9%

Nativity, 2008*

Native-born	69,363
Foreign-born	2,372

Income & Poverty, 2008*

Median household income	$52,667
Median family income	$66,133
Per capita family income	$28,169
Persons in poverty	13.1%

Households & Housing Units, 2008*

Total households	30,647
Family households	18,630
Average household size	2.31
Average family size	2.82
Total housing units	33,281
Owner-occupied	21,545
Median SF home value	$218,400
Renter-occupied	9,102
Median rent	$798

Labor & Employment

Civilian labor force, 2008††	39,091
Unemployment rate	4.9%
Civilian labor force, Dec. 2009††	39,239
Unemployment rate	8.6%
Employed persons 16 years and over by occupation, 2008*	
Managers & professionals	14,076
Service occupations	5,332
Sales & office occupations	9,533
Farming, fishing & forestry	228
Construction & maintenance	3,810
Production & transportation	5,997
Self-employed persons	4,051

Most demographic data is from the Census Bureau's Population Estimates Division
* 2008 American Community Survey
† University of Massachusetts, MISER
†† Massachusetts Department of Revenue

See Introduction for an explanation of all data sources.

Hampden County

Land area (square miles) 618
Water area (square miles)...............16

Population

2000 456,228
2008 (estimate)...................460,840
Male 222,075
Female 238,765
Persons per square mile, 2008........ 745.7
2010 (projected)† 453,909
2020 (projected)† 453,115

Race & Hispanic Origin, 2008

Race
White.........................399,827
Black/African American 43,287
American Indian/Alaska Native.... 1,629
Asian 8,079
Hawaiian Native/Pacific Islander.....887
Two or more races................ 7,131
Hispanic origin 87,344

Age, 2008

Under 5 years 28,495
5 to 13 years 53,037
15 to 44 years 188,188
45 to 64 years 120,289
18 years and over 351,969
65 years and over..................64,235
85 years and over.................. 11,069
Median Age 37.6

Educational Attainment, 2008*

Population 25 years and over....... 301,811
High School graduates or higher ...84.1%
Bachelor's degree or higher 23.4%
Graduate degree...................8.5%

Nativity, 2008*

Native-born 421,809
Foreign-born 39,031

Income & Poverty, 2008*

Median household income.........$48,583
Median family income $60,185
Per capita family income $24,789
Persons in poverty..................15.4%

Households & Housing Units, 2008*

Total households 173,375
Family households.............. 112,144
Average household size............... 2.53
Average family size 3.18
Total housing units 189,933
Owner-occupied 112,076
Median SF home value........$209,500
Renter-occupied................. 61,299
Median rent......................$722

Labor & Employment

Civilian labor force, 2008†† 225,598
Unemployment rate 6.4%
Civilian labor force, Dec. 2009†† ...225,734
Unemployment rate 10.6%
Employed persons 16 years and over by occupation, 2008*
Managers & professionals 68,093
Service occupations..............39,894
Sales & office occupations 55,036
Farming, fishing & forestry..........247
Construction & maintenance 15,748
Production & transportation 30,827
Self-employed persons 12,323

Most demographic data is from the Census Bureau's Population Estimates Division
* 2008 American Community Survey
† University of Massachusetts, MISER
†† Massachusetts Department of Revenue

Hampshire County

Land area (square miles) 529
Water area (square miles)...............16

Population

2000 152,251
2008 (estimate)...................154,983
Male 72,589
Female 82,394
Persons per square mile, 2008........ 293.0
2010 (projected)† 158,015
2020 (projected)† 163,233

Race & Hispanic Origin, 2008

Race
White.........................142,620
Black/African American 3,830
American Indian/Alaska Native......367
Asian 5,551
Hawaiian Native/Pacific Islander......74
Two or more races................2,541
Hispanic origin 6,753

Age, 2008

Under 5 years 6,080
5 to 13 years 11,987
15 to 44 years 75,178
45 to 64 years 40,791
18 years and over 130,158
65 years and over.................. 19,393
85 years and over.................. 3,359
Median Age 35.5

Educational Attainment, 2008*

Population 25 years and over........ 95,812
High School graduates or higher .. 92.9%
Bachelor's degree or higher 43.3%
Graduate degree..................19.3%

Nativity, 2008*

Native-born 143,662
Foreign-born 11,321

Income & Poverty, 2008*

Median household income......... $63,732
Median family income $81,575
Per capita family income $29,047
Persons in poverty..................10.5%

Households & Housing Units, 2008*

Total households 58,894
Family households............... 35,197
Average household size............... 2.31
Average family size 2.86
Total housing units 61,859
Owner-occupied 39,798
Median SF home value........$261,500
Renter-occupied................. 19,096
Median rent......................$869

Labor & Employment

Civilian labor force, 2008†† 88,778
Unemployment rate 4.3%
Civilian labor force, Dec. 2009†† 88,688
Unemployment rate 7.1%
Employed persons 16 years and over by occupation, 2008*
Managers & professionals 38,862
Service occupations.............. 15,517
Sales & office occupations 20,246
Farming, fishing & forestry..........218
Construction & maintenance 6,335
Production & transportation 6,852
Self-employed persons 7,414

Most demographic data is from the Census Bureau's Population Estimates Division
* 2008 American Community Survey
† University of Massachusetts, MISER
†† Massachusetts Department of Revenue

Middlesex County

Land area (square miles) 823
Water area (square miles)...............24

Population

2000 1,465,396
2008 (estimate)................. 1,482,478
Male 724,714
Female 757,764
Persons per square mile, 2008....... 1801.3
2010 (projected)† 1,474,917
2020 (projected)† 1,469,494

Race & Hispanic Origin, 2008

Race
White....................... 1,266,734
Black/African American 63,514
American Indian/Alaska Native.... 3,247
Asian 127,374
Hawaiian Native/Pacific Islander.....957
Two or more races...............20,652
Hispanic origin 85,336

Age, 2008

Under 5 years 88,109
5 to 13 years 159,331
15 to 44 years 619,852
45 to 64 years 406,020
18 years and over 1,161,722
65 years and over................. 191,243
85 years and over..................29,439
Median Age 38.9

Educational Attainment, 2008*

Population 25 years and over......1,017,253
High School graduates or higher ...91.6%
Bachelor's degree or higher 49.2%
Graduate degree...................24.1%

Nativity, 2008*

Native-born 1,214,590
Foreign-born 267,888

Income & Poverty, 2008*

Median household income.........$78,202
Median family income $98,642
Per capita family income $41,009
Persons in poverty.................. 8.2%

Households & Housing Units, 2008*

Total households 566,249
Family households.............. 359,719
Average household size............... 2.52
Average family size 3.14
Total housing units 599,065
Owner-occupied 365,324
Median SF home value........$423,700
Renter-occupied................200,925
Median rent.................. $1,196

Labor & Employment

Civilian labor force, 2008†† 827,598
Unemployment rate 4.3%
Civilian labor force, Dec. 2009†† ... 821,981
Unemployment rate 7.5%
Employed persons 16 years and over by occupation, 2008*
Managers & professionals 404,445
Service occupations............. 110,660
Sales & office occupations 184,053
Farming, fishing & forestry..........852
Construction & maintenance 45,071
Production & transportation 54,067
Self-employed persons 54,682

Most demographic data is from the Census Bureau's Population Estimates Division
* 2008 American Community Survey
† University of Massachusetts, MISER
†† Massachusetts Department of Revenue

©2010 Information Publications, Inc. All rights reserved. Photocopying prohibited. For additional copies, contact the publisher at www.informationpublications.com or (877)544-INFO (4636)

See Introduction for an explanation of all data sources.

Nantucket County

Land area (square miles)	48
Water area (square miles)	256
Population	
2000	9,520
2008 (estimate)	11,215
Male	5,747
Female	5,468
Persons per square mile, 2008	233.6
2010 (projected)†	11,939
2020 (projected)†	14,426
Race & Hispanic Origin, 2008	
Race	
White	9,850
Black/African American	1,122
American Indian/Alaska Native	3
Asian	129
Hawaiian Native/Pacific Islander	9
Two or more races	102
Hispanic origin	649
Age, 2008	
Under 5 years	822
5 to 13 years	1,092
15 to 44 years	5,055
45 to 64 years	2,965
18 years and over	8,866
65 years and over	1,164
85 years and over	142
Median Age	37.7
Educational Attainment, 2000**	
Population 25 years and over	6,976
High School graduates or higher	91.6%
Bachelor's degree or higher	38.4%
Graduate degree	11.4%
Nativity, 2000**	
Native-born	8,761
Foreign-born	759
Income & Poverty, 1999**	
Median household income	$55,522
Median family income	$66,786
Per capita income	$31,314
Persons in poverty	7.5%
Households & Housing Units, 2000**	
Total households	3,699
Family households	2,106
Average household size	2.37
Average family size	2.90
Total housing units	9,210
Owner-occupied	2,334
Median SF home value	$577,500
Renter-occupied	1,365
Median rent	$1,016
Labor & Employment	
Civilian labor force, 2008††	NA
Unemployment rate	NA
Civilian labor force, Dec. 2009††	NA
Unemployment rate	NA
Employed persons 16 years and over by occupation, 2000**	
Managers & professionals	1,638
Service occupations	919
Sales & office occupations	1,300
Farming, fishing & forestry	35
Construction & maintenance	1,214
Production & transportation	345
Self-employed persons	1,387

Most demographic data is from the Census Bureau's Population Estimates Division
** 2000 Decennial Census
† University of Massachusetts, MISER
†† Massachusetts Department of Revenue

Norfolk County

Land area (square miles)	400
Water area (square miles)	44
Population	
2000	650,308
2008 (estimate)	659,909
Male	317,751
Female	342,158
Persons per square mile, 2008	1649.8
2010 (projected)†	654,198
2020 (projected)†	652,440
Race & Hispanic Origin, 2008	
Race	
White	563,796
Black/African American	34,497
American Indian/Alaska Native	1,125
Asian	52,241
Hawaiian Native/Pacific Islander	268
Two or more races	7,982
Hispanic origin	18,453
Age, 2008	
Under 5 years	38,721
5 to 13 years	74,589
15 to 44 years	255,584
45 to 64 years	190,661
18 years and over	511,878
65 years and over	91,744
85 years and over	15,164
Median Age	40.5
Educational Attainment, 2008*	
Population 25 years and over	452,380
High School graduates or higher	93.7%
Bachelor's degree or higher	48.1%
Graduate degree	21.5%
Nativity, 2008*	
Native-born	561,339
Foreign-born	98,570
Income & Poverty, 2008*	
Median household income	$81,444
Median family income	$103,355
Per capita family income	$43,473
Persons in poverty	6.0%
Households & Housing Units, 2008*	
Total households	254,478
Family households	168,291
Average household size	2.52
Average family size	3.12
Total housing units	266,301
Owner-occupied	177,234
Median SF home value	$416,500
Renter-occupied	77,244
Median rent	$1,191
Labor & Employment	
Civilian labor force, 2008††	360,834
Unemployment rate	4.7%
Civilian labor force, Dec. 2009††	359,052
Unemployment rate	7.9%
Employed persons 16 years and over by occupation, 2008*	
Managers & professionals	174,300
Service occupations	41,462
Sales & office occupations	93,486
Farming, fishing & forestry	401
Construction & maintenance	21,706
Production & transportation	20,601
Self-employed persons	22,152

Most demographic data is from the Census Bureau's Population Estimates Division
* 2008 American Community Survey
† University of Massachusetts, MISER
†† Massachusetts Department of Revenue

Plymouth County

Land area (square miles)	661
Water area (square miles)	433
Population	
2000	472,822
2008 (estimate)	492,066
Male	240,454
Female	251,612
Persons per square mile, 2008	744.4
2010 (projected)†	496,053
2020 (projected)†	517,644
Race & Hispanic Origin, 2008	
Race	
White	437,657
Black/African American	40,000
American Indian/Alaska Native	1,339
Asian	6,260
Hawaiian Native/Pacific Islander	267
Two or more races	6,543
Hispanic origin	14,500
Age, 2008	
Under 5 years	29,679
5 to 13 years	58,892
15 to 44 years	192,033
45 to 64 years	141,733
18 years and over	374,224
65 years and over	62,848
85 years and over	9,012
Median Age	39.6
Educational Attainment, 2008*	
Population 25 years and over	329,017
High School graduates or higher	91.8%
Bachelor's degree or higher	31.3%
Graduate degree	11.3%
Nativity, 2008*	
Native-born	455,697
Foreign-born	36,369
Income & Poverty, 2008*	
Median household income	$73,335
Median family income	$85,946
Per capita family income	$32,972
Persons in poverty	6.6%
Households & Housing Units, 2008*	
Total households	176,433
Family households	122,646
Average household size	2.71
Average family size	3.25
Total housing units	193,350
Owner-occupied	136,915
Median SF home value	$358,400
Renter-occupied	39,518
Median rent	$1,071
Labor & Employment	
Civilian labor force, 2008††	262,741
Unemployment rate	5.6%
Civilian labor force, Dec. 2009††	263,399
Unemployment rate	9.5%
Employed persons 16 years and over by occupation, 2008*	
Managers & professionals	92,387
Service occupations	45,411
Sales & office occupations	72,703
Farming, fishing & forestry	656
Construction & maintenance	24,763
Production & transportation	24,119
Self-employed persons	17,872

Most demographic data is from the Census Bureau's Population Estimates Division
* 2008 American Community Survey
† University of Massachusetts, MISER
†† Massachusetts Department of Revenue

©2010 Information Publications, Inc. All rights reserved. Photocopying prohibited. For additional copies, contact the publisher at www.informationpublications.com or (877)544-INFO (4636)

See Introduction for an explanation of all data sources.

Suffolk County

Land area (square miles)	59
Water area (square miles)	62
Population	
2000	689,807
2008 (estimate)	732,684
Male	355,865
Female	376,819
Persons per square mile, 2008	12418.4
2010 (projected)†	731,041
2020 (projected)†	776,811
Race & Hispanic Origin, 2008	
Race	
White	489,036
Black/African American	170,998
American Indian/Alaska Native	3,565
Asian	55,691
Hawaiian Native/Pacific Islander	1,098
Two or more races	12,296
Hispanic origin	132,966
Age, 2008	
Under 5 years	45,831
5 to 13 years	67,757
15 to 44 years	377,818
45 to 64 years	155,620
18 years and over	588,187
65 years and over	78,499
85 years and over	13,115
Median Age	34.2
Educational Attainment, 2008*	
Population 25 years and over	484,928
High School graduates or higher	81.7%
Bachelor's degree or higher	37.5%
Graduate degree	17.3%
Nativity, 2008*	
Native-born	527,304
Foreign-born	205,380
Income & Poverty, 2008*	
Median household income	$51,208
Median family income	$59,629
Per capita family income	$31,464
Persons in poverty	17.8%
Households & Housing Units, 2008*	
Total households	274,043
Family households	135,138
Average household size	2.53
Average family size	3.46
Total housing units	299,036
Owner-occupied	106,264
Median SF home value	$384,800
Renter-occupied	167,779
Median rent	$1,132
Labor & Employment	
Civilian labor force, 2008††	370,174
Unemployment rate	5.2%
Civilian labor force, Dec. 2009††	368,930
Unemployment rate	8.5%
Employed persons 16 years and over by occupation, 2008*	
Managers & professionals	158,619
Service occupations	84,287
Sales & office occupations	91,974
Farming, fishing & forestry	123
Construction & maintenance	21,006
Production & transportation	29,899
Self-employed persons	17,283

Most demographic data is from the Census Bureau's Population Estimates Division
* 2008 American Community Survey
† University of Massachusetts, MISER
†† Massachusetts Department of Revenue

Worcester County

Land area (square miles)	1,513
Water area (square miles)	66
Population	
2000	750,963
2008 (estimate)	783,806
Male	385,009
Female	398,797
Persons per square mile, 2008	518.0
2010 (projected)†	793,336
2020 (projected)†	843,534
Race & Hispanic Origin, 2008	
Race	
White	712,833
Black/African American	29,518
American Indian/Alaska Native	2,368
Asian	28,442
Hawaiian Native/Pacific Islander	668
Two or more races	9,977
Hispanic origin	65,357
Age, 2008	
Under 5 years	48,620
5 to 13 years	90,796
15 to 44 years	324,274
45 to 64 years	212,566
18 years and over	598,976
65 years and over	96,504
85 years and over	16,431
Median Age	38.1
Educational Attainment, 2008*	
Population 25 years and over	522,491
High School graduates or higher	89.0%
Bachelor's degree or higher	33.1%
Graduate degree	12.7%
Nativity, 2008*	
Native-born	698,371
Foreign-born	85,435
Income & Poverty, 2008*	
Median household income	$66,878
Median family income	$79,737
Per capita family income	$31,068
Persons in poverty	8.1%
Households & Housing Units, 2008*	
Total households	292,767
Family households	197,370
Average household size	2.58
Average family size	3.14
Total housing units	317,126
Owner-occupied	199,272
Median SF home value	$282,800
Renter-occupied	93,495
Median rent	$860
Labor & Employment	
Civilian labor force, 2008††	404,241
Unemployment rate	5.8%
Civilian labor force, Dec. 2009††	402,898
Unemployment rate	9.9%
Employed persons 16 years and over by occupation, 2008*	
Managers & professionals	164,956
Service occupations	65,072
Sales & office occupations	98,070
Farming, fishing & forestry	690
Construction & maintenance	33,379
Production & transportation	47,208
Self-employed persons	21,409

Most demographic data is from the Census Bureau's Population Estimates Division
* 2008 American Community Survey
† University of Massachusetts, MISER
†† Massachusetts Department of Revenue

©2010 Information Publications, Inc. All rights reserved. Photocopying prohibited. For additional copies, contact the publisher at www.informationpublications.com or (877)544-INFO (4636)

See Introduction for an explanation of all data sources.

Note: The 2008 American Community Survey (ACS) produced 1-year estimates of demographic data for cities and counties with populations of at least 65,000 – in Massachusetts' case, 15 out of 351 municipalities. The ACS also produces 3-year averages for places with populations over 20,000; these can be found in Appendix E.

Boston
Suffolk County

Population	
Total	613,411
Male	296,410
Female	317,001
Living in group quarters	37,897
percent of total	6.2%
Race & Hispanic Origin	
Race	
White	342,468
Black/African American	148,994
American Indian/Alaskan Native	2,750
Asian	50,797
Hawaiian Native/Pacific Islander	48
Other race	45,496
Two or more races	22,858
Hispanic origin, total	99,208
Mexican	5,901
Puerto Rican	30,415
Cuban	2,158
Other Hispanic	60,734
Age & Nativity	
Under 5 years	39,323
18 years and over	496,109
21 years and over	451,848
65 years and over	62,828
85 years and over	10,605
Median Age	33.3
Native-born	448,265
Foreign-born	165,146
Educational Attainment	
Population 25 years and over	402,706
Less than 9th grade	9.0%
High School grad or higher	83.2%
Bachelor's degree or higher	42.1%
Graduate degree	19.8%
Households	
Total households	232,969
With persons under 18	58,303
With persons over 65	43,899
Family households	110,446
Single-person households	91,905
Persons per household	2.47
Persons per family	3.40
Income & Poverty	
Per capita income	$32,714
Median household income	$51,688
Median family income	$60,543
Persons in poverty	18.7%
H'holds receiving public assistance	7,993
H'holds receiving social security	48,184
Labor & Employment	
Total civilian labor force	354,205
Unemployment rate	7.7%
Employed persons 16 years and over, by occupation	
Managers & professionals	145,868
Service occupations	70,016
Sales & office occupations	75,819
Farming, fishing & forestry	0
Construction & maintenance	14,794
Production & transportation	20,532
Self-employed persons	13,725
Housing Units	
Total	254,403
Single-family units	31,400
Multiple-family units	222,868
Mobile home units	135
Owner-occupied units	85,849
Renter-occupied units	147,120
Median SF home value	$400,100
Median rent	$1,130

Brockton
Plymouth County

Population	
Total	92,492
Male	45,040
Female	47,452
Living in group quarters	2,714
percent of total	2.9%
Race & Hispanic Origin	
Race	
White	51,122
Black/African American	28,540
American Indian/Alaskan Native	210
Asian	1,397
Hawaiian Native/Pacific Islander	0
Other race	7,436
Two or more races	3,787
Hispanic origin, total	9,385
Mexican	935
Puerto Rican	4,146
Cuban	302
Other Hispanic	4,002
Age & Nativity	
Under 5 years	7,441
18 years and over	69,293
21 years and over	66,029
65 years and over	10,614
85 years and over	1,736
Median Age	32.9
Native-born	71,302
Foreign-born	21,190
Educational Attainment	
Population 25 years and over	59,890
Less than 9th grade	6.5%
High School grad or higher	81.8%
Bachelor's degree or higher	16.2%
Graduate degree	3.0%
Households	
Total households	32,723
With persons under 18	14,332
With persons over 65	6,758
Family households	22,749
Single-person households	7,419
Persons per household	2.74
Persons per family	3.12
Income & Poverty	
Per capita income	$21,918
Median household income	$52,145
Median family income	$53,926
Persons in poverty	14.0%
H'holds receiving public assistance	1,923
H'holds receiving social security	8,908
Labor & Employment	
Total civilian labor force	52,284
Unemployment rate	7.3%
Employed persons 16 years and over, by occupation	
Managers & professionals	10,741
Service occupations	12,294
Sales & office occupations	14,255
Farming, fishing & forestry	0
Construction & maintenance	3,781
Production & transportation	7,421
Self-employed persons	2,092
Housing Units	
Total	36,130
Single-family units	17,548
Multiple-family units	18,582
Mobile home units	0
Owner-occupied units	18,827
Renter-occupied units	13,896
Median SF home value	$265,900
Median rent	$954

Brookline
Norfolk County

Population	
Total	65,611
Male	30,575
Female	35,036
Living in group quarters	NA
percent of total	NA
Race & Hispanic Origin	
Race	
White	49,156
Black/African American	1,566
American Indian/Alaskan Native	470
Asian	11,405
Hawaiian Native/Pacific Islander	0
Other race	1,291
Two or more races	1,723
Hispanic origin, total	3,189
Mexican	288
Puerto Rican	561
Cuban	117
Other Hispanic	2,223
Age & Nativity	
Under 5 years	3,750
18 years and over	53,154
21 years and over	51,047
65 years and over	7,814
85 years and over	1,337
Median Age	34.6
Native-born	46,321
Foreign-born	19,290
Educational Attainment	
Population 25 years and over	44,079
Less than 9th grade	1.9%
High School grad or higher	97.0%
Bachelor's degree or higher	82.1%
Graduate degree	51.5%
Households	
Total households	26,985
With persons under 18	8,416
With persons over 65	5,879
Family households	14,785
Single-person households	8,668
Persons per household	2.38
Persons per family	2.94
Income & Poverty	
Per capita income	$61,000
Median household income	$98,324
Median family income	$131,058
Persons in poverty	11.4%
H'holds receiving public assistance	103
H'holds receiving social security	5,031
Labor & Employment	
Total civilian labor force	38,981
Unemployment rate	2.8%
Employed persons 16 years and over, by occupation	
Managers & professionals	28,981
Service occupations	2,229
Sales & office occupations	6,067
Farming, fishing & forestry	0
Construction & maintenance	449
Production & transportation	181
Self-employed persons	2,761
Housing Units	
Total	28,286
Single-family units	5,960
Multiple-family units	22,326
Mobile home units	0
Owner-occupied units	13,407
Renter-occupied units	13,578
Median SF home value	$651,700
Median rent	$1,707

©2010 Information Publications, Inc. All rights reserved. Photocopying prohibited. For additional copies, contact the publisher at www.informationpublications.com or (877)544-INFO (4636)

Note: The 2008 American Community Survey (ACS) produced 1-year estimates of demographic data for cities and counties with populations of at least 65,000 – in Massachusetts' case, 15 out of 351 municipalities. The ACS also produces 3-year averages for places with populations over 20,000; these can be found in Appendix E.

Cambridge

Middlesex County

Population	
Total	96,695
Male	49,148
Female	47,547
Living in group quarters	10,615
percent of total	11.0%
Race & Hispanic Origin	
Race	
White	70,335
Black/African American	8,803
American Indian/Alaskan Native	420
Asian	10,112
Hawaiian Native/Pacific Islander	0
Other race	3,807
Two or more races	3,218
Hispanic origin, total	7,638
Mexican	1,415
Puerto Rican	1,601
Cuban	385
Other Hispanic	4,237
Age & Nativity	
Under 5 years	4,389
18 years and over	83,868
21 years and over	75,916
65 years and over	9,198
85 years and over	2,103
Median Age	30.8
Native-born	72,912
Foreign-born	23,783
Educational Attainment	
Population 25 years and over	64,732
Less than 9th grade	2.7%
High School grad or higher	95.2%
Bachelor's degree or higher	74.7%
Graduate degree	44.2%
Households	
Total households	41,800
With persons under 18	8,079
With persons over 65	7,358
Family households	16,654
Single-person households	17,972
Persons per household	2.06
Persons per family	2.76
Income & Poverty	
Per capita income	$47,938
Median household income	$71,140
Median family income	$94,228
Persons in poverty	13.2%
H'holds receiving public assistance	823
H'holds receiving social security	7,322
Labor & Employment	
Total civilian labor force	56,219
Unemployment rate	4.2%
Employed persons 16 years and over, by occupation	
Managers & professionals	37,959
Service occupations	4,855
Sales & office occupations	9,341
Farming, fishing & forestry	0
Construction & maintenance	340
Production & transportation	1,358
Self-employed persons	2,939
Housing Units	
Total	45,148
Single-family units	4,228
Multiple-family units	40,920
Mobile home units	0
Owner-occupied units	15,953
Renter-occupied units	25,847
Median SF home value	$579,700
Median rent	$1,471

Fall River

Bristol County

Population	
Total	93,066
Male	43,674
Female	49,392
Living in group quarters	2,503
percent of total	2.7%
Race & Hispanic Origin	
Race	
White	83,847
Black/African American	2,226
American Indian/Alaskan Native	140
Asian	3,282
Hawaiian Native/Pacific Islander	0
Other race	1,558
Two or more races	2,013
Hispanic origin, total	3,722
Mexican	NA
Puerto Rican	NA
Cuban	NA
Other Hispanic	NA
Age & Nativity	
Under 5 years	6,007
18 years and over	71,275
21 years and over	67,941
65 years and over	15,004
85 years and over	3,197
Median Age	36.6
Native-born	77,197
Foreign-born	15,869
Educational Attainment	
Population 25 years and over	63,697
Less than 9th grade	16.0%
High School grad or higher	67.2%
Bachelor's degree or higher	14.2%
Graduate degree	4.3%
Households	
Total households	37,024
With persons under 18	11,823
With persons over 65	9,503
Family households	21,924
Single-person households	12,711
Persons per household	2.45
Persons per family	3.21
Income & Poverty	
Per capita income	$19,663
Median household income	$35,161
Median family income	$44,708
Persons in poverty	19.6%
H'holds receiving public assistance	1,790
H'holds receiving social security	12,295
Labor & Employment	
Total civilian labor force	45,606
Unemployment rate	10.3%
Employed persons 16 years and over, by occupation	
Managers & professionals	9,836
Service occupations	10,001
Sales & office occupations	10,594
Farming, fishing & forestry	0
Construction & maintenance	4,626
Production & transportation	5,861
Self-employed persons	2,174
Housing Units	
Total	42,961
Single-family units	9,973
Multiple-family units	32,988
Mobile home units	0
Owner-occupied units	13,859
Renter-occupied units	23,165
Median SF home value	$272,400
Median rent	$656

Framingham

Middlesex County

Population	
Total	69,165
Male	33,405
Female	35,760
Living in group quarters	4,253
percent of total	6.1%
Race & Hispanic Origin	
Race	
White	53,131
Black/African American	2,520
American Indian/Alaskan Native	160
Asian	4,955
Hawaiian Native/Pacific Islander	0
Other race	6,865
Two or more races	1,534
Hispanic origin, total	10,370
Mexican	162
Puerto Rican	2,465
Cuban	290
Other Hispanic	7,453
Age & Nativity	
Under 5 years	4,325
18 years and over	55,147
21 years and over	51,453
65 years and over	9,017
85 years and over	1,386
Median Age	38.1
Native-born	51,438
Foreign-born	17,727
Educational Attainment	
Population 25 years and over	46,595
Less than 9th grade	4.5%
High School grad or higher	90.7%
Bachelor's degree or higher	41.6%
Graduate degree	19.5%
Households	
Total households	26,265
With persons under 18	7,954
With persons over 65	6,088
Family households	17,282
Single-person households	7,404
Persons per household	2.47
Persons per family	3.08
Income & Poverty	
Per capita income	$34,648
Median household income	$70,613
Median family income	$85,191
Persons in poverty	8.6%
H'holds receiving public assistance	725
H'holds receiving social security	6,147
Labor & Employment	
Total civilian labor force	42,384
Unemployment rate	3.6%
Employed persons 16 years and over, by occupation	
Managers & professionals	16,499
Service occupations	6,955
Sales & office occupations	11,351
Farming, fishing & forestry	243
Construction & maintenance	2,826
Production & transportation	2,973
Self-employed persons	3,173
Housing Units	
Total	27,316
Single-family units	13,850
Multiple-family units	13,466
Mobile home units	0
Owner-occupied units	15,787
Renter-occupied units	10,478
Median SF home value	$383,200
Median rent	$1,101

©2010 Information Publications, Inc. All rights reserved. Photocopying prohibited. For additional copies, contact the publisher at www.informationpublications.com or (877)544-INFO (4636)

Note: The 2008 American Community Survey (ACS) produced 1-year estimates of demographic data for cities and counties with populations of at least 65,000 – in Massachusetts' case, 15 out of 351 municipalities. The ACS also produces 3-year averages for places with populations over 20,000; these can be found in Appendix E.

Lawrence

Essex County

Population

Total	72,388
Male	34,985
Female	37,403
Living in group quarters	NA
percent of total	NA

Race & Hispanic Origin

Race	
White	25,851
Black/African American	2,208
American Indian/Alaskan Native	148
Asian	720
Hawaiian Native/Pacific Islander	0
Other race	41,662
Two or more races	1,799
Hispanic origin, total	NA
Mexican	463
Puerto Rican	14,397
Cuban	238
Other Hispanic	34,104

Age & Nativity

Under 5 years	7,839
18 years and over	50,100
21 years and over	46,908
65 years and over	5,425
85 years and over	1,150
Median Age	29.5
Native-born	49,029
Foreign-born	23,359

Educational Attainment

Population 25 years and over	41,619
Less than 9th grade	19.3%
High School grad or higher	66.4%
Bachelor's degree or higher	12.6%
Graduate degree	3.4%

Households

Total households	25,188
With persons under 18	12,127
With persons over 65	3,757
Family households	17,527
Single-person households	6,240
Persons per household	2.85
Persons per family	3.39

Income & Poverty

Per capita income	$16,840
Median household income	$33,684
Median family income	$41,035
Persons in poverty	23.6%
H'holds receiving public assistance	1,709
H'holds receiving social security	4,767

Labor & Employment

Total civilian labor force	35,508
Unemployment rate	7.5%
Employed persons 16 years and over, by occupation	
Managers & professionals	6,619
Service occupations	8,042
Sales & office occupations	7,069
Farming, fishing & forestry	0
Construction & maintenance	2,467
Production & transportation	8,635
Self-employed persons	1,052

Housing Units

Total	27,066
Single-family units	5,240
Multiple-family units	21,826
Mobile home units	0
Owner-occupied units	9,128
Renter-occupied units	16,060
Median SF home value	$255,700
Median rent	$930

Lowell

Middlesex County

Population

Total	97,423
Male	47,928
Female	49,495
Living in group quarters	4,220
percent of total	4.3%

Race & Hispanic Origin

Race	
White	60,212
Black/African American	7,927
American Indian/Alaskan Native	382
Asian	21,715
Hawaiian Native/Pacific Islander	0
Other race	5,843
Two or more races	1,344
Hispanic origin, total	12,148
Mexican	33
Puerto Rican	8,518
Cuban	0
Other Hispanic	3,597

Age & Nativity

Under 5 years	7,398
18 years and over	75,126
21 years and over	69,168
65 years and over	11,139
85 years and over	1,781
Median Age	35.1
Native-born	73,331
Foreign-born	24,092

Educational Attainment

Population 25 years and over	63,104
Less than 9th grade	10.3%
High School grad or higher	79.3%
Bachelor's degree or higher	21.3%
Graduate degree	8.2%

Households

Total households	35,246
With persons under 18	12,188
With persons over 65	7,289
Family households	21,850
Single-person households	10,402
Persons per household	2.64
Persons per family	3.37

Income & Poverty

Per capita income	$23,268
Median household income	$53,250
Median family income	$63,865
Persons in poverty	16.1%
H'holds receiving public assistance	1,290
H'holds receiving social security	8,824

Labor & Employment

Total civilian labor force	52,539
Unemployment rate	6.1%
Employed persons 16 years and over, by occupation	
Managers & professionals	14,827
Service occupations	10,737
Sales & office occupations	10,370
Farming, fishing & forestry	126
Construction & maintenance	3,281
Production & transportation	9,971
Self-employed persons	1,732

Housing Units

Total	39,599
Single-family units	13,163
Multiple-family units	26,436
Mobile home units	0
Owner-occupied units	18,269
Renter-occupied units	16,977
Median SF home value	$255,400
Median rent	$864

Lynn

Essex County

Population

Total	86,466
Male	41,360
Female	45,106
Living in group quarters	NA
percent of total	NA

Race & Hispanic Origin

Race	
White	59,279
Black/African American	10,533
American Indian/Alaskan Native	89
Asian	5,079
Hawaiian Native/Pacific Islander	0
Other race	7,078
Two or more races	4,408
Hispanic origin, total	21,646
Mexican	1,942
Puerto Rican	2,504
Cuban	0
Other Hispanic	17,200

Age & Nativity

Under 5 years	6,207
18 years and over	66,056
21 years and over	62,433
65 years and over	10,535
85 years and over	1,416
Median Age	35.4
Native-born	64,101
Foreign-born	22,365

Educational Attainment

Population 25 years and over	56,715
Less than 9th grade	13.9%
High School grad or higher	75.0%
Bachelor's degree or higher	17.6%
Graduate degree	7.2%

Households

Total households	33,098
With persons under 18	11,511
With persons over 65	7,955
Family households	19,751
Single-person households	11,249
Persons per household	2.55
Persons per family	3.28

Income & Poverty

Per capita income	$22,973
Median household income	$43,216
Median family income	$56,150
Persons in poverty	17.6%
H'holds receiving public assistance	1,683
H'holds receiving social security	10,353

Labor & Employment

Total civilian labor force	44,480
Unemployment rate	9.2%
Employed persons 16 years and over, by occupation	
Managers & professionals	9,921
Service occupations	10,296
Sales & office occupations	11,011
Farming, fishing & forestry	0
Construction & maintenance	3,983
Production & transportation	5,179
Self-employed persons	2,073

Housing Units

Total	35,914
Single-family units	11,934
Multiple-family units	23,980
Mobile home units	0
Owner-occupied units	15,591
Renter-occupied units	17,507
Median SF home value	$290,500
Median rent	$872

©2010 Information Publications, Inc. All rights reserved. Photocopying prohibited. For additional copies, contact the publisher at www.informationpublications.com or (877)544-INFO (4636)

Note: The 2008 American Community Survey (ACS) produced 1-year estimates of demographic data for cities and counties with populations of at least 65,000 – in Massachusetts' case, 15 out of 351 municipalities. The ACS also produces 3-year averages for places with populations over 20,000; these can be found in Appendix E.

New Bedford

Bristol County

Population	
Total	89,396
Male	43,882
Female	45,514
Living in group quarters	3,504
percent of total	3.9%
Race & Hispanic Origin	
Race	
White	74,232
Black/African American	5,667
American Indian/Alaskan Native	547
Asian	544
Hawaiian Native/Pacific Islander	0
Other race	4,755
Two or more races	3,651
Hispanic origin, total	14,302
Mexican	NA
Puerto Rican	NA
Cuban	NA
Other Hispanic	NA
Age & Nativity	
Under 5 years	6,106
18 years and over	69,066
21 years and over	66,445
65 years and over	13,441
85 years and over	2,597
Median Age	36.7
Native-born	73,497
Foreign-born	15,899
Educational Attainment	
Population 25 years and over	61,191
Less than 9th grade	17.5%
High School grad or higher	65.2%
Bachelor's degree or higher	12.8%
Graduate degree	4.5%
Households	
Total households	36,421
With persons under 18	13,033
With persons over 65	8,640
Family households	21,116
Single-person households	12,360
Persons per household	2.36
Persons per family	3.02
Income & Poverty	
Per capita income	$21,760
Median household income	$38,350
Median family income	$46,392
Persons in poverty	23.0%
H'holds receiving public assistance	3,261
H'holds receiving social security	10,062
Labor & Employment	
Total civilian labor force	44,546
Unemployment rate	6.7%
Employed persons 16 years and over, by occupation	
Managers & professionals	9,896
Service occupations	9,164
Sales & office occupations	8,884
Farming, fishing & forestry	267
Construction & maintenance	5,678
Production & transportation	7,652
Self-employed persons	761
Housing Units	
Total	40,455
Single-family units	11,806
Multiple-family units	28,590
Mobile home units	59
Owner-occupied units	15,627
Renter-occupied units	20,794
Median SF home value	$250,200
Median rent	$743

Newton

Middlesex County

Population	
Total	91,342
Male	42,736
Female	48,606
Living in group quarters	7,798
percent of total	8.5%
Race & Hispanic Origin	
Race	
White	78,043
Black/African American	714
American Indian/Alaskan Native	0
Asian	11,202
Hawaiian Native/Pacific Islander	69
Other race	440
Two or more races	874
Hispanic origin, total	3,370
Mexican	NA
Puerto Rican	NA
Cuban	NA
Other Hispanic	NA
Age & Nativity	
Under 5 years	5,523
18 years and over	71,213
21 years and over	64,799
65 years and over	12,150
85 years and over	2,452
Median Age	38.3
Native-born	70,709
Foreign-born	20,633
Educational Attainment	
Population 25 years and over	59,110
Less than 9th grade	2.1%
High School grad or higher	95.9%
Bachelor's degree or higher	72.0%
Graduate degree	42.8%
Households	
Total households	32,586
With persons under 18	11,100
With persons over 65	8,144
Family households	22,793
Single-person households	7,328
Persons per household	2.56
Persons per family	3.01
Income & Poverty	
Per capita income	$56,285
Median household income	$104,493
Median family income	$132,822
Persons in poverty	8.3%
H'holds receiving public assistance	114
H'holds receiving social security	7,324
Labor & Employment	
Total civilian labor force	46,108
Unemployment rate	2.0%
Employed persons 16 years and over, by occupation	
Managers & professionals	32,110
Service occupations	3,499
Sales & office occupations	5,897
Farming, fishing & forestry	0
Construction & maintenance	816
Production & transportation	2,842
Self-employed persons	4,260
Housing Units	
Total	33,744
Single-family units	17,668
Multiple-family units	16,076
Mobile home units	0
Owner-occupied units	22,488
Renter-occupied units	10,098
Median SF home value	$696,300
Median rent	$1,612

Quincy

Norfolk County

Population	
Total	87,859
Male	41,587
Female	46,272
Living in group quarters	NA
percent of total	NA
Race & Hispanic Origin	
Race	
White	64,454
Black/African American	2,787
American Indian/Alaskan Native	60
Asian	18,093
Hawaiian Native/Pacific Islander	0
Other race	1,464
Two or more races	1,001
Hispanic origin, total	3,406
Mexican	309
Puerto Rican	1,868
Cuban	0
Other Hispanic	1,229
Age & Nativity	
Under 5 years	3,289
18 years and over	75,418
21 years and over	72,035
65 years and over	13,288
85 years and over	1,507
Median Age	40.8
Native-born	66,295
Foreign-born	21,564
Educational Attainment	
Population 25 years and over	65,635
Less than 9th grade	4.3%
High School grad or higher	88.4%
Bachelor's degree or higher	35.9%
Graduate degree	12.5%
Households	
Total households	40,525
With persons under 18	8,215
With persons over 65	10,126
Family households	20,967
Single-person households	15,360
Persons per household	2.15
Persons per family	2.89
Income & Poverty	
Per capita income	$34,041
Median household income	$61,158
Median family income	$75,468
Persons in poverty	7.6%
H'holds receiving public assistance	1,118
H'holds receiving social security	11,233
Labor & Employment	
Total civilian labor force	54,990
Unemployment rate	6.5%
Employed persons 16 years and over, by occupation	
Managers & professionals	20,047
Service occupations	8,609
Sales & office occupations	14,469
Farming, fishing & forestry	0
Construction & maintenance	3,408
Production & transportation	4,905
Self-employed persons	2,532
Housing Units	
Total	43,790
Single-family units	14,653
Multiple-family units	29,074
Mobile home units	63
Owner-occupied units	20,175
Renter-occupied units	20,350
Median SF home value	$363,700
Median rent	$1,111

©2010 Information Publications, Inc. All rights reserved. Photocopying prohibited. For additional copies, contact the publisher at www.informationpublications.com or (877)544-INFO (4636)

Note: The 2008 American Community Survey (ACS) produced 1-year estimates of demographic data for cities and counties with populations of at least 65,000 – in Massachusetts' case, 15 out of 351 municipalities. The ACS also produces 3-year averages for places with populations over 20,000; these can be found in Appendix E.

Somerville
Middlesex County

Population

Total	76,430
Male	36,819
Female	39,611
Living in group quarters	3,140
percent of total	4.1%

Race & Hispanic Origin

Race	
White	57,387
Black/African American	3,023
American Indian/Alaskan Native	180
Asian	9,350
Hawaiian Native/Pacific Islander	0
Other race	5,169
Two or more races	1,321
Hispanic origin, total	5,111
Mexican	397
Puerto Rican	622
Cuban	183
Other Hispanic	3,909

Age & Nativity

Under 5 years	3,968
18 years and over	67,122
21 years and over	61,494
65 years and over	6,604
85 years and over	1,291
Median Age	31.1
Native-born	57,207
Foreign-born	19,223

Educational Attainment

Population 25 years and over	53,061
Less than 9th grade	5.3%
High School grad or higher	90.5%
Bachelor's degree or higher	51.9%
Graduate degree	24.8%

Households

Total households	31,070
With persons under 18	6,021
With persons over 65	4,883
Family households	14,179
Single-person households	10,378
Persons per household	2.36
Persons per family	3.04

Income & Poverty

Per capita income	$31,737
Median household income	$58,466
Median family income	$71,341
Persons in poverty	15.8%
H'holds receiving public assistance	317
H'holds receiving social security	5,194

Labor & Employment

Total civilian labor force	52,506
Unemployment rate	6.8%
Employed persons 16 years and over, by occupation	
Managers & professionals	23,500
Service occupations	10,167
Sales & office occupations	10,811
Farming, fishing & forestry	0
Construction & maintenance	2,725
Production & transportation	1,740
Self-employed persons	3,946

Housing Units

Total	32,621
Single-family units	3,568
Multiple-family units	29,053
Mobile home units	0
Owner-occupied units	10,607
Renter-occupied units	20,463
Median SF home value	$448,400
Median rent	$1,285

Springfield
Hampden County

Population

Total	153,386
Male	73,343
Female	80,043
Living in group quarters	10,664
percent of total	7.0%

Race & Hispanic Origin

Race	
White	78,494
Black/African American	31,973
American Indian/Alaskan Native	272
Asian	2,838
Hawaiian Native/Pacific Islander	103
Other race	36,047
Two or more races	3,659
Hispanic origin, total	55,733
Mexican	2,547
Puerto Rican	45,900
Cuban	626
Other Hispanic	6,660

Age & Nativity

Under 5 years	12,185
18 years and over	112,023
21 years and over	102,458
65 years and over	16,429
85 years and over	2,537
Median Age	31.6
Native-born	139,802
Foreign-born	13,584

Educational Attainment

Population 25 years and over	92,554
Less than 9th grade	8.9%
High School grad or higher	77.5%
Bachelor's degree or higher	16.1%
Graduate degree	5.8%

Households

Total households	54,687
With persons under 18	20,255
With persons over 65	12,245
Family households	34,789
Single-person households	16,705
Persons per household	2.61
Persons per family	3.26

Income & Poverty

Per capita income	$18,187
Median household income	$36,652
Median family income	$41,985
Persons in poverty	27.0%
H'holds receiving public assistance	5,195
H'holds receiving social security	14,999

Labor & Employment

Total civilian labor force	71,672
Unemployment rate	15.6%
Employed persons 16 years and over, by occupation	
Managers & professionals	16,071
Service occupations	16,172
Sales & office occupations	14,529
Farming, fishing & forestry	209
Construction & maintenance	3,867
Production & transportation	9,662
Self-employed persons	2,591

Housing Units

Total	63,284
Single-family units	29,740
Multiple-family units	33,347
Mobile home units	197
Owner-occupied units	29,329
Renter-occupied units	25,358
Median SF home value	$161,300
Median rent	$770

Worcester
Worcester County

Population

Total	162,953
Male	80,970
Female	81,983
Living in group quarters	12,289
percent of total	7.5%

Race & Hispanic Origin

Race	
White	128,861
Black/African American	16,376
American Indian/Alaskan Native	614
Asian	7,575
Hawaiian Native/Pacific Islander	0
Other race	5,290
Two or more races	4,237
Hispanic origin, total	33,902
Mexican	2,811
Puerto Rican	18,877
Cuban	346
Other Hispanic	11,868

Age & Nativity

Under 5 years	9,372
18 years and over	130,511
21 years and over	116,936
65 years and over	20,588
85 years and over	4,661
Median Age	35.2
Native-born	126,861
Foreign-born	36,092

Educational Attainment

Population 25 years and over	105,446
Less than 9th grade	7.2%
High School grad or higher	84.9%
Bachelor's degree or higher	27.9%
Graduate degree	11.2%

Households

Total households	65,329
With persons under 18	19,511
With persons over 65	13,815
Family households	36,686
Single-person households	23,213
Persons per household	2.31
Persons per family	3.01

Income & Poverty

Per capita income	$24,535
Median household income	$44,890
Median family income	$52,202
Persons in poverty	14.8%
H'holds receiving public assistance	3,280
H'holds receiving social security	16,405

Labor & Employment

Total civilian labor force	86,349
Unemployment rate	7.9%
Employed persons 16 years and over, by occupation	
Managers & professionals	26,673
Service occupations	16,253
Sales & office occupations	19,599
Farming, fishing & forestry	130
Construction & maintenance	5,315
Production & transportation	11,570
Self-employed persons	2,344

Housing Units

Total	73,721
Single-family units	23,224
Multiple-family units	50,232
Mobile home units	144
Owner-occupied units	29,486
Renter-occupied units	35,843
Median SF home value	$244,200
Median rent	$842

©2010 Information Publications, Inc. All rights reserved. Photocopying prohibited. For additional copies, contact the publisher at www.informationpublications.com or (877)544-INFO (4636)

Note: The 2008 American Community Survey (ACS) produced 3-year estimates of demographic data for cities and counties with populations of at least 20,000 – in Massachusetts' case, 67 out of 351 municipalities. The ACS also produces 1-year averages for places with populations over 65,000; these can be found in Appendix D.

Agawam
Hampden County

Population
Total....28,560
Male....13,917
Female....14,643
Living in group quarters....668
percent of total....2.3%

Race & Hispanic Origin
Race
White....27,615
Black/African American....375
American Indian/Alaskan Native....0
Asian....242
Hawaiian Native/Pacific Islander....0
Other race....190
Two or more races....138
Hispanic origin, total....808
Mexican....NA
Puerto Rican....NA
Cuban....NA
Other Hispanic....NA

Age & Nativity
Under 5 years....1,309
18 years and over....22,801
21 years and over....21,646
65 years and over....4,863
85 years and over....1,352
Median Age....42.8
Native-born....26,528
Foreign-born....2,032

Educational Attainment
Population 25 years and over....20,301
Less than 9th grade....1.5%
High School grad or higher....94.1%
Bachelor's degree or higher....25.6%
Graduate degree....7.9%

Households
Total households....11,317
With persons under 18....3,343
With persons over 65....3,100
Family households....7,376
Single-person households....3,293
Persons per household....2.46
Persons per family....3.06

Income & Poverty
Per capita income....$31,021
Median household income....$64,188
Median family income....$77,223
Persons in poverty....5.4%
H'holds receiving public assistance....105
H'holds receiving social security....3,567

Labor & Employment
Total civilian labor force....16,127
Unemployment rate....3.8%
Employed persons 16 years and over, by occupation
Managers & professionals....5,364
Service occupations....2,347
Sales & office occupations....4,170
Farming, fishing & forestry....0
Construction & maintenance....1,441
Production & transportation....2,189
Self-employed persons....1,233

Housing Units
Total....11,659
Single-family units....7,840
Multiple-family units....3,795
Mobile home units....24
Owner-occupied units....8,740
Renter-occupied units....2,577
Median SF home value....$227,900
Median rent....$777

Arlington
Middlesex County

Population
Total....42,526
Male....19,640
Female....22,886
Living in group quarters....NA
percent of total....NA

Race & Hispanic Origin
Race
White....36,923
Black/African American....821
American Indian/Alaskan Native....0
Asian....3,749
Hawaiian Native/Pacific Islander....0
Other race....106
Two or more races....927
Hispanic origin, total....975
Mexican....NA
Puerto Rican....NA
Cuban....NA
Other Hispanic....NA

Age & Nativity
Under 5 years....2,639
18 years and over....34,037
21 years and over....33,414
65 years and over....6,964
85 years and over....1,122
Median Age....41.5
Native-born....36,446
Foreign-born....6,080

Educational Attainment
Population 25 years and over....31,994
Less than 9th grade....2.1%
High School grad or higher....95.4%
Bachelor's degree or higher....60.6%
Graduate degree....33.2%

Households
Total households....18,717
With persons under 18....5,029
With persons over 65....4,939
Family households....11,064
Single-person households....6,290
Persons per household....2.27
Persons per family....2.93

Income & Poverty
Per capita income....$43,959
Median household income....$80,511
Median family income....$106,924
Persons in poverty....5.1%
H'holds receiving public assistance....283
H'holds receiving social security....5,056

Labor & Employment
Total civilian labor force....24,567
Unemployment rate....3.1%
Employed persons 16 years and over, by occupation
Managers & professionals....14,747
Service occupations....2,240
Sales & office occupations....5,670
Farming, fishing & forestry....0
Construction & maintenance....499
Production & transportation....654
Self-employed persons....1,517

Housing Units
Total....19,760
Single-family units....8,119
Multiple-family units....11,641
Mobile home units....0
Owner-occupied units....11,191
Renter-occupied units....7,526
Median SF home value....$495,500
Median rent....$1,246

Attleboro
Bristol County

Population
Total....44,270
Male....21,536
Female....22,734
Living in group quarters....378
percent of total....0.9%

Race & Hispanic Origin
Race
White....39,451
Black/African American....1,075
American Indian/Alaskan Native....29
Asian....2,335
Hawaiian Native/Pacific Islander....137
Other race....731
Two or more races....512
Hispanic origin, total....2,260
Mexican....253
Puerto Rican....1,026
Cuban....0
Other Hispanic....981

Age & Nativity
Under 5 years....3,075
18 years and over....33,898
21 years and over....32,260
65 years and over....5,031
85 years and over....606
Median Age....37.3
Native-born....39,580
Foreign-born....4,690

Educational Attainment
Population 25 years and over....30,505
Less than 9th grade....5.2%
High School grad or higher....85.5%
Bachelor's degree or higher....28.7%
Graduate degree....8.3%

Households
Total households....16,606
With persons under 18....6,049
With persons over 65....3,526
Family households....11,633
Single-person households....3,810
Persons per household....2.64
Persons per family....3.08

Income & Poverty
Per capita income....$30,563
Median household income....$67,711
Median family income....$83,457
Persons in poverty....6.8%
H'holds receiving public assistance....417
H'holds receiving social security....4,056

Labor & Employment
Total civilian labor force....26,466
Unemployment rate....6.3%
Employed persons 16 years and over, by occupation
Managers & professionals....8,533
Service occupations....3,534
Sales & office occupations....7,317
Farming, fishing & forestry....0
Construction & maintenance....1,959
Production & transportation....3,445
Self-employed persons....1,214

Housing Units
Total....17,870
Single-family units....9,868
Multiple-family units....7,126
Mobile home units....876
Owner-occupied units....11,911
Renter-occupied units....4,695
Median SF home value....$326,200
Median rent....$924

©2010 Information Publications, Inc. All rights reserved. Photocopying prohibited. For additional copies, contact the publisher at www.informationpublications.com or (877)544-INFO (4636)

Note: The 2008 American Community Survey (ACS) produced 3-year estimates of demographic data for cities and counties with populations of at least 20,000 – in Massachusetts' case, 67 out of 351 municipalities. The ACS also produces 1-year averages for places with populations over 65,000; these can be found in Appendix D.

	Barnstable *Barnstable County*	**Belmont** *Middlesex County*	**Beverly** *Essex County*
Population			
Total	44,420	23,964	38,577
Male	21,699	11,505	18,035
Female	22,721	12,459	20,542
Living in group quarters	342	NA	2,893
percent of total	0.8%	NA	7.5%
Race & Hispanic Origin			
Race			
White	39,980	21,223	NA
Black/African American	1,904	188	NA
American Indian/Alaskan Native	479	0	NA
Asian	569	2,250	NA
Hawaiian Native/Pacific Islander	0	0	NA
Other race	798	134	NA
Two or more races	690	169	NA
Hispanic origin, total	1,035	NA	903
Mexican	NA	NA	NA
Puerto Rican	NA	NA	NA
Cuban	NA	NA	NA
Other Hispanic	NA	NA	NA
Age & Nativity			
Under 5 years	1,341	1,709	1,727
18 years and over	36,619	18,244	31,118
21 years and over	35,498	17,756	29,137
65 years and over	9,253	3,682	6,782
85 years and over	1,438	509	1,735
Median Age	44	41.9	42.6
Native-born	39,072	19,452	35,960
Foreign-born	5,348	4,512	2,617
Educational Attainment			
Population 25 years and over	32,632	17,114	27,150
Less than 9th grade	1.5%	1.2%	3.7%
High School grad or higher	93.7%	97.0%	92.6%
Bachelor's degree or higher	36.9%	67.3%	39.2%
Graduate degree	13.9%	38.5%	15.0%
Households			
Total households	19,311	9,547	14,500
With persons under 18	4,814	3,178	4,186
With persons over 65	6,723	2,509	3,777
Family households	12,165	6,537	8,967
Single-person households	5,688	2,423	4,603
Persons per household	2.28	2.48	2.46
Persons per family	2.81	3.01	3.15
Income & Poverty			
Per capita income	$33,976	$52,787	$35,359
Median household income	$61,271	$86,823	$69,650
Median family income	$71,086	$107,745	$86,032
Persons in poverty	6.3%	3.7%	8.4%
H'holds receiving public assistance	350	65	262
H'holds receiving social security	7,094	2,316	4,322
Labor & Employment			
Total civilian labor force	24,168	12,665	20,932
Unemployment rate	4.5%	4.6%	4.2%
Employed persons 16 years and over, by occupation			
Managers & professionals	7,582	7,745	9,219
Service occupations	5,097	1,048	2,636
Sales & office occupations	5,844	2,452	5,518
Farming, fishing & forestry	76	0	15
Construction & maintenance	2,775	363	897
Production & transportation	1,711	473	1,767
Self-employed persons	2,465	1,203	1,287
Housing Units			
Total	26,555	10,032	16,007
Single-family units	22,725	4,808	8,307
Multiple-family units	3,814	5,224	7,626
Mobile home units	16	0	74
Owner-occupied units	15,015	6,079	9,021
Renter-occupied units	4,296	3,468	5,479
Median SF home value	$390,900	$640,800	$396,600
Median rent	$1,129	$1,536	$1,059

©2010 Information Publications, Inc. All rights reserved. Photocopying prohibited. For additional copies, contact the publisher at www.informationpublications.com or (877)544-INFO (4636)

Note: The 2008 American Community Survey (ACS) produced 3-year estimates of demographic data for cities and counties with populations of at least 20,000 – in Massachusetts' case, 67 out of 351 municipalities. The ACS also produces 1-year averages for places with populations over 65,000; these can be found in Appendix D.

	Boston *Suffolk County*	**Braintree** *Norfolk County*	**Brockton** *Plymouth County*
Population			
Total	613,086	33,840	91,956
Male	298,628	16,050	44,097
Female	314,458	17,790	47,859
Living in group quarters	39,623	570	1,994
percent of total	6.5%	1.7%	2.2%
Race & Hispanic Origin			
Race			
White	345,040	30,566	48,674
Black/African American	143,817	704	29,064
American Indian/Alaskan Native	2,588	40	220
Asian	50,197	2,178	2,456
Hawaiian Native/Pacific Islander	453	0	0
Other race	51,824	102	8,019
Two or more races	19,167	250	3,523
Hispanic origin, total	98,417	412	9,086
Mexican	6,789	NA	672
Puerto Rican	29,277	NA	5,214
Cuban	2,012	NA	190
Other Hispanic	60,339	NA	3,010
Age & Nativity			
Under 5 years	36,422	1,624	7,115
18 years and over	497,092	26,211	68,232
21 years and over	454,154	25,027	64,786
65 years and over	62,604	5,714	9,639
85 years and over	9,941	676	1,505
Median Age	33.1	42.7	33.9
Native-born	444,273	30,174	70,470
Foreign-born	168,813	3,666	21,486
Educational Attainment			
Population 25 years and over	402,884	23,866	59,491
Less than 9th grade	8.6%	2.5%	7.4%
High School grad or higher	83.4%	94.3%	82.2%
Bachelor's degree or higher	41.3%	37.6%	16.2%
Graduate degree	19.0%	13.6%	4.4%
Households			
Total households	232,000	12,882	32,773
With persons under 18	56,594	4,276	13,858
With persons over 65	43,742	3,776	6,910
Family households	109,356	8,754	22,053
Single-person households	91,901	3,221	8,280
Persons per household	2.47	2.58	2.75
Persons per family	3.42	3.17	3.28
Income & Poverty			
Per capita income	$31,974	$39,299	$22,401
Median household income	$51,849	$83,314	$51,835
Median family income	$58,902	$101,502	$59,440
Persons in poverty	19.6%	6.1%	12.9%
H'holds receiving public assistance	9,420	255	1,697
H'holds receiving social security	46,064	4,060	7,838
Labor & Employment			
Total civilian labor force	347,300	18,517	50,344
Unemployment rate	7.5%	6.4%	9.4%
Employed persons 16 years and over, by occupation			
Managers & professionals	139,449	7,407	11,610
Service occupations	69,281	2,449	10,447
Sales & office occupations	76,205	4,959	12,446
Farming, fishing & forestry	318	22	0
Construction & maintenance	15,097	1,404	3,825
Production & transportation	20,929	1,083	7,300
Self-employed persons	13,652	711	1,930
Housing Units			
Total	255,082	13,475	35,487
Single-family units	30,423	8,923	16,948
Multiple-family units	224,495	4,447	18,524
Mobile home units	104	41	15
Owner-occupied units	88,363	9,948	18,908
Renter-occupied units	143,637	2,934	13,865
Median SF home value	$419,500	$383,800	$294,700
Median rent	$1,139	$1,161	$979

©2010 Information Publications, Inc. All rights reserved. Photocopying prohibited. For additional copies, contact the publisher at www.informationpublications.com or (877)544-INFO (4636)

Note: The 2008 American Community Survey (ACS) produced 3-year estimates of demographic data for cities and counties with populations of at least 20,000 – in Massachusetts' case, 67 out of 351 municipalities. The ACS also produces 1-year averages for places with populations over 65,000; these can be found in Appendix D.

	Brookline *Norfolk County*	Burlington *Middlesex County*	Cambridge *Middlesex County*
Population			
Total	62,255	23,060	93,635
Male	28,736	11,048	46,936
Female	33,519	12,012	46,699
Living in group quarters	1,929	NA	8,875
percent of total	3.1%	NA	9.5%
Race & Hispanic Origin			
Race			
White	49,449	19,013	64,061
Black/African American	1,677	603	10,922
American Indian/Alaskan Native	199	0	352
Asian	8,464	2,852	12,380
Hawaiian Native/Pacific Islander	0	21	0
Other race	1,276	265	3,068
Two or more races	1,190	306	2,852
Hispanic origin, total	3,341	515	6,338
Mexican	325	NA	1,200
Puerto Rican	798	NA	1,184
Cuban	308	NA	305
Other Hispanic	1,910	NA	3,649
Age & Nativity			
Under 5 years	3,572	1,395	4,369
18 years and over	51,252	17,939	81,304
21 years and over	49,270	17,402	75,332
65 years and over	7,320	3,904	9,587
85 years and over	1,282	451	1,691
Median Age	35.5	41.2	31.8
Native-born	46,971	19,406	68,508
Foreign-born	15,284	3,654	25,127
Educational Attainment			
Population 25 years and over	43,119	16,568	64,913
Less than 9th grade	1.6%	1.4%	2.8%
High School grad or higher	97.1%	94.7%	94.3%
Bachelor's degree or higher	78.4%	46.4%	71.7%
Graduate degree	47.1%	20.2%	42.7%
Households			
Total households	26,401	8,767	41,302
With persons under 18	6,771	3,097	7,614
With persons over 65	5,527	2,841	7,562
Family households	14,348	6,447	16,857
Single-person households	8,349	1,951	17,503
Persons per household	2.28	2.63	2.05
Persons per family	2.82	3.10	2.79
Income & Poverty			
Per capita income	$62,620	$37,850	$43,624
Median household income	$94,476	$88,867	$62,062
Median family income	$132,121	$100,138	$85,458
Persons in poverty	12.8%	3.0%	15.3%
H'holds receiving public assistance	354	106	586
H'holds receiving social security	5,246	2,767	7,336
Labor & Employment			
Total civilian labor force	37,559	13,370	55,573
Unemployment rate	3.3%	5.0%	4.4%
Employed persons 16 years and over, by occupation			
Managers & professionals	25,772	6,034	36,766
Service occupations	2,786	1,295	5,449
Sales & office occupations	7,109	3,763	8,465
Farming, fishing & forestry	0	0	0
Construction & maintenance	383	970	985
Production & transportation	272	645	1,481
Self-employed persons	2,791	756	3,485
Housing Units			
Total	27,426	8,936	45,544
Single-family units	5,737	6,471	4,074
Multiple-family units	21,689	2,465	41,470
Mobile home units	0	0	0
Owner-occupied units	13,952	6,634	16,018
Renter-occupied units	12,449	2,133	25,284
Median SF home value	$658,800	$445,900	$575,400
Median rent	$1,681	$1,511	$1,402

©2010 Information Publications, Inc. All rights reserved. Photocopying prohibited. For additional copies, contact the publisher at www.informationpublications.com or (877)544-INFO (4636)

Note: The 2008 American Community Survey (ACS) produced 3-year estimates of demographic data for cities and counties with populations of at least 20,000 – in Massachusetts' case, 67 out of 351 municipalities. The ACS also produces 1-year averages for places with populations over 65,000; these can be found in Appendix D.

Chelsea
Suffolk County

Population	
Total	34,356
Male	16,045
Female	18,311
Living in group quarters	795
percent of total	2.3%
Race & Hispanic Origin	
Race	
White	19,251
Black/African American	3,093
American Indian/Alaskan Native	13
Asian	677
Hawaiian Native/Pacific Islander	0
Other race	3,737
Two or more races	7,585
Hispanic origin, total	19,262
Mexican	1,914
Puerto Rican	4,109
Cuban	45
Other Hispanic	13,194
Age & Nativity	
Under 5 years	3,072
18 years and over	25,458
21 years and over	24,203
65 years and over	3,916
85 years and over	839
Median Age	33.4
Native-born	21,428
Foreign-born	12,928
Educational Attainment	
Population 25 years and over	22,387
Less than 9th grade	20.7%
High School grad or higher	68.3%
Bachelor's degree or higher	13.4%
Graduate degree	5.2%
Households	
Total households	11,872
With persons under 18	4,500
With persons over 65	2,591
Family households	7,285
Single-person households	4,119
Persons per household	2.83
Persons per family	3.63
Income & Poverty	
Per capita income	$20,206
Median household income	$40,477
Median family income	$48,994
Persons in poverty	20.0%
H'holds receiving public assistance	803
H'holds receiving social security	2,798
Labor & Employment	
Total civilian labor force	17,036
Unemployment rate	10.0%
Employed persons 16 years and over, by occupation	
Managers & professionals	3,606
Service occupations	4,061
Sales & office occupations	3,943
Farming, fishing & forestry	81
Construction & maintenance	990
Production & transportation	2,644
Self-employed persons	538
Housing Units	
Total	12,798
Single-family units	1,790
Multiple-family units	11,008
Mobile home units	0
Owner-occupied units	4,609
Renter-occupied units	7,263
Median SF home value	$343,100
Median rent	$951

Chicopee
Hampden County

Population	
Total	55,775
Male	26,989
Female	28,786
Living in group quarters	1,246
percent of total	2.2%
Race & Hispanic Origin	
Race	
White	48,748
Black/African American	1,514
American Indian/Alaskan Native	125
Asian	849
Hawaiian Native/Pacific Islander	0
Other race	3,804
Two or more races	735
Hispanic origin, total	6,896
Mexican	174
Puerto Rican	5,911
Cuban	49
Other Hispanic	762
Age & Nativity	
Under 5 years	2,856
18 years and over	43,836
21 years and over	41,426
65 years and over	8,650
85 years and over	1,666
Median Age	39
Native-born	50,961
Foreign-born	4,814
Educational Attainment	
Population 25 years and over	37,893
Less than 9th grade	5.7%
High School grad or higher	81.2%
Bachelor's degree or higher	14.7%
Graduate degree	3.7%
Households	
Total households	23,093
With persons under 18	6,084
With persons over 65	6,655
Family households	13,260
Single-person households	8,343
Persons per household	2.36
Persons per family	3.15
Income & Poverty	
Per capita income	$22,809
Median household income	$44,284
Median family income	$57,116
Persons in poverty	12.8%
H'holds receiving public assistance	811
H'holds receiving social security	7,851
Labor & Employment	
Total civilian labor force	29,377
Unemployment rate	8.2%
Employed persons 16 years and over, by occupation	
Managers & professionals	6,923
Service occupations	5,038
Sales & office occupations	7,436
Farming, fishing & forestry	0
Construction & maintenance	2,393
Production & transportation	5,169
Self-employed persons	1,043
Housing Units	
Total	24,577
Single-family units	11,496
Multiple-family units	12,481
Mobile home units	600
Owner-occupied units	14,000
Renter-occupied units	9,093
Median SF home value	$178,600
Median rent	$707

Danvers
Essex County

Population	
Total	25,138
Male	12,190
Female	12,948
Living in group quarters	619
percent of total	2.5%
Race & Hispanic Origin	
Race	
White	NA
Black/African American	NA
American Indian/Alaskan Native	NA
Asian	NA
Hawaiian Native/Pacific Islander	NA
Other race	NA
Two or more races	NA
Hispanic origin, total	NA
Mexican	NA
Puerto Rican	NA
Cuban	NA
Other Hispanic	NA
Age & Nativity	
Under 5 years	1,389
18 years and over	20,108
21 years and over	19,070
65 years and over	4,417
85 years and over	939
Median Age	44.1
Native-born	23,768
Foreign-born	1,370
Educational Attainment	
Population 25 years and over	17,689
Less than 9th grade	4.8%
High School grad or higher	90.9%
Bachelor's degree or higher	41.1%
Graduate degree	16.2%
Households	
Total households	9,681
With persons under 18	2,886
With persons over 65	2,887
Family households	6,700
Single-person households	2,718
Persons per household	2.53
Persons per family	3.12
Income & Poverty	
Per capita income	$36,600
Median household income	$75,332
Median family income	$99,835
Persons in poverty	5.4%
H'holds receiving public assistance	56
H'holds receiving social security	2,888
Labor & Employment	
Total civilian labor force	14,291
Unemployment rate	4.2%
Employed persons 16 years and over, by occupation	
Managers & professionals	6,346
Service occupations	2,042
Sales & office occupations	3,298
Farming, fishing & forestry	79
Construction & maintenance	799
Production & transportation	1,122
Self-employed persons	1,080
Housing Units	
Total	10,217
Single-family units	6,019
Multiple-family units	4,007
Mobile home units	191
Owner-occupied units	7,500
Renter-occupied units	2,181
Median SF home value	$407,300
Median rent	$1,116

©2010 Information Publications, Inc. All rights reserved. Photocopying prohibited. For additional copies, contact the publisher at www.informationpublications.com or (877)544-INFO (4636)

Note: The 2008 American Community Survey (ACS) produced 3-year estimates of demographic data for cities and counties with populations of at least 20,000 – in Massachusetts' case, 67 out of 351 municipalities. The ACS also produces 1-year averages for places with populations over 65,000; these can be found in Appendix D.

	Dedham	Everett	Fall River
	Norfolk County	*Middlesex County*	*Bristol County*
Population			
Total	22,240	39,876	88,587
Male	10,945	20,546	41,484
Female	11,295	19,330	47,103
Living in group quarters	810	254	1,865
percent of total	3.6%	0.6%	2.1%
Race & Hispanic Origin			
Race			
White	20,009	30,381	79,623
Black/African American	1,075	4,929	2,197
American Indian/Alaskan Native	21	0	163
Asian	779	1,866	2,058
Hawaiian Native/Pacific Islander	0	0	0
Other race	78	1,659	2,027
Two or more races	278	1,041	2,519
Hispanic origin, total	572	5,659	4,137
Mexican	NA	670	233
Puerto Rican	NA	382	2,238
Cuban	NA	157	27
Other Hispanic	NA	4,450	1,639
Age & Nativity			
Under 5 years	1,315	2,001	5,252
18 years and over	17,187	31,997	69,519
21 years and over	16,366	30,431	65,961
65 years and over	3,754	4,514	14,049
85 years and over	665	811	2,677
Median Age	42.4	37.2	36.9
Native-born	19,572	26,004	71,946
Foreign-born	2,668	13,872	16,641
Educational Attainment			
Population 25 years and over	15,394	27,480	61,279
Less than 9th grade	1.8%	10.4%	18.1%
High School grad or higher	92.4%	78.4%	66.4%
Bachelor's degree or higher	41.7%	17.3%	14.1%
Graduate degree	17.0%	5.6%	4.2%
Households			
Total households	8,672	14,980	37,106
With persons under 18	2,898	4,528	11,570
With persons over 65	2,549	3,239	9,381
Family households	6,018	9,283	21,746
Single-person households	2,260	4,510	12,790
Persons per household	2.47	2.64	2.34
Persons per family	2.99	3.34	3.04
Income & Poverty			
Per capita income	$40,421	$24,285	$20,024
Median household income	$79,350	$53,151	$35,633
Median family income	$94,922	$61,423	$44,711
Persons in poverty	7.3%	9.9%	18.1%
H'holds receiving public assistance	164	321	1,748
H'holds receiving social security	2,567	3,689	11,257
Labor & Employment			
Total civilian labor force	11,911	23,957	44,193
Unemployment rate	4.3%	7.9%	10.7%
Employed persons 16 years and over, by occupation			
Managers & professionals	5,171	4,582	9,190
Service occupations	1,269	6,375	7,832
Sales & office occupations	3,365	5,661	10,873
Farming, fishing & forestry	0	60	93
Construction & maintenance	973	2,802	4,121
Production & transportation	625	2,578	7,341
Self-employed persons	699	1,248	1,414
Housing Units			
Total	9,084	16,276	41,352
Single-family units	6,839	3,408	8,585
Multiple-family units	2,245	12,868	32,631
Mobile home units	0	0	120
Owner-occupied units	7,090	6,200	13,267
Renter-occupied units	1,582	8,780	23,839
Median SF home value	$403,800	$374,200	$277,600
Median rent	$1,223	$1,117	$641

©2010 Information Publications, Inc. All rights reserved. Photocopying prohibited. For additional copies, contact the publisher at www.informationpublications.com or (877)544-INFO (4636)

Note: The 2008 American Community Survey (ACS) produced 3-year estimates of demographic data for cities and counties with populations of at least 20,000 – in Massachusetts' case, 67 out of 351 municipalities. The ACS also produces 1-year averages for places with populations over 65,000; these can be found in Appendix D.

Fitchburg

Worcester County

Population	
Total	41,433
Male	20,535
Female	20,898
Living in group quarters	2,871
percent of total	6.9%
Race & Hispanic Origin	
Race	
White	34,185
Black/African American	1,838
American Indian/Alaskan Native	18
Asian	1,791
Hawaiian Native/Pacific Islander	0
Other race	2,629
Two or more races	972
Hispanic origin, total	8,581
Mexican	204
Puerto Rican	5,772
Cuban	21
Other Hispanic	2,584
Age & Nativity	
Under 5 years	2,334
18 years and over	32,358
21 years and over	28,781
65 years and over	4,860
85 years and over	672
Median Age	32.6
Native-born	37,288
Foreign-born	4,145
Educational Attainment	
Population 25 years and over	25,373
Less than 9th grade	7.3%
High School grad or higher	81.4%
Bachelor's degree or higher	18.9%
Graduate degree	6.4%
Households	
Total households	15,188
With persons under 18	5,355
With persons over 65	3,391
Family households	9,960
Single-person households	4,170
Persons per household	2.54
Persons per family	3.10
Income & Poverty	
Per capita income	$24,062
Median household income	$49,581
Median family income	$58,791
Persons in poverty	18.0%
H'holds receiving public assistance	539
H'holds receiving social security	4,327
Labor & Employment	
Total civilian labor force	22,228
Unemployment rate	8.5%
Employed persons 16 years and over, by occupation	
Managers & professionals	5,536
Service occupations	3,762
Sales & office occupations	5,437
Farming, fishing & forestry	20
Construction & maintenance	1,448
Production & transportation	4,129
Self-employed persons	722
Housing Units	
Total	17,367
Single-family units	6,564
Multiple-family units	10,724
Mobile home units	79
Owner-occupied units	8,430
Renter-occupied units	6,758
Median SF home value	$223,100
Median rent	$787

Framingham

Middlesex County

Population	
Total	65,157
Male	31,343
Female	33,814
Living in group quarters	3,758
percent of total	5.8%
Race & Hispanic Origin	
Race	
White	47,718
Black/African American	2,599
American Indian/Alaskan Native	180
Asian	4,972
Hawaiian Native/Pacific Islander	0
Other race	8,703
Two or more races	985
Hispanic origin, total	8,177
Mexican	508
Puerto Rican	2,443
Cuban	121
Other Hispanic	5,105
Age & Nativity	
Under 5 years	4,423
18 years and over	51,664
21 years and over	48,393
65 years and over	8,819
85 years and over	1,315
Median Age	38.2
Native-born	48,001
Foreign-born	17,156
Educational Attainment	
Population 25 years and over	45,194
Less than 9th grade	5.4%
High School grad or higher	88.7%
Bachelor's degree or higher	42.9%
Graduate degree	17.4%
Households	
Total households	25,588
With persons under 18	7,968
With persons over 65	5,985
Family households	16,424
Single-person households	7,806
Persons per household	2.40
Persons per family	3.00
Income & Poverty	
Per capita income	$33,075
Median household income	$63,441
Median family income	$80,294
Persons in poverty	8.4%
H'holds receiving public assistance	510
H'holds receiving social security	6,420
Labor & Employment	
Total civilian labor force	37,727
Unemployment rate	4.4%
Employed persons 16 years and over, by occupation	
Managers & professionals	14,549
Service occupations	6,404
Sales & office occupations	9,329
Farming, fishing & forestry	78
Construction & maintenance	2,929
Production & transportation	2,790
Self-employed persons	2,899
Housing Units	
Total	27,128
Single-family units	13,113
Multiple-family units	13,979
Mobile home units	36
Owner-occupied units	14,909
Renter-occupied units	10,679
Median SF home value	$383,700
Median rent	$1,086

Franklin

Norfolk County

Population	
Total	30,869
Male	15,476
Female	15,393
Living in group quarters	NA
percent of total	NA
Race & Hispanic Origin	
Race	
White	NA
Black/African American	NA
American Indian/Alaskan Native	NA
Asian	NA
Hawaiian Native/Pacific Islander	NA
Other race	NA
Two or more races	NA
Hispanic origin, total	449
Mexican	NA
Puerto Rican	NA
Cuban	NA
Other Hispanic	NA
Age & Nativity	
Under 5 years	2,202
18 years and over	22,309
21 years and over	20,780
65 years and over	2,637
85 years and over	263
Median Age	36
Native-born	28,400
Foreign-born	2,469
Educational Attainment	
Population 25 years and over	19,588
Less than 9th grade	1.1%
High School grad or higher	95.5%
Bachelor's degree or higher	46.3%
Graduate degree	15.3%
Households	
Total households	10,741
With persons under 18	4,821
With persons over 65	2,033
Family households	7,876
Single-person households	2,152
Persons per household	2.83
Persons per family	3.34
Income & Poverty	
Per capita income	$37,235
Median household income	$89,659
Median family income	$101,900
Persons in poverty	5.3%
H'holds receiving public assistance	72
H'holds receiving social security	2,067
Labor & Employment	
Total civilian labor force	16,802
Unemployment rate	4.6%
Employed persons 16 years and over, by occupation	
Managers & professionals	8,078
Service occupations	1,962
Sales & office occupations	3,935
Farming, fishing & forestry	16
Construction & maintenance	1,419
Production & transportation	613
Self-employed persons	794
Housing Units	
Total	11,078
Single-family units	7,306
Multiple-family units	3,772
Mobile home units	0
Owner-occupied units	8,767
Renter-occupied units	1,974
Median SF home value	$397,700
Median rent	$1,177

©2010 Information Publications, Inc. All rights reserved. Photocopying prohibited. For additional copies, contact the publisher at www.informationpublications.com or (877)544-INFO (4636)

Note: The 2008 American Community Survey (ACS) produced 3-year estimates of demographic data for cities and counties with populations of at least 20,000 – in Massachusetts' case, 67 out of 351 municipalities. The ACS also produces 1-year averages for places with populations over 65,000; these can be found in Appendix D.

	Gardner (Worcester County)	Gloucester (Essex County)	Haverhill (Essex County)
Population			
Total	21,733	28,215	58,753
Male	11,595	13,451	28,169
Female	10,138	14,764	30,584
Living in group quarters	1,651	NA	596
percent of total	7.6%	NA	1.0%
Race & Hispanic Origin			
Race			
White	19,596	27,232	48,669
Black/African American	1,020	175	2,557
American Indian/Alaskan Native	46	33	178
Asian	376	173	1,262
Hawaiian Native/Pacific Islander	0	0	0
Other race	269	236	4,886
Two or more races	426	366	1,201
Hispanic origin, total	895	300	6,958
Mexican	NA	NA	187
Puerto Rican	NA	NA	3,035
Cuban	NA	NA	75
Other Hispanic	NA	NA	3,661
Age & Nativity			
Under 5 years	1,744	964	4,055
18 years and over	17,330	22,974	44,953
21 years and over	16,583	22,146	42,720
65 years and over	2,940	4,787	6,840
85 years and over	561	581	1,209
Median Age	37.4	45.3	36.2
Native-born	20,487	26,482	53,409
Foreign-born	1,246	1,733	5,344
Educational Attainment			
Population 25 years and over	15,530	20,732	39,881
Less than 9th grade	5.6%	3.6%	4.0%
High School grad or higher	82.1%	90.3%	88.6%
Bachelor's degree or higher	20.3%	32.9%	30.2%
Graduate degree	5.5%	13.4%	8.7%
Households			
Total households	8,404	12,040	23,054
With persons under 18	2,568	3,057	7,793
With persons over 65	2,096	3,500	4,630
Family households	4,981	7,405	14,246
Single-person households	2,567	3,888	6,932
Persons per household	2.39	2.33	2.52
Persons per family	3.02	3.00	3.17
Income & Poverty			
Per capita income	$24,938	$35,651	$29,755
Median household income	$47,630	$60,385	$62,511
Median family income	$63,750	$83,573	$76,688
Persons in poverty	10.4%	6.7%	10.5%
H'holds receiving public assistance	291	266	550
H'holds receiving social security	2,519	3,583	5,842
Labor & Employment			
Total civilian labor force	11,334	15,921	33,131
Unemployment rate	7.7%	4.8%	7.3%
Employed persons 16 years and over, by occupation			
Managers & professionals	2,973	5,659	11,528
Service occupations	2,053	2,827	4,947
Sales & office occupations	2,752	3,387	7,833
Farming, fishing & forestry	99	209	74
Construction & maintenance	1,129	1,444	3,208
Production & transportation	1,457	1,631	3,131
Self-employed persons	485	1,502	1,737
Housing Units			
Total	8,944	13,797	24,562
Single-family units	4,205	7,754	10,608
Multiple-family units	4,599	5,950	13,894
Mobile home units	140	79	60
Owner-occupied units	4,950	8,023	15,052
Renter-occupied units	3,454	4,017	8,002
Median SF home value	$214,700	$393,100	$305,400
Median rent	$676	$1,002	$959

©2010 Information Publications, Inc. All rights reserved. Photocopying prohibited. For additional copies, contact the publisher at www.informationpublications.com or (877)544-INFO (4636)

Note: The 2008 American Community Survey (ACS) produced 3-year estimates of demographic data for cities and counties with populations of at least 20,000 – in Massachusetts' case, 67 out of 351 municipalities. The ACS also produces 1-year averages for places with populations over 65,000; these can be found in Appendix D.

Holyoke
Hampden County

Population	
Total	38,320
Male	18,037
Female	20,283
Living in group quarters	1,504
percent of total	3.9%
Race & Hispanic Origin	
Race	
White	34,245
Black/African American	890
American Indian/Alaskan Native	54
Asian	532
Hawaiian Native/Pacific Islander	0
Other race	2,174
Two or more races	425
Hispanic origin, total	17,671
Mexican	75
Puerto Rican	16,130
Cuban	91
Other Hispanic	1,375
Age & Nativity	
Under 5 years	2,439
18 years and over	28,050
21 years and over	26,931
65 years and over	5,621
85 years and over	1,426
Median Age	35.8
Native-born	36,206
Foreign-born	2,114
Educational Attainment	
Population 25 years and over	24,671
Less than 9th grade	10.1%
High School grad or higher	76.9%
Bachelor's degree or higher	22.1%
Graduate degree	7.6%
Households	
Total households	14,875
With persons under 18	5,620
With persons over 65	3,528
Family households	8,965
Single-person households	4,989
Persons per household	2.48
Persons per family	3.21
Income & Poverty	
Per capita income	$20,047
Median household income	$35,828
Median family income	$41,674
Persons in poverty	29.8%
H'holds receiving public assistance	1,305
H'holds receiving social security	4,714
Labor & Employment	
Total civilian labor force	16,399
Unemployment rate	11.3%
Employed persons 16 years and over, by occupation	
Managers & professionals	4,360
Service occupations	3,137
Sales & office occupations	3,528
Farming, fishing & forestry	17
Construction & maintenance	1,002
Production & transportation	2,501
Self-employed persons	500
Housing Units	
Total	16,235
Single-family units	5,516
Multiple-family units	10,719
Mobile home units	0
Owner-occupied units	6,185
Renter-occupied units	8,690
Median SF home value	$185,900
Median rent	$680

Lawrence
Essex County

Population	
Total	71,234
Male	34,711
Female	36,523
Living in group quarters	468
percent of total	0.7%
Race & Hispanic Origin	
Race	
White	21,522
Black/African American	2,280
American Indian/Alaskan Native	138
Asian	1,773
Hawaiian Native/Pacific Islander	0
Other race	44,099
Two or more races	1,422
Hispanic origin, total	50,438
Mexican	392
Puerto Rican	16,739
Cuban	380
Other Hispanic	32,927
Age & Nativity	
Under 5 years	7,195
18 years and over	49,070
21 years and over	45,661
65 years and over	5,441
85 years and over	946
Median Age	29.8
Native-born	46,498
Foreign-born	24,736
Educational Attainment	
Population 25 years and over	41,126
Less than 9th grade	19.2%
High School grad or higher	63.7%
Bachelor's degree or higher	11.1%
Graduate degree	3.5%
Households	
Total households	24,304
With persons under 18	11,188
With persons over 65	4,010
Family households	16,676
Single-person households	6,405
Persons per household	2.91
Persons per family	3.44
Income & Poverty	
Per capita income	$16,080
Median household income	$32,007
Median family income	$35,452
Persons in poverty	26.7%
H'holds receiving public assistance	1,457
H'holds receiving social security	5,416
Labor & Employment	
Total civilian labor force	32,493
Unemployment rate	7.6%
Employed persons 16 years and over, by occupation	
Managers & professionals	5,987
Service occupations	6,966
Sales & office occupations	6,270
Farming, fishing & forestry	157
Construction & maintenance	2,490
Production & transportation	8,154
Self-employed persons	962
Housing Units	
Total	26,386
Single-family units	4,984
Multiple-family units	21,384
Mobile home units	18
Owner-occupied units	8,794
Renter-occupied units	15,510
Median SF home value	$277,600
Median rent	$916

Leominster
Worcester County

Population	
Total	42,047
Male	20,437
Female	21,610
Living in group quarters	548
percent of total	1.3%
Race & Hispanic Origin	
Race	
White	36,579
Black/African American	1,719
American Indian/Alaskan Native	94
Asian	1,120
Hawaiian Native/Pacific Islander	0
Other race	1,693
Two or more races	842
Hispanic origin, total	4,404
Mexican	88
Puerto Rican	2,113
Cuban	0
Other Hispanic	2,203
Age & Nativity	
Under 5 years	3,369
18 years and over	32,298
21 years and over	30,633
65 years and over	6,208
85 years and over	1,135
Median Age	38.1
Native-born	36,719
Foreign-born	5,328
Educational Attainment	
Population 25 years and over	28,641
Less than 9th grade	5.8%
High School grad or higher	86.3%
Bachelor's degree or higher	21.9%
Graduate degree	7.8%
Households	
Total households	16,302
With persons under 18	5,410
With persons over 65	4,009
Family households	10,914
Single-person households	4,393
Persons per household	2.55
Persons per family	3.11
Income & Poverty	
Per capita income	$27,469
Median household income	$56,713
Median family income	$73,172
Persons in poverty	10.9%
H'holds receiving public assistance	562
H'holds receiving social security	5,013
Labor & Employment	
Total civilian labor force	22,011
Unemployment rate	5.3%
Employed persons 16 years and over, by occupation	
Managers & professionals	6,560
Service occupations	3,478
Sales & office occupations	5,705
Farming, fishing & forestry	18
Construction & maintenance	1,702
Production & transportation	3,381
Self-employed persons	1,341
Housing Units	
Total	17,072
Single-family units	8,554
Multiple-family units	8,148
Mobile home units	370
Owner-occupied units	10,819
Renter-occupied units	5,483
Median SF home value	$257,800
Median rent	$810

©2010 Information Publications, Inc. All rights reserved. Photocopying prohibited. For additional copies, contact the publisher at www.informationpublications.com or (877)544-INFO (4636)

Note: The 2008 American Community Survey (ACS) produced 3-year estimates of demographic data for cities and counties with populations of at least 20,000 – in Massachusetts' case, 67 out of 351 municipalities. The ACS also produces 1-year averages for places with populations over 65,000; these can be found in Appendix D.

Lexington
Middlesex County

Population	
Total	30,065
Male	14,218
Female	15,847
Living in group quarters	580
percent of total	1.9%
Race & Hispanic Origin	
Race	
White	23,944
Black/African American	184
American Indian/Alaskan Native	100
Asian	4,972
Hawaiian Native/Pacific Islander	0
Other race	137
Two or more races	728
Hispanic origin, total	486
Mexican	NA
Puerto Rican	NA
Cuban	NA
Other Hispanic	NA
Age & Nativity	
Under 5 years	1,682
18 years and over	22,244
21 years and over	21,589
65 years and over	5,633
85 years and over	907
Median Age	45.6
Native-born	23,304
Foreign-born	6,761
Educational Attainment	
Population 25 years and over	20,869
Less than 9th grade	1.6%
High School grad or higher	96.8%
Bachelor's degree or higher	76.2%
Graduate degree	49.5%
Households	
Total households	10,878
With persons under 18	4,527
With persons over 65	3,630
Family households	8,841
Single-person households	1,833
Persons per household	2.71
Persons per family	3.05
Income & Poverty	
Per capita income	$61,170
Median household income	$126,960
Median family income	$142,827
Persons in poverty	3.2%
H'holds receiving public assistance	77
H'holds receiving social security	3,164
Labor & Employment	
Total civilian labor force	15,007
Unemployment rate	3.8%
Employed persons 16 years and over, by occupation	
Managers & professionals	10,402
Service occupations	993
Sales & office occupations	2,520
Farming, fishing & forestry	0
Construction & maintenance	237
Production & transportation	281
Self-employed persons	1,642
Housing Units	
Total	11,639
Single-family units	9,466
Multiple-family units	2,173
Mobile home units	0
Owner-occupied units	9,194
Renter-occupied units	1,684
Median SF home value	$691,300
Median rent	$1,841

Lowell
Middlesex County

Population	
Total	98,766
Male	49,469
Female	49,297
Living in group quarters	4,197
percent of total	4.2%
Race & Hispanic Origin	
Race	
White	61,687
Black/African American	5,957
American Indian/Alaskan Native	226
Asian	17,651
Hawaiian Native/Pacific Islander	16
Other race	11,319
Two or more races	1,910
Hispanic origin, total	15,694
Mexican	886
Puerto Rican	10,644
Cuban	145
Other Hispanic	4,019
Age & Nativity	
Under 5 years	7,877
18 years and over	75,124
21 years and over	69,801
65 years and over	10,487
85 years and over	1,546
Median Age	34.4
Native-born	74,924
Foreign-born	23,842
Educational Attainment	
Population 25 years and over	63,587
Less than 9th grade	10.7%
High School grad or higher	77.7%
Bachelor's degree or higher	22.0%
Graduate degree	7.9%
Households	
Total households	36,463
With persons under 18	12,582
With persons over 65	6,959
Family households	22,122
Single-person households	11,423
Persons per household	2.59
Persons per family	3.31
Income & Poverty	
Per capita income	$23,009
Median household income	$50,944
Median family income	$56,878
Persons in poverty	17.5%
H'holds receiving public assistance	1,336
H'holds receiving social security	8,796
Labor & Employment	
Total civilian labor force	51,244
Unemployment rate	6.4%
Employed persons 16 years and over, by occupation	
Managers & professionals	15,252
Service occupations	8,995
Sales & office occupations	10,630
Farming, fishing & forestry	168
Construction & maintenance	3,931
Production & transportation	8,973
Self-employed persons	2,366
Housing Units	
Total	39,927
Single-family units	13,227
Multiple-family units	26,650
Mobile home units	35
Owner-occupied units	18,694
Renter-occupied units	17,769
Median SF home value	$266,600
Median rent	$917

Lynn
Essex County

Population	
Total	87,748
Male	43,048
Female	44,700
Living in group quarters	1,303
percent of total	1.5%
Race & Hispanic Origin	
Race	
White	57,821
Black/African American	12,671
American Indian/Alaskan Native	47
Asian	4,812
Hawaiian Native/Pacific Islander	0
Other race	8,949
Two or more races	3,448
Hispanic origin, total	22,422
Mexican	1,304
Puerto Rican	3,430
Cuban	18
Other Hispanic	17,670
Age & Nativity	
Under 5 years	5,949
18 years and over	65,972
21 years and over	62,892
65 years and over	9,966
85 years and over	1,343
Median Age	34.5
Native-born	62,135
Foreign-born	25,613
Educational Attainment	
Population 25 years and over	56,683
Less than 9th grade	12.7%
High School grad or higher	76.6%
Bachelor's degree or higher	17.9%
Graduate degree	6.1%
Households	
Total households	32,743
With persons under 18	12,113
With persons over 65	7,374
Family households	20,515
Single-person households	10,560
Persons per household	2.64
Persons per family	3.31
Income & Poverty	
Per capita income	$21,241
Median household income	$42,933
Median family income	$50,062
Persons in poverty	18.9%
H'holds receiving public assistance	1,509
H'holds receiving social security	8,653
Labor & Employment	
Total civilian labor force	45,043
Unemployment rate	8.6%
Employed persons 16 years and over, by occupation	
Managers & professionals	9,237
Service occupations	10,072
Sales & office occupations	11,166
Farming, fishing & forestry	184
Construction & maintenance	4,442
Production & transportation	6,064
Self-employed persons	1,977
Housing Units	
Total	36,038
Single-family units	11,320
Multiple-family units	24,657
Mobile home units	61
Owner-occupied units	15,642
Renter-occupied units	17,101
Median SF home value	$306,400
Median rent	$893

©2010 Information Publications, Inc. All rights reserved. Photocopying prohibited. For additional copies, contact the publisher at www.informationpublications.com or (877)544-INFO (4636)

Note: The 2008 American Community Survey (ACS) produced 3-year estimates of demographic data for cities and counties with populations of at least 20,000 – in Massachusetts' case, 67 out of 351 municipalities. The ACS also produces 1-year averages for places with populations over 65,000; these can be found in Appendix D.

Malden
Middlesex County

Population	
Total	56,259
Male	29,700
Female	26,559
Living in group quarters	NA
percent of total	NA
Race & Hispanic Origin	
Race	
White	36,100
Black/African American	7,601
American Indian/Alaskan Native	0
Asian	9,403
Hawaiian Native/Pacific Islander	0
Other race	2,072
Two or more races	1,083
Hispanic origin, total	4,659
Mexican	109
Puerto Rican	984
Cuban	81
Other Hispanic	3,485
Age & Nativity	
Under 5 years	3,411
18 years and over	45,100
21 years and over	43,224
65 years and over	6,067
85 years and over	862
Median Age	36.2
Native-born	35,701
Foreign-born	20,558
Educational Attainment	
Population 25 years and over	39,946
Less than 9th grade	7.4%
High School grad or higher	84.8%
Bachelor's degree or higher	27.7%
Graduate degree	10.7%
Households	
Total households	22,613
With persons under 18	6,616
With persons over 65	4,483
Family households	13,619
Single-person households	7,138
Persons per household	2.48
Persons per family	3.16
Income & Poverty	
Per capita income	$27,851
Median household income	$56,698
Median family income	$69,288
Persons in poverty	11.8%
H'holds receiving public assistance	755
H'holds receiving social security	5,145
Labor & Employment	
Total civilian labor force	33,775
Unemployment rate	7.8%
Employed persons 16 years and over, by occupation	
Managers & professionals	10,330
Service occupations	7,523
Sales & office occupations	7,293
Farming, fishing & forestry	0
Construction & maintenance	2,317
Production & transportation	3,664
Self-employed persons	1,247
Housing Units	
Total	24,312
Single-family units	6,302
Multiple-family units	17,838
Mobile home units	135
Owner-occupied units	10,538
Renter-occupied units	12,075
Median SF home value	$360,400
Median rent	$1,130

Marblehead
Essex County

Population	
Total	20,376
Male	10,153
Female	10,223
Living in group quarters	NA
percent of total	NA
Race & Hispanic Origin	
Race	
White	NA
Black/African American	NA
American Indian/Alaskan Native	NA
Asian	NA
Hawaiian Native/Pacific Islander	NA
Other race	NA
Two or more races	NA
Hispanic origin, total	NA
Mexican	NA
Puerto Rican	NA
Cuban	NA
Other Hispanic	NA
Age & Nativity	
Under 5 years	1,260
18 years and over	15,462
21 years and over	14,845
65 years and over	3,243
85 years and over	312
Median Age	44.7
Native-born	19,049
Foreign-born	1,327
Educational Attainment	
Population 25 years and over	14,310
Less than 9th grade	0.4%
High School grad or higher	98.0%
Bachelor's degree or higher	66.7%
Graduate degree	28.7%
Households	
Total households	8,196
With persons under 18	2,636
With persons over 65	2,321
Family households	5,610
Single-person households	2,384
Persons per household	2.49
Persons per family	3.08
Income & Poverty	
Per capita income	$52,423
Median household income	$100,637
Median family income	$126,893
Persons in poverty	2.8%
H'holds receiving public assistance	90
H'holds receiving social security	2,386
Labor & Employment	
Total civilian labor force	NA
Unemployment rate	NA
Employed persons 16 years and over, by occupation	
Managers & professionals	6,230
Service occupations	987
Sales & office occupations	2,558
Farming, fishing & forestry	40
Construction & maintenance	523
Production & transportation	386
Self-employed persons	1,153
Housing Units	
Total	8,719
Single-family units	6,273
Multiple-family units	2,446
Mobile home units	0
Owner-occupied units	6,439
Renter-occupied units	1,757
Median SF home value	$603,300
Median rent	$1,038

Marlborough
Middlesex County

Population	
Total	35,826
Male	17,642
Female	18,184
Living in group quarters	NA
percent of total	NA
Race & Hispanic Origin	
Race	
White	32,020
Black/African American	618
American Indian/Alaskan Native	23
Asian	1,252
Hawaiian Native/Pacific Islander	0
Other race	1,393
Two or more races	520
Hispanic origin, total	3,449
Mexican	614
Puerto Rican	931
Cuban	99
Other Hispanic	1,805
Age & Nativity	
Under 5 years	2,197
18 years and over	28,551
21 years and over	27,691
65 years and over	4,788
85 years and over	682
Median Age	40.3
Native-born	29,475
Foreign-born	6,351
Educational Attainment	
Population 25 years and over	26,533
Less than 9th grade	2.6%
High School grad or higher	86.2%
Bachelor's degree or higher	39.2%
Graduate degree	14.1%
Households	
Total households	15,056
With persons under 18	4,169
With persons over 65	3,542
Family households	8,430
Single-person households	5,426
Persons per household	2.35
Persons per family	3.16
Income & Poverty	
Per capita income	$38,683
Median household income	$69,382
Median family income	$99,070
Persons in poverty	9.5%
H'holds receiving public assistance	327
H'holds receiving social security	3,916
Labor & Employment	
Total civilian labor force	21,242
Unemployment rate	4.0%
Employed persons 16 years and over, by occupation	
Managers & professionals	9,434
Service occupations	3,824
Sales & office occupations	4,162
Farming, fishing & forestry	21
Construction & maintenance	1,637
Production & transportation	1,319
Self-employed persons	1,326
Housing Units	
Total	16,050
Single-family units	7,699
Multiple-family units	7,880
Mobile home units	471
Owner-occupied units	9,024
Renter-occupied units	6,032
Median SF home value	$354,700
Median rent	$971

©2010 Information Publications, Inc. All rights reserved. Photocopying prohibited. For additional copies, contact the publisher at www.informationpublications.com or (877)544-INFO (4636)

Note: The 2008 American Community Survey (ACS) produced 3-year estimates of demographic data for cities and counties with populations of at least 20,000 – in Massachusetts' case, 67 out of 351 municipalities. The ACS also produces 1-year averages for places with populations over 65,000; these can be found in Appendix D.

Medford
Middlesex County

Population	
Total	53,856
Male	25,452
Female	28,404
Living in group quarters	2,244
percent of total	4.2%
Race & Hispanic Origin	
Race	
White	43,098
Black/African American	5,158
American Indian/Alaskan Native	73
Asian	3,569
Hawaiian Native/Pacific Islander	22
Other race	927
Two or more races	1,009
Hispanic origin, total	3,430
Mexican	269
Puerto Rican	594
Cuban	83
Other Hispanic	2,484
Age & Nativity	
Under 5 years	2,658
18 years and over	45,105
21 years and over	42,491
65 years and over	8,514
85 years and over	1,446
Median Age	38.2
Native-born	42,174
Foreign-born	11,682
Educational Attainment	
Population 25 years and over	38,802
Less than 9th grade	4.7%
High School grad or higher	88.4%
Bachelor's degree or higher	38.8%
Graduate degree	16.3%
Households	
Total households	21,347
With persons under 18	5,263
With persons over 65	6,057
Family households	12,978
Single-person households	6,292
Persons per household	2.42
Persons per family	2.96
Income & Poverty	
Per capita income	$33,421
Median household income	$68,766
Median family income	$79,092
Persons in poverty	8.6%
H'holds receiving public assistance	123
H'holds receiving social security	6,209
Labor & Employment	
Total civilian labor force	31,613
Unemployment rate	5.6%
Employed persons 16 years and over, by occupation	
Managers & professionals	13,542
Service occupations	4,497
Sales & office occupations	7,983
Farming, fishing & forestry	67
Construction & maintenance	1,926
Production & transportation	1,840
Self-employed persons	1,348
Housing Units	
Total	22,945
Single-family units	8,662
Multiple-family units	14,260
Mobile home units	23
Owner-occupied units	12,945
Renter-occupied units	8,402
Median SF home value	$407,700
Median rent	$1,237

Melrose
Middlesex County

Population	
Total	27,790
Male	13,673
Female	14,117
Living in group quarters	NA
percent of total	NA
Race & Hispanic Origin	
Race	
White	NA
Black/African American	NA
American Indian/Alaskan Native	NA
Asian	NA
Hawaiian Native/Pacific Islander	NA
Other race	NA
Two or more races	NA
Hispanic origin, total	NA
Mexican	NA
Puerto Rican	NA
Cuban	NA
Other Hispanic	NA
Age & Nativity	
Under 5 years	1,870
18 years and over	21,247
21 years and over	20,278
65 years and over	4,430
85 years and over	754
Median Age	41
Native-born	24,165
Foreign-born	3,625
Educational Attainment	
Population 25 years and over	19,441
Less than 9th grade	1.3%
High School grad or higher	96.2%
Bachelor's degree or higher	47.3%
Graduate degree	20.0%
Households	
Total households	10,616
With persons under 18	3,428
With persons over 65	2,893
Family households	7,061
Single-person households	3,047
Persons per household	2.56
Persons per family	3.22
Income & Poverty	
Per capita income	$37,061
Median household income	$82,274
Median family income	$101,545
Persons in poverty	4.0%
H'holds receiving public assistance	175
H'holds receiving social security	2,898
Labor & Employment	
Total civilian labor force	14,807
Unemployment rate	3.6%
Employed persons 16 years and over, by occupation	
Managers & professionals	7,612
Service occupations	1,683
Sales & office occupations	3,638
Farming, fishing & forestry	0
Construction & maintenance	974
Production & transportation	365
Self-employed persons	963
Housing Units	
Total	11,251
Single-family units	6,319
Multiple-family units	4,932
Mobile home units	0
Owner-occupied units	7,211
Renter-occupied units	3,405
Median SF home value	$442,400
Median rent	$1,045

Methuen
Essex County

Population	
Total	46,179
Male	22,042
Female	24,137
Living in group quarters	666
percent of total	1.4%
Race & Hispanic Origin	
Race	
White	36,324
Black/African American	592
American Indian/Alaskan Native	50
Asian	1,936
Hawaiian Native/Pacific Islander	26
Other race	5,955
Two or more races	1,296
Hispanic origin, total	9,226
Mexican	176
Puerto Rican	2,925
Cuban	69
Other Hispanic	6,056
Age & Nativity	
Under 5 years	3,025
18 years and over	34,952
21 years and over	33,082
65 years and over	6,247
85 years and over	1,393
Median Age	37.9
Native-born	39,233
Foreign-born	6,946
Educational Attainment	
Population 25 years and over	30,977
Less than 9th grade	6.6%
High School grad or higher	84.3%
Bachelor's degree or higher	23.1%
Graduate degree	7.3%
Households	
Total households	16,583
With persons under 18	6,224
With persons over 65	4,290
Family households	11,093
Single-person households	4,573
Persons per household	2.74
Persons per family	3.41
Income & Poverty	
Per capita income	$27,333
Median household income	$63,537
Median family income	$78,170
Persons in poverty	7.1%
H'holds receiving public assistance	454
H'holds receiving social security	4,737
Labor & Employment	
Total civilian labor force	24,854
Unemployment rate	6.2%
Employed persons 16 years and over, by occupation	
Managers & professionals	8,017
Service occupations	3,617
Sales & office occupations	6,341
Farming, fishing & forestry	37
Construction & maintenance	2,097
Production & transportation	3,200
Self-employed persons	1,533
Housing Units	
Total	17,665
Single-family units	10,374
Multiple-family units	7,249
Mobile home units	42
Owner-occupied units	12,101
Renter-occupied units	4,482
Median SF home value	$327,300
Median rent	$956

©2010 Information Publications, Inc. All rights reserved. Photocopying prohibited. For additional copies, contact the publisher at www.informationpublications.com or (877)544-INFO (4636)

Note: The 2008 American Community Survey (ACS) produced 3-year estimates of demographic data for cities and counties with populations of at least 20,000 – in Massachusetts' case, 67 out of 351 municipalities. The ACS also produces 1-year averages for places with populations over 65,000; these can be found in Appendix D.

Milford

Worcester County

Population

Total	26,216
Male	12,863
Female	13,353
Living in group quarters	411
percent of total	1.6%

Race & Hispanic Origin

Race	
White	23,550
Black/African American	260
American Indian/Alaskan Native	216
Asian	496
Hawaiian Native/Pacific Islander	0
Other race	1,120
Two or more races	574
Hispanic origin, total	1,836
Mexican	29
Puerto Rican	888
Cuban	0
Other Hispanic	919

Age & Nativity

Under 5 years	2,100
18 years and over	20,457
21 years and over	19,586
65 years and over	3,269
85 years and over	666
Median Age	38.1
Native-born	21,165
Foreign-born	5,051

Educational Attainment

Population 25 years and over	18,319
Less than 9th grade	5.7%
High School grad or higher	87.9%
Bachelor's degree or higher	27.5%
Graduate degree	8.6%

Households

Total households	9,575
With persons under 18	3,102
With persons over 65	2,118
Family households	6,506
Single-person households	2,371
Persons per household	2.70
Persons per family	3.24

Income & Poverty

Per capita income	$30,666
Median household income	$62,469
Median family income	$76,775
Persons in poverty	6.1%
H'holds receiving public assistance	179
H'holds receiving social security	2,369

Labor & Employment

Total civilian labor force	15,451
Unemployment rate	5.0%
Employed persons 16 years and over, by occupation	
Managers & professionals	4,911
Service occupations	3,120
Sales & office occupations	3,717
Farming, fishing & forestry	0
Construction & maintenance	1,174
Production & transportation	1,750
Self-employed persons	633

Housing Units

Total	10,174
Single-family units	5,345
Multiple-family units	4,758
Mobile home units	71
Owner-occupied units	5,964
Renter-occupied units	3,611
Median SF home value	$325,900
Median rent	$1,011

Milton

Norfolk County

Population

Total	25,664
Male	12,164
Female	13,500
Living in group quarters	548
percent of total	2.1%

Race & Hispanic Origin

Race	
White	21,673
Black/African American	2,564
American Indian/Alaskan Native	16
Asian	1,047
Hawaiian Native/Pacific Islander	0
Other race	121
Two or more races	243
Hispanic origin, total	669
Mexican	NA
Puerto Rican	NA
Cuban	NA
Other Hispanic	NA

Age & Nativity

Under 5 years	1,674
18 years and over	19,388
21 years and over	18,400
65 years and over	3,841
85 years and over	506
Median Age	41.3
Native-born	22,720
Foreign-born	2,944

Educational Attainment

Population 25 years and over	17,230
Less than 9th grade	2.5%
High School grad or higher	93.7%
Bachelor's degree or higher	53.0%
Graduate degree	23.3%

Households

Total households	9,043
With persons under 18	3,468
With persons over 65	2,902
Family households	6,773
Single-person households	2,116
Persons per household	2.78
Persons per family	3.29

Income & Poverty

Per capita income	$43,083
Median household income	$92,499
Median family income	$114,825
Persons in poverty	2.4%
H'holds receiving public assistance	20
H'holds receiving social security	3,028

Labor & Employment

Total civilian labor force	13,426
Unemployment rate	4.8%
Employed persons 16 years and over, by occupation	
Managers & professionals	6,507
Service occupations	1,882
Sales & office occupations	3,214
Farming, fishing & forestry	30
Construction & maintenance	714
Production & transportation	437
Self-employed persons	710

Housing Units

Total	9,580
Single-family units	7,248
Multiple-family units	2,293
Mobile home units	39
Owner-occupied units	7,328
Renter-occupied units	1,715
Median SF home value	$497,100
Median rent	$1,375

Needham

Norfolk County

Population

Total	28,022
Male	13,260
Female	14,762
Living in group quarters	462
percent of total	1.6%

Race & Hispanic Origin

Race	
White	NA
Black/African American	NA
American Indian/Alaskan Native	NA
Asian	NA
Hawaiian Native/Pacific Islander	NA
Other race	NA
Two or more races	NA
Hispanic origin, total	165
Mexican	NA
Puerto Rican	NA
Cuban	NA
Other Hispanic	NA

Age & Nativity

Under 5 years	1,947
18 years and over	20,355
21 years and over	19,568
65 years and over	4,465
85 years and over	1,102
Median Age	43.4
Native-born	24,832
Foreign-born	3,190

Educational Attainment

Population 25 years and over	18,988
Less than 9th grade	1.5%
High School grad or higher	96.7%
Bachelor's degree or higher	72.1%
Graduate degree	39.5%

Households

Total households	10,213
With persons under 18	4,310
With persons over 65	2,898
Family households	7,640
Single-person households	2,326
Persons per household	2.70
Persons per family	3.20

Income & Poverty

Per capita income	$59,658
Median household income	$123,509
Median family income	$158,635
Persons in poverty	2.8%
H'holds receiving public assistance	131
H'holds receiving social security	2,949

Labor & Employment

Total civilian labor force	13,682
Unemployment rate	3.2%
Employed persons 16 years and over, by occupation	
Managers & professionals	8,826
Service occupations	707
Sales & office occupations	3,320
Farming, fishing & forestry	16
Construction & maintenance	144
Production & transportation	235
Self-employed persons	1,546

Housing Units

Total	10,657
Single-family units	8,131
Multiple-family units	2,513
Mobile home units	13
Owner-occupied units	8,494
Renter-occupied units	1,719
Median SF home value	$656,200
Median rent	$1,410

©2010 Information Publications, Inc. All rights reserved. Photocopying prohibited. For additional copies, contact the publisher at www.informationpublications.com or (877)544-INFO (4636)

Note: The 2008 American Community Survey (ACS) produced 3-year estimates of demographic data for cities and counties with populations of at least 20,000 – in Massachusetts' case, 67 out of 351 municipalities. The ACS also produces 1-year averages for places with populations over 65,000; these can be found in Appendix D.

©2010 Information Publications, Inc. All rights reserved. Photocopying prohibited. For additional copies, contact the publisher at www.informationpublications.com or (877)544-INFO (4636)

New Bedford
Bristol County

Population

Total	95,272
Male	45,302
Female	49,970
Living in group quarters	2,470
percent of total	2.6%

Race & Hispanic Origin

Race	
White	74,719
Black/African American	6,661
American Indian/Alaskan Native	408
Asian	1,243
Hawaiian Native/Pacific Islander	0
Other race	8,645
Two or more races	3,596
Hispanic origin, total	12,810
Mexican	440
Puerto Rican	8,461
Cuban	0
Other Hispanic	3,909

Age & Nativity

Under 5 years	6,978
18 years and over	71,569
21 years and over	68,396
65 years and over	13,426
85 years and over	2,577
Median Age	35.3
Native-born	75,679
Foreign-born	19,593

Educational Attainment

Population 25 years and over	63,352
Less than 9th grade	19.6%
High School grad or higher	64.3%
Bachelor's degree or higher	12.9%
Graduate degree	4.2%

Households

Total households	38,035
With persons under 18	13,670
With persons over 65	9,237
Family households	23,291
Single-person households	12,284
Persons per household	2.44
Persons per family	3.05

Income & Poverty

Per capita income	$20,647
Median household income	$36,809
Median family income	$45,743
Persons in poverty	23.4%
H'holds receiving public assistance	2,815
H'holds receiving social security	11,385

Labor & Employment

Total civilian labor force	45,581
Unemployment rate	7.9%
Employed persons 16 years and over, by occupation	
Managers & professionals	9,862
Service occupations	9,109
Sales & office occupations	9,129
Farming, fishing & forestry	414
Construction & maintenance	5,245
Production & transportation	8,202
Self-employed persons	1,331

Housing Units

Total	41,769
Single-family units	12,580
Multiple-family units	29,073
Mobile home units	116
Owner-occupied units	16,629
Renter-occupied units	21,406
Median SF home value	$256,100
Median rent	$723

Newton
Middlesex County

Population

Total	93,447
Male	44,090
Female	49,357
Living in group quarters	10,613
percent of total	11.4%

Race & Hispanic Origin

Race	
White	79,318
Black/African American	2,746
American Indian/Alaskan Native	0
Asian	8,222
Hawaiian Native/Pacific Islander	112
Other race	1,608
Two or more races	1,441
Hispanic origin, total	3,579
Mexican	347
Puerto Rican	1,028
Cuban	194
Other Hispanic	2,010

Age & Nativity

Under 5 years	5,005
18 years and over	73,332
21 years and over	65,097
65 years and over	12,404
85 years and over	2,226
Median Age	37.9
Native-born	75,445
Foreign-born	18,002

Educational Attainment

Population 25 years and over	58,131
Less than 9th grade	1.5%
High School grad or higher	96.4%
Bachelor's degree or higher	71.2%
Graduate degree	43.3%

Households

Total households	31,879
With persons under 18	11,333
With persons over 65	8,448
Family households	21,835
Single-person households	7,775
Persons per household	2.60
Persons per family	3.11

Income & Poverty

Per capita income	$55,245
Median household income	$108,228
Median family income	$137,493
Persons in poverty	5.6%
H'holds receiving public assistance	379
H'holds receiving social security	7,813

Labor & Employment

Total civilian labor force	47,250
Unemployment rate	2.9%
Employed persons 16 years and over, by occupation	
Managers & professionals	31,448
Service occupations	3,925
Sales & office occupations	7,780
Farming, fishing & forestry	0
Construction & maintenance	1,045
Production & transportation	1,681
Self-employed persons	4,648

Housing Units

Total	33,264
Single-family units	17,905
Multiple-family units	15,359
Mobile home units	0
Owner-occupied units	22,720
Renter-occupied units	9,159
Median SF home value	$702,100
Median rent	$1,570

Northampton
Hampshire County

Population

Total	27,495
Male	11,583
Female	15,912
Living in group quarters	3,129
percent of total	11.4%

Race & Hispanic Origin

Race	
White	24,321
Black/African American	617
American Indian/Alaskan Native	21
Asian	629
Hawaiian Native/Pacific Islander	0
Other race	1,055
Two or more races	852
Hispanic origin, total	2,146
Mexican	62
Puerto Rican	1,439
Cuban	81
Other Hispanic	564

Age & Nativity

Under 5 years	1,135
18 years and over	23,341
21 years and over	21,491
65 years and over	3,188
85 years and over	531
Median Age	37.4
Native-born	25,791
Foreign-born	1,704

Educational Attainment

Population 25 years and over	18,593
Less than 9th grade	1.8%
High School grad or higher	92.8%
Bachelor's degree or higher	51.4%
Graduate degree	26.6%

Households

Total households	11,994
With persons under 18	2,784
With persons over 65	2,251
Family households	5,436
Single-person households	5,072
Persons per household	2.03
Persons per family	2.79

Income & Poverty

Per capita income	$32,514
Median household income	$49,238
Median family income	$68,967
Persons in poverty	12.3%
H'holds receiving public assistance	254
H'holds receiving social security	2,840

Labor & Employment

Total civilian labor force	16,677
Unemployment rate	4.6%
Employed persons 16 years and over, by occupation	
Managers & professionals	8,442
Service occupations	3,008
Sales & office occupations	2,689
Farming, fishing & forestry	0
Construction & maintenance	712
Production & transportation	1,064
Self-employed persons	1,698

Housing Units

Total	12,771
Single-family units	5,846
Multiple-family units	6,853
Mobile home units	72
Owner-occupied units	6,856
Renter-occupied units	5,138
Median SF home value	$265,100
Median rent	$814

Note: The 2008 American Community Survey (ACS) produced 3-year estimates of demographic data for cities and counties with populations of at least 20,000 – in Massachusetts' case, 67 out of 351 municipalities. The ACS also produces 1-year averages for places with populations over 65,000; these can be found in Appendix D.

Norwood
Norfolk County

Population	
Total	28,289
Male	13,601
Female	14,688
Living in group quarters	527
percent of total	1.9%
Race & Hispanic Origin	
Race	
White	24,266
Black/African American	1,165
American Indian/Alaskan Native	42
Asian	1,466
Hawaiian Native/Pacific Islander	0
Other race	1,015
Two or more races	335
Hispanic origin, total	671
Mexican	NA
Puerto Rican	NA
Cuban	NA
Other Hispanic	NA
Age & Nativity	
Under 5 years	1,769
18 years and over	22,507
21 years and over	21,885
65 years and over	4,843
85 years and over	891
Median Age	40.7
Native-born	22,705
Foreign-born	5,584
Educational Attainment	
Population 25 years and over	20,207
Less than 9th grade	3.5%
High School grad or higher	92.2%
Bachelor's degree or higher	38.5%
Graduate degree	13.8%
Households	
Total households	11,373
With persons under 18	3,446
With persons over 65	3,279
Family households	7,314
Single-person households	3,264
Persons per household	2.44
Persons per family	3.01
Income & Poverty	
Per capita income	$34,052
Median household income	$72,490
Median family income	$86,932
Persons in poverty	6.8%
H'holds receiving public assistance	97
H'holds receiving social security	3,320
Labor & Employment	
Total civilian labor force	16,583
Unemployment rate	5.1%
Employed persons 16 years and over, by occupation	
Managers & professionals	6,586
Service occupations	2,673
Sales & office occupations	3,807
Farming, fishing & forestry	0
Construction & maintenance	1,322
Production & transportation	1,343
Self-employed persons	634
Housing Units	
Total	12,140
Single-family units	5,496
Multiple-family units	6,644
Mobile home units	0
Owner-occupied units	6,677
Renter-occupied units	4,696
Median SF home value	$407,400
Median rent	$1,229

Peabody
Essex County

Population	
Total	50,562
Male	23,795
Female	26,767
Living in group quarters	640
percent of total	1.3%
Race & Hispanic Origin	
Race	
White	46,478
Black/African American	794
American Indian/Alaskan Native	21
Asian	994
Hawaiian Native/Pacific Islander	0
Other race	1,572
Two or more races	703
Hispanic origin, total	2,451
Mexican	70
Puerto Rican	497
Cuban	60
Other Hispanic	1,824
Age & Nativity	
Under 5 years	2,685
18 years and over	40,522
21 years and over	38,579
65 years and over	9,771
85 years and over	1,799
Median Age	43.2
Native-born	44,304
Foreign-born	6,258
Educational Attainment	
Population 25 years and over	35,874
Less than 9th grade	3.9%
High School grad or higher	88.8%
Bachelor's degree or higher	29.5%
Graduate degree	9.8%
Households	
Total households	19,658
With persons under 18	5,567
With persons over 65	6,835
Family households	12,393
Single-person households	6,150
Persons per household	2.54
Persons per family	3.26
Income & Poverty	
Per capita income	$29,473
Median household income	$63,069
Median family income	$80,382
Persons in poverty	6.9%
H'holds receiving public assistance	317
H'holds receiving social security	7,154
Labor & Employment	
Total civilian labor force	27,399
Unemployment rate	6.2%
Employed persons 16 years and over, by occupation	
Managers & professionals	8,770
Service occupations	4,736
Sales & office occupations	7,788
Farming, fishing & forestry	25
Construction & maintenance	2,038
Production & transportation	2,352
Self-employed persons	1,422
Housing Units	
Total	20,897
Single-family units	10,773
Multiple-family units	9,474
Mobile home units	650
Owner-occupied units	13,473
Renter-occupied units	6,185
Median SF home value	$377,300
Median rent	$1,085

Pittsfield
Berkshire County

Population	
Total	45,058
Male	21,480
Female	23,578
Living in group quarters	1,784
percent of total	4.0%
Race & Hispanic Origin	
Race	
White	40,703
Black/African American	1,881
American Indian/Alaskan Native	72
Asian	623
Hawaiian Native/Pacific Islander	0
Other race	545
Two or more races	1,234
Hispanic origin, total	1,583
Mexican	105
Puerto Rican	532
Cuban	37
Other Hispanic	909
Age & Nativity	
Under 5 years	2,374
18 years and over	36,053
21 years and over	34,323
65 years and over	8,157
85 years and over	982
Median Age	41.3
Native-born	42,708
Foreign-born	2,350
Educational Attainment	
Population 25 years and over	32,283
Less than 9th grade	2.9%
High School grad or higher	88.8%
Bachelor's degree or higher	25.1%
Graduate degree	10.1%
Households	
Total households	20,266
With persons under 18	5,774
With persons over 65	5,829
Family households	11,595
Single-person households	7,538
Persons per household	2.14
Persons per family	2.75
Income & Poverty	
Per capita income	$26,280
Median household income	$43,136
Median family income	$57,377
Persons in poverty	16.2%
H'holds receiving public assistance	1,159
H'holds receiving social security	6,616
Labor & Employment	
Total civilian labor force	24,038
Unemployment rate	6.4%
Employed persons 16 years and over, by occupation	
Managers & professionals	7,322
Service occupations	5,339
Sales & office occupations	5,875
Farming, fishing & forestry	0
Construction & maintenance	1,698
Production & transportation	2,277
Self-employed persons	1,476
Housing Units	
Total	22,354
Single-family units	11,476
Multiple-family units	10,656
Mobile home units	222
Owner-occupied units	12,161
Renter-occupied units	8,105
Median SF home value	$162,700
Median rent	$704

©2010 Information Publications, Inc. All rights reserved. Photocopying prohibited. For additional copies, contact the publisher at www.informationpublications.com or (877)544-INFO (4636)

Note: The 2008 American Community Survey (ACS) produced 3-year estimates of demographic data for cities and counties with populations of at least 20,000 – in Massachusetts' case, 67 out of 351 municipalities. The ACS also produces 1-year averages for places with populations over 65,000; these can be found in Appendix D.

Quincy
Norfolk County

Population	
Total	84,832
Male	39,658
Female	45,174
Living in group quarters	1,507
percent of total	1.8%
Race & Hispanic Origin	
Race	
White	61,568
Black/African American	3,492
American Indian/Alaskan Native	68
Asian	17,552
Hawaiian Native/Pacific Islander	203
Other race	702
Two or more races	1,247
Hispanic origin, total	2,376
Mexican	185
Puerto Rican	1,006
Cuban	84
Other Hispanic	1,101
Age & Nativity	
Under 5 years	3,928
18 years and over	71,238
21 years and over	68,638
65 years and over	12,987
85 years and over	1,990
Median Age	39.9
Native-born	63,295
Foreign-born	21,537
Educational Attainment	
Population 25 years and over	63,357
Less than 9th grade	5.8%
High School grad or higher	87.4%
Bachelor's degree or higher	36.9%
Graduate degree	13.9%
Households	
Total households	39,038
With persons under 18	8,791
With persons over 65	9,557
Family households	19,598
Single-person households	15,578
Persons per household	2.13
Persons per family	2.92
Income & Poverty	
Per capita income	$33,477
Median household income	$58,815
Median family income	$75,454
Persons in poverty	9.7%
H'holds receiving public assistance	761
H'holds receiving social security	10,767
Labor & Employment	
Total civilian labor force	50,670
Unemployment rate	6.4%
Employed persons 16 years and over, by occupation	
Managers & professionals	19,629
Service occupations	7,799
Sales & office occupations	12,412
Farming, fishing & forestry	0
Construction & maintenance	3,804
Production & transportation	3,778
Self-employed persons	2,186
Housing Units	
Total	42,052
Single-family units	14,617
Multiple-family units	27,361
Mobile home units	49
Owner-occupied units	19,416
Renter-occupied units	19,622
Median SF home value	$367,100
Median rent	$1,138

Randolph
Norfolk County

Population	
Total	29,223
Male	14,484
Female	14,739
Living in group quarters	NA
percent of total	NA
Race & Hispanic Origin	
Race	
White	14,474
Black/African American	10,209
American Indian/Alaskan Native	47
Asian	3,452
Hawaiian Native/Pacific Islander	0
Other race	819
Two or more races	222
Hispanic origin, total	1,900
Mexican	NA
Puerto Rican	NA
Cuban	NA
Other Hispanic	NA
Age & Nativity	
Under 5 years	1,553
18 years and over	23,393
21 years and over	22,469
65 years and over	3,793
85 years and over	729
Median Age	41
Native-born	21,286
Foreign-born	7,937
Educational Attainment	
Population 25 years and over	20,950
Less than 9th grade	5.3%
High School grad or higher	86.8%
Bachelor's degree or higher	29.8%
Graduate degree	10.3%
Households	
Total households	11,137
With persons under 18	3,746
With persons over 65	2,844
Family households	7,663
Single-person households	3,002
Persons per household	2.60
Persons per family	3.13
Income & Poverty	
Per capita income	$29,726
Median household income	$68,522
Median family income	$76,947
Persons in poverty	4.4%
H'holds receiving public assistance	183
H'holds receiving social security	2,793
Labor & Employment	
Total civilian labor force	17,780
Unemployment rate	6.8%
Employed persons 16 years and over, by occupation	
Managers & professionals	6,224
Service occupations	2,617
Sales & office occupations	4,744
Farming, fishing & forestry	0
Construction & maintenance	858
Production & transportation	2,132
Self-employed persons	716
Housing Units	
Total	11,661
Single-family units	7,568
Multiple-family units	4,093
Mobile home units	0
Owner-occupied units	8,224
Renter-occupied units	2,913
Median SF home value	$333,700
Median rent	$1,113

Reading
Middlesex County

Population	
Total	24,243
Male	11,789
Female	12,454
Living in group quarters	NA
percent of total	NA
Race & Hispanic Origin	
Race	
White	NA
Black/African American	NA
American Indian/Alaskan Native	NA
Asian	NA
Hawaiian Native/Pacific Islander	NA
Other race	NA
Two or more races	NA
Hispanic origin, total	NA
Mexican	NA
Puerto Rican	NA
Cuban	NA
Other Hispanic	NA
Age & Nativity	
Under 5 years	1,395
18 years and over	17,887
21 years and over	17,368
65 years and over	3,420
85 years and over	550
Median Age	41.5
Native-born	23,011
Foreign-born	1,232
Educational Attainment	
Population 25 years and over	16,668
Less than 9th grade	1.4%
High School grad or higher	95.5%
Bachelor's degree or higher	54.0%
Graduate degree	24.1%
Households	
Total households	9,064
With persons under 18	3,158
With persons over 65	2,434
Family households	6,525
Single-person households	2,328
Persons per household	2.64
Persons per family	3.24
Income & Poverty	
Per capita income	$43,557
Median household income	$95,988
Median family income	$118,107
Persons in poverty	2.2%
H'holds receiving public assistance	61
H'holds receiving social security	2,503
Labor & Employment	
Total civilian labor force	13,159
Unemployment rate	4.1%
Employed persons 16 years and over, by occupation	
Managers & professionals	7,069
Service occupations	1,103
Sales & office occupations	3,328
Farming, fishing & forestry	28
Construction & maintenance	636
Production & transportation	456
Self-employed persons	785
Housing Units	
Total	9,268
Single-family units	7,156
Multiple-family units	2,112
Mobile home units	0
Owner-occupied units	8,000
Renter-occupied units	1,064
Median SF home value	$455,500
Median rent	$1,043

©2010 Information Publications, Inc. All rights reserved. Photocopying prohibited. For additional copies, contact the publisher at www.informationpublications.com or (877)544-INFO (4636)

Note: The 2008 American Community Survey (ACS) produced 3-year estimates of demographic data for cities and counties with populations of at least 20,000 – in Massachusetts' case, 67 out of 351 municipalities. The ACS also produces 1-year averages for places with populations over 65,000; these can be found in Appendix D.

Revere
Suffolk County

Population	
Total	56,899
Male	27,553
Female	29,346
Living in group quarters	524
percent of total	0.9%
Race & Hispanic Origin	
Race	
White	44,581
Black/African American	2,620
American Indian/Alaskan Native	363
Asian	3,295
Hawaiian Native/Pacific Islander	0
Other race	4,470
Two or more races	1,570
Hispanic origin, total	10,211
Mexican	1,056
Puerto Rican	1,295
Cuban	36
Other Hispanic	7,824
Age & Nativity	
Under 5 years	4,011
18 years and over	43,931
21 years and over	42,481
65 years and over	8,654
85 years and over	1,522
Median Age	39.4
Native-born	40,516
Foreign-born	16,383
Educational Attainment	
Population 25 years and over	40,519
Less than 9th grade	11.8%
High School grad or higher	76.3%
Bachelor's degree or higher	18.8%
Graduate degree	6.0%
Households	
Total households	20,219
With persons under 18	6,321
With persons over 65	5,760
Family households	12,457
Single-person households	6,047
Persons per household	2.79
Persons per family	3.58
Income & Poverty	
Per capita income	$24,261
Median household income	$49,492
Median family income	$60,403
Persons in poverty	12.4%
H'holds receiving public assistance	799
H'holds receiving social security	6,253
Labor & Employment	
Total civilian labor force	28,968
Unemployment rate	5.2%
Employed persons 16 years and over, by occupation	
Managers & professionals	6,765
Service occupations	5,898
Sales & office occupations	7,651
Farming, fishing & forestry	44
Construction & maintenance	2,839
Production & transportation	4,252
Self-employed persons	2,071
Housing Units	
Total	21,945
Single-family units	6,343
Multiple-family units	15,486
Mobile home units	116
Owner-occupied units	10,395
Renter-occupied units	9,824
Median SF home value	$351,300
Median rent	$1,099

Salem
Essex County

Population	
Total	42,460
Male	20,325
Female	22,135
Living in group quarters	1,137
percent of total	2.7%
Race & Hispanic Origin	
Race	
White	35,176
Black/African American	2,113
American Indian/Alaskan Native	331
Asian	996
Hawaiian Native/Pacific Islander	0
Other race	2,940
Two or more races	904
Hispanic origin, total	5,573
Mexican	434
Puerto Rican	678
Cuban	25
Other Hispanic	4,436
Age & Nativity	
Under 5 years	3,183
18 years and over	33,837
21 years and over	31,760
65 years and over	5,513
85 years and over	1,138
Median Age	36.4
Native-born	35,175
Foreign-born	7,285
Educational Attainment	
Population 25 years and over	29,775
Less than 9th grade	3.9%
High School grad or higher	89.6%
Bachelor's degree or higher	37.5%
Graduate degree	14.1%
Households	
Total households	17,619
With persons under 18	5,246
With persons over 65	4,247
Family households	10,063
Single-person households	6,014
Persons per household	2.35
Persons per family	3.09
Income & Poverty	
Per capita income	$30,314
Median household income	$61,906
Median family income	$75,486
Persons in poverty	7.6%
H'holds receiving public assistance	430
H'holds receiving social security	4,452
Labor & Employment	
Total civilian labor force	25,290
Unemployment rate	5.4%
Employed persons 16 years and over, by occupation	
Managers & professionals	10,070
Service occupations	4,237
Sales & office occupations	5,682
Farming, fishing & forestry	27
Construction & maintenance	1,572
Production & transportation	2,337
Self-employed persons	1,526
Housing Units	
Total	18,810
Single-family units	5,205
Multiple-family units	13,605
Mobile home units	0
Owner-occupied units	9,809
Renter-occupied units	7,810
Median SF home value	$347,100
Median rent	$1,075

Saugus
Essex County

Population	
Total	28,732
Male	13,634
Female	15,098
Living in group quarters	NA
percent of total	NA
Race & Hispanic Origin	
Race	
White	26,763
Black/African American	418
American Indian/Alaskan Native	14
Asian	811
Hawaiian Native/Pacific Islander	0
Other race	180
Two or more races	546
Hispanic origin, total	NA
Mexican	NA
Puerto Rican	NA
Cuban	NA
Other Hispanic	NA
Age & Nativity	
Under 5 years	1,638
18 years and over	22,467
21 years and over	21,627
65 years and over	4,363
85 years and over	517
Median Age	41.2
Native-born	25,651
Foreign-born	3,081
Educational Attainment	
Population 25 years and over	20,160
Less than 9th grade	2.7%
High School grad or higher	92.0%
Bachelor's degree or higher	22.4%
Graduate degree	8.3%
Households	
Total households	10,180
With persons under 18	3,197
With persons over 65	3,007
Family households	7,257
Single-person households	2,469
Persons per household	2.79
Persons per family	3.33
Income & Poverty	
Per capita income	$32,011
Median household income	$68,476
Median family income	$85,269
Persons in poverty	6.3%
H'holds receiving public assistance	125
H'holds receiving social security	2,928
Labor & Employment	
Total civilian labor force	15,521
Unemployment rate	3.6%
Employed persons 16 years and over, by occupation	
Managers & professionals	5,779
Service occupations	2,546
Sales & office occupations	4,111
Farming, fishing & forestry	29
Construction & maintenance	1,092
Production & transportation	1,413
Self-employed persons	671
Housing Units	
Total	10,584
Single-family units	7,045
Multiple-family units	3,461
Mobile home units	78
Owner-occupied units	7,923
Renter-occupied units	2,257
Median SF home value	$376,000
Median rent	$1,204

©2010 Information Publications, Inc. All rights reserved. Photocopying prohibited. For additional copies, contact the publisher at www.informationpublications.com or (877)544-INFO (4636)

Note: The 2008 American Community Survey (ACS) produced 3-year estimates of demographic data for cities and counties with populations of at least 20,000 – in Massachusetts' case, 67 out of 351 municipalities. The ACS also produces 1-year averages for places with populations over 65,000; these can be found in Appendix D.

Somerville

Middlesex County

Population

Total	69,662
Male	32,463
Female	37,199
Living in group quarters	3,175
percent of total	4.6%

Race & Hispanic Origin

Race	
White	52,483
Black/African American	3,059
American Indian/Alaskan Native	404
Asian	6,802
Hawaiian Native/Pacific Islander	151
Other race	5,476
Two or more races	1,287
Hispanic origin, total	5,596
Mexican	372
Puerto Rican	936
Cuban	147
Other Hispanic	4,141

Age & Nativity

Under 5 years	2,905
18 years and over	61,798
21 years and over	57,434
65 years and over	6,649
85 years and over	1,196
Median Age	31.4
Native-born	51,663
Foreign-born	17,999

Educational Attainment

Population 25 years and over	48,888
Less than 9th grade	5.9%
High School grad or higher	89.0%
Bachelor's degree or higher	51.7%
Graduate degree	25.1%

Households

Total households	29,190
With persons under 18	5,119
With persons over 65	5,043
Family households	12,338
Single-person households	10,343
Persons per household	2.28
Persons per family	2.96

Income & Poverty

Per capita income	$32,602
Median household income	$60,674
Median family income	$71,057
Persons in poverty	15.6%
H'holds receiving public assistance	448
H'holds receiving social security	5,438

Labor & Employment

Total civilian labor force	46,956
Unemployment rate	5.5%
Employed persons 16 years and over, by occupation	
Managers & professionals	22,468
Service occupations	7,550
Sales & office occupations	9,466
Farming, fishing & forestry	0
Construction & maintenance	2,433
Production & transportation	2,438
Self-employed persons	2,896

Housing Units

Total	31,662
Single-family units	3,417
Multiple-family units	28,245
Mobile home units	0
Owner-occupied units	10,157
Renter-occupied units	19,033
Median SF home value	$469,000
Median rent	$1,281

Springfield

Hampden County

Population

Total	149,586
Male	70,892
Female	78,694
Living in group quarters	7,888
percent of total	5.3%

Race & Hispanic Origin

Race	
White	76,461
Black/African American	31,815
American Indian/Alaskan Native	373
Asian	3,314
Hawaiian Native/Pacific Islander	31
Other race	33,642
Two or more races	3,950
Hispanic origin, total	52,039
Mexican	2,432
Puerto Rican	43,636
Cuban	418
Other Hispanic	5,553

Age & Nativity

Under 5 years	11,634
18 years and over	110,060
21 years and over	99,790
65 years and over	16,318
85 years and over	1,957
Median Age	32
Native-born	135,336
Foreign-born	14,250

Educational Attainment

Population 25 years and over	90,352
Less than 9th grade	9.9%
High School grad or higher	76.5%
Bachelor's degree or higher	16.4%
Graduate degree	6.2%

Households

Total households	55,116
With persons under 18	19,689
With persons over 65	12,128
Family households	33,947
Single-person households	18,041
Persons per household	2.57
Persons per family	3.28

Income & Poverty

Per capita income	$18,143
Median household income	$34,090
Median family income	$41,478
Persons in poverty	27.1%
H'holds receiving public assistance	4,657
H'holds receiving social security	15,372

Labor & Employment

Total civilian labor force	68,103
Unemployment rate	13.0%
Employed persons 16 years and over, by occupation	
Managers & professionals	16,403
Service occupations	14,688
Sales & office occupations	14,419
Farming, fishing & forestry	348
Construction & maintenance	3,740
Production & transportation	9,619
Self-employed persons	3,077

Housing Units

Total	62,769
Single-family units	27,505
Multiple-family units	34,679
Mobile home units	547
Owner-occupied units	28,357
Renter-occupied units	26,759
Median SF home value	$157,600
Median rent	$726

Stoneham

Middlesex County

Population

Total	21,418
Male	9,831
Female	11,587
Living in group quarters	NA
percent of total	NA

Race & Hispanic Origin

Race	
White	19,759
Black/African American	523
American Indian/Alaskan Native	0
Asian	599
Hawaiian Native/Pacific Islander	0
Other race	205
Two or more races	332
Hispanic origin, total	444
Mexican	NA
Puerto Rican	NA
Cuban	NA
Other Hispanic	NA

Age & Nativity

Under 5 years	1,530
18 years and over	16,922
21 years and over	16,481
65 years and over	4,158
85 years and over	802
Median Age	44.1
Native-born	19,380
Foreign-born	2,038

Educational Attainment

Population 25 years and over	15,716
Less than 9th grade	2.7%
High School grad or higher	90.5%
Bachelor's degree or higher	37.1%
Graduate degree	14.5%

Households

Total households	8,914
With persons under 18	2,725
With persons over 65	2,835
Family households	5,331
Single-person households	3,002
Persons per household	2.36
Persons per family	3.11

Income & Poverty

Per capita income	$35,359
Median household income	$74,367
Median family income	$96,342
Persons in poverty	9.9%
H'holds receiving public assistance	188
H'holds receiving social security	3,108

Labor & Employment

Total civilian labor force	11,355
Unemployment rate	6.7%
Employed persons 16 years and over, by occupation	
Managers & professionals	5,064
Service occupations	1,178
Sales & office occupations	3,056
Farming, fishing & forestry	0
Construction & maintenance	631
Production & transportation	660
Self-employed persons	534

Housing Units

Total	9,467
Single-family units	5,226
Multiple-family units	4,241
Mobile home units	0
Owner-occupied units	6,141
Renter-occupied units	2,773
Median SF home value	$427,000
Median rent	$1,127

©2010 Information Publications, Inc. All rights reserved. Photocopying prohibited. For additional copies, contact the publisher at www.informationpublications.com or (877)544-INFO (4636)

Note: The 2008 American Community Survey (ACS) produced 3-year estimates of demographic data for cities and counties with populations of at least 20,000 – in Massachusetts' case, 67 out of 351 municipalities. The ACS also produces 1-year averages for places with populations over 65,000; these can be found in Appendix D.

Taunton

Bristol County

Population

Total	56,970
Male	27,615
Female	29,355
Living in group quarters	980
percent of total	1.7%

Race & Hispanic Origin

Race	
White	50,489
Black/African American	3,020
American Indian/Alaskan Native	131
Asian	773
Hawaiian Native/Pacific Islander	0
Other race	1,468
Two or more races	1,089
Hispanic origin, total	2,951
Mexican	NA
Puerto Rican	NA
Cuban	NA
Other Hispanic	NA

Age & Nativity

Under 5 years	4,020
18 years and over	43,338
21 years and over	40,955
65 years and over	6,836
85 years and over	874
Median Age	36.1
Native-born	50,996
Foreign-born	5,974

Educational Attainment

Population 25 years and over	38,275
Less than 9th grade	6.6%
High School grad or higher	83.0%
Bachelor's degree or higher	21.0%
Graduate degree	6.7%

Households

Total households	21,752
With persons under 18	8,302
With persons over 65	4,945
Family households	14,540
Single-person households	5,815
Persons per household	2.57
Persons per family	3.10

Income & Poverty

Per capita income	$25,951
Median household income	$57,096
Median family income	$71,115
Persons in poverty	11.9%
H'holds receiving public assistance	865
H'holds receiving social security	5,661

Labor & Employment

Total civilian labor force	32,397
Unemployment rate	4.9%
Employed persons 16 years and over, by occupation	
Managers & professionals	9,271
Service occupations	6,523
Sales & office occupations	7,863
Farming, fishing & forestry	41
Construction & maintenance	2,892
Production & transportation	4,221
Self-employed persons	1,498

Housing Units

Total	23,493
Single-family units	10,560
Multiple-family units	12,060
Mobile home units	873
Owner-occupied units	13,489
Renter-occupied units	8,263
Median SF home value	$297,300
Median rent	$903

Wakefield

Middlesex County

Population

Total	24,647
Male	12,112
Female	12,535
Living in group quarters	NA
percent of total	NA

Race & Hispanic Origin

Race	
White	NA
Black/African American	NA
American Indian/Alaskan Native	NA
Asian	NA
Hawaiian Native/Pacific Islander	NA
Other race	NA
Two or more races	NA
Hispanic origin, total	NA
Mexican	NA
Puerto Rican	NA
Cuban	NA
Other Hispanic	NA

Age & Nativity

Under 5 years	1,338
18 years and over	18,952
21 years and over	18,337
65 years and over	3,257
85 years and over	648
Median Age	41.2
Native-born	23,501
Foreign-born	1,146

Educational Attainment

Population 25 years and over	17,066
Less than 9th grade	1.1%
High School grad or higher	95.9%
Bachelor's degree or higher	48.3%
Graduate degree	16.8%

Households

Total households	9,584
With persons under 18	3,016
With persons over 65	2,293
Family households	6,334
Single-person households	2,649
Persons per household	2.55
Persons per family	3.19

Income & Poverty

Per capita income	$38,979
Median household income	$88,226
Median family income	$105,764
Persons in poverty	2.4%
H'holds receiving public assistance	182
H'holds receiving social security	2,291

Labor & Employment

Total civilian labor force	14,668
Unemployment rate	5.0%
Employed persons 16 years and over, by occupation	
Managers & professionals	6,554
Service occupations	1,468
Sales & office occupations	3,562
Farming, fishing & forestry	10
Construction & maintenance	1,659
Production & transportation	675
Self-employed persons	881

Housing Units

Total	10,254
Single-family units	6,460
Multiple-family units	3,794
Mobile home units	0
Owner-occupied units	6,928
Renter-occupied units	2,656
Median SF home value	$426,800
Median rent	$1,057

Waltham

Middlesex County

Population

Total	59,587
Male	30,723
Female	28,864
Living in group quarters	8,280
percent of total	13.9%

Race & Hispanic Origin

Race	
White	45,969
Black/African American	3,364
American Indian/Alaskan Native	74
Asian	6,116
Hawaiian Native/Pacific Islander	29
Other race	3,373
Two or more races	662
Hispanic origin, total	6,538
Mexican	1,153
Puerto Rican	1,379
Cuban	78
Other Hispanic	3,928

Age & Nativity

Under 5 years	3,205
18 years and over	51,551
21 years and over	45,101
65 years and over	7,030
85 years and over	1,280
Median Age	36.8
Native-born	44,393
Foreign-born	15,194

Educational Attainment

Population 25 years and over	40,246
Less than 9th grade	5.9%
High School grad or higher	88.0%
Bachelor's degree or higher	41.1%
Graduate degree	17.9%

Households

Total households	23,204
With persons under 18	4,955
With persons over 65	4,795
Family households	11,943
Single-person households	9,023
Persons per household	2.21
Persons per family	2.98

Income & Poverty

Per capita income	$31,666
Median household income	$62,620
Median family income	$84,178
Persons in poverty	11.7%
H'holds receiving public assistance	562
H'holds receiving social security	4,787

Labor & Employment

Total civilian labor force	35,906
Unemployment rate	5.3%
Employed persons 16 years and over, by occupation	
Managers & professionals	14,439
Service occupations	5,747
Sales & office occupations	9,283
Farming, fishing & forestry	0
Construction & maintenance	2,169
Production & transportation	2,350
Self-employed persons	1,849

Housing Units

Total	24,923
Single-family units	8,967
Multiple-family units	15,907
Mobile home units	49
Owner-occupied units	10,995
Renter-occupied units	12,209
Median SF home value	$438,300
Median rent	$1,245

©2010 Information Publications, Inc. All rights reserved. Photocopying prohibited. For additional copies, contact the publisher at www.informationpublications.com or (877)544-INFO (4636)

Note: The 2008 American Community Survey (ACS) produced 3-year estimates of demographic data for cities and counties with populations of at least 20,000 – in Massachusetts' case, 67 out of 351 municipalities. The ACS also produces 1-year averages for places with populations over 65,000; these can be found in Appendix D.

Watertown
Middlesex County

Population	
Total	32,023
Male	14,827
Female	17,196
Living in group quarters	1,571
percent of total	4.9%
Race & Hispanic Origin	
Race	
White	28,644
Black/African American	946
American Indian/Alaskan Native	0
Asian	1,897
Hawaiian Native/Pacific Islander	56
Other race	146
Two or more races	334
Hispanic origin, total	1,427
Mexican	205
Puerto Rican	95
Cuban	0
Other Hispanic	1,127
Age & Nativity	
Under 5 years	1,503
18 years and over	27,675
21 years and over	26,033
65 years and over	4,859
85 years and over	859
Median Age	38.9
Native-born	25,610
Foreign-born	6,413
Educational Attainment	
Population 25 years and over	23,834
Less than 9th grade	3.6%
High School grad or higher	93.0%
Bachelor's degree or higher	54.7%
Graduate degree	24.6%
Households	
Total households	13,984
With persons under 18	2,909
With persons over 65	3,279
Family households	6,989
Single-person households	5,123
Persons per household	2.18
Persons per family	2.91
Income & Poverty	
Per capita income	$38,739
Median household income	$70,127
Median family income	$81,613
Persons in poverty	6.8%
H'holds receiving public assistance	211
H'holds receiving social security	3,448
Labor & Employment	
Total civilian labor force	19,276
Unemployment rate	5.2%
Employed persons 16 years and over, by occupation	
Managers & professionals	10,282
Service occupations	1,789
Sales & office occupations	4,495
Farming, fishing & forestry	0
Construction & maintenance	894
Production & transportation	813
Self-employed persons	958
Housing Units	
Total	14,980
Single-family units	3,302
Multiple-family units	11,678
Mobile home units	0
Owner-occupied units	7,218
Renter-occupied units	6,766
Median SF home value	$454,800
Median rent	$1,400

Wellesley
Norfolk County

Population	
Total	30,969
Male	13,258
Female	17,711
Living in group quarters	5,260
percent of total	17.0%
Race & Hispanic Origin	
Race	
White	26,190
Black/African American	319
American Indian/Alaskan Native	11
Asian	3,301
Hawaiian Native/Pacific Islander	0
Other race	529
Two or more races	619
Hispanic origin, total	1,458
Mexican	366
Puerto Rican	148
Cuban	72
Other Hispanic	872
Age & Nativity	
Under 5 years	1,832
18 years and over	23,035
21 years and over	18,767
65 years and over	4,175
85 years and over	629
Median Age	37
Native-born	26,157
Foreign-born	4,812
Educational Attainment	
Population 25 years and over	16,935
Less than 9th grade	1.3%
High School grad or higher	97.3%
Bachelor's degree or higher	78.3%
Graduate degree	44.8%
Households	
Total households	9,488
With persons under 18	4,066
With persons over 65	2,619
Family households	7,044
Single-person households	2,138
Persons per household	2.71
Persons per family	3.22
Income & Poverty	
Per capita income	$64,795
Median household income	$138,772
Median family income	$174,631
Persons in poverty	6.1%
H'holds receiving public assistance	70
H'holds receiving social security	2,631
Labor & Employment	
Total civilian labor force	14,255
Unemployment rate	5.5%
Employed persons 16 years and over, by occupation	
Managers & professionals	8,500
Service occupations	1,214
Sales & office occupations	3,270
Farming, fishing & forestry	0
Construction & maintenance	173
Production & transportation	314
Self-employed persons	1,253
Housing Units	
Total	10,077
Single-family units	7,843
Multiple-family units	2,234
Mobile home units	0
Owner-occupied units	7,425
Renter-occupied units	2,063
Median SF home value	$899,400
Median rent	$1,111

Westfield
Hampden County

Population	
Total	42,101
Male	20,434
Female	21,667
Living in group quarters	2,740
percent of total	6.5%
Race & Hispanic Origin	
Race	
White	39,179
Black/African American	438
American Indian/Alaskan Native	113
Asian	614
Hawaiian Native/Pacific Islander	36
Other race	879
Two or more races	842
Hispanic origin, total	2,410
Mexican	NA
Puerto Rican	NA
Cuban	NA
Other Hispanic	NA
Age & Nativity	
Under 5 years	2,521
18 years and over	32,103
21 years and over	28,945
65 years and over	5,309
85 years and over	977
Median Age	37.2
Native-born	38,922
Foreign-born	3,179
Educational Attainment	
Population 25 years and over	26,768
Less than 9th grade	3.3%
High School grad or higher	89.3%
Bachelor's degree or higher	26.5%
Graduate degree	8.9%
Households	
Total households	15,159
With persons under 18	5,316
With persons over 65	3,867
Family households	10,084
Single-person households	4,084
Persons per household	2.60
Persons per family	3.16
Income & Poverty	
Per capita income	$25,542
Median household income	$51,972
Median family income	$70,037
Persons in poverty	14.1%
H'holds receiving public assistance	446
H'holds receiving social security	4,533
Labor & Employment	
Total civilian labor force	21,044
Unemployment rate	7.6%
Employed persons 16 years and over, by occupation	
Managers & professionals	6,879
Service occupations	3,048
Sales & office occupations	5,612
Farming, fishing & forestry	0
Construction & maintenance	1,408
Production & transportation	2,504
Self-employed persons	794
Housing Units	
Total	15,723
Single-family units	8,666
Multiple-family units	6,626
Mobile home units	420
Owner-occupied units	10,133
Renter-occupied units	5,026
Median SF home value	$228,700
Median rent	$832

©2010 Information Publications, Inc. All rights reserved. Photocopying prohibited. For additional copies, contact the publisher at www.informationpublications.com or (877)544-INFO (4636)

Note: The 2008 American Community Survey (ACS) produced 3-year estimates of demographic data for cities and counties with populations of at least 20,000 – in Massachusetts' case, 67 out of 351 municipalities. The ACS also produces 1-year averages for places with populations over 65,000; these can be found in Appendix D.

West Springfield
Hampden County

Population	
Total	28,473
Male	13,728
Female	14,745
Living in group quarters	NA
percent of total	NA
Race & Hispanic Origin	
Race	
White	26,392
Black/African American	698
American Indian/Alaskan Native	50
Asian	646
Hawaiian Native/Pacific Islander	0
Other race	333
Two or more races	354
Hispanic origin, total	1,294
Mexican	NA
Puerto Rican	NA
Cuban	NA
Other Hispanic	NA
Age & Nativity	
Under 5 years	1,767
18 years and over	22,215
21 years and over	21,181
65 years and over	4,405
85 years and over	620
Median Age	38.9
Native-born	24,383
Foreign-born	4,090
Educational Attainment	
Population 25 years and over	18,967
Less than 9th grade	3.1%
High School grad or higher	86.9%
Bachelor's degree or higher	27.7%
Graduate degree	10.2%
Households	
Total households	11,697
With persons under 18	3,377
With persons over 65	3,021
Family households	6,770
Single-person households	4,075
Persons per household	2.39
Persons per family	3.16
Income & Poverty	
Per capita income	$26,511
Median household income	$49,236
Median family income	$63,704
Persons in poverty	10.2%
H'holds receiving public assistance	628
H'holds receiving social security	3,355
Labor & Employment	
Total civilian labor force	15,361
Unemployment rate	6.2%
Employed persons 16 years and over, by occupation	
Managers & professionals	4,781
Service occupations	2,600
Sales & office occupations	3,825
Farming, fishing & forestry	0
Construction & maintenance	1,254
Production & transportation	1,946
Self-employed persons	673
Housing Units	
Total	12,571
Single-family units	6,211
Multiple-family units	6,221
Mobile home units	139
Owner-occupied units	6,779
Renter-occupied units	4,918
Median SF home value	$213,200
Median rent	$747

Weymouth
Norfolk County

Population	
Total	51,593
Male	24,929
Female	26,664
Living in group quarters	601
percent of total	1.2%
Race & Hispanic Origin	
Race	
White	47,071
Black/African American	1,783
American Indian/Alaskan Native	0
Asian	1,562
Hawaiian Native/Pacific Islander	0
Other race	625
Two or more races	552
Hispanic origin, total	1,132
Mexican	22
Puerto Rican	406
Cuban	16
Other Hispanic	688
Age & Nativity	
Under 5 years	3,213
18 years and over	40,906
21 years and over	39,092
65 years and over	7,745
85 years and over	780
Median Age	40.7
Native-born	47,010
Foreign-born	4,583
Educational Attainment	
Population 25 years and over	37,029
Less than 9th grade	1.1%
High School grad or higher	93.9%
Bachelor's degree or higher	29.6%
Graduate degree	9.0%
Households	
Total households	21,691
With persons under 18	6,254
With persons over 65	5,389
Family households	13,427
Single-person households	6,875
Persons per household	2.35
Persons per family	3.03
Income & Poverty	
Per capita income	$34,869
Median household income	$64,897
Median family income	$82,118
Persons in poverty	6.0%
H'holds receiving public assistance	387
H'holds receiving social security	5,839
Labor & Employment	
Total civilian labor force	29,976
Unemployment rate	4.2%
Employed persons 16 years and over, by occupation	
Managers & professionals	10,324
Service occupations	4,767
Sales & office occupations	8,131
Farming, fishing & forestry	0
Construction & maintenance	3,142
Production & transportation	2,351
Self-employed persons	1,404
Housing Units	
Total	22,843
Single-family units	12,773
Multiple-family units	9,951
Mobile home units	119
Owner-occupied units	14,529
Renter-occupied units	7,162
Median SF home value	$347,200
Median rent	$1,135

Wilmington
Middlesex County

Population	
Total	23,495
Male	11,896
Female	11,599
Living in group quarters	NA
percent of total	NA
Race & Hispanic Origin	
Race	
White	NA
Black/African American	NA
American Indian/Alaskan Native	NA
Asian	NA
Hawaiian Native/Pacific Islander	NA
Other race	NA
Two or more races	NA
Hispanic origin, total	168
Mexican	NA
Puerto Rican	NA
Cuban	NA
Other Hispanic	NA
Age & Nativity	
Under 5 years	1,203
18 years and over	17,501
21 years and over	16,475
65 years and over	2,942
85 years and over	277
Median Age	40.4
Native-born	21,958
Foreign-born	1,537
Educational Attainment	
Population 25 years and over	15,537
Less than 9th grade	1.7%
High School grad or higher	93.4%
Bachelor's degree or higher	30.6%
Graduate degree	9.5%
Households	
Total households	7,456
With persons under 18	3,218
With persons over 65	1,890
Family households	6,306
Single-person households	956
Persons per household	3.13
Persons per family	3.42
Income & Poverty	
Per capita income	$34,239
Median household income	$94,452
Median family income	$100,062
Persons in poverty	3.7%
H'holds receiving public assistance	120
H'holds receiving social security	1,940
Labor & Employment	
Total civilian labor force	13,565
Unemployment rate	6.5%
Employed persons 16 years and over, by occupation	
Managers & professionals	5,002
Service occupations	1,620
Sales & office occupations	3,619
Farming, fishing & forestry	0
Construction & maintenance	1,115
Production & transportation	1,325
Self-employed persons	608
Housing Units	
Total	7,662
Single-family units	6,714
Multiple-family units	948
Mobile home units	0
Owner-occupied units	6,649
Renter-occupied units	807
Median SF home value	$410,500
Median rent	$1,431

©2010 Information Publications, Inc. All rights reserved. Photocopying prohibited. For additional copies, contact the publisher at www.informationpublications.com or (877)544-INFO (4636)

Note: The 2008 American Community Survey (ACS) produced 3-year estimates of demographic data for cities and counties with populations of at least 20,000 – in Massachusetts' case, 67 out of 351 municipalities. The ACS also produces 1-year averages for places with populations over 65,000; these can be found in Appendix D.

	Winchester (Middlesex County)	Winthrop (Suffolk County)	Woburn (Middlesex County)
Population			
Total	22,176	20,886	39,069
Male	10,003	9,582	18,670
Female	12,173	11,304	20,399
Living in group quarters	NA	NA	NA
percent of total	NA	NA	NA
Race & Hispanic Origin			
Race			
White	NA	18,283	33,760
Black/African American	NA	640	1,188
American Indian/Alaskan Native	NA	27	0
Asian	NA	140	2,884
Hawaiian Native/Pacific Islander	NA	0	0
Other race	NA	997	923
Two or more races	NA	799	314
Hispanic origin, total	NA	1,082	1,389
Mexican	NA	NA	NA
Puerto Rican	NA	NA	NA
Cuban	NA	NA	NA
Other Hispanic	NA	NA	NA
Age & Nativity			
Under 5 years	1,613	1,594	2,658
18 years and over	15,925	15,662	30,651
21 years and over	15,335	15,066	29,603
65 years and over	3,602	2,955	6,009
85 years and over	803	389	837
Median Age	42.5	39.9	39.4
Native-born	19,235	18,263	33,106
Foreign-born	2,941	2,623	5,963
Educational Attainment			
Population 25 years and over	14,709	14,497	27,869
Less than 9th grade	0.7%	3.8%	2.4%
High School grad or higher	97.6%	90.4%	91.9%
Bachelor's degree or higher	70.5%	28.6%	32.2%
Graduate degree	42.1%	10.0%	13.0%
Households			
Total households	7,944	7,946	15,337
With persons under 18	3,111	2,501	4,892
With persons over 65	2,301	2,009	4,288
Family households	5,669	4,571	10,233
Single-person households	2,028	2,771	4,255
Persons per household	2.73	2.61	2.54
Persons per family	3.35	3.43	3.14
Income & Poverty			
Per capita income	$62,479	$31,834	$32,804
Median household income	$117,952	$62,500	$73,593
Median family income	$163,847	$75,470	$85,318
Persons in poverty	2.2%	9.6%	5.6%
H'holds receiving public assistance	91	87	333
H'holds receiving social security	2,279	2,143	4,492
Labor & Employment			
Total civilian labor force	10,137	11,112	22,914
Unemployment rate	4.6%	4.1%	5.4%
Employed persons 16 years and over, by occupation			
Managers & professionals	6,864	3,912	8,962
Service occupations	866	1,928	2,692
Sales & office occupations	1,517	3,352	6,176
Farming, fishing & forestry	0	0	0
Construction & maintenance	216	896	1,621
Production & transportation	211	567	2,217
Self-employed persons	970	337	973
Housing Units			
Total	8,170	8,452	16,446
Single-family units	5,873	2,682	8,498
Multiple-family units	2,297	5,770	7,948
Mobile home units	0	0	0
Owner-occupied units	6,648	4,612	9,964
Renter-occupied units	1,296	3,334	5,373
Median SF home value	$708,600	$397,400	$396,200
Median rent	$1,216	$1,171	$1,162

©2010 Information Publications, Inc. All rights reserved. Photocopying prohibited. For additional copies, contact the publisher at www.informationpublications.com or (877)544-INFO (4636)

Note: The 2008 American Community Survey (ACS) produced 3-year estimates of demographic data for cities and counties with populations of at least 20,000 – in Massachusetts' case, 67 out of 351 municipalities. The ACS also produces 1-year averages for places with populations over 65,000; these can be found in Appendix D.

Worcester

Worcester County

Population

Total	163,637
Male	81,185
Female	82,452
Living in group quarters	10,502
percent of total	6.4%

Race & Hispanic Origin

Race	
White	128,478
Black/African American	14,750
American Indian/Alaskan Native	474
Asian	8,911
Hawaiian Native/Pacific Islander	398
Other race	7,272
Two or more races	3,354
Hispanic origin, total	31,596
Mexican	1,997
Puerto Rican	20,039
Cuban	247
Other Hispanic	9,313

Age & Nativity

Under 5 years	9,332
18 years and over	129,647
21 years and over	118,071
65 years and over	20,591
85 years and over	4,099
Median Age	34.4
Native-born	131,011
Foreign-born	32,626

Educational Attainment

Population 25 years and over	105,826
Less than 9th grade	7.3%
High School grad or higher	83.7%
Bachelor's degree or higher	28.2%
Graduate degree	10.6%

Households

Total households	64,929
With persons under 18	20,090
With persons over 65	14,252
Family households	36,683
Single-person households	22,865
Persons per household	2.36
Persons per family	3.05

Income & Poverty

Per capita income	$24,626
Median household income	$44,794
Median family income	$53,333
Persons in poverty	17.5%
H'holds receiving public assistance	3,082
H'holds receiving social security	16,538

Labor & Employment

Total civilian labor force	85,360
Unemployment rate	6.5%
Employed persons 16 years and over, by occupation	
Managers & professionals	25,646
Service occupations	16,928
Sales & office occupations	20,906
Farming, fishing & forestry	77
Construction & maintenance	5,330
Production & transportation	10,961
Self-employed persons	3,588

Housing Units

Total	73,511
Single-family units	23,857
Multiple-family units	49,527
Mobile home units	85
Owner-occupied units	30,296
Renter-occupied units	34,633
Median SF home value	$249,700
Median rent	$837

©2010 Information Publications, Inc. All rights reserved. Photocopying prohibited. For additional copies, contact the publisher at www.informationpublications.com or (877)544-INFO (4636)

Acton-Boxborough

Academic Regional - #600
16 Charter Rd
Acton, MA 01720
978-264-4700

Superintendent............. Stephen Mills
Grade plan............................7-12
Total enrollment '09-10 2,930
Grade 12 enrollment, '09-10 459
Graduation rate 96.6%
Dropout rate.........................1.0%
Per-pupil expenditure.............$12,228
Avg teacher salary $67,514
Student/teacher ratio '08-09 ...... 16.8 to 1
Highly-qualified teachers, '08-09 ... 100.0%
Teachers licensed in assigned subject .99.4%
Students per computer ....NA

Massachusetts Competency Assessment System (MCAS), 2007 results

	English		Math	
	% Prof	CPI	% Prof	CPI
Gr 4	NA	NA	NA	NA
Gr 6	NA	NA	NA	NA
Gr 8	93%	97	83%	92.1
Gr 10	96%	98.8	95%	98.5

Recieves students from:
Acton, Boxborough

Adams-Cheshire

Academic Regional - #603
125 Savoy Road
Cheshire, MA 01225
413-743-2939

Superintendent.............Alfred Skrocki
Grade plan........................ PK-12
Total enrollment '09-10 1,554
Grade 12 enrollment, '09-10 90
Graduation rate 75.2%
Dropout rate.........................9.5%
Per-pupil expenditure............. $11,603
Avg teacher salary $56,912
Student/teacher ratio '08-09 ...... 14.1 to 1
Highly-qualified teachers, '08-09.....97.2%
Teachers licensed in assigned subject 98.2%
Students per computer 6.7

Massachusetts Competency Assessment System (MCAS), 2007 results

	English		Math	
	% Prof	CPI	% Prof	CPI
Gr 4	36%	73.1	29%	71.8
Gr 6	55%	83.7	35%	69.2
Gr 8	77%	91.3	40%	71.5
Gr 10	87%	96.4	70%	87.5

Recieves students from:
Adams, Cheshire, Savoy

Amherst-Pelham

Academic Regional - #605
170 Chestnut Street
Amherst, MA 01002
413-362-1805

Superintendent.............. Maria Geryk
Grade plan............................7-12
Total enrollment '09-10 1,661
Grade 12 enrollment, '09-10 292
Graduation rate 88.6%
Dropout rate.........................5.2%
Per-pupil expenditure............. $16,131
Avg teacher salary $62,552
Student/teacher ratio '08-09 ...... 11.5 to 1
Highly-qualified teachers, '08-09.... 88.7%
Teachers licensed in assigned subject .95.7%
Students per computer 3.1

Massachusetts Competency Assessment System (MCAS), 2007 results

	English		Math	
	% Prof	CPI	% Prof	CPI
Gr 4	NA	NA	NA	NA
Gr 6	NA	NA	NA	NA
Gr 8	90%	96.9	65%	83.3
Gr 10	91%	96	86%	93.2

Recieves students from:
Amherst, Leverett, Pelham, Shutesbury

Ashburnham-Westminster

Academic Regional - #610
11 Oakmont Drive, c/o Office of the Superintendent
Ashburnham, MA 01430
978-827-1434

Superintendent.......... Michael Zapantis
Grade plan........................ PK-12
Total enrollment '09-10 2,388
Grade 12 enrollment, '09-10 174
Graduation rate 90.1%
Dropout rate.........................4.4%
Per-pupil expenditure............. $10,927
Avg teacher salary $64,246
Student/teacher ratio '08-09 ...... 15.3 to 1
Highly-qualified teachers, '08-09.... 95.0%
Teachers licensed in assigned subject 96.9%
Students per computer 3.6

Massachusetts Competency Assessment System (MCAS), 2007 results

	English		Math	
	% Prof	CPI	% Prof	CPI
Gr 4	53%	81.6	41%	77
Gr 6	72%	90	53%	79
Gr 8	90%	96.3	54%	78.9
Gr 10	86%	95	88%	94.9

Recieves students from:
Ashburnham, Westminster

Assabet Valley

Vocational Technical - #801
215 Fitchburg Street
Marlborough, MA 01752
508-485-9430

Superintendent......... Mary Jo Nawrocki
Grade plan............................9-12
Total enrollment '09-10 963
Grade 12 enrollment, '09-10 198
Graduation rate 85.8%
Dropout rate....................... 4.9%
Per-pupil expenditure............. $18,662
Avg teacher salary $66,488
Student/teacher ratio '08-09 .... 9.3 to 1
Highly-qualified teachers, '08-09.....93.6%
Teachers licensed in assigned subject 90.9%
Students per computer 1.6

Massachusetts Competency Assessment System (MCAS), 2007 results

	English		Math	
	% Prof	CPI	% Prof	CPI
Gr 4	NA	NA	NA	NA
Gr 6	NA	NA	NA	NA
Gr 8	NA	NA	NA	NA
Gr 10	75%	91.3	76%	90.8

Recieves students from:
Berlin, Hudson, Marlborough, Maynard, Northborough, Southborough, Westborough

Athol-Royalston

Academic Regional - #615
P.O.Box 968, 1062 Pleasant Street
Athol, MA 01331
978-249-2400

Superintendent............Anthony Polito
Grade plan........................ PK-12
Total enrollment '09-10 1,682
Grade 12 enrollment, '09-10 98
Graduation rate 67.7%
Dropout rate........................16.5%
Per-pupil expenditure............. $11,013
Avg teacher salary $55,015
Student/teacher ratio '08-09 ...... 13.1 to 1
Highly-qualified teachers, '08-09.... 98.7%
Teachers licensed in assigned subject .97.7%
Students per computer 8.8

Massachusetts Competency Assessment System (MCAS), 2007 results

	English		Math	
	% Prof	CPI	% Prof	CPI
Gr 4	27%	68.4	27%	67.4
Gr 6	52%	79	54%	76.7
Gr 8	72%	89.3	27%	55.7
Gr 10	86%	93.9	66%	86.2

Recieves students from:
Athol, Royalston

©2010 Information Publications, Inc. All rights reserved. Photocopying prohibited. For additional copies, contact the publisher at www.informationpublications.com or (877)544-INFO (4636)

School data 2007-2008 except as noted.

©2010 Information Publications, Inc. All rights reserved. Photocopying prohibited. For additional copies, contact the publisher at www.informationpublications.com or (877)544-INFO (4636)

Berkshire Hills

Academic Regional - #618
50 Main Street, PO Box 617
Stockbridge, MA 01262
413-298-4017

Superintendent. . . . . Peter Dillon
Grade plan. PK-12
Total enrollment '09-10 1,377
Grade 12 enrollment, '09-10 176
Graduation rate 80.6%
Dropout rate. 9.1%
Per-pupil expenditure. $14,240
Avg teacher salary $59,614
Student/teacher ratio '08-09 . . . . . . 10.3 to 1
Highly-qualified teachers, '08-09 . . . . .97.9%
Teachers licensed in assigned subject .97.1%
Students per computer 2.5

Massachusetts Competency Assessment System (MCAS), 2007 results

	English		Math	
	% Prof	CPI	% Prof	CPI
Gr 4	38%	74.1	37%	75
Gr 6	78%	94.2	58%	82.5
Gr 8	83%	93.1	43%	71.8
Gr 10	86%	94.5	84%	91.6

Recieves students from:
Great Barrington, Stockbridge, West Stockbridge, Farmingham River Regional

Berlin-Boylston

Academic Regional - #620
215 Main Street
Boylston, MA 01505
508-869-2837

Superintendent. . . . . .Brian McDermott
Grade plan. 7-12
Total enrollment '09-10 444
Grade 12 enrollment, '09-10 89
Graduation rate .94.1%
Dropout rate. 1.5%
Per-pupil expenditure. $12,201
Avg teacher salary $60,917
Student/teacher ratio '08-09 . . . . . . 12.7 to 1
Highly-qualified teachers, '08-09 . . . 100.0%
Teachers licensed in assigned subject 100.0%
Students per computer 4.1

Massachusetts Competency Assessment System (MCAS), 2007 results

	English		Math	
	% Prof	CPI	% Prof	CPI
Gr 4	NA	NA	NA	NA
Gr 6	NA	NA	NA	NA
Gr 8	89%	94.8	51%	74.1
Gr 10	95%	99	84%	95.5

Recieves students from:
Berlin, Boylston

Blackstone Valley

Vocational Technical - #805
65 Pleasant Street
Upton, MA 01568
508-529-7758

Superintendent. . . . . Michael Fitzpatrick
Grade plan. 9-12
Total enrollment '09-10 1,136
Grade 12 enrollment, '09-10 266
Graduation rate .97.2%
Dropout rate. 0.9%
Per-pupil expenditure. $16,400
Avg teacher salary $64,581
Student/teacher ratio '08-09 . . . . . . 11.2 to 1
Highly-qualified teachers, '08-09 . . . . 82.9%
Teachers licensed in assigned subject 88.3%
Students per computer 1.5

Massachusetts Competency Assessment System (MCAS), 2007 results

	English		Math	
	% Prof	CPI	% Prof	CPI
Gr 4	NA	NA	NA	NA
Gr 6	NA	NA	NA	NA
Gr 8	NA	NA	NA	NA
Gr 10	86%	95.4	84%	93.5

Recieves students from:
Bellingham, Blackstone, Douglas, Grafton, Hopedale, Mendon, Milford, Millbury, Millville, Northbridge, Sutton, Upton, Uxbridge

Blackstone-Millville

Academic Regional - #622
175 Lincoln Street
Blackstone, MA 01504
508-883-4400

Superintendent. . . . . Kimberly Shaver-Hood
Grade plan. PK-12
Total enrollment '09-10 2,064
Grade 12 enrollment, '09-10 130
Graduation rate 90.2%
Dropout rate. 4.2%
Per-pupil expenditure. $9,936
Avg teacher salary $58,706
Student/teacher ratio '08-09 . . . . . . 13.9 to 1
Highly-qualified teachers, '08-09 . . . . .96.1%
Teachers licensed in assigned subject .97.4%
Students per computer 3.3

Massachusetts Competency Assessment System (MCAS), 2007 results

	English		Math	
	% Prof	CPI	% Prof	CPI
Gr 4	59%	83.1	56%	83
Gr 6	66%	85.8	56%	78.2
Gr 8	78%	91.8	54%	77.7
Gr 10	89%	96.4	79%	91.3

Recieves students from:
Blackstone, Millville

Blue Hills

Vocational Technical - #806
800 Randolph Street
Canton, MA 02021
781-828-5800

Superintendent. . . . . .Joseph Ciccolo
Grade plan. 9-12
Total enrollment '09-10 842
Grade 12 enrollment, '09-10 196
Graduation rate 92.7%
Dropout rate. 5.0%
Per-pupil expenditure. $20,254
Avg teacher salary $74,125
Student/teacher ratio '08-09 . . . . 9.9 to 1
Highly-qualified teachers, '08-09 . . . . .74.8%
Teachers licensed in assigned subject .91.8%
Students per computer 1.6

Massachusetts Competency Assessment System (MCAS), 2007 results

	English		Math	
	% Prof	CPI	% Prof	CPI
Gr 4	NA	NA	NA	NA
Gr 6	NA	NA	NA	NA
Gr 8	NA	NA	NA	NA
Gr 10	72%	90.3	63%	85.6

Recieves students from:
Avon, Braintree, Canton, Dedham, Holbrook, Milton, Norwood, Randolph, Westwood

Bridgewater-Raynham

Academic Regional - #625
166 Mt. Prospect Street
Bridgewater, MA 02324
508-279-2140

Superintendent. . . . . Jacqueline Forbes
Grade plan. PK-12
Total enrollment '09-10 5,804
Grade 12 enrollment, '09-10 413
Graduation rate 88.0%
Dropout rate. 5.7%
Per-pupil expenditure. $10,358
Avg teacher salary $67,990
Student/teacher ratio '08-09 . . . . . . 18.1 to 1
Highly-qualified teachers, '08-09 . . . . 98.8%
Teachers licensed in assigned subject .99.3%
Students per computer 3.8

Massachusetts Competency Assessment System (MCAS), 2007 results

	English		Math	
	% Prof	CPI	% Prof	CPI
Gr 4	68%	87.5	46%	79.6
Gr 6	77%	91.2	59%	81.6
Gr 8	89%	95.9	54%	77.2
Gr 10	84%	93.8	78%	90.3

Recieves students from:
Bridgewater, Raynham

School data 2007-2008 except as noted.

Bristol County Agricultural

County Agricultural - #910
135 Center Street
Dighton, MA 02715
508-669-6744

Superintendent. . . . . Krista Paynton
Grade plan. 9-12
Total enrollment '09-10 441
Grade 12 enrollment, '09-10 100
Graduation rate 96.2%
Dropout rate. 2.9%
Per-pupil expenditure. $17,817
Avg teacher salary $55,231
Student/teacher ratio '08-09 . . . . . . 12.8 to 1
Highly-qualified teachers, '08-09 . . . 100.0%
Teachers licensed in assigned subject .91.0%
Students per computer 3

Massachusetts Competency Assessment System (MCAS), 2007 results

	English % Prof	English CPI	Math % Prof	Math CPI
Gr 4	NA	NA	NA	NA
Gr 6	NA	NA	NA	NA
Gr 8	NA	NA	NA	NA
Gr 10	86%	95.4	84%	94.3

Recieves students from:
Acushnet, Attleboro, Berkley, Dartmouth, Dighton, Easton, Fairhaven, Fall River, Freetown, Mansfield, New Bedford, North Attleborough, Norton, Raynham, Rehoboth, Seekonk, Somerset, Swansea, Taunton, Westport

Bristol-Plymouth

Vocational Technical - #810
940 County Street
Taunton, MA 02780
508-823-5151

Superintendent. . . . . Richard Gross
Grade plan. 9-12
Total enrollment '09-10 1,206
Grade 12 enrollment, '09-10 276
Graduation rate 92.6%
Dropout rate. 6.6%
Per-pupil expenditure. $14,881
Avg teacher salary $70,798
Student/teacher ratio '08-09 . . . . . . 12.7 to 1
Highly-qualified teachers, '08-09 . . . 100.0%
Teachers licensed in assigned subject 98.9%
Students per computer 3.9

Massachusetts Competency Assessment System (MCAS), 2007 results

	English % Prof	English CPI	Math % Prof	Math CPI
Gr 4	NA	NA	NA	NA
Gr 6	NA	NA	NA	NA
Gr 8	NA	NA	NA	NA
Gr 10	85%	95.2	71%	89.1

Recieves students from:
Berkley, Bridgewater, Middleborough, Raynham, Taunton

Cape Cod Regional

Vocational Technical - #815
351 Pleasant Lake Avenue
Harwich, MA 02645
508-432-4500

Superintendent. . . . . William Fisher
Grade plan. 9-12
Total enrollment '09-10 685
Grade 12 enrollment, '09-10 151
Graduation rate 89.5%
Dropout rate. 6.6%
Per-pupil expenditure. . . . . NA
Avg teacher salary . . . . NA
Student/teacher ratio '08-09 . . . . . . 10.4 to 1
Highly-qualified teachers, '08-09 . . . . 95.4%
Teachers licensed in assigned subject 92.6%
Students per computer 2

Massachusetts Competency Assessment System (MCAS), 2007 results

	English % Prof	English CPI	Math % Prof	Math CPI
Gr 4	NA	NA	NA	NA
Gr 6	NA	NA	NA	NA
Gr 8	NA	NA	NA	NA
Gr 10	76%	91.4	70%	88.1

Recieves students from:
Barnstable, Brewster, Chatham, Dennis, Eastham, Harwich, Leyden, Mashpee, Orleans, Provincetown, Truro, Wellfleet, Yarmouth

Central Berkshire

Academic Regional - #635
PO Box 299
Dalton, MA 01227
413-684-0320

Superintendent. . . . . James Stankiewicz
Grade plan. PK-12
Total enrollment '09-10 1,987
Grade 12 enrollment, '09-10 161
Graduation rate 89.6%
Dropout rate. 5.0%
Per-pupil expenditure. $11,385
Avg teacher salary $61,711
Student/teacher ratio '08-09 . . . . . . 14.1 to 1
Highly-qualified teachers, '08-09 . . . . 95.3%
Teachers licensed in assigned subject .95.1%
Students per computer 3.3

Massachusetts Competency Assessment System (MCAS), 2007 results

	English % Prof	English CPI	Math % Prof	Math CPI
Gr 4	54%	81.4	46%	79
Gr 6	61%	83.9	44%	73
Gr 8	79%	93	51%	75.9
Gr 10	87%	96.2	76%	90.5

Recieves students from:
Becket, Cummington, Dalton, Hinsdale, Peru, Washington, Windsor

Chesterfield-Goshen

Academic Regional - #632
19 Stage Rd
Westhampton, MA 01027
413-527-7200

Superintendent. . . . . Craig Jurgensen
Grade plan. PK-6
Total enrollment '09-10 187
Grade 12 enrollment, '09-10 0
Graduation rate . . . . NA
Dropout rate. . . . . NA
Per-pupil expenditure. $10,315
Avg teacher salary $48,311
Student/teacher ratio '08-09 . . . . . . 11.7 to 1
Highly-qualified teachers, '08-09 . . . . 91.9%
Teachers licensed in assigned subject .93.5%
Students per computer 7

Massachusetts Competency Assessment System (MCAS), 2007 results

	English % Prof	English CPI	Math % Prof	Math CPI
Gr 4	42%	77.6	53%	82.9
Gr 6	54%	79.2	50%	76
Gr 8	NA	NA	NA	NA
Gr 10	NA	NA	NA	NA

Recieves students from:
Chesterfield, Goshen

Concord-Carlisle

Academic Regional - #640
120 Meriam Rd
Concord, MA 01742
978-341-2490

Superintendent. . . . . Diana Rigby
Grade plan. 9-12
Total enrollment '09-10 1,245
Grade 12 enrollment, '09-10 334
Graduation rate 94.4%
Dropout rate. 1.6%
Per-pupil expenditure. $17,486
Avg teacher salary $74,296
Student/teacher ratio '08-09 . . . . . . 13.5 to 1
Highly-qualified teachers, '08-09 . . . . 98.5%
Teachers licensed in assigned subject 100.0%
Students per computer 1.5

Massachusetts Competency Assessment System (MCAS), 2007 results

	English % Prof	English CPI	Math % Prof	Math CPI
Gr 4	NA	NA	NA	NA
Gr 6	NA	NA	NA	NA
Gr 8	NA	NA	NA	NA
Gr 10	96%	98.9	88%	95.2

Recieves students from:
Carlisle, Concord

©2010 Information Publications, Inc. All rights reserved. Photocopying prohibited. For additional copies, contact the publisher at www.informationpublications.com or (877)544-INFO (4636)

School data 2007-2008 except as noted.

Dennis-Yarmouth

Academic Regional - #645
296 Station Avenue
South Yarmouth, MA 02664
508-398-7600

Superintendent..........Carol Woodbury
Grade plan........................ PK-12
Total enrollment '09-10 3,349
Grade 12 enrollment, '09-10 223
Graduation rate 74.0%
Dropout rate......................14.7%
Per-pupil expenditure............ $12,922
Avg teacher salary $57,718
Student/teacher ratio '08-09 ...... 12.1 to 1
Highly-qualified teachers, '08-09.....97.3%
Teachers licensed in assigned subject .99.1%
Students per computer 3.2

Massachusetts Competency Assessment System (MCAS), 2007 results

	English		Math	
	% Prof	CPI	% Prof	CPI
Gr 4	43%	74.2	38%	73.1
Gr 6	63%	84.5	47%	74.5
Gr 8	85%	92.9	50%	74.5
Gr 10	82%	92.4	76%	87.9

Recieves students from:
Dennis, Yarmouth

Dighton-Rehoboth

Academic Regional - #650
2700 Regional Road
North Dighton, MA 02764
508-252-5000

Superintendent.......Kathleen Montagano
Grade plan....................... PK-12
Total enrollment '09-10 3,235
Grade 12 enrollment, '09-10 274
Graduation rate 88.7%
Dropout rate.......................8.5%
Per-pupil expenditure............ $10,037
Avg teacher salary $58,788
Student/teacher ratio '08-09 ...... 15.7 to 1
Highly-qualified teachers, '08-09.....97.7%
Teachers licensed in assigned subject .97.2%
Students per computer 4.1

Massachusetts Competency Assessment System (MCAS), 2007 results

	English		Math	
	% Prof	CPI	% Prof	CPI
Gr 4	62%	85.6	50%	81.7
Gr 6	74%	89.8	58%	83
Gr 8	89%	96.7	55%	79.6
Gr 10	88%	95.8	81%	91.5

Recieves students from:
Dighton, Rehoboth

Dover-Sherborn

Academic Regional - #655
157 Farm Street
Dover, MA 02030
508-785-0036

Superintendent........... Valerie Spriggs
Grade plan.........................6-12
Total enrollment '09-10 1,150
Grade 12 enrollment, '09-10 153
Graduation rate 99.3%
Dropout rate.......................0.0%
Per-pupil expenditure............ $15,690
Avg teacher salary $73,396
Student/teacher ratio '08-09 ...... 11.1 to 1
Highly-qualified teachers, '08-09.....97.0%
Teachers licensed in assigned subject 98.4%
Students per computer 3.5

Massachusetts Competency Assessment System (MCAS), 2007 results

	English		Math	
	% Prof	CPI	% Prof	CPI
Gr 4	NA	NA	NA	NA
Gr 6	90%	95.6	81%	91.1
Gr 8	95%	98.8	77%	90.7
Gr 10	99%	99.6	98%	98.8

Recieves students from:
Dover, Sherborn

Dudley-Charlton

Academic Regional - #658
68 Dudley Oxford Road
Dudley, MA 01571
508-943-6888

Superintendent..............Sean Gilrein
Grade plan....................... PK-12
Total enrollment '09-10 4,348
Grade 12 enrollment, '09-10 300
Graduation rate 87.3%
Dropout rate.......................5.2%
Per-pupil expenditure............. $9,948
Avg teacher salary $58,601
Student/teacher ratio '08-09 ...... 15.5 to 1
Highly-qualified teachers, '08-09.....99.9%
Teachers licensed in assigned subject 98.9%
Students per computer 3.7

Massachusetts Competency Assessment System (MCAS), 2007 results

	English		Math	
	% Prof	CPI	% Prof	CPI
Gr 4	63%	85	63%	86.9
Gr 6	68%	88.4	63%	83.3
Gr 8	87%	95.8	56%	81.1
Gr 10	87%	96.1	74%	88.7

Recieves students from:
Charlton, Dudley

Essex Agricultural Technical

County Agricultural - #913
PO BOX 362
Hathorne, MA 01937
978-774-0050

Superintendent.......... Roger Bourgeois
Grade plan.........................9-12
Total enrollment '09-10 462
Grade 12 enrollment, '09-10 92
Graduation rate 93.3%
Dropout rate...................... 4.8%
Per-pupil expenditure............$22,369
Avg teacher salary $58,176
Student/teacher ratio '08-09 .... 9.9 to 1
Highly-qualified teachers, '08-09... 100.0%
Teachers licensed in assigned subject .97.8%
Students per computer 2.1

Massachusetts Competency Assessment System (MCAS), 2007 results

	English		Math	
	% Prof	CPI	% Prof	CPI
Gr 4	NA	NA	NA	NA
Gr 6	NA	NA	NA	NA
Gr 8	NA	NA	NA	NA
Gr 10	80%	93.2	70%	85.7

Recieves students from:
NA

Farmington River

Academic Regional - #662
555 N Main Street, PO Box 679
Otis, MA 01253
413-269-4466

Superintendent............Joanne Austin
Grade plan........................ PK-6
Total enrollment '09-10 148
Grade 12 enrollment, '09-10 0
Graduation rate ....NA
Dropout rate.........................NA
Per-pupil expenditure............ $15,953
Avg teacher salary $55,119
Student/teacher ratio '08-09 .... 8.3 to 1
Highly-qualified teachers, '08-09... 100.0%
Teachers licensed in assigned subject100.0%
Students per computer 4

Massachusetts Competency Assessment System (MCAS), 2007 results

	English		Math	
	% Prof	CPI	% Prof	CPI
Gr 4	40%	76.3	70%	90
Gr 6	59%	86.8	71%	91.2
Gr 8	NA	NA	NA	NA
Gr 10	NA	NA	NA	NA

Recieves students from:
Otis, Sandisfield; sends grades 7-12 to Lenox and Berkshire Hills

School data 2007-2008 except as noted.

©2010 Information Publications, Inc. All rights reserved. Photocopying prohibited. For additional copies, contact the publisher at www.informationpublications.com or (877)544-INFO (4636)

Franklin County

Vocational Technical - #818
82 Industrial Blvd
Turners Falls, MA 01376
413-863-4239

Superintendent.............Richard Lane
Grade plan..........................9-12
Total enrollment '09-10 512
Grade 12 enrollment, '09-10 121
Graduation rate 93.0%
Dropout rate........................3.5%
Per-pupil expenditure............. $19,375
Avg teacher salary $56,082
Student/teacher ratio '08-09 .... 9.8 to 1
Highly-qualified teachers, '08-09... 100.0%
Teachers licensed in assigned subject .98.1%
Students per computer 1.3

Massachusetts Competency Assessment System (MCAS), 2007 results

	English % Prof	English CPI	Math % Prof	Math CPI
Gr 4	NA	NA	NA	NA
Gr 6	NA	NA	NA	NA
Gr 8	NA	NA	NA	NA
Gr 10	67%	87.2	60%	84.6

Recieves students from:
Bernardston, Buckland, Colrain, Conway, Deerfield, Erving, Gill, Greenfield, Heath, Montague, New Salem, Northflield, Orange, Rowe, Shelburne, Snderlnd, Warwick, Wendell, Whatley

Freetown-Lakeville

Academic Regional - #665
98 Howland Rd
Lakeville, MA 02347
508-923-2000

Superintendent...........John McCarthy
Grade plan..........................5-12
Total enrollment '09-10 1,922
Grade 12 enrollment, '09-10 204
Graduation rate 86.2%
Dropout rate...................... 6.2%
Per-pupil expenditure............. $10,260
Avg teacher salary $60,812
Student/teacher ratio '08-09 ...... 14.1 to 1
Highly-qualified teachers, '08-09.....95.4%
Teachers licensed in assigned subject 98.8%
Students per computer 2

Massachusetts Competency Assessment System (MCAS), 2007 results

	English % Prof	English CPI	Math % Prof	Math CPI
Gr 4	NA	NA	NA	NA
Gr 6	76%	89.9	60%	80.9
Gr 8	90%	96.3	63%	82.4
Gr 10	93%	97.7	83%	93.1

Recieves students from:
Freetown, Lakeville

Frontier

Academic Regional - #670
219 Christian Ln RFD1
South Deerfield, MA 01373
413-665-1155

Superintendent.............. Regina Nash
Grade plan..........................7-12
Total enrollment '09-10 705
Grade 12 enrollment, '09-10 114
Graduation rate 88.6%
Dropout rate...................... 2.9%
Per-pupil expenditure............. $13,707
Avg teacher salary $53,799
Student/teacher ratio '08-09 ...... 11.4 to 1
Highly-qualified teachers, '08-09.....99.7%
Teachers licensed in assigned subject 100.0%
Students per computer 2.5

Massachusetts Competency Assessment System (MCAS), 2007 results

	English % Prof	English CPI	Math % Prof	Math CPI
Gr 4	NA	NA	NA	NA
Gr 6	NA	NA	NA	NA
Gr 8	86%	93.8	62%	81.8
Gr 10	88%	96	88%	94.7

Recieves students from:
Conway, Deerfield, Sunderland, Whatley

Gateway

Academic Regional - #672
12 Littleville Road
Huntington, MA 01050
413-685-1000

Superintendent............David Hopson
Grade plan........................ PK-12
Total enrollment '09-10 1,202
Grade 12 enrollment, '09-10 90
Graduation rate 78.6%
Dropout rate.......................10.7%
Per-pupil expenditure............. $13,454
Avg teacher salary $50,875
Student/teacher ratio '08-09 ...... 12.1 to 1
Highly-qualified teachers, '08-09.... 98.5%
Teachers licensed in assigned subject 100.0%
Students per computer 1.2

Massachusetts Competency Assessment System (MCAS), 2007 results

	English % Prof	English CPI	Math % Prof	Math CPI
Gr 4	48%	76.5	55%	83.8
Gr 6	60%	81.5	54%	73.1
Gr 8	69%	86.2	33%	62.2
Gr 10	94%	98.1	79%	91.8

Recieves students from:
Blandford, Chester, Huntington, Middlefield, Montgomery, Russell, Worthington

Gill-Montague

Academic Regional - #674
35 Crocker Avenue
Turners Falls, MA 01376
413-863-9324

Superintendent................Carl Ladd
Grade plan........................ PK-12
Total enrollment '09-10 1,085
Grade 12 enrollment, '09-10 81
Graduation rate 64.7%
Dropout rate.......................19.8%
Per-pupil expenditure............. $14,113
Avg teacher salary $61,651
Student/teacher ratio '08-09 ...... 11.9 to 1
Highly-qualified teachers, '08-09.... 95.9%
Teachers licensed in assigned subject .97.3%
Students per computer 1.8

Massachusetts Competency Assessment System (MCAS), 2007 results

	English % Prof	English CPI	Math % Prof	Math CPI
Gr 4	42%	76.8	35%	75.9
Gr 6	48%	75.5	35%	66
Gr 8	71%	88.8	27%	58.4
Gr 10	82%	91.9	78%	88.8

Recieves students from:
Erving, Gill, Montague

Greater Fall River

Vocational Technical - #821
251 Stonehaven Rd
Fall River, MA 02723
508-678-2891

Superintendent..........Marta Montleon
Grade plan..........................9-12
Total enrollment '09-10 1,352
Grade 12 enrollment, '09-10 313
Graduation rate 92.6%
Dropout rate...................... 4.0%
Per-pupil expenditure............. $15,706
Avg teacher salary $68,471
Student/teacher ratio '08-09 ...... 10.7 to 1
Highly-qualified teachers, '08-09.....97.7%
Teachers licensed in assigned subject 95.2%
Students per computer 2

Massachusetts Competency Assessment System (MCAS), 2007 results

	English % Prof	English CPI	Math % Prof	Math CPI
Gr 4	NA	NA	NA	NA
Gr 6	NA	NA	NA	NA
Gr 8	NA	NA	NA	NA
Gr 10	76%	92.4	70%	88.4

Recieves students from:
Fall River, Somerset, Swansea, Westport

©2010 Information Publications, Inc. All rights reserved. Photocopying prohibited. For additional copies, contact the publisher at www.informationpublications.com or (877)544-INFO (4636)

School data 2007-2008 except as noted.

Greater Lawrence

Vocational Technical - #823
57 River Rd
Andover, MA 01810
978-686-0194

Superintendent. . . . . Judy DeLucia
Grade plan. 9-12
Total enrollment '09-10 1,195
Grade 12 enrollment, '09-10 273
Graduation rate 75.9%
Dropout rate. 13.8%
Per-pupil expenditure. $20,290
Avg teacher salary $63,907
Student/teacher ratio '08-09 . . . . 8.4 to 1
Highly-qualified teachers, '08-09 . . . . 98.6%
Teachers licensed in assigned subject 96.4%
Students per computer 2.1

Massachusetts Competency Assessment System (MCAS), 2007 results

	English		Math	
	% Prof	CPI	% Prof	CPI
Gr 4	NA	NA	NA	NA
Gr 6	NA	NA	NA	NA
Gr 8	NA	NA	NA	NA
Gr 10	58%	81.5	41%	71

Recieves students from:
Andover, Lawrence, Methuen, North Andover

Greater Lowell

Vocational Technical - #828
250 Pawtucket Blvd
Tyngsborough, MA 01879
978-441-4800

Superintendent. . . . . James Cassin
Grade plan. 9-12
Total enrollment '09-10 2,014
Grade 12 enrollment, '09-10 452
Graduation rate 93.1%
Dropout rate. 4.3%
Per-pupil expenditure. $16,917
Avg teacher salary $66,577
Student/teacher ratio '08-09 . . . . . . 10.7 to 1
Highly-qualified teachers, '08-09 . . . 100.0%
Teachers licensed in assigned subject .97.2%
Students per computer 3.3

Massachusetts Competency Assessment System (MCAS), 2007 results

	English		Math	
	% Prof	CPI	% Prof	CPI
Gr 4	NA	NA	NA	NA
Gr 6	NA	NA	NA	NA
Gr 8	NA	NA	NA	NA
Gr 10	65%	87.3	60%	83.9

Recieves students from:
Dracut, Dunstable, Lowell, Tyngsborough

Greater New Bedford

Vocational Technical - #825
1121 Ashley Blvd
New Bedford, MA 02745
508-998-3321

Superintendent. . . . . Michael Shea
Grade plan. 9-12
Total enrollment '09-10 2,106
Grade 12 enrollment, '09-10 477
Graduation rate 87.6%
Dropout rate. 6.6%
Per-pupil expenditure. $16,298
Avg teacher salary $71,103
Student/teacher ratio '08-09 . . . . . . 10.7 to 1
Highly-qualified teachers, '08-09 . . . . 99.0%
Teachers licensed in assigned subject .94.1%
Students per computer 1.6

Massachusetts Competency Assessment System (MCAS), 2007 results

	English		Math	
	% Prof	CPI	% Prof	CPI
Gr 4	NA	NA	NA	NA
Gr 6	NA	NA	NA	NA
Gr 8	NA	NA	NA	NA
Gr 10	78%	91.5	61%	84.2

Recieves students from:
Dartmouth, Fairhaven, New Bedford

Groton-Dunstable

Academic Regional - #673
P O Box 729
Groton, MA 01450
978-448-5505

Superintendent. . . . . Alan Genovese
Grade plan. PK-12
Total enrollment '09-10 2,798
Grade 12 enrollment, '09-10 196
Graduation rate 95.2%
Dropout rate. 2.4%
Per-pupil expenditure. $10,790
Avg teacher salary $59,446
Student/teacher ratio '08-09 . . . . . . 15.6 to 1
Highly-qualified teachers, '08-09 . . . . 98.6%
Teachers licensed in assigned subject .97.0%
Students per computer 3.4

Massachusetts Competency Assessment System (MCAS), 2007 results

	English		Math	
	% Prof	CPI	% Prof	CPI
Gr 4	76%	90.9	75%	91.6
Gr 6	83%	93.2	79%	90.7
Gr 8	91%	97.7	73%	88.5
Gr 10	96%	98.6	97%	98.8

Recieves students from:
Dunstable, Groton

Hamilton-Wenham

Academic Regional - #675
5 School Street
Wenham, MA 01984
978-468-5310

Superintendent. . . . . Marinel McGrath
Grade plan. PK-12
Total enrollment '09-10 2,026
Grade 12 enrollment, '09-10 173
Graduation rate 94.2%
Dropout rate. 1.6%
Per-pupil expenditure. $12,616
Avg teacher salary $67,953
Student/teacher ratio '08-09 . . . . . . 12.7 to 1
Highly-qualified teachers, '08-09 . . . . 96.7%
Teachers licensed in assigned subject 98.8%
Students per computer 4.7

Massachusetts Competency Assessment System (MCAS), 2007 results

	English		Math	
	% Prof	CPI	% Prof	CPI
Gr 4	67%	89.1	64%	88.7
Gr 6	79%	93.2	74%	87.9
Gr 8	92%	96.9	62%	81.6
Gr 10	96%	98.4	90%	96.7

Recieves students from:
Hamilton, Wenham

Hampden-Wilbraham

Academic Regional - #680
621 Main Street
Wilbraham, MA 01095
413-596-3884

Superintendent. . . . . Maurice O'Shea
Grade plan. PK-12
Total enrollment '09-10 3,600
Grade 12 enrollment, '09-10 276
Graduation rate 92.4%
Dropout rate. 3.2%
Per-pupil expenditure. $10,938
Avg teacher salary $57,118
Student/teacher ratio '08-09 . . . . . . 14.3 to 1
Highly-qualified teachers, '08-09 . . . . . 99.4%
Teachers licensed in assigned subject .99.6%
Students per computer 4.7

Massachusetts Competency Assessment System (MCAS), 2007 results

	English		Math	
	% Prof	CPI	% Prof	CPI
Gr 4	61%	85.2	51%	81.9
Gr 6	84%	93.6	72%	86.5
Gr 8	88%	95.2	63%	83.5
Gr 10	90%	96.2	85%	93.5

Recieves students from:
Hampden, Wilbraham

School data 2007-2008 except as noted.

©2010 Information Publications, Inc. All rights reserved. Photocopying prohibited. For additional copies, contact the publisher at www.informationpublications.com or (877)544-INFO (4636)

Hampshire

Academic Regional - #683
19 Stage Rd
Westhampton, MA 01027
413-527-7200

Superintendent........... Craig Jurgensen
Grade plan.......................... 7-12
Total enrollment '09-10 814
Grade 12 enrollment, '09-10 106
Graduation rate 89.4%
Dropout rate.........................6.5%
Per-pupil expenditure.............$12,224
Avg teacher salary $56,839
Student/teacher ratio '08-09 ...... 12.7 to 1
Highly-qualified teachers, '08-09.....97.8%
Teachers licensed in assigned subject 95.5%
Students per computer 1.5

Massachusetts Competency Assessment System (MCAS), 2007 results

	English		Math	
	% Prof	CPI	% Prof	CPI
Gr 4	NA	NA	NA	NA
Gr 6	NA	NA	NA	NA
Gr 8	75%	89.5	48%	75.2
Gr 10	96%	98.9	95%	98.1

Recieves students from:
Chesterfield, Goshen, Southampton, Westhampton, Williamsburg

Hawlemont

Academic Regional - #685
24 Ashfield Rd
Shelburne Falls, MA 01370
413-625-0192

Superintendent........ Michael Buoniconti
Grade plan......................... PK-6
Total enrollment '09-10 109
Grade 12 enrollment, '09-10 0
Graduation rate ....NA
Dropout rate..........................NA
Per-pupil expenditure.............$13,993
Avg teacher salary $42,024
Student/teacher ratio '08-09 .... 9.8 to 1
Highly-qualified teachers, '08-09... 100.0%
Teachers licensed in assigned subject 100.0%
Students per computer 2

Massachusetts Competency Assessment System (MCAS), 2007 results

	English		Math	
	% Prof	CPI	% Prof	CPI
Gr 4	47%	77.9	47%	75
Gr 6	87%	93.3	73%	86.7
Gr 8	NA	NA	NA	NA
Gr 10	NA	NA	NA	NA

Recieves students from:
Charlemont, Hawley

King Philip

Academic Regional - #690
18 King Street
Norfolk, MA 02056
508-520-7991

Superintendent............Richard Robbat
Grade plan.......................... 7-12
Total enrollment '09-10 2,079
Grade 12 enrollment, '09-10 321
Graduation rate 87.3%
Dropout rate.........................5.1%
Per-pupil expenditure.............$11,059
Avg teacher salary $67,955
Student/teacher ratio '08-09 ...... 16.9 to 1
Highly-qualified teachers, '08-09... 100.0%
Teachers licensed in assigned subject 96.2%
Students per computer ....NA

Massachusetts Competency Assessment System (MCAS), 2007 results

	English		Math	
	% Prof	CPI	% Prof	CPI
Gr 4	NA	NA	NA	NA
Gr 6	NA	NA	NA	NA
Gr 8	84%	93.7	53%	76.9
Gr 10	92%	97.3	82%	92.7

Recieves students from:
Norfolk, Plainville, Wrentham

Lincoln-Sudbury

Academic Regional - #695
390 Lincoln Rd
Sudbury, MA 01776
978-443-9961

Superintendent............Scott Carpenter
Grade plan..........................9-12
Total enrollment '09-10 1,615
Grade 12 enrollment, '09-10 392
Graduation rate 95.4%
Dropout rate.........................1.4%
Per-pupil expenditure.............$15,549
Avg teacher salary $76,022
Student/teacher ratio '08-09 ...... 12.9 to 1
Highly-qualified teachers, '08-09.... 98.7%
Teachers licensed in assigned subject .97.8%
Students per computer 1.6

Massachusetts Competency Assessment System (MCAS), 2007 results

	English		Math	
	% Prof	CPI	% Prof	CPI
Gr 4	NA	NA	NA	NA
Gr 6	NA	NA	NA	NA
Gr 8	NA	NA	NA	NA
Gr 10	94%	97.8	92%	96.5

Recieves students from:
Lincoln, Sudbury

Manchester Essex

Academic Regional - #698
PO BOX 1407
Manchester, MA 01944
978-526-4919

Superintendent............. Marcia O'Neil
Grade plan........................ PK-12
Total enrollment '09-10 1,457
Grade 12 enrollment, '09-10 102
Graduation rate 97.9%
Dropout rate.........................2.1%
Per-pupil expenditure.............$12,998
Avg teacher salary $65,940
Student/teacher ratio '08-09 ...... 13.3 to 1
Highly-qualified teachers, '08-09.... 90.5%
Teachers licensed in assigned subject 96.2%
Students per computer 2.9

Massachusetts Competency Assessment System (MCAS), 2007 results

	English		Math	
	% Prof	CPI	% Prof	CPI
Gr 4	75%	89.7	70%	88.1
Gr 6	84%	95.7	73%	89.3
Gr 8	83%	95.5	66%	84.8
Gr 10	97%	99.3	95%	98.5

Recieves students from:
Essex, Manchester

Marthas Vineyard

Academic Regional - #700
4 Pine St
Vineyard Haven, MA 02568
508-693-2007

Superintendent...............James Weiss
Grade plan..........................9-12
Total enrollment '09-10 699
Grade 12 enrollment, '09-10 163
Graduation rate 89.5%
Dropout rate.........................5.3%
Per-pupil expenditure.............$21,042
Avg teacher salary $69,510
Student/teacher ratio '08-09 .... 9.1 to 1
Highly-qualified teachers, '08-09.....97.5%
Teachers licensed in assigned subject 98.7%
Students per computer 2.4

Massachusetts Competency Assessment System (MCAS), 2007 results

	English		Math	
	% Prof	CPI	% Prof	CPI
Gr 4	NA	NA	NA	NA
Gr 6	NA	NA	NA	NA
Gr 8	NA	NA	NA	NA
Gr 10	84%	94.7	80%	90.6

Recieves students from:
Aquinnah, Chilmark, Edgartown, Oak Bluffs, Tisbury, West Tisbury

©2010 Information Publications, Inc. All rights reserved. Photocopying prohibited. For additional copies, contact the publisher at www.informationpublications.com or (877)544-INFO (4636)

School data 2007-2008 except as noted.

Masconomet

Academic Regional - #705
20 Endicott Rd
Topsfield, MA 01983
978-887-2323

Superintendent............. Anthony Bent
Grade plan.......................... 7-12
Total enrollment '09-10 2,085
Grade 12 enrollment, '09-10 365
Graduation rate 94.5%
Dropout rate........................0.9%
Per-pupil expenditure............. $12,172
Avg teacher salary $66,712
Student/teacher ratio '08-09 ...... 16.6 to 1
Highly-qualified teachers, '08-09... 100.0%
Teachers licensed in assigned subject 99.8%
Students per computer 2.4

Massachusetts Competency Assessment System (MCAS), 2007 results

	English		Math	
	% Prof	CPI	% Prof	CPI
Gr 4	NA	NA	NA	NA
Gr 6	NA	NA	NA	NA
Gr 8	96%	98.8	82%	92.4
Gr 10	95%	97.9	95%	97.8

Recieves students from:
Boxford, Middleton, Topsfield

Mendon-Upton

Academic Regional - #710
150 North Ave
Mendon, MA 01756
508-634-1585

Superintendent........ Antonio Fernandes
Grade plan........................ PK-12
Total enrollment '09-10 2,856
Grade 12 enrollment, '09-10 170
Graduation rate 95.3%
Dropout rate........................2.6%
Per-pupil expenditure............. $10,007
Avg teacher salary $52,224
Student/teacher ratio '08-09 ...... 15.4 to 1
Highly-qualified teachers, '08-09.....97.0%
Teachers licensed in assigned subject 95.2%
Students per computer 4.6

Massachusetts Competency Assessment System (MCAS), 2007 results

	English		Math	
	% Prof	CPI	% Prof	CPI
Gr 4	62%	85	55%	82.6
Gr 6	82%	94.2	66%	84.5
Gr 8	90%	96.5	59%	80.7
Gr 10	93%	98.3	86%	94.8

Recieves students from:
Mendon, Upton

Minuteman

Vocational Technical - #830
758 Marrett Rd
Lexington, MA 02421
781-861-6500

Superintendent........ Edward Bouquillon
Grade plan.......................... 9-12
Total enrollment '09-10 583
Grade 12 enrollment, '09-10 139
Graduation rate 87.1%
Dropout rate........................8.6%
Per-pupil expenditure............. $27,953
Avg teacher salary $74,494
Student/teacher ratio '08-09 ....7.4 to 1
Highly-qualified teachers, '08-09.....97.5%
Teachers licensed in assigned subject 92.9%
Students per computer 1.1

Massachusetts Competency Assessment System (MCAS), 2007 results

	English		Math	
	% Prof	CPI	% Prof	CPI
Gr 4	NA	NA	NA	NA
Gr 6	NA	NA	NA	NA
Gr 8	NA	NA	NA	NA
Gr 10	81%	94.5	70%	86.3

Recieves students from:
Acton, Arlington, Belmont, Bolton, Boxborough, Carlisle, Concord, Dover, Lancaster, Lexington, Lincoln, Needham, Stow, Sudbury, Wayland, Weston

Mohawk Trail

Academic Regional - #717
24 Ashfield Rd
Shelburne Falls, MA 01370
413-625-0192

Superintendent........ Michael Buoniconti
Grade plan........................ PK-12
Total enrollment '09-10 1,130
Grade 12 enrollment, '09-10 85
Graduation rate 78.8%
Dropout rate.......................12.1%
Per-pupil expenditure............. $15,722
Avg teacher salary $53,614
Student/teacher ratio '08-09 ...... 11.4 to 1
Highly-qualified teachers, '08-09.... 96.5%
Teachers licensed in assigned subject .95.7%
Students per computer 3.7

Massachusetts Competency Assessment System (MCAS), 2007 results

	English		Math	
	% Prof	CPI	% Prof	CPI
Gr 4	51%	76.5	48%	79.5
Gr 6	66%	88.2	53%	78.9
Gr 8	69%	88.1	34%	65.5
Gr 10	68%	87.3	67%	82

Recieves students from:
Ashfield, Buckland, Charlemont, Colrain, Hawley, Heath, Plainfield, Rowe, Shelburne

Montachusett

Vocational Technical - #832
1050 Westminster Street
Fitchburg, MA 01420
978-345-9200

Superintendent............ James Culkeen
Grade plan.......................... 9-12
Total enrollment '09-10 1,355
Grade 12 enrollment, '09-10 297
Graduation rate 94.2%
Dropout rate........................4.5%
Per-pupil expenditure............. $16,938
Avg teacher salary $70,353
Student/teacher ratio '08-09 ...... 12.8 to 1
Highly-qualified teachers, '08-09.....93.6%
Teachers licensed in assigned subject 95.2%
Students per computer 2.2

Massachusetts Competency Assessment System (MCAS), 2007 results

	English		Math	
	% Prof	CPI	% Prof	CPI
Gr 4	NA	NA	NA	NA
Gr 6	NA	NA	NA	NA
Gr 8	NA	NA	NA	NA
Gr 10	80%	93.2	77%	92

Recieves students from:
Ashburnham, Ashby, Athol, Barre, Fitchburg, Gardner, Harvard, Holden, Hubbardston, Lunenberg, Petersham, Phillipston, Princeton, Royalston, Sterling, Templeton, Westminster, Winchendon

Mount Greylock

Academic Regional - #715
1781 Cold Spring Rd
Williamstown, MA 01267
413-458-9582

Superintendent............ William Travis
Grade plan.......................... 7-12
Total enrollment '09-10 641
Grade 12 enrollment, '09-10 108
Graduation rate 88.1%
Dropout rate........................6.4%
Per-pupil expenditure............. $14,984
Avg teacher salary $64,018
Student/teacher ratio '08-09 ...... 13.0 to 1
Highly-qualified teachers, '08-09.... 98.9%
Teachers licensed in assigned subject 98.0%
Students per computer 3

Massachusetts Competency Assessment System (MCAS), 2007 results

	English		Math	
	% Prof	CPI	% Prof	CPI
Gr 4	NA	NA	NA	NA
Gr 6	NA	NA	NA	NA
Gr 8	84%	93.1	38%	66
Gr 10	90%	96.7	87%	94.9

Recieves students from:
Lanesborough, New Ashford, Williamstown

©2010 Information Publications, Inc. All rights reserved. Photocopying prohibited. For additional copies, contact the publisher at www.informationpublications.com or (877)544-INFO (4636)

School data 2007-2008 except as noted.

Narragansett

Academic Regional - #720
462 Baldwinville Road
Baldwinville, MA 01436
978-939-5661

Superintendent............... Roseli Weiss
Grade plan........................ PK-12
Total enrollment '09-10 1,575
Grade 12 enrollment, '09-10 115
Graduation rate 81.2%
Dropout rate........................ 9.0%
Per-pupil expenditure............ $10,196
Avg teacher salary $66,188
Student/teacher ratio '08-09 ...... 14.7 to 1
Highly-qualified teachers, '08-09 ... 100.0%
Teachers licensed in assigned subject 100.0%
Students per computer 4

Massachusetts Competency Assessment System (MCAS), 2007 results

	English % Prof	English CPI	Math % Prof	Math CPI
Gr 4	40%	74.2	34%	74.4
Gr 6	55%	83.5	52%	76.3
Gr 8	75%	89.3	42%	70
Gr 10	87%	96.2	74%	90.8

Recieves students from:
Phillipstown, Templeton

Nashoba

Academic Regional - #725
50 Mechanic Street
Bolton, MA 01740
978-779-0539

Superintendent............ Michael Wood
Grade plan........................ PK-12
Total enrollment '09-10 3,433
Grade 12 enrollment, '09-10 250
Graduation rate 93.6%
Dropout rate........................ 2.5%
Per-pupil expenditure............ $12,071
Avg teacher salary $69,388
Student/teacher ratio '08-09 ...... 13.5 to 1
Highly-qualified teachers, '08-09..... 99.6%
Teachers licensed in assigned subject 99.8%
Students per computer 3.2

Massachusetts Competency Assessment System (MCAS), 2007 results

	English % Prof	English CPI	Math % Prof	Math CPI
Gr 4	72%	88.7	58%	85.9
Gr 6	79%	93.3	78%	91.1
Gr 8	91%	96.9	82%	91.9
Gr 10	93%	97.9	90%	95.8

Recieves students from:
Bolton, Lancaster, Stow

Nashoba Valley

Vocational Technical - #852
100 Littleton Road
Westford, MA 01886
978-692-4711

Superintendent........ Judith Klimkiewicz
Grade plan......................... 9-12
Total enrollment '09-10 662
Grade 12 enrollment, '09-10 168
Graduation rate 89.3%
Dropout rate........................ 2.0%
Per-pupil expenditure............ $14,736
Avg teacher salary $59,079
Student/teacher ratio '08-09 ...... 11.5 to 1
Highly-qualified teachers, '08-09.... 96.7%
Teachers licensed in assigned subject 96.4%
Students per computer 2.1

Massachusetts Competency Assessment System (MCAS), 2007 results

	English % Prof	English CPI	Math % Prof	Math CPI
Gr 4	NA	NA	NA	NA
Gr 6	NA	NA	NA	NA
Gr 8	NA	NA	NA	NA
Gr 10	67%	88.6	69%	87.9

Recieves students from:
Chelmsford, Groton, Littleton, Pepperell, Shirley, Townsend, Westford

Nauset

Academic Regional - #660
78 Eldredge Pkwy
Orleans, MA 02653
508-255-8800

Superintendent......... Richard Hoffmann
Grade plan......................... 6-12
Total enrollment '09-10 1,535
Grade 12 enrollment, '09-10 227
Graduation rate 86.9%
Dropout rate........................ 2.5%
Per-pupil expenditure............ $14,848
Avg teacher salary $67,366
Student/teacher ratio '08-09 ...... 11.3 to 1
Highly-qualified teachers, '08-09..... 95.4%
Teachers licensed in assigned subject 98.2%
Students per computer 4

Massachusetts Competency Assessment System (MCAS), 2007 results

	English % Prof	English CPI	Math % Prof	Math CPI
Gr 4	NA	NA	NA	NA
Gr 6	82%	92.3	64%	82.8
Gr 8	84%	93.7	76%	86.7
Gr 10	96%	99	90%	96

Recieves students from:
Brewster, Eastham, Orleans, Truro, Wellfleet

New Salem-Wendell

Academic Regional - #728
18 Pleasant Street
Erving, MA 01344
413-423-3337

Superintendent........... Joan Wickman
Grade plan......................... PK-6
Total enrollment '09-10 144
Grade 12 enrollment, '09-10 0
Graduation rate .... NA
Dropout rate.......................... NA
Per-pupil expenditure............ $12,724
Avg teacher salary $49,993
Student/teacher ratio '08-09 ...... 12.2 to 1
Highly-qualified teachers, '08-09 ... 100.0%
Teachers licensed in assigned subject .97.6%
Students per computer 18.4

Massachusetts Competency Assessment System (MCAS), 2007 results

	English % Prof	English CPI	Math % Prof	Math CPI
Gr 4	53%	83.8	41%	80.9
Gr 6	75%	90.6	94%	96.9
Gr 8	NA	NA	NA	NA
Gr 10	NA	NA	NA	NA

Recieves students from:
New Salem, Wendell

Norfolk County Agricultural

County Agricultural - #915
400 Main Street
Walpole, MA 02081
508-668-0268

Superintendent....... Michael McFarland
Grade plan......................... 9-12
Total enrollment '09-10 470
Grade 12 enrollment, '09-10 102
Graduation rate 96.7%
Dropout rate........................ 0.0%
Per-pupil expenditure............ $19,803
Avg teacher salary $65,861
Student/teacher ratio '08-09 ...... 10.1 to 1
Highly-qualified teachers, '08-09.... 94.5%
Teachers licensed in assigned subject 93.3%
Students per computer 2.4

Massachusetts Competency Assessment System (MCAS), 2007 results

	English % Prof	English CPI	Math % Prof	Math CPI
Gr 4	NA	NA	NA	NA
Gr 6	NA	NA	NA	NA
Gr 8	NA	NA	NA	NA
Gr 10	96%	98.9	89%	96.1

Recieves students from:
Avon, Bellingham, Braintree, Brookline, Canton, Cohasset, Dedham, Dover, Foxborough, Franklin, Holbrook, Medfield, Medway, Millis, Milton, Needham, Norfolk, Norwood, Plainville, Quincy, Randolph, Sharon, Stoughton, Walpole, Wellesley, Westwood, Weymouth, Wrentham

©2010 Information Publications, Inc. All rights reserved. Photocopying prohibited. For additional copies, contact the publisher at www.informationpublications.com or (877)544-INFO (4636)

School data 2007-2008 except as noted.

©2010 Information Publications, Inc. All rights reserved. Photocopying prohibited. For additional copies, contact the publisher at www.informationpublications.com or (877)544-INFO (4636)

North Middlesex

Academic Regional - #735
23 Main Street
Townsend, MA 01469
978-597-8713

Superintendent......... Maureen Marshall
Grade plan........................ PK-12
Total enrollment '09-10 4,074
Grade 12 enrollment, '09-10 298
Graduation rate....................89.1%
Dropout rate....................... 4.8%
Per-pupil expenditure.............. $9,754
Avg teacher salary................ $61,702
Student/teacher ratio '08-09 ...... 14.9 to 1
Highly-qualified teachers, '08-09.... 96.8%
Teachers licensed in assigned subject 98.6%
Students per computer................ 5.6

Massachusetts Competency Assessment System (MCAS), 2007 results

	English		Math	
	% Prof	CPI	% Prof	CPI
Gr 4	53%	81.9	41%	76.9
Gr 6	65%	86.8	61%	82.7
Gr 8	86%	95.9	54%	77.8
Gr 10	90%	96.5	86%	94.1

Recieves students from:
Ashby, Pepperell, Townsend

North Shore

Vocational Technical - #854
P.O. Box 806, 30 Log Bridge Rd
Middleton, MA 01949
978-762-0001

Superintendent.......... Daniel O'Connell
Grade plan.......................... 9-12
Total enrollment '09-10 451
Grade 12 enrollment, '09-10 100
Graduation rate.................. 94.3%
Dropout rate........................1.0%
Per-pupil expenditure............ $22,311
Avg teacher salary...............$64,543
Student/teacher ratio '08-09 .... 8.6 to 1
Highly-qualified teachers, '08-09... 100.0%
Teachers licensed in assigned subject .98.1%
Students per computer................ 1.5

Massachusetts Competency Assessment System (MCAS), 2007 results

	English		Math	
	% Prof	CPI	% Prof	CPI
Gr 4	NA	NA	NA	NA
Gr 6	NA	NA	NA	NA
Gr 8	NA	NA	NA	NA
Gr 10	73%	91	62%	83.3

Recieves students from:
Beverly, Boxford, Danvers, Essex, Gloucester, Hamilton, Lynnfield, Manchester, Marblehead, Middleton, Nahant, Rockport, Salem, Swampscott, Topsfield, Wenham

Northampton-Smith

Independent Vocational - #406
80 Locust Street
Northampton, MA 01060
413-587-1414

Superintendent..........Arthur Apostolou
Grade plan.......................... 9-12
Total enrollment '09-10 464
Grade 12 enrollment, '09-10 108
Graduation rate.................. 86.0%
Dropout rate.......................11.0%
Per-pupil expenditure.............$18,266
Avg teacher salary................ $57,185
Student/teacher ratio '08-09 .... 8.6 to 1
Highly-qualified teachers, '08-09.....91.0%
Teachers licensed in assigned subject 86.9%
Students per computer................ 1.7

Massachusetts Competency Assessment System (MCAS), 2007 results

	English		Math	
	% Prof	CPI	% Prof	CPI
Gr 4	NA	NA	NA	NA
Gr 6	NA	NA	NA	NA
Gr 8	NA	NA	NA	NA
Gr 10	51%	80.7	48%	76.9

Recieves students from:
Northampton

Northboro-Southboro

Academic Regional - #730
53 Parkerville Road
Southborough, MA 01772
508-486-5115

Superintendent........... Charles Gobron
Grade plan.......................... 9-12
Total enrollment '09-10 1,409
Grade 12 enrollment, '09-10 362
Graduation rate.................. 96.4%
Dropout rate........................0.6%
Per-pupil expenditure.............$12,585
Avg teacher salary...............$68,639
Student/teacher ratio '08-09 ...... 13.6 to 1
Highly-qualified teachers, '08-09.... 98.8%
Teachers licensed in assigned subject 99.0%
Students per computer................ 2.4

Massachusetts Competency Assessment System (MCAS), 2007 results

	English		Math	
	% Prof	CPI	% Prof	CPI
Gr 4	NA	NA	NA	NA
Gr 6	NA	NA	NA	NA
Gr 8	NA	NA	NA	NA
Gr 10	94%	97.5	92%	96.5

Recieves students from:
Northborough, Southborough

Northeast Metro

Vocational Technical - #853
100 Hemlock Rd
Wakefield, MA 01880
781-246-0810

Superintendent.............John Crowley
Grade plan.......................... 9-12
Total enrollment '09-10 1,249
Grade 12 enrollment, '09-10 285
Graduation rate.................. 90.4%
Dropout rate........................4.1%
Per-pupil expenditure.............$18,406
Avg teacher salary................ $61,775
Student/teacher ratio '08-09 ...... 10.3 to 1
Highly-qualified teachers, '08-09.....99.1%
Teachers licensed in assigned subject 95.0%
Students per computer................ 2.5

Massachusetts Competency Assessment System (MCAS), 2007 results

	English		Math	
	% Prof	CPI	% Prof	CPI
Gr 4	NA	NA	NA	NA
Gr 6	NA	NA	NA	NA
Gr 8	NA	NA	NA	NA
Gr 10	66%	86.5	57%	79.5

Recieves students from:
Chelsea, Malden, Melrose, North Reading, Reading, Revere, Saugus, Stoneham, Wakefield, Winchester, Winthrop, Woburn

Northern Berkshire

Vocational Technical - #851
70 Hodges Cross Rd
North Adams, MA 01247
413-663-5383

Superintendent............ James Brosnan
Grade plan.......................... 9-12
Total enrollment '09-10 500
Grade 12 enrollment, '09-10 113
Graduation rate.................. 94.3%
Dropout rate........................5.7%
Per-pupil expenditure.............$16,929
Avg teacher salary...............$72,394
Student/teacher ratio '08-09 ...... 11.0 to 1
Highly-qualified teachers, '08-09... 100.0%
Teachers licensed in assigned subject 93.9%
Students per computer................ 1.6

Massachusetts Competency Assessment System (MCAS), 2007 results

	English		Math	
	% Prof	CPI	% Prof	CPI
Gr 4	NA	NA	NA	NA
Gr 6	NA	NA	NA	NA
Gr 8	NA	NA	NA	NA
Gr 10	72%	89.1	73%	87.9

Recieves students from:
Adams, Clarksburg, Florida, Monroe, North Adams, Savoy, Williamstown

School data 2007-2008 except as noted.

Old Colony

Vocational Technical - #855
476 North Avenue
Rochester, MA 02770
508-763-8011

Superintendent	Gary Brown
Grade plan	9-12
Total enrollment '09-10	583
Grade 12 enrollment, '09-10	144
Graduation rate	93.8%
Dropout rate	6.3%
Per-pupil expenditure	$16,425
Avg teacher salary	$79,444
Student/teacher ratio '08-09	11.3 to 1
Highly-qualified teachers, '08-09	100.0%
Teachers licensed in assigned subject	88.9%
Students per computer	2.5

Massachusetts Competency Assessment System (MCAS), 2007 results

	English		Math	
	% Prof	CPI	% Prof	CPI
Gr 4	NA	NA	NA	NA
Gr 6	NA	NA	NA	NA
Gr 8	NA	NA	NA	NA
Gr 10	75%	90.7	69%	87.1

Recieves students from:
Acushnet, Carver, Lakeville, Mattapoisett, Rochester

Old Rochester

Academic Regional - #740
135 Marion Rd
Mattapoisett, MA 02739
508-758-2772

Superintendent	Douglas White
Grade plan	PK-12
Total enrollment '09-10	1,151
Grade 12 enrollment, '09-10	165
Graduation rate	91.0%
Dropout rate	5.2%
Per-pupil expenditure	$13,225
Avg teacher salary	$67,378
Student/teacher ratio '08-09	12.9 to 1
Highly-qualified teachers, '08-09	98.1%
Teachers licensed in assigned subject	94.8%
Students per computer	3.2

Massachusetts Competency Assessment System (MCAS), 2007 results

	English		Math	
	% Prof	CPI	% Prof	CPI
Gr 4	NA	NA	NA	NA
Gr 6	NA	NA	NA	NA
Gr 8	90%	95.4	63%	82.5
Gr 10	91%	97.3	90%	96.5

Recieves students from:
Marion, Mattapoisett, Rochester

Pathfinder

Vocational Technical - #860
240 Sykes Street
Palmer, MA 01069
413-283-9701

Superintendent	Gerald Paist
Grade plan	9-12
Total enrollment '09-10	660
Grade 12 enrollment, '09-10	166
Graduation rate	78.6%
Dropout rate	6.5%
Per-pupil expenditure	$18,075
Avg teacher salary	$57,327
Student/teacher ratio '08-09	7.8 to 1
Highly-qualified teachers, '08-09	85.9%
Teachers licensed in assigned subject	88.7%
Students per computer	1.7

Massachusetts Competency Assessment System (MCAS), 2007 results

	English		Math	
	% Prof	CPI	% Prof	CPI
Gr 4	NA	NA	NA	NA
Gr 6	NA	NA	NA	NA
Gr 8	NA	NA	NA	NA
Gr 10	63%	88.3	63%	86.3

Recieves students from:
Belchertown, Granby, Hardwick, Monson, New Braintree, Palmer, Ware

Pentucket

Academic Regional - #745
22 Main Street
West Newbury, MA 01985
978-363-2280

Superintendent	Paul Livingston
Grade plan	PK-12
Total enrollment '09-10	3,226
Grade 12 enrollment, '09-10	185
Graduation rate	90.5%
Dropout rate	5.0%
Per-pupil expenditure	$10,124
Avg teacher salary	$63,019
Student/teacher ratio '08-09	14.1 to 1
Highly-qualified teachers, '08-09	98.3%
Teachers licensed in assigned subject	98.0%
Students per computer	4.8

Massachusetts Competency Assessment System (MCAS), 2007 results

	English		Math	
	% Prof	CPI	% Prof	CPI
Gr 4	64%	87.1	49%	82.9
Gr 6	79%	92.5	72%	89.2
Gr 8	88%	95.7	71%	86.4
Gr 10	92%	97.5	82%	92.4

Recieves students from:
Groveland, Merrimac, West Newbury

Pioneer Valley

Academic Regional - #750
97 F Sumner Turner Rd
Northfield, MA 01360
413-498-2911

Superintendent	Dayle Doiron
Grade plan	PK-12
Total enrollment '09-10	1,167
Grade 12 enrollment, '09-10	74
Graduation rate	88.1%
Dropout rate	6.0%
Per-pupil expenditure	$13,794
Avg teacher salary	$55,891
Student/teacher ratio '08-09	12.5 to 1
Highly-qualified teachers, '08-09	98.8%
Teachers licensed in assigned subject	97.8%
Students per computer	2.8

Massachusetts Competency Assessment System (MCAS), 2007 results

	English		Math	
	% Prof	CPI	% Prof	CPI
Gr 4	40%	71.9	48%	76.4
Gr 6	55%	81	46%	71.7
Gr 8	78%	91.2	47%	72.4
Gr 10	80%	93.2	73%	84.6

Recieves students from:
Bernardston, Leyden, Northfield, Warwick

Quabbin

Academic Regional - #753
872 South Street
Barre, MA 01005
978-355-4668

Superintendent	Maureen Marshall
Grade plan	PK-12
Total enrollment '09-10	3,012
Grade 12 enrollment, '09-10	239
Graduation rate	82.6%
Dropout rate	8.7%
Per-pupil expenditure	$10,359
Avg teacher salary	$60,627
Student/teacher ratio '08-09	15.2 to 1
Highly-qualified teachers, '08-09	99.0%
Teachers licensed in assigned subject	98.1%
Students per computer	5.9

Massachusetts Competency Assessment System (MCAS), 2007 results

	English		Math	
	% Prof	CPI	% Prof	CPI
Gr 4	38%	75.7	46%	78.9
Gr 6	62%	85.4	54%	77.1
Gr 8	83%	93.3	45%	70.7
Gr 10	85%	94.7	83%	92.7

Recieves students from:
Barre, Hardwick, Hubbardston, New Braintree, Oakham

©2010 Information Publications, Inc. All rights reserved. Photocopying prohibited. For additional copies, contact the publisher at www.informationpublications.com or (877)544-INFO (4636)

School data 2007-2008 except as noted.

Quaboag

Academic Regional - #778
48 High Street, PO Box 1538
Warren, MA 01083
413-436-9256

Superintendent............ Brett Kustigian
Grade plan........................ PK-12
Total enrollment '09-10 1,452
Grade 12 enrollment, '09-10 79
Graduation rate 75.5%
Dropout rate.......................11.8%
Per-pupil expenditure............. $10,114
Avg teacher salary $67,843
Student/teacher ratio '08-09 ...... 14.6 to 1
Highly-qualified teachers, '08-09 .... 98.5%
Teachers licensed in assigned subject 99.0%
Students per computer 2.8

Massachusetts Competency Assessment System (MCAS), 2007 results

	English		Math	
	% Prof	CPI	% Prof	CPI
Gr 4	47%	78	31%	70.1
Gr 6	64%	85.4	46%	72.9
Gr 8	52%	80.5	38%	64.3
Gr 10	86%	94.3	80%	92.5

Recieves students from:
Warren, West Brookfield

Ralph C Mahar

Academic Regional - #755
507 South Main Street
Orange, MA 01364
978-544-2920

Superintendent........Michael Baldassarre
Grade plan.......................... 7-12
Total enrollment '09-10 778
Grade 12 enrollment, '09-10 75
Graduation rate 73.2%
Dropout rate...................... 4.9%
Per-pupil expenditure............. $13,506
Avg teacher salary $48,266
Student/teacher ratio '08-09 ...... 12.1 to 1
Highly-qualified teachers, '08-09 ... 100.0%
Teachers licensed in assigned subject 92.6%
Students per computer 1.6

Massachusetts Competency Assessment System (MCAS), 2007 results

	English		Math	
	% Prof	CPI	% Prof	CPI
Gr 4	NA	NA	NA	NA
Gr 6	NA	NA	NA	NA
Gr 8	73%	88.5	39%	66.3
Gr 10	80%	92.1	66%	86.5

Recieves students from:
New Salem, Orange, Petersham, Wendell

Shawsheen Valley

Vocational Technical - #871
100 Cook Street
Billerica, MA 01821
978-667-2111

Superintendent............. Charles Lyons
Grade plan.......................... 9-12
Total enrollment '09-10 1,300
Grade 12 enrollment, '09-10 296
Graduation rate 94.8%
Dropout rate........................1.6%
Per-pupil expenditure............. $17,756
Avg teacher salary $70,440
Student/teacher ratio '08-09 ...... 10.3 to 1
Highly-qualified teachers, '08-09 .... 98.4%
Teachers licensed in assigned subject 96.8%
Students per computer 2

Massachusetts Competency Assessment System (MCAS), 2007 results

	English		Math	
	% Prof	CPI	% Prof	CPI
Gr 4	NA	NA	NA	NA
Gr 6	NA	NA	NA	NA
Gr 8	NA	NA	NA	NA
Gr 10	90%	96.8	83%	94.3

Recieves students from:
Bedford, Billerica, Burlington, Tewksbury, Wilmington

Silver Lake

Academic Regional - #760
250 Pembroke Street
Kingston, MA 02364
781-585-4313

Superintendent................ John Tuffy
Grade plan........................ PK-12
Total enrollment '09-10 1,903
Grade 12 enrollment, '09-10 294
Graduation rate 90.4%
Dropout rate........................7.9%
Per-pupil expenditure............. $11,898
Avg teacher salary $69,158
Student/teacher ratio '08-09 ...... 13.3 to 1
Highly-qualified teachers, '08-09 .... 96.8%
Teachers licensed in assigned subject 96.5%
Students per computer 3.1

Massachusetts Competency Assessment System (MCAS), 2007 results

	English		Math	
	% Prof	CPI	% Prof	CPI
Gr 4	NA	NA	NA	NA
Gr 6	NA	NA	NA	NA
Gr 8	87%	94.1	56%	77.5
Gr 10	89%	96.5	84%	93.3

Recieves students from:
Halifax, Kingston, Plympton

South Middlesex

Vocational Technical - #829
750 Winter Street
Framingham, MA 01702
508-416-2250

Superintendent............. James Lynch
Grade plan.......................... 9-12
Total enrollment '09-10 642
Grade 12 enrollment, '09-10 145
Graduation rate 87.4%
Dropout rate........................6.3%
Per-pupil expenditure............. $25,965
Avg teacher salary $76,443
Student/teacher ratio '08-09 .... 8.0 to 1
Highly-qualified teachers, '08-09 .... 96.9%
Teachers licensed in assigned subject .93.7%
Students per computer 1.9

Massachusetts Competency Assessment System (MCAS), 2007 results

	English		Math	
	% Prof	CPI	% Prof	CPI
Gr 4	NA	NA	NA	NA
Gr 6	NA	NA	NA	NA
Gr 8	NA	NA	NA	NA
Gr 10	51%	78.1	53%	76.6

Recieves students from:
Ashland, Framingham, Holliston, Hopkinton, Natick

South Shore

Vocational Technical - #873
476 Webster Street
Hanover, MA 02339
781-878-8822

Superintendent............ Charles Homer
Grade plan.......................... 9-12
Total enrollment '09-10 595
Grade 12 enrollment, '09-10 136
Graduation rate 93.3%
Dropout rate........................3.7%
Per-pupil expenditure.................NA
Avg teacher salary ....NA
Student/teacher ratio '08-09 ...... 10.0 to 1
Highly-qualified teachers, '08-09 ... 100.0%
Teachers licensed in assigned subject .89.7%
Students per computer 1.5

Massachusetts Competency Assessment System (MCAS), 2007 results

	English		Math	
	% Prof	CPI	% Prof	CPI
Gr 4	NA	NA	NA	NA
Gr 6	NA	NA	NA	NA
Gr 8	NA	NA	NA	NA
Gr 10	77%	91.4	73%	89.9

Recieves students from:
Abington, Cohasset, Hanover, Hanson, Norwell, Rockland, Scituate, Whitman

School data 2007-2008 except as noted.

©2010 Information Publications, Inc. All rights reserved. Photocopying prohibited. For additional copies, contact the publisher at www.informationpublications.com or (877)544-INFO (4636)

Southeastern

Vocational Technical - #872
250 Foundry Street
South Easton, MA 02375
508-230-1200

Superintendent................ Luis Lopes
Grade plan.......................... 9-12
Total enrollment '09-10 1,257
Grade 12 enrollment, '09-10 277
Graduation rate 84.5%
Dropout rate........................ 9.4%
Per-pupil expenditure............ $17,298
Avg teacher salary $73,134
Student/teacher ratio '08-09 ...... 11.0 to 1
Highly-qualified teachers, '08-09..... 91.1%
Teachers licensed in assigned subject 92.9%
Students per computer 1.6

Massachusetts Competency Assessment System (MCAS), 2007 results

	English		Math	
	% Prof	CPI	% Prof	CPI
Gr 4	NA	NA	NA	NA
Gr 6	NA	NA	NA	NA
Gr 8	NA	NA	NA	NA
Gr 10	68%	88.8	59%	82.9

Recieves students from:
Brockton, East Bridgewater, Easton, Foxborough, Mansfield, Norton, Sharon, Stoughton, West Bridgewater

Southern Berkshire

Academic Regional - #765
PO BOX 339
Sheffield, MA 01257
413-229-8778

Superintendent.........Michael Singleton
Grade plan....................... PK-12
Total enrollment '09-10 900
Grade 12 enrollment, '09-10 58
Graduation rate 75.9%
Dropout rate....................... 10.3%
Per-pupil expenditure............ $13,519
Avg teacher salary $56,814
Student/teacher ratio '08-09 ...... 10.7 to 1
Highly-qualified teachers, '08-09..... 95.7%
Teachers licensed in assigned subject 90.7%
Students per computer 1.7

Massachusetts Competency Assessment System (MCAS), 2007 results

	English		Math	
	% Prof	CPI	% Prof	CPI
Gr 4	47%	81.8	39%	77.5
Gr 6	63%	87.5	43%	72.3
Gr 8	85%	94.5	53%	74.2
Gr 10	78%	92.7	66%	83.8

Recieves students from:
Alford, Egremont, Monterey, Mount Washington, New Marlborough, Sheffield

Southern Worcester County

Vocational Technical - #876
57 Old Muggett Hill Road
Charlton, MA 01507
508-248-5971

Superintendent............David Papagni
Grade plan.......................... 9-12
Total enrollment '09-10 1,115
Grade 12 enrollment, '09-10 266
Graduation rate 93.8%
Dropout rate........................ 3.3%
Per-pupil expenditure............ $14,449
Avg teacher salary $63,438
Student/teacher ratio '08-09 .... 9.9 to 1
Highly-qualified teachers, '08-09.... 94.4%
Teachers licensed in assigned subject 92.8%
Students per computer 2.2

Massachusetts Competency Assessment System (MCAS), 2007 results

	English		Math	
	% Prof	CPI	% Prof	CPI
Gr 4	NA	NA	NA	NA
Gr 6	NA	NA	NA	NA
Gr 8	NA	NA	NA	NA
Gr 10	71%	89.6	67%	85.5

Recieves students from:
Auburn, Charlton, Dudley, North Brookfield, Oxford, Paxton, Rutland, Southbridge, Spencer, Webster

Southwick-Tolland

Academic Regional - #766
86 Powder Mill Road
Southwick, MA 01077
413-569-5391

Superintendent................John Barry
Grade plan....................... PK-12
Total enrollment '09-10 1,797
Grade 12 enrollment, '09-10 141
Graduation rate 88.3%
Dropout rate....................... 8.8%
Per-pupil expenditure............ $10,301
Avg teacher salary $55,042
Student/teacher ratio '08-09 ...... 13.2 to 1
Highly-qualified teachers, '08-09... 100.0%
Teachers licensed in assigned subject 100.0%
Students per computer 3.1

Massachusetts Competency Assessment System (MCAS), 2007 results

	English		Math	
	% Prof	CPI	% Prof	CPI
Gr 4	60%	87.1	57%	85
Gr 6	76%	91.4	62%	83.4
Gr 8	86%	95.1	51%	75.3
Gr 10	86%	95.3	80%	92.7

Recieves students from:
Granville, Southwick, Tolland

Spencer-East Brookfield

Academic Regional - #767
306 Main Street
Spencer, MA 01562
508-885-8500

Superintendent..............Ralph Hicks
Grade plan....................... PK-12
Total enrollment '09-10 1,957
Grade 12 enrollment, '09-10 115
Graduation rate 77.6%
Dropout rate........................ 8.5%
Per-pupil expenditure............ $10,889
Avg teacher salary $60,905
Student/teacher ratio '08-09 ...... 15.3 to 1
Highly-qualified teachers, '08-09..... 99.6%
Teachers licensed in assigned subject 100.0%
Students per computer 2.9

Massachusetts Competency Assessment System (MCAS), 2007 results

	English		Math	
	% Prof	CPI	% Prof	CPI
Gr 4	50%	77.7	43%	77.1
Gr 6	64%	86.1	44%	71.4
Gr 8	77%	90	49%	70.5
Gr 10	80%	93.5	66%	86.2

Recieves students from:
East Brookfield, Spencer

Tantasqua

Academic Regional - #770
320A Brookfield Rd
Fiskdale, MA 01518
508-347-3077

Superintendent............Daniel Durgin
Grade plan.......................... 7-12
Total enrollment '09-10 1,782
Grade 12 enrollment, '09-10 270
Graduation rate 90.2%
Dropout rate........................ 3.8%
Per-pupil expenditure............ $10,989
Avg teacher salary $64,647
Student/teacher ratio '08-09 ...... 12.7 to 1
Highly-qualified teachers, '08-09..... 99.6%
Teachers licensed in assigned subject .99.6%
Students per computer 2.6

Massachusetts Competency Assessment System (MCAS), 2007 results

	English		Math	
	% Prof	CPI	% Prof	CPI
Gr 4	NA	NA	NA	NA
Gr 6	NA	NA	NA	NA
Gr 8	79%	91.1	51%	75
Gr 10	78%	90.8	82%	92

Recieves students from:
Brimfield, Brookfield, Holland, Sturbridge, Wales

©2010 Information Publications, Inc. All rights reserved. Photocopying prohibited. For additional copies, contact the publisher at www.informationpublications.com or (877)544-INFO (4636)

School data 2007-2008 except as noted.

Tri County

Vocational Technical - #878
147 Pond Street
Franklin, MA 02038
508-528-5400

Superintendent..........Barbara Renzoni
Grade plan..........................9-12
Total enrollment '09-10 964
Grade 12 enrollment, '09-10 215
Graduation rate 91.1%
Dropout rate........................3.0%
Per-pupil expenditure............$16,224
Avg teacher salary...............$72,132
Student/teacher ratio '08-09 ...... 10.8 to 1
Highly-qualified teachers, '08-09.....97.2%
Teachers licensed in assigned subject .89.4%
Students per computer 2.6

Massachusetts Competency Assessment System (MCAS), 2007 results

	English		Math	
	% Prof	CPI	% Prof	CPI
Gr 4	NA	NA	NA	NA
Gr 6	NA	NA	NA	NA
Gr 8	NA	NA	NA	NA
Gr 10	82%	93.1	78%	90

Recieves students from:
Franklin, Medfield, Medway, Millis, Norfolk, North Attleborough, Plainville, Seekonk, Sherborn, Walpole, Wrentham

Triton

Academic Regional - #773
112 Elm Street
Byfield, MA 01922
978-465-2397

Superintendent..........Sandra Halloran
Grade plan....................... PK-12
Total enrollment '09-10 3,171
Grade 12 enrollment, '09-10 224
Graduation rate 81.6%
Dropout rate........................7.6%
Per-pupil expenditure............$10,792
Avg teacher salary...............$61,800
Student/teacher ratio '08-09 ...... 13.6 to 1
Highly-qualified teachers, '08-09.... 96.3%
Teachers licensed in assigned subject 94.8%
Students per computer 6.6

Massachusetts Competency Assessment System (MCAS), 2007 results

	English		Math	
	% Prof	CPI	% Prof	CPI
Gr 4	64%	86.2	58%	85.6
Gr 6	81%	94.3	73%	89.4
Gr 8	84%	94.8	54%	79.8
Gr 10	82%	93.7	75%	90.4

Recieves students from:
Newbury, Rowley, Salisbury

Up-Island

Academic Regional - #774
4 Pine Street
Vineyard Haven, MA 02568
508-693-2007

Superintendent..............James Weiss
Grade plan........................ PK-8
Total enrollment '09-10 320
Grade 12 enrollment, '09-10 0
Graduation rate ....NA
Dropout rate.........................NA
Per-pupil expenditure............$21,194
Avg teacher salary...............$70,300
Student/teacher ratio '08-09 .... 8.3 to 1
Highly-qualified teachers, '08-09.....92.1%
Teachers licensed in assigned subject 96.9%
Students per computer 1.6

Massachusetts Competency Assessment System (MCAS), 2007 results

	English		Math	
	% Prof	CPI	% Prof	CPI
Gr 4	68%	88.5	78%	92.6
Gr 6	74%	91	82%	92.9
Gr 8	91%	97.8	74%	92
Gr 10	NA	NA	NA	NA

Recieves students from:
Chilmark, Aquinnah, West Tisbury

Upper Cape Cod

Vocational Technical - #879
220 Sandwich Rd
Bourne, MA 02532
508-759-7711

Superintendent...............Kevin Farr
Grade plan..........................9-12
Total enrollment '09-10 672
Grade 12 enrollment, '09-10 160
Graduation rate 89.8%
Dropout rate........................7.2%
Per-pupil expenditure............$18,571
Avg teacher salary...............$65,036
Student/teacher ratio '08-09 .... 9.9 to 1
Highly-qualified teachers, '08-09... 100.0%
Teachers licensed in assigned subject 92.4%
Students per computer 1.2

Massachusetts Competency Assessment System (MCAS), 2007 results

	English		Math	
	% Prof	CPI	% Prof	CPI
Gr 4	NA	NA	NA	NA
Gr 6	NA	NA	NA	NA
Gr 8	NA	NA	NA	NA
Gr 10	78%	92.2	81%	91.4

Recieves students from:
Bourne, Falmouth, Marion, Sandwich, Wareham

Wachusett

Academic Regional - #775
1745 Main Street, c/o Jefferson School
Jefferson, MA 01522
508-829-1670

Superintendent........ Thomas Pandiscio
Grade plan....................... PK-12
Total enrollment '09-10 7,428
Grade 12 enrollment, '09-10 454
Graduation rate 92.4%
Dropout rate........................3.6%
Per-pupil expenditure.............$9,680
Avg teacher salary...............$59,370
Student/teacher ratio '08-09 ...... 15.6 to 1
Highly-qualified teachers, '08-09.....99.7%
Teachers licensed in assigned subject .99.6%
Students per computer 3.9

Massachusetts Competency Assessment System (MCAS), 2007 results

	English		Math	
	% Prof	CPI	% Prof	CPI
Gr 4	71%	89.8	60%	85.8
Gr 6	78%	91.7	68%	86.2
Gr 8	89%	96.6	66%	84.7
Gr 10	95%	98.6	92%	96.6

Recieves students from:
Holden, Paxton, Princeton, Rutland, Sterling

Whitman-Hanson

Academic Regional - #780
610 Franklin Street
Whitman, MA 02382
781-618-7412

Superintendent..... Ruth Gilbert-Whitner
Grade plan....................... PK-12
Total enrollment '09-10 4,463
Grade 12 enrollment, '09-10 338
Graduation rate 88.5%
Dropout rate........................3.9%
Per-pupil expenditure.............$9,771
Avg teacher salary...............$62,769
Student/teacher ratio '08-09 ...... 16.6 to 1
Highly-qualified teachers, '08-09.....99.1%
Teachers licensed in assigned subject .97.8%
Students per computer 3.4

Massachusetts Competency Assessment System (MCAS), 2007 results

	English		Math	
	% Prof	CPI	% Prof	CPI
Gr 4	58%	83.6	45%	78.1
Gr 6	66%	86.4	53%	76.9
Gr 8	88%	95.2	57%	77.2
Gr 10	81%	94.2	76%	89.4

Recieves students from:
Hanson, Whitman

School data 2007-2008 except as noted.

©2010 Information Publications, Inc. All rights reserved. Photocopying prohibited. For additional copies, contact the publisher at www.informationpublications.com or (877)544-INFO (4636)

Whittier

Vocational Technical - #885
115 Amesbury Line Rd
Haverhill, MA 01830
978-373-4101

Superintendent. . . . . William DeRosa
Grade plan. 9-12
Total enrollment '09-10 1,206
Grade 12 enrollment, '09-10 266
Graduation rate .95.6%
Dropout rate. 1.3%
Per-pupil expenditure. $18,516
Avg teacher salary $66,904
Student/teacher ratio '08-09 . . . . . . 10.1 to 1
Highly-qualified teachers, '08-09. . . . .98.1%
Teachers licensed in assigned subject 96.7%
Students per computer 1.6

Massachusetts Competency Assessment System (MCAS), 2007 results

	English		Math	
	% Prof	CPI	% Prof	CPI
Gr 4	NA	NA	NA	NA
Gr 6	NA	NA	NA	NA
Gr 8	NA	NA	NA	NA
Gr 10	75%	92	76%	91.7

Recieves students from:
Amesbury, Georgetown, Groveland, Haverhill, Ipswich, Merrimack, Newbury, Newburyport, Rowley, Salisbury, West Newbury

©2010 Information Publications, Inc. All rights reserved. Photocopying prohibited. For additional copies, contact the publisher at www.informationpublications.com or (877)544-INFO (4636)

School data 2007-2008 except as noted.

Population, 2008

1.	Middlesex County	1,482,478
2.	Worcester County	783,806
3.	Essex County	736,457
4.	Suffolk County	732,684
5.	Norfolk County	659,909
6.	Bristol County	545,823
7.	Plymouth County	492,066
8.	Hampden County	460,840
9.	Barnstable County	221,049
10.	Hampshire County	154,983
11.	Berkshire County	129,395
12.	Franklin County	71,735
13.	Dukes County	15,527
14.	Nantucket County	11,215

(Census Bureau Population Estimates)

Population, 2000

1.	Middlesex County	1,465,396
2.	Worcester County	750,963
3.	Essex County	723,419
4.	Suffolk County	689,807
5.	Norfolk County	650,308
6.	Bristol County	534,678
7.	Plymouth County	472,822
8.	Hampden County	456,228
9.	Barnstable County	222,230
10.	Hampshire County	152,251
11.	Berkshire County	134,953
12.	Franklin County	71,535
13.	Dukes County	14,987
14.	Nantucket County	9,520

(2000 Decennial Census)

Land Area

1.	Worcester County	1,513
2.	Berkshire County	931
3.	Middlesex County	823
4.	Franklin County	702
5.	Plymouth County	661
6.	Hampden County	618
7.	Bristol County	556
8.	Hampshire County	529
9.	Essex County	501
10.	Norfolk County	400
11.	Barnstable County	396
12.	Dukes County	104
13.	Suffolk County	59
14.	Nantucket County	48

(in square miles)

Population Density, 2008

1.	Suffolk County	12,418.4
2.	Middlesex County	1,801.3
3.	Norfolk County	1,649.8
4.	Essex County	1,470.0
5.	Bristol County	981.7
6.	Hampden County	745.7
7.	Plymouth County	744.4
8.	Barnstable County	558.2
9.	Worcester County	518.0
10.	Hampshire County	293.0
11.	Nantucket County	233.6
12.	Dukes County	149.3
13.	Berkshire County	139.0
14.	Franklin County	102.2

(persons per square mile)

Unemployment Rate, 2008

1.	Bristol County	7.0%
2.	Hampden County	6.4
3.	Barnstable County	5.8
4.	Worcester County	5.8
5.	Essex County	5.6
6.	Plymouth County	5.6
7.	Suffolk County	5.2
8.	Berkshire County	5.1
9.	Franklin County	4.9
10.	Norfolk County	4.7
11.	Hampshire County	4.3
12.	Middlesex County	4.3
13.	Dukes County	4.1
14.	Nantucket County	NA

(Massachusetts Department of Labor)

Per Capita Income, 2008

1.	Norfolk County	$43,473
2.	Middlesex County	41,009
3.	Barnstable County	34,481
4.	Essex County	34,354
5.	Plymouth County	32,972
6.	Suffolk County	31,464
7.	Worcester County	31,068
8.	Hampshire County	29,047
9.	Berkshire County	28,279
10.	Franklin County	28,169
11.	Bristol County	28,034
12.	Hampden County	24,789

(2008 American Community Survey)

Med. Household Income, 2008

1.	Norfolk County	$81,444
2.	Middlesex County	78,202
3.	Plymouth County	73,335
4.	Worcester County	66,878
5.	Essex County	65,562
6.	Hampshire County	63,732
7.	Barnstable County	57,314
8.	Bristol County	56,241
9.	Franklin County	52,667
10.	Suffolk County	51,208
11.	Hampden County	48,583
12.	Berkshire County	44,797

(2008 American Community Survey)

Median Home Value, 2008

1.	Middlesex County	$423,700
2.	Norfolk County	416,500
3.	Barnstable County	393,300
4.	Suffolk County	384,800
5.	Essex County	374,500
6.	Plymouth County	358,400
7.	Bristol County	319,800
8.	Worcester County	282,800
9.	Hampshire County	261,500
10.	Franklin County	218,400
11.	Hampden County	209,500
12.	Berkshire County	208,900

(2008 American Community Survey)

Median Rent, 2008

1.	Middlesex County	$1,196
2.	Norfolk County	1,191
3.	Suffolk County	1,132
4.	Plymouth County	1,071
5.	Barnstable County	1,031
6.	Essex County	964
7.	Hampshire County	869
8.	Worcester County	860
9.	Franklin County	798
10.	Bristol County	783
11.	Hampden County	722
12.	Berkshire County	703

(2008 American Community Survey)

©2010 Information Publications, Inc. All rights reserved. Photocopying prohibited. For additional copies, contact the publisher at www.informationpublications.com or (877)544-INFO (4636)

Population, 2008 (estimate)

1. Boston	609,023	
2. Worcester	175,011	
3. Springfield	150,640	
4. Cambridge	105,596	
5. Lowell	103,615	
6. Brockton	93,007	
7. Quincy	92,339	
8. New Bedford	91,365	
9. Fall River	90,931	
10. Lynn	86,957	
11. Newton	82,139	
12. Somerville	75,662	
13. Lawrence	70,014	
14. Framingham	64,885	
15. Haverhill	61,275	
16. Waltham	60,236	
17. Revere	60,204	
18. Plymouth	55,705	
19. Taunton	55,702	
20. Malden	55,597	
21. Medford	55,573	
22. Chicopee	54,941	
23. Brookline	54,896	
24. Weymouth	53,261	
25. Peabody	51,331	
26. Barnstable	46,184	
27. Methuen	44,055	
28. Attleboro	42,833	
29. Pittsfield	42,652	
30. Billerica	41,844	
31. Chelsea	41,577	
32. Salem	41,256	
33. Leominster	41,055	
34. Arlington	40,993	
35. Westfield	40,608	
36. Fitchburg	40,239	
37. Holyoke	39,947	
38. Beverly	39,343	
39. Marlborough	37,932	
40. Everett	37,353	
41. Woburn	36,871	
42. Amherst	35,565	
43. Braintree	35,294	
44. Chelmsford	34,409	
45. Dartmouth	33,899	
46. Shrewsbury	33,435	
47. Andover	33,418	
48. Falmouth	33,123	
49. Watertown	32,365	
50. Franklin	32,148	
51. Natick	31,880	
52. Lexington	30,272	
53. Gloucester	30,243	
54. Randolph	30,082	
55. Tewksbury	29,543	
56. Dracut	29,501	
57. Needham	28,560	
58. Northampton	28,379	
59. Norwood	28,211	
60. Agawam	28,091	
61. North Attleborough	27,794	
62. North Andover	27,522	
63. Saugus	27,478	
64. West Springfield	27,459	
65. Milford	27,246	
66. Wellesley	27,244	
67. Stoughton	26,927	
68. Danvers	26,762	
69. Melrose	26,708	
70. Milton	26,187	
71. Bridgewater	25,774	
72. Burlington	24,985	
73. Marshfield	24,735	
74. Wakefield	24,717	
75. Dedham	24,630	
76. Mansfield	23,969	
77. Yarmouth	23,778	
78. Belmont	23,291	
79. Easton	23,209	
80. Walpole	23,133	
81. Reading	23,052	
82. Hingham	22,561	
83. Ludlow	22,410	
84. Westford	22,066	
85. Canton	22,048	
86. Winthrop	21,880	
87. Wilmington	21,649	
88. Stoneham	21,471	
89. Wareham	21,221	
90. Middleborough	21,117	
91. Winchester	21,090	
92. Acton	20,797	
93. Gardner	20,682	
94. Sandwich	20,129	
95. Marblehead	19,951	
96. Hudson	19,597	
97. Bourne	19,392	
98. Norton	19,186	
99. Pembroke	18,714	
100. Westborough	18,467	
101. Somerset	18,055	
102. Scituate	17,926	
103. Rockland	17,883	
104. Greenfield	17,828	
105. Grafton	17,553	
106. Newburyport	17,542	
107. Concord	17,450	
108. Sharon	17,373	
109. North Reading	17,272	
110. South Hadley	17,241	
111. Sudbury	17,207	
112. Southbridge	16,852	
113. Abington	16,689	
114. Webster	16,655	
115. Holden	16,608	
116. Amesbury	16,584	
117. Foxborough	16,347	
118. Auburn	16,222	
119. Easthampton	16,195	
120. Swansea	16,155	
121. Fairhaven	16,112	
122. Bellingham	15,900	
123. Ashland	15,807	
124. Westport	15,417	
125. Dennis	15,349	
126. East Longmeadow	15,332	
127. Longmeadow	15,329	
128. Northborough	14,646	
129. Duxbury	14,496	
130. Whitman	14,447	
131. Northbridge	14,383	
132. Hopkinton	14,338	
133. Belchertown	14,233	
134. Mashpee	14,227	
135. Westwood	14,189	
136. East Bridgewater	13,996	
137. Hanover	13,995	
138. Wilbraham	13,970	
139. Clinton	13,965	
140. Swampscott	13,944	
141. Holliston	13,901	
142. North Adams	13,711	
143. Oxford	13,615	
144. Seekonk	13,575	
145. Raynham	13,566	
146. Bedford	13,545	
147. Millbury	13,401	
148. Ipswich	13,219	
149. Wayland	12,996	
150. Palmer	12,933	
151. Medway	12,785	
152. Uxbridge	12,672	
153. Charlton	12,585	
154. Kingston	12,328	
155. Harwich	12,298	
156. Medfield	12,275	
157. Tyngsborough	12,019	
158. Spencer	11,922	
159. Weston	11,711	
160. Carver	11,574	
161. Athol	11,570	
162. Rehoboth	11,474	
163. Lynnfield	11,412	
164. Pepperell	11,382	
165. Nantucket	11,215	
166. Wrentham	11,133	
167. Dudley	11,073	
168. Hull	11,041	
169. Norfolk	11,029	
170. Leicester	10,990	
171. Holbrook	10,644	
172. Groton	10,632	
173. Lakeville	10,515	
174. Acushnet	10,368	
175. Norwell	10,293	
176. Maynard	10,182	
177. Winchendon	10,164	
178. Hanson	10,019	
179. Lunenburg	9,946	
180. Brewster	9,936	

See Introduction for an explanation of all data sources.

©2010 Information Publications, Inc. All rights reserved. Photocopying prohibited. For additional copies, contact the publisher at www.informationpublications.com or (877)544-INFO (4636)

Population, 2008 (estimate)

181.	Ware	9,824
182.	Middleton	9,634
183.	Southborough	9,583
184.	Southwick	9,571
185.	Townsend	9,400
186.	Sturbridge	9,103
187.	Sutton	9,028
188.	Freetown	9,027
189.	Blackstone	9,021
190.	Monson	8,952
191.	Littleton	8,711
192.	Georgetown	8,629
193.	Salisbury	8,417
194.	Montague	8,316
195.	Adams	8,295
196.	West Boylston	8,277
197.	Plainville	8,204
198.	Hamilton	8,155
199.	Boxford	8,131
200.	Lincoln	8,078
201.	Williamstown	7,968
202.	Millis	7,957
203.	Douglas	7,955
204.	Shirley	7,904
205.	Rutland	7,899
206.	Sterling	7,865
207.	Templeton	7,831
208.	Halifax	7,692
209.	Orange	7,688
210.	Rockport	7,612
211.	Ayer	7,399
212.	Westminster	7,391
213.	Great Barrington	7,379
214.	Groveland	7,198
215.	Cohasset	7,169
216.	Lancaster	7,015
217.	Newbury	6,934
218.	Dighton	6,724
219.	Chatham	6,701
220.	West Bridgewater	6,674
221.	Dalton	6,593
222.	Upton	6,584
223.	Merrimac	6,504
224.	Mattapoisett	6,463
225.	Berkley	6,462
226.	Stow	6,446
227.	Granby	6,281
228.	Orleans	6,269
229.	Hopedale	6,142
230.	Topsfield	6,051
231.	Harvard	6,006
232.	Ashburnham	5,974
233.	Southampton	5,970
234.	Lee	5,763
235.	Mendon	5,762
236.	Rowley	5,738
237.	Dover	5,644
238.	Eastham	5,438
239.	Barre	5,431
240.	Hampden	5,400
241.	Rochester	5,268
242.	Manchester-by-the-Sea	5,260
243.	Marion	5,148
244.	Lenox	5,095
245.	Boxborough	5,081
246.	Warren	5,068
247.	Carlisle	4,874
248.	North Brookfield	4,833
249.	Wenham	4,788
250.	Hadley	4,732
251.	Deerfield	4,694
252.	Paxton	4,632
253.	Bolton	4,530
254.	Hubbardston	4,482
255.	Avon	4,300
256.	West Newbury	4,269
257.	Boylston	4,264
258.	Sherborn	4,204
259.	Edgartown	3,932
260.	Tisbury	3,811
261.	West Brookfield	3,806
262.	Oak Bluffs	3,735
263.	Sunderland	3,710
264.	Brimfield	3,708
265.	Nahant	3,498
266.	Princeton	3,475
267.	Provincetown	3,376
268.	Essex	3,333
269.	Dunstable	3,323
270.	Cheshire	3,314
271.	Sheffield	3,309
272.	Hatfield	3,227
273.	Northfield	3,026
274.	Brookfield	3,007
275.	Ashby	2,927
276.	Lanesborough	2,866
277.	Berlin	2,853
278.	Millville	2,845
279.	Plympton	2,785
280.	Wellfleet	2,724
281.	Hardwick	2,649
282.	West Tisbury	2,638
283.	Holland	2,529
284.	Williamsburg	2,509
285.	Bernardston	2,230
286.	Huntington	2,219
287.	Stockbridge	2,217
288.	Truro	2,125
289.	East Brookfield	2,057
290.	Shelburne	2,035
291.	Buckland	1,989
292.	Oakham	1,914
293.	Hinsdale	1,913
294.	Conway	1,896
295.	Wales	1,881
296.	Colrain	1,879
297.	Shutesbury	1,847
298.	Ashfield	1,822
299.	Becket	1,801
300.	Phillipston	1,787
301.	Leverett	1,772
302.	Russell	1,719
303.	Granville	1,686
304.	Clarksburg	1,619
305.	Westhampton	1,576
306.	Richmond	1,572
307.	Whately	1,566
308.	Erving	1,552
309.	New Marlborough	1,508
310.	West Stockbridge	1,432
311.	Otis	1,396
312.	Gill	1,388
313.	Pelham	1,386
314.	Charlemont	1,378
315.	Royalston	1,376
316.	Egremont	1,351
317.	Chesterfield	1,288
318.	Petersham	1,288
319.	Chester	1,287
320.	Worthington	1,272
321.	Blandford	1,270
322.	New Braintree	1,116
323.	Hancock	1,112
324.	Wendell	1,000
325.	New Salem	990
326.	Goshen	974
327.	Chilmark	971
328.	Cummington	964
329.	Monterey	950
330.	Sandisfield	848
331.	Windsor	846
332.	Peru	832
333.	Leyden	801
334.	Heath	798
335.	Warwick	749
336.	Savoy	722
337.	Montgomery	720
338.	Florida	675
339.	Plainfield	591
340.	Middlefield	557
341.	Washington	542
342.	Tolland	457
343.	Alford	392
344.	Aquinnah	357
345.	Rowe	348
346.	Tyringham	339
347.	Hawley	337
348.	New Ashford	247
349.	Mount Washington	136
350.	Monroe	96
351.	Gosnold	83

©2010 Information Publications, Inc. All rights reserved. Photocopying prohibited. For additional copies, contact the publisher at www.informationpublications.com or (877)544-INFO (4636)

See Introduction for an explanation of all data sources.

Population, 2000

1.	Boston	589,141	61.	West Springfield	27,899	121.	Bellingham	15,314
2.	Worcester	172,648	62.	North Andover	27,202	122.	Grafton	14,894
3.	Springfield	152,082	63.	Stoughton	27,149	123.	North Adams	14,681
4.	Lowell	105,167	64.	North Attleborough	27,143	124.	Ashland	14,674
5.	Cambridge	101,355	65.	Melrose	27,134	125.	Abington	14,605
6.	Brockton	94,304	66.	Milford	26,799	126.	Swampscott	14,412
7.	New Bedford	93,768	67.	Wellesley	26,613	127.	Duxbury	14,248
8.	Fall River	91,938	68.	Saugus	26,078	128.	Westport	14,183
9.	Lynn	89,050	69.	Milton	26,062	129.	Westwood	14,117
10.	Quincy	88,025	70.	Danvers	25,212	130.	East Longmeadow	14,100
11.	Newton	83,829	71.	Bridgewater	25,185	131.	Northborough	14,013
12.	Somerville	77,478	72.	Yarmouth	24,807	132.	Whitman	13,882
13.	Lawrence	72,043	73.	Wakefield	24,804	133.	North Reading	13,837
14.	Framingham	66,910	74.	Marshfield	24,324	134.	Holliston	13,801
15.	Waltham	59,226	75.	Belmont	24,194	135.	Wilbraham	13,473
16.	Haverhill	58,969	76.	Reading	23,708	136.	Clinton	13,435
17.	Brookline	57,107	77.	Dedham	23,464	137.	Seekonk	13,425
18.	Malden	56,340	78.	Burlington	22,876	138.	Oxford	13,352
19.	Taunton	55,976	79.	Walpole	22,824	139.	Hopkinton	13,346
20.	Medford	55,765	80.	Mansfield	22,414	140.	Northbridge	13,182
21.	Chicopee	54,653	81.	Easton	22,299	141.	Hanover	13,164
22.	Weymouth	53,988	82.	Stoneham	22,219	142.	Wayland	13,100
23.	Plymouth	51,701	83.	Wilmington	21,363	143.	Ipswich	12,987
24.	Peabody	48,129	84.	Ludlow	21,209	144.	East Bridgewater	12,974
25.	Barnstable	47,821	85.	Winchester	20,810	145.	Belchertown	12,968
26.	Revere	47,283	86.	Canton	20,775	146.	Mashpee	12,946
27.	Pittsfield	45,793	87.	Gardner	20,770	147.	Millbury	12,784
28.	Methuen	43,789	88.	Westford	20,754	148.	Bedford	12,595
29.	Arlington	42,389	89.	Marblehead	20,377	149.	Palmer	12,497
30.	Attleboro	42,068	90.	Wareham	20,335	150.	Medway	12,448
31.	Leominster	41,303	91.	Acton	20,331	151.	Harwich	12,386
32.	Salem	40,407	92.	Sandwich	20,136	152.	Medfield	12,273
33.	Westfield	40,072	93.	Middleborough	19,941	153.	Kingston	11,780
34.	Beverly	39,862	94.	Hingham	19,882	154.	Raynham	11,739
35.	Holyoke	39,838	95.	Bourne	18,721	155.	Spencer	11,691
36.	Fitchburg	39,102	96.	Winthrop	18,303	156.	Lynnfield	11,542
37.	Billerica	38,981	97.	Somerset	18,234	157.	Weston	11,469
38.	Everett	38,037	98.	Greenfield	18,168	158.	Athol	11,299
39.	Woburn	37,258	99.	Hudson	18,113	159.	Charlton	11,263
40.	Marlborough	36,255	100.	Norton	18,036	160.	Carver	11,163
41.	Chelsea	35,080	101.	Westborough	17,997	161.	Uxbridge	11,156
42.	Amherst	34,874	102.	Scituate	17,863	162.	Pepperell	11,142
43.	Chelmsford	33,858	103.	Rockland	17,670	163.	Tyngsborough	11,081
44.	Braintree	33,828	104.	Sharon	17,408	164.	Hull	11,050
45.	Watertown	32,986	105.	Southbridge	17,214	165.	Holbrook	10,785
46.	Falmouth	32,660	106.	South Hadley	17,196	166.	Wrentham	10,554
47.	Natick	32,170	107.	Newburyport	17,189	167.	Leicester	10,471
48.	Shrewsbury	31,640	108.	Concord	16,993	168.	Norfolk	10,460
49.	Andover	31,247	109.	Pembroke	16,927	169.	Maynard	10,433
50.	Randolph	30,963	110.	Sudbury	16,841	170.	Rehoboth	10,172
51.	Dartmouth	30,666	111.	Amesbury	16,450	171.	Acushnet	10,161
52.	Lexington	30,355	112.	Webster	16,415	172.	Brewster	10,094
53.	Gloucester	30,273	113.	Foxborough	16,246	173.	Dudley	10,036
54.	Franklin	29,560	114.	Fairhaven	16,159	174.	Lakeville	9,821
55.	Northampton	28,978	115.	Easthampton	15,994	175.	Norwell	9,765
56.	Needham	28,911	116.	Dennis	15,973	176.	Ware	9,707
57.	Tewksbury	28,851	117.	Auburn	15,901	177.	Winchendon	9,611
58.	Norwood	28,587	118.	Swansea	15,901	178.	Groton	9,547
59.	Dracut	28,562	119.	Longmeadow	15,633	179.	Nantucket	9,520
60.	Agawam	28,144	120.	Holden	15,621	180.	Hanson	9,495

©2010 Information Publications, Inc. All rights reserved. Photocopying prohibited. For additional copies, contact the publisher at www.informationpublications.com or (877)544-INFO (4636)

See Introduction for an explanation of all data sources.

Population, 2000

181. Lunenburg	9,401	241. Marion	5,123	301. Leverett	1,663
182. Townsend	9,198	242. Barre	5,113	302. Russell	1,657
183. Southwick	8,835	243. Lenox	5,077	303. Phillipston	1,621
184. Adams	8,809	244. Boxborough	4,868	304. Richmond	1,604
185. Blackstone	8,804	245. Hadley	4,793	305. Whately	1,573
186. Southborough	8,781	246. Warren	4,776	306. Granville	1,521
187. Montague	8,489	247. Deerfield	4,750	307. New Marlborough	1,494
188. Freetown	8,472	248. Carlisle	4,717	308. Westhampton	1,468
189. Williamstown	8,424	249. North Brookfield	4,683	309. Erving	1,467
190. Monson	8,359	250. Rochester	4,581	310. West Stockbridge	1,416
191. Hamilton	8,315	251. Avon	4,443	311. Pelham	1,403
192. Sutton	8,250	252. Wenham	4,440	312. Otis	1,365
193. Littleton	8,184	253. Paxton	4,386	313. Gill	1,363
194. Lincoln	8,056	254. Sherborn	4,200	314. Charlemont	1,358
195. Boxford	7,921	255. West Newbury	4,149	315. Egremont	1,345
196. Millis	7,902	256. Bolton	4,148	316. Chester	1,308
197. Sturbridge	7,837	257. Boylston	4,008	317. Worthington	1,270
198. Salisbury	7,827	258. Hubbardston	3,909	318. Royalston	1,254
199. Rockport	7,767	259. West Brookfield	3,804	319. Blandford	1,214
200. Middleton	7,744	260. Edgartown	3,779	320. Chesterfield	1,201
201. Plainville	7,683	261. Sunderland	3,777	321. Petersham	1,180
202. Great Barrington	7,527	262. Tisbury	3,755	322. Wendell	986
203. Orange	7,518	263. Oak Bluffs	3,713	323. Cummington	978
204. Halifax	7,500	264. Nahant	3,632	324. Monterey	934
205. West Boylston	7,481	265. Provincetown	3,431	325. New Salem	929
206. Lancaster	7,380	266. Cheshire	3,401	326. New Braintree	927
207. Georgetown	7,377	267. Princeton	3,353	327. Goshen	921
208. Ayer	7,287	268. Brimfield	3,339	328. Windsor	875
209. Cohasset	7,261	269. Sheffield	3,335	329. Chilmark	843
210. Sterling	7,257	270. Essex	3,267	330. Sandisfield	824
211. Douglas	7,045	271. Hatfield	3,249	331. Peru	821
212. Westminster	6,907	272. Brookfield	3,051	332. Heath	805
213. Dalton	6,892	273. Lanesborough	2,990	333. Leyden	772
214. Templeton	6,799	274. Northfield	2,951	334. Warwick	750
215. Newbury	6,717	275. Ashby	2,845	335. Hancock	721
216. West Bridgewater	6,634	276. Dunstable	2,829	336. Savoy	705
217. Chatham	6,625	277. Wellfleet	2,749	337. Florida	676
218. Shirley	6,373	278. Millville	2,724	338. Montgomery	654
219. Rutland	6,353	279. Plympton	2,637	339. Plainfield	589
220. Orleans	6,341	280. Hardwick	2,622	340. Washington	544
221. Mattapoisett	6,268	281. West Tisbury	2,467	341. Middlefield	542
222. Dighton	6,175	282. Williamsburg	2,427	342. Tolland	426
223. Topsfield	6,141	283. Holland	2,407	343. Alford	399
224. Merrimac	6,138	284. Berlin	2,380	344. Rowe	351
225. Granby	6,132	285. Stockbridge	2,276	345. Tyringham	350
226. Groveland	6,038	286. Huntington	2,174	346. Aquinnah	344
227. Lee	5,985	287. Bernardston	2,155	347. Hawley	336
228. Harvard	5,981	288. East Brookfield	2,097	348. New Ashford	247
229. Hopedale	5,907	289. Truro	2,087	349. Mount Washington	130
230. Stow	5,902	290. Shelburne	2,058	350. Monroe	93
231. Berkley	5,749	291. Buckland	1,991	351. Gosnold	86
232. Upton	5,642	292. Hinsdale	1,872		(2000 Decennial Census)
233. Dover	5,558	293. Colrain	1,813		
234. Ashburnham	5,546	294. Shutesbury	1,810		
235. Rowley	5,500	295. Conway	1,809		
236. Eastham	5,453	296. Ashfield	1,800		
237. Southampton	5,387	297. Becket	1,755		
238. Mendon	5,286	298. Wales	1,737		
239. Manchester-by-the-Sea	5,228	299. Clarksburg	1,686		
240. Hampden	5,171	300. Oakham	1,673		

©2010 Information Publications, Inc. All rights reserved. Photocopying prohibited. For additional copies, contact the publisher at www.informationpublications.com or (877)544-INFO (4636)

See Introduction for an explanation of all data sources.

Land Area

1. Plymouth	96.5	61. Townsend	32.9	121. Florida	24.4
2. Middleborough	69.6	62. Groton	32.8	122. Sudbury	24.4
3. Dartmouth	61.6	63. Spencer	32.8	123. Phillipston	24.3
4. Barnstable	60.0	64. Athol	32.6	124. Middlefield	24.2
5. Petersham	54.2	65. Ipswich	32.6	125. Newbury	24.2
6. Belchertown	52.7	66. Sutton	32.4	126. Yarmouth	24.2
7. Sandisfield	52.3	67. Deerfield	32.3	127. Boxford	24.0
8. Blandford	51.7	68. Springfield	32.1	128. Ashby	23.8
9. Westport	50.0	69. Worthington	32.1	129. Duxbury	23.8
10. Boston	48.4	70. Templeton	32.0	130. Mashpee	23.5
11. Sheffield	48.1	71. Wendell	32.0	131. Rowe	23.5
12. Nantucket	47.8	72. Tolland	31.6	132. Bernardston	23.4
13. New Marlborough	47.2	73. Palmer	31.5	133. Leicester	23.4
14. Williamstown	46.9	74. Chesterfield	31.1	134. Hadley	23.3
15. Taunton	46.6	75. Andover	31.0	135. Sharon	23.3
16. Westfield	46.6	76. Fall River	31.0	136. Shelburne	23.3
17. Rehoboth	46.5	77. Southwick	31.0	137. Agawam	23.2
18. Becket	46.3	78. Hawley	30.9	138. Cummington	23.1
19. Great Barrington	45.2	79. Westford	30.6	139. Swansea	23.1
20. New Salem	45.0	80. Sterling	30.5	140. Brewster	23.0
21. Barre	44.3	81. Montague	30.4	141. Adams	22.9
22. Monson	44.3	82. Lakeville	29.9	142. Chicopee	22.9
23. Falmouth	44.2	83. Uxbridge	29.5	143. Stockbridge	22.9
24. Colrain	43.4	84. Lanesborough	29.0	144. Leverett	22.8
25. Winchendon	43.3	85. Leominster	28.9	145. Grafton	22.7
26. Sandwich	43.0	86. Norton	28.7	146. Chelmsford	22.6
27. Charlton	42.5	87. Marshfield	28.5	147. Pepperell	22.6
28. Granville	42.2	88. Easton	28.4	148. Hingham	22.5
29. Royalston	41.9	89. Southampton	28.1	149. Dighton	22.4
30. Hubbardston	41.0	90. Granby	27.9	150. Methuen	22.4
31. Bourne	40.9	91. Fitchburg	27.8	151. Gardner	22.2
32. Pittsfield	40.7	92. Amherst	27.7	152. Mount Washington	22.2
33. Ashfield	40.3	93. Lancaster	27.7	153. Wilbraham	22.2
34. Ashburnham	38.7	94. Attleboro	27.5	154. Wrentham	22.2
35. Hardwick	38.6	95. Bridgewater	27.5	155. Dalton	21.8
36. Washington	37.8	96. Warren	27.5	156. Pembroke	21.8
37. Conway	37.7	97. Ludlow	27.1	157. Greenfield	21.7
38. Worcester	37.6	98. Westhampton	27.1	158. Brockton	21.5
39. Carver	37.5	99. Edgartown	27.0	159. Upton	21.5
40. Sturbridge	37.4	100. Cheshire	26.9	160. Holyoke	21.3
41. Warwick	37.3	101. Franklin	26.7	161. Lenox	21.2
42. Chester	36.7	102. North Andover	26.7	162. Dudley	21.1
43. Freetown	36.6	103. Hopkinton	26.6	163. Marlborough	21.1
44. Douglas	36.4	104. Huntington	26.6	164. North Brookfield	21.1
45. Savoy	35.9	105. Oxford	26.6	165. Oakham	21.1
46. Otis	35.8	106. Shutesbury	26.6	166. Plainfield	21.1
47. Wareham	35.8	107. Monterey	26.5	167. Truro	21.1
48. Hancock	35.7	108. Harvard	26.4	168. Harwich	21.0
49. Westminster	35.5	109. Lee	26.4	169. Dracut	20.9
50. Orange	35.4	110. Lunenburg	26.4	170. Norwell	20.9
51. Princeton	35.4	111. Charlemont	26.1	171. Hinsdale	20.8
52. Rutland	35.3	112. Gloucester	26.0	172. New Braintree	20.7
53. Holden	35.0	113. Billerica	25.9	173. Shrewsbury	20.7
54. Windsor	35.0	114. Peru	25.9	174. Tewksbury	20.7
55. Brimfield	34.7	115. Williamsburg	25.6	175. Dennis	20.6
56. Northampton	34.5	116. Framingham	25.1	176. Mansfield	20.5
57. Northfield	34.4	117. Pelham	25.1	177. Raynham	20.5
58. Ware	34.4	118. West Tisbury	25.0	178. Walpole	20.5
59. Rochester	33.9	119. Concord	24.9	179. West Brookfield	20.5
60. Haverhill	33.3	120. Heath	24.9	180. Westborough	20.5

©2010 Information Publications, Inc. All rights reserved. Photocopying prohibited. For additional copies, contact the publisher at www.informationpublications.com or (877)544-INFO (4636)

See Introduction for an explanation of all data sources.

Land Area

181.	North Adams	20.4
182.	Southbridge	20.4
183.	Whately	20.2
184.	Foxborough	20.1
185.	New Bedford	20.1
186.	Acton	20.0
187.	Bolton	19.9
188.	Wellfleet	19.8
189.	Buckland	19.6
190.	Hampden	19.6
191.	Chilmark	19.1
192.	Richmond	19.0
193.	Canton	18.9
194.	Egremont	18.8
195.	Holliston	18.7
196.	Rowley	18.7
197.	Tyringham	18.7
198.	North Attleborough	18.6
199.	Acushnet	18.5
200.	Bellingham	18.5
201.	Kingston	18.5
202.	Northborough	18.5
203.	West Stockbridge	18.5
204.	Seekonk	18.3
205.	Mendon	18.1
206.	Newton	18.1
207.	Leyden	18.0
208.	South Hadley	17.7
209.	Russell	17.6
210.	Stow	17.6
211.	Goshen	17.4
212.	East Bridgewater	17.2
213.	Northbridge	17.2
214.	Scituate	17.2
215.	Wilmington	17.1
216.	Weston	17.0
217.	Weymouth	17.0
218.	Tyngsborough	16.9
219.	Quincy	16.8
220.	West Springfield	16.7
221.	Beverly	16.6
222.	Littleton	16.6
223.	Berkley	16.5
224.	Dunstable	16.5
225.	Mattapoisett	16.5
226.	Lexington	16.4
227.	Peabody	16.4
228.	Chatham	16.2
229.	Halifax	16.1
230.	Boylston	16.0
231.	Hatfield	16.0
232.	Sherborn	16.0
233.	Stoughton	16.0
234.	Shirley	15.8
235.	Millbury	15.7
236.	Wales	15.7
237.	West Bridgewater	15.7
238.	Hanover	15.6
239.	Brookfield	15.5
240.	Auburn	15.4
241.	Carlisle	15.4
242.	Salisbury	15.4
243.	Dover	15.3
244.	Wayland	15.2
245.	Montgomery	15.1
246.	Natick	15.1
247.	Hanson	15.0
248.	Norfolk	14.8
249.	Plympton	14.8
250.	Paxton	14.7
251.	Hamilton	14.6
252.	Marion	14.6
253.	Milford	14.6
254.	Medfield	14.5
255.	Lincoln	14.4
256.	Sunderland	14.4
257.	Essex	14.2
258.	Orleans	14.2
259.	Southborough	14.1
260.	Eastham	14.0
261.	Gill	14.0
262.	Middleton	14.0
263.	Braintree	13.9
264.	Erving	13.9
265.	Lowell	13.8
266.	Bedford	13.7
267.	New Ashford	13.5
268.	West Newbury	13.5
269.	Easthampton	13.4
270.	Danvers	13.3
271.	Gosnold	13.3
272.	North Reading	13.3
273.	East Longmeadow	13.0
274.	Milton	13.0
275.	Berlin	12.9
276.	Georgetown	12.9
277.	West Boylston	12.9
278.	Clarksburg	12.8
279.	Topsfield	12.7
280.	Waltham	12.7
281.	Woburn	12.7
282.	Needham	12.6
283.	Webster	12.5
284.	Amesbury	12.4
285.	Ashland	12.4
286.	Fairhaven	12.4
287.	Holland	12.4
288.	Millis	12.2
289.	Burlington	11.8
290.	Alford	11.6
291.	Hudson	11.5
292.	Medway	11.5
293.	Plainville	11.1
294.	Saugus	11.0
295.	Westwood	11.0
296.	Blackstone	10.9
297.	Lynn	10.8
298.	Monroe	10.7
299.	Dedham	10.5
300.	Norwood	10.5
301.	Boxborough	10.4
302.	Wellesley	10.2
303.	Lynnfield	10.1
304.	Randolph	10.1
305.	Rockland	10.0
306.	Abington	9.9
307.	Cohasset	9.9
308.	Reading	9.9
309.	East Brookfield	9.8
310.	Provincetown	9.7
311.	Manchester-by-the-Sea	9.3
312.	Ayer	9.0
313.	Longmeadow	9.0
314.	Groveland	8.9
315.	Merrimac	8.5
316.	Newburyport	8.4
317.	Medford	8.1
318.	Salem	8.1
319.	Somerset	8.1
320.	Wenham	7.7
321.	Wakefield	7.5
322.	Holbrook	7.4
323.	Oak Bluffs	7.4
324.	Rockport	7.1
325.	Lawrence	7.0
326.	Whitman	7.0
327.	Brookline	6.8
328.	Tisbury	6.6
329.	Cambridge	6.4
330.	Stoneham	6.1
331.	Winchester	6.0
332.	Revere	5.9
333.	Clinton	5.7
334.	Aquinnah	5.4
335.	Arlington	5.2
336.	Hopedale	5.2
337.	Maynard	5.2
338.	Malden	5.1
339.	Millville	4.9
340.	Belmont	4.7
341.	Melrose	4.7
342.	Marblehead	4.5
343.	Avon	4.4
344.	Somerville	4.1
345.	Watertown	4.1
346.	Everett	3.4
347.	Hull	3.0
348.	Swampscott	3.0
349.	Chelsea	2.2
350.	Winthrop	2.0
351.	Nahant	1.2

(in square miles)

©2010 Information Publications, Inc. All rights reserved. Photocopying prohibited. For additional copies, contact the publisher at www.informationpublications.com or (877)544-INFO (4636)

See Introduction for an explanation of all data sources.

Persons per Square Mile, 2008

1.	Chelsea	18,898.6	61.	Haverhill	1,840.1	121.	Medfield	846.6
2.	Somerville	18,454.1	62.	Marlborough	1,797.7	122.	Northbridge	836.2
3.	Cambridge	16,499.4	63.	Rockland	1,788.3	123.	Blackstone	827.6
4.	Boston	12,583.1	64.	Hudson	1,704.1	124.	Ludlow	826.9
5.	Everett	10,986.2	65.	Longmeadow	1,703.2	125.	Southbridge	826.1
6.	Winthrop	10,940.0	66.	Abington	1,685.8	126.	Northampton	822.6
7.	Malden	10,901.4	67.	Stoughton	1,682.9	127.	Ayer	822.1
8.	Revere	10,204.1	68.	West Springfield	1,644.3	128.	Greenfield	821.6
9.	Lawrence	10,002.0	69.	Billerica	1,615.6	129.	Easton	817.2
10.	Brookline	8,072.9	70.	Shrewsbury	1,615.2	130.	East Bridgewater	813.7
11.	Lynn	8,051.6	71.	Attleboro	1,557.6	131.	Foxborough	813.3
12.	Watertown	7,893.9	72.	Chelmsford	1,522.5	132.	Groveland	808.8
13.	Arlington	7,883.3	73.	North Attleborough	1,494.3	133.	Northborough	791.7
14.	Lowell	7,508.3	74.	Fitchburg	1,447.4	134.	Grafton	773.3
15.	Medford	6,860.9	75.	Holbrook	1,438.4	135.	Barnstable	769.7
16.	Melrose	5,682.6	76.	Tewksbury	1,427.2	136.	Merrimac	765.2
17.	Quincy	5,496.4	77.	Leominster	1,420.6	137.	Falmouth	749.4
18.	Salem	5,093.3	78.	Dracut	1,411.5	138.	Sharon	745.6
19.	Belmont	4,955.5	79.	Amesbury	1,337.4	139.	Norfolk	745.2
20.	Waltham	4,743.0	80.	Webster	1,332.4	140.	Dennis	745.1
21.	Springfield	4,692.8	81.	Fairhaven	1,299.4	141.	Holliston	743.4
22.	Worcester	4,654.5	82.	North Reading	1,298.6	142.	Seekonk	741.8
23.	Swampscott	4,648.0	83.	Westwood	1,289.9	143.	Plainville	739.1
24.	New Bedford	4,545.5	84.	Amherst	1,283.9	144.	Cohasset	724.1
25.	Newton	4,538.1	85.	Ashland	1,274.8	145.	Westford	721.1
26.	Marblehead	4,433.6	86.	Wilmington	1,266.0	146.	Tyngsborough	711.2
27.	Brockton	4,325.9	87.	Agawam	1,210.8	147.	Sudbury	705.2
28.	Hull	3,680.3	88.	Easthampton	1,208.6	148.	Concord	700.8
29.	Stoneham	3,519.8	89.	Franklin	1,204.0	149.	Swansea	699.4
30.	Winchester	3,515.0	90.	Taunton	1,195.3	150.	Weston	688.9
31.	Wakefield	3,295.6	91.	Hopedale	1,181.2	151.	Middleton	688.1
32.	Weymouth	3,133.0	92.	East Longmeadow	1,179.4	152.	Southborough	679.6
33.	Peabody	3,129.9	93.	Mansfield	1,169.2	153.	North Adams	672.1
34.	Randolph	2,978.4	94.	Canton	1,166.6	154.	Georgetown	668.9
35.	Fall River	2,933.3	95.	Gloucester	1,163.2	155.	Norton	668.5
36.	Nahant	2,915.0	96.	Lynnfield	1,129.9	156.	Hanson	667.9
37.	Woburn	2,903.2	97.	Walpole	1,128.4	157.	Kingston	666.4
38.	Norwood	2,686.8	98.	Medway	1,111.7	158.	Raynham	661.8
39.	Wellesley	2,671.0	99.	Andover	1,078.0	159.	Millis	652.2
40.	Framingham	2,585.1	100.	Rockport	1,072.1	160.	West Boylston	641.6
41.	Braintree	2,539.1	101.	Auburn	1,053.4	161.	Wilbraham	629.3
42.	Saugus	2,498.0	102.	Pittsfield	1,048.0	162.	Wenham	621.8
43.	Clinton	2,450.0	103.	Scituate	1,042.2	163.	Duxbury	609.1
44.	Chicopee	2,399.2	104.	Acton	1,039.9	164.	Mashpee	605.4
45.	Beverly	2,370.1	105.	North Andover	1,030.8	165.	Wareham	592.8
46.	Dedham	2,345.7	106.	Hingham	1,002.7	166.	Harwich	585.6
47.	Reading	2,328.5	107.	Bedford	988.7	167.	Millville	580.6
48.	Needham	2,266.7	108.	Yarmouth	982.6	168.	Tisbury	577.4
49.	Somerset	2,229.0	109.	Avon	977.3	169.	Plymouth	577.3
50.	Burlington	2,117.4	110.	South Hadley	974.1	170.	Manchester-by-the-Sea	565.6
51.	Natick	2,111.3	111.	Bridgewater	937.2	171.	Lincoln	561.0
52.	Newburyport	2,088.3	112.	Gardner	931.6	172.	Acushnet	560.4
53.	Whitman	2,063.9	113.	Westborough	900.8	173.	Hamilton	558.6
54.	Milton	2,014.4	114.	Hanover	897.1	174.	Dartmouth	550.3
55.	Danvers	2,012.2	115.	Westfield	871.4	175.	Salisbury	546.6
56.	Methuen	1,966.7	116.	Marshfield	867.9	176.	Hopkinton	539.0
57.	Maynard	1,958.1	117.	Bellingham	859.5	177.	Dudley	524.8
58.	Holyoke	1,875.4	118.	Pembroke	858.4	178.	Littleton	524.8
59.	Milford	1,866.2	119.	Wayland	855.0	179.	Oxford	511.8
60.	Lexington	1,845.9	120.	Millbury	853.6	180.	Oak Bluffs	504.7

©2010 Information Publications, Inc. All rights reserved. Photocopying prohibited. For additional copies, contact the publisher at www.informationpublications.com or (877)544-INFO (4636)

See Introduction for an explanation of all data sources.

Persons per Square Mile, 2008

181. Pepperell	503.6	241. Sturbridge	243.4	301. Phillipston	73.5
182. Wrentham	501.5	242. Lenox	240.3	302. Egremont	71.9
183. Shirley	500.3	243. Winchendon	234.7	303. Shutesbury	69.4
184. Norwell	492.5	244. Essex	234.7	304. Sheffield	68.8
185. Boxborough	488.6	245. Nantucket	234.6	305. Hardwick	68.6
186. Halifax	477.8	246. North Brookfield	229.1	306. Aquinnah	66.1
187. Topsfield	476.5	247. Bolton	227.6	307. Westhampton	58.2
188. Holden	474.5	248. Harvard	227.5	308. Goshen	56.0
189. Bourne	474.1	249. Granby	225.1	309. Pelham	55.2
190. Leicester	469.7	250. Rutland	223.8	310. New Braintree	53.9
191. Sandwich	468.1	251. Berlin	221.2	311. Charlemont	52.8
192. Orleans	441.5	252. Douglas	218.5	312. Chilmark	50.8
193. Brewster	432.0	253. Lee	218.3	313. Conway	50.3
194. Uxbridge	429.6	254. Orange	217.2	314. Montgomery	47.7
195. West Bridgewater	425.1	255. Southampton	212.5	315. Ashfield	45.2
196. Chatham	413.6	256. East Brookfield	209.9	316. Leyden	44.5
197. Palmer	410.6	257. Westminster	208.2	317. Colrain	43.3
198. Ipswich	405.5	258. Holland	204.0	318. Cummington	41.7
199. Mattapoisett	391.7	259. Hadley	203.1	319. Chesterfield	41.4
200. Berkley	391.6	260. Monson	202.1	320. Granville	40.0
201. Eastham	388.4	261. Hatfield	201.7	321. Worthington	39.6
202. Lunenburg	376.7	262. Dunstable	201.4	322. Otis	39.0
203. Dover	368.9	263. Brookfield	194.0	323. Becket	38.9
204. Stow	366.3	264. Plympton	188.2	324. Monterey	35.8
205. Spencer	363.5	265. West Brookfield	185.7	325. Chester	35.1
206. Adams	362.2	266. Warren	184.3	326. Alford	33.8
207. Athol	354.9	267. Williamstown	169.9	327. Royalston	32.8
208. Marion	352.6	268. Great Barrington	163.3	328. Peru	32.1
209. Lakeville	351.7	269. Rochester	155.4	329. Heath	32.0
210. Provincetown	348.0	270. Ashburnham	154.4	330. New Marlborough	31.9
211. Boxford	338.8	271. Edgartown	145.6	331. Wendell	31.3
212. Groton	324.1	272. Deerfield	145.3	332. Hancock	31.1
213. Mendon	318.3	273. Wellfleet	137.6	333. Plainfield	28.0
214. Carlisle	316.5	274. Clarksburg	126.5	334. Florida	27.7
215. West Newbury	316.2	275. Cheshire	123.2	335. Blandford	24.6
216. Paxton	315.1	276. Ashby	123.0	336. Windsor	24.2
217. Southwick	308.7	277. Barre	122.6	337. Petersham	23.8
218. Carver	308.6	278. Wales	119.8	338. Middlefield	23.0
219. Westport	308.3	279. Erving	111.7	339. New Salem	22.0
220. Rowley	306.8	280. Hubbardston	109.3	340. Savoy	20.1
221. Upton	306.2	281. Brimfield	106.9	341. Warwick	20.1
222. Middleborough	303.4	282. West Tisbury	105.5	342. New Ashford	18.3
223. Dalton	302.4	283. Buckland	101.5	343. Tyringham	18.1
224. Dighton	300.2	284. Truro	100.7	344. Sandisfield	16.2
225. Charlton	296.1	285. Gill	99.1	345. Rowe	14.8
226. Newbury	286.5	286. Lanesborough	98.8	346. Tolland	14.5
227. Townsend	285.7	287. Princeton	98.2	347. Washington	14.3
228. Ware	285.6	288. Williamsburg	98.0	348. Hawley	10.9
229. Sutton	278.6	289. Russell	97.7	349. Monroe	9.0
230. Hampden	275.5	290. Stockbridge	96.8	350. Gosnold	6.2
231. Montague	273.6	291. Bernardston	95.3	351. Mount Washington	6.1
232. Belchertown	270.1	292. Hinsdale	92.0		
233. Boylston	266.5	293. Oakham	90.7		
234. Sherborn	262.8	294. Northfield	88.0		
235. Sterling	257.9	295. Shelburne	87.3		
236. Sunderland	257.6	296. Huntington	83.4		
237. Lancaster	253.2	297. Richmond	82.7		
238. Rehoboth	246.8	298. Leverett	77.7		
239. Freetown	246.6	299. Whately	77.5		
240. Templeton	244.7	300. West Stockbridge	77.4		

©2010 Information Publications, Inc. All rights reserved. Photocopying prohibited. For additional copies, contact the publisher at www.informationpublications.com or (877)544-INFO (4636)

See Introduction for an explanation of all data sources.

Unemployment Rate, 2000

1.	Wenham	30.7%
2.	Provincetown	20.0
3.	Hamilton	16.1
4.	Truro	13.9
5.	Monterey	12.3
6.	Norton	12.2
7.	Dartmouth	12.0
8.	Monroe	8.7
9.	New Bedford	8.7
10.	Springfield	8.5
11.	Fitchburg	8.4
12.	Lawrence	8.4
13.	Amherst	8.2
14.	Adams	7.9
15.	Hawley	7.9
16.	Wellfleet	7.6
17.	Lanesborough	7.5
18.	Chelsea	7.3
19.	Boston	7.2
20.	Bourne	7.2
21.	Fall River	7.0
22.	Beverly	6.9
23.	Brockton	6.7
24.	Holyoke	6.7
25.	Bridgewater	6.6
26.	Lowell	6.6
27.	Petersham	6.6
28.	Williamstown	6.3
29.	Worcester	6.3
30.	Lynn	6.2
31.	Cambridge	6.1
32.	Wales	6.1
33.	Pittsfield	6.0
34.	Revere	5.9
35.	Yarmouth	5.9
36.	Montague	5.8
37.	Mount Washington	5.8
38.	Barre	5.7
39.	Cheshire	5.7
40.	North Adams	5.7
41.	Chester	5.6
42.	Granville	5.6
43.	Hancock	5.6
44.	Winchendon	5.6
45.	Erving	5.4
46.	Salem	5.4
47.	Southbridge	5.4
48.	Waltham	5.4
49.	Wareham	5.4
50.	Charlemont	5.3
51.	Southwick	5.3
52.	Heath	5.2
53.	South Hadley	5.2
54.	Warren	5.2
55.	Clinton	5.1
56.	Falmouth	5.1
57.	Warwick	5.1
58.	Becket	5.0
59.	Everett	5.0
60.	Belchertown	4.9
61.	Colrain	4.9%
62.	Dennis	4.9
63.	Eastham	4.9
64.	Gloucester	4.9
65.	Greenfield	4.9
66.	Otis	4.9
67.	Templeton	4.9
68.	Westfield	4.9
69.	Barnstable	4.8
70.	Chicopee	4.8
71.	Lunenburg	4.8
72.	Orange	4.8
73.	Savoy	4.8
74.	Clarksburg	4.7
75.	Sunderland	4.7
76.	Washington	4.7
77.	Wendell	4.7
78.	Whately	4.7
79.	Dudley	4.6
80.	Gardner	4.6
81.	Granby	4.6
82.	North Brookfield	4.6
83.	Rochester	4.6
84.	Shelburne	4.6
85.	Somerset	4.6
86.	Ware	4.6
87.	Webster	4.6
88.	Athol	4.5
89.	Chatham	4.5
90.	Dighton	4.5
91.	Plymouth	4.5
92.	Royalston	4.5
93.	Sherborn	4.5
94.	Middlefield	4.4
95.	Ashland	4.3
96.	Harwich	4.3
97.	Kingston	4.3
98.	Leverett	4.3
99.	Methuen	4.3
100.	Nantucket	4.3
101.	Taunton	4.3
102.	Aquinnah	4.2
103.	Buckland	4.2
104.	Franklin	4.2
105.	Halifax	4.2
106.	Holbrook	4.2
107.	Lenox	4.2
108.	Rutland	4.2
109.	Southampton	4.2
110.	Agawam	4.1
111.	Brookfield	4.1
112.	Conway	4.1
113.	Easthampton	4.1
114.	Hinsdale	4.1
115.	Northampton	4.1
116.	Palmer	4.1
117.	Stockbridge	4.1
118.	West Springfield	4.1
119.	Winthrop	4.1
120.	Edgartown	4.0
121.	Hull	4.0%
122.	Leominster	4.0
123.	Malden	4.0
124.	New Salem	4.0
125.	Plympton	4.0
126.	Russell	4.0
127.	Townsend	4.0
128.	Weymouth	4.0
129.	Bernardston	3.9
130.	Blandford	3.9
131.	Fairhaven	3.9
132.	Monson	3.9
133.	New Marlborough	3.9
134.	North Attleborough	3.9
135.	Ashby	3.8
136.	Deerfield	3.8
137.	Middleborough	3.8
138.	Peabody	3.8
139.	Tolland	3.8
140.	West Stockbridge	3.8
141.	Williamsburg	3.8
142.	Attleboro	3.7
143.	Haverhill	3.7
144.	Huntington	3.7
145.	Milford	3.7
146.	Randolph	3.7
147.	Spencer	3.7
148.	Westport	3.7
149.	Amesbury	3.6
150.	Bellingham	3.6
151.	Ludlow	3.6
152.	Mashpee	3.6
153.	Medford	3.6
154.	Plainville	3.6
155.	Rockport	3.6
156.	Salisbury	3.6
157.	Shirley	3.6
158.	Avon	3.5
159.	Brookline	3.5
160.	Chesterfield	3.5
161.	Framingham	3.5
162.	Mansfield	3.5
163.	Maynard	3.5
164.	Oxford	3.5
165.	Somerville	3.5
166.	Topsfield	3.5
167.	Wellesley	3.5
168.	Bolton	3.4
169.	Goshen	3.4
170.	Lee	3.4
171.	Marlborough	3.4
172.	New Ashford	3.4
173.	New Braintree	3.4
174.	Quincy	3.4
175.	Swansea	3.4
176.	Westborough	3.4
177.	Whitman	3.4
178.	Canton	3.3
179.	Danvers	3.3
180.	Hadley	3.3

©2010 Information Publications, Inc. All rights reserved. Photocopying prohibited. For additional copies, contact the publisher at www.informationpublications.com or (877)544-INFO (4636)

See Introduction for an explanation of all data sources.

Unemployment Rate, 2000

181. Holland	3.3%	241. Hardwick	2.7%	301. Melrose	2.0%
182. Medfield	3.3	242. Hubbardston	2.7	302. Swampscott	2.0
183. Rehoboth	3.3	243. Marshfield	2.7	303. Tewksbury	2.0
184. Sandwich	3.3	244. Millbury	2.7	304. Wayland	2.0
185. Seekonk	3.3	245. Norwood	2.7	305. West Tisbury	2.0
186. Upton	3.3	246. Princeton	2.7	306. Berkley	1.9
187. Wilbraham	3.3	247. Rowe	2.7	307. Douglas	1.9
188. Ashburnham	3.2	248. Shutesbury	2.7	308. Dunstable	1.9
189. Ashfield	3.2	249. Stoughton	2.7	309. Essex	1.9
190. Ayer	3.2	250. East Longmeadow	2.6	310. Georgetown	1.9
191. Gill	3.2	251. Great Barrington	2.6	311. Hopedale	1.9
192. Harvard	3.2	252. Hingham	2.6	312. Lincoln	1.9
193. Longmeadow	3.2	253. Lakeville	2.6	313. Norwell	1.9
194. Raynham	3.2	254. Milton	2.6	314. Reading	1.9
195. Richmond	3.2	255. Pepperell	2.6	315. Sudbury	1.9
196. Saugus	3.2	256. Braintree	2.5	316. Blackstone	1.8
197. Tyngsborough	3.2	257. Brewster	2.5	317. Manchester-by-the-Sea	1.8
198. Walpole	3.2	258. East Bridgewater	2.5	318. Mattapoisett	1.8
199. Billerica	3.1	259. Ipswich	2.5	319. Northborough	1.8
200. Carver	3.1	260. Lexington	2.5	320. Northfield	1.8
201. Dracut	3.1	261. Sheffield	2.5	321. Southborough	1.8
202. Easton	3.1	262. Stow	2.5	322. Tyringham	1.8
203. Lynnfield	3.1	263. Westwood	2.5	323. Westford	1.8
204. Pelham	3.1	264. Wrentham	2.5	324. Littleton	1.7
205. Pembroke	3.1	265. Abington	2.4	325. Rowley	1.7
206. Sutton	3.1	266. Auburn	2.4	326. Sandisfield	1.7
207. Wakefield	3.1	267. Chilmark	2.4	327. Sterling	1.7
208. West Bridgewater	3.1	268. Merrimac	2.4	328. West Newbury	1.7
209. Boxborough	3.0	269. Middleton	2.4	329. Weston	1.7
210. Brimfield	3.0	270. Sharon	2.4	330. Duxbury	1.6
211. Foxborough	3.0	271. Sturbridge	2.4	331. Newbury	1.6
212. Grafton	3.0	272. Watertown	2.4	332. Tisbury	1.6
213. Leyden	3.0	273. Westminster	2.4	333. Boxford	1.5
214. Oak Bluffs	3.0	274. Winchester	2.4	334. Cohasset	1.5
215. Oakham	3.0	275. Andover	2.3	335. Hopkinton	1.5
216. Phillipston	3.0	276. Bedford	2.3	336. Nahant	1.5
217. Uxbridge	3.0	277. Belmont	2.3	337. Wilmington	1.5
218. Woburn	3.0	278. Groton	2.3	338. Cummington	1.4
219. Worthington	3.0	279. Millville	2.3	339. Plainfield	1.4
220. Acushnet	2.9	280. North Andover	2.3	340. Hatfield	1.3
221. Alford	2.9	281. Peru	2.3	341. Westhampton	1.3
222. Hanover	2.9	282. Scituate	2.3	342. Dover	1.2
223. Hanson	2.9	283. Arlington	2.2	343. Groveland	1.2
224. Holden	2.9	284. Charlton	2.2	344. Mendon	1.2
225. Holliston	2.9	285. Florida	2.2	345. Berlin	1.0
226. Needham	2.9	286. Marion	2.2	346. Boylston	0.9
227. Newburyport	2.9	287. Norfolk	2.2	347. North Reading	0.9
228. Newton	2.9	288. West Brookfield	2.2	348. Medway	0.8
229. Northbridge	2.9	289. East Brookfield	2.1	349. Carlisle	0.7
230. Paxton	2.9	290. Freetown	2.1	350. Windsor	0.6
231. Rockland	2.9	291. Lancaster	2.1	351. Gosnold	0.0
232. Shrewsbury	2.9	292. Marblehead	2.1		
233. West Boylston	2.9	293. Montgomery	2.1		
234. Egremont	2.8	294. Natick	2.1		
235. Hudson	2.8	295. Orleans	2.1		
236. Leicester	2.8	296. Stoneham	2.1		
237. Millis	2.8	297. Acton	2.0		
238. Burlington	2.7	298. Concord	2.0		
239. Chelmsford	2.7	299. Dalton	2.0		
240. Dedham	2.7	300. Hampden	2.0		

(2000 Decennial Census)

©2010 Information Publications, Inc. All rights reserved. Photocopying prohibited. For additional copies, contact the publisher at www.informationpublications.com or (877)544-INFO (4636)

See Introduction for an explanation of all data sources.

Unemployment Rate, 2008

1.	Provincetown	28.5%	61.	Plympton	7.8%	121.	Abington	6.7%
2.	Truro	17.1%	62.	West Springfield	7.8%	122.	Dennis	6.7%
3.	Wellfleet	13.9%	63.	Leominster	7.7%	123.	Dover	6.7%
4.	Lawrence	13.1%	64.	New Salem	7.7%	124.	Lanesborough	6.7%
5.	Fairhaven	12.7%	65.	Otis	7.7%	125.	Millbury	6.7%
6.	New Bedford	11.8%	66.	Taunton	7.7%	126.	Shirley	6.7%
7.	Southbridge	11.5%	67.	Ayer	7.6%	127.	Charlemont	6.6%
8.	Yarmouth	10.6%	68.	Hinsdale	7.6%	128.	Essex	6.6%
9.	East Longmeadow	10.1%	69.	Lynn	7.6%	129.	Hudson	6.6%
10.	Freetown	9.7%	70.	New Braintree	7.6%	130.	Hull	6.6%
11.	Springfield	9.7%	71.	Plainville	7.6%	131.	Lakeville	6.6%
12.	Winchendon	9.7%	72.	Rehoboth	7.6%	132.	Lee	6.6%
13.	Deerfield	9.5%	73.	Revere	7.6%	133.	North Brookfield	6.5%
14.	Holyoke	9.5%	74.	Brockton	7.5%	134.	Norton	6.5%
15.	Westport	9.5%	75.	Orleans	7.5%	135.	West Boylston	6.5%
16.	Harwich	9.4%	76.	Spencer	7.5%	136.	Weymouth	6.5%
17.	Templeton	9.4%	77.	West Brookfield	7.5%	137.	Williamsburg	6.5%
18.	Falmouth	9.2%	78.	Auburn	7.4%	138.	Worthington	6.5%
19.	Savoy	9.2%	79.	Braintree	7.4%	139.	Barre	6.4%
20.	Swansea	9.2%	80.	Charlton	7.4%	140.	Berlin	6.4%
21.	Easton	9.1%	81.	Franklin	7.4%	141.	Chilmark	6.4%
22.	North Adams	9.1%	82.	Haverhill	7.4%	142.	Dalton	6.4%
23.	Adams	9.0%	83.	Millville	7.4%	143.	Great Barrington	6.4%
24.	Ashland	9.0%	84.	Plymouth	7.4%	144.	Hanson	6.4%
25.	Barnstable	8.9%	85.	Uxbridge	7.4%	145.	Kingston	6.4%
26.	Gardner	8.9%	86.	Belchertown	7.3%	146.	Milford	6.4%
27.	Chelmsford	8.7%	87.	Dracut	7.3%	147.	Oxford	6.4%
28.	Gloucester	8.7%	88.	Lancaster	7.3%	148.	Pembroke	6.4%
29.	Hardwick	8.7%	89.	North Attleborough	7.3%	149.	Salem	6.4%
30.	Royalston	8.7%	90.	Salisbury	7.3%	150.	Stoughton	6.4%
31.	Tisbury	8.7%	91.	Wales	7.3%	151.	East Bridgewater	6.3%
32.	Cheshire	8.6%	92.	Egremont	7.2%	152.	Erving	6.3%
33.	Shelburne	8.6%	93.	Fall River	7.2%	153.	Granby	6.3%
34.	Ludlow	8.5%	94.	Hubbardston	7.2%	154.	Granville	6.3%
35.	Chelsea	8.4%	95.	Ware	7.2%	155.	Nantucket	6.3%
36.	Everett	8.4%	96.	Worcester	7.2%	156.	Randolph	6.3%
37.	Huntington	8.4%	97.	Duxbury	7.1%	157.	Saugus	6.3%
38.	Lowell	8.4%	98.	Holbrook	7.1%	158.	Westfield	6.3%
39.	Orange	8.4%	99.	Holland	7.1%	159.	Agawam	6.2%
40.	Plainfield	8.4%	100.	Montague	7.1%	160.	Malden	6.2%
41.	Somerset	8.4%	101.	Phillipston	7.1%	161.	Marshfield	6.2%
42.	Webster	8.4%	102.	Southwick	7.1%	162.	Quincy	6.2%
43.	Fitchburg	8.3%	103.	Warren	7.1%	163.	Sandisfield	6.2%
44.	Athol	8.2%	104.	Cohasset	7.0%	164.	Sturbridge	6.2%
45.	Brimfield	8.2%	105.	Greenfield	7.0%	165.	Amesbury	6.1%
46.	Carlisle	8.2%	106.	Lunenburg	7.0%	166.	Merrimac	6.1%
47.	Clarksburg	8.2%	107.	Palmer	7.0%	167.	Oakham	6.1%
48.	Acushnet	8.1%	108.	Rockport	7.0%	168.	Tewksbury	6.1%
49.	Billerica	8.1%	109.	Westminster	7.0%	169.	Bolton	6.0%
50.	Wareham	8.1%	110.	Belmont	6.9%	170.	Boylston	6.0%
51.	Chesterfield	8.0%	111.	Monson	6.9%	171.	Gill	6.0%
52.	Middleborough	8.0%	112.	Rockland	6.9%	172.	Grafton	6.0%
53.	Boston	7.9%	113.	Sandwich	6.9%	173.	Leicester	6.0%
54.	Danvers	7.9%	114.	West Bridgewater	6.9%	174.	New Marlborough	6.0%
55.	Methuen	7.9%	115.	Ashburnham	6.8%	175.	Peabody	6.0%
56.	Seekonk	7.9%	116.	Conway	6.8%	176.	Raynham	6.0%
57.	Arlington	7.8%	117.	Halifax	6.8%	177.	Sterling	6.0%
58.	Mashpee	7.8%	118.	Leyden	6.8%	178.	Sutton	6.0%
59.	Northbridge	7.8%	119.	Pittsfield	6.8%	179.	Upton	6.0%
60.	Oak Bluffs	7.8%	120.	Whitman	6.8%	180.	Wakefield	6.0%

©2010 Information Publications, Inc. All rights reserved. Photocopying prohibited. For additional copies, contact the publisher at www.informationpublications.com or (877)544-INFO (4636)

See Introduction for an explanation of all data sources.

Unemployment Rate, 2008

181. Avon	5.9%
182. Berkley	5.9%
183. Brewster	5.9%
184. Dighton	5.9%
185. Easthampton	5.9%
186. Florida	5.9%
187. Lenox	5.9%
188. Mansfield	5.9%
189. North Reading	5.9%
190. Rochester	5.9%
191. Wendell	5.9%
192. Bernardston	5.8%
193. Beverly	5.8%
194. Newbury	5.8%
195. Norfolk	5.8%
196. Wenham	5.8%
197. Winthrop	5.8%
198. Woburn	5.8%
199. Carver	5.7%
200. Cummington	5.7%
201. Eastham	5.7%
202. Hopedale	5.7%
203. New Ashford	5.7%
204. Norwood	5.7%
205. Rowley	5.7%
206. Rutland	5.7%
207. Stoneham	5.7%
208. Wrentham	5.7%
209. Cambridge	5.6%
210. Dartmouth	5.6%
211. Holden	5.6%
212. Millis	5.6%
213. Nahant	5.6%
214. Petersham	5.6%
215. Russell	5.6%
216. Dedham	5.5%
217. Framingham	5.5%
218. Hampden	5.5%
219. Medford	5.5%
220. Medway	5.5%
221. North Andover	5.5%
222. Attleboro	5.4%
223. Bridgewater	5.4%
224. Goshen	5.4%
225. Hamilton	5.4%
226. Maynard	5.4%
227. Mendon	5.4%
228. Middleton	5.4%
229. South Hadley	5.4%
230. Swampscott	5.4%
231. Tyngsborough	5.4%
232. Westhampton	5.4%
233. Wilbraham	5.4%
234. Wilmington	5.4%
235. Windsor	5.4%
236. Boxford	5.3%
237. Hanover	5.3%
238. Bedford	5.2%
239. Blackstone	5.2%
240. Chester	5.2%
241. Dudley	5.2%
242. Southampton	5.2%
243. Walpole	5.2%
244. Chatham	5.1%
245. East Brookfield	5.1%
246. Hatfield	5.1%
247. Lynnfield	5.1%
248. Marblehead	5.1%
249. Marlborough	5.1%
250. Mattapoisett	5.1%
251. Newburyport	5.1%
252. Northborough	5.1%
253. Norwell	5.1%
254. Scituate	5.1%
255. Sheffield	5.1%
256. Shrewsbury	5.1%
257. Townsend	5.1%
258. Waltham	5.1%
259. Georgetown	5.0%
260. Hadley	5.0%
261. Ipswich	5.0%
262. Littleton	5.0%
263. Milton	5.0%
264. Princeton	5.0%
265. Warwick	5.0%
266. Washington	5.0%
267. Groton	4.9%
268. Manchester-by-the-Sea	4.9%
269. Marion	4.9%
270. Melrose	4.9%
271. Northfield	4.9%
272. Pepperell	4.9%
273. Peru	4.9%
274. Sharon	4.9%
275. Stockbridge	4.9%
276. Stow	4.9%
277. West Stockbridge	4.9%
278. Andover	4.8%
279. Becket	4.8%
280. Buckland	4.8%
281. Dunstable	4.8%
282. Edgartown	4.8%
283. Foxborough	4.8%
284. Medfield	4.8%
285. Reading	4.8%
286. Westborough	4.8%
287. Westford	4.8%
288. Williamstown	4.8%
289. Ashfield	4.7%
290. Canton	4.7%
291. Holliston	4.7%
292. Topsfield	4.7%
293. Tyringham	4.7%
294. Groveland	4.6%
295. Hingham	4.6%
296. Leverett	4.6%
297. Blandford	4.5%
298. Boxborough	4.5%
299. Hopkinton	4.5%
300. Northampton	4.5%
301. Somerville	4.5%
302. Watertown	4.5%
303. Heath	4.4%
304. Paxton	4.4%
305. Rowe	4.4%
306. Sudbury	4.4%
307. Tolland	4.4%
308. Wayland	4.4%
309. Aquinnah	4.3%
310. Bourne	4.3%
311. Clinton	4.3%
312. Colrain	4.3%
313. Concord	4.3%
314. Needham	4.3%
315. Monroe	4.2%
316. Natick	4.2%
317. Shutesbury	4.2%
318. Westwood	4.2%
319. Winchester	4.2%
320. Lexington	4.1%
321. Longmeadow	4.1%
322. Newton	4.1%
323. Sunderland	4.1%
324. West Newbury	4.1%
325. Acton	4.0%
326. Ashby	4.0%
327. Monterey	4.0%
328. Richmond	4.0%
329. Bellingham	3.9%
330. Burlington	3.9%
331. Chicopee	3.9%
332. Harvard	3.9%
333. Montgomery	3.9%
334. West Tisbury	3.9%
335. Whately	3.9%
336. Douglas	3.8%
337. Southborough	3.8%
338. Brookfield	3.7%
339. Sherborn	3.7%
340. Hawley	3.6%
341. Wellesley	3.6%
342. Weston	3.6%
343. Amherst	3.5%
344. Lincoln	3.5%
345. Brookline	3.3%
346. Hancock	3.3%
347. Alford	3.1%
348. Mount Washington	3.1%
349. Pelham	3.0%
350. Gosnold	2.9%
351. Middlefield	2.3%

©2010 Information Publications, Inc. All rights reserved. Photocopying prohibited. For additional copies, contact the publisher at www.informationpublications.com or (877)544-INFO (4636)

See Introduction for an explanation of all data sources.

Average Single-Family Home Assessed Value, FY2010

1. Chilmark	$1,841,890	61. Arlington	$477,218	121. Merrimac	$351,972
2. Weston	$1,400,149	62. Swampscott	$475,930	122. Plainville	$351,007
3. Aquinnah	$1,248,895	63. Gloucester	$475,858	123. Longmeadow	$349,758
4. Edgartown	$1,148,542	64. West Stockbridge	$469,540	124. Chelmsford	$347,659
5. Manchester-by-the-Sea	$1,112,485	65. North Andover	$469,012	125. Grafton	$344,408
6. Dover	$1,071,801	66. Mashpee	$467,482	126. Saugus	$343,052
7. West Tisbury	$1,066,313	67. Newbury	$461,116	127. Framingham	$342,887
8. Lincoln	$1,018,661	68. Ipswich	$456,271	128. Woburn	$341,718
9. Wellesley	$1,009,640	69. Natick	$452,621	129. North Attleborough	$341,432
10. Chatham	$861,926	70. Newburyport	$451,108	130. Sutton	$340,638
11. Cohasset	$858,006	71. Westford	$450,723	131. Yarmouth	$339,537
12. Concord	$835,697	72. Bourne	$446,624	132. Amherst	$334,327
13. Newton	$799,218	73. North Reading	$446,021	133. Pembroke	$333,182
14. Carlisle	$771,254	74. Stow	$445,062	134. Plympton	$332,675
15. Truro	$771,042	75. Norfolk	$444,962	135. Princeton	$332,168
16. Winchester	$762,067	76. Richmond	$439,569	136. Quincy	$330,755
17. Belmont	$757,904	77. Egremont	$435,307	137. East Bridgewater	$329,440
18. Orleans	$751,795	78. Reading	$432,939	138. Salisbury	$328,169
19. Sherborn	$723,985	79. Beverly	$430,457	139. Bridgewater	$327,645
20. Needham	$700,739	80. Hanover	$428,538	140. Raynham	$326,393
21. Lexington	$691,470	81. Dennis	$423,534	141. Hopedale	$326,085
22. Marblehead	$685,562	82. Westborough	$422,996	142. Billerica	$325,397
23. Hingham	$659,994	83. Walpole	$417,956	143. Winthrop	$324,714
24. Alford	$652,551	84. Dunstable	$416,275	144. Tyngsborough	$324,403
25. Oak Bluffs	$640,870	85. Georgetown	$412,477	145. Hanson	$324,316
26. Westwood	$636,918	86. Lenox	$410,607	146. Lakeville	$324,041
27. Boxford	$618,372	87. Great Barrington	$406,276	147. Pelham	$321,727
28. Wayland	$617,648	88. Westport	$405,747	148. Halifax	$321,409
29. Duxbury	$611,353	89. Groton	$403,710	149. Mount Washington	$321,116
30. Marion	$606,290	90. Stoneham	$401,628	150. Norton	$320,469
31. Harvard	$595,195	91. Wrentham	$397,285	151. Maynard	$320,390
32. Wenham	$585,126	92. Wakefield	$395,826	152. Otis	$319,539
33. Medfield	$578,363	93. Melrose	$395,233	153. Leverett	$319,344
34. Norwell	$569,881	94. Easton	$394,948	154. Amesbury	$319,201
35. Wellfleet	$567,314	95. Upton	$394,661	155. Seekonk	$318,320
36. Nahant	$560,265	96. Holliston	$394,464	156. Tolland	$317,043
37. Andover	$548,860	97. Marshfield	$392,400	157. Hudson	$314,755
38. Southborough	$548,620	98. Hull	$390,280	158. Plymouth	$314,154
39. Essex	$545,337	99. Boylston	$389,418	159. Freetown	$312,786
40. Lynnfield	$538,718	100. Rowley	$387,562	160. Abington	$312,264
41. Topsfield	$532,305	101. Dedham	$385,198	161. Salem	$311,918
42. Rockport	$526,739	102. Williamstown	$385,009	162. Peabody	$311,748
43. Milton	$519,035	103. Berlin	$383,436	163. Uxbridge	$311,507
44. Monterey	$519,005	104. Burlington	$383,265	164. West Bridgewater	$311,359
45. Stockbridge	$514,281	105. Dartmouth	$377,859	165. Sterling	$311,328
46. Tyringham	$513,092	106. Sandwich	$376,765	166. Lancaster	$309,536
47. Acton	$512,103	107. Mansfield	$374,519	167. Hadley	$306,965
48. Bedford	$506,620	108. Danvers	$374,517	168. Northampton	$302,155
49. Boxborough	$506,349	109. Ashland	$373,619	169. Paxton	$301,283
50. Scituate	$505,815	110. Mendon	$371,748	170. Pepperell	$301,105
51. Brewster	$500,612	111. Littleton	$370,111	171. Conway	$300,939
52. Hamilton	$492,915	112. Norwood	$368,872	172. Millville	$300,877
53. Falmouth	$492,809	113. Franklin	$368,736	173. Stoughton	$300,498
54. West Newbury	$491,224	114. Braintree	$365,241	174. Acushnet	$300,340
55. Hopkinton	$487,768	115. Medway	$362,246	175. Weymouth	$299,544
56. Eastham	$486,521	116. Groveland	$362,032	176. Milford	$299,354
57. Bolton	$485,135	117. Kingston	$359,435	177. Wilbraham	$295,952
58. Middleton	$479,050	118. Medford	$358,006	178. Middleborough	$294,751
59. Mattapoisett	$478,815	119. Wilmington	$356,075	179. Westhampton	$291,668
60. Harwich	$477,993	120. Rochester	$355,504	180. Shirley	$290,234

©2010 Information Publications, Inc. All rights reserved. Photocopying prohibited. For additional copies, contact the publisher at www.informationpublications.com or (877)544-INFO (4636)

See Introduction for an explanation of all data sources.

Average Single-Family Home Assessed Value, FY2010

181. Northbridge	$288,555	241. Granby	$232,096	301. Springfield	$137,709
182. Whitman	$287,022	242. Clinton	$232,076	302. Barnstable	NA
183. Fairhaven	$284,772	243. Lowell	$231,515	303. Becket	NA
184. Avon	$284,629	244. Easthampton	$229,151	304. Berkley	NA
185. Dracut	$284,026	245. Ashburnham	$228,072	305. Blackstone	NA
186. Deerfield	$283,854	246. Leyden	$227,708	306. Boston	NA
187. Douglas	$283,419	247. Agawam	$226,851	307. Brookline	NA
188. Carver	$282,701	248. Dudley	$226,508	308. Cambridge	NA
189. Wareham	$282,306	249. Auburn	$225,198	309. Canton	NA
190. Attleboro	$281,562	250. Hinsdale	$224,301	310. Chelsea	NA
191. Methuen	$281,335	251. Blandford	$223,957	311. Clarksburg	NA
192. Lunenburg	$281,062	252. West Springfield	$223,945	312. Colrain	NA
193. Swansea	$280,209	253. Chesterfield	$223,423	313. Dighton	NA
194. Southampton	$280,205	254. Lynn	$223,153	314. Everett	NA
195. Sandisfield	$278,230	255. Cummington	$223,110	315. Fall River	NA
196. Sturbridge	$277,918	256. Buckland	$218,605	316. Foxborough	NA
197. Granville	$277,502	257. Ludlow	$218,477	317. Gosnold	NA
198. Williamsburg	$277,290	258. Northfield	$216,645	318. Hancock	NA
199. Holden	$277,156	259. Barre	$215,574	319. Hatfield	NA
200. Sunderland	$276,988	260. Bernardston	$215,080	320. Holbrook	NA
201. West Boylston	$276,357	261. Lanesborough	$213,094	321. Hubbardston	NA
202. Whately	$276,231	262. Dalton	$213,020	322. Lawrence	NA
203. Charlton	$276,208	263. Hawley	$212,233	323. Malden	NA
204. Bellingham	$275,984	264. North Brookfield	$211,013	324. Marlborough	NA
205. Ayer	$275,964	265. Holland	$210,996	325. Millis	NA
206. Hampden	$273,753	266. Gill	$210,389	326. Monroe	NA
207. Haverhill	$272,260	267. Cheshire	$209,708	327. Montague	NA
208. New Braintree	$268,794	268. Washington	$209,413	328. Montgomery	NA
209. Rutland	$267,982	269. Worcester	$206,517	329. Nantucket	NA
210. Randolph	$267,015	270. Windsor	$203,453	330. New Bedford	NA
211. Oakham	$262,292	271. Plainfield	$201,150	331. New Marlborough	NA
212. Brimfield	$262,139	272. Huntington	$200,847	332. Northborough	NA
213. Petersham	$261,832	273. Rowe	$200,845	333. Phillipston	NA
214. East Longmeadow	$260,660	274. Charlemont	$199,973	334. Provincetown	NA
215. New Ashford	$259,425	275. Heath	$198,307	335. Rehoboth	NA
216. Belchertown	$256,549	276. Brockton	$197,037	336. Royalston	NA
217. Worthington	$255,408	277. Goshen	$194,294	337. Russell	NA
218. Southwick	$254,771	278. Winchendon	$194,280	338. Savoy	NA
219. Rockland	$254,027	279. Ware	$194,218	339. Sharon	NA
220. Lee	$252,971	280. Warren	$193,569	340. Sheffield	NA
221. Revere	$250,334	281. Greenfield	$190,928	341. Shrewsbury	NA
222. Webster	$248,626	282. Wales	$190,073	342. Somerset	NA
223. Townsend	$248,492	283. Middlefield	$189,868	343. Somerville	NA
224. Shutesbury	$243,814	284. Templeton	$189,512	344. Sudbury	NA
225. Millbury	$242,801	285. Palmer	$188,955	345. Taunton	NA
226. Ashby	$242,536	286. Pittsfield	$187,519	346. Tewksbury	NA
227. East Brookfield	$242,309	287. Erving	$186,613	347. Tisbury	NA
228. Shelburne	$241,154	288. Fitchburg	$186,056	348. Waltham	NA
229. New Salem	$239,314	289. Holyoke	$184,495	349. Watertown	NA
230. Ashfield	$238,932	290. Southbridge	$183,421	350. Wendell	NA
231. Leominster	$238,471	291. Chicopee	$182,709	351. Westminster	NA
232. Westfield	$236,945	292. Warwick	$181,706		
233. Brookfield	$236,930	293. Gardner	$180,050		
234. Hardwick	$236,660	294. Peru	$177,624		
235. Oxford	$236,496	295. Chester	$176,269		
236. Spencer	$236,431	296. Orange	$164,677		
237. Monson	$235,781	297. Florida	$159,507		
238. West Brookfield	$234,453	298. Athol	$154,121		
239. South Hadley	$232,576	299. Adams	$141,746		
240. Leicester	$232,377	300. North Adams	$138,963		

©2010 Information Publications, Inc. All rights reserved. Photocopying prohibited. For additional copies, contact the publisher at www.informationpublications.com or (877)544-INFO (4636)

See Introduction for an explanation of all data sources.

Average Single-Family Tax Bill, FY2010

Rank	Municipality	Tax Bill
1.	Weston	$15,542
2.	Sherborn	$12,626
3.	Dover	$11,704
4.	Lincoln	$11,684
5.	Carlisle	$11,276
6.	Wayland	$10,982
7.	Concord	$10,939
8.	Wellesley	$10,581
9.	Cohasset	$9,627
10.	Lexington	$9,584
11.	Belmont	$9,216
12.	Wenham	$9,105
13.	Manchester-by-the-Sea	$9,056
14.	Winchester	$8,771
15.	Acton	$8,767
16.	Bolton	$8,543
17.	Harvard	$8,529
18.	Boxborough	$8,370
19.	Westwood	$8,325
20.	Newton	$8,320
21.	Medfield	$8,236
22.	Hamilton	$8,030
23.	Swampscott	$7,843
24.	Southborough	$7,714
25.	Hopkinton	$7,687
26.	Boxford	$7,649
27.	Topsfield	$7,383
28.	Needham	$7,379
29.	Stow	$7,379
30.	Norwell	$7,266
31.	Andover	$7,239
32.	Duxbury	$7,220
33.	Westborough	$7,182
34.	Hingham	$7,108
35.	Milton	$6,929
36.	Lynnfield	$6,917
37.	Essex	$6,686
38.	Bedford	$6,627
39.	Westford	$6,594
40.	Marblehead	$6,561
41.	Holliston	$6,434
42.	Longmeadow	$6,394
43.	Groton	$6,371
44.	West Newbury	$6,347
45.	Norfolk	$6,261
46.	North Reading	$6,008
47.	North Andover	$5,975
48.	Reading	$5,953
49.	Medway	$5,901
50.	Pelham	$5,900
51.	Arlington	$5,779
52.	Hanover	$5,747
53.	Dunstable	$5,740
54.	Amesbury	$5,672
55.	Middleton	$5,672
56.	Amherst	$5,667
57.	Ashland	$5,642
58.	Littleton	$5,415
59.	Scituate	$5,341
60.	Easton	$5,328
61.	Walpole	$5,283
62.	Natick	$5,282
63.	Nahant	$5,278
64.	Chelmsford	$5,267
65.	Ipswich	$5,265
66.	Newburyport	$5,260
67.	Dedham	$5,227
68.	Wrentham	$5,212
69.	Marion	$5,184
70.	Maynard	$5,171
71.	Berlin	$5,127
72.	Princeton	$5,109
73.	Leverett	$5,046
74.	Upton	$5,040
75.	Beverly	$5,006
76.	Plympton	$4,993
77.	Boylston	$4,992
78.	Gloucester	$4,992
79.	Mansfield	$4,992
80.	Framingham	$4,979
81.	Lancaster	$4,974
82.	Mattapoisett	$4,951
83.	Paxton	$4,911
84.	Kingston	$4,867
85.	Rowley	$4,845
86.	Wilbraham	$4,791
87.	Melrose	$4,770
88.	West Tisbury	$4,756
89.	Williamstown	$4,736
90.	Aquinnah	$4,733
91.	Rockport	$4,720
92.	Great Barrington	$4,680
93.	Mendon	$4,636
94.	Stoneham	$4,615
95.	Merrimac	$4,604
96.	Danvers	$4,577
97.	Shutesbury	$4,574
98.	East Longmeadow	$4,530
99.	Tyngsborough	$4,525
100.	Halifax	$4,497
101.	Hull	$4,477
102.	Sterling	$4,449
103.	Franklin	$4,436
104.	West Stockbridge	$4,414
105.	Plainville	$4,412
106.	Hopedale	$4,409
107.	Newbury	$4,390
108.	Quincy	$4,373
109.	Salem	$4,370
110.	Georgetown	$4,364
111.	Hampden	$4,336
112.	Abington	$4,328
113.	Groveland	$4,319
114.	Wakefield	$4,307
115.	Pembroke	$4,295
116.	Grafton	$4,281
117.	Westhampton	$4,270
118.	Sandwich	$4,235
119.	Marshfield	$4,218
120.	Milford	$4,215
121.	Sutton	$4,197
122.	West Boylston	$4,192
123.	Burlington	$4,178
124.	Truro	$4,156
125.	Winthrop	$4,124
126.	Wilmington	$4,106
127.	Holden	$4,102
128.	Hudson	$4,098
129.	East Bridgewater	$4,078
130.	Billerica	$4,077
131.	Lenox	$4,073
132.	West Bridgewater	$4,048
133.	Sturbridge	$4,044
134.	Oak Bluffs	$4,037
135.	Bridgewater	$4,033
136.	Whately	$4,008
137.	Williamsburg	$4,001
138.	Lunenburg	$3,991
139.	Conway	$3,948
140.	Raynham	$3,946
141.	Medford	$3,931
142.	Richmond	$3,921
143.	Uxbridge	$3,909
144.	Plymouth	$3,902
145.	Hanson	$3,885
146.	Orleans	$3,872
147.	Rochester	$3,836
148.	Northampton	$3,819
149.	Carver	$3,814
150.	Belchertown	$3,812
151.	Townsend	$3,804
152.	Pepperell	$3,788
153.	Leyden	$3,780
154.	New Braintree	$3,758
155.	Stoughton	$3,744
156.	Chilmark	$3,739
157.	Randolph	$3,722
158.	Norton	$3,711
159.	Ashburnham	$3,683
160.	Rockland	$3,655
161.	Mashpee	$3,642
162.	Stockbridge	$3,595
163.	West Springfield	$3,583
164.	Shirley	$3,573
165.	North Attleborough	$3,565
166.	Whitman	$3,559
167.	Edgartown	$3,549
168.	Millville	$3,547
169.	Braintree	$3,532
170.	Woburn	$3,527
171.	Sunderland	$3,507
172.	Middleborough	$3,487
173.	Petersham	$3,482
174.	Westfield	$3,478
175.	Haverhill	$3,474
176.	Lanesborough	$3,473
177.	Lynn	$3,466
178.	Southampton	$3,463
179.	Rutland	$3,462
180.	Wellfleet	$3,455

©2010 Information Publications, Inc. All rights reserved. Photocopying prohibited. For additional copies, contact the publisher at www.informationpublications.com or (877)544-INFO (4636)

See Introduction for an explanation of all data sources.

Average Single-Family Tax Bill, FY2010

181. Norwood	$3,442	241. Warwick	$2,936	301. Rowe	$1,048
182. Southwick	$3,424	242. Agawam	$2,935	302. Barnstable	NA
183. Chesterfield	$3,409	243. Tyringham	$2,935	303. Becket	NA
184. Brookfield	$3,383	244. Plainfield	$2,925	304. Berkley	NA
185. Greenfield	$3,376	245. Oxford	$2,909	305. Blackstone	NA
186. Bourne	$3,368	246. Gill	$2,884	306. Boston	NA
187. Granby	$3,368	247. Hadley	$2,861	307. Brookline	NA
188. Deerfield	$3,367	248. Easthampton	$2,844	308. Cambridge	NA
189. Heath	$3,367	249. Palmer	$2,836	309. Canton	NA
190. Dalton	$3,366	250. Huntington	$2,830	310. Chelsea	NA
191. Seekonk	$3,365	251. Charlton	$2,828	311. Clarksburg	NA
192. Harwich	$3,360	252. Blandford	$2,826	312. Colrain	NA
193. Dracut	$3,354	253. Ware	$2,806	313. Dighton	NA
194. Revere	$3,347	254. Holland	$2,787	314. Everett	NA
195. Methuen	$3,337	255. Goshen	$2,782	315. Fall River	NA
196. Douglas	$3,336	256. Southbridge	$2,781	316. Foxborough	NA
197. Bernardston	$3,327	257. Monterey	$2,777	317. Gosnold	NA
198. Falmouth	$3,326	258. Holyoke	$2,764	318. Hancock	NA
199. Weymouth	$3,322	259. Wales	$2,756	319. Hatfield	NA
200. Saugus	$3,321	260. Leicester	$2,726	320. Holbrook	NA
201. Lakeville	$3,312	261. Peru	$2,723	321. Hubbardston	NA
202. Ashby	$3,308	262. Brockton	$2,713	322. Lawrence	NA
203. Bellingham	$3,301	263. Oakham	$2,707	323. Malden	NA
204. Leominster	$3,296	264. Fitchburg	$2,687	324. Marlborough	NA
205. Chatham	$3,293	265. Springfield	$2,685	325. Millis	NA
206. Peabody	$3,273	266. Eastham	$2,681	326. Monroe	NA
207. Millbury	$3,268	267. Gardner	$2,676	327. Montague	NA
208. South Hadley	$3,254	268. Pittsfield	$2,663	328. Montgomery	NA
209. Ludlow	$3,238	269. Barre	$2,662	329. Nantucket	NA
210. Salisbury	$3,236	270. Cummington	$2,659	330. New Bedford	NA
211. Ashfield	$3,235	271. Swansea	$2,656	331. New Marlborough	NA
212. Auburn	$3,229	272. North Brookfield	$2,650	332. Northborough	NA
213. Freetown	$3,222	273. West Brookfield	$2,645	333. Phillipston	NA
214. Lee	$3,190	274. Yarmouth	$2,621	334. Provincetown	NA
215. Ayer	$3,171	275. Hardwick	$2,617	335. Rehoboth	NA
216. Monson	$3,171	276. Washington	$2,601	336. Royalston	NA
217. Charlemont	$3,158	277. Winchendon	$2,564	337. Russell	NA
218. Attleboro	$3,153	278. Westport	$2,544	338. Savoy	NA
219. Acushnet	$3,145	279. Fairhaven	$2,532	339. Sharon	NA
220. Middlefield	$3,139	280. Hinsdale	$2,496	340. Sheffield	NA
221. Worcester	$3,129	281. Chicopee	$2,490	341. Shrewsbury	NA
222. Brimfield	$3,127	282. Webster	$2,429	342. Somerset	NA
223. Worthington	$3,126	283. Sandisfield	$2,401	343. Somerville	NA
224. Hawley	$3,109	284. Spencer	$2,322	344. Sudbury	NA
225. Granville	$3,108	285. Wareham	$2,290	345. Taunton	NA
226. Brewster	$3,104	286. Orange	$2,284	346. Tewksbury	NA
227. Clinton	$3,098	287. Windsor	$2,262	347. Tisbury	NA
228. Avon	$3,097	288. Dennis	$2,232	348. Waltham	NA
229. Lowell	$3,072	289. Templeton	$2,227	349. Watertown	NA
230. Shelburne	$3,058	290. Adams	$2,173	350. Wendell	NA
231. Egremont	$3,021	291. Dudley	$2,168	351. Westminster	NA
232. Northfield	$3,014	292. Mount Washington	$2,129		
233. Buckland	$3,012	293. Athol	$2,050		
234. Warren	$3,006	294. Otis	$2,023		
235. Northbridge	$3,001	295. Cheshire	$1,957		
236. Dartmouth	$2,966	296. New Ashford	$1,774		
237. East Brookfield	$2,954	297. North Adams	$1,729		
238. Chester	$2,951	298. Tolland	$1,509		
239. New Salem	$2,944	299. Erving	$1,308		
240. Alford	$2,936	300. Florida	$1,276		

©2010 Information Publications, Inc. All rights reserved. Photocopying prohibited. For additional copies, contact the publisher at www.informationpublications.com or (877)544-INFO (4636)

See Introduction for an explanation of all data sources.

US Senators from Massachusetts, 111th Congress, 2009-2010

Scott Brown, Republican (term expires 2013)

John Kerry, Democratic (term expires 2015)

US Congressional Representatives from Massachusetts, 111th Congress, 2009-2010

District	Representative	Party
1.	John W. Olver	Democratic
2.	Richard E. Neal	Democratic
3.	James P. McGovern	Democratic
4.	Barney Frank	Democratic
5.	Niki Tsongas	Democratic
6.	John F. Tierney	Democratic
7.	Edward J. Markey	Democratic
8.	Michael E. Capuano	Democratic
9.	Stephen F. Lynch	Democratic
10.	William D. Delahunt	Democratic

Massachusetts State Senators, 2009-2010 Session

	Senator	Party	District
1.	Benjamin Downing	Dem	Berkshire, Hampshire, Franklin
2.	James Timility	Dem	Bristol and Norfolk
3.	Joan Menard	Dem	1st Bristol and Plymouth
4.	Mark Montigny	Dem	2nd Bristol and Plymouth
5.	Robert O'Leary	Dem	Cape and Islands
6.	Steven Baddour	Dem	1st Essex
7.	Frederick Berry	Dem	2nd Essex
8.	Bruce Tarr	Rep	1st Essex and Middlesex
9.	Susan Tucker	Dem	2nd Essex and Middlesex
10.	Thomas McGee	Dem	3rd Essex and Middlesex
11.	Stephen Buoniconti	Dem	Hampden
12.	Gale D. Candaras	Dem	1st Hampden and Hampshire
13.	Michael Knapik	Rep	2nd Hampden and Hampshire
14.	Stanley Rosenberg	Dem	Hampshire and Franklin
15.	Steven Panagiotakos	Dem	1st Middlesex
16.	Patricia D. Jehlen	Dem	2nd Middlesex
17.	Susan Fargo	Dem	3rd Middlesex
18.	Ken Donnelly	Dem	4th Middlesex
19.	Richard Tisei	Rep	Middlesex and Essex
20.	Cynthia Stone Creem	Dem	1st Middlesex and Norfolk
21.	Karen Spilka	Dem	2nd Middlesex and Norfolk
22.	(Vacant)	NA	Middlesex, Suffolk, and Essex
23.	James B. Eldridge	Dem	Middlesex and Worcester
24.	Brian Joyce	Dem	Norfolk, Bristol, and Plymouth
25.	(Vacant)	NA	Norfolk, Bristol, Middlesex
26.	Michael Morrissey	Dem	Norfolk and Plymouth
27.	Therese Murray	Dem	Plymouth and Barnstable
28.	Marc Pacheco	Dem	1st Plymouth and Bristol
29.	Thomas P. Kennedy	Dem	2nd Plymouth and Bristol
30.	Robert Hedlund	Rep	Plymouth and Norfolk
31.	John Hart Jr	Dem	1st Suffolk
32.	Sonia Chang-Diaz	Dem	2nd Suffolk
33.	Anthony Petruccelli	Dem	1st Suffolk and Middlesex
34.	Steven Tolman	Dem	2nd Suffolk and Middlesex
35.	Marian Walsh	Dem	Suffolk and Norfolk
36.	Harriette Chandler	Dem	1st Worcester
37.	Michael O. Moore	Dem	2nd Worcester
38.	Stephen Brewer	Dem	Worcester, Hampden, Hampshire, and Franklin
39.	Jennifer L. Flanagan	Dem	Worcester and Middlesex
40.	Richard T. Moore	Dem	Worcester and Norfolk

©2010 Information Publications, Inc. All rights reserved. Photocopying prohibited. For additional copies, contact the publisher at www.informationpublications.com or (877)544-INFO (4636)

Massachusetts State House of Representatives, 2009-2010 Session

	Representative	Party	District
1.	Cleon H. Turner	Dem	First Barnstable
2.	Demetrius J. Atsalis	Dem	Second Barnstable
3.	Matthew C. Patrick	Dem	Third Barnstable
4.	Sarah Peake	Dem	Fourth Barnstable
5.	Jeffrey Davis Perry	Rep	Fifth Barnstable
6.	Timothy Madden	Dem	Barnstable, Dukes, Nantucket
7.	Daniel E. Bosley	Dem	First Berkshire
8.	Denis E. Guyer	Dem	Second Berkshire
9.	Christopher Speranzo	Dem	Third Berkshire
10.	William Smitty Pignatelli	Dem	Fourth Berkshire
11.	Frederick Barrows	Rep	First Bristol
12.	Bill Bowles	Dem	Second Bristol
13.	James H. Fagan	Dem	Third Bristol
14.	Steven D'Amico	Dem	Fourth Bristol
15.	Patricia A. Haddad	Dem	Fifth Bristol
16.	David B. Sullivan	Dem	Sixth Bristol
17.	Kevin Aguiar	Dem	Seventh Bristol
18.	Michael J. Rodrigues	Dem	Eighth Bristol
19.	John F. Quinn	Dem	Ninth Bristol
20.	William M. Straus	Dem	Tenth Bristol
21.	Robert M. Koczera	Dem	Eleventh Bristol
22.	Stephen R. Canessa	Dem	Twelfth Bristol
23.	Antonio F. Cabral	Dem	Thirteenth Bristol
24.	Elizabeth A. Poirier	Rep	Fourteenth Bristol
25.	Michael A. Costello	Dem	First Essex
26.	Harriett L. Stanley	Dem	Second Essex
27.	Brian S. Dempsey	Dem	Third Essex
28.	Bradford Hill	Rep	Fourth Essex
29.	Ann-Margaret Ferrante	Dem	Fifth Essex
30.	Mary E. Grant	Dem	Sixth Essex
31.	John D. Keenan	Dem	Seventh Essex
32.	Lori Ehrlich	Dem	Eighth Essex
33.	Mark V. Falzone	Dem	Ninth Essex
34.	Robert F. Fennell	Dem	Tenth Essex
35.	Steven M. Walsh	Dem	Eleventh Essex
36.	Joyce A. Spiliotis	Dem	Twelfth Essex
37.	Theodore C. Speliotis	Dem	Thirteenth Essex
38.	David M. Torrisi	Dem	Fourteenth Essex
39.	Linda Dean Campbell	Dem	Fifteenth Essex
40.	(Vacant)	NA	Sixteenth Essex
41.	Barry Finegold	Dem	Seventeenth Essex
42.	Barbara A. L'Italien	Dem	Eighteenth Essex
43.	Stephen Kulik	Dem	First Franklin
44.	Christopher J. Donelan	Dem	Second Franklin
45.	Todd M. Smola	Rep	First Hampden
46.	Brian Ashe	Dem	Second Hampden
47.	Rosemary Sandlin	Dem	Third Hampden
48.	Donald F. Humason Jr	Rep	Fourth Hampden
49.	Michael F. Kane	Dem	Fifth Hampden
50.	James T. Welch	Dem	Sixth Hampden
51.	Thomas M. Petrolati	Dem	Seventh Hampden
52.	Joseph F. Wagner	Dem	Eighth Hampden
53.	Sean Curran	Dem	Ninth Hampden
54.	Cheryl A. Coakley-Rivera	Dem	Tenth Hampden
55.	Benjamin Swan	Dem	Eleventh Hampden
56.	Angelo Puppolo	Dem	Twelfth Hampden
57.	Peter V. Kocot	Dem	First Hampshire
58.	John W. Scibak	Dem	Second Hampshire
59.	Ellen Story	Dem	Third Hampshire
60.	Robert S. Hargraves	Rep	First Middlesex
61.	James Arciero	Dem	Second Middlesex
62.	Kate Hogan	Dem	Third Middlesex
63.	Danielle W. Gregoire	Dem	Fourth Middlesex
64.	David Paul Linsky	Dem	Fifth Middlesex
65.	Pam Richardson	Dem	Sixth Middlesex
66.	Tom Sannicandro	Dem	Seventh Middlesex
67.	Carolyn Dykema	Dem	Eighth Middlesex
68.	Thomas M. Stanley	Dem	Ninth Middlesex
69.	Peter J. Koutoujian	Dem	Tenth Middlesex
70.	Kay Khan	Dem	Eleventh Middlesex
71.	Ruth B. Balser	Dem	Twelfth Middlesex
72.	Thomas P. Conroy	Dem	Thirteenth Middlesex
73.	Cory Atkins	Dem	Fourteenth Middlesex
74.	Jay R. Kaufman	Dem	Fifteenth Middlesex
75.	Thomas A. Golden Jr	Dem	Sixteenth Middlesex
76.	David M. Nangle	Dem	Seventeenth Middlesex
77.	Kevin J. Murphy	Dem	Eighteenth Middlesex
78.	James R. Miceli	Dem	Nineteenth Middlesex
79.	Bradley H. Jones Jr	Rep	Twentieth Middlesex
80.	Charles A. Murphy	Dem	Twenty-first Middlesex

©2010 Information Publications, Inc. All rights reserved. Photocopying prohibited. For additional copies, contact the publisher at www.informationpublications.com or (877)544-INFO (4636)

Massachusetts State House of Representatives, 2009-2010 Session *(con't)*

Representative	Party	District
81. William G. Greene Jr	Dem	Twenty-second Middlesex
82. Sean Garballey	Dem	Twenty-third Middlesex
83. William N. Brownsberger	Dem	Twenty-fourth Middlesex
84. Alice K. Wolf	Dem	Twenty-fifth Middlesex
85. Timothy J. Toomey Jr	Dem	Twenty-sixth Middlesex
86. Denise Provost	Dem	Twenty-seventh Middlesex
87. Stephen S. Smith	Dem	Twenty-eighth Middlesex
88. Jon Hecht	Dem	Twenty-ninth Middlesex
89. James Dwyer	Dem	Thirtieth Middlesex
90. Jason Lewis	Dem	Thirty-first Middlesex
91. Katherine Clark	Dem	Thirty-second Middlesex
92. Christopher G. Fallon	Dem	Thirty-third Middlesex
93. Carl M. Sciortino Jr	Dem	Thirty-fourth Middlesex
94. Paul J. Donato	Dem	Thirty-fifth Middlesex
95. Colleen M. Garry	Dem	Thirty-sixth Middlesex
96. Jennifer Benson	Dem	Thirty-seventh Middlesex
97. Bruce J. Ayers	Dem	First Norfolk
98. A. Stephen Tobin	Dem	Second Norfolk
99. Ronald Mariano	Dem	Third Norfolk
100. James M. Murphy	Dem	Fourth Norfolk
101. Joseph R. Driscoll	Dem	Fifth Norfolk
102. William C. Galvin	Dem	Sixth Norfolk
103. Walter F. Timilty	Dem	Seventh Norfolk
104. Louis L. Kafka	Dem	Eighth Norfolk
105. Richard J. Ross	Rep	Ninth Norfolk
106. James E. Vallee	Dem	Tenth Norfolk
107. Paul McMurtry	Dem	Eleventh Norfolk
108. John H. Rogers	Dem	Twelfth Norfolk
109. Lida E. Harkins	Dem	Thirteenth Norfolk
110. Alice Hanlon Peisch	Dem	Fourteenth Norfolk
111. Frank I. Smizik	Dem	Fifteenth Norfolk
112. Viriato Manuel deMacedo	Rep	First Plymouth
113. Susan Williams Gifford	Rep	Second Plymouth
114. Garrett J. Bradley	Dem	Third Plymouth
115. James Cantwell	Dem	Fourth Plymouth
116. Robert J. Nyman	Dem	Fifth Plymouth
117. Daniel K. Webster	Rep	Sixth Plymouth
118. Allen McCarthy	Dem	Seventh Plymouth
119. David L. Flynn	Dem	Eighth Plymouth
120. Michael Brady	Dem	Ninth Plymouth

Representative	Party	District
121. Christine E. Canavan	Dem	Tenth Plymouth
122. Geraldine Creedon	Dem	Eleventh Plymouth
123. Thomas J. Calter III	Dem	Twelfth Plymouth
124. Carlo Basile	Dem	First Suffolk
125. Eugene L. O'Flaherty	Dem	Second Suffolk
126. Aaron M. Michlewitz	Dem	Third Suffolk
127. Brian P. Wallace	Dem	Fourth Suffolk
128. Marie P. St. Fleur	Dem	Fifth Suffolk
129. Willie Mae Allen	Dem	Sixth Suffolk
130. Gloria L. Fox	Dem	Seventh Suffolk
131. Martha M. Walz	Dem	Eighth Suffolk
132. Byron Rushing	Dem	Ninth Suffolk
133. Michael F. Rush	Dem	Tenth Suffolk
134. Elizabeth A. Malia	Dem	Eleventh Suffolk
135. Linda Dorcena Forry	Dem	Twelfth Suffolk
136. Martin J. Walsh	Dem	Thirteenth Suffolk
137. Angelo M. Scaccia	Dem	Fourteenth Suffolk
138. Jeffrey Sanchez	Dem	Fifteenth Suffolk
139. Kathi-Anne Reinstein	Dem	Sixteenth Suffolk
140. Kevin G. Honan	Dem	Seventeenth Suffolk
141. Michael J. Moran	Dem	Eighteenth Suffolk
142. Robert A. DeLeo	Dem	Nineteenth Suffolk
143. Lewis G. Evangelidis	Rep	First Worcester
144. Robert L. Rice	Dem	Second Worcester
145. Stephen L. DiNatale	Dem	Third Worcester
146. Dennis Rosa	Dem	Fourth Worcester
147. Anne M. Gobi	Dem	Fifth Worcester
148. Geraldo Alicea	Dem	Sixth Worcester
149. Paul K. Frost	Rep	Seventh Worcester
150. Paul Kujawski	Dem	Eighth Worcester
151. George N. Peterson Jr	Rep	Ninth Worcester
152. John V. Fernandes	Dem	Tenth Worcester
153. Karyn E. Polito	Rep	Eleventh Worcester
154. Harold P. Naughton Jr	Dem	Twelfth Worcester
155. Robert P. Spellane	Dem	Thirteenth Worcester
156. James O'Day	Dem	Fourteenth Worcester
157. Vincent A. Pedone	Dem	Fifteenth Worcester
158. John P. Fresolo	Dem	Sixteenth Worcester
159. John J. Binienda	Dem	Seventeenth Worcester
160. Jennifer M. Callahan	Dem	Eighteenth Worcester

©2010 Information Publications, Inc. All rights reserved. Photocopying prohibited. For additional copies, contact the publisher at www.informationpublications.com or (877)544-INFO (4636)

ORDER FORM

S=MA10PA

Title	Qty	Edition	Price	ISBN Number	Standing Order YES	Standing Order NO
State & Municipal Profiles Series						
Almanac of the 50 States 2010		Hardcover	$99	978-0-929960-63-0	☐	☐
		Paperback	$89	978-0-929960-62-3	☐	☐
California Cities, Towns & Counties 2010		Paperback	$135	978-0-911273-54-0	☐	☐
		CD	$135	978-0-911273-55-7	☐	☐
Connecticut Municipal Profiles 2010		Paperback	$95	978-0-941391-38-2	☐	☐
		CD	$95	978-0-941391-39-9	☐	☐
Florida Cities, Towns & Counties 2010		Paperback	$135	978-0-941391-40-5	☐	☐
		CD	$135	978-0-941391-41-2	☐	☐
Massachusetts Municipal Profiles 2010		Paperback	$135	978-0-911273-50-2	☐	☐
		CD	$135	978-0-911273-51-9	☐	☐
The New Jersey Municipal Data Book 2010		Paperback	$135	978-0-911273-52-6	☐	☐
		CD	$135	978-0-911273-53-3	☐	☐
Essential Topics Series						
Energy, Transportation & the Environment: A Statistical Sourcebook and Guide to Government Data 2010		Paperback	$95	978-0-929960-70-8	☐	☐
		CD	$95	978-0-929960-71-5	☐	☐
Health in America: A Statistical Sourcebook and Guide to Government Data 2010		Paperback	$95	978-0-929960-72-2	☐	☐
		CD	$95	978-0-929960-73-9	☐	☐
American Profiles Series						
Black Americans: A Statistical Sourcebook and Guide to Government Data 2010		Paperback	$95	978-0-929960-66-1	☐	☐
		CD	$95	978-0-929960-67-8	☐	☐
Hispanic Americans: A Statistical Sourcebook and Guide to Government Data 2010		Paperback	$95	978-0-929960-68-5	☐	☐
		CD	$95	978-0-929960-69-2	☐	☐
Asian Americans: A Statistical Sourcebook and Guide to Government Data 2010		Paperback	$95	978-0-929960-64-7	☐	☐
		CD	$95	978-0-929960-65-4	☐	☐

Offer and prices valid until 12/31/10

Order Subtotal ______

(Required ONLY for shipments to California) CA Sales Tax ______

Purchase orders accepted from libraries, government agencies, and educational institutions.

Shipping & Handling ______

Prepayment required from all other organizations.

Total ______

Please complete the following shipping and billing information. If paying by credit card or PO please call **(877)544-4636** or fax your completed order form to **(877)544-4635**. To pay by check, please mail this form and your payment to the address below.

Information Publications, Inc.
2995 Woodside Rd., Suite 400-182
Woodside, CA 94062

U.S. Ground Shipping Rates	
Order Subtotal	Shipping & Handling
$0-139	$9
$140-270	$15
$271-400	$19
$401-500	$22
>$500	Call

Call for Int'l or Express Shipping Rates

Shipping Information (UPS/FedEx tracking number sent via email)

Organization Name		
Shipping Contact		
Address (No PO Boxes, please)		
City	State	Zip
Email Address (req'd if want tracking #)	Phone #	

Payment Information (mark choice)

☐ Check	☐ Credit Card ☐ Visa ☐ MC ☐ AMEX	☐ Purchase Order (attach PO to this form)
Check #	CC#	PO #
	Exp Date	

Credit Card Billing Information ☐ Check if same as Shipping Address

Name on Credit Card		
Billing Address of Credit Card		
City	State	Zip
Signature		

ORDER FORM

S=MA10PA

Title	Qty	Edition	Price	ISBN Number	Standing Order YES	Standing Order NO
State & Municipal Profiles Series						
Almanac of the 50 States 2010		Hardcover	$99	978-0-929960-63-0	☐	☐
		Paperback	$89	978-0-929960-62-3	☐	☐
California Cities, Towns & Counties 2010		Paperback	$135	978-0-911273-54-0	☐	☐
		CD	$135	978-0-911273-55-7	☐	☐
Connecticut Municipal Profiles 2010		Paperback	$95	978-0-941391-38-2	☐	☐
		CD	$95	978-0-941391-39-9	☐	☐
Florida Cities, Towns & Counties 2010		Paperback	$135	978-0-941391-40-5	☐	☐
		CD	$135	978-0-941391-41-2	☐	☐
Massachusetts Municipal Profiles 2010		Paperback	$135	978-0-911273-50-2	☐	☐
		CD	$135	978-0-911273-51-9	☐	☐
The New Jersey Municipal Data Book 2010		Paperback	$135	978-0-911273-52-6	☐	☐
		CD	$135	978-0-911273-53-3	☐	☐
Essential Topics Series						
Energy, Transportation & the Environment: A Statistical Sourcebook and Guide to Government Data 2010		Paperback	$95	978-0-929960-70-8	☐	☐
		CD	$95	978-0-929960-71-5	☐	☐
Health in America: A Statistical Sourcebook and Guide to Government Data 2010		Paperback	$95	978-0-929960-72-2	☐	☐
		CD	$95	978-0-929960-73-9	☐	☐
American Profiles Series						
Black Americans: A Statistical Sourcebook and Guide to Government Data 2010		Paperback	$95	978-0-929960-66-1	☐	☐
		CD	$95	978-0-929960-67-8	☐	☐
Hispanic Americans: A Statistical Sourcebook and Guide to Government Data 2010		Paperback	$95	978-0-929960-68-5	☐	☐
		CD	$95	978-0-929960-69-2	☐	☐
Asian Americans: A Statistical Sourcebook and Guide to Government Data 2010		Paperback	$95	978-0-929960-64-7	☐	☐
		CD	$95	978-0-929960-65-4	☐	☐

Offer and prices valid until 12/31/10

Order Subtotal ____________

(Required ONLY for shipments to California) CA Sales Tax ____________

Purchase orders accepted from libraries, government agencies, and educational institutions.

Shipping & Handling ____________

Prepayment required from all other organizations.

Total ____________

Please complete the following shipping and billing information. If paying by credit card or PO please call **(877)544-4636** or fax your completed order form to **(877)544-4635**. To pay by check, please mail this form and your payment to the address below.

Information Publications, Inc.
2995 Woodside Rd., Suite 400-182
Woodside, CA 94062

U.S. Ground Shipping Rates	
Order Subtotal	Shipping & Handling
$0-139	$9
$140-270	$15
$271-400	$19
$401-500	$22
>$500	Call

Call for Int'l or Express Shipping Rates

Shipping Information (UPS/FedEx tracking number sent via email)

Organization Name		
Shipping Contact		
Address (No PO Boxes, please)		
City	State	Zip
Email Address (req'd if want tracking #)	Phone #	

Payment Information (mark choice)	☐ **Check**	☐ **Credit Card** ☐ Visa ☐ MC ☐ AMEX	☐ **Purchase Order** (attach PO to this form)
	Check #	CC#	PO #
		Exp Date	

Credit Card Billing Information ☐ Check if same as Shipping Address

Name on Credit Card		
Billing Address of Credit Card		
City	State	Zip
Signature		